MODERN TOPICS

Feenstra and Taylor's text shows why trade and capital flows have been liberalized and allowed to grow. The text focuses more attention on emerging markets and developing countries—regions that now carry substantial weight in the global economy.

In March 2012, the United States, the European Union, and Japan filed another WTO case against China charging that it applied unfair export restrictions on its rare earth minerals, as well as tungsten and molybdenum. The first step in such a case is for the parties involved (the United States, Europe, and Japan on one side; China on the other) to see whether the charges can be resolved through consultations at the WTO. Those consultations failed to satisfy either side, and in September 2012, the case went to a dispute settlement panel at the WTO. The Chinese government appealed to Article XX of the GATT, which allows for an exception to GATT rules in cases "relating to the conservation of exhaustible natural resources." But the WTO ruled against China, who is expected to appeal.

Regardless of the ultimate outcome of that case, it appears that China has already changed its policies on rare earth minerals. By the end of 2012, China realized that its policy of export quotas for rare earth minerals was not having the desired effect of maintaining high world prices. It therefore shifted away from a strict reliance on export quotas, and introduced subsidies to help producers who were losing money. These new policies are described in **Headlines: China Signals Support for Rare Earths.** The new subsidy policy might also lead to objections from the United States, the European Union, and Japan. But as we have seen earlier in this chapter, it is more difficult for the WTO to control subsidies (which are commonly used in agriculture) than to control export quotas.

A final feature of international trade in rare earth minerals is important to recognize: the mining and processing of these minerals poses an environmental risk, because rare earth minerals are frequently found with radioactive ores like thorium or uranium. Processing these minerals therefore leads to low-grade radioactive waste as a by-product. That aspect of rare earth minerals leads to protests against the establishment of new mines. The Lynas Corporation mine in Australia, mentioned in the Headlines article, processes the minerals obtained there in Malaysia. That processing facility was targeted by protesters in Malaysia, led by a retired math teacher named Tan Bun Teet. Although Mr. Tan and the other protestors did not succeed in preventing the processing facility from being opened, they did delay it and also put pressure on the company to ensure that the radioactive waste would be exported from Malaysia, in accordance with that country's laws. But where will this waste go? This environmental dilemma arises because of the exploding worldwide demand for high-tech products (including your own cell phone), whose manufacturing involves environmental risks. This case illustrates the potential interaction between international trade and the environment, a topic we examine in more detail in the next chapter. ∎

Protesters from the Save Malaysia Stop Lynas group demonstrating outside a hotel in Sydney, Australia.

7 High-Technology Export Subsidies

We turn now to consider high-technology final products. This sector of an economy also receives substantial assistance from government, with examples including subsidies to the aircraft industries in both the United States and Europe. In the United States, subsidies take the form of low-interest loans provided by the Export-Import

 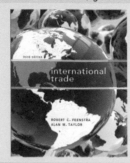  

third edition

international economics

third edition

international economics

ROBERT C. FEENSTRA
University of California, Davis

ALAN M. TAYLOR
University of California, Davis

Worth Publishers
A Macmillan Higher Education Company

Senior Vice President, Editorial and Production: Catherine Woods
Publisher: Charles Linsmeier
Associate Director of Digital Marketing: Scott Guile
Marketing Manager: Tom Digiano
Marketing Assistant: Tess Sanders
Senior Acquisitions Editor: Sarah Dorger
Development Editors: Jane Tufts and Bruce Kaplan
Associate Development Editor: Mary Walsh
Associate Media Editor: Lukia Kliossis
Director of Digital and Print Development: Tracey Kuehn
Associate Managing Editor: Lisa Kinne
Project Editor and Supplements Project Editor: Edgar Bonilla
Senior Designer, Cover and Interior Design: Kevin Kall
Photo Editor: Cecilia Varas
Photo Researchers: Ramon Rivera Moret and Eileen Liang
Production Manager: Barbara Anne Seixas
Supplements Production Manager: Stacey Alexander
Composition, Layout Designer, and Graphics: TSI Graphics
Printing and Binding: RR Donnelley

Cover Photo Credits: © Ocean/Corbis

Library of Congress Control Number: 2013957830

ISBN-13: 978-1-4292-7842-3
ISBN-10: 1-4292-7842-0

Printed in the United States of America

Second printing

Worth Publishers
41 Madison Avenue
New York, NY 10010
www.worthpublishers.com

About the Authors

Bud Harmon

Robert C. Feenstra and **Alan M. Taylor** are Professors of Economics at the University of California, Davis. They each began their studies abroad: Feenstra received his B.A. in 1977 from the University of British Columbia, Canada, and Taylor received his B.A. in 1987 from King's College, Cambridge, U.K. They trained as professional economists in the United States, where Feenstra earned his Ph.D. in economics from the Massachusetts Institute of Technology in 1981 and Taylor earned his Ph.D. in economics from Harvard University in 1992. Feenstra has been teaching international trade at the undergraduate and graduate levels at UC Davis since 1986, where he holds the C. Bryan Cameron Distinguished Chair in International Economics. Taylor teaches international macroeconomics, growth, and economic history at UC Davis, where he also holds appointments as Director of the Center for the Evolution of the Global Economy and Professor of Finance in the Graduate School of Management.

Both Feenstra and Taylor are active in research and policy discussions in international economics. They are research associates of the National Bureau of Economic Research, where Feenstra directs the International Trade and Investment research program. They have both published graduate level books in international economics: *Offshoring in the Global Economy* and *Product Variety and the Gains from Trade* (MIT Press, 2010), by Robert C. Feenstra, and *Global Capital Markets: Integration, Crisis and Growth* (Cambridge University Press, 2004), by Maurice Obstfeld and Alan M. Taylor. Feenstra received the Bernhard Harms Prize from the Institute for World Economics, Kiel, Germany, in 2006, and delivered the Ohlin Lectures at the Stockholm School of Economics in 2008. Taylor was awarded a Guggenheim Fellowship in 2004 and was awarded a Houblon-Norman/George Fellowship by the Bank of England in 2009–10.

Feenstra lives in Davis, California, with his wife, Gail, and has two grown children: Heather, who is a genetics counselor; and Evan, who is a musician and entrepreneur. Taylor also lives in Davis, with his wife, Claire, and has two young children, Olivia and Sebastian.

v

To our parents

Brief Contents

Contents

PART 3
New Explanations for International Trade

PART 5
Introduction to
International
Macroeconomics

Preface

The twenty-first century is an age of unprecedented globalization. In looking at existing texts, we saw that the dramatic economic developments of recent years had not been incorporated into a newly written undergraduate text, and felt the time was ripe to incorporate fresh perspectives, current topics, and up-to-date approaches into the study of international economics. With this book, we have expanded the vision of international economics to encompass the latest theories and events in the world today.

In decades past, international economics was taught differently. There was a much greater emphasis on theory and a strong focus on advanced countries. Policy analysis reflected the concerns of the time, whether strategic trade policy or the Bretton Woods system. Today, the concerns are not the same. In addition to new theoretical developments, there is a much greater emphasis on empirical studies. A wave of applied research in recent years has proved (or refuted) existing theories and taught us important new lessons about the determinants of trade, factor flows, exchange rates, and crises. Trade and capital flows have been liberalized and allowed to grow, and more attention is now devoted to emerging markets and developing countries, regions that now carry substantial weight in the global economy.

Covering new and expanding ground is part of the challenge and excitement of teaching and learning the international economics of the twenty-first century. Our goal is to provide new material that is rigorous enough to meet the challenge yet approachable enough to nurture the excitement. Many of the new topics stand apart from conventional textbook treatments and in the past had been bypassed in lectures or taught through supplementary readings. In our view they deserve a more prominent place in today's curriculum.

We have taught the chapters of this book ourselves several times, and have benefited from the feedback of professors at colleges and universities in the United States and throughout the world. Like us, they have been enthusiastic about the response from students to our fresh, accessible, and up-to-the-minute approach, and we hope that you will enjoy the book, too.

Features

Each chapter includes several features that bring the material alive for the students:

- ❏ **Applications,** which are integrated into the main text and use material that has been covered to illuminate real-world policies, events, and evidence.
- ❏ **Headlines,** which show how topics in the main text relate directly to media coverage of the global economy.
- ❏ **Side Bars,** which include topics that, although not essential, are nonetheless of interest.
- ❏ **Net Work boxes,** located at the end of the chapters with homework problems, provide an opportunity for the students to explore chapter concepts on the Internet.

The book is issued in a variety of formats that allows instructors greater flexibility in tailoring the content to their needs, and may help keep costs down for students.

❏ a combined edition (*International Economics*);

❏ two split editions (*International Trade* and *International Macroeconomics*); and

❏ a brief, combined edition with select chapters that cover international trade and macroeconomics, suitable for a one-semester course (*Essentials of International Economics*).

New in the Third Edition

In this third edition we have thoroughly updated the text, to include new data and Applications, as well as many new Headline features to reflect the rapid changes in international economic news during the last three years. (Chapter numbers in this section refer to the combined book; see later for details on the other editions.) We begin the volume with news of the opening of a Northern Sea route for international trade flows, made possible by the melting of ice in the Arctic Circle. The Northern Sea route reduces the shipping distance between Asia and Europe by about 4,000 nautical miles, as compared with the existing route through the Suez Canal. When this route becomes passable for much of the year, it will likely substantially alter international trade flows. Another item of news has been the migration of refugees from Africa to the Italian island of Lampedusa, covered in Chapter 5, which has created a humanitarian crisis there. In Chapter 8, we discuss the recently expired U.S. tariff against imports of Chinese tires, and argue that the structure of these tariffs led to substantial welfare losses before they expired. Trade policies adopted by the Chinese government receive increased attention, including: export subsidies to solar panels and the resulting antidumping tariffs in the United States (Chapter 9), and Chinese quotas on the export of "rare earth" minerals (Chapter 10). In international macroeconomics, we begin Chapter 12 with news and discussion focusing on the economic crisis in Iceland in 2008. Chapters 13 to 16 include updates to all key macroeconomic data and other revisions to streamline and simplify the presentation. Chapter 18 adds news from recent global macro policy issues (such as the "currency war" debate), retains an application on fiscal stimulus in the United States, and looks at Eurozone issues with news and analysis comparing Poland and Latvia's divergent paths since 2008. Chapter 21 on the euro has been rewritten and expanded to cover the dramatic developments since 2010, including the Greek debt restructuring, assistance programs in Spain, Ireland and Portugal, the Cyprus banking crisis, and the ongoing battle to avert the threats to the very existence of the currency union project.

Finally, in response to the needs and feedback of those instructors who teach a one-semester course that combines international trade and macroeconomics, our text comes in a shorter one-semester *Essentials* version. Again, we have learned from the experiences of faculty teaching this course, and we include 16 chapters most relevant to teaching the one-semester course. The third edition of *Essentials* now includes the chapter on the euro. There is more information on this one-semester version later in the Preface.

Topics and Approaches

Reviewers and class testers have been enthusiastically supportive of the topics we have included in our presentation. Topics covered in *International Economics* and *International Trade* include the offshoring of goods and services (Chapter 7); tariffs and quotas under imperfect competition (Chapter 9); and international agreements on trade, labor, and the environment (Chapter 11). These topics are in addition to core chapters on the Ricardian model (Chapter 2), the specific-factors model (Chapter 3), the Heckscher-Ohlin model (Chapter 4), trade with increasing returns to scale and imperfect competition (Chapter 6), import tariffs and quotas under perfect competition (Chapter 8), and export subsidies (Chapter 10).

Chapters in *International Economics* and *International Macroeconomics* include the gains from financial globalization (Chapter 17 in the combined edition, or Chapter 6 in the *International Macroeconomics* split edition), fixed versus floating regimes (Chapter 19/Chapter 8), exchange-rate crises (Chapter 20/Chapter 9), and the euro (Chapter 21/Chapter 10). These topics are in addition to core chapters on foreign exchange markets and exchange rates in the short run and the long run (Chapters 13–15/Chapters 2–4), the national and international accounts (Chapter 16/Chapter 5), the open economy IS-LM model (Chapter 18/Chapter 7), and a chapter on various applied topics of current interest (Chapter 22/Chapter 11).

In writing our chapters we have made every effort to link them analytically. For example, although immigration and foreign direct investment are sometimes treated as an afterthought in international economics books, we integrate these topics into the discussion of the trade models by covering the movement of labor and capital between countries in Chapter 5. Specifically, we analyze the movement of labor and capital between countries in the short run using the specific-factors model, and explore the long-run implications using the Heckscher-Ohlin model. Chapter 5 therefore builds on the models that the student has learned in Chapters 3 and 4, and applies them to issues at the forefront of policy discussion.

In the macroeconomics section from *International Economics* or *International Macroeconomics*, this analytical linking is seen in the parallel development of fixed and floating exchange rate regimes from the opening introductory tour in Chapter 12 (Chapter 1 in the split edition), through the workings of exchange rates in Chapters 13–15 (Chapters 2–4), the discussion of policy in the IS-LM model of Chapter 18 (Chapter 7), to the discussion of regime choice in Chapter 19 (Chapter 8). Many textbooks discuss fixed and floating regimes separately, with fixed regimes often treated as an afterthought. But given the widespread use of fixed rates in many countries, the rising macro weight of fixed regimes, and the collapse of fixed rates during crises, we think it is more helpful for the student to grapple with the different workings and cost-benefit trade-offs of the two regimes by studying them side by side. This approach also allows us to address numerous policy issues, such as the implications of the trilemma and the optimal choice of exchange rate regime.

In addition to expanding our coverage to include up-to-date theory and policy applications, our other major goal is to present all the material—both new and old—in the most teachable way. To do this, we ensure that all of the material presented rests on firm and up-to-the-minute empirical evidence. We believe this approach is the right way to study economics, and it is our experience, shared with many instructors, that teaching is more effective and more enlivened when students can see not just an elegant derivation in theory but, right next to it, some persuasive evidence of the economic mechanisms under investigation.

The Arrangement of Topics: International Trade

Part 1: Introduction to International Trade

The opening chapter sets the stage by discussing global flows of goods and services through international trade, of people through migration, and of capital through foreign direct investment. The chapter includes maps depicting these flows, so the student can get a feel for which countries have the greatest flows in each case. Historical examples of trade and barriers to trade are also provided. This chapter can serve as a full introductory lecture.

Part 2: Patterns of International Trade

The core models of international trade are presented here: the Ricardian model (Chapter 2), the specific-factors model (Chapter 3), and the Heckscher-Ohlin model (Chapter 4). Some of the topics conventionally included in the specific-factors and Heckscher-Ohlin model, like the effects of changing the endowments of labor or capital, are not covered in those chapters but are instead examined in Chapter 5, which deals with the movement of labor and capital between countries. For example, the "factor price insensitivity" result is deferred to Chapter 5, as is the Rybczynski theorem. By discussing those two results in Chapter 5, we keep the discussion of the Heckscher-Ohlin model more manageable in Chapter 4, which focuses on the Heckscher-Ohlin theorem, the Stolper-Samuelson theorem, and empirical testing of the model. In summary, the ordering of topics among Chapters 3, 4, and 5, and many applications, are new, and these chapters are linked together tightly in their pedagogical approach.

Part 3: New Explanations for International Trade

In this section we cover two relatively new explanations for international trade: increasing returns to scale (Chapter 6), and offshoring (Chapter 7).

Formal models of trade with increasing returns to scale and monopolistic competition have been popular since the early 1980s, but there is no standardized method for presenting this topic in undergraduate textbooks. In Chapter 6, we use the original, graphical discussion from Edward Chamberlin, who introduced the DD and dd curves (which we label in Chapter 6 as simply D and d). The D curve represents the share of the market going to each firm and traces out demand if all firms charge the same prices. In contrast, the d curve is the demand facing a firm when other firms keep their prices constant. The distinction between these two demands is crucial when analyzing the impact of trade liberalization: the d curve clearly shows the incentive for each individual firm to lower its price after trade liberalization, but the steeper D curve shows that when all firms lower prices, then losses occur and some firms must exit.

Chapter 7 is devoted to offshoring, and we have found that students enjoy learning and readily understand this new material. The model we use illustrates a piece of intuition that students grasp easily: the movement of one student from, say, a physics class to an economics class can raise the average grade in *both* classes. Likewise, offshoring can raise the relative wage of skilled workers in both countries. The chapter deals with Paul Samuelson's 2004 critique that offshoring to China or India might be harmful to the United States. That argument is shown to depend on how offshoring affects the U.S. terms of trade: if the terms of trade fall, the United States is worse off, though it still gains overall from international trade. In fact, we argue that the U.S. terms of trade have been rising in recent years, not falling, so Samuelson's argument is hypothetical so far.

Part 4: International Trade Policies

The concluding part of the trade portion of the book is devoted to trade policy: tariffs and quotas under perfect competition (Chapter 8), under imperfect competition (Chapter 9), export subsidies (Chapter 10), and a discussion of international agreements on trade, labor, and the environment (Chapter 11). Our goal is to present this material in a more systematic fashion than found elsewhere, using both very recent and historical applications.

Chapter 8, dealing with tariffs and quotas under perfect competition, is the "bread and butter" of trade policy. We adopt the partial-equilibrium approach, using import demand and export supply curves, along with consumer and producer surplus. Our experience is that students feel very comfortable with this approach from their microeconomics training (so they can usually label the consumer surplus region, for example, in each diagram before the labels are shown). The chapter uses the tariffs applied by President George W. Bush on U.S. steel imports and by President Barack Obama on imported tires from China as motivating cases, which we analyze from both a "small country" and a "large country" perspective.

Chapters 9 and 10 bring in some of the insights from the literature on the strategic role of trade policy, which was developed in the later 1980s and 1990s. Whereas that literature focused on oligopoly interactions between firms, we simplify the analysis in Chapter 9 by focusing on home or foreign monopoly cases. Chapter 10 then presents the duopoly case in the analysis of export subsidies. Most of the theory in these chapters is familiar, but the organization is new, as are many of the applications, including infant industry protection in Chapter 9 and a detailed discussion of export policies in high-technology and resource industries, including rare earth minerals in China, in Chapter 10.

Chapter 11 begins by drawing upon tariffs under perfect competition (from Chapter 8), and showing that large countries have a natural incentive to apply tariffs to move the terms of trade to their advantage. That creates a prisoner's dilemma situation that is overcome by rules in the World Trade Organization. The chapter then moves on to discuss international rules governing labor issues and the environment. Students are especially interested in the environmental applications.

The Arrangement of Topics: International Macroeconomics

Part 5 (Part 1 in *International Macroeconomics*): Introduction to International Macroeconomics

This part consists of Chapter 12 (Chapter 1 in the split edition), which sets the stage by explaining the field and major items of interest with a survey of the three main parts of the book: money and exchange rates, the balance of payments, and the role of policy.

Part 6 (Part 2): Exchange Rates

We depart from the traditional presentation by presenting exchange rates before balance of payments, an approach that we and our students find more logical and appealing. We begin the core macro material with exchange rates because (for macroeconomics) the exchange rate is the key difference between a closed economy and a world of open economies. Our approach, supported by our own experience and that of our reviewers and users, first treats all price topics together in one part, and then moves on to quantity topics.

Chapter 13 (Chapter 2) introduces the basics of exchange rates and the foreign exchange (forex) market (including the principles of arbitrage) and exposes students to real-world data on exchange rate behavior. It describes how the forex market is structured and explains the principles of arbitrage in forex markets. It ends with interest parity conditions, which are then covered in more detail in Chapter 15 (Chapter 4).

Chapter 14 (Chapter 3) presents the monetary approach to the determination of exchange rates in the long run. We cover the long run before the short run because long-run expectations are assumed to be known in the short-run model. Topics include goods market arbitrage, the law of one price, and purchasing power parity. We first develop a simple monetary model (the quantity theory) and then look at the standard monetary model, the Fisher effect, and real interest parity. The chapter ends with discussion of nominal anchors and their relationship to monetary and exchange rate regimes.

Chapter 15 (Chapter 4) presents the asset approach to the determination of exchange rates in the short run. Uncovered interest parity, first introduced in Chapter 13 (Chapter 2), is the centerpiece of the asset approach, and the expected future exchange rate is assumed to be given by the long-run model. Short-run interest rates are explained using a money market model. We show how all the building blocks from the monetary and asset approaches fit together for a complete theory of exchange rate determination. Finally, we explain how the complete theory works for fixed as well as floating regimes, and demonstrate the trilemma.

Part 7 (Part 3): The Balance of Payments

Chapter 16 (Chapter 5 in the split edition) introduces the key macroeconomic quantities: the national and international accounts and the balance of payments (BOP). The BOP is explained as the need for balancing trade on goods, services, and assets (with allowances for transfers). We also introduce external wealth and valuation effects, which are of increasing importance in the world economy.

Chapter 17 (Chapter 6) links the balance of payments to the key question of the costs and benefits of financial globalization, an increasingly important topic. The chapter begins by explaining the significance of the long-run budget constraint and then examines the three key potential benefits of financial globalization: consumptions smoothing, efficient investment, and risk sharing. This chapter allows instructors to present a clear, simplified treatment of the real macroeconomic efficiency gains arising from international trade and payments, a subject often omitted from textbooks.

Chapter 18 (Chapter 7) presents the short-run open economy Keynesian model, which links the balance of payments to output, exchange rates, and macroeconomic policies. We use IS-LM and forex market diagrams, with the interest rate on a common axis. With this presentation, we use tools (IS-LM) that many students have already seen, and avoid inventing new ways to present the same model with new and challenging notation. In this chapter we also discuss fixed and floating rate regimes side by side, not in different chapters. We think it helpful throughout the book to study these regimes in parallel and at this point this presentation leads naturally to the next chapter.

The ordering of Part 7 (Part 3) echoes that of Part 6 (Part 2): we start with definitions, then cover long-run topics (the gains from financial globalization), then move to short-run topics (IS-LM). This ordering of topics allows a smooth transition from some key definitions in Chapter 16 (Chapter 5) to their application at the start of Chapter 17 (Chapter 6), a link that would be impossible if the balance of payments chapter were placed before the coverage of exchange rates.

Part 8 (Part 4) Applications and Policy Issues

Chapter 19 (Chapter 8 in the split edition) confronts one of the major policy issues in international macroeconomics, the choice of fixed versus floating exchange rates. The analysis begins with the two classic criteria for two regions to adopt a fixed exchange rate—high levels of integration and symmetry of economic shocks. The chapter then goes on to consider other factors that could make a fixed exchange rate desirable, especially in developing countries—a need for a credible nominal anchor and the "fear of floating" that results from significant liability dollarization. Empirical evidence is provided for all of these influences. A brief section summarizes the debate over the desirability and possibility of coordination in larger exchange rate systems. Finally, a historical survey uses the tools at hand to understand the evolution of international monetary arrangements since the nineteenth century.

Chapter 20 (Chapter 9) studies exchange rate crises. Before explaining how pegs break, we spend some time studying how pegs work. We begin by focusing on reserve management and the central bank balance sheet, when an economy faces shocks to output, interest rates, and risk premiums. We then extend the framework to consider lender of last resort actions, a structure that allows for more realism. This presentation allows us to discuss recent controversies over reserve accumulation in China and other emerging markets, and also suggests how pegs can fail. The chapter concludes by looking at two models of crises: a first-generation model with ongoing monetized deficits with fixed output and flexible prices, applying the logic of the flexible-price model of Chapter 14 (Chapter 3); and a second-generation model featuring an adverse shock with flexible output and fixed prices, applying the IS-LM-FX model of Chapter 18 (Chapter 7).

Chapter 21 (Chapter 10) discusses common currencies, with particular focus on the euro. We develop the basic optimum currency area (OCA) criteria as an extension of the fixed versus floating analysis of Chapter 19 (Chapter 8). This framework allows us to consider additional economic and political reasons why countries might join a common currency area. We then present empirical evidence to show the differences between the United States and the Eurozone with respect to the OCA criteria and to explain why so many economists believe that the Eurozone currently is not an OCA. A complete explanation of the euro project requires an examination of other forces, which are considered in the remainder of the chapter: the possible endogeneity of the OCA criteria and the role of noneconomic factors. Thus, we examine the essential history, politics, and institutional details of the euro.

Chapter 22 (Chapter 11) is a collection of four "mini chapters" that tackle important topics in macroeconomics. In this edition, these topics are the failure of uncovered interest parity and exchange rate puzzles in the short run (including the carry trade and limits to arbitrage); the failure of purchasing power parity and exchange rates in the long run (including transaction costs and the Balassa-Samuelson effect); the debate over global imbalances (including the savings glut hypothesis and the role of exchange rate adjustments); the problem of default (including a simple model of default as insurance and a discussion of triple crises). We present each of these topics in a self-contained block that can be taught as is or in conjunction with earlier material. The UIP material could be covered with Chapter 13 or 15 (Chapter 2 or 4). The PPP material would nicely augment Chapter 14 (Chapter 3). The global imbalances material could be presented with Chapter 16, 17, or 18 (Chapter 5, 6, or 7). The default topic could be paired with the discussion of currency crises in Chapter 20 (Chapter 9).

Alternative Routes through the Text

Because this book is available as a combined edition and as split volumes, it can be used for several types of courses, as summarized below and in the accompanying table.

A semester-length course in international trade (say, 15 weeks) would start at Chapter 1, but for a shorter, quarter-length course (say, 10 weeks), we suggest skipping Chapter 1 and going straight to the Ricardian model (Chapter 2). Chapters 2, 3 (the specific-factors model), and 4 (the Heckscher-Ohlin model) form the core of trade theory. The movement of labor and capital between countries (Chapter 5) builds on these chapters theoretically, and summarizes the empirical evidence on immigration and foreign direct investment.

The new approaches to international trade covered in Chapters 6 (economies of scale and imperfect competition) and 7 (offshoring) can be taught independently of each other. (A quarter course in international trade may not have time for both chapters.) The final four chapters in international trade deal with trade policy. Chapter 8 (tariffs and quotas under perfect competition) should be discussed in any course regardless of its length. Tariffs and quotas under imperfect competition (Chapter 9) dig more deeply into the effects of trade policy, and are followed by a discussion of export subsidies (Chapter 10). Some or all topics in the final chapter on international agreements can be covered as time permits.

A semester course in international macroeconomics (say, 15 weeks) would start at Chapter 12 in the combined edition (Chapter 1 in the *International Macroeconomics* split edition), but for a shorter quarter-length course (say, 10 weeks), we recommend skipping Chapter 12 (Chapter 1) and going straight to the foreign exchange market presented in Chapter 13 (Chapter 2). Core material on exchange rate theory then follows, with the long run in Chapter 14 (Chapter 3) followed by the short run in Chapter 15 (Chapter 4). Next, come the core definitions of the national and international accounts and the balance of payments, presented in Chapter 16 (Chapter 5). After this point a course with a macro emphasis would cover the costs and benefits of globalization in Chapter 17 (Chapter 6) and IS-LM in Chapter 18 (Chapter 7). To allow time to cover the analysis of crises in Chapter 20 (Chapter 9), the treatment of regime choice in Chapter 19 (Chapter 8) might be combined with a discussion of the euro in Chapter 21 (Chapter 10). Topics from Chapter 22 (Chapter 11) can be selected as time permits: a more finance-oriented course might focus on the first two exchange rate topics; a more macro-oriented course might focus on global imbalances and default. In a semester-length course, there should be time for almost all the topics to be covered.

We recognize that many schools also offer a combined one-semester course in international trade and macroeconomics, sometimes to students outside the economics major. Because of its wealth of applications, this book will serve those students very well. The one-semester *Essentials of International Economics* edition brings together the chapters that are the most important for such a course. The one-semester edition has an introduction in Chapter 1 that incorporates both international trade and

SUGGESTED COURSE OUTLINES	Course Type and Length		
	Trade or Macroeconomics in one term	**International Economics in two terms**	**International Economics in one term**
Chapter Titles	Chapter numbers from *International Trade* version	Chapter numbers from *International Economics*	Chapter numbers from *Essentials of International Economics*
	10 week quarter / 13–15 week semester		
Trade in the Global Economy (*Essentials:* The Global Economy)	— / 1	1	1 (introduces trade and macroeconomics)
Trade and Technology: The Ricardian Model	2 / 2	2	2
Gains and Losses from Trade in the Specific-Factors Model	3 / 3	3	3
Trade and Resources: The Heckscher-Ohlin Model	4 / 4	4	4
Movement of Labor and Capital between Countries	Choose two from 5, 6, 7 / 5	5	5
Increasing Returns to Scale and Monopolistic Competition	/ 6	6	6
Offshoring of Goods and Services	/ 7	7	—
Import Tariffs and Quotas under Perfect Competition	8 / 8	8	7
Import Tariffs and Quotas under Imperfect Competition	9 / 9	9	8
Export Subsidies in Agriculture and High-Technology Industries	10 / 10	10	—
International Agreements: Trade, Labor, and the Environment	As time permits / 11	11	9

	Chapter numbers from *International Macroeconomics* version		
	10 week quarter / 13–15 week semester		
The Global Macroeconomy	— / 1	12	—
Introduction to Exchange Rates and the Foreign Exchange Market	2 / 2	13	10
Exchange Rates I: The Monetary Approach in the Long Run	3 / 3	14	11
Exchange Rates II: The Asset Approach in the Short Run	4 / 4	15	12
National and International Accounts: Income, Wealth, and the Balance of Payments	5 / 5	16	13
The Balance of Payments I: The Gains from Financial Globalization	6 / 6	17	—
The Balance of Payments II: Output, Exchange Rates, and Macroeconomic Policies in the Short Run	7 / 7	18	14
Fixed Versus Floating: International Monetary Experience	Combine with Chapter 8 / 8	19	15
Exchange Rate Crises: How Pegs Work and How They Break	9 / 9	20	—
The Euro	Combine with Chapter 10 / 10	21	16
Topics in International Macroeconomics	1 or 2 topics (as time permits) / 3 or 4 topics (as time permits)	22	—

macroeconomic issues. It then moves to Chapters 2–6 the basic trade chapters, followed by two chapters on tariffs and quotas under perfect competition and under imperfect competition. The international trade section concludes with the chapter on trade agreements and the environment. Those eight chapters (plus the introduction) offer the students a solid perspective on international trade and trade policy. These chapters are followed in the one-semester edition by seven chapters dealing with the core concepts and models in international macroeconomics: the foreign exchange market, the monetary and asset approach to exchange rates, national income accounting, macroeconomic policy, fixed and floating exchange rates, and the euro. This coverage will give students a basic grounding in international macroeconomics.

Supplements and Media

Because technology should never get in the way

At Macmillan Higher Education, we are committed to providing online instructional materials that meet the needs of instructors and students in powerful, yet simple ways—powerful enough to enhance teaching and learning dramatically, yet simple enough to use right away.

We have taken what we have learned from thousands of instructors and the hundreds of thousands of students and created a new generation of Macmillan Higher Education technology—featuring **LaunchPad. LaunchPad** offers our acclaimed content curated and organized for easy assignability in a breakthrough user interface in which power and simplicity go hand in hand.

LaunchPad Units

Curated LaunchPad units make class prep a whole lot easier. Combining a curated collection of multimedia assignments and e-Book content, LaunchPad's interactive units give you a building block to use as is, or as a starting point for your own learning units. An entire unit's worth of work can be assigned in seconds, drastically saving the amount of time it takes for you to have your course up and running.

- ❏ **Everything is assignable.** You can customize the LaunchPad units by adding quizzes and other activities from our vast wealth of resources. You can also add a discussion board, a Dropbox, and RSS feed, with a few clicks. LaunchPad allows you to customize the student experience as much or as little as you would like.

- ❏ **Useful analytics.** The gradebook quickly and easily allows you to look up performance metrics for your whole class, for individual students, and for individual assignments. Having ready access to this information can help in both lecture prep and in making office hours more productive and efficient.

- ❏ **Give students LearningCurve—and get them more engaged with what they are learning.** Powerful adaptive quizzing, a gamelike format, direct links to the e-Book, instant feedback, and the promise of better grades make using LearningCurve a no-brainer. Customized quizzing tailored to each text adapts

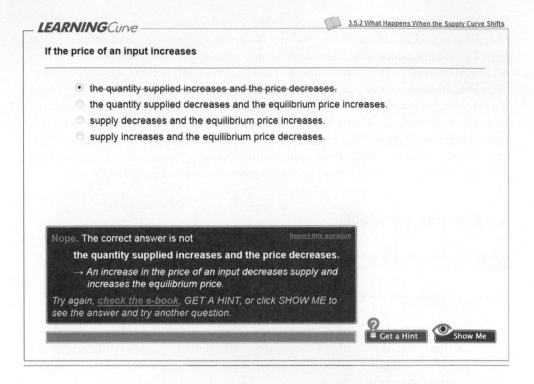

to student responses and provides material at different difficulty levels and topics based on student performance. Students love the simple yet powerful system and instructors can access class reports to help refine lecture content.

❏ **An e-Book that delivers more than content.** Every LaunchPad e-Book comes with powerful study tools for students, video and multimedia content, and easy customization for instructors. Students can search, highlight, and bookmark, making it easier to study and access key content. And instructors can make sure their class gets just the book they want to deliver; they can customize and rearrange chapters, add and share notes and discussions, and link to quizzes, activities, and other resources. In addition, the e-Book will also include links to all research articles and data cited in the text.

❏ **Intuitive interface and design.** Students can be in only two places in LaunchPad—either viewing the home page with their assigned content, or working to complete their assignments. Students' navigation options and expectations are clearly laid out in front of them, at all times ensuring they can never get lost in the system.

❏ **Electronically graded graphing problems** replicate the paper and pencil experience better than any program on the market. Students are asked to draw their response and label each curve. The software automatically grades each response, providing feedback options at the instructor's discretion, including partial credit for incomplete, but not entirely incorrect responses.

❏ **All teaching resources** will be available for instructors within LaunchPad. These will include animated lecture PowerPoint slides with instructor notes, the solutions manual, test bank questions, and more.

Get your feet wet with our graphing tools: Let's imagine a market for Tabloid Newspapers.

Part 1: Select the Line tool and draw a downward-sloping line. Label it "Demand 1". Next, using the same tool, draw an upward-sloping line that intersects "Demand 1" and label it "Supply 1".

Part 2: Use the Double Drop Line tool to identify the price and quantity where the two lines intersect. Label it "Equilibrium 1".

Part 3: With the Line tool, draw a new downward-sloping line that is to the LEFT of "Demand 1". Label it "Demand 2". Use the Double Drop Line tool to show the new equilibrium price and quantity in the global market for this Alien Bigfoot journalism. Label this point "Equilibrium 2."
Feel momentarily happy that demand for sensational stories has fallen, then remember that it's only because of the rise in demand for substitute goods like reality TV.

Continue to play with the graph if you like. We know you are an economist, after all.

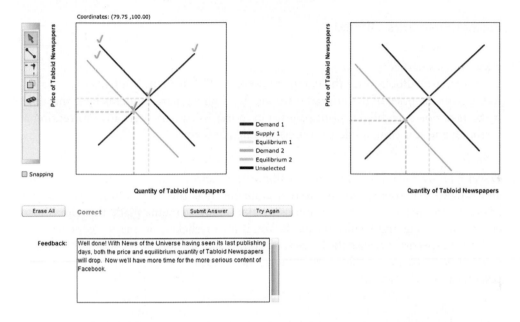

Computerized Test Bank

Diploma was the first software for personal computers that integrated a test-generation program with grade-book software and online testing system. Diploma is now in its fifth generation. The test banks are available for both Windows and Macintosh users.

With Diploma, you can easily create and print test banks and write and edit questions. You can add an unlimited number of questions, scramble questions and distractors, and include figures. Tests can be printed in a wide range of formats. The software's unique synthesis of flexible word-processing and database features creates a program that is extremely intuitive and capable.

Additional Online Offerings

Aplia

www.aplia.com/worth

Worth/Aplia courses are all available with digital textbooks, interactive assignments, and detailed feedback. With Aplia, you retain complete control of and flexibility for your course. You choose the content you want students to cover, and you decide how to organize it. You decide whether online activities are practice (ungraded or graded).

❏ **Extra problem sets** (derived from in-chapter questions in the book) suitable for homework and keyed to specific topics from each chapter

❏ **Regularly updated news analyses**

❏ **Interactive tutorials** to assist with math and graphing

❏ **Instant online reports** that allow instructors to target student trouble areas more efficiently

Further Resources Offered

CourseSmart e-Books

www.coursesmart.com

CourseSmart e-Books offer the complete book in PDF format. Students can save up to 60% off the price of the printed textbook. In CourseSmart, students have the ability to take notes, highlight, print pages, and more. It is great alternative to renting a textbook and it is compatible with most mobile platforms.

i-clicker

Developed by a team of University of Illinois physicists, i-clicker is the most flexible and reliable classroom response system available. It is the only solution created *for educators, by educators*—with continuous product improvements made through direct classroom testing and faculty feedback. You'll love i-clicker, no matter your level of technical expertise, because the focus is on your teaching, not the technology. To learn more about packaging i-clicker with this textbook, please contact your local sales representative or visit www.iclicker.com.

LMS Integration

LaunchPad for *International Economics* can be fully integrated with any campus LMS including such features as single sign-on for students revisiting the site, gradebook integration for all activities completed in LaunchPad, as well as integration of assignments within the campus LMS for certain products. For more information on LMS integration, please contact your local publisher's representative.

Acknowledgments

A book like this would not be possible without the assistance of many people, which we gratefully acknowledge.

First, the renowned team at Worth has spared no effort to help us; their experience and skill in publishing economics textbooks were invaluable. Numerous individuals have been involved with this project, but we must give special mention to a few: the project has been continually and imaginatively guided by acquisitions editor Sarah Dorger, publisher Chuck Linsmeier, development editor Bruce Kaplan, and by marketing manager Tom Digiano, who successfully brought the book to market. Through it all, the manuscript was improved endlessly by our primary development editor, Jane Tufts. We are greatly in their debt.

We have also relied on the assistance of a number of graduate students in collecting data for applications, preparing problems, and proofreading material. We would like to thank Leticia Arroyo Abad, Chang Hong, David Jacks, Alyson Ma, Ahmed Rahman, Seema Sangita, Radek Szulga, and Yingying Xu for their assistance. We are especially grateful to Benjamin Mandel, who has worked on many of the international trade chapters in the first edition; to Philip Luck, who worked on all the chapters in the second edition; and to Charles Liao, who worked on all the trade chapters in the third edition. Thanks also go to Christian Broda, Colin Carter, Michele Cavallo, Menzie Chinn, Sebastian Edwards, Ann Harrison, Mervyn King, Philip Lane, Karen Lewis, Christopher Meissner, Gian Maria Milesi-Ferretti, Michael Pakko, Ugo Panizza, Giovanni Peri, Eswar Prasad, Andrés Rodríguez-Clare, Jay Shambaugh, and Martin Wolf for providing data used in some of the applications and examples.

Special thanks go to Professor Francis Ahking, University of Conneticut, who once again carefully reviewed the page proofs of the entire book.

We have taught the chapters of this book ourselves several times, and have benefited from the feedback of colleagues. For the third edition, we benefited from the suggestions of the following instructors:

Basil Al-Hashimi—*Mesa Community College*

Sam Andoh—*Southern Connecticut State University*

Adina Ardelean—*Santa Clara University*

Joel Auerbach—*Florida Atlantic University*

Mohsen Bahmani-Oskooee—*University of Wisconsin, Milwaukee*

Jeremy Baker—*Owens Community College*

Rita Balaban—*University of North Carolina, Chapel Hill*

Jim Bruehler—*Eastern Illinois University*

Thomas Chaney—*Toulouse School of Economics*

John Chilton—*Virginia Commonwealth University*

Reid Click—*George Washington University*

Catherine Co—*University of Nebraska at Omaha*

Antoinette Criss—*University of South Florida*

Judith Dean—*Brandeis University*

James Devault—*Lafayette College*

Asif Dowla—*St. Mary's College of Maryland*

Justin Dubas—*Texas Lutheran University*

Lee Erickson—*Taylor University*

Xin Fang—*Hawaii Pacific University*

Stephen Grubaugh—*Bentley University*

Ronald Gunderson—*Northern Arizona University*

Chang Hong—*Clark University*

Carl Jensen—*Rutgers University*

Jeff Konz—*University of North Carolina, Asheville*

Robert Krol—*California State University, Northridge*

Dave LaRivee—*United States Air Force Academy*

Daniel Lee—*Shippensburg University*

Yu-Feng (Winnie) Lee—*New Mexico State University*

James Lehman—*Pitzer College*

Carlos Liard-Muriente—*Central Connecticut State University*

Rita Madarassy—*Santa Clara University*

Margaret Malixi—*California State University, Bakersfield*

Steven Matusz—*Michigan State University*

Diego Mendez-Carbajo—*Illinois Wesleyan University*

Kathleen Odell—*Dominican University*

Kerry Pannell—*DePauw University*

Elizabeth Perry-Sizemore—*Randolph College*

Diep Phan—*Beloit College*

Reza Ramazani—*Saint Michael's College*

Artatrana Ratha—*St. Cloud State University*

Raymond Riezman—*University of Iowa*

Helen Roberts—*University of Illinois, Chicago*

Mari L. Robertson—*University of Cincinnati*

Margaretha Rudstrom—*University of Minnesota, Crookston*

Fred Ruppel—*Eastern Kentucky University*

Farhad Saboori—*Albright College*

Jeff Sarbaum—*University of North Carolina, Greensboro*

Mark Scanlan—*Stephen F. Austin State University*

Katherine Schmeiser—*Mount Holyoke College*

Eckhard Siggel—*Concordia University, Montreal*

Annie Voy—*Gonzaga University*

Linda Wilcox Young—*Southern Oregon University*

Zhen Zhu—*University of Central Oklahoma*

For the third edition, we had a wonderful response to a survey focused on our supplements. We want to thank all of the survey respondents:

Ahmed Abou-Zaid—*Eastern Illinois University*

Francis Ahking—*University of Connecticut*

Syed Ahmed—*Cameron University*

Ugur Aker—*Hiram College*

Abiye Alamina—*Bowling Green State University*

Basil Al-Hashimi—*Mesa Community College*

William Amponsah—*Georgia Southern University*

Gary Anders—*Arizona State University*

James Anderson—*Boston College*

Samuel Andoh—*Southern Connecticut State University*

Adina Ardelean—*Santa Clara University*

Ferry Ardiyanto—*Colorado State University*

Iris Au—*University of Toronto, Scarborough*

Joel Auerbach—*Florida Atlantic University*

Sofyan Azaizeh—*University of New Haven*

Chris Azevedo—*University of Central Missouri*

Werner Baer—*University of Illinois, Urbana-Champaign*

Mohsen Bahmani-Oskooee—*University of Wisconsin, Milwaukee*

Scott Baier—*Clemson University*

Jeremy Baker—*Owens Community College*

Rita Balaban—*University of North Carolina, Chapel Hill*

Lila Balla—*St. Louis University*

James Bang—*Saint Ambrose University*

Thomas Baranga—*University of California, San Diego*

Gregory Besharov—*Cornell University*

Joel Blit—*Waterloo University*

Antonio Bojanic—*Humboldt State University*

Bogdan Bonca—*George Washington University*

Russell Boyer—*University of Western Ontario*

Laura Brown—*University of Manitoba*

Jim Bruehler—*Eastern Illinois University*

Joel Bruneau—*University of Saskatchewan, Saskatoon*

Vera Brusentsev—*Swarthmore College*

Hector Butts—*Morris Brown College*

Doyle Butts—*John Brown University*

Andrew Cassey—*Washington State University*

Alberto Cavallo—*Massachusetts Institute of Technology*

Bledi Celiku—*Georgetown University*

Suparna Chakraborty—*Baruch College*

Thomas Chaney—*University of Chicago*

Roberto Chang—*Rutgers University*

John Chilton—*Virginia Commonwealth University*

Michael Clark—*Wesleyan University*

Reid Click—*George Washington University*

Catherine Co—*University of Nebraska, Omaha*

Jim Cobbe—*Florida State University*

Tracy Collins—*North Carolina State University*

AnaMaria Conley—*Regis University*

Matias Cortes—*University of British Columbia*

Antoinette Criss—*University of South Florida*

Anca Cristea—*University of Oregon*

William Crowder—*University of Texas, Arlington*

Wilfrid Csaplar, Jr.—*Bethany College*

Meenakshi Dalal—*Wayne State College*

John Dalton—*Wake Forest University*

Joseph Daniels—*Marquette University*

Amaresh Das—*Southern University at New Orleans*

Kunal Dasgupta—*University of Toronto, St. George Camp*

Judy Dean—*State University of New York, Brockport*

Mamit Deme—*Middle Tennessee State University*

James DeVault—*Lafayette University*

Daniel Dias—*University of Illinois, Urbana-Champaign*

Vaughn Dickson—*University of New Brunswick, Fredericton*

Asif Dowla—*St. Mary's College of Maryland*

Justin Dubas—*Texas Lutheran University*

Anthony Elson—*Johns Hopkins School of Advanced International Studies*

Can Erbil—*Boston College*

Lee Erickson—*Taylor University*

Xin Fang—*Hawaii Pacific University*

Barbara Fischer—*Cardinal Stritch University*

Sherry Forbes—*Sweet Briar College*

David Franck—*University of Tennessee, Martin*

Joseph Friedman—*Temple University*

Diana Fuguitt—*Eckerd College*

Michael Fusillo—*Tufts University*

Stefania Garetto—*Boston University*

Doris Geide-Stevenson—*Weber State University*

Pedro Gete—*Georgetown University*

Soumen Ghosh—*Tennessee State University*

Alex Gialanella—*Manhattanville College*

Harvey Gram—*Queens College, City University of New York*

Jason Grant—*Virginia Tech*

David Griffith—*Austin College*

Elias Grivoyannis—*Yeshiva University*

Stephen Grubaugh—*Bentley College*

Ronald Gunderson—*Northern Arizona University*

Jane Hall—*California State University, Fullerton*

David Harris—*Benedictine College*

Britt Hastey—*Los Angeles City College*

William Hauk—*University of South Carolina*

Denise Hazlett—*Whitman College*

Aldo Heffner—*Northwestern University*

Scott Hegerty—*Northeastern Illinois University*

Ralf Hepp—*Fordham University*

Pablo Hernandez—*Hollins University*

Chang Hong—*Clark University*

David Hummels—*Purdue University*

Brian Hunt—*Georgia State University*

Jamal Husein—*Angelo State University*

Lowell Jacobsen—*Baker University*

Carl Jensen—*Rutgers University*

Michael Jolly—*Ryerson University*

Jason Jones—*Furman University*

Serdar Kabaca—*University of British Columbia*

Mahbubul Kabir—*Lyon College*

Fadhel Kaboub—*Denison University*

Hyunju Kang—*The Ohio State University*

Hugo Kaufmann—*Queens College, City University New York*

Erasmus Kersting—*Villanova University*

Octave Keutiben—*Glendon College*

Farida Khan—*University of Wisconsin, Parkside*

Ali Khan—*Johns Hopkins University*

Chong-Uk Kim—*Sonoma State University*

Colin Knapp—*University of Florida*

Samuel Kohn—*Touro College, Brooklyn*

Jeff Konz—*University of North Carolina, Asheville*

Bill Kosteas—*Cleveland State University*

Robert Krol—*California State University, Northridge*

Kishore Kulkarni—*Metropolitan State Unversity of Denver*

Carsten Lange—*California State Polytechnic University, Pomona*

Harvey Lapan—*Iowa State University*

Dave LaRivee—*United States Air Force Academy*

Daniel Lee—*Shippensburg University*

Yu-Feng Lee—*New Mexico State University*

James Lehman—*Pomona College*

Byron Lew—*Trent University*

Willis Lewis—*Winthrop University*

Carlos Liard-Muriente—*Central Connecticut State University*

Ben Liebman—*St. Joseph's University*

Tony Lima—*California State University, East Bay*

Xuepeng Liu—*Kennesaw State University*

Ricardo Lopez—*Indiana University*

Mary Lovely—*Syracuse University*

Volodymyr Lugovskyy—*Indiana University*

Rita Madarassy—*Westminster College*

Margaret Malixi—*California State University, Bakersfield*

Catherine Mann—*Brandeis University*

Kalina Manova—*Stanford University*

Mary Marchant—*Virginia Tech*

Kathryn Marshall—*California State Polytechnic University, San Luis Obispo*

Tim Mason—*Eastern Illinois University*

Fred May—*Trident Technical College*

Peter Mayer—*University of Wisconsin, Osh Kosh*

Cynthia McCarty—*Jacksonville State University*

Rachel McCulloch—*Brandeis University*

Jerry McElroy—*St. Mary's College*

Diego Mendez-Carbajo—*Illinois Wesleyan University*

Edward Merkel—*Troy University*

Ida Mirzaie—*Ohio State University*

Ilir Miteza—*University of Michigan, Dearborn*

Shahruz Mohtadi—*Suffolk University*

Shalah Mostashari—*University of Iowa*

Rebecca Neumann—*University of Colorado*

Trien Nguyen—*University of Waterloo*

Jasminka Ninkovic—*Emory University*

Shuichiro Nishioka—*West Virginia University*

Dmitri Nizovtsev—*Washburn University*

Stanley Nollen—*Georgetown University*

Joe Nowakowski—*Muskingum University*

Kathleen Odell—*Dominican University*

Constantin Ogloblin—*Georgia Southern University*

Ilaria Ossella-Durbal—*Illinois Wesleyan University*

Tomi Ovaska—*Youngstown State University*

Suleyman Ozmucur—*University of Pennsylvania*

Kerry Pannell—*De Pauw University*

Kit Pasula—*University of British Columbia, Okanagan*

Nina Pavcnik—*Dartmouth College*

Lourenco Paz—*Syracuse University*

Elizabeth Perry-Sizemore—*Randolph College*

Nam Pham—*George Washington University*

Diep Phan—*Beloit College*

Roger Philips—*Concordia University*

Thomas Pieplow—*Athens State University*

Gina Pieters—*University of Minnesota*

Jane Pietrowski—*Mary Baldwin College*

Jeff Pliskin—*Hamilton College*

Jim Polito—*Lonestar College*

Vincenzo Quadrini—*University of Southern California*

Fernando Quijano—*Dickinson State University*

Reza Ramazani—*Saint Michael's College*

Natalia Ramondo—*University of Texas*

Artatrana Ratha—*St. Cloud State University*

James Rauch—*University of California, San Diego*

Arslan Razmi—*University of Massachusetts, Amherst*

Hyuk-jae Rhee—*Michigan State University*

Ray Riezman—*University of Iowa*

Helen Roberts—*University of Illinois, Chicago*

Wade C. Roberts—*University of Utah*

Mari Robertson—*University of Cincinnati*

Malcolm Robinson—*Thomas More College*

Carol Rogers—*Georgetown University*

Michael Rolleigh—*Williams College*

Jacek Rothert—*University of Minnesota, Twin Cities*

Philip Rothman—*East Carolina University*

Jayjit Roy—*Appalachian State University*

Camilo Rubbini—*Indiana University of Pennsylvania*

Margot Rudstrom—*Virginia Secondary School*

Rochelle Ruffer—*Nazareth College*

Fred Ruppel—*Eastern Kentucky University*

David R. Sabiston—*University of Calgary*

Farhad Saboori—*Albright College*

Rupi Saggi—*Southern Methodist University*

Jeff Sarbaum—*University of North Carolina, Greensboro*

Mark Scanlan—*Stephen F. Austin State University*

Georg Schaur—*University of Tennessee, Knoxville*

Katherine Schmeiser—*Mount Holyoke College*

Nicolas Schmitt—*Simon Fraser University*

Peter Schott—*Yale University*

Aberra Senbeta—*Bloomsburg University*

Richard Sicotte—*University of Vermont*

Eckhard Siggel—*Concordia University*

Rajesh Singh—*Iowa State University*

Ken Slaysman—*York College of Pennsylvania*

Constance Smith—*University of Alberta*

Gregor Smith—*Queens University, Kingston*

Julie Smith—*Lafayette College*

David Sobiechowski—*University of Michigan, Dearborn*

Arjun Sondhi—*Wayne State University*

Robert Sonora—*Fort Lewis College*

Charles Staelin—*Smith College*

Paul Stock—*University of Mary Hardin, Baylor*

Edward Stuart—*Northeastern Illinois University*

Chuck Stull—*Michigan State University*

Vera Tabakova—*East Carolina University*

Wendy Takacs—*University of Maryland*

Robert Teitelbaum—*Empire State College*

Tommaso Tempesti—*University of Massachusetts, Lowell*

Richard Torz—*Saint Joseph's College, New York*

Peter Tracey—*University of Calgary*

Richard Trainer—*Nassau Community College*

Arja Turunen-Red—*University of New Orleans*

Geetha Vaidyanathan—*University of North Carolina, Chapel Hill*

Marc von der Ruhr—*Saint Norbert College*

Pablo Vega-Garcia—*George Washington University*

Annie Voy—*Gonzaga University*

Tatsuma Wada—*Wayne State University*

Andreas Waldkirch—*Colby College*

Doug Waldo—*University of Florida*

Rui Wan—*University of Calgary*

Xiao Wang—*University of North Dakota*

Jane Waples—*Memorial University*

Chris Warburton—*John Jay College, City University of New York*

Tonia Warnecke—*Rollins College*

Matt Warning—*University of Puget Sound*

William Watson—*McGill University*

Scott Wentland—*George Mason University*

Mark Wessel—*Carnegie Mellon University*

Ben Widner—*New Mexico State University*

Joan Wiggenhorn—*Barry University*

David Wildasin—*University of Kentucky*

Mark Wohar—*University of Nebraska, Omaha*

Mickey Wu—*Coe College*

Peter Wylie—*University of British Columbia, Okanagan*

Bill Yang—*Georgia Southern University*

Mahmut Yasar—*Emory University*

Hakan Yilmazkuday—*Temple University*

Linda Young—*Southern Oregon University*

Kevin Zhang—*Illinois State University*

Dan Zhao—*Austin College*
Haiwen Zhou—*Old Dominion University*
Zhen Zhu—*University of Central Oklahoma*
Susan Zhu—*Michigan State University*

For the second edition, we benefited from the suggestions of the following reviewers:

Bradley Andrew—*Juniata College*
Damyana Bakardzhieva—*George Washington University*
Mina Baliamoune—*University of North Florida*
Valerie Bencivenga—*University of Texas at Austin*
Emily Blanchard—*University of Virginia*
Nicola Borri—*Boston University*
Drusilla Brown—*Tufts University*
Vera Brusentsev—*University of Delaware*
Colleen Callahan—*American University*
Geoffrey Carliner—*Boston University*
Ron Cronovich—*Carthage College*
Firat Demir—*University of Oklahoma*
Asim Erdilek—*Case Western Reserve University*
John Gilbert—*Utah State University*
William Hauk—*University of South Carolina*
David Hummels—*Purdue University*
Hakan Inal—*Virginia Commonwealth University*
Alan Isaac—*American University*
Robert Jerome—*James Madison University*
Grace Johnson—*Oklahoma State University, Tulsa*
Kathy Kelly—*University of Texas at Arlington*
Bill Kosteas—*Cleveland State University*
Ricardo Lopez—*Indiana University*

Volodymyr Lugovskyy—*Georgia Tech*
Nicolas Magud—*University of Oregon*
Keith Malone—*University of North Alabama*
Maria Maniagurria—*University of Wisconsin, Madison*
Catherine Mann—*Brandeis University*
Steven J. Matusz—*Michigan State University*
Fabio Mendez—*University of Arkansas*
William Mertens—*University of Colorado at Boulder*
Rebecca Neumann—*University of Wisconsin, Milwaukee*
Emanuel Ornelas—*London School of Economics*
Perry Patterson—*Wake Forest University*
Masha Rahnama—*Texas Tech University*
Michael Rinkus—*Walsh College*
Sheikh Shahnawaz—*University of Southern California*
David Sobiechowski—*University of Michigan, Dearborn*
Steve Steib—*University of Tulsa*
Nicholas Stratis—*Florida State University*
Edward Tower—*Duke University*
Elizabeth Wheaton—*Southern Methodist University*
Peter Wylie—*University of British Columbia, Okanagan*

We would like to thank the following instructors for sharing their ideas with us in the development of the first edition. These colleagues were enthusiastic about the reception of their students to our fresh approach.

Joshua Aizenman—*University of California, Santa Cruz*
Scott Baier—*Clemson University*
Paul Bergin—*University of California, Davis*
Matilde Bombardini—*University of British Columbia, Vancouver*
Drusilla Brown—*Tufts University*
Avik Chakraborty—*University of Tennessee, Knoxville*
Gordon Hanson—*University of California, San Diego*
James Harrigan—*University of Virginia*
Takeo Hoshi—*University of California, San Diego*
David Hummels—*Purdue University*

Samuel Kortum—*University of Chicago*
John McLaren—*University of Virginia*
Robert Murphy—*Boston College*
Constantin Ogloblin—*Georgia Southern University*
Kevin O'Rourke—*Trinity College, Dublin*
Sanjay Paul—*Elizabethtown College*
Priya Ranjan—*University of California, Irvine*
Andrés Rodriguez-Clare—*Pennsylvania State University*
Katheryn Russ—*University of California, Davis*
Stephen Stageberg—*University of Mary Washington*
Bruce Wydick—*University of San Francisco*
Stephen Yeaple—*Pennsylvania State University*

A huge number of colleagues were very helpful in reviewing the first-edition manuscript. We wish to thank the following reviewers:

Joshua Aizenman—*University of California, Santa Cruz*

Mohsen Bahmani-Oskooee—*University of Wisconsin, Milwaukee*

Scott Baier—*Clemson University*

Richard Baillie—*Michigan State University*

Joe Bell—*Missouri State University*

Paul Bergin—*University of California, Davis*

Robert Blecker—*American University*

Roger Butters—*University of Nebraska, Lincoln*

Francisco Carrada-Bravo—*Arizona State University*

Menzie Chinn—*University of Wisconsin, Madison*

Richard Chisik—*Florida International University*

Ann Davis—*Marist College*

Robert Driskill—*Vanderbilt University*

James Fain—*Oklahoma State University*

David H. Feldman—*The College of William & Mary*

Diane Flaherty—*University of Massachusetts, Amherst*

Jean-Ellen Giblin—*Fashion Institute of Technology*

Bill Gibson—*University of Vermont*

Thomas Grennes—*North Carolina State University*

Gordon Hanson—*University of California, San Diego*

Mehdi Haririan—*Bloomsburg University*

James Harrigan—*University of Virginia*

Takeo Hoshi—*University of California, San Diego*

Douglas Irwin—*Dartmouth College*

Michael Klein—*Tufts University*

Kala Krishna—*Pennsylvania State University*

Maria Kula—*Roger Williams University*

Ricardo Lopez—*Indiana University*

Mary Lovely—*Syracuse University*

Barbara Lowrey—*University of Maryland*

Steven Matusz—*Michigan State University*

Jose Mendez—*Arizona State University*

Shannon Mitchell—*Virginia Commonwealth University*

Farshid Mojaver Hosseini—*University of California, Davis*

Marc A. Muendler—*University of California, San Diego*

Maria Muniagurria—*University of Wisconsin, Madison*

Robert Murphy—*Boston College*

Ranganath Murthy—*Bucknell University*

Kanda Naknoi—*Purdue University*

Constantin Ogloblin—*Georgia Southern University*

Kevin O'Rourke—*Trinity College, Dublin*

Kerry Pannell—*DePauw University*

Jaishankar Raman—*Valparaiso University*

Raymond Robertson—*Macalester College*

Andrés Rodriguez-Clare—*Pennsylvania State University*

Hadi Salehi-Esfahani—*University of Illinois at Urbana-Champaign*

Andreas Savvides—*Oklahoma State University*

Till Schreiber—*The College of William & Mary*

Gunjan Sharma—*University of Missouri, Columbia*

John Subrick—*George Mason University*

Mark P. Taylor—*University of Warwick*

Linda Tesar—*University of Michigan, Ann Arbor*

Geetha Vaidyanathan—*University of North Carolina at Greensboro*

Kristin Van Gaasbeck—*California State University, Sacramento*

Gary Wells—*Clemson University*

Mark Wohar—*University of Nebraska, Omaha*

Susan Wolcott—*State University of New York, Binghamton*

Bin Xu—*China Europe International Business School*

Stephen Yeaple—*Pennsylvania State University*

We received useful feedback from focus group participants. We would like to thank the following individuals:

Mohsen Bahmani-Oskooee—*University of Wisconsin, Milwaukee*

Roger Butters—*University of Nebraska, Lincoln*

Francisco Carrada-Bravo—*Arizona State University*

Mitchell Charkiewicz—*Central Connecticut State University*

Menzie Chinn—*University of Wisconsin, Madison*

Carl Davidson—*Michigan State University*

Ann Davis—*Marist College*

Robert Driskill—*Vanderbilt University*

Eric Fisher—*California Polytechnic State University, San Luis Obispo*

Diane Flaherty—*University of Massachusetts, Amherst*

Bill Gibson—*University of Vermont*

Thomas Grennes—*North Carolina State University*

Mehdi Haririan—*Bloomsburg University*

Andreas Hauskrecht—*Indiana University*

Andrew Hughes-Hallett—*Vanderbilt University*

Eckhard Janeba—*University of Mannheim*

Mary Lovely—*Syracuse University*

Marc Melitz—*Harvard University*

Norman Miller—*Miami University of Ohio*

Shannon Mitchell—*Virginia Commonwealth University*

Ranganath Murthy—*Bucknell University*

Rebecca Neumann—*University of Wisconsin, Milwaukee*

Constantin Ogloblin—*Georgia Southern University*

Lucjan Orlowski—*Sacred Heart University*

Jeff Pliskin—*Hamilton College*

Francisca Richter—*Cleveland State University*

Hadi Salehi-Esfahani—*University of Illinois at Urbana-Champaign*

Bin Xu—*China Europe International Business School*

We would like to thank the following individuals who provided feedback on the initial preliminary version of the first edition of our text:

Scott Baier—*Clemson University*

Paul Bergin—*University of California, Davis*

Luisa Blanco Raynal—*Pepperdine University*

James Cassing—*University of Pittsburgh*

Ted Fu—*Stanford University*

James Harrigan—*University of Virginia*

David Hummels—*Purdue University*

Farshid Mojaver Hosseini—*University of California, Davis*

Maria Muniagurria—*University of Wisconsin, Madison*

Kanda Naknoi—*Purdue University*

Raymond Robertson—*Macalester College*

Andrés Rodriguez-Clare—*Pennsylvania State University*

Jeffrey Rosensweig—*Emory University*

Jennifer Steele—*University of Texas at Austin*

Asha Sundaram—*Syracuse University*

Kristin Van Gaasbeck—*California State University, Sacramento*

Wolfgang Keller—*University of Colorado at Boulder*

We would like to thank the following instructors who have aided us in the preparation and extensive review of the ancillary package. This list of contributors and reviewers is comprehensive of those who have contributed across editions at this time and will continue to grow as new resources are developed.

Francis Ahking—*University of Connecticut*

Ron Davies—*University College, Dublin*

Justin Dubas—*Texas Lutheran University*

Chang Hong—*Clark University*

Anthony Lima—*California State University, East Bay*

Alyson Ma—*University of San Diego*

Terry Monson—*Michigan Technological University*

Robert Murphy—*Boston College*

Sanjay Paul—*Elizabethtown College*

Jaishankar Raman—*Valparaiso University*

Rajesh Singh—*Iowa State University*

Millicent Sites—*Carson-Newman College*

Alexandre Skiba—*University of Wyoming*

Robert Sonora—*Fort Lewis College*

Marie Truesdell—*Marian College*

Kristin Van Gaasbeck—*California State University, Sacramento*

Stephen Yeaple—*Pennsylvania State University*

We would also like to thank our families, especially Claire and Gail, for their sustained support during the time we have devoted to writing this book.

Finally, you will see an accompanying picture of children in Ciudad Darío, Nicaragua, with their teacher, in the classroom of a small schoolhouse that was built for them by Seeds of Learning (www.seedsoflearning.org), a nonprofit organization dedicated to improving educational opportunities in rural Latin America. A portion of the royalties from this book go toward supporting the work of Seeds of Learning.

ROBERT C. FEENSTRA

ALAN M. TAYLOR

Davis, California
December 2013

Sixth-grade class with their teacher in La Carreta #2 school in Ciudad Darío, Nicaragua.

third edition

international economics

Trade in the Global Economy

The emergence of China, India, and the former communist-bloc countries implies that the greater part of the earth's population is now engaged, at least potentially, in the global economy. There are no historical antecedents for this development.

Ben Bernanke, chairman of the U.S. Federal Reserve, 2006

The main losers in today's very unequal world are not those who are too much exposed to globalization. They are those who have been left out.

Kofi Annan, former secretary general of the United Nations, 2000

In August 2009, the ships *Beluga Fraternity* and *Beluga Foresight* made a historic voyage through the Northern Sea Route of the Arctic Ocean, accompanied by a Russian nuclear icebreaker. These ships carried power-plant components from South Korea, around the top of Russia, to the Siberian port of Novy, where the cargo was unloaded. The ships continued westward to the city of Rotterdam in the Netherlands. This was one of the first times that commercial ships had successfully navigated this northern route through the Arctic Circle, and it was made possible by the shrinkage of Arctic ice in recent years. It is believed that global warming is causing the Arctic ice to melt, which will open up new shipping lanes through the Arctic Ocean.

In this historical milestone, we see that global climate change can have important consequences for **international trade,** by which we mean the movement of goods (such as cargo) and services (such as the shipping of the cargo) across borders. To move goods from South Korea (or elsewhere in Asia) to Europe would normally involve a trip through the Suez Canal (in the Middle East) at much greater cost. The Northern Sea Route is shorter than the Suez Canal route by about 4,000 nautical miles. If the Northern Sea Route becomes passable for much of the year, then we would expect that the amount of trade from Asia to Europe will increase.

In this book, we will study international trade in goods and services and will learn the economic forces that determine what that trade looks like: what products are traded; who trades them; at what quantities and prices they are traded; and what the

Melting icebergs in Disko Bay, Greenland

benefits and costs of trade are. We will also learn about the policies that governments use to shape trade patterns among countries.

Why should we care about international trade? Many people believe that international trade creates opportunities for countries to grow and thrive. The manufacture of goods exported from China, for example, creates employment for many millions of workers there. The same is true for exports from the United States and European countries. It is not just large countries that potentially benefit from trade; smaller countries, too, are affected. In Greenland, for example, higher temperatures due to global warming have exposed deposits of "rare earth" minerals, such as lanthanum and neodymium, which are used in cell phones and other high-tech devices. Because of international trade, Greenland is expected to benefit from exporting these rare earth minerals to meet global demand. But such benefits can also bring difficult social change and challenges, as the traditional lifestyle of fishing becomes less crucial to Greenland's economy. In this book we will explore both the opportunities and challenges created by international trade for different groups in society.

Let's begin by looking at a very broad picture of international trade. What country was the world's largest exporter of goods in 2012? If you guessed China, you are right: since 2009, it overtook Germany as the top exporter. In 2012, China sold around $2.0 trillion in goods to other countries, ahead of the $1.6 trillion exported by the second-place country, the United States. The third largest exporter of goods was Germany, which exported $1.5 trillion in goods.

These numbers reveal only part of the trade picture, however, because in addition to exporting goods, countries also export services. In 2012 the United States exported $0.6 trillion in services (including business services, education of foreign students, travel by foreigners, and so forth). If we combine exports in goods and services, then in 2012 the world's largest exporter was the United States at $2.2 trillion, followed by China, Germany, the United Kingdom, and Japan.

Nations trade goods for many reasons, the most obvious of which is that they can get products from abroad that are cheaper or of higher quality than those they can produce at home. For example, Germany was the largest exporter of goods up until 2009, a position that reflected its world-class technologies for producing high-quality manufactured goods, such as cars like the BMW and Mercedes-Benz. China, on the other hand, can produce goods more cheaply than most industrial countries. The United States has both the technology to produce high-quality manufactured goods and the ability to produce agricultural goods very cheaply (because of its abundant land resources as well as government policies).

In the first part of this book, we develop a number of models that help us understand the reasons that countries trade goods and services. In addition, we investigate **migration,** the flow of people across borders as they move from one country to another, and **foreign direct investment (FDI),** the flow of capital across borders when a firm owns a company in another country. All three types of flows between countries—of products (goods and services), people, and capital—are so common today that we take them for granted. When you go into a store to purchase an item, for example, it is possible that it was made in another country, the store itself might be foreign-owned, and the salesperson who assists you may be an immigrant. Why are these international flows so common? What are the consequences of these flows for the countries involved? And what actions do governments take to make their countries more or less open to trade, migration, and FDI? These are the questions we address.

1 International Trade

This section begins our study of international economics by defining some important terms and summarizing the overall trends in world trade.

The Basics of World Trade

Countries buy and sell goods and services from one another constantly. An **export** is a product sold from one country to another, and an **import** is a product bought by one country from another. We normally think of exports and imports as goods that are shipped between countries, but for services that is not necessarily the case. Construction services, for example, are performed on-site in the importing country rather than being shipped. Travel and tourism are large categories of service exports that also occur on-site: the money spent by a U.S. visitor to the Eiffel Tower is a service export of France, and a Chinese visitor to the Grand Canyon adds to U.S. service exports.

A country's **trade balance** is the difference between its total value of exports and its total value of imports (usually including both goods and services). Countries that export more than they import, such as China in recent years, run a **trade surplus,** whereas countries that import more than they export, such as the United States, run a **trade deficit.** In addition to keeping track of the overall trade balance for a country with the rest of the world, we often see reported in the newspaper the **bilateral trade balance,** meaning the difference between exports and imports between two countries. The U.S. bilateral trade balance with China, for example, has been a trade deficit of more than $200 billion every year between 2005 and 2012.

In the models developed to understand international trade, we are not concerned with whether a country has a trade deficit or surplus but just assume that each country has balanced trade, with exports equal to imports. There are two reasons why we make this assumption. First, economists believe that an overall trade deficit or surplus arises from macroeconomic conditions, such as the overall levels of spending and savings in an economy—countries with high spending and low savings will run a trade deficit. (Macroeconomic conditions are studied in the second half of this book that deals with international macroeconomics.)

Second, the interpretation of a trade deficit or surplus is problematic when we focus on the bilateral trade balance between two countries, such as the United States and China. To see what the problem is, think about the U.S. import of a particular good from China, such as the iPhone (see **Headlines: Sum of iPhone Parts: Trade Distortion).**

In 2010, the iPhone 3GS was valued at about $179 when it was shipped from China to the United States, and it sold for about $500 in the United States. However only $6.50 of that amount reflects the value of Chinese labor used in the assembly.[1] The rest of the $172.50 export value was actually imported into China from other countries, including: $60 for the flash memory, display module, and touch screen from Toshiba in Japan; $23 for the processor chip and memory from Samsung in Korea; $29 for the camera and transmitting and receiving devices from Infineon in Germany, and so on. Nevertheless, the entire $179 is counted as an export from China to the United States. This example shows that the bilateral trade deficit or surplus between countries is a slippery concept. It doesn't really make sense to count the entire $179 iPhone as a Chinese export to the United States, as is done in official trade statistics, when only $6.50 is the **value-added** in China; that is, the difference between the value of the iPhone when it leaves China and the cost of parts and materials purchased in China and imported from other countries. That shortcoming of official statistics gives us a good reason to not focus on the bilateral trade deficit or surplus between countries, even though that number is often reported in the media.

The iPhone example illustrates how the manufacturing required for a single final product is often spread across many countries. That so many countries can be involved in manufacturing a final product and its components is a new phenomenon that illustrates the drop in transportation and communication costs in the modern world economy. In the past, trade occurred in more standardized goods (such as raw materials) that were shipped long distances, but were not shipped back-and-forth between countries during the manufacturing process. This new feature of world trade and production, often called **offshoring,** is discussed later in the book; here, we present the idea by looking at how trade patterns have changed over time.

[1] See Yuqing Xing and Neal Detert, "How the iPhone Widens the United States Trade Deficit with the People's Republic of China," Asian Development Bank Institute, Working Paper no. 257, December 2010 (revised May 2011), from which the estimates in this paragraph are drawn. They cite: A. Rassweiler, "iPhone 3G S Carries $178.96 BOM and Manufacturing Cost, iSuppli Teardown Reveals," *iSuppli*, 24, June 2009.

HEADLINES

Sum of iPhone Parts: Trade Distortion

Although the iPhone sold in the United States is assembled in China, most of its value comes from parts made in other countries. Counting its full value as a U.S. import from China therefore exaggerates the size of the U.S. trade deficit with China.

One widely touted solution for current U.S. economic woes is for America to come up with more of the high-tech gadgets that the rest of the world craves. Yet two academic researchers have found that Apple Inc.'s iPhone—one of the most iconic U.S. technology products—actually added $19 billion to the U.S. trade deficit with China last year. How is this possible?

. . . Though the iPhone is entirely designed and owned by a U.S. company, and is made largely of parts produced in other countries, it is physically assembled in China. Both countries' trade statistics therefore consider the iPhone a Chinese export to the U.S. So a U.S. consumer who buys what is often considered an American product will add to the U.S. trade deficit with China. The result is that according to official statistics, "even high-tech products invented by U.S. companies will not increase U.S. exports,". . . . This isn't a problem with high-tech products, but with how exports and imports are measured . . .

The new research adds to a growing technical debate about traditional trade statistics that could have big real-world consequences. Conventional trade figures are the basis for political battles waging in Washington and Brussels over what to do about China's currency policies and its allegedly unfair trading practices. But there is a growing belief that the practice of assuming every product shipped from one country is entirely produced by that country may need to be adjusted. "What we call 'Made in China' is indeed assembled in China, but what makes up the commercial value of the product comes from the numerous countries that preceded its assembly in China in the global value chain," Pascal Lamy, the director-general of the World Trade Organization, said in a speech in October. "The concept of country of origin for manufactured goods has gradually become obsolete." Mr. Lamy said that if trade statistics were adjusted to reflect the actual value contributed to a product by different countries, the size of the U.S. trade deficit with China—$226.88 billion, according to U.S. figures—would be cut in half. That

Products like the Apple iPhone are often assembled in China from components made in many other countries.

means, he argued, that political tensions over trade deficits are probably larger than they should be.

Source: Excerpted from Andrew Batson, "Sum of iPhone Parts: Trade Distortion," The Wall Street Journal, December 16, 2010, p. 3. Reprinted with permission of The Wall Street Journal, Copyright © 2010 Dow Jones & Company, Inc. All Rights Reserved Worldwide.

APPLICATION

Is Trade Today Different from the Past?

Is the type of trade today different from that in the past? The answer to this question is *yes*. Not only is there more international trade today than in the past, but the type of trade has also changed. We can see the changes in the type of trade by organizing imports and exports into four categories, depending on their use in the economy: (1) foods, feeds, and beverages; (2) industrial supplies and materials (raw materials like chemicals and petroleum and basic processed goods, such as steel, newsprint, and textiles); (3) capital goods (durable goods including aircraft, cars, computers, machinery, and so forth); (4) finished consumer goods (all finished household goods, except cars and computers, but including the iPhone). The percentage of U.S. imports and exports accounted for by these four categories from 1925 to 2010 is shown in Figure 1-1, with U.S. imports in panel (a) and exports in panel (b).

In Figure 1-1(a), we see that U.S. trade has shifted away from agriculture and raw materials and toward manufactured goods, as shown by the declining shares of foods, feeds, and beverages and industrial supplies and materials. Together, these two categories of traded goods accounted for 90% of imports in 1925 but only about 40%

FIGURE 1-1

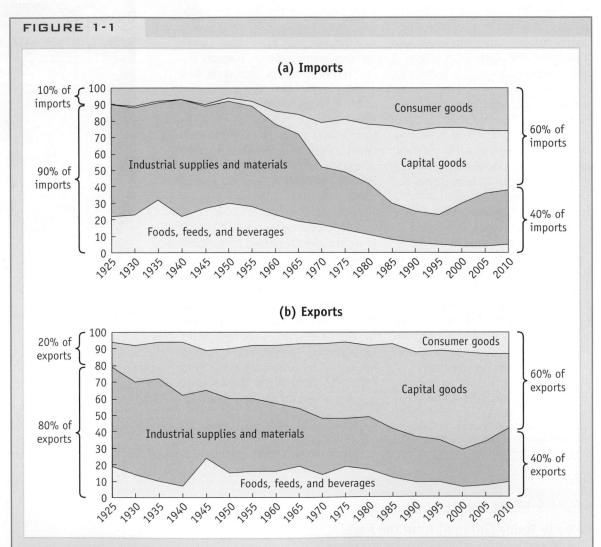

The Changing Face of U.S. Import and Export Industries, 1925–2010 The types of goods imported and exported by the United States have changed drastically over the past century. Foods, feeds, and beverages and industrial supplies were 90% of imports in 1925, but represented only 40% in 2010. These categories' shares of exports have also fallen from 80% in 1925 to 40% in 2010. Capital plus consumer goods plus automobiles have increased from 10% of imports in 1925 to 60% of imports in 2010. Exports of these goods have likewise increased from 20% in 1925 to 60% in 2010.

Source: Bureau of Economic Analysis.

in 2010. Figure 1-1(b) shows that the export share of these same categories also fell from about 80% to 40% over that time.

Figure 1-1(a) also shows that the imports of capital goods plus consumer goods have increased from 10% in 1925 to 60% in 2010. In Figure 1-1(b), we see that the export of capital plus consumer goods has likewise increased from about 20% of exports in 1925 to about 60% of exports in 2010. Capital goods and consumer products (including the iPhone) are the types of goods that are most likely to have a portion of their production process sent overseas through offshoring. The fact that the share of trade in these products has increased shows that the type of trade today has changed greatly from the past.

Map of World Trade

To show the flow of exports and imports around the world, we use the map in Figure 1-2, which shows trade in billions of dollars for 2010. That year about $16.8 trillion in goods crossed international borders. (Because trade in services is harder to measure between countries, we do not include it in Figure 1-2.) The amount

FIGURE 1-2

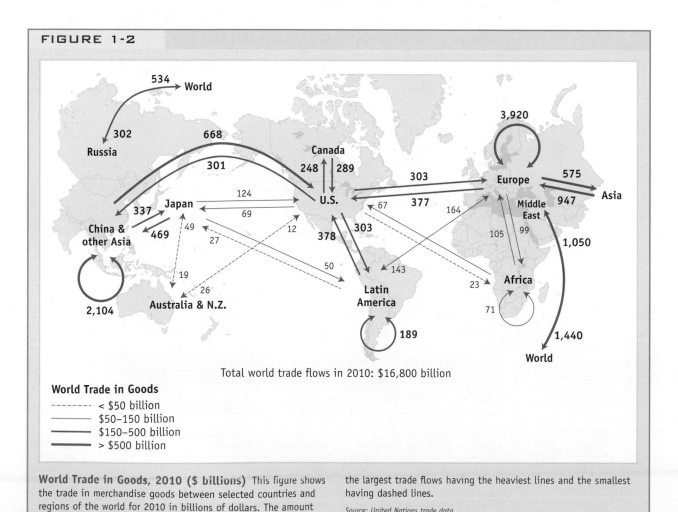

Total world trade flows in 2010: $16,800 billion

World Trade in Goods
- - - - - - - - < $50 billion
——————— $50–150 billion
——————— $150–500 billion
——————— > $500 billion

World Trade in Goods, 2010 ($ billions) This figure shows the trade in merchandise goods between selected countries and regions of the world for 2010 in billions of dollars. The amount of trade in goods is illustrated by the width of the lines, with the largest trade flows having the heaviest lines and the smallest having dashed lines.

Source: United Nations trade data.

of trade in goods is illustrated by the width of the lines, with the largest trade flows having the heaviest lines and the smallest having dashed lines. For large trade flows, we usually draw two lines indicating the direction of each trade flow. For smaller amounts of trade, we draw a single dashed line, with the amount of the trade flows shown on each arrow. The trade flows within certain regions, such as Europe, are described by a circle, with the total amount of trade shown.

European and U.S. Trade The largest amount of trade shown in Figure 1-2 is the flow of goods within Europe, which was $3.9 trillion in 2010, or almost one-quarter (23%) of world trade! This fact is shown in Table 1-1 as internal trade within Europe. The European countries trade a great deal with one another because there are so many countries located there and because it is easy to ship from one country to another. Furthermore, trade is high because **import tariffs** (taxes on international trade) are low. The European Union is a group of countries within Europe that have zero tariffs on imports from one another. That group of countries expanded from 15 to 25 members in 2004, with two more countries joining in 2007, so most of the European countries trade with each other at zero tariffs.[2]

In addition to large trade flows among the European countries, there are also large trade flows between the United States and Europe. The United States exported $303 billion of goods to Europe in 2010 and imported $377 billion of goods from Europe. If we add those flows to the trade flow within Europe, we find that Europe and the United States account for about $4.6 trillion, or 27%, of the $16.8 trillion in world trade flows. This fact is also recorded in Table 1-1, and it shows that a large amount

---

TABLE 1-1

Shares of World Trade, Accounted for by Selected Regions, 2010 This table shows the share of trade within each region, or the share of exports from each region, as a percentage of total world trade in 2010. Europe and the Americas combined account for about one-half (51%) of world exports, and Asia accounts for another one-third (34%) of world exports.

	Share of World Trade (%)		Share of World Trade (%)
Europe (internal trade)	23	Asia (exports)	34
Europe (internal) plus trade with the U.S.	27	Middle East and Russia (exports)	12
Americas (internal trade)	8	Africa (exports)	2
Europe and the Americas (exports)	51	Australia and New Zealand (exports)	1.6

Note: The shares of world trade are calculated from Figure 1-2, as explained in the text. The Americas includes North, Central, and South America and the Caribbean. Exports for the Middle East and Russia also include exports for the Commonwealth of Independent States, which consists of Azerbaijan, Armenia, Belarus, Georgia, Kazakhstan, Kyrgyzstan, Moldova, Russia, Tajikistan, Turkmenistan, Uzbekistan, and Ukraine.

Source: United Nations trade data.

---

[2] Prior to 2004, the European Union consisted of 15 countries: Belgium, France, Germany, Italy, Luxembourg, and the Netherlands (founding members in 1952); Denmark, Ireland, and the United Kingdom (added in 1973); Greece (added in 1981); Portugal and Spain (added in 1986); and Austria, Finland, and Sweden (added in 1995). On May 1, 2004, 10 more countries were added: Cyprus, the Czech Republic, Estonia, Hungary, Lithuania, Latvia, Malta, Poland, Slovakia, and Slovenia. In January 2007 Bulgaria and Romania joined. In addition to zero tariffs, countries within the European Union have many common economic regulations, and some of them share a currency (the euro).

of world trade occurs between countries that are similar in their levels of advanced industrialization and great wealth. Why do these countries trade so much with one another?

The many differences among European countries and between Europe and the United States explain, in part, the trade between them. The first model of trade we study in the next chapter, called the Ricardian model, was initially used to explain trade between England and Portugal based on their difference in climate. Despite such differences, however, industrialized countries like the United Kingdom and the United States have many similarities in their consumption patterns and in their ability to produce goods and services. Why, then, do "similar" countries trade so much with one another? We try to answer that question in a later chapter, by arguing that even similar countries have enough variety in the goods they produce (such as different models of cars or types of cheese) that it is natural for them to trade with one another.

Trade in the Americas There is also a large amount of trade recorded within the Americas; that is, between North America, Central America, South America, and the Caribbean. In 2010 the United States exported $248 billion to Canada and imported $289 billion from Canada. In addition, the United States exported $303 billion to Latin America (which consists of Mexico, Central and South America, and the Caribbean) and imported $378 billion from Latin America. If we add together these trade flows, plus the amounts that Canada trades with Latin America and Latin America trades internally, we get $1.4 trillion as the total trade in goods within the Americas in 2010, or another 8% of world trade.

So trade within the Americas is about one-third of trade within Europe, and the vast majority of that trade is within the North American Free Trade Area, consisting of Canada, the United States, and Mexico. There is a proposal to extend free trade with the United States to many of the other countries that border the Pacific Ocean in the Trans-Pacific Partnership. There is also a proposal for a free trade area between the United States and the European Union in the Trans-Atlantic Trade and Investment Partnership. We study the consequences of free trade areas for the countries included, and for the countries left out, in a later chapter.

If we add the trade flows within the Americas to those within Europe and also include all other exports of these two regions to the rest of the world, we find that these combined regions account for $8.5 trillion in exports, or about one-half (51%) of the $16.8 trillion in world trade. This finding is also recorded in Table 1-1.

Trade with Asia Very large trade flows are also shown in Figure 1-2 to and from Asia. For example, Europe exported $575 billion to the Asian countries in 2010 and imported $947 billion. The United States exported $69 billion to Japan and $301 billion to the rest of Asia and imported about twice as much from each of these regions.

If we break up Asian exports to the United States, the largest exporting country is China (selling $383 billion in 2010), followed by Japan ($124 billion), South Korea ($51 billion), and Taiwan ($37 billion). India, Indonesia, Thailand, Vietnam, and the other Asian countries export smaller amounts. The exports from all of Asia to the United States totaled $792 billion in 2010.

All the exports from Asia totaled about $5.7 trillion in 2010, or about one-third (34%) of world trade, as shown in Table 1-1. Remember that this total includes only trade in goods and omits trade in services, which is becoming increasingly important. India, for example, performs a wide range of services such as accounting, customer support, computer programming, and research and development tasks for firms in the United States and Europe. Because these services are performed for U.S. and European firms in another country, they are considered service exports from the country in which the services are performed. In the quote at the beginning of the chapter, Ben Bernanke, the chairman of the U.S. Federal Reserve, points out that the entrance of China, India, and the former Communist-bloc countries into the world economy has led to a level of globalization that exceeds anything we have seen in the past.

Why does Asia trade so much? There are many answers to this question. One answer is that wages in many Asian countries are much lower than in the industrialized world. China's low wages allow it to produce goods cheaply and then export them. But why are Chinese wages so low? One explanation is that Chinese workers are less productive (the Ricardian model presented in the next chapter explains wages in that way). Low wages cannot explain why Japan exports so much, however. Japan's wages are very high because its workers are very productive; its exports to Europe and the United States are large because its highly skilled workforce and large amount of capital (factories and machines) make it possible for Japan to produce high-quality goods in abundance. Conversely, its scarcity of raw materials explains why it imports those goods from resource-rich countries such as Australia, Canada, and the United States. Trade patterns based on the amounts of labor, capital, and natural resources found in each country are explained by the Heckscher-Ohlin trade model, the topic of a later chapter.

Other Regions The Middle East sells oil to many countries, earning $1.5 trillion in export revenues and spending $1.1 trillion on imports. Like the Middle East, Russia also has reserves of oil and natural gas, which countries in Europe rely on and that are an important source of export revenue for Russia. In 2010 Russia earned $534 billion in its export sales and spent $302 billion on imports. The exports of the Middle East and Russia combined (together with countries around Russia like Azerbaijan, Kazakhstan, Kyrgyzstan, Uzbekistan, Tajikistan, and Turkmenistan) total $2 trillion, or another 12% of world trade.

And then there is Africa. The European nations have the closest trade links with Africa, reflecting both their proximity and the former colonial status of some African countries. Europe exported $99 billion and imported $105 billion from Africa in 2010, as compared with African trade with the United States, which totaled $90 billion, mostly in U.S. imports. Internal trade within Africa is also small: only $71 billion in 2010. Adding up all its exports, the continent of Africa accounts for only 2% of world trade, a very small number given Africa's huge land mass and population.

In the quote at the start of the chapter, Kofi Annan, former secretary general of the United Nations, expresses the view that Africa's growth out of poverty will depend on its developing greater linkages with the world economy through trade. A thorough treatment of the difficulties faced by African and other least-developed countries is beyond the scope of this book, and we recommend that the interested reader consult a textbook on development economics. But the lessons we draw from our examination of international trade and trade policy will still hold for the African countries.

The export percentages shown in Table 1-1 add up to 100% (being careful not to add Europe and the Americas twice), once we include trade at the bottom of the world: Australia and New Zealand export $270 billion (accounting for 1.6%

of world exports) and import $242 billion. You do not need to know all the specific percentages shown in Table 1-1, but an understanding of the broad picture (such as which regions trade the most) will be useful as we undertake our study of international trade.

Trade Compared with GDP

So far, we have discussed the value of trade crossing international borders. But there is a second way that trade is often reported, and that is as a ratio of trade to a country's **gross domestic product (GDP),** the value of all final goods produced in a year. For the United States, the average value of imports and exports (for goods and services) expressed relative to GDP was 15% in 2010. Most other countries have a higher ratio of trade to GDP, as shown in Table 1-2.

At the top of the list are Hong Kong (China) and Singapore, where the amount of trade exceeds their GDP![3] These two countries are important shipping and processing centers, so they are importing goods, processing them, and then exporting the final product to other countries. As in our iPhone example, the value-added involved in the exports ($6.50 for each iPhone) can be much less than the total value of exports ($179). That explains why the total amount that countries trade can be greater than their GDP. At the bottom of the list are the United States and Japan, which are very large in economic size; Pakistan, which is only starting to engage in international trade; and Brazil and Argentina, which are far away from other importing countries.

So even though the United States is among the world's largest exporters and importers, it is nearly the smallest trading nation of the countries shown in Table 1-2 when trade is measured as a percent of a country's GDP. What is the reason for this inverse relationship? Very large countries tend to have a lot of trade among states or provinces *within* their borders, but that trade is not counted as part of international trade. Other countries that are not quite as large as the United States but are close to their major trading partners, such as Germany, the United Kingdom, Italy, and Spain, and Canada and Mexico, tend to appear in the middle of the list in Table 1-2. Smaller countries with close neighbors, such as Hong Kong, Singapore, Malaysia, and the smaller European nations, will have more trade spilling across their borders and have the highest ratios of trade to GDP.

---

[3] Hong Kong (China) has been a part of the People's Republic of China since July 1, 1997, but its trade statistics are measured separately, so we list Hong Kong in Table 1-2 as a distinct region.

TABLE 1-2

Trade/GDP Ratio in 2010 This table shows the ratio of total trade to GDP for each country, where trade is calculated as (Imports + Exports)/2, including both merchandise goods and services. Countries with the highest ratios of trade to GDP tend to be small in economic size and are often important centers for shipping goods, like Hong Kong (China) and Singapore. Countries with the lowest ratios of trade to GDP tend to be very large in economic size, like Japan and the United States, or are not very open to trade because of trade barriers or their distance from other countries.

Country	Trade/GDP (%)	GDP ($ billion)
Hong Kong (China)	216	229
Singapore	193	213
Malaysia	85	247
Hungary	83	129
Thailand	68	319
Austria	52	377
Denmark	48	313
Sweden	46	463
Switzerland	46	552
Germany	44	3,284
Norway	35	418
United Kingdom	32	2,256
Mexico	31	1,035
Canada	30	1,577
China	29	5,931
Spain	28	1,380
Italy	28	2,044
South Africa	27	364
Greece	27	292
France	27	2,549
Russian Federation	26	1,488
India	25	1,684
Turkey	24	731
Indonesia	24	708
Venezuela	23	394
Argentina	20	369
Pakistan	17	176
Japan	15	5,488
United States	15	14,419
Brazil	11	2,143

Source: World Development Indicators, The World Bank.

Barriers to Trade

Table 1-2 shows the differences across countries in the amount of trade relative to GDP, but this ratio changes over time. There are many reasons, aside from country size, for the amount of trade to change. Those reasons include import tariffs, taxes that countries charge on imported goods; transportation costs of shipping from one country to another; events, such as wars and natural disasters, that lead to reduced trade; and so on. The term **trade barriers** refers to all factors that influence the amount of goods and services shipped across international borders. To see how these trade barriers have changed over time, Figure 1-3 graphs the ratio of trade in goods and services to GDP for a selection of countries for which historical data are available: Australia, Canada, Japan, the United Kingdom, the United States, and an average of countries in continental Europe (Denmark, France, Germany, Italy, Norway, and Sweden).[4]

"First Golden Age" of Trade

The period from 1890 until World War I (1914–1918) is sometimes referred to as a "golden age" of international trade. Those years saw dramatic improvements in transportation, such as the steamship and the railroad, that allowed for a great increase in the amount of international trade. Figure 1-3 shows this increase in the ratio of trade to GDP between 1890 and World War I. The United Kingdom reached the highest ratio of trade to GDP (30%), while Australia, Canada, and the average of European countries all exceeded 20% at their peaks (shown in 1913 or 1920). Japan reached a ratio of trade to GDP of 15%, while the United States achieved 7.5%, which was low in comparison with other countries (as expected for a large country) but still high by the United States' historical standards.

Interwar Period   In the aftermath of World War I, the ratio of trade to GDP fell in all countries, a decline that was made worse by the Great Depression, which began in 1929, and World War II, which began in Europe in 1939. During the Great Depression, the United States adopted high tariffs called the Smoot-Hawley tariffs, named after Senator Reed Smoot from Utah and Representative Willis C. Hawley from Oregon. Signed into law in June 1930, the Smoot-Hawley Tariff Act raised tariffs to as high as 60% on many categories of imports.

These tariffs were applied by the United States to protect farmers and other industries, but they backfired by causing other countries to retaliate. Canada retaliated by applying high tariffs of its own against the United States; France used **import quotas,** a limitation on the quantity of an imported good allowed into a country, to restrict imports from the United States; Britain gave preferences to goods available from its former colonies; and other countries reacted, too. As reported by one economic historian:[5]

> A groundswell of resentment spread around the world and quickly led to retaliation. Italy objected to duties on hats and bonnets of straw, wool-felt hats, and olive oil; Spain reacted sharply to increases on cork and onions; Canada took umbrage at increases on maple sugar and syrup, potatoes, cream, butter, buttermilk,

---

[4] Because historical data on trade in services are not available, in Figure 1-3 we include trade in services starting in 1950.
[5] Charles Kindleberger, 1989, "Commercial Policy between the Wars." In P. Mathias and S. Pollard, eds., *The Cambridge Economic History of Europe*, Vol. VIII (Cambridge, UK: Cambridge University Press), p. 170.

FIGURE 1-3

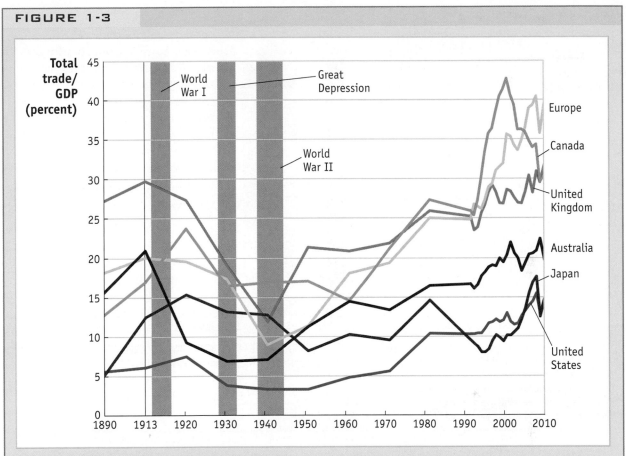

Trade in Goods and Services Relative to GDP This diagram shows total trade in merchandise goods and services for each country (i.e., the average of imports and exports) divided by gross domestic product (GDP). There was a considerable increase in the ratio of trade to GDP between 1890 and 1913. This trend ended by World War I and the Great Depression, and it took many years to regain the same level of trade. Most of the industrial countries shown did not reach the level of trade prevailing in 1913 until the 1970s. Some countries—such as Australia and the United Kingdom—did not reach their earlier levels until the end of the century. The financial crisis in 2008–2009 led to a fall in trade relative to GDP for most countries.

Source: Revised from Robert C. Feenstra, Fall 1998, "Integration of Trade and Disintegration of Production in the Global Economy," Journal of Economic Perspectives, 31–50.

and skimmed milk. Switzerland was moved to boycott American typewriters, fountain pens, motor cars, and films because of increased duties on watches, clocks, embroidery, cheese and shoes. . . . Retaliation was begun long before the [Smoot-Hawley] bill was enacted into law in June 1930.

The response of these countries, initially against the United States and then against one another, led to a dramatic increase in worldwide tariffs during the interwar period. The average worldwide tariff for 35 countries from 1860 to 2010 is shown in Figure 1-4. We see that the average tariff fluctuated around 15% from 1860 to 1914. After World War I, however, the average tariff rose because of the Smoot-Hawley Tariff Act and the reaction by other countries, reaching about 25% by 1933. The high tariffs led to a dramatic fall in world trade in the interwar period, with large costs to the United States and the world economy. These costs are one reason that the Allied countries met together after World War II to develop international agreements to

FIGURE 1-4

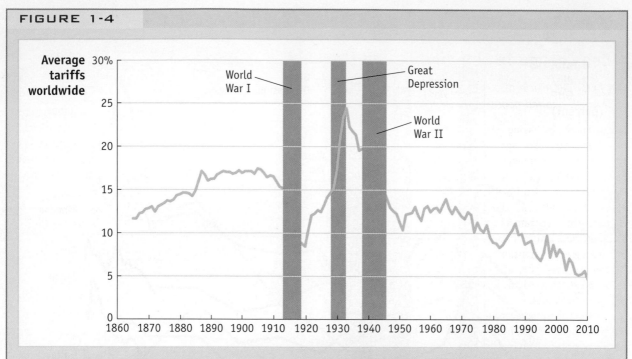

Average Worldwide Tariffs, 1860–2010 This diagram shows the world average tariff for 35 countries from 1860 to 2010. The average tariff fluctuated around 15% from 1860 to 1913. After World War I, however, the average tariff rose sharply because of the Smoot-Hawley Tariff Act in the United States and the reaction by other countries, reaching 25% by 1933. Since the end of World War II, tariffs have fallen.

Source: Updated from Michael A. Clemens and Jeffrey G. Williamson, 2004, "Why Did the Tariff-Growth Correlation Change after 1950?" Journal of Economic Growth, 9(1), 5–46.

keep tariffs low, such as the General Agreement on Tariffs and Trade, now known as the World Trade Organization. Later in this book, we study tariffs and other trade policies in more detail and the international institutions that govern their use. The lesson from the interwar period is that high tariffs reduce the amount of trade and impose large costs on the countries involved.

"Second Golden Age" of Trade

It took many years for the world economy to regain the same level of global integration that existed before World War I. From Figure 1-3, we can see that some countries (the United Kingdom, Europe, and Australia) began increasing trade immediately after the end of World War II in 1945, so their ratio of trade to GDP was much higher in 1950 than it was in 1940. Some countries did not show an increase until after 1950 and others not until after 1960. In addition to the end of World War II and tariff reductions under the General Agreement on Tariffs and Trade, improved transportation costs contributed to the growth in trade. The shipping container, invented in 1956, allowed goods to be moved by ship, rail, and truck more cheaply than before (see **Headlines: A Sea Change in Shipping 50 Years Ago**). As a result of all these factors, world trade grew steadily after 1950 in dollar terms and as a ratio to GDP. For this reason, the period after 1950 is called the "second golden age" of trade and globalization.

HEADLINES

A Sea Change in Shipping 50 Years Ago

The following article discusses the invention of the shipping container 50 years ago, which allowed goods to be shipped between countries at a much lower cost.

Globalization is having an anniversary. It was 50 years ago that Malcom McLean, an entrepreneur from North Carolina, loaded a ship with 58 35-foot containers and sailed from Newark, N.J., to Houston. He wasn't the only one to suggest that containers might make shipping more efficient. But he was the first to design a transportation system around the packaging of cargo in huge metal boxes that could be loaded and unloaded by cranes.

Container shipping eventually replaced the traditional "break-bulk" method of handling crates, barrels and bags, and stowing them loose in a ship's hold, a system in use since the days of the Phoenicians. Replacing break-bulk with cargo containers dramatically reduced shipping costs, reinvigorating markets and fueling the world economy. . . .

In 1959, according to Matson Research, the industry was loading and unloading 0.627 tons per man hour. By 1976, with container shipping well established, the figure was 4,234 tons per man hour. A ship's time in port shrank from three weeks to 18 hours. In 1950, an average commercial vessel could carry 10,000 tons at a speed of 16 knots.

With container shipping, the average commercial vessel carried 40,000 tons at a speed of 23 knots, Matson says. The numbers are even larger today. A vessel capable of carrying 6,600 20-foot containers can carry 77,000 tons at up to 24.8 knots.

"Containerization has transformed global trade in manufactured goods as dramatically as jet planes have changed the way we travel and the Internet has changed the way we communicate," said Joseph Bonney, editor of the *Journal of Commerce*, the bible of the shipping industry. "The Asian economic miracle of the last two decades could not have happened without the efficient transportation that containerized shipping provides."

A fully loaded container ship can carry thousands of containers.

Source: Excerpted from George Raine, "A Sea Change in Shipping: 50 Years Ago, Container Ships Altered the World," San Francisco Chronicle, February 5, 2006, electronic edition.

Many of the countries shown in Figure 1-3 have substantially exceeded the peak levels of trade relative to GDP that prevailed just before or after World War I. Canada's trade ratio grew from 24% in 1920 to 43% by 2000, and then back down to 30% in 2010 (due to reduced exports of natural gas). The average of European countries increased from 20% in 1913 to 39% in 2010. Likewise, the U.S. trade ratio grew from 7.5% in 1920 to 15% by 2010. A few countries, such as Australia and the United Kingdom, have only recently achieved the level of trade relative to GDP that they had prior to World War I and are now in a position to surpass that level. For the world as a whole, the ratio of trade to GDP in 2010 was about 30%, up from 20% in 1980 and 12% in 1970.

Near the end of the decade, in the years just before 2010, we see a fall in the ratios of trade to GDP for several countries in Figure 1-3. What happened to cause this slow-down in trade? In the fall of 2008 there was a financial crisis in the United States that quickly spread to other countries.[6] The crisis had a substantial impact on the amount of international trade, because it sent many countries into recessions that led to a fall in both exports and imports. This fall in trade is illustrated in the final years shown in Figure 1-3, with signs of a recovery of trade in most countries by 2010. Still, it will take some years more for the world economy to again reach a level of trade, or ratio of trade to GDP, that is as high as that achieved before the financial crisis.

2   Migration and Foreign Direct Investment

In addition to examining the reasons for and effects of international trade (the flow of goods and services between countries), we will also analyze migration, the movement of people across borders, and foreign direct investment, the movement of capital across borders. All three of these flows affect the economy of a nation that opens its borders to interact with other nations.

Map of Migration

In Figure 1-5, we show a map of the number of migrants around the world. The values shown are the number of people in 2005 (this is the most recent year for which these data are available) who were living (legally or illegally) in a country other than the one in which they were born. For this map, we combine two different sources of data: (1) the movement of people from one country to another, reported for just the Organisation for Economic Co-operation and Development (OECD) countries and shown by arrows from one country to another[7], and (2) the number of foreign-born located in each region (but without data on their country of origin), shown by the bold arrows from World into Asia, Africa, and Latin America.[8]

In 2005 there were 62 million foreign-born people living in the OECD countries. But that was less than one-third of the total number of foreign-born people worldwide, which was 195 million. These figures show that unlike trade (much of which occurs between the OECD countries), the majority of immigration occurs *outside* the OECD between countries that are less wealthy. Asia, for example, was home to 53.1 million migrants in 2005, and Africa was home to 17.1 million migrants. Latin America has 6.9 million foreign-born people living there. We expect that many of

---

[6] The full, detailed story of the financial crisis is beyond the scope of this book. But in simplified terms, the reason this crisis occurred was that the prices for homes rose from 1997 to 2005, and then fell substantially from 2006 up to 2009. As a result, many homeowners started to default on (i.e., stop paying) their mortgages, and banks began foreclosing on and taking possession of the homes. Mortgage defaults meant that the loans made by the banks became worth much less—they became worth only the value at which the house could be sold, which was often far less than the price for which the house had been purchased. Banks making mortgages therefore lost a great deal of money, and these losses spread throughout the whole financial system in the United States and abroad.

[7] The Organization for Economic Cooperation and Development (OECD) consists of 30 member countries, including most European countries as well as Australia, Canada, Japan, Mexico, South Korea, and the United States. See the complete list of countries at http://www.oecd.org.

[8] Data on total immigration for major regions are available from the United Nations at http://www.esa.un.org/migration.

FIGURE 1-5

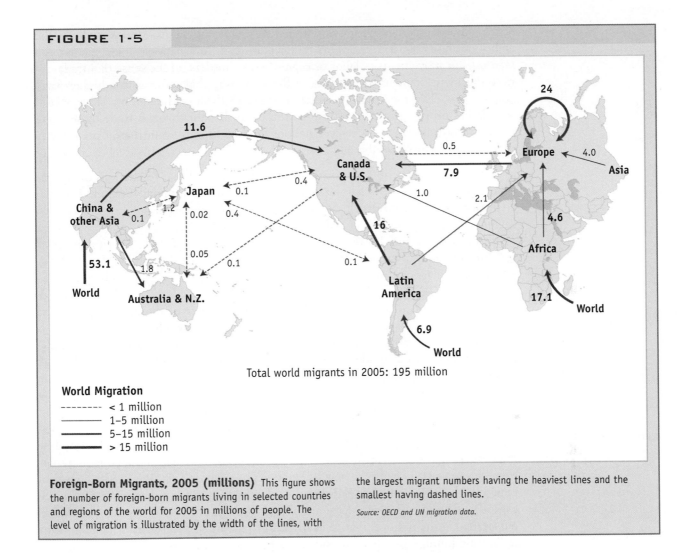

Total world migrants in 2005: 195 million

World Migration

-------- < 1 million
———— 1–5 million
━━━━ 5–15 million
━━━ > 15 million

Foreign-Born Migrants, 2005 (millions) This figure shows the number of foreign-born migrants living in selected countries and regions of the world for 2005 in millions of people. The level of migration is illustrated by the width of the lines, with the largest migrant numbers having the heaviest lines and the smallest having dashed lines.

Source: OECD and UN migration data.

these immigrants come from the same continent where they are now living but have had to move from one country to another for employment or other reasons such as famine and war.[9]

Given the choice, these migrants would probably rather move to a high-wage, industrial country. But people cannot just move to another country as can the goods and services that move in international trade. All countries have restrictions on who can enter and work there. In many OECD countries, these restrictions are in place because policy makers fear that immigrants from low-wage countries will drive down the wages for a country's own less skilled workers. Whether or not that fear is justified, immigration is a hotly debated political issue in many countries, including Europe and the United States. As a result, the flow of people between countries is *much less* free than the flow of goods.

---

[9] The United Nations data on migrants include refugees. Of the 50.3 million migrants in Asia in 2000, 8.8 million were refugees; of the 16.5 million migrants in Africa, 3.6 million were refugees; and of the 6.3 million migrants in Latin America, 500,000 were refugees.

The limitation on migration out of the low-wage countries is offset partially by the ability of these countries to export products instead. International trade can act as a *substitute* for movements of labor or capital across borders, in the sense that trade can raise the living standard of workers in the same way that moving to a higher-wage country can. The increased openness to trade in the world economy since World War II has provided opportunities for workers to benefit through trade by working in export industries, even when restrictions on migration prevent them from directly earning higher incomes abroad.

European and U.S. Immigration We have just learned that restrictions on migration, especially into the wealthier countries, limit the movement of people between countries. Let us see how such restrictions are reflected in recent policy actions in two regions: the European Union and the United States.

Prior to 2004 the European Union (EU) consisted of 15 countries in western Europe, and labor mobility was very open between them.[10] On May 1, 2004, 10 more countries of central Europe were added: Cyprus, the Czech Republic, Estonia, Hungary, Latvia, Lithuania, Malta, Poland, Slovakia, and Slovenia. These countries had per capita incomes that were only about one-quarter of the average per capita incomes in those western European countries that were already EU members. This large difference in wages created a strong incentive for labor migration. In principle, citizens from these newly added countries were permitted to work anywhere in the EU. As shown in Figure 1-5, in 2005 there were 24 million people from Europe living in an EU country in which they were not born. In practice, however, fears of this impending inflow of labor led to policy disagreements among the countries involved.

Germany and Austria, which border some of the new member countries, argued for a 7-year moratorium on allowing labor mobility from new members, if desired by the host countries. Britain and Ireland, on the other hand, promised to open up their countries to workers from the new EU members. In January 2007 two more countries joined the EU: Romania and Bulgaria. Legal immigration from these countries in the expanded EU, together with legal and illegal immigration from other countries, has put strains on the political system in Britain. All major political parties spoke in favor of limiting immigration from outside the EU, and this issue may have contributed to the ousting of the Labour Party in Britain in the election of May 2010.

A second example of recent migration policy is from the United States. As shown in Figure 1-5, there were 16 million people from Latin America living in the United States and Canada in 2005, and the largest group of these migrants is Mexicans living in the United States. It is estimated that today close to 13 million Mexicans are living in the United States, about half legally and half illegally. This number is more than 10% of Mexico's population of 115 million. The concern that immigration will drive down wages applies to Mexican migration to the United States and is amplified by the exceptionally high number of illegal immigrants. It is no surprise, then, that immigration policy is a frequent topic of debate in the United States.

There is a widespread perception among policy makers in the United States that the current immigration system is not working and needs to be fixed. In 2007 President George W. Bush attempted an immigration reform, but it was not supported by the

---

[10] Those 15 countries are detailed in footnote 2.

Congress. During his first term as president, Barack Obama also promised to pursue immigration reform. But that promise had to wait for other policy actions, most notably the health-care reform bill and the reform of the financial system following the 2008–2009 crisis, both of which delayed the discussion of immigration. As President Obama began his second term in 2013, he again promised action on immigration reform, and that idea is supported by members of both parties in the United States. As of the time of writing, it remains to be seen what type of immigration bill will be enacted during President Obama's administration.

Map of Foreign Direct Investment

As mentioned earlier in the chapter, foreign direct investment (FDI) occurs when a firm in one country owns (in part or in whole) a company or property in another country. Figure 1-6 shows the principal stocks of FDI in 2010, with the magnitude of the stocks illustrated by the width of the lines. As we did for migration, we again combine two sources of information: (1) stocks of FDI found in the OECD countries

FIGURE 1-6

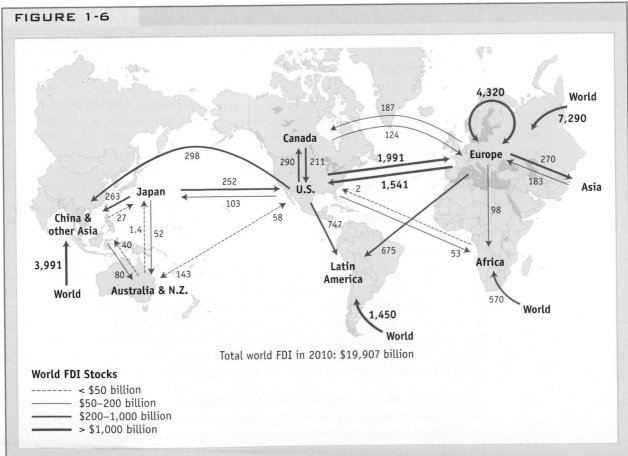

Stock of Foreign Direct Investment, 2010 ($ billions)
This figure shows the stock of foreign direct investment between selected countries and regions of the world for 2010 in billions of dollars. The stock of investment is illustrated by the width of the lines, with the largest stocks having the heaviest lines and the smallest having dashed lines.

Source: OECD and UN foreign investment data.

that are owned by another country, shown by arrows from the country of ownership to the country of location, and (2) FDI stocks from anywhere in the world found in Africa, Asia, Europe, and Latin America.

In 2010 the total value of FDI stocks located in the OECD countries or owned by those countries was $17 trillion. That value is 85% of the total world stock of FDI, which was $19.9 trillion in 2010. So unlike our findings for immigration, the vast majority of FDI is located in or owned by firms in the OECD countries. The concentration of FDI among wealthy countries is even more pronounced than the concentration of international trade flows. The FDI stock in Africa ($570 billion) is just over one-third of the stock in Latin America ($1,450 billion), which in turn is less than one-half of the FDI into China and other Asian countries ($3,991 billion). Most of this FDI is from industrial countries, but Chinese firms have begun to acquire land in Africa and Latin America for agriculture and resource extraction, as well as purchase companies in the industrial countries, as we discuss below.

FDI can be described in one of two ways: horizontal FDI or vertical FDI.

Horizontal FDI The majority of FDI occurs between industrial countries, when a firm from one industrial country owns a company in another industrial country. We refer to these flows between industrial countries as **horizontal FDI.** Recent examples have occurred in the automobile industry, such as the 2009 purchase of Chrysler by Fiat, an Italian firm.

There are many reasons why companies want to acquire firms in another industrial country. First, having a plant abroad allows the parent firm to avoid any tariffs from exporting to a foreign market because it can instead produce and sell locally in that market. For example, as early as the 1950s and 1960s, American auto manufacturers produced and sold cars in Europe to avoid having to pay any tariffs. In the 1980s and 1990s many Japanese auto firms opened plants in the United States to avoid U.S. import quotas (restrictions on the amount imported). Today, more Japanese cars are built in the United States than are imported from Japan.

Second, having a foreign subsidiary abroad also provides improved access to that economy because the local firms will have better facilities and information for marketing products. For example, Toyota Motor Sales U.S.A. is a wholly owned subsidiary of Toyota Motor Corporation in Japan and markets Toyota cars and trucks in the United States. Many other foreign firms selling in the United States have similar local retail firms. Third, an alliance between the production divisions of firms allows technical expertise to be shared and avoids possible duplication of products. Examples are the American and Canadian divisions of General Motors, Ford, and Chrysler, which have operated plants specializing in different vehicles on both sides of the border (in Detroit, Michigan, and Windsor, Ontario) for decades. There are many reasons for horizontal FDI, which is really just a way for a firm to expand its business across international borders.

Vertical FDI The other form of FDI occurs when a firm from an industrial country owns a plant in a developing country, which we call **vertical FDI.** Low wages are the principal reasons that firms shift production abroad to developing countries. In the traditional view of FDI, firms from industrial economies use their technological expertise and combine this with inexpensive labor in developing countries to produce goods for the world market. This is a reasonable view of FDI in China, although as we have already seen, much of worldwide FDI does not fit this traditional view because it is between industrial countries.

In addition to taking advantage of low wages, firms have entered the Chinese market to avoid tariffs and acquire local partners to sell there. For example, China formerly had high tariffs on automobile imports, so many auto producers from the United States, Germany, and Japan established plants there, always with a Chinese partner, enabling them to sell more easily in that market. China joined the World Trade Organization in 2001, which means that it has reduced its tariffs on nearly all imports, including automobiles. Nevertheless, the foreign automobile firms are planning to remain and are now beginning to export cars from China.

European and U.S. FDI Turning back now to Figure 1-6, the largest stocks of FDI are within Europe; these stocks amounted to $11.6 trillion in 2010, or more than one-half of the world total, with $4.3 trillion coming from other European countries. In addition, the horizontal FDI from Europe to the United States ($1.5 trillion) and that from the United States to Europe ($2.0 trillion) are very substantial. An example of a European direct investment in the United States was the merger of the German company Daimler-Benz (which produces the Mercedes-Benz car) and Chrysler Corporation in 1998, resulting in the firm DaimlerChrysler. That deal lasted for fewer than 10 years, however, and in May 2007 DaimlerChrysler sold the Chrysler firm back to an American financial company, Cerberus Capital Management, so Chrysler returned to American ownership. Then, in 2009, Chrysler was again sold to a European automobile firm, Fiat. An example of American direct investment in Europe was Ford Motor Company's acquisition of the British firm Jaguar (in 1989) and the Swedish firm Volvo (in 1999). The United States consistently ranks as the top country for both inbound and outbound FDI stocks ($2.5 trillion and $4.3 trillion in 2010, respectively), followed by the United Kingdom and then France.

Adding up the stocks within Europe and between Europe and the United States, we find that they total $7.9 trillion, or more than one-third (39%) of the world total. That share is even larger than the roughly one-quarter (27%) of worldwide trade that occurs within Europe and between Europe and the United States (see Table 1-1). This finding illustrates that the greatest amount of FDI is horizontal FDI between the industrial countries.

FDI in the Americas There are also substantial amounts of FDI shown in Figure 1-6 among the United States, Canada, and Latin America. The United States had a stock of direct investments of $290 billion in Canada in 2010, and Canada invested $211 billion in the United States. The United States had a stock of direct investments of $747 billion in Latin America, principally in Mexico. Brazil and Mexico are two of the largest recipients of FDI among developing countries, after China. In 2010 Mexico had a FDI stock of $265 billion, and Brazil had a stock of $514 billion, accounting for about one-half of the total $1,450 billion in FDI to Latin America. These are examples of vertical FDI, prompted by the opportunity to produce goods at lower wages than in the industrial countries.

FDI with Asia The direct investments between the United States and Japan and between Europe and Japan are horizontal FDI. In addition to Japan, the rest of Asia shows a large amount of FDI in Figure 1-6. The United States had direct investments of $298 billion in the rest of Asia, especially China, while Europe had a direct investment of $270 billion in Asia. These stocks are also examples of vertical FDI, foreign direct investment from industrial to developing countries, to take advantage of low wages.

China has become the largest recipient country for FDI in Asia and the second largest recipient of FDI in the world (after the United States). The FDI stock in China and Hong Kong was $1,476 billion in 2010, which accounts for 37% of the total FDI into China and the rest of Asia ($4.0 trillion). There is some "double counting" in these numbers for China and Hong Kong because Hong Kong itself has direct investment in mainland China, which is funded in part by businesses on the mainland. This flow of funds from mainland China to Hong Kong and then back to China is called "round tripping," and it is estimated that one-quarter to one-half of FDI flowing into China is funded that way.

Notice in Figure 1-6 that Asia has direct investment into the United States and Europe, or what we might call "reverse-vertical FDI." Contrary to the traditional view of FDI, these are companies from developing countries buying firms in the industrial countries. Obviously, these companies are not going after low wages in the industrial countries; instead, they are acquiring the technological knowledge of those firms, which they can combine with low wages in their home countries. A widely publicized example was the purchase of IBM's personal computer division by Lenovo, a Chinese firm. What expertise did Lenovo acquire from this purchase? According to media reports, Lenovo will acquire the management and international expertise of IBM and will even hire IBM executives to run the business. Instead of using FDI to acquire inexpensive labor, Lenovo has engaged in FDI to acquire expensive and highly skilled labor, which is what it needs to succeed in the computer industry.

Another example of reverse-vertical FDI from China is the 2009 purchase of Volvo (formerly a Swedish company) from Ford Motor Company, by the Chinese automaker Geely. In a later chapter, we will discuss how automobile companies from the United States, Europe, and Japan entered the automobile industry in China by buying partial ownership in Chinese firms, which allowed the Chinese firms to learn from their foreign partners. That process of learning the best technology continues in the case of Geely purchasing Volvo from Ford, but now it is the Chinese firm that is doing the buying rather than the American, European, or Japanese firms.

In addition to acquiring technical knowledge, Chinese firms have been actively investing in foreign companies whose products are needed to meet the growing demand of its 1.3 billion people. A recent example is the proposed purchase of the American firm Smithfield Foods, one of the largest producers of pork in the United States, by the Chinese firm Shuanghui International. Rising incomes have led to increased demand for pork in China, exceeding that country's own ability to supply it. This example illustrates the more general trend of Chinese companies investing in natural resource and infrastructure projects around the world. As reported in *The New York Times*:[11]

> [The proposed purchase of Smithfield] fulfills a major ambition of the Chinese government, to encourage companies to venture abroad by acquiring assets, resources and technical expertise. In North America, Africa and Australia, Chinese companies, flush with cash, are buying up land and resources to help a country that is plagued by water shortages and short of arable land, a situation exacerbated by a long running property and infrastructure boom.

---

[11] Michael J. de la Merced and David Barboza, "China, In Need of Pork, to Buy U.S. Supplier," May 30, 2013, *The New York Times*, p. B6.

As China continues to industrialize, which will raise the income of its consumers and the ability of its firms to invest overseas, we can expect that its firms and government will continue to look beyond its borders to provide for the needs of its population.

3 Conclusions

Globalization means many things: the flow of goods and services across borders, the movement of people and firms, the spread of culture and ideas among countries, and the tight integration of financial markets around the world. Although it might seem as if such globalization is new, international trade and the integration of financial markets were also very strong in the period before World War I. The war and the Great Depression disrupted these global linkages. Since World War II world trade has grown rapidly again, even faster than the growth in world GDP, so that the ratio of trade to world GDP has risen steadily. International institutions established after World War II have promoted the growth in trade: the General Agreement on Tariffs and Trade (now known as the World Trade Organization), the International Monetary Fund, the United Nations, and the World Bank were all established in the postwar years to promote freer trade and economic development.

Migration across countries is not as free as international trade, and all countries have restrictions on immigration because of the fear that the inflow of workers will drive down wages. That fear is not necessarily justified. We argue in a later chapter that immigrants can sometimes be absorbed into a country with no change in wages. FDI is largely unrestricted in the industrial countries but often faces some restrictions in developing countries. China, for example, requires approval of all foreign investments and until recently, required that foreign firms have a local partner. Typically, firms invest in developing countries to take advantage of lower wages in those countries. Investments in developing countries and industrial countries enable firms to spread their business and knowledge of production processes across borders. Migration and FDI are further aspects of the globalization that has become so widespread today.

KEY POINTS

1. The trade balance of a country is the difference between the value of its exports and the value of its imports, and is determined by macroeconomic conditions in the country.

2. The type of goods being traded between countries has changed from the period before World War I, when standardized goods (raw materials and basic processed goods like steel) were predominant. Today, the majority of trade occurs in highly processed consumer and capital goods, which might cross borders several times during the manufacturing process.

3. A large portion of international trade is between industrial countries. Trade within Europe and trade between Europe and the United States accounts for roughly one-quarter of total world trade.

4. Many of the trade models we study emphasize the differences between countries, but it is also possible to explain trade between countries that are similar. Similar countries will trade different varieties of goods with one another.

5. Larger countries tend to have smaller shares of trade relative to GDP because so much of their trade occurs internally. Hong Kong (China) and Singapore have ratios of trade to GDP that exceed 100%, whereas the United States' ratio of trade to GDP in 2010 was 15%.

6. The majority of world migration occurs into developing countries as a result of restrictions on immigration into wealthier, industrial countries.

7. International trade in goods and services acts as a substitute for migration and allows workers to improve their standard of living through working in export industries, even when they cannot migrate to earn higher incomes.

8. The majority of world FDI occurs between industrial countries. In 2010 more than one-third of the world stock of FDI was within Europe or between Europe and the United States, and 85% of the world stock of FDI was into or out of the OECD countries.

KEY TERMS

international trade, p. 1
migration, p. 3
foreign direct investment (FDI), p. 3
export, p. 3
import, p. 3
trade balance, p. 3

trade surplus, p. 3
trade deficit, p. 4
bilateral trade balance, p. 4
value-added, p. 4
offshoring, p. 4
import tariffs, p. 8

gross domestic product (GDP), p. 11
trade barriers, p. 12
import quotas, p. 12
horizontal FDI, p. 20
vertical FDI, p. 20

PROBLEMS

1. Figures 1-2 and 1-6 rely on data from 2010, and Figure 1-5 relies on data from 2005, to map worldwide trade, migration, and FDI. Updated data for migration and FDI were not available at the time this chapter was written, but it is available for worldwide trade. In this question, you are asked to update the numbers for world trade shown in Table 1-1.

   a. Go to the World Trade Organization's website at http://www.wto.org, and look for its trade data under "Documents and resources" then "International trade statistics." Look for the most recent edition of its *International Trade Statistics* publication, then go to "Trade by region," and find the Excel spreadsheet with "Intra- and interregional merchandise trade." Print out this table.

      If you cannot find the website or spreadsheet, use the 2011 table for "Intra- and Inter-Regional Merchandise Trade" that

   appears below to answer the following questions.[12]

   b. From this table, what is the total amount of trade within Europe? What percentage of total world trade is this?

   c. What is the total amount of trade (in either direction) between Europe and North America? Add that to the total trade within Europe, and calculate the percentage of this to the world total.

   d. What is the total amount of trade within the Americas (i.e., between North America, Central America, South America, and within each of these regions)? What percentage of total world trade is this?

   e. What is the total value of exports from Europe and the Americas, and what percentage of the world total is this?

   f. What is the total value of exports from Asia, and what percentage of the world total is this?

---

[12] The trade statistics for 2011 were obtained from Table I-4 at: http://www.wto.org/english/res_e/statis_e/its2012_e/its12_world_trade_dev_e.htm.

g. What is the total value of exports from the Middle East and the Commonwealth of Independent States,[13] and what percentage of the world total is this?

h. What is the total value of exports from Africa, and what percentage of the world total is this?

i. How do your answers to (b) through (h) compare with the shares of worldwide trade shown in Table 1-1?

2. The quotation from Federal Reserve Chairman Ben Bernanke at the beginning of the chapter is from a speech that he delivered in Jackson Hole, Wyoming, on August 25, 2006, titled "Global Economic Integration: What's New and What's Not?" The full transcript of the speech is available at http://www.federalreserve.gov/newsevents/speech/bernanke20060825a.htm. Read this speech and answer the following questions:

a. List three ways in which international trade today does not differ from the trade that occurred before World War I.

b. List three ways in which international trade today does differ from the trade that occurred before World War I.

Intra- and Inter-Regional Merchandise Trade, 2011 ($ billions)

Region of Origin	North America	South and Central America	Europe	CIS	Africa	Middle East	Asia	World
World	2,923	749	6,881	530	538	672	5,133	17,816
North America	1,103	201	382	15	37	63	476	2,282
South and Central America	181	200	138	8	21	18	169	750
Europe	480	119	4,667	234	199	194	639	6,612
Commonwealth of Independent States (CIS)	43	11	409	154	12	24	117	789
Africa	102	19	205	2	77	21	146	594
Middle East	107	10	158	6	38	110	660	1,251
Asia	906	189	922	110	152	242	2,926	5,538

Source: WTO, International Trade Statistics 2012.

NET WORK

The World Trade Organization is a good source for international trade statistics. Go to its website at http://www.wto.org, and look for trade data under "Documents and resources." Look for the most recent edition of its *International Trade Statistics* publication, and find the value for world trade in goods and in services for the most recent year provided.

[13] The Commonwealth of Independent States consists of Azerbaijan, Armenia, Belarus, Georgia, Kazakhstan, Kyrgyzstan, Moldova, Russia, Tajikistan, Turkmenistan, Ukraine, and Uzbekistan.

Trade and Technology: The Ricardian Model

England exported cloth in exchange for wine, because, by so doing her industry was rendered more productive to her; she had more cloth and wine than if she had manufactured both for herself; and Portugal imported cloth and exported wine, because the industry of Portugal could be more beneficially employed for both countries in producing wine. . . .

It would therefore be advantageous for [Portugal] to export wine in exchange for cloth. This exchange might even take place, notwithstanding that the commodity imported by Portugal could be produced there with less labour than in England.

David Ricardo, *On the Principles of Political Economy and Taxation*, 1821

Comparative advantage is the best example of an economic principle that is undeniably true yet not obvious to intelligent people.

Paul Samuelson, "The Way of an Economist," 1969[1]

Pick any manufactured product, and you will most likely find that it is traded among a number of countries. Let's choose snowboards as an example. In 2012 the United States **imported** (i.e., purchased from other countries) $33.3 million of snowboards from 18 different countries; Table 2-1 identifies the 12 countries with the highest dollar amount of snowboard sales to the United States.

At the top of the list in Table 2-1 is China, **exporting** (i.e., selling to another country) more than $19 million worth of snowboards to the United States. The second largest exporter to the United States is Austria, selling just over $10 million in 2012. These two countries sell considerably more than the next country on the list,

---

[1] Samuelson, Paul A. 1969. "The Way of an Economist." *In International Economic Relations: Proceedings of the Third Congress of the International Economic Association*, edited by Paul A. Samuelson (London: Macmillan), pp. 1–11.

TABLE 2-1

U.S. Imports of Snowboards, 2012

Rank	Country	Value of Imports ($ thousands)	Quantity of Snowboards (thousands)	Average Price ($/board)
1	China	19,560	400.6	49
2	Austria	10,479	93.6	112
3	Taiwan	2,108	46.5	45
4	Canada	362	23.2	16
5	Tunisia	337	2.0	171
6	Spain	285	1.9	151
7	Switzerland	42	0.2	226
8	Netherlands	42	0.3	159
9	Slovenia	27	0.2	121
10	Italy	24	0.2	140
11	Poland	16	0.1	155
12	France	15	0.1	126
13–18	All other countries	46	1.2	40
	Total	33,343	570	58

Source: U.S. Department of Commerce and the U.S. International Trade Commission.

Taiwan (which sold $2 million of snowboards to the United States). The fourth largest exporter in 2012 was Canada, selling $362,000 of snowboards to the United States.

Then, a group consisting of mostly European countries—Spain, Switzerland, the Netherlands, Slovenia, Italy, Poland and France, as well as Tunisia, a country on the north coast of Africa that is a former colony of France—sold between $15,000 and $337,000 each to the United States. Another six countries (the Czech Republic, Mexico, Hong Kong, Australia, Germany, and Japan), sold smaller amounts. This rather long list of countries raises a question: With all the manufacturing capability in the United States, why does it purchase snowboards from these countries at all instead of producing them domestically?

The first chapters of this book look at various reasons why countries trade goods with one another. These reasons include:

- Differences in the **technology** used in each country (i.e., differences in each country's ability to manufacture products)
- Differences in the total amount of **resources** (including labor, capital, and land) found in each country
- Differences in the costs of **offshoring** (i.e., producing the various parts of a good in different countries and then assembling it in a final location)
- The **proximity** of countries to one another (i.e., how close they are to one another)

In this chapter, we focus on the first of these reasons as an explanation for trade—technology differences across countries. This explanation is often called the **Ricardian model** because it was proposed by the nineteenth-century economist David Ricardo.

Where did Shaun White's snowboard come from?

This model explains how the level of a country's technology affects the wages paid to labor, such that countries with better technologies have higher wages. This, in turn, helps to explain how a country's technology affects its **trade pattern,** the products that it imports and exports.

1 Reasons for Trade

Besides technology differences across countries, which is the focus of the Ricardian model, there are many other reasons why countries trade goods. Before we get into the details of the Ricardian model, let's briefly explore the other reasons for trade.

Proximity

The proximity of countries is a reason for trade primarily because it affects the costs of transportation. Countries that are near one another will usually have lower shipping costs added to the cost of their traded goods. The proximity of countries to one another helps to explain why Canada is among the top exporters of snowboards to the United States and why Canada is the United States' largest trading partner overall. There are many other examples of how the closeness of countries affects trade partners. The largest trading partner of many European countries is another European country, and the largest trading partner of many Asian countries is Japan or China.

Sometimes neighboring countries take advantage of their proximity by joining into a **free-trade area,** in which the countries have no restrictions on trade between them.

Resources

Proximity is only a partial explanation for trade patterns. As you can see in Table 2-1, Austria sells about three times the value of snowboards to the United States as does Canada, despite being farther away, and Mexico (included among "All other countries" in Table 2-1) sells only $12,000 of snowboards to the United States. Why do Austria and Canada rank higher than Mexico in their sales of snowboards to the United States? Among other reasons, Austria and Canada have cold climates and mountains, making skiing and snowboarding more popular than in Mexico. In many cases, the local production of (and expertise for) ski and snowboard equipment develops as a result of being in a place where snow sports are common. This local production occurs because of either high demand for equipment or the ready supply of a complementary good (such as a snowy mountain). This is an example of how the geography of a country (mountains and climate, in this case) affects its exports. Ski resorts can also be found in many of the other countries listed in Table 2-1, including Switzerland, Slovenia, Italy, Poland, and France.

Geography includes the **natural resources** (such as land and minerals) found in a country, as well as its **labor resources** (labor of various education and skill levels) and **capital** (machinery and structures). A country's resources are often collectively called its **factors of production,** the land, labor, and capital used to produce goods and services. In the next two chapters, we study how the resources of a country influence its trade patterns and how trade leads to economic gains or losses for different factors of production.

In some cases, a country can export a good without having any advantage in the natural resources needed to produce it. One example is "icewine," which is a type of wine invented in Germany but now also produced in the Niagara Falls region of Canada and the United States (see **Side Bar: Can Comparative Advantage Be Created? The Case of "Icewine"**). Neither Taiwan nor Mexico has many mountains with ski resorts, so what explains their exports of snowboards? A hint is provided by noticing that the wholesale price of a snowboard purchased by the United States from these countries is very low: Taiwan sold snowboards to the United States for $45 and Mexico's wholesale price was just $13. These prices are very low compared with the highest-priced countries shown, which are Switzerland ($226), Tunisia ($171), the Netherlands ($159), and Poland ($155). The low prices from Taiwan and Mexico indicate that the snowboards they sell to the United States are either lower-quality or unfinished boards imported into the United States for further processing. This type of trade in unfinished goods is an example of *offshoring*, a process in which a company spreads its production activities across several countries and trades semifinished products among them. The snowboards coming into the United States from Mexico (at $13) and Canada (at $16) are probably semifinished.

Absolute Advantage

We've now explained some possible reasons for many countries to export snowboards to the United States, but we haven't yet explained the imports from China, the largest exporter of snowboards to the United States, and from the Netherlands, the eighth

SIDE BAR

Can Comparative Advantage Be Created? The Case of "Icewine"

In Ricardo's original example of trade between Portugal and England, he gave Portugal an absolute advantage in both wine and cloth, based on its favorable climate. England would find it very difficult to grow grapes for wine and not so difficult to produce cloth, so it had a comparative advantage in cloth. This raises the question: What if a new technology could be discovered that would allow England to produce world-class grapes and wine? Would it be possible for it to create a new comparative advantage in wine?

Something like this occurred in the Niagara Falls region of Canada, which sells a product called "icewine." First developed in Germany in 1794 (when Ricardo was 21 years old), icewine is produced by allowing grapes to freeze on the vine. Freezing concentrates the sugars and flavors of the grapes, which are picked by hand and then processed into a sweet dessert wine. In 1983 several wineries in the Niagara Falls region of Canada experimented with producing this wine, and it has since taken off to become a local specialty. The cold climate of Niagara Falls offers an advantage in producing icewine, because the temperature should be −10°C to −13°C before picking. The yield from this process is very low—an entire vine might make only one bottle—which is why it is sold in half-bottles. But demand is high because of the unique flavor of this wine, and

Harvesting frozen grapes to make icewine.

the half-bottles often sell for $50 or more. Icewine is now also being produced in the Okanagan Valley region of British Columbia, Canada, which similarly enjoys a climate warm enough in the summer to grow grapes and cold enough in the winter to freeze them. Will England ever be able to develop this wine? If so, the comparative advantage between England and Portugal in Ricardo's original model might be reversed!

largest exporter in 2012 and the country with one of the highest wholesale prices, $159. The Netherlands has no mountains at all, so natural resources are not the reason that it exports snowboards. The Netherlands is, however, known for having very high-quality manufactured products, such as those made by the electronics firm Philips. That is also true for its neighboring country Germany (included among "All other countries" in Table 2-1), which sold only 3 snowboards to the United States in 2012 at an average price of $876 each! That price indicates that the snowboards must be of very high quality and that Germany has the world's most advanced *technology* for producing snowboards. In fact, Germany is recognized as a world leader in the methods used to produce many goods, including chemicals, machine tools, motor vehicles, and steel products. When a country has the best technology for producing a good, it has an **absolute advantage** in the production of that good. Germany has an absolute advantage in many industries, and it produces high-quality goods. But if Germany has an absolute advantage in producing snowboards, why does the United States import so many more snowboards from China, which uses less advanced technologies than Germany in most industries?

Furthermore, although Germany is a world leader in many technologies, so is the United States. So why should the United States import snowboards from Germany or China at all? Why doesn't it just produce all the snowboards it needs with U.S. technology and factors of production?

Comparative Advantage

These questions indicate that absolute advantage is not, in fact, a good explanation for trade patterns. This is one of the key lessons from this chapter. Instead, **comparative advantage** is the primary explanation for trade among countries. To get an idea of what comparative advantage means, let us consider the example of trade between Portugal and England, as described by David Ricardo (see **Side Bar: David Ricardo and Mercantilism**).

To keep things simple, Ricardo considered just two commodities: wine and cloth. Ricardo allowed Portugal to have an absolute advantage in the production of both goods. Portugal's absolute advantage may reflect, for example, its more favorable climate for growing grapes and raising sheep. Even though Portugal can produce wine and cloth more easily than England, England is still able to produce both cloth and wine, but it is *relatively more difficult* to produce wine in England than cloth—as any visitor to England will know, it lacks the steady sunshine needed to produce good grapes! Based on these assumptions, Ricardo argued that England would have a comparative advantage in producing cloth and would export cloth to Portugal, whereas Portugal would have comparative advantage in producing wine and would export wine to England.

SIDE BAR

David Ricardo and Mercantilism

David Ricardo (1772–1823) was one of the great classical economists, and the first model we study in this book is named after him. At the time that Ricardo was writing, there was a school of economic thought known as *mercantilism*. Mercantilists believed that exporting (selling goods to other countries) was good because it generated gold and silver for the national treasury and that importing (buying goods from other countries) was bad because it drained gold and silver from the national treasury. To ensure that a country exported a lot and imported only a little, the mercantilists were in favor of high *tariffs* (taxes that must be paid at the border when a good is imported). The mercantilist school of thought was discredited shortly after the time that Ricardo wrote, but some of these old ideas are still advocated today. For example, the United States sometimes insists that other countries should buy more from its companies and sometimes restricts import purchases from other countries; proponents of these ideas are called "mercantilists."

Ricardo was interested in showing that countries could benefit from international trade without having to use tariffs and without requiring exports to be higher than imports. He considered a case that contrasted sharply with what mercantilists believed to be best for a nation: in his writings about trade, Ricardo assumed that the value of exports equaled the value of imports (a situation called *balanced trade*) and that countries engaged in *free trade*, with no tariffs or other restrictions to limit the flow of goods across borders. Under these assumptions, can international trade benefit every country? Ricardo showed that it could. All countries gain from trade by exporting the goods in which they have comparative advantage.

Ricardo's ideas are so important that it will take some time to explain how and why they work. It is no exaggeration to say that many of the major international institutions in the world today, including the United Nations, the World Bank, and the World Trade Organization, are founded at least in part on the idea that free trade between countries brings gains for all trading partners. This idea comes from the writings of David Ricardo (and Adam Smith, a great classical economist of the eighteenth century).

David Ricardo.

From this example, we can see that a country has comparative advantage in producing those goods that it produces best *compared with* how well it produces other goods. That is, Portugal is better at producing wine than cloth, and England is better at producing cloth than wine, even though Portugal is better than England at producing both goods. This is the idea behind the quotation from Ricardo at the start of the chapter—it is advantageous for Portugal to import cloth from England because England has a comparative advantage in cloth. In our snowboard example, we would expect that China has a disadvantage compared with Germany or the United States in producing many manufactured goods, but it is still better at producing snowboards than some other goods, so it is able to export snowboards to the United States.

It will take us most of the chapter to explain the concept of comparative advantage and why it works as an explanation for trade patterns. As indicated by the other quotation at the beginning of the chapter, from Nobel laureate Paul Samuelson, this concept is far from obvious, and students who master it will have come a long way in their study of international trade.

2 Ricardian Model

In developing the Ricardian model of trade, we will work with an example similar to that used by Ricardo; instead of wine and cloth, however, the two goods will be wheat and cloth. Wheat and other grains (including barley, rice, and so on) are major exports of the United States and Europe, while many types of cloth are imported into these countries. In our example, the home country (we will call it just "Home") will end up with this trade pattern, exporting wheat and importing cloth.

The Home Country

To simplify our example, we will ignore the role of land and capital and suppose that both goods are produced with labor alone. In Home, one worker can produce 4 bushels of wheat or 2 yards of cloth. This production can be expressed in terms of the **marginal product of labor (MPL)** for each good. Recall from your study of microeconomics that the marginal product of labor is the extra output obtained by using one more unit of labor.[2] In Home, one worker produces 4 bushels of wheat, so $MPL_W = 4$. Alternatively, one worker can produce 2 yards of cloth, so $MPL_C = 2$.

Home Production Possibilities Frontier Using the marginal products for producing wheat and cloth, we can graph Home's **production possibilities frontier (PPF)**. Suppose there are $\overline{L} = 25$ workers in the home country (the bar over the letter L indicates our assumption that the amount of labor in Home stays constant). If all these workers were employed in wheat, they could produce $Q_W = MPL_W \cdot \overline{L} = 4 \cdot 25 = 100$ bushels. Alternatively, if they were all employed in cloth, they could produce $Q_C = MPL_C \cdot \overline{L} = 2 \cdot 25 = 50$ yards. The production possibilities frontier is a straight line between these two points at the corners, as shown in Figure 2-1. The straight-line PPF, a special feature of the Ricardian model, follows from the assumption that

[2] A special assumption of the Ricardian model is that there are no diminishing returns to labor, so the marginal product of labor is constant. That assumption will no longer be made in the next chapter, when we introduce capital and land, along with labor, as factors of production.

FIGURE 2-1

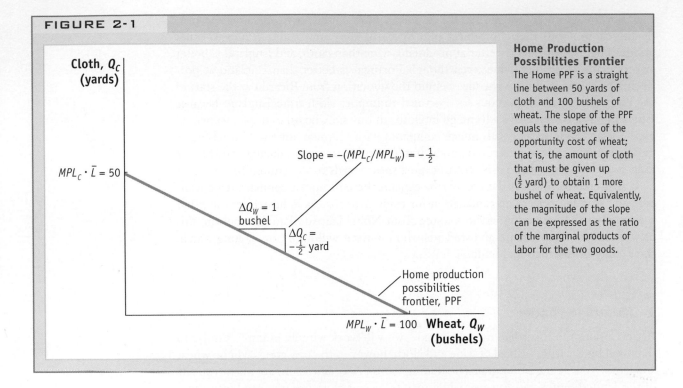

Home Production Possibilities Frontier
The Home PPF is a straight line between 50 yards of cloth and 100 bushels of wheat. The slope of the PPF equals the negative of the opportunity cost of wheat; that is, the amount of cloth that must be given up ($\frac{1}{2}$ yard) to obtain 1 more bushel of wheat. Equivalently, the magnitude of the slope can be expressed as the ratio of the marginal products of labor for the two goods.

the marginal products of labor are *constant*. That is, regardless of how much wheat or cloth is already being produced, one extra hour of labor yields an additional 4 bushels of wheat or 2 yards of cloth. There are *no diminishing returns* in the Ricardian model because it ignores the role of land and capital.

Given this property, the slope of the PPF in Figure 2-1 can be calculated as the ratio of the quantity of cloth produced to the quantity of wheat produced at the corners, as follows:

$$\text{Slope of PPF} = -\frac{50}{100} = -\frac{MPL_C \cdot \overline{L}}{MPL_W \cdot \overline{L}} = -\left(\frac{MPL_C}{MPL_W}\right) = -\frac{1}{2}$$

Ignoring the minus sign, the slope equals the ratio of marginal products of the two goods. The slope is also the **opportunity cost** of wheat, the amount of cloth that must be given up to obtain one more unit of wheat.[3] To see this, suppose that Q_W is increased by 1 bushel. It takes one worker to produce 4 bushels of wheat, so increasing Q_W by 1 bushel means that one-quarter of a worker's time must be withdrawn from the cloth industry and shifted into wheat production. This shift would reduce cloth output by $\frac{1}{2}$ yard, the amount of cloth that could have been produced by one-quarter of a worker's time. Thus, yard of cloth is the opportunity cost of obtaining 1 more bushel of wheat and is the slope of the PPF.

Home Indifference Curve With this production possibilities frontier, what combination of wheat and cloth will Home actually produce? The answer depends on

---

[3] Notice that the slope of the PPF is the opportunity cost of the good on the *horizontal* axis—wheat, in this case.

the country's demand for each of the two goods. There are several ways to represent demand in the Home economy, but we will start by using **indifference curves.** Each indifference curve shows the combinations of two goods, such as wheat and cloth, that a person or economy can consume and be equally satisfied.

In Figure 2-2, the consumer is indifferent between points A and B, for example. Both of these points lie on an indifference curve U_1 associated with a given level of satisfaction, or utility. Point C lies on a higher indifference curve U_2, indicating that it gives a higher level of utility, whereas point D lies on a lower indifference curve U_0, indicating that it gives a lower level of utility. It is common to use indifference curves to reflect the utility that an individual consumer receives from various consumption points. In Figure 2-2, we go a step further, however, and apply this idea to an entire country. That is, the indifference curves in Figure 2-2 show the preferences of an entire country. The combinations of wheat and cloth on U_0 give consumers in the country lower utility than the combinations on indifference curve U_1, which in turn gives lower utility than the combinations of wheat and cloth on U_2.

Home Equilibrium   In the absence of international trade, the production possibilities frontier acts like a budget constraint for the country, and with perfectly competitive markets, the economy will produce at the point of highest utility subject to the limits imposed by its PPF. The point of highest utility is at point A in Figure 2-2, where Home consumes 25 yards of cloth and 50 bushels of wheat. This bundle of goods gives Home the highest level of utility possible (indifference curve U_1) given the limits of its PPF. Notice that Home could produce at other points such as point D,

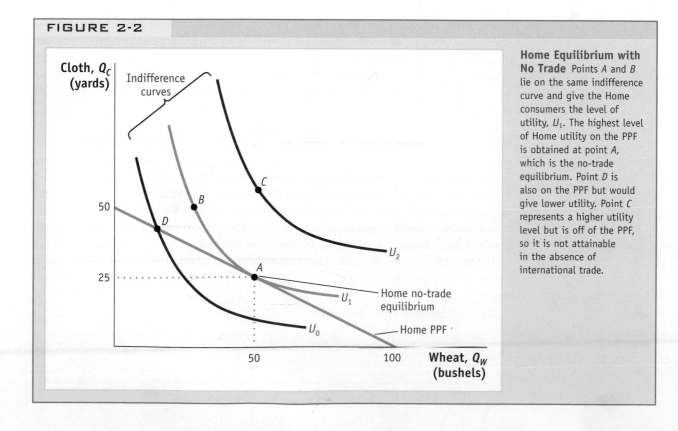

FIGURE 2-2

Home Equilibrium with No Trade   Points A and B lie on the same indifference curve and give the Home consumers the level of utility, U_1. The highest level of Home utility on the PPF is obtained at point A, which is the no-trade equilibrium. Point D is also on the PPF but would give lower utility. Point C represents a higher utility level but is off of the PPF, so it is not attainable in the absence of international trade.

but this point would give a lower level of utility than point A (i.e., point D would offer lower utility because U_0 is lower than U_1). Other consumption points, such as C, would give higher levels of utility than point A but cannot be obtained in the absence of international trade because they lie outside of Home's PPF.

We will refer to point A as the "no-trade" or the "pre-trade" equilibrium for Home.[4] What we really mean by this phrase is "no *international* trade." The Home country is able to reach point A by having its own firms produce wheat and cloth and sell these goods to its own consumers. We are assuming that there are many firms in each of the wheat and cloth industries, so the firms act under perfect competition and take the market prices for wheat and cloth as given. The idea that perfectly competitive markets lead to the highest level of well-being for consumers—as illustrated by the highest level of utility at point A—is an example of the "invisible hand" that Adam Smith (1723–1790) wrote about in his famous book *The Wealth of Nations*. Like an invisible hand, competitive markets lead firms to produce the amount of goods that results in the highest level of well-being for consumers.

Opportunity Cost and Prices Whereas the slope of the PPF reflects the opportunity cost of producing one more bushel of wheat, under perfect competition the opportunity cost of wheat should also equal the relative price of wheat, as follows from the economic principle that price reflects the opportunity cost of a good. We can now check that this equality between the opportunity cost and the relative price of wheat holds at point A.

Wages We solve for the prices of wheat and cloth using an indirect approach, by first reviewing how wages are determined. In competitive labor markets, firms hire workers up to the point at which the cost of one more hour of labor (the wage) equals the value of one more hour of production. In turn, the value of one more hour of labor equals the amount of goods produced in that hour (the marginal product of labor) times the price of the good (P_W for the price of wheat and P_C for the price of cloth). That is to say, in the wheat industry, labor will be hired up to the point at which the wage equals $P_W \cdot MPL_W$, and in the cloth industry labor will be hired up to the point at which the wage equals $P_C \cdot MPL_C$.

If we assume that labor is perfectly free to move between these two industries and that workers will choose to work in the industry for which the wage is highest, then wages must be equalized across the two industries. If the wages were not the same in the two industries, laborers in the low-wage industry would have an incentive to move to the high-wage industry; this would, in turn, lead to an abundance of workers and a decrease in the wage in the high-wage industry and a scarcity of workers and an increase in the wage in the low-wage industry. This movement of labor would continue until wages are equalized between the two industries.

We can use the equality of the wage across industries to obtain the following equation:

$$P_W \cdot MPL_W = P_C \cdot MPL_C$$

By rearranging terms, we see that

$$P_W/P_C = MPL_C/MPL_W$$

---

[4] We also refer to point A as the "autarky equilibrium," because "autarky" means a situation in which the country does not engage in international trade.

The right-hand side of this equation is the slope of the production possibilities frontier (the opportunity cost of obtaining one more bushel of wheat) and the left-hand side of the equation is the **relative price** of wheat, as we will explain in the next paragraph. This equation says that the relative price of wheat (on the left) and opportunity cost of wheat (on the right) must be equal in the no-trade equilibrium at point A.

To understand why we measure the relative price of wheat as the ratio P_W/P_C, suppose that a bushel of wheat costs \$3 and a yard of cloth costs \$6. Then \$3/\$6 = $\frac{1}{2}$, which shows that the relative price of wheat is $\frac{1}{2}$, that is, $\frac{1}{2}$ of a yard of cloth (or half of \$6) must be given up to obtain 1 bushel of wheat (the price of which is \$3). A price ratio like P_W/P_C always denotes the relative price of the good in the numerator (wheat, in this case), measured in terms of how much of the good in the denominator (cloth) must be given up. In Figure 2-2, the slope of the PPF equals the relative price of wheat, the good on the *horizontal axis*.

The Foreign Country

Now let's introduce another country, Foreign, into the model. We will assume that Foreign's technology is inferior to Home's so that it has an absolute *disadvantage* in producing both wheat and cloth as compared with Home. Nevertheless, once we introduce international trade, we will still find that Foreign will trade with Home.

Foreign Production Possibilities Frontier Suppose that one Foreign worker can produce 1 bushel of wheat ($MPL^*_W = 1$), or 1 yard of cloth ($MPL^*_C = 1$), whereas recall that a Home worker can produce 4 bushels of wheat or 2 yards of cloth. Suppose that there are $\overline{L}^* = 100$ workers available in the Foreign country. If all these workers were employed in wheat, they could produce $MPL^*_W \cdot \overline{L}^* = 100$ bushels, and if they were all employed in cloth, they could produce $MPL^*_C \cdot \overline{L}^* = 100$ yards. Foreign's production possibilities frontier (PPF) is thus a straight line between these two points, with a slope of –1, as shown in Figure 2-3.

You might find it helpful to think of the Home country in our example as the United States or Europe and the Foreign country as the "rest of the world." Empirical evidence supports the idea that the United States and Europe have the leading technologies in many goods and an absolute advantage in the production of both wheat and cloth. Nevertheless, they import much of their clothing and textiles from abroad, especially from Asia and Latin America. Why does the United States or Europe import these goods from abroad when they have superior technology at home? To answer this question, we want to focus on the *comparative advantage* of Home and Foreign in producing the two goods.

Comparative Advantage In Foreign, it takes one worker to produce 1 bushel of wheat or 1 yard of cloth. Therefore, the opportunity cost of producing 1 yard of cloth is 1 bushel of wheat. In Home, one worker produces 2 yards of cloth or 4 bushels of wheat. Therefore, Home's opportunity cost of a bushel of wheat is $\frac{1}{2}$ a yard of cloth, and its opportunity cost of a yard of cloth is 2 bushels of wheat. Based on this comparison, Foreign has a *comparative advantage in producing cloth* because its opportunity cost of cloth (which is 1 bushel of wheat) is *lower* than Home's opportunity cost of cloth (which is 2 bushels of wheat). Conversely, Home has a *comparative advantage in producing wheat* because Home's opportunity cost of wheat (which is $\frac{1}{2}$ yard of cloth) is lower than Foreign's (1 yard of cloth). In general, a country has a comparative advantage in a good when it has a lower opportunity cost of producing it than does

FIGURE 2-3

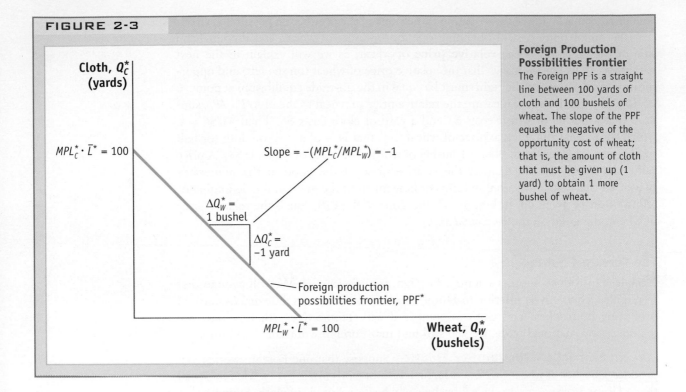

Foreign Production Possibilities Frontier The Foreign PPF is a straight line between 100 yards of cloth and 100 bushels of wheat. The slope of the PPF equals the negative of the opportunity cost of wheat; that is, the amount of cloth that must be given up (1 yard) to obtain 1 more bushel of wheat.

the other country. Notice that Foreign has a comparative advantage in cloth even though it has an absolute disadvantage in both goods.

As before, we can represent Foreign's preferences for wheat and cloth with indifference curves like those shown in Figure 2-4. With competitive markets, the economy will produce at the point of highest utility for the country, point A^*, which is the no-trade equilibrium in Foreign. The slope of the PPF, which equals the opportunity cost of wheat, also equals the relative price of wheat.[5] Therefore, in Figure 2-4, Foreign's no-trade relative price of wheat is $P_W^*/P_C^* = 1$. Notice that this relative price *exceeds* Home's no-trade relative price of wheat, which is $P_W/P_C = \frac{1}{2}$. This difference in these relative prices reflects the comparative advantage that Home has in the production of wheat.[6]

APPLICATION

Comparative Advantage in Apparel, Textiles, and Wheat

The U.S. textile and apparel industries face intense import competition, especially from Asia and Latin America. Employment in this industry in the United States fell by more than 80%, from about 1.7 million people in 1990 to about 300,000 in 2011.

---

[5] Remember that the slope of the PPF (ignoring the minus sign) equals the relative price of the good on the *horizontal* axis—wheat in Figure 2-4. Foreign has a steeper PPF than Home as shown in Figure 2-2, so Foreign's relative price of wheat is higher than Home's. The inverse of the relative price of wheat is the relative price of cloth, which is lower in Foreign.

[6] Taking the reciprocal of the relative price of wheat in each country, we also see that Foreign's no-trade relative price of cloth is $P_C^*/P_W^* = 1$, which is less than Home's no-trade relative price of cloth, $P_C/P_W = 2$. Therefore, Foreign has a comparative advantage in cloth.

FIGURE 2-4

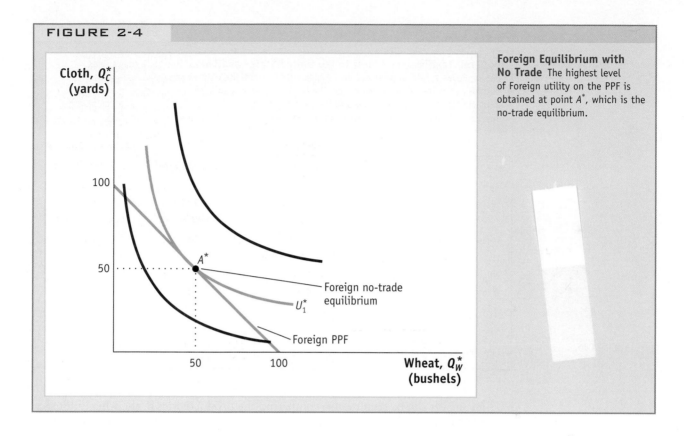

Foreign Equilibrium with No Trade The highest level of Foreign utility on the PPF is obtained at point A^*, which is the no-trade equilibrium.

An example of this import competition can be seen in one U.S. fabric manufacturer, Burlington Industries, which announced in January 1999 that it would reduce its production capacity by 25% because of increased imports from Asia. Burlington closed seven plants and laid off 2,900 people, approximately 17% of its domestic force. After the layoffs, Burlington Industries employed 17,400 people in the United States. Despite these reductions in employment, textiles and apparel remains an important industry in some cities: Los Angeles had about 2,500 business establishments in the apparel industry in 2010, and New York had about 800.[7]

The average sales per employee for all U.S. apparel producers was $56,000 in 2010, as shown in Table 2-2. The textile industry, producing the fabric and material inputs for apparel, is even more productive, with annual sales per employee of $165,000 in the United States. In comparison, the average employee in China produces $23,000 of sales per year in the apparel industry and $27,000 in the textile industry. Thus, an employee in the United States produces $56,000/$23,000 = 2.4 times more apparel sales than an employee in China and $165,000/$27,000 = 6.1 times more textile sales. This ratio is shown in Table 2-2 in the column labeled "Absolute Advantage." It illustrates how much more productive U.S. labor is in these industries relative to Chinese labor. The United States clearly has an absolute advantage in both these industries, so why does it import so much of its textiles and apparel from Asia, including China?

---

[7] These facts and many more about the apparel industry in the United States can be found at: http://www.bls.gov/spotlight/2012/fashion/ (accessed March 2, 2013).

TABLE 2-2

Apparel, Textiles, and Wheat in the United States and China This table shows sales per employee for the apparel and textile industries in the United States and China, as well as bushels per worker in producing wheat. The United States has an absolute advantage in all these products (as shown by the numbers in the right-hand column of the table), but it has a comparative advantage in producing wheat (as shown by the numbers in the bottom rows of the table).

	United States	China	Absolute Advantage
	Sales/Employee	Sales/Employee	U.S./China Ratio
Apparel	$56,000	$23,000	2.4
Textiles	$165,000	$27,000	6.1
	Bushels/Worker	Bushels/Worker	U.S./China Ratio
Wheat	12,260	300	41
	Comparative Advantage		
Wheat/apparel ratio	0.22	0.01	
Wheat/textile ratio	0.07	0.01	

Note: Data are for 2010.

Source: U.S. apparel and textile data from U.S. Bureau of Labor Statistics. U.S. wheat data from USDA Wheat Yearbook 2010. All China data from China Statistical Yearbook 2010.

The answer can be seen by also comparing the productivities in the wheat industry. The typical wheat farm in the United States grows more than 12,000 bushels of wheat per worker (by which we mean either the farmer or an employee). In comparison, the typical wheat farm in China produces only 300 bushels of wheat per worker, so the U.S. farm is 12,260/300 = 41 times more productive! The United States clearly has an *absolute advantage* in the textile and apparel and wheat industries.

But China has the *comparative advantage* in both apparel and textiles, as illustrated by the rows labeled "Comparative Advantage." Dividing the marginal product of labor in wheat by the marginal product of labor in apparel give us the *opportunity cost of apparel*. In the United States, for example, this ratio is 12,260/$56,000 = 0.22 bushels/$, indicating that 0.22 bushels of wheat must be foregone to obtain an extra dollar of sales in apparel. In textiles, the U.S. ratio is 12,260/$165,000 = 0.07 bushels/$, so that 0.07 bushels of wheat must be foregone to obtain an extra dollar in textile sales. These ratios are much smaller in China: only 300/$23,000 or 300/$27,000 ≈ 0.01 bushels of wheat must be foregone to obtain $1 of extra sales in either textiles or apparel. As a result, China has a lower opportunity cost of both textiles and apparel than the United States, which explains why it exports those goods, while the United States exports wheat, just as predicted by the Ricardian model. ■

3 Determining the Pattern of International Trade

Now that we have examined each country in the absence of trade, we can start to analyze what happens when goods are traded between them. We will see that a country's no-trade relative price determines which product it will export and which it will import when trade is opened. Earlier, we saw that the no-trade relative price in each country equals its opportunity cost of producing that good. Therefore, the pattern of exports and imports is determined by the opportunity costs of production in each country, or by each country's pattern of comparative advantage. This section examines why this is the case and details each country's choice of how much to produce, consume, and trade of each good.

International Trade Equilibrium

The differences in no-trade prices across the countries create an opportunity for international trade between them. In particular, producers of cloth in Foreign, where the relative price of cloth is $P_C^*/P_W^* = 1$, would want to export cloth to Home, where the relative price, $P_C/P_W = 2$, is higher. Conversely, producers of wheat in Home, where the relative price of wheat is $P_W/P_C = \frac{1}{2}$, would want to export wheat to Foreign, where the relative price of $P_W^*/P_C^* = 1$ is higher. The trade pattern that we expect to arise, then, is that *Home will export wheat*, and *Foreign will export cloth*. Notice that both countries export the good in which they have a comparative advantage, which is what the Ricardian model predicts.

To solidify our understanding of this trade pattern, let's be more careful about explaining where the two countries would produce on their PPFs under international trade and where they would consume. As Home exports wheat, the quantity of wheat sold at Home falls, and this condition bids up the price of wheat in the Home market. As the exported wheat arrives in the Foreign wheat market, more wheat is sold there, and the price of wheat in the Foreign market falls. Likewise, as Foreign exports cloth, the price of cloth in Foreign will be bid up and the price of cloth in Home will fall. The two countries are in an **international trade equilibrium,** or just "trade equilibrium," for short, when the relative price of wheat is the same in the two countries, which means that the relative price of cloth is also the same in both countries.[8]

To fully understand the international trade equilibrium, we are interested in two issues: (1) determining the relative price of wheat (or cloth) in the trade equilibrium and (2) seeing how the shift from the no-trade equilibrium to the trade equilibrium affects production and consumption in both Home and Foreign. Addressing the first issue requires some additional graphs, so let's delay this discussion for a moment and suppose for now that the relative price of wheat in the trade equilibrium is established at a level between the pre-trade prices in the two countries. This assumption is consistent with the bidding up of export prices and bidding down of import prices, as discussed previously. Since the no-trade prices were $P_W/P_C = \frac{1}{2}$ in Home and $P_W^*/P_C^* = 1$ in Foreign, let's suppose that the world relative price of wheat is between these two values, say, at $\frac{2}{3}$. Given the change in relative prices from their pre-trade level to the international trade equilibrium, what happens to production and consumption in each of the two countries?

Change in Production and Consumption The world relative price of wheat that we have assumed is higher than Home's pre-trade price ($\frac{2}{3} > \frac{1}{2}$). This relationship between the pre-trade and world relative prices means that Home producers of wheat can earn more than the opportunity cost of wheat (which is 1/2) by selling their wheat to Foreign. For this reason, Home will shift its labor resources toward the production

---

[8] Notice that if the relative price of wheat P_W/P_C is the same in the two countries, then the relative price of cloth, which is just its inverse (P_C/P_W), is also the same.

of wheat and produce more wheat than it did in the pre-trade equilibrium (point A in Figure 2-5). To check that this intuition is correct, let us explore the incentives for labor to work in each of Home's industries.

Recall that Home wages paid in the wheat industry equal $P_W \cdot MPL_W$, and wages paid in the cloth industry equal $P_C \cdot MPL_C$. We know that the relative price of wheat in the trade equilibrium is $P_W/P_C = \frac{2}{3}$, that the marginal product of labor in the Home wheat industry is $MPL_W = 4$, and that the marginal product of labor in the Home cloth industry is $MPL_C = 2$. We can plug these numbers into the formulas for wages to compute the *ratio* of wages in the two industries as

$$\frac{P_W \cdot MPL_W}{P_C \cdot MPL_C} = \left(\frac{2}{3}\right)\left(\frac{4}{2}\right) = \frac{8}{6} > 1, \text{ so that } P_W \cdot MPL_W > P_C \cdot MPL_C$$

This formula tells us that with the world relative price of wheat, wages paid in Home's wheat industry ($P_W \cdot MPL_W$) are greater than those paid in its cloth industry ($P_C \cdot MPL_C$). Accordingly, all of Home's workers will want to work in the wheat industry, and no cloth will be produced. With trade, the Home economy

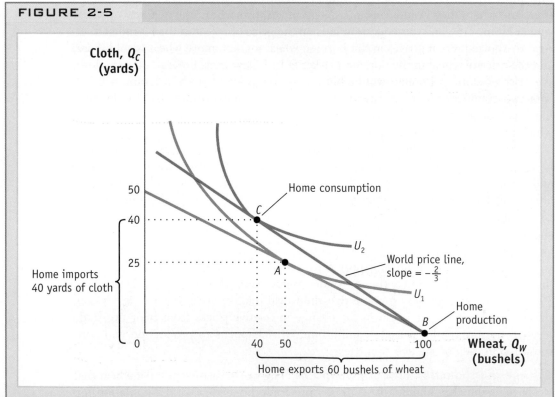

FIGURE 2-5

Home Equilibrium with Trade With a world relative price of wheat of $\frac{2}{3}$, Home production will occur at point B. Through international trade, Home is able to export each bushel of wheat it produces in exchange for $\frac{2}{3}$ yard of cloth. As wheat is exported, Home moves up the world price line, BC. Home consumption occurs at point C, at the tangent intersection with indifference curve, U_2, since this is the highest possible utility curve on the world price line. Given these levels of production and consumption, we can see that total exports are 60 bushels of wheat in exchange for imports of 40 yards of cloth and also that Home consumes 10 fewer bushels of wheat and 15 more yards of cloth relative to its pre-trade levels.

will be fully specialized in wheat production, as occurs at production point B in Figure 2-5.[9]

International Trade Starting at the production point B, Home can export wheat at a relative price of $\frac{2}{3}$. This means that for 1 bushel of wheat exported to Foreign, it receives $\frac{2}{3}$ yard of cloth in exchange. In Figure 2-5, we can trace out its international trades by starting at point B and then exchanging 1 bushel of wheat for $\frac{2}{3}$ yard of cloth, another bushel of wheat for $\frac{2}{3}$ yard of cloth, and so on. From point B, this traces out the line toward point C, with slope $-\frac{2}{3}$. We will call the line starting at point B (the production point) and with a slope equal to the negative of the world relative price of wheat, the **world price line,** as shown by BC. The world price line shows the range of *consumption possibilities* that a country can achieve by specializing in one good (wheat, in Home's case) and engaging in international trade (exporting wheat and importing cloth). We can think of the world price line as a new budget constraint for the country under international trade.

Notice that this budget constraint (the line BC) lies *above* Home's original PPF. The ability to engage in international trade creates consumption possibilities for Home that were not available in the absence of trade, when the consumption point had to be on Home's PPF. Now, Home can choose to consume at any point on the world price line, and utility is maximized at the point corresponding to the intersection with highest indifference curve, labeled C with a utility of U_2. Home obtains a higher utility with international trade than in the absence of international trade (U_2 is higher than U_1); the finding that Home's utility increases with trade is our first demonstration of the **gains from trade,** by which we mean the ability of a country to obtain higher utility for its citizens under free trade than with no trade.

Pattern of Trade and Gains from Trade Comparing production point B with consumption point C, we see that Home is exporting $100 - 40 = 60$ bushels of wheat, in exchange for 40 yards of cloth imported from Foreign. If we value the wheat at its international price of $\frac{2}{3}$, then the value of the exported wheat is $\frac{2}{3} \cdot 60 = 40$ yards of cloth, and the value of the imported cloth is also 40 yards of cloth. Because Home's exports equal its imports, this outcome shows that Home's trade is balanced.

What happens in Foreign when trade occurs? Foreign's production and consumption points are shown in Figure 2-6. The world relative price of wheat ($\frac{2}{3}$) is less than Foreign's pre-trade relative price of wheat (which is 1). This difference in relative prices causes workers to leave wheat production and move into the cloth industry. Foreign specializes in cloth production at point B^*, and from there, trades along the world price line with a slope of (negative) $\frac{2}{3}$, which is the relative price of wheat. That is, Foreign exchanges $\frac{2}{3}$ yard of cloth for 1 bushel of wheat, then $\frac{2}{3}$ yard of cloth for another 1 bushel of wheat, and so on repeatedly, as it moves down the world price line B^*C^*. The consumption point that maximizes Foreign's utility is C^*, at which point 60 units of each good are consumed and utility is U_2^*. Foreign's utility is greater than it was in the absence of international trade (U_2^* is a higher indifference curve than U_1^*), as is true for Home. Therefore, both countries gain from trade.

---

[9] The fully specialized economy (producing only wheat) is a special feature of the Ricardian model because of its straight-line production possibilities frontier.

FIGURE 2-6

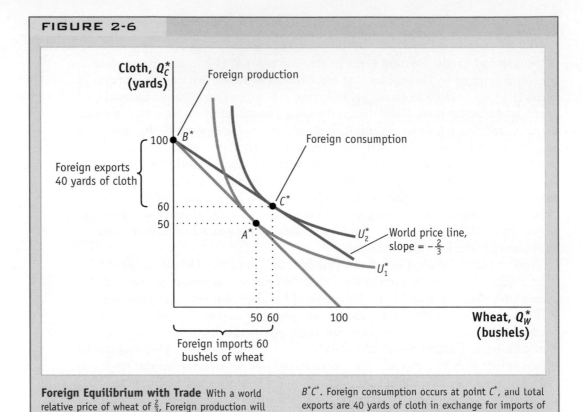

Foreign Equilibrium with Trade With a world relative price of wheat of $\frac{2}{3}$, Foreign production will occur at point B^*. Through international trade, Foreign is able to export $\frac{2}{3}$ yard of cloth in exchange for 1 bushel of wheat, moving down the world price line, B^*C^*. Foreign consumption occurs at point C^*, and total exports are 40 yards of cloth in exchange for imports of 60 bushels of wheat. Relative to its pre-trade wheat and cloth consumption (point A^*), Foreign consumes 10 more bushels of wheat and 10 more yards of cloth.

Foreign produces 100 yards of cloth at point B^*: it consumes 60 yards itself and exports $100 - 60 = 40$ yards of cloth in exchange for 60 bushels of wheat imported from Home. This trade pattern is exactly the opposite of Home's, as must be the case. In our two-country world, everything leaving one country must arrive in the other. We see that Home is exporting wheat, in which it has a comparative advantage (Home's opportunity cost of wheat production is $\frac{1}{2}$ yard of cloth compared with 1 yard in Foreign). Furthermore, Foreign is exporting cloth, in which it has a comparative advantage (Foreign's opportunity cost of cloth production is 1 bushel of wheat compared with 2 bushels in Home). This outcome confirms that *the pattern of trade is determined by comparative advantage*, which is the first lesson of the Ricardian model. We have also established that there are *gains from trade for both countries*, which is the second lesson.

These two conclusions are often where the Ricardian model stops in its analysis of trade between countries, but the story is incomplete because we have not yet determined the level of wages across countries. We have seen that with trade, the relative price of each good converges to a single equilibrium price in both countries. Does the same occur with wages? As we now show, this is not the case. Wage levels differ across countries with trade, and wages are determined by *absolute* advantage, not *comparative* advantage. This is a third, less emphasized lesson from the Ricardian model, which we explore next.

Solving for Wages Across Countries To understand how wages are determined, we go back to microeconomics. In competitive labor markets, firms will pay workers the value of their marginal product. Home produces and exports wheat, so we can think of Home workers being paid in terms of that good: their real wage is $MPL_W = 4$ bushels of wheat. We refer to this payment as a "real" wage because it is measured in terms of a good that workers consume and not in terms of money. The workers can then sell the wheat they earn on the world market at the relative price of $P_W/P_C = \frac{2}{3}$. Thus, their real wage in terms of units of cloth is $(P_W/P_C) \cdot MPL_W = \frac{2}{3} \cdot 4 = \frac{8}{3}$ yard. Summing up, the Home wage is[10]

$$\text{Home wage} = \begin{cases} MPL_W = 4 \text{ bushels of wheat} \\ \text{or} \\ (P_W/P_C) \cdot MPL_W = \frac{8}{3} \text{ yard of cloth} \end{cases}$$

What happens to Foreign wages? Foreign produces and exports cloth, and the real wage is $MPL_C^* = 1$ yard of cloth. Because cloth workers can sell the cloth they earn for wheat on the world market at the price of $\frac{3}{2}$, their real wage in terms of units of wheat is $(P_C^*/P_W^*) \cdot MPL_C^* = \frac{3}{2} \cdot 1 = \frac{3}{2}$ bushel. Thus, the Foreign wage is[11]

$$\text{Foreign wage} = \begin{cases} (P_C^*/P_W^*) \cdot MPL_C^* = \frac{3}{2} \text{ bushels of wheat} \\ \text{or} \\ MPL_C^* = 1 \text{ yard of cloth} \end{cases}$$

Foreign workers earn less than Home workers as measured by their ability to purchase either good. This fact reflects Home's absolute advantage in the production of both goods.

Absolute Advantage As our example shows, wages are determined by absolute advantage: Home is paying higher wages because it has better technology in both goods. In contrast, the pattern of trade in the Ricardian model is determined by comparative advantage. Indeed, these two results go hand in hand—the only way that a country with poor technology can export at a price others are willing to pay is by having low wages.

This statement might sound like a pessimistic assessment of the ability of less developed countries to pay reasonable wages, but it carries with it a silver lining: as a country develops its technology, its wages will correspondingly rise. In the Ricardian model, a logical consequence of technological progress is that workers will become better off through receiving higher wages. In addition, as countries engage in international trade, the Ricardian model predicts that their real wages will rise.[12] We do not have to look very hard to see examples of this outcome in the world. Per capita income in China in 1978, just as that nation began to open up to international trade,

---

[10] Recall that without international trade, Home wages were $MPL_W = 4$ bushels of wheat or $MPL_C = 2$ yards of cloth. Home workers are clearly better off with trade because they can afford to buy the same amount of wheat as before (4 bushels) but more cloth ($\frac{8}{3}$ yards instead of 2 yards). This is another way of demonstrating the gains from trade.

[11] Without international trade, Foreign wages were $MPL_W^* = 1$ bushel of wheat or $MPL_C^* = 1$ yard of cloth. Foreign workers are also better off with trade because they can afford to buy the same amount of cloth (1 yard) but more wheat ($\frac{3}{2}$ bushels instead of 1 bushel).

[12] That result is shown by the comparison of real wages in the trade equilibrium as compared with the no-trade equilibrium in each country, as is done in the previous two footnotes.

is estimated to have been $755 (all numbers are in 2005 dollars), whereas 32 years later in 2010, per capita income in China had risen by nearly 10 times to $7,437. Likewise for India, per capita income more than tripled from $1,040 in 1978 to $3,477 in 2010.[13] Many people believe that the opportunity for these countries to engage in international trade has been crucial in raising their standard of living. As our study of international trade proceeds, we will try to identify the conditions that have allowed China, India, and many other developing countries to improve their standards of living through trade.

APPLICATION

Labor Productivity and Wages

The close connection between wages and labor productivity is evident by looking at data across countries. Labor productivity can be measured by the *value-added per hour* in manufacturing. Value-added is the difference between sales revenue in an industry and the costs of intermediate inputs (e.g., the difference between the value of a car and the cost of all the parts used to build it). Value-added then equals the payments to labor and capital in an industry. In the Ricardian model, we ignore capital, so we can measure labor productivity as value-added divided by the number of hours worked, or value-added per hour.

In Figure 2-7, we show the value-added per hour in manufacturing in 2010 for several different countries. The United States has the highest level of productivity and Taiwan has the lowest for the countries shown. Figure 2-7 also shows the wages

FIGURE 2-7

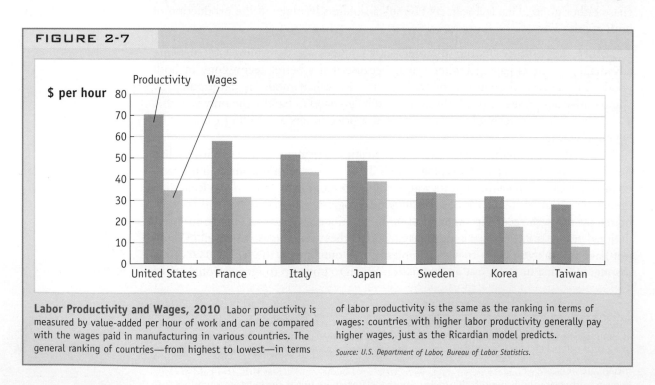

Labor Productivity and Wages, 2010 Labor productivity is measured by value-added per hour of work and can be compared with the wages paid in manufacturing in various countries. The general ranking of countries—from highest to lowest—in terms of labor productivity is the same as the ranking in terms of wages: countries with higher labor productivity generally pay higher wages, just as the Ricardian model predicts.

Source: U.S. Department of Labor, Bureau of Labor Statistics.

---

[13] These values are expressed in 2005 dollars and are taken from the Penn World Table version 7.1, http://pwt.econ.upenn.edu, averaging Version 1 and Version 2 for China.

per hour paid in each country. These are somewhat less than value-added per hour because value-added is also used to pay capital. We see that the highest productivity countries shown—the United States and France—have higher wages than the lowest productivity countries shown—South Korea and Taiwan. But the middle countries—Italy, Japan, and Sweden—have wages at or above the U.S. level, despite having lower productivity. That is because the wage being used includes the *benefits* received by workers, in the form of medical benefits, Social Security, and so on. Many European countries and Japan have higher social benefits than the United States. Although including benefits distorts the comparison between wages and productivity, we still see from Figure 2-7 that higher productivity countries tend to have higher wages, broadly speaking, as the Ricardian model predicts. The connection between productivity and wages is also evident if we look at countries over time. Figure 2-8 shows that the general upward movement in labor productivity is matched by upward movement in wages, also as the Ricardian model predicts. ■

4 Solving for International Prices

In Figures 2-5 and 2-6, we assumed that the world relative price of wheat was $\frac{2}{3}$ and that at this level Home's exports of wheat just equaled Foreign's imports of wheat (and vice versa for cloth). Now let's dig a little deeper to show how the world price is determined.

To determine the world relative price of wheat, we will use supply and demand curves. Home exports wheat, so we will derive a Home **export supply curve,** which shows the amount it wants to export at various relative prices. Foreign imports wheat, so we will derive a Foreign **import demand curve,** which shows the amount of wheat that it will import at various relative prices. The international trade equilibrium is the quantity and relative price at which Home exports equal Foreign imports of wheat. This equality occurs where the Home export supply curve intersects the Foreign import demand curve.

Home Export Supply Curve

In panel (a) of Figure 2-9, we repeat Figure 2-5, which shows the trade equilibrium for Home with production at point B and consumption at point C. At the world relative price of $P_W/P_C = \frac{2}{3}$, Home exports 60 bushels of wheat (the difference between wheat production of 100 and consumption of 40). We can use these numbers to construct a new graph, the Home export supply curve of wheat, shown in panel (b). The vertical axis in panel (b) measures the relative price of wheat and the horizontal axis measures the exports of wheat. The points B and C in panel (a), with the relative price of $P_W/P_C = \frac{2}{3}$ and Home exports of 60 bushels of wheat, now appear as point C' in panel (b), with $P_W/P_C = \frac{2}{3}$ on the vertical axis and Home wheat exports of 60 bushels on the horizontal axis. This is our first point on the Home export supply curve.

To derive other points on the export supply curve, consider the no-trade equilibrium in panel (a), which is shown by production and consumption at point A. The no-trade relative price of wheat is $\frac{1}{2}$ (the slope of Home's PPF), and Home exports of wheat are zero because there is no international trade. So the point A in panel (a) can be graphed at point A' in panel (b), with a relative price of $P_W/P_C = \frac{1}{2}$ and zero Home exports of wheat. This gives us a second point on the Home export supply curve.

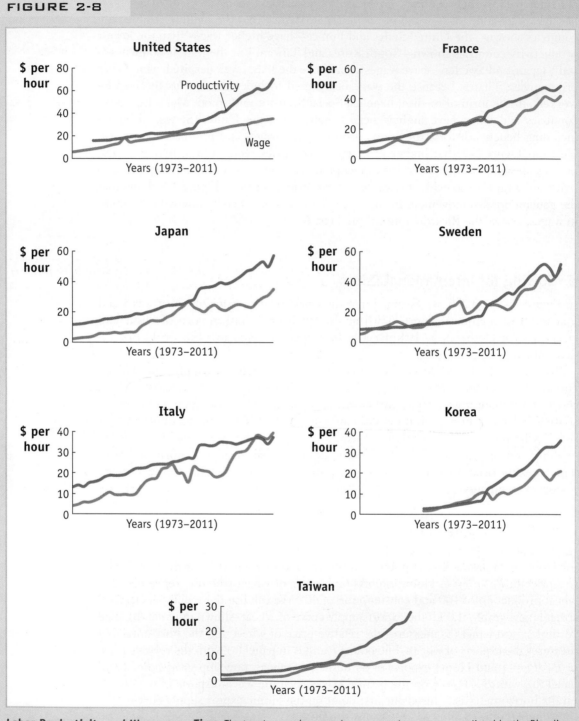

FIGURE 2-8

Labor Productivity and Wages over Time The trends in labor productivity and wages can also be graphed over time. The general upward movement in labor productivity is matched by upward movements in wages, as predicted by the Ricardian model.

Source: U.S. Department of Labor, Bureau of Labor Statistics.

FIGURE 2-9

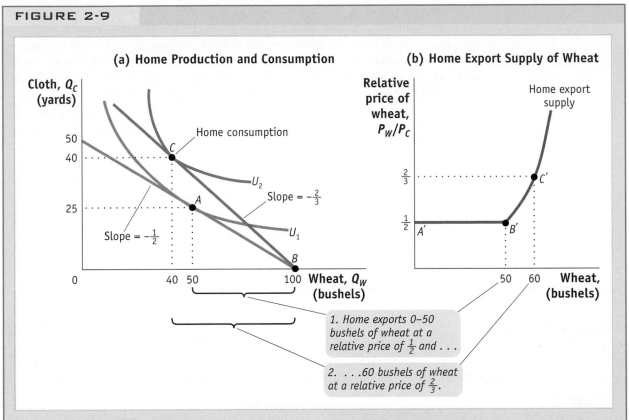

(a) Home Production and Consumption

Cloth, Q_C (yards)

Home consumption

50
40 ⋯⋯⋯⋯⋯⋯ C

U_2

Slope = $-\frac{2}{3}$

25 ⋯⋯⋯⋯ A

Slope = $-\frac{1}{2}$

U_1

B

0   40 50   100 **Wheat, Q_W**
                              (bushels)

(b) Home Export Supply of Wheat

Relative price of wheat, P_W/P_C

Home export supply

$\frac{2}{3}$ ⋯⋯⋯⋯⋯⋯⋯ C'

$\frac{1}{2}$ A' B'

                    50 60 **Wheat,**
                              (bushels)

1. Home exports 0–50 bushels of wheat at a relative price of $\frac{1}{2}$ and . . .

2. . . .60 bushels of wheat at a relative price of $\frac{2}{3}$.

Home Export Supply Panel (a) repeats Figure 2-5 showing the trade equilibrium for Home with production at point B and consumption at point C. Panel (b) shows the Home export supply of wheat. When the relative price of wheat is $\frac{1}{2}$, Home will export any amount of wheat between 0 and 50 bushels, along the segment $A'B'$ of the Home export supply curve. For relative prices above $\frac{1}{2}$, Home exports more than 50 bushels, along the segment $B'C'$. For example, at the relative price of $\frac{2}{3}$, Home exports 60 bushels of wheat.

To get a third point, let us keep the relative price of wheat at $P_W/P_C = \frac{1}{2}$, as in the no-trade equilibrium, but now allow Home to export some wheat in exchange for cloth at this price. Home consumption remains at point A in panel (a), but production can shift from that point. The reason that production can shift to another point on the PPF is that, with the relative price $P_W/P_C = \frac{1}{2}$, the wages of workers are equal in wheat and cloth. This result was shown in our earlier discussion. With wages equal in the two industries, workers are willing to shift between them, so any point on the PPF is a possible production point. Consider, for example, production at point B in panel (a), where all workers have shifted into wheat and no cloth is produced. With the relative price $P_W/P_C = \frac{1}{2}$, consumption is still at point A, so the difference between points A and B is the amount of wheat that Home is exporting and the amount of cloth Home is importing. That is, Home exports 50 bushels of wheat (the difference between production of 100 and consumption of 50) and imports 25 yards of cloth (the difference between production of 0 and consumption of 25). Therefore, the relative price of $P_W/P_C = \frac{1}{2}$, with wheat exports of 50, is another point on the Home export supply curve, shown by B' in panel (b).

Joining up points A', B', and C', we get a Home export supply curve that is flat between A' and B', and then rises between B' and C' and beyond. The flat portion of the export supply curve is a special feature of the Ricardian model that occurs because the PPF is a straight line. That is, with the relative price of $P_W/P_C = \frac{1}{2}$, production can occur anywhere along the PPF as workers shift between industries; meanwhile, consumption is fixed at point A, leading to all the export levels between A' and B' in panel (b). As the relative price of wheat rises above $\frac{1}{2}$, production remains fixed at point B in panel (a), but the consumption point changes, rising above point A. With the relative price $P_W/P_C = \frac{2}{3}$, for example, consumption is at point C. Then Home exports of wheat are calculated as the difference between production at B and consumption at C. Graphing the various relative prices above and the bushels of wheat exported at each price, we get the upward-sloping Home export supply curve between B' and C' in panel (b).

Foreign Import Demand Curve   In Foreign we will again focus on the wheat market and construct an import demand curve for wheat. In panel (a) of Figure 2-10, we repeat Figure 2-6, which shows the Foreign trade equilibrium with production at point B^* and consumption at point C^*. At the world relative price of $P_W/P_C = \frac{2}{3}$,

FIGURE 2-10

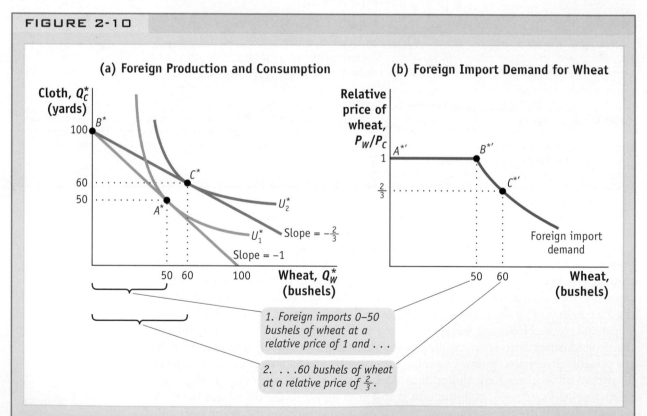

(a) Foreign Production and Consumption

(b) Foreign Import Demand for Wheat

1. Foreign imports 0–50 bushels of wheat at a relative price of 1 and . . .

2. . . .60 bushels of wheat at a relative price of $\frac{2}{3}$.

Foreign Import Demand Panel (a) repeats Figure 2-6, showing the Foreign trade equilibrium with production at point B^* and consumption at point C^*. Panel (b) shows Foreign import demand for wheat. When the relative price of wheat is 1, Foreign will import any amount of wheat between 0 and 50 bushels, along the segment $A^{*'}B^{*'}$ of the Foreign import demand curve. For relative prices below 1, Foreign imports more than 50 bushels, along the segment $B^{*'}C^{*'}$. For example, at the relative price of $\frac{2}{3}$, Foreign imports 60 bushels of wheat.

Foreign imports 60 bushels of wheat (the difference between wheat consumption of 60 and production of 0). These numbers are graphed as point $C^{*\prime}$ in panel (b), where we have the relative price of wheat on the vertical axis and the Foreign imports of wheat on the horizontal axis.

Other points on Foreign's import demand curve can be obtained in much the same way as we did for Home. For example, the no-trade equilibrium in Foreign is shown by production and consumption at point A^* in panel (a), with the relative price of wheat equal to 1 (the slope of Foreign's PPF) and zero imports (since there is no international trade). This no-trade equilibrium is graphed as point $A^{*\prime}$ in panel (b). Keeping the relative price of wheat fixed at 1 in Foreign, production can shift away from point A^* in panel (a). This can occur because, as we argued for Home, wages are the same in Foreign's wheat and cloth industries when the relative price is at its no-trade level, so workers are willing to move between industries. Keeping Foreign consumption fixed at point A^* in panel (a), suppose that all workers shift into the cloth industry, so that production is at point B^*. Then Foreign imports of wheat are 50 bushels (the difference between Foreign consumption of 50 and production of zero), as shown by point $B^{*\prime}$ in panel (b).

Joining up points $A^{*\prime}$, $B^{*\prime}$, and $C^{*\prime}$, we get an import demand curve that is flat between $A^{*\prime}$ and $B^{*\prime}$ and then falls between $B^{*\prime}$ and $C^{*\prime}$ and beyond. The flat portion of the Foreign import demand curve is once again a special feature of the Ricardian model that occurs because the PPF is a straight line. As we investigate other trade models in the following chapters, in which the production possibilities frontiers are curved rather than straight lines, the export supply and import demand curves will no longer have the flat portions. A general feature of these export supply and import demand curves is that they begin at the no-trade relative price for each country and then slope up (for export supply) or down (for import demand).

International Trade Equilibrium

Now that we have derived the Home export supply curve and the Foreign import demand curve, we can put them together in a single diagram, shown in Figure 2-11. The intersection of these two curves at point C' gives the international trade equilibrium, the equilibrium relative price of wheat at which the quantity of Home exports just equals Foreign imports. In Figure 2-11, the equilibrium relative price of wheat is $P_W/P_C = \frac{2}{3}$. This graph looks just like the supply equals demand equilibria that you have seen in other economics classes, except that Figure 2-11 now refers to the *world* market for wheat rather than the market in a single country. That is, Home's export supply of wheat is the *excess* of the total Home supply over the quantity demanded by Home consumers, whereas Foreign import demand is the excess of total Foreign demand over the quantity supplied by Foreign suppliers. The intersection of these excess supply and demand curves, or export supply and import demand curves in Figure 2-11, determines the relative price of wheat that clears the world market, that is, at which the desired sales of Home equal the desired purchases by Foreign.

The Terms of Trade The price of a country's exports divided by the price of its imports is called the **terms of trade.** Because Home exports wheat, (P_W/P_C) is its terms of trade. Notice that an increase in the price of wheat (Home's export) or a fall in the price of cloth (Home's import) would both *raise* its terms of trade. Generally, an increase in the terms of trade is good for a country because it is earning more for its

FIGURE 2-11

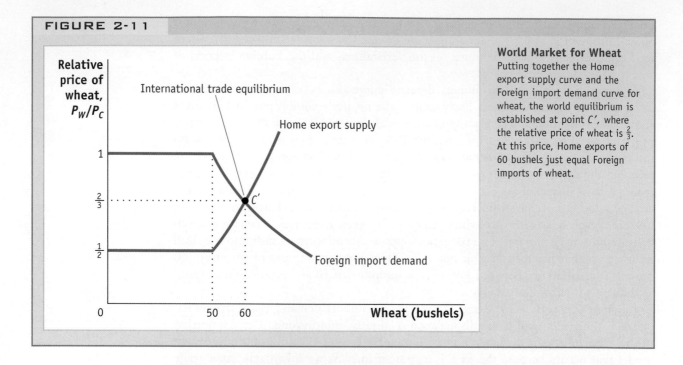

World Market for Wheat
Putting together the Home export supply curve and the Foreign import demand curve for wheat, the world equilibrium is established at point C', where the relative price of wheat is $\frac{2}{3}$. At this price, Home exports of 60 bushels just equal Foreign imports of wheat.

exports or paying less for its imports, thus making it better off. Foreign exports cloth, so (P_C/P_W) is its terms of trade. In this case, having a higher price for cloth (Foreign's export) or a lower price for wheat (Foreign's import) would make the Foreign country better off.

APPLICATION

The Terms of Trade for Primary Commodities

What has happened over time to the terms of trade? Writing in the 1950s, the Latin American economist Raúl Prebisch and the British economist Hans Singer each put forward the hypothesis that the price of *primary commodities* (i.e., agricultural products and minerals) would decline over time relative to the price of manufactured goods. Because primary commodities are often exported by developing countries, this would mean that the terms of trade in developing countries would decline over time.

There are several reasons why the Prebisch-Singer hypothesis might be true. First, it is well known that as people or countries become richer, they spend a smaller share of their income on food.[14] This means that as world income grows, the demand for food will decline relative to the demand for manufactured goods. Therefore, the price of agricultural products can also be expected to decline relative to manufactured goods. Second, for mineral products, it may be that industrialized countries continually find substitutes for the use of minerals in their production of manufactured products. For example, much less steel is used in cars today because automobile producers

---

[14] This relationship is known as Engel's law after the nineteenth-century German statistician Ernst Engel. It is certainly true for purchases of food eaten at home but might not hold for dining out. As your income rises, you might spend a constant or even increasing share of your budget on restaurant food.

have shifted toward the use of plastic and aluminum in the body and frame. We can think of the substitution away from mineral products as a form of technological progress, and as it proceeds, it can lead to a fall in the price of raw minerals.

However, there are also several reasons why the Prebisch-Singer hypothesis may not be true. First, technological progress in manufactured goods can certainly lead to a fall in the price of these goods as they become easier to produce (e.g., think of the reduction in prices of many electronic goods, such as MP3 and DVD players). This is a fall in the terms of trade for industrialized countries rather than developing countries. Second, at least in the case of oil exports, the Organization of Petroleum Exporting Countries (OPEC) has managed to keep oil prices high by restricting supplies on the world market. This has resulted in an increase in the terms of trade for oil-exporting countries, which includes developing and industrialized nations.

Data on the relative price of primary commodities are shown in Figure 2-12.[15] This study considered 24 primary commodities from 1900 to 1998 and measured their world price relative to the overall price of manufactured goods. Of the 24 commodities, one-half of them showed a decline in their relative price for 50% or more of that period, including aluminum, cotton, hides, palm oil, rice, sugar, rubber, wheat, and wool. This evidence provides some support for the Prebisch-Singer hypothesis. Several examples of these commodities, with declining relative prices, are shown in panel (a) of Figure 2-12.

However, there are also a number of primary commodities whose prices increased for significant periods of time, or showed no consistent trend over the century. Commodities that had increasing relative prices for 50% or more of that period include beef, lamb, timber, tin, and tobacco. Several of these commodities are shown in panel (b) of Figure 2-12. Finally, commodities that had no consistent trend in their relative prices between the beginning and end of the century include bananas, coffee, copper, and zinc. Several of these are shown in panel (c) of Figure 2-12. From these results for different commodities, we should conclude that there are some that follow the pattern predicted by Prebisch and Singer, with falling prices relative to manufacturing. This is not a general rule, however, and other primary commodities have had increasing or no consistent change in their prices. ■

5 Conclusions

The Ricardian model was devised to respond to the mercantilist idea that exports are good and imports are bad. Not so, said David Ricardo, and to prove his point, he considered an example in which trade between two countries (England and Portugal) is balanced; that is, the value of imports equals the value of exports for each country. The reason that England and Portugal trade with each other in Ricardo's example is that their technologies for producing wine and cloth are different. Portugal has an absolute advantage in both goods, but England has a comparative advantage in cloth. That is, the opportunity cost of producing cloth in England (measured by how much wine would have to be given up) is lower than in Portugal. Based on this comparative advantage, the no-trade relative price of cloth is also lower in England

---

[15] These results are provided by Neil Kellard and Mark E. Wohar, 2006, "Trends and Persistence in Primary Commodity Prices," *Journal of Development Economics*, 79, February, 146–167.

FIGURE 2-12

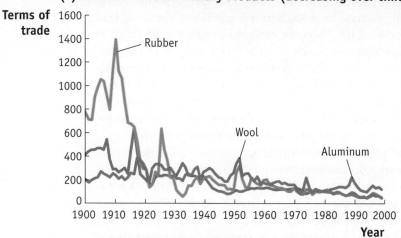

(a) Relative Price of Primary Products (decreasing over time)

Rubber

Wool

Aluminum

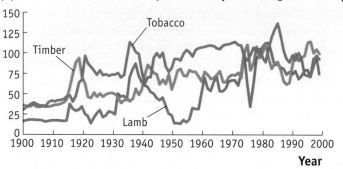

(b) Relative Price of Primary Products (increasing over time)

Tobacco

Timber

Lamb

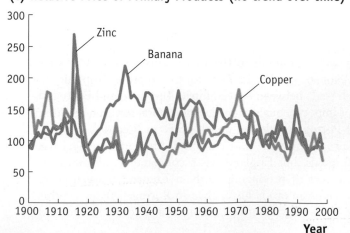

(c) Relative Price of Primary Products (no trend over time)

Zinc

Banana

Copper

Relative Price of Primary Commodities
Many developing countries export primary commodities (i.e., agricultural products and minerals), whereas industrial countries export manufactured products. Shown here are the prices of various primary commodities relative to an overall manufacturing price, from 1900 to 1998. The relative prices of some primary commodities have fallen over time (panel a), whereas other commodities have had rising relative prices (panel b). Other commodity prices show no consistent trend over time (panel c).

than in Portugal. When trade is opened, cloth merchants in England export to Portugal, where they can obtain a higher price, and wine vintners in Portugal export to England. Thus, the pattern of trade is determined by comparative advantage, and both countries gain from trade.

For simplicity, the Ricardian model is presented with just a single factor of production—labor. We have used a lesson from microeconomics to solve for wages as the marginal product of labor times the price of each good. It follows from this relationship that the ratio of wages across countries is determined by the marginal product of labor in the goods being produced and by the prices of those goods. Because wages depend on the marginal products of labor in each country, we conclude that wages are determined by absolute advantage—a country with better technology will be able to pay higher wages. In addition, wages depend on the prices prevailing on world markets for the goods exported by each country. We have defined the "terms of trade" as the price of a country's exports divided by the price of its imports. Generally, having higher terms of trade (because of high export prices or low import prices) will lead to higher real wages and therefore will benefit workers.

The fact that only labor is used in the Ricardian model, with a constant marginal product of labor, makes it special. Because of this assumption, the PPF in the Ricardian model is a straight line, and the export supply and import demand curves each have a flat segment. These special properties do not occur in other models we consider in the following chapters, where in addition to labor, industries will use capital and land. Once we allow for the more realistic assumption of several factors of production, the gains from trade become more complicated. Even if there are overall gains for a country, some factors of production might gain as other factors of production lose due to opening trade. That is the topic we explore in the next chapter.

KEY POINTS

1. A country has comparative advantage in producing a good when the country's opportunity cost of producing the good is lower than the opportunity cost of producing the good in another country.

2. The pattern of trade between countries is determined by comparative advantage. This means that even countries with poor technologies can export the goods in which they have comparative advantage.

3. All countries experience gains from trade. That is, the utility of an importing or exporting country is at least as high as it would be in the absence of international trade.

4. The level of wages in each country is determined by its absolute advantage; that is, by the amount the country can produce with its labor. This result explains why countries with poor technologies are still able to export: their low wages allow them to overcome their low productivity.

5. The equilibrium price of a good on the world market is determined at the point where the export supply of one country equals the import demand of the other country.

6. A country's terms of trade equal the price of its export good divided by the price of its import good. A rise in a country's terms of trade makes it better off because it is exporting at higher prices or importing at lower prices.

KEY TERMS

import, p. 27
export, p. 27
technology, p. 28
resources, p. 28
offshoring, p. 28
proximity, p. 28
Ricardian model, p. 28
trade pattern, p. 29
free-trade area, p. 30
natural resources, p. 30

labor resources, p. 30
capital, p. 30
factors of production, p. 30
absolute advantage, p. 31
comparative advantage, p. 32
marginal product of labor (MPL),
   p. 33
production possibilities frontier
   (PPF), p. 33
opportunity cost, p. 34

indifference curves, p. 35
utility, p. 35
relative price, p. 37
international trade equilibrium,
   p. 41
world price line, p. 43
gains from trade, p. 43
export supply curve, p. 47
import demand curve, p. 47
terms of trade, p. 51

PROBLEMS

1. At the beginning of the chapter, there is a brief quotation from David Ricardo; here is a longer version of what Ricardo wrote:

   > England may be so circumstanced, that to produce the cloth may require the labour of 100 men for one year; and if she attempted to make the wine, it might require the labour of 120 men for the same time. . . . To produce the wine in Portugal, might require only the labour of 80 men for one year, and to produce the cloth in the same country, might require the labour of 90 men for the same time. It would therefore be advantageous for her to export wine in exchange for cloth. This exchange might even take place, notwithstanding that the commodity imported by Portugal could be produced there with less labour than in England.

   Suppose that the amount of labor Ricardo describes can produce 1,000 yards of cloth or 1,000 bottles of wine, in either country. Then answer the following:

   a. What is England's marginal product of labor in cloth and in wine, and what is Portugal's marginal product of labor in cloth and in wine? Which country has absolute advantage in cloth, and in wine, and why?

   b. Use the formula $P_W/P_C = MPL_C/MPL_W$ to compute the no-trade relative price of wine in each country. Which country has comparative advantage in wine, and why?

2. Suppose that each worker in the Home country can produce three cars or two TVs. Assume that Home has four workers.

   a. Graph the production possibilities frontier for the Home country.

   b. What is the no-trade relative price of cars at Home?

3. Suppose that each worker in the Foreign country can produce two cars or three TVs. Assume that Foreign also has four workers.

   a. Graph the production possibilities frontier for the Foreign country.

   b. What is the no-trade relative price of cars in Foreign?

   c. Using the information provided in Problem 2 regarding Home, in which good does Foreign have a comparative advantage, and why?

4. Suppose that in the absence of trade, Home consumes nine cars and two TVs, while Foreign consumes two cars and nine TVs. Add the indifference curve for each country to the figures in Problems 2 and 3. Label the production possibilities frontier (PPF), indifference curve (U_1), and the no-trade equilibrium consumption and production for each country.

5. Now suppose the world relative price of cars is $P_C/P_{TV} = 1$.

   a. In what good will each country specialize? Briefly explain why.

b. Graph the new world price line for each country in the figures in Problem 4, and add a new indifference curve (U_2) for each country in the trade equilibrium.

c. Label the exports and imports for each country. How does the amount of Home exports compare with Foreign imports?

d. Does each country gain from trade? Briefly explain why or why not.

6. Answer the following questions using the information given by the accompanying table:

	Home Country	Foreign Country	Absolute Advantage
Number of bicycles produced per hour	4	2	?
Number of snowboards produced per hour	6	8	?
Comparative advantage	?	?	

a. Complete the table for this problem in the same manner as Table 2-2.

b. Which country has an absolute advantage in the production of bicycles? Which country has an absolute advantage in the production of snowboards?

c. What is the opportunity cost of bicycles in terms of snowboards at Home? What is the opportunity cost of bicycles in terms of snowboards in Foreign?

d. Which product will Home export, and which product does Foreign export? Briefly explain why.

7. Assume that Home and Foreign produce two goods, TVs and cars, and use the information below to answer the following questions:

In the No-Trade Equilibrium

Home Country		Foreign Country	
$Wage_{TV} = 12$	$Wage_C = ?$	$Wage^*_{TV} = ?$	$Wage^*_C = 6$
$MPL_{TV} = 2$	$MPL_C = ?$	$MPL^*_{TV} = ?$	$MPL^*_C = 1$
$P_{TV} = ?$	$P_C = 4$	$P^*_{TV} = 3$	$P^*_C = ?$

a. What is the marginal product of labor for TVs and cars in the Home country? What is the no-trade relative price of TVs at Home?

b. What is the marginal product of labor for TVs and cars in the Foreign country? What is the no-trade relative price of TVs in Foreign?

c. Suppose the world relative price of TVs in the trade equilibrium is $P_{TV}/P_C = 1$. Which good will each country export? Briefly explain why.

d. In the trade equilibrium, what is the real wage at Home in terms of cars and in terms of TVs? How do these values compare with the real wage in terms of either good in the no-trade equilibrium?

e. In the trade equilibrium, what is the real wage in Foreign in terms of TVs and in terms of cars? How do these values compare with the real wage in terms of either good in the no-trade equilibrium?

f. In the trade equilibrium, do Foreign workers earn more or less than those at Home, measured in terms of their ability to purchase goods? Explain why.

8. Why do some low-wage countries, such as China, pose a threat to manufacturers in industrial countries, such as the United States, whereas other low-wage countries, such as Haiti, do not?

Answer Problems 9 to 11 using the chapter information for Home and Foreign.

9. a. Suppose that the number of workers doubles in Home. What happens to the Home PPF and what happens to the no-trade relative price of wheat?

b. Suppose that there is technological progress in the wheat industry such that Home can produce more wheat with the same amount of labor. What happens to the Home PPF, and what happens to the relative price of wheat? Describe what would happen if a similar change occurred in the cloth industry.

10. a. Using Figure 2-5, show that an increase in the relative price of wheat from its world relative price of $\frac{2}{3}$ will raise Home's utility.

b. Using Figure 2-6, show that an increase in the relative price of wheat from its world relative price of $\frac{2}{3}$ will lower Foreign's utility. What is Foreign's utility when the world relative price of wheat reaches 1, and what happens in Foreign when the world relative price of wheat rises above that level?

11. *(This is a harder question.)* Suppose that the Home country is much larger than the Foreign country. For example, suppose we double the number of workers at Home from 25 to 50. Then Home is willing to export up to 100 bushels of wheat at its no-trade price of $P_W/P_C = \frac{1}{2}$ rather than 50 bushels of wheat as shown in Figure 2-11. In the following, we draw a new version of Figure 2-11, with the larger Home country.

   a. From this figure, what is the new world relative price of wheat (at point D)?

   b. Using this new world equilibrium price, draw a new version of the trade equilibrium in Home and in Foreign, and show the production point and consumption point in each country.

   c. Are there gains from trade in both countries? Explain why or why not.

12. Using the results from Problem 11, explain why the Ricardian model predicts that Mexico would gain more than the United States when the two countries signed the North American Free Trade Agreement, establishing free trade between them.

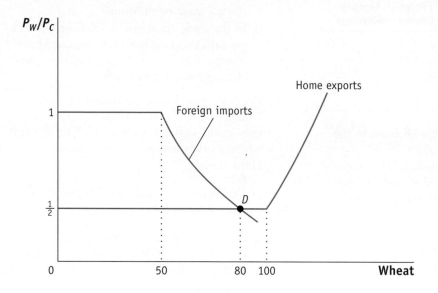

Gains and Losses from Trade in the Specific-Factors Model

The time has come, the awaited day, a historic day in which Bolivia retakes absolute control of our natural resources.

Evo Morales, President of Bolivia, 2006[1]

If we do not take action, those who have the most reason to be dissatisfied with our present rate of growth will be tempted to seek shortsighted and narrow solutions—to resist automation, to reduce the work week to 35 hours or even lower, to shut out imports, or to raise prices in a vain effort to obtain full capacity profits on under-capacity operations. But these are all self-defeating expedients which can only restrict the economy, not expand it.

President John F. Kennedy, New York Economic Club, 1962

Over the span of three years, 2003 to 2005, Bolivia had three presidents. This rapid succession at the highest level of government was largely a result of public dissatisfaction with the distribution of gains that had come from exporting natural gas. Many people, including the indigenous Aymara Indians, believed that most of these gains had gone to multinational oil corporations, with little distributed to the citizens of the country in which the gas deposits and refineries are located.

Violent protests in September 2003 led to the resignation of President Gonzalo Sánchez de Lozada, who was replaced by Carlos Mesa, a writer and television journalist. He promised to respect the views of the indigenous people of Bolivia and in July 2004 held a referendum on whether the country should export natural gas. The referendum included provisions to ensure that more of the profits from natural gas exports would go to the Bolivian government rather than to foreign companies. With these assurances, the referendum passed, and in May 2005 taxes on foreign oil companies were sharply

---

[1] Speech from the San Alberto field operated by Petrobras, "Bolivia Nationalizes Natural Gas Industry," *USA Today*, May 1, 2006.

AP Photos/Dado Galdieri

Evo Morales and his supporters.

increased. But many protestors wanted more and forced President Mesa to resign within the year. Elections were held again in December 2005, and Evo Morales scored a decisive victory, becoming the first Aymara Indian elected to president in Bolivia's 180-year history. In May 2006 he nationalized the gas industry, which meant that all natural gas resources were placed under the control of the state-owned energy company. With this policy change, foreign investors lost their majority ownership claims to gas fields, pipelines, and refineries that they had built and lost a significant portion of the profits from the sales of Bolivian natural gas. This drastic step, which was criticized heavily by foreign governments, was supported by people in Bolivia. Because of this and other popular policies, Evo Morales was re-elected in 2009 for another five-year term. As of 2013, the gas industry in Bolivia is still largely owned by the state.

The Bolivian experience illustrates the difficulty of ensuring that all people within a country share in the gains from trade. Despite the abundant natural gas resources along with other minerals such as silver, tin and lithium—used to make car batteries—many of the local population remained in poverty. The difficulty of sharing these gains among Bolivia's citizenry makes the export of gas a contentious issue. Although the export of natural gas clearly generated gains for the foreign-owned and state-owned companies that sold the resources, the indigenous peoples did not historically share in those gains.

A new constitution in 2009 gave indigenous peoples control over natural resources in their territories. Companies from Japan and Europe made deals with the Morales government to extract this resource, but the government ensured that the gains flowed to the local population through poverty reduction programs. Since 2009, Bolivia has experienced high economic growth, averaging 4.7% over the past five years. There has been substantial migration from indigenous rural locations to cities such as El Alto, which was formerly the site of violent protests, but now is host to thriving small businesses owned by men and women.[2]

A key lesson from this chapter is that in most cases, opening a country to trade generates winners *and* losers. In general, the gains of those who benefit from trade exceed the losses of those who are harmed, and in this sense there are overall gains from trade. That was a lesson from the Ricardian model in the last chapter. But our argument in the last chapter that trade generates gains for *all* workers was too simple because, in the Ricardian model, labor is the only factor of production. Once we make the more realistic assumption that capital and land are also factors of production, then trade generates gains for some factors and losses for others. Our goal in this chapter is to determine who gains and who loses from trade and under what circumstances.

The model we use to analyze the role of international trade in determining the earnings of labor, land, and capital assumes that one industry (agriculture) uses labor and land and the other industry (manufacturing) uses labor and capital. This model is sometimes called the **specific-factors model** because land is *specific* to the agriculture sector and capital is *specific* to the manufacturing sector; labor is used in both sectors, so it is not specific to either one. The idea that land is specific to agriculture and that capital is specific to manufacturing might be true in the short run but does not really hold in the long run. In later chapters, we develop a long-run model, in which capital

---

[2] You can read more about this case in Simon Romero, "In Bolivia, Untapped Bounty Meets Nationalism," *New York Times*, February 3, 2009, and Sara Shahriari, "The Booming World: Bolivia," *The Guardian*, December 20, 2012, from which this paragraph is drawn.

and other resources can be shifted from use in one industry to use in another. For now we focus on the short-run specific-factors model, which offers many new insights about the gains from trade beyond those obtained from the Ricardian model.

1 Specific-Factors Model

We address the following question in the specific-factors model: How does trade affect the earnings of labor, land, and capital? We have already seen from our study of the Ricardian model that when a country is opened to free trade, the relative price of exports rises and the relative price of imports falls. Thus, the question of how trade affects factor earnings is really a question of how changes in *relative prices* affect the earnings of labor, land, and capital. The idea we develop in this section is that the earnings of *specific* or *fixed factors* (such as capital and land) rise or fall primarily because of changes in relative prices (i.e., specific factor earnings are the most sensitive to relative price changes) because in the short run they are "stuck" in a sector and cannot be employed in other sectors. In contrast, mobile factors (such as labor) can offset their losses somewhat by seeking employment in other industries.

As in our study of international trade in Chapter 2, we look at two countries, called Home and Foreign. We first discuss the Home country.

The Home Country

Let us call the two industries in the specific-factors model "manufacturing" and "agriculture." Manufacturing uses labor and capital, whereas agriculture uses labor and land. In each industry, increases in the amount of labor used are subject to **diminishing returns;** that is, the marginal product of labor declines as the amount of labor used in the industry increases. Figure 3-1, panel (a), plots output against the amount

---

FIGURE 3-1

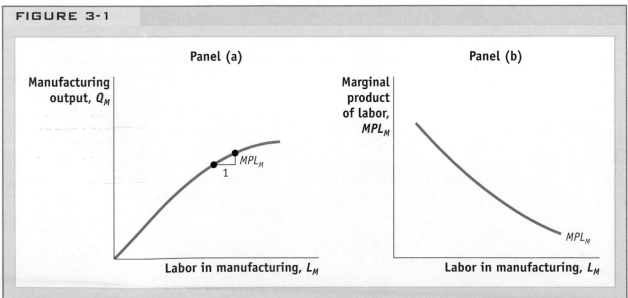

Panel (a)

Manufacturing output, Q_M

MPL_M

1

Labor in manufacturing, L_M

Panel (b)

Marginal product of labor, MPL_M

MPL_M

Labor in manufacturing, L_M

Panel (a) Manufacturing Output As more labor is used, manufacturing input increases, but it does so at a diminishing rate. The slope of the curve measures the marginal product of labor, which declines as the quantity of labor used in manufacturing increases.

Panel (b) Diminishing Marginal Product of Labor An increase in the amount of labor used in manufacturing lowers the marginal product of labor.

of labor used in production, and shows diminishing returns for the manufacturing industry. As more labor is used, the output of manufacturing goes up, but it does so at a diminishing rate. The slope of the curve in Figure 3-1 measures the marginal product of labor, which declines as labor increases.

Figure 3-1, panel (b), graphs MPL_M, the marginal product of labor in manufacturing, against the labor used in manufacturing L_M. This curve slopes downward due to diminishing returns. Likewise, in the agriculture sector (not drawn), the marginal product of labor MPL_A also diminishes as the amount of labor used in agriculture L_A increases.

Production Possibilities Frontier Combining the output for the two industries, manufacturing and agriculture, we obtain the production possibilities frontier (PPF) for the economy (Figure 3-2). Because of the diminishing returns to labor in both sectors, the PPF is *bowed out* or concave with respect to the graph's origin. (You may recognize this familiar shape from your introductory economics class.)

By using the marginal products of labor in each sector, we can determine the slope of the PPF. Starting at point A in Figure 3-2, suppose that one unit of labor leaves agriculture and enters manufacturing so that the economy's new output is at point B. The drop in agricultural output is MPL_A, and the increase in manufacturing output is MPL_M. The slope of the PPF between points A and B is the negative of the ratio of marginal products, or $-MPL_A/MPL_M$. This ratio can be interpreted as the opportunity cost of producing one unit of manufacturing, the cost of one unit of manufacturing in terms of the amount of food (the agricultural good) that would need to be given up to produce it.

Opportunity Cost and Prices As in the Ricardian model, the slope of the PPF, which is the opportunity cost of manufacturing, also equals the relative price of manufacturing. To understand why this is so, recall that in competitive markets, firms hire labor up to the point at which the cost of one more hour of labor (the wage) equals

---

FIGURE 3-2

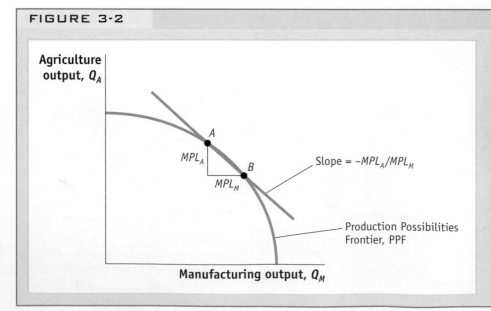

Production Possibilities Frontier The production possibilities frontier shows the amount of agricultural and manufacturing outputs that can be produced in the economy with labor. Its slope equals $-MPL_A/MPL_M$, the ratio of the marginal products of labor in the two industries. The slope of the PPF can be interpreted as the opportunity cost of the manufacturing output—it is the amount of the agricultural good that would need to be given up to obtain one more unit of output in the manufacturing sector.

the value of one more hour of labor in terms of output. In turn, the value of one more hour of labor equals the amount of goods produced in that hour (the marginal product of labor) times the price of the good. In manufacturing, labor will be hired to the point at which the wage W equals the price of manufacturing P_M times the marginal product of labor in manufacturing MPL_M.

$$W = P_M \cdot MPL_M$$

Similarly, in agriculture, labor will be hired to the point at which the wage W equals the price of agriculture P_A times the marginal product of labor in agriculture MPL_A.

$$W = P_A \cdot MPL_A$$

Because we are assuming that labor is free to move between sectors, the wages in these two equations must be equal. If the wage were not the same in both sectors, labor would move to the sector with the higher wage. This movement would continue until the increase in the amount of labor in the high-wage sector drove down the wage, and the decrease in amount of labor in the low-wage sector drove up the wage, until the wages were equal. By setting the two wage equations equal, we obtain $P_M \cdot MPL_M = P_A \cdot MPL_A$, and by rearranging terms, we get

$$(P_M/P_A) = (MPL_A/MPL_M)$$

This equation shows that the relative price of manufacturing (P_M/P_A) equals the opportunity cost of manufacturing (MPL_A/MPL_M), the slope of the production possibilities frontier. These relative prices also reflect the value that Home consumers put on manufacturing versus food. In the absence of international trade, the equilibrium for the Home economy is at point A in Figure 3-3, where the relative price of manufacturing (P_M/P_A) equals the slope of the PPF as well as the slope of the indifference curve for a representative consumer with utility of U_1. The intuition for the

---

FIGURE 3-3

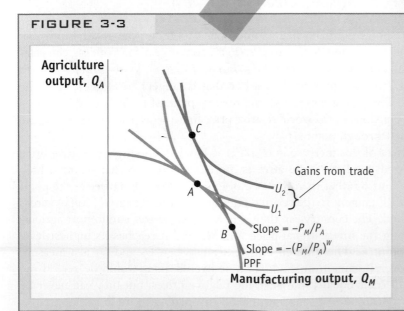

Increase in the Relative Price of Manufactures In the absence of international trade, the economy produces and consumes at point A. The relative price of manufactures, P_M/P_A, is the slope of the line tangent to the PPF and indifference curve, U_1, at point A. With international trade, the economy is able to produce at point B and consume at point C. The world relative price of manufactures, $(P_M/P_A)^W$, is the slope of the line BC. The rise in utility from U_1 to U_2 is a measure of the gains from trade for the economy.

no-trade equilibrium is exactly the same as for the Ricardian model in Chapter 2: equilibrium occurs at the tangency of the PPF and the consumer's indifference curve. This point on the PPF corresponds to the highest possible level of utility for the consumer.

The Foreign Country

In this chapter, we do not discuss the Foreign country in any detail. Instead, we simply assume that the no-trade relative price of manufacturing in Foreign (P_M^*/P_A^*) differs from the no-trade price (P_M/P_A) at Home. There are several reasons why these prices can differ. In the previous chapter, we showed how differences in productivities across countries cause the no-trade relative prices to differ across countries. That is the key assumption, or starting point, of the Ricardian model. Another reason for relative prices to differ, which we have not yet investigated, is that the amounts of labor, capital, or land found in the two countries are different. (That will be the key assumption of the Heckscher-Ohlin model, which we discuss in the next chapter.)

For now, we will not explain why the no-trade relative prices differ across countries but will take it for granted that this is not unusual. For the sake of focusing on one case, let us assume that the Home no-trade relative price of manufacturing is *lower* than the Foreign relative price, $(P_M/P_A) < (P_M^*/P_A^*)$. This assumption means that Home can produce manufactured goods relatively cheaper than Foreign, or, equivalently, that Home has a comparative advantage in manufacturing.

Overall Gains from Trade

Starting at the no-trade equilibrium point A in Figure 3-3, suppose that the Home country opens up to international trade with Foreign. Once trade is opened, we expect that the world equilibrium relative price, that is, the relative price in *all* countries $(P_M/P_A)^W$, will lie between the no-trade relative prices in the two countries, so

$$(P_M/P_A) < (P_M/P_A)^W < (P_M^*/P_A^*)$$

This equation shows us that when Home opens to trade, the relative price of manufacturing will *rise*, from (P_M/P_A) to $(P_M/P_A)^W$; conversely, for Foreign, the relative price of manufacturing will *fall*, from (P_M^*/P_A^*) to $(P_M/P_A)^W$. With trade, the world relative price $(P_M/P_A)^W$ is represented by a line that is tangent to Home's PPF, line BC in Figure 3-3. The increase in the Home relative price of manufactured goods is shown by the steeper slope of the world relative price line as compared with the Home no-trade price line (through point A).

What is the effect of this increase in (P_M/P_A) at Home? The higher relative price of the manufactured good at Home attracts more workers into that sector, which now produces at point B rather than A. As before, production takes place at the point along the Home PPF tangent to the relative price line, where equality of wages across industries is attained. The country can then export manufactures and import agricultural products along the international price line BC, and it reaches its highest level of utility, U_2, at point C. The difference in utility between U_2 and U_1 is a measure of the country's overall gains from trade. (These overall gains would be zero if the relative prices with trade equaled the no-trade relative prices, but they can never be negative—a country can never be made worse off by opening to trade.)

Notice that the good whose relative price goes up (manufacturing, for Home) is exported and the good whose relative price goes down (agriculture, for Home) is imported. By exporting manufactured goods at a higher price and importing food at a lower price, Home is better off than it was in the absence of trade. To measure the gains from trade, economists rely on the price increases for exports and the price decreases for imports to determine how much extra consumption a country can afford. The following application considers the magnitude of the overall gains from trade in historical cases in which the gains have been measured.

APPLICATION

How Large Are the Gains from Trade?

How large are the overall gains from trade? There are a few historical examples of countries that have moved from **autarky** (i.e., no trade) to free trade, or vice versa, quickly enough that we can use the years before and after this shift to estimate the gains from trade.

One such episode in the United States occurred between December 1807 and March 1809, when the U.S. Congress imposed a nearly complete halt to international trade at the request of President Thomas Jefferson. A complete stop to all trade is called an **embargo.** The United States imposed its embargo because Britain was at war with Napoleon, and Britain wanted to prevent ships from arriving in France that might be carrying supplies or munitions. As a result, Britain patrolled the eastern coast of the United States and seized U.S. ships that were bound across the Atlantic. To safeguard its own ships and possibly inflict economic losses on Britain, the United States declared a trade embargo for 14 months from 1807 to 1809. The embargo was not complete, however; the United States still traded with some countries, such as Canada and Mexico, that didn't have to be reached by ship.

As you might expect, U.S. trade fell dramatically during this period. Exports (such as cotton, flour, tobacco, and rice) fell from about $49 million in 1807 to $9 million in 1809. The drop in the value of exports reflects both a drop in the quantity exported and a drop in the price of exports. Recall that in Chapter 2 we defined the terms of trade of a country as the price of its export goods divided by the price of its import goods, so a drop in the price of U.S. exports is a fall in its terms of trade, which is a loss for the United States. According to one study, the cost of the trade embargo to the United States was about 5% of gross domestic product (GDP). That is, U.S. GDP was 5% lower than it would have been without the trade embargo. The cost of the embargo was offset somewhat because trade was not completely eliminated and because some U.S. producers were able to shift their efforts to producing goods (such as cloth and glass) that had previously been imported. Thus, we can take 5% of GDP as a lower estimate of what the gains from trade for the United States would have been relative to a situation with no trade.

Is 5% of GDP a large or small number? It is large when we think that a recession that reduced GDP by 5% in one year would be regarded as a very deep downturn.[3] To get another perspective, instead of comparing the costs of the embargo with overall GDP, we can instead compare them with the size of U.S. exports, which were 13% of

---

[3] The most severe downturn ever in the United States was the Great Depression of the 1930s. U.S. real GDP fell each year between 1929 and 1933 by an average of 9% per year and then began to recover. It was not until 1939 that the United States regained the same level of real GDP that it had in 1929.

GDP before the embargo. Taking the ratio of these numbers, we conclude that the cost of the embargo was more than one-third of the value of exports.

Another historical case was Japan's rapid opening to the world economy in 1854, after 200 years of self-imposed autarky. In this case, military action by Commodore Matthew Perry of the United States forced Japan to open up its borders so that the United States could establish commercial ties. When trade was opened, the prices of Japanese exports to the United States (such as silk and tea) rose, and the prices of U.S. imports (such as woolens) fell. These price movements were a terms-of-trade gain for Japan, very much like the movement from the no-trade point A in Figure 3-3 to a trade equilibrium at points B and C. According to one estimate, Japan's gains from trade after its opening were 4 to 5% of GDP.[4] The gains were not one-sided, however; Japan's trading partners—such as the United States—also gained from being able to trade in the newly opened markets. ■

2 Earnings of Labor

Because there are overall gains from trade, *someone* in the economy must be better off, but not *everyone* is better off. The goal of this chapter is to explore how a change in relative prices, such as that shown in Figure 3-3, feeds back into the earnings of workers, landowners, and capital owners. We begin our study of the specific-factors model by looking at what happens to the wages earned by labor when there is an increase in the relative price of manufactures.

Determination of Wages

To determine wages, it is convenient to take the marginal product of labor in manufacturing (MPL_M), which was shown in Figure 3-1, panel (b), and the marginal product of labor in agriculture (MPL_A), and put them in one diagram.

First, we add the amount of labor used in manufacturing L_M and the amount used in agriculture L_A to give us the total amount of labor in the economy $\overline{L}$:

$$L_M + L_A = \overline{L}$$

Figure 3-4 shows the total amount of labor $\overline{L}$ on the horizontal axis. The amount of labor used in manufacturing L_M is measured from left (0_M) to right, while the amount of labor used in agriculture L_A is measured from right (0_A) to left. Each point on the horizontal axis indicates how much labor is used in manufacturing (measured from left to right) and how much labor is used in agriculture (measured from right to left). For example, point L indicates that $0_M L$ units of labor are used in manufacturing and $0_A L$ units of labor are used in agriculture, which adds up to $\overline{L}$ units of labor in total.

The second step in determining wages is to multiply the marginal product of labor in each sector by the price of the good in that sector (P_M or P_A). As we discussed earlier, in competitive markets, firms will hire labor up to the point at which the cost of one more hour of labor (the wage) equals the value of one more hour in production,

[4] Daniel M. Bernhofen and John C. Brown, March 2005, "Estimating the Comparative Advantage Gains from Trade," *American Economic Review*, 95(1), 208–225.

FIGURE 3-4

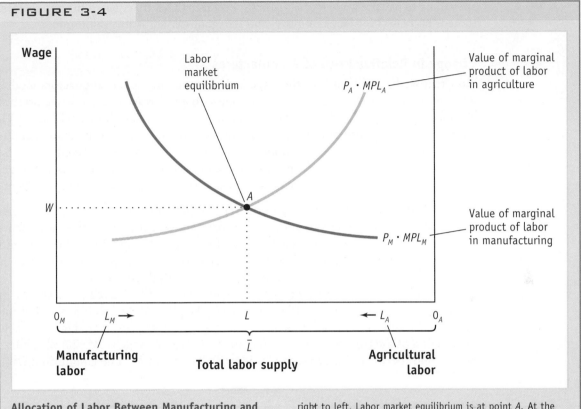

Allocation of Labor Between Manufacturing and Agriculture The amount of labor used in manufacturing is measured from left to right along the horizontal axis, and the amount of labor used in agriculture is measured from right to left. Labor market equilibrium is at point A. At the equilibrium wage of W, manufacturing uses $0_M L$ units of labor and agriculture uses $0_A L$ units.

which is the marginal product of labor times the price of the good. In each industry, then, labor will be hired until

$$W = P_M \cdot MPL_M \text{ in manufacturing}$$

$$W = P_A \cdot MPL_A \text{ in agriculture}$$

In Figure 3-4, we draw the graph of $P_M \cdot MPL_M$ as downward-sloping. This curve is basically the same as the marginal product of labor MPL_M curve in Figure 3-1, panel (b), except that it is now multiplied by the price of the manufactured good. When we draw the graph of $P_A \cdot MPL_A$ for agriculture, however, it slopes upward. This is because we are measuring the labor used in agriculture L_A from *right* to *left* in the diagram: the marginal product of labor in agriculture falls as the amount of labor increases (moving from right to left).

Equilibrium Wage The equilibrium wage is found at point A, the intersection of the curves $P_M \cdot MPL_M$ and $P_A \cdot MPL_A$ in Figure 3-4. At this point, $0_M L$ units of labor are used in manufacturing, and firms in that industry are willing to pay the wage $W = P_M \cdot MPL_M$. In addition, $0_A L$ units of labor are used in agriculture, and farmers are willing to pay the wage $W = P_A \cdot MPL_A$. Because wages are equal in the two sectors, there is no reason for labor to move, and the labor market is in equilibrium.

Change in Relative Price of Manufactures

Now that we have shown how the wage is determined in the specific-factors model, we want to ask how the wage *changes* in response to an increase in the relative price of manufactures. That is, as the relative price of manufactures rises (shown in Figure 3-3), and the economy shifts from its no-trade equilibrium at point A to its trade equilibrium with production and consumption at points B and C, what is the effect on the earnings of each factor of production? In particular, what are the changes in the wage, and in the earnings of capital owners in manufacturing and landowners in agriculture?

Effect on the Wage An increase in the relative price of manufacturing P_M/P_A can occur due to either an increase in P_M or a decrease in P_A. Both these price movements will have the same effect on the **real wage;** that is, on the amount of manufactures and food that a worker can afford to buy. For convenience, let us suppose that the price of manufacturing P_M rises, while the price of agriculture P_A does not change.

When P_M rises, the curve $P_M \cdot MPL_M$ shifts up to $P'_M \cdot MPL_M$, as shown in Figure 3-5. The vertical rise in this curve is exactly $\Delta P_M \cdot MPL_M$, as illustrated in the diagram. (We use the symbol Δ, delta, to stand for the *change* in a variable.) The new intersection of the two curves occurs at point B, where the wage is W' and the allocation of labor between the two sectors is identified by point L'. The equilibrium wage

FIGURE 3-5

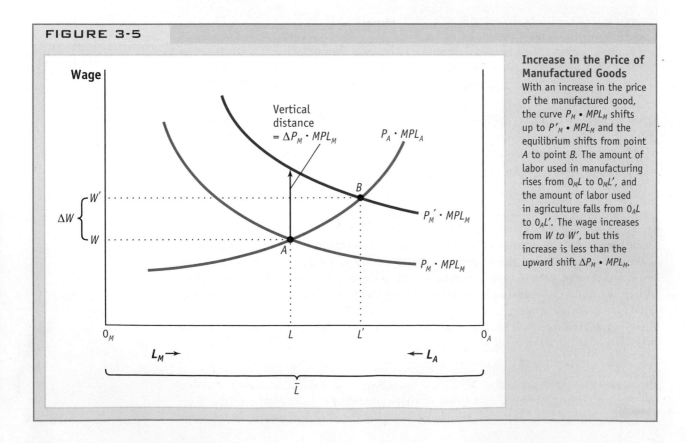

Increase in the Price of Manufactured Goods
With an increase in the price of the manufactured good, the curve $P_M \cdot MPL_M$ shifts up to $P'_M \cdot MPL_M$ and the equilibrium shifts from point A to point B. The amount of labor used in manufacturing rises from $0_M L$ to $0_M L'$, and the amount of labor used in agriculture falls from $0_A L$ to $0_A L'$. The wage increases from W to W', but this increase is less than the upward shift $\Delta P_M \cdot MPL_M$.

has risen from W to W', the amount of labor used in the manufacturing sector has increased from $0_M L$ to $0_M L'$, and the amount of labor used in agriculture has fallen from $0_A L$ to $0_A L'$.

Effect on Real Wages The fact that the wage has risen does not really tell us whether workers are better off or worse off in terms of the amount of food and manufactured goods they can buy. To answer this question, we have to take into account any change in the prices of these goods. For instance, the amount of food that a worker can afford to buy with his or her hourly wage is W/P_A.[5] Because W has increased from W to W' and we have assumed that P_A has not changed, workers can afford to buy more food. In other words, the real wage has increased in terms of food.

The amount of the manufactured good that a worker can buy is measured by W/P_M. While W has increased, P_M has also increased, so at first glance we do not know whether W/P_M has increased or decreased. However, Figure 3-5 can help us figure this out. Notice that as we've drawn Figure 3-5, the increase in the wage from W to W' is less than the vertical increase $\Delta P_M \cdot MPL_M$ that occurred in the $P_M \cdot MPL_M$ curve. We can write this condition as

$$\Delta W < \Delta P_M \cdot MPL_M$$

To see how W/P_M has changed, divide both sides of this equation by the initial wage W (which equals $P_M \cdot MPL_M$) to obtain

$$\frac{\Delta W}{W} < \frac{\Delta P_M \cdot MPL_M}{P_M \cdot MPL_M} = \frac{\Delta P_M}{P_M}$$

where the final ratio is obtained because we canceled out MPL_M in the numerator and denominator of the middle ratio. The term $\Delta W/W$ in this equation is the *percentage change in wages*. For example, suppose the initial wage is $8 per hour and it rises to $10 per hour. Then $\Delta W/W = \$2/\$8 = 0.25$, which is a 25% increase in the wage. Similarly, the term $\Delta P_M/P_M$ is the *percentage change in the price of manufactured goods*. When $\Delta W/W < \Delta P_M/P_M$, then the percentage increase in the wage is *less than* the percentage increase in the price of the manufactured good. This inequality means that the amount of the manufactured good that can be purchased with the wage has fallen, so the *real wage in terms of the manufactured good W/P_M* has decreased.[6]

Overall Impact on Labor We have now determined that as a result of our assumption of an increase in the relative price of manufactured goods, the *real wage in terms of food has increased and the real wage in terms of the manufactured good has decreased*. In this case, we assumed that the increase in relative price was caused by an increase in the price of manufactures with a constant price of agriculture. Notice, though, that if we had assumed a constant price of manufactures and a decrease in the price of agriculture (taken together, an increase in the relative price of manufactures), then we would have arrived at the same effects on the real wage in terms of both products.

---

[5] For example, suppose that you earn $8 per hour, and your favorite snack costs $2. Then you could afford to buy $\$8/\$2 = 4$ of these snacks after working for one hour.

[6] For example, suppose that the manufactured good is compact discs (CDs), which initially cost $16 and then rise in price to $24. The increase in the price of CDs is $8, and so the percentage increase in the price of CDs is $\Delta P_M/P_M = \$8/\$16 = 0.50 = 50\%$. Suppose also that the wage has increased from $8 to $10 per hour, or 25%. Using the initial prices, by working one hour, you could afford to buy $W/P_M = \$8/\$16 = 0.5$, or one-half of a CD. Using the new prices, by working one hour, you can afford to buy $W/P_M = \$10/\$24 = 0.42$, or about four-tenths of a CD. So, your real wage measured in terms of CDs has gone down.

Is labor better off or worse off after the price increase? We cannot tell. People who spend most of their income on manufactured goods are worse off because they can buy fewer manufactured goods, but those who spend most of their income on food are better off because more food is affordable. The bottom line is that in the specific-factors model, the increase in the price of the manufactured good has an ambiguous effect on the real wage and therefore an *ambiguous* effect on the well-being of workers.

The conclusion that we cannot tell whether workers are better off or worse off from the opening of trade in the specific-factors model might seem wishy-washy to you, but it is important for several reasons. First, this result is different from what we found in the Ricardian model of Chapter 2, in which the real wage increases with the opening of trade so that workers are always unambiguously better off than they are in the absence of trade.[7] In the specific-factors model, that is no longer the case; the opening of trade and the shift in relative prices raise the real wage in terms of one good but lower it in terms of the other good. Second, our results for the specific-factors model serve as a warning against making unqualified statements about the effect of trade on workers, such as "Trade is bad for workers" or "Trade is good for workers." Even in the specific-factors model, which is simplified by considering only two industries and not allowing capital or land to move between them, we have found that the effects of opening trade on the real wage are complicated. In reality, the effect of trade on real wages is more complex still.

Unemployment in the Specific-Factors Model We have ignored one significant, realistic feature in the specific-factors model: unemployment. You may often see news stories about workers who are laid off because of import competition and who face a period of unemployment. Despite this outcome, most economists do not believe that trade necessarily harms workers overall. It is true that we have ignored unemployment in the specific-factors model: the labor employed in manufacturing L_M plus the labor employed in agriculture L_A always sums to the total labor supply $\overline{L}$, which means that there is no unemployment. One of the reasons we ignore unemployment in this model is that it is usually treated as a macroeconomic phenomenon, caused by business cycles, and it is hard to combine business cycle models with international trade models to isolate the effects of trade on workers. But the other, simpler reason is that even when people are laid off because of import competition, many of them find new jobs within a reasonable period, and sometimes they find jobs with *higher* wages, as shown in the next application. Therefore, even if we take into account spells of unemployment, once we recognize that workers can find new jobs—possibly in export industries that are expanding—then we still cannot conclude that trade is necessarily good or bad for workers.

In the two applications that follow, we look at some evidence from the United States on the amount of time it takes to find new jobs and on the wages earned, and at attempts by governments to compensate workers who lose their jobs because of import competition. This type of compensation is called **Trade Adjustment Assistance (TAA)** in the United States.

---

[7] The only situation in which workers do not gain from trade in the Ricardian model is if the Home country is very large, as discussed in Problem 11 of Chapter 2, such that the international relative price equals the no-trade relative price. In that case, Home workers are no better off from international trade but also no worse off.

APPLICATION

Manufacturing and Services in the United States: Employment and Wages Across Sectors

Although the specific-factors model emphasizes manufacturing and agriculture, the amount of labor devoted to agriculture in most industrialized countries is small. A larger sector in industrialized countries is that of **services,** which includes wholesale and retail trade, finance, law, education, information technology, software engineering, consulting, and medical and government services. In the United States and most industrial countries, the service sector is larger than the manufacturing sector and much larger than the agriculture sector.

In Figure 3-6, we show employment in the manufacturing sector of the United States, both in terms of the number of workers employed in it and as a percentage of total employment in the economy. Using either measure, employment in manufacturing has been falling over time; given zero or negative growth in the agriculture sector, this indicates that the service sector has been growing. In Figure 3-7, we show the real wages earned by production—or blue-collar—workers in manufacturing, in all private services, and in information services (a subset of private services).[8] While wages were

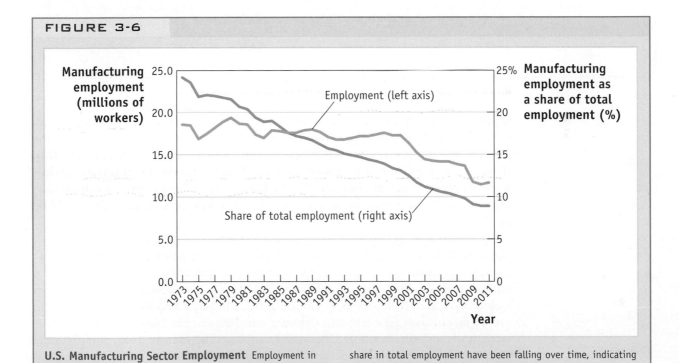

FIGURE 3-6

U.S. Manufacturing Sector Employment Employment in the U.S. manufacturing sector is shown on the left axis, and the share of manufacturing employment in total U.S. employment is shown on the right axis. Both manufacturing employment and its share in total employment have been falling over time, indicating that the service sector has been growing.

Source: Economic Report of the President, 2012, Table B46.

---

[8] The real wages shown in Figure 3-7 are measured relative to consumer prices in 2012 and represent the average hourly earnings for *production* workers, those workers involved in the assembly of services or products. Production workers are sometimes called "blue-collar" workers and typically earn hourly wages. The other category of workers, *nonproduction* workers, includes managers and all those who work at a desk. They are sometimes called "white-collar" workers and typically earn annual salaries instead of hourly wages.

FIGURE 3-7

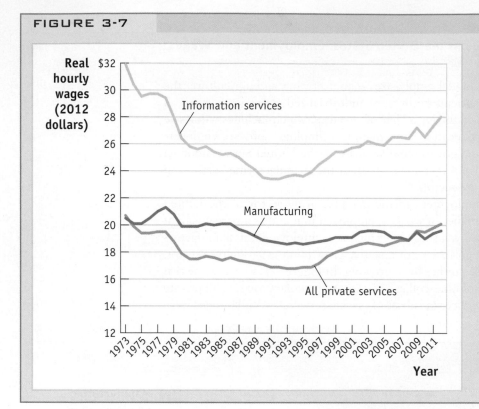

Real Hourly Earnings of Production Workers This chart shows the real wages (in constant 2012 dollars) earned by production workers in U.S. manufacturing, in all private services, and in information services (a subset of all private services). While wages were slightly higher in manufacturing than in all private services from 1974 through 2007, all private service wages have been higher since 2008. This change is due in part to the effect of wages in the information service industry, which are substantially higher than those in manufacturing. Real wages for production workers fell in most years between 1979 and 1995 but have risen only slightly in manufacturing and by more in the service sector since then.

Source: http://www.bls.gov, Historical Data for the "B" Tables of the Employment Situation Release.

slightly higher in manufacturing than in private services from 1974 through 2007, all private service wages have been higher since 2008. This change is due in part to the effect of wages in the *information service* industry, which are substantially higher than those in manufacturing. For example, average hourly earnings in all private services were $19.90 per hour in 2012 and slightly lower—$19.60 per hour—in manufacturing overall. But in information services, average wages were much higher—$28.00 per hour.

In both manufacturing and services, many workers are *displaced* or laid off each year and need to look for other jobs. In the three years from January 2009 to December 2011, for example, about 1.2 million workers were displaced in manufacturing and 2.6 million in all service industries, as shown in Table 3-1. Of those laid off in manufacturing, 56% were reemployed by January 2012, and about two-thirds of these (65%) earned less in their new jobs and only one-third earned the same or more. For services, while a similar fraction 57% were reemployed by January 2012, slightly more than one-half of these (51%) earned the same or more in their new jobs. So the earnings of those displaced in the service sectors do not suffer as much as the earnings of workers displaced from manufacturing.

There are four lessons that we can take away from this comparison of employment and wages in manufacturing and services. First, wages differ across different sectors in the economy, so our theoretical assumption that wages are the same in agriculture and manufacturing is a simplification. Second, many workers are displaced each year and must find jobs elsewhere. Some of these workers may be laid off due to competition from imports, but there are other reasons, too—for instance, products that used to be

TABLE 3-1

Job Losses in Manufacturing and Service Industries, 2009–2011 This table shows the number of displaced (or laid-off) workers in manufacturing and service industries from 2009 to 2011. More than one half (56%) of the workers displaced from 2009 to 2011 were reemployed by January 2012, with about two-thirds earning less in their new jobs in manufacturing and only one-third earning the same or more. But in service industries, about one-half of the workers reemployed earned less in their new jobs with the other half earning the same or more.

Industry	Total Displaced Workers (thousands) January 2009–December 2011	Workers Reemployed by January 2012	PERCENTAGES	
			Of the Workers Reemployed:	
			Earn Less in New Job	Earn Same or More in New Job
Total	6,121	56%	54%	46%
Manufacturing industries	1,183	56%	65%	35%
Service industries	2,613	57%	49%	51%

Source: U.S. Bureau of Labor Statistics.

purchased go out of fashion, firms reorganize as computers and other technological advances become available, and firms change locations. Third, more than one-half of displaced workers find a new job within two or three years but not necessarily at the same wage. Typically, older workers (age 45 to 64) experience earnings losses when shifting between jobs, whereas younger workers (age 25 to 44) are often able to find a new job with the same or higher wages. Finally, when we measure wages in real terms by adjusting for inflation in the price of consumer goods, we see that real wages for all production workers fell in most years between 1979 and 1995 (we examine the reasons for that fall in later chapters). The real wages for production workers in manufacturing have risen only slightly since then, while the real wages for service workers have risen by more, so that workers in services now have higher earnings than those in manufacturing on average (and especially so for workers in information services). ■

APPLICATION

Trade Adjustment Assistance Programs: Financing the Adjustment Costs of Trade

Should the government step in to compensate workers who are looking for jobs or who do not find them in a reasonable period? The unemployment insurance program in the United States provides some compensation, regardless of the reason for the layoff. In addition, the *Trade Adjustment Assistance (TAA)* program offers additional unemployment insurance payments and health insurance to workers who are laid off because of import competition and who are enrolled in a retraining program. The quotation from President Kennedy at the beginning of the chapter comes from a speech he made introducing the TAA program in 1962. He believed that this program was needed to compensate those Americans who lost their jobs due to international trade. Since 1993 there has also been a special TAA program under the North American Free Trade Agreement

(NAFTA) for workers who are laid off as a result of import competition from Mexico or Canada.[9] Recently, as part of the jobs stimulus bill signed by President Obama on February 17, 2009, workers in the service sector (as well as farmers) who lose their jobs due to trade can now also apply for TAA benefits. This extension is described in **Headlines: Services Workers Are Now Eligible for Trade Adjustment Assistance.**

Other countries also have programs like TAA to compensate those harmed by trade. A particularly interesting example occurred with the unification of East and West Germany on June 30, 1990. On that date, all barriers to trade between the countries were removed as well as all barriers to the movement of labor and capital between the two regions. The pressure from labor unions to achieve wage parity (equality) between the East and West meant that companies in former East Germany were faced with wages that were far above what they could afford to pay. According to one estimate, only 8% of former East German companies would be profitable at the higher wages paid in the West. In the absence of government intervention, it could be expected that severe bankruptcy and unemployment would result, leading to massive migration of East German workers to the former West Germany.

Economists studying this situation proposed that deep wage subsidies, or "flexible employment bonuses," should be given in former East Germany, thereby allowing factories to employ their workers while paying only a fraction of their wages. Furthermore, they argued that the wage subsidies would essentially pay for themselves because without them the government would have to provide unemployment insurance on a massive scale to the people left without jobs.[10] As it turns out, wage subsidies of this type were not used, and unemployment in the East and migration to the West continue to be challenging policy issues for the united Germany. According to the 2011 census and recent studies, the East–West differences still remain with the East having higher unemployment and lower wages than found in the West of Germany.[11] ■

3 Earnings of Capital and Land

Let us now return to the specific-factors model. We have found that with the opening of trade and an increase in the relative price of manufactures, there are overall gains for the country, but labor does not necessarily gain. What about the gains to the other factors of production, either the capital used in manufacturing or the land used in agriculture? Capital and land are the two specific factors of production that cannot shift between the two industries; let us now look at the effect of the increase in the relative price of manufactures on the earnings of these specific factors.

Determining the Payments to Capital and Land

In each industry, capital and land earn what is left over from sales revenue after paying labor. Labor (L_M and L_A) earns the wage W, so total payments to labor in manufacturing are $W \cdot L_M$ and in agriculture are $W \cdot L_A$. By subtracting the payments to labor

---

[9] We discuss the North American Free Trade Agreement in a later chapter and provide more details there on how many workers applied for benefits under the NAFTA-TAA program.

[10] George Akerlof, Andrew Rose, Janet Yellen, and Helga Hessenius, 1991, "East Germany in from the Cold: The Economic Aftermath of Currency Union," *Brookings Papers on Economic Activity*, Vol. 1, 1–87.

[11] See Jeevan Vasagar, "Germany Still Split East-West", *Los Angeles Times*, June 1, 2013.

HEADLINES

Services Workers Are Now Eligible for Trade Adjustment Assistance

President Kennedy first introduced Trade Adjustment Assistance (TAA) in the United States in 1962, for workers in manufacturing. This article described how it was extended in 2009 to include service workers. The TAA program was reauthorized by the 2011 U.S. Congress through the end of 2013, and we can expect its continued reauthorization in the future to support workers who are displaced by trade.

In today's era of global supply chains, high-speed Internet connection, and container shipping, Kennedy's concerns remain relevant: technology and trade mean growth, innovation and better living standards, but also change and instability. (Research early in this decade typically found that international competition accounted for about 2 percent of layoffs.) But while concerns may be permanent, specific programs and policies fade unless they adapt to changing times. And despite its periodic update, until this week TAA remained designed for an older world. Most notably, it barred support for services workers facing Internet-based competition. . . .

In this context, yesterday's . . . bill signing contained the first fundamental change to the TAA program in a

half-century. An accord three years in the making, overseen by Senators Max Baucus (D-MT) and Charles Grassley (R-IA), reshapes TAA for the 21st century. The new program, set out in 184 pages of legal text, has three basic changes:

- More workers are eligible: Service-industry employees will be fully eligible for TAA services, making the program relevant to the high-tech economy. So will workers whose businesses move abroad, regardless of the destination. The reform also eases eligibility for farmers and fishermen.

- They get more help: The reform raises training support from $220 million to $575 million, hikes support

for health insurance from 65 percent to 80 percent of premiums, gives states $86 million a year to pay for TAA caseworkers, creates a $230 million program to support communities dealing with plant closure, and triples support for businesses managing sudden trade competition.

- They are more likely to know their rights: The bill also creates a special Labor Department TAA office to ensure that eligible workers know their options.

Kennedy's innovation is thus adapted to the 21st-century economy, guaranteeing today's workers the support their grandparents enjoyed. A bit of good news, in a year when it is all too rare.

Source: Excerpted from Progressive Policy Institute trade fact of the week, "Services Workers Are Now Eligible for Trade Adjustment Assistance," February 18, 2009.

from the sales revenue earned in each industry, we end up with the payments to capital and to land. If Q_M is the output in manufacturing and Q_A is the output in agriculture, the revenue earned in each industry is $P_M \cdot Q_M$ and $P_A \cdot Q_A$, and the payments to capital and to land are

$$\text{Payments to capital} = P_M \cdot Q_M - W \cdot L_M$$

$$\text{Payments to land} = P_A \cdot Q_A - W \cdot L_A$$

It will be useful to take these payments one step further and break them down into the earnings of each unit of capital and land. To do so, we need to know the quantity of capital and land. We denote the quantity of land used in agriculture as T acres and the quantity of capital (number of machines) used in manufacturing as K. Thus, the earnings of one unit of capital (a machine, for instance), which we call R_K, and the earnings of an acre of land, which we call R_T, are calculated as

$$R_K = \frac{\text{Payments to capital}}{K} = \frac{P_M \cdot Q_M - W \cdot L_M}{K}$$

$$R_T = \frac{\text{Payments to land}}{T} = \frac{P_A \cdot Q_A - W \cdot L_A}{T}$$

Economists call R_K the **rental on capital** and R_T the **rental on land.** The use of the term "rental" does not mean that the factory owners or farmers rent their machines or land from someone else, although they could. Instead, the rental on machines and land reflects what these factors of production earn during a period when they are used in manufacturing and agriculture. Alternatively, the rental is the amount these factors *could* earn if they were rented to someone else over that same time.

There is a second way to calculate the rentals, which will look similar to the formula we have used for wages. In each industry, wages reflect the marginal product of labor times the price of the good, $W = P_M \cdot MPL_M = P_A \cdot MPL_A$. Similarly, capital and land rentals can be calculated as

$$R_K = P_M \cdot MPK_M \text{ and } R_T = P_A \cdot MPT_A$$

where MPK_M is the marginal product of capital in manufacturing, and MPT_A is the marginal product of land in agriculture. These marginal product formulas give the same values for the rentals as first calculating the payments to capital and land, as we just did, and then dividing by the quantity of capital and land. We will use both approaches to obtain rental values, depending on which is easiest.

Change in the Real Rental on Capital   Now that we understand how the rentals on capital and land are determined, we can look at what happens to them when the price of the manufactured good P_M rises, holding constant the price in agriculture P_A. From Figure 3-5, we know that the wage rises throughout the economy and that labor shifts from agriculture into manufacturing. As more labor is used in manufacturing, the marginal product of capital rises because each machine has more labor to work it. In addition, as labor leaves agriculture, the marginal product of land falls because each acre of land has fewer laborers to work it. The general conclusion is that *an increase in the quantity of labor used in an industry will raise the marginal product of the factor specific to that industry, and a decrease in labor will lower the marginal product of the specific factor.* This outcome does not contradict the law of diminishing returns, which states that an increase in labor will lower the marginal product *of labor* because now we are talking about how a change in labor affects the marginal product of *another factor.*

Using the preceding formulas for the rentals, we can summarize the results so far with

$$P^M \uparrow \Rightarrow \left\{ \begin{array}{l} L_M \uparrow, \text{ so that } MPK_M = R_K/P_M \uparrow \\ \\ L_A \downarrow, \text{ so that } MPT_A = R_T/P_A \downarrow \end{array} \right\}$$

That is, the increase in the marginal product of capital in manufacturing means that R_K/P_M also increases. Because R_K is the rental for capital, R_K/P_M is the amount of the manufactured good that can be purchased with this rent. Thus, the fact that R_K/P_M

increases means that the real rental on capital in terms of the manufactured good has gone up. For the increase in the real rental on capital to occur even though the price of the manufactured good has gone up, too, the percentage increase in R_K must be greater than the percentage increase in P_M.[12]

The amount of food that can be purchased by capital owners is R_K/P_A. Because R_K has increased, and P_A is fixed, R_K/P_A must also increase; in other words, the real rental on capital in terms of food has also gone up. Because capital owners can afford to buy more of both goods, they are clearly better off when the price of the manufactured good rises. Unlike labor, whose real wage increased in terms of one good but fell in terms of the other, capital owners clearly gain from the rise in the relative price of manufactured goods.

Change in the Real Rental on Land Let us now consider what happens to the landowners. With labor leaving agriculture, the marginal product of each acre falls, so R_T/P_A also falls. Because R_T is the rental on land, R_T/P_A is the amount of food that can be purchased with this rent. The fact that R_T/P_A falls means that the real rental on land in terms of food has gone down, so landowners cannot afford to buy as much food. Because the price of food is unchanged while the price of the manufactured good has gone up, landowners will not be able to afford to buy as much of the manufactured good either. Thus, landowners are clearly worse off from the rise in the price of the manufactured good because they can afford to buy less of both goods.

Summary The real earnings of capital owners and landowners move in opposite directions, an outcome that illustrates a general conclusion: *an increase in the relative price of an industry's output will increase the real rental earned by the factor specific to that industry but will decrease the real rental of factors specific to other industries.* This conclusion means that the specific factors used in export industries will generally gain as trade is opened and the relative price of exports rises, but the specific factors used in import industries will generally lose as trade is opened and the relative price of imports falls.

Numerical Example

We have come a long way in our study of the specific-factors model and conclude by presenting a numerical example of how an increase in the relative price of manufactures affects the earnings of labor, capital, and land. This example reviews the results we have obtained so far using actual numbers. Suppose that the manufacturing industry has the following payments to labor and capital:

Manufacturing: Sales revenue $= P_M \cdot Q_M = \$100$

Payments to labor $= W \cdot L_M = \$60$

Payments to capital $= R_K \cdot K = \$40$

Notice that 60% of sales revenue in manufacturing goes to labor, and 40% goes to capital.

---

[12] For example, if the price of manufactured goods rises by 6% and the rental on capital rises by 10%, then owners of capital can afford to buy 4% more of the manufactured good.

In agriculture, suppose that the payments to labor and land are as follows:

Agriculture: Sales revenue $= P_A \cdot Q_A = \$100$

Payments to labor $= W \cdot L_A = \$50$

Payments to land $= R_T \cdot T = \$50$

In the agriculture industry, we assume that land and labor each earn 50% of the sales revenue.

An increase in the relative price of manufactures P_M/P_A can be caused by an increase in P_M or a decrease in P_A. To be specific, suppose that the price of manufactures P_M rises by 10%, whereas the price of agriculture P_A does not change at all. We have found in our earlier discussion that $\Delta W/W$, the percentage change in the wage, will be between the percentage change in these two industry prices. So let us suppose that $\Delta W/W$, is 5%. We summarize these output and factor price changes as follows:

Manufacturing: Percentage increase in price $= \Delta P_M/P_M = 10\%$

Agriculture: Percentage increase in price $= \Delta P_A/P_A = 0\%$

Both industries: Percentage increase in the wage $= \Delta W/W = 5\%$

Notice that the increase in the wage applies in both industries because wages are always equalized across sectors.

Change in the Rental on Capital   Our goal is to use the preceding data for manufacturing and agriculture to compute the change in the rental on capital and the change in the rental on land. Let's start with the equation for the rental on capital, which was computed by subtracting wage payments from sales revenue and then dividing by the amount of capital:

$$R_K = \frac{\text{Payments to capital}}{K} = \frac{P_M \cdot Q_M - W \cdot L_M}{K}$$

If the price of manufactured goods rises by $\Delta P_M > 0$, holding constant the price in agriculture, then the change in the rental is

$$\Delta R_K = \frac{\Delta P_M \cdot Q_M - \Delta W \cdot L_M}{K}$$

We want to rewrite this equation using percentage changes, like $\Delta P_M/P_M$, $\Delta W/W$, and $\Delta R_K/R_K$. To achieve this, divide both sides by R_K and rewrite the equation as

$$\frac{\Delta R_K}{R_K} = \frac{(\Delta P_M/P_M) \cdot P_M \cdot Q_M - (\Delta W/W) \cdot W \cdot L_M}{R_K \cdot K}$$

You can cancel terms in this equation to check that it is the same as before.

The term $\Delta P_M/P_M$ in this equation is the percentage change in the price of manufacturing, whereas $\Delta W/W$ is the percentage change in the wage. Given this information, along with the preceding data on the payments to labor, capital, and sales revenue, we can compute the percentage change in the rental on capital:

$$\frac{\Delta R_K}{R_K} = \frac{(10\% \cdot 100 - 5\% \cdot 60)}{40} = 17.5\%$$

We see that the percentage increase in the rental on capital, 17.5%, *exceeds* the percentage increase in the relative price of manufacturing, 10% (so $\Delta R_K / R_K > \Delta P_M / P_M > 0$). This outcome holds no matter what numbers are used in the preceding formula, provided that the percentage increase in the wage is less than the percentage increase in the price of the manufactured good (as proved in Figure 3-5).

Change in the Rental on Land We can use the same approach to examine the change in the rental on land. Continuing to assume that the price of the manufactured good rises, while the price in agriculture stays the same ($\Delta P_A = 0$), the change in the land rental is

$$\Delta R_T = \frac{0 \cdot Q_A - \Delta W \cdot L_A}{T}$$

Because the wage is increasing, $\Delta W > 0$, it follows immediately that the *rental on land is falling*, $\Delta R_T < 0$. The percentage amount by which it falls can be calculated by rewriting the above equation as

$$\frac{\Delta R_T}{R_T} = -\frac{\Delta W}{W} \left(\frac{W \cdot L_A}{R_T \cdot T} \right)$$

Using these earlier data for agriculture in this formula, we get

$$\frac{\Delta R_T}{R_T} = -5\% \left(\frac{50}{50} \right) = -5\%$$

In this case, the land rent falls by the same percentage amount that the wage increases. This equality occurs because we assumed that labor and land receive the same share of sales revenue in agriculture (50% each). If labor receives a higher share of revenue than land, then the rent on land will fall even more; if it receives a lower share, then the rent on land won't fall as much.

General Equation for the Change in Factor Prices By summarizing our results in a single equation, we can see how all the changes in factor and industry prices are related. Under the assumption that the price of the manufactured good increased but the price of the agricultural good did not change, we have shown the following:

$$\underbrace{\Delta R_T / R_T < 0}_{\substack{\text{Real rental} \\ \text{on land falls}}} < \underbrace{\Delta W / W < \Delta P_M / P_M}_{\substack{\text{Change in the real} \\ \text{wage is ambiguous}}} < \underbrace{\Delta R_K / R_K}_{\substack{\text{Real rental} \\ \text{on capital rises}}}, \text{ for an increase in } P_M$$

In other words, wages rise but not as much as the percentage increase in the price of the manufactured good; the rental on capital (which is specific to the manufacturing sector) rises by more than the manufacturing price, so capital owners are better off; and the rental on land (which is the specific factor in the other sector) falls, so landowners are worse off.

What happens if the price of the manufactured good falls? Then the inequalities are reversed, and the equation becomes

$$\underbrace{\Delta R_K / R_K < \Delta P_M / P_M}_{\substack{\text{Real rental} \\ \text{on capital falls}}} < \underbrace{\Delta W / W < 0}_{\substack{\text{Change in the real} \\ \text{wage is ambiguous}}} < \underbrace{\Delta R_T / R_T}_{\substack{\text{Real rental} \\ \text{on land rises}}}, \text{ for a decrease in } P_M$$

In this case, wages fall but by less than the percentage decrease in the manufactured good; the rental on capital (which is specific to the manufacturing sector) falls by more than the manufacturing price, so capital owners are worse off; and the rental on land (which is the specific factor in the other sector) rises, so landowners are better off.

What happens if the *price of the agricultural good rises*? You can probably guess based on the previous example that this change will benefit land and harm capital. The equation summarizing the changes in all three factor earnings becomes

$$\underbrace{\Delta R_K/R_K < 0}_{\substack{\text{Real rental} \\ \text{on capital falls}}} < \underbrace{\Delta W/W}_{\substack{\text{Change in the real} \\ \text{wage is ambiguous}}} < \underbrace{\Delta P_A/P_A < \Delta R_T/R_T}_{\substack{\text{Real rental} \\ \text{on land rises}}}, \text{ for an increase in } P_A$$

Note that it is the specific factor in the agricultural sector that gains and the specific factor in manufacturing that loses. The general result of these summary equations is that *the specific factor in the sector whose relative price has increased gains, the specific factor in the other sector loses, and labor is "caught in the middle," with its real wage increasing in terms of one good but falling in terms of the other.* These equations summarize the response of all three factor prices in the short run, when capital and land are specific to each sector but labor is mobile.

What It All Means

Our results from the specific-factors model show that the earnings of *specific factors* change the most from changes in relative prices due to international trade. Regardless of which good's price changes, the earnings of capital and land show the most extreme changes in their rentals, whereas the changes in the wages paid to labor are in the middle. Intuitively, these extreme changes in factor prices occur because in the short run the specific factors are not able to leave their sectors and find employment elsewhere. Labor benefits by its opportunity to move between sectors and earn the same wage in each, but the interests of capital and land are opposed to each other: one gains and the other loses. This suggests that we ought to be able to find real-world examples in which a change in international prices leads to losses for either capitalists or landowners. There are many such examples, and we discuss one in the next application.

▪ APPLICATION

Prices in Agriculture

At the end of the previous chapter, we discussed the Prebisch-Singer hypothesis, which states that the prices of primary commodities tend to fall over time. Although we argued that this hypothesis does not hold for all primary commodities, it does hold for some agricultural goods: the relative prices of cotton, palm oil, rice, sugar, rubber, wheat, and wool declined for more than half the years between 1900 and 1998. Generally, agricultural prices fall as countries become more efficient at growing crops and begin exporting them. From our study of the specific-factors model, it will be landowners (i.e., farmers) who lose in real terms from this decline in the relative price of agricultural products. On the other hand, capital owners gain in real terms, and changes in the real wage are ambiguous. Faced with declining real earnings in the agriculture sector, governments and other groups often take actions to prevent the incomes of farmers from falling.

Coffee Prices An example of an agricultural commodity with particularly volatile prices is coffee. The price of coffee on world markets fluctuates a great deal from year to year because of weather and also because of the entry of new suppliers in Brazil and new supplying countries such as Vietnam. The movements in the real wholesale price of coffee (measured in 2012 dollars) are shown in Figure 3-8. Wholesale prices were at a high of $3.58 per pound in 1986, then fell to a low of 87¢ per pound in 1992, rose to $2.08 in 1994–95, and then fell to 59¢ per pound in 2001. Since 2001 there has been a sustained increase in both price and quantity, implying a shift in import demand. By 2011 prices had risen to $2.15 per pound. These dramatic fluctuations in prices create equally large movements in the real incomes of farmers, making it difficult for them to sustain a living. The very low prices in 2001 created a crisis in the coffee-growing regions of Central America, requiring humanitarian aid for farmers and their families. The governments of coffee-growing regions in Central America and Asia cannot afford to protect their coffee farmers by propping up prices, as do the industrial countries.

According to the specific-factors model, big fluctuations in coffee prices are extremely disruptive to the real earnings of landowners in coffee-exporting developing countries, many of whom are small farmers and their families. Can anything be

FIGURE 3-8

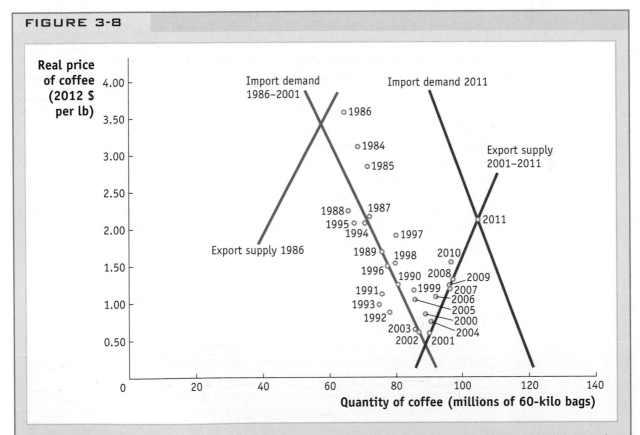

World Coffee Market, 1984–2011 Real wholesale prices for coffee have fluctuated greatly on world markets. Using 2012 dollars, prices were at a high of $3.58 per pound in 1986, fell to 87¢ per pound in 1992, rose to $2.08 in 1994–95, and then fell to 59¢ per pound in 2001. Since 2001 there has been a sustained increase in both price and quantity, implying a shift

in import demand. By 2011 prices had risen to $2.15 per pound. Correspondingly, the quantity of world coffee exports was at a low in 1986 (65 million bags) and at a high in 2011 (105 million bags), as supplies from Brazil and Vietnam increased.

Source: International Coffee Organization, http://www.ico.org.

Groups like TransFair USA ensure coffee farmers like Jesus Lopez Hernandez, pictured here, a more stable source of income over time.

done to avoid the kind of boom-and-bust cycle that occurs regularly in coffee markets?

Fair-Trade Coffee One idea that is gaining appeal is to sell coffee from developing countries directly to consumers in industrial countries, thereby avoiding the middlemen (such as local buyers, millers, exporters, shippers, and importers) and ensuring a minimum price for the farmers. You may have seen "fair-trade" coffee at your favorite coffeehouse. This coffee first appeared in the United States in 1999, imported by a group called TransFair USA that is committed to passing more of the profits back to the growers. TransFair USA is an example of a nongovernmental organization that is trying to help farmers by raising prices, and the consumer gets the choice of whether to purchase this higher-priced product. In addition to coffee, TransFair USA has been applying its Fair Trade label to imports of cocoa, tea, rice, sugar, bananas, mangoes, pineapples, and grapes.

World coffee prices recovered in 2005, which meant that groups like TransFair USA faced a dilemma: the fair-trade prices that they had guaranteed to farmers were actually less than the world price of coffee. The accompanying article **Headlines: Rise in Coffee Prices—Great for Farmers, Tough on Co-ops** describes how some farmers were tempted to break their contracts with local co-ops (at fixed, fair-trade prices) to deliver coffee to local middlemen at prevailing world prices. TransFair USA and similar organizations purchase coffee at higher than the market price when the market is low (as in 2001), but in other years (like 2005) the fair-trade price is below the market price. Essentially, TransFair USA is offering farmers a form of *insurance* whereby the fair-trade price of coffee will not fluctuate too much, ensuring them a more stable source of income over time. By protecting farmers against the boom-and-bust cycle of fluctuating prices, they are able to enjoy greater gains from trade by exporting their coffee. So when you consider buying a cup of fair-trade coffee at your favorite coffeehouse, you are supporting coffee farmers who rely on the efforts of groups like TransFair USA to raise their incomes, and applying the logic of the specific-factors model, all at the same time! ■

4   Conclusions

In the Ricardian model of Chapter 2, we showed that free trade could never make a country worse off, and in most cases free trade would make it better off. This result remains true when we add land and capital as factors of production, in addition to labor. Provided that the relative price with international trade differs from the no-trade relative price, then a country gains from international trade. This conclusion does not mean, however, that each and every factor of production gains. On the contrary, we have shown in this chapter that the change in relative prices due to the opening of trade creates winners and losers. Some factors of production gain in real terms and other factors of production lose. To demonstrate this result, we have used a short-run model, in which labor is mobile between sectors, but land and capital are each specific to their sectors.

HEADLINES

Rise in Coffee Prices—Great for Farmers, Tough on Co-ops

TransFair USA guarantees a minimum purchase price for coffee farmers, acting as insurance against a falling market price. But during periods when the market price is rising, it is challenging to ensure that farmers deliver their coffee.

During winter and spring of the 2005 harvest, a dilemma surfaced in rural areas of Central America and Mexico. Fairtrade cooperative managers found it increasingly difficult to get members to deliver coffee to their own organization at fair-trade prices. The co-op managers were holding contracts that were set months before at fixed fair-trade prices of $1.26 per pound, but now the world coffee price was higher. Growers were seeing some of the highest prices paid in five years, and the temptation was great to sell their coffee to the highest local bidder, instead of delivering it as promised to their own co-ops.

In most cases, the co-ops' leaders were able to convince farmers to deliver coffee, but often based on arguments of loyalty, as the fair-trade fixed price was now lower than the premium prices being offered by the local middleman. It was not the model that the founders of fair-trade coffee pricing had envisioned when they created the program.

"It's worth noting that we were pleased to see prices rise in late 2004," says Christopher Himes, TransFair USA's Director of Certification and Finance. "This price rise, in conjunction with the impact fair trade was already having, increased the income and living standards of coffee farmers around the world. The most challenging thing during this time for TransFair USA was the speed with which the local differentials [between the fair-trade price and the world price] rose in Indonesia. They quickly skyrocketed to 80 cents [per pound] or higher, making the market value of farmers' coffee higher than that of some of the . . . fair-trade contracts."

Source: David Griswold, http://www.FreshCup.com, June 2005.

Classical economists believed that, in the short run, factors of production that could not move between industries would lose the most from trade. We have found that this is true for the factor that is specific to the import-competing industry. That industry suffers a drop in its relative price because of international trade, which leads to a fall in the real rental on the specific factor in that industry. On the other hand, the specific factor in the export industry—whose relative price rises with the opening of trade—enjoys an increase in its real rental. Labor is mobile between the two industries, which allows it to avoid such extreme changes in its wage—real wages rise in terms of one good but fall in terms of the other good, so we cannot tell whether workers are better off or worse off after a country opens to trade.

Economists have carefully proved that, in theory, the gains of individuals due to opening trade exceed the losses. This result means that, in principle, the government should be able to tax the winners and compensate the losers so that everyone is better off because of trade. In practice, it is very difficult to design programs to achieve that level of compensation. In this chapter, we looked at one compensation program—Trade Adjustment Assistance—that is used in the United States and other countries to compensate people who are laid off because of import competition. There are many other policies (such as import tariffs and quotas) that are intended to protect individuals from the effect of price changes resulting from international trade, and we examine these policies later in the book.

KEY POINTS

1. Opening a country to international trade leads to overall gains, but in a model with several factors of production, some factors of production will lose.

2. The fact that some people are harmed because of trade sometimes creates social tensions that may be strong enough to topple governments. A recent example is Bolivia, where the citizens in the early 2000s could not agree on how to share the gains from exporting natural gas.

3. In the specific-factors model, factors of production that cannot move between industries will gain or lose the most from opening a country to trade. The factor of production that is specific to the import industry will lose in real terms, as the relative price of the import good falls. The factor of production that is specific to the export industry will gain in real terms, as the relative price of the export good rises.

4. In the specific-factors model, labor can move between the industries and earns the same wage in each. When the relative price of either good changes, then the real wage rises when measured in terms of one good but falls when measured in terms of the other good. Without knowing how much of each good workers prefer to consume, we cannot say whether workers are better off or worse off because of trade.

5. Economists do not normally count the costs of unemployment as a loss from trade because people are often able to find new jobs. In the United States, for example, about two-thirds of people laid off from manufacturing or services companies find new jobs within two or three years, although sometimes at lower wages.

6. Trade Adjustment Assistance policies are intended to compensate those who are harmed because of trade by providing additional income during the period of unemployment. Recently, the Trade Adjustment Assistance program in the United States was expanded to include workers laid off because of trade in service industries.

7. Even when many people are employed in export activities, such as those involved in coffee export from certain developing countries, fluctuations in the world market price can lead to large changes in income for growers and workers.

KEY TERMS

specific-factors model, p. 60
diminishing returns, p. 61
autarky, p. 65
embargo, p. 65

real wage, p. 68
Trade Adjustment Assistance (TAA), p. 70
services, p. 71

rental on capital, p. 76
rental on land, p. 76

PROBLEMS

1. Why is the specific-factors model referred to as a short-run model?

2. Figure 3-7 presents wages in the manufacturing and services sectors for the period 1973 to 2012. Is the difference in wages across sectors consistent with either the Ricardian model studied in Chapter 2 or the specific-factors model? Explain why or why not.

3. In the gains from trade diagram in Figure 3-3, suppose that instead of having a rise in the relative price of manufactures, there is instead a fall in that relative price.

   a. Starting at the no-trade point A in Figure 3-3, show what would happen to production and consumption.

   b. Which good is exported and which is imported?

c. Explain why the overall gains from trade are still positive.

4. Starting from equilibrium in the specific-factors model, suppose the price of manufactured goods falls so that wages fall from W' to W in Figure 3-5.

 a. Show that the percentage fall in the wage is less than the percentage fall in the price of manufacturing so that the real wage of labor in terms of manufactured goods goes up.

 b. What happens to the real wage of labor in terms of agriculture?

 c. Are workers better off, worse off, or is the outcome ambiguous?

5. Use the information given here to answer the following questions:

 Manufacturing:

   Sales revenue = $P_M \cdot Q_M = 150$
   Payments to labor = $W \cdot L_M = 100$
   Payments to capital = $R_K \cdot K = 50$

 Agriculture:

   Sales revenue = $P_A \cdot Q_A = 150$
   Payments to labor = $W \cdot L_A = 50$
   Payments to land = $R_T \cdot T = 100$

 Holding the price of manufacturing constant, suppose the increase in the price of agriculture is 10% and the increase in the wage is 5%.

 a. Determine the impact of the increase in the price of agriculture on the rental on land and the rental on capital.

 b. Explain what has happened to the real rental on land and the real rental on capital.

6. If instead of the situation given in Problem 5, the price of manufacturing were to fall by 10%, would landowners or capital owners be better off? Explain. How would the decrease in the price of manufacturing affect labor? Explain.

7. Read the article by Lori G. Kletzer and Robert E. Litan, "A Prescription to Relieve Worker Anxiety," *Policy Brief* 01-2 (Washington, D.C.: Peterson Institute for International Economics), available online at http://www.iie.com/publications/pb/pb.cfm?researchid=70, which refers to the

U.S. recession of 2000 and 2001. Then answer the following:

 a. Under the version of Trade Adjustment Assistance (TAA) in the United States that they refer to, how many extra weeks of unemployment insurance are workers eligible for? What two criteria must workers meet to qualify for this extra unemployment insurance?

 b. Consider the proposal for "wage insurance" that Kletzer and Litan make in their article. What criteria would workers need to qualify for this insurance? What amount of extra income would they receive from the insurance?

 c. If Kletzer and Litan's new plan for "wage insurance" had been adopted by the United States, what would have been the budgetary cost in 1999, when unemployment was 4.2%? How does this compare with the amount that is now spent on unemployment insurance?

8. In the specific-factors model, assume that the price of agricultural goods decreases while the price of manufactured goods is unchanged ($\Delta P_A/P_A < 0$ and $\Delta P_M/P_M = 0$). Arrange the following terms in ascending order:

 $\Delta R_T/R_T \quad \Delta R_K/R_K \quad \Delta P_A/P_A \quad \Delta P_M/P_M \quad \Delta W/W$

 Hint: Try starting with a diagram like Figure 3-5, but change the price of agricultural goods instead.

9. Suppose two countries, Canada and Mexico, produce two goods: timber and televisions. Assume that land is specific to timber, capital is specific to televisions, and labor is free to move between the two industries. When Canada and Mexico engage in free trade, the relative price of televisions falls in Canada and the relative price of timber falls in Mexico.

 a. In a graph similar to Figure 3-5, show how the wage changes in Canada due to a fall in the price of televisions, holding constant the price of timber. Can we predict that change in the real wage?

 b. What is the impact of opening trade on the rentals on capital and land in Canada? Can we predict that change in the real rentals on capital and land?

c. What is the impact of opening trade on the rentals on capital and land in Mexico? Can we predict that change in the real rentals on capital and land?

d. In each country, has the specific factor in the export industry gained or lost and has the specific factor in the import industry gained or lost?

10. Home produces two goods, computers and wheat, for which capital is specific to computers, land is specific to wheat, and labor is mobile between the two industries. Home has 100 workers and 100 units of capital but only 10 units of land.

a. Draw a graph similar to Figure 3-1 with the output of wheat on the vertical axis and the labor in wheat on the horizontal axis. What is the relationship between the output of wheat and the marginal product of labor in the wheat industry as more labor is used?

b. Draw the production possibilities frontier for Home with wheat on the horizontal axis and computers on the vertical axis.

c. Explain how the price of wheat relative to computers is determined in the absence of trade.

d. Reproduce Figure 3-4 with the amount of labor used in wheat measuring from left to right along the horizontal axis and the amount of labor used in computers moving in the reverse direction.

e. Assume that due to international trade, the price of wheat rises. Analyze the effect of the increase in the price of wheat on the allocation of labor between the two sectors.

11. Similar to Home in Problem 10, Foreign also produces computers and wheat using capital, which is specific to computers; land, which is specific to wheat; and labor, which is mobile between the two sectors. Foreign has 100 workers and 100 units of land but only 10 units of capital. It has the same production functions as Home.

a. Will the no-trade relative price of wheat be higher in Home or in Foreign? Explain why you expect this outcome.

b. When trade is opened, what happens to the relative price of wheat in Foreign and to the relative price of wheat in Home?

c. Based on your answer to (b), predict the effect of opening trade on the rental on land in each country, which is specific to wheat. What about the rental on capital, which is specific to computers?

12. In the text, we learned that workers displaced by import competition are eligible for compensation through the Trade Adjustment Assistance program. Firms are also eligible for support through Trade Adjustment Assistance for Firms, a federal program that provides financial assistance to manufacturers affected by import competition. Go to http://www.taacenters.org to read about this program, and answer the following:

a. What criteria does a firm have to satisfy to quality for benefits?

b. What amount of money is provided to firms, and for what purpose?

c. Provide an argument for and an argument against the continued funding of this federal program.

N E T W O R K

The Bureau of Labor Statistics regularly releases information on the changes in employment, wages, and displacement of workers at http://www.bls.gov. Find one recent announcement and summarize that information. How does the information in that announcement compare with the trends in the Application on pages 71–73 on employment and wages in manufacturing and services?

Trade and Resources:
The Heckscher-Ohlin Model

God did not bestow all products upon all parts of the earth, but distributed His gifts over different regions, to the end that men might cultivate a social relationship because one would have need of the help of another. And so He called commerce into being, that all men might be able to have common enjoyment of the fruits of the earth, no matter where produced.

Libanius (AD 314–393), *Orations* (III)

Nature, by giving a diversity of geniuses, climates, and soils, to different nations, has secured their mutual intercourse and commerce. . . . The industry of the nations, from whom they import, receives encouragement: Their own is also [i]ncreased, by the sale of the commodities which they give in exchange.

David Hume, *Essays, Moral, Political, and Literary*, 1752,
Part II, Essay VI, "On the Jealousy of Trade"

In Chapter 2, we examined U.S. imports of snowboards. We argued there that the resources found in a country would influence its pattern of international trade. Canada's export of snowboards to the United States reflects its mountains and cold climate, as do the exports of snowboards to the United States from Austria, Spain, Switzerland, Slovenia, Italy, Poland, and France. Because each country's resources are different and because resources are spread unevenly around the world, countries have a reason to trade the goods made with these resources. This is an old idea, as shown by the quotations at the beginning of this chapter; the first is from the fourth-century Greek scholar Libanius, and the second is from the eighteenth-century philosopher David Hume.

In this chapter, we outline the **Heckscher-Ohlin model**, a model that assumes that trade occurs because countries have different resources. This model contrasts with the Ricardian model, which assumed that trade occurs because countries use their technological comparative advantage to specialize in the production of different goods. The model is named after the Swedish economists Eli Heckscher, who wrote about his views of international trade in a 1919 article, and his student Bertil Ohlin, who further developed these ideas in his 1924 dissertation.

The Heckscher-Ohlin model was developed at the end of a "golden age" of international trade (as described in Chapter 1) that lasted from about 1890 until 1914, when World War I started. Those years saw dramatic improvements in transportation: the steamship and the railroad allowed for a great increase in the amount of international trade. For these reasons, there was a considerable increase in the ratio of trade to GDP between 1890 and 1914. It is not surprising, then, that Heckscher and Ohlin would want to explain the large increase in trade that they had witnessed in their own lifetimes. The ability to transport machines across borders meant that they did not look to differences in technologies across countries as the reason for trade, as Ricardo had done. Instead, they assumed that technologies were the same across countries, and they used the uneven distribution of resources across countries to explain trade patterns.

Even today, there are many examples of international trade driven by the land, labor, and capital resources found in each country. Canada, for example, has a large amount of land and therefore exports agricultural and forestry products, as well as petroleum; the United States, Western Europe, and Japan have many highly skilled workers and much capital and these countries export sophisticated services and manufactured goods; China and other Asian countries have a large number of workers and moderate but growing amounts of capital and they export less sophisticated manufactured goods; and so on. We study these and other examples of international trade in this chapter.

Our first goal is to describe the Heckscher-Ohlin model of trade. The specific-factors model that we studied in the previous chapter was a short-run model because capital and land could not move between the two industries we looked at. In contrast, the Heckscher-Ohlin model is a long-run model because all factors of production can move between industries. It is difficult to deal with three factors of production (labor, capital, and land) in both industries, so, instead, we assume that there are just two factors (labor and capital).

After predicting the long-run pattern of trade between countries using the Heckscher-Ohlin model, our second goal is to examine the empirical evidence on the Heckscher-Ohlin model. Although you might think it is obvious that a country's exports will be based on the resources the country has in abundance, it turns out that this prediction does not always hold true in practice. To obtain better predictions from the Heckscher-Ohlin model, we extend it in several directions, first by allowing for more than two factors of production and second by allowing countries to differ in their technologies, as in the Ricardian model. Both extensions make the predictions from the Heckscher-Ohlin model match more closely the trade patterns we see in the world economy today.

The third goal of the chapter is to investigate how the opening of trade between the two countries affects the payments to labor and to capital in each of them. We use the Heckscher-Ohlin model to predict which factor(s) gain when international trade begins and which factor(s) lose.

1 Heckscher-Ohlin Model

In building the Heckscher-Ohlin model, we suppose there are two countries, Home and Foreign, each of which produces two goods, computers and shoes, using two factors of production, labor and capital. Using symbols for capital (K) and labor (L), we can add up the resources used in each industry to get the total for the economy. For example, the amount of capital Home uses in shoes K_S, plus the amount of capital used in computers K_C, adds up to the total capital available in the economy $\overline{K}$, so that $K_C + K_S = \overline{K}$. The same applies for Foreign: $K_C^* + K_S^* = \overline{K}^*$. Similarly, the amount of labor Home uses in shoes L_S, and the amount of labor used in computers L_C, add up to the total labor in the economy $\overline{L}$, so that $L_C + L_S = \overline{L}$. The same applies for Foreign: $L_C^* + L_S^* = \overline{L}^*$.

Assumptions of the Heckscher-Ohlin Model

Because the Heckscher-Ohlin (HO) model describes the economy in the long run, its assumptions differ from those in the short-run specific-factors model of Chapter 3:

Assumption 1: Both factors can move freely between the industries.

This assumption implies that if both industries are actually producing, then capital must earn the same rental R in each of them. The reason for this result is that if capital earned a higher rental in one industry than the other, then all capital would move to the industry with the higher rental and the other industry would shut down. This result differs from the specific-factors model in which capital in manufacturing and land in agriculture earned different rentals in their respective industries. But like the specific-factor model, if both industries are producing, then all labor earns the same wage W in each of them.

Our second assumption concerns how the factors are combined to make shoes and computers:

Assumption 2: Shoe production is labor-intensive; that is, it requires more labor per unit of capital to produce shoes than computers, so that $L_S/K_S > L_C/K_C$.

Another way to state this assumption is to say that computer production is capital-intensive; that is, more capital per worker is used to produce computers than to produce shoes, so that $K_C/L_C > K_S/L_S$. The idea that shoes use more labor per unit of capital, and computers use more capital per worker, matches how most of us think about the technologies used in these two industries.

In Figure 4-1, the demands for labor relative to capital in each industry (L_C/K_C and L_S/K_S) are graphed against the wage relative to the rental on capital, W/R (or the wage-rental ratio). These two curves slope down just like regular demand curves: as W/R rises, the quantity of labor demanded relative to the quantity of capital demanded falls. As we work through the HO model, remember that these are *relative* demand curves for labor; the "quantity" on the horizontal axis is the ratio of labor to capital used in production, and the "price" is the ratio of the labor wage to the capital rental. Assumption 2 says that the relative demand curve in shoes, L_S/K_S in Figure 4-1, lies to the right of the relative demand curve in computers L_C/K_C, because shoe production is more labor-intensive.

Whereas the preceding assumptions have focused on the production process within each country, the HO model requires assumptions that apply across countries as well. Our next assumption is that the amounts of labor and capital found in Home and Foreign are different:

FIGURE 4-1

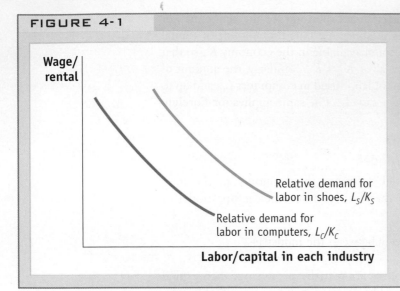

Labor Intensity of Each Industry The demand for labor relative to capital is assumed to be higher in shoes than in computers, $L_S/K_S > L_C/K_C$. These two curves slope down just like regular demand curves, but in this case, they are *relative* demand curves for labor (i.e., demand for labor divided by demand for capital).

Assumption 3: Foreign is <u>labor-abundant,</u> by which we mean that the labor–capital ratio in Foreign exceeds that in Home, $\overline{L}^*/\overline{K}^* > \overline{L}/\overline{K}$. Equivalently, Home is capital-abundant, so that $\overline{K}/\overline{L} > \overline{K}^*/\overline{L}^*$.

There are many reasons for labor, capital, and other resources to differ across countries: countries differ in their geographic size and populations, previous waves of immigration or emigration may have changed a country's population, countries are at different stages of development and so have differing amounts of capital, and so on. If we are considering land in the HO model, Home and Foreign will have different amounts of usable land due to the shape of their borders and to differences in topography and climate. In building the HO model, we do not consider why the amounts of labor, capital, or land differ across countries but simply accept these differences as important determinants of why countries engage in international trade.

Assumption 3 focuses on a particular case, in which <u>Foreign is labor-abundant and Home is capital-abundant.</u> This assumption is true, for example, if Foreign has a larger workforce than Home ($\overline{L}^* > \overline{L}$) and Foreign and Home have equal amounts of capital, $\overline{K}^* = \overline{K}$. Under these circumstances, $\overline{L}^*/\overline{K}^* > \overline{L}/\overline{K}$, so Foreign is labor-abundant. Conversely, the capital–labor ratio in Home exceeds that in Foreign, $\overline{K}/\overline{L} > \overline{K}^*/\overline{L}^*$, so the Home country is capital-abundant.

Assumption 4: The final outputs, shoes and computers, can be traded freely (i.e., without any restrictions) between nations, but labor and capital do not move between countries.

In this chapter, we do not allow labor or capital to move between countries. We relax this assumption in the next chapter, in which we investigate the movement of labor between countries through immigration as well as the movement of capital between countries through foreign direct investment.

Our final two assumptions involve the technologies of firms and tastes of consumers across countries:

Assumption 5: The technologies used to produce the two goods are identical across the countries.

This assumption is the opposite of that made in the Ricardian model (Chapter 2), which assumes that technological differences across countries are the reason for trade. It is not realistic to assume that technologies are the same across countries because often the technologies used in rich versus poor countries are quite different (as described in the following application). Although assumption 5 is not very realistic, it allows us to focus on a single reason for trade: the different amounts of labor and capital found in each country. Later in this chapter, we use data to test the validity of the HO model and find that the model performs better when assumption 5 is not used.

Our final assumption is as follows:

Assumption 6: Consumer tastes are the same across countries, and preferences for computers and shoes do not vary with a country's level of income.

That is, we suppose that a poorer country will buy fewer shoes and computers, but will buy them in the same ratio as a wealthier country facing the same prices. Again, this assumption is not very realistic: consumers in poor countries do spend more of their income on shoes, clothing, and other basic goods than on computers, whereas in rich countries a higher share of income can be spent on computers and other electronic goods than on footwear and clothing. Assumption 6 is another simplifying assumption that again allows us to focus attention on the differences in resources as the sole reason for trade.

APPLICATION

Are Factor Intensities the Same Across Countries?

One of our assumptions for the Heckscher-Ohlin (HO) model is that the same good (shoes) is labor-intensive in both countries. Specifically, we assume that in both countries, shoe production has a higher labor–capital ratio than does computer production. Although it might seem obvious that this assumption holds for shoes and computers, it is not so obvious when comparing other products, say, shoes and call centers.

In principle, all countries have access to the same technologies for making footwear. In practice, however, the machines used in the United States are different from those used in Asia and elsewhere. While much of the footwear in the world is produced in developing nations, the United States retains a small number of shoe factories. New Balance, which manufactures sneakers, has five plants in the New England states, and 25% of the shoes it sells in North America are produced in the United States. One of their plants is in Norridgewock, Maine, where employees operate computerized equipment that allows one person to do the work of six.[1] This is a far cry from the plants in Asia that produce shoes for Nike, Reebok, and

Despite its nineteenth-century exterior, this New Balance factory in Maine houses advanced shoe-manufacturing technology.

---

[1] This description of the New Balance plant is drawn from Aaron Bernstein, "Low-Skilled Jobs: Do They Have to Move?" *BusinessWeek*, February 26, 2001, 94–95.

other U.S. producers. Because Asian plants use older technology (such as individual sewing machines), they use more workers to operate less productive machines.

In call centers, on the other hand, technologies (and, therefore, factor intensities) are similar across countries. Each employee works with a telephone and a personal computer, so call centers in the United States and India are similar in terms of the amount of capital per worker that they require. The telephone and personal computer, costing several thousand dollars, are much less expensive than the automated manufacturing machines in the New Balance plant in the United States, which cost tens or hundreds of thousands of dollars. So the manufacture of footwear in the New Balance plant is capital-intensive as compared with a U.S. call center. In India, by contrast, the sewing machine used to produce footwear is cheaper than the computer used in the call center. So footwear production in India is labor-intensive as compared with the call center, which is the opposite of what holds in the United States. This example illustrates a **reversal of factor intensities** between the two countries.

The same reversal of factor intensities is seen when we compare the agricultural sector across countries. In the United States, agriculture is capital-intensive. Each farmer works with tens of thousands of dollars in mechanized, computerized equipment, allowing a farm to be maintained by only a handful of workers. In many developing countries, however, agriculture is labor-intensive. Farms are worked by many laborers with little or no mechanized equipment. The reason that this labor-intensive technology is used in agriculture in developing nations is that capital equipment is expensive relative to the wages earned.

In assumption 2 and Figure 4-1, we assume that the labor–capital ratio (L/K) of one industry exceeds that of the other industry *regardless of the wage-rental ratio* (W/R). That is, whether labor is cheap (as in a developing country) or expensive (as in the United States), we are assuming that the same industry (shoes, in our example) is labor-intensive in both countries. This assumption may not be true for footwear or for agriculture, as we have just seen. In our treatment of the HO model, we ignore the possibility of factor intensity reversals. The reason for ignoring these is to get a definite prediction from the model about the pattern of trade between countries so that we can see what happens to the price of goods and the earnings of factors when countries trade with one another. ■

No-Trade Equilibrium

In assumption 3, we outlined the difference in the amount of labor and capital found at Home and in Foreign. Our goal is to use these differences in resources to predict the pattern of trade. To do this, we begin by studying the equilibrium in each country in the absence of trade.

Production Possibilities Frontiers To determine the no-trade equilibria in Home and Foreign, we start by drawing the production possibilities frontiers (PPFs) in each country as shown in Figure 4-2. Under our assumptions that Home is capital-abundant and that computer production is capital-intensive, Home is capable of producing more computers than shoes. The Home PPF drawn in panel (a) is skewed in the direction of computers to reflect Home's greater capability to produce computers. Similarly, because Foreign is labor-abundant and shoe production is labor-intensive, the Foreign PPF shown in panel (b) is skewed in the direction of shoes, reflecting Foreign's greater capability to produce shoes. These particular shapes for the PPFs are reasonable given the assumptions we have made. When we continue our study of the Heckscher-Ohlin (HO) model in Chapter 5, we prove that the PPFs must take

FIGURE 4-2

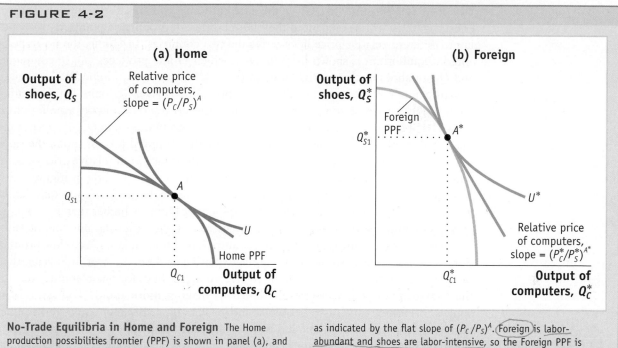

(a) Home

(b) Foreign

No-Trade Equilibria in Home and Foreign The Home production possibilities frontier (PPF) is shown in panel (a), and the Foreign PPF is shown in panel (b). Because Home is capital-abundant and computers are capital-intensive, the Home PPF is skewed toward computers. Home preferences are summarized by the indifference curve, U, and the Home no-trade (or autarky) equilibrium is at point A, with a low relative price of computers, as indicated by the flat slope of $(P_C/P_S)^A$. Foreign is labor-abundant and shoes are labor-intensive, so the Foreign PPF is skewed toward shoes. Foreign preferences are summarized by the indifference curve, U^*, and the Foreign no-trade equilibrium is at point A^*, with a higher relative price of computers, as indicated by the steeper slope of $(P_C^*/P_S^*)^{A^*}$.

this shape.[2] For now, we accept these shapes of the PPF and use them as the starting point for our study of the HO model.

Indifference Curves Another assumption of the HO model (assumption 6) is that consumer tastes are the same across countries. As we did in the Ricardian model, we graph consumer tastes using indifference curves. Two of these curves are shown in Figure 4-2 (U and U^* for Home and Foreign, respectively); one is tangent to Home's PPF, and the other is tangent to Foreign's PPF. Notice that these indifference curves are the same shape in both countries, as required by assumption 6. They are tangent to the PPFs at different points because of the distinct shapes of the PPFs just described.

The slope of an indifference curve equals the amount that consumers are willing to pay for computers measured in terms of shoes rather than dollars. The slope of the PPF equals the opportunity cost of producing one more computer in terms of shoes given up. When the slope of an indifference curve equals the slope of a PPF, the relative price that consumers are willing to pay for computers equals the opportunity cost of producing them, so this point is the no-trade equilibrium.[3] The common slope of the indifference curve and PPF at their tangency equals the relative price of computers P_C/P_S. A steeply sloped price line implies a high relative price of computers, whereas a flat price line implies a low relative price for computers.

---

[2] See Problem 7 in Chapter 5.
[3] Remember that the slope of an indifference curve or PPF reflects the relative price of the good on the *horizontal* axis, which is computers in Figure 4-2.

No-Trade Equilibrium Price Given the differently shaped PPFs, the indifference curves of each country will be tangent to the PPFs at different production points, corresponding to different relative price lines across the two countries. In Home, the no-trade or autarky equilibrium is shown by point A, at which Home produces Q_{C1} of computers and Q_{S1} of shoes at the relative price of $(P_C/P_S)^A$. Because the Home PPF is skewed toward computers, the slope of the Home price line $(P_C/P_S)^A$ is quite flat, indicating a low relative price of computers. In Foreign, the no-trade or autarky equilibrium is shown by point A^* at which Foreign produces Q_{C1}^* of computers and Q_{S1}^* of shoes at the relative price of $(P_C^*/P_S^*)^{A^*}$. Because the Foreign PPF is skewed toward shoes, the slope of the Foreign price line $(P_C^*/P_S^*)^{A^*}$ is quite steep, indicating a high relative price of computers. Therefore, the result from comparing the no-trade equilibria in Figure 4-2 is that the *no-trade relative price of computers at Home is lower than in Foreign.* (Equivalently, we can say that the no-trade relative price of shoes at Home is higher than in Foreign.)

These comparisons of the no-trade prices reflect the differing amounts of labor found in the two countries: the Foreign country has abundant labor, and shoe production is labor-intensive, so the no-trade relative price of shoes is lower in Foreign than in Home. That Foreigners are willing to give up more shoes for one computer reflects the fact that Foreign resources are suited to making more shoes. The same logic applies to Home, which is relatively abundant in capital. Because computer production is capital-intensive, Home has a lower no-trade relative price of computers than Foreign. Thus, Home residents need to give up fewer shoes to obtain one computer, reflecting the fact that their resources are suited to making more computers.

Free-Trade Equilibrium

We are now in a position to determine the pattern of trade between the countries. To do so, we proceed in several steps. First, we consider what happens when the world relative price of computers is above the no-trade relative price of computers at Home, and trace out the Home export supply of computers. Second, we consider what happens when the world relative price is *below* the no-trade relative price of computers in Foreign, and trace out the Foreign import demand for computers. Finally, we put together the Home export supply and Foreign import demand to determine the equilibrium relative price of computers with international trade.

Home Equilibrium with Free Trade The first step is displayed in Figure 4-3. We have already seen in Figure 4-2 that the no-trade relative price of computers is lower in Home than in Foreign. Under free trade, we expect the equilibrium relative price of computers to lie between the no-trade relative prices in each country (as we already found in the Ricardian model of Chapter 2). Because the no-trade relative price of computers is lower at Home, the free-trade equilibrium price will be above the no-trade price at Home. Therefore, panel (a) of Figure 4-3 shows the Home PPF with a free-trade or world relative price of computers, $(P_C/P_S)^W$, higher than the no-trade Home relative price, $(P_C/P_S)^A$, shown in panel (a) of Figure 4-2.

The no-trade equilibrium at Home, point A, has the quantities (Q_{C1}, Q_{S1}) for computers and shoes, shown in Figure 4-2. At the higher world relative price of computers, Home production moves from point A, (Q_{C1}, Q_{S1}), to point B in Figure 4-3, (Q_{C2}, Q_{S2}), with more computers and fewer shoes. Thus, with free trade, Home produces fewer shoes and specializes further in computers to take advantage of higher world relative prices of computers. Because Home can now engage in trade at the world relative price,

FIGURE 4-3

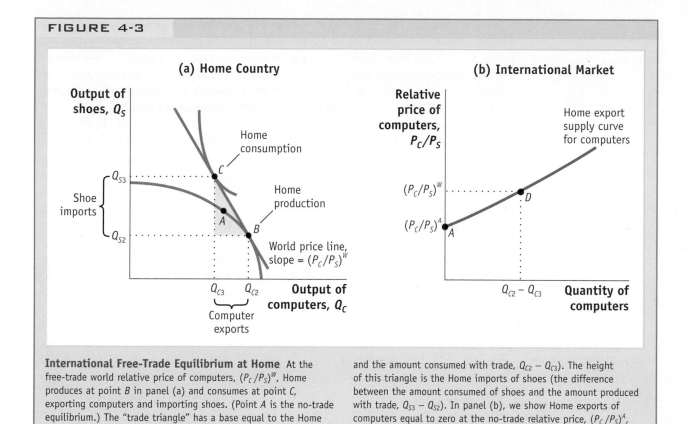

International Free-Trade Equilibrium at Home At the free-trade world relative price of computers, $(P_C/P_S)^W$, Home produces at point B in panel (a) and consumes at point C, exporting computers and importing shoes. (Point A is the no-trade equilibrium.) The "trade triangle" has a base equal to the Home exports of computers (the difference between the amount produced and the amount consumed with trade, $Q_{C2} - Q_{C3}$). The height of this triangle is the Home imports of shoes (the difference between the amount consumed of shoes and the amount produced with trade, $Q_{S3} - Q_{S2}$). In panel (b), we show Home exports of computers equal to zero at the no-trade relative price, $(P_C/P_S)^A$, and equal to $(Q_{C2} - Q_{C3})$ at the free-trade relative price, $(P_C/P_S)^W$.

Home's consumption can now lie on any point along the world price line through B with slope $(P_C/P_S)^W$. The highest Home utility is obtained at point C, which is tangent to the world price line $(P_C/P_S)^W$ and has the quantities consumed (Q_{C3}, Q_{S3}).

We can now define the Home "trade triangle," which is the triangle connecting points B and C, shown in panel (a) of Figure 4-3. Point B is where Home is producing and point C is where it is consuming, and the line connecting the two points represents the amount of trade at the world relative price. The base of this triangle is the Home exports of computers (the difference between the amount produced and the amount consumed with trade, or $Q_{C2} - Q_{C3}$). The height of this triangle is the Home imports of shoes (the difference between the amount consumed of shoes and the amount produced with trade, or $Q_{S3} - Q_{S2}$).

In panel (b) of Figure 4-3, we graph the Home exports of computers against their relative price. In the no-trade equilibrium, the Home relative price of computers was $(P_C/P_S)^A$, and exports of computers were zero. This no-trade equilibrium is shown by point A in panel (b). Under free trade, the relative price of computers is $(P_C/P_S)^W$, and exports of computers are the difference between the amount produced and amount consumed with trade, or $(Q_{C2} - Q_{C3})$. This free-trade equilibrium is shown by point D in panel (b). Joining up points A and D, we obtain the Home export supply curve of computers. It is upward-sloping because at higher relative prices as compared with the no-trade price, Home is willing to specialize further in computers to export more of them.

Foreign Equilibrium with Free Trade We proceed in a similar fashion for the Foreign country. In panel (a) of Figure 4-4, the Foreign no-trade equilibrium is at point A^*, with the high equilibrium relative price of computers $(P_C^*/P_S^*)^{A^*}$. Because the Foreign no-trade relative price was higher than at Home, and we expect the free-trade relative price to lie between, it follows that the free-trade or world equilibrium price of computers $(P_C/P_S)^W$ is lower than the no-trade Foreign price $(P_C^*/P_S^*)^{A^*}$.

At the world relative price, Foreign production moves from point A^*, (Q_{C1}^*, Q_{S1}^*), to point B^*, (Q_{C2}^*, Q_{S2}^*), with more shoes and fewer computers. Thus, with free trade, Foreign specializes further in shoes and produces fewer computers. Because Foreign can now engage in trade at the world relative price, Foreign's consumption can now lie on any point along the world price line through B^* with slope $(P_C/P_S)^W$. The highest Foreign utility is obtained at point C^*, which is tangent to the world price line $(P_C/P_S)^W$ and has the quantities consumed (Q_{C3}^*, Q_{S3}^*). Once again, we can connect points B^* and C^* to form a "trade triangle." The base of this triangle is Foreign imports of computers (the difference between consumption of computers and production with trade, or $Q_{C3}^* - Q_{C2}^*$), and the height is Foreign exports of shoes (the difference between production and consumption with trade, or $Q_{S2}^* - Q_{S3}^*$).

FIGURE 4-4

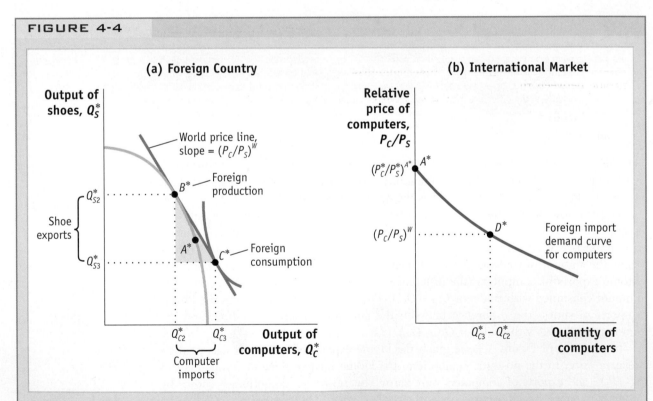

(a) Foreign Country

(b) International Market

International Free-Trade Equilibrium in Foreign At the free-trade world relative price of computers, $(P_C/P_S)^W$, Foreign produces at point B^* in panel (a) and consumes at point C^*, importing computers and exporting shoes. (Point A^* is the no-trade equilibrium.) The "trade triangle" has a base equal to Foreign imports of computers (the difference between the consumption of computers and the amount produced with trade, $Q_{C3}^* - Q_{C2}^*$). The height of this triangle is Foreign exports of shoes (the difference between the production of shoes and the amount consumed with trade, $Q_{S2}^* - Q_{S3}^*$). In panel (b), we show Foreign imports of computers equal to zero at the no-trade relative price, $(P_C^*/P_S^*)^{A^*}$, and equal to $(Q_{C3}^* - Q_{C2}^*)$ at the free-trade relative price, $(P_C/P_S)^W$.

In panel (b) of Figure 4-4, we graph Foreign's imports of computers against its relative price. In the no-trade equilibrium, the Foreign relative price of computers was $(P_C^*/P_S^*)^{A^*}$, and imports of computers were zero. This no-trade equilibrium is shown by the point A^* in panel (b). Under free trade, the relative price of computers is $(P_C/P_S)^W$, and imports of computers are the difference between the amount produced and amount consumed with trade, or $(Q_{C3}^* - Q_{C2}^*)$. This free-trade equilibrium is shown by the point D^* in panel (b). Joining up points A^* and D^*, we obtain the Foreign import demand curve for computers. It is downward-sloping because at lower relative prices as compared with no-trade, Foreign specializes more in shoes and exports these in exchange for computers.

Equilibrium Price with Free Trade As we see in Figure 4-5, the equilibrium relative price of computers with free trade is determined by the intersection of the Home export supply and Foreign import demand curves, at point D (the same as point D in Figure 4-3 or D^* in Figure 4-4). At that relative price, the quantity of computers that the Home country wants to export equals the quantity of computers that Foreign wants to import; that is, $(Q_{C2} - Q_{C3}) = (Q_{C3}^* - Q_{C2}^*)$. Because exports equal imports, there is no reason for the relative price to change and so this is a **free-trade equilibrium.** Another way to see the equilibrium graphically is to notice that in panel (a) of Figures 4-3 and 4-4, the trade triangles of the two countries are identical in size—the quantity of computers one country wants to sell is the same as the quantity the other country wants to buy.

Pattern of Trade Using the free-trade equilibrium, we have determined the pattern of trade between the two countries. Home exports computers, the good that uses intensively the factor of production (capital) found in abundance at Home. Foreign exports shoes, the good that uses intensively the factor of production (labor) found in abundance there. This important result is called the **Heckscher-Ohlin theorem.**

FIGURE 4-5

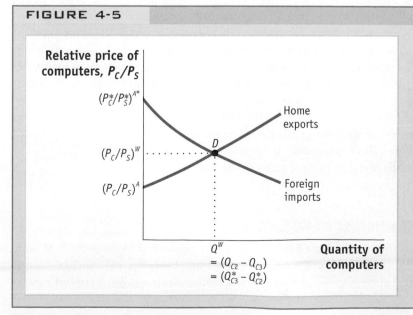

Determination of the Free-Trade World Equilibrium Price The world relative price of computers in the free-trade equilibrium is determined at the intersection of the Home export supply and Foreign import demand, at point D. At this relative price, the quantity of computers that Home wants to export, $(Q_{C2} - Q_{C3})$, just equals the quantity of computers that Foreign wants to import, $(Q_{C3}^* - Q_{C2}^*)$.

Heckscher-Ohlin Theorem: With two goods and two factors, each country will export the good that uses intensively the factor of production it has in abundance and will import the other good.

It is useful to review the assumptions we made at the beginning of the chapter to see how they lead to the Heckscher-Ohlin theorem.

Assumption 1: Labor and capital flow freely between the industries.
Assumption 2: The production of shoes is labor-intensive as compared with computer production, which is capital-intensive.
Assumption 3: The amounts of labor and capital found in the two countries differ, with Foreign abundant in labor and Home abundant in capital.
Assumption 4: There is free international trade in goods.
Assumption 5: The technologies for producing shoes and computers are the same across countries.
Assumption 6: Tastes are the same across countries.

Assumptions 1 to 3 allowed us to draw the PPFs of the two countries as illustrated in Figure 4-2, and in conjunction with assumptions 5 and 6, they allowed us to determine that the no-trade relative price of computers in Home was lower than the no-trade relative price of computers in Foreign; that is, $(P_C/P_S)^A$ was less than $(P_C^*/P_S^*)^{A^*}$. This key result enabled us to determine the starting points for the Home export supply curve for computers (point A) and the Foreign import demand curve for computers (point A^*) in panel (b) of Figures 4-3 and 4-4. Using those starting points, we put together the upward-sloping Home export supply curve and downward-sloping Foreign import demand curve. We see from Figure 4-5 that the relative price of computers in the free-trade equilibrium lies between the no-trade relative prices (which confirms the expectation we had when drawing Figures 4-3 and 4-4).

Therefore, when Home opens to trade, its relative price of computers rises from the no-trade equilibrium relative price $(P_C/P_S)^A$, to the free-trade equilibrium price $(P_C/P_S)^W$, giving Home firms an incentive to export computers. That is, higher prices give Home an incentive to produce more computers than it wants to consume, and export the difference. Similarly, when Foreign opens to trade, its relative price of computers falls from the no-trade equilibrium price $(P_C^*/P_S^*)^{A^*}$, to the trade equilibrium price $(P_C/P_S)^W$, encouraging Foreign consumers to import computers from Home. That is, lower prices give Foreign an incentive to consume more computers than it wants to produce, importing the difference.

You might think that the Heckscher-Ohlin theorem is somewhat obvious. It makes sense that countries will export goods that are produced easily because the factors of production are found in abundance. It turns out, however, that this prediction does not always work in practice, as we discuss in the next section.

2 Testing the Heckscher-Ohlin Model

The first test of the Heckscher-Ohlin theorem was performed by economist Wassily Leontief in 1953, using data for the United States from 1947. We will describe his test below and show that he reached a surprising conclusion, which is called **Leontief's paradox.** After that, we will discuss more recent data for many countries that can be used to test the Heckscher-Ohlin model.

Leontief's Paradox

To test the Heckscher-Ohlin theorem, Leontief measured the amounts of labor and capital used in all industries needed to produce $1 million of U.S. exports and to produce $1 million of imports into the United States. His results are shown in Table 4-1.

Leontief first measured the amount of capital and labor required in the production of $1 million worth of U.S. exports. To arrive at these figures, Leontief measured the labor and capital used *directly* in the production of final good exports in each industry. He also measured the labor and capital used *indirectly* in the industries that produced the intermediate inputs used in making the exports. From the first row of Table 4-1, we see that $2.55 million worth of capital was used to produce $1 million of exports. This amount of capital seems much too high, until we recognize that what is being measured is the total stock, which exceeds that part of the capital stock that was actually used to produce exports that year:

TABLE 4-1

Leontief's Test Leontief used the numbers in this table to test the Heckscher-Ohlin theorem. Each column shows the amount of capital or labor needed to produce $1 million worth of exports from, or imports into, the United States in 1947. As shown in the last row, the capital–labor ratio for exports was less than the capital–labor ratio for imports, which is a paradoxical finding.

	Exports	Imports
Capital ($ millions)	2.55	3.1
Labor (person-years)	182	170
Capital/labor ($/person)	14,000	18,200

Source: Wassily Leontief, 1953, "Domestic Production and Foreign Trade: The American Capital Position Re-examined," Proceedings of the American Philosophical Society, 97, September, 332–349. Reprinted in Richard Caves and Harry G. Johnson, eds., 1968, Readings in International Economics (Homewood, IL: Irwin).

the capital used that year would be measured by the depreciation on this stock. For labor, 182 person-years were used to produce the exports. Taking the ratio of these, we find that each person employed (directly or indirectly) in producing exports was working with $14,000 worth of capital.

Turning to the import side of the calculation, Leontief immediately ran into a problem—he could not measure the amount of labor and capital used to produce imports because he didn't have data on foreign technologies. To get around this difficulty, Leontief did what many researchers have done since—he simply used the data on U.S. technology to calculate estimated amounts of labor and capital used in imports from abroad. Does this approach invalidate Leontief's test of the Heckscher-Ohlin model? Not really, because the Heckscher-Ohlin model assumes that technologies are the same across countries, so Leontief is building this assumption into the calculations needed to test the theorem.

Using U.S. technology to measure the labor and capital used directly and indirectly in producing imports, Leontief arrived at the estimates in the last column of Table 4-1: $3.1 million of capital and 170 person-years were used in the production of $1 million worth of U.S. imports, so the capital–labor ratio for imports was $18,200 per worker. Notice that this amount *exceeds* the capital–labor ratio for exports of $14,000 per worker.

Leontief supposed correctly that in 1947 the United States was abundant in capital relative to the rest of the world. Thus, from the Heckscher-Ohlin theorem, Leontief expected that the United States would export capital-intensive goods and import labor-intensive goods. What Leontief actually found, however, was just the opposite: the capital–labor ratio for U.S. imports was *higher* than the capital–labor ratio found for U.S. exports! This finding contradicted the Heckscher-Ohlin theorem and came to be called Leontief's paradox.

Explanations A wide range of explanations has been offered for Leontief's paradox, including the following:

- U.S. and foreign technologies are not the same, in contrast to what the Heckscher-Ohlin theorem and Leontief assumed.

- By focusing only on labor and capital, Leontief ignored land abundance in the United States.

- Leontief should have distinguished between high-skilled and low-skilled labor (because it would not be surprising to find that U.S. exports are intensive in high-skilled labor).

- The data for 1947 may be unusual because World War II had ended just two years earlier.

- The United States was not engaged in completely free trade, as the Heckscher-Ohlin theorem assumes.

Several of the additional possible explanations for the Leontief paradox depend on having more than two factors of production. The United States is abundant in land, for example, and that might explain why in 1947 it was exporting labor-intensive products: these might have been agricultural products, which use land intensively and, in 1947, might also have used labor intensively. By ignoring land, Leontief was therefore not performing an accurate test of the Heckscher-Ohlin theorem. Alternatively, it might be that the United States was mainly exporting goods that used skilled labor. This is certainly true today, with the United States being a leading exporter of high-technology products, and was probably also true in 1947. By not distinguishing between high-skilled versus low-skilled labor, Leontief was again giving an inaccurate picture of the factors of production used in U.S. trade.

Research in later years aimed to redo the test that Leontief performed, while taking into account land, high-skilled versus low-skilled labor, checking whether the Heckscher-Ohlin theorem holds in other years, and so on. We now discuss the data that can be used to test the Heckscher-Ohlin theorem in a more recent year—2010.

Factor Endowments in 2010

In Figure 4-6, we show the country shares of six factors of production and world GDP in 2010, broken down by select countries (the United States, China, Japan, India, Germany, the United Kingdom, France, and Canada) and then the rest of the world. To determine whether a country is abundant in a certain factor, we compare the country's share of that factor with its share of world GDP. If its share of a factor exceeds its share of world GDP, then we conclude that the country is **abundant in that factor,** and if its share in a certain factor is less than its share of world GDP, then we conclude that the country is **scarce in that factor.** This definition allows us to calculate factor abundance in a setting with as many factors and countries as we want.

Capital Abundance For example, in the first bar graph of Figure 4-6, we see that in 2010, 17.1% of the world's physical capital was located in the United States, with 16.9% located in China, 7.7% in Japan, 3.9% in India, 4.3% in Germany, and so on. When we compare these numbers with the final bar in the graph, which shows each country's percentage of world GDP, we see that in 2010 the United States had 19.1% of world GDP, China had 14.4%, Japan 5.6%, India 6.1%, Germany 4.0%, and so on. Because the United States had 17.1% of the world's capital and 19.1% of world GDP, we can conclude that the United States was scarce in physical capital in 2010. China, on the other hand, is abundant in physical capital: it has 16.9% of the world's capital and produces 14.4% of the world's GDP. Indeed, it is the rapid accumulation

FIGURE 4-6

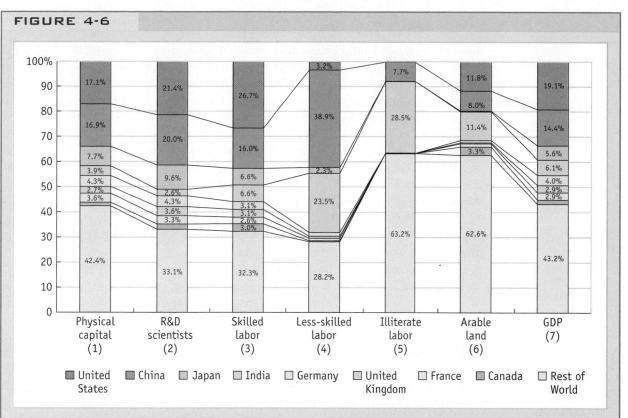

Country Factor Endowments, 2010 Shown here are country shares of six factors of production in the year 2010, for eight selected countries and the rest of the world. In the first bar graph, we see that 17.1% of the world's physical capital in 2010 was located in the United States, with 16.9% located in China, 7.7% located in Japan, and so on. In the final bar graph, we see that in 2010 the United States had 19.1% of world GDP, China had 14.4%, Japan had 5.6%, and so on. When a country's factor share is larger than its share of GDP, then the country is abundant in that factor, and when a country's factor share is less than its share of GDP, then the country is scarce in that factor.

Notes:
(1) From PWT (Penn World Trade) version 8.0 (University of Groningen and University of California, Davis).

(2) The product of R&D researchers per million and total population (World Bank, World Development Indicators).
(3) Labor force with tertiary education (World Bank, World Development Indicators).
(4) Labor force with primary and/or secondary education (World Bank, World Development Indicators).
(5) The product of one minus the adult literacy rate and the adult population (World Bank, World Development Indicators).
(6) Hectares of arable land (World Bank, World Development Indicators).
(7) Gross domestic product converted to 2010 dollars using purchasing power parity rates (PWT version 8.0, University of Groningen and University of California, Davis).

of capital in China during the past decade that has now made the United States relatively scarce in this factor (because as China accumulates more capital, the U.S. share of the world's capital falls).[4] Japan had 7.7% of the world's capital and 5.6% of world GDP in 2010, so it was also abundant in capital, as was Germany (with 4.3% of the world's capital and 4.0% of world GDP). The opposite holds for India, and the group of countries included in the rest of the world: their shares of world capital were less than their shares of GDP, so they were scarce in capital.

---

[4] In 2000, China had a much smaller share of the world's physical capital—just 8.7% as compared with 16.9% in 2010. So China's share nearly doubled, while the U.S. share fell from 24.0% to 17.1%.

Labor and Land Abundance We can use a similar comparison to determine whether each country is abundant in R&D scientists, in types of labor distinguished by skill, in arable land, or any other factor of production. For example, the United States was abundant in R&D scientists in 2010 (with 21.4% of the world's total as compared with 19.1% of the world's GDP) and also skilled labor (workers with more than a high school education) but was scarce in less-skilled labor (workers with a high school education or less) and illiterate labor. India was scarce in R&D scientists (with 2.6% of the world's total as compared with 6.1% of the world's GDP) but abundant in skilled labor, semiskilled labor, and illiterate labor (with shares of the world's total that exceed its GDP share). Canada was abundant in arable land (with 3.3% of the world's total as compared with 1.7% of the world's GDP), as we would expect. But the United States was scarce in arable land (11.8% of the world's total as compared with 19.1% of the world's GDP). That is a surprising result because we often think of the United States as a major exporter of agricultural commodities, so from the Heckscher-Ohlin theorem, we would expect it to be land-abundant.

Another surprising result in Figure 4-6 is that China was abundant in R&D scientists: it had 20.0% of the world's R&D scientists, as compared with 14.4% of the world's GDP in 2010. This finding also seems to contradict the Heckscher-Ohlin theorem, because we think of China as exporting greater quantities of basic manufactured goods, not research-intensive manufactured goods. These observations regarding R&D scientists (a factor in which both the United States and China were abundant) and land (in which the United States was scarce) can cause us to question whether an R&D scientist or an acre of arable land has the same productivity in all countries. If not, then our measures of factor abundance are misleading: if an R&D scientist in the United States is more productive than his or her counterpart in China, then it does not make sense to just compare each country's share of these with each country's share of GDP; and likewise, if an acre of arable land is more productive in the United States than in other countries, then we should not compare the share of land in each country with each country's share of GDP. Instead, we need to make some adjustment for the differing productivities of R&D scientists and land across countries. In other words, we need to abandon the original Heckscher-Ohlin assumption of identical technologies across countries.

Differing Productivities Across Countries

Leontief himself suggested that we should abandon the assumption that technologies are the same across countries and instead allow for differing productivities, as in the Ricardian model. Remember that in the original formulation of the paradox, Leontief had found that the United States was exporting labor-intensive products even though it was capital-abundant at that time. One explanation for this outcome would be that labor is highly productive in the United States and less productive in the rest of the world. If that is the case, then the **effective labor force** in the United States, the labor force times its productivity (which measures how much output the labor force can produce), is much larger than it appears to be when we just count people. If this is true, perhaps the United States is abundant in *skilled* labor after all (like R&D scientists), and it should be no surprise that it is exporting labor-intensive products.

We now explore how differing productivities can be introduced into the Heckscher-Ohlin model. In addition to allowing labor to have a differing productivity across countries, we can also allow capital, land, and other factors of production to have differing productivity across countries.

Measuring Factor Abundance Once Again To allow factors of production to differ in their productivities across countries, we define the **effective factor endowment** as the actual amount of a factor found in a country times its productivity:

Effective factor endowment = Actual factor endowment • Factor productivity

The amount of an effective factor found in the world is obtained by adding up the effective factor endowments across all countries. Then to determine whether a country is abundant in a certain factor, we compare the country's share of that *effective* factor with its share of world GDP. If its share of an effective factor exceeds its share of world GDP, then we conclude that the country is **abundant in that effective factor;** if its share of an effective factor is less than its share of world GDP, then we conclude that the country is **scarce in that effective factor.** We can illustrate this approach to measuring effective factor endowments using two examples: R&D scientists and arable land.

Effective R&D Scientists The productivity of an R&D scientist depends on the laboratory equipment, computers, and other types of material with which he or she has to work. R&D scientists working in different countries will not necessarily have the same productivities because the equipment they have available to them differs. A simple way to measure the equipment they have available is to use a country's *R&D spending per scientist*. If a country has more R&D spending per scientist, then its productivity will be higher, but if there is less R&D spending per scientist, then its productivity will be lower. To measure the effective number of R&D scientists in each country, we take the total number of scientists and multiply that by the R&D spending per scientist:

Effective R&D scientists = Actual R&D scientists • R&D spending per scientist

Using the R&D spending per scientist in this way to obtain effective R&D scientists is one method to correct for differences in the productivity of scientists across countries. It is not the only way to make such a correction because there are other measures that could be used for the productivity of scientists (e.g., we could use scientific publications available in a country, or the number of research universities). The advantage of using R&D spending per scientist is that this information is collected annually for many countries, so using this method to obtain a measure of effective R&D scientists means that we can easily compare the share of each country with the world total.[5] Those shares are shown in Figure 4-7.

In the first bar graph of Figure 4-7, we repeat from Figure 4-6 each country's share of world R&D scientists, not corrected for productivity differences. In the second bar graph, we show each country's share of effective scientists, using the R&D spending per scientist to correct for productivity. The United States had 21.4% of the world's total R&D scientists in 2010 (in the first bar) but 24.8% of the world's effective scientists (in the second bar). So the United States was more abundant in effective R&D

[5] Notice that by correcting the number of R&D scientists by the R&D spending per scientist, we end up with the total R&D spending in each country: Effective R&D scientists = Actual R&D scientists • R&D spending per scientist = Total R&D spending. So a country's share of effective R&D scientists equals its share of world R&D spending.

FIGURE 4-7

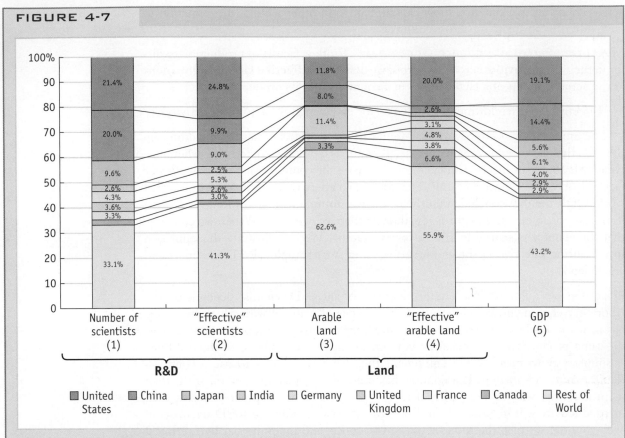

"Effective" Factor Endowments, 2010 Shown here are country shares of R&D scientists and land in 2010, using first the information from Figure 4-6, and then making an adjustment for the productivity of each factor across countries to obtain the "effective" shares. China was abundant in R&D scientists in 2010 (since it had 20.0% of the world's R&D scientists as compared with 14.4% of the world's GDP) but scarce in effective R&D scientists (because it had 9.9% of the world's effective R&D scientists as compared with 14.4% of the world's GDP). The United States was scarce in arable land when using the number of acres (since it had 11.8% of the world's land as compared with 19.1% of the world's GDP) but neither scarce nor abundant in effective land (since it had 20.0% of the world's effective land, which nearly equaled its share of the world's GDP).

Notes:
(1) The product of R&D researchers per million and total population (World Bank, World Development Indicators).
(2) R&D expenditure in units of purchasing power parity (World Bank, World Development Indicators, and PWT version 8.0, University of Groningen).
(3) Hectares of arable land (World Bank, World Development Indicators).
(4) Productivity adjustment based on agriculture TFP (Total Factor Productivity) estimation.
(5) Gross domestic product converted to 2010 dollars using purchasing power parity rates (PWT version 8.0, University of Groningen).

scientists in 2010 than it was in the number of scientists. Likewise, Germany had a greater share of effective scientists, 5.3%, as compared with its share of R&D scientists, which was 4.3%. But China's share of R&D scientists fell by half when correcting for productivity, from a 20.0% share in the number of R&D scientists to a 9.9% share in effective R&D scientists. Since China's share of world GDP was 14.4% in 2010, it became scarce in effective R&D scientists once we made this productivity correction.

China has increased its spending on R&D in recent years and now exceeds the level of R&D spending in Japan. It is also investing heavily in universities, many of which offer degrees in science and engineering. Even when compared with the United

States, China is taking the lead in some areas of R&D. An example is in research on "green" technologies, such as wind and solar power. We will discuss government subsidies in China for solar panels in a later chapter. As described in **Headlines: China Drawing High-Tech Research from U.S.,** the Silicon Valley firm Applied Materials has recently established a research laboratory in China and has many contracts to sell solar equipment there. Applied Materials was attracted to China by a combination of inexpensive land and skilled labor. For all these reasons, we should expect that China's share of effective R&D scientists will grow significantly in future years.

Effective Arable Land As we did for R&D scientists, we also need to correct arable land for its differing productivity across countries. To make this correction, we use a measure of agricultural productivity in each country. Then the effective amount of arable land found in a country is

$$\text{Effective arable land} = \text{Actual arable land} \cdot \text{Productivity in agriculture}$$

HEADLINES

China Drawing High-Tech Research from U.S.

Applied Materials, a well-known firm in Silicon Valley, recently announced plans to establish a large laboratory in Xi'an, China, as described in this article.

XI'AN, China—For years, many of China's best and brightest left for the United States, where high-tech industry was more cutting-edge. But Mark R. Pinto is moving in the opposite direction. Mr. Pinto is the first chief technology officer of a major American tech company to move to China. The company, Applied Materials, is one of Silicon Valley's most prominent firms. It supplied equipment used to perfect the first computer chips. Today, it is the world's biggest supplier of the equipment used to make semiconductors, solar panels and flat-panel displays.

In addition to moving Mr. Pinto and his family to Beijing in January, Applied Materials, whose headquarters are in Santa Clara, Calif., has just built its newest and largest research labs here. Last week, it even held its an-nual shareholders' meeting in Xi'an. It is hardly alone. Companies—and their engineers—are being drawn here more and more as China develops a high-tech economy that increasingly competes directly with the United States. . . .

Not just drawn by China's markets, Western companies are also attracted to China's huge reservoirs of cheap, highly skilled engineers—and the subsidies offered by many Chinese cities and regions, particularly for green energy companies. Now, Mr. Pinto said, researchers from the United States and Europe have to be ready to move to China if they want to do cutting-edge work on solar manufacturing because the new Applied Materials complex here is the only research center that can fit an entire solar panel assembly line. "If you really want to have an impact on this field, this is just such a tremendous laboratory," he said. . . .

Locally, the Xi'an city government sold a 75-year land lease to Applied Materials at a deep discount and is reimbursing the company for roughly a quarter of the lab complex's operating costs for five years, said Gang Zou, the site's general manager. The two labs, the first of their kind anywhere in the world, are each bigger than two American football fields. Applied Materials continues to develop the electronic guts of its complex machines at laboratories in the United States and Europe. But putting all the machines together and figuring out processes to make them work in unison will be done in Xi'an. The two labs, one on top of the other, will become operational once they are fully outfitted late this year. . . .

We will not discuss here the exact method for measuring productivity in agriculture, except to say that it compares the output in each country with the inputs of labor, capital, and land: countries with higher output as compared with inputs are the more productive, and countries with lower output as compared with inputs are the less productive. The United States has very high productivity in agriculture, whereas China has lower productivity.

In the third bar graph of Figure 4-7, we repeat from Figure 4-6 each country's share of arable land, not corrected for productivity differences. In the fourth bar graph, we show each country's share of effective arable land in 2010, corrected for productivity differences. The United States had 11.8% of the world's total arable land (in the third bar), as compared with 19.1% of the world's GDP (in the final bar), so it was scarce in land in 2010 without making any productivity correction. But when measured by effective arable land, the United States had 20.0% of the world's total (in the fourth bar), as compared with 19.1% of the world's GDP (in the final bar). These two numbers are so close that we should conclude *the United States was neither abundant nor scarce in effective arable land*: its share of the world's total approximately equaled its share of the world's GDP.

How does this conclusion compare with U.S. trade in agriculture? We often think of the United States as a major exporter of agricultural goods, but this pattern is changing. In Table 4-2, we show the U.S. exports and imports of food products and total agricultural trade. This table shows that U.S. food trade has fluctuated between positive and negative net exports since 2000, which is consistent with our finding that the United States is neither abundant nor scarce in land. Total agricultural trade (including nonfood items like cotton) continues to have positive net exports, however.

TABLE 4-2

U.S. Food Trade and Total Agricultural Trade, 2000–2012 This table shows that U.S. food trade has fluctuated between positive and negative net exports since 2000, which is consistent with our finding that the United States is neither abundant nor scarce in land. Total agricultural trade (including nonfood items like cotton) has positive net exports, however.

	2000	2002	2004	2006	2008	2010	2012
U.S. food trade (billions of U.S. dollars)							
Exports	41.4	43.2	50.0	57.8	97.4	92.3	132.9
Imports	41.4	44.7	55.7	68.9	81.3	86.6	101.2
Net exports	0.0	−1.5	−5.7	−11.1	16.1	5.7	31.7
U.S. agricultural trade (billions of U.S. dollars)							
Exports	51.3	53.1	61.4	70.9	115.3	115.8	141.3
Imports	39.2	42.0	54.2	65.5	80.7	81.9	102.9
Net exports	12.1	11.1	7.2	5.5	34.6	33.9	38.4

Source: Total agricultural trade compiled by USDA using data from Census Bureau, U.S. Department of Commerce. U.S. food trade data provided by the USDA, Foreign Agricultural Service.

Leontief's Paradox Once Again

Our discussion of factor endowments in 2010 shows that it is possible for countries to be abundant in more that one factor of production: the United States and Japan are both abundant in physical capital and R&D scientists, and the United States is also abundant in skilled labor (see Figure 4-6). We have also found that it is sometimes important to correct that actual amount of a factor of production for its productivity, obtaining the effective factor endowment. Now we can apply these ideas to the United States in 1947 to reexamine the Leontief paradox.

Using a sample of 30 countries for which GDP information is available in 1947, the U.S. share of those countries' GDP was 37%. That estimate of the U.S. share of "world" GDP is shown in the last bar graph of Figure 4-8. To determine whether the United States was abundant in physical capital or labor, we need to estimate its share of the world endowments of these factors.

Capital Abundance It is hard to estimate the U.S. share of the world capital stock in the postwar years. But given the devastation of the capital stock in Europe and Japan due to World War II, we can presume that the U.S. share of world capital was more than 37%. That estimate (or really a "guesstimate") means that the U.S. share of world capital exceeds the U.S. share of world GDP, so that the United States was abundant in capital in 1947.

Labor Abundance What about the abundance of labor for the United States? If we do not correct labor for productivity differences across countries, then the population

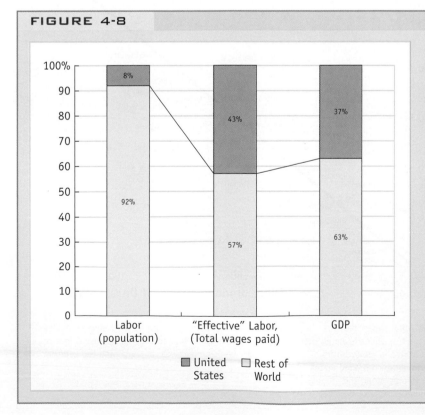

FIGURE 4-8

Labor Endowment and GDP for the United States and Rest of World, 1947 Shown here are the share of labor, "effective" labor, and GDP of the United States and the rest of the world (measured by 30 countries for which data are available) in 1947. The United States had only 8% of the world's population, as compared with 37% of the world's GDP, so it was very scarce in labor. But when we measure effective labor by the total wages paid in each country, then the United States had 43% of the world's effective labor as compared with 37% of GDP, so it was abundant in effective labor.

Source: Author's own calculations.

of each country is a rough measure of its labor force. The U.S. share of population for the sample of 30 countries in 1947 was very small, about 8%, which is shown in the first bar graph of Figure 4-8. This estimate of labor abundance is much less than the U.S. share of GDP, 37%. According to that comparison, the United States was scarce in labor (its share of that factor was less than its share of GDP).

Labor Productivity Using the U.S. share of population is not the right way to measure the U.S. labor endowment, however, because it does not correct for differences in the productivity of labor across countries. A good way to make that correction is to use wages paid to workers as a measure of their productivity. To illustrate why this is a good approach, in Figure 4-9 we plot the wages of workers in various countries and the estimated productivity of workers in 1990. The vertical axis in Figure 4-9 measures wages earned across a sample of 33 countries, measured relative to (i.e., as a percentage of) the United States. Only one country—Canada—has wages higher than those in the United States (probably reflecting greater union pressure in that country). All other countries have lower wages, ranging from Austria and Switzerland

FIGURE 4-9

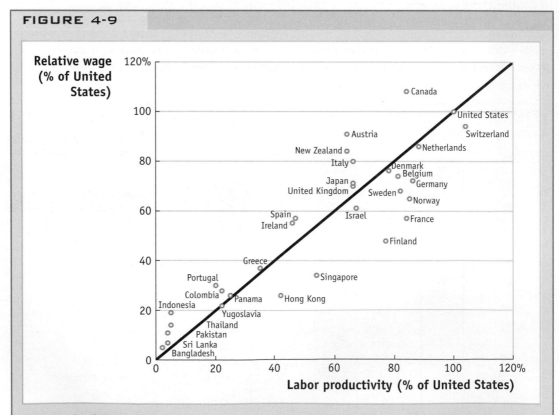

Labor Productivity and Wages Shown here are estimated labor productivities across countries, and their wages, relative to the United States in 1990. Notice that the labor and wages were highly correlated across countries: the points roughly line up along the 45-degree line. This close connection between wages and labor productivity holds for the data in 1990, and we expect that it also held in 1947, so that we can use wages to adjust for labor productivity in explaining the Leontief paradox.

Source: Daniel Trefler, 1993, "International Factor Price Differences: Leontief was Right!" Journal of Political Economy, 101(6), December, 961–987.

with wages that are about 95% of the U.S. wage, to Ireland, France, and Finland, with wages at about 50% of the U.S. level, to Bangladesh and Sri Lanka, with wages at about 5% of the U.S. level.

The horizontal axis in Figure 4-9 measures labor productivity in various countries relative to that in the United States. For example, labor productivity in Canada is 80% of that in the United States; labor productivity in Austria and New Zealand is about 60% of that in the United States; and labor productivity in Indonesia, Thailand, Pakistan, Sri Lanka, and Bangladesh is about 5% of that in the United States. Notice that the labor productivities (on the horizontal axis) and wages (on the vertical axis) are highly correlated across countries: the points in Figure 4-9 line up approximately along the 45-degree line. This close connection between wages and labor productivity holds for the data in 1990 and, we expect that it also held in 1947, so that we can use wages to adjust for labor productivity in explaining the Leontief Paradox.

Effective Labor Abundance As suggested by Figure 4-9, wages across countries are strongly correlated with the productivity of labor. Going back to the data for 1947, which Leontief used, we use the wages earned by labor to measure the productivity of labor in each country. Then the *effective* amount of labor found in each country equals the actual amount of labor times the wage. Multiplying the amount of labor in each country by average wages, we obtain total wages paid to labor. That information is available for 30 countries in 1947, and we have already found that the United States accounted for 37% of the GDP of these countries, as shown in the final bar in Figure 4-8. Adding up total wages paid to labor across the 30 countries and comparing it with the United States, we find that the United States accounted for 43% of wages paid to labor in these 30 countries, as shown in the bar labeled "effective" labor. By comparing this estimate with the United States share of world GDP of 37% in 1947, we see that the United States was abundant in effective labor, taking into account the differing productivity of labor across countries. So not only was the United States abundant in capital, it was also abundant in effective—or skilled—labor in 1947, just as we have also found for the year 2010!

Summary In Leontief's test of the Heckscher-Ohlin theorem, he found that the capital–labor ratio for exports from the United States in 1947 was less than the capital–labor ratio for imports. That finding seemed to contradict the Heckscher-Ohlin theorem if we think of the United States as being capital-abundant: in that case, it should be exporting capital-intensive goods (with a high capital–labor ratio). But now we have found that the United States was abundant in *both* capital *and* labor in 1947, once we correct for the productivity of labor by using its wage. Basically, the relatively low population and number of workers in the United States are boosted upward by high U.S. wages, making the effective labor force seem much larger—large enough so that the U.S. share of worldwide wages even exceeds its share of GDP.

Such a finding means the United States was *also* abundant in effective—or skilled—labor in 1947, just as it is today. Armed with this finding, it is not surprising that Leontief found exports from the United States in 1947 used relatively less capital and more labor than did imports: that pattern simply reflects the high productivity of labor in the United States and its abundance of this effective factor. As Leontief himself proposed, once we take into account differences in the productivity of factors across countries, there is no "paradox" after all, at least in the data for 1947. For more recent years, too, taking account of factor productivity differences across countries is important when testing the Heckscher-Ohlin theorem.

3 Effects of Trade on Factor Prices

In the Heckscher-Ohlin model developed in the previous sections, Home exported computers and Foreign exported shoes. Furthermore, we found in our model that the relative price of computers *rose* at Home from the no-trade equilibrium to the trade equilibrium (this higher relative price with trade is why computers are exported). Conversely, the relative price of computers *fell* in Foreign from the no-trade equilibrium to the trade equilibrium (this lower relative price with trade is why computers are imported abroad). The question we ask now is how the changes in the relative prices of goods affect the wage paid to labor in each country and the rental earned by capital. We begin by showing how the wage and rental are determined, focusing on Home.

Effect of Trade on the Wage and Rental of Home

To determine the wage and rental, we go back to Figure 4-1, which showed that the quantity of labor demanded relative to the quantity of capital demanded in each industry at Home depends on the relative wage at Home W/R. We can use these relative demands for labor in each industry to derive an economy-wide relative demand for labor, which can then be compared with the economy-wide relative supply of labor $\overline{L}/\overline{K}$. By comparing the economy-wide relative demand and supply, just as we do in any supply and demand context, we can determine Home's relative wage. Moreover, we can evaluate what happens to the relative wage when the Home relative price of computers rises after Home starts trading.

Economy-Wide Relative Demand for Labor To derive an economy-wide relative demand for labor, we use the conditions that the quantities of labor and capital used in each industry add up to the total available labor and capital: $L_C + L_S = \overline{L}$ and $K_C + K_S = \overline{K}$. We can divide total labor by total capital to get

$$\underbrace{\frac{\overline{L}}{\overline{K}}}_{\substack{\text{Relative} \\ \text{supply}}} = \frac{L_C + L_S}{\overline{K}} = \underbrace{\frac{L_C}{K_C} \cdot \left(\frac{K_C}{\overline{K}}\right) + \frac{L_S}{K_S} \cdot \left(\frac{K_S}{\overline{K}}\right)}_{\substack{\text{Relative} \\ \text{demand}}}$$

The left-hand side of this equation is the economy-wide supply of labor relative to capital, or relative supply. The right-hand side is the economy-wide demand for labor relative to capital, or relative demand. The relative demand is a weighted average of the labor–capital ratio in each industry. This weighted average is obtained by multiplying the labor–capital ratio for each industry, L_C/K_C and L_S/K_S, by the terms $K_C/\overline{K}$ and $K_S/\overline{K}$, the shares of total capital employed in each industry. These two terms must add up to 1, $(K_C/\overline{K}) + (K_S/\overline{K}) = 1$, because capital must be employed in one industry or the other.

The determination of Home's equilibrium relative wage is shown in Figure 4-10 as the intersection of the relative supply and relative demand curves. The supply of labor relative to the supply of capital, the relative supply $(\overline{L}/\overline{K})$, is shown as a vertical line because the total amounts of labor and capital do not depend on the relative wage; they are fixed by the total amount of factor resources in each country. Because the relative demand (the *RD* curve in the graph) is an average of the L_C/K_C and L_S/K_S curves from Figure 4-1, it therefore lies *between* these two curves. The point at which relative demand intersects relative supply, point A, tells us that the wage relative to

FIGURE 4-10

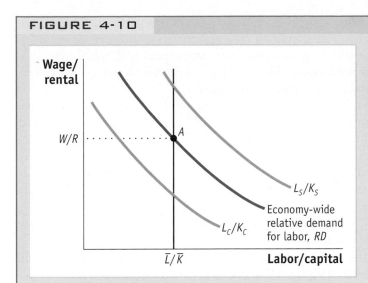

Determination of Home Wage/Rental The economy-wide relative demand for labor, *RD,* is an average of the L_C/K_C and L_S/K_S curves and lies between these curves. The relative supply, $\overline{L}/\overline{K}$, is shown by a vertical line because the total amount of resources in Home is fixed. The equilibrium point *A,* at which relative demand *RD* intersects relative supply $\overline{L}/\overline{K}$, determines the wage relative to the rental, *W/R.*

the rental is *W/R* (from the vertical axis). Point *A* describes an equilibrium in the labor and capital markets and combines these two markets into a single diagram by showing relative supply equal to relative demand.

Increase in the Relative Price of Computers When Home opens itself to trade, it faces a higher relative price of computers; that is, P_C/P_S increases at Home. We illustrate this higher relative price using Home's production possibilities frontier in Figure 4-11. At the no-trade or autarky equilibrium, point *A,* the relative price of computers is $(P_C/P_S)^A$ and the computer industry produces Q_{C1}, while the shoe

FIGURE 4-11

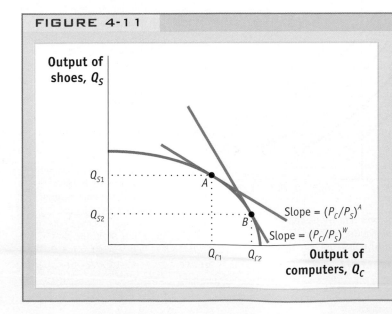

Increase in the Price of Computers Initially, Home is at a no-trade equilibrium at point *A* with a relative price of computers of $(P_C/P_S)^A$. An increase in the relative price of computers to the world price, as illustrated by the steeper world price line, $(P_C/P_S)^W$, shifts production from point *A* to *B*. At point *B*, there is a higher output of computers and a lower output of shoes, $Q_{C2} > Q_{C1}$ and $Q_{S2} < Q_{S1}$.

industry produces Q_{S1}. With a rise in the relative price of computers to $(P_C/P_S)^W$, the computer industry increases its output to Q_{C2}, and the shoe industry decreases its output to Q_{S2}. With this shift in production, labor and capital both move from shoe production to computer production. What is the effect of these resource movements on the relative supply and relative demand for labor?

The effects are shown in Figure 4-12. Relative supply $\overline{L}/\overline{K}$ is the same as before because the total amounts of labor and capital available in Home have not changed. The relative demand for labor changes, however, because capital has shifted to the computer industry. This shift affects the terms used in the weighted average: $(K_C/\overline{K})$ rises and $(K_S/\overline{K})$ falls. The relative demand for labor in the economy is now more weighted toward computers and less weighted toward the shoe industry. In Figure 4-12, the change in the weights shifts the relative demand curve from RD_1 to RD_2. The curve shifts in the direction of the relative demand curve for computers, and the equilibrium moves from point A to B.

The impacts on all the variables are as follows. First, the relative wage W/R falls from $(W/R)_1$ to $(W/R)_2$, reflecting the fall in the relative demand for labor as both factors move into computer production from shoe production. Second, the lower relative wage induces *both* industries to hire more workers per unit of capital (a move down along their relative demand curves). In the shoe industry, for instance, the new, lower relative wage $(W/R)_2$ intersects the relative demand curve for labor L_S/K_S at a point

FIGURE 4-12

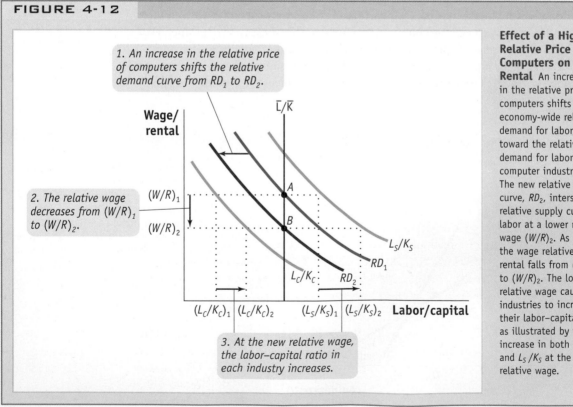

1. An increase in the relative price of computers shifts the relative demand curve from RD_1 to RD_2.

2. The relative wage decreases from $(W/R)_1$ to $(W/R)_2$.

3. At the new relative wage, the labor–capital ratio in each industry increases.

Effect of a Higher Relative Price of Computers on Wage/ Rental An increase in the relative price of computers shifts the economy-wide relative demand for labor, RD_1, toward the relative demand for labor in the computer industry, L_C/K_C. The new relative demand curve, RD_2, intersects the relative supply curve for labor at a lower relative wage $(W/R)_2$. As a result, the wage relative to the rental falls from $(W/R)_1$ to $(W/R)_2$. The lower relative wage causes both industries to increase their labor–capital ratios, as illustrated by the increase in both L_C/K_C and L_S/K_S at the new relative wage.

corresponding to a higher L/K level than the initial relative wage $(W/R)_1$. That is, $(L_S/K_S)_2 > (L_S/K_S)_1$, and the same argument holds for the computer industry. As a result, the labor–capital ratio rises in both shoes and computers.

How is it possible for the labor–capital ratio to rise in *both* industries when the amount of labor and capital available in total is fixed? The answer is that more labor per unit of capital is released from shoes than is needed to operate that capital in computers (because computers require fewer workers per machine). As the relative price of computers rises, computer output rises while shoe output falls, and labor is "freed up" to be used more in both industries. In terms of our earlier equation for relative supply and relative demand, the changes in response to the increase in the relative price of computers P_C/P_S are

$$\underbrace{\frac{\overline{L}}{\overline{K}}}_{\substack{\text{Relative supply} \\ \text{No change}}} = \underbrace{\frac{L_C}{K_C} \cdot \left(\frac{K_C}{\overline{K}}\right) + \frac{L_S}{K_S} \cdot \left(\frac{K_S}{\overline{K}}\right)}_{\substack{\text{Relative demand} \\ \text{No change in total}}}$$

$$\quad\quad\quad\quad\quad\quad \uparrow \quad \uparrow \quad\quad \uparrow \quad\ \downarrow$$

The relative supply of labor has not changed, so relative demand for labor cannot change overall. Since some of the individual components of relative demand have increased, other components must decrease to keep the overall relative demand the same. After the rise in the price of computers, even more capital will be used in the computer industry ($K_C/\overline{K}$ rises while $K_S/\overline{K}$ falls) because the output of computers rises and the output of shoes falls. This shift in weights on the right-hand side pulls down the overall relative demand for labor (this is necessarily true since $L_C/K_C < L_S/K_S$ by assumption). But because the relative supply on the left-hand side doesn't change, another feature must increase the relative demand for labor: this feature is the increased labor–capital ratios in *both* industries. In this way, relative demand continues to equal relative supply at point B, and at the same time, the labor–capital ratios have risen in both industries.

Determination of the Real Wage and Real Rental

To summarize, we have found that an increase in the relative price of computers—which are capital-intensive—leads to a fall in the relative wage (W/R). In turn, the decrease in the relative wage leads to an increase in the labor–capital ratio used in each industry (L_C/K_C and L_S/K_S). Our goal in this section is to determine who gains and who loses from these changes. For this purpose, it is not enough to know how the *relative* wage changes; instead, we want to determine the change in the *real wage* and *real rental*; that is, the change in the quantity of shoes and computers that each factor of production can purchase. With the results we have already obtained, it will be fairly easy to determine the change in the real wage and real rental.

Change in the Real Rental Because the labor–capital ratio increases in both industries, the marginal product of capital also increases in both industries. This is because there are more people to work with each piece of capital. This result follows from our earlier argument that when a machine has more labor to work it, it will be more productive, and the marginal product of capital will go up. In both industries, the rental on capital is determined by its marginal product and by the prices of the goods:

$$R = P_C \cdot MPK_C \text{ and } R = P_S \cdot MPK_S$$

Because capital can move freely between industries in the long run, the rental on capital is equalized across them. By using the result that both marginal products of capital increase and by rearranging the previous equations, we see that

$$MPK_C = R/P_C \uparrow \text{ and } MPK_S = R/P_S \uparrow$$

Remember that R/P_C measures that quantity of computers that can be purchased with the rental, whereas R/P_S measures the quantity of shoes that can be bought with the rental. When both of these go up, the real rental on capital (in terms of either good) *increases*. Therefore, capital owners are clearly better off when the relative price of computers increases. Notice that computer manufacturing is the capital-intensive industry, so the more general result is that *an increase in the relative price of a good will benefit the factor of production used intensively in producing that good.*

Change in the Real Wage To understand what happens to the real wage when the relative price of computers rises, we again use the result that the labor–capital ratio increases in *both* industries. The law of diminishing returns tells us that the marginal product of labor must fall in both industries (since there are more workers on each machine). In both industries, the wage is determined by the marginal product of labor and the prices of the goods:

$$W = P_C \cdot MPL_C \text{ and } W = P_S \cdot MPL_S$$

Using the result that the marginal product of labor falls in both industries, we see that

$$MPL_C = W/P_C \downarrow \text{ and } MPL_S = W/P_S \downarrow$$

Therefore, the quantity of computers that can be purchased with the wage (W/P_C) and the quantity of shoes that can be purchased with the wage (W/P_S) both fall. These decreases mean that the real wage (in terms of either good) is *reduced*, and labor is clearly worse off because of the increase in the relative price of computers.

We can summarize our results with the following theorem, first derived by economists Wolfgang Stolper and Paul Samuelson.

Stolper-Samuelson Theorem: In the long run, when all factors are mobile, an increase in the relative price of a good will increase the real earnings of the factor used intensively in the production of that good and decrease the real earnings of the other factor.

For our example, the **Stolper-Samuelson theorem** predicts that when Home opens to trade and faces a higher relative price of computers, the real rental on capital in Home rises and the real wage in Home falls. In Foreign, the changes in real factor prices are just the reverse. When Foreign opens to trade and faces a lower relative price of computers, the real rental falls and the real wage rises. Remember that Foreign is abundant in labor, so our finding that labor is better off there, but worse off at Home, means that workers in the labor-abundant country gain from trade but workers in the capital-abundant country lose. In addition, capital in the capital-abundant country (Home) gains, and capital in the labor-abundant country loses. These results are sometimes summarized by saying that in the Heckscher-Ohlin model, *the abundant factor gains from trade, and the scarce factor loses from trade.*[6]

Changes in the Real Wage and Rental: A Numerical Example

To illustrate the Stolper-Samuelson theorem, we use a numerical example to show how much the real wage and rental can change in response to a change in price. Suppose that the computer and shoe industries have the following data:

Computers: Sales revenue $= P_C \cdot Q_C = 100$

Earnings of labor $= W \cdot L_C = 50$

Earnings of capital $= R \cdot K_C = 50$

Shoes: Sales revenue $= P_S \cdot Q_S = 100$

Earnings of labor $= W \cdot L_S = 60$

Earnings of capital $= R \cdot K_S = 40$

Notice that shoes are more labor-intensive than computers: the share of total revenue paid to labor in shoes ($60/100 = 60\%$) is more than that share in computers ($50/100 = 50\%$).

When Home and Foreign undertake trade, the relative price of computers rises. For simplicity we assume that this occurs because the price of computers P_C rises, while the price of shoes P_S does not change:

Computers: Percentage increase in price $= \Delta P_C/P_C = 10\%$

Shoes: Percentage increase in price $= \Delta P_S/P_S = 0\%$

Our goal is to see how the increase in the relative price of computers translates into long-run changes in the wage W paid to labor and the rental on capital R. Remember that the rental on capital can be calculated by taking total sales revenue in each industry, subtracting the payments to labor, and dividing by the amount of capital. This calculation gives us the following formulas for the rental in each industry:[7]

$$R = \frac{P_C \cdot Q_C - W \cdot L_C}{K_C}, \text{ for computers}$$

$$R = \frac{P_S \cdot Q_S - W \cdot L_S}{K_S}, \text{ for shoes}$$

The price of computers has risen, so $\Delta P_C > 0$, holding fixed the price of shoes, $\Delta P_S = 0$. We can trace through how this affects the rental by changing P_C and W in the previous two equations:

$$\Delta R = \frac{\Delta P_C \cdot Q_C - \Delta W \cdot L_C}{K_C}, \text{ for computers}$$

$$\Delta R = \frac{0 \cdot Q_C - \Delta W \cdot L_S}{K_S}, \text{ for shoes}$$

[6] This result follows logically from combining the Heckscher-Ohlin theorem with the Stolper-Samuelson theorem.
[7] Remember that because of factor mobility, the rental is the same in each industry, but it is helpful here to derive two separate equations for the percentage change in rental by industry.

It is convenient to work with percentage changes in the variables. For computers, $\Delta P_C/P_C$ is the percentage change in price. Similarly, $\Delta W/W$ is the percentage change in the wage, and $\Delta R/R$ is the percentage change in the rental of capital. We can introduce these terms into the preceding formulas by rewriting them as

$$\frac{\Delta R}{R} = \left(\frac{\Delta P_C}{P_C}\right)\left(\frac{P_C \cdot Q_C}{R \cdot K_C}\right) - \left(\frac{\Delta W}{W}\right)\left(\frac{W \cdot L_C}{R \cdot K_C}\right), \text{ for computers}$$

$$\frac{\Delta R}{R} = -\left(\frac{\Delta W}{W}\right)\left(\frac{W \cdot L_S}{R \cdot K_S}\right), \text{ for shoes}$$

(You should cancel terms in these equations to check that they are the same as before.)
Now we'll plug the above data for shoes and computers into these formulas:

$$\frac{\Delta R}{R} = 10\% \cdot \left(\frac{100}{50}\right) - \left(\frac{\Delta W}{W}\right)\left(\frac{50}{50}\right), \text{ for computers}$$

$$\frac{\Delta R}{R} = -\left(\frac{\Delta W}{W}\right)\left(\frac{60}{40}\right), \text{ for shoes}$$

Our goal is to find out by how much rental and wage change given changes in the relative price of the final goods, so we are trying to solve for two unknowns ($\Delta R/R$ and $\Delta W/W$) from the two equations given here. A good way to do this is to reduce the two equations with two unknowns into a single equation with one unknown. This can be done by subtracting one equation from the other, as follows:

$$\frac{\Delta R}{R} = 10\% \cdot \left(\frac{100}{50}\right) - \left(\frac{\Delta W}{W}\right)\left(\frac{50}{50}\right), \text{ for computers}$$

Minus: $\quad \dfrac{\Delta R}{R} = 0 - \left(\dfrac{\Delta W}{W}\right)\left(\dfrac{60}{40}\right), \text{ for shoes}$

Equals: $\quad 0 = 10\% \cdot \left(\dfrac{100}{50}\right) + \left(\dfrac{\Delta W}{W}\right)\left(\dfrac{20}{40}\right)$

Simplifying the last line, we get $0 = 20\% + \left(\dfrac{\Delta W}{W}\right)\left(\dfrac{1}{2}\right)$, so that

$$\left(\frac{\Delta W}{W}\right) = \left(\frac{-20\%}{\frac{1}{2}}\right) = -40\%, \text{ is the change in wages}$$

So when the price of computers increases by 10%, the wage falls by 40%. With the wage falling, labor can no longer afford to buy as many computers (W/P_C has fallen since W is falling and P_C has increased) or as many pairs of shoes (W/P_S has fallen since W is falling and P_S has not changed). In other words, the *real wage* measured in terms of either good has *fallen*, so labor is clearly worse off.

To find the change in the rental paid to capital ($\Delta R/R$), we can take our solution for $\Delta W/W = -40\%$, and plug it into the equation for the change in the rental in the shoes sector:[8]

---

[8] You should check that you get the same answer if instead you plug the change in the wage into the formula for the change in the rental in the computer sector.

$$\frac{\Delta R}{R} = -\left(\frac{\Delta W}{W}\right)\left(\frac{60}{40}\right) = 40\% \cdot \left(\frac{60}{40}\right) = 60\%, \text{ change in rental}$$

The rental on capital increases by 60% when the price of computers rises by 10%, so the rental increases even more (in percentage terms) than the price. Because the rental increases by more than the price of computers in percentage terms, it follows that (R/P_C) rises: owners of capital can afford to buy more computers, even though their price has gone up. In addition, they can afford to buy more shoes (R/P_S also rises, since R rises and P_S is constant). Thus, the real rental measured in terms of either good has *gone up*, and capital owners are clearly better off.

General Equation for the Long-Run Change in Factor Prices The long-run results of a change in factor prices can be summarized in the following equation:

$$\underbrace{\Delta W/W < 0}_{\substack{\text{Real wage}\\\text{falls}}} < \underbrace{\Delta P_C/P_C}_{\substack{\text{Real rental}\\\text{increases}}} < \Delta R/R, \text{ for an increase in } P_C$$

That is, the increase in the price of computers (10%) leads to an even larger increase in the rental on capital (60%) and a decrease in the wage (−40%). If, instead, the price of computers falls, then these inequalities are reversed, and we get

$$\underbrace{\Delta R/R < \Delta P_C/P_C}_{\substack{\text{Real rental}\\\text{falls}}} < \underbrace{0 < \Delta W/W}_{\substack{\text{Real wage}\\\text{increases}}}, \text{ for an decrease in } P_C$$

What happens if the relative price of shoes increases? From the Stolper-Samuelson theorem, we know that this change will benefit labor, which is used intensively in shoe production, and will harm capital. The equation summarizing the changes in factor earnings when the price of shoes increases is

$$\underbrace{\Delta R/R < 0}_{\substack{\text{Real rental}\\\text{falls}}} < \underbrace{\Delta P_S/P_S}_{\substack{\text{Real wage}\\\text{increases}}} < \Delta W/W, \text{ for an increase in } P_S$$

These equations relating the changes in product prices to changes in factor prices are sometimes called the "magnification effect" because they show how changes in the prices of goods have *magnified effects* on the earnings of factors: even a modest fluctuation in the relative prices of goods on world markets can lead to exaggerated changes in the long-run earnings of both factors. This result tells us that some groups—those employed intensively in export industries—can be expected to support opening an economy to trade because an increase in export prices increases their real earnings. But other groups—those employed intensively in import industries—can be expected to oppose free trade because the decrease in import prices decreases their real earnings. The following application examines the opinions that different factors of production have taken toward free trade.

APPLICATION

Opinions Toward Free Trade

Countries sometimes conduct a survey about their citizens' attitudes toward free trade. A survey conducted in the United States by the National Elections Studies (NES) in 1992 included the following question:

Some people have suggested placing new limits on foreign imports in order to protect American jobs. Others say that such limits would raise consumer prices and hurt American exports. Do you favor or oppose placing limits on imports, or haven't you thought much about this?

Respondents to the survey could either answer that they "favor" placing limits on imports, meaning that they do not support free trade, or that they "oppose" limits on imports, meaning that they support free trade. How do these answers compare with characteristics of the respondents, such as their wages, skills, or the industries in which they work?

According to the specific-factors model, in the short run we do not know whether labor will gain or lose from free trade, but we do know that the specific factor in the export sector gains, and the specific factor in the import sector loses. Think about an extension of this model, in which, in addition to their wage, labor also earns some part of the rental on the specific factor in their industry. This assumption is true for farmers, for example, who work in agriculture and may own their land; it can also be true for workers in manufacturing if their salary includes a bonus that is based on the profits earned by capital. In those situations, we would expect that workers in export industries will support free trade (since the specific factor in that industry gains), but workers in import-competing industries will be against free trade (since the specific factor in that industry loses). In the short run, then, the *industry of employment* of workers will affect their attitudes toward free trade.

In the long-run Heckscher-Ohlin (HO) model, however, the industry of employment should not matter. According to the Stolper-Samuelson theorem, an increase in the relative price of exports will benefit the factor of production used intensively in exports and harm the other factor, regardless of the industry in which these factors of production actually work (remember that each factor of production earns the same wage or rental across industries in the long run). In the United States, export industries tend to use high-skilled labor intensively for research and development and other scientific work. An increase in the relative price of exports will benefit high-skilled labor in the long run, regardless of whether these workers are employed in export-oriented industries or import-competing industries. Conversely, an increase in the relative price of exports will harm low-skilled labor, regardless of where these workers are employed. In the long run, then, the *skill level* of workers should determine their attitudes toward free trade.

In the 1992 NES survey, the industry of employment was somewhat important in explaining the respondents' attitudes toward free trade, but their skill level was much more important.[9] That is, workers in export-oriented industries are somewhat more likely to favor free trade, with those in import-competing industries favoring import restrictions, but this statistical relationship is not strong. A much more important determinant of the attitudes toward free trade is the skill level of workers, as measured by their wages or their years of education. Workers with lower wages or fewer years of education are more likely to favor import restrictions, whereas those with higher wages and more years of education favor free trade. This finding suggests that the respondents to the survey are basing their answer on their *long-run* earnings, as

[9] See Kenneth F. Scheve and Matthew J. Slaughter, 2001, "What Determines Individual Trade-Policy Preferences?" *Journal of International Economics*, 54, 267–292.

predicted by the HO model and Stolper-Samuelson theorem, rather than on their short-run industry of employment, as predicted by the specific-factors model.

There is an interesting extension to these findings, however. The survey also asked respondents whether they owned a home. It turns out that people who own homes in communities in which the local industries face a lot of import competition are much more likely to oppose free trade. Examples of this are towns in the northeastern states where people have been employed by textile mills, or in the midwestern states where people have been employed by automobile, steel, and other heavy industries. But people who own homes in communities in which the industries benefit from export opportunities, such as the high-tech areas in Boston or in Silicon Valley, California, are much more likely to support free trade. We can think of a house as a specific factor, since it cannot move locations. So the attitudes in this part of the NES survey conform to the short-run specific-factors model: people are very concerned about the asset value of their homes, just as the owners of specific factors in our model are concerned about the rental earned by the factor of production they own. ■

4 Conclusions

The Heckscher-Ohlin framework is one of the most widely used models in explaining trade patterns. It isolates the effect of different factor endowments across countries and determines the impact of these differences on trade patterns, relative prices, and factor returns. This approach is a major departure from the view that technology differences determine trade patterns as we saw in the Ricardian model and is also a departure from the short-run specific-factors model that we studied in Chapter 3.

In this chapter, we have investigated some empirical tests of the Heckscher-Ohlin theorem; that is, tests to determine whether countries actually export the goods that use their abundant factor intensively. The body of literature testing the theorem originates in Leontief's puzzling finding that U.S. exports just after World War II were relatively labor-intensive. Although the original formulation of his test did not seem to support the Heckscher-Ohlin theorem, later research has reformulated the test to measure the effective endowments of labor, capital, and other factors found in each country. Using this approach, we found that the United States was abundant in effective labor, and we also presume that it was abundant in capital. The United States had a positive factor content of net exports for both labor and capital in 1947, which is consistent with the finding of Leontief, so there was really no "paradox" after all.

By focusing on the factor intensities among goods (i.e., the relative amount of labor and capital used in production), the Heckscher-Ohlin (HO) model also provides clear guidance as to who gains and who loses from the opening of trade. In the specific-factors model, an increase in the relative price of a good leads to real gains for the specific factor used in that industry, losses for the other specific factor, and an ambiguous change in the real wage for labor. In contrast, the HO model predicts real gains for the factor used intensively in the export good, whose relative price goes up with the opening of trade, and real losses for the other factor. Having just two factors, both of which are fully mobile between the industries, leads to a very clear prediction about who gains and who loses from trade in the long run. Conclusion

KEY POINTS

1. In the Heckscher-Ohlin model, we assume that the technologies are the same across countries and that countries trade because the available resources (labor, capital, and land) differ across countries.

2. The Heckscher-Ohlin model is a long-run framework, so labor, capital, and other resources can move freely between the industries.

3. With two goods, two factors, and two countries, the Heckscher-Ohlin model predicts that a country will export the good that uses its abundant factor intensively and import the other good.

4. The first test of the Heckscher-Ohlin model was made by Leontief using U.S. data for 1947. He found that U.S. exports were less capital-intensive and more labor-intensive than U.S. imports. This was a paradoxical finding because the United States was abundant in capital.

5. The assumption of identical technologies used in the Heckscher-Ohlin model does not hold in practice. Current research has extended the empirical tests of the Heckscher-Ohlin model to allow for many factors and countries, along with differing productivities of factors across countries. When we allow for different productivities of labor in 1947, we find that the United States is abundant in effective—or skilled—labor, which explains the Leontief paradox.

6. According to the Stolper-Samuelson theorem, an increase in the relative price of a good will cause the real earnings of labor and capital to move in opposite directions: the factor used intensively in the industry whose relative price goes up will find its earnings increased, and the real earnings of the other factor will fall.

7. Putting together the Heckscher-Ohlin theorem and the Stolper-Samuelson theorem, we conclude that a country's abundant factor gains from the opening of trade (because the relative price of exports goes up), and its scarce factor loses from the opening of trade.

KEY TERMS

Heckscher-Ohlin model, p. 87
reversal of factor intensities, p. 92
free-trade equilibrium, p. 97
Heckscher-Ohlin theorem, p. 97
Leontief's paradox, p. 98

abundant in that factor, p. 100
scarce in that factor, p. 100
effective labor force, p. 102
effective factor endowment, p. 103

abundant in that effective factor, p. 103
scarce in that effective factor, p. 103
Stolper-Samuelson theorem, p. 114

PROBLEMS

1. This problem uses the Heckscher-Ohlin model to predict the direction of trade. Consider the production of handmade rugs and assembly line robots in Canada and India.

   a. Which country would you expect to be relatively labor-abundant, and which is capital-abundant? Why?

   b. Which industry would you expect to be relatively labor-intensive, and which is capital-intensive? Why?

   c. Given your answers to (a) and (b), draw production possibilities frontiers for each country.

   Assuming that consumer preferences are the same in both countries, add indifference curves and relative price lines (without trade) to your PPF graphs. What do the slopes of the price lines tell you about the direction of trade?

   d. Allowing for trade between countries, redraw the graphs and include a "trade triangle" for each country. Identify and label the vertical and horizontal sides of the triangles as either imports or exports.

2. Leontief's paradox is an example of testing a trade model using actual data observations. If

Leontief had observed that the amount of labor needed per \$1 million of U.S. exports was 100 person-years instead of 182, would he have reached the same conclusion? Explain.

3. Suppose there are drastic technological improvements in shoe production at Home such that shoe factories can operate almost completely with computer-aided machines. Consider the following data for the Home country:

Computers: Sales revenue = $P_C Q_C = 100$

Payments to labor = $WL_C = 50$

Payments to capital = $RK_C = 50$

Percentage increase in the price = $\Delta P_C/P_C = 0\%$

Shoes: Sales revenue = $P_S Q_S = 100$

Payments to labor = $WL_S = 5$

Payments to capital = $RK_S = 95$

Percentage increase in the price = $\Delta P_S/P_S = 50\%$

a. Which industry is capital-intensive? Is this a reasonable question, given that some industries are capital-intensive in some countries and labor-intensive in others?

b. Given the percentage changes in output prices in the data provided, calculate the percentage change in the rental on capital.

c. How does the magnitude of this change compare with that of labor?

d. Which factor gains in real terms, and which factor loses? Are these results consistent with the Stolper-Samuelson theorem?

4. Using the information in the chapter, suppose Home doubles in size, while Foreign remains the same. Show that an equal proportional increase in capital and labor at Home will change the relative price of computers, wage, rental on capital, and the amount traded but not the pattern of trade.

5. Using a diagram similar to Figure 4-12, show the effect of a decrease in the relative price of computers in Foreign. What happens to the wage relative to the rental? Is there an increase in the labor–capital ratio in each industry? Explain.

6. Suppose when Russia opens to trade, it imports automobiles, a capital-intensive good.

a. According to the Heckscher-Ohlin theorem, is Russia capital-abundant or labor-abundant? Briefly explain.

b. What is the impact of opening trade on the real wage in Russia?

c. What is the impact of opening trade on the real rental on capital?

d. Which group (capital owner or labor) would support policies to limit free trade? Briefly explain.

7. In Figure 4-3, we show how the movement from the no-trade equilibrium point A to a trade equilibrium at a higher relative price of computers leads to an upward-sloping export supply, from points A to D in panel (b).

a. Suppose that the relative price of computers continues to rise in panel (a), and label the production and consumption points at several higher prices.

b. In panel (b), extend the export supply curve to show the quantity of exports at the higher relative prices of computers.

c. What happens to the export supply curve when the price of computers is high enough? Can you explain why this happens? *Hint:* An increase in the relative price of a country's export good means that the country is richer because its terms of trade have improved. Explain how that can lead to fewer exports as their price rises.

8. On March 2, 2013, Tajikistan successfully negotiated terms to become a member of the World Trade Organization. Consequently, countries such as those in western Europe are shifting toward free trade with Tajikistan. What does the Stolper-Samuelson theorem predict about the impact of the shift on the real wage of low-skilled labor in western Europe? In Tajikistan?

9. The following are data on U.S. exports and imports in 2012 at the two-digit Harmonized Tariff Schedule (HTS) level. Which products do you think support the Heckscher-Ohlin theorem? Which products are inconsistent?

HTS Level	Product	Export ($ billions)	Import ($ billions)
22	Beverages	6.4	19.2
30	Pharmaceutical products	38.0	64.1
52	Cotton	8.2	1.1
61	Apparel	1.4	41.1
64	Footwear	0.8	23.7
72	Iron and steel	22.0	29.0
74	Copper	9.3	10.2
85	Electric machinery	105.0	289.0
87	Vehicles	122.3	240.0
88	Aircraft	95.8	24.2
94	Furniture	8.7	44.3
95	Toys	4.4	27.0

Source: International Trade Administration, U.S. Department of Commerce.

10. Following are data for soybean yield, production, and trade for 2010–2011:

Suppose that the countries listed in the table are engaged in free trade and that soybean production is land-intensive. Answer the following:

a. In which countries does land benefit from free trade in soybeans? Explain.

b. In which countries does land lose from free trade in soybeans? Explain.

c. In which countries does the move to free trade in soybeans have little or no effect on the land rental? Explain.

	Yield (metric ton/hectare)	Production (100,000 metric ton)	Export (100,000 metric ton)	Imports (100,000 metric ton)
Australia	1.71	0.29	0.025	0.007
Brazil	3.12	748.2	258	1.18
Canada	2.75	42.5	27.8	2.42
China	1.89	144	1.64	570
France	2.95	1.23	0.24	5.42
Japan	1.60	2.19	0.0006	34.6
Mexico	1.32	2.05	0.001	37.7
Russian Federation	1.48	17.6	0.008	10.7
United States	2.79	831	423	4.45

Source: Food and Agriculture Organization.

11. According to the Heckscher-Ohlin model, two countries can equalize wage differences by either engaging in international trade in goods or allowing high-skilled and low-skilled labor to freely move between the two countries. Discuss whether this is true or false, and explain why.

12. According to the standard Heckscher-Ohlin model with two factors (capital and labor) and two goods, movement of Turkish migrants to Germany would decrease the amount of capital-intensive products produced in Germany. Discuss whether this is true or false, and explain why.

NETWORK

See the New Balance plant in Skowhegan, Maine, at http://www.youtube.com/watch?v=ittvWwCS5QI. What shoes are produced there, and what is the "Super Team 33"?

5

Movement of Labor and Capital Between Countries

Amidst growing dissent, housing and job shortages as well as a plummeting economy, Cuban Premier Fidel Castro withdrew his guards from the Peruvian embassy in Havana on April 4, 1980. . . . Less than 48 hours after the guards were removed, throngs of Cubans crowded into the lushly landscaped gardens at the embassy, requesting asylum. . . . By mid-April, Carter issued a Presidential Memorandum allowing up to 3,500 refugees sanctuary in the U.S. . . . But the Carter Administration was taken by surprise when on April 21, refugees started arriving on Florida's shores—their numbers would eventually reach 125,000.

"Memories of Mariel, 20 Years Later"[1]

If you're a foreign student who wants to pursue a career in science or technology, or a foreign entrepreneur who wants to start a business with the backing of American investors, we should help you do that here. Because if you succeed, you'll create American businesses and American jobs. You'll help us grow our economy. You'll help us strengthen our middle class.

President Barack Obama, Del Sol High School, Las Vegas, January 29, 2013

From May to September 1980, boatloads of refugees from Cuba arrived in Miami, Florida. For political reasons, Fidel Castro had allowed them to leave freely from the port of Mariel, Cuba, during that brief period. Known as "the Mariel boat lift," this influx of about 125,000 refugees to Miami increased the city's Cuban population by 20% and its overall population by about 7%. The widespread unemployment of many of the refugees during the summer of 1980 led many people to expect that the wages of other workers in Miami would be held down by the Mariel immigrants.

Not surprisingly, the refugees were less skilled than the other workers in Miami, as is confirmed by looking at their wages: the immigrants initially earned about

---

[1] Judy L. Silverstein, "Memories of Mariel, 20 Years Later," *U.S. Coast Guard Reservist*, 47(3), April/May 2000, electronic edition.

one-third less than other Cubans in Miami. What is surprising, however, is that this influx of low-skilled immigrants does not appear to have pulled down the wages of other less skilled workers in Miami.[2] The wages for low-skilled workers in Miami essentially followed national trends over this period, despite the large inflow of workers from Cuba. This finding seems to contradict the prediction of basic supply and demand theory—that a higher supply of workers should bid down their wage and that restricting immigration will raise the wages for local workers. The fact that wages in Miami did not respond to the inflow of Mariel refugees calls for an explanation, which is one goal of this chapter.

A similar outcome occurred in a more recent case of sudden migration, the emigration of Russian Jews to Israel after 1989, when the Soviet Union relaxed its restrictions on such departures. From late 1989 to 1996, some 670,000 Russian Jews immigrated to Israel, which increased the population in Israel by 11% and its workforce by 14%. This wave of immigration was especially notable because the Russian immigrants were more highly skilled than the existing Israeli population. But despite this large influx of immigrants, the relative wages of high-skilled workers in Israel actually *rose* during the 1990s. Careful studies of this episode can find little or no negative impact of the Russian immigrants on the wages of other high-skilled workers.[3]

These emigrations were of different types of workers—the Cuban workers were low-skilled and the Russian emigrants high-skilled—but they share the finding that large inflows of workers need not depress wages in the areas where they settle. In other cases of large-scale migration—such as occurred from Europe to America during the 1800s and 1900s—wages did indeed fall because of the inflow of immigrants. So the Mariel boat lift and Russian immigration to Israel should be seen as special: they are cases in which the economic principles of supply and demand do not at first glance work as we would expect them to.

In this chapter, we begin our study of the movement of labor across countries by explaining the case in which immigration leads to a fall in wages, as we normally expect. The model we use is the **specific-factors model,** the short-run model introduced in Chapter 3. That model allows labor to move between industries but keeps capital and land specific to each industry. To study migration, we allow labor to move between countries as well as industries, while still keeping capital and land specific to each industry.

Next, we use the long-run Heckscher-Ohlin model, from Chapter 4, in which capital and land can also move between industries. In the long run, an increase in labor *will not* lower the wage, as illustrated by the Mariel boat lift to Miami and the Russian immigration to Israel. This outcome occurs because industries have more time to respond to the inflow of workers by adjusting their outputs. It turns out that by adjusting industry output enough, the economy can absorb the new workers without changing the wage for existing workers. The explanation for this surprising outcome relies on the assumption that industries are able to sell their outputs on international markets.

To give a brief idea of how this long-run explanation will work, think about the highly skilled scientists and engineers emigrating from Russia to Israel. The only way

---

[2] See David Card, January 1990, "The Impact of the Mariel Boatlift on the Miami Labor Market," *Industrial Labor Relations Review*, 43(2), 245–257.
[3] See Neil Gandal, Gordon Hanson, and Matthew Slaughter, 2004, "Technology, Trade and Adjustment to Immigration in Israel," *European Economic Review*, 48(2), 403–428.

to employ the large number of these workers at the going wages would be to increase the number of scientific and engineering projects in which Israeli companies are engaged. Where does the demand for these new projects come from? It is unlikely this demand would be generated in Israel alone, and more likely that it would come from Israeli *exports* to the rest of the world. We see then that the ability of Israel to export products making use of the highly skilled immigrants is essential to our explanation: with international demand, it is possible for the Russian immigrants to be fully employed in export activities without lowering wages in Israel. Likewise, with the influx of low-skilled Cuban immigrants to Miami, many of whom could work in the textile and apparel industry or in agriculture, it is the ability of Florida to export those products that allows the workers to be employed at the going wages.

The effect of immigration on wages can be quite different in the short run and in the long run. In this chapter we demonstrate that difference, and discuss government policies related to immigration. Policies to restrict or to allow immigration are an important part of government regulation in every country, including the United States. As President Obama began his second term as President in 2013, one of his goals was to achieve a reform of immigration policies. We discuss why reforms are needed in the United States and what they might achieve.

After studying what happens when labor moves across countries, we study the effects of foreign direct investment (FDI), the movement of capital across countries. FDI occurs when a company from one country owns a company in another country. We conclude the chapter by discussing the gains to the source and destination countries, and to the world, from the movement of labor or capital between countries.

1 Movement of Labor Between Countries: Migration

We begin with the examples of labor migration described by the Mariel boat lift and the Russian migration to Israel. We can think of each migration as a movement of labor from the Foreign country to the Home country. What is the impact of this movement of labor on wages paid at Home? To answer this question, we make use of our work in Chapter 3, in which we studied how the wages paid to labor and the rentals paid to capital and land are determined by the prices of the goods produced. The prices of goods themselves are determined by supply and demand in world markets. In the analysis that follows, we treat the prices of goods as fixed and ask how the Home wage and the rentals paid to capital and land change as labor moves between countries.

Effects of Immigration in the Short Run: Specific-Factors Model

We begin our study of the effect of factor movements between countries by using the specific-factors model we learned in Chapter 3 to analyze the short run, when labor is mobile among Home industries, but land and capital are fixed. After that, we consider the long run, when all factors are mobile among industries at Home.

Determining the Wage Figure 5-1 shows a diagram that we used in Chapter 3 to determine the equilibrium wage paid to labor. The horizontal axis measures the total amount of labor in the economy $\overline{L}$, which consists of the labor used in manufacturing L_M and the amount used in agriculture L_A:

$$L_M + L_A = \overline{L}$$

FIGURE 5-1

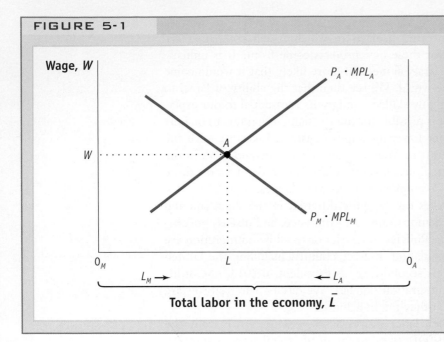

Home Labor Market The Home wage is determined at point A, the intersection of the marginal product of labor curves $P_M \cdot MPL_M$ and $P_A \cdot MPL_A$ in manufacturing and agriculture, respectively. The amount of labor used in manufacturing is measured from left to right, starting at the origin 0_M, and the amount of labor used in agriculture is measured from right to left, starting at the origin 0_A. At point A, $0_M L$ units of labor are used in manufacturing and $0_A L$ units of labor are used in agriculture.

In Figure 5-1, the amount of labor used in manufacturing L_M is measured from left (0_M) to right, and the amount of labor used in agriculture L_A is measured from right (0_A) to left.

The two curves in Figure 5-1 take the marginal product of labor in each sector and multiply it by the price (P_M or P_A) in that sector. The graph of $P_M \cdot MPL_M$ is downward-sloping because as more labor is used in manufacturing, the marginal product of labor in that industry declines, and wages fall. The graph of $P_A \cdot MPL_A$ for agriculture is upward-sloping because we are measuring the labor used in agriculture L_A from *right to left* in the diagram: as more labor is used in agriculture (moving from right to left), the marginal product of labor in agriculture falls, and wages fall.

The equilibrium wage is at point A, the intersection of the marginal product curves $P_M \cdot MPL_M$ and $P_A \cdot MPL_A$ in Figure 5-1. At this point, $0_M L$ units of labor are used in manufacturing, and firms in that industry are willing to pay the wage $W = P_M \cdot MPL_M$. In addition, $0_A L$ units of labor are used in agriculture, and farmers are willing to pay the wage $W = P_A \cdot MPL_A$. Because wages are equal in the two sectors, there is no reason for labor to move between them, and the Home labor market is in equilibrium.

In the Foreign country, a similar diagram applies. We do not draw this but assume that the equilibrium wage abroad W^* is less than W in Home. This assumption would apply to the Cuban refugees, for example, who moved to Miami and to the Russian emigrants who moved to Israel to earn higher wages as well as to enjoy more freedom. As a result of this difference in wages, workers from Foreign would want to immigrate to Home and the Home workforce would increase by an amount ΔL, reflecting the number of immigrants.

Effect of Immigration on the Wage in Home The effects of immigration are shown in Figure 5-2. Because the number of workers at Home has grown by ΔL, we expand the size of the horizontal axis from $\overline{L}$ to $\overline{L}' = \overline{L} + \Delta L$. The right-most point on the horizontal axis, which is the origin 0_A for the agriculture industry, shifts to the

FIGURE 5-2

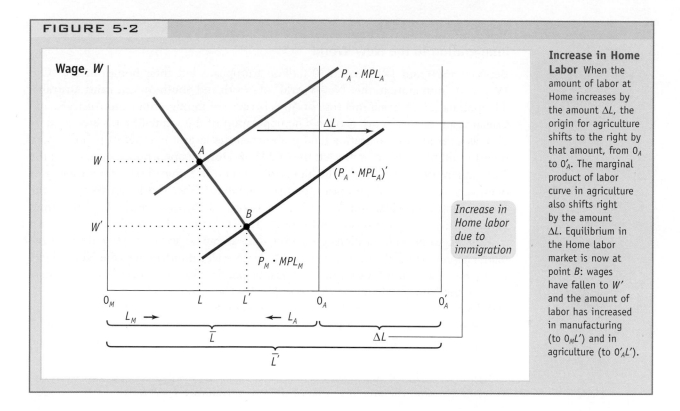

Increase in Home Labor When the amount of labor at Home increases by the amount ΔL, the origin for agriculture shifts to the right by that amount, from 0_A to $0'_A$. The marginal product of labor curve in agriculture also shifts right by the amount ΔL. Equilibrium in the Home labor market is now at point B: wages have fallen to W' and the amount of labor has increased in manufacturing (to $0_M L'$) and in agriculture (to $0'_A L'$).

right by the amount ΔL. As this origin moves rightward, it carries along with it the marginal product curve $P_A \cdot MPL_A$ for the agriculture industry (because the marginal product of labor curve is graphed relative to its origin). That curve shifts to the right by exactly the amount ΔL, the increase in the Home workforce. There is no shift in the marginal product curve $P_M \cdot MPL_M$ for the manufacturing industry because the origin 0_M for manufacturing has not changed.[4]

The new equilibrium Home wage is at point B, the intersection of the marginal product curves. At the new equilibrium, the wage is lower. Notice that the extra workers ΔL arriving at Home are shared between the agriculture and manufacturing industries: the number of workers employed in manufacturing is now $0_M L'$, which is higher than $0_M L$, and the number of workers employed in agriculture is $0'_A L'$, which is also higher than $0_A L$.[5] Because both industries have more workers but fixed amounts of capital and land, the wage in both industries declines due to the diminishing marginal product of labor.

We see, then, that the specific-factors model predicts that an inflow of labor will lower wages in the country in which the workers are arriving. This prediction has been confirmed in numerous episodes of large-scale immigration, as described in the applications that follow.

---

[4] If, instead, we had added labor to the left-hand side of the graph, the origin and marginal product curve for manufacturing would have shifted and those of agriculture would have remained the same, yielding the same final results as in Figure 5-2—the wage falls and both industries use more labor.
[5] We know that the number of workers employed in agriculture rises because the increase in workers in manufacturing, from $0_M L$ to $0_M L'$, is less than the total increase in labor ΔL.

APPLICATION

Immigration to the New World

Between 1870 and 1913, some 30 million Europeans left their homes in the "Old World" to immigrate to the "New World" of North and South America and Australia. The population of Argentina rose by 60% because of immigration, and Australia and Canada gained 30% more people. The population of the United States increased by 17% as a result of immigration (and it absorbed the largest number of people, more than 15 million). The migrants left the Old World for the opportunities present in the New and, most important, for the higher real wages. In Figure 5-3, we show an index of average real wages in European countries and in the New World (an average of the United States, Canada, and Australia).[6] In 1870 real wages were nearly three times higher in the New World than in Europe—120 as compared with 40.

Real wages in both locations grew over time as capital accumulated and raised the marginal product of labor. But because of the large-scale immigration to the New World, wages grew more slowly there. By 1913, just before the onset of World War I, the wage index in the New World was at 160, so real wages had grown by $(160 - 120)/120 = 33\%$ over 43 years. In Europe, however, the wage index reached 75 by 1913, an increase of $(75 - 40)/40 = 88\%$ over 43 years. In 1870 real wages in the New World were three times as high as those in Europe, but by 1913 this wage gap was substantially reduced, and

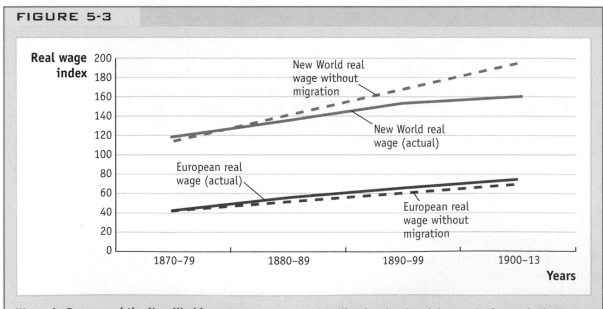

FIGURE 5-3

Wages in Europe and the New World Large-scale migration from Europe to the New World in America and Australia closed the wage gap between the two locations. In 1870 wages in the New World were almost three times as high as wages in Europe, whereas in 1910 they were about twice as high. Migration also slowed the growth of wages in the New World relative to what they would have been without migration and allowed for slightly faster growth of wages in Europe.

Source: Alan M. Taylor and Jeffrey G. Williamson, 1997, "Convergence in the Age of Mass Migration," European Review of Economic History, 1, April, 27–63.

---

[6] From Alan M. Taylor and Jeffrey G. Williamson, 1997, "Convergence in the Age of Mass Migration," *European Review of Economic History*, 1, April, 27–63.

wages in the New World were only about twice as high as those in Europe. Large-scale migration therefore contributed to a "convergence" of real wages across the continents.

In Figure 5-3, we also show estimates of what real wages would have been if migration had not occurred. Those estimates are obtained by calculating how the marginal product of labor would have grown with capital accumulation but without the immigration. Comparing the actual real wages with the no-migration estimates, we see that the growth of wages in the New World was slowed by immigration (workers arriving), while wages in Europe grew slightly faster because of emigration (workers leaving). ■

APPLICATION

Immigration to the United States and Europe Today

The largest amount of migration is no longer from Europe to the "New World." Instead, workers from developing countries immigrate to wealthier countries in the European Union and North America, when they can. In many cases, the immigration includes a mix of low-skilled workers and high-skilled workers. During the 1960s and 1970s, some European countries actively recruited guest workers, called *gastarbeiters* in West Germany, to fill labor shortages in unskilled jobs. Many of these foreign workers have remained in Germany for years, some for generations, so they are no longer "guests" but long-term residents. At the end of 1994, about 2.1 million foreigners were employed in western Germany, with citizens of Turkey, the former Yugoslavia, Greece, and Italy representing the largest groups.

Today, the European Union has expanded to include many of the countries in Eastern Europe, and in principle there is free migration within the European Union. In practice, it can still be difficult for countries to absorb all the workers who want to enter, whether they come from inside or outside the Union. A recent example from Europe is the inflow of migrants from Northern Africa, especially from Tunisia and Libya. During 2011 and 2012, some 58,000 migrants escaped unrest in Africa and sailed on small boats to the island of Lampedusa in Italy. That inflow of migrants has created a situation not unlike the "Mariel boat lift" situation several decades ago in the United States, as discussed at the beginning of the chapter. The inflow has strained the ability of the European Union to maintain passport-free migration between countries. As described in **Headlines: Call for Return of Border Controls in Europe,** these migrants were not welcome to move freely from Italy to France, where some of them had families or friends.

Immigrants from Tunisia, Africa arrive in Lampedusa, Italy on March 27, 2011.

In the United States, there is a widespread perception among policy makers that the current immigration system is not working and needs to be fixed. A new immigration bill was debated in the U.S. Congress in 2013. As described in **Headlines: The Economic Windfall of Immigration Reform,** there are several issues that this bill needs to address, related to both illegal and legal immigration.

It is estimated that there are about 12 million illegal immigrants in the United States, many of them from Mexico. Gaining control over U.S. borders is one goal of immigration policy, but focusing on that goal alone obscures the fact that the majority of immigrants who enter the United States each year are legal.

HEADLINES

Call for Return of Border Controls in Europe

In 2011, Nicolas Sarkozy, the French president at the time, and Silvio Berlusconi, the Italian prime minister at the time, called for limits on passport-free travel among European Union countries in response to the flood of North African immigrants entering Italy through the island of Lampedusa.

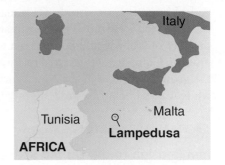

Nicolas Sarkozy and Silvio Berlusconi are expected to call on Tuesday for a partial reintroduction of national border controls across Europe, a move that would put the brakes on European integration and curb passport-free travel for more than 400 million people in 25 countries.

The French president and the Italian prime minister are meeting in Rome after weeks of tension between their two countries over how to cope with an influx of more than 25,000 immigrants fleeing revolutions in north Africa. The migrants, mostly Tunisian, reached the EU by way of Italian islands such as Lampedusa, but many hoped to get work in France where they have relatives and friends.

Earlier this month, Berlusconi's government outraged several EU governments, including France, by offering the migrants temporary residence permits which, in principle, allowed them to travel to other member states under the Schengen agreement. An Italian junior minister said on Sunday that Rome had so far issued some 8,000 permits and expected the number would rise to 11,000.

Launched in 1995, Schengen allows passport-free travel in most of the EU, Switzerland, Norway and Iceland. But the documents issued by the Italian authorities are only valid if the holders can show they have the means to support themselves, and French police

have rounded up or turned back an unknown number of migrants in recent days.

On 17 April, Paris blocked trains crossing the frontier at Ventimiglia in protest at the Italian initiative. "Rarely have the two countries seemed so far apart," said Le Monde in an editorial on Monday.

Yet, with both leaders under pressure from the far right, French and Italian officials appear to have agreed a common position on amending Schengen so that national border checks can be reintroduced in "special circumstances".

Source: Excerpted from John Hooper and Ian Traynor, "Sarkozy and Berlusconi to call for return of border controls in Europe," The Guardian, April 25 2011, electronic edition. Copyright Guardian News & Media Ltd 2011.

Persons seeking to legally enter the United States sometimes must wait a very long time, because under current U.S. law, migrants from any one foreign country cannot number more than 7% of the total legal immigrants into the United States each year. Giovanni Peri, the author of "The Economic Windfall of Immigration Reform" article, proposes that businesses should be allowed to compete for migrants who have the skills needed for the jobs that the businesses have to offer. Firms could, for example, compete by bidding for temporary work permits in auctions. After obtaining the work permits, the firms could then sell them to other firms.[7] In this way, the permits would eventually be bought by the firms that valued them most highly, promoting efficiency in the flow of migrants.

Such an auction scheme could be used for seasonal agricultural workers, for example, some of whom legally enter the United States under the H-2A visa program. An

---

[7] The proposal to auction work permits is discussed at greater length in: Giovanni Peri, "Rationalizing U.S. Immigration Policy: Reforms for Simplicity, Fairness, and Economic Growth," Discussion paper 2012–01, The Hamilton Project, Washington D.C. May 2012. A video presentation is available at: http://www.hamiltonproject.org/multimedia/video/u.s._immigration_policy_-_roundtable_a_market-based_approach_to_immigr/.

HEADLINES

The Economic Windfall of Immigration Reform

Writing during the U.S. debate over immigration reform in 2013, Professor Giovanni Peri discusses three principles that reform should follow. He argues that there are large gains from increasing the supply of highly-skilled immigrants to the United States, by allowing firms to bid for temporary work permits.

After months of acrimony, it now appears that immigration reform, and a comprehensive one at that, is within reach. While most of the debates have been about the immediate consequences of any change in policy, the goal should be to promote economic growth over the next 40 years.

Much of the reform debate has centered around granting legal status to undocumented immigrants, conditional upon payment of fees and back taxes. From an economic point of view, this will likely have only a modest impact, especially in the short run. Yet the problem of undocumented immigrants is likely to come back unless we find better ways to legally accommodate new immigrants. Much larger economic gains are achievable if we reorganize the immigration system to do that, following three fundamental principles.

The first is simplification. The current visa system is the accumulation of many disconnected provisions. Some

rules, set in the past—such as the 7% limit on permanent permits to any nationality—are arbitrary and produce delays, bottlenecks and inefficiencies. . . . A more rational approach would have the government set overall targets and simple rules for temporary and permanent working permits, deciding the balance between permits in "skilled" and "unskilled" jobs. But the government should not micromanage permits, rules and limits in specific occupations. Employers compete to hire immigrants, and they are best suited at selecting the individuals who will be the most productive in the jobs that are needed.

The second important principle is that the number of temporary work visas should respond to the demand for labor. Currently the limited number of these visas is set with no consideration for economic conditions. Their number is rarely revised. In periods of high demand, the economic incentives to bypass the limits

and hire undocumented workers are large. . . . [W]e propose that temporary permits to hire immigrants should be made tradable and sold by the government in auctions to employers. Such a "cap and trade" system would ensure efficiency. The auction price of permits would signal the demand for immigrants and guide the upward and downward adjustment of the permit numbers over years.

The third principle governing immigration reform is that scientists, engineers and innovators are the main drivers of productivity and of economic growth. . . . I have found in a study published in January that foreign scientists and engineers brought into this country under the H1B visa program have contributed to 10%–20% of the yearly productivity growth in the U.S. during the period 1990–2010. This allowed the GDP per capita to be 4% higher that it would have been without them—that's an aggregate increase of output of $615 billion as of 2010.

Source: Excerpted from Giovanni Peri, "The Economic Windfall of Immigration Reform," The Wall Street Journal, *February 13th 2013. p. A15. Reprinted with permission of The Wall Street Journal, Copyright © (2013) Dow Jones & Company, Inc. All Rights Reserved Worldwide.*

auction could also expand the existing H-1B visa program for engineers, scientists, and other skilled workers needed in high-technology industries. The H-1B program was established during the Clinton administration to attract highly skilled immigrants to the United States, and it continues today. According to this article, the inflow of highly skilled immigrants on H-1B visas can explain 10% to 20% of the yearly productivity growth in the United States, as discussed later in the chapter.

The potential competition that immigrants create for U.S. workers with the same educational level is illustrated in Figure 5-4. On the vertical axis we show the share of immigrants (legal and illegal) as a percentage of the total workforce in the United States with that educational level. For example, from the first bar we see that immigrants account for 40% of the total number of workers in the United States that do not have a high-school education (the remaining 60% are U.S. born). Many of those

FIGURE 5-4

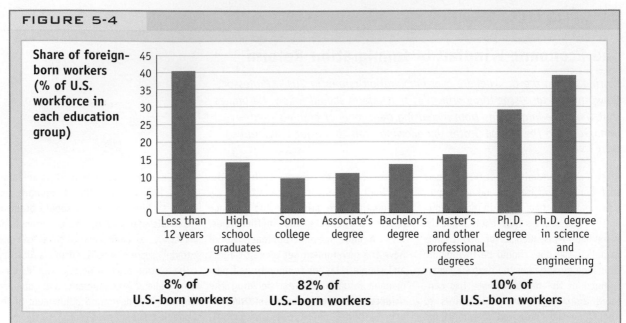

Share of Foreign-Born Workers in U.S. Workforce, 2010 This figure shows the share of foreign-born workers in the U.S. workforce, categorized by educational level. For example, among workers with 0 to 11 years of education, about 40% were foreign-born. At the other end of the spectrum, the foreign-born make up 16% of workers with Master's and professional degrees, almost 30% of those with Ph.D.'s, and almost 40% of those with Ph.D.'s in science and engineering. In the middle educational levels (high school and college graduates), there are much smaller shares of foreign-born workers, ranging from 10% to 15%. On the horizontal axis, we show the share of U.S.-born workers in each educational group. Only about 8% to 10% of U.S.-born workers are categorized in each of the low-education and high-education groups; most U.S.-born workers are either high school graduates or college graduates.

Source: 2010 American Community Survey, U.S. Census Bureau.

immigrants without a high-school education are illegal, but we do not know the exact number. We know, however, that the share of high-school dropouts in the U.S.-born workforce is quite small: only 8% of workers born in the United States do not have a high-school education. That percentage is shown on the horizontal axis of Figure 5-4. So, even though illegal immigrants attract much attention in the U.S. debate over immigration, those immigrants with less than high-school education are competing with a small share of U.S.-born workers.

As we move to the next bars in Figure 5-4, the story changes. A large portion of U.S.-born workers—82% as shown on the horizontal axis—have completed high school education, may have started college, or graduated with an Associate's or Bachelor's degree. The shares of these educational groups that are composed of immigrants are quite small, ranging between 10% and 15% (the remainder being U.S.-born workers). So in these middle levels of education, immigrants are not numerous enough to create a significant amount of competition with U.S.-born workers for jobs.

At the other end of the spectrum, 10% of U.S.-born workers have Master's degrees or Ph.D.'s. Within this high-education group, foreign-born Master's-degree holders make up 16% of the U.S. workforce, and foreign-born Ph.D.'s make up nearly 30%, of the U.S. workforce. Furthermore, an even higher fraction of foreign-born immigrants, close to 40%, have Ph.D.'s in science and engineering fields (with slightly more than 60% being U.S. born). To summarize, Figure 5-4 shows that immigrants into the United States compete primarily with workers at the lowest and highest ends of the educational levels and much less with the majority of U.S.-born workers with mid-levels of education.

If we extend the specific-factors model to allow for several types of labor distinguished by educational level but continue to treat capital and land as fixed, then the greatest negative impact of immigration on wages would be for the lowest- and highest-educated U.S. workers. That prediction is supported by estimates of the effect of immigration on U.S. wages: from 1990 to 2006, immigration led to a fall in wages of 7.8% for high school dropouts and 4.7% for college graduates. But the impact of immigration on the wages of the majority of U.S. workers (those with mid-levels of education) is much less: wages of high school graduates decreased by 2.2% from 1990 to 2006, and wages of individuals with less than four years of college decreased by less than 1%. The negative impact of immigration on wages is thus fairly modest for most workers and is offset when capital moves between industries, as discussed later in the chapter. ■

Other Effects of Immigration in the Short Run

The United States and Europe have both welcomed foreign workers into specific industries, such as agriculture and the high-tech industry, even though these workers compete with domestic workers in those industries. This observation suggests that there must be benefits to the industries involved. We can measure the potential benefits by the payments to capital and land, which we refer to as "rentals." We saw in Chapter 3 that there are two ways to compute the rentals: either as the earnings left over in the industry after paying labor or as the marginal product of capital or land times the price of the good produced in each industry. Under either method, the owners of capital and land benefit from the reduction in wages due to immigration.

Rentals on Capital and Land   Under the first method for computing the rentals, we take the revenue earned in either manufacturing or agriculture and subtract the payments to labor. If wages fall, then there is more left over as earnings of capital and land, so these rentals are higher. Under the second method for computing rentals, capital and land earn their marginal product in each industry times the price of the industry's good. As more labor is hired in each industry (because wages are lower), the marginal products of capital and land both increase. The increase in the marginal product occurs because each machine or acre of land has more workers available to it, and that machine or acre of land is therefore more productive. So under the second method, too, the marginal products of capital and land rise and so do their rentals.

From this line of reasoning, we should not be surprised that owners of capital and land often support more open borders, which provide them with foreign workers who can be employed in their industries. The restriction on immigration in a country should therefore be seen as a compromise between entrepreneurs and landowners who might welcome the foreign labor; local unions and workers who view migrants as a potential source of competition leading to lower wages; and the immigrant groups themselves, who if they are large enough (such as the Cuban population in Miami) might also have the ability to influence the political outcome on immigration policy.

Effect of Immigration on Industry Output   One final effect of labor immigration is its effect on the output of the industries. In Figure 5-2, the increase in the labor force due to immigration led to more workers being employed in each of the industries: employment increased from 0_ML to $0_ML'$ in manufacturing and from 0_AL to

$0'_A L'$ in agriculture. With more workers and the same amount of capital or land, the output of both industries rises. This outcome is shown in Figure 5-5—immigration leads to an outward shift in the production possibilities frontier (PPF). With constant prices of goods (as we assumed earlier, because prices are determined by world supply and demand), the output of the industries rises from point A to point B.

Although it may seem obvious that having more labor in an economy will increase the output of both industries, it turns out that this result depends on the short-run nature of the specific-factors model, when capital and land in each industry are fixed. If instead these resources can move between the industries, as would occur in the long run, then the output of one industry will increase but that of the other industry will decline, as we explain in the next section.

Effects of Immigration in the Long Run

We turn now to the long run, in which all factors are free to move between industries. Because it is complicated to analyze a model with three factors of production—capital, land, and labor—all of which are fully mobile between industries, we will ignore land and assume that only labor and capital are used to produce two goods: computers and shoes. The long-run model is just like the Heckscher-Ohlin model studied in the previous chapter except that we now allow labor to move between countries. (Later in the chapter, we allow capital to move between the countries.)

The amount of capital used in computers is K_C, and the amount of capital used in shoe production is K_S. These quantities add up to the total capital available in the economy: $K_C + K_S = \overline{K}$. Because capital is fully mobile between the two sectors in the

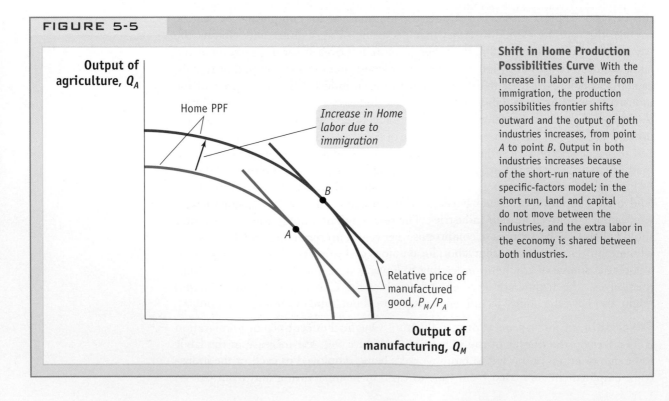

FIGURE 5-5

Shift in Home Production Possibilities Curve With the increase in labor at Home from immigration, the production possibilities frontier shifts outward and the output of both industries increases, from point A to point B. Output in both industries increases because of the short-run nature of the specific-factors model; in the short run, land and capital do not move between the industries, and the extra labor in the economy is shared between both industries.

long run, it must earn the same rental R in each. The amount of labor used to manufacture computers is L_C, and the labor used in shoe production is L_S. These amounts add up to the total labor in the economy, $L_C + L_S = \overline{L}$, and all labor earns the same wage of W in both sectors.

In our analysis, we make the realistic assumption that more labor per machine is used in shoe production than in computer production. That assumption means that shoe production is labor-intensive compared with computer production, so the labor–capital ratio in shoes is higher than it is in computers: $L_S/K_S > L_C/K_C$. Computer production, then, is capital-intensive compared with shoes, and the capital–labor ratio is higher in computers: $K_C/L_C > K_S/L_S$.

The PPF for an economy producing shoes and computers is shown in Figure 5-6. Given the prices of both goods (determined by supply and demand in world markets), the equilibrium outputs are shown at point A, at the tangency of the PPF and world relative price line. Our goal in this section is to see how the equilibrium is affected by having an inflow of labor into Home as a result of immigration.

"You seem familiar, yet somehow strange— are you by any chance Canadian?"

Box Diagram To analyze the effect of immigration, it is useful to develop a new diagram to keep track of the amount of labor and capital used in each industry. Shown as a "box diagram" in Figure 5-7, the length of the top and bottom horizontal axes is the total amount of labor $\overline{L}$ at Home, and the length of the right and left vertical axes is the total amount of capital $\overline{K}$ at Home. A point like point A in the diagram indicates that $0_S L$ units of labor and $0_S K$ units of capital are used in shoes, while $0_C L$ units of labor and $0_C K$ units of capital are used in computers. Another way to express this is that the line $0_S A$ shows the amount of labor and capital used in shoes and the line $0_C A$ shows the amount of labor and capital used in computers.

FIGURE 5-6

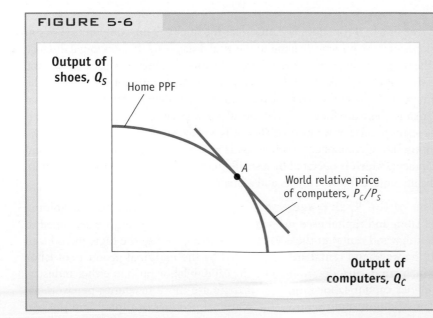

Production Possibilities Frontier Shown here is the production possibilities frontier (PPF) between two manufactured goods, computers and shoes, with initial equilibrium at point A. Domestic production takes place at point A, which is the point of tangency between the world price line and the PPF.

FIGURE 5-7

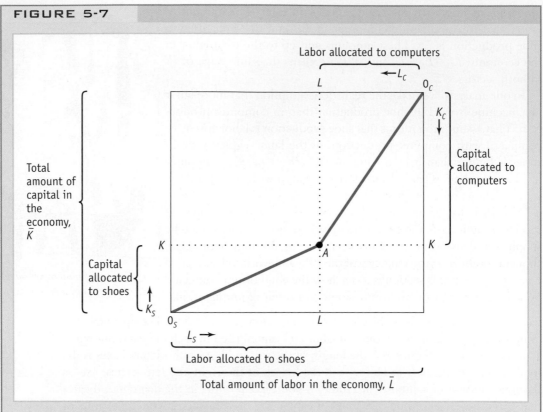

Allocation of Labor and Capital in a Box Diagram The top and bottom axes of the box diagram measure the amount of labor, $\bar{L}$, in the economy, and the side axes measure the amount of capital, $\bar{K}$. At point A, $0_S L$ units of labor and $0_S K$ units of capital are used in shoe production, and $0_C L$ units of labor and $0_C K$ units of capital are used in computers. The K/L ratios in the two industries are measured by the slopes of $0_S A$ and $0_C A$, respectively.

Notice that the line $0_S A$ for shoes is flatter than the line $0_C A$ for computers. We can calculate the slopes of these lines by dividing the vertical distance by the horizontal distance (the rise over the run). The slope of $0_S A$ is $0_S K / 0_S L$, the capital–labor ratio used in the shoe industry. Likewise, the slope of $0_C A$ is $0_C K / 0_C L$, the capital–labor ratio for computers. The line $0_S A$ is flatter than $0_C A$, so the capital–labor ratio in the shoe industry is less than that in computers; that is, there are fewer units of capital per worker in the shoe industry. This is precisely the assumption that we made earlier. It is a realistic assumption given that the manufacture of computer components such as semiconductors requires highly precise and expensive equipment, which is operated by a small number of workers. Shoe production, on the other hand, requires more workers and a smaller amount of capital.

Determination of the Real Wage and Real Rental In addition to determining the amount of labor and capital used in each industry in the long run, we also need to determine the wage and rental in the economy. To do so, we use the logic introduced in Chapter 3: the wage and rental are determined by the marginal products of labor and capital, which are in turn determined by the capital–labor ratio in either industry. If there is a higher capital–labor ratio (i.e., if there are more machines per worker), then by the law of diminishing returns, the marginal product of capital and the real rental must be lower. Having more machines per worker means that the marginal product of labor (and hence the real wage) is higher because each worker is more productive. On the other hand, if there is a higher labor–capital ratio (more workers per machine), then the marginal product of labor must be lower because of diminishing returns, and hence the real wage is lower, too. In addition, having more workers per machine means that the marginal product of capital and the real rental are both higher.

The important point to remember is that each amount of labor and capital used in Figure 5-7 along line $0_S A$ corresponds to a particular capital–labor ratio for shoe manufacture and therefore a particular real wage and real rental. We now consider how the labor and capital used in each industry will change due to immigration at Home. Although the total amount of labor and capital used in each industry changes, we will show that the capital–labor ratios are unaffected by immigration, which means that the immigrants can be absorbed with no change at all in the real wage and real rental.

Increase in the Amount of Home Labor Suppose that because of immigration, the amount of labor at Home increases from $\overline{L}$ to $\overline{L}' = \overline{L} + \Delta L$. This increase expands the labor axes in the box diagram, as shown in Figure 5-8. Rather than allocating $\overline{L}$ labor and $\overline{K}$ capital between the two industries, we must now allocate $\overline{L}'$ labor and

FIGURE 5-8

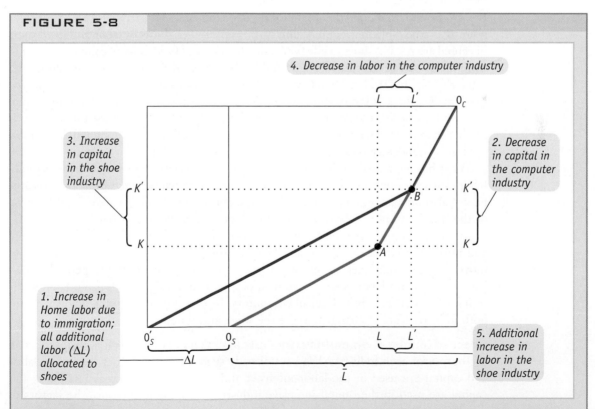

Increase in Home Labor With an increase in Home labor from $\overline{L}$ to $\overline{L} + \Delta L$, the origin for the shoe industry shifts from 0_S to $0'_S$. At point B, $0'_S L'$ units of labor and $0'_S K'$ units of capital are used in shoes, whereas $0_C L'$ units of labor and $0_C K'$ units of capital are used in computers. In the long run, industry outputs adjust so that the capital–labor ratios in each industry at point B (the slopes of $0'_S B$ and $0_C B$) are unchanged from the initial equilibrium at point A (the slopes of $0_S A$ and $0_C A$). To achieve this outcome, all new labor resulting from immigration is allocated to the shoe industry, and capital and *additional* labor are transferred from computers to shoes, keeping the capital–labor ratio in both industries unchanged.

$\overline{K}$ capital. The question is how much labor and capital will be used in each industry so that the total amount of both factors is fully employed?

You might think that the only way to employ the extra labor is to allocate more of it to both industries (as occurred in the short-run specific-factors model). This outcome would tend to lower the marginal product of labor in both industries and therefore lower the wage. But it turns out that such an outcome will not occur in the long-run model because when capital is also able to move between the industries, industry outputs will adjust to keep the capital–labor ratios in each industry constant. Instead of allocating the extra labor to both industries, all the extra labor (ΔL) will be allocated to shoes, the *labor*-intensive industry. Moreover, along with that extra labor, some capital is withdrawn from computers and allocated to shoes. To maintain the capital–labor ratio in the computer industry, some labor will also leave the computer industry, along with the capital, and go to the shoe industry. Because all the new workers in the shoe industry (immigrants plus former computer workers) have the same amount of capital to work with as the shoe workers prior to immigration, the capital–labor ratio in the shoe industry stays the same. *In this way, the capital–labor ratio in each industry is unchanged and the additional labor in the economy is fully employed.*

This outcome is illustrated in Figure 5-8, where the initial equilibrium is at point A. With the inflow of labor due to immigration, the labor axis expands from $\overline{L}$ to $\overline{L} + \Delta L$, from 0_S to $0'_S$, and the origin for the shoe industry shifts from 0_S to $0'_S$. Consider point B as a possible new equilibrium. At this point, $0'_S L'$ units of labor and $0'_S K'$ units of capital are used in shoes, while $0_C L'$ units of labor and $0_C K'$ units of capital are used in computers. Notice that the lines $0_S A$ and $0'_S B$ are parallel and have the same slope, and similarly, the lines $0_C A$ and $0_C B$ have the same slope. The extra labor has been employed by *expanding* the amount of labor and capital used in shoes (the line $0'_S B$ is longer than $0_S A$) and *contracting* the amount of labor and capital used in computers (the line $0_C B$ is smaller than $0_C A$). That the lines have the same slope means that the capital–labor ratio used in each industry is exactly the same before and after the inflow of labor.

What has happened to the wage and rentals in the economy? Because the capital–labor ratios are unchanged in both industries, the marginal products of labor and capital are also unchanged. Therefore, the wage and rental do not change at all because of the immigration of labor! This result is very different from what happens in the short-run specific-factors model, which showed that immigration depressed the wage and raised the rental on capital and land. In the long-run model, when capital can move between industries, an inflow of labor has no impact on the wage and rental. Instead, the extra labor is employed in shoes, by combining it with capital and additional labor that has shifted out of computers. In that way, the capital–labor ratios in both industries are unchanged, as are the wage and rental.

Effect of Immigration on Industry Outputs What is the effect of immigration on the output of each industry? We have already seen from Figure 5-8 that more labor and capital are used in the labor-intensive industry (shoes), whereas less labor and capital are used in the capital-intensive industry (computers). Because the factors of production both increase or both decrease, it follows that the output of shoes expands and the output of computers contracts.

This outcome is shown in Figure 5-9, which shows the outward shift of the PPF due to the increase in the labor endowment at Home. Given the prices of computers and shoes, the initial equilibrium was at point A. At this point, the slope of the PPF equals the relative price of computers, as shown by the slope of the line tangent to the

FIGURE 5-9

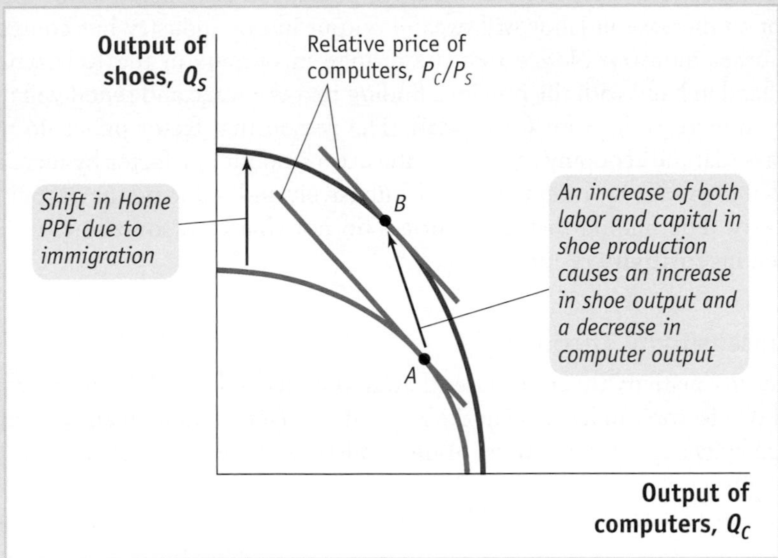

The Long-Run Effect on Industry Outputs of an Increase in Home Labor With an increase in the amount of labor at Home, the PPF shifts outward. The output of shoes increases, while the output of computers declines as the equilibrium moves from point A to B. The prices of goods have not changed, so the slopes of the PPFs at points A and B (i.e., the relative price of computers) are equal.

PPF. With unchanged prices for the goods, and more labor in the economy, the equilibrium moves to point *B*, with greater output of shoes but reduced output of computers. Notice that the slope of the PPFs at points *A* and *B* is identical because the relative price of computers is unchanged. As suggested by the diagram, the expansion in the amount of labor leads to an uneven outward shift of the PPF—it shifts out more in the direction of shoes (the labor-intensive industry) than in the direction of computers. This asymmetric shift illustrates that the new labor is employed in shoes and that this additional labor pulls capital and additional labor out of computers in the long run, to establish the new equilibrium at point *B*. *The finding that an increase in labor will expand one industry but contract the other holds only in the long run; in the short run, as we saw in Figure 5-5, both industries will expand.* This finding, called the **Rybczynski theorem,** shows how much the long-run model differs from the short-run model. The long-run result is named after the economist T. N. Rybczynski, who first discovered it.

Rybczynski Theorem

The formal statement of the Rybczynski theorem is as follows: in the Heckscher-Ohlin model with two goods and two factors, an increase in the amount of a factor found in an economy will increase the output of the industry using that factor intensively and decrease the output of the other industry.

We have proved the Rybczynski theorem for the case of immigration, in which labor in the economy grows. As we find later in the chapter, the same theorem holds when capital in the economy grows: in this case, the industry using capital intensively expands and the other industry contracts.[8]

---

[8] Furthermore, the Rybczynski theorem can be used to compare the output of the same industry across two countries, where the two countries have identical technologies but differing factor endowments as in the Heckscher-Ohlin model. See Problem 7 at the end of the chapter.

Effect of Immigration on Factor Prices The Rybczynski theorem, which applies to the long-run Heckscher-Ohlin model with two goods and two factors of production, states that an increase in labor will expand output in one industry but contract output in the other industry. Notice that the change in outputs in the Rybczynski theorem goes hand in hand with the previous finding that the wage and rental will not change due to an increase in labor (or capital). The reason that factor prices do not need to change is that the economy can absorb the extra amount of a factor by increasing the output of the industry using that factor intensively and reducing the output of the other industry. The finding that factor prices do not change is sometimes called the **factor price insensitivity** result.

Factor Price Insensitivity Theorem

The factor price insensitivity theorem states that: in the Heckscher-Ohlin model with two goods and two factors, an increase in the amount of a factor found in an economy can be absorbed by changing the outputs of the industries, without any change in the factor prices.

The applications that follow offer evidence of changes in output that absorb new additions to the labor force, as predicted by the Rybczynski theorem, without requiring large changes in factor prices, as predicted by the factor price insensitivity result.

APPLICATION

The Effects of the Mariel Boat Lift on Industry Output in Miami

Now that we have a better understanding of long-run adjustments due to changes in factor endowments, let us return to the case of the Mariel boat lift to Miami in 1980. We know that the Cuban refugees were less skilled than the average labor force in Miami. According to the Rybczynski theorem, then, we expect some unskilled-labor–intensive industry, such as footwear or apparel, to expand. In addition, we expect that some skill-intensive industry, such as the high-tech industry, will contract. Figure 5-10 shows how this prediction lines up with the evidence from Miami and some comparison cities.[9]

Panel (a) of Figure 5-10 shows real value-added in the apparel industry for Miami and for an average of comparison cities. **Real value-added** measures the payments to labor and capital in an industry corrected for inflation. Thus, real value-added is a way to measure the output of the industry. We divide output by the population of the city to obtain real value-added per capita, which measures the output of the industry adjusted for the city size.

Panel (a) shows that the apparel industry was declining in Miami and the comparison cities before 1980. After the boat lift, the industry continued to decline but at a slower rate in Miami; the trend of output per capita for Miami has a smaller slope (and hence a smaller rate of decline in output) than that of the trend for comparison cities from 1980 onward. Notice that there is an increase in industry output in Miami from 1983 to 1984 (which may be due to new data collected that year), but even when averaging this out as the trend lines do, the industry decline in Miami is slightly

---

[9] Figure 5-10 and the material in this application are drawn from Ethan Lewis, 2004, "How Did the Miami Labor Market Absorb the Mariel Immigrants?" Federal Reserve Bank of Philadelphia Working Paper No. 04-3.

FIGURE 5-10

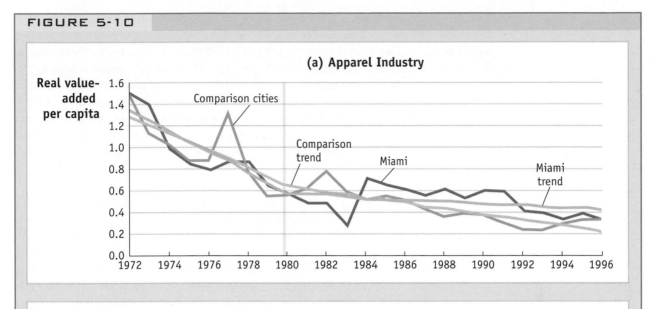

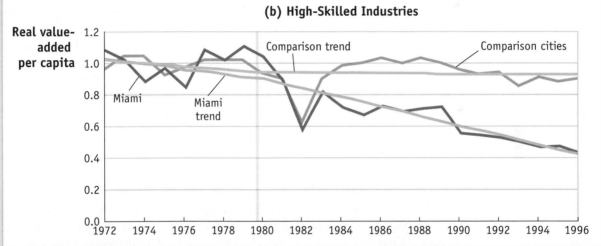

Industry Value-Added in Miami Shown here are real value-added in the apparel industry and in high-skilled industries (measured relative to the city population), for Miami and an average of comparison cities. In panel (a), with the inflow of refugees from Cuba in 1980, real value-added in the apparel industry in Miami rose from 1983 to 1984, and the trend decline of this industry in Miami was slower (i.e., value-added did not fall as fast) after 1980 than in the comparison cities. In panel (b), real value-added in Miami in high-skilled industries fell faster after 1980 than in the comparison cities. Both these findings are consistent with the Rybczynski theorem.

Source: Ethan Lewis, 2004, "How Did the Miami Labor Market Absorb the Mariel Immigrants?" Federal Reserve Bank of Philadelphia Working Paper No. 04–3.

slower than in the comparison cities after 1980. This graph provides some evidence of the Rybczynski theorem at work: the reduction in the apparel industry in Miami was slower than it would have been without the inflow of immigrants.

What about the second prediction of the Rybczynski theorem: Did the output of any other industry in Miami fall because of the immigration? Panel (b) of Figure 5-10 shows that the output of a group of skill-intensive industries (including motor vehicles, electronic equipment, and aircraft) fell more rapidly in Miami after 1980. These data may also provide some evidence in favor of the Rybczynski theorem. However, it also happened that with the influx of refugees, there was a flight of homeowners away from Miami, and some of these were probably high-skilled workers. So the decline in the group of skill-intensive industries, shown in panel (b), could instead be due to this population decline. The change in industry outputs in Miami provides some evidence in favor of the Rybczynski theorem. Do these changes in industry outputs in Miami also provide an adequate explanation for why wages of unskilled workers did not decline, or is there some other explanation? An alternative explanation for the finding that wages did not change comes from comparing the use of computers in Miami with national trends. Beginning in the early 1980s, computers became increasingly used in the workplace. The adoption of computers is called a "skill-biased technological change." That is, computers led to an increase in the demand for high-skilled workers and reduced the hiring of low-skilled workers. This trend occurred across the United States and in other countries.

In Miami, however, computers were adopted somewhat more slowly than in cities with similar industry mix and ethnic populations. One explanation for this finding is that firms in many industries, not just apparel, employed the Mariel refugees and other low-skilled workers rather than switching to computer technologies. Evidence to support this finding is that the Mariel refugees were, in fact, employed in many industries. Only about 20% worked in manufacturing (5% in apparel), and the remainder worked in service industries. The idea that the firms may have slowed the adoption of new technologies to employ the Mariel emigrants is hard to prove conclusively, however. We suggest it here as an alternative to the Rybczynski theorem to explain how the refugees could be absorbed across many industries rather than just in the industries using unskilled labor, such as apparel. ■

APPLICATION

Immigration and U.S. Wages, 1990–2006

In 1980, the year of the Mariel boat lift, the percentage of foreign-born people in the U.S. population was 6.2%. The percentage grew to 9.1% in 1990 and then to 13.0% in 2005, so there was slightly more than a doubling of foreign-born people in 25 years.[10] That period saw the greatest recent increase in foreign-born people in the United States, and by 2010 the percentage had grown only slightly more, to 13.5%. How did the wave of immigration prior to 2006 affect U.S. wages?

Part A of Table 5-1 reports the estimated impact of the immigration from 1990 to 2006 on the wages of various workers, distinguished by their educational level. The first row in part A summarizes the estimates from the specific-factors model, when capital and land are kept fixed within all industries. As we discussed in an earlier application, the greatest negative impact of immigration is on native-born workers with less than 12 years of education, followed by college graduates, and then followed by high school graduates and those with some college. Overall, the average impact of immigration on U.S. wages over the period of 1990–2006 was –3.0%. That is, wages fell by 3.0%, consistent with the specific-factors model.

[10] This information on foreign-born people is available from the United Nations, at http://www.esa.un.org/migration.

TABLE 5-1

Immigration and Wages in the United States This table shows the estimated effect of immigration on the wages of workers, depending on their educational level, from 1990–2006. Short-run estimates hold capital and land fixed, while long-run estimates allow capital to adjust so that the capital/labor ratio and real rental are constant in the economy. Part A shows the impact of immigration assuming that U.S.-born and foreign-born workers are perfect substitutes. Immigration has the greatest impact on workers with very low or high levels of education and only a small impact on those workers with middle levels of education (12 to 15 years). The impact is even smaller in the long run, when capital adjusts to keep the real rental on capital fixed. Part B shows long-run estimates when U.S.-born and foreign-born workers in the U.S. are imperfect substitutes. In this case, immigrants compete especially strongly with other foreign-born workers by lowering their wages, and can potentially complement the activities of U.S.-born workers.

	PERCENTAGE CHANGE IN THE WAGE OF WORKERS WITH EDUCATIONAL LEVEL				
	Less Than 12 Years	High School Graduate	Some College	College Graduates	Overall Average
Part A: Effect of Immigration on All U.S. Workers					
Method:					
Short run	−7.8	−2.2	−0.9	−4.7	−3.0
Long run	−4.7	0.9	2.2	−1.7	0.1
Part B: Long-Run Effect of Immigration, by Type of Worker					
Type of Worker:					
U.S. born	0.3	0.4	0.9	0.5	0.6
Foreign born	−4.9	−7.0	−4.0	−8.1	−6.4

Sources: Gianmarco I. P. Ottaviano and Giovanni Peri, 2012, "Rethinking The Effect Of Immigration On Wages," Journal of the European Economic Association, European Economic Association, vol. 10(1), 152–197; and Gianmarco I.P. Ottaviano and Giovanni Peri, 2008, "Immigration and National Wages: Clarifying the Theory and the Empirics." National Bureau of Economic Research working paper no. 14188, Tables 7–8.

A different story emerges, however, if instead of keeping capital fixed, we hold constant the capital–labor ratio in the economy and the real rental on capital. Under this approach, we allow capital to grow to accommodate the inflow of immigrants, so that there is no change in the real rental. This approach is similar to the long-run model we have discussed, except that we now distinguish several types of labor by their education levels. In the second row of part A, we see that total U.S. immigration had a negative impact on workers with the lowest and highest levels of education and a *positive* impact on the other workers (due to the growth in capital). With these new assumptions, we see that the average U.S. wage rose by 0.1% because of immigration (combined with capital growth), rather than falling by 3.0%.

The finding that the average U.S. wage is nearly constant in the long run (rising by just 0.1%) is similar to our long-run model in which wages do not change because of immigration. However, the finding that some workers gain (wages rise for the middle education levels) and others lose (wages fall for the lowest and the highest education levels) is different from our long-run model. There are two reasons for this outcome. First, as we already noted, Table 5-1 categorizes workers by different education levels. Even when the *overall* capital–labor ratio is fixed, and the real rental on capital is fixed, it is still possible for the wages of workers with certain education levels to change. Second, we can refer back to the U-shaped pattern of immigration shown in

Figure 5-4, where the fraction of immigrants in the U.S. workforce is largest for the lowest and highest education levels. It is not surprising, then, that these two groups face the greatest loss in wages due to an inflow of immigrants.

We can dig a little deeper to better understand the long-run wage changes in part A. In part A, we assumed that U.S.-born workers and foreign-born workers in each education level are perfect substitutes, that is, they do the same types of jobs and have the same abilities. In reality, evidence shows that U.S. workers and immigrants often end up doing different types of jobs, even when they have similar education. In part B of Table 5-1, we build in this realistic feature by treating U.S.-born workers and foreign-born workers in each education level as imperfect substitutes. Just as the prices of goods that are imperfect substitutes (for example, different types of cell phones) can differ, the wages of U.S.-born and foreign-born workers with the same education can also differ. This modification to our assumptions leads to a substantial change in the results.

In part B of Table 5-1, we find that immigration now raises the wages of all U.S.-born workers in the long run, by 0.6% on average. That slight rise occurs because the U.S-born and foreign-born workers are doing different jobs that can complement one another. For example, on a construction site, an immigrant worker with limited language skills can focus on physical tasks, while a U.S. worker can focus on tasks involving personal interaction. Part B shows another interesting outcome: the 1990–2006 immigration had the greatest impact on the wages of all other foreign-born workers, whose wages fell by an average of 6.4% in the long run. When we allow for imperfect substitution between U.S.-born and foreign-born workers, immigrants compete especially strongly with other foreign-born workers, and can potentially complement the activities of U.S.-born workers. Contrary to popular belief, immigrants don't necessarily lower the wages for U.S. workers with similar educational backgrounds. Instead, immigrants can raise wages for U.S. workers if the two groups are doing jobs that are complementary. ■

2 Movement of Capital Between Countries: Foreign Direct Investment

To continue our examination of what happens to wages and rentals when factors can move across borders, we turn now to look at how capital can move from one country to another through **foreign direct investment (FDI),** which occurs when a firm from one country owns a company in another country. How much does the company have to own for foreign direct investment to occur? Definitions vary, but the Department of Commerce in the United States uses 10%: if a foreign company acquires 10% or more of a U.S. firm, then that is counted as an FDI inflow to the United States, and if a U.S. company acquires 10% or more of a foreign firm, then that is counted as an FDI outflow from the United States.

When a company builds a plant in a foreign country, it is sometimes called "greenfield FDI" (because we imagine the site for the plant starting with grass on it). When a firm buys an existing foreign plant, it is called "acquisition FDI" (or sometimes "brownfield FDI"). Having capital move from high-wage to low-wage countries to earn a higher rental is the traditional view of FDI, and the viewpoint we take in this chapter.[11]

---

[11] As discussed in Chapter 1, there are many instances of FDI that do not fit with this traditional view.

Greenfield Investment

Our focus in this section will be on greenfield investment; that is, the building of new plants abroad. We model FDI as a movement of capital between countries, just as we modeled the movement of labor between countries. The key question we ask is: How does the movement of capital into a country affect the earnings of labor and capital there? This question is similar to the one we asked for immigration, so the earlier graphs that we developed can be modified to address FDI.

FDI in the Short Run: Specific-Factors Model

We begin by modeling FDI in the short run, using the specific-factors model. In that model, the manufacturing industry uses capital and labor and the agriculture industry uses land and labor, so as capital flows into the economy, it will be used in manufacturing. The additional capital will raise the marginal product of labor in manufacturing because workers there have more machines with which to work. Therefore, as capital flows into the economy, it will shift out the curve $P_M \cdot MPL_M$ for the manufacturing industry as shown in panel (a) of Figure 5-11.

Effect of FDI on the Wage As a result of this shift, the equilibrium wage increases, from W to W'. More workers are drawn into the manufacturing industry, and the labor used there increases from $0_M L$ to $0_M L'$. Because these workers are pulled out of agriculture, the labor used there shrinks from $0_A L$ to $0_A L'$ (measuring from right to left).

FIGURE 5-11

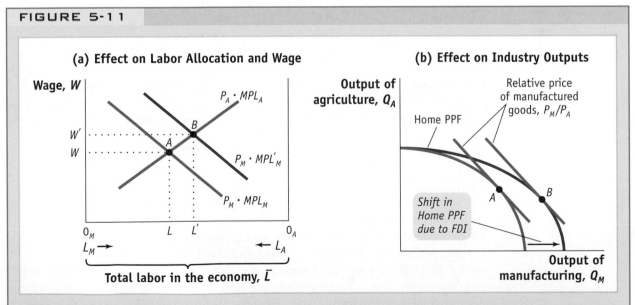

(a) Effect on Labor Allocation and Wage

(b) Effect on Industry Outputs

Increase in the Capital Stock in the Short Run In panel (a), an inflow of capital into the manufacturing sector shifts out the marginal product of labor curve in that sector. The equilibrium in the labor market moves from point A to B, and the wage increases from W to W'. Labor used in the manufacturing industry increases from $0_M L$ to $0_M L'$. These workers are pulled out of agriculture, so the labor used there shrinks from $0_A L$ to $0_A L'$.

In panel (b), with the inflow of capital into manufacturing, and the extra labor used in that sector, the output of manufacturing increases. Because labor has been drawn out of agriculture, the output of that sector falls. These changes in outputs are shown by the outward shift of the PPF (due to the increase in capital) and the movement from point A to point B.

Effect of FDI on the Industry Outputs It is easy to determine the effect of an inflow of FDI on industry outputs. Because workers are pulled out of agriculture, and there is no change in the amount of land used there, output of the agriculture industry must fall. With an increase in the number of workers used in manufacturing and an increase in capital used there, the output of the manufacturing industry must rise. These changes in output are shown in panel (b) of Figure 5-11 by the outward shift of the production possibilities frontier. At constant prices for goods (i.e., the relative price lines have the same slope before and after the increase in capital), the equilibrium outputs shift from point A to point B, with more manufacturing output and less agricultural output.

Effect of FDI on the Rentals Finally, we can determine the impact of the inflow of capital on the rental earned by capital and the rental earned by land. It is easiest to start with the agriculture industry. Because fewer workers are employed there, each acre of land cannot be cultivated as intensively as before, and the marginal product of land must fall. One way to measure the rental on land T is by the value of its marginal product, $R_T = P_A \cdot MPT_A$. With the fall in the marginal product of land (MPT_A), and no change in the price of agricultural goods, the rental on land falls.

Now let us consider manufacturing, which uses more capital and more labor than before. One way to measure the rental on capital is by the value of the marginal product of capital, or $R_K = P_M \cdot MPK_M$. Using this method, however, it is difficult to determine how the rental on capital changes. As capital flows into manufacturing, the marginal product of capital falls because of diminishing returns. That effect reduces the rental on capital. But as labor is drawn into manufacturing, the marginal product of capital tends to rise. So we do not know at first glance how the rental on capital changes overall.

Fortunately, we can resolve this difficulty by using another method to measure the rental on capital. We take the revenue earned in manufacturing and subtract the payments to labor. If wages are higher, and everything else is the same, then there must be a reduced amount of funds left over as earnings of capital, so the rental is lower.

Let us apply this line of reasoning more carefully to see how the inflow of FDI affects the rental on capital. In Figure 5-12, we begin at point A and then assume the capital stock expands because of FDI. Suppose we hold the wage constant, and let the labor used in manufacturing expand up to point C. Because the wage is the same at points A and C, the marginal product of labor in manufacturing must also be the same (since the wage is $W = P_M \cdot MPL_M$). The only way that the marginal product of labor can remain constant is for each worker to have the same amount of capital to work with as he or she had before the capital inflow. In other words, the capital–labor ratio in manufacturing L_M/K_M must be the same at points A and C: the expansion of capital in manufacturing is just matched by a proportional expansion of labor into manufacturing. But if the capital–labor ratio in manufacturing is identical at points A and C, then the marginal product of capital must also be equal at these two points (because each machine has the same number of people working on it). Therefore, the rental on capital, $R_K = P_M \cdot MPK_M$, is also equal at points A and C.

Now let's see what happens as the manufacturing wage increases while holding constant the amount of capital used in that sector. The increase in the wage will move us up the curve $P_M \cdot MPL'_M$ from point C to point B. As the wage rises, less labor is used in manufacturing. With less labor used on each machine in manufacturing, the marginal product of capital and the rental on capital must fall. This result confirms

FIGURE 5-12

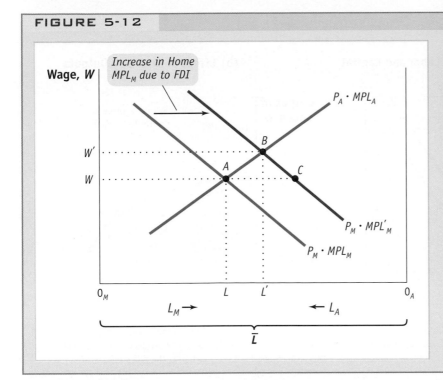

The Effect of an Increase in Capital Stock on the Rental on Capital By carefully tracing through how the capital–labor ratio in manufacturing is affected by the movement from A to C (where wages and hence the capital–labor ratio do not change), and then the movement from C to B (where wages and the capital–labor ratio both increase), we conclude that the rental on capital is lower at point B than at point A. Therefore, the rental on capital declines when the capital stock increases through FDI.

our earlier reasoning: when wages are higher and the amount of capital used in manufacturing is the same, then the earnings of capital (i.e., its rental) must be lower. Because the rental on capital is the same at points A and C but is lower at point B than C, the overall effect of the FDI inflow is to reduce the rental on capital. We learned previously that the FDI inflow also reduces the rental on land, so both rentals fall.

FDI in the Long Run

The results of FDI in the long run, when capital and labor can move between industries, differ from those we saw in the short-run specific-factors model. To model FDI in the long run, we assume again that there are two industries—computers and shoes—both of which use two factors of production: labor and capital. Computers are capital-intensive as compared with shoes, meaning that K_C/L_C exceeds K_S/L_S.

In panel (a) of Figure 5-13, we show the initial allocation of labor and capital between the two industries at point A. The labor and capital used in the shoe industry are $0_S L$ and $0_S K$, so this combination is measured by the line $0_S A$. The labor and capital used in computers are $0_C L$ and $0_C K$, so this combination is measured by the line $0_C A$. That amount of labor and capital used in each industry produces the output of shoes and computers shown by point A on the PPF in panel (b).

Effect of FDI on Outputs and Factor Prices An inflow of FDI causes the amount of capital in the economy to increase. That increase expands the right and left sides of the box in panel (a) of Figure 5-13 and shifts the origin up to $0'_C$. The new allocation of factors between the industries is shown at point B. Now the labor and capital used in the shoe industry are measured by $0_S B$, which is shorter than the line $0_S A$. Therefore, less labor and less capital are used in the production of footwear, and shoe

FIGURE 5-13

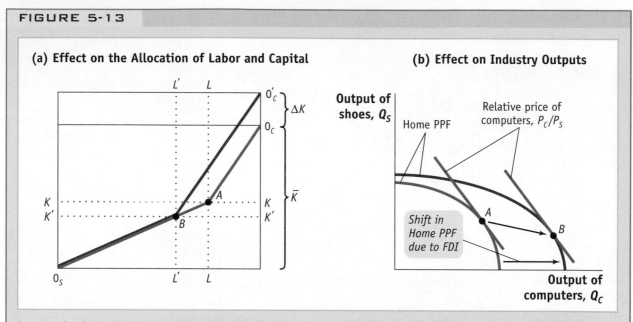

(a) Effect on the Allocation of Labor and Capital

(b) Effect on Industry Outputs

Increase in the Capital Stock in the Long Run In panel (a), the top and bottom axes of the box diagram measure the amount of labor in the economy, and the right and left axes measure the amount of capital. The initial equilibrium is at point A. When there is an inflow of capital, the equilibrium moves to point B. Similar to the box diagram for immigration (Figure 5-8), the K/L ratios remain unchanged by allocating the new capital, as well as additional capital and labor from shoes, to computers. In panel (b), with the increase in the amount of capital at Home from increased FDI, the PPF shifts outward. The output of computers increases while the output of shoes declines as the equilibrium moves from point A to B. Because the prices of goods have not changed, the slopes of the PPFs at points A and B are equal.

output falls. The labor and capital used in computers are measured by $0'_C B$, which is longer than the line $0_C A$. Therefore, more labor and more capital are used in computers, and the output of that industry rises.

The change in outputs of shoes and computers is shown by the shift from point A to point B in panel (b) of Figure 5-13. In accordance with the Rybczynski theorem, the increase in capital through FDI has increased the output of the capital-intensive industry (computers) and reduced the output of the labor-intensive industry (shoes). Furthermore, this change in outputs is achieved *with no change* in the capital–labor ratios in either industry: the lines $0'_C B$ and $0_S B$ have the same slopes as $0_C A$ and $0_S A$, respectively.

Because the capital–labor ratios are unchanged in the two industries, the wage and the rental on capital are also unchanged. Each person has the same amount of capital to work with in his or her industry, and each machine has the same number of workers. The marginal products of labor and capital are unchanged in the two industries, as are the factor prices. This outcome is basically the same as that for immigration in the long run: in the long-run model, an inflow of *either* factor of production will leave factor prices unchanged.

When discussing immigration, we found cases in which wages were reduced (the short-run prediction) and other cases in which wages have been constant (the long-run prediction). What about for foreign direct investment? Does it tend to lower rentals or leave them unchanged? There are fewer studies of this question, but we next consider an important application for Singapore.

The Effect of FDI on Rentals and Wages in Singapore

For many years, Singapore has encouraged foreign firms to establish subsidiaries within its borders, especially in the electronics industry. For example, many hard disks are manufactured in Singapore by foreign companies. In 2005 Singapore had the fourth largest amount of FDI in the world (measured by stock of foreign capital found there), following China, Mexico, and Brazil, even though it is much smaller than those economies.[12] As capital in Singapore has grown, what has happened to the rental and to the wage?

One way to answer this question is to estimate the marginal product of capital in Singapore, using a production function that applies to the entire economy. The overall capital–labor ratio in Singapore has grown by about 5% per year from 1970 to 1990. Because of diminishing returns, it follows that the marginal product of capital (equal to the real rental) has fallen, by an average of 3.4% per year as shown in part A of Table 5-2. At the same time, each worker has more capital to work with, so the marginal product of labor (equal to the real wage) has grown by an average of

---

TABLE 5-2

Real Rental and Wages in Singapore This table shows the growth rate in the real rental and real wages in Singapore, depending on the method used to construct these factor prices. In part A, a production function approach is used to construct the factor prices, and the real rental falls over time because of the growth in capital. As a result, implied productivity growth is negative. In part B, the rental and wages are constructed from data on payments to capital and labor in Singapore, and real wages grow over time, while the real rental either grows or falls slightly. As a result, implied productivity growth is positive.

	ANNUAL GROWTH RATE (%)		
	Real Rental	**Real Wages**	**Implied Productivity**
Part A: Using Production Function and Marginal Products			
Period:			
1970–1980	−5.0	2.6	−1.5
1980–1990	−1.9	0.5	−0.7
1970–1990	−3.4	1.6	−1.1
Part B: Using Calculated Rental and Actual Wages			
Interest Rate Used and Period:			
Bank lending rate (1968–1990)	1.6	2.7	2.2
Return on equity (1971–1990)	−0.2	3.2	1.5
Earnings-price ratio (1973–1990)	−0.5	3.6	1.6

Sources: Part A from Alwyn Young, 1995, "The Tyranny of Numbers: Confronting the Statistical Realities of the East Asian Growth Experience," Quarterly Journal of Economics, 110(3), August, 641–680.

Part B from Chang-Tai Hsieh, 2002, "What Explains the Industrial Revolution in East Asia? Evidence from the Factor Markets," American Economic Review, 92(3), 502–526.

---

[12] In 2005, China had $318 billion in foreign capital, with another $533 billion in Hong Kong; Mexico had $210 billion; Brazil $202 billion; and Singapore $189 billion, which was 7% of the total foreign capital in developing countries.

1.6% per year, as also shown in part A. These estimates of the falling rental and rising wage are consistent with the short-run specific-factors model.

But there is a second way to calculate a rental on capital besides using the marginal product. Under this second approach, we start with the price P_K of some capital equipment. If that equipment were rented rather than purchased, what would its rental be? Let us suppose that the rental agency needs to make the same rate of return on renting the capital equipment that it would make if it invested its money in some financial asset, such as a savings account in a bank or the stock market. If it invested P_K and the asset had the interest rate of i, then it could expect to earn $P_K \cdot i$ from that asset. On the other hand, if it rents out the equipment, then that machinery also suffers wear and tear, and the rental agency needs to recover that cost, too. If d is the rate of depreciation of the capital equipment (the fraction of it that is used up each year), then to earn the same return on a financial asset as from renting out the equipment, the rental agency must receive $P_K \cdot (i + d)$. This formula is an estimate of R, the rental on capital. Dividing by an overall price index P, the real rental is

$$\frac{R}{P} = \frac{P_K}{P} \cdot (i + d)$$

In part B of Table 5-2, we show the growth rate in the real rental, computed from this formula, which depends on the interest rate used. In the first row, we use the bank lending rate for i, and the computed real rental grows by 1.6% per year. In the next rows, we use two interest rates from the stock market: the return on equity (what you would earn from investing in stocks) and the earnings–price ratio (the profits that each firm earns divided by the value of its outstanding stocks). In both these latter cases, the calculated real rental falls slightly over time, by 0.2% and 0.5% per year, much less than the fall in the real rental in part A. According to the calculated real rentals in part B, there is little evidence of a downward fall in the rentals over time.

In part B, we also show the real wage, computed from actual wages paid in Singapore. Real wages grow substantially over time—between 2.7% and 3.6% per year, depending on the exact interest rate and period used. This is not what we predicted from our long-run model, in which factor prices would be unchanged by an inflow of capital, because the capital–labor ratios are constant (so the marginal product of labor would not change). That real wages are growing in Singapore, with little change in the real rental, is an indication that there is *productivity growth* in the economy, which leads to an increase in the marginal product of labor *and* in the real wage.

We will not discuss how productivity growth is actually measured[13] but just report the findings from the studies in Table 5-2: in part B, productivity growth is between 1.5% and 2.2% per year, depending on the period, but in part A, productivity growth is negative! The reason that productivity growth is so much higher in part B is because the average of the growth in the real wage and real rental is rising, which indicates that productivity growth has occurred. In contrast, in part A the average of the growth in the real wage and real rental is zero or negative, indicating that no productivity growth has occurred.

The idea that Singapore might have zero productivity growth contradicts what many people believe about its economy and the economies of other fast-growing Asian countries, which were thought to exhibit "miraculous" growth during this period. If productivity growth is zero or negative, then all growth is due only to capital accumulation,

---

[13] The calculation of productivity growth is discussed in Problem 10.

and FDI has no spillover benefits to the local economy. Positive productivity growth, as shown in part B, indicates that the free-market policies pursued by Singapore stimulated innovations in the manufacture of goods that have resulted in higher productivity and lower costs. This is what many economists and policy makers believe happened in Singapore, but this belief is challenged by the productivity calculations in part A. Which scenario is correct—zero or positive productivity growth for Singapore—is a source of ongoing debate in economics. Read the item **Headlines: The Myth of Asia's Miracle** for one interpretation of the growth in Singapore and elsewhere in Asia. ■

3 Gains from Labor and Capital Flows

Foreign investment and immigration are both controversial policy issues. Most countries impose limits on FDI at some time in their development but later become open to foreign investment. Nearly all countries impose limits on the inflow of people. In

HEADLINES

The Myth of Asia's Miracle

A CAUTIONARY FABLE: Once upon a time, Western opinion leaders found themselves both impressed and frightened by the extraordinary growth rates achieved by a set of Eastern economies. Although those economies were still substantially poorer and smaller than those of the West, the speed with which they had transformed themselves from peasant societies into industrial powerhouses, their continuing ability to achieve growth rates several times higher than the advanced nations, and their increasing ability to challenge or even surpass American and European technology in certain areas seemed to call into question the dominance not only of Western

power but of Western ideology. The leaders of those nations did not share our faith in free markets or unlimited civil liberties. They asserted with increasing self-confidence that their system was superior: societies that accepted strong, even authoritarian governments and were willing to limit individual liberties in the interest of the common good, take charge of their economics, and sacrifice short-run consumer interests for the sake of long-run growth would eventually outperform the increasingly chaotic societies of the West. And a growing minority of Western intellectuals agreed.

The gap between Western and Eastern economic performance eventually be-

came a political issue. The Democrats recaptured the White House under the leadership of a young, energetic new president who pledged to "get the country moving again"—a pledge that, to him and his closest advisers, meant accelerating America's economic growth to meet the Eastern challenge.

The time, of course, was the early 1960s. The dynamic young president was John F. Kennedy. The technological feats that so alarmed the West were the launch of Sputnik and the early Soviet lead in space. And the rapidly growing Eastern economies were those of the Soviet Union and its satellite nations.

Were you tricked by this fable? Did you think that the "Eastern economies" that the author, Paul Krugman, referred to in the beginning were the Asian economies? Krugman is using this rhetorical trick to suggest that the high growth of the Asian economies is not too different from the growth of the Soviet Union in the 1950s and 1960s, which was due to capital accumulation but without much productivity growth. Other economists disagree and believe that Asian growth is due in significant part to improved productivity, in addition to capital accumulation.

Source: Excerpted from Paul Krugman, 1994, "The Myth of Asia's Miracle," Foreign Affairs, November/December, 63–79. Reprinted by permission of FOREIGN AFFAIRS, November/December. Copyright 1994 by the Council on Foreign Relations, Inc. www.ForeignAffairs.com.

the United States, controls on immigration were first established by the Quota Law of 1921, which limited the number of people arriving annually from each country of origin. The Immigration and Nationality Act Amendments of 1965 revised the country-specific limits and allowed immigration on a first-come, first-served basis, up to an annual limit, with special allowances for family members and people in certain occupations. Subsequent revisions to the immigration laws in the United States have established penalties for employers who knowingly hire illegal immigrants, have allowed some illegal immigrants to gain citizenship, or have tightened border controls and deported other illegal immigrants.

Why is immigration so controversial? A glance at articles in the newspaper or on the Internet will show that some groups oppose the spending of public funds on immigrants, such as for schooling, medical care, or welfare. Other groups fear the competition for jobs created by the inflow of foreign workers. We have already seen that immigration creates gains and losses for different groups, often lowering the wage for workers in similar jobs but providing benefits to firms hiring these workers.

This finding raises the important question: Does immigration provide an overall gain to the host country, not including the gains to the immigrants themselves? We presume that the immigrants are better off from higher wages in the country to which they move.[14] But what about the other workers and owners of capital and land in the host country? In the short run, we learned that workers in the host country face competition from the immigrants and receive lower wages, while owners of capital and land benefit from immigration. When we add up these various gains and losses, are there "overall gains" to the destination country, in the same way as we have found overall gains from trade? Fortunately, this answer turns out to be yes.

Immigration benefits the host country in the specific-factors model, not including the income of the immigrants themselves. If we include the immigrant earnings with Foreign income, then we find that emigration benefits the Foreign country, too. The same argument can be made for FDI. An inflow of capital benefits the host country, not including the extra earnings of foreign capital. By counting those extra earnings in Foreign income, then FDI also benefits the source country of the capital. After showing these theoretical results, we discuss how large the overall gains from immigration or FDI flows might be in practice.

Gains from Immigration

To measure the gains from immigration, we will use the specific-factors model. In Figure 5-14, we measure the *world* amount of labor on the horizontal axis, which equals $\overline{L} + \overline{L}^*$. The number of workers in the Home country $\overline{L}$ is measured from left (the origin 0) to right. The number of workers in Foreign $\overline{L}^*$ is measured from right (0^*) to left. Each point on the horizontal axis indicates how many workers are located in the two countries. For example, point L indicates that $0L$ workers are located in Home, and 0^*L workers are located in the Foreign country.

Wages at Home and Abroad We already know from our discussion earlier in the chapter that as immigrants enter the Home country, the wage is reduced. In Figure 5-14, we graph this relationship as a downward-sloping line labeled "Home

---

[14] This ignores cases in which the immigrants regret the decision to move because of hardship in making the passage or discrimination once they arrive.

FIGURE 5-14

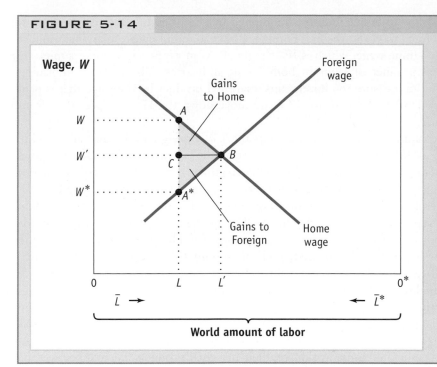

World Labor Market Initially, Home has $0L$ workers and Foreign has 0^*L workers. The Home wage is W, as determined at point A, which is higher than the Foreign wage W^* at A^*. Workers will move from Foreign to Home to receive higher wages. The equilibrium with full migration is at point B, where wages are equalized at W'. The gain to Home from migration is measured by triangle ABC, and triangle A^*BC represents the gains to Foreign.

wage." With Home workers of $0L$ before immigration, the wage is W at point A. If Foreign workers enter and the Home labor force grows to $0L'$, then the Home wage is reduced to W' at point B. The downward-sloping "Home wage" line illustrates the inverse relationship between the number of Home workers and their wage. You can think of this line as a labor demand curve, not for a single industry, but for the economy as a whole.

Similarly, in the Foreign country, there is an inverse relationship between the numbers of workers and their wage. Before any emigration, the labor force in Foreign is 0^*L, and we show the wage at W^* at point A^*. That is lower than the Home wage of W, so some workers will want to migrate from Foreign to Home. Remembering that we measure the Foreign workers from right (0^*) to left, when the labor force abroad shrinks from 0^*L to $0^*L'$, the Foreign wages rise from W^* to W' at point B. We see that as Foreign workers leave, it benefits those left behind by raising their wages.

We will refer to point B as the **equilibrium with full migration.** At this point, the wages earned at Home and abroad are equalized at W'. It would certainly take a long time for migration to lead to complete wage equality across countries. In our discussion of emigration from the Old World to the New, we saw in Figure 5-3 that real wages in the New World were still twice as high as wages in Europe even after 40 years of large-scale migration. So the equilibrium with full migration is reached only in the very long run. The question we want to answer is whether this migration has benefited the workers (not including the immigrants), labor, and capital in the Home country. In addition, we want to know whether migration has benefited the Foreign country, including the migrants.

Gains for the Home Country To determine whether there are overall gains for Home, we need to measure the contribution of each Foreign worker to the output of one good or the other in that country. This measurement is easy to do. The marginal product of labor in either industry (multiplied by the price of shoes or computers) equals the Home wage. So the first Foreign worker to migrate has a marginal product equal to the Home wage, which is W at point A. As more Foreign workers migrate, the marginal product of labor in both Home industries falls due to diminishing returns. We can measure the immigrants' marginal product by the wage that is paid at Home, which falls from W to W' as we move down the Home wage curve from point A to B.

At the equilibrium with full migration, point B, *all* Foreign immigrants are paid the Home wage of W'. But all Foreign workers except the last one to enter had a marginal product of labor that is above W': the first Foreign worker had a marginal product of W, and the later Foreign immigrants have lower marginal products, ranging from W to W'. Therefore, their contribution to the output of goods in the Home economy *exceeds* the wage that they are paid. The first Foreign immigrant had a marginal product of W but receives the wage W', so the gain to the Home economy from having that worker is $(W - W')$. Likewise, each immigrant to come later has a marginal product between W and W' but is still paid the wage W', so the difference between their marginal products and wages is a gain for the Home economy.

Adding the gains to the Home economy from the Foreign workers, we end up with the triangle ABC, which represents the Home gains as a result of full immigration. The reason for these gains is the law of diminishing returns: as more Foreign immigrants enter the Home workforce, their marginal products fall, and because the wage equals the marginal product of the last worker, it must be less than the marginal products of the earlier immigrants. This economic logic guarantees gains to the Home country from migration.

Gains for the Foreign Country Now consider the Foreign country. To assess the overall gains from emigration, we include the wages received by the migrants who left in calculating Foreign income. These wages are often returned to their families (see **Side Bar: Immigrants and Their Remittances**), but even if they are not, we still incorporate the wages earned by the immigrants in our measure of Foreign income because that is from where the migrants originally came.

In the absence of any emigration, the Foreign wage is W^*, the marginal product of labor in either industry abroad (multiplied by the price of that product in Foreign). As Foreign workers emigrate, the marginal product of labor remaining in Foreign rises, and the Foreign wage rises from W^* to W' (or from points A^* to B in Figure 5-14). Each of these higher marginal products or wages—between W^* and W'—equals the drop in Foreign output (of either good) from having workers leave.

Under full migration, all Foreign migrants earn the wage W' in the Home country. Notice that this wage is *higher* than their Foreign marginal products of labor, which are between W^* and W'. The difference between the wage earned by the migrants and their Foreign marginal products equals the gain to Foreign. Adding up the gains over all Foreign emigrants, we obtain the triangle A^*BC. This gain represents the earnings of the emigrants over and above the drop in output that occurs when they leave Foreign.

World Gains from Migration Combining the gains to the Home and Foreign countries, we obtain the triangular region ABA^*, the world gains from immigration. This magnitude is not too difficult to measure in practice. Turning the triangle on its side, its base equals $(W - W^*)$, the difference in the Home and Foreign wage in the

SIDE BAR

Immigrants and Their Remittances

Immigrants often send a substantial portion of their earnings back home, which we refer to as "remittances." According to estimates from the World Bank, remittances to developing countries were $406 billion in 2012, up from $372 billion in 2011. In 2011, official aid to foreign governments was $156 billion, less than half the amount of remittances from immigrants back to their home countries. The countries receiving the largest amount of remittances in 2011 were India ($64 billion), China ($62 billion), Mexico ($24 billion), and the Philippines ($23 billion). As a share of GDP, however, remittances are highest in smaller and lower-income countries, including Tajikistan (31%), Lesotho (29%), Samoa (23%), Kyrgyz Republic (21%), and Nepal and Tonga (20% each). In 2011, there were about 215 million immigrant workers in the world, so the remittances of $372 billion translate into each immigrant worker sending home approximately $1,800.

In Table 5-3, we show the remittances received by some developing countries in 2010, as compared with their net foreign aid. For all countries except Sudan, the income sent home by emigrants is a larger source of income than official aid. Sudan was experiencing a humanitarian crisis in 2010 so official aid was high. Remittances and official aid are especially important in other African countries, too.

The fact that emigrants return some of their income back home may not be enough to compensate their home countries for the loss of their labor. To calculate any gain to the home countries from the emigration of their workers, we need to include *all the earnings* of the emigrants in their home countries' income. In reality, however, emigrants do not send all of their income home, so the countries they leave can lose from their outflow. Consider, for example, the case of highly educated migrants. In 2000 there were 1 million Indian-born people with college educations living in the 30 wealthy countries of the Organisation for Economic Co-operation and Development (OECD). That amounts to 4.3% of India's large number of college graduates. In 2008, 53% of Indian-born migrants living in the OECD had a postsecondary education. For Asia as a whole, 38% of migrants living in the OECD had a postsecondary education. But for some individual countries, the outflow is much larger. Almost 47% of Ghana's college-educated labor force lives in OECD countries, and for Guyana, the percentage is 89%.[15] Unless these migrants return most of their earnings back home, those countries lose from the outflow of these highly educated workers.

To address this concern, Jagdish Bhagwati, an Indian-born economist now at Columbia University in New York, has proposed that countries impose a "brain-drain tax" on the outflow of educated workers. The idea is to tax the earnings of people living outside the countries in which they were born and, through an organization such as the United Nations, return the proceeds from the tax to the countries that lose the most workers. In that way, countries with an outflow of educated workers would be compensated, at least in part, for the outflow. A brain-drain tax has been widely debated, but so far it has not been used in practice.

TABLE 5-3

Workers' Remittances and Net Foreign Aid, 2010 Shown here are the remittances received by various countries from their citizens working abroad. In many cases, these remittances are larger than the official aid received by the countries. An exception was Sudan, which was experiencing a humanitarian crisis in 2010 so aid was high.

Country	Remittances Received ($ millions)	Net Aid Received ($ millions)
Albania	924	305
Bangladesh	10,836	1,415
Brazil	2,076	661
Colombia	4,023	901
Croatia	342	151
Dominican Republic	2,998	175
India	53,043	2,806
Mexico	21,303	471
Morocco	6,423	993
Sudan	1,291	2,076
Vietnam	8,000	2,940

Source: World Development Indicators, The World Bank.

---

[15] These percentages are obtained from "Fruit that falls far from the tree," *The Economist*, November 3, 2005, which draws on a World Bank study, and from the 2008 OECD Migration Outlook.

absence of any migration. The height of the triangle is $(L' - L)$, the number of foreign workers that would emigrate in the equilibrium with full migration. So the area of the triangle is $\frac{1}{2}(W - W^*) \cdot (L' - L)$. To solve for the area, we need to know the difference in wages before any migration and the number of people who would emigrate.

One way to think about the world gains from migration is that they equal the *increase in world GDP due to immigration.* To understand why this is so, think about the first person to migrate from Foreign to Home. That person earns the wage W^* in Foreign, which equals his or her marginal product times the price in the industry in which he or she works. When this individual leaves Foreign, GDP in that country falls by W^*. Once he or she moves to Home, he or she earns W, which again reflects the marginal product times the industry price. So W equals the increase in Home GDP when the immigrant begins working. The difference between the Home and Foreign wages therefore equals the net increase in world GDP due to migration. By adding up this amount across all migrants, we obtain the triangular region ABA^*, the increase in world GDP and the world gains due to migration.

In practice, however, there are other costs that immigrants bear that would make the gains from immigration less than the increase in world GDP. Immigrants often face sizable moving costs, including the psychological costs of missing their families and home countries as well as monetary payments to traffickers of illegal immigrants. These costs should be subtracted from the increase in GDP to obtain the net gains. Because all the moving costs are hard to quantify, however, in the next application we measure the net gains from immigration by the increase in Home or world GDP.

APPLICATION

Gains from Migration

How large are the gains from immigration? For the United States, a study by the economist George Borjas puts the net gain from immigration at about 0.1% of GDP (one-tenth of 1% of GDP). That value is obtained by using a stock of immigrants equal to 10% of the workforce in the United States and assuming that the immigrants compete for the same jobs as U.S. workers. If instead we assume the immigrants are lower-skilled on average than the U.S. population, then the low-skilled immigrants can complement the higher-skilled U.S. population, and the gains from immigration in the United States are somewhat higher, up to 0.4% of GDP. These estimates are shown in the first row of Table 5-4. The net gains to the United States in this case equal the increase in U.S. GDP.

Borjas's estimates for the U.S. gains from immigration may seem small, but lying behind these numbers is a larger shift in income from labor to capital and landowners. Labor loses from immigration, while capital and landowners gain, and the net effect of all these changes in real income is the gain in GDP that Borjas estimates. For the net gain of 0.1% of U.S. GDP due to immigration, Borjas estimates that capital would gain 2% and domestic labor would lose 1.9% of GDP. These figures lead him to conclude, "The relatively small size of the immigration surplus [that is, the gain in GDP]—particularly when compared to the very large wealth transfers caused by immigration [that is, the shift in income from labor to capital]—probably explains why the debate over immigration policy has usually focused on the potentially harmful labor market impacts rather than the overall increase in native income."

TABLE 5-4

Gains from Immigration The results from several studies of immigration are shown in this table. The second column shows the amount of immigration (as a percentage of the Home labor force), and the third column shows the increase in Home GDP or the increase in GDP of the region.

	AMOUNT OF IMMIGRATION	
	Percent of Home labor	Increase in GDP (%)
Part A: Calculation of Home Gains		
Study used:		
Borjas (1995, 1999), U.S. gains	10	0.1–0.4
Kremer and Watt (2006), Household workers	7	1.2–1.4
Peri, Shih, and Sparber (2013)	(24% of STEM workers*)	4.0
Part B: Calculation of Regional Gains		
Study used:		
Walmsley and Winters (2005),		
From developed to developing countries	3	0.6
Klein and Ventura (2009),		
Enlargement of the European Union†		
After 10 years	0.8–1.8	0.2–0.7
After 25 years	2.5–5.0	0.6–1.8
After 50 years	4.8–8.8	1.7–4.5
Common Labor Market in NAFTA†		
After 10 years	1.0–2.4	0.1–0.4
After 25 years	2.8–5.5	0.4–1.0
After 50 years	4.4–9.1	1.3–3.0

*STEM workers: scientists, technology professionals, engineers, and mathematicians

† All numbers are an estimated range.

Sources: George Borjas, 1995, "The Economic Benefits from Immigration," Journal of Economic Perspectives, 9(2), 3–22.

George Borjas, 1999, "The Economic Analysis of Immigration." In Orley Ashenfelter and David Card, eds., Handbook of Labor Economics, Vol. 3A (Amsterdam: North Holland), pp. 1697–1760. Paul Klein and Gustavo Ventura, 2009, "Productivity Differences and the Dynamic Effects of Labour Movements," Journal of Monetary Economics, 56(8), November, 1059–1073.

Michael Kremer and Stanley Watt, 2006, "The Globalization of Household Production," Harvard University.

Giovanni Peri, Kevin Shih, and Chad Sparber, 2013, "STEM Workers, H1B Visa and productivity in U.S. Cities," University of California, Davis.

Terrie Louise Walmsley and L. Alan Winters, 2005, "Relaxing the Restrictions on the Temporary Movement of Natural Persons: A Simulation Analysis," Journal of Economic Integration, 20(4), December, 688–726.

Other calculations suggest that the overall gains from immigration could be larger than Borjas's estimates. In the second row of Table 5-4, we report figures from a study by Kremer and Watt that focuses on just one type of immigrant: household workers. Foreign household workers, who are primarily female, make up 10% or more of the labor force in Bahrain, Kuwait, and Saudi Arabia, and about 7% of the labor force in Hong Kong and Singapore. The presence of these household workers often allows another member of that household—typically, a highly educated woman—to seek employment in her Home country. Thus, the immigration of low-skilled household workers allows for an increase in the high-skilled supply of individuals at Home, generating higher Home GDP as a result. It is estimated that this type of immigration, if it accounts for 7% of the workforce as in some countries, would increase Home GDP by approximately 1.2% to 1.4%.

Another larger estimate of the gains from immigration was obtained in a study by Giovanni Peri, who wrote **Headlines: The Economic Windfall of Immigration Reform,** seen earlier in the chapter. Peri and his co-authors measured the inflow of foreign workers to the United States who are scientists, technology professionals, engineers, or mathematicians—or STEM workers, for short. The H-1B visa program has allowed between 50,000 and 150,000 of these immigrants to enter the United States annually since 1991. Many have remained in the country as permanent residents. By 2010, foreign-born STEM workers accounted for 1.1% of the population in major cities in the United States, and accounted for 24% of the total STEM workers (foreign or U.S.-born) found in these cities. Peri and his co-authors measured the productivity gains to these cities from having this inflow of foreign talent, and they found that the gains were substantial: as mentioned in the earlier Headlines article, they found that 10% to 20% of the productivity growth in these cities can be explained by the presence of the foreign STEM workers. These productivity gains can come from new start-up technology companies, patents for new inventions, and so on. Adding up these productivity gains over time, the presence of the foreign STEM workers accounted for a 4% increase in GDP in the United States by 2010.

In part B of Table 5-4, we report results from estimates of gains due to migration for several regions of the world. The first study, by Walmsley and Winters, found that an increase in labor supply to developed countries of 3%, as a result of immigration from the developing countries, would create world gains of 0.6% of world GDP. This calculation is similar to the triangle of gains ABA^* shown in Figure 5-14. The next study, by Klein and Ventura, obtains larger estimates of the world gains by modeling the differences in technology across countries. Under this approach, wealthier regions have higher productivity, so an immigrant moving there will be more productive than at home. This productivity increase is offset somewhat by a skill loss for the immigrant (since the immigrant may not find the job for which he or she is best suited, at least initially). Nevertheless, the assumed skill loss is less than the productivity difference between countries, so immigrants are always more productive in the country to which they move.

In their study, Klein and Ventura considered the recent enlargement of the European Union (EU) from 15 countries to 25.[16] Workers from the newly added Eastern European countries are, in principle, permitted to work anywhere in the EU. Klein and Ventura assumed that the original 15 EU countries are twice as productive as the newly added countries. During the first 10 years, they found that the population of those 15 EU countries increased by an estimated 0.8% to 1.8%, and the combined GDP in the EU increased by 0.2% to 0.7%. The range of these estimates comes from different assumptions about the skill losses of immigrants when they move, and from the psychological costs of their moving, which slow down the extent of migration. As time passed, however, more people flowed from Eastern to Western Europe, and GDP continued to rise. Klein and Ventura estimated that in 25 years the combined GDP of the EU will increase by 0.6% to 1.8%, and that over 50 years, the increase in GDP would be 1.7% to 4.5%.

---

[16] Prior to 2004, the European Union consisted of 15 countries: Belgium, France, Germany, Italy, Luxembourg, and the Netherlands (founding members in 1952); Denmark, Ireland, and the United Kingdom (added in 1973); Greece (added in 1981); Portugal and Spain (added in 1986); and Austria, Finland, and Sweden (added in 1995). On May 1, 2004, 10 more countries were added: Cyprus, the Czech Republic, Estonia, Hungary, Lithuania, Latvia, Malta, Poland, Slovakia, and Slovenia.

Next, Klein and Ventura considered a common labor market within the North American Free Trade Area (NAFTA), established in 1994, which consists of Canada, Mexico, and the United States. Although NAFTA allows for free international trade between these countries, labor mobility is not free. So the experiment that Klein and Ventura considered allowed workers from Mexico to migrate freely to the United States and Canada, which are assumed to have workers who are 1.7 times as productive as those from Mexico. During the first 10 years, they predicted that the population of the United States and Canada would increase by an estimated 1.0% to 2.4% due to the immigration from Mexico, and the combined GDP in the NAFTA region would increase by 0.1% to 0.4%. After 25 years, they estimated that the combined GDP of the region would increase by 0.4% to 1.0%, and over 50 years, the increase in GDP would be 1.3% to 3.0%. These estimates are hypothetical because they assume free mobility of labor within the NAFTA countries, which did not occur. In the next chapter we will discuss some other estimates of the gains due to NAFTA, based on the actual experience of the countries involved with free international trade, but without free labor mobility.

Gains from Foreign Direct Investment

A diagram very similar to Figure 5-14 can be used to measure the gains from FDI. In Figure 5-15, we show the world amount of capital on the horizontal axis, which equals $\overline{K} + \overline{K}^*$. The rental earned in each country is on the vertical axis. With $0K$ units of capital employed at Home (measured from left to right), the Home rental is R, determined at point A. The remaining capital 0^*K (measured from right to left) is in Foreign, and the Foreign rental is R^*, determined at point A^*.

FIGURE 5-15

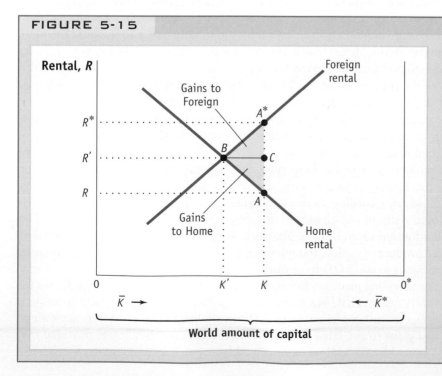

World Capital Market With OK units of capital at Home, the Home rental is R at point A. The remaining capital 0^*K is in Foreign, and the Foreign rental is R^* at point A^*. Capital will move from Home to Foreign to receive a higher rental. The equilibrium with full capital flows is at point B, where rentals are equalized at R'. Triangle ABC measures the gains to Home from the capital outflow, and triangle A^*BC measures the gains to Foreign.

Because the Foreign rental is higher than that at Home, capital will flow from Home to Foreign. As it enters Foreign, the additional capital will reduce the marginal product of capital and bid down the rental. Likewise, as capital leaves Home, the marginal product of capital will increase, and the Home rental will be bid up. The equilibrium with full capital flows is at point B, where rentals are equalized at R'. Similar to what we found in the case of immigration, the gains to Home from the capital outflow is the triangle ABC, while the gains to Foreign is the triangle A^*BC, and the world gains are A^*BA. ■

4 Conclusions

Immigration, the movement of workers between countries, potentially affects the wages in the host country in which the workers arrive. In the short-run specific-factor model, a larger supply of workers due to immigration will lower wages. Most immigrants into the United States have either the lowest or the highest amounts of education. As a result, after an inflow of labor from other countries, the wages of these two groups of workers fall in the short run. The majority of U.S. workers, those with mid-levels of education, are not affected that much by immigration. Moreover, the arrival of immigrants is beneficial to owners of capital and land in the specific-factors model. As wages are reduced in the short run, the rentals on capital and land will rise. This result helps to explain why landowners lobby for programs to allow agricultural workers to immigrate at least temporarily, and why other industries support increased immigration, such as H1-B visas for workers in the high-technology and other professional industries.

In a long-run framework, when capital can move between industries, the fall in wages will not occur. Instead, the industries that use labor intensively can expand and other industries contract, so that the immigrants become employed without any fall in wages. This change in industry outputs is the main finding of the Rybczynski theorem. The evidence from the Mariel boat lift in 1980 suggests that a readjustment of industry outputs along these lines occurred in Miami after the arrival of immigrants from Cuba: the output of the apparel industry fell by less than predicted from other cities, whereas the output of some skill-intensive industries fell by more than predicted.

The movement of capital between countries is referred to as foreign direct investment (FDI) and has effects analogous to immigration. In the short run, the entry of foreign capital into a country will lower the rental on capital, raise wages, and lower the rental on land. But in the long run, when capital and land can move between industries, these changes in the wage and rentals need not occur. Instead, industry outputs can adjust according to the Rybczynski theorem so that the extra capital is fully employed without any change in the wage or rentals. Evidence from Singapore suggests that foreign capital can be absorbed without a large decline in the rental or the marginal product of capital, though this is an area of ongoing debate in economics.

Both immigration and FDI create world gains as labor and capital move from countries with low marginal products to countries with high marginal products. Gains for the host country are created because the inflow of labor and capital is paid an amount that is less than its full contribution to GDP in the host country. At the same time, there are also gains to the labor and capital in the country they leave, provided that the income earned by the emigrants or capital is included in that country's welfare.

KEY POINTS

1. Holding the amount of capital and land fixed in both industries, as in the specific-factors model, immigration leads to a fall in wages. This was the case, for example, with the mass migration to the New World in the nineteenth century.

2. As wages fall because of immigration, the marginal products of the specific factors (capital and land) rise, and therefore their rentals also increase.

3. Fixing the amount of capital and land in a country is a reasonable assumption in the short run, but in the longer run, firms will move capital between industries, which will change the effect of immigration on wages and rentals.

4. In a long-run model with two goods and two factors, both of which are perfectly mobile between the industries, additional labor from immigration will be absorbed entirely by the labor-intensive industry. Furthermore, the labor-intensive industry will also absorb additional capital and labor from the capital-intensive industry, so its capital–labor ratio does not change in the long run. Because the capital–labor ratio in each industry does not change, the wage and rentals remain the same as well. This results in what is known as factor price insensitivity.

5. According to the Rybczynski theorem, immigration will lead to an increase in output in the labor-intensive industry and a decrease in the output of the capital-intensive industry. This result is different from that of the short-run specific-factors model, in which immigration leads to increased output in both industries.

6. Besides trade in goods and the movement of labor, another way that countries interact with one another is through investment. When a company owns property, plant, or equipment in another country, it is called foreign direct investment, or FDI.

7. In the short run, FDI lowers the rentals on capital and land and raises wages. In the long run, the extra capital can be absorbed in the capital-intensive industry without any change in the wage or rental.

8. According to the Rybczynski theorem, FDI will lead to an increase in the output of the capital-intensive industry and a decrease in the output of the labor-intensive industry.

9. The movement of capital and labor generates overall gains for both the source and host countries, provided that the income of the emigrants is included in the source country's welfare. Hence, there are global gains from immigration and FDI.

KEY TERMS

specific-factors model, p. 124
Rybczynski theorem, p. 139
factor price insensitivity, p. 140
real value-added, p. 140
foreign direct investment (FDI), p. 144
equilibrium with full migration, p. 153

PROBLEMS

1. In the short-run specific-factors model, examine the impact on a small country following a natural disaster that decreases it population. Assume that land is specific to agriculture and capital is specific to manufacturing, whereas labor is free to move between the two sectors.

   a. In a diagram similar to Figure 5-2, determine the impact of the decrease in the workforce on the output of each industry and the equilibrium wage.

   b. What happens to the rentals on capital and land?

2. How would your answer to Problem 1 change if instead we use the long-run model, with shoes and computers produced using labor and capital?

3. Consider an increase in the supply of labor due to immigration, and use the long-run model. Figure 5-8 shows the box diagram and the leftward shift of the origin for the shoe industry. Redraw this diagram but instead shift to the right the origin for computers. That is, expand the labor axis by the amount ΔL but shift it to the right rather than to the left. With the new diagram, show how the amount of labor and capital in shoes and computers is determined, without any change in factor prices. Carefully explain what has happened to the amount of labor and capital used in each industry and to the output of each industry.

4. In the short-run specific-factors model, consider a decrease in the stock of land. For example, suppose a natural disaster decreases the quantity of arable land used for planting crops.

   a. Redraw panel (a) of Figure 5-11 starting from the initial equilibrium at point A.

   b. What is the effect of this change in land on the quantity of labor in each industry and on the equilibrium wage?

   c. What is the effect on the rental on land and the rental on capital?

   d. Now suppose that the international community wants to help the country struck by the natural disaster and decides to do so by increasing its level of FDI. So the rest of the world increases its investment in physical capital in the stricken country. Illustrate the effect of this policy on the equilibrium wage and rentals.

5. According to part A of Table 5-1, what education level loses most (i.e., has the greatest decrease in wage) from immigration to the United States? Does this result depend on keeping the rental on capital constant? Explain why or why not.

6. Suppose that computers use 2 units of capital for each worker, so that $K_C = 2 \cdot L_C$, whereas shoes use 0.5 unit of capital for each worker, so that $K_S = 0.5 \cdot L_S$. There are 100 workers and 100 units of capital in the economy.

   a. Solve for the amount of labor and capital used in each industry.

Hint: The box diagram shown in Figure 5-7 means that the amount of labor and capital used in each industry must add up to the total for the economy, so that

$$K_C + K_S = 100 \text{ and } L_C + L_S = 100$$

Use the facts that $K_C = 2 \cdot L_C$ and $K_S = 0.5 \cdot L_S$ to rewrite these equations as

$$2 \cdot L_C + 0.5 \cdot L_S = 100 \text{ and } L_C + L_S = 100$$

Use these two equations to solve for L_C and L_S, and then calculate the amount of capital used in each industry using $K_C = 2 \cdot L_C$ and $K_S = 0.5 \cdot L_S$.

   b. Suppose that the number of workers increases to 125 due to immigration, keeping total capital fixed at 100. Again, solve for the amount of labor and capital used in each industry. *Hint:* Redo the calculations from part (a), but using $L_C + L_S = 125$.

   c. Suppose instead that the amount of capital increases to 125 due to FDI, keeping the total number of workers fixed at 100. Again solve for the amount of labor and capital used in each industry. *Hint:* Redo the calculations from part (a), using $K_C + K_S = 125$.

   d. Explain how your results in parts (b) and (c) are related to the Rybczynski theorem.

Questions 7 and 8 explore the implications of the Rybczynski theorem and the factor price insensitivity result for the Heckscher-Ohlin model from Chapter 4.

7. In this question, we use the Rybczynski theorem to review the derivation of the Heckscher-Ohlin theorem.

   a. Start at the no-trade equilibrium point A on the Home PPF in Figure 4-2, panel (a). Suppose that through immigration, the amount of labor in Home grows. Draw the new PPF, and label the point B where production would occur with the same prices for goods. *Hint:* You can refer to Figure 5-9 to see the effect of immigration on the PPF.

   b. Suppose that the only difference between Foreign and Home is that Foreign has more labor. Otherwise, the technologies used to produce each good are the same across countries. Then how does the Foreign PPF compare with the new Home PPF (including immigration) that you drew in part (a)? Is point B the no-trade equilibrium in Foreign? Explain why or why not.

c. Illustrate a new point A^* that is the no-trade equilibrium in Foreign. How do the relative no-trade prices of computers compare in Home and Foreign? Therefore, what will be the pattern of trade between the countries, and why?

8. Continuing from Problem 7, we now use the factor price insensitivity result to compare factor prices across countries in the Heckscher-Ohlin model.

a. Illustrate the international trade equilibrium on the Home and Foreign production possibilities frontiers. *Hint:* You can refer to Figure 4-3 to see the international trade equilibrium.

b. Suppose that the only difference between Foreign and Home is that Foreign has more labor. Otherwise, the technologies used to produce each good are the same across countries. Then, according to the factor price insensitivity result, how will the wage and rental compare in the two countries?

c. Call the result in part (b) "factor price equalization." Is this a realistic result? *Hint:* You can refer to Figure 4-9 to see wages across countries.

d. Based on our extension of the Heckscher-Ohlin model at the end of Chapter 4, what is one reason why the factor price equalization result does not hold in reality?

9. Recall the formula from the application "The Effect of FDI on Rentals and Wages in Singapore." Give an intuitive explanation for this formula for the rental rate. *Hint:* Describe one side of the equation as a marginal benefit and the other as a marginal cost.

10. In Table 5-2, we show the growth in the real rental and real wages in Singapore, along with the implied productivity growth. One way to calculate the productivity growth is to take the average of the growth in the real rental and real wage. The idea is that firms can afford to pay

more to labor and capital if there is productivity growth, so in that case real factor prices should be growing. But if there is no productivity growth, then the average of the growth in the real rental and real wage should be close to zero.

To calculate the average of the growth in the real factor prices, we use the shares of GDP going to capital and labor. Specifically, we multiply the growth in the real rental by the capital share of GDP and add the growth in the real wage multiplied by the labor share of GDP. Then answer the following:

a. For a capital-rich country like Singapore, the share of capital in GDP is about one-half and the share of labor is also one-half. Using these shares, calculate the average of the growth in the real rental and real wage shown in each row of Table 5-2. How do your answers compare with the productivity growth shown in the last column of Table 5-2?

b. For an industrialized country like the United States, the share of capital in GDP is about one-third and the share of labor in GDP is about two-thirds. Using these shares, calculate the average of the growth in the real rental and real wage shown in each row of Table 5-2. How do your answers now compare with the productivity growth shown in the last column?

11. Figure 5-14 is a supply and demand diagram for the world labor market. Starting at points A and A^*, consider a situation in which some Foreign workers migrate to Home but not enough to reach the equilibrium with full migration (point B). As a result of the migration, the Home wage decreases from W to $W'' > W'$, and the Foreign wage increases from W^* to $W^{**} < W'$.

a. Are there gains that accrue to the Home country? If so, redraw the graph and identify the magnitude of the gains for each country. If not, say why not.

b. Are there gains that accrue to the Foreign country? If so, again show the magnitude of these gains in the diagram and also show the world gains.

12. A housekeeper from the Philippines is contemplating immigrating to Singapore in search of higher wages. Suppose the housekeeper earns approximately $2,000 annually and expects to find a job in Singapore worth approximately $5,000 annually for a period of three years. Furthermore, assume that the cost of living in Singapore is $500 more per year than at home.

a. What can we say about the productivity of housekeepers in Singapore versus the Philippines? Explain.
b. What is the total gain to the housekeeper from migrating?
c. Is there a corresponding gain for the employer in Singapore? Explain.

N E T WORK

Immigration is frequently debated in the United States and other countries. Find a recent news report dealing with immigration policy in the United States, and briefly summarize the issues discussed.

6

Increasing Returns to Scale and Monopolistic Competition

Foreign trade, then, . . . [is] highly beneficial to a country, as it increases the amount and variety of the objects on which revenue may be expended.
David Ricardo, *On the Principles of Political Economy and Taxation*, Chapter 7

The idea that a simple government policy [free trade between Canada and the United States] could raise productivity so dramatically is to me truly remarkable.
Professor Daniel Trefler, University of Toronto, 2005

1 Basics of Imperfect Competition

2 Trade Under Monopolistic Competition

3 The North American Free Trade Agreement

4 Intra-Industry Trade and the Gravity Equation

5 Conclusions

In Chapter 2, we looked at data for U.S. snowboard imports and considered the reasons why the United States imports this product from so many different countries. Now we look at another sporting good that the United States imports *and exports* in large quantities to illustrate how a country can both buy a product and sell it to other countries. In 2012 the United States imported golf clubs from 25 countries and exported them to 74 countries. In Table 6-1, we list the 12 countries that sell the most golf clubs to the United States and the 12 countries to which the United States sells the most golf clubs. The table also lists the amounts bought or sold and their average wholesale prices.

In panel (a), we see that China sells the most clubs to the United States, providing $385 million worth of golf clubs at an average price of $27 each. Next is Mexico, selling $45 million of clubs at an average wholesale price of $70 each.[1] Vietnam comes next, exporting $26 million of clubs at an average price of $51, followed by Japan, Taiwan, and Thailand, each of which sells golf clubs to the United States with an

---

[1] Actually, if you divide the value of imported clubs from Mexico by the quantity reported in Table 6-1, you will get an average price of $338. That number seems too high for the price of individual golf clubs (suggesting that either the value or the quantity is misreported in 2012), so we have instead used the average price of imported clubs from Mexico in 2011, which was $70.

TABLE 6-1

U.S. Imports and Exports of Golf Clubs, 2012 This table shows the value, quantity, and average price for golf clubs imported into and exported from the United States. Many of the same countries both sell golf clubs to and buy golf clubs from the United States, illustrating what we call intra-industry trade.

(a) IMPORTS

Rank	Country	Value of Imports ($ thousands)	Quantity of Golf Clubs (thousands)	Average Price ($/club)
1	China	385,276	14,482	27
2	Mexico	44,725	132	70
3	Vietnam	25,579	504	51
4	Japan	9,180	47	197
5	Taiwan	7,830	69	114
6	Thailand	1,705	12	143
7	Hong Kong	1,043	40	26
8	Canada	376	16	23
9	Germany	96	5	18
10	United Kingdom	71	12	6
11	South Korea	28	3	9
12	Belgium	24	1	19
13–25	Various countries	31	11	3
	All 25 countries	475,966	18,083	26

(b) EXPORTS

Rank	Country	Value of Imports ($ thousands)	Quantity of Golf Clubs (thousands)	Average Price ($/club)
1	Japan	37,943	326	117
2	Canada	18,916	275	69
3	Korea	18,047	149	121
4	Australia	10,563	132	80
5	Hong Kong	9,996	78	128
6	United Kingdom	8,079	97	84
7	Singapore	4,427	39	115
8	Netherlands	1,977	14	142
9	South Africa	1,513	20	75
10	Mexico	1,403	15	91
11	Argentina	1,070	12	88
12	New Zealand	1,068	14	77
13–74	Various countries	6,525	83	79
	All 74 countries	121,575	1,253	97

Source: U.S. International Trade Commission Interactive Tariff and Trade DataWeb at http://dataweb.usitc.gov/.

average price exceeding $100. The higher average prices of golf clubs from these three countries as compared with Chinese and Vietnamese clubs most likely indicate that the clubs sold by Japan, Taiwan, and Thailand are of much higher quality. The clubs from the other top-selling countries have wholesale prices below $30. In total, the United States imported $476 million of golf clubs in 2012.

On the export side, shown in panel (b), the top destination for U.S. clubs is Japan, followed by Canada and South Korea. Notice that these three countries are also among the top 12 countries selling golf clubs to the United States. The average price for U.S. exports varies between $69 and $142 per club, higher than the price of all the imported clubs, except those from Mexico, Japan, Taiwan, and Thailand, which suggests that the United States is exporting high-quality clubs.

Many of the countries that sell to the United States also buy from the United States: 6 of the top 12 selling countries were also among the top 12 countries buying U.S. golf clubs in 2012. Of the 25 selling countries, 24 also bought U.S. golf clubs (the only country that sold clubs to the United States but did not also buy them was Bangladesh). Why does the United States export and import golf clubs to and from the same countries? The answer to this question is one of the "new" explanations for trade that we study in this chapter and the next. The Ricardian model (Chapter 2) and the Heckscher-Ohlin model (Chapter 4) explained why nations would either import or export a good, but those models do not predict the simultaneous import and export of a product, as we observe for golf clubs and many other goods.

To explain why countries import and export the same product, we need to change some assumptions made in the Ricardian and Heckscher-Ohlin models. In those models, we assumed that markets were perfectly competitive, which means there are many small producers, each producing a homogeneous (identical) product, so none of them can influence the market price for the product. As we know just from walking down the aisles in a grocery or department store, most goods are **differentiated goods;** that is, they are not identical. Based on price differences in Table 6-1, we can see that the traded golf clubs are of different types and quality. So in this chapter, we drop the assumption that the goods are homogeneous, as in perfect competition, and instead assume that goods are differentiated and allow for **imperfect competition,** in which case firms can influence the price that they charge.

The new explanation for trade explored in this chapter involves a type of imperfect competition called **monopolistic competition,** which has two key features. The first feature, just mentioned, is that the goods produced by different firms are differentiated. By offering different products, firms are able to exert some control over the price they can charge for their particular product. Because the market in which the firms operate is not a perfectly competitive one, they do not have to accept the market price, and by increasing their price, they do not lose all their business to competitors. On the other hand, because these firms are not monopolists (i.e., they are not the only firm that produces this type of product), they cannot charge prices as high as a monopolist would. When firms produce differentiated products, they retain some ability to set the price for their product, but not as much as a monopolist would have.

The second feature of monopolistic competition is **increasing returns to scale,** by which we mean that the average costs for a firm fall as more output is produced. For this reason, firms tend to specialize in the product lines that are most successful—by selling more of those products, the average cost for the production of the successful products falls. Firms can lower their average costs by selling more in their home markets but can possibly attain even lower costs from selling more in foreign markets through exporting. So increasing returns to scale create a reason for trade to occur even when the trading countries are similar in their technologies and factor endowments. Increasing returns to scale set the monopolistic competition trade model apart from the logic of the Ricardian and Heckscher-Ohlin models.

In this chapter, we describe a model of trade under monopolistic competition that incorporates product differentiation and increasing returns to scale. After describing the monopolistic competition model, the next goal of the chapter is to discuss how this model helps explain trade patterns that we observe today. In our golf club example, countries specialize in different varieties of the same type of product and trade them; this type of trade is called **intra-industry trade** because it deals with imports and exports in the same industry. The monopolistic competition model explains this trade pattern and also predicts that larger countries will trade more with one another. Just as the force of gravity is strongest between two large objects, the monopolistic competition model implies that large countries (as measured by their GDP) should trade the most.[2] There is a good deal of empirical evidence to support this prediction, which is called the **gravity equation.**

The monopolistic competition model also helps us to understand the effects of **free-trade agreements,** in which free trade occurs among a group of countries. In this chapter, we use the North American Free Trade Agreement (NAFTA) to illustrate the predictions of the monopolistic competition model. The policy implications of free-trade agreements are discussed in a later chapter.

1 Basics of Imperfect Competition

Monopolistic competition incorporates some aspects of a monopoly (firms have control over the prices they charge) and some aspects of perfect competition (many firms are selling). Before presenting the monopolistic competition model, it is useful to review the case of monopoly, which is a single firm selling a product. The monopoly firm faces the industry demand curve. After that, we briefly discuss the case of **duopoly,** when there are two firms selling a product. Our focus will be on the demand facing each of the two firms. Understanding what happens to demand in a duopoly will help us understand how demand is determined when there are many firms selling differentiated products, as occurs in monopolistic competition.

Monopoly Equilibrium

In Figure 6-1, the industry demand curve is shown by D. For the monopolist to sell more, the price must fall, and so the demand curve slopes downward. This fall in price means that the extra revenue earned by the monopolist from selling another unit is less than the price of that unit—the extra revenue earned equals the price charged for that unit *minus* the fall in price times the quantity sold of all earlier units. The extra revenue earned from selling one more unit is called the **marginal revenue** and is shown by the curve MR in Figure 6-1. The marginal revenue curve lies below the demand curve D because the extra revenue earned from selling another unit is less than the price.

---

[2] If you have read Chapter 1, you will know that large countries do indeed trade the most, as seen in the map of world trade.

FIGURE 6-1

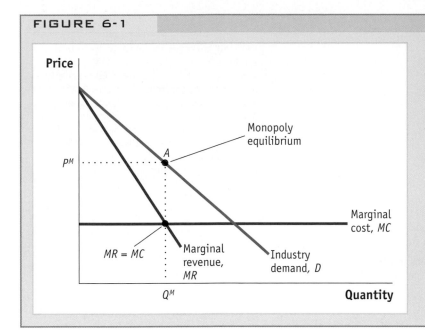

Monopoly Equilibrium The monopolist chooses the profit-maximizing quantity, Q^M, at which marginal revenue equals marginal cost. From that quantity, we trace up to the demand curve and over to the price axis to see that the monopolist charges the price P^M. The monopoly equilibrium is at point A.

To maximize its profit, the monopolist sells up to the point at which the marginal revenue *MR* earned from selling one more unit equals the **marginal cost** *MC* of producing one more unit. In Figure 6-1, the marginal cost curve is shown by *MC*. Because we have assumed, for simplicity, that marginal costs are constant, the *MC* curve is flat, although this does not need to be the case. To have marginal revenue equal marginal costs, the monopolist sells the quantity Q^M. To find the profit-maximizing price the monopolist charges, we trace up from quantity Q^M to point A on the demand curve and then over to the price axis. The price charged by the monopolist P^M is the price that allows the monopolist to earn the highest profit and is therefore the monopoly equilibrium.

Demand with Duopoly

Let us compare a monopoly with a duopoly, a market structure in which two firms are selling a product. We will not solve for the duopoly equilibrium but will just study how the introduction of a second firm affects the demand facing each of the firms. Knowing how demand is affected by the introduction of a second firm helps us understand how demand is determined when there are many firms, as there are in monopolistic competition.

In Figure 6-2, the industry faces the demand curve D. If there are two firms in the industry and they charge the same price, then the demand curve facing each firm is $D/2$. For example, if both firms charged the price P_1, then the industry demand is at point A, and each firm's demand is at point B on curve $D/2$. The two firms share the market equally, each selling exactly one-half of the total market demand, $Q_2 = Q_1/2$.

If one firm charges a price different from the other firm, however, the demand facing both firms changes. Suppose that one firm charges a lower price P_2, while the other firm keeps its price at P_1. If the firms are selling the same homogeneous product, then the firm charging the lower price would get all the demand (shown by point C), which

FIGURE 6-2

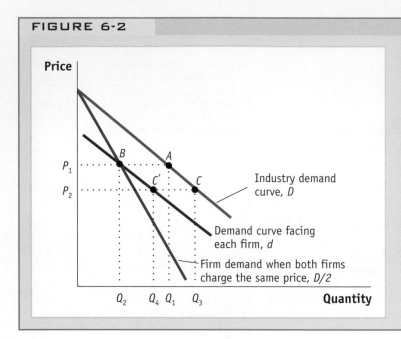

Demand Curves with Duopoly When there are two firms in the market and they both charge the same price, each firm faces the demand curve $D/2$. At the price P_1, the industry produces Q_1 at point A and each firm produces $Q_2 = Q_1/2$ at point B. If both firms produce identical products and one firm lowers its price to P_2, all consumers will buy from that firm only; the firm that lowers its price will face the demand curve, D, and sell Q_3 at point C. Alternatively, if the products are differentiated, the firm that lowers its price will take some, but not all, sales from the other firm; it will face the demand curve, d, and at P_2 it will sell Q_4 at point C'.

is Q_3 at the price P_2. Now suppose that the products are not homogeneous but instead are differentiated. In that case, the firm with the lower price P_2 will capture more of the market than the firm with the higher price P_1, but will not capture the entire market. Because the products are not precisely the same (for instance, in our golf club example the higher-priced club is of better quality than the less expensive club), some consumers will still want to buy the other firm's product even though its price is higher. The firm selling at the lower price P_2 now sells the quantity Q_4, for example, at point C'.

The demand curve d is the demand curve for the firm that lowered its price from P_1 to P_2, even though the other firm held its price at P_1. As we have illustrated, the demand curve d is *flatter* than the demand curve $D/2$. This means that each firm faces a more elastic demand curve than $D/2$: when only one firm lowers its price, it increases its quantity sold by more than when all firms lower their prices. Not only does the quantity demanded in the industry increase, but in addition, the firm that lowers its price takes away some of the quantity demanded from the other firm. In summary, the demand curve d facing each firm producing in a duopoly is more elastic than the demand curve $D/2$ each faces when the firms charge the same price.

2 Trade Under Monopolistic Competition

We begin our study of monopolistic competition by carefully stating the assumptions of the model.

Assumption 1: Each firm produces a good that is similar to but differentiated from the goods that other firms in the industry produce.

Because each firm's product is somewhat different from the goods of the other firms, a firm can raise its price without losing all its customers to other firms. Thus, each firm faces a downward-sloping demand curve for its product and has some control over the price it charges. This is different from perfect competition, in which all firms produce exactly the same product and therefore must sell at exactly the same market-determined price.

Assumption 2: There are many firms in the industry.

The discussion of duopoly demand in the previous section helps us to think about the demand curve facing a firm under monopolistic competition, when there are many firms in the industry. If the number of firms is N, then D/N is the share of demand that each firm faces when the firms are all charging the same price. When only one firm lowers its price, however, it will face a flatter demand curve d. We will begin describing the model by focusing on the demand curve d and later bring back the demand curve D/N.

The first two assumptions are about the demand facing each firm; the third assumption is about each firm's cost structure:

Assumption 3: Firms produce using a technology with increasing returns to scale.

The assumptions underlying monopolistic competition differ from our usual assumptions on firm costs by allowing for increasing returns to scale, a production technology in which the average costs of production fall as the quantity produced increases. This relationship is shown in Figure 6-3, in which average costs are labeled AC. The assumption that average costs fall as quantity increases means that marginal costs, labeled MC, must be *below* average costs. Why? Think about whether a new student coming into your class will raise or lower the class average grade. If the new student's average is below the existing class average, then when he or she enters, the class average will fall. In the same way, when MC is less than AC, then AC must be falling.[3]

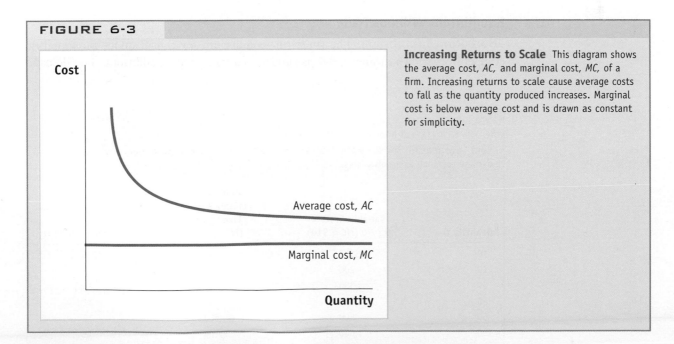

FIGURE 6-3

Increasing Returns to Scale This diagram shows the average cost, AC, and marginal cost, MC, of a firm. Increasing returns to scale cause average costs to fall as the quantity produced increases. Marginal cost is below average cost and is drawn as constant for simplicity.

Cost

Average cost, AC

Marginal cost, MC

Quantity

---

[3] For simplicity, we assume that marginal costs are constant, but this need not be the case.

Numerical Example As an example of the cost curves in Figure 6-3, suppose that the firm has the following cost data:

$$\text{Fixed costs} = \$100$$

$$\text{Marginal costs} = \$10 \text{ per unit}$$

Given these costs, the average costs for this firm for various quantities are as shown in Table 6-2.

Notice that as the quantity produced rises, average costs fall and eventually become close to the marginal costs of $10 per unit, as shown in Figure 6-3.

Assumption 3 means that average cost is above marginal cost. Assumption 1 means that firms have some control over the price they charge, and these firms charge a price that is also above marginal cost (we learn why in a later section).

Whenever the price charged is above average cost, a firm earns **monopoly profit.** Our final assumption describes what happens to profits in a monopolistically competitive industry in the long run:

Assumption 4: Because firms can enter and exit the industry freely, monopoly profits are zero in the long run.

Recall that under perfect competition, we assume there are many firms in the industry and that in a long-run equilibrium each firm's profit must be zero. In monopolistic competition, there is the same requirement for a long-run equilibrium. We assume that firms can enter and exit the industry freely; this means that firms will enter as long as it is possible to make monopoly profits, and as more firms enter, the profit per firm falls. This condition leads to a long-run equilibrium in which profit for each firm is zero, just as in perfect competition!

Equilibrium Without Trade

Short-Run Equilibrium The short-run equilibrium for a firm under monopolistic competition, shown in Figure 6-4, is similar to a monopoly equilibrium. The demand

---

TABLE 6-2

Cost Information for the Firm This table illustrates increasing returns to scale, in which average costs fall as quantity rises.

Quantity Q	Variable Costs = $Q \cdot MC$ ($MC = \$10$)	Total Costs = Variable Costs + Fixed Costs ($FC = \$100$)	Average Costs = Total Costs/Quantity
10	$100	$200	$20
20	200	300	15
30	300	400	13.3
40	400	500	12.5
50	500	600	12
100	1,000	1,100	11
Large Q	$10 \cdot Q$	$10 \cdot Q + 100$	Close to 10

FIGURE 6-4

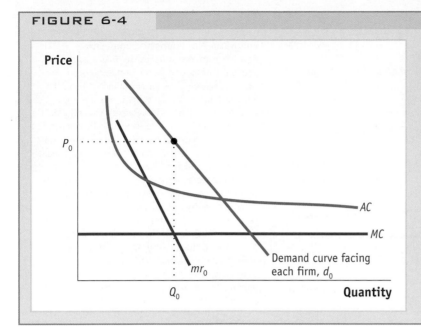

Short-Run Monopolistic Competition Equilibrium without Trade The short-run equilibrium under monopolistic competition is the same as a monopoly equilibrium. The firm chooses to produce the quantity Q_0 at which the firm's marginal revenue, mr_0, equals its marginal cost, MC. The price charged is P_0. Because price exceeds average cost, the firm makes a monopoly profit.

curve faced by each firm is labeled d_0, the marginal revenue curve is labeled mr_0, and the marginal cost curve of each firm is shown by MC. Each firm maximizes profit by producing Q_0, the quantity at which marginal revenue equals marginal cost. Tracing up from this quantity to the demand curve shows that the price charged by the firms is P_0. Because the price exceeds average costs at the quantity Q_0, the firm earns monopoly profit.

Long-Run Equilibrium In a monopolistically competitive market, new firms continue to enter the industry as long as they can earn monopoly profits. In the long run, the entry of new firms draws demand away from existing firms, causing demand curve d_0 to shift to the left until no firm in the industry earns positive monopoly profits (Figure 6-5). Moreover, when new firms enter and there are more product varieties available to consumers, the d_0 curve faced by each firm becomes more elastic, or flatter. We expect the d_0 curve to become more elastic as more firms enter because each product is similar to the other existing products; therefore, as the number of close substitutes increases, consumers become more price sensitive.

New firms continue to enter the industry until the price charged by each firm is on the average cost curve and monopoly profit is zero. At this point, the industry is in a long-run equilibrium, with no reason for any further entry or exit. The long-run equilibrium without trade is shown in Figure 6-5. Again, the demand curve for the firm is labeled d, with the short-run demand curve denoted d_0 and the long-run demand curve denoted d_1 (with corresponding marginal revenue curve mr_1). Marginal revenue equals marginal cost at quantity Q_1. At this quantity, all firms in the industry charge price P^A. The price P^A equals average cost at point A, where the demand curve d_1 is tangent to the average cost curve. Because the price equals average costs, the firm is earning zero monopoly profit and there is no incentive for firms to enter or exit the industry. Thus, point A is the firm's (and the industry's) long-run equilibrium without trade. Notice that the long-run equilibrium curve d_1 is to the left of and more elastic (flatter) than the short-run curve d_0.

FIGURE 6-5

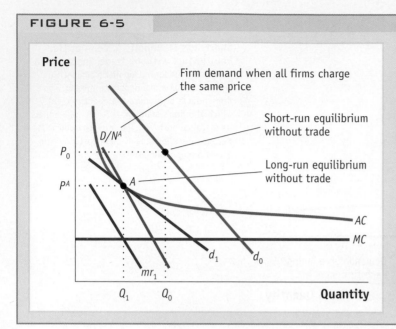

Long-Run Monopolistic Competition Equilibrium Without Trade Drawn by the possibility of making profits in the short-run equilibrium, new firms enter the industry and the firm's demand curve, d_0, shifts to the left and becomes more elastic (i.e., flatter), shown by d_1. The long-run equilibrium under monopolistic competition occurs at the quantity Q_1 where the marginal revenue curve, mr_1 (associated with demand curve d_1), equals marginal cost. At that quantity, the no-trade price, P^A, equals average costs at point A. In the long-run equilibrium, firms earn zero monopoly profits and there is no entry or exit. The quantity produced by each firm is less than that in short-run equilibrium (Figure 6-4). Q_1 is less than Q_0 because new firms have entered the industry. With a greater number of firms and hence more varieties available to consumers, the demand for each variety d_1 is less then d_0. The demand curve D/N^A shows the no-trade demand when all firms charge the same price.

Before we allow for international trade, we need to introduce another curve into Figure 6-5. The firm's demand curve d_1 shows the quantity demanded depending on the price charged by that firm, holding the price charged by all other firms fixed. In contrast, there is another demand curve that shows the quantity demanded from each firm when all firms in the industry charge the *same price*. This other demand curve is the total market demand D divided by the number of firms in the absence of trade N^A. In Figure 6-5, we label the second demand curve as D/N^A. We omit drawing total industry demand D itself so we do not clutter the diagram.

The demand curve d_1 is flatter, or more elastic, than the demand curve D/N^A. We discussed why that is the case under duopoly (see Figure 6-2) and can review the reason again now. Starting at point A, consider a drop in the price by just one firm, which increases the quantity demanded along the d_1 curve for that firm. The demand curve d_1 is quite elastic, meaning that the drop in price leads to a large increase in the quantity purchased because customers are attracted away from other firms. If instead all firms drop their price by the same amount, along the curve D/N^A, then each firm will not attract as many customers away from other firms. When all firms drop their prices equally, then the increase in quantity demanded from each firm along the curve D/N^A is less than the increase along the firm's curve d_1. Thus, demand is less elastic along the demand curve D/N^A, which is why it is steeper than the d_1 curve. As we proceed with our analysis of opening trade under monopolistic competition, it will be helpful to keep track of both of these demand curves.

Equilibrium with Free Trade

Let us now allow for free trade between Home and Foreign in this industry. For simplicity, we assume that Home and Foreign countries are exactly the same, with the same number of consumers, the same factor endowments, the same technology and cost curves, and the same number of firms in the no-trade equilibrium. If there were no increasing returns to scale, there would be no reason at all for international trade to occur. Under the Ricardian model, for example, countries with identical technologies would not trade because their no-trade relative prices would be equal. Likewise, under the Heckscher-Ohlin model, countries with identical factor endowments would not trade because their no-trade relative prices would be the same. Under monopolistic competition, however, two identical countries will still engage in international trade because increasing returns to scale exist.

Short-Run Equilibrium with Trade We take as given the number of firms in the no-trade equilibrium in each country N^A and use this number of firms to determine the short-run equilibrium with trade. Our starting point is the long-run equilibrium without trade, as shown by point A in Figure 6-5 and reproduced in Figure 6-6. When we allow free trade between Home and Foreign, the number of consumers available to each firm doubles (because there is an equal number of consumers in each country) as does the number of firms (because there is an equal number of firms in each country). Because there are not only twice as many consumers but also twice as many firms, the demand curve D/N^A is the same as it was before, $2D/2N^A = D/N^A$. In other words, point A is still on the demand curve D/N^A, as shown in Figure 6-6.

Free trade doubles the number of firms, which also doubles the product varieties available to consumers. With a greater number of product varieties available to consumers, their demand for each individual variety will be *more elastic*. That is, if one firm drops its price below the no-trade price P^A, then it can expect to attract an even greater number of customers away from other firms. Before trade the firm would attract additional Home customers only, but after trade it will attract additional Home and Foreign consumers. In Figure 6-6, this consumer response is shown by the firm's new demand curve d_2, which is more elastic than its no-trade demand curve d_1. As a result, the demand curve d_2 is no longer tangent to the average cost curve at point A

FIGURE 6-6

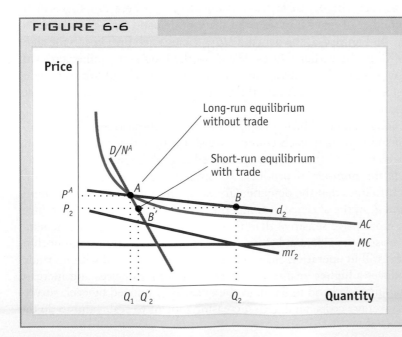

Short-Run Monopolistic Competition Equilibrium with Trade When trade is opened, the larger market makes the firm's demand curve more elastic, as shown by d_2 (with corresponding marginal revenue curve, mr_2). The firm chooses to produce the quantity Q_2 at which marginal revenue equals marginal costs; this quantity corresponds to a price of P_2. With sales of Q_2 at price P_2, the firm will make monopoly profits because price is greater than AC. When *all* firms lower their prices to P_2, however, the relevant demand curve is D/N^A, which indicates that they can sell only Q'_2 at price P_2. At this short-run equilibrium (point B'), price is less than average cost and all firms incur losses. As a result, some firms are forced to exit the industry.

but is *above* average costs for prices below P^A. The new demand curve d_2 has a corresponding marginal revenue curve mr_2, as shown in Figure 6-6.

With the new demand curve d_2 and new marginal revenue curve mr_2, the firm again needs to choose its profit-maximizing level of production. As usual, that level will be where marginal revenue equals marginal cost at Q_2. When we trace from Q_2 up to point B on the firm's demand curve d_2, then over to the price axis, we see that the firm will charge P_2. Because P_2 is above average cost at point B, the firm will make a positive monopoly profit. We can see clearly the firm's incentive to lower its price: at point A it earns zero monopoly profit and at point B it earns positive profit. Producing Q_2 and selling it at P_2 is the firm's profit-maximizing position.

This happy scenario for the firm is not the end of the story, however. *Every* firm in the industry (in both Home and Foreign) has the same incentive to lower its price in the hope of attracting customers away from all the other firms and earning monopoly profit. When all firms lower their prices at the same time, however, the quantity demanded from each firm increases along the demand curve D/N^A, not along d_2. Remember that the D/N^A curve shows the demand faced by each firm when all firms in the industry charge the same price. With the prices of all firms lowered to P_2, they will each sell the quantity Q'_2 at point B' rather than their expected sales of Q_2 at point B. At point B', the price charged is *less than* average costs, so every firm is incurring a loss. In the short-run equilibrium with trade, firms lower their prices, expecting to make profits at point B, but end up making losses at point B'.

Point B' is not the long-run equilibrium because the losses will bankrupt some firms and cause them to exit from the industry. This exit will increase demand (both d and D/N^A) for the remaining firms and decrease the number of product varieties available to consumers. To understand where the new long-run equilibrium occurs, we turn to a new diagram.

Long-Run Equilibrium with Trade Due to the exit of firms, the number of firms remaining in each country after trade is less than it was before trade. Let us call the number of firms in each country after trade is opened N^T, where $N^T < N^A$. This reduction in the number of firms increases the share of demand facing each one, so that $D/N^T > D/N^A$. In Figure 6-7, the demand D/N^T facing each firm lies to the right of the demand D/N^A in the earlier figures. We show the long-run equilibrium with trade at point C. At point C, the demand curve d_3 facing an individual firm is tangent to the average cost curve AC. In addition, the marginal revenue curve mr_3 intersects the marginal cost curve MC.

How does this long-run equilibrium compare to that without trade? First of all, despite the exit of some firms in each country, we still expect that the world number of products, which is $2N^T$ (the number produced in each country N^T times two countries), exceeds the number of products N^A available in each country before trade, $2N^T > N^A$. It follows that the demand curve d_3 facing each firm must be more elastic than demand d_1 in the absence of trade: the availability of imported products makes consumers more price sensitive than they were before trade, so the demand curve d_3 is more elastic than demand d_1 in Figure 6-5. At free-trade equilibrium (point C), each firm still in operation charges a lower price than it did with no trade, $P^W < P^A$, and produces a higher quantity, $Q_3 > Q_1$. The drop in prices and increase in quantity for each firm go hand in hand: as the quantity produced by each surviving firm increases, average costs fall due to increasing returns to scale, and so do the prices charged by firms.

FIGURE 6-7

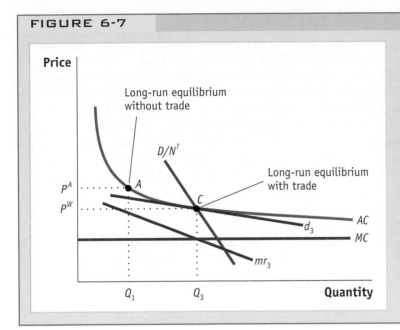

Long-Run Monopolistic Competition Equilibrium with Trade The long-run equilibrium with trade occurs at point C. At this point, profit is maximized for each firm producing Q_3 (which satisfies $mr_3 = MC$) and charging price P^W (which equals AC). Because monopoly profit is zero when price equals average cost, no firms enter or exit the industry. Compared with the long-run equilibrium without trade (Figure 6-5), d_3 (along with mr_3) has shifted out as domestic firms exited the industry and has become more elastic due to the greater total number of varieties with trade, $2N^T > N^A$. Compared with the long-run equilibrium without trade at point A, the trade equilibrium at point C has a lower price and higher sales by all surviving firms.

Gains from Trade The long-run equilibrium at point C has two sources of gains from trade for consumers. First, the price has fallen as compared with point A, so consumers benefit for that reason. A good way to think about this drop in the price is that it reflects increasing returns to scale, with average costs falling as the output of firms rises. The drop in average costs is a rise in productivity for these surviving firms because output can be produced more cheaply. So consumers gain from the drop in price, which is the result of the rise in productivity.

There is a second source of gains from trade to consumers. We assume that consumers obtain higher surplus when there are more product varieties available to buy, and hence the increase in variety is a source of gain for consumers. Within each country, some firms exit the market after trade begins, so fewer product varieties are produced by the remaining domestic firms. However, because consumers can buy products from both Home and Foreign firms, the *total* number of varieties available with trade is greater than the number of varieties available in any one country before trade, $2N^T > N^A$. Thus, in addition to the drop in prices, there is an added consumer gain from the availability of additional product varieties.

Adjustment Costs from Trade Against these long-run gains from trade, there are short-run adjustment costs as some firms in each country shut down and exit the industry. The workers in those firms will experience a spell of unemployment as they look for new jobs. Over the long run, however, we expect these workers to find new positions, so we view these costs as temporary. We do not build these adjustment costs into the model because they are short-term, but we are still interested in how large these costs might be in practice. To compare the short-run adjustment costs with the long-run gains from trade, we next look at the evidence from Canada, Mexico, and the United States under the North American Free Trade Agreement. We will see that the predictions of the monopolistic competition model hold reasonably well in each case.

3 The North American Free Trade Agreement

The idea that free trade will expand the range of products available to consumers is not new—it is even mentioned by David Ricardo in the quote at the beginning of this chapter. But the ability to carefully model the effects of trade under monopolistic competition is new and was developed in research during the 1980s by Professors Elhanan Helpman, Paul Krugman, and the late Kelvin Lancaster. That research was not just theoretical but was used to shed light on free-trade agreements, which guarantee free trade among a group of countries. In 1989, for example, Canada and the United States entered into a free-trade agreement, and in 1994 they were joined by Mexico in the North American Free Trade Agreement (NAFTA). The potential for Canadian firms to expand their output (and enjoy lower average costs) by selling in the United States and Mexico was a key factor in Canada's decision to enter into these free-trade agreements. The quote from the Canadian economist Daniel Trefler at the beginning of the chapter shows that there was indeed a rise in productivity in Canada because of the free-trade agreements. We use NAFTA to illustrate the gains and costs predicted by the monopolistic competition model.

Gains and Adjustment Costs for Canada Under NAFTA

Studies in Canada dating back to the 1960s predicted substantial gains from free trade with the United States because Canadian firms would expand their scale of operations to serve the larger market and lower their costs. A set of simulations based on the monopolistic competition model performed by the Canadian economist Richard Harris in the mid-1980s influenced Canadian policy makers to proceed with the free-trade agreement with the United States in 1989. Enough time has passed since then to look back and see how Canada has fared under the trade agreements with the United States and Mexico.

Headlines: The Long and the Short of the Canada-U.S. Free Trade Agreement describes what happened in Canada. Using data from 1988 to 1996, Professor Daniel Trefler of the University of Toronto found short-run adjustment costs of 100,000 lost jobs, or 5% of manufacturing employment. Some industries that faced particularly large tariff cuts saw their employment fall by as much as 15%. These are very large declines in employment. Over time, however, these job losses were more than made up for by the creation of new jobs elsewhere in manufacturing, so there were no long-run job losses as a result of the free-trade agreement.

What about long-run gains? Trefler found a large positive effect on the productivity of firms, with productivity rising as much as 18% over eight years in the industries most affected by tariff cuts, or a compound growth rate of 2.1% per year. For manufacturing overall, productivity rose by 6%, for a compound growth rate of 0.7% per year. The difference between these two numbers, which is 2.1 − 0.7 = 1.4% per year, is an estimate of how free trade with the United States affected the Canadian industries most affected by the tariff cuts over and above the impact on other industries. The productivity growth in Canada allowed for a modest rise in real earnings of 2.4% over the eight-year period for production workers, or 0.3% per year. We conclude that the prediction of the monopolistic competition model that surviving firms increase their productivity is confirmed for Canadian manufacturing. Those productivity gains led to a fall in prices for consumers and a rise in real earnings for workers, which demonstrates the first source of the gains from trade. The second source of gains from trade—increased product variety for Canadian consumers—was not measured in the

HEADLINES

The Long and the Short of the Canada-U.S. Free Trade Agreement

University of Toronto Professor Daniel Trefler studied the short-run effect of the Canada–United States Free Trade Agreement on employment in Canada, and the long-run effect on productivity and wages.

There is good news and bad news in regard to the Canada/U.S. Free Trade Agreement. The good news is that the deal, especially controversial in Canada, has raised productivity in Canadian industry since it was implemented on January 1, 1989, benefiting both consumers and stakeholders in efficient plants. The bad news is that there were also substantial short-run adjustment costs for workers who lost their jobs and for stakeholders in plants that were closed because of new import competition or the opportunity to produce more cheaply in the south. "One cannot understand current debates about freer trade without understanding this conflict" between the costs and gains that flow from trade liberalization, notes Daniel Trefler in "The Long and Short of the Canada-U.S. Free Trade Agreement"

(NBER Working Paper No. 8293). His paper looks at the impact of the FTA on a large number of performance indicators in the Canadian manufacturing sector from 1989 to 1996. In the one-third of industries that experienced the largest tariff cuts in that period, ranging between 5 and 33 percent and averaging 10 percent, employment shrunk by 15 percent, output fell 11 percent, and the number of plants declined 8 percent. These industries include the makers of garments, footwear, upholstered furniture, coffins and caskets, fur goods, and adhesives. For manufacturing as a whole, the comparable numbers are 5, 3, and 4 percent, respectively, Trefler finds. "These numbers capture the large adjustment costs associated with reallocating resources out of protected, inefficient, low-end manufacturing," he notes.

Since 1996, manufacturing employment and output have largely rebounded in Canada. This suggests that some of the lost jobs and output were reallocated to high-end manufacturing. On the positive side, the tariff cuts boosted labor productivity (how much output is produced per hour of work) by a compounded annual rate of 2.1 percent for the most affected industries and by 0.6 percent for manufacturing as a whole, Trefler calculates. . . . Surprisingly, Trefler writes, the tariff cuts raised annual earnings slightly. Production workers' wages rose by 0.8 percent per year in the most affected industries and by 0.3 percent per year for manufacturing as a whole. The tariff cuts did not effect earnings of higher-paid non-production workers or weekly hours of production workers.

Source: Excerpted from David R. Francis, "Canada Free Trade Agreement," NBER Digest, September 1, 2001, http://www.nber.org/digest/sep01/w8293.html. This paper by Daniel Trefler was published in the American Economic Review, *2004, 94(4), pp. 870–895.*

study by Professor Trefler but has been estimated for the United States, as discussed later in this chapter.

Gains and Adjustment Costs for Mexico Under NAFTA

In the mid-1980s Mexican President Miguel de la Madrid embarked on a program of economic liberalization that included land reform and greater openness to foreign investment. Tariffs with the United States were as high as 100% on some goods, and there were many restrictions on the operations of foreign firms. De la Madrid believed that the economic reforms were needed to boost growth and incomes in Mexico. Joining NAFTA with the United States and Canada in 1994 was a way to ensure the permanence of the reforms already under way. Under NAFTA, Mexican tariffs on U.S. goods declined from an average of 14% in 1990 to 1% in 2001.[4] In

---

[4] Trade was not completely free in 2001 because the tariff reductions under NAFTA were phased in for periods as long as 15 years. Tariff cuts in the agriculture sector in Mexico had the longest phase-in period.

addition, U.S. tariffs on Mexican imports fell as well, though from levels that were much lower to begin with in most industries.

How did the fall in tariffs under NAFTA affect the Mexican economy? We will review the evidence on productivity and wages below, but first, you should read **Headlines: NAFTA Turns 15, Bravo!** This editorial was written in 2009, the fifteenth anniversary of the beginning of NAFTA, and appeared in a U.S.-based

HEADLINES

NAFTA Turns 15, Bravo!

This editorial discussed the impact of NAFTA on the U.S. and Mexican economies. It appeared in a U.S.-based pro-business publication focusing on Latin-American businesses.

As Americans and Mexicans celebrated the start of a new year yesterday, they had reason to celebrate another milestone as well: The North American Free Trade Agreement (NAFTA) turned 15. Despite the slowdown in both the U.S. and Mexican economies, trade between the two nations was expected to set a new record last year. In the first half of 2008, U.S.-Mexico trade grew by 9.6 percent to $183.7 billion. That follows a record $347 billion in trade in 2007. Compare that to the $81.5 billion in total two-way trade in 1993, the last year before NAFTA was implemented.

NAFTA has without a doubt been the primary reason for that success. It dramatically opened up Mexico's economy to U.S. goods and investments, helping boost revenues for many U.S. companies. At the same time, Mexican companies were able to get duty-free access to the world's largest market, resulting in more sales and more jobs there. The trade growth has meant benefits for both consumers and companies on each side of the border.

While China clearly dominates many of the products we buy in U.S. stores these days, Mexico also plays an important role. Mexico ranks third behind Canada and China among the top exporters to the U.S. market. But Mexico beats China when it comes to buying U.S. goods. During the first ten months last year [2008], Mexico imported U.S. products worth $129.4 billion—or more than twice the $61.0 billion China (with a much larger economy) bought from us. . . .

NAFTA has benefited consumers in the U.S. through greater choice of products, in terms of selection, quality, and price, including many that are less expensive than pre-NAFTA. . . . NAFTA has allowed U.S. manufacturing giants from General Motors to General Electric to use economies of scale for their production lines. Prior to NAFTA, GM's assembly plants in Mexico assembled small volumes of many products, which resulted in high costs and somewhat inferior quality, says Mustafa Mohatarem, GM's chief economist. Now its plants in Mexico specialize in few high-volume products, resulting in low cost and high quality, he points out. The result benefits both U.S. and Mexican consumers. . . .

To be sure, NAFTA is not perfect. For one, it didn't even touch on Mexico's sensitive oil sector, which should have been part of a comprehensive free trade agreement. Neither did it offer any teeth when it came to violations. For example, the shameful U.S. disregard for the NAFTA regulations on allowing Mexican trucks to enter the United States. Only in September last year [2008], as part of a pilot program by the Bush Administration, did the first Mexican trucks enter the United States—after a delay of eight years . . . thanks to opposition from U.S. unions and lawmakers. . . . Many economists also are critical of NAFTA's labor and environmental side agreements, which President Bill Clinton negotiated in order to support the treaty.

However, all in all NAFTA has been of major benefit for both the United States and Mexico. Any renegotiation of NAFTA, as president-elect Barack Obama pledged during last year's campaign, would negatively harm both economies just as they now suffer from economic recession. It would also harm our relations with Mexico, our top trading partner in Latin America. Hopefully, pragmatism will win the day in Washington, D.C. this year, as our new president aims to find a way to get the U.S. economy back on track. Leaving NAFTA alone would be a good start.

In the meantime, we congratulate NAFTA on its 15 years. *Feliz Cumpleaños.*

Source: Editors, Latin Business Chronicle, *January 2, 2009, electronic edition.*

pro-business publication focusing on Latin-American businesses. It makes a number of arguments in favor of NAFTA that we have also discussed, including increasing returns to scale and product variety for consumers. But it also points out some defects of NAFTA, including the tardiness of the United States in allowing an open border for trucks from Mexico, and the environmental and labor side agreements (discussed in a later chapter). Even after 15 years, Mexican trucks were not permitted into the United States, and this fact led Mexico to retaliate by imposing tariffs on some U.S. goods. Two years later, in 2011, the United States finally agreed to allow Mexican trucks to cross the border to deliver goods.[5] In **Headlines: Nearly 20 Years After NAFTA, First Mexican Truck Arrives In U.S. Interior,** we describe this milestone in the economic relations between the United States and Mexico.

Productivity in Mexico As we did for Canada, let us investigate the impact of NAFTA on productivity in Mexico. In panel (a) of Figure 6-8, we show the growth in labor productivity for two types of manufacturing firms: the maquiladora plants, which are close to the border and produce almost exclusively for export to the United States, and all other nonmaquiladora manufacturing plants in Mexico.[6] The

HEADLINES

Nearly 20 Years After NAFTA, First Mexican Truck Arrives In U.S. Interior

A truck crosses the border between Mexico and the United States on October 21, 2011.

On October 21, 2011, the first big-rig truck from Mexico crossed the border into Laredo, Texas, under a trucking program that was agreed to in NAFTA but that took 17 years to implement.

Nearly two decades after the passage of the North American Free Trade Agreement, the first Mexican truck ventured into the U.S. under provisions of the controversial treaty. With little fanfare, a white tractor-trailer with Mexican license plates entered the courtyard of the Atlas Copco facility in Garland, Texas on Saturday afternoon to unload a Mexico-manufactured metal structure for drilling oil wells.

The delivery marked the first time that a truck from Mexico reached the U.S. interior under the 17-year-old trade agreement, which was supposed to give trucks from the neighboring countries access to highways on both sides of the border. The Obama administration signed an agreement with Mexico to end the long dispute over the NAFTA provision in July that also removes $2 billion in duties on American goods. "We were prepared for this a long time ago because we met the requirements and complied with the rules of cross-border transportation, which made us earn the trust of American companies," said Gerardo Aguilar, a manager for "Transportes Olympic," the only Mexican company authorized to operate its trucks in the U.S. The long-delayed door-to-door delivery was launched with a bi-national ceremony Friday to mark the truck's crossing at the international bridge "World Trade" in Laredo, Tex., the entry point for 40 percent of products imported from Mexico.

Source: The Huffington Post, http://www.huffingtonpost.com/2011/10/24/nearly-20-years-after-nafta-first-mexican-arrives-in-us-interior_n_1028630.html, First Posted: 10/24/11 06:08 PM ET Updated: 12/24/11 05:12 AM ET

---

[5] The U.S. spending bill signed by President Obama in 2009 eliminated a pilot program that would have allowed Mexican long-haul trucks to transport cargo throughout the United States. In retaliation, Mexico imposed tariffs on $2.4 billion worth of American goods. See Elisabeth Malkin, "Nafta's Promise, Unfulfilled," *The New York Times*, March 24, 2009, electronic edition.

[6] Labor productivity for the maquiladoras is real value-added per worker and for non-maquiladoras is real output per worker. Both are taken from Gary C. Hufbauer and Jeffrey J. Schott, 2005, *NAFTA Revisited: Achievements and Challenges* (Washington, D.C.: Peterson Institute for International Economics), Table 1-9, p. 45.

maquiladora plants should be most affected by NAFTA. In panel (b), we also show what happened to real wages and real incomes.

For the maquiladora plants in panel (a), productivity rose 45% from 1994 (when Mexico joined NAFTA) to 2003, a compound growth rate of 4.1% per year for more than nine years. For the non-maquiladora plants, productivity rose overall by 25% from 1994 to 2003, 2.5% per year. The difference between these two numbers, which is 1.6% per year, is an estimate of the impact of NAFTA on the productivity of the maquiladora plants over and above the increase in productivity that occurred in the rest of Mexico.

Real Wages and Incomes Real wages in the maquiladora and non-maquiladora plants are shown in panel (b) of Figure 6-8. From 1994 to 1997, there was a fall of more than 20% in real wages in both sectors, despite a rise in productivity in the non-maquiladora sector. This fall in real wages is not what we expect from the monopolistic competition model, so why did it occur?

Shortly after Mexico joined NAFTA, it suffered a financial crisis that led to a large devaluation of the peso. It would be incorrect to attribute the peso crisis to Mexico's joining NAFTA, even though both events occurred the same year. Prior to 1994 Mexico followed a fixed exchange-rate policy, but in late 1994 it switched to a flexible exchange-rate regime instead, and the peso devalued to much less than its former fixed value. Details about exchange-rate regimes and the reasons for switching from

FIGURE 6-8

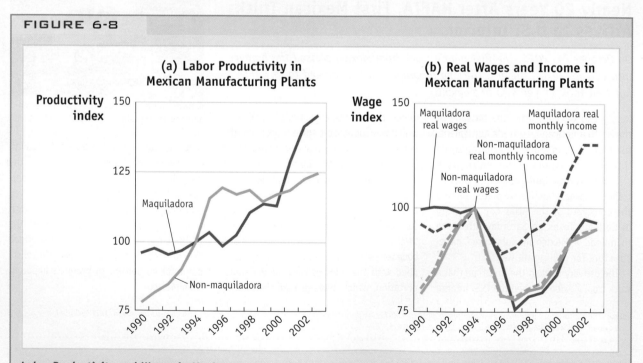

Labor Productivity and Wages in Mexico Panel (a) shows labor productivity for workers in the maquiladora Mexican manufacturing plants and for workers in non-maquiladora plants in the rest of Mexico. Panel (b) shows wages and monthly income for workers in maquiladora and non-maquiladora plants. Productivity and real monthly income grew faster in the maquiladora plants because of increased trade with the United States.

Source: Gary C. Hufbauer and Jeffrey J. Schott, 2005, NAFTA Revisited: Achievements and Challenges (Washington, D.C.: Peterson Institute for International Economics), p. 45.

a fixed to flexible exchange rate are covered in international macroeconomics. For now, the key idea is that when the peso's value falls, it becomes more expensive for Mexico to import goods from the United States because the peso price of imports goes up. The Mexican consumer price index also goes up, and as a result, real wages for Mexican workers fall.

The maquiladora sector, located beside the U.S. border, was more susceptible to the exchange-rate change and did not experience much of a gain in productivity over that period because of the increased cost of inputs imported from the United States. Workers in both the maquiladora and non-maquiladora sectors had to pay higher prices for imported goods, which is reflected in higher Mexican consumer prices. So the decline in real wages for workers in both sectors is similar. This decline was short-lived, however, and real wages in both sectors began to rise again in 1998. By 2003 real wages in both sectors had risen to nearly equal their value in 1994. This means that workers in Mexico did not gain or lose because of NAFTA on average: the productivity gains were not shared with workers, which is a disappointing finding, but real wages at least recovered from the effects of the peso crisis.

The picture is somewhat better if instead of real wages, we look at real monthly income, which includes higher-income employees who earn salaries rather than wages.[7] In panel (b), for the non-maquiladora sector, the data on real wages and real monthly income move together closely. But in the maquiladora sector, real monthly incomes were indeed higher in 2003 than in 1994, indicating some gains for workers in the manufacturing plants most affected by NAFTA. This conclusion is reinforced by other evidence from Mexico, which shows that higher-income workers fared better than unskilled workers in the maquiladora sector and better than workers in the rest of Mexico.[8] From this evidence, the higher-income workers in the maquiladora sector gained most from NAFTA in the long run.

Adjustment Costs in Mexico When Mexico joined NAFTA, it was expected that the short-run adjustment costs would fall especially hard on the agricultural sector in Mexico, such as the corn industry, because it would face strong import competition from the United States. For that reason, the tariff reductions in agriculture were phased in over 15 years. The evidence to date suggests that the farmers growing corn in Mexico did not suffer as much as was feared.[9] There were several reasons for this outcome. First, the poorest farmers do not sell the corn they grow but consume it themselves and buy any extra corn they need. These farmers benefited from cheaper import prices for corn from the United States. Second, the Mexican government was able to use subsidies to offset the reduction in income for other corn farmers. Surprisingly, the total production of corn in Mexico rose following NAFTA instead of falling.

Turning to the manufacturing sector, we should again distinguish the maquiladora and non-maquiladora plants. For the maquiladora plants, employment grew rapidly following NAFTA, from 584,000 workers in 1994 to a peak of 1.29 million workers in

---

[7] Wage data refer to production workers who are involved in assembly-line and similar activities. Income data refer to all employees, including production and nonproduction workers. Monthly income includes payment from profit-sharing by firms and a Christmas bonus, which are common in Mexico.

[8] Gordon H. Hanson, 2007, "Globalization, Labor Income and Poverty in Mexico." In Ann Harrison, ed., *Globalization and Poverty* (Chicago: University of Chicago Press; Washington, D.C.: National Bureau of Economic Research [NBER]), pp. 417–452.

[9] See Margaret McMillan, Alix Peterson Zwane, and Nava Ashraf, 2007, "My Policies or Yours: Does OECD Support for Agriculture Increase Poverty in Developing Countries?" In Ann Harrison, ed., *Globalization and Poverty* (Chicago: University of Chicago Press; Washington, D.C.: NBER), pp. 183–232.

2000. After that, however, the maquiladora sector entered a downturn, due to several factors: the United States entered a recession, reducing demand for Mexican exports; China was competing for U.S. sales by exporting products similar to those sold by Mexico; and the Mexican peso became overvalued, making it difficult to export abroad. For all these reasons, employment in the maquiladora sector fell after 2000, to 1.1 million workers in 2003. It is not clear whether we should count this decline in employment as a short-run adjustment cost due to NAFTA, nor is it clear how long it will take the maquiladora sector to recover. What is apparent is that the maquiladora sector faces increasing international competition (not all due to NAFTA), which can be expected to raise the volatility of its output and employment, and that volatility can be counted as a cost of international trade for workers who are displaced.

Gains and Adjustment Costs for the United States Under NAFTA

Studies on the effects of NAFTA on the United States have not estimated its effects on the productivity of American firms, perhaps because Canada and Mexico are only two of many export markets for the United States, and it would be hard to identify the impact of their tariff reductions. Instead, to measure the long-run gains from NAFTA and other trade agreements, researchers have estimated the second source of gains from trade: the expansion of import varieties available to consumers. For the United States, we will compare the long-run gains to consumers from expanded product varieties with the short-run adjustment costs from exiting firms and unemployment.

Expansion of Variety to the United States To understand how NAFTA affected the range of products available to American consumers, Table 6-3 shows the variety of goods Mexico exported to the United States in 1990 and 2001. To interpret these numbers, start with the 1990 export variety in agriculture of 42%. That figure means that 42% of all the agricultural products the United States imported in 1990, from any country, also came from Mexico. For instance, avocados, bananas, cucumbers, and tomatoes imported from various Central or South American countries were also imported to the United States from Mexico. Measuring the variety of products Mexico exported to the United States does not take into account *the amount* that Mexico sells of each product; rather, it counts the *number* of different types of products Mexico

TABLE 6-3

Mexico's Export Variety to the United States, 1990–2001 This table shows the extent of variety in Mexican exports to the United States, by industry. From 1990 to 2001, export variety grew in every industry, as U.S. tariffs were reduced due to NAFTA. All figures are percentages.

	Agriculture	Textiles and Garments	Wood and Paper	Petroleum and Plastics	Mining and Metals	Machinery and Transport	Electronics	Average
1990	42%	71%	47%	55%	47%	66%	40%	52%
2001	51	83	63	73	56	76	66	67
Annual growth	1.9	1.4	2.6	2.5	1.7	1.3	4.6	2.2

Source: Robert Feenstra and Hiau Looi Kee, 2007, "Trade Liberalization and Export Variety: A Comparison of Mexico and China," The World Economy, 30(1), 5–21.

sells to the United States as compared with the total number of products the United States imports from all countries.

From 1990 to 2001, the range of agricultural products that Mexico exported to the United States expanded from 42 to 51%. That compound growth rate of 1.9% per year is close to the average annual growth rate for export variety in all industries shown in the last column of Table 6-3, which is 2.2% per year. Export variety grew at a faster rate in the wood and paper industry (with a compound growth rate of 2.6% per year), petroleum and plastics (2.5% growth), and electronics (4.6% growth). The industries in which there has traditionally been a lot of trade between the United States and Mexico—such as machinery and transport (including autos) and textiles and garments—have slower growth in export variety because Mexico was exporting a wide range of products in these industries to the United States even before joining NAFTA.

The increase in the variety of products exported from Mexico to the United States under NAFTA is a source of gains from trade for American consumers. The United States has also imported more product varieties over time from many other countries, too, especially developing countries. According to one estimate, the total number of product varieties imported into the United States from 1972 to 2001 has increased by four times. Furthermore, that expansion in import variety has had the same beneficial impact on consumers as a reduction in import prices of 1.2% per year.[10] That equivalent price reduction is a measure of the gains from trade due to the expansion of varieties exported to the United States from all countries.

Unfortunately, we do not have a separate estimate of the gains from the growth of export varieties from Mexico alone, which averages 2.2% per year from Table 6-3. Suppose we use the same 1.2% price reduction estimate for Mexico that has been found for all countries. That is, we assume that the growth in export variety from Mexico leads to the same beneficial impact on U.S. consumers as a reduction in Mexican import prices of 1.2% per year, or about one-half as much as the growth in export variety itself. In 1994, the first year of NAFTA, Mexico exported $50 billion in merchandise goods to the United States and by 2001 this sum had grown to $131 billion. Using $90 billion as an average of these two values, a 1.2% reduction in the prices for Mexican imports would save U.S. consumers $90 billion · 1.2% = $1.1 billion per year. We will assume that all these savings are due to NAFTA, though even without NAFTA, there would likely have been some growth in export variety from Mexico.

It is crucial to realize that these consumer savings are *permanent* and that they *increase over time* as export varieties from Mexico continue to grow. Thus, in the first year of NAFTA, we estimate a gain to U.S. consumers of $1.1 billion; in the second year a gain of $2.2 billion, equivalent to a total fall in prices of 2.4%; in the third year a gain of $3.3 billion; and so on. Adding these up over the first nine years of NAFTA, the total benefit to consumers was $49.5 billion, or an average of $5.5 billion per year. In 2003, the tenth year of NAFTA, consumers would gain by $11 billion as compared with 1994. This gain will continue to grow as Mexico further increases the range of varieties exported to the United States.

[10] Christian Broda and David E. Weinstein, 2006, "Globalization and the Gains from Variety," *Quarterly Journal of Economics*, 121(2), May, 541–585.

Adjustment Costs in the United States Adjustment costs in the United States come as firms exit the market because of import competition and the workers employed by those firms are temporarily unemployed. One way to measure that temporary unemployment is to look at the claims under the U.S. **Trade Adjustment Assistance (TAA)** provisions. The TAA program offers assistance to workers in manufacturing who lose their jobs because of import competition. As we discussed in Chapter 3, the North American Free Trade Agreement included a special extension of TAA to workers laid off due to import competition because of NAFTA.

By looking at claims under that program, we can get an idea of the unemployment caused by NAFTA, one of the short-run costs of the agreement. From 1994 to 2002, some 525,000 workers, or about 58,000 per year, lost their jobs and were certified as adversely affected by trade or investment with Canada or Mexico under the NAFTA-TAA program.[11] As a result, these workers were entitled to additional unemployment benefits. This number is probably the most accurate estimate we have of the temporary unemployment caused by NAFTA.

How large is the displacement of 58,000 workers per year due to NAFTA? We can compare this number with overall job displacement in the United States. Over the three years from January 1999 to December 2001, 4 million workers were displaced, about one-third of whom were in manufacturing. So the annual number of workers displaced in manufacturing was 4 million $\cdot (\frac{1}{3}) \cdot (\frac{1}{3}) = 444,000$ workers per year. Thus, the NAFTA layoffs of 58,000 workers were about 13% of the total displacement in manufacturing, which is a substantial amount.

Rather than compare the displacement caused by NAFTA with the total displacement in manufacturing, however, we can instead evaluate the wages lost by displaced workers and compare this amount with the consumer gains. In Chapter 3 (see **Application: Manufacturing and Services**), we learned that about 56% of workers laid off in manufacturing during the 2009–2011 period were reemployed within three years (by January 2012). That estimate of the fraction of workers reemployed within three years has been somewhat higher—66%—during earlier recessions. Some workers are reemployed in less than three years; for some, it takes longer. To simplify the problem, suppose that the *average* length of unemployment for laid-off workers is three years.[12] Average yearly earnings for production workers in manufacturing were $31,000 in 2000, so each displaced worker lost $93,000 in wages (three times the workers' average annual income).[13] Total lost wages caused by displacement would be 58,000 workers displaced per year times $93,000, or $5.4 billion per year during the first nine years of NAFTA.

These private costs of $5.4 billion are nearly equal to the average welfare gains of $5.5 billion per year due to the expansion of import varieties from Mexico from 1994 to 2002, as computed previously. But the gains from increased product variety *continue and grow over time* as new imported products become available to American consumers. Recall from the previous calculation that the gains from the ongoing

---

[11] The information in this paragraph is drawn from Gary Clyde Hufbauer and Jeffrey J. Schott, 2006, *NAFTA Revisited: Achievements and Challenges* (Washington, D.C.: Peterson Institute for International Economics), pp. 38–42.

[12] We show in Problem 8 at the end of the chapter that this assumption is accurate.

[13] We are not considering the additional losses if the new job has lower wages than earned previously.

expansion of product varieties from Mexico were $11 billion in 2003, the tenth year of NAFTA, or twice as high as the $5.4 billion costs of adjustment. As the consumer gains continue to grow, adjustment costs due to job losses fall. Thus, the consumer gains from increased variety, when summed over years, considerably exceed the private losses from displacement. This outcome is guaranteed to occur because the gains from expanded import varieties occur *every year* that the imports are available, whereas labor displacement is a temporary phenomenon.

The calculation we have made shows that the gains to U.S. consumers from greater import variety from Mexico, when summed over time, are more than the private costs of adjustment. In practice, the actual compensation received by workers is much less than their costs of adjustment. In 2002 the NAFTA–TAA program was consolidated with the general TAA program in the United States, so there is no further record of layoffs as a result of NAFTA. Under the Trade Act of 2002, the funding for TAA was increased from $400 million to $1.2 billion per year and some other improvements to the program were made, such as providing a health-care subsidy for laid-off workers. In addition, as part of the jobs stimulus bill signed by President Obama on February 17, 2009, workers in the service sector (as well as farmers) who lose their jobs due to trade can now also apply for TAA benefits, as was discussed in Chapter 3. It would be desirable to continue to expand the TAA program to include more workers who face layoffs due to increased global competition.

Summary of NAFTA In this section, we have been able to measure, at least in part, the long-run gains and short-run costs from NAFTA for Canada, Mexico, and the United States. The monopolistic competition model indicates two sources of gains from trade: the rise in productivity due to expanded output by surviving firms, which leads to lower prices, and the expansion in the overall number of varieties of products available to consumers with trade, despite the exit of some firms in each country. For Mexico and Canada, we measured the long-run gains by the improvement in productivity for exporters as compared with other manufacturing firms. For the United States, we measured the long-run gains using the expansion of varieties from Mexico, and the equivalent drop in price faced by U.S. consumers. It is clear that for Canada and the United States, the long-run gains considerably exceed the short-run costs. The picture is less optimistic for Mexico because the gains have not been reflected in the growth of real wages for production workers (due in part to the peso crisis). The real earnings of higher-income workers in the maquiladora sector have risen, however, so they have been the principal beneficiaries of NAFTA so far.

4 Intra-Industry Trade and the Gravity Equation

In the monopolistic competition model, countries both import and export different varieties of differentiated goods. This result differs from the Ricardian and Heckscher-Ohlin models that we studied in Chapters 2 and 4: in those models, countries either export or import a good but do not export and import the same good simultaneously. Under monopolistic competition, countries will specialize in producing different varieties of a differentiated good and will trade those varieties back and forth. As we saw from the example of golf clubs at the beginning of the chapter, this is a common trade pattern that we call intra-industry trade.

Index of Intra-Industry Trade

To develop the idea of intra-industry trade, consider the U.S. imports and exports of the goods shown in Table 6-4. In 2012 the United States imported $1,731 million in vaccines and exported $2,514 million. When the amounts of imports and exports are similar for a good, as they are for vaccines, it is an indication that much of the trade in that good is intra-industry trade. The **index of intra-industry** trade tells us what proportion of trade in each product involves both imports and exports: a high index (up to 100%) indicates that an equal amount of the good is imported and exported, whereas a low index (0%) indicates that the good is either imported or exported but not both.

The formula for the index of intra-industry trade is

$$(\text{Index of intra-industry trade}) = \frac{\text{Minimum of imports and exports}}{\frac{1}{2}(\text{Imports} + \text{exports})}$$

For vaccines, the minimum of imports and exports is $1,731 million, and the average of imports and exports is $\frac{1}{2}(1,731 + 2,514) = \$2,123$ million. So $\frac{1731}{2123} = 82\%$ of the U.S. trade in vaccines is intra-industry trade; that is, it involves both exporting and importing of vaccines.

In Table 6-4, we show some other examples of intra-industry trade in other products for the United States. In addition to vaccines, products such as whiskey and frozen orange juice have a high index of intra-industry trade. These are all examples of highly differentiated products: for vaccines and whiskey, each exporting country sells products that are different from those of other exporting countries, including the United States. Even frozen orange juice is a differentiated product, once we realize that it is imported and exported in different months of the year. So it is not surprising

TABLE 6-4

Index of Intra-Industry Trade for the United States, 2012 Shown here are value of imports, value of exports, and the index of intra-industry trade for a number of products. When the value of imports is similar to the value of exports, such as for vaccines, whiskey, and frozen orange juice, then the index of intra-industry trade is highest, and when a product is mainly imported or exported (but not both), then the index of intra-industry trade is lowest.

Product	Value of Imports ($ millions)	Value of Export ($ millions)	Index of Intra-Industry Trade (%)
Vaccines	1,731	2,514	82
Whiskey	1,457	1,008	82
Frozen orange juice	24	16	81
Natural gas	8,292	4,346	69
Mattresses	195	59	46
Golf clubs	476	122	41
Small cars	77,086	19,478	40
Apples	169	826	34
Sunglasses	1,287	248	32
Golf carts	12	137	16
Telephones	615	38	12
Large passenger aircraft	4,588	84,171	10
Men's shorts	768	7	2

Source: U.S. International Trade Commission, Interactive Tariff and Trade DataWeb, at http://dataweb.usitc.gov/.

that we both export and import these products. On the other hand, products such as men's shorts, large passenger aircraft, telephones, and golf carts have a low index of intra-industry trade. These goods are either mainly imported into the United States (like men's shorts and telephones) or mainly exported (like large passenger aircraft and golf carts). Even though these goods are still differentiated, we can think of them as being closer to fitting the Ricardian or Heckscher-Ohlin model, in which trade is determined by comparative advantage, such as having lower relative costs in one country because of technology or resource abundance. To obtain a high index of intra-industry trade, it is necessary for the good to be differentiated *and* for costs to be similar in the Home and Foreign countries, leading to both imports and exports.

The Gravity Equation

The index of intra-industry trade measures the degree of intra-industry trade for a product but does not tell us anything about the total amount of trade. To explain the value of trade, we need a different equation, called the "gravity equation." This equation was given its name by a Dutch economist and Nobel laureate, Jan Tinbergen. Tinbergen was trained in physics, so he thought about the trade between countries as similar to the force of gravity between objects: Newton's universal law of gravitation states that objects with larger mass, or that are closer to each other, have a greater gravitational pull between them. Tinbergen's gravity equation for trade states that countries with larger GDPs, or that are closer to each other, have more trade between them. Both these equations can be explained simply—even if you have never studied physics, you will be able to grasp their meanings. The point is that just as the force of gravity is strongest between two large objects, the monopolistic competition model predicts that large countries (as measured by their GDP) should trade the most with one another. There is much empirical evidence to support this prediction, as we will show.

Newton's Universal Law of Gravitation Suppose that two objects each have mass M_1 and M_2 and are located distance d apart. According to Newton's universal law of gravitation, the force of gravity F_g between these two objects is

$$F_g = G \cdot \frac{M_1 \cdot M_2}{d^2}$$

where G is a constant that tells us the magnitude of this relationship. The larger each object is, or the closer they are to each other, the greater is the force of gravity between them.

The Gravity Equation in Trade The equation proposed by Tinbergen to explain trade between countries is similar to Newton's law of gravity, except that instead of the mass of two objects, we use the GDP of two countries, and instead of predicting the force of gravity, we are predicting the amount of trade between them. The gravity equation in trade is

$$\text{Trade} = B \cdot \frac{GDP_1 \cdot GDP_2}{dist^n}$$

where Trade is the amount of trade (measured by imports, exports, or their average) between two countries, GDP_1 and GDP_2 are their gross domestic products, and *dist* is the distance between them. Notice that we use the exponent n on distance, $dist^n$, rather than $dist^2$ as in Newton's law of gravity, because we are not sure of the precise relationship between distance and trade. The term B in front of the gravity equation is a constant that indicates the relationship between the "gravity term" (i.e., $GDP_1 \cdot GDP_2/dist^n$) and Trade. It can also be interpreted as summarizing the effects of all factors (other than size and distance) that influence the amount of trade between two countries; such factors include tariffs (which would lower the amount of trade and reduce B), sharing a common border (which would increase trade and raise B), and so on.

According to the gravity equation, the larger the countries are (as measured by their GDP), or the closer they are to each other, the greater is the amount of trade between them. This connection among economic size, distance, and trade is an implication of the monopolistic competition model that we have studied in this chapter. The monopolistic competition model implies that larger countries trade the most for two reasons: larger countries export more because they produce more product varieties, and they import more because their demand is higher. Therefore, larger countries trade more in both exports and imports.

Deriving the Gravity Equation To explain more carefully why the gravity equation holds in the monopolistic competition model, we can work through some algebra using the GDPs of the various countries. Start with the GDP of Country 1, GDP_1. Each of the goods produced in Country 1 is a differentiated product, so they are different from the varieties produced in other countries. Every other country will demand the goods of Country 1 (because they are different from their home-produced goods), and the amount of their demand will depend on two factors: (1) the relative size of the importing country (larger countries demand more) and (2) the distance between the two countries (being farther away leads to higher transportation costs and less trade).

To measure the relative size of each importing country, we use its share of world GDP. Specifically, we define Country 2's share of world GDP as $Share_2 = GDP_2/GDP_W$. To measure the transportation costs involved in trade, we use distance raised to a power, or $dist^n$. Using these definitions, exports from Country 1 to Country 2 will equal the goods available in Country 1 (GDP_1), times the relative size of Country 2 ($Share_2$), divided by the transportation costs between them ($dist^n$), so that

$$\text{Trade} = \frac{GDP_1 \cdot Share_2}{dist^n} = \left(\frac{1}{GDP_W}\right)\frac{GDP_1 \cdot GDP_2}{dist^n}$$

This equation for the trade between Countries 1 and 2 looks similar to the gravity equation, especially if we think of the term $(1/GDP_W)$ as the constant term B. We see from this equation that the trade between two countries will be proportional to their relative sizes, measured by the product of their GDPs (the greater the size of the countries, the larger is trade), and inversely proportional to the distance between them (the smaller the distance, the larger is trade). The following application explores how well the gravity equation works in practice.

APPLICATION

The Gravity Equation for Canada and the United States

We can apply the gravity equation to trade between any pair of countries, or even to trade between the provinces or states of one country and another. Panel (a) of Figure 6-9 shows data collected on the value of trade between Canadian provinces and U.S. states in 1993. On the horizontal axis, we show the gravity term:

$$\text{Gravity term} = \frac{GDP_1 \cdot GDP_2}{dist^{1.25}}$$

where GDP_1 is the gross domestic product of a U.S. state (in billions of U.S. dollars), GDP_2 is the gross domestic product of a Canadian province (in billions of U.S. dollars), and *dist* is the distance between them (in miles). We use the exponent 1.25 on the distance term because it has been shown in other research studies to describe the relationship between distance and trade value quite well. The horizontal axis is

FIGURE 6-9

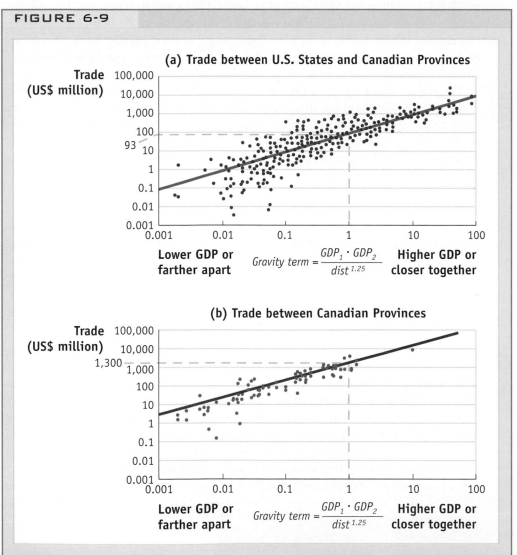

Gravity Equation for the United States and Canada, 1993 Plotted in these figures are the dollar value of exports in 1993 and the gravity term (plotted in log scale). Panel (a) shows these variables for trade between 10 Canadian provinces and 30 U.S. states. When the gravity term is 1, for example, the amount of trade between a province and state is $93 million. Panel (b) shows these variables for trade between 10 Canadian provinces. When the gravity term is 1, the amount of trade between the provinces is $1.3 billion, 14 times larger than between a province and a state. These graphs illustrate two important points: there is a positive relationship between country size (as measured by GDP) and trade volume, and there is much more trade within Canada than between Canada and the United States.

Source: Author's calculations using data from James A. Anderson and Eric van Wincoop, 2003, "Gravity with Gravitas: A Solution to the Border Puzzle," American Economic Review, 170–192.

plotted as a logarithmic scale, with values from 0.001 to 100. A higher value along the horizontal axis indicates either a large GDP for the trading province and state or a smaller distance between them.

The vertical axis in Figure 6-9 shows the 1993 value of exports (in millions of U.S. dollars) between a Canadian province and U.S. state or between a U.S. state and Canadian province; this is the value of trade for the province–state pair. That axis is also plotted as a logarithmic scale, with values from $0.001 million (or $1,000) to $100,000 million (or $100 billion) in trade. There are 30 states and 10 provinces included in the study, so there are a total of 600 possible trade flows between them (though some of those flows are zero, indicating that no exporting takes place). Each of the points in panel (a) represents the trade flow and gravity term between one state and one province.

We can see from the set of points in panel (a) that states and provinces with a higher gravity term between them (measured on the horizontal axis) also tend to have more trade (measured on the vertical axis). That strong, positive relationship shown by the set of points in panel (a) demonstrates that the gravity equation holds well empirically. Panel (a) also shows the "best fit" straight line through the set of points, which has the following equation:

$$\text{Trade} = 93\,\frac{GDP_1 \cdot GDP_2}{dist^{1.25}}$$

The constant term $B = 93$ gives the best fit to this gravity equation for Canadian provinces and U.S. states. When the gravity term equals 1, as illustrated in panel (a), then the predicted amount of trade between that state and province is $93 million. The closest example to this point is Alberta and New Jersey. In 1993 there were $94 million in exports from Alberta to New Jersey and they had a gravity term of approximately 1.

Trade Within Canada Because the gravity equation works well at predicting international trade between provinces and states in different countries, it should also work well at predicting trade *within* a country, or *intra-national* trade. To explore this idea, panel (b) of Figure 6-9 graphs the value of exports (in millions of U.S. dollars) between any two Canadian provinces, along with the gravity term for those provinces. The scale of the axes in panel (b) is the same as in panel (a). From panel (b), we again see that there is a strong, positive relationship between the gravity term between two provinces (measured on the horizontal axis) and their trade (measured on the vertical axis). The "best fit" straight line through the set of points has the following equation:

$$\text{Trade} = 1{,}300 \cdot \frac{GDP_1 \cdot GDP_2}{dist^{1.25}}$$

That is, the constant term $B = 1,300$ gives the best fit to this gravity equation for Canadian provinces. When the gravity term equals 1, as illustrated in panel (b), then the predicted amount of trade between two provinces is $1,300 million, or $1.3 billion. The closest example to this combination is between British Columbia and Alberta: in 1993 their gravity term was approximately 1.3 and British Columbia exported $1.4 billion of goods to Alberta.

Comparing the gravity equation for international trade between Canada and the United States with the gravity equation for intra-national trade in Canada, the constant term for Canadian trade is much bigger—1,300 as compared with 93. Taking the ratio of these two constant terms (1,300/93 = 14), we find that on average there is 14 times more trade *within* Canada than occurs across the border! That number is even higher if we consider an earlier year, 1988, just before Canada and the United States signed the Canada–U.S. Free Trade Agreement in 1989. In 1988 intra-national trade within Canada was 22 times higher than international trade between Canada and the United States.[14] Even though that ratio fell from 1988 to 1993 because of the free-trade agreement between Canada and the United States, it is still remarkable that there is so much more trade *within* Canada than across the border, or more generally, so much more intra-national than international trade.

The finding that trade across borders is less than trade within countries reflects all the barriers to trade that occur between countries. Factors that make it easier or more difficult to trade goods between countries are often called **border effects,** and they include the following:

- Taxes imposed when imported goods enter into a country, **tariffs**
- Limits on the number of items allowed to cross the border, **quotas**
- Other administrative rules and regulations affecting trade, including the time required for goods to clear customs
- Geographic factors such as whether the countries share a border
- Cultural factors such as whether the countries have a common language that might make trade easier

In the gravity equation, all the factors that influence the amount of trade are reflected in the constant B. As we have seen, the value of this constant differs for trade within a country versus trade between countries. In later chapters, we explore in detail the consequences of tariffs, quotas, and other barriers to trade. The lesson from the gravity equation is that such barriers to trade can potentially have a large impact on the amount of international trade as compared with intra-national trade. ■

5 Conclusions

When firms have differentiated products and increasing returns to scale, the potential exists for gains from trade above and beyond those that we studied in earlier chapters under perfect competition. We have demonstrated these additional gains using a model of monopolistic competition. In this model, trade will occur even between countries that are identical because the potential to sell in a larger market will induce firms to lower their prices below those charged in the absence of trade. When all firms lower their prices, however, some firms are no longer profitable and exit the market. The remaining firms expand their output, lowering their average costs through increasing returns to scale. The reduction in average costs lowers the prices charged by firms, creating gains for consumers in the importing country. In addition, because each firm produces a differentiated product, trade between countries allows for the importing of product varieties that are different from those produced domestically, creating a second source of gains for consumers.

---

[14] That conclusion comes from John McCallum, 1995, "National Borders Matter," *American Economic Review*, 615–623. The 1993 data used in Figure 6-9 derive from James A. Anderson and Eric van Wincoop, 2003, "Gravity with Gravitas: A Solution to the Border Puzzle," *American Economic Review*, 170–192.

When some firms have to exit the market, short-run adjustment costs arise within this model because of worker displacement. Using examples from Canada, Mexico, and the United States, we have argued that the short-run adjustment costs are less than the long-run gains. Regional trade agreements like the North American Free Trade Agreement (NAFTA) are a good application of the monopolistic competition model. Another application is the "gravity equation," which states that countries that are larger or closer to one another will trade more. That prediction is supported by looking at data on trade between countries. Research has also shown that trade within countries is even larger than trade between countries.

KEY POINTS

1. The monopolistic competition model assumes differentiated products, many firms, and increasing returns to scale. Firms enter whenever there are profits to be earned, so profits are zero in the long-run equilibrium.

2. When trade opens between two countries, the demand curve faced by each firm becomes more elastic, as consumers have more choices and become more price sensitive. Firms then lower their prices in an attempt to capture consumers from their competitors and obtain profits. When all firms do so, however, some firms incur losses and are forced to leave the market.

3. Introducing international trade under monopolistic competition leads to additional gains from trade for two reasons: (i) lower prices as firms expand their output and lower their average costs and (ii) additional imported product varieties available to consumers. There are also short-run adjustment costs, such as unemployment, as some firms exit the market.

4. The assumption of differentiated goods helps us to understand why countries often import and export varieties of the same type of good. That outcome occurs with the model of monopolistic competition.

5. The gravity equation states that countries with higher GDP, or that are close, will trade more. In addition, research has shown that there is more trade within countries than between countries.

KEY TERMS

differentiated goods, p. 167
imperfect competition, p. 167
monopolistic competition, p. 167
increasing returns to scale, p. 167
intra-industry trade, p. 168
gravity equation, p. 168
free-trade agreements, p. 168

duopoly, p. 168
marginal revenue, p. 168
marginal cost, p. 169
monopoly profit, p. 172
Trade Adjustment Assistance
   (TAA), p. 186

index of intra-industry trade,
   p. 188
border effects, p. 193
tariffs, p. 193
quotas, p. 193

PROBLEMS

1. Explain how increasing returns to scale in production can be a basis for trade.

2. Why is trade within a country greater than trade between countries?

3. Starting from the long-run equilibrium without trade in the monopolistic competition model, as illustrated in Figure 6-5, consider what happens when the Home country begins trading

with two other identical countries. Because the countries are all the same, the number of consumers in the world is three times larger than in a single country, and the number of firms in the world is three times larger than in a single country.

a. Compared with the no-trade equilibrium, how much does industry demand D increase? How much does the number of firms (or product varieties) increase? Does the demand curve D/N^A still apply after the opening of trade? Explain why or why not.

b. Does the d_1 curve shift or pivot due to the opening of trade? Explain why or why not.

c. Compare your answer to (b) with the case in which Home trades with only one other identical country. Specifically, compare the elasticity of the demand curve d_1 in the two cases.

d. Illustrate the long-run equilibrium with trade, and compare it with the long-run equilibrium when Home trades with only one other identical country.

4. Starting from the long-run trade equilibrium in the monopolistic competition model, as illustrated in Figure 6-7, consider what happens when industry demand D increases. For instance, suppose that this is the market for cars, and lower gasoline prices generate higher demand D.

a. Redraw Figure 6-7 for the Home market and show the shift in the D/N^T curve and the new short-run equilibrium.

b. From the new short-run equilibrium, is there exit or entry of firms, and why?

c. Describe where the new long-run equilibrium occurs, and explain what has happened to the number of firms and the prices they charge.

5. Our derivation of the gravity equation from the monopolistic competition model used the following logic:

(i) Each country produces many products.
(ii) Each country demands all of the products that every other country produces.
(iii) Thus, large countries demand more imports from other countries.

The gravity equation relationship does not hold in the Heckscher-Ohlin model. Explain how the logic of the gravity equation breaks down in the Heckscher-Ohlin model; that is, which of the statements just listed is no longer true in the Heckscher-Ohlin model?

6. The United States, France, and Italy are among the world's largest producers. To answer the following questions, assume that their markets are monopolistically competitive, and use the gravity equation with $B = 93$ and $n = 1.25$.

	GDP in 2012 ($ billions)	Distance from the United States (miles)
France	2,776	5,544
Italy	2,196	6,229
United States	14,991	—

a. Using the gravity equation, compare the expected level of trade between the United States and France and between the United States and Italy.

b. The distance between Paris and Rome is 694 miles. Would you expect more French trade with Italy or with the United States? Explain what variable (i.e., country size or distance) drives your result.

7. What evidence is there that Canada is better off under the free-trade agreement with the United States?

8. In the section "Gains and Adjustment Costs for the United States Under NAFTA," we calculated the lost wages of workers displaced because of NAFTA. Prior experience in the manufacturing sector shows that about two-thirds of these workers obtain new jobs within three years. One way to think about that reemployment process is that one-third of workers find jobs in the first year, and another one-third of remaining unemployed workers find a job each subsequent year. Using this approach, in the table that follows, we show that one-third of workers get a job in the first year (column 2), leaving two-thirds of workers unemployed (column 4). In the second year, another $\left(\frac{1}{3}\right) \cdot \left(\frac{2}{3}\right) = \frac{2}{9}$ of workers get a job (column 2), so that $\frac{1}{3} + \frac{2}{9} = \frac{5}{9}$ of the workers are employed (column 3). That leaves $1 - \frac{5}{9} = \frac{4}{9}$ of the workers unemployed (column 4) at the end of the second year.

Year	Fraction Finding Job	Total Fraction Employed	Total Fraction Unemployed
1	$\frac{1}{3}$	$\frac{1}{3}$	$1 - \frac{1}{3} = \frac{2}{3}$
2	$\frac{1}{3} \cdot \frac{2}{3} = \frac{2}{9}$	$\frac{1}{3} + \frac{2}{9} = \frac{5}{9}$	$1 - \frac{5}{9} = \frac{4}{9}$
3	$\frac{1}{3} \cdot \frac{4}{9} = \frac{4}{27}$		
4			
5			
6	$\frac{1}{3} \cdot \left(\frac{2}{3}\right)^{Year-1}$		

a. Fill in two more rows of the table using the same approach as for the first two rows.

b. Notice that the fraction of workers finding a job each year (column 2) has the formula

$$\text{Fraction finding job} = \frac{1}{3} \cdot \left(\frac{2}{3}\right)^{Year-1}$$

Using this formula, fill in six more values for the fraction of workers finding a job (column 2), up to year 10.

c. To calculate the average spell of unemployment, we take the fraction of workers finding jobs (column 2), multiply it by the years of unemployment (column 1), and add up the result over all the rows. By adding up over 10 rows, calculate what the average spell of unemployment is. What do you expect to get when adding up over 20 rows?

d. Compare your answer to (c) with the average three-year spell of unemployment on page 186. Was that number accurate?

9. a. Of two products, rice and paintings, which product do you expect to have a higher index of intra-industry trade? Why?

b. Access the U.S. TradeStats Express website at http://tse.export.gov/. Click on "National Trade Data" and then "Global Patterns of U.S. Merchandise Trade." Under the "Product" section, change the item to rice (HS 1006) and obtain the export and import values. Do the same for paintings (HS 9701); then calculate the intra-industry trade index for rice and paintings in 2012. Do your calculations confirm your expectation from part (a)? If your answers did not confirm your expectation, explain.

N E T W O R K

In this chapter, we included the editorial **Headlines: NAFTA Turns 15, Bravo!** There were many other editorials written in 2009, for the fifteenth anniversary of NAFTA, and more written since then. Find another editorial about NAFTA on the Web, and summarize the pro and con arguments for the organization.

Offshoring of Goods and Services

One facet of increased services trade is the increased use of offshore outsourcing in which a company relocates labor-intensive service-industry functions to another country. . . . When a good or service is produced more cheaply abroad, it makes more sense to import it than to make or provide it domestically.

Economic Report of the President, 2004, p. 229

Increasing numbers of Americans . . . perceive offshoring . . . as an actual or potential threat to their jobs or to their wages even if they hold onto their jobs.

Jagdish Bhagwati and Alan S. Blinder, 2007, *Offshoring of American Jobs*

The American people deserve a tax code that . . . lowers incentives to move jobs overseas, and lowers tax rates for businesses and manufacturers that are creating jobs right here in the United States of America. That's what tax reform can deliver.

President Barack Obama, State of the Union address, February 12, 2013

I f you take the battery out of your cell phone to see where the phone was produced, you will likely see several countries listed inside. Motorola, for example, is a U.S. company that produces some of its cell phones in Singapore using batteries and a battery charger made in China. Nokia is a Finnish company that produces some of its American-sold cell phones in the United States using batteries made in Japan and software that was written in India. Apple produces its iPhone in facilities found in China, Taiwan, Thailand, Malaysia, Singapore, South Korea, the Czech Republic, Philippines, and the United States. A vast array of products, including simple toys like the Barbie doll and sophisticated items like airplanes and personal computers, consist of materials, parts, components, and services that are produced in numerous countries. The following excerpt from a *New York Times* article illustrates this observation:[1]

---

[1] Louis Uchitelle, "Why Hasn't a Weak Dollar Slowed Imports?" *New York Times*, April 8, 2005, online edition.

General Electric in the United States and Snechma of France . . . jointly manufacture the jet engine for Boeing's 737 and Airbus's 320. G.E. makes the "hot section" at its plant in Cincinnati, while Snechma manufactures the giant fans in France. They ship these components to each other and each partner does the final assembly of the engines for its customers. In addition, G.E. makes smaller jet engines for the commuter planes that Bombardier makes in Canada and Embraer makes in Brazil. The engines are exported to those countries, but 24 percent of the value of the engines comes from components imported from Japan.

The provision of a service or the production of various parts of a good in different countries that are then used or assembled into a final good in another location is called **foreign outsourcing** or, more simply, **offshoring.** We will not worry about the subtle distinction between these two terms in this chapter (see **Side Bar: "Foreign Outsourcing" Versus "Offshoring"**); we'll use "offshoring" because it has become most commonly used by economists.[2]

Offshoring is a type of international trade that differs from the type of trade analyzed in the Ricardian and Heckscher-Ohlin models; the goods traded in those models were final goods. Offshoring is trade in *intermediate inputs*, which can sometimes cross borders several times before being incorporated into a final good that can be sold domestically or abroad. Offshoring is a relatively new phenomenon in world trade.[3] The amount of world trade relative to the GDPs of countries was high even in the late nineteenth and early twentieth centuries. But it is unlikely that a good would have crossed borders multiple times at several stages of production because the costs of transportation and communication were too high. Today, however, these costs have fallen so much that it is now economical to combine the labor and capital resources of several countries to produce a good or service. Indeed, if you have ever called for help with your laptop, chances are that you have spoken with someone at a call center in India, which shows just how low the costs of communication have become!

Is offshoring different from the type of trade examined in the Ricardian and Heckscher-Ohlin models? From one point of view, the answer is no. Offshoring allows a company to purchase inexpensive goods or services abroad, just as consumers can purchase lower-priced goods from abroad in the Ricardian and Heckscher-Ohlin models. This is what the quote from the *Economic Report of the President* at the beginning of the chapter suggests: with offshoring we import those goods and services that are cheaper to produce abroad. From another point of view, however, offshoring is different. Companies now have the opportunity to send *a portion* of their activities to other countries. The jobs associated with those activities leave the United States, and by paying lower wages abroad, U.S. firms lower their costs and pass on these savings to consumers. Offshoring results in lower prices but changes the mix of jobs located in the United States. Higher-skilled workers in the United States, engaged in activities

[2] Both "foreign outsourcing" and "offshoring" have been coined recently to describe this new type of international trade. The earliest known use of the word "outsourcing" is a quotation from an American auto executive in the *Journal of the Royal Society of Arts,* 1979, who said, "We are so short of professional engineers in the motor industry that we are having to outsource design work to Germany" (William Safire, "On Language," *New York Times Magazine,* March 21, 2004, p. 30).
[3] There is also the concept of *domestic outsourcing,* which occurs when a company decides to shift some of its production activities from one location to another within the same country. In this text, outsourcing always means *foreign outsourcing.*

SIDE BAR

"Foreign Outsourcing" Versus "Offshoring"

In discussions of foreign outsourcing, we often hear the term "offshoring." The quote from the *Economic Report of the President* at the beginning of the chapter combined these terms as "offshore outsourcing." Is there a difference between "foreign outsourcing" and "offshoring"?

The term "offshoring" is sometimes used to refer to a company moving some of its operations overseas but retaining ownership of those operations. In other words, the company moves some operations offshore but does not move production outside of its own firm. Intel, for example, produces microchips in China and Costa Rica using subsidiaries that it owns. Intel has engaged in foreign direct investment (FDI) to establish these offshore subsidiaries.

Mattel, on the other hand, arranges for the production of the Barbie doll in several different countries. Unlike Intel, however, Mattel does not actually own the firms in those countries.

Furthermore, Mattel lets these firms purchase their inputs (like the hair and cloth for the dolls) from whichever sources are most economical. Mattel is engaging in foreign outsourcing as it contracts with these firms abroad but has not done any FDI.

Dell is an intermediate case. Dell assembles its computers overseas in firms it does not own, so it is outsourcing rather than offshoring the assembly. However, Dell exercises careful control over the inputs (such as computer parts) that these overseas firms use. Dell outsources the assembly but monitors the overseas firms closely to ensure the high quality of the computers being assembled.

In this chapter, we will not worry about the distinction between "offshoring" and "foreign outsourcing"; we'll use the term "offshoring" whenever the components of a good or service are produced in several countries, regardless of who owns the plants that provide the components or services.

---

such as marketing and research, will be combined with less skilled workers abroad, engaged in assembling products. In a sense, offshoring is similar to immigration in that U.S. firms are able to employ foreign workers, even though those workers do not have to leave their home countries.

The first goal of this chapter is to examine in detail the phenomenon of offshoring and describe in what ways it differs from trade in final products. We discuss how offshoring affects the demand for high-skilled and low-skilled labor and the wages paid to those workers. Since the early 1980s, there has been a significant change in the pattern of wage payments in the United States and other countries—the wages of skilled workers have been rising relative to those of less skilled workers. We examine whether this change in relative wages is the result of offshoring or whether there are other explanations for it.

A second goal of the chapter is to discuss the gains from offshoring. We argue that offshoring creates gains from trade, similar to those seen from the trade of final goods in the Ricardian or Heckscher-Ohlin models. But having overall gains from trade for a country does not necessarily mean that every person in the country gains. As the second quote at the beginning of the chapter shows, many workers are fearful that their jobs and wages are threatened by offshoring. We focus attention on how offshoring affects high-skilled versus low-skilled workers.

A third goal of the chapter is to examine the response to offshoring in the United States. The final quotation at the beginning of the chapter, from the 2013 State of the Union address by President Obama, indicates that he proposes to limit tax breaks to companies engaged in offshoring. Many economists would disagree with this proposal, and argue instead that offshoring has overall benefits. We examine these arguments and also discuss the newest trend of "inshoring" activities back into the United States.

1 A Model of Offshoring

To develop a model of offshoring, we need to identify all the activities involved in producing and marketing a good or service. These activities are illustrated in Figure 7-1. Panel (a) describes the activities in the order in which they are performed (starting with research and development [R&D] and ending with marketing and after-sales service). For instance, in producing a television, the design and engineering are developed first; components such as wiring, casing, and screens are manufactured next; and finally the television is assembled into its final version and sold to consumers.

For the purpose of building a model of offshoring, however, it is more useful to line up the activities according to the ratio of high-skilled/low-skilled labor used, as in panel (b). We start with the less skilled activities, such as the manufacture and assembly of simple components (like the case or the electric cord for the television), then move to more complex components (like the screen). Next are the supporting service activities such as accounting, order processing, and product service (sometimes called "back-office" activities because the customer does not see them). Finally, we come to activities that use more skilled labor, such as marketing and sales ("front-office" activities), and those that use the most skilled labor such as R&D.

Value Chain of Activities

The whole set of activities that we have illustrated in Figures 7-1(a) and 7-1(b) is sometimes called the **value chain** for the product, with each activity adding more

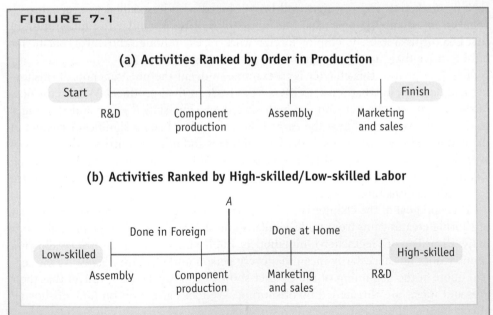

FIGURE 7-1

(a) Activities Ranked by Order in Production

Start | R&D | Component production | Assembly | Marketing and sales | Finish

(b) Activities Ranked by High-skilled/Low-skilled Labor

A

Done in Foreign | Done at Home

Low-skilled | Assembly | Component production | Marketing and sales | R&D | High-skilled

The Value Chain of a Product Any product has many different activities involved in its manufacture. Panel (a) lists some of these activities for a given product in the order in which they occur. The value chain in (b) lists these same activities in order of the amount of high-skilled/low-skilled labor used in each. In panel (b), the assembly activity, on the left, uses the least skilled labor, and R&D, on the right, uses the most skilled labor. Because we assume that the relative wage of skilled labor is higher at Home and that trade and capital costs are uniform across activities, there is a point on the value chain, shown by line A, below which all activities are offshored to Foreign and above which all activities are performed at Home.

value to the combined product. All these activities do not need to be done in one country—a firm can transfer some of these activities abroad by offshoring them when it is more economical to do so. By lining up the activities in terms of the relative amount of skilled labor they require, we can predict which activities are likely to be transferred abroad. This prediction depends on several assumptions, which follow.

Relative Wage of Skilled Workers Let W_L be the wage of low-skilled labor in Home and W_H the wage of high-skilled labor. Similarly, let W_L^* and W_H^* be the wages of low-skilled and high-skilled workers in Foreign. Our first assumption is that Foreign wages are less than those at Home, $W_L^* < W_L$ and $W_H^* < W_H$, and that the *relative wage* of low-skilled labor is lower in Foreign than at Home, so $W_L^*/W_H^* < W_L/W_H$. This assumption is realistic because low-skilled labor in developing countries receives especially low wages.

Costs of Capital and Trade As the firm considers sending some activities abroad, it knows that it will lower its labor costs because wages in Foreign are lower. However, the firm must also take into account the extra costs of doing business in Foreign. In many cases, the firm pays more to capital through (1) higher prices to build a factory or higher prices for utilities such as electricity and fuel; (2) extra costs involved in transportation and communication, which will be especially high if Foreign is still developing roads, ports, and telephone capabilities; and (3) the extra costs from tariffs if Foreign imposes taxes on goods (such as component parts) when they come into the country. We lump together costs 2 and 3 into what we call "trade costs."

Higher capital and trade costs in Foreign can prevent a Home firm from offshoring all its activities abroad. In making the decision of what to offshore, the Home firm will balance the savings from lower wages against the extra costs of capital and trade.

Our second assumption is that these extra costs apply *uniformly* across all the activities in the value chain; that is, these extra costs add, say, 10% to each and every component of operation in Foreign as compared with Home. Unlike our assumption about relative wages in Home and Foreign, this assumption is a bit unrealistic. For instance, the extra costs of transportation versus those of communication are quite different in countries such as China and India; good roads for transport have developed slowly, while communications technology has developed rapidly. As a result, technology in telephones is advanced in those countries, so cell phones are often cheaper there than in the United States and Europe. In this case, the higher infrastructure costs will affect the activities that rely on transportation more than activities that rely on communication.

Slicing the Value Chain Now suppose that the Home firm with the value chain in Figure 7-1, panel (b), considers transferring some of these activities from Home to Foreign. Which activities will be transferred? Based on our assumptions that $W_L^*/W_H^* < W_L/W_H$ and that the extra costs of capital and trade apply uniformly, it makes sense for the firm to send abroad the activities that are the least skilled and labor-intensive and keep at Home the activities that are the most skilled and labor-intensive. Looking at Figure 7-1, all activities to the left of the vertical line A might be done in Foreign, for example, whereas those activities to the right of the vertical line will be done in Home. We can refer to this transfer of activities as "slicing the value chain."[4]

---

[4] This term is drawn from Paul Krugman, 1995, "Growing World Trade: Causes and Consequences," *Brookings Papers on Economic Activity*, 1.

Activities to the left of line A are sent abroad because the cost savings from paying lower wages in Foreign are greatest for activities that require less skilled labor. Because the extra costs of capital and trade are uniform across activities, the cost savings on wages are most important in determining which activities to transfer and which to keep at Home.

Relative Demand for Skilled Labor Now that we know the division of activities between Home and Foreign, we can graph the demand for labor in each country, as illustrated in Figure 7-2. For Home, we add up the demand for high-skilled labor H and low-skilled labor L for all the activities to the right of line A in Figure 7-1, panel (b). Taking the ratio of these, in panel (a) we graph the relative demand for skilled labor at Home H/L against the relative wage W_H/W_L. This relative demand curve slopes downward because a higher relative wage for skilled labor would cause Home firms to substitute less skilled labor in some activities. For example, if the relative wage of skilled labor increased, Home firms might hire high school rather than college graduates to serve on a sales force and then train them on the job.

In Foreign, we add up the demand for high-skilled labor H^* and for low-skilled labor L^* for all the activities to the left of line A^*. Panel (b) graphs the relative demand for skilled labor in Foreign H^*/L^* against the relative wage W_H^*/W_L^*. Again, this curve slopes downward because a higher relative wage for skilled labor would cause Foreign firms to substitute less skilled labor in some activities. In each country, we can add a relative supply curve to the diagram, which is upward-sloping because a higher relative wage for skilled labor causes more skilled individuals to enter this industry. For instance, if the high-skilled wage increases relative to the low-skilled wage in either

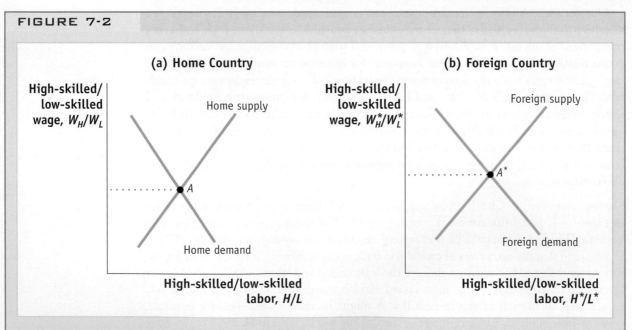

FIGURE 7-2

(a) Home Country

High-skilled/low-skilled wage, W_H/W_L

Home supply

Home demand

High-skilled/low-skilled labor, H/L

(b) Foreign Country

High-skilled/low-skilled wage, W_H^*/W_L^*

Foreign supply

A^*

Foreign demand

High-skilled/low-skilled labor, H^*/L^*

Relative Demand and Supply for High-Skilled/Low-Skilled Labor In panel (a), we show the relative demand and supply for skilled labor at Home, H/L, depending on the relative wage, W_H/W_L. The equilibrium relative wage at Home is determined at A. In panel (b), we show the relative demand and supply for skilled labor in Foreign, H^*/L^*, depending on the relative wage, W_H^*/W_L^*. The Foreign equilibrium is at point A^*.

country, then individuals will invest more in schooling to equip themselves with the skills necessary to earn the higher relative wage.

The intersection of the relative demand and relative supply curves, at points A and A^*, gives the equilibrium relative wage in this industry in each country and the equilibrium relative employment of high-skilled/low-skilled workers. Starting at these points, next we study how the equilibrium changes as Home offshores more activities to Foreign.

Changing the Costs of Trade

Suppose now that the costs of capital or trade in Foreign fall. For example, the North American Free Trade Agreement (NAFTA) lowered tariffs charged on goods crossing the U.S.–Mexico border. This fall in trade costs made it easier for U.S. firms to offshore to Mexico. And even before NAFTA, Mexico had liberalized the rules concerning foreign ownership of capital there, thereby lowering the cost of capital for U.S. firms. Another example is India, which in 1991 eliminated many regulations that had been hindering businesses, communications, and foreign investment. Before 1991 it was difficult for a new business to start, or even to secure a phone or fax line in India; after 1991 the regulations on domestic and foreign-owned business were simplified, and communication technology improved dramatically with cell phones and fiber-optic cables. These policy changes made India more attractive to foreign investors and firms interested in offshoring.

Change in Home Labor Demand and Relative Wage When the costs of capital or trade decline in Foreign, it becomes desirable to shift more activities in the value chain from Home to Foreign. Figure 7-3 illustrates this change with the shift of the dividing line from A to B. The activities between A and B, which used to be done at Home, are now done in Foreign. As an example, consider the transfer of television production from the United States to Mexico. As U.S. firms first shifted manufacturing to Mexico, the chassis of the televisions were constructed there. Later on, electronic circuits were constructed in Mexico, and later still the picture tubes were manufactured there.[5]

FIGURE 7-3

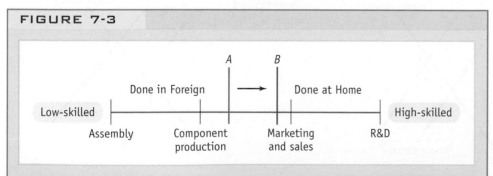

Offshoring on the Value Chain As the costs of capital or trade fall in the Foreign country, a Home firm will find it profitable to offshore more activities. Offshoring shifts the dividing line between Home and Foreign production from A to B. The activities between A and B, which formerly were done at Home, are now done in Foreign. Notice that these activities are more skill-intensive than the activities formerly done in Foreign (to the left of A) but less skill-intensive than the activities now done at Home (to the right of B).

---

[5] Martin Kenney and Richard Florida, 1994, "Japanese Maquiladoras: Production Organization and Global Commodity Chains," *World Development*, 22(1), 27–44.

How does this increase in offshoring affect the relative demand for skilled labor in each country? First consider the Home country. Notice that the activities no longer performed at Home (i.e., those between *A* and *B*) are *less* skill-intensive than the activities still done there (those to the right of *B*). This means that the activities now done at Home are more skilled and labor-intensive, on average, than the activities formerly done at Home. For this reason, the relative demand for skilled labor at Home will increase, and the Home demand curve will shift to the right, as shown in Figure 7-4, panel (a). Note that this diagram does not show the *absolute* quantity of labor demanded, which we expect would fall for both high-skilled and low-skilled labor when there is more offshoring; instead, we are graphing the *relative* demand for high-skilled/low-skilled labor, which increases because the activities still done at Home are more skill-intensive than before the decrease in trade and capital costs. With the increase in the relative demand for skilled labor, the equilibrium will shift from point *A* to point *B* at Home; that is, the relative wage of skilled labor will increase because of offshoring.

Change in Foreign Labor Demand and Relative Wage Now let's look at what happens in Foreign when Home offshores more of its production activities to Foreign. How will offshoring affect the relative demand for labor and relative wage in Foreign? As we saw in Figure 7-3, the activities that are newly offshored to Foreign (those between *A* and *B*) are *more* skill-intensive than the activities that were initially

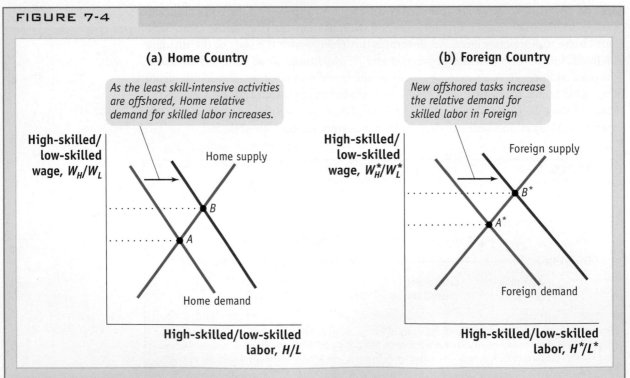

FIGURE 7-4

(a) Home Country

As the least skill-intensive activities are offshored, Home relative demand for skilled labor increases.

High-skilled/low-skilled wage, W_H/W_L

Home supply

Home demand

High-skilled/low-skilled labor, H/L

(b) Foreign Country

New offshored tasks increase the relative demand for skilled labor in Foreign

High-skilled/low-skilled wage, W_H^*/W_L^*

Foreign supply

Foreign demand

High-skilled/low-skilled labor, H^*/L^*

Change in the Relative Demand for High-Skilled/Low-Skilled Labor With greater offshoring from Home to Foreign, some of the activities requiring less skill that were formerly done at Home are now done abroad. It follows that the relative demand for skilled labor at Home increases, and the relative wage rises from point *A* to point *B*. The relative demand for skilled labor in Foreign also increases because the activities shifted to Foreign are more skill-intensive than those formerly done there. It follows that the relative wage for skilled labor in Foreign also rises, from point *A** to point *B**.

offshored to Foreign (those to the left of A). This means that the range of activities now done in Foreign is more skilled and labor-intensive, on average, than the set of activities formerly done there. For this reason, the relative demand for skilled labor in Foreign also increases, and the Foreign demand curve shifts to the right, as shown in panel (b) of Figure 7-4. With this increase in the relative demand for skilled labor, the equilibrium shifts from point A^* to point B^*. As a result of Home's increased offshoring to Foreign, then, the relative wage of skilled labor increases in Foreign. The conclusion from our model is that both countries experience an increase in the relative wage of skilled labor because of increased offshoring.

It might seem surprising that a shift of activities from one country to the other can increase the relative demand for skilled labor in *both* countries. An example drawn from your classroom experience might help you to understand how this can happen. Suppose you have a friend who is majoring in physics but is finding it difficult: she is scoring below average in a physics class that she is taking. So you invite her to join you in an economics class, and it turns out that your friend has a knack for economics: she scores above average in that class. How does your friend's transfer from physics to economics affect the class averages? Because she was performing below average in the physics class, when she leaves the class, her departure raises the class average (computed now using the students still there, not including her). Because your friend performs better than average in the economics class, her arrival raises the class average there, too (computed using everyone, including your friend). Thus, your friend's move from one class to another raises the average in both classes.

This result is just like the logic of the offshoring model: as activities in the middle of the value chain are shifted from Home to Foreign, they raise the relative demand for skilled labor in both countries because these activities are the *least* skill-intensive of those formerly done at Home but the *most* skill-intensive of tasks done in Foreign. That is why the relative demand for skilled labor increases in both countries, along with the relative wage of skilled labor. This result is one of the most important predictions from our offshoring model and it would not occur in our earlier models of trade, such as the Heckscher-Ohlin model.[6] We now turn to evidence from the United States and Mexico to see whether this prediction is borne out.

APPLICATION

Change in Relative Wages Across Countries

Since the early 1980s, the wages of high-skilled workers have risen relative to those of low-skilled workers in many countries. The relative wage of skilled workers in industrial countries (such as the United States, Australia, Canada, Japan, Sweden, and the United Kingdom) and in developing countries (such as Hong Kong, Chile, and Mexico) has increased. Our offshoring model predicts that the relative wage of skilled workers will rise in *both* the country doing the offshoring and the country receiving the new activities. At first glance, that prediction seems to be consistent with the change in wages that has actually occurred. Let us dig more deeply, however, using evidence from the United States and Mexico, to see what the change in wages has been and whether it is due to offshoring.

---

[6] The Heckscher-Ohlin model tells us that the factor prices in the two countries will move toward equality when they open trade. So the wage relative to the capital rental will move in different directions in the two countries due to the opening of trade, not in the same direction.

Change in Relative Wages in the United States

To measure the wages of skilled and low-skilled workers, we can use data from the manufacturing sector on "production" and "nonproduction" workers. As their name suggests, production workers are involved in the manufacture and assembly of goods, whereas nonproduction workers are involved in supporting service activities. Firms are required to report wages for both types of workers. We could also call these two types of workers "blue collar" and "white collar." Generally, nonproduction workers require more education, and so we will treat these workers as "high-skilled," whereas the production workers are treated here as "low-skilled" workers.[7]

Relative Wage of Nonproduction Workers Figure 7-5 shows the average annual earnings of nonproduction workers relative to production workers (analogous to the ratio of high-skilled to low-skilled wages, or W_H/W_L) in U.S. manufacturing from 1958 to 2010. We see that relative earnings moved erratically from 1958 to 1967, and that from 1968 to about 1982, relative wages were on a downward trend. It is generally accepted that the relative wage fell during this period because of an increase in the supply of college graduates, skilled workers who moved into nonproduction jobs (the increase in supply would bring down the nonproduction wage, so the relative wage would also fall).

FIGURE 7-5

Relative Wage of Nonproduction/Production Workers, U.S. Manufacturing This diagram shows the average wage of nonproduction workers divided by the average wage of production workers in U.S. manufacturing. This ratio of wages moved erratically during the 1960s and 1970s, although showing some downward trend. This trend reversed itself during the 1980s and 1990s, when the relative wage of nonproduction workers increased until 2000. This trend means that the relative wage of production, or low-skilled, workers fell during the 1980s and 1990s. In more recent years, the relative wage has become quite volatile, falling erratically until 2004, then rising to 2010.

Source: Annual Survey of Manufactures and National Bureau of Economic Research (NBER) productivity database, updated from U.S. Bureau of the Census.

---

[7] This distinction is far from perfect, however. Nonproduction workers include clerical and custodial staff, for example, who may be less skilled than some production workers.

Starting in 1982, however, this trend reversed itself and the relative wage of nonproduction workers increased steadily to 2000. Since that time the relative wage fell erratically until 2004, and then rose again to 2010.

Relative Employment of Nonproduction Workers In Figure 7-6, we see that there was a steady increase in the ratio of nonproduction to production workers employed in U.S. manufacturing until about 1992. Such a trend indicates that firms were hiring fewer production, or low-skilled workers, relative to nonproduction workers. During the 1990s the ratio of nonproduction to production workers fell until 1998, after which relative employment rose again.

The increase in the relative supply of college graduates from 1968 to 1982 is consistent with the reduction in the relative wage of nonproduction workers, as shown in Figure 7-5, and with the increase in their relative employment, as shown in Figure 7-6. After 1982, however, the story changes. We would normally think that the rising relative wage of nonproduction workers should have led to a shift in employment *away* from nonproduction workers, but it did not; as shown in Figure 7-6, the relative employment of nonproduction workers continued to rise from 1980 to about 1992, then fell until 1998. How can there be both an increase in the relative wage and an increase in the relative employment of nonproduction workers? The only explanation consistent with these facts is that during the 1980s there was an *outward shift* in the relative demand for nonproduction (skilled)

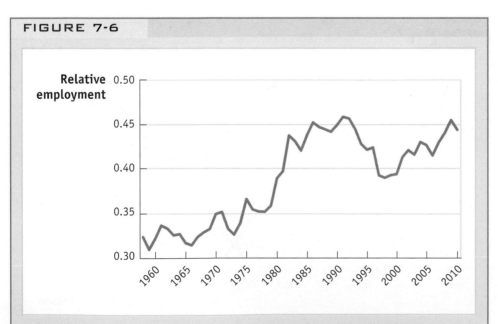

FIGURE 7-6

Relative Employment of Nonproduction/Production Workers, U.S. Manufacturing This diagram shows the employment of nonproduction workers in U.S. manufacturing divided by the employment of production workers. There was a steady increase in the ratio of nonproduction to production workers employed in U.S. manufacturing until the early 1990s. That trend indicates firms were hiring fewer production workers relative to nonproduction workers. During the 1990s there was a fall in the ratio of nonproduction to production workers until 1998, and then a rise again thereafter.

Source: Annual Survey of Manufactures and NBER productivity database, updated from U.S. Bureau of the Census.

workers, which led to a simultaneous increase in their relative employment *and* in their wages.

This conclusion is illustrated in Figure 7-7, in which we plot the relative wage of nonproduction workers and their relative employment from 1979 to 1990. As we have already noted, both the relative wage and relative employment of nonproduction workers rose during the 1980s. The only way this pattern can be consistent with a supply and demand diagram is if the relative demand curve for skilled labor increases, as illustrated. This increased demand would lead to an increase in the relative wage for skilled labor and an increase in its relative employment, the pattern seen in the data for the United States.

Explanations What factors can lead to an increase in the relative demand for skilled labor? One explanation is offshoring. An increase in demand for high-skilled workers, at the expense of low-skilled workers, can arise from offshoring, as shown by the rightward shift in the relative demand for skilled labor in Figure 7-4, panel (a). The evidence from the manufacturing sector in the United States is strongly consistent with our model of offshoring.

There is, however, a second possible explanation for the increase in the relative demand for skilled workers in the United States. In the 1980s personal computers began to appear in the workplace. The addition of computers in the workplace can increase the demand for skilled workers to operate them. The shift in relative demand

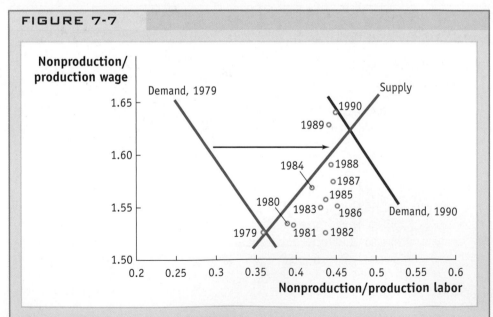

FIGURE 7-7

Supply and Demand for Nonproduction/ Production Workers in the 1980s This diagram shows the average wage of nonproduction workers divided by the average wage of production workers on the vertical axis, and on the horizontal axis the employment of nonproduction workers divided by the employment of production workers. Both the relative wage and the relative employment of nonproduction, or skilled, workers rose in U.S. manufacturing during the 1980s, indicating that the relative demand curve must have shifted to the right.

Source: NBER productivity database.

toward skilled workers because of the use of computers and other high-tech equipment is called **skill-biased technological change.** Given these two potential explanations for the same observation, how can we determine which of these factors was most responsible for the actual change in wages?

Answering this question has been the topic of many research studies in economics. The approach that most authors take is to measure skill-biased technological change and offshoring in terms of some underlying variables. For skill-biased technological change, for example, we might use the amount of computers and other high-technology equipment used in manufacturing industries. For offshoring, we could use the imports of intermediate inputs into manufacturing industries. By studying how the use of high-tech equipment and the imports of intermediate inputs have grown and comparing this with the wage movements in industries, we can determine the contribution of each factor toward explaining the wage movements.

The results from one study of this type are shown in Table 7-1. The goal of this study was to explain two observations. First, it sought to explain the increase in the share of **total wage payments** going to nonproduction (high-skilled) labor in U.S. manufacturing industries from 1979 to 1990 (part A). Because wage payments equal the wage times the number of workers hired, this statistic captures both the rising relative wage and the rising relative employment of skilled workers. Second, the study analyzed the increase in the *relative wage* of nonproduction labor in particular over the same period (part B).[8]

The study considered two possible explanations for the two observations: offshoring and the use of high-tech equipment such as computers. Offshoring was measured as the intermediate inputs imported by each industry. For example, the U.S. auto industry builds seats, dashboards, and other car parts in Mexico and then imports these for assembly in the United States. In addition, high-technology equipment can be measured in two ways: either as a fraction of the total capital equipment installed in each industry or as a fraction of new investment in capital that is devoted to computers and other high-tech devices. In the first method, high-tech equipment is measured as a fraction of the capital *stock*, and in the second method, high-tech equipment is measured as a fraction of the annual *flow* of new investment. In the early 1980s a large portion of the flow of new investment in some industries was devoted to computers and other high-tech devices, but a much smaller fraction of the capital stock consisted of that equipment. In Table 7-1, we report results from both measures because the results differ depending on which measure is used.

Using the first measure of high-tech equipment (as a fraction of the capital stock), the results in the first row of part A show that between 20% and 23% of the increase in the share of wage payments going to the nonproduction workers can be explained by offshoring, and between 8% and 12% of that increase can be explained by the growing use of high-tech capital. The remainder is unexplained by these two factors. Thus, using the first measure of high-tech equipment, it appears that offshoring was more important than high-tech capital in explaining the change in relative demand for skilled workers.

---

[8] To illustrate the distinction between parts A and B, consider the following example. If nonproduction workers earn $25 per hour and 5 are hired, and production workers earn $10 per hour and 20 are hired, then the total wage payments are $25 • 5 + $10 • 20 = $325, and the relative wage of nonproduction labor is $25/$10 = 2.5. In contrast, the share of total wage payments going to nonproduction workers is then $125/$325 = 38%, which equals the actual, average share of wages going to nonproduction workers in U.S. manufacturing from 1979 to 1990.

TABLE 7-1

Increase in the Relative Wage of Nonproduction Labor in U.S. Manufacturing, 1979–1990 This table shows the estimated effects of offshoring and the use of high-technology equipment on the wages earned by nonproduction (or skilled) workers. Part A focuses on how these two variables affect the share of wage payments going to nonproduction workers. Part B shows how these two variables affect the relative wage of nonproduction workers.

| | PERCENT OF TOTAL INCREASE EXPLAINED BY EACH FACTOR | |
	Offshoring	High-Technology Equipment
Part A: Share of Wage Payments Going to Nonproduction Workers		
Measurement of high-tech equipment:		
As a share of the capital stock	20–23	8–12
As a share of capital flow (i.e., new investment)	13	37
Part B: Relative Wage of Nonproduction/Production Workers		
Measurement of high-tech equipment:		
As a share of the capital stock	21–27	29–32
As a share of capital flow (i.e., new investment)	12	99

Source: Robert C. Feenstra and Gordon H. Hanson, August 1999, "The Impact of Outsourcing and High-Technology Capital on Wages: Estimates for the United States, 1979–1990," Quarterly Journal of Economics, 114(3), 907–940.

The story is different, however, if we instead use offshoring and the second measure of high-tech equipment (a fraction of new investment), as shown in the second row of part A. In that case, offshoring explains only 13% of the increase in the nonproduction share of wages, whereas high-tech investment explains 37% of that increase. So we see from these results that both offshoring and high-tech equipment are important explanations for the increase in the relative wage of skilled labor in the United States, but which one is *most* important depends on how we measure the high-tech equipment.

In part B, we repeat the results but now try to explain the increase in the relative wage of nonproduction workers. Using the first measure of high-tech equipment (a fraction of the capital stock), the results in the first row of part B show that between 21% and 27% of the increase in the relative wage of nonproduction workers can be explained by offshoring, and between 29% and 32% of that increase can be explained by the growing use of high-tech capital. In the second row of part B, we use the other measure of high-tech equipment (a fraction of new investment). In that case, the large spending on high-tech equipment in new investment can explain *nearly all* (99%) of the increased relative wage for nonproduction workers, leaving little room for offshoring to play much of a role (it explains only 12% of the increase in the relative wage). These results are lopsided enough that we might be skeptical of using new investment to measure high-tech equipment and therefore prefer the results in the first rows of parts A and B, using the capital stocks.

Summing up, we conclude that both offshoring and high-tech equipment explain the increase in the relative wage of nonproduction/production labor in U.S. manufacturing, but it is difficult to judge which is more important because the results depend on how we measure the high-tech equipment.

Change in Relative Wages in Mexico

Our model of offshoring predicts that the relative wage of skilled labor will rise in *both* countries. We have already seen (in Figure 7-5) that the relative wage of nonproduction (skilled) labor rises in the United States. But what about for Mexico?

In Figure 7-8, we show the relative wage of nonproduction/production labor in Mexico from 1964 to 2000. The data used in Figure 7-8 come from the census of industries in Mexico, which occurred infrequently, so there are only a few turning points in the graph in the early years. We can see that the relative wage of nonproduction workers fell from 1964 to 1984, then rose until 1996, leveling out thereafter. The fall in the relative wage from 1964 to 1984 is similar to the pattern in the United States and probably occurred because of an increased supply of skilled labor in the workforce. More important, the rise in the relative wage of nonproduction workers from 1984 to 1996 is also similar to what happened in the United States and illustrates the prediction of our model of offshoring: that relative wages move in the *same* direction in both countries.

The leveling off of the relative wage of nonproduction workers in Mexico occurred in 1996, two years after the North American Free Trade Agreement (NAFTA) established free trade between the United States, Canada, and Mexico. The tariff reductions on imports from Mexico to the United States began in 1994 and were phased in over the next ten years. Tariffs on imports from the United States and other countries

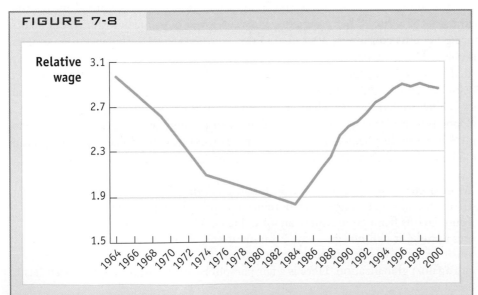

FIGURE 7-8

Relative Wage of Nonproduction/Production Workers, Mexico Manufacturing This diagram shows the wage of nonproduction workers in the manufacturing sector of Mexico divided by the wage of production workers. After declining during the 1960s and 1970s, this relative wage began to move upward in the mid-1980s, at the same time that the relative wage of nonproduction workers was increasing in the United States (see Figure 7-5). The relative wage in Mexico continued to rise until 1996, two years after NAFTA began, and then leveled out.

Sources: Robert C. Feenstra and Gordon H. Hanson, May 1997, "Foreign Direct Investment and Relative Wages: Evidence from Mexico's Maquiladoras," Journal of International Economics, 4, 371–393; and Gerardo Esquivel and José Antonio Rodríguez-López, 2003, "Technology, Trade, and Wage Inequality in Mexico Before and After NAFTA," Journal of Development Economics, 72, 543–565.

into Mexico had been reduced much earlier, however—right around the 1984 turning point that we see in Figure 7-8. According to one study:[9]

> In 1985, in the midst of the debt crisis and as a result of the collapse of the oil price, Mexico initiated an important process of trade liberalization. In that year, Mexico implemented a considerable unilateral reduction in trade barriers and announced its intention to participate in the General Agreement on Tariffs and Trade (GATT).

The average tariff charged by Mexico fell from 23.5% in 1985 to 11.0% in 1988, and the range of goods subject to tariffs was reduced. After 1985, Mexico also became much more open to the establishment of manufacturing plants by foreign (especially American) firms.

Summing up, the changes in relative prices in the United States and Mexico match each other during the period from 1964 to 1984 (with relative wages falling) and during the period from 1984 to 1996 (with relative wages rising in both countries). Offshoring from the United States to Mexico rose from 1984 to 1996, so the rise in relative wages matches our prediction from the model of offshoring. ■

2 The Gains from Offshoring

We have shown that offshoring can shift the relative demand for labor and therefore raise the relative wage for skilled workers. Because the relative wage for low-skilled workers is the reciprocal of the high-skilled relative wage, it falls in both countries. High-skilled labor gains and low-skilled labor loses in relative terms. On the other hand, the ability of firms to relocate some production activities abroad means that their costs are reduced. In a competitive market, lower costs mean lower prices, so off-shoring benefits consumers. Our goal in this section is to try to balance the potential losses faced by some groups (low-skilled labor) with the gains enjoyed by others (high-skilled labor and consumers). Our argument in previous chapters on the Ricardian and Heckscher-Ohlin models has been that international trade generates more gains than losses. Now we have to ask whether the same is true for offshoring.

One answer to this question comes from a surprising source. The Nobel laureate Paul Samuelson has been among the foremost proponents of global free trade, but in 2004 he had the following to say about the gains from foreign outsourcing:[10]

> Most noneconomists are fearful when an emerging China or India, helped by their still low real wages, outsourcing and miracle export-led developments, cause layoffs from good American jobs. This is a hot issue now, and in the coming decade, it will not go away. Prominent and competent mainstream economists enter in the debate to educate and correct warm-hearted protestors who are against globalization. Here is a fair paraphrase of the argumentation that has been used. . . .
>
> Yes, good jobs may be lost here in the short run. But still total U.S. net national product *must, by the economic laws of comparative advantage, be raised in the long run (and in China, too)*. The gains of the winners from free trade, properly measured,

[9] Gerardo Esquivel and José Antonio Rodríguez-López, 2003, "Technology, Trade, and Wage Inequality in Mexico Before and After NAFTA," *Journal of Development Economics*, 72, pp. 546–547.
[10] Paul Samuelson, Summer 2004, "Where Ricardo and Mill Rebut and Confirm Arguments of Mainstream Economists Supporting Globalization," *Journal of Economic Perspectives*, 18(3), 135–146.

work out to exceed the losses of the losers. . . . Correct economic law recognizes that some American groups can be hurt by dynamic free trade. But correct economic law vindicates the word "creative" destruction by its proof that the gains of the American winners are big enough to more than compensate the losers.

Does this paraphrase by Samuelson sound familiar? You can find passages much like it in this chapter and earlier ones, saying that the gains from trade exceed the losses. But listen to what Samuelson says next:

The last paragraph can be only an innuendo. For it is dead wrong about [the] *necessary* surplus of winnings over losings.

So Samuelson seems to be saying that the winnings for those who gain from trade *do not necessarily* exceed the losses for those who lose. How can this be? His last statement seems to contradict much of what we have learned in this book. Or does it?

Simplified Offshoring Model

To understand Samuelson's comments, we can use a simplified version of the offshoring model we have developed in this chapter. Instead of having many activities involved in the production of a good, suppose that there are only *two* activities: components production and research and development (R&D). Each of these activities uses high-skilled and low-skilled labor, but we assume that components production uses low-skilled labor intensively and that R&D uses skilled labor intensively. As in our earlier model, we assume that the costs of capital are equal in the two activities and do not discuss this factor. Our goal will be to compare a no-trade situation with an equilibrium with trade through offshoring, to determine whether there are overall gains from trade.

Suppose that the firm has a certain amount of high-skilled (H) and low-skilled (L) labor to devote to components and R&D. It is free to move these workers between the two activities. For example, scientists could be used in the research lab or could instead be used to determine the best method to produce components; similarly, workers who are assembling components can instead assist with the construction of full-scale models in the research lab. Given the amount of high-skilled and low-skilled labor used in total, we can graph a production possibilities frontier (PPF) for the firm between components and R&D activities, as shown in Figure 7-9. This PPF looks just like the production possibilities frontier for a country, except that now we apply it to a single firm. Points on the PPF, such as *A*, correspond to differing amounts of high-skilled and low-skilled labor used in the components and R&D activities. Moving left from point *A* to another point on the PPF, for example, would involve shifting some high-skilled and low-skilled labor from the production of components into the research lab.

Production in the Absence of Offshoring

Now that we have the PPF for the firm, we can analyze an equilibrium for the firm, just as we have previously done for an entire economy. Suppose initially that the firm cannot engage in offshoring of its activities. This assumption means that the component production and R&D done at Home are used to manufacture a final product at

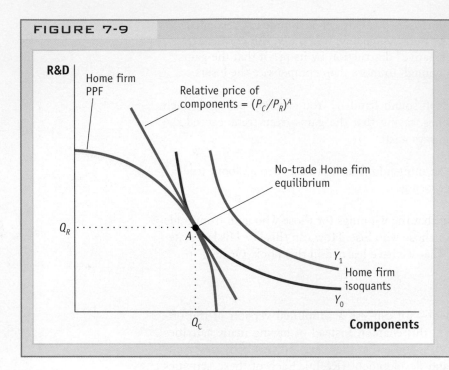

FIGURE 7-9

No-Trade Equilibrium for the Home Firm The PPF shows the combinations of components and R&D that can be undertaken by a firm with a given amount of labor and capital. In the absence of offshoring, the firm produces at A, using quantities Q_C of components and Q_R of R&D to produce amount Y_0 of the final good. The line tangent to the isoquant through point A measures the value that the firm puts on components relative to R&D, or their relative price, $(P_C/P_R)^A$. Amount Y_1 of the final good cannot be produced in the absence of offshoring because it lies outside the PPF for the firm.

Home: it cannot assemble any components in Foreign, and likewise, it cannot send any of its R&D results abroad to be used in a Foreign plant.

The two production activities are used to produce a final good. To determine how much of the final good is produced, we can use **isoquants.** An isoquant is similar to a consumer's indifference curve, except that instead of utility, it illustrates the production of the firm; it is a curve along which the output of the firm is constant despite changing combinations of inputs. Two of these isoquants are labeled as Y_0 and Y_1 in Figure 7-9. The quantity of the final good Y_0 can be produced using the quantity Q_C of components and the quantity Q_R of R&D, shown at point A in the figure. Notice that the isoquant Y_0 is tangent to the PPF at point A, which indicates that this isoquant is the highest amount of the final good that can be produced using any combination of components and R&D on the PPF. The quantity of the final good Y_1 cannot be produced in the absence of offshoring because it lies outside the PPF. Thus, point A is the amount of components and R&D that the firm chooses in the absence of offshoring or what we will call the "no-trade" or "autarky" equilibrium for short.

Through the no-trade equilibrium A in Figure 7-9, we draw a line with the slope of the isoquant at point A. The slope of the isoquant measures the value, or price, that the firm puts on components relative to R&D. We can think of these prices as internal to the firm, reflecting the marginal costs of production of the two activities. An automobile company, for example, would be able to compute the extra labor and other inputs needed to produce some components of a car and that would be its internal price of components P_C. Similarly, it could compute the marginal cost of developing one more prototype of a new vehicle, which is the internal price of R&D or P_R. The slope of the price line through point A is the price of components relative to the price of R&D, $(P_C/P_R)^A$, in the absence of offshoring.[11]

---

[11] Recall that the slope of a price line is the relative price of the good on the horizontal axis, which is Components in Figure 7-9.

Equilibrium with Offshoring Now suppose that the firm can import and export its production activities through offshoring. For example, some of the components could be done in a Foreign plant and then imported by the Home firm. Alternatively, some R&D done at Home can be exported to a Foreign plant and used there. In either case, the quantity of the final good is no longer constrained by the Home PPF. Just as in the Ricardian and Heckscher-Ohlin models, in which a higher level of utility (indifference curve) can be obtained if countries specialize and trade with each other, here a higher level of production (isoquant) is possible by trading intermediate activities.

We refer to the relative price of the two activities that the Home firm has available through offshoring as the world relative price or $(P_C/P_R)^{W1}$. Let us assume that the world relative price of components is cheaper than Home's no-trade relative price, $(P_C/P_R)^{W1} < (P_C/P_R)^A$. That assumption means the Home firm can import components at a lower relative price than it can produce them itself. The assumption that $(P_C/P_R)^{W1} < (P_C/P_R)^A$ is similar to the assumption we made in the previous section, that the relative wage of low-skilled labor is lower in Foreign, $W_L^*/W_H^* < W_L/W_H$. With a lower relative wage of low-skilled labor in Foreign, the components assembly will also be cheaper in Foreign. It follows that Home will want to offshore components, which are cheaper abroad, while the Home firm will be exporting R&D (i.e., offshoring it to Foreign firms), which is cheaper at Home.

The Home equilibrium with offshoring is illustrated in Figure 7-10. The world relative price of components is tangent to the PPF at point B. Notice that the world

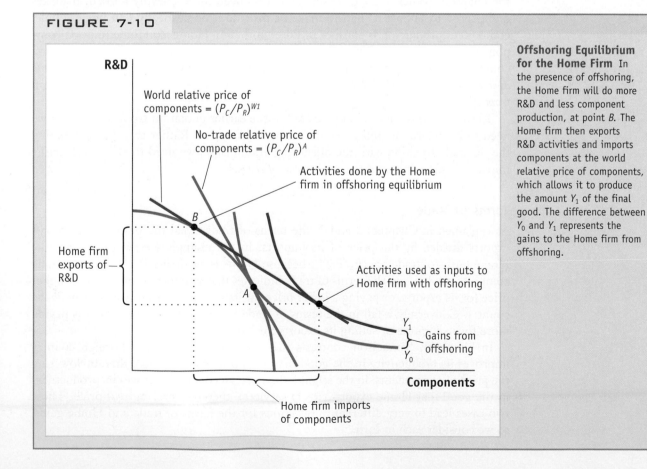

FIGURE 7-10

R&D

World relative price of components = $(P_C/P_R)^{W1}$

No-trade relative price of components = $(P_C/P_R)^A$

Activities done by the Home firm in offshoring equilibrium

B

Home firm exports of R&D

Activities used as inputs to Home firm with offshoring

A

C

Y_1

Gains from offshoring

Y_0

Components

Home firm imports of components

Offshoring Equilibrium for the Home Firm In the presence of offshoring, the Home firm will do more R&D and less component production, at point B. The Home firm then exports R&D activities and imports components at the world relative price of components, which allows it to produce the amount Y_1 of the final good. The difference between Y_0 and Y_1 represents the gains to the Home firm from offshoring.

relative price line is *flatter* than the no-trade relative price line at Home. The flattening of the price line reflects the lower world relative price of components as compared with the no-trade relative price at Home. As a result of this fall in the relative price of components, the Home firm undertakes more R&D and less component production, moving from point *A* to point *B* on its PPF.

Starting at point *B* on its PPF, the Home firm now exports R&D and imports components, moving along the relative price line to point *C*. Therefore, through offshoring the firm is able to move off of its PPF to point *C*. At that point, the isoquant labeled Y_1 is tangent to the world price line, indicating that the maximum amount of the final good Y_1 is being produced. Notice that this production of the final good exceeds the amount Y_0 that the Home produced in the absence of offshoring.

Gains from Offshoring Within the Firm The increase in the amount of the final good produced—from Y_0 to Y_1—is a measure of the gains from trade to the Home firm through offshoring. Using the same total amount of high-skilled and low-skilled labor at Home as before, the company is able to produce more of the final good through its ability to offshore components and R&D. Because more of the final good is produced with the same overall amount of high-skilled and low-skilled labor available in Home, the Home company is more productive. Its costs of production fall, and we expect that the price of its final product also falls. The gains for this company are therefore spread to consumers, too.

For these reasons, we agree with the quote about offshoring at the beginning of the chapter: "When a good or service is produced more cheaply abroad, it makes more sense to import it than to make or provide it domestically." In our example, component production is cheaper in Foreign than in Home, so Home imports components from Foreign. There are overall gains from offshoring. That is our first conclusion: *when comparing a no-trade situation to the equilibrium with offshoring, and assuming that the world relative price differs from that at Home, there are always gains from offshoring.*

To see how this conclusion is related to the earlier quotation from Samuelson, we need to introduce one more feature into our discussion. Rather than just comparing the no-trade situation with the offshoring equilibrium, we need to also consider the impact of offshoring on a country's *terms of trade*.

Terms of Trade

As explained in Chapters 2 and 3, the terms of trade equal the price of a country's exports divided by the price of its imports. In the example we are discussing, the Home terms of trade are $(P_R/P_C)^{W1}$, because Home is exporting R&D and importing components. A rise in the terms of trade indicates that a country is obtaining a higher price for its exports, or paying a lower price for its imports, both of which benefit the country. Conversely, a fall in the terms of trade harms a country because it is paying more for its imports or selling its exports for less.

In his paper, Samuelson contrasts two cases. In the first, the Foreign country improves its productivity in the good that it exports (components), thereby lowering the price of components; in the second, the Foreign country improves its productivity in the good that Home exports (R&D services), thereby lowering *that* price. These two cases lead to very different implications for the terms of trade and Home gains, so we consider each in turn.

Fall in the Price of Components Turning to Figure 7-11, let the Home country start at the equilibrium with offshoring shown by points B and C. From that situation, suppose there is a *fall* in the relative price of component production. That price might fall, for instance, if the Foreign country improves its productivity in components, thereby lowering the price paid by Home for this service. Because components are being imported by Home, a fall in their price is a *rise* in the Home terms of trade, to $(P_R/P_C)^{W2}$. Let us trace how this change in the terms of trade will affect the Home equilibrium.

Because of the fall in the relative price of components, the world price line shown in Figure 7-11 becomes *flatter*. Production will shift to point B', and by exporting R&D and importing components along the world price line, the firm ends up at point C'. Production of the final good at point C' is Y_2, which exceeds the production Y_1 in the initial equilibrium with offshoring.[12] Thus, the Home firm enjoys *greater* gains from offshoring when the price of components falls. This is the first case considered by Samuelson, and it reinforces our conclusions that offshoring leads to overall gains.

FIGURE 7-11

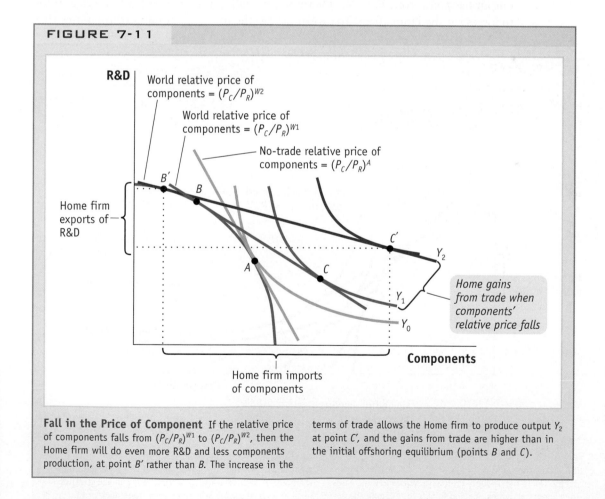

Fall in the Price of Component If the relative price of components falls from $(P_C/P_R)^{W1}$ to $(P_C/P_R)^{W2}$, then the Home firm will do even more R&D and less components production, at point B' rather than B. The increase in the terms of trade allows the Home firm to produce output Y_2 at point C', and the gains from trade are higher than in the initial offshoring equilibrium (points B and C).

---

[12] Notice that the fall in the relative price of components leads to an increase in the amount of components imported but that the amount of R&D exported from Home does not necessarily increase. You are asked to explore this case further in Problem 9 at the end of the chapter.

Fall in the Price of R&D We also need to consider the second case identified by Samuelson, and that is when there is a fall in the price of R&D services rather than components. This is what Samuelson has in mind when he argues that offshoring might allow developing countries, such as India, to gain a comparative advantage in those activities in which the United States formerly had comparative advantage. As Indian companies like Wipro (an information technology services company headquartered in Bangalore) engage in more R&D activities, they are directly competing with American companies exporting the same services. So this competition can lower the world price of R&D services.

In Figure 7-12, we reproduce Figure 7-10, including the Home no-trade equilibrium at point A and the Home production point B with offshoring. Starting at point B, a fall in the world relative price of R&D will lead to a *steeper* price line (because the slope of the price line is the world relative price of components, which increases when P_R *falls*). At the new price $(P_C/P_R)^{W3}$, Home shifts production to point B'' and, by exporting R&D and importing components, moves to point C''. Notice that final output has *fallen* from Y_1 to Y_3. Therefore, the fall in the price of R&D services leads to losses for the Home firm. To explain where the losses are coming from, notice that

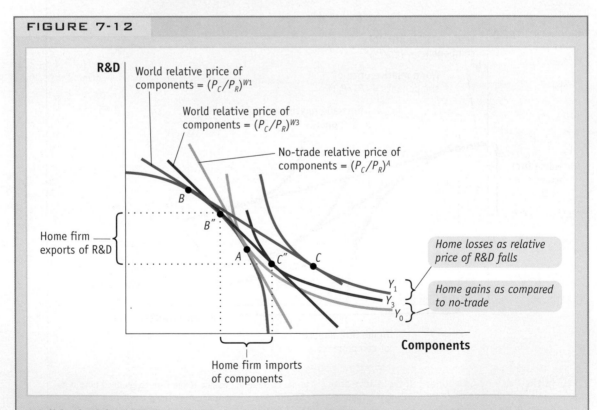

FIGURE 7-12

A Fall in the Price of R&D A fall in the relative price of R&D makes the world price line steeper, $(P_C/P_R)^{W3}$. As a result, the Home firm reduces its R&D activities and increases its components activities, moving from B to B'' along the PPF. At the new world relative price, the Home firm faces a terms-of-trade loss and can no longer export each unit of R&D for as many components as it could in the initial offshoring equilibrium. The final good output is reduced from Y_1 to Y_3 at point C''. Notice that the final good output, Y_3, is still higher than output without trade, Y_0. After the fall in the relative price of R&D, there are still gains from trade relative to no-trade (point A) but losses relative to the initial offshoring equilibrium (points B and C).

Home is exporting R&D and importing components in the initial offshoring equilibrium (points B and C), so its terms of trade are the price of R&D divided by the price of components (P_R/P_C). With the fall in the price of R&D, the Home terms of trade have *worsened*, and Home is worse off compared with its initial offshoring equilibrium. Samuelson's point is that the United States *could* be worse off if China or India becomes more competitive in, and lowers the prices of, the products that the United States itself is exporting, such as R&D services. This is theoretically correct. Although it may be surprising to think of the United States being in this position, the idea that a country will suffer when its terms of trade fall is familiar to us from developing-country examples (such as the Prebisch-Singer hypothesis) in earlier chapters.

Furthermore, notice that final output of Y_3 is still higher than Y_0, the no-offshoring output. *Therefore, there are still Home gains from offshoring at C″ as compared with the no-trade equilibrium at A.* It follows that Home can never be worse off with trade as compared with no trade. Samuelson's point is that a country is worse off when its terms of trade fall, even though it is still better off than in the absence of trade. With the fall in the terms of trade, some factors of production will lose and others will gain, but in this case the gains of the winners are not enough to compensate the losses of the losers. Our simple model of offshoring illustrates Samuelson's point.

The offshoring that occurred from the United States in the 1980s and the 1990s often concerned manufacturing activities. But today, the focus is frequently one of the newer forms of offshoring, the offshoring of **business services** to foreign countries. Business services are activities such as accounting, auditing, human resources, order processing, telemarketing, and after-sales service, like getting help with your computer. Firms in the United States are increasingly transferring these activities to India, where the wages of educated workers are much lower than in the United States. This is the sort of competition that Samuelson had in mind when he spoke of China and India improving their productivity and comparative advantage in activities that the United States already exports. The next application discusses the magnitude of service exports and also the changes in their prices.

APPLICATION

U.S. Terms of Trade and Service Exports

Because Samuelson's argument is a theoretical one, the next step is to examine the evidence for the United States. If the United States has been facing competition in R&D and the other skill-intensive activities that we export, then we would expect the terms of trade to fall. Conversely, if the United States has been offshoring in manufacturing, then the opportunity to import lower-priced intermediate inputs should lead to a rise in the terms of trade.

Merchandise Prices To evaluate these ideas, we make use of data on the terms of trade for the United States. In Figure 7-13, we first show the terms of trade for the United States for merchandise goods (excluding petroleum), which is the gold line.[13] The terms of trade for goods fell from 1990 to 1994 but then rose to 2008,

---

[13] Merchandise goods include agriculture, mining, and manufacturing. We have excluded petroleum because its world price is determined by conditions such as shortages and wars and behaves quite differently from the prices of other merchandise goods.

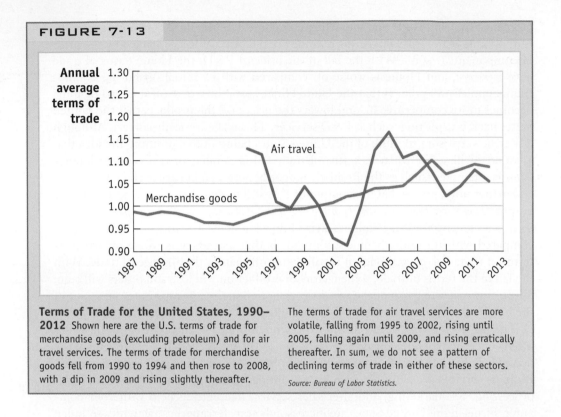

FIGURE 7-13

Terms of Trade for the United States, 1990–2012 Shown here are the U.S. terms of trade for merchandise goods (excluding petroleum) and for air travel services. The terms of trade for merchandise goods fell from 1990 to 1994 and then rose to 2008, with a dip in 2009 and rising slightly thereafter.

The terms of trade for air travel services are more volatile, falling from 1995 to 2002, rising until 2005, falling again until 2009, and rising erratically thereafter. In sum, we do not see a pattern of declining terms of trade in either of these sectors.

Source: Bureau of Labor Statistics.

with a dip in 2009 and a slight rise thereafter. The overall improvement in the merchandise terms of trade shows that we are able to import intermediate inputs (and also import final goods) at lower prices over time. This rise in the terms of trade means that there are increasing gains from trade in merchandise goods for the United States.

Service Prices For trade in services, such as finance, insurance, and R&D, it is very difficult to measure their prices in international trade. These services are tailored to the buyer and, as a result, there are not standardized prices. For this reason, we do not have an overall measure of the terms of trade in services. There is one type of service, however, for which it is relatively easy to collect international prices: air travel. The terms of trade in air travel equal the price that foreigners pay for travel on U.S. airlines (a service export) divided by the price that Americans pay on foreign airlines (a service import). In Figure 7-13, we also show the U.S. terms of trade in air travel that are available since 1995. The terms of trade in air travel are quite volatile, falling from 1995 to 2002, rising until 2005, falling again until 2009, and rising erratically thereafter. For this one category of services, the terms of trade improvement from 2002 to 2005 indicates growing gains from trade for the United States, the same result we found for merchandise goods. Summing up, there is no evidence to date that the falling terms of trade that Samuelson is concerned about have occurred for the United States.

Service Trade What about other traded services? Although standard prices are not available, data on the *amount* of service exports and imports for the United States are collected annually. These data are shown in Table 7-2 for 2011. The

United States runs a substantial surplus in services trade, with exports of $587 billion and imports of $393 billion. Categories of service exports that exceed imports include several types of business, professional, and technical services (but in computer and information services, the United States now runs a deficit); education (which is exported when a foreign student studies in the United States); financial services; travel; and royalties and license fees (which are collected from foreign firms when they use U.S. patents and trademarks or are paid abroad when we use foreign patents). The fact that exports exceed imports in many categories in Table 7-2 means that the United States has a comparative advantage in traded services. Indeed, the U.S. surplus in business, professional, and technical services is among the highest in the world, similar to that of the United Kingdom and higher than that of Hong Kong and India. London is a world financial center and competes with New York and other U.S. cities, which explains the high trade surplus of the United Kingdom, whereas Hong Kong is a regional hub for transportation and offshoring to China. The combined trade balance in computer and information services, insurance and financial services for the United

TABLE 7-2		
U.S. Trade in Services, 2011 ($ millions) This table shows U.S. exports and imports in the major categories of services trade for 2011.		
	Exports	**Imports**
Computer and information services	15,501	24,538
Management and consulting services	32,169	24,823
R&D and testing services	23,364	22,360
Operational leasing	7,142	1,922
Other business, professional, and technical services	56,240	31,130
Total business, professional, and technical services	$134,416	$104,773
Education	22,726	5,888
Financial services	74,055	16,207
Insurance services	15,477	56,619
Telecommunications	12,650	7,690
Total other private services	$270,193	$191,973
Travel	116,115	78,651
Passenger fares	36,631	31,109
Other transporation	43,064	54,711
Royalties and license fees	120,836	36,620
Other services	62,633	11,917
Total private services	$586,839	$393,065

Source: U.S. Bureau of Economic Analysis.

States, the United Kingdom, and India since 1970 are graphed in Figure 7-14.

The U.S. surplus in these categories of services has been growing since about 1985, with an occasional dip, and exceeded the trade surplus of the United Kingdom, its chief competitor, up until about 2000. Since then the surpluses of the United Kingdom and of the United States have been quite similar. India's surplus began growing shortly after 2000 and derives entirely from its exports of computer and information services. In 2010 the combined U.S. surplus in computers, insurance, and financial services ($122 billion) was three times larger than that of India ($37 billion), and about the same as of the United Kingdom ($108 billion).

What will these surpluses look like a decade or two from now? It is difficult to project, but notice in Figure 7-14 that in approximately 2000, as the Indian surplus began growing, the U.S. surplus dipped to become more similar to that of the United Kingdom. The Indian trade surplus is entirely due to its exports of computer and information services—a category in which the United States also has strong net exports. So even though the Indian trade surplus is still much smaller than that of the United States, it appears to pose a competitive challenge to the United States. It is at least possible that in a decade or two, India's overall surplus in service exports could overtake that of the United States. Only time will tell whether the United States will eventually face the same type of competition from India in its service exports that it has already faced for many years from the United Kingdom. ■

FIGURE 7-14

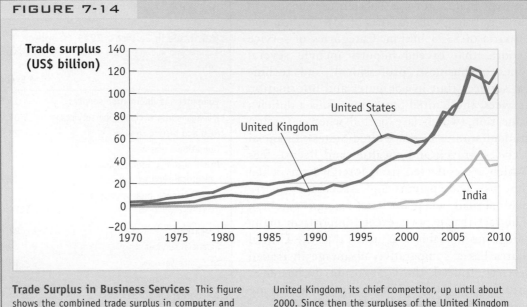

Trade Surplus in Business Services This figure shows the combined trade surplus in computer and information services, insurance, and financial services for the United States, the United Kingdom, and India from 1970 to 2010. The U.S. surplus in these categories of services has been growing since about 1985, with an occasional dip, and exceeded the trade surplus of the United Kingdom, its chief competitor, up until about 2000. Since then the surpluses of the United Kingdom and of the United States have been similar. India's surplus began growing around 2000 and is based entirely on its exports of computer and information services.

Source: World Bank World Development Indicators.

3 The Politics and Future of Offshoring

Offshoring is controversial and is often the topic of political debate. In February 2004 the first quote at the beginning of this chapter appeared in the *Economic Report of the President*. The writer of that sentence, Harvard economist N. Gregory Mankiw, who was chairman of the Council of Economic Advisors, also said that "outsourcing is just a new way of doing international trade. More things are tradable than were tradable in the past, and that's a good thing." Those comments were widely criticized by the Democrats and Republicans alike, and Professor Mankiw later apologized in a letter to the House of Representatives, writing, "My lack of clarity left the wrong impression that I praised the loss of U.S. jobs."

In the Democratic primary elections of 2007 and in the presidential campaign of 2008, this topic came up again. Senators Barack Obama and Hillary Clinton both promised that, if elected, they would end tax breaks for companies earning profits overseas:[14]

> **Obama, Nov. 3, 2007:** When I am president, I will end the tax giveaways to companies that ship our jobs overseas, and I will put the money in the pockets of working Americans, and seniors, and homeowners who deserve a break.

---

[14] These quotations and some material that follows are taken from http://www.factcheck.org/2008/02/oil-and-gas-company-tax-breaks/ (accessed August 23, 2013).

Clinton, Nov. 19, 2007: And we are going to finally close the tax loopholes and stop giving tax breaks to companies that ship jobs overseas. Enough with outsourcing American jobs using taxpayer dollars.

To what tax breaks were Mr. Obama and Ms. Clinton referring? The United States taxes corporate profits at 35%, a high rate when compared with the corporate tax rates in other countries. Profit earned by overseas subsidiaries of U.S. companies, however, goes untaxed by the U.S. government provided that such a subsidiary stays overseas and does not appear on the books of the parent company in the United States. That tax provision gives U.S. multinational companies an incentive to use these funds overseas for further investment in the subsidiary, but it does not necessarily lead them to move jobs overseas in the first place. Eventually, when these profits are moved back to the parent company in the United States, they are taxed at the normal rate.

President Obama recently announced that he would follow through on his campaign pledge to end the tax break on overseas profits of multinational firms, as indicated by the quotation at the beginning of this chapter: "The American people deserve a tax code that . . . lowers incentives to move jobs overseas, and lowers tax rates for businesses and manufacturers that are creating jobs right here in the United States of America. That's what tax reform can deliver." That change in policy does not have much support from economists. One strongly worded response comes from Matthew Slaughter, Professor at Dartmouth College, in **Headlines: How to Destroy American Jobs.** He cites evidence that U.S. multinationals have added roughly as many jobs in the United States as they have added abroad, and argues that these jobs in the United States depend on the ability of the multinationals to offshore other jobs.

In addition to the employment statistics, Professor Slaughter also cites evidence that U.S. multinational firms conducted nearly 90% of all private-sector R&D in the United States, and that these firms account for the majority of U.S. productivity gains.

Direct evidence on the positive impact of offshoring on productivity comes from another source, a 2005 study of the offshoring of material inputs and services by U.S. manufacturing firms in the 1990s.[15] Over the eight years from 1992 to 2000, that study found that service offshoring can explain between 11% and 13% of the total increase in productivity within the U.S. manufacturing sector. In addition, the offshoring of material inputs explains between 3% and 6% of the increase in manufacturing productivity. Combining these effects, offshoring explains between 15% and 20% of overall productivity growth in the manufacturing sector. Evidence of this type makes economists reluctant to impose additional taxes on U.S. companies that engage in offshoring, because of the possible adverse effects on productivity here in the United States.

On the other hand, changes in economic conditions that lead firms to *voluntarily* bring some activities back home would be viewed favorably by most economists. There is some evidence that economic conditions have changed in that direction, as

---

[15] Mary Amiti and Shang-Jin Wei, 2005, "Service Offshoring, Productivity, and Employment: Evidence from the United States," International Monetary Fund, IMF Working Paper 05/238; and 2006, "Service Offshoring and Productivity: Evidence from the United States," National Bureau of Economic Research (NBER) Working Paper No. 11926.

HEADLINES

How to Destroy American Jobs

This article argues that offshoring by multinational companies supports an increase in jobs at home, and that these jobs would be lost by policies to restrict offshoring.

Deep in the president's budget released Monday [February 1, 2010] appear a set of proposals headed "Reform U.S. International Tax System." If these proposals are enacted, U.S.-based multinational firms will face $122.2 billion in tax increases over the next decade. This is a natural follow-up to President Obama's sweeping plan announced last May [2009] entitled "Leveling the Playing Field: Curbing Tax Havens and Removing Tax Incentives for Shifting Jobs Overseas."

The fundamental assumption behind these proposals is that U.S. multinationals expand abroad only to "export" jobs out of the country. Thus, taxing their foreign operations more would boost tax revenues here and create desperately needed U.S. jobs. This is simply wrong. These tax increases would not create American jobs, they would destroy them.

Academic research, including most recently that done by Harvard's Mihir Desai and Fritz Foley and University of Michigan's James Hines, has consistently found that expansion abroad by U.S. multinationals tends to support jobs based in the U.S. More investment and employment abroad are strongly associated with more investment and employment in American parent companies.

When parent firms based in the U.S. hire workers in their foreign affiliates, the skills and occupations of these workers are often complementary; they aren't substitutes. More hiring abroad stimulates more U.S. hiring. For example, as Wal-Mart has opened stores abroad, it has created hundreds of U.S. jobs for workers to coordinate the distribution of goods worldwide. The expansion of these foreign affiliates—whether to serve foreign customers, or to save costs—also expands the overall scale of multinationals.

Expanding abroad also allows firms to refine their scope of activities. For example, exporting routine production means that employees in the U.S. can focus on higher value-added tasks such as R&D, marketing and general management. The total impact of this process is much richer than an overly simplistic story of exporting jobs. But the ultimate proof lies in the empirical evidence.

Consider total employment spanning 1988 through 2007 (the most recent year of data available from the U.S. Bureau of Economic Analysis). Over that time, employment in affiliates rose by 5.3 million—to 11.7 million from 6.4 million. Over that same period, employment in U.S. parent companies increased

by nearly as much—4.3 million—to 22 million from 17.7 million. Indeed, research repeatedly shows that foreign-affiliate expansion tends to expand U.S. parent activity. . . .

The major policy challenge facing the U.S. today is not just to create jobs, but to create high-paying private-sector jobs linked to investment and trade. Which firms can create these jobs? U.S.-based multinationals. They—along with similarly performing U.S. affiliates of foreign-based multinationals—have long been among the strongest companies in the U.S. economy.

These two groups of firms accounted for the majority of the post-1995 acceleration in U.S. productivity growth, the foundation of rising standards of living for everyone. They tend to create high-paying jobs—27.5 million in 2007. . . . And these firms also conducted $240.2 billion in research and development, a remarkable 89.2% of all U.S. private-sector R&D.

To climb out of the recession, we need to create millions of the kinds of jobs that U.S. multinationals tend to create. Economic policy on all fronts should be encouraging job growth by these firms. The proposed international-tax reforms do precisely the opposite.

Source: Matthew J. Slaughter, "How to Destroy American Jobs," Wall Street Journal, February 3, 2010, p. A17.

described in **Headlines: Caterpillar Joins "Onshoring" Trend.** In 2010, General Electric joined this trend by moving the manufacturing of a water heater from China to Louisville, Kentucky, and in late 2012 Apple Computer announced that it would be bringing some jobs back to the United States by building some Macintosh computers locally.[16] A combination of higher wages in China, higher transportation costs

---

[16] Charles Fishman, "The Insourcing Boom," *Atlantic Magazine*, December 2012, and Catherine Rampell and Nick Wingfield, "In Shift of Jobs, Apple Will Make Some Macs in U.S.," *New York Times*, December 6, 2012.

HEADLINES

Caterpillar Joins "Onshoring" Trend

Some American companies have found it advantageous to take activities they had previously shifted overseas and move them back home, in what is called "onshoring."

Caterpillar, Inc. is considering relocating some heavy-equipment overseas production to a new U.S. plant, part of a growing movement among manufacturers to bring more operations back home—a shift that will likely spark fierce competition among states for new manufacturing jobs. The trend, known as onshoring or reshoring, is gaining momentum as a weak U.S. dollar makes it costlier to import products from overseas. Manufacturers are also counting on White House jobs incentives, as well as their ability to negotiate lower prices from U.S. suppliers who were hurt by the downturn and willing to bargain.

After a decade of rapid globalization, economists say companies are seeing disadvantages of offshore production, including shipping costs, complicated logistics, and quality issues. Political unrest and theft of intellectual property pose additional risks. "If you want to keep your supply chain tight, it's hard to do that with a 16-hour plane ride from Shanghai to Ohio," said Cliff Waldman, an econo-mist with the Manufacturers Alliance/ MAPI, a public policy and economics research group in Arlington, Virginia.

General Electric Co. said last June it would move production of some water heaters from China to its facility in Louisville, Kentucky, starting in 2011. A GE spokeswoman said a 2005 labor agreement under which new employees would be paid $13 an hour, [instead of the] nearly $20 an hour [they once made], "enabled us to be more competitive."

Source: Kris Maher and Bob Tita, "Caterpillar Joins 'Onshoring' Trend," The Wall Street Journal, *March 11, 2010, p. A17. Reprinted with permission of The Wall Street Journal, Copyright © (2010) Dow Jones & Company, Inc. All Rights Reserved Worldwide.*

due to rising oil prices, and U.S. unions that are more willing to compromise with management, has led these and other companies to "onshore" their activities back to the United States. This trend has also occurred because companies are finding that communication with overseas suppliers can be slow and costly.

The Future of U.S. Comparative Advantage

Just as in our model of this chapter, the recent "onshoring" trend shows that companies usually avoid offshoring *all* activities from the United States: the extra communication and trade costs involved need to be balanced against the lower foreign wages to find the right amount of offshoring. Most often companies find it advantageous to keep some activities in the United States (such as those using more highly skilled labor or relying on close communication with customers) and move other activities abroad (using less skilled labor and involving more routine activities). The fear sometimes expressed in the popular press that offshoring threatens the elimination of most manufacturing and service jobs in the United States is overstated. The ability to offshore a portion of the production process allows other activities to remain in the United States.

A good example to illustrate this point is the offshoring of medical services. The transcription of doctors' notes from spoken to written form was one of the first service activities offshore to India. Since then, other types of medical services have also been offshored, and a *New York Times* article in 2003 identified the reading of X-rays—or radiology—as the next area that could shift overseas: "It turns out that even American radiologists, with their years of training and annual salaries of $250,000 or more, worry about their jobs moving to countries with lower wages, in much the same way that garment knitters, blast-furnace operators and data-entry clerks do. . . . Radiology may just be the start of patient care performed overseas."[17]

It turns out, however, that the types of radiology jobs that can potentially be transferred overseas are very limited.[18] Radiology is a high-paying profession precisely because the reading of X-rays is difficult and takes years of training and practice to perfect. X-rays are normally analyzed in the same hospital where the patient is being treated. In a few cases of specific diseases, such as the reading of mammograms for breast cancer, it is possible that the work can be outsourced (i.e., performed outside the hospital), either domestically or offshore. Firms known as "nighthawks" already provide some outsourcing services to hospitals, principally during nighttime hours. Nighthawk firms are headquartered in the United States but have radiologists at offshore sites, including Australia, Israel, Spain, and India. These nighttime services allow smaller hospitals that cannot afford a full-time night radiologist to obtain readings during evening hours, and allow the nighthawk firms to keep their radiologists fully employed by combining the demand from multiple hospitals.

The offshoring to nighthawk firms is a natural response to the round-the-clock demand for hospital services but less-than-full-time demand for radiologists on-site. Often these nighttime services are used only for preliminary reads, leading to immediate treatment of patients; the X-ray image is then read again by the staff radiologist in the United States the next day. That is, in many cases, the services being outsourced are not directly competing for the daytime jobs but, instead, are complements to these U.S. jobs.

Radiology is under no imminent threat from outsourcing because the profession involves decisions that cannot be codified in written rules. Much of the radiologist's knowledge is gained from reading countless X-rays with complex images and shadows, and the ability to recognize patterns cannot easily be passed on to another person or firm. It follows that the work cannot be offshored except for the nighttime activities of nighthawk firms, which actually work in conjunction with the daytime activities in major hospitals.

In every profession there will always be jobs that cannot be performed by someone who is not on-site. For many of the service activities listed in Table 7-2, the United States will continue to have comparative advantage even while facing foreign competition. In many manufacturing industries, the United States will continue to maintain some activities at home, such as R&D and marketing, even while shifting a portion of the production process abroad. Finally, we should recognize that the ability to offshore to Mexico or India ultimately makes the U.S. companies involved more profitable and therefore better able to withstand foreign competition.

4 Conclusions

In this chapter, we have studied a type of trade that is becoming increasingly important: offshoring, by which we mean the shifting of some production activities to another country, while other production activities are kept at Home. Rather than

---

[17] Andrew Pollack, "Who's Reading Your X-Ray?" *New York Times*, November 16, 2003, section 3, pp. 1, 9.
[18] The material in the following paragraphs is drawn from Frank Levy and Ari Goelman, "Offshoring and Radiology," presented at the Brookings Institute Trade Forum, May 12–13, 2005.

trading final goods, like wheat for cloth as in the Ricardian model of Chapter 2, or computers for shoes as in the Heckscher-Ohlin model of Chapter 4, with offshoring each good can be produced in stages in several countries and then assembled in a final location.

In the model of offshoring we presented, because low-skilled labor is relatively cheap abroad, it makes sense for Home to offshore to the Foreign country those activities that are less skill-intensive, while keeping at Home those activities that are more skill-intensive. "Slicing" the value chain in this way is consistent with the idea of comparative advantage, because each country is engaged in the activities for which its labor is relatively cheaper. From *both* the Home and Foreign point of view, the ratio of high-skilled/low-skilled labor

in value chain activities goes up. A major finding of this chapter, then, is that an increase in offshoring will raise the relative demand (and hence relative wage) for skilled labor in *both* countries.

In a simplified model in which there are only two activities, we found that a fall in the world price of the low-skilled and labor-intensive input will lead to gains to the Home firm from offshoring. But in contrast, a fall in the price of the skilled labor-intensive input would lead to losses to the Home firm, as compared with the prior trade equilibrium. Such a price change is a terms-of-trade loss for Home, leading to losses from the lower relative price of exports. So even though Home gains overall from offshoring (producing at least as much as it would in a no-offshoring equilibrium), it is still the case that competition in the input being exported by Home will make it worse off.

We concluded the chapter by exploring offshoring in service activities, a topic that has received much attention in the media recently. Offshoring from the United States to Mexico consists mainly of low-skilled jobs; offshoring from the United States to India consists of higher-skilled jobs performed by college-educated Indians. This new type of offshoring has been made possible by information and communication technologies (such as the Internet and fiber-optic cables) and has allowed cities like Bangalore, India, to establish service centers for U.S. companies. These facilities not only answer questions from customers in the United States and worldwide, they are also engaged in accounting and finance, writing software, R&D, and many other skilled business services.

The fact that it is not only *possible* to shift these activities to India but *economical* to do so shows how new technologies make possible patterns of international trade that would have been unimaginable a decade ago. Such changes show "globalization" at work. Does the offshoring of service activities pose any threat to white-collar workers in the United States? There is no simple answer. On the one hand, we presented evidence that service offshoring provides productivity gains, and therefore gains from trade, to the United States. But as always, having gains from trade does not mean that everyone gains: there can be winners and losers. For service offshoring, it is possible that skilled workers will see a potential reduction in their wages, just as low-skilled labor bore the brunt of the impact from offshoring in the 1980s. Nevertheless, it is still the case that the United States, like the United Kingdom and other European countries, continues to have a comparative advantage in exporting various types of business services. Although India is making rapid progress in the area of computer and information services, there are still many types of service activities that need be done locally and cannot be outsourced. One likely prediction is that the activities in the United States that cannot be codified in written rules and procedures, and that benefit from face-to-face contact as well as proximity to other highly skilled individuals in related industries, will continue to have comparative advantage.

KEY POINTS

1. The provision of a service or the production of various parts of a good in different countries for assembly into a final good in another location is called foreign outsourcing or offshoring.

2. We can apply the same ideas that we developed for trade in final goods among countries to the trade of intermediate offshored activities. For instance, if low-skilled labor is relatively inexpensive in the Foreign country, then the activities that are least skill-intensive will be offshored there, and Home will engage in the activities that are more skill-intensive.

3. We can also predict what happens to relative wages of skilled labor when there is a change in trading costs and more offshoring. Our model predicts that the relative demand for skilled labor *increases in both countries*. This result helps to explain the observation that relative wages

have been increasing in the United States and in other countries at the same time.

4. In an overall sense, there are gains from offshoring, because the specialization of countries in different production activities allows firms in both countries to produce a higher level of final goods. That increase in output represents a productivity gain, and the gains from trade.

5. With service offshoring, it is possible that a country like India will have rising productivity in activities in which the United States has comparative advantage, such as R&D. Rising productivity in India would lead to a fall in the price of R&D, which is a terms-of-trade loss for the United States. For that reason, the United States could lose due to service offshoring, though it still gains as compared with a situation of no offshoring at all.

KEY TERMS

foreign outsourcing, p. 198
offshoring, p. 198
value chain, p. 200

skill-biased technological change, p. 209
total wage payments, p. 209

isoquants, p. 214
business services, p. 219

PROBLEMS

1. Consider an offshoring model in which the hours of labor used in four activities in the United States and Mexico are as follows: Note that labor hours in Mexico are twice those in the United States, reflecting Mexico's lower productivity. Also note that the ratio of high-skilled to low-skilled labor used in each activity increases as we move to the right, from 1/5 in assembly, to 10/1 in R&D. Suppose that the wage of U.S.

low-skilled workers is $10 per hour and that of high-skilled workers is $25 per hour, and that the wage of Mexican low-skilled workers is $1 per hour and that of high-skilled workers is $5 per hour (these values are made up to be convenient, not realistic). Also suppose that the trade costs are 25%, 30%, or 50%, which means that an additional 25%, 30%, or 50% is added to the costs of offshoring to Mexico.

Hours of Labor Used in Each Activity (per unit of output):

	Assembly	Component Production	Office Services	R&D
Low-skilled labor	Mexico: 20	Mexico: 12	Mexico: 8	Mexico: 4
	U.S.: 5	U.S.: 3	U.S.: 2	U.S.: 1
High-skilled labor	Mexico: 4	Mexico: 4	Mexico: 8	Mexico: 40
	U.S.: 1	U.S.: 1	U.S.: 2	U.S.: 10
High-skilled/low-skilled ratio	1/5	1/3	1/1	10/1

a. Fill in the blank cells in the following table by computing the costs of production of each activity in each country (two cells are filled in for you):

	Assembly	Component Production	Office Services	R&D
Mexico	$40			
United States				
Imported by United States from Mexico, Trade Costs = 25%				
Imported by United States from Mexico, Trade Costs = 30%	$52			
Imported by United States from Mexico, Trade Costs = 50%				

b. With trade costs of 50%, where is the value chain sliced? That is, which activities are cheaper to import from Mexico and which are cheaper to produce in the United States?

c. With trade costs of 30%, and then 25%, where is the value chain sliced?

2. Consider an offshoring model in which Home's skilled labor has a higher relative wage than Foreign's skilled labor and in which the costs of capital and trade are uniform across production activities.

   a. Will Home's offshored production activities be high or low on the value chain for a given product? That is, will Home offshore production activities that are skilled and labor-intensive, or low-skilled and labor-intensive? Explain.

   b. Suppose that Home uniformly increases its tariff level, effectively increasing the cost of importing all goods and services from abroad. How does this affect the slicing of the value chain?

   c. Draw relative labor supply and demand diagrams for Home and Foreign showing the effect of this change. What happens to the relative wage in each country?

3. Consider a U.S. firm's production of automobiles, including research and development and component production.

   a. Starting from a no-trade equilibrium in a PPF diagram, illustrate the gains from offshoring if the United States has a comparative advantage in component production.

   b. Now suppose that advances in engineering abroad decrease the relative price of research and development. Illustrate this change on your diagram and state the implications for production in the United States.

c. Does the U.S. firm gain from advances in research and development abroad? Explain why or why not.

4. Consider the model of a firm that produces final goods using R&D and components as inputs, with cost data as follows:

Components: Total costs of production = $P_C \cdot Q_C = 100$

Earnings of high-skilled labor = $W_H \cdot H_C = 10$

Earnings of low-skilled labor = $W_L \cdot L_C = 40$

Earnings of capital = $R \cdot K_C = 50$

Share of total costs paid to high-skilled labor = $10/100 = 10\%$

Share of total costs paid to low-skilled labor = $40/100 = 40\%$

R&D: Total costs of R&D = $P_R \cdot Q_R = 100$

Earnings of high-skilled labor = $W_H \cdot H_R = 40$

Earnings of low-skilled labor = $W_L \cdot L_R = 10$

Earnings of capital = $R \cdot K_R = 50$

Share of total costs paid to high-skilled labor = $40/100 = 40\%$

Share of total costs paid to low-skilled labor = $10/100 = 10\%$

a. In which factor(s) is components intensive? In which factor(s) is R&D intensive?
b. Suppose that due to the opening of trade, the price of components fall by $\Delta P_C/P_C = -10\%$, while the price of R&D remains unchanged, $\Delta P_R/P_R = 0$. Using the hint below, calculate the change in the wage of skilled and low-skilled labor.

Hint: We follow a procedure similar to that used in Chapter 4 when calculating the change in factor prices in the Heckscher-Ohlin model.

First, write the total costs in each activity as consisting of the payments to labor and capital:

$P_C \cdot Q_C = R \cdot K_C + W_H \cdot H_C + W_L \cdot L_C$, for components

$P_R \cdot Q_R = R \cdot K_R + W_H \cdot H_R + W_L \cdot L_R$, for R&D

Because we assume that 50% of costs in either components or R&D is always paid to capital, then $R \cdot K_C = 0.5(P_C \cdot Q_C)$ and $R \cdot K_R = 0.5(P_R \cdot Q_R)$, so we can rewrite the above two equations as

$0.5(P_C \cdot Q_C) = W_H \cdot H_C + W_L \cdot L_C$, for components

$0.5(P_R \cdot Q_R) = W_H \cdot H_R + W_L \cdot L_R$, for R&D

Taking the change in these equations:

$0.5(\Delta P_C \cdot Q_C) = \Delta W_H \cdot H_C + \Delta W_L \cdot L_C$, for components

$0.5(\Delta P_R \cdot Q_R) = \Delta W_H \cdot H_R + \Delta W_L \cdot L_R$, for R&D

Dividing the equations by $(\Delta P_C \cdot Q_C)$ and $(\Delta P_R \cdot Q_R)$, respectively, we can rewrite the equations as

$$0.5\left[\frac{\Delta P_C}{P_C}\right] = \left(\frac{\Delta W_H}{W_H}\right)\left(\frac{W_H \cdot H_C}{P_C \cdot Q_C}\right) + \left(\frac{\Delta W_L}{W_L}\right)\left(\frac{W_L \cdot L_C}{P_C \cdot Q_C}\right),$$
for components

$$0.5\left[\frac{\Delta P_R}{P_R}\right] = \left(\frac{\Delta W_H}{W_H}\right)\left(\frac{W_H \cdot H_R}{P_R \cdot Q_R}\right) + \left(\frac{\Delta W_L}{W_L}\right)\left(\frac{W_L \cdot L_R}{P_R \cdot Q_R}\right),$$
for R&D

Use the cost shares and price change data in these formulas to get

$$-5\% = \left(\frac{\Delta W_H}{W_H}\right)\left(\frac{10}{100}\right) + \left(\frac{\Delta W_L}{W_L}\right)\left(\frac{40}{100}\right),$$
for components

$$0 = \left(\frac{\Delta W_H}{W_H}\right)\left(\frac{40}{100}\right) + \left(\frac{\Delta W_L}{W_L}\right)\left(\frac{10}{100}\right),$$
for R&D

Now solve these two equations for the change in the high-skilled wage ($\Delta W_H/W_H$), and the change in the low-skilled wage ($\Delta W_L/W_L$).

c. What has happened to the *relative wage* of high-skilled/low-skilled labor? Does this match the predictions of the offshoring model in this chapter?

5. Consider the model of a firm that produces final goods using R&D and components as inputs, with cost data as follows:

Components: Total costs of production = $P_C \cdot Q_C = 100$

Earnings of high-skilled labor = $W_H \cdot H_C = 25$

Earnings of low-skilled labor = $W_L \cdot L_C = 25$

Earnings of capital = $R \cdot K_C = 50$

Share of total costs paid to high-skilled labor = 25/100 = 25%

Share of total costs paid to low-skilled labor = 25/100 = 25%

R&D: Total costs of R&D = $P_R \cdot Q_R = 100$

Earnings of high-skilled labor = $W_H \cdot H_R = 30$

Earnings of low-skilled labor = $W_L \cdot L_R = 20$

Earnings of capital = $R \cdot K_R = 50$

Share of total costs paid to high-skilled labor = 30/100 = 30%

Share of total costs paid to low-skilled labor = 20/100 = 20%

a. In which factor(s) is components intensive? In which factor(s) is research intensive?

b. Suppose that due to the opening of trade, the relative price of R&D increases, $\Delta P_R/P_R = 10\%$, whereas the price of components stays unchanged, $\Delta P_C/P_C = 0$. Calculate the change in the relative wage of high-skilled and low-skilled labor.

c. What has happened to the *relative wage* of high-skilled/low-skilled labor? How does this result compare to Problem 4, and explain why it is similar or different.

6. The following diagram shows what happened to the relative wage and relative demand for skilled labor in the U.S. manufacturing sector during the 1990s. These points are plotted using the data

from Figures 7-5 and 7-6. To interpret this diagram, let us think about the offshoring of service activities done by nonproduction workers.

a. Suppose that the nonproduction workers providing service activities being offshored, such as call centers, earn a *lower* wage in the United States than other *nonproduction* workers. As the amount of offshoring increases, what will happen to the *average* wage of the nonproduction workers remaining in the United States? What happens to the relative wage of nonproduction/production workers? Is this outcome consistent with the diagram?

b. As the service activities are offshored, what happens to the U.S. employment of nonproduction workers? What happens to the relative employment of nonproduction/production workers? Is this outcome also consistent with the diagram?

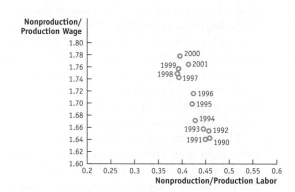

7. Read the following excerpt, and using what you have learned in this chapter, discuss how offshoring creates opportunities for the countries involved.

Sudhakar Shenoy, chief executive of Information Management Consultants (IMC) in Reston, makes an effective pitch for offshoring.

Several years ago IMC saw a market developing for software that would allow biotech companies to make better and faster use of the new human genome research. Doing it here, Shenoy calculated, would cost several million dollars, which he figured would have priced the product too high for most customers. But by having a small group of engineers at IMC's Indian subsidiary do much of the coding work, he was able to bring the project in at $500,000. The result: IMC now has a thriving line of business in bioinformatics, with major clients and a growing payroll of six-figure PhDs here. And there are more engineers than ever—six here for every one in India.

But that's only part of the good-news story. In Pune, where IMC's Indian operations are located, an airport under construction will require lots of U.S. engineering, design and electronics. At the same time, IMC's Indian engineers, who earned annual salaries of $3,500 a decade ago, now command up to $12,000—enough to buy all manner of imported consumer goods.

Source: Excerpted from Steven Pearlstein, "Still Short of the Offshoring Ideal," *Washington Post*, March 12, 2004.

8. The quote from the 2004 *Economic Report of the President* at the beginning of the chapter generated a lot of controversy that year, as discussed at the beginning of section 3 here. The chairman of the Council, N. Gregory Mankiw, made the following additional comments in a speech while presenting the report: "Outsourcing is just a new way of doing international trade. More things are tradable than were tradable in the past, and that's a good thing."

Those statements quickly led to reactions from both Democratic and Republican members of Congress. Tom Daschle, then the Democratic Senate minority leader, said, "If this is the administration's position, they owe an apology to every worker in America." Dennis Hastert, then Republican Speaker of the House, said, "Outsourcing can be a problem for American workers and the American economy." John Kerry, the 2004 Democratic presidential candidate, referred to businesses that offshored as "Benedict Arnold corporations." In response, Mankiw clarified his earlier comments: "My lack of clarity left the wrong impression that I praised the loss of U.S. jobs."

Although you might feel that these statements just represented a squabble between politicians trying to score points during a presidential campaign, it is still worth trying to sort out who gains and who loses from offshoring.

a. Why does Mankiw say that "outsourcing is a good thing"? Who is it good for in the

United States? Are there overall gains for the United States? Explain with a diagram.

b. Later in this chapter, Paul Samuelson is quoted as saying that there is no "necessary surplus of winnings over losings" due to offshoring. Use Figure 7-12 to carefully explain why Samuelson says this.

9. In Figure 7-11, we saw that a fall in the relative price of components leads to an increase in the amount of components imported but that the amount of R&D exported from Home does not necessarily increase. To explore this further, complete the following:

a. Let the relative price of components continue to fall in Figure 7-11, and show in a graph what happens to the equilibrium point on the isoquant for the final good.

b. Now draw another graph that has the relative price of components on the vertical axis and the imports of components on the horizontal axis. Start at the no-trade relative price of components, where imports are zero. Then label the various world relative prices of components on the vertical axis, and graph the quantity of imports at each price. Can we be sure that the import demand curve slopes downward?

c. Now draw a new graph that has the relative price of R&D on the vertical axis and the exports of R&D on the horizontal axis. Start at the no-trade relative price of R&D, where exports are zero. Then label the various world relative prices of R&D on the vertical axis, and graph the quantity of exports at each price. When the relative price of R&D is high enough, what do you notice about the export supply curve?

10. Why might it be relatively easier for a developing country like India to export service activities through offshoring than to participate in the global economy by producing manufacturing components?

11. It is widely noted that even though China is the favored destination for manufacturing offshoring, it is far behind India in the business of offshored services. What differences between these two countries might account for this observation?

Import Tariffs and Quotas Under Perfect Competition

Over a thousand Americans are working today because we stopped a surge in Chinese tires.
President Barack Obama, State of the Union Address, January 24, 2012

I take this action to give our domestic steel industry an opportunity to adjust to surges in foreign imports, recognizing the harm from 50 years of foreign government intervention in the global steel market, which has resulted in bankruptcies, serious dislocation, and job loss.
President George W. Bush, in press statement announcing new "safeguard" tariffs on imported steel, March 5, 2002

On September 27, 2012, a tariff of 35% on U.S. imports of tires made in China expired, meaning that these products were no longer taxed as they crossed the U.S. border. The end of that tariff hardly made the news at all, especially as compared with the headlines when President Barack Obama first announced the tariff three years earlier, on September 11, 2009. At that time, the tariff was seen as a victory for the United Steelworkers, the union that represents American tire workers, but it was opposed by many economists as well as by a number of American tire-manufacturing companies. By approving this tariff in 2009, it is believed that President Obama won additional support from the labor movement for the health-care bill that would be considered later that year.

The tariff on Chinese-made tires announced by President Obama was not the first instance of a U.S. President—of either party—approving an import tariff soon after being elected. During the 2000 presidential campaign, George W. Bush promised that he would consider implementing a tariff on imports of steel. That promise was made for political purposes: It helped Bush secure votes in Pennsylvania, West Virginia, and Ohio, states that produce large amounts of steel. After he was elected, the U.S. tariffs on steel were increased in March 2002, though they were removed less than two years later, as we discuss later in this chapter.

The steel and tire tariffs are examples of **trade policy,** a government action meant to influence the amount of international trade. In earlier chapters, we learned that the opening of trade normally creates both winners and losers. Because the gains from trade are unevenly spread, it follows that firms, industries, and labor unions often feel that the government should do something to help maximize their gains or limit their losses from international trade. That "something" is trade policy, which includes the use of **import tariffs** (taxes on imports), **import quotas** (quantity limits on imports), and **export subsidies** (meaning that the seller receives a higher price than the buyer pays). In this chapter, we begin our investigation of trade policies by focusing on the effects of tariffs and quotas in a perfectly competitive industry. In the next chapter, we continue by discussing the use of import tariffs and quotas when the industry is imperfectly competitive.

President Obama and President Bush could not just put tariffs on imports of tires made in China and foreign steel. Rather, they had to follow the rules governing the use of tariffs that the United States and many other countries have agreed to follow. Under these rules, countries can temporarily increase tariffs to safeguard an industry against import competition. This "safeguard" rationale was used to increase the U.S. tariffs on steel and tires. The international body that governs these rules is called the World Trade Organization (WTO); its precursor was the General Agreement on Tariffs and Trade (GATT). This chapter first looks briefly at the history and development of the WTO and GATT.

Once the international context for setting trade policy has been established, the chapter examines in detail the most commonly used trade policy, the tariff. We explain the reasons why countries apply tariffs and the consequences of these tariffs on the producers and consumers in the importing and exporting countries. We show that import tariffs typically lead to welfare losses for "small" importing countries, by which we mean countries that are too small to affect world prices. Following that, we examine the situation for a "large" importing country, meaning a country that is a large enough buyer for its tariff to affect world prices. In that case, we find that the importing country can possibly gain by applying a tariff, but only at the expense of the exporting countries.

A third purpose of the chapter is to examine the use of an import quota, which is a limit on the quantity of a good that can be imported from a foreign country. Past examples of import quotas in the United States include limits on the imports of agricultural goods, automobiles, and steel. More recently, the United States and Europe imposed temporary quotas on the import of textile and apparel products from China. We note that, like a tariff, an import quota often imposes a cost on the importing country. Furthermore, we argue that the cost of quotas can sometimes be even greater than the cost of tariffs. For that reason, the use of quotas has been greatly reduced under the WTO, though they are still used in some cases.

Throughout this chapter, we assume that firms are perfectly competitive. That is, each firm produces a homogeneous good and is small compared with the market, which comprises many firms. Under perfect competition, each firm is a price taker in its market. In the next chapter, we learn that tariffs and quotas have different effects in imperfectly competitive markets.

1 A Brief History of the World Trade Organization

As we discussed in Chapter 1, during the period between the First and Second World Wars, unusually high tariffs between countries reduced the volume of world trade. When peace was reestablished following World War II, representatives of the Allied countries met on several occasions to discuss the rebuilding of Europe and issues such as high trade barriers and unstable exchange rates. One of these conferences, held in Bretton Woods, New Hampshire, in July 1944, established the International Monetary Fund (IMF) and the International Bank for Reconstruction and Development, later known as the World Bank. A second conference held at the Palais des Nations, in Geneva, Switzerland, in 1947 established the General Agreement on Tariffs and Trade (GATT), the purpose of which was to reduce barriers to international trade between nations.[1]

Under the GATT, countries met periodically for negotiations, called "rounds," to lower trade restrictions between countries. Each round is named for the country in which the meeting took place. The Uruguay Round of negotiations, which lasted from 1986 to 1994, established the World Trade Organization (WTO) on January 1, 1995. The WTO is a greatly expanded version of the GATT. It keeps most of the GATT's earlier provisions but adds rules that govern an expanded set of global interactions (including trade in services and intellectual property protection) through binding agreements. The most recent round of WTO negotiations, the Doha Round, began in Doha, Qatar, in November 2001.

Although the goal of the WTO is to keep tariffs low, it allows countries to charge a higher tariff on a specific import under some conditions. In **Side Bar: Key Provisions of the GATT,** we show some of the articles of the GATT that still govern trade in the WTO. Some of the main provisions are as follows:

1. A nation must extend the same tariffs to all trading partners that are WTO members. Article I of the GATT, the "most favored nation" clause, states that every country belonging to the WTO must be treated the same: if a country imposes low tariffs on one trading partner, then those low tariffs must be extended to every other trading partner belonging to the WTO.[2]

2. Tariffs may be imposed in response to unfair trade practices such as **dumping.** As we discuss in the next chapter, "dumping" is defined as the sale of export goods in another country at a price less than that charged at home, or alternatively, at a price less than costs of production and shipping. Article VI of the GATT states that an importing country may impose a tariff on goods being dumped into its country by a foreign exporter.

3. Countries should not limit the quantity of goods and services that they import. Article XI states that countries should not maintain quotas against imports. We discuss exceptions to this rule later in this chapter.

4. Countries should declare export subsidies provided to particular firms, sectors, or industries. Article XVI deals with export subsidies, benefits such as tax

---

[1] A history of the GATT is provided in Douglas A. Irwin, Petros C. Mavroidis, and Alan O. Sykes, 2008, *The Genesis of the GATT* (New York: Cambridge University Press).

[2] In the United States, the granting of most favored nation trade status to a country is now called "normal trade relations" because most countries now belong to the WTO and enjoy that status.

breaks or other incentives for firms that produce goods specifically for export. The article states that countries should notify each other of the extent of subsidies and discuss the possibility of eliminating them. During the Doha Round of WTO negotiations, the elimination of agricultural subsidies has recently been discussed.

5. Countries can temporarily raise tariffs for certain products. Article XIX, called the **safeguard provision** or the **escape clause,** is our focus in this chapter. Article XIX lists the conditions under which a country can temporarily raise tariffs on particular products. It states that a country can apply a tariff when it imports "any product . . . in such increased quantities and under such conditions as to cause or threaten serious injury to domestic producers." In other words, the importing country can temporarily raise the tariff when domestic producers are suffering due to import competition.

   The steel tariff of 2002–2004 is an example of a tariff that was applied by the United States under Article XIX of the GATT (and the tire tariff of 2009–2012 was applied under a related provision that focused on U.S. imports from China, discussed later in the chapter). European governments strenuously objected to the steel tariffs, however, and filed a complaint against the United States with the WTO. A panel at the WTO ruled in favor of the European countries. This ruling entitled them to retaliate against the United States by putting tariffs of their own on some $2.2 billion worth of U.S. exports. This pressure from Europe, along with pressure from companies in the United States that had been purchasing the cheaper imported steel, led President Bush to remove the steel tariffs in December 2003. Later in the chapter, we discuss the steel tariff in more detail, and see how Article XIX of the GATT is reflected in U.S. trade laws.

6. **Regional trade agreements** are permitted under Article XXIV of the GATT. The GATT recognizes the ability of blocs of countries to form two types of regional trade agreements: (i) **free-trade areas,** in which a group of countries voluntarily agrees to remove trade barriers between themselves, and (ii) **customs unions,** which are free-trade areas in which the countries also adopt identical tariffs between themselves and the rest of the world. We discuss regional trade agreements in a later chapter.

2 The Gains from Trade

In earlier chapters, we demonstrated the gains from trade using a production possibilities frontier and indifference curves. We now instead demonstrate the gains from trade using Home demand and supply curves, together with the concepts of **consumer surplus** and **producer surplus.** You may already be familiar with these concepts from an earlier economics course, but we provide a brief review here.

Consumer and Producer Surplus

Suppose that Home consumers have the demand curve D in panel (a) of Figure 8-1 and face the price of P_1. Then total demand is D_1 units. For the last unit purchased, the consumer buying it values that unit at close to its purchase price of P_1, so he or

SIDE BAR

Key Provisions of the GATT

ARTICLE I

General Most-Favoured-Nation Treatment

1. With respect to customs duties . . . and with respect to all rules and formalities in connection with importation and exportation . . . any advantage, favour, privilege or immunity granted by any contracting party to any product originating in or destined for any other country shall be accorded immediately and unconditionally to the like product originating in or destined for the territories of all other contracting parties. . . .

ARTICLE VI

Anti-Dumping and Countervailing Duties

1. The contracting parties recognize that dumping, by which products of one country are introduced into the commerce of another country at less than the normal value of the products, is to be condemned if it causes or threatens material injury to an established industry. . . . [A] product is to be considered . . . less than its normal value, if the price of the product exported from one country to another

   a. is less than the comparable price . . . for the like product when destined for consumption in the exporting country, or,
   b. in the absence of such domestic price, is less than either
      i) the highest comparable price for the like product for export to any third country in the ordinary course of trade, or
      ii) the cost of production of the product in the country of origin plus a reasonable addition for selling cost and profit. . . .

ARTICLE XI

General Elimination of Quantitative Restrictions

1. No prohibitions or restrictions other than duties, taxes or other charges, whether made effective through quotas, import or export licenses or other measures, shall be instituted or maintained by any contracting party on the importation of any product of the territory of any other contracting party or on the exportation or sale for export of any product destined for the territory of any other contracting party. . . .

ARTICLE XVI

Subsidies

1. If any contracting party grants or maintains any subsidy, including any form of income or price support, which operates directly or indirectly to increase exports of any product from, or to reduce imports of any product into, its territory, it shall notify the contracting parties in writing of the extent and nature of the subsidization. In any case in which it is determined that serious prejudice to the interests of any other contracting party is caused or threatened by any such subsidization, the contracting party granting the subsidy shall, upon request, discuss with the other contracting party . . . the possibility of limiting the subsidization.

ARTICLE XIX

Emergency Action on Imports of Particular Products

1.
   a. If, as a result of unforeseen developments and of the effect of the obligations incurred by a contracting party under this Agreement, including tariff concessions, any product is being imported into the territory of that contracting party in such increased quantities and under such conditions as to cause or threaten serious injury to domestic producers in that territory of like or directly competitive products, the contracting party shall be free, in respect of such product, and to the extent and for such time as may be necessary to prevent or remedy such injury, to suspend the obligation in whole or in part or to withdraw or modify the concession. . . .

ARTICLE XXIV

Territorial Application—Frontier Traffic—Customs Unions and Free-Trade Areas

4. The contracting parties recognize the desirability of increasing freedom of trade by the development, through voluntary agreements, of closer integration between the economies of the countries party to such agreements. They also recognize that the purpose of a customs union or of a free-trade area should be to facilitate trade between the constituent territories and not to raise barriers to the trade of other contracting parties with such territories.

5. Accordingly, the provisions of this Agreement shall not prevent [the formation of customs unions and free-trade areas, provided that:]
   a. . . . the duties [with outside parties] shall not on the whole be higher or more restrictive than the general incidence of the duties . . . prior to the formation. . . .

Source: http://www.wto.org/english/docs_e/legal_e/gatt47_01_e.htm#articleI.

she obtains little or no surplus over the purchase price. But for all the earlier units purchased (from 0 to D_1 units), the consumers valued the product at *higher than* its purchase price: the consumers' willingness to pay for the product equals the height of the demand curve. For example, the person buying unit D_2 would have been willing to pay the price of P_2, which is the height of the demand curve at that quantity. Therefore, that individual obtains the surplus of $(P_2 - P_1)$ from being able to purchase the good at the price P_1.

For each unit purchased before D_1, the value that the consumer places on the product exceeds the purchase price of P_1. Adding up the surplus obtained on each unit purchased, from 0 to D_1, we can measure consumer surplus (CS) as the shaded region below the demand curve and above the price P_1. This region measures the satisfaction that consumers receive from the purchased quantity D_1, over and above the amount $P_1 \cdot D_1$ that they have paid.

Panel (b) of Figure 8-1 illustrates producer surplus. This panel shows the supply curve of an industry; the height of the curve represents the firm's marginal cost at each level of production. At the price of P_1, the industry will supply S_1. For the last unit supplied, the price P_1 equals the marginal cost of production for the firm supplying that unit. But for all earlier units supplied (from 0 to S_1 units), the firms were able to produce those units at a marginal cost *less than* the price P_1. For example, the firm supplying unit S_0 could produce it with a marginal cost of P_0, which is the height of the supply curve at that quantity. Therefore, that firm obtains the producer surplus of $(P_1 - P_0)$ from being able to sell the good at the price P_1.

FIGURE 8-1

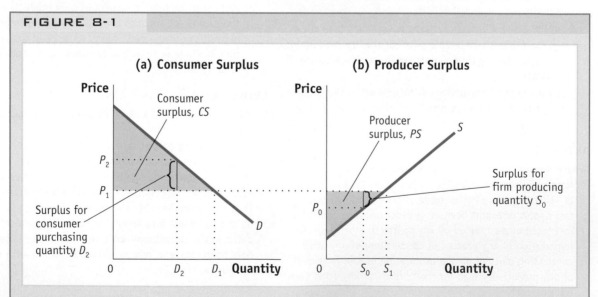

(a) Consumer Surplus

(b) Producer Surplus

Consumer and Producer Surplus In panel (a), the consumer surplus from purchasing quantity D_1 at price P_1 is the area below the demand curve and above that price. The consumer who purchases D_2 is willing to pay price P_2 but has to pay only P_1. The difference is the consumer surplus and represents the satisfaction of consumers over and above the amount paid. In panel (b), the producer surplus from supplying the quantity S_1 at the price P_1 is the area above the supply curve and below that price. The supplier who supplies unit S_0 has marginal costs of P_0 but sells it for P_1. The difference is the producer surplus and represents the return to fixed factors of production in the industry.

For each unit sold before S_1, the marginal cost to the firm is less than the sale price of P_1. Adding up the producer surplus obtained for each unit sold, from 0 to S_1, we obtain producer surplus (PS) as the shaded region in panel (b) above the supply curve and below the price of P_1. It is tempting to think of producer surplus as the profits of firms, because for all units before S_1, the marginal cost of production is less than the sale price of P_1. But a more accurate definition of producer surplus is that it equals the *return to fixed factors of production in the industry*. That is, producer surplus is the difference between the sales revenue $P_1 \cdot S_1$ and the total variable costs of production (i.e., wages paid to labor and the costs of intermediate inputs). If there are fixed factors such as capital or land in the industry, as in the specific-factors model we studied in Chapter 3, then producer surplus equals the returns to these fixed factors of production. We might still loosely refer to this return as the "profit" earned in the industry, but it is important to understand that producer surplus is not *monopoly profit*, because we are assuming perfect competition (i.e., zero monopoly profits) throughout this chapter.[3]

Home Welfare

To examine the effects of trade on a country's welfare, we consider once again a world composed of two countries, Home and Foreign, with each country consisting of producers and consumers. Total Home welfare can be measured by adding up consumer and producer surplus. As you would expect, the greater the total amount of Home welfare, the better off are the consumers and producers overall in the economy. To measure the gains from trade, we will compare Home welfare in no-trade and free-trade situations.

No Trade In panel (a) of Figure 8-2, we combine the Home demand and supply curves in a single diagram. The no-trade equilibrium occurs at the autarky price of P^A, where the quantity demanded equals the quantity supplied, of Q_0. Consumer surplus is the region above the price of P^A and below the demand curve, which is labeled as CS in panel (a) and also shown as area a in panel (b). Producer surplus is the area below the price of P^A and above the supply curve, which is labeled as PS in panel (a) and also shown as area $(b+c)$ in panel (b). So the sum of consumer surplus and producer surplus is the area between the demand and supply curves, or $CS + PS =$ area $(a+b+c)$. That area equals Home welfare in the market for this good in the absence of international trade.

Free Trade for a Small Country Now suppose that Home can engage in international trade for this good. As we have discussed in earlier chapters, the world price P^W is determined by the intersection of supply and demand in the world market. Generally, there will be many countries buying and selling on the world market. We will suppose that the Home country is a **small country,** by which we mean that it is small in comparison with all the other countries buying and selling this product. For that reason, Home will be a *price taker* in the world market: it faces the fixed world price of P^W, and its own level of demand and supply for this product has no influence on the world price. In panel (b) of Figure 8-2, we assume that the world price P^W is *below* the Home no-trade price of P^A. At the lower price, Home demand will increase

[3] Recall from Chapter 6 that under imperfect competition, firms can influence the price of their goods and hence earn positive monopoly profits.

FIGURE 8-2

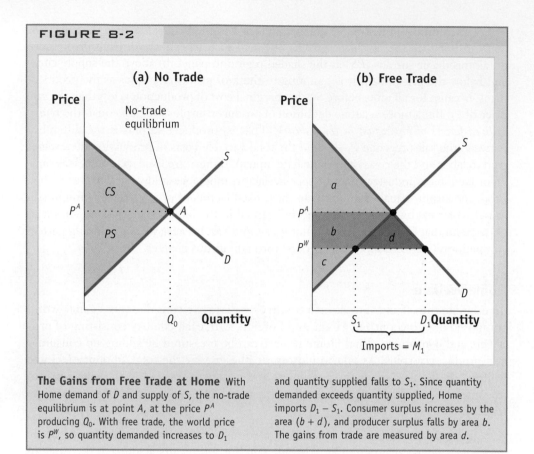

(a) No Trade

Price

No-trade equilibrium

CS

P^A ⋯⋯⋯⋯⋯⋯⋯ A

PS

S

D

Q_0 **Quantity**

(b) Free Trade

Price

a

P^A ⋯⋯⋯⋯⋯⋯

b d

P^W ⋯⋯⋯⋯

c

S

D

S_1 D_1**Quantity**

Imports = M_1

The Gains from Free Trade at Home With Home demand of D and supply of S, the no-trade equilibrium is at point A, at the price P^A producing Q_0. With free trade, the world price is P^W, so quantity demanded increases to D_1 and quantity supplied falls to S_1. Since quantity demanded exceeds quantity supplied, Home imports $D_1 - S_1$. Consumer surplus increases by the area $(b + d)$, and producer surplus falls by area b. The gains from trade are measured by area d.

from Q_0 under no trade to D_1, and Home supply will decrease from Q_0 under no trade to S_1. The difference between D_1 and S_1 is *imports* of the good, or $M_1 = D_1 - S_1$. Because the world price P^W is below the no-trade price of P^A, the Home country is an importer of the product at the world price. If, instead, P^W were above P^A, then Home would be an exporter of the product at the world price.

Gains from Trade Now that we have established the free-trade equilibrium at price P^W, it is easy to measure Home welfare as the sum of consumer and producer surplus with trade, and compare it with the no-trade situation. In panel (b) of Figure 8-2, Home consumer surplus at the price P^W equals the area $(a + b + d)$, which is the area below the demand curve and above the price P^W. In the absence of trade, consumer surplus was the area a, so the drop in price from P^A to P^W has increased consumer surplus by the amount $(b + d)$. Home consumers clearly gain from the drop in price.

Home firms, on the other hand, suffer a decrease in producer surplus from the drop in price. In panel (b), Home producer surplus at the price P^W equals the area c, which is the area above the supply curve and below the price P^W. In the absence of trade, producer surplus was the area $(b + c)$, so the drop in price from P^A to P^W has decreased producer surplus by the amount b. Home firms clearly lose from the drop in price.

Comparing the gains of consumers, $(b + d)$, with the losses of producers, area b, we see that consumers gain more than the producers lose, which indicates that total

Home welfare (the sum of consumer surplus and producer surplus) has gone up. We can calculate the total change in Home welfare due to the opening of trade by adding the *changes* in consumer surplus and producer surplus:

Rise in consumer surplus:	$+ (b + d)$
Fall in producer surplus:	$- b$
Net effect on Home welfare:	**$+d$**

The area d is a measure of the *gains from trade* for the importing country due to free trade in this good. It is similar to the gains from trade that we have identified in earlier chapters using the production possibilities frontier and indifference curves, but it is easier to measure: the triangle d has a base equal to free-trade imports $M_1 = D_1 - S_1$, and a height that is the drop in price, $P^A - P^W$, so the gains from trade equal the area of the triangle, $\frac{1}{2} \cdot (P^A - P^W) \cdot M_1$. Of course, with many goods being imported, we would need to add up the areas of the triangles for each good and take into account the net gains on the export side to determine the overall gains from trade for a country. Because gains are positive for each individual good, after summing all imported and exported goods, the gains from trade are still positive.

Home Import Demand Curve

Before introducing a tariff, we use Figure 8-3 to derive the **import demand curve,** which shows the relationship between the world price of a good and the quantity of imports demanded by Home consumers. We first derived this curve in Chapter 2,

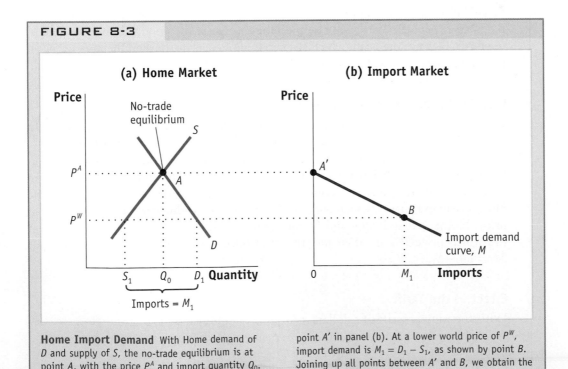

FIGURE 8-3

(a) Home Market   **(b) Import Market**

Home Import Demand With Home demand of D and supply of S, the no-trade equilibrium is at point A, with the price P^A and import quantity Q_0. Import demand at this price is zero, as shown by the point A' in panel (b). At a lower world price of P^W, import demand is $M_1 = D_1 - S_1$, as shown by point B. Joining up all points between A' and B, we obtain the import demand curve, M.

for the Ricardian model. We now briefly review the derivation of the import demand curve before analyzing the effect of an import tariff on prices and welfare.

In panel (a) of Figure 8-3, we again show the downward-sloping Home demand curve (D) and the upward-sloping Home supply curve (S). The no-trade equilibrium is at point A, which determines Home's no-trade equilibrium price P^A, and its no-trade equilibrium quantity of Q_0. Because quantity demanded equals quantity supplied, there are zero imports of this product. Zero imports is shown as point A' in panel (b).

Now suppose the world price is at P^W, below the no-trade price of P^A. At the price of P^W, the quantity demanded in Home is D_1, but the quantity supplied by Home suppliers is only S_1. Therefore, the quantity imported is $M_1 = D_1 - S_1$, as shown by the point B in panel (b). Joining points A' and B, we obtain the downward-sloping import demand curve M.

Notice that the import demand curve applies for all prices *below* the no-trade price of P^A in Figure 8-3. Having lower prices leads to greater Home demand and less Home supply and, therefore, positive imports. What happens if the world price is *above* the no-trade price? In that case, the higher price would lead to greater Home supply and less Home demand, so Home would become an exporter of the product.

3 Import Tariffs for a Small Country

We can now use this supply and demand framework to show what happens when a small country imposes a tariff. As we have already explained, an importing country is "small" if its tariff does not have any effect on the world price of the good on which the tariff is applied. As we will see, the Home price of the good will increase due to the tariff. Because the tariff (which is a tax) is applied at the border, the price charged to Home consumers will increase by the amount of the tariff.

Free Trade for a Small Country

In Figure 8-4, we again show the free-trade equilibrium for the Home country. In panel (b), the Foreign export supply curve X^* is horizontal at the world price P^W. The horizontal export supply curve means that Home can import any amount at the price P^W without having an impact on that price. The free-trade equilibrium is determined by the intersection of the Foreign export supply and the Home import demand curves, which is point B in panel (b), at the world price P^W. At that price, Home demand is D_1 and Home supply is S_1, shown in panel (a). Imports at the world price P^W are then just the difference between demand and supply, or $M_1 = D_1 - S_1$.

Effect of the Tariff

With the import tariff of t dollars, the export supply curve facing the Home country shifts up by exactly that amount, reflecting the higher price that must be paid to import the good. The shift in the Foreign export supply curve is analogous to the shift in domestic supply caused by a sales tax, as you may have seen in earlier economics courses; it reflects an effective increase in the costs of the firm. In

FIGURE 8-4

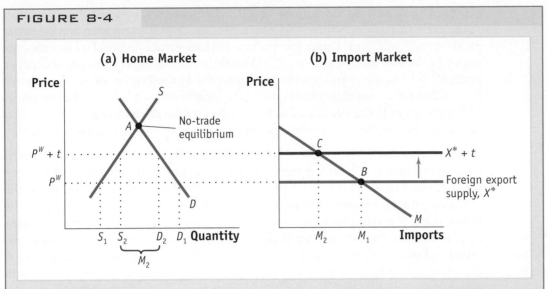

(a) Home Market

(b) Import Market

Tariff for a Small Country Applying a tariff of t dollars will increase the import price from P^W to $P^W + t$. The domestic price of that good also rises to $P^W + t$. This price rise leads to an increase in Home supply from S_1 to S_2, and a decrease in Home demand from D_1 to D_2, in panel (a). Imports fall due to the tariff, from M_1 to M_2 in panel (b). As a result, the equilibrium shifts from point B to C.

panel (b) of Figure 8-4, the export supply curve shifts up to $X^* + t$. The intersection of the post-tariff export supply curve and the import demand curve now occurs at the price of $P^W + t$ and the import quantity of M_2. The import tariff has reduced the amount imported, from M_1 under free trade to M_2 under the tariff, because of its higher price.

We assume that the imported product is identical to the domestic alternative that is available. For example, if the imported product is a women's cruiser bicycle, then the Home demand curve D in panel (a) is the demand for women's cruisers, and the Home supply curve is the supply of women's cruisers. When the import price rises to $P^W + t$, then we expect that the Home price for locally produced bicycles will rise by the same amount. This is because at the higher import price of $P^W + t$, the quantity of cruisers demanded at Home falls from its free-trade quantity of D_1 to D_2. At the same time, the higher price will encourage Home firms to increase the quantity of cruisers they supply from the free-trade quantity of S_1 to S_2. As firms increase the quantity they produce, however, the marginal costs of production rise. The Home supply curve (S) reflects these marginal costs, so the Home price will rise along the supply curve until Home firms are supplying the quantity S_2, at a marginal cost just equal to the import price of $P^W + t$. Since marginal costs equal $P^W + t$, the price charged by Home firms will also equal $P^W + t$, and the domestic price will equal the import price.

Summing up, Home demand at the new price is D_2, Home supply is S_2, and the difference between these are Home imports of $M_2 = D_2 - S_2$. Foreign exporters still receive the "net-of-tariff" price (i.e., the Home price minus the tariff) of P^W, but Home consumers pay the higher price $P^W + t$. We now investigate how the rise in the Home price from P^W to $P^W + t$ affects consumer surplus, producer surplus, and overall Home welfare.

Effect of the Tariff on Consumer Surplus In Figure 8-5, we again show the effect of the tariff of t dollars, which is to increase the price of the imported and domestic good from P^W to $P^W + t$. Under free trade, consumer surplus in panel (a) was the area under the demand curve and above P^W. With the tariff, consumers now pay the higher price, $P^W + t$, and their surplus is the area under the demand curve and above the price $P^W + t$. The fall in consumer surplus due to the tariff is the area between the two prices and to the left of Home demand, which is $(a + b + c + d)$ in panel (a) of Figure 8-5. This area is the amount that consumers lose due to the higher price caused by the tariff.

Effect of the Tariff on Producer Surplus We can also trace the impact of the tariff on producer surplus. Under free trade, producer surplus was the area above the supply curve in panel (a) and below the price of P^W. With the tariff, producer surplus is the area above the supply curve and below the price $P^W + t$: since the tariff increases the Home price, firms are able to sell more goods at a higher price, thus increasing their surplus. We can illustrate this rise in producer surplus as the amount between the two prices and to the left of Home supply, which is labeled as a in panel (a). This area is the amount that Home firms gain because of the higher price caused by the tariff. As we have just explained, the rise in producer surplus should be thought of as an increase in the return to fixed factors (capital or land) in the industry. Sometimes we even think of labor as a partially fixed factor because the skills learned in one industry cannot necessarily be transferred to other industries. In that case, it is reasonable to think that the increase in Home producer surplus can also benefit Home workers in the import-competing industry, along with capital and land, but this benefit comes at the expense of consumer surplus.

Effect of the Tariff on Government Revenue In addition to affecting consumers and producers, the tariff also affects government revenue. The amount of revenue collected is the tariff t times the quantity of imports $(D_2 - S_2)$. In Figure 8-5, panel (a), this revenue is shown by the area c. The collection of revenue is a gain for the government in the importing country.

Overall Effect of the Tariff on Welfare We are now in a position to summarize the impact of the tariff on the welfare of the Home importing country, which is the sum of producer surplus, consumer surplus, and government revenues. Thus, our approach is to *add up* these impacts to obtain a net effect. In adding up the loss of consumers and the gains of producers, one dollar of consumer surplus is the same as one dollar of producer surplus or government revenue. In other words, we do not care whether the consumers facing higher prices are poor or rich, and do not care whether the specific factors in the industry (capital, land, and possibly labor) earn a lot or a little. Under this approach, transferring one dollar from consumer to producer surplus will have no impact on overall welfare: the decrease in consumer surplus will cancel out the increase in producer surplus.

You may object to this method of evaluating overall welfare, and feel that a dollar taken away from a poor consumer and given to a rich producer represents a net loss of overall welfare, rather than zero effect, as in our approach. We should be careful in evaluating the impact of tariffs on different income groups in the society, especially for poor countries or countries with a high degree of inequality among income groups. But for now we ignore this concern and simply add up consumer surplus, producer surplus, and government revenue. Keep in mind that under this approach we are just evaluating the *efficiency* of tariffs and not their effect on equity (i.e., how fair the tariff is to one group versus another).

FIGURE 8-5

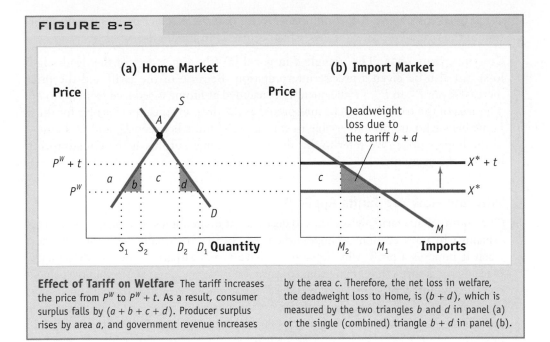

(a) Home Market

(b) Import Market

Effect of Tariff on Welfare The tariff increases the price from P^W to $P^W + t$. As a result, consumer surplus falls by $(a + b + c + d)$. Producer surplus rises by area a, and government revenue increases by the area c. Therefore, the net loss in welfare, the deadweight loss to Home, is $(b + d)$, which is measured by the two triangles b and d in panel (a) or the single (combined) triangle $b + d$ in panel (b).

The overall impact of the tariff in the small country can be summarized as follows:

Fall in consumer surplus:	$-(a + b + c + d)$
Rise in producer surplus:	$+ a$
Rise in government revenue:	$+ c$
Net effect on Home welfare:	$-(b + d)$

In Figure 8-5(b), the triangle $(b + d)$ is the *net welfare loss* in a small importing country due to the tariff. We sometimes refer to this area as a **deadweight loss,** meaning that it is not offset by a gain elsewhere in the economy. Notice that in panel (a) the area a, which is a gain for producers, just cancels out that portion of the consumer surplus loss; the area a is effectively a transfer from consumers to producers via the higher domestic prices induced by the tariff. Likewise, area c, the gain in government revenue, also cancels out that portion of the consumer surplus loss; this is a transfer from consumers to the government. Thus, the area $(b + d)$ is the remaining loss for consumers that is not offset by a gain elsewhere. This deadweight loss is measured by the two triangles, b and d, in panel (a), or by the combined triangle $(b + d)$ in panel (b). The two triangles b and d of deadweight loss can each be given a precise interpretation, as follows.

Production Loss Notice that the base of triangle b is the net increase in Home supply due to the tariff, from S_1 to S_2. The height of this triangle is the increase in marginal costs due to the increase in supply. The unit S_1 was produced at a marginal cost equal to P^W, which is the free-trade price, but every unit above that amount is produced with higher marginal costs. The fact that marginal costs exceed the world price means that this country is producing the good inefficiently: it would be cheaper to import it rather than produce the extra quantity at home. The area of triangle b equals the increase in marginal costs for the extra units produced and can be interpreted as the **production loss** (or the *efficiency loss*) for the economy due to producing at marginal costs above the world price. Notice that the production loss is only a portion of the overall deadweight loss, which is $(b + d)$ in Figure 8-5.

Consumption Loss The triangle d in panel (a) (the other part of the deadweight loss) can also be given a precise interpretation. Because of the tariff and the price increase from P^W to $P^W + t$, the quantity consumed at Home is reduced from D_1 to D_2. The area of the triangle d can be interpreted as the drop in consumer surplus for those individuals who are no longer able to consume the units between D_1 and D_2 because of the higher price. We refer to this drop in consumer surplus as the **consumption loss** for the economy.

Why and How Are Tariffs Applied?

Our finding that a tariff always leads to deadweight losses for a small importing country explains why most economists oppose the use of tariffs. If a small country suffers a loss when it imposes a tariff, why do so many have tariffs as part of their trade policies? One answer is that a developing country does not have any other source of government revenue. Import tariffs are "easy to collect" because every country has customs agents at major ports checking the goods that cross the border. It is easy to tax imports, even though the deadweight loss from using a tariff is typically higher than the deadweight loss from using "hard-to-collect" taxes, such as income taxes or value-added taxes. These taxes are hard to collect because they require individuals and firms to honestly report earnings, and the government cannot check every report (as they can check imports at the border). Still, to the extent that developing countries recognize that tariffs have a higher deadweight loss, we would expect that over time they would shift away from such easy-to-collect taxes. That is exactly what has occurred, according to one research study.[4] The fraction of total tax revenue collected from "easy to collect" taxes such as tariffs fell during the 1980s and 1990s, especially in developing countries, whereas the fraction of revenue raised from "hard to collect" taxes rose over this same period.

A second reason why tariffs are used even though they have a deadweight loss is politics. The tariff benefits the Home producers, as we have seen, so if the government cares more about producer surplus than consumer surplus, it might decide to use the tariff despite the deadweight loss it incurs. Indeed, the benefits to producers (and their workers) are typically more concentrated on specific firms and states than the costs to consumers, which are spread nationwide. This is our interpretation of the tariff that President George W. Bush granted to the steel industry from 2002 to 2004: its benefits were concentrated in the steel-producing states of Pennsylvania, West Virginia, and Ohio, and its costs to consumers—in this case, steel-using industries—were spread more widely.[5] For the tariff on tires imported from China granted by President Barack Obama from 2009 to 2012, the argument is a bit different. This tariff was

---

[4] Joshua Aizenman and Yothin Jinjarak, January 2006, "Globalization and Developing Countries—A Shrinking Tax Base?" National Bureau of Economic Research (NBER) Working Paper No. 11933.

[5] Although the steel tariff was used to obtain votes from the steel-producing states, it also served another political purpose. In 2002 President George W. Bush faced a vote on whether the president should be granted "fast-track authority" to negotiate trade agreements with other countries. Fast-track authority allows the president to present a new trade agreement to the Congress for an up-or-down vote within 90 days, without having the terms of the trade agreement revised by the Congress. This authority expires every five years. In 2002 the steel tariff prompted some members of Congress to vote in favor of fast-track authority, which passed in Congress by only two votes. More recently, fast-track authority, also called "trade promotion authority," was not renewed by Congress and was allowed to lapse on July 1, 2007.

requested by the United Steelworkers, the union who represents workers in the U.S. tire industry, and it was expected to benefit those workers. But U.S. tire producers did not support the tariff because many of them were already manufacturing tires in other countries—especially China—and this tariff made it more costly for them to do so.

In both the steel and tire cases, the president was not free to impose just any tariff, but had to follow the rules of the GATT discussed earlier in this chapter. Recall that Article XIX of the GATT, known as the "safeguard" or "escape clause," allows a temporary tariff to be used under certain circumstances. GATT Article XIX is mirrored in U.S. trade law. In **Side Bar: Safeguard Tariffs,** we list the key passages for two sections of the Trade Act of 1974, as amended, both of which deal with safeguard tariffs.

First, Section 201 states that a tariff can be requested by the president, by the House of Representatives, by the Senate, or by any other party such as a firm or union that files a petition with the U.S. International Trade Commission (ITC). That commission determines whether rising imports have been "a substantial cause of serious injury, or threat thereof, to the U.S. industry. . . ." The commission then makes a recommendation to the president who has the final authority to approve or veto the tariff. Section 201 goes further in defining a "substantial cause" as a "cause that is important and not less than any other cause." Although this kind of legal language sounds obscure, it basically means that rising imports have to be *the most important* cause of injury to justify import protection. The steel tariff used by President Bush met this criterion, but as we see in later chapters, many other requests for tariffs do not meet this criterion and are not approved.

SIDE BAR

Safeguard Tariffs

The U.S. Trade Act of 1974, as amended, describes conditions under which tariffs can be applied in the United States, and it mirrors the provisions of the GATT and WTO. Two sections of the Trade Act of 1974 deal with the use of "safeguard" tariffs:

Section 201

Upon the filing of a petition. . . , the request of the President or the Trade Representative, the resolution of either the Committee on Ways and Means of the House of Representatives or the Committee on Finance of the Senate, or on its own motion, the [International Trade] Commission shall promptly make an investigation to determine whether an article is being imported into the United States in such increased quantities as to be a *substantial cause of serious injury, or the threat thereof, to the domestic industry* producing an article like or directly competitive with the imported article.

. . . For purposes of this section, the term "substantial cause" means a cause which is *important and not less than any other cause.*

Section 421

Upon the filing of a petition . . . the United States International Trade Commission . . . shall promptly make an investigation to determine whether products of the People's Republic of China are being imported into the United States in such increased quantities or under such conditions as to *cause or threaten to cause market disruption to the domestic producers* of like or directly competitive products.

. . . (1) For purposes of this section, *market disruption* exists whenever imports of an article like or directly competitive with an article produced by a domestic industry are increasing rapidly, either absolutely or relatively, so as to be a *significant cause of material injury, or threat of material injury, to the domestic industry.*

(2) For purposes of paragraph (1), the term "significant cause" refers to a cause which contributes significantly to the material injury of the domestic industry, *but need not be equal to or greater than any other cause.*

Source: http://www.law.cornell.edu/uscode/text/19/2252 and http://www.law.cornell.edu/uscode/text/19/2451

A second, more recent amendment to the Trade Act of 1974 is Section 421 that applies only to China. This provision was added by the United States as a condition to China's joining the WTO in 2001.[6] Because the United States was worried about exceptional surges in imports from China, it drafted this legislation so that tariffs could be applied in such a case. Under Section 421, various groups can file a petition with the U.S. International Trade Commission, which makes a recommendation to the president. The commission must determine whether rising imports from China cause "market disruption" in a U.S. industry, which means "a significant cause of material injury, or threat of material injury, to the domestic industry." Furthermore, the term "significant cause" refers to "a cause which contributes significantly to the material injury of the domestic industry, but need not be equal to or greater than any other cause." Again, the legal language can be hard to follow, but it indicates that tariffs can be applied even when rising imports from China *are not the most important* cause of injury to the domestic industry. Section 421 can therefore be applied under weaker conditions than Section 201, and it was used by President Obama to justify the tariff on tires imported from China.

APPLICATION

U.S. Tariffs on Steel and Tires

The U.S. steel and tire tariffs highlight the political motivation for applying tariffs despite the deadweight losses associated with them. We can use our small-country model introduced previously to calculate a rough estimate of how costly these tariffs were in terms of welfare. Although the United States may not be a small country

when it comes to its influence on import and export prices, it is a good starting point for our analysis, and we will examine the large-country case in the next section. For now, we stay with our small-country model and illustrate the dead-weight loss due to a tariff with the U.S. steel tariff in place from March 2002 to December 2003. After that calculation, we compare the steel tariff with the more recent tariff on tires.

To fulfill his campaign promise to protect the steel industry, President George W. Bush requested that the ITC initiate a Section 201 investigation into the steel industry. This was one of the few times that a president had initiated a Section 201 action; usually, firms or unions in an industry apply to the ITC for import protection. After investigating, the ITC determined that the conditions of Section 201 and Article XIX were met and recommended that tariffs be put in place to protect the U.S. steel industry. The tariffs recommended by the ITC varied across products, ranging from 10% to 20% for the first year, as shown in Table 8-1, and then falling over time so as to be eliminated after three years.

---

[6] Section 421 was added to U.S. trade law for 12 years, and was due to expire on December 11, 2013.

TABLE 8-1

U.S. ITC Recommended and Actual Tariffs for Steel Shown here are the tariffs recommended by the U.S. International Trade Commission for steel imports, and the actual tariffs that were applied in the first year.

Product Category	U.S. ITC Recommendation (First Year, %)	Actual U.S. Tariff (First Year, %)
Carbon and Alloy Flat Products		
Slab	20	30
Flat products	20	30
Tin mill products	U*	30
Carbon and Alloy Long Products		
Hot-rolled bar	20	30
Cold-finished bar	20	30
Rebar	10	15
Carbon and Alloy Tubular Products		
Tubular products	?**	15
Alloy fittings and flanges	13	13
Stainless and Tool Steel Products		
Stainless steel bar	15	15
Stainless steel rod	?**	15
Stainless steel wire	U*	8

* Uncertain—the ITC was divided on whether a tariff should be used.

** A specific recommendation was not made by the U.S. ITC.

Source: Robert Read, 2005, "The Political Economy of Trade Protection: The Determinants and Welfare Impact of the 2002 U.S. Emergency Steel Safeguard Measures," The World Economy, 1119–1137.

The ITC decision was based on several factors.[7] First, imports had been rising and prices were falling in the steel industry from 1998 to early 2001, leading to substantial losses for U.S. firms. Those losses, along with falling investment and employment, met the condition of "serious injury." An explanation given by the ITC for the falling import prices was that the U.S. dollar appreciated substantially prior to 2001: as the dollar rises in value, foreign currencies become cheaper and so do imported products such as steel, as occurred during this period. To meet the criterion of Section 201 and Article XIX, rising imports need to be a "substantial cause" of serious injury, which is defined as "a cause which is important and not less than any other cause." Sometimes another cause of injury to U.S. firms can be a domestic recession, but that was not the case in the years preceding 2001, when demand for steel products was rising.[8]

President Bush accepted the recommendation of the ITC but applied even higher tariffs, ranging from 8% to 30%, as shown in Table 8-1, with 30% tariffs applied to

---

[7] We focus here on the ITC conclusions for flat-rolled carbon steel, from U.S. International Trade Commission, 2001, Steel: Investigation No. TA-201-73, Volume I, Publication 3479, Washington, D.C.

[8] A short recession began in the United States in March 2001 and ended eight months later, in November 2001.

the most commonly used steel products (such as flat-rolled steel sheets and steel slab). Initially, the tariffs were meant to be in place for three years and to decline over time. Knowing that U.S. trading partners would be upset by this action, President Bush exempted some countries from the tariffs on steel. The countries exempted included Canada, Mexico, Jordan, and Israel, all of which have free-trade agreements with the United States, and 100 small developing countries that were exporting only a very small amount of steel to the United States.

Deadweight Loss Due to the Steel Tariff To measure the deadweight loss due to the tariffs levied on steel, we need to estimate the area of the triangle $b + d$ in Figure 8-5(b). The base of this triangle is the change in imports due to the tariffs, or $\Delta M = M_1 - M_2$. The height of the triangle is the increase in the domestic price due to the tariff, or $\Delta P = t$. So the deadweight loss equals

$$DWL = \frac{1}{2} \cdot t \cdot \Delta M$$

It is convenient to measure the deadweight loss relative to the value of imports, which is $P^W \cdot M$. We will also use the percentage tariff, which is t/P^W, and the percentage change in the quantity of imports, which is $\%\Delta M = \Delta M/M$. The deadweight loss relative to the value of imports can then be rewritten as

$$\frac{DWL}{P^W \cdot M} = \frac{1}{2} \cdot \frac{t \cdot \Delta M}{P^W \cdot M} = \frac{1}{2} \cdot \left(\frac{t}{P^W} \right) \cdot \%\Delta M$$

For the tariffs on steel, the most commonly used products had a tariff of 30%, so that is the percentage increase in the price: $t/P^W = 0.3$. It turns out that the quantity of steel imports also fell by 30% the first year after the tariff was imposed, so that $\%\Delta M = 0.3$. Therefore, the deadweight loss is

$$\frac{DWL}{P^W \cdot M} = \frac{1}{2} (0.3 \cdot 0.3) = 0.045, \text{ or } 4.5\% \text{ of the import value}$$

The value of steel imports that were affected by the tariff was about $4.7 billion in the year prior to March 2002 and $3.5 billion in the year after March 2002, so average imports over the two years were $\frac{1}{2}(4.7 + 3.5) = \$4.1$ billion (these values do not include the tariffs).[9]

If we apply the deadweight loss of 4.5% to the average import value of $4.1 billion, then the dollar magnitude of deadweight loss is 0.045 · 4.1 billion = $185 million. As we discussed earlier, this deadweight loss reflects the net annual loss to the United States from applying the tariff. If you are a steelworker, then you might think that the price of $185 million is money well spent to protect your job, at least temporarily. On the other hand, if you are a consumer of steel, then you will probably object to the higher prices and deadweight loss. In fact, many of the U.S. firms that purchase steel—such as firms producing automobiles—objected to the tariffs and encouraged President Bush to end them early. But the biggest objections to the tariffs came from exporting countries whose firms were affected by the tariffs, especially the European countries. ■

---

[9] The drop in imports of 30% corresponds to a fall in import value of $1.2 billion (since 1.2/4.1 ≈ 0.30, or 30%).

Response of the European Countries The tariffs on steel most heavily affected Europe, Japan, and South Korea, along with some developing countries (Brazil, India, Turkey, Moldova, Romania, Thailand, and Venezuela) that were exporting a significant amount of steel to the United States. These countries objected to the restriction on their ability to sell steel to the United States.

The countries in the European Union (EU) therefore took action by bringing the case to the WTO. They were joined by Brazil, China, Japan, South Korea, New Zealand, Norway, and Switzerland. The WTO has a formal **dispute settlement procedure** under which countries that believe that the WTO rules have not been followed can bring their complaint and have it evaluated. The WTO evaluated this case and, in early November 2003, ruled that the United States had failed to sufficiently prove that its steel industry had been harmed by a sudden increase in imports and therefore did not have the right to impose "safeguard" tariffs.

The WTO ruling was made on legal grounds: that the United States had essentially failed to prove its case (i.e., its eligibility for Article XIX protection).[10] But there are also economic grounds for doubting the wisdom of the safeguard tariffs in the first place. Even if we accept that there might be an argument on equity or fairness grounds for temporarily protecting an industry facing import competition, it is hard to argue that such protection should occur because of a change in exchange rates. The U.S. dollar appreciated for much of the 1990s, including the period before 2001 on which the ITC focused, leading to much lower prices for imported steel. But the appreciation of the dollar also lowered the prices for *all other* import products, so many other industries in the United States faced import competition, too. On fairness grounds, there is no special reason to single out the steel industry for protection.

The WTO ruling entitled the European Union and other countries to retaliate against the United States by imposing tariffs of their own against U.S. exports. The European countries quickly began to draw up a list of products—totaling some $2.2 billion in U.S. exports—against which they would apply tariffs. The European countries naturally picked products that would have the greatest negative impact on the United States, such as oranges from Florida, where Jeb Bush, the president's brother, was governor.

The threat of tariffs being imposed on these products led President Bush to reconsider the U.S. tariffs on steel. On December 5, 2003, he announced that they would be suspended after being in place for only 19 months rather than the three years as initially planned. This chain of events illustrates how the use of tariffs by an importer can easily lead to a response by exporters and a **tariff war.** The elimination of the steel tariffs by President Bush avoided such a retaliatory tariff war.

Tariff on Tires The tariff on tires imported from China, announced by President Obama on September 11, 2009, was requested by the United Steel, Paper and Forestry, Rubber, Manufacturing, Energy, Allied Industrial, and Service Workers International Union (or the United Steelworkers, for short), the union that represents American

---

[10] One of the legal reasons for the WTO ruling was that imports of flat-rolled steel into the United States had fallen from 1998 to 2001, so this product did not meet the requirement that imports had to be increasing to receive Article XIX protection. Even though imports of other steel products were rising, flat-rolled steel was considered one of the most important imported products.

tire workers. On April 20, 2009, they filed a petition with the U.S. ITC for import relief under Section 421 of U.S. trade law. As discussed in **Side Bar: Safeguard Tariffs,** this section of U.S. trade law enables tariffs to be applied against products imported from China if the imports are "a significant cause of material injury" to the U.S. industry. A majority of the ITC commissioners felt that rising imports from China of tires for cars and light trucks fit this description and recommended that tariffs be applied for a three-year period. Their recommendation was for tariffs of 55% in the first year, 45% in the second year, and 35% in the third year (these tariffs would be in addition to a 4% tariff already applied to U.S. tire imports).

President Obama decided to accept this recommendation from the ITC, which was the first time that a U.S. President accepted a tariff recommendation under Section 421. From 2000 to 2009, there had been six other ITC investigations under Section 421, and in four of these cases a majority of commissioners voted in favor of tariffs. But President George W. Bush declined to apply tariffs in all these cases. In accepting the recommendation to apply tariffs on tires, however, President Obama reduced the amount of the tariff to 35% in the first year starting September 26, 2009, 30% in the second year, and 25% in the third year, with the tariff expiring on September 27, 2012.

We've already noted one key difference between the tariff on tires and the earlier tariff on steel: the tire tariff was applied to imports from a single country—China—under Section 421 of U.S. trade law, whereas the steel tariff was applied against many countries under Section 201. For this reason we will refer to the tariff on tires applied against China as a **discriminatory tariff,** meaning a tariff that is applied to the imports from a specific country. Notice that a discriminatory tariff violates the "most favored nation" principle of the WTO and GATT (see **Sidebar: Key Provisions of the GATT**), which states that all members of the WTO should be treated equally. It was possible for the United States to apply this discriminatory tariff against China because Section 421 was negotiated as a condition for China entering the WTO.

A second difference between these cases is that steel producers in the United States supported that tariff, but no U.S. tire producers joined in the request for the tariff on tires. There are 10 producers of tires in the United States, and seven of them—including well-known firms like Goodyear, Michelin, Cooper, and Bridgestone—also produce tires in China and other countries. These firms naturally did not want the tariff put in place because it would harm rather than help them.

There are also a number of similarities in the two cases. As occurred in steel, the tariff on tires led to retaliation. China responded with actual or potential tariffs on products such as chicken feet (a local delicacy), auto parts, certain nylon products, and even passenger cars. For its part, the United States went on to apply new tariffs on steel pipe imported from China, and also investigated several other products. Another similarity with the steel case is that China made an official complaint to the WTO under its dispute settlement procedure, just as the European countries did in the steel case. China claimed that the "significant cause of material injury" conditions of Section 421 had not been met. China also questioned whether it was legal under the WTO for the United States to apply a discriminatory tariff. Unlike the steel case, the WTO concluded that the United States was justified in applying the tariff on tires.

The final comparison we make between the steel and tire tariffs focuses on the calculation of the deadweight losses. Because the tariff on tires was applied against only one country—China—you might think that it would have a lower deadweight loss that the steel tariff, which was applied against many countries selling to the United

States. It turns out that the opposite is true: the tariff on tires had a *higher* deadweight loss than that tariff on steel, precisely because it was a discriminatory tariff that was applied against only one country. To explain this surprising outcome, we will make use of Figure 8-6.

A Discriminatory Tariff We suppose that China can sell any amount of tires to the United States at the price of P^W in Figure 8-6. What is new in this figure is the treatment of the *other* countries exporting to the United States. We represent these countries by the upward-sloping supply curve X^*, which is added onto U.S. supply of S to obtain total supply from all countries other than China of $S + X^*$.

Under free trade, the price for tires is P^W and the supply from the United States is S_1. Supply from the United States and exporting countries other than China is $S_1 + X_1^*$, while China exports the difference between $S_1 + X_1^*$ and demand of D_1. When the tariff of t is applied against China, the price of tires rises to $P^W + t$, supply from the United States rises to S_2. Supply from the United States and exporting countries other than China rises to $S_2 + X_2^*$. China exports the difference between $S_2 + X_2^*$ and demand of D_2. Because the price has risen to $P^W + t$, both U.S. producers and exporting countries other than China are selling more (moving along their supply curves) while China must be selling less (because the other countries are selling more and total demand has gone down).

So far the diagram looks only a bit different from our treatment of the tariff in Figure 8-5. But when we calculate the effect of the tariff on welfare in the United States, we find a new result. We will not go through each of the steps in calculating the change in consumer and producer surplus, but will focus on tariff revenue and the difference with our earlier treatment in Figure 8-5. The key idea to keep in mind is that the tariff applies only to China, and not to other exporting countries. So with

FIGURE 8-6

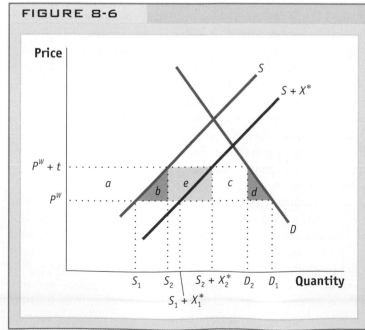

Effect of the Tariff on Tires The tariff on tires increases the price of tires from China from P^W to $P^W + t$. The supply from the United States is shown by S, and the supply from other exporting countries by X^*. As a result of the tariff, these two sources of supply increase from $S_1 + X_1^*$ to $S_2 + X_2^*$; China supplies the rest of the market up to demand D_1. Because the other exporting countries do not face the tariff, they collect area e from the higher prices charged in the U.S. market. Therefore, the deadweight loss from the tariff is $(b + d + e)$.

the increase in the price of tires from P^W to $P^W + t$, the other exporting countries get to keep that higher price: it is not collected from these countries as tariff revenue. Under these circumstances, the amount of tariff revenue is only the quantity that China exports (the difference between $S_2 + X_2^*$ and demand of D_2) times the tariff t, which is the area shown by c. In comparison, the area shown by e is the increase in the price charged by *other* exporters times their exports of X_2^*. Area e is not collected by the U.S. government as tariff revenue, and becomes part of the deadweight loss for the United States. The total deadweight loss for the U.S. is then $(b + d + e)$, which exceeds the deadweight loss of $(b + d)$ that we found in Figure 8-5. The reason that the deadweight loss has gone up is that other exporters are selling for a higher price in the United States, and the government does not collect any tariff revenue from them.

Deadweight Loss Due to the Tire Tariff Figure 8-6 shows that a discriminatory tariff applied against just one country has a higher deadweight loss, of $(b + d + e)$, than an equal tariff applied against all exporting countries, in which case the deadweight loss is just $(b + d)$ as we found in Figure 8-5. To see whether this theoretical result holds in practice, we can compare the tariff on tires with the tariff on steel. In the end, we will find that the tariff on tires was costlier to the United States because other countries—especially Mexico and other countries from Asia—were able to sell more tires to the United States at higher prices.

The effect of the tariff on the percentage of U.S. import value coming from China and other countries is shown in Figure 8-7. Just before the tariff was imposed in September 2009, imports into the United States were evenly divided with one-third coming from China, one-third from other Asian countries, and one-third from Canada, Mexico, and all other countries. The lowest area in the graph represents the value of imports from China. We can see that Chinese imports dropped in the fourth quarter (Q4) of 2009, after the tariff began in September, and rose again in the fourth quarter (Q4) of 2012, after the tariff ended in September of that year. The value of imports from China fell from about 33% of overall imports to 15% when the tariff began, and rose from about 12% of overall imports to 22% after the tariff ended. But this 18 percentage point decline in imports from China when the tariff began was substantially made up by increased imports from other Asian countries. We can see this result by looking at the next area shown in the graph, above China, which represents imports from all other Asian countries. When adding up the Chinese and other Asian imports, we obtain about 60% of the total imports, and while this percentage varies to some extent when the tariff begins and ends, it varies much less than does the percentage imported from China itself. In other words, other Asian countries made up for the reduction in China exports by increasing their own exports; similarly, Mexico (included within the top area in the graph) also increased its exports to the United States during the time the tariff was applied.

This increase in sales from other Asian countries and Mexico is consistent with Figure 8-6, which shows that sales from other exporters increase from X_1^* to X_2^* due to the tariff on China. The evidence also indicates that these other exporters were able to charge higher prices for the tires they sold to the United States. For car tires, the average price charged by countries other than China increased from $54 to $64 during the times of the tariff, while for light truck tires, the average prices increased from $76 to $90. Both these increases are higher than we would expect from inflation during 2009–12. As shown in Figure 8-6, these price increases for other exporters occur because they are competing with Chinese exporters who must pay the tariff.

FIGURE 8-7

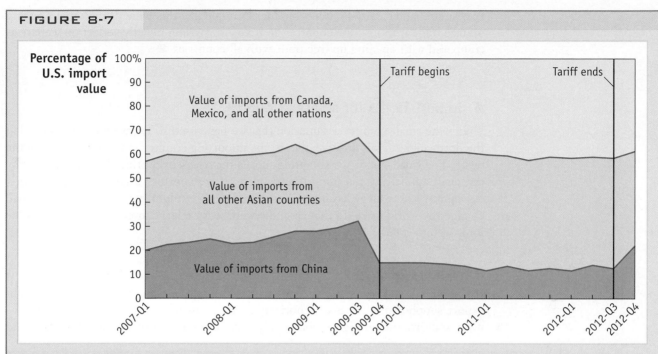

U.S. Imports of Tires The tariff applied to U.S. imports of tires began in the fourth quarter of 2009 (2009Q4) and ended in the third quarter of 2012 (2012Q3). The value of imports from China fell from about 33% of overall imports to 15% when the tariff began, and rose from about 12% of overall imports to 22% when the tariff ended. This decline in imports from China was substantially made up by increased imports from other Asian countries and Mexico, which exported more to the United States.

An estimate of the area *e*—which is the total increase in the amount paid to tire exporters other than China—is $716 million per year for imports of car tires and another $101 million per year for imports of light truck tires, totaling $817 million per year.[11] This is in addition to the deadweight loss (*b* + *d*). This area *e* for the tire tariff substantially exceeds the deadweight loss for the steel tariff of $185 million per year that we calculated above. So we see that a discriminatory tariff, applied against just one exporting country, can be more costly then an equal tariff applied against all exporters.

At the beginning of the chapter we included a quote from President Obama in his State of the Union address in 2012, in which he said that "over a thousand Americans are working today because we stopped a surge in Chinese tires." Although 1,000 jobs in the tire industry is roughly the estimate of how many jobs were saved, we have shown that these jobs came at a very high cost because the tariff was discriminatory.[12]

[11] See Gary Clyde Hufbauer and Sean Lowry, 2012, "U.S. Tire Tariffs: Saving Few Jobs at High Cost," Peterson Institute for International Economics, Policy Brief no. PB12-9.
[12] According to Gary Clyde Hufbauer and Sean Lowry, 2012, cited in the previous footnote, there were 1,200 jobs saved in the tire industry. But taking the area *e* cost of $817 million and dividing it by 1,200 jobs gives an annual cost per job of $681,000, which is many times more than the annual earnings of a tire worker. So the discriminatory tariff was an expensive way to save these jobs.

In a later chapter we will discuss another example like this which shows that opening up free trade with just one country can have a surprising negative effect on welfare as compared with opening up free trade with all countries. ■

4 Import Tariffs for a Large Country

Under the small-country assumption that we have used so far, we know for sure that the deadweight loss is positive; that is, the importing country is always harmed by the tariff. The small-country assumption means that the world price P^W is unchanged by the tariff applied by the importing country. If we consider a large enough importing country or a **large country,** however, then we might expect that its tariff will change the world price. In that case, the welfare for a large importing country can be improved by a tariff, as we now show.

Foreign Export Supply

If the Home country is large, then we can no longer assume that it faces a Foreign export supply curve X^* that is horizontal at the given world price P^W. Instead, we need to derive the Foreign export supply curve using the Foreign market demand and

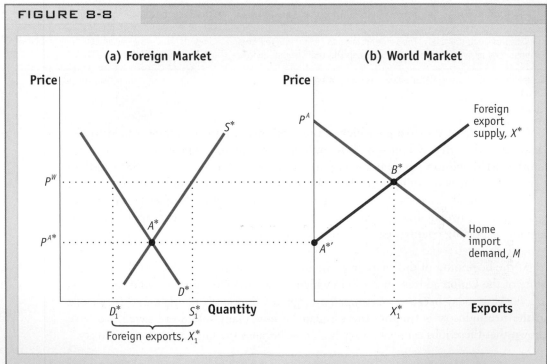

FIGURE 8-8

Foreign Export Supply In panel (a), with Foreign demand of D^* and Foreign supply of S^*, the no-trade equilibrium in Foreign is at point A^*, with the price of P^{A*}. At this price, the Foreign market is in equilibrium and Foreign exports are zero—point A^* in panel (a) and point $A^{*\prime}$ in panel (b), respectively. When the world price P^W is higher than Foreign's no-trade price, the quantity supplied by Foreign, S^*_1, exceeds the quantity demanded by Foreign, D^*_1, and Foreign exports $X^*_1 = S^*_1 - D^*_1$. In panel (b), joining up points $A^{*\prime}$ and B^*, we obtain the upward-sloping export supply curve X^*. With the Home import demand of M, the world equilibrium is at point B^*, with the price P^W.

supply curves. In panel (a) of Figure 8-8, we show the Foreign demand curve D^* and supply curve S^*. These intersect at the point A^*, with a no-trade equilibrium price of P^{A*}. Because Foreign demand equals supply at that price, Foreign exports are zero, which we show by point $A^{*\prime}$ in panel (b), where we graph Foreign exports against their price.

Now suppose the world price P^W is above the Foreign no-trade price of P^{A*}. At the price of P^W, the Foreign quantity demanded is lower, at D_1^* in panel (a), but the quantity supplied by Foreign firms is larger, at S_1^*. Because Foreign supply exceeds demand, Foreign will export the amount $X_1^* = S_1^* - D_1^*$ at the price of P^W, as shown by the point B^* in panel (b). Drawing a line through points $A^{*\prime}$ and B^*, we obtain the upward-sloping Foreign export supply curve X^*.

We can then combine the Foreign export supply curve X^* and Home import demand curve M, which is also shown in panel (b). They intersect at the price P^W, the world equilibrium price. Notice that the Home import demand curve starts at the no-trade price P^A on the price axis, whereas the Foreign export supply curve starts at the price P^{A*}. As we have drawn them, the Foreign no-trade price is lower, $P^{A*} < P^A$. In Chapters 2 to 5 of this book, a country with comparative advantage in a good would have a lower no-trade relative price and would become an exporter when trade was opened. Likewise, in panel (b), Foreign exports the good since its no-trade price P^{A*} is lower than the world price, and Home imports the good since its no-trade price P^A is higher than the world price. So the world equilibrium illustrated in panel (b) is similar to that in some of the trade models presented in earlier chapters.

Effect of the Tariff

In panel (b) of Figure 8-9, we repeat the Home import demand curve M and Foreign export supply curve X^*, with the world equilibrium at B^*. When Home applies a tariff of t dollars, the cost to Foreign producers of supplying the Home market is t more than it was before. Because of this increase in costs, the Foreign export supply curve shifts up by exactly the amount of the tariff, as shown in panel (b) with the shift from X^* to $X^* + t$. The $X^* + t$ curve intersects import demand M at point C, which establishes the Home price (including the tariff) paid by consumers. On the other hand, the Foreign exporters receive the net-of-tariff price, which is directly below the point C by exactly the amount t, at point C^*. Let us call the price received by Foreign exporters P^*, at point C^*, which is the new world price.

The important feature of the new equilibrium is that the price Home pays for its imports, $P^* + t$, rises by *less than* the amount of the tariff t as compared with the initial world price P^W. The reason that the Home price rises by less than the full amount of the tariff is that the price received by Foreign exporters, P^*, has fallen as compared with the initial world price P^W. So, Foreign producers are essentially "absorbing" a part of the tariff, by lowering their price from P^W (in the initial free-trade equilibrium) to P^* (after the tariff).

In sum, we can interpret the tariff as driving a wedge between what Home consumers pay and what Foreign producers receive, with the difference (of t) going to the Home government. As is the case with many taxes, the amount of the tariff (t) is shared by both consumers and producers.

FIGURE 8-9

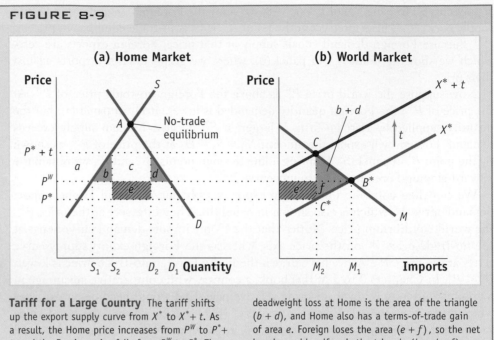

(a) Home Market
(b) World Market

Tariff for a Large Country The tariff shifts up the export supply curve from X^* to $X^* + t$. As a result, the Home price increases from P^W to $P^* + t$, and the Foreign price falls from P^W to P^*. The deadweight loss at Home is the area of the triangle $(b + d)$, and Home also has a terms-of-trade gain of area e. Foreign loses the area $(e + f)$, so the net loss in world welfare is the triangle $(b + d + f)$.

Terms of Trade In Chapter 2, we defined the **terms of trade** for a country as the ratio of export prices to import prices. Generally, an improvement in the terms of trade indicates a gain for a country because it is either receiving more for its exports or paying less for its imports. To measure the Home terms of trade, we want to use the net-of-tariff import price P^* (received by Foreign firms) since that is the total amount transferred from Home to Foreign for each import. Because this price has fallen (from its initial world price of P^W), it follows that the Home terms of trade have increased. We might expect, therefore, that the Home country gains from the tariff in terms of Home welfare. To determine whether that is the case, we need to analyze the impact on the welfare of Home consumers, producers, and government revenue, which we do in Figure 8-9.

Home Welfare In panel (a), the Home consumer price increases from P^W to $P^* + t$, which makes consumers worse off. The drop in consumer surplus is represented by the area between these two prices and to the left of the demand curve D, which is shown by $(a + b + c + d)$. At the same time, the price received by Home firms rises from P^W to $P^* + t$, making Home firms better off. The increase in producer surplus equals the area between these two prices, and to the left of the supply curve S, which is the amount a. Finally, we also need to keep track of the changes in government revenue. Revenue collected from the tariff equals the amount of the tariff (t) times the new amount of imports, which is $M_2 = D_2 - S_2$. Therefore, government revenue equals the area $(c + e)$ in panel (a).

By summing the change in consumer surplus, producer surplus, and government revenue, we obtain the overall impact of the tariff in the large country, as follows:

Fall in consumer surplus:	$-(a + b + c + d)$
Rise in producer surplus:	$+ a$
Rise in government revenue:	$+ (c + e)$
Net effect on Home welfare:	$+ e - (b + d)$

The triangle $(b + d)$ is the deadweight loss due to the tariff (just as it is for a small country). But for the large country, there is also a source of gain—the area e—that offsets this deadweight loss. If e exceeds $(b + d)$, then Home is better off due to the tariff; if e is less than $(b + d)$, then Home is worse off.

Notice that the area e is a rectangle whose height is the fall in the price that Foreign exporters receive, the difference between P^W and P^*. The base of this rectangle equals the quantity of imports, M_2. Multiplying the drop in the import price by the quantity of imports to obtain the area e, we obtain a precise measure of the **terms-of-trade gain** for the importer. If this terms-of-trade gain exceeds the deadweight loss of the tariff, which is $(b + d)$, then Home gains from the tariff.

Thus, we see that a large importer might gain by the application of a tariff. We can add this to our list of reasons why countries use tariffs, in addition to their being a source of government revenue or a tool for political purposes. However, for the large country, any net gain from the tariff comes at the expense of the Foreign exporters, as we show next.

Foreign and World Welfare While Home might gain from the tariff, Foreign, the exporting country, definitely loses. In panel (b) of Figure 8-9, the Foreign loss is measured by the area $(e + f)$. We should think of $(e + f)$ as the loss in Foreign producer surplus from selling fewer goods to Home at a lower price. Notice that the area e is the terms-of-trade gain for Home but an equivalent terms-of-trade *loss* for Foreign; Home's gain comes at the expense of Foreign. In addition, the large-country tariff incurs an extra deadweight loss of f in Foreign, so the combined total outweighs the benefits to Home. For this reason, we sometimes call a tariff imposed by a large country a "beggar thy neighbor" tariff.

Adding together the change in Home welfare and Foreign welfare, the area e cancels out and we are left with a *net loss* in world welfare of $(b + d + f)$, the triangle in panel (b). This area is a deadweight loss for the world. The terms-of-trade gain that Home has extracted from the Foreign country by using a tariff comes at the expense of the Foreign exporters, and in addition, there is an added world deadweight loss. The fact that the large-country tariff leads to a world deadweight loss is another reason that most economists oppose the use of tariffs.

Optimal Tariff for a Large Importing Country We have found that a large importer might gain by the application of tariffs, but have yet to determine what *level* of tariff a country should apply in order to maximize welfare. It turns out there is a shortcut method we can use to evaluate the effect of the tariff on the welfare of a large importing country. The shortcut method uses the concept of the **optimal tariff.**

The optimal tariff is defined as the tariff that leads to the maximum increase in welfare for the importing country. For a large importing country, a small tariff initially increases welfare because the terms-of-trade gain exceeds the deadweight loss. That is, the area of the rectangle e in panel (a) of Figure 8-9 exceeds the area of the triangle $(b + d)$ in panel (b) when the tariff is small enough. The reason for this is that both the height and base of the triangle $(b + d)$ shrink to zero when the tariff is very small, so the area of the triangle is very small indeed; but for the rectangle e, only the height shrinks to zero when the tariff is small, so the area of the rectangle exceeds that of the triangle. By this mathematical reasoning, the Home gains are positive—$e > (b + d)$—when the Home tariff is sufficiently small.

In Figure 8-10, we graph Home welfare against the level of the tariff. Free trade is at point B, where the tariff is zero. A small increase in the tariff, as we have just noted, leads to an *increase* in Home welfare (because the terms-of-trade gain exceeds the deadweight loss). Therefore, starting at point B, the graph of Home welfare must be upward-sloping. But what if the tariff is very large? If the tariff is too large, then welfare will fall *below* the free-trade level of welfare. For example, with a prohibitive tariff so high that no imports are purchased at all, then the importer's welfare will be at the no-trade level, shown by point A. So while the graph of welfare must be increasing for a small tariff from point B, as the tariff increases, welfare eventually falls past the free-trade level at point B' to the no-trade welfare at point A.

Given that points B and A are both on the graph of the importer's welfare (for free trade and no trade, respectively) and that welfare must be rising after point B, it follows that there must be a highest point of welfare, shown by point C. At this point, the importer's welfare is highest because the difference between the terms-of-trade gain and deadweight loss is maximized. We will call the tariff at that point the "optimal tariff." For increases in the tariff beyond its optimal level (i.e., between points C and A), the importer's welfare falls because the deadweight loss due to the tariff overwhelms the terms-of-trade gain. But whenever the tariff is below its optimal level, between points B and C, then welfare is higher than its free-trade level because the terms-of-trade gain exceeds the deadweight loss.

Optimal Tariff Formula It turns out that there is a simple formula for the optimal tariff. The formula depends on the elasticity of Foreign export supply, which we call E_X^*. Recall that the elasticity of any supply curve is the percentage increase in supply caused by a percentage increase in price. Likewise, the elasticity of the Foreign export supply curve is the percentage change in the quantity exported in response to a percent change in the world price of the export. If the export supply curve is very steep, then there is

FIGURE 8-10

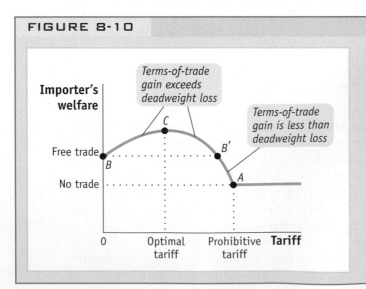

Tariffs and Welfare for a Large Country For a large importing country, a tariff initially increases the importer's welfare because the terms-of-trade gain exceeds the deadweight loss. So the importer's welfare rises from point B. Welfare continues to rise until the tariff is at its optimal level (point C). After that, welfare falls. If the tariff is too large (greater than at B'), then welfare will fall below the free-trade level. For a prohibitive tariff, with no imports at all, the importer's welfare will be at the no-trade level, at point A.

little response of the quantity supplied, and so the elasticity E_X^* is low. Conversely, if the export supply curve is very flat, there is a large response of the quantity supplied due to a change in the world price, and so E_X^* is high. Recall also that a small importing country faces a perfectly horizontal, or perfectly elastic, Foreign export supply curve, which means that the elasticity of Foreign export supply is infinite.

Using the elasticity of Foreign export supply, the optimal tariff equals

$$\text{optimal tariff} = \frac{1}{E_X^*}$$

That is, the optimal tariff (measured as a percentage) equals the inverse of the elasticity of Foreign export supply. For a small importing country, the elasticity of Foreign export supply is infinite, and so the optimal tariff is zero. That result makes sense, since any tariff higher than zero leads to a deadweight loss for the importer (and no terms-of-trade gain), so the best tariff to choose is zero, or free trade.

For a large importing country however, the Foreign export supply is less than infinite, and we can use this formula to compute the optimal tariff. As the elasticity of Foreign export supply decreases (which means that the Foreign export supply curve is steeper), the optimal tariff is higher. The reason for this result is that with a steep Foreign export supply curve, Foreign exporters will lower their price more in response to the tariff.[13] For instance, if E_X^* decreases from 3 to 2, then the optimal tariff increases from $\frac{1}{3} = 33\%$ to $\frac{1}{2} = 50\%$, reflecting the fact that Foreign producers are willing to lower their prices more, taking on a larger share of the tariff burden. In that case, the Home country obtains a larger terms-of-trade increase and hence the optimal level of the tariff is higher.

APPLICATION

U.S. Tariffs on Steel Once Again

Let us return to the U.S. tariff on steel, and reevaluate the effect on U.S. welfare in the large-country case. The calculation of the deadweight loss that we did earlier in the application assumed that the United States was a small country, facing fixed world prices for steel. In that case, the 30% tariff on steel was fully reflected in U.S. prices, which rose by 30%. But what if the import prices for steel in the United States did not rise by the full amount of the tariff? If the United States is a large enough importer of steel, then the Foreign export price will fall and the U.S. import price will rise by less than the tariff. It is then possible that the United States gained from the tariff.

To determine whether the United States gained from the tariff on steel products, we can compute the deadweight loss (area $b + d$) and the terms-of-trade gain (area e) for each imported steel product using the optimum tariff formula.

Optimal Tariffs for Steel Let us apply this formula to the U.S. steel tariffs to see how the tariffs applied compare with the theoretical optimal tariff. In Table 8-2, we show various steel products along with their respective elasticities of export supply to the United States. By taking the inverse of each export supply elasticity, we obtain the optimal tariff. For example, alloy steel flat-rolled products (the first item) have a low

---

[13] See Problem 3 at the end of the chapter, where you will show that steeper export supply leads Foreign to absorb more of the tariff.

TABLE 8-2

Optimal Tariffs for Steel Products This table shows optimal tariffs for steel products, calculated with the elasticity formula.

Product Category	Elasticity of Export Supply	Optimal Tariff (%)	Actual Tariff (%)
Alloy steel flat-rolled products	0.27	370	30
Iron and steel rails and railway track	0.80	125	0
Iron and steel bars, rods, angles, shapes	0.80	125	15–30
Ferrous waste and scrap	17	6	0
Iron and steel tubes, pipes, and fittings	90	1	13–15
Iron and nonalloy steel flat-rolled products	750	0	0

Source: Elasticities of export supply provided by Christian Broda and David Weinstein, May 2006, "Globalization and the Gains from Variety," Quarterly Journal of Economics, 121(2), 541–585.

export supply elasticity, 0.27, so they have a very high optimal tariff of 1/0.27 = 3.7 = 370%. In contrast, iron and nonalloy steel flat-rolled products (the last item) have a very high export supply elasticity of 750, so the optimal tariff is 1/750 ≈ 0%. Products between these have optimal tariffs ranging from 1% to 125%.

In the final column of Table 8-2, we show the actual tariffs that were applied to these products. For alloy steel flat-rolled products (the first item), the actual tariff was 30%, which is far below the optimal tariff. That means the terms-of-trade gain for that product was higher than the deadweight loss: the tariff is on the portion of the welfare graph between B and C in Figure 8-10, and U.S. welfare is above its free-trade level. The same holds for iron and steel bars, rods, angles, and shapes, for which the tariffs of 15% to 30% are again less than their optimal level, so the United States obtains a terms-of-trade gain that exceeds the deadweight loss. However, for iron and steel tubes, pipes, and fittings, the U.S. tariffs were 13% to 15%, but the optimal tariff for that product was only 1%. Because of the very high elasticity of export supply, the United States has practically no effect on the world price, so the deadweight loss for that product exceeds the terms-of-trade gain.

To summarize, for the three product categories in Table 8-2 to which the United States applied tariffs, in two products the terms-of-trade gain exceeded the deadweight loss, so U.S. welfare rose due to the tariff, but in a third case the deadweight loss was larger, so U.S. welfare fell due to the tariff. The first two products illustrate the large-country case for tariffs, in which the welfare of the importer can rise because of a tariff, whereas the third product illustrates the small-country case, in which the importer loses from the tariff.

From the information given in Table 8-2, we do not know whether the United States gained or lost overall from the steel tariffs: that calculation would require adding up the gains and losses due to the tariff over all imported steel products, which we have not done. But in the end, we should keep in mind that any rise in U.S. welfare comes at the expense of exporting countries. Even if there were an overall terms-of-trade gain for the United States when adding up across all steel products, that gain would be at the expense of the European countries and other steel exporters. As we have already discussed, the steel exporters objected to the U.S. tariffs at the WTO and were entitled to apply *retaliatory* tariffs of their own against U.S. products. If these tariffs had been applied, they would have eliminated and reversed any U.S. gain. By removing the tariffs in less than two years, the United States avoided a costly tariff war. Indeed, that is one of the main goals of the WTO: by allowing exporting countries to retaliate with tariffs, the WTO prevents importers from using optimal tariffs to their own advantage. In a later chapter, we show more carefully how such a tariff war will end up being costly to all countries involved. ■

5 Import Quotas

On January 1, 2005, China was poised to become the world's largest exporter of textiles and apparel. On that date, a system of worldwide import quotas known as the **Multifibre Arrangement (MFA)** was abolished. Import quotas are a restriction on the amount of a particular good that one country can purchase from another country. Under the Multifibre Arrangement, begun in 1974, import quotas restricted the amount of nearly every textile and apparel product that was imported to Canada, the European countries, and the United States. These countries limited their textile imports to protect their own domestic firms producing those products. With the end of the MFA, China was ready to enjoy greatly increased exports—but this did not occur. The threat of import competition from China led the United States and Europe to negotiate *new* temporary import quotas with China, as we discuss in this section.

Besides the MFA, there are many other examples of import quotas. For example, since 1993 Europe had a quota on the imports of bananas that allowed for a greater number of bananas to enter from its former colonies in Africa than from Latin America. In 2005 that quota was simplified and converted into a tariff, even though that tariff still discriminated among countries based on their colonial past. Then, in 2009, Europe agreed to reduce the tariff on Latin American bananas, effectively bringing to an end this "banana war," which had lasted for more than 15 years (see **Headlines: Banana Wars**). Another example is the quota on U.S. imports of sugar, which is still in place despite calls for its removal (see **Headlines: Sugar Could Sweeten U.S. Australia Trans-Pacific Trade Talks**). In this section, we explain how quotas affect the importing and exporting countries and examine the differences between quotas and tariffs. Like a tariff, an import quota often imposes a welfare cost on the importing country. But we will find that quotas can often lead to higher welfare losses for the importer than tariffs do.

Import Quota in a Small Country

Applying an import quota for a small country is similar to applying a tariff, so we can use the graphs developed earlier in the chapter to analyze quotas, too.

Free-Trade Equilibrium In panel (a) of Figure 8-11, we show the Home demand curve D and the Home supply curve S. At the free-trade world price of P^W, Home quantity demanded is D_1 and quantity supplied is S_1, so imports are $M_1 = D_1 - S_1$. The import demand curve $M = D - S$ is shown in panel (b). The assumption that the Home country is small means that the fixed world price P^W is not affected by the import quota, so under free trade, the Foreign export supply curve X^* is

FIGURE 8-11

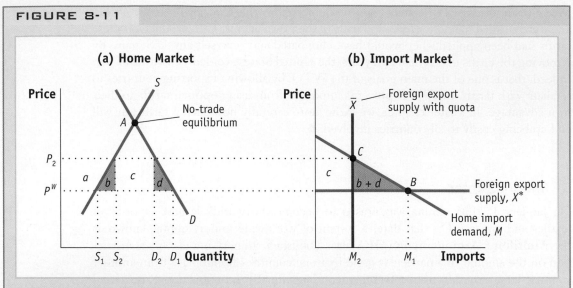

(a) Home Market

(b) Import Market

Quota for a Small Country Under free trade, the Foreign export supply curve is horizontal at the world price, P^W, and the free-trade equilibrium is at point B with imports of M_1. Applying an import quota of $M_2 < M_1$ leads to the vertical export supply curve $\bar{X}$—with the equilibrium at point C. The quota increases the import price from P^W to P_2. There would be the same impact on price and quantities if instead of the quota, a tariff of $t = P_2 - P^W$ had been used.

a horizontal line at the world price P^W. The Home import demand curve M and Foreign export supply curve X^* intersect at point B, resulting in the free-trade level of imports, M_1.

Effect of the Quota Now suppose that an import quota of $M_2 < M_1$ is imposed, meaning that the quantity imported cannot exceed this amount. This quota effectively establishes a vertical export supply curve labeled as $\bar{X}$ in panel (b), which fixes the import quantity at M_2. The vertical export supply curve now intersects import demand at point C, which establishes the Home price of P_2. In panel (a), the price of P_2 leads firms to increase the quantity supplied to S_2 and consumers to decrease their quantity demanded to D_2.

The import quota therefore leads to an increase in the Home price and a reduction in Home imports, just like a tariff. Furthermore, notice that there would be an equivalent effect on the import price and quantity if instead of the quota, the government had imposed an import tariff of $t = P_2 - P^W$. That is, the tariff of $t = P_2 - P^W$ would raise the Home price to P_2 and reduce imports to the level M_2. We conclude that for every level of the import quota, there is an **equivalent import tariff** that would lead to the same Home price and quantity of imports.[14]

Effect on Welfare As we have shown, the quota leads to an increase in the Home price. The rise in the price for consumers leads to a fall in consumer surplus. That fall is measured by the area between the prices P_2 and P^W and to the left of the demand curve, which is the area $(a + b + c + d)$ in panel (a) of Figure 8-11. On the other hand, the increase in the price facing Home producers leads to a gain in producer surplus.

---

[14] As we show in the next chapter, this conclusion depends on our assumption of perfect competition and does not hold without that assumption.

HEADLINES

Banana Wars

This article discusses a well-known example of a quota that applied to European imports of bananas. The quota and discriminatory tariff on bananas from Latin America finally ended in late 2009.

I can hardly believe the banana wars are over. The dispute started back in 1993 when the European Union set quotas favoring banana imports from Ivory Coast, the Windward Islands and other former colonies at the expense of imports from Latin America. American banana companies and the Latin American countries where they grow their bananas sued the E.U., accusing it of rigging an unfair trade deal, first under the GATT and then under the W.T.O.

The suit dragged on for years, and at several points threatened to spark an all-out trade war between Washington and Europe. In 1999, after a meeting on Kosovo was hijacked by the banana crisis, the secretary of state then, Madeleine Albright, declared in exasperation: "I never in my life thought I would spend so much time on bananas."

It finally ended this month when the E.U. said it would continue to grant tariff-free access to its former colonies but would reduce tariffs on Latin American bananas by 35 percent over seven years. The United States and Latin American producers agreed to drop their case. After all the roiling, what strikes me now is how little people seem to care. That says a lot about how attitudes toward trade have changed.

When this started, trade was trumpeted as the single most important tool for development. Europe insisted that its special treatment of its former colonies was central to its post-imperial responsibilities. The United States and Latin American countries vowed to hold the line for free trade—over bananas at least—to make it a tool of development for all.

Today nobody talks about bananas. Stalled global trade talks (remember Doha?) barely get mentioned. There are a lot of problems out there, including the collapse of world trade in the wake of the global recession and the looming threat of protectionism. Yet there has also been a rethinking about trade's supposed silver bullet role in economic development.

China's growth stands as a beacon for the power of trade. But others that have hitched their economic strategy to trade, like Mexico, have found prosperity elusive. Despite growing banana exports, both the Latin American banana exporters and Europe's impoverished former colonies remain poor.

One thing we have learned over the past 15 years is that trade is necessary but not sufficient for development. Countries also need investment in infrastructure, technology and human capital. They need credit. They need legitimate institutions—like clean courts to battle monopolies—and help building them. Putting up a few barriers against banana imports, or tearing a few of them down, can't do it all.

That gain is measured by the area between the prices P_2 and P^W and to the left of the supply curve, which is the area a in Figure 8-11(a). These two welfare effects are the same as would occur under a tariff.

The quota and tariff differ, however, in terms of area c, which would be collected as government revenue under a tariff. Under the quota, this area equals the difference between the domestic price P_2 and the world price P^W, times the quantity of imports M_2. Therefore, whoever is actually importing the good will be able to earn the difference between the world price P^W and the higher Home price P_2 by selling the imports in the Home market. We call the difference between these two prices the *rent* associated with the quota, and hence the area c represents the total **quota rents**. There are four possible ways that these quota rents can be allocated:

1. Giving the Quota to Home Firms First, **quota licenses** (i.e., permits to import the quantity allowed under the quota system) can be given to Home firms, which are then able to import at the world price P^W and sell locally at P_2, earning the difference

HEADLINES

Sugar Could Sweeten U.S. Australia Trans-Pacific Trade Talks

This article discusses the reasons for a sugar quota in the United States, which has been in place since before World War II. Under current negotiations for the Trans-Pacific Partnership, Australia has asked the United States to reconsider this quota and allow more exports from Australia.

Australia's sugar growers and investors could end up with a sweeter deal under the upcoming Trans-Pacific Partnership negotiations as the U.S. faces growing calls to put its long-standing sugar import restrictions on the table. The U.S. has been leading the wide-ranging regional talks, which aim to eliminate barriers to trade between the world's largest economy and some of the fastest-growing markets. In all, the 11 countries in the talks—which include Australia—account for one-third of U.S. trade. . . . [The] U.S. may finally be forced to reconsider the limits on sugar imports it has had in place since before the start of the Second World War.

To be sure, sugar is a sticky subject in the U.S. That's not only because it's already the world's largest importer of sugar, buying from more than 40 countries, the largest market for sweeteners or because, with annual production in excess of 8 million short tons, it's also one of the world's largest producers. It's because the sugar industry—which employs around 142,000 people and generates nearly $20 billion a year, according to lobby group the American Sugar Alliance—is extremely politically vocal and represents important votes in key swing states. For this reason the industry has been able to keep trade barriers intact that, for decades, kept domestic prices at roughly double the world price until about 5 years ago.

. . . [A]s the world's third-largest sugar exporter, Australia stands to reap significant benefits if the U.S. relaxes its regulations. Tom Earley, vice president for Agralytica Consulting, estimates there's an annual shortfall of more than 1 million metric tons in the U.S. that isn't met by fixed quotas and so would be up for grabs under any changes. "Australian negotiators are saying everything should be on the table and that makes sense to me," he said. "At the end of the day everything is on the table." . . . A spokesman for Australia's Department of Agriculture, Fisheries and Forestry said the U.S. remains a "valued market for the Australian sugar industry, despite volumes being constrained." The government "continues to press for increased sugar access to the U.S., although this remains a difficult issue for both countries," he added.

between these as rents. An example of this is the dairy industry in the United States, in which U.S. producers of cheese receive licenses to import from abroad. With home firms earning the rents c, the net effect of the quota on Home welfare is

Fall in consumer surplus:	$-(a + b + c + d)$
Rise in producer surplus:	$+a$
Quota rents earned at Home	$+c$
Net effect on Home welfare:	$-(b + d)$

We see from this calculation that the net effect on Home welfare is a loss of amount $(b + d)$. That loss is the same as what we found in Section 3 of this chapter for the loss of a tariff in a small country. As in that section, we still refer to $(b + d)$ as a deadweight loss.

2. Rent Seeking One complication of simply giving valuable quota licenses to Home firms is that these firms may engage in some kind of inefficient activities to obtain them. For example, suppose that Home firms are producing batteries and import the chemical needed as an input. If licenses for the imported chemicals are allocated in proportion to each firm's production of batteries in the previous years, then the Home firms will likely produce more batteries than they can sell (and at lower quality) *just to obtain the import licenses for the following year*. Alternatively, firms might engage in bribery or other lobbying activities to obtain the licenses. These kinds of inefficient activities done to obtain quota licenses are called **rent seeking.** It has been suggested that the waste of resources devoted to rent-seeking activities could be as large as the value of rents themselves so that the area c would be wasted rather than accrue to Home firms. If rent seeking occurs, the welfare loss due to the quota would be

Fall in consumer surplus:	$-(a + b + c + d)$
Rise in producer surplus:	$+a$
Net effect on Home welfare:	$-(b + c + d)$

The waste of resources due to rent seeking leads to a fall in Home welfare of $(b + c + d)$, which is larger than that for a tariff. It is often thought that rent seeking is more severe in some developing countries where rules are not well enforced and officials are willing to take bribes in exchange for the licenses.

3. Auctioning the Quota A third possibility for allocating the rents that come from the quota is for the government of the importing country to auction off the quota licenses. This occurred in Australia and New Zealand during the 1980s. In Australia, the auctions covered imports of textiles, apparel, footwear, and motor vehicles. The quota auctions used for imports of textiles and apparel in Australia were an alternative to the Multifibre Arrangement (MFA). Auctions of import quotas have also been proposed in the United States but have never actually occurred.[15] In a well-organized, competitive auction, the revenue collected should exactly equal the value of the rents, so that area c would be earned by the Home government. Using the auction method to allocate quota rents, the net loss in domestic welfare due to the quota becomes

Fall in consumer surplus:	$-(a + b + c + d)$
Rise in producer surplus:	$+a$
Auction revenue earned at Home	$+c$
Net effect on Home welfare:	$-(b + d)$

The net effect on Home welfare in this case is the deadweight loss of $(b + d)$, which is once again the same loss as incurred from a tariff.

4. "Voluntary" Export Restraint The final possibility for allocating quota rents is for the government of the importing country to give authority for implementing the quota to the government of the *exporting* country. Because the exporting

---

[15] The proposals to auction import quotas in the United States were made during the 1980s; see C. Fred Bergsten, 1987, *Auction Quotas and United States Trade Policy* (Washington, D.C.: Peterson Institute for International Economics). Government auctions have occurred in the United States for bandwidth in radio frequencies and also for off-shore oil drilling.

country allocates the quota among its own producers, this is sometimes called a **"voluntary" export restraint (VER), or a "voluntary" restraint agreement (VRA).** In the 1980s the United States used this type of arrangement to restrict Japanese automobile imports. In that case, Japan's Ministry of International Trade and Industry (MITI), a government agency that implements Japan's trade policies, told each Japanese auto manufacturer how much it could export to the United States. In this case, the quota rents are earned by foreign producers, so the loss in Home welfare equals

Fall in consumer surplus:	$-(a + b + c + d)$
Rise in producer surplus:	$+a$
Net effect on Home welfare:	$-(b + c + d)$

The VER gives a higher net loss $(b + c + d)$ for the importer than does a tariff because the quota rents are earned by foreign exporters. This result raises the question of why VERs are used at all. One answer is that by giving the quota rents to firms in the exporting country that country is much less likely to retaliate by adopting import tariffs or quotas of its own. In other words, the transfer of quota rents to the exporter becomes a way to avoid a tariff or quota war.

Costs of Import Quotas in the United States Table 8-3 presents some estimates of the home deadweight losses, along with the quota rents, for major U.S. quotas in the years around 1985. In all cases except dairy, the rents were earned by foreign exporters. We discuss the case of automobiles in the next chapter, for which the quota rents earned by foreigners range from $2 billion to $8 billion. Textiles and apparel also had very large quota rents and U.S. deadweight losses (about $5 billion each) under the MFA. In addition, the MFA imposed large losses on the Foreign exporting countries, due to rent-seeking activities by exporters to obtain the quota permits. Adding up the costs shown in Table 8-3, the total U.S. deadweight loss from these quotas was in the range of $8 billion to $12 billion annually in the mid-1980s, whereas the quota rents transferred to foreigners were another $7 billion to $17 billion annually.

Some, but not all, of these costs for the United States are no longer relevant today. The quota in automobiles ceased being applied after 1987 because Japanese producers built plants in the United States and therefore reduced their imports. The quotas in the steel industry were replaced by the "safeguard" tariffs that President Bush temporarily imposed from 2002 to 2003. But the quotas used in sugar remain, and while the MFA expired on January 1, 2005, it has been replaced by a new set of quotas with China. There is the prospect of continuing losses for the United States due to quotas in these industries, as we discuss in the next application to textiles and apparel.

TABLE 8-3

Annual Cost of U.S. Import Protection ($ billions)
Shown here are estimates of the deadweight losses and quota rents due to U.S. import quotas in the 1980s, for the years around 1985. Many of these quotas are no longer in place today.

	U.S. Deadweight Loss (area $b + d$)	Quota Rents (area c)
Automobiles	0.2–1.2	2.2–7.9
Dairy	1.4	0.25*
Steel	0.1–0.3	0.7–2.0
Sugar	0.1	0.4–1.3
Textiles and apparel	4.9–5.9	4.0–6.1
Import tariffs	1.2–3.4	0
Total	7.9–12.3	7.3–17.3

* In dairy the quota rents are earned by U.S. importers and so are not included in the total.

Source: Robert Feenstra, Summer 1992, "How Costly Is Protectionism?" Journal of Economic Perspectives, 159–178.

CHAPTER 8 ■ IMPORT TARIFFS AND QUOTAS UNDER PERFECT COMPETITION **269**

APPLICATION

China and the Multifibre Arrangement

One of the founding principles of GATT was that countries should not use quotas to restrict imports (see Article XI of **Side Bar: Key Provisions of the GATT**). The Multifibre Arrangement (MFA), organized under the auspices of the GATT in 1974, was a major exception to that principle and allowed the industrial countries to restrict imports of textile and apparel products from the developing countries. Importing countries could join the MFA and arrange quotas bilaterally (i.e., after negotiating with exporters) or unilaterally (on their own). In practice, the import quotas established under the MFA were very detailed and specified the amount of each textile and apparel product that each developing country could sell to countries including Canada, Europe, and the United States.

Although the amount of the quotas was occasionally revised upward, it did not keep up with the increasing ability of new supplying countries to sell. Under the Uruguay Round of WTO negotiations held from 1986 to 1994, developing countries were able to negotiate an end to this system of import quotas. The MFA expired on January 1, 2005. The biggest potential supplier of textile and apparel products was China, so the expiration of the MFA meant that China could export as much as it wanted to other countries—or so it thought. The potential for a huge increase in exports from China posed a problem for many other countries. Some developing countries expected that rising exports from China would compete with their own export of apparel items, on which many workers depended for their livelihood. The large producers in importing countries were also concerned with the potential rise in Chinese exports because it could lead to the loss of jobs for their own workers in textiles and apparel.

Growth in Exports from China Immediately after January 1, 2005, exports of textiles and apparel from China grew rapidly. For example, exports of Chinese tights and pantyhose to the European Union increased by 2,000% in January and February, as compared with a year earlier; imports of pullovers and jerseys from China jumped nearly 1,000%; and imports of trousers more than tripled. Overall in 2005, China's textile and apparel imports to the United States rose by more than 40% as compared with the year before, as shown in Figure 8-12, where we include the top 20 exporters to the U.S. market.[16] In panel (a), we show the change in the value of textile and apparel imports from each country. The surge of imports from China came at the expense of some higher-cost exporters, such as South Korea, Hong Kong, and Taiwan, whose exports to the United States declined by 10% to 20%.

In panel (b) of Figure 8-12, we show the percentage change in the prices of textiles and apparel products from each country, depending on whether the products were "constrained goods," subject to the MFA quota before January 1, 2005. China has the largest drop in prices from 2004 to 2005, 38% in the "constrained goods" categories. Many other countries also experienced a substantial fall in their prices due to the end of the MFA quota: 18% for Pakistan; 16% for Cambodia; and 8% to 9% for the Philippines, Bangladesh, India, Indonesia, and Sri Lanka. A drop in price due to the removal of the import quota is exactly what we predict from the theory, as we move

---

[16] Figure 8-12 and the welfare estimates in the following paragraphs are from James Harrigan and Geoffrey Barrows, 2009, "Testing the Theory of Trade Policy: Evidence from the Abrupt End of the Multifibre Arrangement," *The Review of Economics and Statistics*, vol. 91(2), pp. 282–294.

FIGURE 8-12

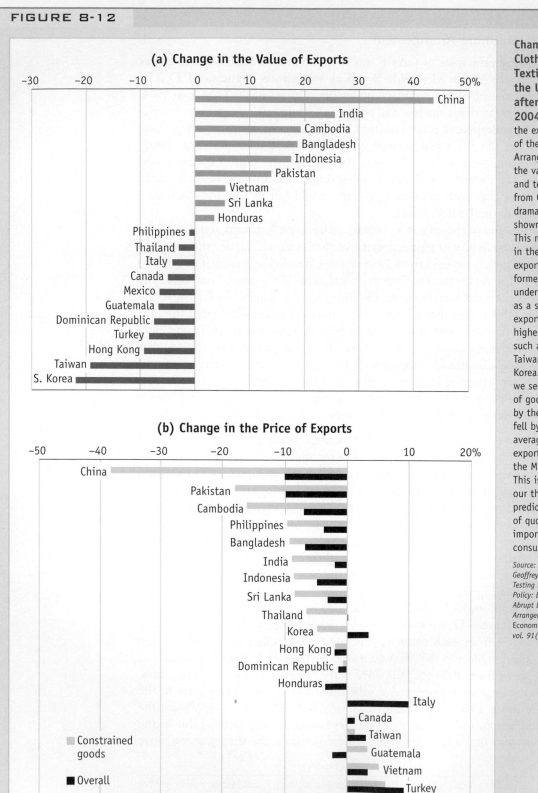

Changes in Clothing and Textile Exports to the United States after the MFA, 2004–2005 After the expiration of the Multifibre Arrangement (MFA), the value of clothing and textile exports from China rose dramatically, as shown in panel (a). This reflects the surge in the quantity of exports that were formerly constrained under the MFA as well as a shift to Chinese exports from other, higher-cost producers such as Hong Kong, Taiwan, and South Korea. In panel (b), we see that the prices of goods constrained by the MFA typically fell by more than the average change in export prices after the MFA's expiry. This is exactly what our theory of quotas predicts: The removal of quotas lowers import prices for consumers.

Source: James Harrigan and Geoffrey Barrows, 2009, Testing the Theory of Trade Policy: Evidence from the Abrupt End of the Multifibre Arrangement, The Review of Economics and Statistics, vol. 91(2), pp. 282–294.

from the price P_2 in Figure 8-11 to the free-trade price P^W. Surprisingly, a few countries in Figure 8-12 show increases in their prices, such as Mexico. However, less than 1% of Mexico's sales of textiles and apparel to the United States were constrained by the quota, so that price increase does not appear to be due to the removal of the MFA.

Welfare Cost of MFA Given the drop in prices in 2005 from countries selling to the United States, it is possible to estimate the welfare loss due to the MFA. The United States did not auction the quota licenses for textiles and apparel so the quota rents were earned by foreign exporting firms. That means the welfare loss for the United States due to the MFA is the area $(b + c + d)$ in Figure 8-11. Using the price drops from 2004 to 2005, that area is estimated to be in the range of $6.5 billion to $16.2 billion in 2005.[17] The simple average of these estimates is $11.4 billion as the total cost to the United States. To put that welfare loss in perspective, there were 111 million households in the United States in 2005, and the typical household spent about $1,400 on apparel. Dividing the loss of $11.4 billion by the 111 million households, we obtain about $100 per household, or 7% of their annual spending on apparel as the welfare cost of the MFA.[18]

Import Quality Besides the overall decline in prices, there was also an interesting pattern to the price drops: the prices of textile and apparel products dropped the most (in percentage terms) for the lower-priced items. So, an inexpensive T-shirt coming from China and priced at $1 had a price drop of more than 38% (more than 38¢), whereas a more expensive item priced at $10 experienced a price drop of less than 38% (less than $3.80). As a result, U.S. demand shifted toward the lower-priced items imported from China: there was "quality downgrading" in the exports from China.

To understand why this quality downgrading occurred, it is easiest to think about the problem in reverse: when a quota like the MFA is applied, what is the effect on quality? The MFA, like most other quotas, was applied to the *quantity* of the import sent to each country: it was applied to yards of cloth, or number of shirts, or dozens of pairs of socks, and so on. Faced with a quota of that type, the exporting firm would have an incentive to *upgrade* the type of cloth, shirts, or socks that it sells, since selling a higher value for the same quantity will still meet the quota limitation. So when the MFA starts, we expect to see "quality upgrading" in the exports for each country. By the same logic, when the MFA was removed, there was "quality downgrading" in the exports from China to the United States and exports from other countries, too.

Reaction of the United States and Europe The surge in exports from China to the United States and Europe was short-lived, however. The European Union threatened to impose new quotas on Chinese exports, and in response, China agreed on June 11, 2005, to "voluntary" export restraints that would limit its growth of textile exports to about 10% per year through the end of 2008. For the United States, the ability to negotiate a new system of quotas with China had been guaranteed by a special agreement with China when it joined the WTO in 2001. Under this agreement, China was limited to a 7.5% annual growth in its textile exports to the United States, from 2005 to 2008. This temporary

---

[17] Notice that this range of estimates for 2005 is comparable with (but wider than) the range of estimates for the welfare costs of textiles and apparel in Table 8-3, which is $8.9 billion to $12 billion for 1985, obtained by adding up the deadweight loss and the quota rents.

[18] In comparison, there were 737,000 U.S. workers in the textile and apparel industries in 2004, with an average annual salary of $31,500. If we divide the total loss of $11.4 billion by all these workers, we obtain about $15,500 per job protected in the U.S. industry, or about one-half of the annual salary of each worker.

quota expired at the end of 2008, at which time we might have expected the U.S. textile and apparel industry to renew its call for quota protection once again. But because of the worldwide recession, Chinese exports in this industry were much lower in 2009 than they had been in earlier years. For that reason, China indicated that it would not accept any further limitation on its ability to export textile and apparel products to the United States and to Europe, and both these quotas expired. ■

6 Conclusions

A tariff on imports is the most commonly used trade policy tool. In this chapter, we have studied the effect of tariffs on consumers and producers in both importing and exporting countries. We have looked at several different cases. First, we assumed that the importing country is so small that it does not affect the world price of the imported good. In that case, the price faced by consumers and producers in the importing country will rise by the full amount of the tariff. With a rise in the consumer price, there is a drop in consumer surplus; and with a rise in the producer price, there is a gain in producer surplus. In addition, the government collects revenue from the tariff. When we add together all these effects—the drop in consumer surplus, gain in producer surplus, and government revenue collected—we still get a *net loss* for the importing country. We have referred to that loss as the deadweight loss resulting from the tariff.

The fact that a small importing country always has a net loss from a tariff explains why most economists oppose the use of tariffs. Still, this result leaves open the question of why tariffs are used. One reason that tariffs are used, despite their deadweight loss, is that they are an easy way for governments to raise revenue, especially in developing countries. A second reason is politics: the government might care more about protecting firms than avoiding losses for consumers. A third reason is that the small-country assumption may not hold in practice: countries may be large enough importers of a product so that a tariff will affect its world price. In this large-country case, the decrease in imports demanded due to the tariff causes foreign exporters to lower their prices. Of course, consumer and producer prices in the importing country still go up, since these prices include the tariff, but they rise by less than the full amount of the tariff. We have shown that if we add up the drop in consumer surplus, gain in producer surplus, and government revenue collected, it is possible for a small tariff to generate welfare gains for the importing country.

Still, any gain for the importer in this large-country case comes at the expense of the foreign exporters. For that reason, the use of a tariff in the large-country case is sometimes called a "beggar thy neighbor" policy. We have found that the drop in the exporter's welfare due to the tariff is greater than the gain in the importer's welfare. Therefore, the world loses overall because of the tariff. This is another reason that most economists oppose their use.

In addition to an import tariff, we have also studied import quotas, which restrict the quantity of imports into a country. The WTO has tried to limit the use of import quotas and has been somewhat successful. For example, the Multifibre Arrangement (MFA) was a complex system of quotas intended to restrict the import of textiles and apparel into many industrialized countries. It was supposed to end on January 1, 2005, but both the United States and the European Union then established new quotas against imports of textiles and apparel from China, which expired at the end of 2008. The United States continues to have a quota on imports of sugar, and up until very recently, the European Union had a quota and then a discriminatory tariff on imports of bananas (that "banana war" has now ended). These are some of the best-known import quotas, and there are other examples, too.

Under perfect competition, the effect of applying an import quota is similar to the effect of applying an import tariff: they both lead to an increase in the domestic price in the importing country, with a loss for consumers and a gain for producers. One difference, however, is that under a tariff the government in the importing country collects revenue, whereas under a quota, whoever is able to bring in the import earns the difference between the domestic and world prices, called "quota rents." For example, if firms in the importing country have the licenses to bring in imports, then they earn the quota rents. Alternatively, if resources are wasted by firms trying to capture these rents, then there is an additional deadweight loss. It is more common, however, for the foreign exporters to earn the quota rents, as occurs under a "voluntary" export restraint, administered by the foreign government. A fourth possibility is that the government in the importing country auctions the quota licenses, in which case it earns the equivalent of the quota rents as auction revenue; this case is identical to the tariff in its welfare outcome.

KEY POINTS

1. The government of a country can use laws and regulations, called "trade policies," to affect international trade flows. An import tariff, which is a tax at the border, is the most commonly used trade policy.

2. The rules governing trade policies in most countries are outlined by the General Agreement on Tariffs and Trade (GATT), an international legal convention adopted after World War II to promote increased international trade. Since 1995 the new name for the GATT is the World Trade Organization (WTO).

3. In a small country, the quantity of imports demanded is assumed to be very small compared with the total world market. For this reason, the importer faces a fixed world price. In that case, the price faced by consumers and producers in the importing country will rise by the full amount of the tariff.

4. The use of a tariff by a small importing country always leads to a net loss in welfare. We call that loss the "deadweight loss."

5. A discriminatory tariff, which is applied against just one exporting country (such as the tariff on tires applied against China), has a higher deadweight loss than an equal tariff applied against all exporters.

6. In a large country, the decrease in imports demanded due to the tariff causes foreign exporters to lower their prices. Consumer and producer prices in the importing country still go up, since these prices include the tariff, but they rise by less than the full amount of the tariff (since the exporter price falls).

7. The use of a tariff for a large country can lead to a net gain in welfare because the price charged by the exporter has fallen; this is a terms-of-trade gain for the importer.

8. The "optimal tariff" is the tariff amount that maximizes welfare for the importer. For a small country, the optimal tariff is zero since any tariff leads to a net loss. For a large country, however, the optimal tariff is positive.

9. The formula for the optimal tariff states that it depends inversely on the foreign export supply elasticity. If the foreign export supply elasticity is high, then the optimal tariff is low, but if the foreign export supply elasticity is low, then the optimal tariff is high.

10. "Import quotas" restrict the quantity of a particular import, thereby increasing the domestic price, increasing domestic production, and creating a benefit for those who are allowed to import the quantity allotted. These benefits are called "quota rents."

11. Assuming perfectly competitive markets for goods, quotas are similar to tariffs since the restriction in the amount imported leads to a higher domestic price. However, the welfare implications of quotas are different from those of tariffs depending on who earns the quota rents. These rents might be earned by firms in the importing country (if they have the licenses to import the good), or by firms in the exporting country (if the foreign government administers the quota), or by the government in the importing country (if it auctions off the quota licenses). The last case is most similar to a tariff, since the importing government earns the revenue.

KEY TERMS

trade policy, p. 234
import tariff, p. 234
import quota, p. 234
export subsidy, p. 234
dumping, p. 235
safeguard provision, p. 236
escape clause, p. 236
regional trade agreements, p. 236
free-trade areas, p. 236
customs unions, p. 236
consumer surplus, p. 236
producer surplus, p. 236

small country, p. 239
import demand curve, p. 241
deadweight loss, p. 245
production loss, p. 245
consumption loss, p. 246
dispute settlement procedure, p. 251
tariff war, p. 251
discriminatory tariff, p. 252
large country, p. 256
terms of trade, p. 258
terms-of-trade gain, p. 259

optimal tariff, p. 259
Multifibre Arrangement (MFA), p. 263
equivalent import tariff, p. 264
quota rents, p. 265
quota licenses, p. 265
rent seeking, p. 267
"voluntary" export restraint (VER), p. 268
"voluntary" restraint agreement (VRA), p. 268

PROBLEMS

1. The following questions refer to **Side Bar: Key Provisions of the GATT.**

   a. If the United States applies a tariff to a particular product (e.g., steel) imported from one country, what is the implication for its steel tariffs applied to all other countries according to the "most favored nation" principle?

   b. Is Article XXIV an exception to most favored nation treatment? Explain why or why not.

   c. Under the GATT articles, instead of a tariff, can a country impose a quota (quantitative restriction) on the number of goods imported? What has been one exception to this rule in practice?

2. Consider a small country applying a tariff t to imports of a good like that represented in Figure 8-5.

   a. Suppose that the country decides to *reduce* its tariff to t'. Redraw the graphs for the Home and import markets and illustrate this change. What happens to the quantity and price of goods produced

at Home? What happens to the quantity of imports?

   b. Are there gains or losses to domestic consumer surplus due to the reduction in tariff? Are there gains or losses to domestic producer surplus due to the reduction in tariff? How is government revenue affected by the policy change? Illustrate these on your graphs.

   c. What is the overall gain or loss in welfare due to the policy change?

3. Consider a large country applying a tariff t to imports of a good like that represented in Figure 8-9.

   a. How does the export supply curve in panel (b) compare with that in the small-country case? Explain why these are different.

   b. Explain how the tariff affects the price paid by consumers in the *importing* country and the price received by producers in the *exporting* country. Use graphs to illustrate how the prices are affected if (i) the export supply curve is very elastic (flat) or (ii) the export supply curve is inelastic (steep).

4. Consider a large country applying a tariff t to imports of a good like that represented in Figure 8-9. How does the size of the terms-of-trade gain compare with the size of the deadweight loss when (i) the tariff is very small and (ii) the tariff is very large? Use graphs to illustrate your answer.

5. a. If the foreign export supply is perfectly elastic, what is the optimal tariff Home should apply to increase welfare? Explain.

   b. If the foreign export supply is less than perfectly elastic, what is the formula for the optimal tariff Home should apply to increase welfare?

   c. What happens to Home welfare if it applies a tariff higher than the optimal tariff?

6. Rank the following in ascending order of Home welfare and justify your answers. If two items are equivalent, indicate this accordingly.

   a. Tariff of t in a small country corresponding to the quantity of imports M

   b. Tariff of t in a large country corresponding to the same quantity of imports M

   c. Tariff of t' in a large country corresponding to the quantity of imports $M' > M$

7. Rank the following in ascending order of Home welfare and justify your answers. If two items are equivalent, indicate this accordingly.

   a. Tariff of t in a small country corresponding to the quantity of imports M

   b. Quota with the same imports M in a small country, with quota licenses distributed to Home firms and no rent seeking

   c. Quota of M in a small country with quota licenses auctioned to Home firms

   d. Quota of M in a small country with the quota given to the exporting firms

   e. Quota of M in a small country with quota licenses distributed to rent-seeking Home firms

8. Why did President George W. Bush suspend the U.S. tariffs on steel 17 months ahead of schedule?

9. What provision of U.S. trade law was used by President Barack Obama to apply a tariff on tires imported from China? Does this provision make it easier or harder to apply a tariff than Section 201?

10. No U.S. tire producers joined in the request for the tariff on tires in 2009. Rather, the petition for a tariff on tires imported from China was brought by the United Steelworkers of America, the union who represents workers in the tire industry. Why did major tire manufacturers operating in the United States, such as Goodyear, Michelin, Cooper, and Bridgestone, not support the tariff?

11. Suppose Home is a small country. Use the graphs below to answer the questions.

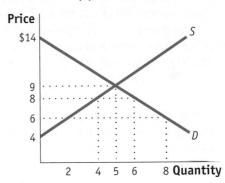

(a) Home Market

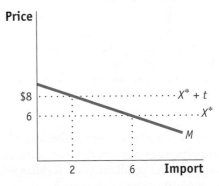

(b) Import Market

   a. Calculate Home consumer surplus and producer surplus in the absence of trade.

   b. Now suppose that Home engages in trade and faces the world price, $P^* = \$6$. Determine the consumer and producer surplus under free trade. Does Home benefit from trade? Explain.

   c. Concerned about the welfare of the local producers, the Home government imposes a tariff in the amount of $2 (i.e., $t = \$2$). Determine the net effect of the tariff on the Home economy.

12. Refer to the graphs in Problem 11. Suppose that instead of a tariff, Home applies an import quota limiting the amount Foreign can sell to 2 units.

   a. Determine the net effect of the import quota on the Home economy if the quota licenses are allocated to local producers.

   b. Calculate the net effect of the import quota on Home welfare if the quota rents are earned by Foreign exporters.

   c. How do your answers to parts (a) and (b) compare with part (c) of Problem 11?

13. Consider a small country applying a tariff t as in Figure 8-5. Instead of a tariff on *all* units imported, however, we will suppose that the tariff applies only to *imports* in excess of some quota amount M' (which is less than the total imports). This is called a "tariff-rate quota" (TRQ) and is commonly used on agricultural goods.

   a. Redraw Figure 8-5, introducing the quota amount M'. Remember that the tariff applies only to imports *in excess* of this amount. With this in mind, what is the rectangle of tariff revenue collected? What is the rectangle of quota rents? Explain briefly what quota rents mean in this scenario.

   b. How does the use of a TRQ rather than a tariff at the same rate affect Home welfare? How does the TRQ, as compared with a tariff at the same rate, affect Foreign welfare? Does it depend on who gets the quota rents?

   c. Based on your answer to (b), why do you think TRQs are used quite often?

14. Consider the following hypothetical information pertaining to a country's imports, consumption, and production of T-shirts following the removal of the MFA quota:

	With MFA	Without MFA (Free Trade)
World price ($/shirt)	2.00	2.00
Domestic price ($/shirt)	2.50	2.00
Domestic consumption (million shirts/year)	100	125
Domestic production (million shirts/year)	75	50
Imports (million shirts/year)	25	75

   a. Graph the effects of the quota removal on domestic consumption and production.

   b. Determine the gain in consumer surplus from the removal of the quota.

   c. Determine the loss in producer surplus from the removal of the quota.

   d. Calculate the quota rents that were earned under the quota.

   e. Determine how much the country has gained from removal of the quota.

15. Suppose that a producer in China is constrained by the MFA to sell a certain number of shirts, regardless of the type of shirt. For a T-shirt selling for $2.00 under free trade, the MFA quota leads to an increase in price to $2.50. For a dress shirt selling for $10.00, the MFA will also lead to an increase in price.

	With MFA	Without MFA (Free Trade)
Domestic price of T-shirt ($/shirt)	2.50	2.00
Domestic price of dress shirt ($/shirt)	?	10.00

   a. Suppose that the MFA leads to an increase in the price of dress shirts from $10 to $11. Will the producer be willing to export both T-shirts and dress shirts? (Remember that only a fixed number of shirts can be exported, but of any type.) Explain why or why not.

   b. For the producer to be willing to sell *both* T-shirts and dress shirts, what must be the price of dress shirts under the MFA?

   c. Based on your answer to part (b), calculate the price of dress shirts *relative* to T-shirts before and after the MFA. What has happened to the relative price due to the MFA?

   d. Based on your answer to part (c), what will happen to the relative demand in the United States for dress shirts versus T-shirts from this producer due to the MFA?

   e. Thinking now of the total export bundle of this producer, does the MFA lead to quality upgrading or downgrading? How about the removal of the MFA?

N E T W O R K

Go to http://www.wto.org/ and find out how many countries belong to the WTO. Which countries joined most recently?

Go to http://www.usitc.gov/trade_remedy/about_global_safeguard_inv.htm and read about Section 201 and Section 421 of U.S. Trade Act of 1974. What are the differences between these sections? What are some recent cases?

Import Tariffs and Quotas Under Imperfect Competition

We've brought trade cases against China at nearly twice the rate as the last administration—and it's made a difference. . . . But we need to do more. . . . Tonight, I'm announcing the creation of a Trade Enforcement Unit that will be charged with investigating unfair trading practices in countries like China.

President Barack Obama, State of the Union Address, January 24, 2012

If the case of heavyweight motorcycles is to be considered the only successful escape-clause [tariff], it is because it caused little harm and it helped Harley-Davidson get a bank loan so it could diversify.
John Suomela, chief economist, U.S. International Trade Commission, 1993[1]

1 Tariffs and Quotas with Home Monopoly

2 Tariffs with Foreign Monopoly

3 Dumping

4 Policy Response to Dumping

5 Infant Industry Protection

6 Conclusions

In a recent survey of economists, 87% agreed with the statement "tariffs and import quotas usually reduce general economic welfare."[2] It is no exaggeration to say that this belief has been a guiding principle of the international institutions established to govern the world economy since World War II, especially the World Trade Organization. That belief is the message from the previous chapter, which showed that the application of tariffs and quotas will reduce welfare for a small country. We also found that although a large country might gain from the application of a tariff, that gain would come at the expense of its trading partners, so the *world* as a whole would still lose. So there is really no good economic argument for the use of tariffs or quotas.

Still, you might wonder if that is really the whole story. We gave several recent examples of tariffs and quotas in the previous chapter, and there are many more examples if we look to countries at earlier stages in their development. For example, during

[1] Cited in Douglas A. Irwin, 2002, *Free Trade under Fire* (Princeton, NJ: Princeton University Press), pp. 136–137.
[2] Robert Whaples and Jac C. Heckelman, 2005, "Public Choice Economics: Where Is There Consensus?" *American Economist*, 49(1), pp. 66–78.

the 1800s the United States had average tariff rates that fluctuated between 10% and 50%. These tariff rates were at times even higher than the Smoot-Hawley tariff that was applied during the Great Depression and peaked at 25%. Likewise, countries that industrialized after World War II, like Japan, South Korea, and Taiwan, started with high tariffs and quotas that were eliminated only slowly and incompletely. More recently, China had very high tariffs before it joined the World Trade Organization in 2001, and it still enjoys tariffs in some industries that are well above those in the United States or Europe.

These observations can lead us to wonder if there are some arguments in favor of tariffs that are missing from our treatment in the previous chapter, which dealt with perfect competition. Do the effects of trade policies differ when markets are imperfectly competitive? We explore the answer to this question in this chapter and the next.

This question received a good deal of attention from trade economists in the 1980s, in a body of research that became known as **strategic trade policy.** The idea of strategic trade policy was that government trade policies could give a strategic advantage to Home firms in imperfectly competitive markets that would enable them to compete more effectively with Foreign firms. Initially, the economists writing in this area thought that their research would challenge the idea that free trade is best for a country. As more research was done, however, supporters of strategic trade policy theory realized that the new arguments were limited in their scope: in some cases, the use of tariffs or quotas would backfire and harm the Home country, and in other cases, their use would give results similar to the large country case we analyzed in the previous chapter. We will give examples of both outcomes.

When countries use strategic trade policies to try to give advantage to their own firms, other countries trading with them often regard these policies as "unfair" and may respond to these policies in some way. That is the idea behind the first quotation at the beginning of the chapter from President Barack Obama, who announced in 2012 that the United States would establish a special "Trade Enforcement Unit that will be charged with investigating unfair trading practices in countries like China." In the previous chapter we already discussed one trade policy recently used by the United States against China: the tariff on imports of Chinese tires (in effect from September 2009 to September 2012). In this chapter we discuss other examples, including tariffs recently imposed by the United States against imports of solar panels from China. To explore strategic trade policy, we need to abandon the assumption that markets are perfectly competitive, an assumption that was central to the treatment of the tariff and quota in the previous chapter. Instead, we need to allow for imperfect competition, which we defined in Chapter 6 as the market conditions that exist when firms have influence over the price that they charge and can charge a price above marginal costs for their goods. Recall that imperfect competition can arise when there is a small number of producers, as in a monopoly or oligopoly, or if products are differentiated from one another, as we assumed in our model of monopolistic competition in Chapter 6. In this chapter, we use the extreme case of a single producer—a Home or Foreign monopoly—to see how tariffs and quotas affect prices, trade, and welfare. In practice, imperfectly competitive industries often have more than one firm, but focusing on the monopoly case will give us the clearest sense of how the effects of these policy tools differ from those under perfect competition.

In this chapter, we begin by analyzing the effects of tariffs and quotas under the assumption of a Home monopoly. In the perfectly competitive framework of the previous chapter, quotas and tariffs have an equivalent impact on Home prices. In imperfectly competitive markets, however, these two trade policy instruments have *different* effects on Home prices, so the choice of which, if any, trade policy to implement must take these different effects into account.

The second case we analyze is a Foreign monopoly that exports to the Home market. We analyze the effect of an import tariff applied by the Home country and find that the tariff has effects similar to those in the large-country case under perfect competition (described in the previous chapter) in which the Home country can potentially gain from the tariff. A specific example of a Foreign monopolist is the Foreign **discriminating monopoly,** which charges a lower price to Home than to firms in its own local market and is therefore **dumping** its product into the Home market. A tariff applied against the Foreign discriminating monopoly is called an **antidumping duty.** Because of the special way in which antidumping duties are applied, they are unlikely to result in gains for the Home country and instead result in losses.

The final case we analyze is an **infant industry** at Home, by which we mean an industry that is too young to have achieved its lowest costs. Often these industries comprise a small number of firms. In our analysis, we assume there is only one firm, so it is again a case of Home monopoly. The special feature of this Home firm is that it cannot compete effectively under free trade, because the world price is below its minimum cost of production today, so the firm makes a loss. But by increasing its output today, the firm will learn how to produce its output more efficiently, and therefore have lower costs in the future, so that it can compete profitably at the world price. One way to achieve this end is for the government to step in and offer assistance—such as with a tariff—that will help the firm to survive long enough to achieve lower, world-competitive costs. This policy is called an "infant industry tariff."

Although we include the infant industry tariff argument in this chapter on strategic trade policy, it is actually a much older argument, dating back to the writings of John Stuart Mill (1806–1873). We will give several examples of infant industries, including the automobile industry in China, which imposed very high tariffs and quotas on foreign cars before it joined the WTO in 2001. We also use this argument to analyze the tariff used in the 1980s to protect Harley-Davidson motorcycles in the United States. The key policy question for an infant industry is whether a government should impose a temporary tariff today, to protect infant industry from competition, thereby keeping it in business long enough for it to learn how to achieve lower costs (and thus competitive prices) in the future.

1 Tariffs and Quotas with Home Monopoly

To illustrate the effect of tariffs and quotas under imperfect competition, we start with the example of a Home monopolist—a single firm selling a homogeneous good. In this case, free trade introduces many more firms selling the same good into the Home market, which eliminates the monopolist's ability to charge a price higher than its marginal cost (the free-trade equilibrium results in a perfectly competitive Home market). As we will show, tariffs and quotas affect this trade equilibrium differently because of their impact on the Home monopoly's **market power,** the extent to which a firm can set its price. With a tariff, the Home monopolist still competes against a large number of importers and so its market power is limited. With an import quota, on the other hand, once the quota limit is reached, the monopolist is the only producer able to sell in the Home market; hence, the Home monopolist can exercise its market power once again. This section describes the Home equilibrium with and without trade and explains this difference between tariffs and quotas.

No-Trade Equilibrium

We begin by showing in Figure 9-1 the no-trade equilibrium with a Home monopoly. The Home demand curve is shown by D, and because it is downward-sloping, as the monopolist sells more, the price will fall. This fall in price means that the extra revenue earned by the monopolist from selling one more unit is less than the price: the extra revenue earned equals the price charged for that unit *minus* the fall in price times the quantity sold of all earlier units. The extra revenue earned from selling one more unit, the **marginal revenue**, is shown by curve MR in Figure 9-1.

To maximize its profits, the monopolist produces at the point where the marginal revenue MR earned from selling one more unit equals the marginal cost MC of producing one more unit. As shown in Figure 9-1, the monopolist produces quantity Q^M. Tracing up from Q^M to point A on the demand curve and then over to the price axis, the price charged by the monopolist is P^M. This price enables the monopolist to earn the highest profits and is the monopoly equilibrium in the absence of international trade.

Comparison with Perfect Competition We can contrast the monopoly equilibrium with the perfect competition equilibrium in the absence of trade. Instead of a single firm, suppose there are many firms in the industry. We assume that all these firms combined have the same cost conditions as the monopolist, so the industry marginal cost is identical to the monopolist's marginal cost curve of MC. Because a perfectly competitive industry will produce where price equals marginal cost, the

FIGURE 9-1

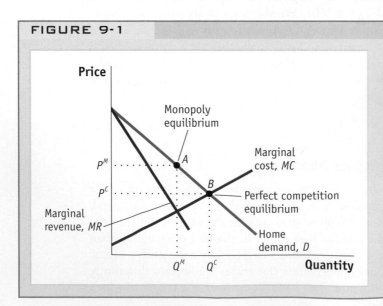

No-Trade Equilibrium In the absence of international trade, the monopoly equilibrium at Home occurs at the quantity Q^M, where marginal revenue equals marginal cost. From that quantity, we trace up to the demand curve at point A, and the price charged is P^M. Under perfect competition, the industry supply curve is MC, so the no-trade equilibrium would occur where demand equals supply (point B), at the quantity Q^C and the price P^C.

MC curve is also the industry supply curve. The no-trade equilibrium under perfect competition occurs where supply equals demand (the quantity Q^C and the price P^C). The competitive price P^C is less than the monopoly price P^M, and the competitive quantity Q^C *is* higher than the monopoly quantity Q^M. This comparison shows that in the absence of trade, the monopolist restricts its quantity sold to increase the market price. Under free trade, however, the monopolist cannot limit quantity and raise price, as we investigate next.

Free-Trade Equilibrium

Suppose now that Home engages in international trade. We will treat Home as a "small country," which means that it faces the fixed world price of P^W. In Figure 9-2, we draw a horizontal line at that price and label it as X^*, the Foreign export supply curve. At that price, Foreign will supply any quantity of imports (because Home is a small country, the Foreign export supply is perfectly elastic). Likewise, the Home monopolist can sell as much as it desires at the price of P^W (because it is able to export at the world price) but cannot charge any more than that price at Home. If it charged a higher price, Home consumers would import the product instead. Therefore, the Foreign supply curve of X^* is *also* the new demand curve facing the Home monopolist: the original no-trade Home demand of D no longer applies.

Because this new demand curve facing the Home monopolist is horizontal, the Home firm's new marginal revenue curve is the same as the demand curve, so $X^* = MR^*$. To understand why this is so, remember that marginal revenue equals the price earned from selling one more unit *minus* the fall in price times the quantity sold of all earlier units. For a horizontal demand curve, there is no fall in price from selling more because additional units sell for P^W, the same price for which the earlier units sell. Thus, marginal revenue is the price earned from selling another unit, P^W. Therefore,

FIGURE 9-2

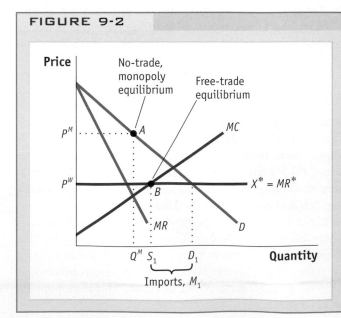

Home Monopoly's Free-Trade Equilibrium Under free trade at the fixed world price P^W, Home faces Foreign export supply of X^* at that price. Because the Home firm cannot raise its price above P^W without losing all its customers to imports, X^* is now also the demand curve faced by the Home monopolist. Because the price is fixed, the marginal revenue MR^* is the same as the demand curve. Profits are maximized at point B, where marginal revenue equals marginal costs. The Home firm supplies S_1, and Home consumers demand D_1. The difference between these is imports, $M_1 = D_1 - S_1$. Because the Home monopoly now sets its price at marginal cost, the same free-trade equilibrium holds under perfect competition.

the demand curve X^* facing the Home monopolist is identical to the marginal revenue curve; the no-trade marginal revenue of MR no longer applies.

To maximize profits under the new free-trade market conditions, the monopolist will set marginal revenue equal to marginal cost (point B in Figure 9-2) and will supply S_1 at the price P^W. At the price P^W, Home consumers demand D_1, which is more than the Home supply of S_1. The difference between demand and supply is Home imports under free trade, or $M_1 = D_1 - S_1$.

Comparison with Perfect Competition Let us once again compare this monopoly equilibrium with the perfect competition equilibrium, now with free trade. As before, we assume that the cost conditions facing the competitive firms are the same as those facing the monopolist, so the industry supply curve under perfect competition is equal to the monopolist's marginal cost curve of MC. With free trade and perfect competition, the industry will supply the quantity S_1, where the price P^W equals marginal cost, and consumers will demand the quantity D_1 at the price P^W. Under free trade for a small country, then, a Home monopolist produces the same quantity and charges the same price as a perfectly competitive industry. The reason for this result is that free trade for a small country eliminates the monopolist's control over price; that is, its market power. It faces a horizontal demand curve, equal to marginal revenue, at the world price of P^W. Because the monopolist has no control over the market price, it behaves just as a competitive industry (with the same marginal costs) would behave.

This finding that free trade eliminates the Home monopolist's control over price is an extra source of gains from trade for the Home consumers because of the reduction in the monopolist's market power. We have already seen this extra gain in Chapter 6, in which we first discussed monopolistic competition. There we showed that with free trade, a monopolistically competitive firm faces more-elastic demand curves for its differentiated product, leading it to expand output and lower its prices. The same result holds in Figure 9-2, except that now we have assumed that the good produced by the Home monopolist and the imported good are homogeneous products, so they sell at exactly the same price. Because the Home good and the import are homogeneous, the demand curve X^* facing the Home monopolist in Figure 9-2 is perfectly elastic, leading the monopolist to behave in the same way under free trade as in a competitive industry.

Effect of a Home Tariff

Now suppose the Home country imposes a tariff of t dollars on imports, which increases the Home price from P^W to $P^W + t$. In Figure 9-3, the effect of the tariff is to raise the Foreign export supply curve from X^* to $X^* + t$. The Home firm can sell as much as it desires at the price of $P^W + t$ but cannot charge any more than that price. If it did, the Home consumers would import the product. Thus, the Foreign supply curve of $X^* + t$ is also the new demand curve facing the Home monopolist.

Because this new demand curve is horizontal, the new marginal revenue curve is once again the same as the demand curve, so $MR^* = X^* + t$. The reasoning for this result is similar to the reasoning under free trade: with a horizontal demand curve, there is no fall in price from selling more, so the Home firm can sell as much as it desires at the price of $P^W + t$. So the demand curve $X^* + t$ facing the Home monopolist is identical to its marginal revenue curve.

FIGURE 9-3

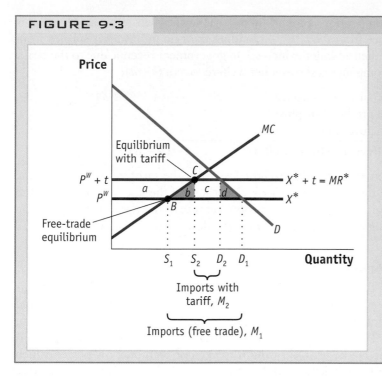

Imports with tariff, M_2

Imports (free trade), M_1

Tariff with Home Monopoly Initially under free trade at the fixed world price P^W, the monopolist faces the horizontal demand curve (and marginal revenue curve) X^*, and profits are maximized at point B. When a tariff t is imposed, the export supply curve shifts up since Foreign firms must charge $P^W + t$ in the Home market to earn P^W. This allows the Home monopolist to increase its domestic price to $P^W + t$, but no higher, since otherwise it would lose all its customers to imports. The result is fewer imports, M_2, because Home supply S increases and Home demand D decreases. The deadweight loss of the tariff is measured by the area $(b + d)$. This result is the same as would have been obtained under perfect competition because the Home monopolist is still charging a price equal to its marginal cost.

To maximize profits, the monopolist will once again set marginal revenue equal to marginal costs, which occurs at point C in Figure 9-3, with the price $P^W + t$ and supply of S_2. At the price $P^W + t$, Home consumers demand D_2, which is more than Home supply of S_2. The difference between demand and supply is Home imports, $M_2 = D_2 - S_2$. The effect of the tariff on the Home monopolist relative to the free-trade equilibrium is to raise its production from S_1 to S_2 and its price from P^W to $P^W + t$. The supply increase in combination with a decrease in Home demand reduces imports from M_1 to M_2.

Comparison with Perfect Competition Let us compare this monopoly equilibrium with the tariff to what would happen under perfect competition. The tariff-inclusive price facing a perfectly competitive industry is $P^W + t$, the same price faced by the monopolist. Assuming that the industry supply curve under perfect competition is the same as the monopolist's marginal cost MC, the competitive equilibrium is where price equals marginal cost, which is once again at the quantity S_2 and the price $P^W + t$. So with a tariff, a Home monopolist produces the same quantity and charges the same price as would a perfectly competitive industry. This result is similar to the result we found under free trade. This similarity occurs because the tariff still limits the monopolist's ability to raise its price: it can raise the price to $P^W + t$ but no higher because otherwise consumers will import the product. Because the monopolist has limited control over its price, it behaves in the same way a competitive industry would when facing the tariff.

Home Loss Due to the Tariff Because the tariff and free-trade equilibria are the same for a Home monopoly and a perfectly competitive industry, the deadweight loss from the tariff is also the same. As we learned in the previous chapter, the deadweight loss under perfect competition is found by taking the total fall in consumer surplus due to the rise in price from P^W to $P^W + t$, adding the gain in producer surplus from the rise in price, and then adding the increase in government revenue due to the tariff. Summing all these components shows a net welfare loss of $(b + d)$:

Fall in consumer surplus:	$-(a + b + c + d)$
Rise in producer surplus:	$+a$
Rise in government revenue:	$+c$
Net effect on Home welfare:	**$-(b + d)$**

Under Home monopoly, the deadweight loss from the tariff is the same. Home consumers still have the loss of $(a + b + c + d)$ because of the rise in price, while the Home monopolist gains the amount a in profits because of the rise in price. With the government collecting area c in tariff revenue, the deadweight loss is still area $(b + d)$.

Effect of a Home Quota

Let us now contrast the tariff with an import quota imposed by the Home government. As we now show, the quota results in a higher price for Home consumers, and therefore a larger Home loss, than would a tariff imposed on the same equilibrium quantity of imports. The reason for the higher costs is that the quota creates a "sheltered" market for the Home firm, allowing it to exercise its monopoly power, which leads to higher prices than under a tariff. Economists and policy makers are well aware of this additional drawback to quotas, which is why the WTO has encouraged countries to replace many quotas with tariffs.

To show the difference between the quota and tariff with a Home monopoly, we use Figure 9-4, in which the free-trade equilibrium is at point B and the tariff equilibrium is at point C (the same points that appear in Figure 9-3). Now suppose that instead of the tariff, a quota is applied. We choose the quota so that it equals the imports under the tariff, which are M_2. Since imports are fixed at that level, the effective demand curve facing the Home monopolist is the demand curve D *minus* the amount M_2. We label this effective demand curve $D - M_2$. Unlike the situation under the tariff, the monopolist now retains the ability to influence its price: it can choose the optimal price and quantity along $D - M_2$. We graph the marginal revenue curve MR for the effective demand curve $D - M_2$. The profit-maximizing position for the monopolist is where marginal revenue equals marginal cost, at point E, with price P_3 and supply S_3.

Let us now compare the tariff equilibrium, at point C, with the quota equilibrium, at point E. It will definitely be the case that the price charged under the quota is higher, $P_3 > P^W + t$. The higher price under the quota reflects the ability of the monopolist to raise its price once the quota amount has been imported. The higher price occurs even though the quota equilibrium *has the same level of imports as the tariff*, M_2. Therefore, the effects of a tariff and a quota are no longer equivalent as they were under perfect competition: the quota enables a monopolist to exercise its market power and raise its price.

What about the quantity produced by the monopolist? Because the price is higher under the quota, the monopolist will definitely produce a lower quantity under the quota, $S_3 < S_2$. What is more surprising, however, is that it is even possible that the quota could lead to a fall in output as compared with free trade: in Figure 9-4, we have shown $S_3 < S_1$. This is not a necessary result, however, and instead we could

FIGURE 9-4

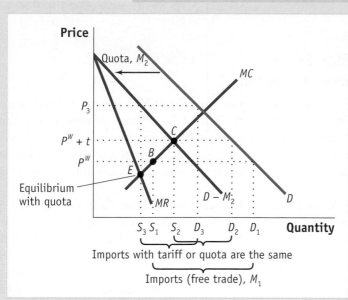

Effect of Quota with Home Monopoly Under free trade, the Home monopolist produces at point B and charges the world price of P^W. With a tariff of t, the monopolist produces at point C and charges the price of $P^W + t$. Imports under the tariff are $M_2 = D_2 - S_2$. Under a quota of M_2, the demand curve shifts to the left by that amount, resulting in the demand $D - M_2$ faced by the Home monopolist. That is, after M_2 units are imported, the monopolist is the only firm able to sell at Home, and so it can choose a price anywhere along the demand curve $D - M_2$. The marginal revenue curve corresponding to $D - M_2$ is MR, and so with a quota, the Home monopolist produces at point E, where MR equals MC. The price charged at point E is $P_3 > P^W + t$, so the quota leads to a higher Home price than the tariff.

have drawn the MR curve so that $S_3 > S_1$. It is surprising that the case $S_3 < S_1$ is even possible because it suggests that workers in the industry would *fail to be protected* by the quota; that is, employment could fall because of the reduction in output under the quota. We see, then, that the quota can have undesirable effects as compared with a tariff when the Home industry is a monopoly.

Home Loss Due to the Quota Our finding that Home prices are higher with a quota than with a tariff means that Home consumers suffer a greater fall in surplus because of the quota. On the other hand, the Home monopolist earns higher profit from the quota because its price is higher. We will not make a detailed calculation of the deadweight loss from the quota with Home monopoly because it is complicated. We can say, however, that the deadweight loss will always be *higher* for a quota than for a tariff because the Home monopolist will always charge a higher price. That higher price benefits the monopolist but harms Home consumers and creates an extra deadweight loss because of the exercise of monopoly power.

Furthermore, the fact that the Home monopolist is charging a higher price also increases the quota rents, which we defined in the previous chapter as the ability to import goods at the world price and sell them at the higher Home price (in our example, this is the difference between P_3 and P^W times the amount of imports M_2). In the case of Home monopoly, the quota rents are greater than government revenue would be under a tariff. Recall that quota rents are often given to Foreign countries in the case of "voluntary" export restraints, when the government of the exporting country implements the quota, or else quota rents can even be wasted completely when rent-seeking activities occur. In either of these cases, the increase in quota rents adds to Home's losses if the rents are given away or wasted.

In the next application, we examine a quota used in the United States during the 1980s to restrict imports of Japanese cars. Because the car industry has a small number of producers, it is imperfectly competitive. So our predictions from the case of monopoly discussed previously can serve as a guide for what we expect in the case of Home oligopoly.

APPLICATION

U.S. Imports of Japanese Automobiles

A well-known case of a "voluntary" export restraint (VER) for the United States occurred during the 1980s, when the U.S. limited the imports of cars from Japan. To understand why this VER was put into place, recall that during the early 1980s, the United States suffered a deep recession. That recession led to less spending on durable goods (such as automobiles), and as a result, unemployment in the auto industry rose sharply.

In 1980 the United Automobile Workers and Ford Motor Company applied to the International Trade Commission (ITC) for protection under Article XIX of the General Agreement on Tariffs and Trade (GATT) and Section 201 of U.S. trade laws. As described in the previous chapter, Section 201 protection can be given when increased imports are a "substantial cause of serious injury to the domestic industry," where "substantial cause" must be "not less than any other cause." In fact, the ITC determined that the U.S. recession was a more important cause of injury to the auto industry than increased imports. Accordingly, it did not recommend that the auto industry receive protection.

With this negative determination, several members of Congress from states with auto plants continued to pursue import limits by other means. In April 1981 Senators John Danforth from Missouri and Lloyd Bentsen from Texas introduced a bill in the U.S. Senate to restrict imports. Clearly aware of this pending legislation, the Japanese government announced on May 1 that it would "voluntarily" limit Japan's export of automobiles to the U.S. market. For the period April 1981 to March 1982, this limit was set at 1.83 million autos. After March 1984 the limit was raised to 2.02 million and then to 2.51 million vehicles annually. By 1988 imports fell *below* the VER limit because Japanese companies began assembling cars in the United States.

We are interested in whether American producers were able to exercise their monopoly power and raise their prices under the quota restriction. We are also interested in how much import prices increased. To measure the increase in import prices, we need to take into account a side effect of the 1980 quota: it led to an increase in the features of Japanese cars being sold in the United States such as size, weight, horsepower, and so on, or what we call an increase in quality.[3] The overall increase in auto import prices during the 1980s needs to be broken up into the increases due to (1) the quality upgrading of Japanese cars; (2) the "pure" increase in price because of the quota, which equals the quota rents; and (3) any price increase that would have occurred anyway, even if the auto industry had not been subject to protection.

Price and Quality of Imports The impact of the VER on the price of Japanese cars is shown in Figure 9-5. Under the VER on Japanese car imports, the average price rose from $5,150 to $8,050 between 1980 and 1985. Of that $2,900 increase, $1,100

---

[3] The previous chapter discusses the quality effect of a U.S. import quota on Chinese textile and apparel exports to the United States.

FIGURE 9-5

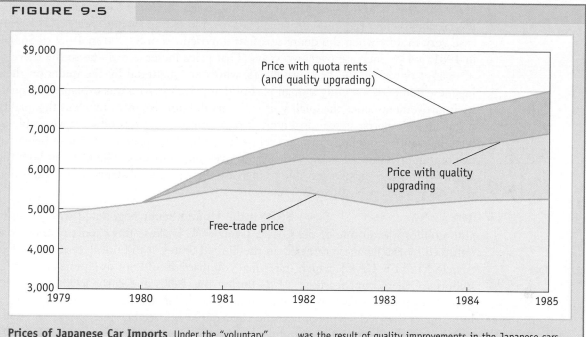

Prices of Japanese Car Imports Under the "voluntary" export restraint (VER) on Japanese car imports, the average price rose from $5,150 to $8,050 between 1980 and 1985. Of that $2,900 increase, $1,100 was the result of quota rent increases earned by Japanese producers. Another $1,650 was the result of quality improvements in the Japanese cars, which became heavier and wider, with improved horsepower, transmissions, and so on. The remaining $150 is the amount that import prices would have risen under free trade.

was the result of quota rents earned by Japanese producers in 1984 and 1985. Another $1,650 was from quality improvements in the Japanese cars, which became heavier and wider, with improved horsepower, transmissions, and so on. The remaining $150 is the amount that import prices would have risen under free trade.

Quota Rents If we multiply the quota rents of $1,100 per car by the imports of about 2 million cars, we obtain total estimated rents of $2.2 billion, which is the lower estimate of the annual cost of quota rents for automobiles. The upper estimate of $7.9 billion comes from also including the increase in price for European cars sold in the United States. Although European cars were not restricted by a quota, they did experience a significant increase in price during the quota period; that increase was due to the reduced competition from Japanese producers.

The Japanese firms benefited from the quota rents that they received. In fact, their stock prices *rose* during the VER period, though only after it became clear that the Japanese Ministry of International Trade and Industry would administer the quotas to each producer (so that the Japanese firms would capture the rents). Moreover, because each producer was given a certain number of cars it could export to the United States, but no limit on the value of the cars, producers had a strong incentive to export more expensive models. That explains the quality upgrading that occurred during the quota, which was when Japanese producers started exporting more luxurious cars to the United States.

Price of U.S. Cars What happened to the prices of American small cars during this period? Under the VER on Japanese car imports, the average price of U.S. cars rose very rapidly when the quota was first imposed: from $4,200 in 1979 to $6,000 in 1981, a 43% increase over two years. That price increase was due to the exercise of market power by the U.S. producers, who were sheltered by the quota on their Japanese competitors. Only a small part of that price increase was explained by quality improvements since the quality of U.S. cars did not rise by as much as the quality of Japanese imports, as seen in Figure 9-6. So the American producers were able to benefit from the quota by raising their prices, and the Japanese firms also benefited by combining a price increase with an improvement in quality. The fact that both the Japanese and U.S. firms were able to increase their prices substantially indicates that the policy was very costly to U.S. consumers.

The GATT and WTO The VER that the United States negotiated with Japan in automobiles was outside of the GATT framework: because this export restraint was enforced by the Japanese rather than the United States, it did not necessarily violate Article XI of the GATT, which states that countries should not use quotas to restrict imports. Other countries used VERs during the 1980s and early 1990s to restrict imports in products such as automobiles and steel. All these cases were exploiting a loophole in the GATT agreement whereby a quota enforced by the *exporter* was not a violation of the GATT. This loophole was closed when the WTO was established in 1995. Part of the WTO agreement states that "a Member shall not seek, take or maintain any voluntary export restraints, orderly marketing arrangements or any other

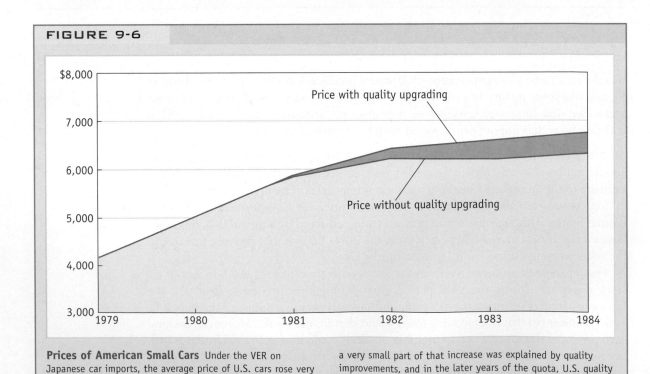

FIGURE 9-6

Prices of American Small Cars Under the VER on Japanese car imports, the average price of U.S. cars rose very rapidly when the quota was first imposed: from $4,200 in 1979 to $6,000 in 1981, or a 43% increase over two years. Only a very small part of that increase was explained by quality improvements, and in the later years of the quota, U.S. quality did not rise by as much as it did in the Japanese imports.

similar measures on the export or the import side. These include actions taken by a single Member as well as actions under agreements, arrangements and understandings entered into by two or more Members."[4] As a result of this rule, VERs can no longer be used unless they are a part of some other agreement in the WTO.[5] ■

2 Tariffs with Foreign Monopoly

So far in this chapter, we have studied the effects of a tariff or quota under Home monopoly. For simplicity, we have focused on the case in which the Home country is small, meaning that the world price is fixed. Let us now examine a different case, in which we treat the Foreign exporting firm as a monopoly. We will show that applying a tariff under a Foreign monopoly leads to an outcome similar to that of the large-country case in the previous chapter; that is, the tariff will lower the price charged by the Foreign exporter. In contrast to the small-country case, a tariff may now benefit the Home country.

Foreign Monopoly

To focus our attention on the Foreign monopolist selling to the Home market, we will assume that there is no competing Home firm, so the Home demand D in Figure 9-7 is supplied entirely by exports from the Foreign monopolist. This assumption is not very realistic because normally a tariff is being considered when there is also a Home firm. But ignoring the Home firm will simplify our analysis while still helping us to understand the effect of an imperfectly competitive Foreign exporter.

Free-Trade Equilibrium In addition to the Home demand of D in Figure 9-7, we also show Home marginal revenue of MR. Under free trade, the Foreign monopolist maximizes profits in its export market where Home marginal revenue MR equals Foreign marginal cost MC^*, at point A in Figure 9-7. It exports the amount X_1 to the Home market and charges the price of P_1.

Effect of a Tariff on Home Price If the Home country applies an import tariff of t dollars, then the marginal cost for the exporter to sell in the Home market increases to $MC^* + t$. With the increase in marginal costs, the new intersection with marginal revenue occurs at point B in Figure 9-7, and the import price rises to P_2.

Under the case we have drawn in Figure 9-7, where the MR curve is steeper than the demand curve, the increase in price from P_1 to P_2 is *less than* the amount of the tariff t. In other words, the vertical rise along the MR curve caused by the tariff (the vertical distance from point A to B, which is the tariff amount) corresponds to a smaller vertical rise moving along the demand curve (the difference between P_1 and P_2). In this case, the net-of-tariff price received by the Foreign exporter, which is $P_3 = P_2 - t$, has *fallen* from its previous level of P_1 because the price rises by less than the tariff. Since the Home country is paying a lower net-of-tariff price P_3 for its import, it has experienced a terms-of-trade gain as a result of the tariff.

---

[4] From Article 11, "Prohibition and Elimination of Certain Measures," of the WTO Agreement on Safeguards.
[5] An example is the quota in textiles that the United States negotiated with China in 2005, which was allowed under the provisions of China's entry into the WTO, as discussed in the previous chapter.

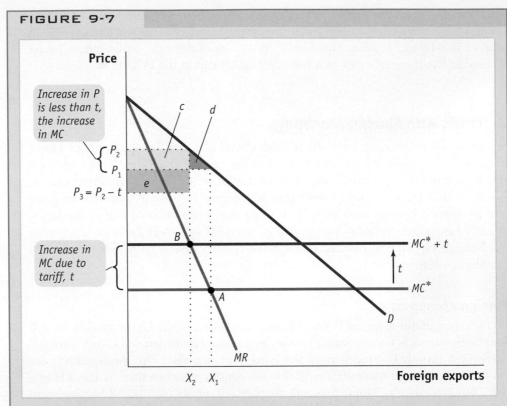

FIGURE 9-7

Tariff with a Foreign Monopoly Under free trade, the Foreign monopolist charges prices P_1 and exports X_1, where marginal revenue MR equals marginal cost MC^*. When an antidumping duty of t is applied, the firm's marginal cost rises to $MC^* + t$, so the exports fall to X_2 and the Home price rises to P_2. The decrease in consumer surplus is shown by the area $c + d$, of which c is collected as a portion of tax revenues. The net-of-tariff price that the Foreign exporter receives falls to $P_3 = P_2 - t$. Because the net-of-tariff price has fallen, the Home country has a terms-of-trade gain, area e. Thus, the total welfare change depends on the size of the terms-of-trade gain e relative to the deadweight loss d.

The effect of the tariff applied against a Foreign monopolist is similar to the effect of a tariff imposed by a large country (analyzed in the previous chapter). There we found that a tariff would lower the price charged by Foreign firms because the quantity of exports decreased, so Foreign marginal costs also fell. Now that we have assumed a Foreign monopoly, we get the same result but for a different reason. The marginal costs of the monopolist are constant at MC^* in Figure 9-7, or $MC^* + t$ including the tariff. The rise in marginal costs from the tariff leads to an increase in the tariff-inclusive Home price as the quantity of Home imports falls, but the monopolist chooses to increase the Home price by *less than* the full amount of the tariff. In that way, the quantity exported to Home does not fall by as much as it would if the Foreign firm increased its price by the full amount of the tariff. So, the Foreign firm is making a strategic decision to absorb part of the tariff itself (by lowering its price from P_1 to P_3) and pass through only a portion of the tariff to the Home price (which rises from P_1 to P_2).

Summary To preserve its sales to Home, the Foreign monopolist chooses to increase the Home price by less than the amount of the tariff. This result depends on having MR steeper than D, as shown in Figure 9-7. It is not necessarily the case that MR is steeper than D for all demand curves, but this is usually how we draw them. In the case of a straight-line demand curve such as the one drawn in Figure 9-7, for example, the marginal revenue curve is exactly twice as steep as the demand curve.[6] In this case, the Home import price rises by exactly half of the tariff amount, and the Foreign export price falls by exactly half of the tariff amount.

Effect of the Tariff on Home Welfare With the rise in the Home price from P_1 to P_2, consumers are worse off. The decline in consumer surplus equals the area between the two prices and to the left of the demand curve, which is $(c + d)$ in Figure 9-7. The increase in the Home price would in principle benefit Home firms, but we have assumed for simplicity that there is no Home producer, so we do not need to keep track of the change in Home producer surplus. We do need to take account of tariff revenue collected by the Home government, however. Tariff revenue equals the amount of the tariff t times Foreign exports X_2, which is area $(c + e)$. Therefore, the effect of the tariff on Home welfare is

Fall in Home consumer surplus:	$-(c + d)$
Rise in Home government revenue:	$+(c + e)$
Net change in Home welfare:	**$+(e - d)$**

We can interpret the area e as the terms-of-trade gain for the Home country, whereas the area d is the deadweight loss from the tariff. If the terms-of-trade gain exceeds the deadweight loss, $e > d$, then Home gains overall by applying a tariff, similar to the result we found for a large country in the previous chapter. As we discussed there, we can expect the terms-of-trade gain to exceed the deadweight loss when the tariff is small, so that Home welfare initially rises for small tariffs. Welfare then reaches some maximum level and then falls as the tariff is increased beyond its optimal level. The same results apply when a tariff is placed against a Foreign monopolist, provided that the marginal revenue curve is steeper than demand, as we have assumed.

To illustrate how a tariff can affect the prices charged by a Foreign monopolist in practice, we once again use the automobile industry as an example. Because there are a small number of firms in that industry, it is realistic to expect them to respond to a tariff in the way that a Foreign monopolist would.

APPLICATION

Import Tariffs on Japanese Trucks

We have found that in the case of a Foreign monopolist, Home will experience a terms-of-trade gain from a small tariff. The reason for this gain is that the Foreign firm will lower its net-of-tariff price to avoid too large an increase in the price paid by consumers in the importing country. To what extent do Foreign exporters actually behave that way?

To answer this question, we can look at the effects of the 25% tariff on imported Japanese compact trucks imposed by the United States in the early 1980s and still in place today. The history of how this tariff came to be applied is an interesting story. Recall from the application earlier in the chapter that in 1980 the United Automobile

---

[6] You are asked to show this result in Problem 6.

Workers and Ford Motor Company applied for a tariff under Article XIX of the GATT and Section 201 of U.S. trade law. They were turned down for the tariff, however, because the International Trade Commission determined that the U.S. recession was a more important cause of injury in the auto industry than growing imports. For cars, the "voluntary" export restraint (VER) with Japan was pursued. But for compact trucks imported from Japan, it turned out that another form of protection was available.

At that time, most compact trucks from Japan were imported as cab/chassis with some final assembly needed. These were classified as "parts of trucks," which carried a tariff rate of only 4%. But another category of truck—"complete or unfinished trucks"—faced a tariff rate of 25%. That unusually high tariff was a result of the "chicken war" between the United States and West Germany in 1962. At that time, Germany joined the European Economic Community (EEC) and was required to adjust its external tariffs to match those of the other EEC countries. This adjustment resulted in an increase in its tariff on imported U.S. poultry. In retaliation, the United States increased its tariffs on trucks and other products, so the 25% tariff on trucks became a permanent item in the U.S. tariff code.

That tariff created an irresistible opportunity to reclassify the Japanese imports and obtain a substantial increase in the tariff, which is exactly what the U.S. Customs Service did with prodding from the U.S. Congress. Effective August 21, 1980, imported cab/chassis "parts" were reclassified as "complete or unfinished" trucks. This reclassification raised the tariff rate on all Japanese trucks from 4% to 25%, which remains in effect today.

How did Japanese exporters respond to the tariff? According to one estimate, the tariff on trucks was only *partially* reflected in U.S. prices: of the 21% increase, only 12% (or about 60% of the increase) was passed through to U.S. consumer prices; the other 9% (or about 40% of the increase) was absorbed by Japanese producers.[7] Therefore, this tariff led to a terms-of-trade gain for the United States, as predicted by our theory: for a straight-line demand curve (as in Figure 9-7), marginal revenue is twice as steep, and the tariff will lead to an equal increase in the Home import price and decrease in the Foreign export price.[8] The evidence for Japanese trucks is not too different from what we predict in that straight-line case.

Notice that the terms-of-trade gain from the tariff applied on a Foreign monopolist is similar to the terms-of-trade gain from a tariff applied by a "large" country, as we discussed in the previous chapter. In both cases, the Foreign firm or industry absorbs part of the tariff by lowering its price, which means that the Home price rises by less than the full amount of the tariff. If the terms-of-trade gain, measured by the area *e* in Figure 9-7 exceed the deadweight loss *d*, then the Home country gains from the tariff. This is our first example of strategic trade policy that leads to a potential gain for Home.

In principle, this potential gain arises from the tariff that the United States has applied on imports of compact trucks, and that is still in place today. But some economists feel that this tariff has the undesirable side effect of encouraging the U.S. automobile industry to focus on the sales of trucks, since compact trucks have higher

---

[7] Robert Feenstra, 1989, "Symmetric Pass-Through of Tariffs and Exchange Rates under Imperfect Competition: An Empirical Test," *Journal of International Economics*, 27(1/2), 25–45.
[8] You are asked to derive this relationship numerically in Problem 7 at the end of the chapter.

prices because of the tariff.[9] That strategy by U.S. producers can work when gasoline prices are low, so consumers are willing to buy trucks. At times of high prices, however, consumers instead want fuel-efficient cars, which have not been the focus of the American industry. So high fuel prices can lead to a surge in imports and fewer domestic sales, exactly what happened after the oil price increase of 1979 and again in 2008, just before the financial crisis. Some industry experts believe that these factors contributed to the losses faced by the American industry during the crisis, as explained in **Headlines: The Chickens Have Come Home to Roost.** ■

HEADLINES

The Chickens Have Come Home to Roost

This article discusses the history of the 25% tariff that still applies to U.S. imports of lightweight trucks. The author argues that this tariff caused some of the difficulties in the U.S. automobile industry today.

Although we call them the big three automobile companies, they have basically specialized in building trucks. This left them utterly unable to respond when high gas prices shifted the market towards hybrids and more fuel efficient cars.

One reason is that Americans like to drive SUVs, minivans and small trucks when gasoline costs $1.50 to $2.00 a gallon. But another is that the profit margins have been much higher on trucks and vans because the US protects its domestic market with a twenty-five percent tariff. By contrast, the import tariff on regular automobiles is just 2.5 percent and US duties from tariffs on all imported goods are just one percent of the overall value of merchandise imports. Since many of the inputs used to assemble trucks are not subject to tariffs anywhere near 25 percent—US tariffs on all goods average only 3.5 percent—the effective protection and subsidy equivalent of this policy has been huge.

It is no wonder much of the initial foray by Japanese transplants to the US involved setting up trucks assembly plants, no wonder that Automakers only put three doors on SUVs so they can qualify as vans and no wonder that Detroit is so opposed to the US-Korea Free Trade Agreement that would eventually allow trucks built in Korea Duty-Free access to the US market.

What accounts for this distinctive treatment of trucks? An accident of history that shows how hard it is for the government to withdraw favors even when they have no sound policy justification.

It all comes down to the long forgotten chicken wars of the 1960s. In 1962, when implementing the European Common Market, the Community denied access to US chicken producers. In response after being unable to resolve the issue diplomatically, the US responded with retaliatory tariffs that included a twenty five percent tariffs on trucks that was aimed at the German Volkswagen

Combi-Bus that was enjoying brisk sales in the US.

Since the trade (GATT) rules required that retaliation be applied on a nondiscriminatory basis, the tariffs were levied on all truck-type vehicles imported from all countries and have never been removed. Over time, the Germans stopped building these vehicles and today the tariffs are mainly paid on trucks coming from Asia. The tariffs have bred bad habits, steering Detroit away from building high-quality automobiles towards trucks and trucklike cars that have suddenly fallen into disfavor.

If Congress wants an explanation for why the big three have been so uncompetitive it should look first at the disguised largess it has been providing them with for years. It has taken a long time—nearly 47 years—but it seems that eventually the chickens have finally come home to roost.

Source: Robert Lawrence, guest blogger on Dani Rodrik's weblog, posted May 4, 2009. http://www.rodrik.typepad.com/dani_rodriks_weblog/2009/05/the-chickens-have-come-home-to-roost.html.

---

[9] Larger trucks and SUVs imported into the United States do not have this tariff, but there is another reason why U.S. firms sell many of these products: fuel-economy regulations, which apply to cars but not to trucks or SUVs. These regulations require that the fleet of cars and light trucks sold by U.S. firms meet a certain average fuel economy, which is expensive for the firms to achieve. Since larger trucks and SUVs do not have to meet the same standard, they are cheaper to produce.

3 Dumping

With imperfect competition, firms can charge *different* prices across countries and will do so whenever that pricing strategy is profitable. Recall that we define imperfect competition as the firm's ability to influence the price of its product. With international trade, we extend this idea: not only can firms charge a price that is higher than their marginal cost, they can also choose to charge different prices in their domestic market than in their export market. This pricing strategy is called **price discrimination** because the firm is able to choose how much different groups of customers pay. To discriminate in international trade, there must be some reason that consumers in the high-price market cannot import directly from the low-cost market; for example, that reason could be transportation costs or tariffs between the markets.

Dumping occurs when a foreign firm sells a product abroad at a price that is either less than the price it charges in its local market, or less than its average cost to produce the product. Dumping is common in international trade, even though the rules of the World Trade Organization (WTO) discourage this activity. Under the rules of the WTO, an importing country is entitled to apply a tariff any time a foreign firm dumps its product on a local market. Such a tariff is called an antidumping duty. We study antidumping duties in detail in the next section. In this section, we want to ask the more general question: Why do firms dump at all? It might appear at first glance that selling abroad at prices less than local prices or less than the average costs of production must be unprofitable. Is that really the case? It turns out the answer is no. It can be profitable to sell at low prices abroad, even at prices lower than average cost.

Discriminating Monopoly To illustrate how dumping can be profitable, we use the example of a Foreign monopolist selling both to its local market and exporting to Home. As described previously, we assume that the monopolist is able to charge different prices in the two markets; this market structure is sometimes called a discriminating monopoly. The diagram for a Foreign discriminating monopoly is shown in Figure 9-8. The local demand curve for the monopolist is D^*, with marginal revenue MR^*. We draw these curves as downward-sloping for the monopolist because to induce additional consumers to buy its product, the monopolist lowers its price (downward-sloping D^*), which decreases the revenue received from each additional unit sold (downward-sloping MR^*).

In the export market, however, the Foreign firm will face competition from other firms selling to the Home market. Because of this competition, the firm's demand curve in the export market will be more elastic; that is, it will lose more customers by raising prices than it would in its local market. If it faces enough competition in its export market, the Foreign monopolist's export demand curve will be horizontal at the price P, meaning that it cannot charge more than the competitive market price. If the price for exports is fixed at P, selling more units does not depress the price or the extra revenue earned for each unit exported. Therefore, the marginal revenue for exports equals the price, which is labeled as P in Figure 9-8.

Equilibrium Condition We can now determine the profit-maximizing level of production for the Foreign monopolist, as well as its prices in each market. For the discriminating monopoly, profits are maximized when the following condition holds:

$$MR = MR^* = MC^*$$

FIGURE 9-8

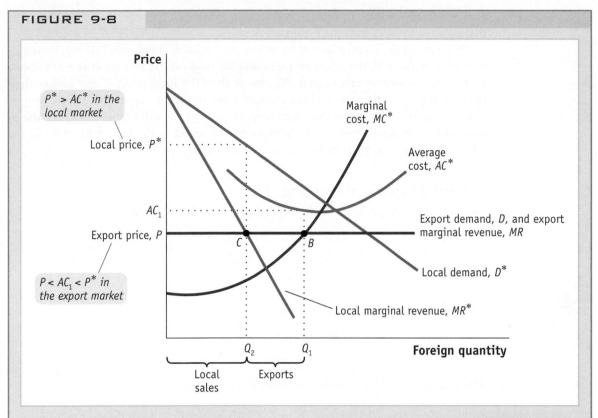

Foreign Discriminating Monopoly The Foreign monopoly faces different demand curves and charges different prices in its local and export markets. Locally, its demand curve is D^* with marginal revenue MR^*. Abroad, its demand curve is horizontal at the export price, P, which is also its marginal revenue of MR. To maximize profits, the Foreign monopolist chooses to produce the quantity Q_1 at point B, where local marginal cost equals marginal revenue in the export market, $MC^* = MR$. The quantity sold in the local market, Q_2 (at point C), is determined where local marginal revenue equals export marginal revenue, $MR^* = MR$. The Foreign monopolist sells Q_2 to its local market at P^*, and $Q_1 - Q_2$ to its export market at P. Because $P < P^*$ (or alternatively $P < AC_1$), the firm is dumping.

This equation looks similar to the condition for profit maximization for a single-market monopolist, which is marginal revenue equals marginal cost, except that now the marginal revenues should also be equal in the two markets.

We illustrate this equilibrium condition in Figure 9-8. If the Foreign firm produces quantity Q_1, at point B, then the marginal cost of the last unit equals the export marginal revenue MR. But not all of the supply Q_1 is exported; some is sold locally. The amount sold locally is determined by the equality of the firm's local marginal revenue MR^* with its export marginal revenue MR (at point C), *and* the equality of its local marginal cost MC^* with MR (at point B). All three variables equal P, though the firm charges the price P^* (by tracing up the Foreign demand curve) to its local consumers. Choosing these prices, the profit-maximization equation just given is satisfied, and the discriminating monopolist is maximizing profits across both markets.

The Profitability of Dumping The Foreign firm charges P^* to sell quantity Q_2 in its local market (from Q_2, we go up to the local demand curve D^* and across to the price). The local price exceeds the price P charged in the export market. Because the

Foreign firm is selling the same product at a lower price to the export market, it is dumping its product into the export market.

What about the comparison of its export price with average costs? At total production of Q_1 at point B, the firm's average costs are read off the average cost curve above that point, so average costs equal AC_1, lower than the local price P^* but higher than the export price P. Because average costs AC_1 are above the export price P, the firm is also dumping according to this cost comparison. But we will argue that the Foreign firm still earns positive profits from exporting its good at the low price of P. To see why that is the case, we turn to a numerical example.

Numerical Example of Dumping

Suppose the Foreign firm has the following cost and demand data:

$$
\begin{aligned}
\text{Fixed costs} &= \$100 \\
\text{Marginal costs} &= \$10 \text{ per unit} \\
\text{Local price} &= \$25 \\
\text{Local quantity} &= 10 \\
\text{Export price} &= \$15 \\
\text{Export quantity} &= 10
\end{aligned}
$$

The profits earned from selling in its local market are

$$\underbrace{(\$25 \cdot 10)}_{\text{Revenue}} - \underbrace{\$10 \cdot 10}_{\substack{\text{Variable} \\ \text{cost}}} - \underbrace{\$100}_{\substack{\text{Fixed} \\ \text{cost}}} = \underbrace{\$50}_{\text{Profits}}$$

Notice that the average costs for the firms are

$$\text{Average costs} = \frac{\$200}{10} = \$20$$

Now suppose that this firm sells an additional 10 units abroad, at the price of $15, which is less than its average cost of production. It is *still* worthwhile to sell these extra units because profits become

$$\underbrace{(\$25 \cdot 10 + \$15 \cdot 10)}_{\text{Revenue}} - \underbrace{\$10 \cdot 20}_{\substack{\text{Variable} \\ \text{cost}}} - \underbrace{\$100}_{\substack{\text{Fixed} \\ \text{cost}}} = \underbrace{\$100}_{\text{Profits}}$$

Profits have increased because the extra units are sold at $15 but produced at a *marginal cost* of $10, which is less than the price received in the export market. Therefore, each unit exported will increase profits by the difference between the price and marginal costs. Thus, even though the export price is less than average costs, profits still rise from dumping in the export market.

4 Policy Response to Dumping

In the previous section, we learned that dumping is not unusual: a Foreign monopolist that discriminates between its local and export markets by charging different prices in each can end up charging a lower price in its export market. Furthermore, the price it charges in its export market might be less than its average cost of production and still be profitable. Our interest now is in understanding the policy response in the Home importing country.

Antidumping Duties

Under the rules of the WTO, an importing country is entitled to apply a tariff—called an antidumping duty—any time that a foreign firm is dumping its product. An imported product is being dumped if its price is below the price that the exporter charges in its own local market; if the exporter's local price is not available, then dumping is determined by comparing the import price to (1) a price charged for the product in a third market or (2) the exporter's average costs of production.[10] If one of these criteria is satisfied, then the exporting firm is dumping and the importing country can respond with antidumping duty. The amount of the antidumping duty is calculated as the difference between the exporter's local price and the "dumped" price in the importing country.

There are many examples of countries applying antidumping duties. In 2006 the European Union applied tariffs of 10% to 16.5% on shoes imported from China and 10% on shoes imported from Vietnam. These antidumping duties were justified because of the low prices at which the imported shoes are sold in Europe. These duties expired in 2011. A recent example of antidumping duties from the United States are those applied to the imports of solar panels from China, discussed next.

APPLICATION

United States Imports of Solar Panels from China

Since November 2012, the United States has applied antidumping duties on the imports of solar panels from China. In addition to the antidumping duties, another tariff—called a **countervailing duty**—has been applied against imports of solar panels from China. A countervailing duty is used when the Foreign government subsidizes its own exporting firms so that they can charge lower prices for their exports. We will examine export subsidies in the next chapter. For now, we'll just indicate the amount of the subsidy provided by the Chinese government to their firms that export solar panels. Later in the chapter, we'll discuss the type of subsidies the U.S. government provides to American producers of solar panels.

In October 2011, seven U.S. companies led by SolarWorld Industries America, based in Hillsboro, Oregon, filed a trade case against Chinese exporters of photovoltaic cells, or solar panels. These U.S. companies argued that the Chinese firms were dumping solar panels into the United States —that is, they were exporting them at less than the costs of production—and also that these firms were receiving substantial export subsidies from the Chinese government. These twin claims of dumping and of export subsidies triggered several investigations by the U.S. Department of Commerce and the International Trade Commission (ITC), to determine the U.S. response.

The ITC completed its first investigation in December 2011, and made a preliminary finding that the U.S. companies bringing the trade case had been harmed—or "materially injured"—by the U.S. imports of solar panels from China. From 2009 to 2011, imports of solar panels from China increased by four times, and their value grew from $640 million to more than $3 billion. During this period, several American solar

---

[10] See Article VI of the GATT in Side Bar: Key Provisions of the GATT in the previous chapter.

panel producers went bankrupt, so it was not surprising that the ITC found material injury due to imports.

Following the ITC's investigation, the U.S. Department of Commerce held two inquiries during 2012 to determine the extent of dumping and the extent of Chinese export subsidies. It is particularly difficult to determine the extent of dumping when the exporting firm is based in a nonmarket economy like China, because it is hard to determine the market-based costs of the firms. To address this difficulty, the Department of Commerce looked at the costs of production in another exporting country—Thailand—and used those costs to estimate what market-based costs in China would be.[11] In a preliminary ruling in May 2012, and a later ruling in October 2012, the Department of Commerce found that a group of affiliated producers, all owned by Suntech Power Holdings, Co., Ltd., were selling in the United States at prices 32% below costs, and that a second group of producers were selling at 18% below costs. The 32% and 18% gaps include an export subsidy of about 11%. Because there was an additional export subsidy of 4% to 6% paid to the Chinese producers that was not reflected in the 32% and 18% gaps between costs and prices, tariffs of 36% were recommended for the first group of producers, and tariffs of 24% were recommended for the others.

In November 2012, the ITC made a final determination of material injury to the U.S. solar panel industry, and the tariffs went into effect. Not all American producers supported these tariffs, however, because they raised costs for firms such as SolarCity Corp., which finances and installs rooftop solar systems. These firms are the consumers of the imported solar panels and they face higher prices as a result of the tariffs. Despite the tariffs, the installation of solar panels is a thriving industry in the United States today, and the higher prices protect the remaining U.S. manufacturers of solar panels. ■

Strategic Trade Policy? The purpose of an antidumping duty is to raise the price of the dumped good in the importing Home country, thereby protecting the domestic producers of that good. There are two reasons for the Home government to use this policy. The first reason is that Foreign firms are acting like discriminating monopolists, as we discussed above. Then because we are dealing with dumping by a Foreign monopolist, we might expect that the antidumping duty, which is a tariff, will lead to a terms-of-trade gain for the Home country. That is, we might expect that the Foreign monopolist will absorb part of the tariff through lowering its own price, as was illustrated in Figure 9-7. It follows that the rise in the consumer price in the importing country is less than the full amount of the tariff, as was illustrated in the application dealing with Japanese compact trucks.

Does the application of antidumping duties lead to a terms-of-trade gain for the Home country, making this another example of strategic trade policy that can potentially benefit the Home country? In the upcoming analysis, we'll find that the answer to this question is "no," and that the antidumping provisions of U.S. trade law are *overused* and create a much greater cost for consumers and larger deadweight loss than does the less frequent application of tariffs under the safeguard provision, Article XIX of the GATT.[12]

---

[11] The Chinese industry instead wanted the Department of Commerce to use the costs of producing solar panels in India as an estimate of what the market-based Chinese costs would be. Because the costs in India are presumably lower than costs in Thailand, it would be less likely that the Chinese exporters would be found to be dumping.

[12] See Article XIX of the GATT in Side Bar: Key Provisions of the GATT in the previous chapter.

A second reason for the Home government to use an antidumping duty is because of **predatory dumping.** Predatory dumping refers to a situation in which a Foreign firm sells at a price below its average costs with the intention of causing Home firms to suffer losses and, eventually, to leave the market because of bankruptcy. Predatory pricing behavior can occur within a country (between domestic firms), but when it occurs across borders between a Foreign and Home firm, it is called dumping. Economists generally believe that such predatory behavior is rare: the firm engaged in the predatory pricing behavior must believe that it can survive its own period of losses (due to low prices) for longer than the firm or firms it is trying to force out of the market. Furthermore, the other firms must have no other option except to exit the market even though the firm using the predatory pricing can survive. If we are truly dealing with a case of predatory dumping, then the discussion that follows (about the effect of an antidumping duty) does not really apply. Instead, we need to consider a more complicated model in which firms are deciding whether to enter and remain in the market. In the next chapter's discussion of export subsidies, we analyze such a model. In this chapter, we focus on dumping by a discriminating Foreign monopoly and the effect of an antidumping duty in that case.

Comparison with Safeguard Tariff It is important to recognize that the tariff on compact trucks, discussed in the earlier application, was not an antidumping duty. Rather, it was a **safeguard tariff** applied under Section 201 of the U.S. tariff code, or Article XIX of the GATT. Because the tariff on trucks was increased in the early 1980s and has not been changed since, it fits our assumption that Foreign firms treat the tariff as fixed. That assumption does not hold for antidumping duties, however, because Foreign exporting firms can *influence* the amount of an antidumping duty by their own choice of prices. In fact, the evidence shows that Foreign firms often change their prices and *increase* the price charged in the importing country even before an antidumping tariff is applied. To see why this occurs, let us review how the antidumping duty is calculated.

Calculation of Antidumping Duty The amount of an antidumping duty is calculated based on the Foreign firm's local price. If its local price is $10 (after converting from Foreign's currency to U.S. dollars), and its export price to the Home market is $6, then the antidumping tariff is calculated as the difference between these prices, $4 in our example. This method of calculating the tariff creates an incentive for the Foreign firm to *raise* its export price even before the tariff is applied so that the duty will be lower. If the Foreign firm charges an export price of $8 instead of $4 but maintains its local price of $10, then the antidumping tariff would be only $2. Alternatively, the Foreign firm could charge $10 in its export market (the same as its local price) and avoid the antidumping tariff altogether!

Thus, the calculation of an antidumping duty creates a strong incentive for Foreign firms to raise their export prices to reduce or avoid the duty. This increase in the import price results in a terms-of-trade *loss* for the Home country. Such an increase in the import price is illustrated in Figure 9-9 as the rise from price P_1 to P_2. This price increase leads to a gain for Home firms of area a, but a loss for Home consumers of area $(a + b + c + d)$. There is no revenue collected when the duty is not imposed, so the net loss for the Home country is area $(b + c + d)$. This loss is higher than the deadweight loss from a tariff (which is area $b + d$) and illustrates the extra costs associated with the threat of an antidumping duty.

FIGURE 9-9

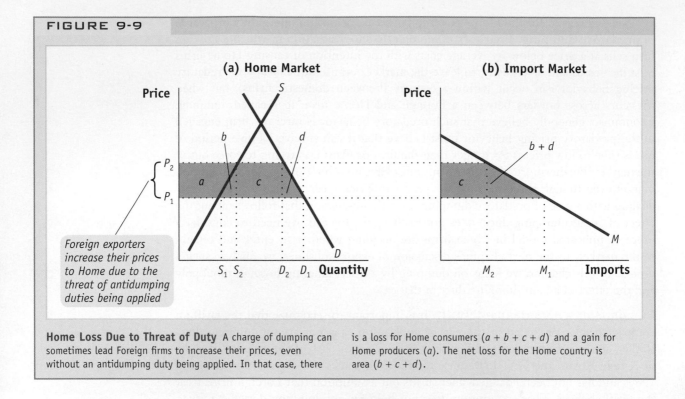

(a) Home Market

Price

P_2
P_1

b d S

a c

S_1 S_2 D_2 D_1 **Quantity**

D

Foreign exporters increase their prices to Home due to the threat of antidumping duties being applied

(b) Import Market

Price

$b + d$

c

M_2 M_1 **Imports**

M

Home Loss Due to Threat of Duty A charge of dumping can sometimes lead Foreign firms to increase their prices, even without an antidumping duty being applied. In that case, there is a loss for Home consumers $(a + b + c + d)$ and a gain for Home producers (a). The net loss for the Home country is area $(b + c + d)$.

Furthermore, the fact that Foreign firms will raise their prices to reduce the potential duty gives Home firms an incentive to charge Foreign firms with dumping, even if none is occurring: just the *threat* of an antidumping duty is enough to cause Foreign firms to raise their prices and reduce competition in the market for that good. As the following application shows, these incentives lead to excessive filings of antidumping cases.

APPLICATION

Antidumping Duties Versus Safeguard Tariffs

In the previous chapter, we discussed the "safeguard" provision in Article XIX of the GATT **(Side Bar: Key Provisions of the GATT)** and Section 201 of U.S. trade law. This provision, which permits temporary tariffs to be applied, is used infrequently. As shown in Table 9-1, from 1980 to 1989, only 19 safeguard (also called "escape clause") cases were filed in the United States. In the following decade there were only nine, and from 2000 to 2011 only three such cases were filed. In each case, the U.S. International Trade Commission (ITC) must determine whether rising imports are the "most important cause of serious injury, or threat thereof, to the domestic industry." Of the 31 cases filed from 1980 to 2011, the ITC made a *negative* recommendation (i.e., it did not approve the tariff requests) in 16, or about one-half the cases. One of those negative recommendations was for the tariff on Japanese compact trucks discussed in the earlier application: the ITC made a negative recommendation for both cars and trucks in 1980, but trucks still obtained a tariff by reclassifying the type of trucks being imported.

TABLE 9-1

Import Protection Cases in the United States, 1980–2011 This table shows the use of safeguard tariffs as compared with antidumping duties in the United States. Safeguard tariffs are used much less often.

Safeguard or Escape Clause Cases

			TOTAL 1980–2011		
Total 1980–1989	Total 1990–1999	Total 2000–2011	Negative ITC Ruling	Affirmative ITC Ruling*	Affirmative U.S. President Decision
19	9	3	16	12	9

China-Specific Safeguard Cases

			TOTAL 1980–2011		
Total 1980–1989	Total 1990–1999	Total 2000–2011	Negative ITC Ruling	Affirmative ITC Ruling	Affirmative U.S. President Decision
NA	NA	7	2	5	1

Antidumping Cases

			TOTAL 1980–2011		
Total 1980–1989	Total 1990–1999	Total 2000–2011	Duty Levied	Case Rejected	Cases Withdrawn
468	428	332	548	456	148

In addition to the 12 affirmative ITC safeguard cases, there were two ties and one terminated case.

NA—not applicable since the China specific safeguard began in 2001.

Sources: Wendy Hansen and Thomas J. Prusa, 1995, "The Road Most Taken: The Rise of Title VII Protection," The World Economy, 295–313. Update for 1989 to 1994 from I. M. Destler, 2005, American Trade Politics, Washington, D.C.: Peterson Institute for International Economics, pp. 149, 165. Updated for 1995 to 2011 from Chad P. Bown, 2011, "Global Antidumping Database," available at www.brandeis.edu/~cbown/global_ad/ .

The ITC made an affirmative ruling for protection in 12 cases, which then went for a final ruling to the President, who recommended import protection in only nine cases.[13] An example of a positive recommendation was the tariff on the import of steel, as discussed in the previous chapter, and the tariff imposed on heavyweight motorcycles, discussed later in this chapter. That only 31 cases were brought forward in three decades, and that tariffs were approved by the President in only nine cases, shows how infrequently this trade provision is used.

In the next panel of Table 9-1, we show the number of China-specific safeguard cases. This new trade provision, discussed in the previous chapter, took effect in 2001. Since that time, seven cases have been filed, of which two were denied by the ITC and five were approved. Of these five approved tariffs, the President also ruled in favor only once—the tariff imposed on imports of tires from China, approved by President Obama in 2009 and in effect until 2012.

---

[13] In addition to the 12 affirmative ITC safeguard cases, there were two ties and one terminated case.

The infrequent use of the safeguard provision can be contrasted with the many cases of antidumping duties. The cases filed in the United States under this provision are also listed in Table 9-1, which shows that the number of antidumping cases vastly exceeds safeguard cases. From 1980 to 1989 and from 1990 to 1999, there were more than 400 antidumping cases filed in the United States. In the next 12 years, 2000 to 2011, there were more than 300 antidumping cases, bringing the total number of antidumping cases filed from 1980 to 2011 to more than 1,200!

To have antidumping duties applied, a case must first go to the U.S. Department of Commerce (DOC), which rules on whether imports are selling domestically at "less than fair value"; that is, below the price in their own market or below the average cost of making them. These rulings were positive in 93% of cases during this period. The case is then brought before the ITC, which must rule on whether imports have caused "material injury" to the domestic industry (defined as "harm that is not inconsequential, immaterial, or unimportant"). This criterion is much easier to meet than the "substantial cause of serious injury" provision for a safeguard tariff, and as a result, the ITC more frequently rules in favor of antidumping duties. Furthermore, the application of duties does not require the additional approval of the President. Of the 1,200 antidumping cases filed from 1980 to 2011, about 450 were rejected and another 550 had duties levied.

The remaining 150 antidumping cases (or 148 to be precise, shown at the bottom of Table 9-1) fall into a surprising third category: those that are *withdrawn* prior to a ruling by the ITC. It turns out that the U.S. antidumping law actually permits U.S. firms to withdraw their case and, acting through an intermediary at the DOC, agree with the foreign firm on the level of prices and market shares! As we would expect, these withdrawn and settled cases result in a significant increase in market prices for the importing country.

Why do firms make claims of dumping so often? If a dumping case is successful, a duty will be applied against the Foreign competitor, and the import price will increase. If the case is withdrawn and settled, then the Foreign competitor will also raise its price. Even if the case is not successful, imports often decline while the DOC or ITC is making an investigation, and the smaller quantity of imports also causes their price to rise. So regardless of the outcome of a dumping case, the increase in the price of Foreign imports benefits Home firms by allowing them to charge more for their own goods. As a result, Home producers have a strong incentive to file for protection from dumping, whether it is occurring or not.

Because of the large number of antidumping cases and because exporting firms raise their prices to avoid the antidumping duties, this trade policy can be quite costly. According to one estimate, the annual cost to the United States from its antidumping policies is equivalent to the deadweight loss of a 6% uniform tariff applied across all imports.[14] ■

5 Infant Industry Protection

We now turn to the final application of tariffs that we will study in this chapter, and that is a tariff applied to an industry that is too young to withstand foreign competition, and so will suffer losses when faced with world prices under free trade. Given

---

[14] Kim Ruhl, "Antidumping in the Aggregate," New York University Stern School of Business, 2012.

time to grow and mature, the industry will be able to compete in the future. The only way that a firm in this industry could cover its losses today would be to borrow against its future profits. But if banks are not willing to lend to this firm—perhaps because it is small and inexperienced—then it will go bankrupt today unless the government steps in and offers some form of assistance, such as with a tariff or quota. This argument is called the "infant industry case" for protection. Although we include the infant industry tariff argument in this chapter on strategic trade policy, the idea of protecting a young industry dates back to the writings of John Stuart Mill (1806–1873).

To analyze this argument and make use of our results from the previous sections, we assume there is only one Home firm, so it is again a case of Home monopoly. The special feature of this Home firm is that increasing its output today will lead to lower costs in the future because it will learn how to produce its output more efficiently and at a lower cost. The question, then, is whether the Home government should intervene with a temporary protective tariff or quota today, so that the firm can survive long enough to achieve lower costs and higher profits in the future.

There are two cases in which infant industry protection is potentially justified. First, protection may be justified if a tariff today leads to an increase in Home output that, in turn, helps the firm learn better production techniques and reduce costs in the future. This is different from increasing returns to scale as discussed in Chapter 6. With increasing returns to scale, lower costs arise from producing farther down along a decreasing average cost curve; while a tariff might boost Home production and lower costs, removing the tariff would reduce production to its initial level and still leave the firm uncompetitive at world prices. For infant industry protection to be justified, the firm's learning must *shift down* the entire average cost curve to the point where it is competitive at world prices in the future, even without the tariff.

If the firm's costs are going to fall in the future, then why doesn't it simply borrow today to cover its losses and pay back the loan from future profits? Why does it need import protection to offset its current losses? The answer was already hinted at above: banks may be unwilling to lend to this firm because they don't know with certainty that the firm will achieve lower costs and be profitable enough in the future to repay the loan. In such a situation, a tariff or quota offsets an imperfection in the market for borrowing and lending (the capital market). What is most essential for the infant industry argument to be valid is not imperfect competition (a single Home firm), but rather, this imperfection in the Home capital market.

A second case in which import protection is potentially justified is when a tariff in one period leads to an increase in output and reductions in future costs *for other firms in the industry,* or even for firms in other industries. This type of **externality** occurs when firms learn from each other's successes. For instance, consider the high-tech semiconductor industry. Each firm innovates its products at a different pace, and when one firm has a technological breakthrough, other firms benefit by being able to copy the newly developed knowledge. In the semiconductor industry, it is not unusual for firms to mimic the successful innovations of other firms, and benefit from a **knowledge spillover.** In the presence of spillovers, the infant industry tariff promotes a positive externality: an increase in output for one firm lowers the costs for everyone. Because firms learn from one another, each firm on its own does not have much incentive to invest in learning by increasing its production today. In this case, a tariff is needed to offset this externality by increasing production, allowing for these spillovers to occur among firms so that there are cost reductions.

As both of these cases show, the infant industry argument supporting tariffs or quotas depends on the existence of some form of **market failure.** In our first example, the market does not provide loans to the firm to allow it to avoid bankruptcy; in the second, the firm may find it difficult to protect its intellectual knowledge through patents, which would enable it to be compensated for the spillover of knowledge to others. These market failures create a potential role for government policy. In practice, however, it can be very difficult for a government to correct market failure. If the capital market will not provide loans to a firm because it doesn't think the firm will be profitable in the future, then why would the government have better information about that firm's future prospects? Likewise, in the case of a spillover of knowledge to other firms, we cannot expect the government to know the extent of spillovers. Thus, we should be skeptical about the ability of government to distinguish the industries that deserve infant industry protection from those that do not.

Furthermore, even if either of the two conditions we have identified to potentially justify infant industry protection hold, these market failures do not guarantee that the protection will be worthwhile—we still need to compare the future benefits of protection (which are positive) with its costs today (the deadweight losses). So while some form of market failure is a *prerequisite* condition for infant industry protection to be justified, we will identify two further conditions below that must be satisfied for the protection to be successful. With these warnings in mind, let's look at how infant industry protection can work.

Free-Trade Equilibrium

In panel (a) of Figure 9-10, we show the situation a Home firm faces today, and in panel (b) we show its situation in the future. We assume that the Home country is small and therefore faces a fixed world price. As discussed earlier in the chapter, even a Home monopolist will behave in the same manner as a perfectly competitive industry under free trade, assuming that they have the same marginal costs. We also assume that any increase in the firm's output today leads to a reduction in costs in the future (i.e., a downward shift in the firm's average cost curve).

Equilibrium Today With free trade today, the Home firm faces the world price of P^W (which, you will recall from earlier in this chapter, is also its marginal revenue curve) and will produce to the point at which its marginal cost of production equals P^W. The Home firm therefore supplies the quantity S_1. To verify that S_1 is actually the Home supply, however, we need to check that profits are not negative at this quantity. To do so, we compare the firm's average costs with the price. The average cost curve is shown as AC in panel (a), and at the supply of S_1, average costs are much higher than the price P^W. That means the Home firm is suffering losses and would shut down today instead of producing S_1.

Tariff Equilibrium

To prevent the firm from shutting down, the Home government could apply an import tariff or quota to raise the Home price. Provided that the Home firm increases its output in response to this higher price, we assume that this increased size allows the firm to learn better production techniques so that its future costs are reduced. Given the choice of an import tariff or quota to achieve this goal, the Home government should

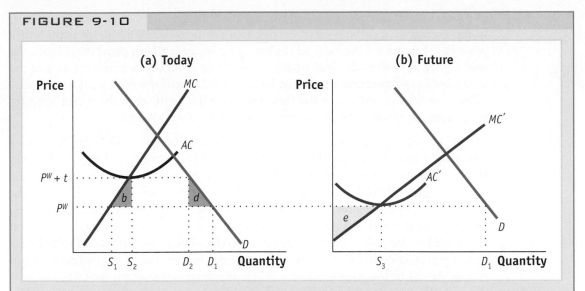

FIGURE 9-10

Infant Industry Protection In the situation today (panel a), the industry would produce S_1, the quantity at which $MC = P^W$. Because P^W is less than average costs at S_1, the industry would incur losses at the world price of P^W and would be forced to shut down. A tariff increases the price from P^W to $P^W + t$, allowing the industry to produce at S_2 (and survive) with the net loss in welfare of $(b + d)$. In panel (b), producing today allows the average cost curve to fall through learning to AC'. In the future, the firm can produce the quantity S_3 at the price P^W without tariff protection and earn producer surplus of e.

definitely choose the tariff. The reason is that when a Home monopolist is faced with a quota rather than a tariff, it will produce *less* output under the quota so that it can further raise its price. The decrease in output leads to additional deadweight loss today, as discussed earlier in the chapter. Furthermore, because we have assumed that the firm's learning depends on how much it produces and output is lower under the quota, there would be less learning and a smaller reduction in future costs under a quota than a tariff. For both reasons, a tariff is a better policy than a quota when the goal is to nurture an infant industry.

Equilibrium Today If the government applies an import tariff of t dollars today, the Home price increases from P^W to $P^W + t$. We assume that the government sets the tariff high enough so that the new Home price, $P^W + t$, just covers the infant industry's average costs of production. At this new price, the firm produces the quantity S_2 in panel (a). As illustrated, the price $P^W + t$ exactly equals average costs, AC, at the quantity S_2, so the firm is making zero profits. Making zero profits means that the Home firm will continue to operate.

Equilibrium in the Future With the firm producing S_2 today rather than S_1, it can learn about better production methods and lower its costs in the future. The effect of learning on production costs is shown by the downward shift of the average cost curve from AC in panel (a) to AC' in panel (b).[15] The lower average costs in the future mean that the firm can produce quantity S_3 without tariff protection at the world price P^W

---

[15] The marginal cost curve might also shift down, from MC in panel (a) to MC' in panel (b), although that shift is not essential to our argument.

in panel (b) and still cover its average costs. We are assuming that the downward shift in the average cost curve is large enough that the firm can avoid losses at the world price P^W. If that is not the case—if the average cost curve AC' in panel (b) is above the world price P^W—then the firm would be unable to avoid losses in the future and the infant industry protection would not be successful. But if the temporary tariff today allows the firm to operate in the future without the tariff, then the infant industry protection has satisfied the *first condition* to be judged successful.

Effect of the Tariff on Welfare The application of the tariff today leads to a deadweight loss, and in panel (a), the deadweight loss is measured by the triangles $(b + d)$. But we also need to count the gain from having the firm operating in the future. In panel (b) of Figure 9-10, the producer surplus earned in the future by the firm is shown by the region e. We should think of the region e as the present value (i.e., the discounted sum over time) of the firm's future producer surplus; it is this amount that would be forgone if the firm shut down today. The *second condition* for the infant industry protection to be successful is that the deadweight loss $(b + d)$ when the tariff is used should be less than the area e, which is present value of the firm's future produce surplus when it no longer needs the tariff.

To evaluate whether the tariff has been successful, it needs to satisfy both conditions: the firm has to be able to produce without losses and without needing the tariff in the future; and the future gains in producer surplus need to exceed the current deadweight loss from the tariff. To evaluate the second criterion, we need to compare the future gain of e with the deadweight loss today of $(b + d)$. If e exceeds $(b + d)$, then the infant industry protection has been worthwhile, but if e is less than $(b + d)$, then the costs of protection today do not justify the future benefits. The challenge for government policy is to try to distinguish worthwhile cases (those for which future benefits exceed present costs) from those cases that are not. In the application that follows, we will see whether the governments of China, Brazil, and the United States have been able to distinguish between these cases.

APPLICATION

Examples of Infant Industry Protection

There are many examples of infant industry protection in practice, and we will consider four: (1) policies used in the United States, Europe, and in China to support the solar panel industry; (2) a U.S. tariff imposed to protect Harley-Davidson motorcycles in the United States during the 1980s; (3) a complete ban on imports imposed from 1977 to the early 1990s to protect the computer industry in Brazil; and (4) tariffs and quotas imposed to protect the automobile industry in China, which were reduced when China joined the WTO in 2001.

Government Policies in the Solar Panel Industry

Many countries subsidize the production or installation of photovoltaic cells (solar panels). In the United States, there are tax credits available to consumers who install solar panels on their home. This type of policy is common in other countries, too, and can be justified because the generation of electricity using solar panels does not lead to any pollution, in contrast to the generation of electricity by the burning of fossil fuels (coal, natural gas, and oil), which emits carbon dioxide and other pollutants. Earlier in this chapter we introduced the concept of an externality, which is an economic activity that imposes costs on other firms or consumers. Pollution is the leading example of an externality, and too much pollution will be emitted unless the government takes some action. Giving a subsidy to users of solar panels, because these households and businesses use less electricity from fossil fuels, is one way to limit the amount of pollution arising from electricity generation.

So subsidies for the use of solar panels are a way to correct an externality and, on their own, should not be viewed as a form of infant industry protection. But countries use other policies to encourage the production (not just the use) of solar panels in their own country. In the United States, the government gives tax breaks and low-interest loans or loan guarantees to companies that produce solar panels. One example of a loan guarantee was to the U.S. company Solyndra, which received a $535 million loan guarantee from the U.S. Department of Energy in 2009. The guarantee meant that the U.S. government would repay the loan if Solyndra could not, so that banks making loans to Solyndra did not face any risk. That policy can be viewed as a type of infant industry protection: giving the loan guarantee in the hope that the company will be profitable in the future. But Solyndra subsequently went bankrupt in 2011, and President Obama was widely criticized for this loan guarantee. This example illustrates how difficult it is to know whether a company protected by some form of infant industry protection will actually become profitable in the future, which is one of the conditions for the infant industry protection to be successful.

China has also pursued policies to encourage the production of solar panels, and especially to encourage their export. We discussed the use of export subsidies in China in an earlier application dealing with U.S. imports of solar panels from China. We discuss export subsidies in more detail in the next chapter, but for now you should think of them as similar to import tariffs: the export subsidy raises the price received by firms, just like an import tariff, and also carries a deadweight loss. So our discussion of infant industry protection applies equally well to export subsidies: these infant-industry policies are successful if (1) the industry becomes profitable in the future, after the export subsidy is removed; and (2) the deadweight loss of the subsidy is less than the future profits earned by the industry.

As we have already learned about the use of loan guarantees in the United States (where Solyndra went bankrupt), export subsidies also don't always work out as planned. In China, for example, the extensive use of subsidies led to vast overcapacity in the industry, which in turn led to the bankruptcy of the key Chinese firm, Suntech Power Holdings, whose main subsidiary in Beijing went bankrupt in March 2013. The Suntech-affiliated firms were named in the antidumping and countervailing duty case brought by the American companies in 2011 as having the lowest prices in the United States. The fact that some of these firms have gone bankrupt indicates that the Chinese export subsidies were not successful in leading them to be profitable. Other firms have survived and are still producing in China, but their exports to the United States are limited by the antidumping and countervailing duties now applied by the United States. Furthermore, the European Union is now contemplating stiff antidumping penalties against Chinese firms, as discussed in **Headlines: Solar Flares.** Ironically, the company in Europe calling for these duties is SolarWorld, whose U.S. subsidiary filed the trade case against Chinese exporters of solar panels in the United States. If these European duties are enacted, more Chinese firms could go bankrupt. For these various reasons, it appears that the Chinese subsidies to the solar panel industry have not been successful.

Still, we should recognize that this industry is still young and future years could bring further changes. Some experts believe that the industry might now migrate to Taiwan, where it would not face the U.S. tariffs applied against China. On the other hand, the Chinese industry itself will be helped by subsidies to the installation of solar panels in China, which the government is now starting to use rather than only relying on export subsidies. And in the United States and Europe, there are still a number of producers of solar panels, as well as a strong industry involved with the installation of either locally produced or imported panels, and this industry will continue to create demand for solar panels built in China or elsewhere in Asia. Given the state of the worldwide solar panel industry, it is too early to say for sure what the long-term impact of the U.S., European, and Chinese policies will be.

U.S. Tariff on Heavyweight Motorcycles

Harley-Davidson does not really fit the usual description of an "infant" industry: the first plant opened in 1903 in Milwaukee, Wisconsin, and it was owned and operated by William Harley and the three Davidson brothers. Until the late 1970s it did not face intense import competition from Japanese producers; but by the early 1980s, Harley-Davidson was on the verge of bankruptcy. Even though it had been around since 1903, Harley-Davidson had many of the characteristics we associate with an infant industry: the inability to compete at the international price today and (as we will see) the potential for lower costs in the future. By including this case in our discussion of infant industries,

HEADLINES

Solar Flares

This article discusses the solar energy industry in Europe, and a recent proposal by the European Union to impose antidumping duties against China.

Four years ago, in the midst of Europe's solar energy boom, Wacker Chemie opened a new polysilicon factory in its sprawling chemicals facility in the small Bavarian town of Burghausen. There, in a production hall as large as an aircraft hangar but as clean as a laboratory, ultra-pure ingots of polysilicon—the most basic ingredient in photovoltaic cells—take shape in custom-built reactors heated to more than 1,000C. These days, the boom is over and Wacker's factory, with its 2,400 workers, is looking vulnerable. The company has been caught in what is shaping up to be a decisive trade fight between Europe and China and Wacker executives are worried about collateral damage.

Last September the EU launched its biggest ever investigation, probing billions of euros of imports of Chinese solar equipment. This week Karel De Gucht, the EU trade commissioner, urged that provisional duties averaging 47 per cent be imposed on the country's exports of solar panels for dumping, or selling products below cost, in Europe. For Wacker, the fear is that such measures will backfire by pushing up solar equipment prices for consumers and further undermining an industry already under pressure in Europe. Adding to their unease is the likelihood that Wacker will be first in line for Chinese retaliation. Late last year—just weeks after the EU opened its investigation—Beijing launched its own probe into Europe's polysilicon manufacturers. "This simply does not make sense," says Rudolf Staudigl, Wacker's chief executive, who is pleading with Brussels to hold fire. "If tariffs are implemented, Europe will be damaged more than China."

The case has risen to the highest political levels, with Angela Merkel, the German chancellor, last year calling for a negotiated solution amid concerns that the confrontation could precipitate a full-blown trade war.

we are able to make a precise calculation of the effect of the tariffs on consumers and producers to determine whether the infant industry protection was successful.

In 1983 Harley-Davidson, the legendary U.S.-based motorcycle manufacturer, was in trouble. It was suffering losses due to a long period of lagging productivity combined with intense competition from Japanese producers. Two of these producers, Honda and Kawasaki, not only had plants in the United States but also exported Japan-made goods to the United States. Two other Japanese producers, Suzuki and Yamaha, produced and exported their products from Japan. In the early 1980s these four Japanese firms were engaged in a global price war that spilled over into the U.S. market, and inventories of imported heavyweight cycles rose dramatically in the United States. Facing this intense import competition, Harley-Davidson applied to the International Trade Commission (ITC) for Section 201 protection.

As required by law, the ITC engaged in a study to determine the source of injury to the industry, which in this case was identified as heavyweight (more than 700 cc) motorcycles. Among other factors, it studied the buildup of inventories by Japanese producers in the United States. The ITC determined that there was more than nine months' worth of inventory of Japanese motorcycles already in the United States, which could depress the prices of heavyweight cycles and threaten bankruptcy for Harley-Davidson. As a result, the ITC recommended to President Ronald Reagan that import protection be placed on imports of heavyweight motorcycles. This case is interesting because it is one of the few times that the *threat* of injury by imports has been used as a justification for tariffs under Section 201 of U.S. trade law.

President Ronald Reagan visits the Harley-Davidson plant.

Reprinted by permission of the York Daily Record/York Sunday News

President Reagan approved the recommendation from the ITC, and tariffs were imposed on imports of heavyweight motorcycles. These tariffs were initially very high, but they declined over five years. The initial tariff, imposed on April 16, 1983, was 45%; it then fell annually to 35%, 20%, 15%, and 10% and was scheduled to end in April 1988. In fact, Harley-Davidson petitioned the ITC to end the tariff one year early, after the 15% rate expired in 1987, by which time it had cut costs and introduced new and very popular products so that profitability had been restored. Amid great fanfare, President Reagan visited the Harley-Davidson plant in Milwaukee, Wisconsin, and declared that the tariff had been a successful case of protection.

Calculation of Deadweight Loss Was the tariff on heavyweight motorcycles really successful? To answer this, we need to compare the deadweight loss of the tariff with the future gain in producer surplus. In our discussion of the steel tariff in the previous chapter, we derived a formula for the deadweight loss from using a tariff, measured relative to the import value:

$$\frac{DWL}{P \cdot M} = \tfrac{1}{2} \cdot \left(\frac{t}{P^W}\right) \cdot \%\Delta M = \tfrac{1}{2}\,(0.45 \cdot 0.17) = 0.038, \text{ or } 3.8\%$$

We can calculate the average import sales from 1982 to 1983 as (452 + 410)/2 = $431 million. Multiplying the percentage loss by average imports, we obtain the deadweight loss in 1983 of 0.038 × 431 = $16.3 million. That deadweight loss is reported in the last column of Table 9-2, along with the loss for each following year. Adding up these deadweight losses, we obtain a total loss of $112.5 million over the four years that the tariff was used.[16]

Future Gain in Producer Surplus To judge whether the tariff was effective, we need to compare the deadweight loss of $112.5 million with the *future* gain in producer surplus (area *e* in Figure 9-10). How can we assess these future gains? We can use a technique that economists favor: we can evaluate the future gains in producer surplus by examining the stock market value of the firm around the time that the tariff was removed.

During the time that the tariff was in place, the management of Harley-Davidson reduced costs through several methods: implementing a "just-in-time" inventory system, which means producing inventory on demand rather than having excess amounts in warehouses; reducing the workforce (and its wages); and implementing "quality circles," groups of assembly workers who volunteer to meet together to discuss workplace improvements, along with a "statistical operator control system" that allowed employees to evaluate the quality of their output. Many of these production techniques were copied from Japanese firms. The company also introduced a new engine. These changes allowed Harley-Davidson to transform losses during the period from 1981 to 1982 into profits for 1983 and in following years.

In July 1986 Harley-Davidson became a public corporation and issued stock on the American Stock Exchange: 2 million shares at $11 per share, for a total offering of $22 million. It also issued debt of $70 million, which was to be repaid from future profits. In June 1987 it issued stock again: 1.23 million shares at $16.50 per share, for a total offering of $20.3 million. The sum of these stock and debt issues is $112.3 million, which we can interpret as the present discounted value of the producer surplus of the firm. This estimate of area *e* is nearly equal to the consumer surplus loss,

TABLE 9-2

U.S. Imports of Heavyweight Motorcycles This table shows the effects of the tariff on imports of heavyweight motorcycles in the United States.

Year	Import Sales ($ millions)	Import Quantity	% Fall in Imports (from 1982)	Tariff (%)	Net Loss/ Average Sales (%)	Deadweight Loss (% millions)
1982	452	164,000				
1983	410	139,000	17	45	3.8	16.3
1984	179	80,000	69	35	12.1	38.4
1985	191	72,000	78	20	7.8	25.2
1986	152	43,000	116	15	8.7	26.4
January–March 1987	59	14,000	98	15	7.3	6.3
Total, 1983–1987						112.5

Source: Heavy Weight Motorcycles. *Report to the President on Investigation No. TA-203-17, under Section 203 of the Trade Act of 1974. U.S. International Trade Commission, June 1987, and author's calculations.*

[16] This calculation is not quite accurate because we have used the calendar years 1983 to 1986 rather than the 12 months from April of each year to March of the next year, during which the tariff was effective.

$112.5 million, in Table 9-2. Within a month after the second stock offering, however, the stock price rose from $16.50 to $19 per share. Using that price to evaluate the outstanding stock of 3.23 million, we obtain a stock value of $61 million, plus $70 million in repaid debt, to obtain $131 million as the future producer surplus.

By this calculation, the future gain in producer surplus from tariff protection to Harley-Davidson ($131 million) exceeds the deadweight loss of the tariff ($112.5 million). Furthermore, since 1987 Harley-Davidson has become an even more successful company. Its sales and profits have grown every year, and many model changes have been introduced, so it is now the Japanese companies that copy Harley-Davidson. By March 2005 Harley-Davidson had actually surpassed General Motors in its stock market value: $17.7 billion versus $16.2 billion. Both of these companies suffered losses during the financial crisis of 2008 and 2009, but Harley-Davidson continued to operate as usual (with a stock market value of $4.3 billion in mid-2009), whereas General Motors declared bankruptcy and required a government bailout (its stock market value fell to less than $0.5 billion). Although both companies can be expected to recover after the crisis, it is clear that General Motors—which once had the world's highest stock market value—has been surpassed by Harley-Davidson.

Was Protection Successful? Does this calculation mean that the infant industry protection was successful? A complete answer to that question involves knowing what would have happened if the tariff had *not* been put in place. When we say that infant industry protection is successful if the area e of future producer surplus gain ($131 million) exceeds the deadweight loss ($112.5 million), we are assuming that the firm would not have survived at all without the tariff protection. That assumption may be true for Harley-Davidson. It is well documented that Harley-Davidson was on the brink of bankruptcy from 1982 to 1983. Citibank had decided that it would not extend more loans to cover Harley's losses, and Harley found alternative financing on December 31, 1985, just one week before filing for bankruptcy.[17] If the tariff saved the company, then this was clearly a case of successful infant industry protection.

On the other hand, even if Harley-Davidson had not received the tariff and had filed for bankruptcy, it might still have emerged to prosper again. Bankruptcy does not mean that a firm stops producing; it just means that the firm's assets are used to repay all possible debts. Even if Harley-Davidson had gone bankrupt without the tariff, some or all of the future gains in producer surplus might have been realized. So we cannot be certain whether the turnaround of Harley-Davidson required the use of the tariff.[18]

Despite all these uncertainties, it still appears that the tariff on heavyweight motorcycles bought Harley-Davidson some breathing room. This is the view expressed by the chief economist at the ITC at that time, in the quotation at the beginning of the chapter: "If the case of heavyweight motorcycles is to be considered the only successful escape-clause [tariff], it is because it caused little harm and it helped Harley-Davidson get a bank loan so it could diversify."[19] We agree with this assessment

---

[17] See Peter C. Reid, 1990, *Made Well in America: Lessons from Harley-Davidson on Being the Best* (New York: McGraw-Hill).

[18] The chairman of Harley-Davidson stated in 1987 that the tariff had not actually helped the company that much because the Japanese producers were able to downsize some of their motorcycles to 699 cc engine size, and thereby avoid the tariff (*Wall Street Journal*, March 20, 1987, p. 39).

[19] John Suomela, chief economist at the U.S. International Trade Commission, as cited in Douglas A. Irwin, 2002, *Free Trade under Fire* (Princeton, NJ: Princeton University Press), pp. 136–137.

that the harm caused by the tariff was small compared with the potential benefits of avoiding bankruptcy, which allowed Harley-Davidson to become the very successful company that it is today.

Computers in Brazil

There are many cases in which infant industry protection has not been successful. One well-known case involves the computer industry in Brazil. In 1977 the Brazilian government began a program to protect domestic firms involved in the production of personal computers (PCs). It was thought that achieving national autonomy in the computer industry was essential for strategic military reasons. Not only were imports of PCs banned, but domestic firms also had to buy from local suppliers whenever possible, and foreign producers of PCs were not allowed to operate in Brazil.

The Brazilian ban on imports lasted from 1977 to the early 1990s. This was a period of rapid innovations in PC production worldwide, with large drops in the cost of computing power. In Figure 9-11, we show the effective price of computing power in the United States and Brazil between 1982 and 1992, which fell very rapidly in both countries. The price we are graphing is "effective" because it is not just the retail price of a new PC but a price index that reflects the improvements over time in the PC's speed of calculations, storage capacity, and so on.

FIGURE 9-11

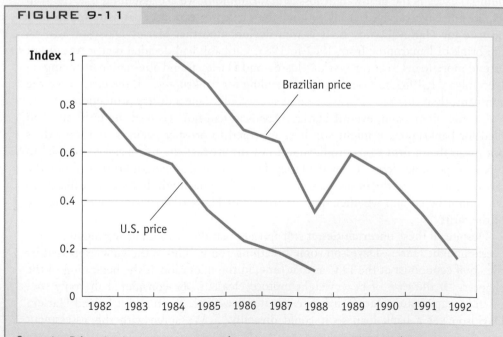

Computer Prices in the United States and Brazil, 1982–1992 This diagram shows the effective price of computer power in the United States and Brazil. Both prices fell very rapidly because of technological improvements, but the drop in the U.S. price exceeded that of the Brazilian price. The difference between the two prices is a measure of the technology gap between Brazil and the United States in the production of personal computers.

Source: Eduardo Luzio and Shane Greenstein, November 1995, "Measuring the Performance of a Protected Infant Industry: The Case of Brazilian Microcomputers," Review of Economics and Statistics, 77(4), 622–633.

Prices in Brazil Brazilian firms were adept at reverse engineering the IBM PCs being sold from the United States. But the reverse engineering took time, and the fact that Brazilian firms were required to use local suppliers for many parts within the computers added to the costs of production. We can see from Figure 9-11 that Brazil *never achieved the same low prices* as the United States. By 1992, for example, the effective prices in Brazil were between the prices that had been achieved in the United States four or five years earlier. The persistent gap between the prices in Brazil and the United States means that Brazil was never able to produce computers at competitive prices without tariff protection. This fact alone means that the infant industry protection was not successful.

Consumer and Producer Surplus In Table 9-3, we show the welfare calculation for Brazil, as well as other details of the PC industry. Local sales peaked at about $750 million in 1986, and the following year, the Brazilian prices rose to within 20% of those in the United States. But that is as close as the Brazilian industry ever got to world prices. In 1984 prices in Brazil were nearly double those in the United States, which led to a producer surplus gain of $29 million but a consumer surplus loss in Brazil of $80 million. The net loss was therefore $80 million – $29 million = $51 million, which was 0.02% of Brazilian gross domestic product (GDP) that year. By 1986 the net loss had grown to $164 million, or 0.06% of GDP. This net loss was the deadweight loss from the tariff during the years it was in place. The industry was never able to produce in the absence of tariffs, so there are no future gains (like area *e* in Figure 9-10) that we can count against those losses.

Other Losses The higher prices in Brazil imposed costs on Brazilian industries that relied on computers in manufacturing, as well as on individual users, and they became increasingly dissatisfied with the government's policy. During his campaign in 1990, President Fernando Collor de Mello promised to abolish the infant industry protection for personal computers, which he did immediately after he was elected.

A number of reasons have been given for the failure of this policy to develop an efficient industry in Brazil: imported materials such as silicon chips were expensive to obtain, as were domestically produced parts that local firms were required to use; in addition, local regulations limited the entry of new firms into the industry. Whatever

TABLE 9-3

Brazilian Computer Industry This table shows the effects of the government ban on imports of personal computers into Brazil.

Year	Sales ($ millions)	Brazil/U.S. Price (%)	Producer Surplus Gain ($ millions)	Consumer Surplus Loss ($ millions)	Net Loss ($ millions)	Net Loss (% of GDP)
1984	126	189	29	80	51	0.02
1985	384	159	70	179	109	0.04
1986	746	143	113	277	164	0.06
1987	644	119	50	112	62	0.02
1988	279	127	29	68	39	0.01

Source: Eduardo Luzio and Shane Greenstein, November 1995, "Measuring the Performance of a Protected Infant Industry: The Case of Brazilian Microcomputers," Review of Economics and Statistics, 77(4), 622–633.

the reasons, this case illustrates how difficult it is to successfully nurture an infant industry and how difficult it is for the government to know whether temporary protection will allow an industry to survive in the future.

Protecting the Automobile Industry in China

The final example of infant industry protection that we discuss involves the automobile industry in China. In 2009, China overtook the United States as the largest automobile market in the world (measured by domestic sales plus imports). Strong competition among foreign firms located in China, local producers, and import sales have resulted in new models and falling prices so that the Chinese middle class can now afford to buy automobiles. In 2009, there were over 13 million vehicles sold in China, as compared with 10.4 million cars and light trucks sold in the United States. Four years later in 2013, the Chinese industry is poised to reach another milestone by producing more cars than Europe, as described in **Headlines: Milestone for China Car Output.**

Growth in automotive production and sales has been particularly strong since 2001, when China joined the World Trade Organization (WTO). With its accession to the WTO, China agreed to reduce its tariffs on foreign autos, which were as high as 260% in the early 1980s, then fell from 80% to 100% by 1996, and 25% by July 2006. The tariff on automobile parts was further cut from 25% to 10% in 2009. China has loosened its import quotas, as well. Those tariffs and quotas, in addition to restrictions at the province and city level on what type of cars could be sold, had limited China's imports and put a damper on the auto industry in that country. Prices were high and foreign producers were reluctant to sell their newest models to China. That situation has changed dramatically. Now, foreign firms scramble to compete in China with their latest designs and are even making plans to export cars from China. Is the Chinese automobile industry a successful case of infant industry protection? Are the benefits

HEADLINES

Milestone for China Car Output

China is poised to produce more cars than Europe in 2013 for the first time, hitting a landmark in the country's rise in the automobile industry and underlining the difficulties for the European vehicle sector as it faces a challenging 12 months. China is in 2013 set to make 19.6 million cars and other light vehicles such as small trucks compared with 18.3 million in Europe . . . In 2012, on the basis of motor industry estimates, Europe made 18.9 million cars and related vehicles, comfortably ahead of China's tally of 17.8 million. . . . With global sales valued at about $1.3 trillion a year, the car industry is one of the best bellwethers of world economic conditions.

According to the data, Europe will in 2013 make just over a fifth of the world's cars—a figure that is well down on the 35 per cent it recorded in 2001. In 1970 nearly one in every two cars made in the world originated from a factory in Europe—which is generally recognized as the place where the global auto industry began with the unveiling of a rudimentary three-wheeler in 1885 by the German inventor Karl Benz. Car production in China in 2013 is likely to be 10 times higher than in 2000—when its share of global auto manufacturing was just 3.5 per cent as opposed to a likely 23.8 per cent in 2013.

Source: Excerpted from "Milestone for China Car Output," Financial Times, January 2, 2013, p. 11. From the Financial Times © The Financial Times Limited 2013. All Rights Reserved.

gained by the current production and export of cars greater than the costs of the tariffs and quotas imposed in the past? To answer this, we begin by briefly describing the history of the Chinese auto industry.

Production in China Beginning in the early 1980s, China permitted a number of joint ventures between foreign firms and local Chinese partners. The first of these in 1983 was Beijing Jeep, which was a joint venture between American Motors Corporation (AMC—later acquired by Chrysler Corporation) and a local firm in Beijing. The following year, Germany's Volkswagen signed a 25-year contract to make passenger cars in Shanghai, and France's Peugeot agreed to another passenger car project to make vehicles in Guangzhou.

Although joint venture agreements provided a window for foreign manufacturers to tap the China market, there were limits on their participation. Foreign manufacturers could not own a majority stake in a manufacturing plant—Volkswagen's venture took the maximum of 50% foreign ownership. The Chinese also kept control of distribution networks for the jointly produced automobiles. These various regulations, combined with high tariff duties, helped at least some of the new joint ventures achieve success. Volkswagen's Shanghai plant was by the far the winner under these rules, and it produced more than 200,000 vehicles per year by the late 1990s, more than twice as many as any other plant. Volkswagen's success was also aided by some Shanghai municipal efforts. Various restrictions on engine size, as well as incentives offered to city taxi companies that bought Volkswagens, helped ensure that only Volkswagen's models could be sold in the Shanghai market; essentially, the Shanghai Volkswagen plant had a local monopoly.

That local monopoly has been eroded by entry into the Shanghai market, however. A recent example occurred in early 2009, when General Motors opened two new plants in Shanghai, at a cost of $1.5 billion and $2.5 billion each. General Motors is a leading producer in China, and locally produced 1.8 million of the 13 million vehicles sold in China in 2009. In fact, its profits from the Chinese market were the only bright spot on its global balance sheet that year, and served to offset some of its losses in the American market, as described in **Headlines: Shanghai Tie-Up Drives Profits for GM.**

Cost to Consumers The tariffs and quotas used in China kept imports fairly low throughout the 1990s, ranging from a high of 222,000 cars imported in 1993 to a low of 27,500 imports in 1998 and 160,000 cars in 2005. Since tariffs were in the range of 80% to 100% by 1996, import prices were approximately doubled because of the tariffs. But the quotas imposed on auto imports probably had at least as great an impact on prices of imports *and* domestically produced cars. Our analysis earlier in the chapter showed that quotas have a particularly large impact on domestic prices when the Home firm is a monopoly. That situation applied to the sales of Volkswagen's joint venture in Shanghai, which enjoyed a local monopoly on the sales of its vehicles.

HEADLINES

Shanghai Tie-Up Drives Profits for GM

This article discusses how partnerships in China have helped GM's profits.

If General Motors believes in God, it must be thanking Him right now for China.

Mainland Chinese sales were by far the brightest spot in GM's universe last year: sales in China rose 66 per cent while US sales fell by 30 per cent. One in four GM cars is now made in China. Even those cars made in Detroit were partly designed in Shanghai. GM managed to offload distressed assets to Chinese companies: the loss-making, environment-harming Hummer was sold to a previously unknown heavy equipment manufacturer, Sichuan Tengzhong

[this sale was, however, blocked by the Chinese government in February 2010], and Beijing Automotive (BAIC) took some Saab technology off GM's hands. Perhaps most importantly of all, though, China agreed last year to bankroll GM's expansion in Asia.

In exchange for a deal to sell Chinese minicommercial vehicles in India, GM agreed to give up the 50-50 ownership of its leading mainland joint venture, Shanghai General Motors, ceding 51 percent majority control to its Chinese partner, Shanghai Automotive Industry

Corp (SAIC). The Sino-American partnership said this would be only the first of many such deals. Will observers one day look back at that deal and say that was the day GM signed over its future to the Chinese? And does that deal demonstrate how China can save GM—or hint that it might gobble it up? "The quick answer is that Chinese consumers have already saved GM," says Klaus Paur of TNS auto consultancy in Shanghai, referring to stratospheric Chinese auto sales last year.

Source: "Shanghai Tie-Up Drives Profits for GM," by Patti Waldmeir, Financial Times, January 21, 2010. From the Financial Times © The Financial Times Limited 2010. All Rights Reserved.

The effect of this local monopoly was to substantially increase prices in the Shanghai market. In Figure 9-12, we show the estimated markups of price over marginal costs for autos sold in China from 1995 to 2001, by various producers. The markups for Shanghai Volkswagen are the highest, reaching a high of 54% in 1998 and then falling to 28% in 2001, for an average of 42% for the period from 1995 to 2001. In comparison, the average markup charged by Tianjin Auto was 19%, and the average markup charged by Shanghai GM was 14%. All the other producers shown in Figure 9-12 have even lower markups.

From this evidence, it is clear that Shanghai Volkswagen was able to substantially raise its prices because of the monopoly power granted by the local government. Furthermore, the Jetta and Audi models produced by Shanghai Volkswagen during the 1990s were outdated models. That plant had the highest production through 2001, despite its high prices and outdated models, so a large number of consumers in the Shanghai area and beyond bore the costs of that local protection. This example illustrates how a Home monopoly can gain from protection at the expense of consumers. The example also illustrates how protection can stifle the incentive for firms to introduce the newest models and production techniques.

Gains to Producers For the tariffs and quotas used in China to be justified as infant industry protection, they should lead to a large enough drop in future costs so that the protection is no longer needed. China has not reached that point entirely, since it still imposes a tariff of 25% on autos, and a 10% tariff on auto parts. These tariff rates are much lower than in the past but still substantially protect the local market. So it is premature to point to the Chinese auto industry as a successful case of infant industry protection. Still, there are some important lessons that can be

FIGURE 9-12

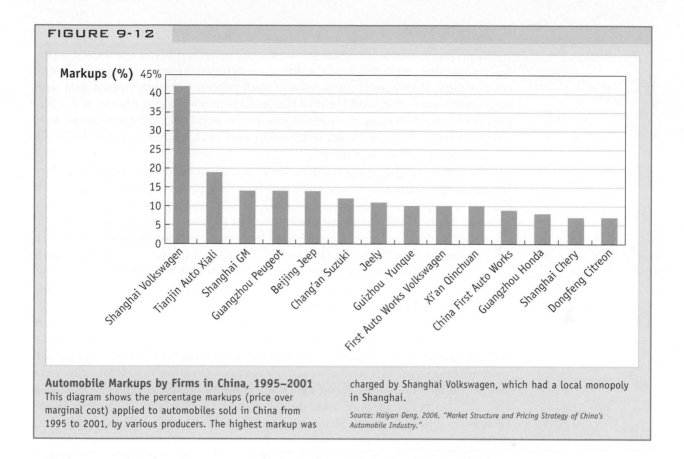

Automobile Markups by Firms in China, 1995–2001
This diagram shows the percentage markups (price over marginal cost) applied to automobiles sold in China from 1995 to 2001, by various producers. The highest markup was charged by Shanghai Volkswagen, which had a local monopoly in Shanghai.

Source: Haiyan Deng, 2006, "Market Structure and Pricing Strategy of China's Automobile Industry."

learned from its experience. First, there is no doubt that past protection contributed to the inflow of foreign firms to the Chinese market. All the foreign auto companies that entered China prior to its WTO accession in 2001 did so under high levels of protection, so that acquiring a local partner was the only way to sell locally: tariffs were too high to allow significant imports to China. As a result, local costs fell as Chinese partners gained from the technology transferred to them by their foreign partners. We can conclude that tariff protection combined with the ownership restrictions for joint ventures has led to a great deal of learning and reduced costs by the Chinese partners.

Second, at least as important as the tariffs themselves is the rapid growth of income in China, which has led to a boom in domestic sales. It is that rapid growth in income that has led China to overtake the United States to become the largest automobile market in the world measured by sales in 2009, and with production exceeding that of Europe in 2013. Tariffs have contributed to the inflow of foreign investment, but it is now the consumers in China who are forcing firms to offer the newest models built with the most efficient techniques. For now, we must leave open the question of whether the high tariffs and quotas in China are responsible for the current success of its auto industry, or whether they just resulted in high prices and lagging model designs that slowed the development of the industry. It will be some years before researchers can look back at the development of this industry and identify the specific causes of its success. ■

6 Conclusions

In the previous chapter, we discussed the use of import tariffs and quotas under perfect competition and highlighted the difference between the small-country and large-country cases. With perfect competition, a small importing country loses from a tariff (because it cannot affect world prices), but the large importing country can potentially gain from a tariff (because the tariff depresses the world price). Import quotas have effects similar to those of import tariffs under perfect competition, so we often refer to quotas and tariffs as "equivalent."

We can contrast the results obtained under perfect competition with the results we learned in this chapter, in which we assume imperfect competition—either Home or Foreign monopoly. Under Home monopoly, the effects of a tariff and quota are very different. With a tariff, the Home monopolist can increase its price by the amount of the tariff (as would a competitive industry) but cannot exercise its monopoly power. With an import quota, however, the Home firm is able to charge a higher price than it could with a tariff because it enjoys a "sheltered" market. So the import quota leads to higher costs for Home consumers than the tariff, and these two policies are no longer "equivalent," as they are under perfect competition.

Under Foreign monopoly, the results are similar to those of the large-country case analyzed in the previous chapter: the tariff leads to a fall in the price received by the Foreign monopolist, so the price paid by Home consumers rises by *less than* the full amount of the tariff. The tariff is shared between an increase in the Home price and a decrease in the Foreign price, and the Home importer obtains a terms-of-trade gain. For small tariffs, the terms-of-trade gain exceeds the deadweight loss, and the Home country gains from the tariff. So this is a case where the use of a tariff as strategic trade policy can benefit the Home country, but at the expense of the Foreign firm.

A specific example of a tariff applied against a Foreign monopoly occurs when the Foreign firm is a discriminating monopoly and it dumps its output into Home at a lower price than it charges in its own local market. When dumping occurs, the importing country is permitted by WTO rules to respond with a tariff, which is called an antidumping duty. In principle, we might expect Home to gain from the duty because the Foreign firm will lower its price (as occurs for a tariff applied against a Foreign monopolist). But we have argued that the potential for Home gains from the antidumping duty are unlikely to arise because of special features in the way these duties are applied. Instead, the expected outcome from antidumping duties is that Foreign exporters raise prices even when a duty is *not* applied, leading to Home losses. Because of these losses, the use of antidumping duties as strategic trade policy is not effective.

Another topic discussed in this chapter is the infant industry case for protection. We studied four industries as examples of infant industry protection: solar panels in the United States and China, Harley-Davidson motorcycles in the United States, computers in Brazil, and automobiles in China. Both the United States and China provide various type of subsidies for the production or use of solar panels, and the United States has recently applied antidumping and countervailing duties on these imports from China. The solar panel industry is suffering from overcapacity on a global scale and firms in both countries have gone bankrupt. So the policies applied have not yet led to the long-term profitability of firms in either country. The tariff given to protect Harley-Davidson motorcycles in the United States during the 1980s appears to have been successful because Harley-Davidson survived and has become very profitable. For computers in Brazil, the ban on imports during the 1980s was not successful because the industry was never able to learn enough from the world leaders to reach the same level of efficiency and competitive prices. Finally, automobile production in China has grown rapidly and overtaken production in Europe, but it is still protected by a 25% tariff, so it is too early to judge whether this is a successful case of infant industry protection. In addition, the rapid growth in the domestic income of Chinese consumers has been at least as important as past tariffs to the recent growth in production and sales.

KEY POINTS

1. Free trade will lead a Home monopoly in a small country to act in the same way as a perfectly competitive industry and charge a price equal to marginal cost. Therefore, competition from imports eliminates the monopoly power of the Home firm.

2. Quotas are not equivalent to tariffs when the Home firm is a monopolist. Because a quota limits the number of imports, the Home monopolist can charge higher prices than under a tariff, which results in greater costs to consumers.

3. When a tariff is applied against a Foreign monopolist, the results are similar to those of the large-country case analyzed in the previous chapter: the Foreign monopolist increases the price in the importing country by less than the full amount of the tariff and allows its own net-of-tariff price to fall. Hence, the tariff is shared between an increase in the Home price and a decrease in the Foreign price, a terms-of-trade gain for Home.

4. Dumping is the practice of a Foreign firm exporting goods at a price that is below its own domestic price or below its average cost of production. If the price charged for the exported good is above the firm's marginal cost, then dumping is profitable. We expect to observe dumping when the Foreign firm is acting like a discriminating monopolist.

5. Countries respond to dumping by imposing antidumping duties on imports. Antidumping duties are calculated as the difference between a Foreign firm's local price (or average costs) and its export price. To reduce or avoid the antidumping duties, Foreign firms can raise their export prices. That increase in price is a terms-of-trade loss for the importer and occurs because the Foreign firm can influence the duty.

6. In the United States and other countries, the use of antidumping tariffs far exceeds the use of safeguard tariffs. It is easy for domestic firms to bring a charge of dumping, and in many cases upholding the charge results in an increase in foreign prices and a decrease in competition for the domestic firm. The excessive use of antidumping cases also invites other countries to respond with their own charges of dumping.

7. An infant industry is a firm that requires protection to compete at world prices today. When a government applies a temporary tariff, it expects that costs for the firm or the industry overall will fall due to learning, thereby allowing it to compete at world prices in the future.

KEY TERMS

strategic trade policy, p. 280
discriminating monopoly, p. 281
dumping, p. 281
antidumping duty, p. 281
infant industry, p. 281

market power, p. 281
marginal revenue, p. 282
price discrimination, p. 296
countervailing duty, p. 299
predatory dumping, p. 301

safeguard tariff, p. 301
externality, p. 305
knowledge spillover, p. 305
market failure, p. 306

PROBLEMS

1. Figure 9-1 shows the Home no-trade equilibrium under perfect competition (with the price P^C) and under monopoly (with the price P^M). In this problem, we compare the welfare of Home consumers in these two situations.

   a. Under perfect competition, with the price P^C, label the triangle of consumer surplus and the triangle of producer surplus. Outline the area of total Home surplus (the sum of consumer surplus and producer surplus).

   b. Under monopoly, with the price P^M, label the consumer surplus triangle.

   c. Producer surplus is the same as the profits earned by the monopolist. To measure this, label the point in Figure 9-1 where the MR curve intersects MC at point B'. For selling the units between zero and Q^M, marginal costs rise along the MC curve, up to B'. The monopolist earns the difference between the price P^M and MC for each unit sold. Label the difference between the price and the MC curve as producer surplus, or profits.

   d. Outline the area of total Home surplus with a Home monopoly.

   e. Compare your answers to parts (a) and (d), and outline what the difference between these two areas is. What is this difference called and why?

2. Figure 9-2 shows the free-trade equilibrium under perfect competition and under monopoly (both with the price P^W). In this problem, we compare the welfare of Home consumers in the no-trade situation and under free trade.

   a. Under perfect competition, with the price P^W, label the triangle of consumer surplus and the triangle of producer surplus. Outline the area of total Home surplus (the sum of consumer surplus and producer surplus).

   b. Based on your answers to part (a) in this problem and part (a) of the last problem, outline the area of gains from free trade under perfect competition.

   c. Under monopoly, still with the price P^W, again label the triangle of consumer surplus and the triangle of producer surplus.

   d. Based on your answers to part (c) in this problem and part (d) in the last problem, outline the area of gains from free trade under Home monopoly.

   e. Compare your answers to parts (b) and (d). That is, which area of gains from trade is higher and why?

3. Rank the following in ascending order of Home welfare and justify your answers. If two items are equivalent, indicate this accordingly.

   a. Tariff t in a small country with perfect competition

   b. Tariff t in a small country with a Home monopoly

   c. Quota with the same imports M in a small country, with a Home monopoly

   d. Tariff t in a country facing a Foreign monopoly

4. Refer to the prices of Japanese auto imports under the VER (Figure 9-5) and answer the following:

   a. What component of the price of imported automobiles from Japan rose the most over the period 1980 to 1985?

   b. Sketch how Figures 9-5 and 9-6 might have looked if the United States had applied a tariff to Japanese auto imports instead of the VER (with the same level of imports). In words, discuss how the import prices and U.S. prices might have compared under a tariff and the VER.

   c. Which policy—a tariff or the VER—would have been least costly to U.S. consumers?

5. In this problem, we analyze the effects of an import quota applied by a country facing a Foreign monopolist. In Figure 9-7, suppose that the Home country applies an import quota of X_2, meaning that the Foreign firm cannot sell any more than that amount.

   a. To achieve export sales of X_2, what is the highest price that the Foreign firm can charge?

   b. At the price you have identified in part (a), what is the Home consumer surplus?

   c. Compare the consumer surplus you identify in part (b) with the consumer surplus under free trade. Therefore, outline in Figure 9-7 the Home losses due to the quota. *Hint:* Remember that there is no Home firm, so you do not need to take into account Home producer surplus or tariff revenue. Assume that quota rents go to Foreign firms.

d. Based on your answer to (c), which has the greater loss to the Home country—a tariff or a quota, leading to the same level of sales X_2 by the Foreign firm?

6. Suppose that the demand curve for a good is represented by the straight line

$$P = 10 - Q$$

Fill in the missing information in the following chart:

Quantity	Price	Total Revenue	Marginal Revenue
0			NA
1			
2			
3			
4			
5			
6			
7			
8			
9			
10			

a. Draw a graph containing both the demand curve and marginal revenue curve.

b. Is the marginal revenue curve a straight line as well? What is the slope of the marginal revenue curve? How does that slope compare with that of the demand curve?

c. Does the marginal revenue curve contain negative values over the specified range of quantities? Explain why or why not.

7. Consider the case of a Foreign monopoly with no Home production, shown in Figure 9-7. Starting from free trade at point A, consider a $10 tariff applied by the Home government.

a. If the demand curve is linear, as in Problem 6, what is the shape of the marginal revenue curve?

b. How much does the tariff-inclusive Home price increase because of the tariff, and how

much does the net-of-tariff price received by the Foreign firm fall?

c. Discuss the welfare effects of implementing the tariff. Use a graph to illustrate under what conditions, if any, there is an increase in Home welfare.

8. Suppose the Home firm is considering whether to enter the Foreign market. Assume that the Home firm has the following costs and demand:

Fixed costs	=	$140
Marginal costs	=	$10 per unit
Local price	=	$25
Local quantity	=	20
Export price	=	$15
Export quantity	=	10

a. Calculate the firm's total costs from selling only in the local market.

b. What is the firm's average cost from selling only in the local market?

c. Calculate the firm's profit from selling only in the local market.

d. Should the Home firm enter the Foreign market? Briefly explain why.

e. Calculate the firm's profit from selling to both markets.

f. Is the Home firm dumping? Briefly explain.

9. Suppose that in response to a *threatened* antidumping duty of t, the Foreign monopoly raises its price by the amount t.

a. Illustrate the losses for the Home country.

b. How do these losses compare with the losses from a safeguard tariff of the amount t, applied by the Home country against the Foreign monopolist?

c. In view of your answers to (a) and (b), why are antidumping cases filed so often?

10. Why is it necessary to use a market failure to justify the use of infant industry protection?

11. What is a positive externality? Explain the argument of knowledge spillovers as a potential reason for infant industry protection.

12. If infant industry protection is justified, is it better for the Home country to use a tariff or a quota, and why?

13. Figures A, B, and C are taken from a paper by Chad Bown: "The Pattern of Antidumping and Other Types of Contingent Protection" (World Bank, PREM Notes No. 144, October 21, 2009), and updated from Chad Bown, 2012, "Global Antidumping Database," available at http://econ.worldbank.org/ttbd/

   a. Figure A shows the number of newly initiated trade remedy investigations, including safeguard (SF), China safeguard (CSF), antidumping (AD), and countervailing duty (CVD) (a countervailing duty is used when foreign firms receive a subsidy from their government, and then the CVD prevents them from charging lower prices in the importing country). Each bar shows the number of new cases in each quarter of the year (Q1, Q2, etc.) for 2007 through Q1 of 2012. The number of cases is graphed separately for developing countries and developed countries. What does this graph tell us about what has happened to the number of such cases since 2007? What might have caused this pattern?

   b. Figure B shows the number of safeguard (SF) tariff initiations by WTO members. Since 1995 what three years saw the largest numbers of safeguards? What might explain these increases? (Hint: Consider the U.S. business cycle over these years.)

   c. According to Figure B, year 2002 had the most safeguard actions by WTO members. How many action were started that year, and what U.S. safeguard case that year was discussed in this chapter?

   d. Figure C shows the number of newly initiated antidumping (AD) investigations, for quarters of the year from 2007 through Q1 of 2012. Compare the number of cases in this graph with Figure A, which included safeguard (SF), China safeguard (CSF), antidumping (AD), and countervailing duty (CVD). What can you conclude about the total number of SF, CSF, and CVD cases as compared with the number of AD cases?

FIGURE A

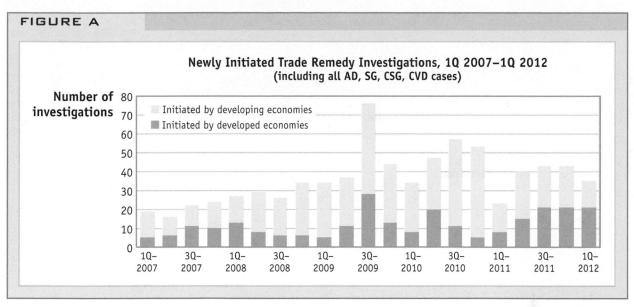

Newly Initiated Trade Remedy Investigations, 1Q 2007–1Q 2012
(including all AD, SG, CSG, CVD cases)

FIGURE B

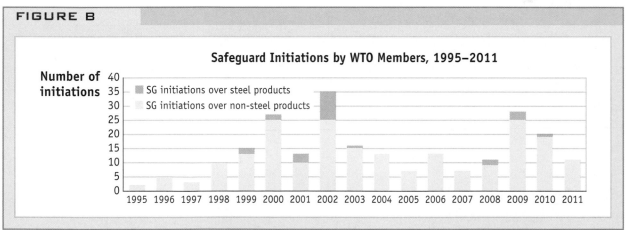

Safeguard Initiations by WTO Members, 1995–2011

FIGURE C

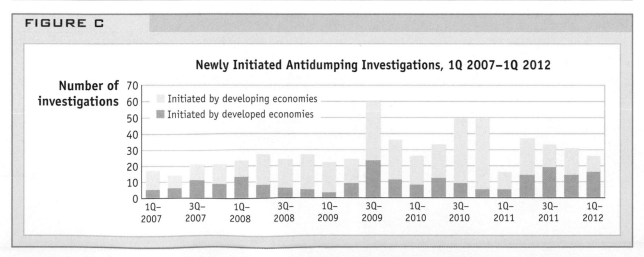

Newly Initiated Antidumping Investigations, 1Q 2007–1Q 2012

Source: Bown, Chad P., 2009, "The Pattern of Antidumping and Other Types of Contingent Protection," World Bank, PREM Notes No. 144, 21 October. Updated from Bown, Chad P. (2012) "Global Antidumping Database," available at http://econ.worldbank.org/ttbd/.

10

Export Policies in Resource and High-Technology Industries

The Middle East has its oil, China has rare earth.
  Deng Xiaoping, architect of China's economic reforms, Southern Tour of China, 1992

After more than a decade, the Doha round of global trade talks finally produced a deal. The package agreed to in Bali on Saturday [December 7, 2013] is significantly less ambitious than what the representatives who convened in [Doha,] Qatar in 2001 had in mind . . . With developing and rich countries at loggerheads over sensitive topics such as agricultural duties, the World Trade Organization built around a package of "trade facilitation" measures that could be more easily agreed upon.
                                        Financial Times, editorial, December 9, 2013, p.10.

On July 21, 2008, representatives of the 152 countries belonging to the World Trade Organization (WTO) met in Geneva, Switzerland, to discuss reforms of the world trading system. Like earlier meetings in Seattle (1999), Cancún, Mexico (2003), and Hong Kong (2005), this meeting was marked by large-scale protests. Groups including farmers from South Korea and fishermen from the Philippines objected to the impact that agricultural reforms could have on lowering food prices, thereby threatening their livelihoods. Farmers in South Korea, along with those in Japan, Europe, and the United States, benefit from an intricate system of tariffs (taxes on imports) and subsidies (payments to exporters) that keeps prices for their crops high but in some cases lowers prices in the rest of the world. The lower world price hurts farmers in land-rich developing countries such as Brazil, India, China, and some African nations by making it harder for them to export their own agricultural products. On the other hand, the lower world prices are a benefit to land-poor developing countries that must import agricultural products. Consumers in those countries will be hurt if prices end up rising as a result of agricultural reforms in the WTO.

  The first goal of this chapter is to explain subsidy policies that affect resource-based industries (such as agriculture, mining, and fuel production) and high-tech industries.

Police fight rioters outside the World Trade Organization's meeting. Most of the protesters were South Korean farmers worried about rice imports.

The primary reason that countries subsidize exports is political, but there are other reasons as well. For example, agricultural subsidies benefit a group in society (such as farmers) that the government wants to support. Such subsidies occur in the United States, Europe, Japan, South Korea, and many other countries. Because these subsidies are costly to the governments of these countries and because they harm exporters from land-rich developing countries, many countries attending the Doha Round of WTO negotiations (2001–present) advocated for the removal of agricultural subsidies. In exchange for the removal of subsidies, it was expected that land-poor developing countries would lower their tariffs on agricultural goods. This complex negotiation (which involved agriculture in many countries) ultimately failed, and the 2008 Geneva meeting of the Doha Round broke up without agreement. More recently, in December 2013 a much smaller deal to streamline customs procedures was agreed to in Bali, Indonesia, but without agreement on agricultural subsidies, as indicated in the quote at the beginning of the chapter.[1] In this chapter, we describe the tentative agreements to reduce agricultural subsidies made at the 2005 Hong Kong meeting of the WTO, and the issues that could not be resolved which led to the breakup of the 2008 Geneva meeting.

Export subsidies are not the only kind of policy that is used to influence trade in resource-based industries such as agriculture, mining, and fuel extraction. The second goal of this chapter is to explain the effect of two policies, export tariffs and export quotas, on the countries that use them. To raise government revenue, some countries impose export tariffs, taxes applied by the exporting country when a good leaves the country.[2] Argentina, for example, charges export tariffs on many agricultural and resource exports. In 2011 the tariffs were 35% on soybeans, 30% on sunflower meal and oil, 23% on wheat, 20% on corn, and 20% on biodiesel (vegetable oil–based diesel fuel). Another trade policy that can sometimes benefit companies is an export quota, a restriction on the amount that producers are allowed to export. China, for example, applied quotas on firms exporting "rare earth" minerals in 2011 and 2012, which led to a substantial increase in the price of these minerals.

The third goal of the chapter is to examine how governments can strategically use export subsidies to bolster domestic companies and industries. Instead of being used to support a particular industry or to raise revenue for the government, some subsidies are meant to give a domestic industry a strategic advantage in international competition. Some high-technology industries, such as Airbus in Europe and Boeing in the United States, receive generous government subsidies, which often leads to political friction. Legislators often believe that subsidies to high-tech industries will raise those industries' profits and benefit the exporting country.

In this chapter, we assess the arguments for and against the various export policies by examining their effects on prices, the amount of trade, and welfare.

---

[1] "Trade facilitation" measures, referred to in the quote, mean the streamlining of customs procedures so as to increase the flow of international trade.
[2] In the United States, export tariffs are prohibited by Clause 5 of the U.S. Constitution.

1 WTO Goals on Agricultural Export Subsidies

In Table 10-1, we describe the agreements made at the Hong Kong meeting of the WTO in December 2005. These agreements were never ratified by the legislatures in the countries involved, however, so it is best to think of them as goals that have not yet been achieved rather than definite outcomes. Four of the items deal with agricultural subsidies and tariffs, which were the focus of that meeting.

Agricultural Export Subsidies

An **export subsidy** is payment to firms for every unit exported (either a fixed amount or a fraction of the sales price). Governments give subsidies to encourage domestic

TABLE 10-1

Agreements Made at the Hong Kong WTO Meeting, December 2005 This table shows the agreements made at the 2005 WTO meeting in Hong Kong, which had as its major focus the subsidies provided to agricultural products. This meeting was part of the Doha Round of WTO negotiations, which have not yet been concluded.

Issue	Decision Made in Hong Kong	Unresolved in Hong Kong
Agricultural export subsidies	Abolition by end of 2013, with a "substantial part" scrapped before 2011, and parallel elimination of indirect subsidies.	Must agree [on] value of indirect subsidies and detailed phase-out programs.
Domestic farm supports	Agreement to classify WTO members in three bands based on their level of domestic farm support (top—European Union, middle—United States and Japan, bottom—everyone else).	Must agree [on] size of subsidy reduction and rules to stop countries from shifting trade-distorting subsidies into categories sheltered from deep cuts.
Agricultural tariffs	Agreement on four tiers (different for rich and poor countries) and on a mechanism allowing poor nations to raise duties to counter import surges.	Must decide size of tariff cuts and number and treatment of "sensitive" and "special" products.
Cotton Agreement	Agreement to eliminate export subsidies in 2006 and grant unrestricted access for cotton exports from West African producers and other least developed countries (LDCs).	United States will have the "objective" of cutting its $4 billion subsidies to cotton growers further and faster than the still-to-be-agreed-upon overall reduction for domestic farm supports.
Industrial goods	Agreement on formula and on a "comparably high level of ambition" for tariff cuts in agriculture and industrial goods so rich nations do not demand more cuts than they give.	Must agree [on] key elements of formula, how much to cut, flexibilities for developing countries, and role of sectoral negotiations.
Services	Some negotiating guidelines for trade in services agreed upon . . .	The European Union is pressing for liberalization timing targets opposed by developing countries; poor nations want rich ones to accept more temporary service workers.
Development	Duty-free, quota-free access extended to 97% of product[s] . . . from least developed countries by 2008, allowing significant exclusions (e.g., U.S. textiles imports). More pledges of aid for trade.	Must agree [on] other measures to strengthen special treatment provisions for poor countries.

Source: Guy de Jonquières, "Tentative Steps Forward Seen as Better Than None at All," Financial Times, December 19, 2005, p. 2.

firms to produce more in particular industries. As shown in Table 10-1, the member countries of the WTO agreed to abolish all export subsidies in agriculture by the end of 2013, though as mentioned above, this goal has not yet been achieved. Some agricultural exporters, such as Brazil, India, and China, had pushed for an earlier end to the subsidies but faced stiff opposition from many European countries. Europe maintains a system of agricultural subsidies known as the **Common Agricultural Policy (CAP).** For example, to help its sugar growers, the CAP pays farmers up to 50 euros per ton of harvested sugar beets, which is five times the world market price. Because of the subsidy, European farmers can afford to sell the sugar made from their sugar beets at a much lower price than the world market price. As a result, the sugar beet subsidy makes Europe a leading supplier of sugar worldwide, even though countries in more temperate or tropical climates have a natural comparative advantage. Other countries maintain agricultural subsidies that are just as generous. The United States, for example, pays cotton farmers to grow more cotton and then subsidizes agribusiness and manufacturers to buy the American cotton, so both the production *and* the sale of cotton receive subsidies. Japan allows 10% of the approximately 7 million tons of milled rice it consumes annually to enter into the country tariff-free but imposes a 500% tariff on any rice in excess of this 10% limit. There are many other examples of agricultural protection like this from countries all over the world.

Indirect Subsidies Included in the Hong Kong export subsidy agreement is the parallel elimination of **indirect subsidies** to agriculture, including food aid from developed to poor countries and other exports by state-sponsored trading companies in advanced countries. Europe has already eliminated its food aid subsidies and argues that *cash aid* to poor countries is much more effective; the United States continues to export agricultural commodities as aid. Later in the chapter, we explore the argument made by the European Union that cash aid is more effective than food aid in assisting developing countries.

Domestic Farm Supports Another item mentioned in the Hong Kong agreement is **domestic farm supports,** which refers to any assistance given to farmers, even if it is not directly tied to exports. Such domestic assistance programs can still have an indirect effect on exports by lowering the costs (and hence augmenting the competitiveness) of domestic products. The Hong Kong agreement is only a first step toward classifying the extent of such programs in each country, without any firm commitment as to when they might be eliminated.

Cotton Subsidies Finally, export subsidies in cotton received special attention because that crop is exported by many low-income African countries and is highly subsidized in the United States. The United States agreed to eliminate these export subsidies, but that action has not yet occurred because the Hong Kong agreement was never ratified. Subsidies to the cotton industry remain a contentious issue between the United States and other exporting countries, such as Brazil.

Other Matters from the Hong Kong WTO Meeting

Issues that are related to export subsidies were also discussed at the 2005 Hong Kong meeting, in addition to the elimination of the subsidies themselves. One of these issues is the use of tariffs as a response to other countries' use of subsidies. As we now explain, that issue is so contentious that it led to the breakup of the subsequent meeting in Geneva in 2008 and threatens to derail the Doha Round of negotiations.

Tariffs in Agriculture Export subsidies applied by large countries depress world prices, so that exporting countries can expect tariffs to be imposed on the subsidized products when they are imported by other countries. The agriculture-exporting developing countries pushed for a dramatic reduction in these and other agriculture-related tariffs, especially by importing industrial countries, but were not able to obtain such a commitment in Hong Kong.

These discussions continued three years later in Geneva. At that time, the developing country food importers wanted two special provisions allowing them to limit the amount by which tariffs would be lowered. First, they wanted a list of "special products" that would be completely exempt from tariff reductions. Second, they wanted a "special safeguard mechanism" that could be applied to all other agricultural products. Under this mechanism, tariffs could be temporarily raised whenever imports suddenly rose or their prices suddenly fell.

Recall from Chapter 8 that Article XIX of the GATT allows for such a "safeguard tariff," and that there are specific rules allowing for its use mainly in manufactured goods (see **Side Bar: Key Provisions of the GATT** in Chapter 8). The "special safeguard mechanism" in agriculture likewise requires that countries agree on the exact conditions under which it would be used. The problem in Hong Kong was that countries could not agree on the conditions under which a safeguard tariff could be temporarily applied. Likewise, the negotiators at the Geneva meeting could not agree on how many agricultural products could be treated as "special" by the importing countries, and exempt from any tariff cuts. These conflicts led to the breakdown of the Geneva talks in 2008, but must eventually be resolved before the Doha Round of negotiations can be concluded.

Issues Involving Trade in Industrial Goods and Services Other issues were also discussed in Hong Kong, as listed in Table 10-1. To achieve further cuts in the tariffs on industrial goods, there was agreement in principle to use some formula for the cuts, but the exact nature of that formula was left for future negotiation. There was also an agreement to discuss opening trade in service sectors, which would benefit the industrial countries and their large service industries. The developing countries are expected to make some future offers to open their markets to trade in services, but in return they will expect wealthy countries to accept more temporary immigrant workers in their service sectors. Finally, there was agreement to allow 97% of imported products from the world's 50 least developed countries (LDCs) to enter WTO member markets tariff free and duty free. The United States already allows duty-free and tariff-free access for 83% of products from those 50 countries, and under this agreement, the United States would extend that access to nearly all products. Omitted from this agreement, however, are textile imports into the United States from LDCs because the United States wants to protect its domestic textile producers from low-priced imports from countries such as Bangladesh and Cambodia. This is not surprising, given our discussion of the United States' sensitivity to low-cost imports in the clothing and textiles industries, as illustrated by the history of quotas on clothing imports (see Chapter 8).

2 Export Subsidies in a Small Home Country

To see the effect of export subsidies on prices, exports, and welfare, we begin with a small Home country that faces a fixed world price for its exports. Following that, we see how the outcomes differ when the Home country is large enough to affect world prices.

Consider a small country exporting sugar. The Home no-trade equilibrium is at point A in Figure 10-1. With free trade, Home faces the world price of sugar P^W. In panel (a) of Figure 10-1, the quantity supplied in Home at that price is S_1 and the quantity demanded is D_1 tons of sugar. Because quantity demanded is less than quantity supplied, the Home country exports $X_1 = S_1 - D_1$ tons under free trade. That quantity of exports is shown as point B in panel (b) corresponding to the free-trade price of P^W. By determining the level of exports at other prices, we can trace out the Home export supply curve X.

Impact of an Export Subsidy

Now suppose that because the government wishes to boost the exports of the domestic sugar producers, each ton of sugar exported receives a subsidy of s dollars from the government. Panel (a) of Figure 10-1 traces the effect of this subsidy on the domestic economy. With an export subsidy of s dollars per ton, exporters will receive $P^W + s$ for

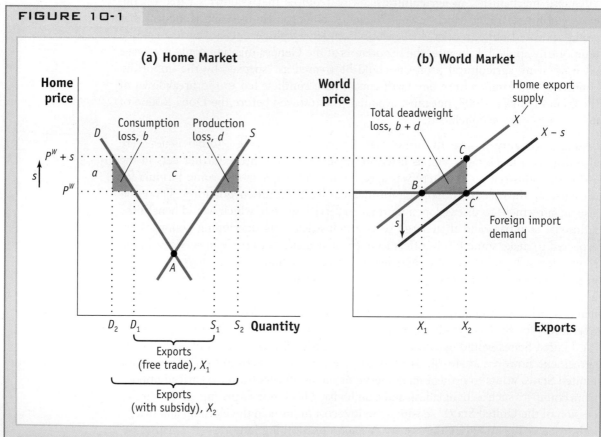

Export Subsidy for a Small Country Applying a subsidy of s dollars per unit exported will increase the price that Home exporters receive from P^W to $P^W + s$. As a result, the domestic price of the similar good will also rise by that amount. This price rise leads to an increase in Home quantity supplied from S_1 to S_2 and a decrease in Home quantity demanded from D_1 to D_2, in panel (a). Exports rise as a result of the subsidy, from X_1 to X_2 in panel (b). The Home export supply curve shifts down by exactly the amount of the subsidy since the marginal cost of a unit of exports decreases by exactly s. As in the case of a tariff, the deadweight loss as a result of the subsidy is the triangle $(b + d)$, the sum of consumer loss b and producer loss d.

each ton exported rather than the lower free-trade price P^W. Because they are allowed to export any amount they want at the subsidized price, the Home firms will not accept a price less than $P^W + s$ for their domestic sales: if the domestic price was less than $P^W + s$, the firms would just export all their sugar at the higher price. Thus, the domestic price for sugar must rise to $P^W + s$ so that it equals the export price received by Home firms.

Notice that with the domestic sugar price rising to $P^W + s$, Home consumers could in principle *import* sugar at the price of P^W rather than buy it from local firms. To prevent imports from coming into the country, we assume that the Home government has imposed an import tariff equal to (or higher than) the amount of the export subsidy. This is a realistic assumption. Many subsidized agricultural products that are exported are also protected by an import tariff to prevent consumers from buying at lower world prices. We see that the combined effect of the export subsidy and import tariff is to raise the price paid by Home consumers and received by Home firms.

With the price rising to $P^W + s$, the quantity supplied in Home increases to S_2, while the quantity demanded falls to D_2 in panel (a). Therefore, Home exports increase to $X_2 = S_2 - D_2$. The change in the quantity of exports can be thought of in two ways as reflected by points C and C' in panel (b). On one hand, if we were to measure the *Home price* P^W on the vertical axis, point C is on the original Home export supply curve X: that is, the rise in Home price has resulted in a *movement along* Home's initial supply curve from point B to C since the quantity of exports has increased with the Home price.

On the other hand, with the vertical axis of panel (b) measuring the *world price* and given our small-country assumption that the world price is fixed at P^W, the increase in exports from X_1 to X_2 because of the subsidy can be interpreted as a *shift* of the domestic export supply curve to $X - s$, which includes point C'. Recall from Chapter 8 that the export supply curve shifts by precisely the amount of the tariff. Here, because the export subsidy is like a negative tariff, the Home export supply curve shifts down by exactly the amount s. In other words, the subsidy allows firms to sell their goods to the world market at a price exactly s dollars lower *at any point* on the export supply curve; thus, the export supply curve shifts down. According to our small-country assumption, Home is a price taker in the world market and thus always sells abroad at the world price P^W; the only difference is that with the subsidy, Home exports higher quantities.

Summary From the domestic perspective, the export subsidy increases both the price and quantity of exports, a movement along the domestic export supply curve. From the world perspective, the export subsidy results in an increase in export supply and, given an unchanged world price (because of the small-country assumption), the export supply curve shifts down by the amount of the subsidy s. As was the case with a tariff, the subsidy has driven a wedge between what domestic exporters receive ($P^W + s$ at point C) and what importers abroad pay (P^W at point C').

Impact of the Subsidy on Home Welfare Our next step is to determine the impact of the subsidy on the welfare of the exporting country. The rise in Home price lowers consumer surplus by the amount $(a + b)$ in panel (a). That is the area between the two prices (P^W and $P^W + s$) and underneath the demand curve D. On the other hand, the price increase raises producer surplus by the amount $(a + b + c)$, the area between the two prices (P^W and $P^W + s$), and above the supply curve S. Finally, we need to determine the effect on government revenue. The export subsidy costs the government s per unit exported, or $s \cdot X_2$ in total. That revenue cost is shown by the area $(b + c + d)$.

Adding up the impact on consumers, producers, and government revenue, the overall impact of the export subsidy is

Fall in consumer surplus:	$-(a + b)$
Rise in producer surplus:	$+(a + b + c)$
Fall in government revenue:	$-(b + c + d)$
Net effect on Home welfare:	$-(b + d)$

The triangle $(b + d)$ in panel (b) is the net loss or **deadweight loss** due to the subsidy in a small country. The result that an export subsidy leads to a deadweight loss for the exporter is similar to the result that a tariff leads to a deadweight loss for an importing country. As with a tariff, the areas b and d can be given precise interpretations. The triangle d equals the increase in marginal costs for the extra units produced because of the subsidy and can be interpreted as the **production loss** or the *efficiency loss* for the economy. The area of the triangle b can be interpreted as the drop in consumer surplus for those individuals no longer consuming the units between D_1 and D_2, which we call the **consumption loss** for the economy. The combination of the production and consumption losses is the deadweight loss for the exporting country.

3 Export Subsidies in a Large Home Country

Now suppose that the Home country is a large enough seller on international markets so that its subsidy affects the world price of the sugar (e.g., this occurs with European sugar subsidies and U.S. cotton subsidies). This large-country case is illustrated in Figure 10-2. In panel (b), we draw the Foreign import demand curve M^* as downward-sloping because changes in the amount exported, as will occur when Home applies a subsidy, now affect the world price.

Under free trade, the Home and world price is P^W. At this price, Home exports $X_1 = S_1 - D_1$, and the world export market is in equilibrium at the intersection of Home export supply X and Foreign import demand M^*. Home and Foreign consumers pay the same price for the good, P^W, which is the world price.

Effect of the Subsidy

Suppose that Home applies a subsidy of s dollars per ton of sugar exported. As we found for the small country, a subsidy to Home export production is shown as a downward shift of the Home export supply curve in panel (b) by the amount s; the vertical distance between the original export supply curve X and the new export supply curve $X - s$ is precisely the amount of the subsidy s. The new intersection of Home export supply, $X - s$, and Foreign import demand M^* corresponds to a new world price of P^*, decreased from the free-trade world price P^W, and a Home price $P^* + s$, increased from the free-trade price P^W. Furthermore, the equilibrium with the subsidy now occurs at the export quantity X_2 in panel (b), increased from X_1.

In Chapter 2, we defined the *terms of trade* for a country as the ratio of export prices to import prices. Generally, a fall in the terms of trade indicates a loss for a country because it is either receiving less for exports or paying more for imports. We have

FIGURE 10-2

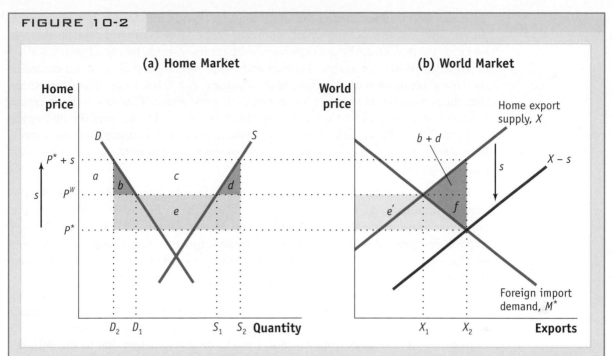

Export Subsidy for a Large Country Panel (a) shows the effects of the subsidy at Home. The Home price increases from P^W to $P^* + s$, Home quantity demanded decreases from D_1 to D_2, and Home quantity supplied increases from S_1 to S_2. The deadweight loss for Home is the area of triangle $(b + d)$, but Home also has a terms-of-trade loss of area e. In the world market, the Home subsidy shifts out the export supply curve from X to $X - s$ in panel (b). As in the small-country case, the export supply curve shifts down by the amount of the subsidy, reflecting the lower marginal cost of exports. As a result, the world price falls from P^W to P^*. The Foreign country gains the consumer surplus area e', so the world deadweight loss due to the subsidy is the area $(b + d + f)$. The extra deadweight loss f arises because only a portion of the Home terms-of-trade loss is a Foreign gain.

found that with the export subsidy, Foreign consumers pay a lower price for Home exports, which is therefore a fall in the Home terms of trade but a gain in the Foreign terms of trade. We should expect, therefore, that the Home country will suffer an overall loss because of the subsidy but that Foreign consumers will gain. To confirm these effects, let's investigate the impact of the subsidy on Home and Foreign welfare.

Home Welfare In panel (a) of Figure 10-2, the increase in the Home price from P^W to $P^* + s$ reduces consumer surplus by the amount $(a + b)$. In addition, the increase in the price benefits Home firms, and producer surplus rises by the amount $(a + b + c)$. We also need to take into account the cost of the subsidy. Because the amount of the subsidy is s, and the amount of Home exports (after the subsidy) is $X_2 = S_2 - D_2$, it follows that the revenue cost of the subsidy to the government is the area $(b + c + d + e)$, which equals $s \cdot X_2$ (the government pays s for every unit exported). Therefore, the overall impact of the subsidy in the large country can be summarized as follows:

Fall in consumer surplus:	$-(a + b)$
Rise in producer surplus:	$+(a + b + c)$
Fall in government revenue:	$-(b + c + d + e)$
Net effect on Home welfare:	$-(b + d + e)$

In the world market, panel (b), the triangle $(b + d)$ is the deadweight loss due to the subsidy, just as it is for a small country. For the large country, however, there is an extra source of loss, the area e, which is the terms-of-trade loss to Home: $e = e' + f$ in panel (b). When we analyze Foreign and world welfare, it will be useful to divide the Home terms-of-trade loss into two sections, e' and f, but from Home's perspective, the terms-of-trade welfare loss is just their sum, area e. This loss is the decrease in export revenue because the world price has fallen to P^*; Home loses the difference between P^W and P^* on each of X_2 units exported. So a large country loses even more from a subsidy than a small country because of the reduction in the world price of its exported good.

Foreign and World Welfare While Home definitely loses from the subsidy, the Foreign importing country definitely gains. Panel (b) of Figure 10-2 illustrates the consumer surplus benefit to Foreign of the Home subsidy; the price of Foreign imports decreases and Foreign's terms of trade improves. The change in consumer surplus for Foreign is area e', the area below its import demand curve M^* and between the free-trade world price P^W and the new world price (with subsidy) P^*.

When we combine the total Home consumption and production losses $(b + d)$ plus the Home terms-of-trade loss e, and subtract the Foreign terms-of-trade gain e', there is an overall deadweight loss for the world, which is measured by the area $(b + d + f)$ in panel (b). The area f is the additional world deadweight loss due to the subsidy, which arises because the terms-of-trade loss in Home is not completely offset by a terms-of-trade gain in Foreign.

Because there is a transfer of terms of trade from Home to Foreign, the export subsidy might seem like a good policy tool for large wealthy countries seeking to give aid to poorer countries. However, this turns out not to be the case. The deadweight loss f means that using the export subsidy to increase Home production and send the excess exported goods overseas (as was the case for food aid, discussed earlier as an example of an indirect subsidy) is an inefficient way to transfer gains from trade among countries. It would be more efficient to simply give cash aid in the amount of the Home terms-of-trade loss to poor importers, a policy approach that, because it does not change the free-trade levels of production and consumption in either country, would avoid the deadweight loss $(b + d + f)$ associated with the subsidy. This argument is made by the European countries, which, several years ago, eliminated transfers of food as a form of aid and switched to cash payments. The United States has now agreed to make the same policy change, as discussed in the following application.

APPLICATION

Who Gains and Who Loses?

Now that we have studied the effect of export subsidies on world prices and trade volume in theory, we return to the agreements of the Hong Kong meeting of the WTO in December 2005 and ask: Which countries will gain and which will lose when export subsidies (including the "indirect" subsidies like food aid) are ever eliminated?

Gains The obvious gainers from this action will be current agricultural exporters in developing countries such as Brazil, Argentina, Indonesia, and Thailand, along with potential exporters such as India and China. These countries will gain from the rise in world prices as agricultural subsidies by the industrialized countries—especially

Europe and the United States—are eliminated. These countries will gain even more when and if an agreement is reached on the elimination of agricultural tariffs in the industrial countries, including Japan and South Korea, that protect crops such as rice. Both of these actions will also benefit the industrial countries themselves, which suffer both a deadweight loss *and* a terms-of-trade loss from the combination of export subsidies and import tariffs in agriculture. Farmers in the industrial countries who lose the subsidies will be worse off, and the government might choose to offset that loss with some type of adjustment assistance. In the United States and Europe, however, it is often the largest farmers who benefit the most from subsidy programs, and they may be better able to adjust to the elimination of subsidies (through switching to other crops) than small farmers.

Losses Which countries will lose from the elimination of export subsidies? To the extent that the elimination of export subsidies leads to higher world prices, as we expect from our analysis (in Figure 10-2, the price would rise from P^* to P^W), then the food-importing countries, typically the poorer non-food-producing countries, will lose. This theoretical result is confirmed by several empirical studies. One study found that the existing pattern of agricultural supports (tariffs and subsidies) raises the per capita income of two-thirds of 77 developing nations, including most of the poorest countries, such as Burundi and Zambia.[3] This result is illustrated in Figure 10-3. Panel (a) shows net agricultural exports graphed against countries' income per capita over the period 1990 to 2000. The poorer countries (i.e., those lower on the income scale on the horizontal axis) export more agricultural products and therefore would benefit from a rise in their prices. But for *food* exports in panel (b), rather than *total agricultural* exports (which includes non-food items like cotton), it is the middle-income countries that export the most. Panel (c) shows that poor countries are *net importers* of essential food items such as corn, rice, and wheat (summarized as "cereal exports") and would be harmed by an increase in their world price. Many of the world's poorest individuals depend on cereal crops for much of their diet and would be especially hard hit by any increase in those prices.

Food Aid What about indirect subsidies such as food aid? The United States has been a principal supplier of food aid, which it uses for both humanitarian purposes and to get rid of surpluses of food products at home. No country will argue with the need for donations in cases of starvation, as have occurred recently in the Darfur region of Sudan and in 1984 in Ethiopia, but the United States also provides food shipments to regions without shortages, an action that can depress local prices and harm local producers. European countries stopped this practice many years ago and argue that it is better to instead have United Nations relief agencies buy food from local farmers in poor regions and then distribute it to the poorest individuals in a country. In this way, the European countries boost production in the country and help to feed its poorest citizens. In the Hong Kong talks, the European Union insisted that the indirect subsidies to regions without shortages be eliminated.

---

[3] Margaret McMillan, Alix Peterson Zwane, and Nava Ashraf, 2007, "My Policies or Yours: Have OECD Agricultural Policies Affected Incomes in Developing Countries?" In Ann Harrison, *Globalization and Poverty* [Chicago: University of Chicago Press and National Bureau of Economic Research (NBER)], pp. 183–232.

FIGURE 10-3

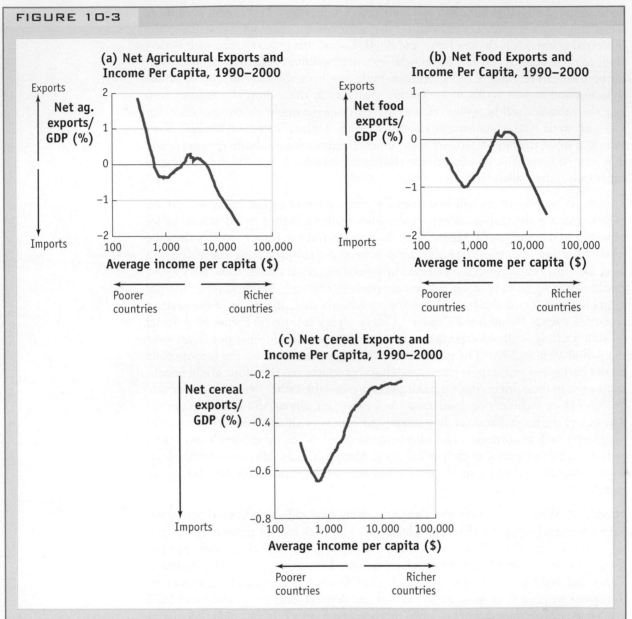

Agriculture, Food, and Cereal Exports Panel (a) shows net agricultural exports graphed against countries' income per capita. The poorer countries export more agricultural products overall and would thus benefit from a rise in the prices due to the removal of subsidies. On the other hand, panel (b) shows that it is middle-income countries that export the most food. Panel (c) shows that poor countries are net *importers* of essential food items (cereals) such as corn, rice, and wheat and would be harmed by an increase in their world price.

Source: Margaret McMillan, Alix Peterson Zwane, and Nava Ashraf, 2007, "My Policies or Yours: Have OECD Agricultural Policies Affected Incomes in Developing Countries?" In Ann Harrison, Globalization and Poverty *(Chicago: University of Chicago Press and NBER), pp. 183–232.*

Even though the proposals from the Hong Kong talks were never ratified and the elimination of tariff and subsidies in agriculture has not occurred, the Doha Round of negotiations is still ongoing and some progress has been made toward the goal of replacing food aid with efforts to increase production. In 2009, the Group of Eight

(G8)[4] countries pledged to increase funding for agricultural development by $12 billion per year, as described in **Headlines: G8 Shifts Focus from Food Aid to Farming.** This pledge represents a shift in focus away from food aid and toward agricultural sustainability in developing countries. As the Headlines article describes, this approach is a major shift in focus for the United States, where 20 times more money has been spent on food aid than on projects to increase local production.

Despite this announcement, however, many observers remain skeptical that the funding for agricultural development in poor countries will be forthcoming. After the G8 summit many editorials appeared challenging these countries to follow through on their pledges. We include one of these editorials in **Headlines: Hunger and Food Security Back on Political Agenda;** this one written by the chairman of the European Food Security Group, a network of 40 European nongovernmental organizations. ■

HEADLINES

G8 Shifts Focus from Food Aid to Farming

This article announces a new "food security initiative" from the G8 countries, who promised billions of dollars to assist farmers in developing countries. As the next Headlines article describes, however, not all observers believe that these funds will be forthcoming, despite the overwhelming need for the assistance.

The G8 countries will this week announce a "food security initiative," committing more than $12 [billion] for agricultural development over the next three years, in a move that signals a further shift from food aid to long-term investments in farming in the developing world.

The US and Japan will provide the bulk of the funding, with $3–$4 [billion] each, with the rest coming from Europe and Canada, according to United Nations officials and Group of Eight diplomats briefed on the "L'Aquila Food Security Initiative." Officials said it would more than triple spending. . . .

The G8 initiative underscores Washington's new approach to fighting global hunger, reversing a two-decades-old policy focused almost exclusively on food aid. Hillary Clinton, US secretary of state, and Tom Vilsack, the agriculture secretary, have both highlighted the shifting emphasis in recent speeches.

"For too long, our primary response [to fight hunger] has been to send emergency [food] aid when the crisis is at its worst," Ms. Clinton said last month. "This saves lives, but it doesn't address hunger's root causes. It is, at best, a short-term fix."

Washington's shift could prove contentious in the US, as its farmers are the largest exporters of several crops, including soyabean and corn. The US is the world's largest donor of food aid—mainly crops grown by US farmers, costing more than $2 [billion] last year.

The Chicago Council on Global Affairs, a think-tank, estimates that Washington spends 20 times more on food aid than on long-term schemes in Africa to boost local food production. US annual spending on African farming projects topped $400 [million] in the 1980s, but by 2006 had dwindled to $60 [million], the council said in a report this year. . . .

Source: Excerpted from Javier Blas, "G8 Shifts Focus from Food Aid to Farming," Financial Times, *July 6, 2009, p. 1. From the* Financial Times © *The Financial Times Limited 2009. All Rights Reserved.*

---

[4] The G8 countries consist of Canada, France, Germany, Italy, Japan, Russia, the United Kingdom, and the United States. In addition, the European Union as a whole is represented at the G8.

HEADLINES

Hunger and Food Security Back on Political Agenda

This article expresses skepticism that the promises of the G8 countries for billions of dollars to assist farmers in developing countries will be forthcoming.

Global food security is a political and economic priority for the first time since the early 1970s. That should be the key message from the decision by the G8 group of leading economic nations to endorse a "food security initiative" at their meeting in Italy this week. But this welcome decision needs to be followed up by further significant policy change at national and international level if food security is to be achieved for the world's growing population over the coming decades. . . .

It is reported that the initiative will involve a commitment of $12 billion for agricultural development over the next three years. But before giving three cheers for the G8, two critical questions must be answered. Is the $12 billion additional resources or a repackaging of existing commitments? How can this initiative feed into sustained policy change aimed at increasing food security at household, national and global level?

Policy change is necessary in many countries which are currently food insecure. Investment in agricultural and rural development has been shamefully neglected over the past 30 years. Donors, including the World Bank, also bear responsibility for this. There must now be an acceptance that budget allocations to agriculture must increase and must be sustained. . . . The history of such summits is not good: the gap between the promises and subsequent actions is great. At the first such summit in 1974, Dr. Henry Kissinger made the pledge that "within 10 years, no child will go to bed hungry."

The G8 food security initiative at least provides a positive backdrop to the summit. It should provide an opportunity to many developing countries to commit to the type of policy change necessary to increase their own food security. With one billion hungry people in the world, with growing populations and with the threat that climate change presents to agricultural production capacity, such a commitment is both critical and urgent. It is good politics and good economics to do so.

Source: Excerpted from Tom Arnold, "Hunger and Food Security Back on Political Agenda," The Irish Times, July 8, 2009, electronic edition.

4 Production Subsidies

The agreements reached in Hong Kong in 2005 distinguish between export subsidies in agriculture—which will be eliminated—and all other forms of domestic support that increase production (e.g., tax incentives and other types of subsidies). The agreements make this distinction because other forms of agricultural support are expected to have less impact on exports than direct subsidies. Therefore, there is less impact on other countries from having domestic support programs as compared with export subsidies. To illustrate this idea, let's examine the impact of a "production subsidy" in agriculture for both a small and a large country.

Suppose the government provides a subsidy of *s* dollars for *every unit* (e.g., ton of sugar in our example) that a Home firm produces. This is a **production subsidy** because it is a subsidy to every unit produced and not just to units that are exported. There are several ways that a government can implement such a subsidy. The government might guarantee a minimum price to the farmer, for example, and make up the difference between the minimum price and any lower price for which the farmer sells.

Alternatively, the government might provide subsidies to users of the crop to purchase it, thus increasing demand and raising market prices; this would act like a subsidy to every unit produced. As mentioned earlier, the United States has used both methods to support its cotton growers.

These policies all fall under Article XVI of the GATT (see **Side Bar: Key Provisions of the GATT** in Chapter 8). Article XVI states that partner countries should be notified of the extent of such subsidies, and when possible, they should be limited. In Hong Kong, the WTO members further agreed to classify countries according to the extent of such subsidies, with the European Union classified as having a high level of production subsidies, the United States and Japan having a middle level, and all other countries having low subsidies (see Table 10-1). Future discussion will determine the timing and extent of cuts in these production subsidies.

Effect of a Production Subsidy in a Small Home Country

To illustrate the effect of a production subsidy, we begin with a small country that faces a fixed world price of P^W. In Figure 10-4, panel (a), the production subsidy of s increases the price received by Home producers to $P^W + s$ and increases Home's quantity supplied from S_1 to S_2. The quantity *demanded* at Home does not change,

FIGURE 10-4

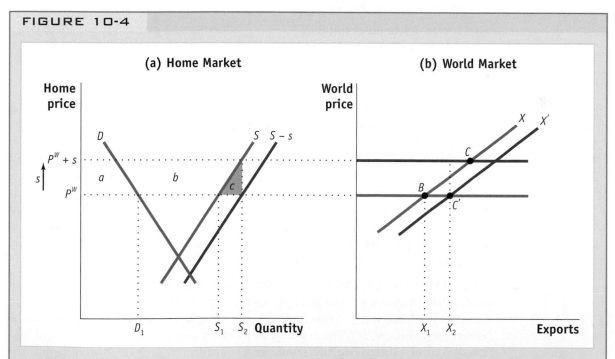

Production Subsidy for a Small Country In panel (a), applying a production subsidy of s dollars per unit produced will increase the price that Home firms receive from P^W to $P^W + s$. This price rise leads to an increase in Home quantity supplied from S_1 to S_2. The consumer price at Home is not affected because the production subsidy does not distinguish between items sold at Home or exported (firms therefore continue to charge the world price at Home), so the quantity demanded stays at D_1. The deadweight loss of the subsidy for a small country is the area c. In panel (b), exports rise as a result of the production subsidy, from X_1 to X_2, though the increase in exports is less than for the export subsidy because, for the production subsidy, quantity demanded does not change at Home.

however, because producers *continue to charge the world price* at Home. This is the case (in contrast to the export subsidy) because Home producers receive a subsidy regardless of whom they sell to (domestic consumers or Foreign consumers through exporting). So with a production subsidy, Home producers charge the world price to Foreign consumers and receive the extra subsidy from the government and likewise charge the world price to Home consumers, and again receive the extra subsidy. In contrast, for an export subsidy, Home firms receive the subsidy *only* for export sales and not for domestic sales.

Because the price for Home consumers with the production subsidy is still P^W, there is no change in the quantity demanded at Home, which remains at D_1. In panel (b), we see that the production subsidy increases the quantity of exports from $X_1 = S_1 - D_1$ to $X_2 = S_2 - D_1$. Because demand is not affected, the production subsidy increases exports by less than an export subsidy would. That result occurs because the quantity demanded decreases with an export subsidy due to higher Home prices, leading to greater Home exports. In contrast, with the production subsidy, the quantity demanded at Home is unchanged, so exports do not rise as much.

Home Welfare With the increase in the price received by Home producers, from P_W to $P_W + s$, there is a corresponding rise in producer surplus of the amount $(a + b)$ in panel (a). The government revenue cost of the subsidy is the entire area $(a + b + c)$, which equals the amount of the subsidy s, times Home production S_2. So the overall impact of the production subsidy is

Change in consumer surplus:	*none* (because demand is not affected)
Rise in producer surplus:	$+ (a + b)$
Fall in government revenue:	$- (a + b + c)$
Net effect on Home welfare:	$- c$

The deadweight loss caused by the production subsidy in a small country, area c, is less than that caused by the export subsidy in Figure 10-1, which is area $(b + d)$. The reason that the production subsidy has a lower deadweight loss than the export subsidy is that consumer decisions have not been affected at all: Home consumers still face the price of P^W. The production subsidy increases the quantity supplied by Home producers, just as an export subsidy does, but the production subsidy does so without raising the price for Home consumers. The only deadweight loss is in production inefficiency: the higher subsidized price encourages Home producers to increase the amount of production at higher marginal costs (i.e., farther right along the supply curve) than would occur in a market equilibrium without the subsidy.

Targeting Principle Our finding that the deadweight loss is lower for the production subsidy makes it a better policy instrument than the export subsidy to achieve an increase in Home supply. This finding is an example of the **targeting principle:** *to achieve some objective, it is best to use the policy instrument that achieves the objective most directly.* If the objective of the Home government is to increase cotton supply, for example, and therefore benefit cotton growers, it is better to use a production subsidy than an export subsidy. Of course, the benefits to cotton growers come at the expense of government revenue.

There are many examples of this targeting principle in economics. To limit the consumption of cigarettes and improve public health, the best policy is a tax on cigarette purchases, as many countries use. To reduce pollution from automobiles, the best policy would be a tax on gasoline, the magnitude of which is much higher in Europe than in the United States. And, to use an example from this book, to compensate people for losses from international trade, it is better to provide trade adjustment assistance directly (discussed in Chapter 3) to those affected than to impose an import tariff or quota.

Effect of the Production Subsidy in a Large Home Country

We will not draw the large-country case in detail but will use Figure 10-4 to briefly explain the effects of a production subsidy on prices, exports, and welfare. When the price for Home producers rises from P^W to $P^W + s$, the quantity of the exported good supplied increases from S_1 to S_2. Because demand has not changed, exports increase by exactly the same amount as the quantity supplied by domestic producers. We show that increase in exports by the outward shift of the export supply curve, from X to X' in panel (b). As mentioned previously, the rise in the quantity of exports due to the production subsidy, from point B to C' in Figure 10-4, is *less than* the increase in the quantity of exports for the export subsidy, from point B to C' shown in Figure 10-1. With the export subsidy, the price for Home producers *and* consumers rose to $P^W + s$, so exports increased because of both the rise in quantity supplied and the drop in quantity demanded. As a result, the export subsidy shifted down the Home export supply curve by exactly the amount s in Figure 10-1. In contrast, with a production subsidy, exports rise only because Home quantity supplied increases so that export supply shifts down by an amount less than s in Figure 10-4.

If we drew a downward-sloping Foreign import demand curve in panel (b), then the increase in supply as a result of the production subsidy would lower the world price. But that drop in world price would be *less than* the drop that occurred with the export subsidy because the increase in exports under the production subsidy is less.

Summary Production subsidies in agriculture still lower world prices, but they lower prices by less than export subsidies. For this reason, the WTO is less concerned with eliminating production subsidies and other forms of domestic support for agriculture. These policies have a smaller impact on world prices and, as we have also shown, a smaller deadweight loss as compared with that of export subsidies.

5 Export Tariffs

Export and production subsidies are not the only policies that countries use to influence trade in certain products. Some countries apply **export tariffs**—which are taxes applied by the exporting country when a good leaves the country. As we saw in the introduction to this chapter, Argentina applies export tariffs on many of its agricultural products. Mozambique charges a tariff on exports of diamonds, and Thailand charges a tariff on exports of teak wood. The main purpose of these export tariffs is to raise revenue for the government; farmers and other companies do not benefit from the export tariffs, because they pay the tax.

In this section we look at how export tariffs affect the overall welfare of the exporting country, taking into account the effects on consumers, producers, and government revenue. We start with the case of a small exporting country, facing fixed world prices. Following that, we look at how the outcome differs when the country is large enough to affect world prices.

Impact of an Export Tariff in a Small Country

Consider a small country (like Argentina) that exports soybeans. The Home no-trade equilibrium is shown at point A in panel (a) of Figure 10-5. With free trade, Home faces a world price of soybeans of P^W pesos (we are using the currency of Argentina). At that price, the quantity supplied at Home is S_1 and the quantity demanded is D_1 in panel (a), so Home will export soybeans. The quantity of exports is $X_1 = S_1 - D_1$, which is shown by point B in panel (b). So far, the free trade equilibrium in Figure 10-5 is the same as that in Figure 10-1, which showed the impact of an export subsidy. But the two figures will change when we consider the effects of an export tariff.

Now suppose that the government applies a tariff of t pesos to the exports of soybeans. Instead of receiving the world price of P^W, producers will instead receive the price of $P^W - t$ for their exports, because the government collects t pesos. If the price they receive at Home is any higher than this amount, then producers will sell only in the Home market and not export at all. As a result there would be an oversupply at Home and the local price would fall. Thus, in equilibrium, the Home price must also fall to equal the export price of $P^W - t$.

FIGURE 10-5

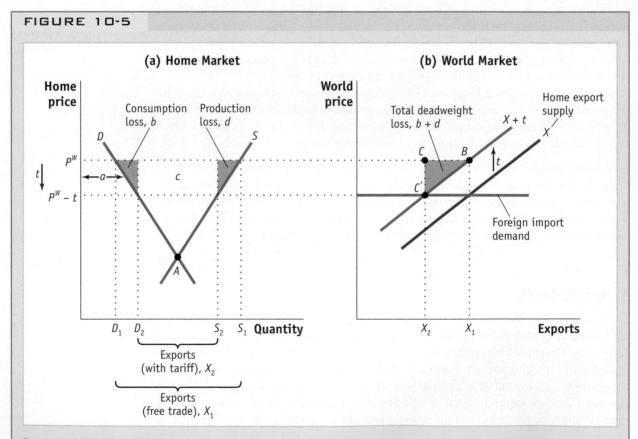

Export Tariff for a Small Country Panel (a): Applying an export tariff of t pesos per unit exported decreases the price that Home exporters receive from P^W to $P^W - t$. As a result, the domestic price of the similar good also falls by that amount. This price fall leads to a decrease in Home quantity supplied from S_1 to S_2, and an increase in Home quantity demanded from D_1 to D_2, in panel (a). Exports fall due to the tariff, from X_1 to X_2. Panel (b): The Home export supply curve shifts up by the amount of the tariff because the marginal cost of a unit of exports increases by exactly t. The deadweight loss due to the subsidy is the triangle $(b + d)$, the sum of the consumption loss b and production loss d.

With the price falling to $P^W - t$, the quantity supplied in Home falls to S_2, and the quantity demanded increases to D_2 in panel (a). Therefore, Home exports fall to $X_2 = S_2 - D_2$. The change in the quantity of exports can be thought of as a leftward, or upward, shift of the export supply curve in panel (b), where we measure the *world price* rather than the Home price on the vertical axis. The export supply curve shifts up by the amount of the tariff t. This result is analogous to what happened when we introduced a subsidy in Figure 10-1. In that case, the export supply curve fell by the amount of the subsidy s.

The new intersection of supply and demand in the world market is at point C in panel (b), with exports of X_2. Alternatively, on the original export supply curve X, exports of X_2 occur at the point C' and the domestic price of $P^W - t$.

Impact of the Export Tariff on Small Country Welfare We can now determine the impact of the tariff on the welfare of the small exporting country. Since the Home price falls because of the export tariff, consumers benefit. The rise in consumer surplus is shown by area a in panel (a). Producers are worse off, however, and the fall in producer surplus is shown by the amount $(a + b + c + d)$. The government collects revenue from the export tariff, and the amount of revenue equals the amount of the tariff t times exports of X_2, area c.

Adding up the impact on consumers, producers, and government revenue, the overall impact of the export tariff on the welfare of a small exporting country is:

Rise in consumer surplus:	$+ a$
Fall in producer surplus:	$- (a + b + c + d)$
Rise in government revenue:	$+ c$
Net effect on Home welfare:	$- (b + d)$

To sum up, the export tariff for a small country has a deadweight loss of $(b + d)$. (This outcome is similar to the results of the import tariff that we studied in Chapter 8 and the export subsidy we studied earlier in this chapter.) That loss can be broken up into two components. The triangle b in panel (a) is the consumption loss for the economy. It occurs because as consumers increase their quantity from D_1 to D_2, the amount that they value these extra units varies between P^W and $P^W - t$, along their demand curve. The true cost to the economy of these extra units consumed is always P^W. Therefore, the value of the extra units is less than their cost to the economy, indicating that there is a deadweight loss.

Triangle d is the production loss for the economy. It occurs because as producers reduce their quantity from S_1 to S_2, the marginal cost of supplying those units varies between P^W and $P^W - t$, along their supply curve. But the true value to the economy of these extra units consumed is always P^W, because that is the price at which they could be exported without the tariff. Therefore, the value of the forgone units exceeds their cost to the economy, indicating again that there is a deadweight loss.

Impact of an Export Tariff in a Large Country

We have shown that the export tariff in a small country leads to a decline in overall welfare. Despite that, some governments—especially in developing countries—find that export tariffs are a convenient way to raise revenue, because it is very easy to apply the tax at border stations as goods leave the country. The fact that the economy overall suffers a loss does not prevent governments from using this policy.

What happens in a large exporting country? Does an export tariff still produce an overall loss? Recall from Chapter 8 that an import tariff in a large country would lead to an overall *gain* rather than a loss, provided that the tariff is not too high. This gain arises because the import tariff reduces demand for the imported product, and therefore lowers its price, which leads to a terms-of-trade gain. In this section, we see that an export tariff also leads to a terms-of-trade gain. That result occurs because an export tariff reduces the amount supplied to the world market, and therefore increases the price of the export product, which is a terms-of-trade gain.

Figure 10-6 illustrates the effect of an export tariff for a large country. Under free trade the price of soybeans is P^W, which is at the intersection of Home export supply X and Foreign import demand M^* in panel (b). When the government applies a tariff of t pesos to soybean exports, the Home export supply curve shifts up by exactly the amount of the tariff from X to $X + t$. The new intersection of the Home export supply curve and the Foreign import demand curve occurs at point C, and the world price has risen from P^W to P^*.

The price P^* is paid by Foreign buyers of soybeans and includes the export tariff. The Foreign import demand curve M^* is downward sloping rather than horizontal as it was in Figure 10-5 for a small country. Because the Foreign import demand curve slopes downward, the price P^* is greater than P^W but not by as much as the tariff t, which equals the upward shift in the export supply curve. Home receives price $P^* - t$,

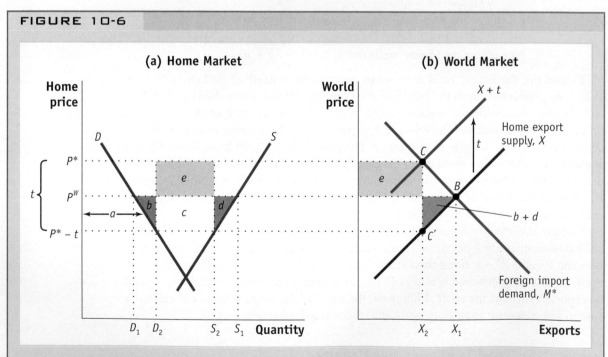

FIGURE 10-6

(a) Home Market

(b) World Market

Export Tariff for a Large Country The tariff shifts up the export supply curve from X to $X + t$, in panel (b). As a result, the world price increases from P^W to P^*. But this increase in the world price is less than the upward shift in export supply of t. It follows that the Home price decreases from P^W to $P^* - t$, in panel (a). Home quantity demanded increases from D_1 to D_2, and Home quantity supplied decreases from S_1 to S_2. The deadweight loss for Home is the area of triangle $(b + d)$. Because world price rises from P^W to P^*, Home also has a terms-of-trade gain of area e.

which is measured net of the export tariff. Because P^* has risen above P^W by less than the amount t, it follows that $P^* - t$ falls below P^W, as shown in panel (a).

Impact of the Export Tariff on Large Country Welfare We can now determine the impact of the tariff on the welfare of the large exporting country. Home consumer and producers faced the free trade price of P^W under free trade, but face the lower price of $P^* - t$ once the tariff is applied. The rise in consumer surplus is shown by area a in panel (a) and the fall in producer surplus is shown by area $(a + b + c + d)$. The revenue the government collects from the export tariff equals the amount of the tariff t times exports of X_2, by area $(c + e)$.

Adding up the impacts on consumers, producers, and government revenue, the overall impact of the export tariff on the welfare of a large exporting country is:

Rise in consumer surplus:	$+ a$
Fall in producer surplus:	$- (a + b + c + d)$
Rise in government revenue:	$+ (c + e)$
Net effect on Home welfare:	$e - (b + d)$

Compared with the effect of an export tariff for a small country, we find that the net effect on large-country Home welfare can be positive rather than negative, as long as $e < (b + d)$. The amount $(b + d)$ is still the deadweight loss; area e is the *terms-of-trade gain* due to the export tariff. In either panel of Figure 10-6, this terms-of-trade gain is measured by the rise in the price paid by Foreign purchasers of soybeans, from P^W to P^*, multiplied by the amount of exports X_2. This terms-of-trade gain is the "extra" money that Home receives from exporting soybeans at a higher price. If the terms-of-trade gain exceeds the deadweight loss, then the Home country gains overall from applying the tariff.

To sum up, the effect of an export tariff is most similar to that of an import tariff because it leads to a terms-of-trade gain. In Chapter 8 we argued that for an import tariff that is not too high, the terms-of-trade gain e would always exceed the deadweight loss $(b + d)$. That argument applies here, too, so that for export tariffs that are not too high, the terms-of-trade gain e exceeds the deadweight loss and Home country gains. In Chapter 8 we stressed that this terms-of-trade gain came at the expense of the Foreign country, which earns a lower price for the product it sells under an import tariff. Similarly, the Foreign country loses under an export tariff because it is paying a higher price for the product it is buying. So, just as we called an import tariff a *beggar-thy-neighbor policy*, the same idea applies to export tariffs because they harm the Foreign country. These results are the opposite of those we found for an export subsidy, which for a large Home country always leads to a terms-of-trade loss for Home and a benefit for Foreign buyers.

6 Export Quotas

The finding that a large country can gain from an export tariff gives a government an added reason to use this policy, in addition to earning the tariff revenue. There is one other export policy that also benefits the large country applying it: an **export quota,** which is a limit on the amount that firms are allowed to export. The most well-known system of export quotas in the world today is the system used by the Organization of

Petroleum Exporting Countries (OPEC), which includes six countries in the Middle East, four in Africa, and two in South America. OPEC sets limits on the amount of oil that can be exported by each country, and by limiting oil exports in this way, it keeps world petroleum prices high. Those high prices benefit not only OPEC's member countries, but also other oil-exporting countries that do not belong to OPEC. (At the same time, the high prices clearly harm oil-importing countries). The oil companies themselves benefit from the export quotas because they earn the higher prices. Thus, the export quota is different from an export tariff (which is, in effect, a tax on firms that lowers their producer surplus).

We can use Figure 10-7 to illustrate the effect of an export quota. This figure is similar to Figure 10-6 because it deals with a large exporting country. Initially under free trade, the world trade price occurs at the intersection of Home export supply X and Foreign import demand M^*, at point B in panel (b) with exports of X_1. Now suppose that the Home country imposes a quota that limits its exports to the quantity $\overline{X} < X_1$. We can think of the export supply curve as a vertical line at the amount $\overline{X}$. A vertical line at $\overline{X}$ would intersect Foreign import demand at the point C, leading to a higher world price of $P_2^* > P^W$.

That higher world price is earned by the Home producers. But because they export less ($\overline{X}$ rather than the free trade amount X_1), they sell more locally. Local sales can be found by subtracting exports of $\overline{X}$ from the Home supply curve in panel (a), shifting the remaining Home supply left to the curve labeled $S - \overline{X}$. The intersection of

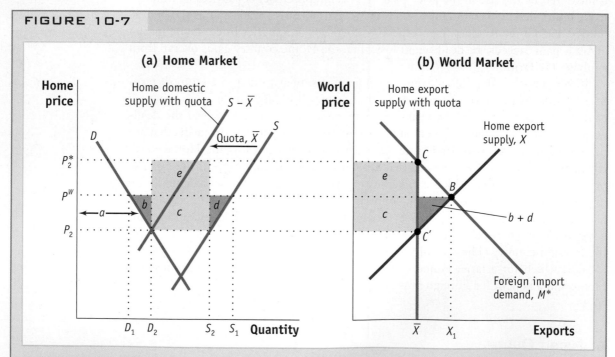

FIGURE 10-7

(a) Home Market

(b) World Market

Export Quota for a Large Country The export quota leads to a vertical export supply curve above the quantity $\overline{X}$ in panel (b). As a result, the world price increases from P^W to P_2^*. Because Home firms can export only the amount $\overline{X}$, the remaining home supply curve shifts left by that amount, as shown by $S - \overline{X}$. This remaining Home supply intersects Home demand at the price P_2 in panel (a), which is lower than the initial world price of P^W. This increase in the world price is less than the upward shift in export supply of t. The deadweight loss for Home is the area of triangle $(b + d)$, while Home firms earn the quota rents of area $(c + e)$.

this remaining Home supply with Home demand occurs at the price P_2 in panel (a), which is lower than the initial world price of P^W. As we found for the export tariff in Figure 10-6, the fall in the Home price leads to an increase in Home demand from D_1 to D_2. That quantity is the amount that Home firms supply to the local market. The *total* amount supplied by Home firms is $D_2 + \overline{X} = S_2$, which has fallen in relation to the free-trade supply of S_1. So we see that a side-effect of the export quota is to limit the total sales of Home firms.

Let's compare the welfare effects of the export quota with those of the export tariff. Home consumers gain the same amount of consumer surplus a due to lower domestic prices. The change in producer surplus is more complicated. If producers earned the lower price of P_2 on *all* their quantity sold, as they do with the export tariff, then they would lose $(a + b + c + d)$ in producer surplus. But under the export quota they also earn rents of $(c + e)$ on their export sales, which offsets the loss in producer surplus. These rents equal the difference between the Home and world prices, $P_2^* - P_2$, times the amount exported $\overline{X}$. A portion of these rents—the area e—is the rise in the world price times the amount exported, or the terms-of-trade gain for the exporter; the remaining amount of rents—the area c—offsets some of the loss in producer surplus. The government does not collect any revenue under the export quota, because the firms themselves earn rents from the higher export prices.

The overall impact of the export quota is:

Rise in consumer surplus:	$+ a$
Fall in producer surplus:	$- (a + b + c + d)$
Rise in rents earned by producers:	$+ (c + e)$
Rise in government revenue:	0
Net effect on Home welfare:	$e - (b + d)$

To summarize, the overall effect of the export quota on the Home country welfare is the same as the export tariff, with a net effect on welfare of $e - (b + d)$. If this amount is positive, then Home gains from the export quota. The effects of the quota on Home firms and the government differ from those of the tariff. Under the export tariff the Home government earns revenue of $(c + e)$, while under the export quota that amount is earned instead as quota rents by Home firms.

This conclusion is the same as the one we reached in Chapter 8, when we examined the ways that import quotas can be allocated. One of those ways was by using a "voluntary" export restraint (VER), which is put in place by the exporting country rather than the importing country. The VER and the export quota are the same idea with different names. In both cases, the restriction on exports raises the world price. Firms in the exporting country can sell at that higher world price, so they earn the quota rents, with no effect on government revenue. In the following application, we look at how China used export quotas to limit its export of some mineral products.

APPLICATION

Chinese Export Policies in Mineral Products

Like many developing countries, China uses a wide variety of export policies. Export tariffs ranging from 10% to 40% are applied to steel products, for example, which create a source of revenue for the government. In addition, China has applied both tariffs and quotas to its exports of mineral products. The policies that China has applied to mineral exports have attracted international attention recently, since some of these minerals are essential to the production of goods in other countries. As we saw in Figures 10-6 and 10-7, export tariffs and export quotas both increase the world price, making it more expensive for other countries to obtain a product and at the same time benefiting the exporting country with a terms-of-trade gain.

In 2009, the United States, the European Union, and Mexico filed a case against China at the World Trade Organization (WTO), charging that the export tariffs and export quotas that China applied on bauxite, zinc, yellow phosphorus, and six other industrial minerals, distorted the pattern of international trade.[5] Export restrictions of this type are banned under Article XI of the General Agreement on Tariffs and Trade (see **Side Bar: Key Provisions of the GATT,** Chapter 8). When China joined the WTO in 2001, it was required to eliminate its export restrictions, including those on minerals. But an exception to Article XI states that this rule does not apply to "export prohibitions or restrictions temporarily applied to prevent or relieve critical shortages of foodstuffs or other products essential to the exporting contracting party." For example, a country facing a food shortage can restrict its food exports to keep the food at home. In its response to this 2009 case, China claimed that this exception applied to its exports of industrial minerals; China claimed that it was restricting its exports of the minerals because they were needed by Chinese industries using these products (such as the solar panel industry), and also because the export quota would limit the total amount sold of these precious resources and leave more in the ground for future use. But in July 2011, the WTO ruled that this exception did not apply to China's exports of these products, and that it must remove its export restrictions on industrial minerals. China filed an appeal, but the WTO reaffirmed the ruling again in January 2012.

This legal battle at the WTO was closely watched around the world, because shortly after the case was filed in 2009, China also started applying export quotas to other mineral products: "rare earth" minerals, such as lanthanum (used in batteries and lighting) and neodymium (used in making permanent magnets, which are found in high-tech products ranging from smartphones to hybrid cars to wind turbines).[6] At that time, China controlled more than 95% of the world production and exports of these minerals. The export quotas applied by China contributed to a rise in the world prices of these products. For example, the price of lanthanum went from $6 per kilogram in 2009 to $60 in 2010 to $151 in 2011, and then back down to $36 in 2012. The high world prices made it profitable for other nations to supply the minerals: Australia opened a mine and the United States reopened a mine in the Mojave Desert that had closed a decade earlier for environmental reasons. The U.S. mine includes deposits of light rare earth elements, such as neodymium, as well as the heavy rare elements terbium, yttrium, and dysprosium (which are needed to manufacture wind turbines and solar cells).[7] These new sources of supply led to the price drop in 2012.

---

[5] The six other minerals are coke, fluorspar, magnesium, manganese, silicon carbide, and silicon metal. The information in this paragraph and the next is drawn from Keith Bradsher, "In Victory for the West, W.T.O. Orders China to Stop Export Taxes on Minerals," *The New York Times*, January 30, 2012, and "Rare Earth Trade Case Against China May Be Too Late" *The New York Times*, March 13, 2012.

[6] There are 17 rare earth minerals, consisting of the 15 lanthanides along with yttrium and scandium. The material in this paragraph is drawn from Jacob Marder, "The Rare Earth Metal Industry," University of California, Davis.

[7] See Kyle Wiens, "A Visit to the Only American Mine for Rare Earth Metals", *The Atlantic*, February 21, 2012, electronic edition.

In March 2012, the United States, the European Union, and Japan filed another WTO case against China charging that it applied unfair export restrictions on its rare earth minerals, as well as tungsten and molybdenum. The first step in such a case is for the parties involved (the United States, Europe, and Japan on one side; China on the other) to see whether the charges can be resolved through consultations at the WTO. Those consultations failed to satisfy either side, and in September 2012, the case went to a dispute settlement panel at the WTO. The Chinese government appealed to Article XX of the GATT, which allows for an exception to GATT rules in cases "relating to the conservation of exhaustible natural resources." But the WTO ruled against China, who is expected to appeal.

Regardless of the ultimate outcome of that case, it appears that China has already changed its policies on rare earth minerals. By the end of 2012, China realized that its policy of export quotas for rare earth minerals was not having the desired effect of maintaining high world prices. It therefore shifted away from a strict reliance on export quotas, and introduced subsidies to help producers who were losing money. These new policies are described in **Headlines: China Signals Support for Rare Earths.** The new subsidy policy might also lead to objections from the United States, the European Union, and Japan. But as we have seen earlier in this chapter, it is more difficult for the WTO to control subsidies (which are commonly used in agriculture) than to control export quotas.

A final feature of international trade in rare earth minerals is important to recognize: the mining and processing of these minerals poses an environmental risk, because rare earth minerals are frequently found with radioactive ores like thorium or uranium. Processing these minerals therefore leads to low-grade radioactive waste as a by-product. That aspect of rare earth minerals leads to protests against the establishment of new mines. The Lynas Corporation mine in Australia, mentioned in the Headlines article, processes the minerals obtained there in Malaysia. That processing facility was targeted by protesters in Malaysia, led by a retired math teacher named Tan Bun Teet. Although Mr. Tan and the other protestors did not succeed in preventing the processing facility from being opened, they did delay it and also put pressure on the company to ensure that the radioactive waste would be exported from Malaysia, in accordance with that country's laws. But where will this waste go? This environmental dilemma arises because of the exploding worldwide demand for high-tech products (including your own cell phone), whose manufacturing involves environmental risks. This case illustrates the potential interaction between international trade and the environment, a topic we examine in more detail in the next chapter. ■

Protesters from the Save Malaysia Stop Lynas group demonstrating outside a hotel in Sydney, Australia.

7 High-Technology Export Subsidies

We turn now to consider high-technology final products. This sector of an economy also receives substantial assistance from government, with examples including subsidies to the aircraft industries in both the United States and Europe. In the United States, subsidies take the form of low-interest loans provided by the Export-Import

HEADLINES

China Signals Support for Rare Earths

China has changed its rare earths policy amid fears that its hard line on producers threatens its dominance of the global market for 17 key substances found in items from smartphones to missiles. In a move that Beijing describes as "promoting orderly development", China will provide direct subsidies to revive struggling producers—a tacit acknowledgment of the strategic importance of the industry. The subsidies represent a significant shift in China's policy of the past two years, which focused on restricting production of rare earths, closing down illegal mines, and tightening control

of exports. These moves led to price fluctuations and slowing global demand.

Chen Zhanheng, of the China Rare Earths Industry Association, said the move would help the large, state-controlled rare earths companies the government is trying to promote. "In the long run, the policy can promote resource protection and effective utilisation of rare earths," said Mr. Chen. "[The subsidy] is aimed at supporting technological upgrades, energy conservation and environmental protection."

. . . Beijing's near monopoly in the strategic sector has raised concerns

in Washington and Tokyo, particularly when China suspended rare earths shipments to Japan during a diplomatic dispute in 2010. That incident, combined with broader concerns about the reliability of Chinese supply, triggered a surge of investment in mines outside China, several of which are set to start producing next year. Lynas Corporation, an Australia-based miner, announced yesterday that its first shipment of rare earths ore had arrived in Malaysia, where it has a processing facility expected to start producing the substances in the first half of 2013.

Source: Excerpted from "China signals support for rare earths," Financial Times, Nov. 23, 2012, p. 14. From the Financial Times © The Financial Times Limited [2012]. All Rights Reserved.

Bank to foreign firms or governments that want to purchase aircraft from Seattle-based Boeing. (The Export-Import Bank is a U.S. government agency that finances export-related projects.) On the European side, government support for research and development and other subsidies are given to Airbus, which produces parts and assembles its finished products in a number of European countries. In Japan and South Korea, direct subsidies have been given to high-tech manufacturing firms that achieve certain targets for increasing their export sales. High-tech subsidies are given by many other countries, too.

Why do governments support their high-technology industries? In the case of agricultural products, subsidies are instituted primarily because of the political clout of those industries. Although politics plays a role in subsidies for high-tech industries, governments also subsidize these industries because they may create benefits that spill over to other firms in the economy. That is, governments believe that high-tech industry produces a positive **externality.** This argument for a subsidy is similar to the infant industry argument used to justify protective tariffs (see Chapter 9), except that the protection is applied to an export industry rather than an import-competing industry.

"Strategic" Use of High-Tech Export Subsidies

In addition to the spillover argument for export subsidies, governments and industries also argue that export subsidies might give a **strategic advantage** to export firms that are competing with a small number of rivals in international markets. By a strategic advantage, we mean that the subsidized industry can compete more effectively with its rivals on the world market. Think of the aircraft industry, which currently has just two producers of large, wide-bodied airplanes: Boeing in the United States and Airbus in Europe. Each of these firms receives some type of subsidy from its government. If high-tech subsidies allow firms to compete more effectively and earn more profits in international markets, and if the extra profits are more than the amount of the subsidy, then the exporting country will obtain an overall benefit from the export subsidy, similar to the benefit that comes from a large country applying a tariff.

To examine whether countries can use their subsidies strategically, we use the assumption of **imperfect competition.** We already used this assumption in Chapter 9, in which we considered the cases of Home monopoly and Foreign monopoly. Now we allow for two firms in the market, which is called a **duopoly.** In that case, each firm can set the price and quantity of its output (and hence maximize its profits) based on the price and quantity decisions of the other firm. When a government uses subsidies to affect this interaction between firms and to increase the profits of its own domestic firm, the government is said to be acting strategically. In this section, we examine the effects of strategic export subsidies to determine whether profits of the exporting firm will rise enough to offset the cost of the subsidy to the government.

Because we now assume that certain high-tech industries operate in imperfectly competitive markets, we need to use a different set of tools to model their supply decisions than we have used thus far in this chapter. To capture the strategic decision making of two firms, we use **game theory,** the modeling of strategic interactions (games) between firms as they choose actions that will maximize their returns. The main goal in this section is to model the strategic interaction of high-tech firms in Home and Foreign, and then to see the impact of export subsidies on their respective decisions and payoffs.

To examine the effect of an export subsidy, we start with the free-trade situation, before any subsidies are in place. Suppose there are two firms that are competing for sales of a new type of aircraft. For example, Airbus sells the double-decker A380, and Boeing sells a smaller aircraft called the 787 Dreamliner (discussed later in the chapter). For convenience, we focus on the decision of each firm to produce a relatively new aircraft that competes with the other firm for sales to the rest of the world. By ignoring sales to firms in their own countries, we will not have to keep track of consumer surplus in the United States or Europe. Instead, the measure of welfare for these countries will depend only on the profits earned by Boeing or Airbus from their sales to the rest of the world.

Payoff Matrix In Figure 10-8, we show a **payoff matrix** for Boeing and Airbus, each of which has to decide whether to produce the new aircraft. Each quadrant of the matrix shows the profit earned by Boeing in the lower-left corner and the profits of Airbus in the upper-right corner. When both firms produce (upper-left quadrant), their prices are reduced through competition, and they both end up making negative profits (i.e., losses) of $5 million.[8]

If Airbus produces the new aircraft and Boeing does not (lower-left quadrant), then Boeing earns nothing, whereas Airbus, the only supplier, earns high profits of $100 million. Conversely, if Boeing produces and Airbus does not (upper-right quadrant), Airbus earns nothing, and Boeing, now the only supplier, earns high profits of $100 million. Finally, if both firms choose not to produce (lower-right quadrant), then they both earn profits of 0.

---

[8] The numbers we are using in the payoff matrix are made up for convenience, but they illustrate the idea of competition between the firms for the sale of a new aircraft.

Nash Equilibrium With the pattern of payoffs shown in Figure 10-8, we want to determine what the outcome of this game between the two firms will be. At first glance, this seems like a difficult problem. It is hard for each firm to decide what to do without knowing whether the other firm is going to produce. To solve this problem, we use the concept of the Nash equilibrium, named after John Nash, a winner of the Nobel Prize in economics.[9]

The idea of a **Nash equilibrium** is that each firm must make its own best decision, taking as given each possible action of the rival firm. When each firm is acting that way, the outcome of the game is a Nash equilibrium. That is, the action of each player is the best possible response to the action of the other player.

Best Strategy for Boeing To determine the Nash equilibrium, we proceed by checking each quadrant of the payoff matrix. Let us look at Boeing's possible strategies, starting with the case in which its rival, Airbus, chooses to produce. If Boeing knows that Airbus will produce, then Boeing needs to decide whether to produce. If Boeing produces, then it earns –$5 million (in the upper-left quadrant); if Boeing does not produce, then it earns 0 (in the lower-left quadrant). Therefore, if Airbus produces, then Boeing is better off *not* producing. This finding proves that having both firms produce is not a Nash equilibrium. Boeing would never stay in production, since it prefers to drop out of the market whenever Airbus produces.

Best Strategy for Airbus Let's continue with the case in which Boeing does not produce but Airbus does (lower-left quadrant of Figure 10-8). Is this the best strategy for Airbus? To check this, suppose that Airbus chooses instead not to produce. That would move us from the lower-left quadrant to the lower-right quadrant in Figure 10-8, meaning that Airbus's profits fall from $100 million to 0. This outcome is worse for Airbus, so it would not change its decision: it would still choose to produce. We conclude that the decision illustrated in the lower-left quadrant, with Airbus producing and Boeing not producing, is a Nash equilibrium because each firm is making its best decision given what the other is doing. When Airbus produces, then Boeing's best response is not to produce, and when Boeing does not produce, then Airbus's best response is to produce. There is no reason for either firm to change its behavior from the Nash equilibrium.

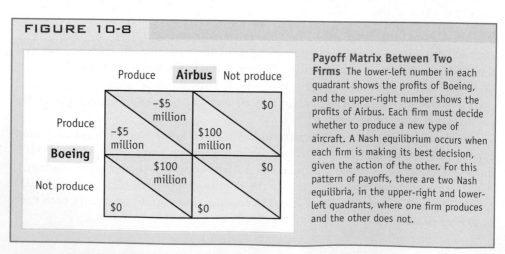

FIGURE 10-8

Payoff Matrix Between Two Firms The lower-left number in each quadrant shows the profits of Boeing, and the upper-right number shows the profits of Airbus. Each firm must decide whether to produce a new type of aircraft. A Nash equilibrium occurs when each firm is making its best decision, given the action of the other. For this pattern of payoffs, there are two Nash equilibria, in the upper-right and lower-left quadrants, where one firm produces and the other does not.

---

[9] The book and movie *A Beautiful Mind* describes the career of John Nash.

Multiple Equilibria Is it possible to find more than one Nash equilibrium? To check for this, we need to check the other quadrants in Figure 10-8. Let us try the case in the upper-right quadrant, where Boeing produces but Airbus does not. Consider Airbus making the decision to produce or not, given that Boeing produces, or Boeing making the decision to produce or not, given that Airbus does not produce. Using the same logic we have already gone through, you can confirm that neither firm would want to change the decision it has made as seen in the upper-right quadrant: if either firm changed its choice, its profits would fall. If Boeing decides not to produce, then its profits fall to 0 (from the upper-right to the lower-right quadrant), whereas if Airbus decides to produce, its profits fall to –$5 million (from the upper-right to the upper-left quadrant). So we conclude that the upper-right quadrant, with Boeing producing and Airbus not producing, is *also* a Nash equilibrium. When Boeing produces, then Airbus's best response is to not produce, and when Airbus does not produce, then Boeing's best response is to produce. Finally, by applying the same logic to the other quadrants, we can confirm that there are no more Nash equilibria.

When there are two Nash equilibria, there must be some force from outside the model that determines in which equilibrium we are. An example of one such force is the **first mover advantage,** which means that one firm is able to decide whether to produce before the other firm. If Boeing had this advantage, it would choose to produce, and Airbus, as the second mover, would not produce, so we would be in the upper-right quadrant. Let us suppose that is the Nash equilibrium from which we start. Because Airbus is not producing, it is making zero profits. In this situation, the government in Europe might want to try to change the Nash equilibrium so that Airbus would instead earn positive profits. That is, by providing subsidies to Airbus, we want to determine whether the payoffs in the matrix change such that the Nash equilibrium also changes.

The type of subsidy we consider in our model is a cash payment to Airbus. In practice, however, subsidies are of many kinds: Boeing has benefited from U.S. military contracts, where the research and development (R&D) done for those contracts has been used in its civilian aircraft, too. Airbus, on the other hand, has benefited from direct R&D subsidies to defray the "launch costs" of getting a new aircraft off the ground. Both companies have benefited from low-cost loans provided by their governments to purchasers of aircraft. Later in the chapter, we examine in more detail actual export subsidies that are used in the aircraft industry.

Effect of a Subsidy to Airbus

Suppose the European governments provide a subsidy of $25 million to Airbus. With this subsidy in place, Airbus's profits will increase by $25 million when it produces. In Figure 10-9, we add that amount to the payoffs for Airbus and check to see whether the Nash equilibria have changed. Recall that the free-trade Nash equilibria occur when one firm produces and the other does not.

Best Strategy for Airbus Let us start with the free-trade Nash equilibrium in which Boeing produces but Airbus does not (upper-right quadrant) and see whether it changes when Airbus receives a government subsidy. After the subsidy, that option is no longer a Nash equilibrium: if Boeing is producing, then Airbus is now better off by *also* producing because then it receives a $25 million subsidy from the government. With the subsidy, it will now earn $20 million ($5 million in negative profits plus the $25 million subsidy) even when Boeing produces. Recall that in the original situation, if Boeing produced,

FIGURE 10-9

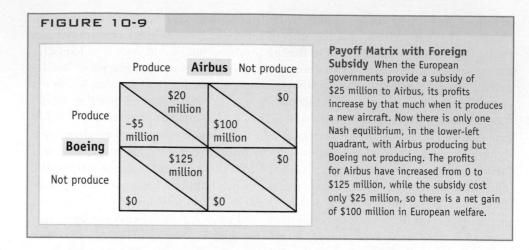

Payoff Matrix with Foreign Subsidy When the European governments provide a subsidy of $25 million to Airbus, its profits increase by that much when it produces a new aircraft. Now there is only one Nash equilibrium, in the lower-left quadrant, with Airbus producing but Boeing not producing. The profits for Airbus have increased from 0 to $125 million, while the subsidy cost only $25 million, so there is a net gain of $100 million in European welfare.

then Airbus would not choose to produce because otherwise it would lose $5 million. With the subsidy, Airbus now earns $20 million by producing instead of losing $5 million.

Best Strategy for Boeing Is this new position a Nash equilibrium? To answer that, we need to see whether Boeing would still be making the right decision given that Airbus is producing. When Airbus produces, Boeing loses $5 million when it produces (upper-left quadrant) but loses nothing when it does not produce (lower-left quadrant). Therefore, Boeing will want to drop out of the market. Once Boeing makes the decision not to produce, Airbus's decision doesn't change. It still chooses to produce, but its payoff increases dramatically from $20 million to $125 million, and we move to the lower-left quadrant, with Airbus producing and Boeing not.

Nash Equilibrium You can readily check that the lower-left quadrant is a unique Nash equilibrium: each firm is making its best decision, given the action of the other. Furthermore, it is the *only* Nash equilibrium. The effect of the European governments' subsidy has been to shift the equilibrium from having Boeing as the only producer (where we started, in the upper-right quadrant) to having Airbus as the only producer (in the lower-left quadrant).

European Welfare The European subsidy has had a big impact on the equilibrium of the game being played between the two firms. But can we necessarily conclude that Europe is better off? To evaluate that, we need to add up the welfare of the various parties involved, much as we did earlier in the chapter.

The calculation of European welfare is simplified, however, because of our assumption that production is for export to the rest of the world. From Europe's point of view, we do not need to worry about the effect of the subsidy on consumer surplus in its own market. The only two items left to evaluate, then, are the profits for Airbus from its sales to the rest of the world and the cost of the subsidy to the European government.

Airbus's profits have increased from 0 (when it was not producing but Boeing was) to $125 million (now that Airbus is producing but Boeing is not). The revenue cost of the subsidy to Europe is $25 million. Therefore, the net effect of the subsidy on European welfare is

Rise in producer surplus:	+ 125
Fall in government revenue:	− 25
Net effect on European welfare:	**+ 100**

In this case, the subsidy led to a net gain in European welfare because the increase in profits for Airbus is more than the cost of the subsidy.[10]

Subsidy with Cost Advantage for Boeing

Our finding that the subsidy can raise European welfare depends on the numbers we assumed so far, however. Let us now consider another case in which Boeing has a cost advantage over Airbus. In this case, we assume that the cost advantage is the result not of U.S. subsidies but of U.S. comparative advantage in aircraft production.

When Boeing has a cost advantage in aircraft production, the payoff matrix is as shown in Figure 10-10. Boeing earns profits of $5 million when both firms produce and profits of $125 million when Airbus does not produce. There is now only one Nash equilibrium, and it is in the upper-right quadrant in which Boeing produces and Airbus does not. The alternative free-trade Nash equilibrium in Figure 10-8 (in which Airbus produces and Boeing does not) is no longer a Nash equilibrium because—with the cost advantage we are now assuming Boeing has, even if Airbus chooses to produce—it is better for Boeing to produce and earn profits of $5 million than not produce and earn 0 profits.

Now suppose, once again, that the European governments provide a $25 million subsidy to Airbus. We add that amount to the payoffs of Airbus when it produces (still assuming that Boeing has a cost advantage over Airbus), as shown in Figure 10-11.

Best Strategy for Airbus Let's see how the subsidy has affected the previous Nash equilibrium in which Boeing produces and Airbus does not (upper-right quadrant). Given that Boeing produces, the decision not to produce is no longer the best one for Airbus: with the subsidy now in place and Boeing producing, Airbus's best decision is to produce and to earn profits of $20 million (upper-left quadrant) rather than 0.

Best Strategy for Boeing Is this new position a Nash equilibrium? Once again, we need to check to see whether, given Airbus's new post-subsidy decision to produce, Boeing is still making the right decision. Given that Airbus produces, then Boeing earns profits of $5 million when it produces and 0 when it does not. Therefore,

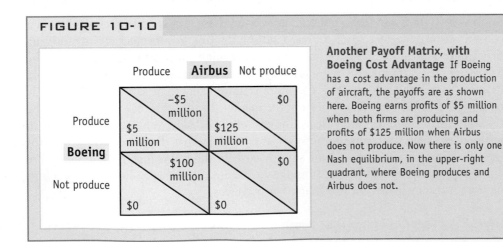

FIGURE 10-10

Another Payoff Matrix, with Boeing Cost Advantage If Boeing has a cost advantage in the production of aircraft, the payoffs are as shown here. Boeing earns profits of $5 million when both firms are producing and profits of $125 million when Airbus does not produce. Now there is only one Nash equilibrium, in the upper-right quadrant, where Boeing produces and Airbus does not.

[10] Notice that if the initial equilibrium was one in which Airbus produced and Boeing did not, then the only effect of the subsidy would be to make this equilibrium unique; it would not change the decision of either firm. Moreover, the effect on total European welfare would be zero because the subsidy would be just a transfer from the European government to Airbus.

FIGURE 10-11

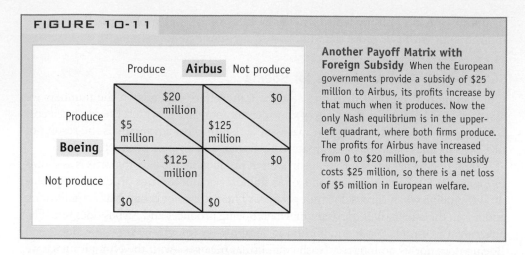

Another Payoff Matrix with Foreign Subsidy When the European governments provide a subsidy of $25 million to Airbus, its profits increase by that much when it produces. Now the only Nash equilibrium is in the upper-left quadrant, where both firms produce. The profits for Airbus have increased from 0 to 20 million, but the subsidy costs $25 million, so there is a net loss of $5 million in European welfare.

Boeing will stay in the market, and we have proved that having both firms produce is a Nash equilibrium.

European Welfare Once Again When Boeing has a cost advantage, the European subsidy allows Airbus to enter the market, but it *has not* resulted in the exit of Boeing as it did in the earlier no-cost-advantage scenario. Let us evaluate the effect on European welfare under these circumstances.

Airbus's profits have increased from 0 (when it was not producing, but Boeing was) to 20 (now that both firms are producing). The revenue cost of the subsidy to Europe is still 25. Therefore, the net effect of the subsidy on European welfare is

Rise in producer profits:	+ 20
Fall in government revenue:	− 25
Net effect on European welfare:	**− 5**

When Boeing has a cost advantage, then, the subsidy leads to a *net loss* in European welfare because the increase in profits for Airbus is less than the cost of the subsidy.

Summary The lesson that we should draw from these various examples is that under conditions of imperfect competition, a subsidy by one government to its exporting firm might increase welfare for its nation, but it might not. Although profits for the exporting firm certainly rise, there is an increase in welfare only if profits rise by more than the cost of the subsidy. This condition is more likely to be satisfied if the subsidy leads to the *exit* of the other firm from the market. In that case, the profits earned by the single firm could very well exceed the cost of the subsidy. When both firms remain in the market after the subsidy, however, it is unlikely that the increase in profits for the subsidized firm will exceed the subsidy cost. In the following application, we are especially interested in whether subsidies in the aircraft industry have kept one firm out of a market segment in which another produces.

APPLICATION

Subsidies to Commercial Aircraft

In the large passenger aircraft industry, there have been just three competitors: Boeing and McDonnell-Douglas in the United States and Airbus in Europe. The former two companies merged on August 1, 1997, so the industry effectively became a duopoly.

The United States and Europe have used various types of subsidies to support their respective firms. First, there are indirect subsidies that arise because in the production of civilian and military aircraft, the research and development (R&D) for the military versions effectively subsidize R&D for the civilian aircraft. These indirect subsidies have benefited both McDonnell-Douglas and Boeing in the United States. Second, the government might directly subsidize the R&D costs of a new aircraft, as Europe subsidizes R&D at Airbus. Third, the government can subsidize the interest rates that aircraft buyers pay when they borrow money to purchase aircraft. Europe and the United States both provide such low-interest loans, for instance, through the Export-Import Bank in the United States as mentioned previously.

1992 Agreement Recognizing that these subsidies are ultimately costly, the United States and the European Community reached an agreement to limit them in 1992. The main features of this agreement are summarized in Table 10-2. Development subsidies are limited to 33% of the total development costs of a new aircraft, and it is expected that the aircraft manufacturers will repay these subsidies at the government interest rate. In addition, the agreement limits indirect (military) subsidies to not more than 4% of any firm's annual sales, prohibits production subsidies, and limits the ability of government agencies to subsidize the interest rate on purchases of aircraft. According to one estimate, this agreement reduced subsidies by between 7.5% and 12.5% of the costs of production. As a result of the reduction in subsidies, prices for aircraft rose by somewhere between 3.1% and 8.8%. This agreement between the United States and Europe benefited the countries' governments because they no longer had to spend the money on the subsidies, and most likely also benefited the aircraft companies because prices rose, but the higher prices led to welfare losses for the purchasing countries.

The Superjumbo There are recent claims that the terms of the 1992 agreement were violated by Airbus as it launched its newest aircraft: the double-decker A380, which is even larger than the Boeing 747 and will compete directly with the 747 in long flights. This "superjumbo" aircraft carries up to 555 passengers and consists of two passenger decks for its entire length. Its first test flight in Europe took place in April 2005, and its first commercial flight to the United States was in March 2007. The expenditures to develop the A380 are estimated to have been $12 billion, one-third of which the governments of France, Germany, the Netherlands, Belgium, Spain, Finland, and the United Kingdom are expected to pay. The European governments provided some $3.5 billion in low-interest loans to cover development costs. In 2005 both the United States and the European Union filed countercomplaints at the World Trade Organization (WTO) regarding illegal subsidies by the other party to their respective aircraft producers. Europe was accused of "illegally" subsidizing the A380, while the United States was accused of subsidizing the development of Boeing's 787 commercial jet. The complaints at the WTO have been going on since 2004, as discussed in **Headlines: EU Seeks $12 billion from U.S. over Boeing Aid.**

Both Airbus and Boeing have filed cases against each other at the WTO, claiming that the subsidies given for the A380 and the 787 aircraft violated the terms of the 1992 Agreement on Trade in Civil Aircraft. In bringing the initial case to the WTO in 2004, the United States declared that it would no longer abide by the 1992 Agreement, which the United States felt had outlived its usefulness. Over the years, the WTO has ruled in favor of both companies, finding that the European Union gave up to $18 billion in subsidized financing to Airbus, while the United States

---

TABLE 10-2

Provisions of the 1992 Agreement between the United States and the European Community on Trade in Civil Aircraft This table shows the major provisions of a 1992 agreement between the United States and Europe that limited the subsidies provided to the development and production of civilian aircraft.

Aircraft Covered
- All aircraft of 100 seats or larger are subject to the provisions of the agreement.

Direct Support Levels
- Funds advanced by governments for aircraft development may not exceed 33% of total development costs and are to be provided only to programs in which there is a reasonable expectation of recoupment within 17 years.

Interest Rates
- Airbus will repay the first 25% of total development costs at the government cost of borrowing within 17 years of first disbursement; the remaining 8% will be repaid at the government cost of borrowing plus 1% within 17 years of first disbursement.

Indirect Supports
- Both sides agree that indirect (i.e., military) supports should neither confer unfair advantage on manufacturers of civil aircraft nor lead to distortions in international trade in such aircraft.
- Identifiable benefits from indirect support are limited to 3% of the value of industry-wide turnover in each signatory and 4% of the value of each firm's annual sales. Benefits will primarily be calculated as cost reductions in the development of a civil aircraft program realized from technology acquired through government R&D programs.

Escape Clause on Emergency Aid
- Either side can temporarily derogate from the agreement, with the exception of the development support provisions, if survival and financial viability of an aircraft manufacturer are in jeopardy. Any such withdrawal would require consultations with representatives of the other side, full disclosure of information to justify the withdrawal, and full explanation of the remedy to be used.

Production Supports
- No further production subsidies are allowed.

Dispute Settlement Mechanisms
- Both sides will consult at least twice a year to ensure the functioning of the agreement. Either side may request consultations related to the agreement at any time. Such consultations must be held no later than 30 days after they are requested.

Source: Excerpted from Laura D'Andrea Tyson, 1992, Who's Bashing Whom? Trade Conflict in High Technology Industries (Washington, D.C.: Peterson Institute for International Economics).

---

gave up to $4 billion in subsidized financing to Boeing. Both governments are now requesting that they be permitted to apply "countermeasures" against the other countries, which means that they can apply tariffs against products imported from those countries in retaliation for the subsidies. We do not know at this point whether these tariffs will be permitted, and it will probably be years before this complex case is ever resolved at the WTO.

National Welfare Will the development subsidies provided by the European governments to the Airbus A380 increase their national welfare? From the theory presented previously, that outcome is more likely to happen if Airbus is the only firm producing in that market. And such is the case, because Boeing did not try to produce a double-decker aircraft to compete with the A380. Instead, it modified its 747 jumbo jet model to compete with the A380, and it focused its R&D on its new 787 Dreamliner, a midsized (250-passenger), wide-bodied aircraft.

Because Boeing did not enter the market with its own double-decker aircraft, it is possible that the profits earned by Airbus will be large enough to cover the subsidy costs, the criterion for an increase in national welfare. But that outcome is certainly not guaranteed. The profits earned by Airbus on the A380 will depend on how many aircraft are sold and at what price. Airbus has stated that it needs to produce at least

250 planes to cover its development costs but that it expects to sell 1,500 A380s over the next 20 years. As of April 2013, it had delivered 101 of 262 aircraft ordered and was experiencing a slow-down in new orders because of small cracks discovered in the aircraft wings. These cracks have been traced to faulty brackets connecting the wings to the body, and all A380 aircraft in operation will be serviced to repair this defect. Boeing believes that market demand for the A380 superjumbo will not exceed 700 aircraft over the next 20 years. It remains to be seen whether the subsidies provided by the European Union for the A380 will ultimately pay off.

Boeing has its own share of difficulties with the production of the 787 Dreamliner, which was initially scheduled for delivery in 2008, but did not make its first flight until December 15, 2009. Boeing outsourced many of the components of the 787 to firms in other countries, but then had difficulty in assembling these components back in the United States, which led to the delay in its delivery. Then, in January 2013, there were battery fires in two

787 aircraft owned by Japan Air and United Airlines. Those fires led to the grounding of all 787 aircraft until the battery problem could be addressed and solved. The planes were allowed to fly again in June 2013. Finally, note that Airbus has produced a competitor for the 787 Dreamliner, the A350 wide-bodied jet, which had its maiden take-off on June 14, 2013. Boeing and Airbus will be in direct competition for customers for these new aircraft. France, Germany, and Britain pledged $4.1 billion in launch funding for the A350, and it remains to be seen whether this funding will lead to another legal case at the WTO. The fact that both firms are producing a new midsized, wide-bodied aircraft makes it less likely that either country will recoup the subsidies provided and experience a rise in national welfare from the subsidies. ■

The Boeing 787 (top) and the Airbus A350 (bottom) will compete in the wide-body aircraft market.

8 Conclusions

Countries use export subsidies in a wide range of industries, including agriculture, mining, and high technology. For agriculture, the underlying motivation for the export subsidies is to prop up food prices, thereby raising the real incomes of farmers. This motivation was also discussed at the end of Chapter 3 using the specific-factors model. In this chapter, we used supply and demand curves to analyze the effect of export subsidies, but obtain the same result as in the specific-factors model: export subsidies raise prices for producers, thereby increasing their real income (in the specific-factors model) and their producer surplus (using supply curves).

Shifting income toward farmers comes with a cost to consumers, however, because of the higher food prices in the exporting country. When we add up the loss in consumer surplus, the gain in producer surplus, and the revenue cost of the subsidy, we obtain a net loss for the exporting country as a result of the subsidy. This deadweight loss is similar to that from a tariff in a small country. On the other hand, for a large country, an import tariff and an export subsidy have different welfare implications. Both policies lead to a rise in domestic prices (of either the import good or the export good) and a fall in world prices. For an export subsidy, however, the fall in world prices is a terms-of-trade loss for the exporting country. This means that applying an export subsidy in a large exporting country leads to even greater losses than applying

HEADLINES

EU Seeks $12 billion from US over Boeing Aid

The EU has asked the World Trade Organisation for permission to levy up to $12bn in punitive tariffs against US goods for Washington's failure to dismantle illegal subsidies for Boeing, the aircraft maker. The EU request is the highest on record for so-called countermeasures in a WTO trade case and marks the latest turn in a eight year, tit-for-tat fight between the world's largest civil aircraft. . . .

The US in December made a similar demand for up to $10bn in countermeasures against the EU after it complained that European governments had not complied with a WTO ruling to remove illegal subsidies for Airbus. Under WTO rules, countermeasures allow a govern-

ment to raise tariffs on goods from another country to recoup damages. The US and EU have previously hit politically sensitive items, such as Florida orange juice and French cheese.

The Boeing-Airbus dispute dates back to 2004, when each government filed complaints at the WTO, saying the other had lavished vast amounts of illegal subsidies on its civil aircraft maker, such as cheap financing, tax breaks, defense contracts and research and development aid. After years of litigation, both sides were ultimately found to have been guilty, although the sums for Airbus, at about $18bn, were more than four-times higher.

Nkenge Harmon, a spokeswoman for the US trade representative, said: "It is

truly difficult to see how the EU characterises the finding against the US as the "worst loss" ever. "The WTO found that the EU granted $18bn in subsidised financing, which caused 342 lost sales for the United States. The WTO found $2bn to $4bn, mostly in subsidised research, against the United States, with 118 lost sales for Airbus," she added. . . .

Airbus said the company was "grateful to the EU Commission for taking consequential action," and urged Boeing to come to the bargaining table. "We regret that Boeing continues a legal battle that should have long been resolved by a mutual agreement. We made offers time and again but are ready to fight it through if the other side wishes to do so."

it to a small country: there is no possibility of gain, as we found for a large-country import tariff.

The losses arising from an export subsidy, for either a small or a large country, are less severe when we instead consider production subsidies. A production subsidy provides a farmer with an extra payment for every unit produced, regardless of whether it is sold at home or abroad. So consumer prices do not change from their world level. Since consumer prices are not affected, exports increase only because domestic supply increases. In other words, the excess supply in response to production subsidies will indirectly spill over into international markets but production subsidies do not exclusively subsidize those exports (as export subsidies do). For these reasons, the losses arising from production subsidies in an exporting country are less severe than the losses arising from export subsidies. At the Hong Kong meeting of the WTO in December 2005, countries agreed to eliminate export subsidies in agriculture by 2013, but that agreement was not ratified and has not been implemented. In addition, the countries made a much weaker agreement for production subsidies and other domestic farm supports.

The losses experienced by an exporting country due to subsidies are reversed when countries instead use export tariffs, as occurs for some natural resource products. With export tariffs in a large country, the exporter obtains a terms-of-trade gain through restricting supply of its exports and driving up the world price. This terms-of-trade gain comes at the expense of its trade partners who are buying the products, so like an import tariff, and export tariff is a "beggar thy neighbor" policy.

The losses experienced by an exporting country due to subsidies also change when we consider high-technology industries, operating under imperfect competition. In this chapter, we examined an international duopoly (two firms) producing a good for sale in the rest of the world: Boeing and Airbus, competing for sales of a new aircraft. We showed that it is *possible* for an export subsidy to lead to gains for the exporting country, by increasing the profits earned by the exporting firms by more than the cost of the subsidy. But that result often requires the subsidy to force the other firm out of the market, which does not necessarily occur. In this case, if both firms stay in the market and are subsidized by their governments, then it is unlikely that the subsidies are in the national interest of either the United States or the European Union; instead, the countries purchasing the aircraft gain because of the lower price, while the United States and Europe lose as a result of the costs of the subsidies.

KEY POINTS

1. An export subsidy leads to a fall in welfare for a small exporting country facing a fixed world price. The drop in welfare is a deadweight loss and is composed of a consumption and production loss, similar to an import tariff for a small country.

2. In the large-country case, an export subsidy lowers the price of that product in the rest of the world. The decrease in the export price is a terms-of-trade loss for the exporting country. Therefore, the welfare of the exporters decreases because of both the deadweight loss of the subsidy and the terms-of-trade loss. This is in contrast to the effects of an import tariff in the large-country case, which generates a terms-of-trade gain for the importing country.

3. Export subsidies applied by a large country create a benefit for importing countries in the rest of the world, by lowering their import prices. Therefore, the removal of these subsidy programs has an adverse affect on those countries. In fact, many of the poorest countries are net food importers that will face higher prices as agricultural subsidies in the European Union and the United States are removed.

4. Production subsidies to domestic producers also have the effect of increasing domestic production. However, consumers are unaffected by these subsidies. As a result, the deadweight loss of a production subsidy is less than that for an equal export subsidy, and the terms-of-trade loss is also smaller.

5. Export tariffs applied by a large country create a terms-of-trade gain for these countries, by raising the price of their export product. In addition, the export tariff creates a deadweight loss. If the terms-of-trade gain exceeds the deadweight loss, then the exporting countries gain overall.

6. It is common for countries to provide subsidies to their high-technology industries because governments believe that these subsidies can create a strategic advantage for their firms in international markets. Because these industries often have only a few global competitors, we use game theory (the study of strategic interactions) to determine how firms make their decisions under imperfect competition.

7. A Nash equilibrium is a situation in which each player is making the best response to the action of the other player. In a game with multiple Nash equilibria, the outcome can depend on an external factor, such as the ability of one player to make the first move.

8. Export subsidies can affect the Nash equilibrium of a game by altering the profits of the firms. If a subsidy increases the profits to a firm by more than the subsidy cost, then it is worthwhile for a government to undertake the subsidy. As we have seen, though, subsidies are not always worthwhile unless they can induce the competing firm to exit the market altogether, which may not occur.

KEY TERMS

export subsidy, p. 329
Common Agricultural Policy (CAP), p. 330
indirect subsidies, p. 330
domestic farm supports, p. 330
deadweight loss, p. 334
production loss, p. 334

consumption loss, p. 334
production subsidy, p. 340
targeting principle, p. 342
export tariff, p. 343
export quota, p. 347
externality, p. 352
strategic advantage, p. 352

imperfect competition, p. 353
duopoly, p. 353
game theory, p. 353
payoff matrix, p. 353
Nash equilibrium, p. 354
first mover advantage, p. 355

PROBLEMS

1. Describe the impact of each of the following goals from the Hong Kong WTO meeting on (i) domestic prices and welfare of the country taking the action and (ii) world prices and welfare for the partner countries.

   a. Elimination of agriculture export subsidies
   b. Reduction of agricultural tariffs
   c. Duty-free, quota-free access for 97% of goods originating in the world's least developed countries

2. Consider a large country with export subsidies in place for agriculture. Suppose the country changes its policy and decides to cut its subsidies in half.

   a. Are there gains or losses to the large country, or is it ambiguous? What is the impact on domestic prices for agriculture and on the world price?
   b. Suppose a small food-importing country abroad responds to the lowered subsidies by lowering its tariffs on agriculture by the same amount. Are there gains or losses to the small country, or is it ambiguous? Explain.
   c. Suppose a large food-importing country abroad reciprocates by lowering its tariffs on agricultural goods by the same amount. Are there gains or losses to this large country, or is it ambiguous? Explain.

3. Suppose Home is a small exporter of wheat. At the world price of $100 per ton, Home growers export 20 tons. Now suppose the Home government decides to support its domestic producer with an export subsidy of $40 per ton. Use the following figure to answer these questions.

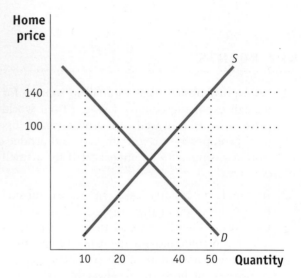

   a. What is the quantity exported under free trade and with the export subsidy?
   b. Calculate the effect of the export subsidy on consumer surplus, producer surplus, and government revenue.
   c. Calculate the overall net effect of the export subsidy on Home welfare.

4. Refer to Problem 3. Rather than a small exporter of wheat, suppose that Home is a large country. Continue to assume that the free-trade world price is $100 per ton and that the Home government provides the domestic producer with an export subsidy in the amount of $40 per ton. Because of the export subsidy, the local price increases to $120, while the foreign market price declines to $80 per ton. Use the following figure to answer these questions.

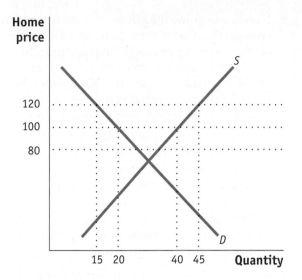

a. Relative to the small-country case, why does the new domestic price increase by less than the amount of the subsidy?

b. Calculate the effect of the export subsidy on consumer surplus, producer surplus, and government revenue.

c. Calculate the overall net effect of the export subsidy on Home welfare. Is the large country better or worse off as compared to the small country with the export subsidy? Explain.

5. Refer to Problem 3. Suppose Home is a small exporter of wheat. At the world price of $100 per ton, Home growers export 20 tons. But rather than an export subsidy, suppose the Home government provides its domestic producer with a production subsidy of $40 per ton. Use the following figure to answer these questions.

a. What is the quantity exported with the production subsidy?

b. Calculate the effect of the production subsidy on consumer surplus, producer surplus, and government revenue.

c. Calculate the overall net effect of the production subsidy on Home welfare. Is the cost of the production subsidy more or less than the cost of the export subsidy for the small country? Explain.

6. Explain why the WTO is more concerned with the use of direct export subsidies than production subsidies in achieving the same level of domestic support.

7. Boeing and Airbus are the world's only major producers of large, wide-bodied aircrafts. But with the cost of fuel increasing and changing demand in the airline industry, the need for smaller regional jets has increased. Suppose that both firms must decide whether they will produce a smaller plane. We will assume that Boeing has a slight cost advantage over Airbus in both large and small planes, as shown in the payoff matrix below (in millions of U.S. dollars). Assume that each producer chooses to produce only large, only small, or no planes at all.

   a. What is the Nash equilibrium of this game?

   b. Are there multiple equilibria? If so, explain why. *Hint*: Guess at an equilibrium and then check whether either firm would want to change its action, given the action of the other firm. Remember that Boeing can change only its own action, which means moving up or down a column, and likewise, Airbus can change only its own action, which means moving back or forth on a row.

8. Refer to Problem 7. Now suppose the European government wants Airbus to be the sole producer in the lucrative small-aircraft market. Then answer the following:

   a. What is the minimum amount of subsidy that Airbus must receive when it produces small aircraft to ensure that outcome as the unique Nash equilibrium?

   b. Is it worthwhile for the European government to undertake this subsidy?

9. Here we examine the effects of domestic sales taxes on the market for exports, as an example of the "targeting principle." For example, in the domestic market, there are heavy taxes on the purchase of cigarettes. Meanwhile, the United States has several very large cigarette companies that export their products abroad.

   a. What is the effect of the sales tax on the quantity of cigarette exports from the United States? *Hint:* Your answer should parallel the case of production subsidies but for a consumption tax instead.

   b. How does the change in exports, if any, due to the sales tax compare with the effect of an export subsidy on cigarettes?

10. Refer to Problem 9. Based on your answer there, would foreign countries have a reason to object to the use of a sales tax on cigarettes by the United States? Based on your knowledge of the GATT/WTO provisions (see **Side Bar: Key Provisions of the GATT** in Chapter 8), are foreign countries entitled to object to the use of such a tax?

11. To improve national welfare, a large country would do better to implement an export subsidy rather than an import tariff. Is this true or false? Explain why.

12. Who gains and who loses when governments in Europe and the United States provide subsidies to Airbus and Boeing?

13. Provide motivations for the use of export subsidies. Does your answer depend on whether firms compete under perfect or imperfect competition?

		Airbus		
		Large planes	Small planes	Not produce
Boeing	Large planes	10 / −5	115 / 125	115 / 0
	Small planes	150 / 100	15 / 0	150 / 0
	Not produce	0 / 100	0 / 125	0 / 0

1•2•3•4•5•6•7•8•9•10•**11**•12•13•14•15•16•17•18•19•20•21•22

International Agreements: Trade, Labor, and the Environment

Seattle was a riot, they tried to pin on us.
But we didn't show up, with gas and billy clubs
An un-armed mass of thousands, just trying to be heard.
But there are no world leaders that want to hear our words.
Lyrics from "Seattle Was a Riot" by the punk-rock band Anti-Flag, 1999

We now have a Copenhagen Accord which I think contains a number of very significant elements.
. . . But not an accord that is legally binding. Not an accord that, at this moment, pins down in-
dustrialised countries to individual targets. Not an accord that at this stage specifies what major
developing countries will do.
Yvo de Boer, Executive Secretary of the United Nations Framework
Convention on Climate Change, December 19, 2009

1 International Trade Agreements

2 International Agreements on Labor Issues

3 International Agreements on the Environment

4 Conclusions

In 1999 policy makers from around the world met in Seattle, Washington, to discuss the next round of trade negotiations under the World Trade Organization (WTO). But the meeting never achieved that goal because it was disrupted by large groups of protesters who filled the streets. The protest at times turned violent (as described in the lyrics above from "Seattle Was a Riot"). The scale of these protests took many people by surprise; after all, discussions about trade reform had been occurring since the General Agreement on Tariffs and Trade (GATT) was formed in 1947, but never before had there been such an organized protest against it. What explains this grass-roots movement against the WTO?

In past rounds of negotiations, the GATT and now the WTO have been successful in lowering tariffs in most sectors of its members' economies. The barriers to trade remaining for the WTO to address now go beyond tariffs and involve issues of national interest that are indirectly related to trade. One of those issues is the environment. Most countries have national laws governing environmental

367

In protests at the 1999 meeting of the World Trade Organization in Seattle, Washington, environmentalists dressed as turtles and other endangered species that had been affected by recent WTO rulings.

issues, such as the use of pesticides or genetically modified organisms, the protection of endangered species, the extent to which firms can release pollutants into the atmosphere, the harvesting of renewable and nonrenewable resources, and so on. Inevitably, some of these rules will also affect international trade, and that is where the WTO comes in. Under the Uruguay Round of negotiations (1986–1994), the WTO toughened its own rules governing the extent to which national laws can affect international trade. Countries that believed they were excluded from a foreign market because of unreasonable environmental standards there could bring a dispute before the WTO, where a panel of judges in Geneva would rule on the case. In principle, the panel's ruling would be binding on the countries involved.

The new WTO rules governing environmental regulations infuriated grassroots groups in the United States and abroad. Just before the Seattle meeting, these environmental groups formed a coalition with union leaders, religious groups, third-world activists, and others who believed that the WTO might threaten the interests of those whom they represent. In addition, a wide range of political groups—from conservatives to anarchists—believed it was undesirable for a WTO panel in Geneva to make rulings that would affect U.S. regulations. Members of all these groups gathered in Seattle to voice their dissatisfaction with the WTO. The environmentalists dressed as dolphins, turtles, and other endangered species that had been affected by recent WTO rulings. The scenes of these costumed creatures marching arm in arm with steelworkers gave an entirely new image to protests against the WTO.

Protesters at the U.N. climate change conference, Copenhagen, December 2009.

Protests over the environment were also evident at a meeting 10 years later, in December 2009, held in Copenhagen, Denmark. Called the Copenhagen Climate Summit, this international meeting was supposed to establish binding reductions for countries' emissions of greenhouse gases. Hundreds of protesters were arrested and thousands more attended rallies, some dressed as polar bears and panda bears to highlight the threat of global warming to the habitat of those animals. Although expectations for the summit were high, the meeting unfortunately broke up without any binding commitments from countries to reduce their greenhouse gas emissions, as indicated in the quotation at the beginning of the chapter from Yvo de Boer, who was, at the time, Executive Secretary of the United Nations Framework Convention on Climate Change.[1]

The goal of this chapter is to examine why international agreements like those negotiated under the WTO for trade, and those negotiated for environmental reasons like the Copenhagen Climate Summit, are needed. We begin by reviewing the reasons why international agreements dealing with tariffs are needed. As we discussed in an earlier chapter, countries that are large can influence

---

[1] Two months after the Copenhagen Climate Summit, Mr. Yvo de Boer resigned his position.

the price they pay for imports by applying an import tariff: the tariff increases the import price for consumers in the large country but lowers the price received by foreign exporting firms. The reduction in the price received by exporters is a **terms-of-trade gain** for the importing country. In this chapter, we show that when two or more countries apply tariffs against one another in an attempt to capture this terms-of-trade gain, they both end up losing. The terms-of-trade gain for one country is canceled by the use of a tariff in another country, so both countries wind up losing as a result of the tariffs.

To avoid such losses, international agreements to reduce tariffs and move toward free trade are needed. These international agreements take several forms. The WTO is a **multilateral agreement,** involving many countries, with agreement to lower tariffs between all the members. There are also smaller **regional trade agreements,** involving several countries, often located near one another. The North American Free Trade Agreement (NAFTA) and the European Union are both examples of regional trade agreements, which lead to free trade among the countries who are parties to the agreement. A recent example is an agreement between China and the Association of Southeast Asian Nations (ASEAN) for the China–ASEAN free-trade area. That agreement eliminated tariffs on 90% of products traded between China and six members of ASEAN—Brunei, Indonesia, Malaysia, Philippines, Singapore, and Thailand—on January 1, 2010, with the remaining four countries of the association (Cambodia, Laos, Myanmar, and Vietnam) added by 2015. This Asian free-trade area covers nearly 1.9 billion people, or more than one-quarter of the world's population. In economic terms, it is the third largest free-trade area in the world, after the European Union (covering about 500 million people) and NAFTA (covering 444 million people).

Many new regional trade agreements that span vast regions are currently being considered. The Trans-Pacific Partnership is a proposed free-trade agreement between Australia, Brunei, Chile, Canada, Japan, Malaysia, Mexico, New Zealand, Peru, Singapore, the United States, Vietnam and South Korea. The Trans-Atlantic Trade and Investment partnership is a proposed agreement between the United States and the European Union. A Europe-Japan free-trade area is also under consideration. All of these proposed free-trade areas are a response to the failure of the Doha Round of WTO negotiations. As we saw in the last chapter, the Doha Round has foundered over the issue of agricultural tariffs and subsidies. Although it will still be difficult to bargain over the use of these policies in a Trans-Pacific, Trans-Atlantic, or Europe–Japan free-trade area, we can expect that it will be easier than when *all* the 159 members of the WTO are involved in the negotiations, as they have been in the Doha Round.

In addition to eliminating tariffs on trade, regional and multilateral trade agreements often address broader issues. For example, the NAFTA agreement has two other "side agreements": one involves the rights of workers in each country, and the other involves the environment. In this chapter, we discuss the extent to which NAFTA and other labor agreements protect the rights of workers, and then we discuss international agreements on the environment. Rulings at the WTO have an indirect impact on the environment, which is what concerned many protesters in Seattle. But other international agreements, such as that attempted at the Copenhagen Climate Summit and its precursor, the Kyoto Protocol, have a more direct impact. Both of these agreements were intended to reduce carbon dioxide emissions worldwide and therefore slow global warming. We argue that for "global" pollutants such as carbon dioxide, countries do not fully recognize the environmental costs of their economic activity. So, we need international agreements to ensure that countries recognize these environmental costs. Such agreements are in the best interests of the world community, even though they are hard to achieve.

1 International Trade Agreements

When countries seek to reduce trade barriers between themselves, they enter into a **trade agreement**—a pact to reduce or eliminate trade restrictions. Multilateral trade agreements occur among a large set of countries, such as the members of the WTO, that have negotiated many "rounds" of trade agreements. Under the **most favored nation principle** of the WTO, the lower tariffs agreed to in multilateral negotiations must be extended *equally* to all WTO members (see Article I in **Side Bar: Key Provisions of the GATT,** in Chapter 8). Countries joining the WTO enjoy the low tariffs extended to all member countries but must also agree to lower their own tariffs.

The WTO is an example of a multilateral trade agreement, which we analyze first in this section. To demonstrate the logic of multilateral agreements, we assume for simplicity that there are only two countries in the world that enter into an agreement; however, the theoretical results that we obtain also apply when there are many countries. The important feature of multilateral agreements is that no countries are *left out* of the agreement.

Following our discussion of multilateral agreements, we analyze regional trade agreements that occur between smaller groups of countries and find that the implications of regional trade agreements differ from those of multilateral trade agreements. When entering into a regional trade agreement, countries agree to eliminate tariffs between themselves but do not reduce tariffs against the countries left out of the agreement. For example, the United States has many regional trade agreements, including those with Israel, Jordan, Chile, with the countries of Central America and the Dominican Republic (through an agreement called CAFTA-DR), and new agreements being planned with South Korea, Panama, and Colombia, which have not been ratified.[2] In South America, the countries of Argentina, Brazil, Paraguay, Uruguay, and Venezuela belong to a free-trade area called Mercosur. In fact, there are more than 200 free-trade agreements worldwide, which some economists feel threaten the WTO as the major forum for multilateral trade liberalization.

The Logic of Multilateral Trade Agreements

Before we begin our analysis of the effects of multilateral trade agreements, let's review the effects of tariffs imposed by large countries under perfect competition.

Tariffs for a Large Country In Figure 11-1, we show the effects of a large-country (Home) tariff, repeated from an earlier chapter. We previously found that a tariff leads to a deadweight loss for Home, which is the sum of consumption and production

---

[2] The free-trade agreements with these three countries were negotiated by President George W. Bush before leaving office in January 2009, but not ratified by Congress. President Obama mentioned these agreements in his State of the Union address on January 27, 2010, saying that: "we will strengthen our trade relations in Asia and with key partners like South Korea and Panama and Colombia."

losses, of area $(b + d)$ in Figure 11-1. In addition, the tariff leads to a terms-of-trade gain for Home, which is area e, equal to the reduction in Foreign price due to the tariff, $(P^W - P^*)$, multiplied by the amount of Home imports under the tariff, $(D_2 - S_2)$. If Home applies an optimal tariff, then its terms-of-trade gain exceeds its deadweight loss, so that $e > (b + d)$. Panel (b) shows that for the rest of the world (which in our two-country case is just Foreign), the tariff leads to a deadweight loss f from producing an inefficiently low level of exports relative to free trade, and a terms-of-trade loss e due to the reduction in its export prices. That is, the Home terms-of-trade gain comes at the expense of an equal terms-of-trade loss e for Foreign, plus a Foreign deadweight loss f.

Payoff Matrix This quick review of the welfare effects of a large-country tariff under perfect competition can be used to derive some new results. Although our earlier analysis indicated that it is optimal for large countries to impose small positive tariffs, that rationale ignored the strategic interaction among *multiple* large countries. If every country imposes even a small positive tariff, is it still optimal behavior for each country individually? We can use game theory to model the strategic choice of whether to apply a tariff, and use a payoff matrix to determine the Nash equilibrium outcome for each country's tariff level. A Nash equilibrium occurs when each player is taking the action that is the best response to the action of the other player (i.e., yielding the highest payoff).

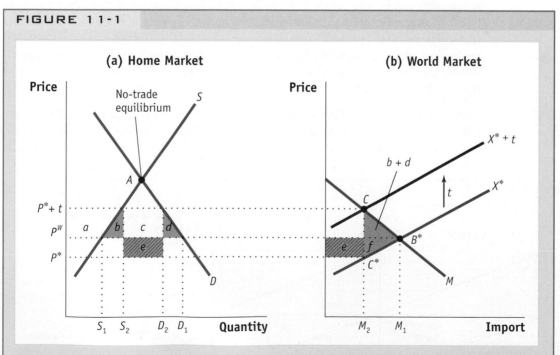

FIGURE 11-1

(a) Home Market   **(b) World Market**

Tariff for a Large Country The tariff shifts up the export supply curve from X^* to $X^* + t$. As a result, the Home price increases from P^W to $P^* + t$, and the Foreign price falls from P^W to P^*. The deadweight loss at Home is the area of the triangle $(b + d)$, and Home also has a terms-of-trade gain of area e. Foreign loses the area $(e + f)$, so the net loss in world welfare is the triangle $(b + d + f)$.

In Figure 11-2, we show a payoff matrix between the Home and Foreign countries (both large), each of which has to decide whether to impose a tariff against the other country. Each quadrant of the matrix includes Home's payoff in the lower-left corner and Foreign's payoff in the upper-right corner. We will start with a situation of free trade and then measure the change in welfare for Home or Foreign by applying a tariff. For convenience, we will also assume that the two countries are exactly the same size, so their payoffs are symmetric.

Free Trade When both countries do not impose tariffs, we are in a free-trade situation, shown in the upper-left quadrant. For convenience, let us write the payoffs for the two countries under free trade as zero, which means that we will measure the payoffs in any other situation as *relative to* free trade.

Tariffs First, suppose that Home imposes a tariff but Foreign does not. Then the Home payoff as compared with free trade is $e - (b + d)$ (which is positive for an optimal tariff), and the Foreign payoff is $-(e + f)$, the terms-of-trade and deadweight losses described previously. These payoffs are shown in the lower-left quadrant of the matrix. Now suppose that Foreign imposes a tariff but Home does not. Because we have assumed that the Home and Foreign countries are the same size, they have the same potential payoffs from using a tariff. Under these circumstances, the Foreign payoff from its own tariff is $e - (b + d) > 0$, and the Home payoff is the loss $-(e + f)$. These two payoffs are shown in the upper-right quadrant of the matrix.

Finally, suppose that *both* countries impose optimal tariffs and that the tariffs are the same size. Then the terms-of-trade gain that each country gets from its own tariff is canceled out by the terms-of-trade loss it suffers because of the other country's tariff. In that case, neither country gets any terms-of-trade gain but both countries still suffer a deadweight loss. That deadweight loss is $(b + d)$ from each country's own tariffs plus area f, the deadweight loss from the other country's tariff. The total deadweight loss for each country is $-(b + d + f)$, as shown in the lower-right quadrant of the matrix.

Prisoner's Dilemma The pattern of payoffs in Figure 11-2 has a special structure called the **prisoner's dilemma.** The "prisoner's dilemma" refers to a game in which two accomplices are caught for a crime that they committed, and each has to decide

FIGURE 11-2

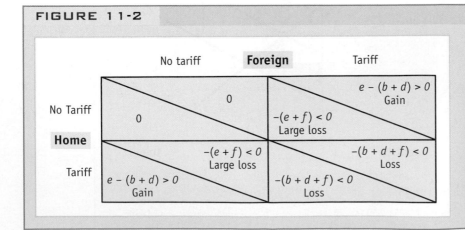

Payoffs in a Tariff Game This payoff matrix shows the welfare of the Home and Foreign countries as compared with free trade (upper-left quadrant in which neither country applies a tariff). Welfare depends on whether one or both countries apply a tariff. The structure of payoffs is similar to the "prisoner's dilemma" because both countries suffer a loss when they both apply tariffs, and yet this is the unique Nash equilibrium.

whether to confess. They are kept in separate cells, so they cannot communicate with each other. If one confesses and the other does not, then the person confessing will get a much lighter jail sentence and is better off than taking the chance of being found guilty in a trial. But if they both confess, then they both go to jail for the full sentence. This is like the pattern in Figure 11-2, in which each country acting on its own has an incentive to apply a tariff, but if they both apply tariffs, they will both be worse off.

Nash Equilibrium The only Nash equilibrium in Figure 11-2 is for both countries to apply a tariff (lower-right quadrant). Starting at that point, if either country eliminates its tariff, then it loses $(e + f)$ as compared with free trade, rather than $(b + d + f)$. Because we know that $e > (b + d)$ for an optimal tariff, it follows that each country acting on its own is worse off by moving to free trade (i.e., removing its tariff). That is, the loss $(e + f)$ is greater than the loss $(b + d + f)$. As a result, the Nash equilibrium is for both countries to apply a tariff.

But, like having both prisoners confess, the outcome for both countries when each country applies a tariff is bad. They both suffer the deadweight losses that arise from their own tariff and their partner's tariff, without any terms-of-trade gain. The Nash equilibrium in this case leads to an outcome that is undesirable for both countries even though it is the best outcome for each country given that the other country is imposing a tariff.

Trade Agreement This bad outcome can be avoided if the countries enter into some kind of trade agreement. In an earlier chapter, for example, we saw how the WTO dispute-settlement mechanism came into play when the steel tariffs applied by President Bush became problematic for the United States' trading partners. The European Union (EU) filed a case at the WTO objecting to these tariffs, and it was ruled that the tariffs did not meet the criterion for a safeguard tariff. As a result, the WTO ruled that European countries could *retaliate* by imposing tariffs of their own against U.S. exports. The threat of these tariffs led President Bush to eliminate the steel tariffs ahead of schedule, and the outcome moved from both countries potentially applying tariffs to both countries having zero tariffs.

Thus, the WTO mechanism eliminated the prisoner's dilemma by providing an incentive to remove tariffs; the outcome was in the preferred upper-left quadrant of the payoff matrix in Figure 11-2, rather than the original Nash equilibrium in the lower-right quadrant. The same logic comes into play when countries agree to join the WTO. They are required to reduce their own tariffs, but in return, they are also assured of receiving lower tariffs from other WTO members. That assurance enables countries to mutually reduce their tariffs and move closer to free trade.

Regional Trade Agreements

Under regional trade agreements, several countries eliminate tariffs among themselves but maintain tariffs against countries outside the region. Such regional trade agreements are permitted under Article XXIV of the GATT (see **Side Bar: Key Provisions of the GATT,** in Chapter 8). That article states that countries can enter into such agreements provided they do not jointly increase their tariffs against outside countries.

Although they are authorized by the GATT, regional trade agreements contradict the most favored nation principle, which states that every country belonging to the GATT/WTO should be treated equally. The countries included in a regional trade agreement are treated better (because they face zero tariffs) than the countries excluded. For this reason, regional trade agreements are sometimes called **preferential trade agreements,** to emphasize that the member countries are favored over other countries. Despite this violation of the most favored nation principle, regional trade agreements are permitted because it is thought that the removal of trade barriers among expanding groups of countries is one way to achieve freer trade worldwide.

Regional trade agreements can be classified into two basic types: free-trade areas and customs unions.

Free-Trade Area A **free-trade area** is a group of countries agreeing to eliminate tariffs (and other barriers to trade) among themselves but keeping whatever tariffs they formerly had with the rest of the world. In 1989 Canada entered into a free-trade agreement with the United States known as the Canada–U.S. Free Trade Agreement. Under this agreement, tariffs between the two countries were eliminated over the next decade. In 1994, Canada and the United States entered into an agreement with Mexico called the North American Free Trade Agreement (NAFTA). NAFTA created free trade among all three countries. Each of these countries still has its own tariffs with all other countries of the world.

Customs Union A **customs union** is similar to a free-trade area, except that in addition to eliminating tariffs among countries in the union, the countries within a customs union also agree to a *common* schedule of tariffs with each country outside the union. Examples of customs unions include the countries in the EU and the signatory countries of Mercosur in South America. All countries in the EU have identical tariffs with respect to each outside country; the same holds for the countries in Mercosur.[3]

Rules of Origin The fact that the countries in a free-trade area do not have common tariffs for outside countries, as do countries within a customs union, leads to an obvious problem with free-trade areas: if China, for example, wants to sell a good to Canada, what would prevent it from first exporting the good to the United States or Mexico, whichever has the lowest tariff, and then shipping it to Canada? The answer is that free-trade areas have complex **rules of origin** that specify what type of goods can be shipped duty-free within the free-trade area.

A good entering Mexico from China, for example, is not granted duty-free access to the United States or Canada, unless that good is first incorporated into another product in Mexico, giving the new product enough "North American content" to qualify for duty-free access. So China or any other outside country cannot just choose the lowest-tariff country through which to enter North America. Rather, products can be shipped duty-free between countries only if most of their production occurred within North America. To determine whether this criterion has been satisfied, the rules of origin must specify—for each and every product—how much of its production (as determined by value-added or the use of some key inputs) took place in North

---

[3] When new countries enter the EU or Mercosur, they must adjust their outside tariffs to the customs union level. Sometimes that will mean *increasing* a tariff on an outside member, as occurred when West Germany joined the European Economic Community in 1962. Germany increased the tariff that it charged on imported U.S. poultry, to be in accordance with the tariffs charged by the European Economic Community on U.S. imports, and in retaliation, the United States increased its tariffs on trucks and other products imported from Germany. This episode became known as the "chicken war." The tariff of 25% on trucks applied by the United States became a permanent item in the U.S. tariff code and today applies to compact trucks imported by the United States from Japan (see Application: Import Tariffs on Japanese Trucks in an earlier chapter).

America. As you can imagine, it takes many pages to specify these rules for each and every product, and it is said that the rules of origin for NAFTA take up more space in the agreement than all other considerations combined!

Notice that these rules are not needed in a customs union because in that case the tariffs on outside members are the same for all countries in the union: there is no incentive to import a good into the lowest-tariff country. So why don't countries just create a customs union, making the rules of origin irrelevant? The answer is that modifying the tariffs applied against an outside country is a politically sensitive issue. The United States, for example, might want a higher tariff on textiles than Canada or Mexico, and Mexico might want a higher tariff on corn. NAFTA allows each of these three countries to have its own tariffs for each commodity on outside countries. So despite the complexity of rules of origin, they allow countries to enter into a free-trade agreement without modifying their tariffs on outside countries.

Now that we understand the difference between free-trade areas and customs unions, let us set that difference aside and focus on the main economic effects of regional trade agreements, by which we mean free-trade areas or customs unions.

Trade Creation and Trade Diversion

When a regional trade agreement is formed and trade increases between member countries, the increase in trade can be of two types. The first type of trade increase, **trade creation,** occurs when a member country imports a product from another member country that formerly it produced for itself. In this case, there is a gain in consumer surplus for the importing country (by importing greater amounts of goods at lower prices) and a gain in producer surplus for the exporting country (from increased sales). These gains from trade are analogous to those that occur from the opening of trade in the Ricardian or Heckscher-Ohlin models. No other country inside or outside the trade agreement is affected because the product was not traded before. Therefore, trade creation brings welfare gains for both countries involved.

The second reason for trade to increase within a regional agreement is **trade diversion,** which occurs when a member country imports a product from another member country that it formerly imported *from a country outside of the new trade region.* The article **Headlines: China-ASEAN Treaty Threatens Indian Exporters** gives an example of trade diversion that could result from the free-trade agreement between China and the ASEAN countries, which was implemented on January 1, 2010.

Numerical Example of Trade Creation and Diversion

To illustrate the potential for trade diversion, we use an example from NAFTA, in which the United States might import auto parts from Mexico that it formerly imported from Asia.[4] Let us keep track of the gains and losses for the countries involved. Asia will lose export sales to North America, so it suffers a loss in producer surplus in its exporting industry. Mexico gains producer surplus by selling the auto parts. The problem with this outcome is that Mexico is not the most efficient (lowest cost) producer of auto parts: we know that Asia is more efficient because that is

---

[4] The largest exporters of auto parts to the United States currently are Canada, Mexico, and Japan. So the Asian country in this example can be thought of as Japan. In the future, however, China is expected to become a major exporter of auto parts, especially for the labor-intensive parts now produced in Mexico.

HEADLINES

China-ASEAN Treaty Threatens Indian Exporters

This article discusses the China–ASEAN free-trade area, which was implemented on January 1, 2010. By eliminating tariffs between China and the ASEAN countries, this free-trade area will make it more difficult for India to export to those countries, which is an example of trade diversion.

BEIJING—Indian exporters are faced with a new challenge as the free trade agreement between China and members of the Association of Southeast Asian Nations became operational on Friday. It will mean nearly zero duty trade between several Asian nations making it difficult for Indian businesses to sell a range of products.

India has been planning to enlarge its trade basket to include several commodities that are now supplied to China by ASEAN countries. These products include fruits, vegetables and grains. Indian products, which will face 10–12 per cent import duty [tariff], may find it extremely difficult to survive the competition from ASEAN nations. China is cutting tariffs on imports from ASEAN nations from an average of 9.8 per cent to about 0.1 per cent. The original members of ASEAN—Brunei, Indonesia, Malaysia, the Philippines, Singapore and Thailand—have also agreed to dramatically cut import duty on Chinese products from an average of 12.8 per cent to just 0.6 per cent. The newly created free-trade area involves 11 countries will a total population of 1.9 billion and having a combined gross domestic product of $6 trillion.

The successful implementation of the FTA is bound to force New Delhi to expatiate similar trade agreements with countries in the ASEAN region besides China. India is in the process of discussing trade agreements with several countries including China. New Delhi has also inked agreements with Beijing on the supply of fruits, vegetables and Basmati rice. But they remain to be implemented. At present, 58 per cent of Indian exports to China consists of iron ore with very little component of value added goods. India has been trying to widen the trade basket to include manufactured goods, fruits and vegetables. This effort might be severely hit because goods from ASEAN nations will now cost much less to the Chinese consumer. . . .

Source: Excerpted from Saibal Dasgupta, "China-ASEAN Treaty Threatens Indian Exporters," January 3, 2010. The Times of India. © Bennett, Coleman & Co. Ltd. All Rights Reserved.

where the United States initially purchased its auto parts. Because the United States is importing from a less efficient producer, there is some potential loss for the United States due to trade diversion. We can determine whether this is indeed the case by numerically analyzing the cases of trade creation and trade diversion.

Suppose that the costs to the United States of importing an auto part from Mexico or from Asia are as shown in Table 11-1. The rightmost columns show the total costs of the part under free trade (zero tariff), with a 10% tariff and 20% tariff, respectively. Under free trade, the auto part can be produced in Mexico for $20 or in Asia for $19. Thus, Asia is the most efficient producer. If the United States purchased the part from an American supplier, it would cost $22, as shown in the last row of the table. With a tariff of 10%, the costs of importing from Mexico or Asia are increased to $22 and $20.90, respectively. Similarly, a 20% tariff would increase the cost of importing to $24 and $22.80, respectively. Under NAFTA, however, the cost of importing from Mexico is $20 regardless of the tariff.

With the data shown in Table 11-1, we can examine the effect of NAFTA on each country's welfare. First, suppose that the tariff applied by the United States is 20%, as shown in the last column. Before NAFTA, it would have cost $24 to import the auto part from Mexico, $22.80 to import it from Asia, and $22 to produce it locally in the United States. Before NAFTA, then, producing the part in the United States for $22 is the cheapest option. With the tariff of 20%, therefore, there are no imports of this auto part into the United States.

Trade Creation When Mexico joins NAFTA, it pays no tariff to the United States, whereas Asia continues to have a 20% tariff applied against it. After NAFTA, the United States will import the part from Mexico for $20 because the price is less than the U.S. cost of $22. Therefore, all the auto parts will be imported from Mexico. This is an example of trade creation. The United States clearly gains from the lower cost of the auto part; Mexico gains from being able to export to the United States; and Asia neither gains nor loses, because it never sold the auto part to the United States to begin with.

Trade Diversion Now suppose instead that the U.S. tariff on auto parts is 10% (the middle column of Table 11-1). Before NAFTA, the United States can import the auto part from Mexico for $22 or from Asia for $20.90. It still costs $22 to produce the part at home. In this

TABLE 11-1

Cost of Importing an Automobile Part This table shows the cost to the United States of purchasing an automobile part from various source countries, with and without tariffs. If there is a 20% tariff on all countries, then it would be cheapest for the United States to buy the auto part from itself (for $22). But when the tariff is eliminated on Mexico after NAFTA, then the United States would instead buy from that country (for $20), which illustrates the idea of trade creation. If instead we start with a 10% tariff on all countries, then it would be cheapest for the United States to buy from Asia (for $20.90). When the tariff on Mexico is eliminated under NAFTA, then the United States would instead buy there (for $20), illustrating the idea of trade diversion.

	U.S. Tariff		
	0%	10%	20%
From Mexico, before NAFTA	$20	$22	$24
From Asia, before NAFTA	$19	$20.90	$22.80
From Mexico, after NAFTA	$20	$20	$20
From Asia, after NAFTA	$19	$20.90	$22.80
From the United States	$22	$22	$22

case, the least-cost option is for the United States to import the auto part from Asia. When Mexico joins NAFTA, however, this outcome changes. It will cost $20 to import the auto part from Mexico duty-free, $20.90 to import it from Asia subject to the 10% tariff, and $22 to produce it at home. The least-cost option is to import the auto part from Mexico. Because of the establishment of NAFTA, the United States *switches* the source of its imports from Asia to Mexico, an example of trade diversion.

Producer surplus in Asia falls because it loses its export sales to the United States, whereas producer surplus in Mexico rises. What about the United States? Before NAFTA, it imported from Asia at a price of $20.90, of which 10% (or $1.90 per unit) consisted of the tariff. The net-of-tariff price that Asia received for the auto parts was $19. After NAFTA the United States instead imports from Mexico, at the price of $20, but it does not collect any tariff revenue at all. So the United States gains 90¢ on each unit from paying a lower price, but it also loses $1.90 in tariff revenue from not purchasing from Asia. From this example, it seems that importing the auto part from Mexico is not a very good idea for the United States because it no longer collects tariff revenue. To determine the overall impact on U.S. welfare, we can analyze the same example in a graph.

Trade Diversion in a Graph

In Figure 11-3, we show the free-trade price of the auto part from Asia as P_{Asia}, and the free-trade export supply curve from Asia as the horizontal line labeled S_{Asia}. By treating this price as fixed, we are supposing that the United States is a small country relative to the potential supply from Asia. Inclusive of the tariff, the cost of imported parts from Asia becomes $P_{Asia} + t$, and the supply curve is $S_{Asia} + t$. The free-trade supply from Mexico is shown as the upward-sloping curve labeled S_{Mex}; inclusive of the tariff, the supply curve is $S_{Mex} + t$.

FIGURE 11-3

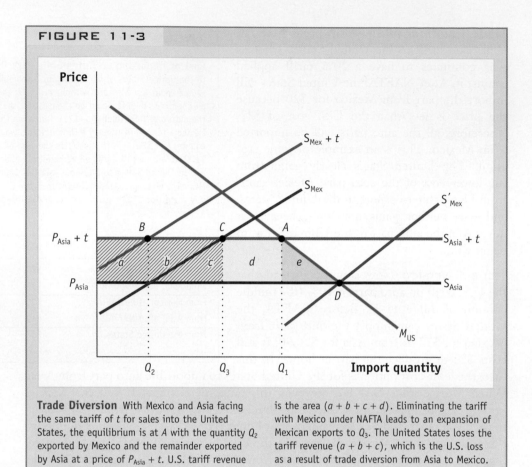

Trade Diversion With Mexico and Asia facing the same tariff of t for sales into the United States, the equilibrium is at A with the quantity Q_2 exported by Mexico and the remainder exported by Asia at a price of $P_{Asia} + t$. U.S. tariff revenue is the area $(a + b + c + d)$. Eliminating the tariff with Mexico under NAFTA leads to an expansion of Mexican exports to Q_3. The United States loses the tariff revenue $(a + b + c)$, which is the U.S. loss as a result of trade diversion from Asia to Mexico.

Before NAFTA, both Mexico and Asia face the same tariff of t. So the equilibrium imports occur at point A, where the quantity imported is Q_1 and the tariff-inclusive price to the United States is $P_{Asia} + t$. Of the total imports Q_1, the amount Q_2 comes from Mexico at point B, since under perfect competition these imports have the same tariff-inclusive price as those from Asia. Thus, tariff revenue is collected on imports from both Mexico and Asia, so the total tariff revenue is the area $(a + b + c + d)$ in Figure 11-3.

After Mexico joins NAFTA, it is able to sell to the United States duty-free. In that case, the relevant supply curve is S_{Mex}, and imports from Mexico expand to Q_3 at point C. Notice that the price charged by Mexico at point C still equals the tariff-inclusive price from Asia, which is $P_{Asia} + t$, even though Mexican imports do not have any tariff. Mexico charges that price because its marginal costs have risen along its supply curve, so even though the tariff has been removed, the price of its imports to the United States has not changed.

Because the imports from Mexico enter the United States duty-free, the United States loses tariff revenue of $t \cdot Q_3$, which is the area $(a + b + c)$ in Figure 11-3. The price of imports to the United States has not changed, so the United States is worse off due to NAFTA by the loss in its tariff revenue. Mexico is better off because of the increase in its producer surplus from charging the price $P_{Asia} + t$, without paying any tariff on its expanded amount of exports. Mexico's producer surplus rises by $(a + b)$, the area to the left of the supply curve S_{Mex}. If we add together the changes in U.S. and Mexican welfare, the combined change in their welfare is

Loss in U.S. tariff revenue:	$-(a + b + c)$
Gain in Mexico's producer surplus:	$+(a + b)$
Combined effect due to NAFTA:	$-c$

So we see that the combined welfare of the United States and Mexico actually *falls* as a result of NAFTA. This is a very counterintuitive result because we normally expect that countries will be better off when they move toward free trade. Instead, in this example, we see that one of the countries within the regional agreement is worse off (the United States), and so much so that its fall in welfare exceeds the gains for Mexico, so that their combined welfare falls!

Interpretation of the Loss This is one of the few instances in this textbook in which a country's movement toward free trade makes that country worse off. What is the reason for this result? Asia is the most efficient producer of auto parts in this example for units $Q_3 - Q_2$: its marginal costs equal P_{Asia} (not including the tariff). By diverting production to Mexico, the marginal costs of Mexico's extra exports to the United States rise from P_{Asia} (which is the marginal cost at quantity Q_2, not including the tariff) to $P_{Asia} + t$ (which is Mexico's marginal cost at quantity Q_3). Therefore, the United States necessarily loses from trade diversion, and by more than Mexico's gain.

The combined loss to the United States and Mexico of area c can be interpreted as the average difference between Mexico's marginal cost (rising from P_{Asia} to $P_{Asia} + t$) and Asia's marginal cost (P_{Asia}), multiplied by the extra imports from Mexico. This interpretation of the net loss area c is similar to the "production loss" or "efficiency loss" due to a tariff for a small country. However, in this case, the net loss comes from *removing* a tariff among the member countries of a regional agreement rather than from adding a tariff.

What you should keep in mind in this example of the adverse effects of trade diversion is that the tariff between the United States and Mexico was removed, but the tariff against imports of auto parts from Asia was maintained. So it is really only a halfway step toward free trade. We have shown that this halfway step can be bad for the countries involved rather than good. This effect of trade diversion explains why some economists oppose regional trade agreements but support multilateral agreements under the WTO.

Not All Trade Diversion Creates a Loss We should stress that the loss due to a regional trade agreement in this example is not a *necessary* result, but a *possible* result, depending on our assumptions of Mexico's marginal costs. There could also be a gain to the importing country. In Figure 11-3, for example, suppose that after joining NAFTA, Mexico has considerable investment in the auto parts industry, and its supply curve shifts to S'_{Mex} rather than S_{Mex}. Then equilibrium imports to the United States will occur at point D, at the price P_{Asia}, and Mexico will *fully* replace Asia as a supplier of auto parts. As compared with the initial situation with the tariff, the United States will lose all tariff revenue of area $(a + b + c + d)$. But the import price drops to P_{Asia}, so it has a gain in consumer surplus of area $(a + b + c + d + e)$. Therefore, the net change in U.S. welfare is

Gain in consumer surplus:	$+(a + b + c + d + e)$
Loss in tariff revenue:	$-(a + b + c + d)$
Net effect on U.S. welfare:	$+e$

The United States experiences a net gain in consumer surplus in this case, and Mexico's producer surplus rises because it is exporting more.

This case combines elements of trade diversion (Mexico has replaced Asia) and trade creation (Mexico is exporting more to the United States than total U.S. imports before NAFTA). Thus, we conclude that NAFTA and other regional trade agreements have the potential to create gains among their members, *but only if the amount of trade creation exceeds the amount of trade diversion*. In the following application we look at what happened to Canada and the United States when free trade opened between them, to see whether the extent of trade creation for Canada exceeded the amount of trade diversion.

APPLICATION

Trade Creation and Diversion for Canada

In 1989, Canada formed a free-trade agreement with the United States and, five years later, entered into the North American Free Trade Agreement with the United States and Mexico. Research by Professor Daniel Trefler at the University of Toronto has analyzed the effect of these free-trade agreements on Canadian manufacturing industries. As summarized in Chapter 6, initially there was unemployment in Canada, but that was a short-term result. A decade after the free-trade agreement with the United States, employment in Canadian manufacturing had recovered and that sector also enjoyed a boom in productivity.

In his research, Trefler also estimated the amount of trade creation versus trade diversion for Canada in its trade with the United States. He found that the reduction in Canadian tariffs on U.S. goods increased imports of those goods by 54%. This increase was trade creation. However, since Canada was now buying more tariff-free goods from the United States, those tariff reductions reduced Canadian imports from the rest of the world by 40% (trade diversion). To compare these amounts, keep in mind that imports from the United States make up 80% of all Canadian imports, whereas imports from the rest of the world make up the remaining 20%. So the 54% increase in imports from the United States should be multiplied (or weighted) by its 80% share in overall Canadian imports to get the amount of trade creation. Likewise, the 40% reduction in imports from the rest of the world should be multiplied by its 20% share in Canadian imports to get trade diversion. Taking the difference between the trade created and diverted, we obtain

$$\underbrace{80\%}_{\substack{\text{Share of} \\ \text{U.S. imports}}} \times \underbrace{54\%}_{\substack{\text{Increase in} \\ \text{U.S. imports}}} - \underbrace{20\%}_{\substack{\text{Share of} \\ \text{other imports}}} \times \underbrace{40\%}_{\substack{\text{Decrease in} \\ \text{other imports}}} \approx 35\% > 0$$

Because this calculation gives a positive number, Trefler concludes that trade creation exceeded trade diversion when Canada and the United States entered into the free-trade agreement. Therefore, Canada definitely gained from the free-trade agreement with the United States. ■

2 International Agreements on Labor Issues

Regional agreements often include issues other than tariffs and trade. For example, the NAFTA agreement included two side agreements that were negotiated by President Clinton to help ensure its passage through the U.S. Congress. One side agreement dealt with the environment (discussed later in this chapter), and the other dealt with labor issues.

We use the term **labor standards** to refer to all issues that directly affect workers, including occupational health and safety, child labor, minimum wages, and so on. Labor standards were included in NAFTA to satisfy several groups. First, consumers and policy makers are often concerned with the working conditions in factories abroad and want to avoid "sweat shop" conditions that exploit workers. Second, unions in the industrial countries are also concerned with these conditions, partly because of solidarity with foreign workers and partly because of the concern that poor labor standards abroad will create more competition for U.S. workers (imports will be cheaper because manufacturers don't have to spend as much on safer working conditions and other labor standards).

Economists are sometimes skeptical about such concerns for foreign workers, however, and view attempts to enforce minimum labor standards as a form of "disguised protection" in the industrial countries. For example, the Indian economist T. N. Srinivasan of Yale University states, "The demand for linkage between trading rights and observance of standards with respect to the environment and labor would seem to arise largely from protectionist motives."[5] Likewise, the World Bank writes, "The real danger of using trade sanctions as an instrument for promoting basic rights is that the trade-standards linkage could become highjacked by protectionist interests attempting to preserve activities rendered uncompetitive by cheaper imports."[6] The former prime minister of Malaysia, Mahathir bin Mohammed, goes even further: "Western countries openly propose to eliminate the competitive edge of East Asia. . . . [T]he professed concern about workers welfare is motivated by selfish interest . . . to put as many obstacles as possible in the way of anyone attempting to catch up and compete with the West."[7] Whether you agree with these sentiments or not, economics teaches that we need to be careful that enforcing labor standards abroad does not worsen the situation for foreign workers by leading to unemployment. We discuss below some examples in which such an outcome has occurred.

Labor Side Agreement Under NAFTA

The labor side agreement negotiated under NAFTA does not change the existing labor laws in these countries but is meant to improve the *enforcement* of such laws. If one country believes that another is failing to enforce its own laws in these areas, then a complaint can be brought before a commission of the North American Agreement on Labor Cooperation (NAALC), which includes representatives from each country and which attempts to resolve the dispute through consultation and cooperation. Although many cases deal with conditions in the *maquiladora* plants in Mexico, operating just south of the Mexico–U.S. border, complaints have also been brought against the United States, as with a case in 1998 involving farm workers picking apples in the State of Washington, for example.[8] In that case, the petitioners in Mexico charged that

[5] T. N. Srinivasan, 1994, "International Labor Standards Once Again." In U.S. Department of Labor, Bureau of International Affairs, *International Labor Standards and Global Economic Integration: Proceedings of a Symposium* (Washington, D.C.), p. 36. All quotations in this paragraph are cited in Richard B. Freeman, 1996, "International Labor Standards and World Trade: Friends or Foes?" In Jeffrey J. Schott, ed., *The World Trading System: Challenges Ahead* (Washington, D.C.: Peterson Institute for International Economics), Chap. 5.
[6] World Bank, *World Development Report*, 1995, p. 79.
[7] *International Herald Tribune*, May 17, 1994, p. 6.

the United States failed to protect the rights of workers, especially migrant labor. The resolution of this case, reached in 2000, called for "planned outreach sessions at which these issues were to be discussed with migrant workers as well as a public forum for workers, unions, employers, and government officials."[9]

Critics of the NAALC agreement have argued that the procedures for resolving disputes are slow and include major exceptions that render them ineffective. For example, a study at the University of California, Los Angeles, concluded, "The NAALC has failed to protect workers' rights to safe jobs and is in danger of fading into oblivion."[10] Others argue that the agreement has created an institutional forum in which unions and labor activists from the three countries can build solidarity and that even the review of cases alone can lead firms to modify their practices.

Other Labor Agreements

Besides the labor side agreement in NAFTA, there are many other examples of international agreements that monitor the conditions of workers in foreign countries. Unions and other organizations are concerned with issues such as job safety, the right of workers to unionize, workers' entitlement to breaks and not being forced to work overtime, and so on. In some cases, the pressure from unions and grassroots organizations can lead to positive changes in the situation faced by workers in other countries. Consumers also have an important role to play through their purchasing power: if consumers are more likely to buy a product that has been produced using methods that respect the rights of workers, then companies will implement such methods more quickly.

Consumer Responsibility How much do consumers value the idea that the clothing they purchase is made under conditions that do not exploit foreign workers? A survey conducted by the National Bureau of Economic Research asked people to respond to this question, with the results shown in Table 11-2.[11]

Individuals in the first group, Sample A, were asked whether they cared about "the condition of workers who make the clothing they buy," and 84% responded that they care a lot or somewhat. Then they were asked, "How much more would you be willing to pay for items made under good working conditions," for items worth $10 and $100. The premium they were willing to pay was $2.80 for a $10 item and $15 for a $100 item.

Individuals in the second group, Sample B, were asked about the premium they would pay for a T-shirt made under "good" conditions, but also about the discount needed to buy a T-shirt made under "bad" conditions. In this group, 84% said that they would choose an identically priced alternative to a T-shirt "with a nice logo" if local students told them that the one with the nice logo was made under poor working conditions. Furthermore, 65% said they would not buy the T-shirt made under

[8] The annual reports of the North American Commission for Labor Cooperation are available at http://www.naalc.org; choose "Publications" and then "Annual Reports."
[9] See the summary of this and other NAALC cases in Joel Solomon, 2001, "Trading Away Rights: The Unfulfilled Promise of NAFTA's Labor Side Agreement," http://www.hrw.org.
[10] "NAFTA's Labor Side Agreement: Fading into Oblivion? An Assessment of Workplace Health and Safety Cases," March 2004, UCLA Center for Labor Research and Education.
[11] See Kimberly Ann Elliott and Richard B. Freeman, 2003, "White Hats or Don Quixotes: Human Rights Vigilantes in the Global Economy." In Richard B. Freeman, Joni Hersch, and Lawrence Mishel, eds., *Emerging Labor Market Institutions for the 21st Century* [Chicago: University of Chicago Press for the National Bureau of Economic Research (NBER)]; and Kimberly Ann Elliott and Richard B. Freeman, 2003, *Can Labor Standards Improve under Globalization?* (Washington, D.C.: Peterson Institute for International Economics), Chap. 2.

TABLE 11-2

Survey Responses This table summarizes the responses from a survey conducted by the National Bureau of Economic Research that asked individuals their attitudes toward an item made under good working conditions and under poor working conditions.

Sample A

Consumers who say they care about the condition of workers who make the clothing they buy:	
A lot	46%
Somewhat	38%
Only a little	8%
Not at all (or no response)	8%
Consumers willing to pay more for an item if assured it was made under good working conditions:	81%
Additional amount willing to pay for $10 item	$2.80
Additional amount willing to pay for $100 item	$15

Sample B

Would choose an alternative to a T-shirt "with a nice logo" that local students say is made under poor working conditions if alternative is the same price	84%
Would not buy T-shirt made under poor working conditions at all	65%
Would buy T-shirt made under poor working conditions at average discount of	$4.30
Would pay more for T-shirt if came with assurance it was made under good conditions	78%
Average additional amount would pay (including as zeros those who did not offer to pay more or were inconsistent)	$1.83

Source: Kimberly Ann Elliott and Richard B. Freeman, 2003, Can Labor Standards Improve under Globalization? *(Washington, D.C.: Peterson Institute for International Economics), Chap. 2, Table 2.1, Sample A.*

---

poor working conditions at all. Among the 35% who were willing to consider buying it, the average discount to buy it was $4.30, whereas the premium they were willing to pay if assured the T-shirt was made under good conditions was $1.83.

The results of this survey highlight several interesting observations about people's attitudes toward labor standards. One such observation is that consumers have a downward-sloping demand curve for labor standards; that is, many people are willing to pay at least a small amount to ensure good labor standards (or simply switch to an alternative with the same price), though relatively few are willing to pay a lot. For example, for a higher-priced good, consumers were willing to pay a smaller percentage of its value to ensure good

Global Sweatshop conditions.

labor conditions. A second observation is that individuals had to receive a higher discount to purchase a shirt made under poor conditions than they were willing to pay for a shirt made under good conditions. This finding indicates that consumers are more worried about potential losses (paying more) than potential gains (the discount), which is a commonly observed characteristic of consumer behavior. Results similar to those reported in Table 11-2 have also been found in larger-scale surveys of consumers in the United States and the United Kingdom. We conclude that a sizable number of consumers are willing to adjust their shopping patterns in response to the conditions faced by foreign workers.

Corporate Responsibility Because of the pressure from consumers and unions, corporations have started to monitor and improve the conditions in their overseas plants and the plants of their overseas subcontractors. One example of this monitoring is reported in **Headlines: Wal-Mart Orders Chinese Suppliers to Lift Standards.**

HEADLINES

Wal-Mart Orders Chinese Suppliers to Lift Standards

In response to criticism from activists in the United States, Wal-Mart has established strict labor and environmental standards that its overseas suppliers must follow. This article reports on these standards for factories in China.

Wal-Mart, the world's biggest retailer, yesterday told its Chinese suppliers to meet strict environmental and social standards or risk losing its business. "Meeting social and environmental standards is not optional," Lee Scott, Wal-Mart's chief executive, told a gathering of more than 1,000 suppliers in Beijing. "A company that cheats on overtime and on the age of its labour, that dumps its scraps and its chemicals in our rivers, that does not pay its taxes or honour its contracts will ultimately cheat on the quality of its products."

Wal-Mart has been pursuing a drive to improve its reputation on environmental and social issues over the past three years in response to growing criticism in the US over issues that include labour conditions in its supplier factories. . . . The requirements include a clear demonstration of compliance with Chinese environmental laws, an improvement of 20 per cent in energy efficiency at the company's 200 largest China suppliers and disclosure of the names and addresses of every factory involved in the production process. The company will require a 25 per cent rise in the efficiency of energy-intensive products such as flat-screen TVs by 2011.

Walmart insisted that its factories in China meet strict guidelines on both labor and environmental standards, or lose its business.

There are times, however, when this monitoring is inadequate and poor conditions for workers lead to disastrous outcomes. Sad examples are the fires in garment factories in Bangladesh and Pakistan in 2012 that killed or injured hundreds of workers, and the collapse of a garment factory in Bangladesh in 2013 that killed more than 1,000 workers. These were among the worst industrial accidents ever in the two countries, and they led to a storm of international criticism over worker safety. According to news reports, workers were unable to exit the burning factories because of locked fire escapes, leading to charges of criminal negligence for the owners and managers. It was also reported that both the factories in Pakistan and Bangladesh had passed recent safety inspections without serious violations. So the monitoring by the countries' governments and by the companies buying from these factories—including Walmart and other major U.S. and European retailers—was not enough to prevent these disasters.

Country Responsibility After disasters like the burned and collapsed factories in Bangladesh and Pakistan happen, what additional steps can be taken beyond the improved monitoring of these buildings? One idea recommended by Sanchita Saxena of the University of California, Berkeley, is to reduce the tariff on imports from these countries, as described in **Headlines: American Tariffs, Bangladeshi Deaths.** She points out that Bangladesh faces a high tariff (15.3%) on its garment exports to the United States, which account for about 90% of its exports. This high tariff lowers the profits earned in the garment industry in Bangladesh, along with the wages of workers and the ability of firms to make improvements. It is ironic that this high tariff is charged on Bangladesh's largest export item, when nearly all of its other exports enter the United States duty free. The European Union includes garments and textiles in the duty-free items imported from Bangladesh. It would seem to be a humanitarian gesture for the United States to eliminate the tariff on garments from Bangladesh, which, in conjunction with improved monitoring of factories, could improve the conditions of workers there.

Shortly after the collapse of the factory in Bangladesh in 2013, however, the United States took an action in the opposite direction. Rather than reducing the tariff charged on garment imports from Bangladesh, it *increased* the tariff changed on other items imported from Bangladesh. This action was taken in an attempt to force the country to improve its monitoring of its factories. As described in **Headlines: U.S. Suspends Bangladesh's Preferential Trade Status,** President Barack Obama dropped Bangladesh from the list of countries eligible for a program known as the Generalized System of Preferences (GSP), which grants low tariffs to the least-developed countries. In eliminating Bangladesh's GSP status, President Obama cited the lack of progress being made in bringing worker rights to that country. The article describes this move as "symbolic" because it affects only a very small percentage of trade from Bangladesh, whose principal export to the United States is garments, which do not qualify for low tariffs under the GSP. Still, this action is meant to send a strong signal to the Bangladeshi government that greater attention must be paid to worker safety.

How effective will this action by the United States government be in changing the conditions for workers in Bangladesh? To answer this question, we can look at earlier cases in which the United States has raised tariffs. Several U.S. trade laws give the President the power to *withhold* trade privileges from countries that do not give their workers basic rights, including the right to organize. One study showed that these provisions have been used by the President 32 times from 1985 to 1994, but only one-half of the cases are judged to have been effective in improving workers' rights.[12]

There are two problems with trying to withhold trade privileges. First, denying preferences to a foreign country across all industries is a very broad foreign policy action, when the problems may occur only in particular companies. Second, these laws involve a comparison of U.S. labor standards with those found abroad and the judgment that foreign practices are inadequate. Many people believe that countries should choose their own domestic policies, even when they conflict with established norms abroad, and that countries should not impose their preferences on one another.[13]

An alternative approach to government sanctions is for nongovernmental organizations (NGOs) to take actions that limit undesirable sweatshop activities. According to one research study focusing on Indonesia, actions by NGOs are actually more effective than government action.[14] This study showed that when the U.S. government threatened to withdraw tariff privileges for Indonesia, the minimum wage was doubled in real terms. That increase in the wage reduced the employment of unskilled workers by as much as 10%, so these workers were harmed. The antisweatshop activism by NGOs targeted at textile, apparel, and footwear plants raised real wages as well, by ensuring that plants paid the minimum wage. But this activism did not reduce employment to the same extent. Plants targeted by activists were more likely to close, but those losses were offset by employment gains at surviving plants, which benefited

---

[12] Kimberly Ann Elliott and Richard B. Freeman, 2003, *Can Labor Standards Improve under Globalization?* (Washington, D.C.: Peterson Institute for International Economics), p. 79.
[13] An important example here is child labor, which is avoided in industrial countries but may be necessary for families' survival in developing countries.
[14] Ann Harrison and Jason Scorse, May 2004, "Moving Up or Moving Out? Anti-Sweatshop Activists and Labor Market Outcomes," NBER Working Paper No. 10492.

HEADLINES

American Tariffs, Bangladeshi Deaths

The collapse of garment factories in Bangladesh in 2013 killed more than 1,000 workers. As a response, Sanchita Saxena of the University of California, Berkeley, proposes that the United States should reduce the tariff on garment imports from Bangladesh and other Asian countries.

The fire that killed 112 workers at a garment factory in the suburbs of Bangladesh's capital last month was a stark reminder of the human costs of producing and consuming cheap clothes. While American officials have condemned poor safety conditions at the factory and have urged the Bangladeshi government to raise wages and improve working conditions, the United States can do much more: It should bring down high tariffs on imports from Bangladesh and other Asian countries, which put pressure on contractors there to scrimp on labor standards in order to stay competitive.

The United States imported more than $4 billion worth of apparel and textiles from Bangladesh last year. So it has an interest in giving the country's garment industry some financial room with which to improve conditions for the three million employees, most of them female, who work in the industry. Monitoring systems have, in many cases, achieved progress at the higher levels of the industry: the contractors that deal directly with American retailers. But oversight is lax, and conditions particularly dire, in factories run by subcontractors, like the Tazreen Fashions factory, the site of the deadly blaze on Nov. 24.

A bill introduced in Congress in 2009 by Representative Jim McDermott, Democrat of Washington, could have improved the situation by including Bangladesh, Cambodia, Laos, Nepal, Pakistan and Sri Lanka on the list of developing countries, like Mexico, that receive duty-free access to the American market as a result of free-trade agreements. But the bill never even made it to committee, and Bangladesh still faces a cost squeeze that is ultimately felt most acutely on those lowest on the production chain, especially the lowest-paying subcontractors, among whom corruption is endemic. It takes its greatest toll on workers.

The distortions created by the current trade policy are striking. In the United States federal fiscal year that ended in September 2011, Bangladesh exported $5.10 billion in goods to the United States, of which less than 10 percent were eligible for exemption from import duties. On the rest, Bangladesh had to pay at least 15.3 percent in tariffs. The tariffs were equivalent to imposing a $4.61 tax on every person in Bangladesh, a country with a per-capita annual income of $770.

This year, according to news accounts, Bangladesh will have paid more than $600 million annually in American tariffs, even as the United States Agency for International Development said it was committed to $200 million in development aid to Bangladesh. Of course, no free trade legislation is controversy-free. One argument against reducing restrictions on Bangladeshi imports is that it might hurt even poorer countries, in sub-Saharan Africa, that enjoy duty-free access under a 2000 law, the African Growth and Opportunity Act. But studies have shown that extending duty-free access to South Asian goods would have negligible costs, yield huge benefits for Bangladesh's economy and have minimal negative impact on African exports.

Bangladesh's government and industries have a moral duty to prevent catastrophes like the November fire from ever occurring again. They need to insist that factory operators meet safety standards, that inspections are conducted honestly and that recommendations are enforced. But leveling the playing field of international trade could advance all of these goals. International brands like Tommy Hilfiger, Gap, H&M, Target and Walmart demand low prices and fast turnaround. In that context, high tariffs work against the goals of fair-labor standards and factory safety.

In the fire's aftermath, it's tempting to focus only on local corruption and lax labor standards. But there have been positive changes in recent years; labor groups, businesses, nongovernmental organizations and even some international buyers have formed coalitions to improve safety at many factories. In a survey I conducted of garment workers at established factories, 62 percent said labor conditions had improved. But for improvements in workers' well-being to have lasting effect, tariffs on exports to the United States, the world's largest consumer market, must be eased.

HEADLINES

U.S. Suspends Bangladesh's Preferential Trade Status

Instead of reducing tariffs on imports from Bangladesh, President Obama increased the tariff on certain products by suspending the "preferential" trade treatment given to Bangladesh and other developing countries. The change in tariffs does not apply to garments, however, which already face high U.S. tariffs.

The U.S. suspended its preferential trade treatment for Bangladesh on Thursday [June 27, 2013], a largely symbolic move to punish the country for poor labor practices that attracted worldwide attention after a garment factory collapsed in April, killing more than 1,100 workers.

President Barack Obama carved the South Asian country from a trade framework that eliminates certain U.S. import duties for select developing economies. The suspension, which will begin in about 60 days, is expected to raise U.S. import duties on some Bangladeshi goods, including golf equipment and ceramics, but would have little effect on the garment industry, which dominates the country's international trade. The decision marks a victory for U.S. labor leaders, who have criticized the labor laws and worker safety in Bangladesh.

AFL-CIO President Richard Trumka said the suspension "sends an important message to our trading partners." Sen. Robert Menendez, chairman of the Senate Foreign Relations Committee, which held a hearing this month on labor issues in Bangladesh, hailed the move, saying, "We cannot and will not look the other way while workers are subjected to unsafe conditions." . . .

from the growth in exports in these industries. So there was no significant decline in employment from the pressure exerted by NGOs.

The message of this study is that pressure from the U.S. government to raise wages by withholding trade privileges was too blunt a tool to be effective, whereas the actions of NGOs, which were better targeted at particular plants, resulted in higher wages with little or no net loss in employment. In addition, the pressure from activists can sometimes make U.S. companies more willing to reveal their foreign plants, as Nike has done, thereby making them open to monitoring.

Living Wage The final question we can ask about labor issues is whether it is fair to expect foreign firms to pay a **living wage** to their workers; that is, a wage above the norm in the developing country. This issue is perhaps the most controversial part of labor standards because it involves a difficult judgment: How high should foreign wages be to make them acceptable to activists in industrial countries? Economists have a ready answer: the wages should be as high as the market will allow, and not any higher. Raising wages above their equilibrium level will very likely lead to unemployment. In extreme cases, workers laid off from manufacturing jobs in developing countries might be forced into prostitution or other illegal activities that are far worse than the low-wage factory positions they held.

These types of concerns lead many economists and policy makers to reject calls for a "living wage." But this rejection *does not* mean that we should abandon other types of labor standards. Workers in all countries are entitled to conditions that are safe and clean, honesty in payment, the right to unionize, and so on. Consumers, corporations, and unions all play an important role in advocating for such conditions in foreign countries, and that advocacy needs to continue. The enforcement of labor standards can ensure that workers benefit from trade without being exploited in the workplace.

3 | International Agreements on the Environment

Many of the protesters at the 1999 Seattle meeting of the World Trade Organization (WTO), shown in the photo at the start of this chapter, were concerned about how WTO rulings affect the environment. The WTO does not directly address environmental issues; other international agreements, called **multilateral environmental agreements,** deal specifically with the environment. There are some 200 multilateral environmental agreements, including the Convention on International Trade in Endangered Species (CITES) and the Montreal Protocol on Substances that Deplete the Ozone Layer (which has eliminated the use of chlorofluorocarbons which deplete the ozone layer). But the WTO still indirectly affects the environment as the protesters in Seattle were well aware. We begin by clarifying the role of the GATT and WTO in environmental issues.

Environmental Issues in the GATT and WTO

In an earlier chapter (see **Side Bar: Key Provisions of the GATT** in Chapter 8), we summarized some of the founding articles of the General Agreement on Tariffs and Trade (GATT). Not mentioned there was Article XX, known as the "green provision." Article XX allows countries to adopt their own laws in relation to environmental issues, provided that these laws are applied uniformly to domestic and foreign producers so that the laws do not discriminate against imports.

In its full text, Article XX of the GATT states that "subject to the requirement that such measures are not applied in a manner which would constitute a . . . disguised restriction on international trade, nothing in this Agreement shall be construed to prevent the adoption or enforcement by any contracting party of measures: . . . (b) necessary to protect human, animal or plant life or health; . . . (g) relating to the conservation of exhaustible natural resources if such measures are made effective in conjunction with restrictions on domestic production or consumption."

If the provisions of the GATT and WTO permit countries to apply their own environmental regulations, why were people dressed as turtles and dolphins protesting WTO rulings at the 1999 Seattle meetings? To understand the concerns of these protesters, we need to dig into the details of some specific GATT/WTO cases, summarized in Table 11-3.[15]

Tuna–Dolphin Case In 1991, before the WTO was formed, Mexico brought a GATT case against the United States. The reason for the case was that the United States had banned imports of tuna from Mexico because Mexican fishermen did not catch tuna using nets that safeguarded against the accidental capture of dolphins. The U.S. Marine Mammal Protection Act requires that U.S. tuna fishermen use nets that are safe for dolphins, and by Article XX(g) of the GATT, the United States reasoned that the same requirement could be extended to Mexican fishermen. But the U.S. ban on imports of tuna from Mexico ran afoul of the GATT.

GATT concluded that the United States could not ban the import of tuna because the United States applied the import restriction to the *production process*

---

[15] These cases are drawn from Jeffrey A. Frankel, November 2003, "The Environment and Globalization," NBER Working Paper No. 10090. Environmental cases are summarized on the WTO webpage at http://www.wto.org/English/tratop_e/envir_e/edis00_e.htm, and details are also provided at the Trade and Environmental Database at the American University, http://www.american.edu/TED/ted.htm.

TABLE 11-3

Environmental Cases at the GATT and WTO This table shows the outcome of environmental cases ruled upon by the General Agreement on Tariffs and Trade (GATT) and the World Trade Organization (WTO).

Case	Issue	Outcome
Tuna-Dolphin In 1991 Mexico appealed to the GATT against a U.S. ban on Mexican tuna imports.	The United States put a ban on imports of tuna from Mexico that were not caught with nets which were safe for dolphins (as required in the United States under the Marine Mammal Protection Act).	In 1992 the GATT ruled in favor of Mexico that the U.S. import ban violated GATT rules. But the strong consumer response led to labeling of imported tuna as "dolphin friendly."
Shrimp-Turtle In 1996 India, Malaysia, Pakistan, and Thailand appealed to the WTO against a U.S. ban on shrimp imports.	The United States put a ban on imports of shrimp from India, Malaysia, Pakistan, and Thailand that were not caught with nets safe for sea turtles (as required in the United States under the Species Act).	In 1998 the WTO ruled in favor of India, Malaysia, Pakistan, and Thailand that the U.S. import ban violated WTO rules. But the United States could still require these exporting countries to use turtle-safe nets, provided that adequate notice and consultation were pursued.
Gasoline In 1994 Venezuela and Brazil appealed to the GATT against a U.S. ban on gasoline imports.	The United States put a ban on imports of gasoline from Venezuela and Brazil because the gas exceeded the maximum amount allowed of a smog-causing chemical (under the U.S. Clean Air Act).	In 1996 the WTO ruled in favor of Venezuela and Brazil that the U.S. import restriction violated equal treatment of domestic and foreign producers. The United States adjusted the rules to be consistent with the WTO and still pursued its own clean air goals.
Biotech Food In 2003 the United States appealed to the WTO that Europe was keeping out genetically modified food and crops.	Since 1998 no imports of genetically modified food or crops had been approved in the European Union.	In 2006 the WTO ruled that the European actions violated the principle that import restrictions must be based on "scientific risk assessments." Labeling and consumer concerns in Europe will still limit such imports.

Source: Updated from Jeffrey A. Frankel, 2005, "The Environment and Globalization." In Michael Weinstein, ed., Globalization: What's New, (New York: Columbia University Press), pp. 129–169. Reprinted in R. Stavins, ed., 2005, Economics of the Environment (New York: W. W. Norton), pp. 361–398.

method and not the product itself. The idea that the production process could not be a basis for a trade restriction was a principle of GATT that was upheld in this case. In addition, the GATT panel ruled that "GATT rules did not allow one country to take trade action for the purpose of attempting to enforce its own domestic laws in another country—even to protect animal health or exhaustible natural resources." Both of these conclusions were a blow to environmentalists interested in protecting the dolphins, and this is the reason that some of the Seattle protesters were dressed as dolphins.

Even though the GATT panel ruled in favor of Mexico and against the United States in this case, the strong consumer response led to the dolphins being protected.

Interested parties in the United States and Mexico worked out a system of labeling that now appears on cans of tuna in the United States, declaring the product to be "dolphin-safe." Since 1990 the major companies have sold only this "dolphin friendly" product from Mexico, and the labeling procedure was found to be consistent with GATT. So despite the initial ruling against the United States, the outcome of this case has had the desired effect of protecting dolphins in Mexican waters (in addition to the protection they already received in U.S. waters).

Shrimp–Turtle Case In 1996, just after the WTO was formed, a second closely related case arose involving shrimp and sea turtles. In this case, India, Malaysia, Pakistan, and Thailand appealed to the WTO against a U.S. ban on shrimp imports. The United States had banned imports of shrimp from these countries because they were not caught with nets that were safe for sea turtles, as required in the United States under the Endangered Species Act of 1987. Again, by Article XX(g) of the GATT, the United States reasoned that the same requirement could be extended against fishermen from these Asian countries.

Although this case has a number of similarities to the earlier tuna–dolphin case, the outcome at the WTO was different. The WTO still ruled against the United States, but in this case it *did not rule* against the principle that one country could restrict imports based on the production process method used in another country. On the contrary, the WTO ruled that the United States was consistently applying its laws to American and Asian producers in requiring that turtle-safe nets be used. The problem with the U.S. import ban was that it was applied without due notice and consultation with the exporting countries involved, which did not allow the countries sufficient time to employ turtle-safe devices. In other words, the WTO ruling against the United States was on narrow, technical grounds and not on the principle of protecting endangered species in foreign waters.

In many ways, this WTO ruling was more favorable to environmentalists than the earlier tuna–dolphin ruling at the GATT. The WTO panel explicitly recognized that "the conservation of exhaustible natural resources" referred to in Article XX(g) applies to living resources, especially if they are threatened with extinction. After the United States allowed more flexibility in its regulations and made good-faith efforts to develop an agreement with the Asian producers, the laws requiring the use of turtle-safe nets for exporters were found to be consistent with the WTO in a 2001 ruling.

Gasoline from Venezuela and Brazil A third GATT/WTO case that involves environmental issues was brought against the United States by Venezuela and Brazil in 1994. The United States had restricted imports of gasoline from these countries because the gas did not meet the requirements of the U.S. Clean Air Act (which mandates a maximum amount of certain smog-causing chemicals). In this case, the WTO ruled in 1996 that the United States violated the principle that national and foreign producers should be treated equally. The issue was that refineries in the United States were given a three-year grace period to meet the Clean Air Act goals, whereas that grace period was not extended to refineries abroad. So the U.S. import restriction discriminated against the refineries in Venezuela and Brazil.

This gasoline case is often seen as a loss for environmentalists, but economists would argue that U.S. regulations were in fact acting like "disguised protection" against the import of Venezuelan gasoline. From the perspective of promoting free trade and treating foreign producers fairly, the WTO was correct in ruling against the

United States. The United States was not blocked by the WTO in pursuing clean air goals, but it had to modify its requirements so that they were applied equally to U.S. and foreign producers.

Biotech Food in Europe A final case concerns whether food that has been genetically modified can be imported into Europe. In 2003 the United States (joined by Argentina and Canada) appealed to the WTO that the European Union (EU) was keeping out genetically modified food and crops. Since 1998 no such imports had been approved in the EU, though it denied that there was any "moratorium" on these imports. Rather, Europe claimed that it needed more time to study the health effects of genetically modified organisms and was not approving such imports for precautionary reasons.

The WTO ruled in 2006 that the European actions violated the principle that import restrictions must be based on "scientific risk assessments." That is, countries cannot keep out imports based on precautionary reasons but must have some scientific evidence to back up the import restriction. Despite this ruling, the EU can use consumer labeling to allow the buyers to decide whether to purchase foods that have been genetically modified. As in our earlier discussion of the labeling of U.S. tuna imports from Mexico, it is expected that the labeling of genetically modified organisms in Europe will allow consumers to exert their power in limiting purchases of these foods if they so choose. Since 2006, Europe has approved the import of about 50 genetically modified food products, most for animal feed imports.

Summary of GATT/WTO Cases The cases in Table 11-3 show that WTO rulings have not adversely affected the environment: in the tuna–dolphin case, the reaction of consumers in the United States was enough to ensure that dolphin-safe nets were used in Mexico; in the shrimp–turtle case, the WTO did not object to the principle of requiring foreign countries to use the same turtle-friendly nets as do the U.S. companies; in the gasoline case, the imports from Venezuela and Brazil had to meet the requirements of the Clean Air Act, after the same grace period given to U.S. firms; and in the case of biotech foods, labeling in Europe is expected to limit such imports if consumers so choose.

These outcomes have led some observers to conclude that even though environmentalists have lost some specific cases at the WTO, they have gained the upper hand in ensuring that environmental concerns are respected: environmentalists may have lost some battles, but they have won the war! This conclusion does not mean that environmental concerns can now be dropped. On the contrary, the lobbying activity of environmental groups, including the costumed protesters at the Seattle meetings, has been important in shifting public opinion and WTO rulings in directions that support the environment and such lobbying activities should continue to be pursued.

Does Trade Help or Harm the Environment?

Having clarified the role of the WTO in resolving specific cases brought between particular countries, let us turn to the more general question of whether trade helps or harms the environment. Many of the protesters at the 1999 WTO meetings in Seattle believed that trade is bad for the environment and that is why they demonstrated. The cases we reviewed above show that these protests can lead to increased regard for environmental protection in WTO decisions. But these cases do not answer the question of whether free trade is good or bad for the environment. To address that question, we need to introduce the idea of externalities.

Externalities An **externality** occurs when one person's production or consumption of a good affects another person. Externalities can be positive, such as when one firm's discoveries from research and development (R&D) are used by other firms, or negative, such as when the production of a good leads to pollution. Closely related to the concept of externalities is the idea of **market failure,** which means that the positive or negative effects of the externality on other people are not paid for. For example, when the discovery of one firm is freely copied by another firm, there is a failure of the second firm to pay for the knowledge; and when a firm freely pollutes, there is a failure of that firm to pay penalties for the adverse effects of the pollution or to clean up that pollution.

In your intermediate microeconomics course, you learned that externalities can lead to outcomes that are not desirable from a social point of view. For example, if discoveries are freely copied, then a firm will invest too little in its R&D; and if pollution is not penalized, then a firm will pollute too much. The solution in both cases is to add some government regulations that essentially "create a market" for the cost or benefit of the externality. To encourage firms to undertake R&D, for example, nearly all governments support a patent system that allows the inventor of a new product to earn profits from its sales without fear of being copied, at least for some period. The ability of firms to patent their discoveries encourages more R&D, which is socially beneficial. To combat pollution, many countries regulate the emissions of their industries, and assess fines when these regulations are disregarded. These regulations lead to less pollution, which is again socially beneficial. These examples show how government action can improve the outcomes in the presence of externalities.

Externalities and Trade When we introduce international trade, we focus on understanding how trade interacts with externality: does trade lead to more of a negative externality, making the outcome worse, or offset it, making the outcome better? If it is too difficult to directly control the externality, perhaps because it requires coordinated action on the part of many governments, then there might be an argument to take action by controlling the amount of trade instead. As we will now show, there are some cases in which having more trade reduces the externality and raises welfare, but other cases in which having less trade is needed to achieve that outcome. The answer to the question "does free trade help or harm the environment?" is that it all depends, and either case is possible.

To show that either case is possible, we use Figure 11-4. In panels (a) and (b) we show the Home demand curve D and supply curve S for an industry. (You can ignore the curves SMC and SMB for now.) In the absence of international trade, the autarky (no-trade) price is at P^A, and the quantities demanded and supplied are equal at Q_0. With international trade, we assume that the world price is fixed at the level P^W, less than the autarky price. The quantity demanded rises to D_1 and the quantity supplied falls to S_1, and the difference between them equals imports of $M_1 = D_1 - S_1$.

It is easy to determine the gains to this country from opening trade. With the fall in price from P^A to P^W, consumer surplus rises by the area a (in red) + b (in blue) and producer surplus falls by the area a. The combined effect on consumers and producers (what we call the *private* gains from trade) is area b. That outcome is the same as the outcome we saw in Figure 8-2. When we introduce externalities into the picture, however, this conclusion will change.

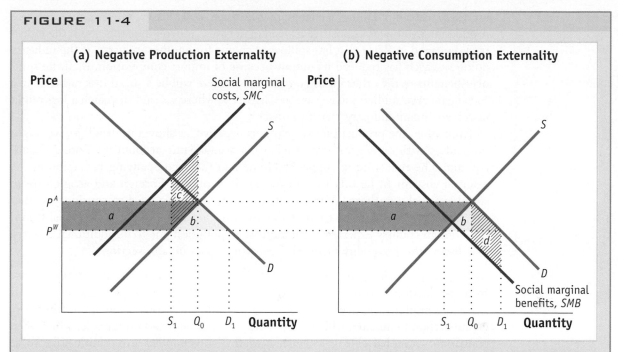

FIGURE 11-4

(a) Negative Production Externality

(b) Negative Consumption Externality

Externalities and the Gains from Trade Panel (a) illustrates a negative production externality, which means that the social marginal cost curve, *SMC*, lies above the private marginal cost (supply) curve *S*. With free trade, the price falls from P^A to P^W and Home supply falls from Q_0 to S_1. As a result, the social cost of the externality is reduced by area *c*, which measures a social gain that is additional to the private gains from trade, area *b*. Panel (b) illustrates a negative consumption externality, which means that the social marginal benefits, *SMB*, lie below the private marginal benefit (demand) curve *D*. The vertical distance between the *SMB* and *D* curve, times the quantity consumed, reflects the social cost of the externality. With free trade Home demand increases from Q_0 to D_1. As a result, the social cost of the externality increases by area *d*. That area is a social cost that offsets the private gains from trade, area *b*.

Negative Production Externalities The supply curve *S* shown in both panels of Figure 11-4 represents the marginal costs of production for firms, or what we call "private" marginal costs. When there is an externality then the true marginal costs for society, the "social" marginal costs, differ from the private marginal costs. When there is a negative production externality such as pollution, then the social marginal costs are higher than the private marginal costs, because the pollution is imposing an extra cost on society. This extra cost of pollution for each unit of quantity produced is measured by the vertical distance between the social marginal cost curve, labeled by *SMC* in panel (a), and the private marginal cost curve, *S*.

When trade is opened, we have already argued that the quantity supplied by the Home industry falls from Q_0 to S_1. This fall in production reduces the social cost of pollution. We can measure the reduction in the social cost by the fall in production times the distance between the *SMC* and *S* curves. In other words, the shaded area *c* in panel (a) is the reduction in the social cost of pollution. This reduced social cost should be counted as a gain. This social cost gain is added to the private gains from trade (area *b*), so the total gains from trade in this case is the amount ($b + c$). When there is a negative production externality at Home, then, free trade reduces the externality as compared with autarky and leads to additional social gains.

If we change our assumptions, however, the opening of trade will not necessarily lead to an additional gain. There are a number of cases in which the external cost increases instead of falling, a change that leads to social losses. For example, suppose production externality is positive instead of negative, as would be the case if the industry is engaged in R&D that has spillover benefits for another industry. If the industry doing research has reduced its output because of import competition, then the spillover benefits to the other industry will fall and there will be a social loss rather than a social gain. We studied such a case in Chapter 9, where we said that such a loss might justify an "infant industry" tariff to offset it.

Even when the production externality is negative, as shown in panel (a), we might not end up with *world* gains from trade when we take into account the Foreign country, too. The reduction in supply at Home and the accompanying reduction in the external cost might be offset by an *increase* in supply in Foreign and an increase in social external cost there. With pollution, for example, we need to consider whether the reduction in pollution at Home due to lower local supply is really a social gain if the Foreign country experiences an increase in pollution due to its additional exports. We discuss this possibility further in real-world cases in later sections.

Negative Consumption Externalities In addition to the externality that can arise from production, it is possible that the consumption of a good leads to an externality. An example is the consumption of automobiles that use gasoline, and therefore create carbon monoxide, which contributes to smog and carbon dioxide, which then contribute to global climate change. Negative consumption externalities like these mean that the true, social benefit of consuming the good, measured by curve *SMB*, is less than the private benefit from consumption as measured curve D, which shows the price that consumers are willing to pay. For example, in panel (b) of Figure 11-4 consumers are willing to pay the price P^W to consume the amount D_1. That the *SMB* curve lies *below* the demand curve D indicates that the social value of consuming D_1 is less than P^W. The vertical distance between the *SMB* and D curve, times the quantity consumed, reflects the *social cost* of the externality.

With free trade, the quantity demanded rises from Q_0 to D_1. This rise in consumption increases the social cost of pollution. We can measure the increase in the social cost by the rise in the quantity consumed times the distance between the *SMB* and demand curves. So the shaded area d in panel (b) is the increase in the social cost of pollution. This increase in the social cost is a loss for the country, which should be counted against the private gains from trade, area b. If $b > d$ then the country still gains from trade, but if $b < d$ then the country loses from trade overall, because the increase in the social cost of the externality overwhelms the private gains.

In the next sections, we look at a series of examples that illustrate both production and consumption externalities, and the idea that free trade can either help or harm the environment.

Examples of the Environmental Impact of Trade

U.S. Trade Restrictions in Sugar and Ethanol The United States maintains an import quota on sugar. The import quota leads to higher prices for American buyers, both consumers and firms, who pay domestic prices that can be as high as twice the world price. One source of demand for imported sugarcane comes from firms that are producing ethanol, an alternative (or additive) to gasoline that can be produced from sugar or corn. Because of the high import price for sugarcane, however, these firms instead purchase corn from American farmers, who are themselves subsidized by the

U.S. government. As a result of the quota for sugar imports and the subsidies for corn production, much more corn than sugar is used to produce ethanol.

The problem with this arrangement is that producing ethanol from corn is much less energy-efficient than producing it from sugarcane. Corn depletes the soil and needs fertilizers in order to grow, which themselves use energy in their production. Because the net energy savings by making ethanol from corn and using it as a gasoline substitute are poor, it would be better to use sugarcane to produce ethanol, *if* it could be purchased at world prices. Alternatively, the United States would benefit from importing ethanol directly from Brazil, where it is manufactured from abundant sugarcane. But up until 2012, the United States had a tariff of 54 cents per gallon on imported ethanol, limiting what U.S. gasoline producers could purchase from abroad.

Applying this example to Figure 11-4, in panel (a) we can think of the supply curve *S* as representing the U.S. ethanol industry. There is a negative production externality because the U.S. ethanol industry makes ethanol from corn rather than sugar (thereby using more energy). The tariff on ethanol made that externality worse because it limited imports and led to more U.S. production. So free trade in ethanol would be a better policy: it would lead to the usual gains from trade (area *b*) plus a reduced social cost of the externality (area *c*).

In fact, the United States followed that policy by eliminating the import tariff on ethanol on January 1, 2012. As a result, imports from Brazil rose dramatically, and in 2012 the United States imported 9.6 million barrels of ethanol from Brazil. At the same time, U.S. production of ethanol from corn slowed, leading to reduced environmental costs. These facts line up well with predictions from Figure 11-4, and show that allowing free trade in ethanol has reduced the externality and brought a social gain.

Still, ethanol trade between the United States and Brazil is far from perfect. As pointed out by *The Financial Times*, while the United States imported 9.6 million barrels of ethanol from Brazil, it also *exported* two million barrels to Brazil in 2012.[16] Aside from being processed from different raw materials (corn versus sugar), these barrels of ethanol are identical to the users, so there is a waste of energy in shipping the ethanol in both directions. The reason for this "two-way" trade in ethanol is that fuel companies in the United States are required by government regulation to use both ethanol made from corn and ethanol made from other sources, which in practice is made up by imports from Brazil. Those regulations led to an excess of the U.S.-produced corn ethanol, which was then sold at a discounted price back to Brazil. This "two-way" trade is a clear indication of a social waste, which can be eliminated by improved regulations in the United States.

U.S. Automobile VER The tariff on ethanol is not the only case in which a U.S. trade restriction has worked to harm the environment. In an earlier chapter, we discussed the "voluntary" export restraint (VER) on exports of Japanese cars to the United States, which began in 1981. The VER limited the number of cars that Japanese firms could export each year, but not their value, so there was an incentive for the Japanese firms to export larger and/or more luxurious models. As the quality of the Japanese cars rose, so did the engine size and weight of the vehicles; as a result, the average gas mileage of the imported cars fell.

---

[16] Greg Meyer, "Ethanol: Logic of circular biofuel trade comes into question," *The Financial Times*, May 16, 2013, electronic edition.

The impact of the VER on gas mileage is shown in Figure 11-5 which shows data on Japanese imported cars from 1979 to 1982, before and after the VER began. The horizontal axis shows the change in the quantity sold (in percent) between these years, and the vertical axis shows the gas mileage of each model. The data show that the luxury models with the lowest gas mileage—such as the Maxima, Cressida, and Mazda 626—experienced the greatest increase in sales between these years. Sales went up despite the limit on total imports because the prices of these more luxurious models did not rise as much as the prices of the economy models. U.S. consumers shifted their purchases toward the luxury models, and because those models had worse gas mileage, the VER increased the use of energy and led to greater carbon emissions from the vehicles, therefore harming the environment.

Applying this example to Figure 11-4 panel (b) we can think of the demand curve D as coming from U.S. consumers. The use of automobiles has a negative consumption externality because the carbon emissions contribute to smog and global climate change. But that externality was *smaller* for imported Japanese cars in the early 1980s (think of this as a positive externality for imported cars compared with domestically produced cars). So free trade would have reduced the external cost of pollution, leading to an additional source of social gain. In contrast, the VER made the externality worse by leading to an increase in imported cars with worse gas mileage.

The Tragedy of the Commons

The two previous examples, dealing with trade in ethanol and automobiles, illustrate how free trade can be good for the environment. We now turn to two other

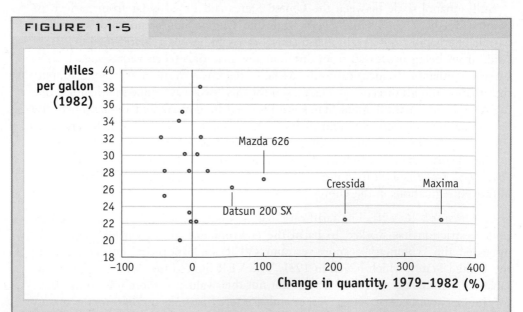

FIGURE 11-5

U.S. Imports of Japanese Autos This figure uses data on Japanese imported cars from 1979 to 1982, before and after the "voluntary" export restraint with Japan began. The horizontal axis shows the change in the quantity sold (in percent) between these years, and the vertical axis shows the gas mileage of each model. The models with the lowest mileage—such as the Maxima, Cressida, and Mazda 626—experienced the greatest increase in sales between these years.

cases in which free trade has harmed the environment by leading to overharvesting of a resource. Economists believe that this outcome can occur whenever people are competing for the same resource stock (fish, for example) and refer to this phenomenon as the **tragedy of the commons.** When a resource is treated as **common property** that anyone can harvest, it will be subject to overuse and its stocks will diminish rapidly over time as each producer seeks to use as much of the resource as it can. International trade can make the tragedy of the commons worse by directing global demand toward the resources of a particular country or region so that there is even more overuse of the resource under free trade.

In terms of Figure 11-4, the tragedy of the commons illustrates a negative consumption externality that arises because of a resource is limited. International trade increases the demand for the limited good and therefore worsens the consumption externality, as shown in panel (b). When it is not possible to control the externality directly by limiting the amount of the resource being consumed, then nations should act to restrict the amount of trade.

Trade in Fish Because of overharvesting, many species of fish are no longer commercially viable and, in some extreme cases, are close to extinction. Examples include the Atlantic cod, tuna in the Mediterranean, and sturgeon in European and Asian waters. According to one scientific study, 29% of fish and seafood species have collapsed; that is, their catch declined by 90% or more between 1950 and 2003. The same authors writing in 2009 found that the "exploitation rates" of some species had fallen, but that "63% of assessed fish stocks worldwide still require rebuilding, and even lower exploitation rates are needed to reverse the collapse of vulnerable species."[17]

The fundamental cause of the overharvesting of fish is not that the resource is traded internationally but that it is treated as common property by the people who are harvesting it. If instead there was a system of international rules that assigned property rights to the fish and limited the harvest of each nation, then the overharvesting could be avoided. One country acting on its own does not have enough incentive to control its fish harvest if other countries do not also enact controls. In the absence of international controls, international trade will make the tragedy of the commons in the global fishing industry worse.

International agreements for fish and other endangered species are arranged through the Convention on International Trade in Endangered Species (CITES). According to information at www.cites.org, CITES has protected 5,000 species of animals and 29,000 species of plants against overexploitation through international trade. In 2013, for example, five types of sharks were added to the CITES list of protected species.

Trade in Buffalo The fish trade is not the only case in which international trade has interacted with the tragedy of the commons to result in the near extinction of a species. An historical case from America occurred with the slaughter of the Great Plains buffalo in a 10-year period from 1870 to 1880. Various reasons are often given for the slaughter: the railroad allowed hunters to reach the Great Plains easier; the buffalo were killed by the U.S. military in its fight against Native Americans; and climate change on the Great Plains—a wet period up to the 1850s followed by 30 years

---

[17] Juliet Eilperin, "World's Fish Supply Running Out, Researchers Warn," *Washington Post*, November 3, 2006, p. A01, citing an article from *Science*; and Boris Worm, et al., "Rebuilding Global Fisheries," *Science* 2009, 325, pp. 578–585.

of drought—combined with overhunting by Native Americans. But recent research has uncovered a new reason that dominates all others for the slaughter of the buffalo: an invention in London circa 1871 that allowed the buffalo hides to be tanned for industrial use (such as for belts), creating a huge demand from Europe for the hides.[18] As a result, the price of hides increased in America, and the vast majority of untanned hides were exported to Europe for use in industry.

An estimate of the import of untanned hides from the United States to the United Kingdom and France is shown in Figure 11-6. These estimates come from comparing import demand in the United Kingdom and France with demand in Canada, where the invention allowing buffalo hides to be tanned for industrial use was not known. We are therefore looking at the *extra* demand in the United Kingdom and France after the invention was put to use. We can see from Figure 11-6 that the amount of imports into these countries (in excess of imports into Canada) was small or negative before 1871, but then grew rapidly and peaked in 1875. That year the United Kingdom and France combined imported more than 1 million hides and, over the entire period from 1871 to 1878, imported some 3.5 million hides, which can plausibly account for

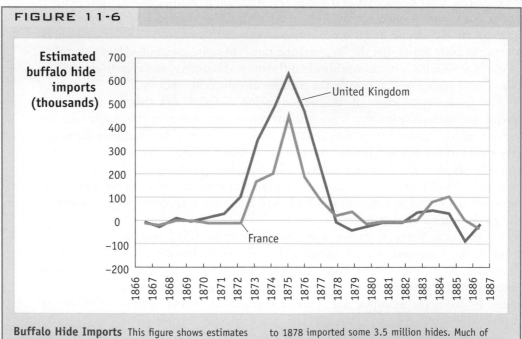

FIGURE 11-6

Buffalo Hide Imports This figure shows estimates of the imports to the United Kingdom and France of buffalo hides from the United States. The amount of imports into these countries (in excess of imports to Canada) was small or negative before 1871, but then grew rapidly and peaked in 1875. That year the United Kingdom and France combined imported more than 1 million hides and over the entire period from 1871 to 1878 imported some 3.5 million hides. Much of this trade volume can be attributed to an invention in London in 1871 that allowed buffalo hides to be tanned for industrial use.

Source: M. Scott Taylor, March 2007, "Buffalo Hunt: International Trade and the Virtual Extinction of the North American Bison," NBER Working Paper No. 12969.

---

[18] See M. Scott Taylor, March 2007, "Buffalo Hunt: International Trade and the Virtual Extinction of the North American Bison," NBER Working Paper No. 12969.

the slaughter of the entire Great Plains herd.[19] A further slight increase in imports in the 1880s likely reflects hides from the Northern herd of buffalo in the United States.

Figure 11-6 shows convincingly that international trade, combined with the innovation in tanning technology in London and the absence of any property rights over the buffalo, was responsible for the slaughter of the buffalo. That is a sad result of market forces and one that we want to avoid today through agreements such as CITES. We now turn to two final examples of trade policy cases being discussed in the world today that have environmental implications. In contrast to the slaughter of the buffalo or the overharvesting of fish, it is more challenging in these final examples to determine the social costs or benefits of international trade.

Trade in Solar Panels In Chapter 9, we discussed the production and export of solar panels. When consumers install solar panels there is a *positive consumption externality*, because this source of electricity does not rely on the burning of fossils fuels, which emits carbon and contributes to global climate change. In terms of Figure 11-4 panel (b), the *SMB* curve would be drawn *above* the demand curve rather than below it. Free trade in solar panels would lead to an extra social gain, because with increased Home consumption of solar panels, the benefit from the consumption externality grows. There would be two sources of gains from trade: the private gains from trade (area *b*), and an extra area of social gains (like area *d*, but measured with *SMB* drawn above the *D* curve).

In principle, the extra social gains that come from free trade are even larger when one country subsidizes the production of solar panels and exports more panels at lower prices. That is what the United States and the European Union (EU) believe that China has done. But rather than accept the low-priced solar panels, with the positive consumption externality, these countries have threatened to apply tariffs against China. Why are these countries not willing to import solar panels at the lowest possible price and in this way get the greatest social gain from not burning fossil fuels, as environmentalists would prefer?

There are two answers to this question. The first is that the positive consumption externality from using solar panels is a *global* externality: using sunshine rather than fossil fuel generates fewer carbon emissions and therefore reduces the risks from global climate change. Because this benefit applies to everyone on the globe and not just to one nation's population, an importing country might not be willing to accept low-priced solar panels when the social benefits are so diffuse, particularly when the imported low-price solar panels threaten local producers.

The second related reason comes from the competitive threat to Home producers from the low-priced imports. In addition to the political pressure to help Home producers, the governments of the United States and the EU might believe that maintaining this industry at Home has spillover benefits to other American and European industries. In other words, U.S. and European policy makers might believe that there is a *positive production externality* in manufacturing solar panels, because that manufacturing will lead to knowledge that can be applied elsewhere. The difficulty for policy makers is to correctly identify the extent of these potential knowledge spillovers, especially compared with the social benefits from using solar panels. Put simply, is it more important to encourage knowledge spillovers by protecting the solar

---

[19] The import data for the United Kingdom and France are in pounds, so these estimates of imports assume that each four hides weigh 112 pounds.

panel industry in the U.S. and EU through tariffs, or to encourage the greatest use of solar panels in these countries by allowing low-price imports from China? That is the dilemma faced by the United States and the EU with regard to the imports of solar panels from China.

Trade in Rare Earth Minerals In Chapter 10, we discussed policies used by China in its export of rare earth minerals. During 2009–11, China used export quotas to restrict the sale of these minerals, leading to higher world prices. As a result, a mine was opened in Australia and a mine in the Mojave Desert of the United States was re-opened. The U.S. mine had been closed in 2002 because of a spill of radioactive fluid from a pipeline. Rare earth minerals are often found in the presence of radioactive elements such as thorium and uranium, so the processing of these minerals leads to low-grade radioactive waste. It is this by-product of the processing of rare earth minerals that leads to environmental concerns. The ore from the Australian mine is processed in Malaysia, leading to worry in that country about the safe handling of the radioactive waste: see **Headlines: China Signals Support for Rare Earths,** in Chapter 10. Other countries that have deposits of these minerals include Greenland (as discussed in the beginning of Chapter 1) and some African countries.

Regardless of the country in which they are processed, the processing of rare earth minerals has a negative production externality, as we examined in panel (a) of Figure 11-4. It would be difficult to limit the amount demanded of these minerals, because they are used in so many high-tech products. So from an environmental point of view, the most important matter is to regulate the disposal of the radioactive by-product.

China has begun to make efforts in that direction, as discussed in the **Headlines** article in Chapter 10. But as a newly industrialized country, China does not have the same level of environmental regulation as found in the United States or Australia. We can expect the processing activities of the mines in the Mohave Desert to be closely monitored, especially the treatment of the radioactive waste. But it is troubling that the company that owns the mine in Australia, Lynas Corporation, has chosen to process the ore in Malaysia. That concern has led to the protests of activists in Malaysia (as discussed in Chapter 10). Similar to the policies that ensure the safety of workers discussed earlier in this chapter, monitoring the disposal of radioactive waste from rare earth minerals will probably involve a combination of consumer protests, corporate responsibility, and government policies across countries.

International Agreements on Pollution

Pollution is a by-product of many manufacturing activities. The tragedy of the commons applies to pollution, too, because companies and countries can treat the air and water as a common-property resource, allowing pollutants to enter it without regard for where these pollutants end up. Pollution is an international issue because it can often cross borders in the water or atmosphere. We will use the term "global pollutants" for substances that cross country borders. Examples include chlorofluorocarbons (CFCs), which result in a depletion of the ozone layer in the atmosphere, and carbon dioxide (CO_2), which contributes to global warming. In contrast, we use the term "local pollutants" for substances that, for the most part, stay within a country. An example is smog, which is caused by the carbon monoxide in factory emissions and automobile exhaust.

Global Pollutants For global pollutants, a prisoner's dilemma similar to that illustrated in Figure 11-2 for tariffs again applies. Because the pollution crosses international borders, each country does not face the full cost of its own pollution. It follows that there is little incentive to regulate global pollutants. In the absence of regulation, however, countries will end up with the bad outcome of having too much global pollution, so international agreements are needed to control the amount.

Payoff Matrix To make this argument more carefully, in Figure 11-7 we show the payoff matrix for two countries, each of which decides whether to regulate the emissions of a pollutant. The regulations could take the form of limits on how much of the pollutant an industry can emit, which means that the industry must install special equipment to reduce its emissions, at its own expense. Each quadrant of the matrix includes Home's payoff in the lower-left corner and Foreign's payoff in the upper-right corner. We start with a situation of regulation and then measure the change in welfare for Home or Foreign when there are no pollution regulations (or when pollution regulations are not enforced).

Starting in the upper-left cell, when both countries regulate emissions of the pollutant, consumers are better off as compared with no regulations, while producers are worse off because of the expense of the regulations. If one country—say, Home—decides not to regulate, then its producers would gain because they no longer have to install the extra equipment to reduce emissions, but consumers in Home and Foreign would lose if regulations are not used because of the extra pollution. The outcome is similar if Foreign decides not to regulate: its producers gain, and consumers in both countries lose. Finally, if neither country regulates, then there is a large loss for consumers from the extra pollution and a small gain for producers due to the cost savings from not installing the equipment (this gain is small because neither producer is subject to the regulations, so competition can eliminate most of their gains).

Nash Equilibrium Let us use the structure of payoffs in Figure 11-7 to determine the Nash equilibrium. Start in the upper-left quadrant, where both countries regulate their pollution emissions. If either country deviates from this position and does not

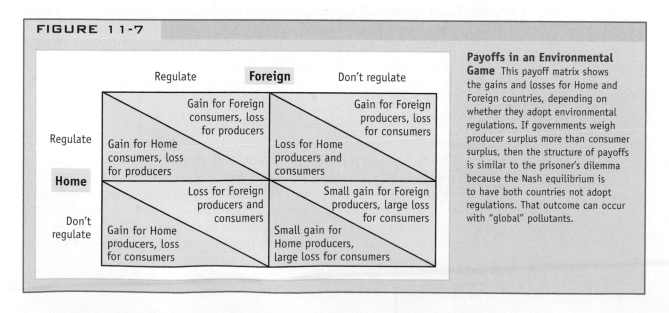

FIGURE 11-7

	Regulate	**Foreign**	Don't regulate

Regulate

Gain for Foreign consumers, loss for producers

Gain for Home consumers, loss for producers

Gain for Foreign producers, loss for consumers

Loss for Home producers and consumers

Home

Don't regulate

Loss for Foreign producers and consumers

Gain for Home producers, loss for consumers

Small gain for Foreign producers, large loss for consumers

Small gain for Home producers, large loss for consumers

Payoffs in an Environmental Game This payoff matrix shows the gains and losses for Home and Foreign countries, depending on whether they adopt environmental regulations. If governments weigh producer surplus more than consumer surplus, then the structure of payoffs is similar to the prisoner's dilemma because the Nash equilibrium is to have both countries not adopt regulations. That outcome can occur with "global" pollutants.

regulate, it will experience a gain for producers and a loss for consumers. If pollution is local, then the country might realize that the costs to consumers outweigh the gains to producers. That is why the Environmental Protection Agency (EPA) in the United States regulates the pollution from factories and from cars: the gains to consumers from reducing pollution outweigh the costs to producers.

In the case of global pollution, however, this calculation changes. If a country's pollution crosses international borders, as with CO_2 emissions, then the perceived gains to a country's *own* consumers from regulating the pollution may be less than the costs to producers. In that case, neither country will want to stay in the regulated quadrant in the upper left of Figure 11-7 and will have an incentive *not* to regulate its global pollution. Given that one country does not regulate its global pollution, the other country will have an even greater incentive not to regulate: if Home does not regulate in Figure 11-7 so that we are in the bottom row, then Foreign's best decision will likely be not to regulate either because the additional loss to its consumers will be offset by a gain to producers.[20]

Thus, the payoffs shown in Figure 11-7 can lead us to a situation in which neither country regulates pollution, in the lower-right quadrant, despite the large losses to consumers. That outcome is similar to the prisoner's dilemma that we discussed for the tariff game (Figure 11-2): both countries can end up with a bad outcome (with high tariffs or high pollution), even though they are individually making their best decisions. Just like the tariff game, multilateral agreements are needed to ensure that countries end up instead in the upper-left quadrant, with both countries regulating the global pollution.

Multilateral Agreements One example of an international agreement is the Montreal Protocol on Substances that Deplete the Ozone Layer, which has successfully eliminated the use of CFCs. In that case, the scientific evidence showing that CFCs were creating a "hole" in the ozone layer above Australia and New Zealand was conclusive. In addition, the CFCs that were used in refrigerators, air conditioners, and other appliances could be replaced with alternative chemicals at relatively low cost. So it was not that difficult to get all countries to agree to a ban on the use of CFCs, which began in 1989 and has already reduced the damage to the ozone layer. A more difficult case is that of global warming, which is regulated by an agreement known as the Kyoto Protocol, and more recently by the Copenhagen Accord, as discussed in our final application.

APPLICATION

The Kyoto Protocol and the Copenhagen Accord

In December 1997, representatives from many nations met in Kyoto, Japan, to discuss nonbinding targets for reducing emissions of greenhouse gases. The principal greenhouse gas is CO_2, which is released by cars, factories, home heating, the generation of electricity through coal plants, and basically nearly every activity that involves combustion. CO_2 creates a "greenhouse" effect, whereby heat is trapped inside the atmosphere, slightly increasing the earth's temperature. Even small increases in temperature can have dramatic consequences through the melting of ice caps, which raises

---

[20] In the problems at the end of the chapter, you are asked to work through examples using specific numbers for the gains and losses in Figure 11-7, to determine the Nash equilibrium.

the level of oceans; changes weather patterns; affects agriculture, tourism, and other economic activities; endangers species; and may have even worse consequences.

The **Kyoto Protocol** built on the United Nations' 1992 treaty on climate change, which was ratified by 189 countries, including the United States. Five years later, in 1997, the Kyoto Protocol established specific targets for reduction in greenhouse gas emissions: the industrial countries should cut their emissions of greenhouse gases by a collective 5.2% less than their 1990 levels (which is estimated to be a reduction of 29% from what 2010 levels are predicted to occur without the agreement). Targets for individual countries range from an 8% reduction for the European Union, 7% for the United States, 6% for Japan, 0% for Russia, and permitted increases for Australia and Iceland. In addition, a market for emissions targets was established so that Russia, for example, could sell its credits to other countries if it produces less than its 1990 level of greenhouse gases.

More than 160 countries have ratified this agreement, including about 40 industrial countries. Russia ratified the treaty on November 18, 2004, bringing the amount of greenhouse gases accounted for by the members to more than 55% of the world total. The treaty then took effect three months later, on February 16, 2005. However, the United States did not ratify this treaty and is the only large industrial country not to join the effort. Why did the United States refuse to join, and what actions can be taken instead to reduce global emissions?

There are four reasons often given to explain why the United States did not join the Kyoto Protocol:[21] (1) although the evidence toward global warming is strong, we still do not understand all the consequences of policy actions; (2) the United States is the largest emitter of greenhouse gases and meeting the Kyoto targets would negatively affect its economy; (3) Kyoto failed to include the developing countries, especially China and India; (4) there are other ways to pursue reductions in greenhouse gas emissions.

The first point has become less plausible over time, as the evidence for and consequences of global warming become more apparent. The second point is true: the United States is the largest emitter of greenhouse gases (because of its very large economy), and meeting the Kyoto goals would certainly impose significant costs on the economy. The costs to the United States would probably be higher than the costs to Germany, for example, because East Germany had plants that were highly polluting in 1990 that have now been shut down. The percentage reduction in German pollution is calculated from a baseline that includes the highly polluting plants, whereas the percentage reduction in the United States is calculated from a baseline using plants that were already polluting less in 1990, due to U.S. regulations.

Nevertheless, the fact that costs are high should not prevent countries from trying to reduce greenhouse gas emissions. A 2006 report by the Stern Commission in the United Kingdom argues that the costs of *not* reducing greenhouse gas emissions are unacceptably high: as high as "the great wars and the economic depression of the first half of the twentieth century" and damage from climate change that is potentially irreversible.[22]

---

[21] These reasons are all mentioned in a speech given by President George W. Bush to the United Nations in 2001. See "In the President's Words: 'A Leadership Role on the Issue of Climate Change,'" *New York Times*, June 12, 2001, electronic edition.

[22] "The Economics of Climate Change," available at http://www.hm-treasury.gov.uk, as cited in Martin Wolf, "A Compelling Case for Action to Avoid a Climatic Catastrophe," *Financial Times*, November 1, 2006, p. 13.

The third point—that the Kyoto Protocol leaves out developing countries such as China and India—is perhaps the major reason why the United States did not ratify the treaty. Just as in the prisoner's dilemma game illustrated in Figure 11-7, if one player does not regulate its emissions, then there is less incentive for the other player to also regulate. For this reason, the Copenhagen Climate Summit, held in Copenhagen in December 2009, brought together all the major countries with an interest in climate change—119 nations in total—to try and hammer out a new agreement. Unfortunately, the meeting ended with only modest goals, called the **Copenhagen Accord:** a recognition that further increases in global average temperature should be kept below 2 degrees centigrade; an agreement that industrialized countries will submit goals for greenhouse gas emissions reductions, while developing countries will communicate their efforts in this regard; and the establishment of a fund to finance the needs of developing countries in fighting the effect of climate change. But as indicated in **Headlines: Dismal Outcome at Copenhagen Fiasco,** these goals come without any firm means to enforce them.

The **Headlines** article recognizes that action on global climate change requires global cooperation. But the multilateral deal that was attempted at Copenhagen is not the only way to go. Countries can and should pursue domestic policies that limit greenhouse gas emissions. Europe already has a well-functioning market for carbon emissions, which allows companies and countries to buy and sell credits for such emissions. The United States is considering the same type of market under a "cap and trade" system, which puts a cap (upper limit) on the carbon emissions of each firm, but allows them to trade credits with other firms. Although China does not yet envisage such a system, it is making another type of contribution by focusing on alternative energy, becoming the world's largest producer and exporter of solar panel cells and wind turbines. Furthermore, in March 2010, China and India agreed to join the Copenhagen Accord, as has the United States and more than 100 other countries. These actions show that the modest goals of the Copenhagen Accord have made it easier for countries to join that agreement than the earlier, binding limits of the Kyoto Protocol. Even though this accord does not include a means of enforcement, it could form the basis for future international cooperation on climate change.

4 Conclusions

Throughout this book, we have referred to international agreements on trade, including multilateral agreements such as the GATT and WTO and regional agreements such as NAFTA. In this chapter, we have explored the rationale for these agreements more carefully, and discussed areas other than trade—such as labor standards and the environment—that these agreements encompass.

The first issue we addressed is why international agreements are needed at all. The answer is that there are strong temptations for countries to use tariffs for their own benefit, or to avoid adopting environmental regulations, as occurs when countries do not face the costs of their own global pollutants. In these situations, countries have an incentive to use tariffs or not regulate, but when all countries act in this manner, they end up losing: the outcome can be high tariffs or high pollution. This outcome can occur because the countries are in a "prisoner's dilemma" in which the Nash equilibrium leads both parties to act in ways that seem right taken on their own but result in

HEADLINES

Dismal Outcome at Copenhagen Fiasco

In the introduction to the chapter, we discussed the Copenhagen Climate Summit, held in December 2009, which was intended to establish new guidelines for reductions in greenhouse gas emissions. The summit did not achieve that goal, unfortunately, and this article discusses possible next steps.

The [Copenhagen Accord] agreement cobbled together by the US, China, India, Brazil and South Africa is merely an expression of aims. It recognises the scientific case for keeping the rise in global temperatures to 2°C. It calls on developed countries to provide $100 [billion] a year in support of poor nations' efforts by 2020, but without saying who pays what to whom. It appears to commit none of the signatories to anything.

. . . Climate change requires global cooperation, to be sure, because the global stock of greenhouse gases is the driver. Collective action is essential. The free-rider problem is obvious and has to be addressed. But the maximalist approach to this, a global treaty with binding caps on emissions, is going to

be extraordinarily difficult to achieve. Even if the will were there, enforcing the caps would be a problem, as the Kyoto Protocol amply attests. If the maximalist model can be revived in time for next December's [2010] scheduled conference in Mexico, well and good: the key thing, though, is that progress should not be held hostage to it. The need is for greater pragmatism and flexibility.

The US and China can take the lead. In Copenhagen, friction between the two was evident, with the US calling for independent verification of emissions reductions, and China resisting infringements of its sovereignty. In fact the two countries are not so far apart: the US Congress is as jealous of national sovereignty, and as wary of international obligations, as

China. Both countries should lead by example, with unilateral low-cost carbon-abatement policies already announced or under consideration: cap and trade in the US, measures to reduce carbon intensity in China. The international framework need not insist on lock-step agreement. Above all, it should not obstruct policies that push the right way. . . .

Generous aid to developing countries for greenhouse gas abatement is warranted, but should be negotiated separately. Again, the need is to unpack the problem into manageable pieces. Copenhagen has shown the limits to the current approach. Reviving international co-operation is of paramount importance. This can best be done by asking less of it.

Source: Lex Team, "Dismal outcome at Copenhagen fiasco," Financial Times, December 20, 2009. From the Financial Times © The Financial Times Limited 2009. All Rights Reserved.

a poor outcome (i.e., both use tariffs or pollute). International agreements are needed to avoid these bad equilibria and restore a free-trade or low-pollution outcome.

A second issue we have addressed is that *halfway* steps toward the complete use of markets (as with complete free trade) can also have bad results. We found that such an outcome was a possibility with regional trade agreements, also called "preferential trade agreements," if the amount of trade diversion caused by the agreement is more than the amount of trade creation. Because preferential trade agreements provide zero tariffs only to the countries included in the agreement but maintain tariffs against all outside countries, they are a halfway step toward free trade. Countries that are not members of the agreement are worse off from being excluded. We have also shown that such agreements *might* make the member countries worse off, too, because the lowest-cost producers can be excluded from the agreement.

Another case in which a halfway step toward open markets can make countries worse off is with the overharvesting of resources. We have argued that in the absence of property rights for an exhaustible resource such as fish, opening countries to free trade can lead to even more harvesting of the resource, to the point of near extinction or extinction. That outcome is bad for the exporting country, at least, and illustrates a negative externality in consumption. So free trade *in the absence of well-defined property rights* can lead to losses. Economists think of this case as opening one market (i.e., free trade between countries) without having a properly functioning market for the resource (no property rights). Viewed in that way, the overharvesting of an exhaustible resource is similar to trade diversion in a regional trade agreement, since the trade agreement also opens one market (i.e., free trade between member countries) without having complete free trade (tariffs are applied against the nonmember countries). Both overharvesting and trade diversion are bad outcomes that arise in settings in which markets are not functioning properly.

Finally, we have argued that actions by consumers, unions, and firms to improve labor standards and the environment are important. Such actions, including the protests at the 1999 WTO meetings, *have* made a difference in the rulings of the WTO in environmental cases: although environmentalists have lost some battles at the WTO, some observers believe they have won the war. We can also expect that such actions make a difference to the labor standards enjoyed by workers and the environmental safeguards used by firms.

KEY POINTS

1. There are two primary types of free-trade agreements: multilateral and regional. Multilateral agreements are negotiated among large groups of countries (such as all countries in the WTO) to reduce trade barriers among them, whereas regional agreements operate among a smaller group of countries, often in the same region.

2. Under perfect competition, we can analyze the benefits of multilateral agreements by considering the Nash equilibrium of a two-country game in which the countries are deciding whether to apply a tariff. The unique Nash equilibrium for two large countries is to apply tariffs against each other, which is an example of a "prisoner's dilemma." By using an agreement to remove tariffs, both countries become better off by eliminating the deadweight losses of the tariffs.

3. Regional trade agreements are also known as preferential trade agreements, because they give preferential treatment (i.e., free trade) to the countries included within the agreement, but maintain tariffs against outside countries. There are two types of regional trade agreements: free-trade areas (such as NAFTA) and customs unions (such as the European Union).

4. The welfare gains and losses that arise from regional trade agreements are more complex than those that arise from multilateral trade agreements because only the countries included within the agreement have zero tariffs, while tariffs are maintained against the countries outside the agreement. Under a free-trade area, the countries within the regional trade agreement each have their own tariffs against outside countries; whereas under a customs union, the countries within the regional trade agreement have the same tariffs against outside countries.

5. Trade creation occurs when a country within a regional agreement imports a product from another member country that formerly it produced for itself. In this case, there is a welfare gain for both the buying and the selling country.

6. Trade diversion occurs when a member country imports a product from another member country that it formerly imported from a country outside of the new trade region. Trade diversion leads to losses for the former exporting country and possibly for the importing country and the new trading region as a whole.

7. Labor standards refer to all issues that directly affect workers, including occupational health and safety, child labor, minimum wages, the right to unionize, and so on. The enforcement of labor standards is sometimes included within trade agreements and is an issue on which consumer groups and unions often demand action.

8. The WTO does not deal directly with the environment, but environmental issues come up as the WTO is asked to rule on specific cases. A review of these cases shows that the WTO has become friendlier to environmental considerations in its rulings.

9. In the presence of externalities, international trade might make a negative externality worse, bringing a social cost that offsets the private gains from trade. International trade can also reduce a negative externality, leading to a social gain that is in addition to the private gains from trade. From this logic and from real-world examples, we conclude that free trade can help or hurt the environment.

10. International agreements on the environment are needed for the same reasons that agreements on tariffs are needed—to avoid a prisoner's dilemma type of outcome, which is bad for all countries. The Kyoto Protocol of 2005 had only limited success because the United States did not agree to participate, and developing countries such as China and India were excluded. The Copenhagen Accord of 2009 also did not achieve international commitments with firm enforcement, but at least the United States, China, India, and more than 100 other countries have agreed to participate.

KEY TERMS

terms-of-trade gain, p. 369
multilateral agreement, p. 369
regional trade agreement, p. 369
trade agreement, p. 370
most favored nation principle,
 p. 370
prisoner's dilemma, p. 372
preferential trade agreements,
 p. 374

free-trade area, p. 374
customs union, p. 374
rules of origin, p. 374
trade creation, p. 375
trade diversion, p. 375
labor standards, p. 381
living wage, p. 387
multilateral environmental
 agreements, p. 388

externality, p. 392
market failure, p. 392
tragedy of the commons, p. 397
common property, p. 397
Kyoto Protocol, p. 403
Copenhagen Accord, p. 404

PROBLEMS

1. a. How is a customs union different from a free-trade area? Provide examples of each.

   b. Why do some economists prefer multilateral trade agreements over regional trade agreements?

2. Figure 11-2 shows the tariff game among large countries.

   a. Redraw the payoff matrix for a game between a large and small country.
   b. What is/are the Nash equilibrium/equilibria, assuming that the large country applies an optimal tariff?
   c. What does your answer to (b) tell you about the role of the WTO in a situation like this?

3. Consider the following variation of Table 11-1 for the U.S. semiconductor market:

	U.S. TARIFF		
	0%	10%	20%
From Canada, before NAFTA	$46	$W	$55.2
From Asia, before NAFTA	$42	$X	$Y
From Canada, after NAFTA	$46	$Z	$Z
From Asia, after NAFTA	$42	$X	$Y
From the United States	$47	$47	$47

a. Fill in the values for W, X, Y, and Z.
b. Suppose that before NAFTA, the United States had a 20% tariff on imported semiconductors. Which country supplied the U.S. market? Is it the lowest-cost producer?

c. After NAFTA, who supplies the U.S. market? Has either trade creation or diversion occurred because of NAFTA? Explain.

d. Now suppose that before NAFTA, the United States had a 10% tariff on imported semiconductors. Then repeat parts (b) and (c).

e. In addition to the assumptions made in (d), consider the effect of an increase in high-technology investment in Canada due to NAFTA, allowing Canadian firms to develop better technology. As a result, *three years after the initiation of NAFTA*, Canadian firms can begin to sell their products to the United States for $46. What happens to the U.S. trade pattern three years after NAFTA? Has either trade creation or diversion occurred because of NAFTA? Explain.

4. Assume that Thailand and India are potential trading partners of China. Thailand is a member of ASEAN but India is not. Suppose the import price of textiles from India (P_{India}) is 50 per unit under free trade and is subject to a 20% tariff. As of January 1st 2010, China and Thailand entered into the China–ASEAN free-trade area, eliminating tariffs on Thai imports. Use the following figure to answer these questions:

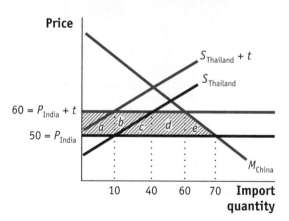

a. Before the China–ASEAN free-trade area, how much does China import from each trading partner? What is the import price? Calculate the tariff revenue.

b. After the China–ASEAN free-trade area, how much does China import from each trade partner? What is the import price? What is the total tariff revenue of China?

c. Based on your answer to part (b), what is the impact of the China–ASEAN free-trade area on the welfare of China?

d. What is the effect of the China–ASEAN free-trade area on the welfare of Thailand and India?

e. As mentioned in the **Headlines: China-ASEAN Treaty Threatens Indian Exporters,** the China–ASEAN agreement may lead to a similar one between China and India. How would this affect China's imports from each country? What would be the effect on welfare in China, Thailand, and India if such an agreement was signed?

5. Redraw the graph of trade diversion (Figure 11-3) with the S'_{Mex} curve intersecting the M_{US} curve *between* points A and D.

a. When the United States and Mexico join NAFTA, who supplies auto parts to the United States? Does the United States import a larger quantity of auto parts after NAFTA; that is, does trade creation occur?

b. What is the change in government revenue compared with before NAFTA?

c. Is the United States better off for joining NAFTA?

6. Refer to the survey in Table 11-2 regarding consumers' attitudes toward working conditions.

a. Fill in the survey questions for yourself and at least five friends.

b. Average your results, and compare them with those in Table 11-2. Are there any consistent differences in the answers from your friends and those in Table 11-2?

c. Do the answers from your friends show the following two characteristics?

   i. Many people are willing to pay at least a small amount to ensure good labor standards (or simply switch to an alternative with the same price), though relatively few are willing to pay a lot.

   ii. Individuals had to receive a higher discount to purchase a T-shirt made under poor conditions than they were willing to pay for a T-shirt made under good conditions.

   Explain whether these characteristics apply to your friends or not.

7. Using Table 11-3, explain why environmentalists have "lost the battle but won the war" in their dealings with the WTO. Refer to specific WTO cases in your answer.

8. Refer to Figure 11-4 when answering this question.

   a. Redraw Figure 11-4, panel (a), assuming that the production externality is positive so that the SMC curve lies below the supply curve. Label the area c that reflects the change in the cost of the externality when trade is opened. Is this area an additional social gain from free trade or an offsetting cost?

   Can you think of a real-world example of this case?

   b. Redraw Figure 11-4, panel (b), assuming that the consumption externality is positive so that the SMB curve lies above the demand curve. Label the area d that arises when trade is opened, and explain why this area is an additional social gain from free trade. (You can refer to the discussion of solar panels earlier in the chapter.)

9. Refer to following variations of the payoff matrix for the environmental game shown in Figure 11-7. In this problem, a number is assigned to represent the welfare level of each outcome for Home and Foreign.

   a. First, consider the case of global pollution in which the government puts more weight on producer profits than consumer well-being when calculating welfare (this is so since a portion of consumer costs are borne by the other country). How can you tell that the government favors producers over consumers from the following payoff matrix? What is the Nash equilibrium for this environmental game? Is it a prisoner's dilemma? Briefly explain.

   (Figure: Foreign / Home payoff matrix. Regulate/Regulate: 80, 80. Regulate(Home)/Don't(Foreign): 100,50. Don't/Regulate: 50,100. Don't/Don't: 70,70.)

   b. Next, consider the case of local pollution in which the government puts more weight on consumer well-being than producer profits

when calculating welfare. How can you tell that the government favors consumers over producers from the following payoff matrix? What is the Nash equilibrium for this environmental game? Is it a prisoner's dilemma? Briefly explain.

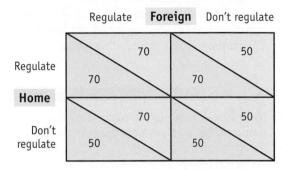

(Figure: Foreign / Home payoff matrix. Regulate/Regulate: 70,70. Regulate/Don't: 50,70. Don't/Regulate: 70,50. Don't/Don't: 50,50.)

Longer study questions: The following questions ask you to consider a real-life situation involving international trade agreements, dealing with trade, labor, or the environment. For each question, you are asked to develop an "agree" or "disagree" position on each situation. These situations are drawn from recent press reports, which are available in the instructor's manual. You can research the issues on the Web and also rely on any relevant information from this textbook. Your instructor might ask you to answer these questions individually, in pairs, or in groups for presentation in class.

10. In 2007, several members of Congress in the United States proposed that any further trade negotiations be accompanied by a "grand bargain" on labor standards. The problem with this action is that the current labor practices of the United States sometimes run afoul of the guidelines of the International Labour Organization (ILO), which would open up the United States to criticism and potentially sanctions from that agency. The article "Why a 'Grand Deal' on Labor Could End Trade Talks" describes these concerns and argues that such a "grand deal" would be a mistake for the United States. A full-text version of this article is available at http://www.iie.com/publications/opeds/oped.cfm?ResearchID=716.

Answer the following: Do you agree or disagree with the proposal for the United States to pursue a "grand deal" on labor standards, bringing its own laws into line with those of the International Labour Organization?

11. In March 2007 it was announced that several restaurants in the greater San Francisco area would no longer provide bottled water to their patrons to save on the environmental costs of transporting that water: do an Internet search for the phrase "bottled water backlash" to find articles about the San Francisco restaurants and other companies taking this action. Instead, these companies would install filtering equipment that would allow them to serve local water. Although these actions are intended to be more environmentally friendly, they will affect firms and countries that sell bottled water. One of these countries is Fiji, which obtains a major portion of its export earnings from bottled water.

Answer the following: Do you agree or disagree with the actions taken by the restaurants in San Francisco?

NET WORK

Do an Internet search for "corporate responsibility" to find an example of a corporation or group of companies that is adopting procedures to protect workers' rights or the environment. Briefly describe the procedures being adopted.

The Global Macroeconomy

So much of barbarism, however, still remains in the transactions of most civilized nations, that almost all independent countries choose to assert their nationality by having, to their inconvenience and that of their neighbors, a peculiar currency of their own.

John Stuart Mill

Neither a borrower nor a lender be; / For loan oft loseth both itself and friend. / And borrowing dulls the edge of husbandry.

Polonius, in William Shakespeare's *Hamlet*

History, in general, only informs us of what bad government is.

Thomas Jefferson

International macroeconomics is devoted to the study of large-scale economic interactions among interdependent economies. It is international because a deeper exploration of the interconnections among nations is essential to understanding how the global economy works. It is macroeconomic because it focuses on key economy-wide variables, such as exchange rates, prices, interest rates, income, wealth, and the current account. In the chapters that follow, we use familiar macroeconomic ideas to examine the main features of the global macroeconomy.

The preceding quotations indicate that the broad range of topics and issues in international macroeconomics can be reduced to three key elements: the world has many monies (not one), countries are financially integrated (not isolated), and in this context economic policy choices are made (but not always very well).

- **Money** John Stuart Mill echoes the complaints of many exasperated travelers and traders when he bemoans the profusion of different monies around the world. Mill's vision of a world with a single currency is even more distant today: in his day, the number of currencies was far smaller than the more than 150 currencies in use today. Why do all these monies exist, and what purposes do they serve? How do they affect the working of our global economy? What are the causes and consequences of the changing value of one currency against another? Do the benefits of having a national currency outweigh the costs?

■ **Finance** William Shakespeare's Polonius would surely be distressed by the sight of the mounting debts owed by the United States and other borrower countries to the rest of world. For him, happiness meant financial isolation, with income exactly equal to expenditure. Over the centuries, however, this has been a minority view among individuals and among nations. Today, the scale of international financial transactions has risen to record levels as capital has become ever more mobile internationally. Why do all these transactions occur, and what purposes do they serve? Who lends to whom, and why? Why are some debts paid but not others? Does the free flow of finance have costs as well as benefits?

■ **Policy** Thomas Jefferson's assessment of government may be extreme, but looking at economic outcomes around the world today, it surely contains some truth. If government policies were always optimal, recessions never happened, currencies never crashed, and debts were never in default . . . well, that would be a nice world to inhabit. The reality—all too apparent after the global financial crisis of 2008—is that policy making is frequently not optimal, even at the best of times in the best-run countries. And in the worst run countries, poverty, underinvestment, hyperinflation, crises, and debt problems are common events. How do exchange rates and international capital flows affect an economy? How can policy makers avoid bad economic outcomes and formulate better monetary and fiscal policies? What are the trade-offs for each policy decision? Is there even a single "right" approach to the many intricate economic problems facing interdependent nations?

Many fundamental questions like these must be answered if we are to understand the economic world around us. To that end, the chapters that follow combine economic theory with compelling empirical evidence to explain the workings of today's global macroeconomy. This introductory chapter briefly explains the road ahead.

1 Foreign Exchange: Currencies and Crises

In most branches of economics, and even in the study of international trade, it is common to assume that all goods are priced in a common currency. Despite this unrealistic assumption, such analysis delivers important insights into the workings of the global economy.

In the real world, however, countries have different currencies, and a complete understanding of how a country's economy works requires that we study the *exchange rate*, the price of foreign currency. Because products and investments move across borders, fluctuations in exchange rates have significant effects on the relative prices of home and foreign goods (such as autos and clothing), services (such as insurance and tourism), and assets (such as equities and bonds). We start our analysis of the global economy with the theory of exchange rates, and learn how and why they fluctuate. In later chapters, we'll see why exchange rates matter for economic outcomes and why they are an important focus of economic policy making.

How Exchange Rates Behave

In studying exchange rates, it is important to understand the types of behavior that any theory of exchange rate determination must explain. Figure 12-1 illustrates some basic facts about exchange rates. Panel (a) shows the exchange rate of China with the United States, in yuan per U.S. dollar ($).[1] Panel (b) shows the exchange rate of the United States with the Eurozone, in U.S. dollars per euro.

The behavior of the two exchange rates is very different. The yuan–dollar rate is almost flat. In fact, for many years it was literally unchanged, day after day, at 8.28 yuan/$. Finally, on July 23, 2005, it dropped exactly 2%. Then it followed a fairly smooth, slow downward trend for a while: by September 2008 (when the global financial crisis began), it had fallen a further 15%. After the crisis, it reverted to a flat line once again at 6.83 yuan/$, and then on June 21, 2010, it resumed a gradual slow decline. During the period shown, the daily average absolute change in the exchange rate was less than five-hundredths of one percent (0.05%).

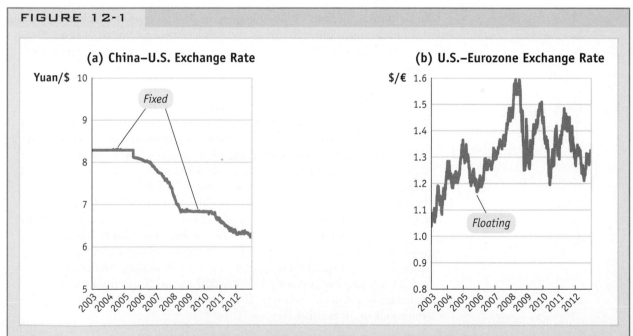

FIGURE 12-1

Major Exchange Rates The chart shows two key exchange rates from 2003 to 2012. The China–U.S. exchange rate varies little and would be considered a fixed exchange rate, despite a period when it followed a gradual trend. The U.S.–Eurozone exchange rate varies a lot and would be considered a floating exchange rate.

Note: For comparative purposes, the two vertical scales have the same proportions: the maximum is twice the minimum.

Source: oanda.com.

---

[1] The Chinese yuan is also known as the *renminbi* ("people's currency").

100 Chinese yuan, U.S. dollars, Eurozone euros

In contrast, the euro–dollar exchange rate experienced much wider fluctuations over the same period. On a *daily* basis, the average absolute change in this exchange rate was one-third of one percent (0.33%), about 6 or 7 times as large as the average change in the yuan–dollar rate.

Based on such clearly visible differences in exchange rate behavior, economists divide the world into two groups of countries: those with **fixed** (or *pegged*) **exchange rates** and those with **floating** (or *flexible*) **exchange rates**. In Figure 12-1, China's exchange rate with the United States would be considered fixed. It was officially set at a fixed exchange rate with the dollar until July 2005, and again in 2008–10, but even at other times its very limited range of movement was so controlled that it was effectively "fixed."[2] In contrast, the euro–dollar exchange rate is a floating exchange rate, one that moves up and down over a much wider range.

Key Topics How are exchange rates determined? Why do some exchange rates fluctuate sharply in the short run, while others remain almost constant? What explains why exchange rates rise, fall, or stay flat in the long run?

Why Exchange Rates Matter

Changes in exchange rates affect an economy in two ways:

■ Changes in exchange rates cause a change in the international relative prices of goods. That is, one country's goods and services become more or less expensive relative to another's when expressed in a common unit of currency. For example, in 2011 *Spiegel* interviewed one Swiss cheesemaker:

> When Hans Stadelmann talks about currency speculators, it seems like two worlds are colliding. . . . Five men are working at the boilers, making the most popular Swiss cheese in Germany according to a traditional recipe . . . then there are the international financial markets, that abstract global entity whose actors have decided that the Swiss franc is a safe investment and, in doing so, have pushed the currency's value to record levels. . . . A year back, one euro was worth 1.35 francs. Two weeks ago, the value was 1-to-1. This presents a problem for Stadelmann. About 40% of his products are exported, most of them to EU countries. In order to keep his earnings level in francs, he's being forced to charge higher prices in euros—and not all of his customers are willing to pay them. 'I'm already selling less, and I'm afraid it's going to get much worse,' Stadelmann says. And it's not just his company he's worried about. 'I get my milk from 50 small family farmers,' he says. 'If I close up shop, I'd be destroying the livelihoods of 50 families.'"[3]

■ Changes in exchange rates can cause a change in the international relative prices of assets. These fluctuations in wealth can then affect firms, governments, and individuals. For example, in June 2010, Swiss investors held $397 billion of U.S. securities, when $1 was worth 1.05 Swiss francs (SFr). So these

---

[2] At the time of writing, in early 2013, the yuan–dollar exchange rate has started to hold stable again in the face of another global economic slowdown.
[3] Christian Teevs, "The Surging Franc: Swiss Fear the End of Economic Paradise," Spiegel Online (http://www.spiegel.de), August 25, 2011.

assets were worth 1.05 times 397, or SFr 417 billion. One year later $1 was worth only SFr 0.85, so the same securities would have been worth just 0.85 times 397 or SFr 337 billion, all else equal. That capital loss of SFr 80 billion (about 20%) came about purely because of exchange rate changes. Although other factors affect securities values in domestic transactions with a single currency, all cross-border transactions involving two currencies are strongly affected by exchange rates as well.[4]

Key Topics How do exchange rates affect the real economy? How do changes in exchange rates affect international prices, the demand for goods from different countries, and hence the levels of national output? How do changes in exchange rates affect the values of foreign assets, and hence change national wealth?

When Exchange Rates Misbehave

Even after studying how exchange rates behave and why they matter, we still face the challenge of explaining one type of event that is almost guaranteed to put exchange rates front and center in the news: an **exchange rate crisis.** In such a crisis, a currency experiences a sudden and pronounced loss of value against another currency, following a period in which the exchange rate had been fixed or relatively stable.

One of the most dramatic currency crises in recent history occurred in Argentina from December 2001 to January 2002. For a decade, the Argentine peso had been fixed to the U.S. dollar at a one-to-one rate of exchange. But in January 2002, the fixed exchange rate became a floating exchange rate. A few months later, 1 Argentine peso, which had been worth one U.S. dollar prior to 2002, had fallen in value to just $0.25 (equivalently, the price of a U.S. dollar rose from 1 peso to almost 4 pesos).

The drama was not confined to the foreign exchange market. The Argentine government declared a then-record **default** (i.e., a suspension of payments) on its $155 billion of debt; the financial system was in a state of near closure for months; inflation climbed; output collapsed and unemployment soared; and more than 50% of Argentine households fell below the poverty line. At the height of the crisis, violence flared and the country had five presidents in the space of two weeks.

Argentina's experience was extreme but hardly unique. Exchange rate crises are fairly common. Figure 12-2 lists 27 exchange rate crises in the 12-year period from 1997 to 2011. In almost all cases, a fairly stable exchange rate experienced a large and sudden change. The year 1997 was especially eventful, with seven crises, five of them in East Asia. The Indonesian rupiah lost 49% of its U.S. dollar value, but severe collapses also occurred in Thailand, Korea, Malaysia, and the Philippines. Other notable crises during this period included Liberia in 1998, Russia in 1998, and Brazil in 1999. More recently, Iceland and Ukraine saw their exchange rates crash during the global financial crisis of 2008 (see **Headlines: Economic Crisis in Iceland**).

Crisis episodes display some regular patterns. Output typically falls, banking and debt problems emerge, households and firms suffer. In addition, political turmoil often ensues. Government finances worsen and embarrassed authorities may appeal for external help from international organizations, such as the **International Monetary Fund (IMF)** or **World Bank,** or other entities. The economic setbacks

---

[4] Data for this example are based on the U.S. Treasury TIC report, June 30, 2011.

FIGURE 12-2

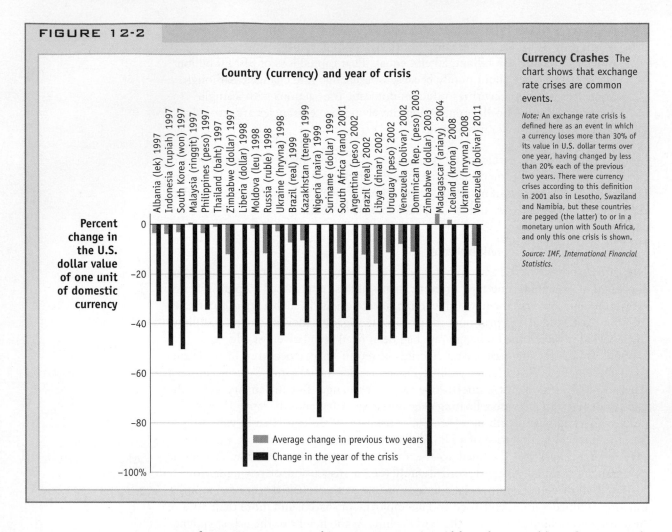

Currency Crashes The chart shows that exchange rate crises are common events.

Note: An exchange rate crisis is defined here as an event in which a currency loses more than 30% of its value in U.S. dollar terms over one year, having changed by less than 20% each of the previous two years. There were currency crises according to this definition in 2001 also in Lesotho, Swaziland and Namibia, but these countries are pegged (the latter) to or in a monetary union with South Africa, and only this one crisis is shown.

Source: IMF, International Financial Statistics.

are often more pronounced in poorer countries. Although we could confine our study of exchange rates to normal times, the frequent and damaging occurrence of crises obliges us to pay attention to these abnormal episodes, too.

Key Topics Why do exchange rate crises occur? Are they an inevitable consequence of deeper fundamental problems in an economy or are they an avoidable result of "animal spirits"—irrational forces in financial markets? Why are these crises so economically and politically costly? What steps might be taken to prevent crises, and at what cost?

Summary and Plan of Study

International macroeconomists frequently refer to the exchange rate as "the single most important price in an open economy." If we treat this statement as more than self-promotion, we should learn why it might be true. In our course of study, we will explore the factors that determine the exchange rate, how the exchange rate affects the economy, and how crises occur.

Our study of exchange rates proceeds as follows: in Chapter 13, we learn about the structure and operation of the markets in which foreign currencies are traded.

HEADLINES

....

Economic Crisis in Iceland

International macroeconomics can often seem like a dry and abstract subject, but it must be remembered that societies and individuals can be profoundly shaken by the issues we will study. This article was written just after the start of the severe economic crisis that engulfed Iceland in 2008, following the collapse of its exchange rate, a financial crisis, and a government fiscal crisis. Real output per person shrank by more than 10%, and unemployment rose from 1% to 9%. Five years later a recovery was just beginning to take shape.

Reykjavik—The crisis that brought down Iceland's economy in late 2008 threw thousands of formerly well-off families into poverty, forcing people like Iris to turn to charity to survive.

Each week, up to 550 families queue up at a small white brick warehouse in Reykjavik to receive free food from the Icelandic Aid to Families organisation, three times more than before the crisis.

Rutur Jonsson, a 65-year-old retired mechanical engineer, and his fellow volunteers spend their days distributing milk, bread, eggs and canned food donated by businesses and individuals or bought in bulk at the supermarket.

"I have time to spend on others and that's the best thing I think I can do," he said as he pre-packed grocery bags full of produce.

In a small, close-knit country of just 317,000 people, where everyone knows everyone, the stigma of accepting a hand-out is hard to live down and of the dozens of people waiting outside the food bank in the snow on a dreary March afternoon, Iris is the only one willing to talk.

"It was very difficult for me to come here in the beginning. But now I try not to care so much anymore," said the weary-looking 41-year-old, who lost her job in a pharmacy last summer, as she wrung her hands nervously.

The contrast is brutal with the ostentatious wealth that was on display across the island just two years ago, as a hyperactive banking sector flooded the small, formerly fishing-based economy with fast cash.

Back then, the biggest worry for many Icelanders was who had the nicest SUV, or the most opulent flat.

But today visible signs of poverty are quickly multiplying in the Nordic island nation, despite its generous welfare state, as the middle class is increasingly hit by unemployment, which is up from one to nine per cent in about a year, and a large number of defaults on mortgages.

Icelanders who lose their job are initially entitled to benefits worth 70 per cent of their wages—but the amount dwindles fast the longer they are without work. Coupled with growing debt, the spike in long-term unemployment is taking a heavy toll.

"The 550 families we welcome here represent about 2,700 people, and the number keeps going up. And we think it will keep growing until next year, at least," said Asgerdur Jona Flosadottir, who manages the Reykjavik food bank.

For Iris, the fall came quickly.

She is struggling to keep up with payments on two car loans, which she took out in foreign currencies on what proved to be disastrous advice from her bank, and which have tripled since the kronur's collapse.

Threatened in November with eviction from her home in the village of Vogar, some 40 kilometres (25 miles) southwest of Reykjavik, she managed to negotiate a year's respite with her bank.

"I feel very bad and I am very worried," she said, running her fingers

Protesters outside the Icelandic parliament in Reykjavik demand that the government do more to improve conditions for the recently poor.

Continued on next page

through her long, brown hair.

"I've thought about going abroad, but decided to stay because friends have come forward to guarantee my loans," she added sadly, before leaving with a friend who was driving her back home.

To avoid resorting to charity, many other Icelanders are choosing to pack their bags and try for a new future abroad, with official statistics showing the country's biggest emigration wave in more than a century is underway.

"I just don't see any future here. There isn't going to be any future in this country for the next 20 years," laments Anna Margret Bjoernsdottir, a 46-year-old single mother who is preparing to move to Norway in June if she is unable to ward off eviction from her home near Reykjavik.

For those left behind, a growing number are having trouble scraping together enough money to put decent food on their children's plates.

While only a minority have been forced to seek out food banks to feed their families, some parents admit to going hungry to feed their children.

"I must admit that with the hike in food prices, my two sons eat most of what my husband and I bring home," Arna Borgthorsdottir Cors confessed in a Reykjavik cafe.

"We get what is left over," she says.

Source: Excerpted from Marc Preel, "Iceland's new poor line up for food," AFP, 8 April 2010.

Chapters 14 and 15 present the theory of exchange rates. Chapter 16 discusses how exchange rates affect international transactions in assets. We examine the short-run impact of exchange rates on the demand for goods in Chapter 18, and with this understanding Chapter 19 examines the trade-offs governments face as they choose between fixed and floating exchange rates. Chapter 20 covers exchange rate crises in detail and Chapter 21 covers the euro, a common currency used in many countries. Chapter 22 presents further exploration of some exchange rate topics.

2 Globalization of Finance: Debts and Deficits

Financial development is a defining characteristic of modern economies. Households' use of financial instruments such as credit cards, savings accounts, and mortgages is taken for granted, as is the ability of firms and governments to use the products and services offered in financial markets. A few years ago, very little of this financial activity spilled across international borders; countries were very nearly closed from a financial standpoint. Today many countries are more open: financial globalization has taken hold around the world, starting in the economically advanced countries and spreading to many emerging market countries.

Although you might expect that you need many complex and difficult theories to understand the financial transactions between countries, such analysis requires only the application of familiar household accounting concepts such as income, expenditure, and wealth. We develop these concepts at the national level to understand how flows of goods, services, income, and capital make the global macroeconomy work. We can then see how the smooth functioning of international finance can make countries better off by allowing them to lend and borrow. Along the way, we also find that financial interactions are not always so smooth. Defaults and other disruptions in financial markets can mean that the potential gains from globalization are not so easily realized in practice.

Deficits and Surpluses: The Balance of Payments

Do you keep track of your finances? If so, you probably follow two important figures: your income and your expenditure. The difference between the two is an important number: if it is positive, you have a surplus; if it is negative, you have a deficit. The number tells you if you are living within or beyond your means. What would you do with a surplus? The extra money could be added to savings or used to pay down debt. How would you handle a deficit? You could run down your savings or borrow and go into deeper debt. Thus, imbalances between income and expenditure require you to engage in financial transactions with the world outside your household.

At the national level, we can make the same kinds of economic measurements of **income, expenditure, deficit,** and **surplus,** and these important indicators of economic performance are the subject of heated policy debate. For example, Table 12-1 shows measures of U.S. national income and expenditure since 1991 in billions of U.S. dollars. At the national level, the income measure is called *gross national disposable income;* the expenditure measure is called *gross national expenditure.* The difference between the two is a key macroeconomic aggregate called the *current account.*

Since posting a small surplus in 1991, the U.S. deficit on the current account (a negative number) has grown much larger and at times it has approached $1 trillion per year, although it fell markedly in the latest recession. That is, U.S. income has not been high

TABLE 12-1

Income, Expenditure, and the Current Account The table shows data for the United States from 1990 to 2011 in billions of U.S. dollars. During this period, in all but one year U.S. expenditure exceeded income, with the U.S. current account in deficit. The last (small) surplus was in 1991.

	Income *Gross National Disposable Income*	Expenditure *Gross National Expenditure*	Difference *Current Account*
1990	$5,803	$5,878	−$75
1991	6,027	6,019	8
1992	6,330	6,375	−46
1993	6,653	6,732	−79
1994	7,063	7,178	−115
1995	7,400	7,505	−105
1996	7,821	7,935	−114
1997	8,304	8,434	−129
1998	8,751	8,955	−205
1999	9,324	9,616	−292
2000	9,923	10,334	−410
2001	10,266	10,657	−392
2002	10,618	11,070	−452
2003	11,130	11,646	−516
2004	11,847	12,472	−625
2005	12,605	13,346	−741
2006	13,348	14,147	−798
2007	14,026	14,742	−716
2008	14,322	15,001	−679
2009	13,980	14,362	−382
2010	14,562	15,011	−449
2011	15,178	15,644	−466
2012	15,771	16,245	−474

Source: U.S. National Income and Product Accounts, Tables 1.1.5 and 4.1, April 2013, bea.gov.

enough to cover U.S. expenditure in these years. How did the United States bridge this deficit? It engaged in financial transactions with the outside world and borrowed the difference, just as households do.

Because the world *as a whole* is a closed economy (we can't borrow from outer space, as yet), it is impossible for the world to run a deficit. If the United States is a net borrower, running a current account deficit with income less than expenditure, then the rest of the world must be a net lender to the United States, running surpluses with expenditure less than income. Globally, the world's finances must balance in this way, even if individual countries and regions have surpluses or deficits. Figure 12-3

FIGURE 12-3

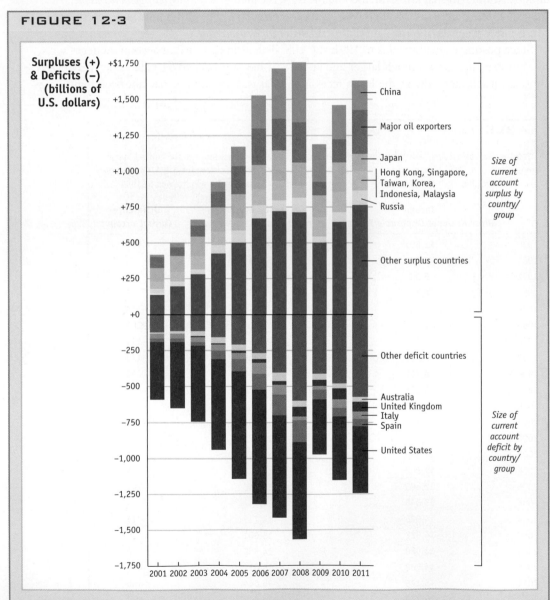

Global Imbalances For more than a decade, the United States current account deficit has accounted for about half of all deficits globally. Major offsetting surpluses have been seen in Asia (e.g., China and Japan) and in oil-exporting countries.

Source: IMF, World Economic Outlook, October 2012.

shows the massive scale of some of these recent imbalances, dramatically illustrating the impact of financial globalization.

Key Topics How do different international economic transactions contribute to current account imbalances? How are these imbalances financed? How long can they persist? Why are some countries in surplus and others in deficit? What role do current account imbalances perform in a well-functioning economy? Why are these imbalances the focus of so much policy debate?

Debtors and Creditors: External Wealth

To understand the role of wealth in international financial transactions, we revisit our household analogy. Your total **wealth** or net worth is equal to your assets (what others owe you) minus your liabilities (what you owe others). When you run a surplus, and save money (buying assets or paying down debt), your total wealth, or net worth, tends to rise. Similarly, when you have a deficit and borrow (taking on debt or running down savings), your wealth tends to fall. We can use this analysis to understand the behavior of nations. From an international perspective, a country's net worth is called its *external wealth* and it equals the difference between its foreign assets (what it is owed by the rest of the world) and its foreign liabilities (what it owes to the rest of the world). Positive external wealth makes a country a creditor nation (other nations owe it money); negative external wealth makes it a debtor nation (it owes other nations money).

Changes in a nation's external wealth can result from imbalances in its current account: external wealth rises when a nation has a surplus, and falls when it has a deficit, all else equal. For example, a string of U.S. current account deficits, going back to the 1980s, has been a major factor in the steady decline in U.S. external wealth, as shown in Figure 12-4, panel (a). The United States was generally a creditor nation until the mid-1980s when it became a debtor nation. More recently, by the end of 2012, the United States was the world's largest debtor, with external wealth equal to −$4,416 billion.[5] Argentina, another country with persistent current account deficits in the 1990s, also saw its external wealth decline, as panel (b) shows.

A closer look at these figures shows that there must be other factors that affect external wealth besides expenditure and income. For example, in years in which the United States ran deficits, its external wealth sometimes went up, not down. How can this be? Let us return to the household analogy. If you have ever invested in the stock market, you may know that even in a year when your expenditure exceeds your income, you may still end up wealthier because the value of your stocks has risen. For example, if you run a deficit of $1,000, but the value of your stocks rises by $10,000, then, on net, you are $9,000 wealthier. If the stocks' value falls by $10,000, your wealth will fall by $11,000. Again, what is true for households is true for countries: their external wealth can be affected by **capital gains** (or, if negative, capital losses) on investments, so we need to think carefully about the complex causes and consequences of external wealth.

We also have to remember that a country can gain not only by having the value of its assets rise but also by having the value of its liabilities fall. Sometimes, liabilities fall because of market fluctuations; at other times they fall as a result of a deliberate action such as a nation deciding to default on its debts. For example, in 2002 Argentina

[5] Based on preliminary data released by bea.gov on March 26, 2013.

FIGURE 12-4

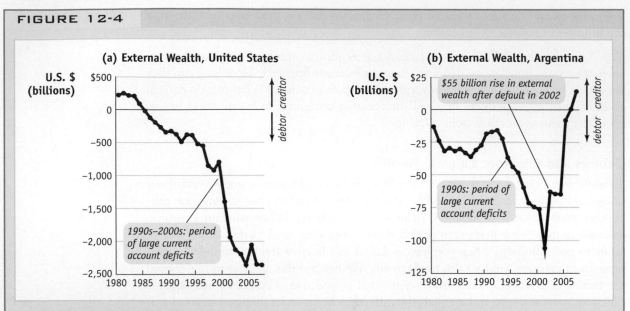

(a) External Wealth, United States

(b) External Wealth, Argentina

External Wealth A country's net credit position with the rest of the world is called external wealth. The time series charts show levels of external wealth from 1980 to 2007 for the United States in panel (a) and Argentina in panel (b). All else equal, deficits cause external wealth to fall; surpluses (and defaults) cause it to rise.

Source: Philip R. Lane and Gian Maria Milesi-Ferretti, 2007, "The External Wealth of Nations Mark II: Revised and Extended Estimates of Foreign Assets and Liabilities, 1970–2004," Journal of International Economics, 73(2), 223–250 (and updates).

announced a record default on its government debt by offering to pay about 30¢ for each dollar of debt in private hands. The foreigners who held most of this debt lost about $55 billion. At the same time, Argentina gained about $55 billion in external wealth, as shown by the sudden jump in Figure 12-4, panel (b). Thus, you don't have to run a surplus to increase external wealth—external wealth rises not only when creditors are paid off but also when they are blown off.

Key Topics What forms can a nation's external wealth take and does the composition of wealth matter? What explains the level of a nation's external wealth and how does it change over time? How important is the current account as a determinant of external wealth? How does it relate to the country's present and future economic welfare?

Darlings and Deadbeats: Defaults and Other Risks

The 2002 Argentine government's debt default was by no means unusual. The following countries (among many others) have defaulted (sometimes more than once) on private creditors since 1980: Argentina (twice), Chile, Dominican Republic (twice), Ecuador, Greece, Indonesia, Mexico, Nigeria, Pakistan, Peru (twice), Philippines, Russia (twice), South Africa (twice), Ukraine, and Uruguay (twice).[6] Dozens more countries could be added to the list if we expanded the definition of default to include the inability to make payments on loans from international financial institutions like

---

[6] The list is limited to privately issued bond and bank debts since 1980. Data from Eduardo Levy Yeyati and Ugo G. Panizza, January 2011, "The Elusive Costs of Sovereign Defaults," *Journal of Development Economics*, 94(1) 95–105, except for the more recent case of Greece.

the World Bank. (These debts may be continually rolled over, thus avoiding default by a technicality. In some cases, such loans are eventually forgiven, so they do not fall into the "default" category.)

Defaults highlight a peculiar risk of international finance: creditors may be poorly protected in foreign jurisdictions. Sovereign governments can repudiate debt without legal penalty or hurt creditors in other ways such as by taking away their assets or changing laws or regulations after investments have already been made.

International investors try to avoid these risks as much as possible by careful assessment and monitoring of debtors. For example, any financial misbehavior by a nation or firm usually ends up on a credit report: a "grade A" credit score means easy access to low-interest loans; a "grade C" score means more limited credit and very high interest rates. Advanced countries usually have good credit ratings, but emerging markets often find themselves subject to lower ratings.

In one important type of credit rating, countries are also rated on the quality of the bonds they issue to raise funds. Such bonds are rated by agencies such as Standard & Poor's (S&P): bonds rated BBB– or higher are considered high-grade or *investment-grade* bonds and bonds rated BB+ and lower are called *junk bonds*. Poorer ratings tend to go hand in hand with higher interest rates. The difference between the interest paid on a safe "benchmark" U.S. Treasury bond and the interest paid on a bond issued by a nation associated with greater risk is called **country risk**. Thus, if U.S. bonds pay 3% and another country pays 5% per annum on its bonds, the country risk is +2%.

For example, on September 28, 2012, the *Financial Times* reported that relatively good investment-grade governments such as Poland (grade A–) and Brazil (BBB) carried a country risk of +1.15% and +0.67% respectively, relative to U.S. Treasuries. Governments with junk grades such as Indonesia (grade BB+) and Turkey (BB) had to pay higher interest rates, with a country risk of 1.66% and 2.69%, respectively. Finally, Argentina, a country still technically in default, had bonds trading so cheaply (unrated, and considered beyond junk) they carried a massive +58% of country risk.

Key Topics Why do countries default? And what happens when they do? What are the determinants of risk premiums? How do risk premiums affect macroeconomic outcomes such as output, wealth, and exchange rates?

Summary and Plan of Study

International flows of goods, services, income, and capital allow the global macroeconomy to operate. In our course of study, we build up our understanding gradually, starting with basic accounting and measurement, then moving on to the causes and consequences of imbalances in the flows and the accumulations of debts and credits. Along the way, we learn about the gains from financial globalization, as well as some of its potential risks.

In Chapter 16, we learn how international transactions enter into a country's national income accounts. Chapter 17 considers the helpful functions that imbalances can play in a well-functioning economy in the long run, and shows us the potential long-run benefits of financial globalization. Chapter 18 then explores how imbalances play a role in short-run macroeconomic adjustment and in the workings of the monetary and fiscal policies that are used to manage a nation's aggregate demand. In Chapter 19, we learn that assets traded internationally are often denominated in different currencies and see how wealth can be sensitive to exchange rate changes and what macroeconomic effects this might have. Chapter 20 examines the implications of risk premiums for exchange rates, and shows that exchange rate crises and default crises are linked. Chapter 22 explores in more detail topics such as global imbalances and default.

3 Government and Institutions: Policies and Performance

In theory, one could devise a course of study in international economics without reference to government, but the result might not shed much light on reality. As we know from other courses in economics, and as we have already started to see in this chapter, government actions influence economic outcomes in many ways by making decisions about exchange rates, macroeconomic policies, whether to pay (or not pay) their debts, and so on.

To gain a deeper understanding of the global macroeconomy, we can look at government activity on several distinct levels. We will study **policies,** direct government actions, including familiar textbook topics like monetary and fiscal policy. However, economists also consider the broader context of rules and norms, or the **regimes** in which policy choices are made. At the broadest level, research also focuses on **institutions,** a term that refers to the overall legal, political, cultural, and social structures that influence economic and political actions.

To conclude this brief introduction to international macroeconomics, we highlight three important features of the broad macroeconomic environment that play an important role in the remainder of this book: the rules that a government decides to apply to restrict or allow capital mobility; the decision that a government makes between a fixed and a floating exchange rate regime; and the institutional foundations of economic performance, such as the quality of governance that prevails in a country.

Integration and Capital Controls: The Regulation of International Finance

The United States is seen as one of the most financially open countries in the world, fully integrated into the global capital market. This is mostly true, but in recent years the U.S. government has blocked some foreign investment in ports, oil, and airlines. These are exceptional cases in the United States, but in many countries there are numerous, severe restrictions on cross-border financial transactions.

It is important to remember that globalization does not occur in a political vacuum. Globalization is often viewed as a technological phenomenon, a process driven by innovations in transport and communications such as container shipping and the Internet. But international economic integration has also occurred because some governments have allowed it to happen. In the past 60 years, international trade has grown as trade barriers have been slowly dismantled. More recently, many nations have encouraged international capital movement by lifting restrictions on financial transactions.

Figure 12-5 documents some of the important features of the trend toward financial globalization since 1970. Panel (a) employs an index of financial openness, where 0% means fully closed with tight capital controls and 100% means fully open with no controls. The index is compiled from measures of restriction on cross-border financial transactions. The average value of the index is shown for three groups of countries that will play an important role in our analysis:

FIGURE 12-5

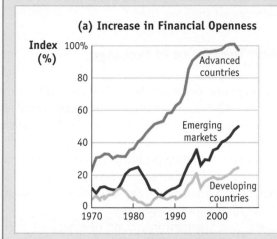

(a) Increase in Financial Openness

Index (%)

Advanced countries

Emerging markets

Developing countries

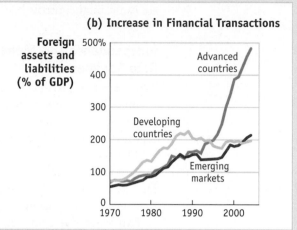

(b) Increase in Financial Transactions

Foreign assets and liabilities (% of GDP)

Advanced countries

Developing countries

Emerging markets

Financial Globalization Since the 1970s, many restrictions on international financial transactions have been lifted, as shown by the time series chart in panel (a). The volume of transactions has also increased dramatically, as shown in panel (b). These trends have been strongest in the advanced countries, followed by the emerging markets and the developing countries.

Sources: Philip R. Lane and Gian Maria Milesi-Ferretti, 2007, "The External Wealth of Nations Mark II: Revised and Extended Estimates of Foreign Assets and Liabilities, 1970–2004," Journal of International Economics 73(2), 223–250 (and updates); Menzie D. Chinn and Hiro Ito, 2006, "What Matters for Financial Development? Capital Controls, Institutions, and Interactions," Journal of Development Economics, 81(1), 163–192 (and updates). Country classifications are an extended version of those developed by M. Ayhan Kose, Eswar Prasad, Kenneth S. Rogoff, and Shang-Jin Wei, 2006, "Financial Globalization: A Reappraisal," NBER Working Paper No. 12484.

■ **Advanced countries**—countries with high levels of income per person that are well integrated into the global economy

■ **Emerging markets**—middle-income countries that are growing and becoming more integrated into the global economy

■ **Developing countries**—low-income countries that are not yet well integrated into the global economy

Using these data to gauge policy changes over the past three decades, we can see that the trend toward financial openness started first, and went the furthest, in the advanced countries, with a rapid shift toward openness evident in the 1980s, when many countries abolished capital controls that had been in place since World War II. We can also see that in the 1990s, emerging markets also started to become more financially open and, to a lesser degree, so did some developing countries.

What were the consequences of these policy changes? Panel (b) shows that as the world became more financially open, the extent of cross-border financial transactions (total foreign assets and liabilities expressed as a fraction of output) increased by a factor of 10 or more. As one might expect, this trend has gone the furthest in the more financially open advanced countries, but the emerging markets and developing countries follow a similar path.

Key Topics Why have so many countries made the choice to pursue policies of financial openness? What are the potential economic benefits of removing capital

Evading control: For years, Zimbabwe imposed capital controls. In theory, U.S. dollars could be traded for Zimbabwe dollars only through official channels at an official rate. On the street, the reality was different.

HALLDOR KOLBEINS/AFP/Getty Images

controls and encouraging openness? If there are benefits, why has this policy change been so slow to occur since the 1970s? Are there any costs that offset the benefits? If so, can capital controls benefit the country that imposes them?

Independence and Monetary Policy: The Choice of Exchange Rate Regimes

There are two broad categories of exchange rate behavior: fixed regimes and floating regimes. How common is each type? Figure 12-6 shows that there are many countries operating under each kind of regime. Because fixed and floating are both common regime choices, we have to understand both.

The choice of exchange rate regime is a major policy problem. If you have noticed the attention given by journalists and policy makers in recent years to the exchange rate movements of the dollar, euro, yen, pound, yuan, and other currencies, you know that these are important issues in debates on the global economy.

Exploring the evidence on exchange rate fluctuations, their origins, and their impact is a major goal of this book. On an intuitive level, whether we are confused travelers fumbling to change money at the bank or importers and exporters trying to conduct business in a predictable way, we have a sense that exchange rate fluctuations, especially if drastic, can impose real economic costs. If every country fixed its exchange rate, we could avoid those costs. Or, taking the argument to an extreme, if we had a single world currency, we might think that all currency-related transaction costs could be avoided. With more than 150 different currencies in existence today, however, we are very far from such a monetary utopia!

The existence of multiple currencies in the world dates back centuries, and for a country to possess its own currency has long been viewed as an almost essential aspect of sovereignty. Without control of its own national currency, a government's freedom to pursue its own monetary policy is sacrificed automatically. However, it still remains to be seen how beneficial monetary independence is.

Despite the profusion of currencies, we also see newly emerging forms of monetary organization. Some groups of countries have sought to simplify their transactions through the adoption of a **common currency** with shared policy responsibility. The

FIGURE 12-6

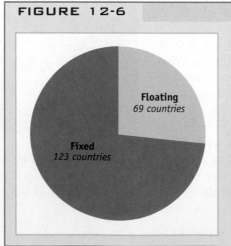

Exchange Rate Regimes The pie chart shows a classification of exchange rate regimes around the world using the most recent data from the year 2010.

Notes: The fixed category includes: No separate legal tender, Pre announced peg or currency board arrangement, Pre announced horizontal band that is narrower than or equal to +/−2%, De facto peg, Pre announced crawling peg, Pre announced crawling band that is narrower than or equal to +/−2%, De facto crawling peg, De facto crawling band that is narrower than or equal to +/−2%

The floating category includes: Pre announced crawling band that is wider than or equal to +/−2%, De facto crawling band that is narrower than or equal to +/−5%, Moving band that is narrower than or equal to +/−2% (i.e., allows for both appreciation and depreciation over time), Managed floating, Freely floating, Freely falling, and Dual market in which parallel market data is missing.

Source: Ilzetzki, Ethan, Carmen M. Reinhart and Kenneth S. Rogoff, 2010, "Exchange Rate Arrangements Entering the 21st Century: Which Anchor Will Hold?" See the next chapter for more details.

Floating
69 countries

Fixed
123 countries

most notable example is the Eurozone, a subset of the European Union that in 2013 comprised 17 countries, but with more members expected to join at some point in the future. Still other countries have chosen to use currencies over which they have no policy control, as with the recent cases of **dollarization** in El Salvador and Ecuador.

Key Topics Why do so many countries insist on the "barbarism" of having their own currency (as John Stuart Mill put it)? Why do some countries create a common currency or adopt another nation's currency as their own? Why do some of the countries that have kept their own currencies maintain a fixed exchange rate with another currency? And why do others permit their exchange rate to fluctuate over time, making a floating exchange rate their regime choice?

Institutions and Economic Performance: The Quality of Governance

Going beyond specific policy choices, economists also consider the broader institutional context in which such choices are made. The legal, political, social, cultural, ethical, and religious structures of a society can influence the environment for economic prosperity and stability, or poverty and instability.

Figure 12-7 shows evidence on the importance of the quality of a nation's institutions or "governance" using an average or composite of measures on six dimensions: voice and accountability, political stability, government effectiveness, regulatory quality, rule of law, and control of corruption. The figure shows that, across countries, institutional quality is strongly correlated with economic outcomes (see **Headlines: The Wealth of Nations**).

First, we see that better institutions are correlated with more **income per capita** in panel (a). A government that is unaccountable, unstable, ineffective, unpredictable, corrupt, and not based on laws is unlikely to encourage commerce, business, investment, or innovation. The effects of institutions on economic prosperity are very large. In the advanced countries at the top right of the figure, income per person is more than 50 times larger than in the poorest developing countries at the bottom left, probably the largest gap between rich and poor nations we have ever seen in history. Economists refer to this unequal outcome as "The Great Divergence."

We also see that better institutions are correlated with less **income volatility** (i.e., smaller fluctuations in the growth of income per capita, measured by the standard deviation). This result is shown in panel (b) and may also reflect the unpredictability of economic activity in poorly governed economies. There may be periodic shifts in political power, leading to big changes in economic policies. Or there may be internal conflict between groups that sporadically breaks out and leads to conflict over valuable economic resources. Or the state may be too weak to ensure that essential policies to stabilize the economy (such as bank regulation) are carried out.

Recent research has documented these patterns and has sought to show that causality runs from institutions to outcomes and to explore the possible sources of institutional variation. Institutional change is typically very slow, taking decades or even centuries, because vested interests may block efficiency-enhancing reforms. Thus, as the institutional economist Thorstein Veblen famously pointed out, "Institutions are products of the past process, are adapted to past circumstances, and are therefore never in full accord with the requirements of the present." Consequently, influential recent research seeks to find the roots of institutional (and income) divergence in factors such as:

FIGURE 12-7

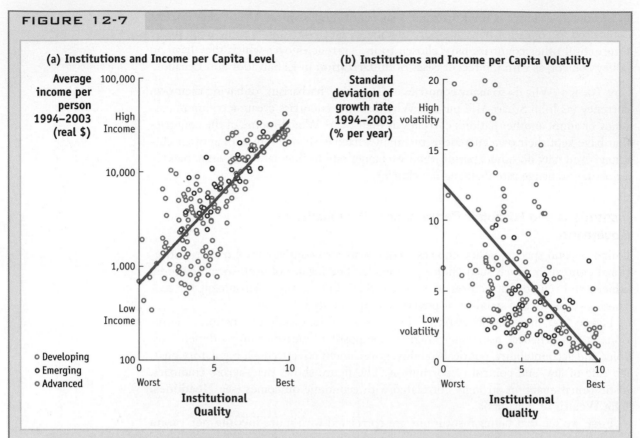

Institutions and Economic Performance The scatterplots show how the quality of a country's institutions is positively correlated with the level of income per capita (panel a), and inversely correlated with the volatility of income per capita (panel b). In each case, the line of best fit is shown.

Source: Real GDP per capita from Penn World Tables. Institutional quality from Daniel Kaufmann, Aart Kraay, and Massimo Mastruzzi, September 2006, "Governance Matters V: Governance Indicators for 1996–2005," World Bank Policy Research.

- Actions of colonizing powers (helpful in setting up good institutions in areas settled by Europeans but harmful in tropical areas where Europeans did not transplant their own institutions, but instead supported colonizers and local elites with a strong interest in extracting revenue or resources);

- Types of legal codes that different countries developed (British common law generally resulted in better outcomes than codes based on continental civil law);

- Resource endowments (tropical regions being more suitable for slave-based economies, elite rule, and high inequality; temperate regions being more suited to small-scale farming, decentralized democracy, and better governance).[7]

[7] Daron Acemoglu, Simon Johnson, and James A. Robinson, December 2001, "The Colonial Origins of Comparative Development: An Empirical Investigation," *American Economic Review*, 91(5), 1369–1401. Stanley L. Engerman and Kenneth L. Sokoloff, 1997, "Factor Endowments, Institutions, and Differential Paths of Growth among New World Economies: A View from Economic Historians of the United States," in Stephen Haber, ed., *How Latin America Fell Behind* (Stanford, Calif.: Stanford University Press). Rafael La Porta, Florencio Lopez-de-Silanes, Andrei Shleifer, and Robert Vishny, April 1999, "The Quality of Government," *Journal of Law, Economics and Organization*, 15(1), 222–279.

Key Topics Governance explains large differences in countries' economic outcomes. Poor governance generally means that a country is poorer, subject to more damaging macroeconomic and political shocks, and cannot conduct policy in a reliable and consistent way. These characteristics force us to think carefully about how to formulate optimal policies and policy regimes in rich and poor countries. One size may not fit all, and policies that work well in a stable well-governed country may be less successful in an unstable developing country with poor governance.

Summary and Plan of Study

The functioning of the global macroeconomy is affected in many ways by the actions of governments. Throughout this book, we must pay attention to the possible actions that governments might take and try to understand their possible causes and consequences.

Chapter 15 explores the finding that if a country is financially open, then a fixed exchange rate is incompatible with monetary policy autonomy. Because both goals may be desirable, policy makers are often reluctant to face up to the difficult trade-offs implied by financial globalization. Chapter 17 explores the economic rationales for financial liberalization: If financial openness has clear economic benefits, why are countries slow to liberalize? We explore exchange rate regime choice in detail in Chapter 19 and study the trade-offs involved. Then, in Chapter 20, we study crises, and find that if a country's policy makers cling to fixed exchange rates, there is a risk of suffering costly crises. The remarkable Euro project, discussed in Chapter 21, throws these issues into sharper perspective in the one region of the world where economic integration has arguably progressed the furthest in recent decades—but where the recent economic crisis has been most severe. The main lessons of our study are that policy makers need to acknowledge trade-offs, formulate sensible goals, and exercise careful judgment when deciding when and how to financially open their economies. Sadly, history shows that, all too often, they don't.

HEADLINES

....

The Wealth of Nations

Social scientists have sought for centuries to understand the essential conditions that enable a nation to achieve prosperity. In The Wealth of Nations, *Adam Smith said: "Little else is requisite to carry a state to the highest degree of opulence from the lowest barbarism, but peace, easy taxes, and a tolerable administration of justice; all the rest being brought about by the natural course of things." The following article discusses the poor quality of governance in developing countries and the obstacle this poses to economic development.*

It takes 200 days to register a new business in Haiti and just two in Australia. This contrast perfectly encapsulates the gulf between one of the world's poorest countries and one of the richest. A sophisticated mar-ket economy is a uniquely powerful engine of prosperity. Yet, in far too many poor countries, the law's delays and the insolence of office prevent desperately needed improvements in economic performance.

That makes [the 2005] "World Development Report" among the most important the World Bank has ever produced.[*] It is about how to make market economies work. . . . The report is based on two big research projects: surveys of

Continued on next page

the investment climate . . . in 53 countries; and the "doing business" project, which identifies obstacles to business in 130 countries. . . . The argument starts with growth. As the report rightly notes: "With rising populations, economic growth is the only sustainable mechanism for increasing a society's standard of living." Happily, "investment climate improvements in China and India have driven the greatest reductions in poverty the world has ever seen." . . . Governmental failure is the most important obstacle business faces. Inadequate enforcement of contracts, inappropriate regulations, corruption, rampant crime and unreliable infrastructure can cost 25 per cent of sales. This is more than three times what businesses typically pay in taxes. Similarly, when asked to enumerate the obstacles they face, businesses list policy uncertainty, macroeconomic instability, taxes and corruption at the head of the list. What do these have in common? Incompetence and malfeasance by governments is again the answer. . . .

In many developing countries, the requirement is not less government but more and better directed government. What does this involve? Four requirements are listed: a reduction in the "rent-seeking" that affects all countries but mars developing countries to an extreme extent; credibility in the making and execution of policy; the fostering of public trust and legitimacy; and the tailoring of policy responses to what works in local conditions.

One of the conclusions the report rightly draws from this list is that reform is not a one-off event but a process. What is involved is not just discrete and

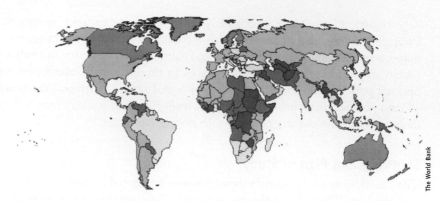

The World Bank

Green means grow: The map above shows the World Bank's composite Worldwide Governance Indicator in 2005. The index measures voice and accountability, political stability, government effectiveness, regulatory quality, rule of law, and control of corruption. Green indicates a country that is in the top 25% based on this measure; yellow, the next 25%; orange, the next 25%; and red, the bottom 25%. Dark green and dark red are the top and bottom 10%, respectively. The prosperity in Europe, North America, Australasia, and Japan coincides with the best institutions of governance; the poverty in so much of Africa and parts of Asia with the poorest ones.

well-known policy changes (such as lower tariffs) but the fine-tuning of policy and the evolution of institutions. This is why, it suggests, the credibility of the government's journey, as in China, may be more important than the details of policy at each stage along the way.

Turning these broad objectives into specific policy is a tricky business. The Bank describes its core recommendation as "delivering the basics." These are: stability and security, which includes protection of property. . . , facilitating contract enforcement, curbing crime and compensating for expropriation; better regulation and taxation, which means focusing intervention where it is needed, broadening the tax base and lowering tax rates, and reducing barriers to trade; better finance and infrastructure, which requires both more competition and better regulation; and transforming labour market regulation, to foster

skills, while avoiding the counterproductive interventions that so often destroy employment in the formal sector. . . .

The world's wealthy countries can also help by lifting their many barriers to imports from developing countries and by targeting aid on improving the investment climate.

Governments then are both the disease and the cure. This is why development is so hard and so slow. The big advance is in the richness of our understanding of what makes an economy thrive. But that understanding also demonstrates the difficulties. The Bank's recognition of the nature of the disease is at least a first step towards the cure.

A Better Investment Climate for Everyone, World Development Report 2005. Oxford University Press and the World Bank.

4 Conclusions

Today's global macroeconomy is an economic system characterized by increasingly integrated markets for goods, services, and capital. To effectively study macroeconomic outcomes in this context, we must understand the economic linkages between different countries—their currencies, their trade, their capital flows, and so on. Only then can we begin to understand some of the most important economic phenomena in the world today, such as the fluctuations in currencies, the causes of crises, the determinants of global imbalances, the problems of economic policy making, and the origins of the growing gap between rich and poor countries.

KEY POINTS

1. Countries have different currencies, and the price at which these currencies trade is known as the exchange rate. In learning what determines this exchange rate and how the exchange rate is linked to the rest of the economy, we confront various questions: Why do some countries have fixed exchange rates and others floating? Why do some go from one to the other, often in response to a crisis? Why do some countries have no currency of their own?

2. When countries are financially integrated, it allows them to decouple their level of income from their level of expenditure; the difference between the two is the current account. An important goal is to understand what determines the current account and how the current account is linked to the rest of a nation's economy. Along the way, we learn how a country's current account affects its wealth, how its credits and debts are settled, and how the current account changes.

3. Countries differ in the quality of their policy choices and in the quality of the deeper institutional context in which policies are made. In studying international macroeconomic interactions and events, it is essential to understand how policy regimes and institutions affect policy choices and economic outcomes. How does quality of governance affect economic outcomes? Why might some policies, such as a fixed exchange rate, work better in some contexts than others? Do country characteristics affect the costs and benefits of financial globalization?

KEY TERMS

fixed exchange rate, p. 414
floating exchange rate, p. 414
exchange rate crisis, p. 415
default, p. 415
International Monetary Fund (IMF), p. 415
World Bank, p. 415
income, p. 419

expenditure, p. 419
deficit, p. 419
surplus, p. 419
wealth, p. 421
capital gains, p. 421
country risk, p. 423
policies, p. 424
regimes, p. 424

institutions, p. 424
advanced countries, p. 425
emerging markets, p. 425
developing countries, p. 425
common currency, p. 426
dollarization, p.427
income per capita, p. 427
income volatility, p. 427

PROBLEMS

1. The data in Table 12-1 end in 2011. Visit the U.S. Bureau of Economic Analysis at bea.gov to find information for the latest full calendar year (or for the last four quarters). What is the latest estimate of the size of the annual U.S. current account deficit in billions of dollars?

2. The data in Figure 12-1 end in 2012. Visit oanda.com (or another site with daily exchange rate data) and download data on the same exchange rates (yuan per dollar and dollar per euro) for the past 12 months. What are the rates today? What were they a year ago? By what percentage amount did the rates change? Do you think the rates are floating or fixed? Why?

3. The data in Figure 12-3 end in the year 2011. Find the IMF's World Economic Outlook Databases. (*Hint:* Try searching "world economic outlook databases.") Use this interactive tool to obtain the latest data on current accounts in U.S. dollars for all countries (actual data or IMF estimates). Which countries had the 10 largest deficits last year? Which countries had the 10 largest surpluses last year?

4. Visit the *Financial Times* website (at ft.com click on "Market data") to download data for country risk today. (*Hint:* Try searching "FT high-yield emerging markets.") Which three emerging market countries have the highest spreads on their U.S. dollar debt? Which three have the lowest?

5. The map at the end of the chapter shows the World Bank's composite governance indicator. The World Bank has prepared other indicators to measure institutional differences among countries. Use the Internet to find the World Bank's "Ease of Doing Business Map." (*Hint:* Again, try an Internet search.) Do you notice a correlation between the ease of doing business and the overall governance indicator? Can you find countries that rank high on the Ease of Doing Business indicator but low on the governance indicator? Are these countries rich or poor? (*Hint:* Look up their GNI per person at the World Bank by searching "world bank GNI per capita.")

6. The charts on page 433 show the growth of real GDP per capita in three pairs of geographically adjacent countries: North and South Korea, Argentina and Chile, Zimbabwe and Botswana (using data from the Penn World Table).

    (a) Which country in each pair experienced faster growth in GDP per capita? Which one is now richest?
    (b) The World Bank's World Governance Indicators for each country in 2000 were as shown in the table above (higher is better):

    Based on these data, do you think institutions can explain the divergent outcomes in these countries? Explain. Why do you think it helps to compare countries that are physically contiguous?

7. Visit one of the many websites that lists all of the current exchange rates between different currencies around the world. Try a financial newspaper's site such as ft.com (follow the links to "Market Data," and then "Currencies"), or try websites devoted to foreign exchange market data such as oanda.com or xe.com (dig down; don't just look at the major currency tables). According to these lists, how many distinct currencies exist around the world today? Are some currencies used in more than one country?

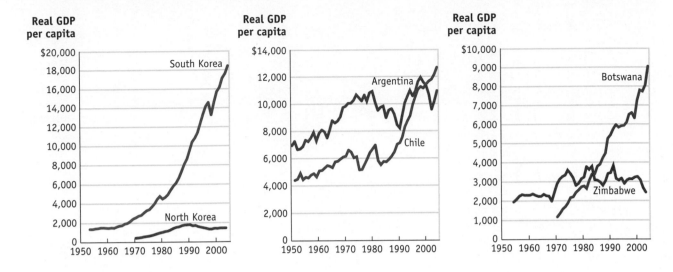

	Control of Corruption	Government Effectiveness	Political Stability and Absence of Violence	Rule of Law	Regulatory Quality	Voice and Accountability
South Korea	0.37	0.63	0.49	0.64	0.47	0.76
North Korea	−0.93	−1.10	−0.66	−1.08	−1.70	−2.02
Chile	1.56	1.34	0.85	1.31	1.38	0.56
Argentina	−0.34	0.28	0.48	0.17	0.45	0.44
Botswana	1.02	0.98	0.90	0.67	0.79	0.78
Zimbabwe	−0.87	−1.13	−1.21	−0.74	−1.61	−0.97

Introduction to Exchange Rates and the Foreign Exchange Market

The chapter on the Fall of the Rupee you may omit. It is somewhat too sensational.
Miss Prism, in Oscar Wilde's *The Importance of Being Earnest*, 1895

The people who benefit from roiling the world currency market are speculators and as far as I am concerned they provide not much useful value.
Paul O'Neill, U.S. Secretary of the Treasury, 2002

Every few years, George, an American, takes a vacation in Paris. To make purchases in Paris, he buys foreign currency, or *foreign exchange*. He can purchase euros, the currency used in France, by trading his U.S. dollars for euros in the *market for foreign exchange* at the prevailing market *exchange rate*. In 2003, 1 euro could be purchased for $1.10, so the €100 he spent on a night at the hotel cost him $110 in U.S. currency. In 2007, 1 euro cost $1.32, so each night at the same hotel (where the room price hadn't changed) made a $132 dent in his vacation budget. In 2012, the cost of 1 euro had fallen back a little to $1.25: not as high as in 2007, but still expensive enough in dollar terms to make George think about vacationing in northern California, where he might find equally good hotels, restaurants, fine food, and wine at prices that were more affordable.

Tourists like George are not the only people affected by exchange rates. Exchange rates affect large flows of international trade by influencing the prices in different currencies of the imported goods and services we buy and the exported goods and services we sell. Foreign exchange also facilitates massive flows of international investment, which include the direct investments made by multinationals in overseas firms as well as the stock and bond trades made by individual investors and fund managers seeking to diversify their portfolios.

Individual foreign exchange transactions are far removed from deep macroeconomic and political consequences. In the aggregate, however, activity in the foreign exchange market can be responsible for "sensational" events (and we are not being ironic as was Oscar Wilde in the chapter opening quote) and can arouse strong passions (Paul O'Neill is only one of many to criticize the activities of foreign exchange traders). In the foreign exchange market, trillions of dollars are traded each day and the economic implications of shifts in the market can be dramatic. In times of crisis, the fates of nations and their leaders seem to hang, in part, on the state of the currency market. Why is that so?

In this chapter, we begin to study the nature and impact of activity in the foreign exchange market. We first survey exchange rate basics: the key definitions of exchange rates and related concepts. We then examine the evidence to see how exchange rates behave in the real world and establish some basic facts about exchange rate behavior that require explanation. We next look at the workings of the foreign exchange market, including the role of private participants, as well as interventions by governments. Finally, we look in detail at how foreign exchange markets work, and we emphasize two key market mechanisms: *arbitrage* and *expectations*.

1 Exchange Rate Essentials

An **exchange rate** (E) is the price of some foreign currency expressed in terms of a home (or domestic) currency. Because an exchange rate is the relative price of two currencies, it may be quoted in either of two ways:

1. The number of home currency units that can be exchanged for one unit of foreign currency. For example, if the United States is considered home, the dollar–euro exchange rate might be $1.15 per euro (or 1.15 $/€). To buy one euro, you would have to pay $1.15.

2. The number of foreign currency units that can be exchanged for one unit of home currency. For example, the 1.15$/€ exchange rate can also be expressed as €0.87 per U.S. dollar (or 0.87 €/$). To buy one dollar, you would have to pay €0.87.

Knowing the format in which exchange rates are quoted is essential to avoid confusion, so we now establish a systematic rule, even if it is arbitrary.

Defining the Exchange Rate

It is common practice to quote the prices of items traded, whether goods or assets, as units of home currency per unit purchased. In the United States, coffee might be sold at 10 dollars per pound ($/lb); in France, at 20 euros per kilogram (€/kg).[1]

The usual way to quote the price of foreign currency is no different: units of home currency per unit of foreign currency. Confusion may arise because the price then depends on the perspective of the observer. Consider the dollar–euro exchange rate. For the U.S. citizen, who is accustomed to prices expressed as $/unit, the price of a foreign currency (say, the euro) is in terms of $/€. For someone in the Eurozone, however, the convention is to quote prices as €/unit, so €/$ would be the natural choice.

To avoid confusion, we must specify which country is the home country and which is foreign. Throughout the remaining chapters of this book, when we refer to a par-

---

[1] Coffee prices could also be quoted as 0.1 lb/$ or 0.05 kg/€, but this format is not the norm.

ticular country's exchange rate, we will quote it in terms of units of home currency per unit of foreign currency. For example, Denmark's exchange rate with the Eurozone is quoted as Danish krone per euro (or kr/€).

From now on, $E_{1/2}$ will denote the exchange rate in units of country 1 currency per unit of country 2 currency; it is the rate at which country 1's currency can be exchanged for one unit of country 2's currency. For example, $E_{\$/\epsilon}$ is the U.S. exchange rate (against the euro) in U.S. dollars per euro. In our previous example, $E_{\$/\epsilon}$ was 1.15 $/€.

We see different expressions of the same exchange rate all the time—even on the same page in the same publication! So it is important to keep things straight. Table 13-1 presents a typical display of exchange rate information as one might see it in the financial press.[2] Column (1) shows the reported price of U.S. dollars in various currencies (e.g., €/$); columns (2) and (3) show, respectively, the price of euros (e.g., $/€) and British pounds sterling (e.g., $/£) on the publication date of December 31, 2012.[3] Thus, the first three entries show the Canadian dollar's exchange rate against the U.S. dollar, the euro, and the pound. For comparison, columns (4) to (6) show the same rates one year earlier.

TABLE 13-1

Exchange Rate Quotations This table shows major exchange rates as they might appear in the financial media. Columns (1) to (3) show rates on December 31, 2012. For comparison, columns (4) to (6) show rates on December 31, 2011. For example, column (1) shows that at the end of 2012, one U.S. dollar was worth 0.996 Canadian dollars, 5.659 Danish krone, 0.759 euros, and so on. The euro-dollar rates appear in bold type.

Country (currency)	Currency Symbol	EXCHANGE RATES ON DECEMBER 31, 2012			EXCHANGE RATES ON DECEMBER 31, 2011 *ONE YEAR PREVIOUSLY*		
		(1)	(2)	(3)	(4)	(5)	(6)
		Per $	Per €	Per £	Per $	Per €	Per £
Canada (dollar)	C$	0.996	1.313	1.619	1.018	1.322	1.582
Denmark (krone)	DKr	5.659	7.461	9.199	5.725	7.432	8.898
Euro (euro)	€	**0.759**	—	1.233	**0.770**	—	1.197
Japan (yen)	¥	86.47	114.00	140.55	76.94	99.88	119.57
Norway (krone)	NKr	5.565	7.337	9.046	5.968	7.747	9.275
Sweden (krona)	SKr	6.506	8.577	10.575	6.855	8.899	10.65
Switzerland (franc)	SFr	0.915	1.207	1.488	0.935	1.214	1.453
United Kingdom (pound)	£	0.615	0.811	—	0.644	0.835	—
United States (dollar)	$	—	**1.318**	1.626	—	**1.298**	1.554

Source: Currencies data archive at markets.ft.com.

---

[2] These are typically *midrange* or *central* interbank rates—an end-of-day average of buying and selling rates by banks in the market. As we discuss later in the chapter, such rates do not allow for the differences or *spreads*, between the prices at which currencies are bought and sold. In any market in which intermediaries are present, commissions and fees push buying prices above selling prices.
[3] The currency's price in terms of itself equals 1 and is omitted.

The four bold entries in this table correspond to the dollar–euro exchange rate. On December 31, 2012, for example, the euro was quoted at $1.318 per euro. According to our definition, this is the price from the U.S. perspective and it is sometimes called the *American terms*. Conversely, the dollar is quoted at €0.759 per dollar, the *European terms*.

We write these exchange rates using mathematical symbols as follows, with care given to the explicit expression of the relevant units:

$$E_{\$/€} = 1.318 = \text{U.S. exchange rate (American terms)}$$

$$E_{€/\$} = 0.759 = \text{Eurozone exchange rate (European terms)}$$

Just as there is complete equivalence when we express the relative price of coffee and dollars at 10 $/lb or 0.1 lb/$, the price of the euro in terms of dollars always equals the reciprocal (or inverse) of the price of dollars in terms of euros. Hence,

$$E_{\$/€} = \frac{1}{E_{€/\$}}$$

In our example,

$$1.318 = \frac{1}{0.759}$$

Similar calculations and notations apply to any pair of currencies.

Appreciations and Depreciations

Like many financial tables, Table 13-1 includes information on how prices have changed over time. Over the previous 12 months, the Eurozone exchange rate *decreased* from $E_{€/\$} = 0.770$ a year before to $E_{€/\$} = 0.759$ on December 31, 2012. The value of the euro relative to the dollar went up—fewer euros were needed to buy one dollar. This change is often described by saying that the euro got "stronger" or "strengthened" against the dollar.

Symmetrically, the value of the dollar in euro terms also changed. We see this by computing the reciprocal American terms. Over the same year, the U.S exchange rate *increased* from $E_{\$/€} = 1/0.770 = 1.298$ a year before to $E_{\$/€} = 1/0.759 = 1.318$ on December 31, 2012. The value of the dollar relative to the euro went down—more dollars were needed to buy one euro. This change is often described by saying that the dollar got "weaker" or "weakened" against the euro.

If one currency buys more of another currency, we say it has experienced an **appreciation**—its value has *risen*, *appreciated*, or *strengthened*. If a currency buys less of another currency, we say it has experienced a **depreciation**—its value has *fallen*, *depreciated*, or *weakened*.

In our example, we can understand appreciation and depreciation from both the U.S. and European perspective; this lesson generalizes to all other currency pairs.

In U.S. terms, the following holds true:

- When the U.S. exchange rate $E_{\$/€}$ *rises*, more dollars are needed to buy one euro. The price of one euro goes up in dollar terms, and the U.S. dollar experiences a depreciation.

- When the U.S. exchange rate $E_{\$/€}$ *falls*, fewer dollars are needed to buy one euro. The price of one euro goes down in dollar terms, and the U.S. dollar experiences an appreciation.

Similarly, in European terms, the following holds true:

■ When the Eurozone exchange rate $E_{€/\$}$ *rises*, the price of one dollar goes up in euro terms and the euro experiences a depreciation.

■ When the Eurozone exchange rate $E_{€/\$}$ *falls*, the price of one dollar goes down in euro terms and the euro experiences an appreciation.

If the dollar is appreciating against the euro, the euro must simultaneously be depreciating against the dollar. Because they are the reciprocal of each other, changes in $E_{\$/€}$ and $E_{€/\$}$ must always move in opposite directions.

It may seem confusing or counterintuitive that a fall in the U.S. exchange rate means the dollar is appreciating. Yet it is reasonable because we express the price of foreign currency in dollars, just as we express the prices of other goods. When the price of coffee falls from \$10 to \$9 per pound, it seems sensible to say that coffee is depreciating or falling in value—but relative to what? The dollars—the currency in which the price is denominated. Conversely, dollars are *appreciating* against coffee because it takes fewer dollars to buy the same amount of coffee! If we keep this analogy in mind, it makes sense that when the dollar price of a euro falls, the dollar has appreciated against the euro.

Exchange rate humor.

In addition to knowing whether a currency has appreciated or depreciated, we are often interested in knowing the size of an appreciation or depreciation. To do this, we can calculate the proportional or fractional change in the foreign-currency value of the home currency. This proportional change is usually expressed in percentage terms.

In the previous example, we would describe these changes as follows:

■ In 2011, at time t, the dollar value of the euro was $E_{\$/€,t} = \$1.298$.

■ In 2012, at time $t + 1$, the dollar value of the euro was $E_{\$/€,t+1} = \$1.318$.

■ The change in the dollar value of the euro was $\Delta E_{\$/€,t} = 1.318 - 1.298 = +\$0.020$.

■ The percentage change was $\Delta E_{\$/€,t}/E_{\$/€,t} = +0.020/1.298 = +1.54\%$.

■ Thus, the euro *appreciated* against the dollar by 1.54%.

Similarly, over the same year:

■ In 2011, at time t, the euro value of the dollar was $E_{€/\$,t} = €0.770$.

■ In 2012, at time $t + 1$, the euro value of the dollar was $E_{€/\$,t+1} = €0.759$.

■ The change in the euro value of the dollar was $\Delta E_{€/\$,t} = 0.759 - 0.770 = -€0.011$.

■ The percentage change was $\Delta E_{€/\$,t}/E_{€/\$,t} = -0.011/0.770 = -1.43\%$.

■ Thus, the dollar *depreciated* against the euro by 1.43%.

Note that the size of one country's appreciation (here 1.54%) does not exactly equal the size of the other country's depreciation (here 1.43%). For small changes, however, the opposing movements are *approximately* equal. For example, if the

U.S. terms move slightly from $1.00 to $1.01 per euro, the European terms move from €1.00 to €0.99099; a 1% euro appreciation is approximately a 1% dollar depreciation.[4]

Multilateral Exchange Rates

Our discussion of exchange rates has focused on the simplest type of exchange rate between two countries or currencies, what economists refer to as a *bilateral* exchange rate. In reality, we live in a world of many countries and many currencies, and it is of great practical importance to ask whether a particular currency has strengthened or weakened not just against one other currency, but against other currencies in general.

The answer is not always obvious. It could, and very often is, the case that the U.S. dollar may be depreciating against some currencies, while remaining fixed or appreciating against others. To aggregate these different trends in bilateral exchange rates into one measure, economists calculate *multilateral* exchange rate changes for baskets of currencies using *trade weights* to construct an average of all the bilateral changes for each currency in the basket. The resulting measure is called the change in the **effective exchange rate.**

For example, suppose 40% of Home trade is with country 1 and 60% is with country 2; Home's currency appreciates 10% against 1 but depreciates 30% against 2. To calculate the change in Home's effective exchange rate, we multiply each exchange rate change by the corresponding trade share and then add up: $(-10\% \cdot 40\%) + (30\% \cdot 60\%) = (-0.1 \cdot 0.4) + (0.3 \cdot 0.6) = -0.04 + 0.18 = 0.14 = +14\%$. In this example, Home's effective exchange rate has depreciated by 14%.

In general, suppose there are N currencies in the basket, and Home's trade with the N partners is $\text{Trade} = \text{Trade}_1 + \text{Trade}_2 + \ldots + \text{Trade}_N$. Applying trade weights to each bilateral exchange rate change, the home country's effective exchange rate ($E_{\text{effective}}$) will change according to the following weighted average:

$$\frac{\Delta E_{\text{effective}}}{E_{\text{effective}}} = \underbrace{\frac{\Delta E_1}{E_1}\frac{\text{Trade}_1}{\text{Trade}} + \frac{\Delta E_2}{E_2}\frac{\text{Trade}_2}{\text{Trade}} + \ldots + \frac{\Delta E_N}{E_N}\frac{\text{Trade}_N}{\text{Trade}}}$$

Trade-weighted average of bilateral nominal exchange rate changes

Many discussions among policy makers and within the financial press focus on the effective exchange rate. An especially contentious topic in the last decade has been the path of the United States' effective exchange rate, shown in Figure 13-1. Since 2002,

---

[4] In general, suppose that the home exchange rate is a, so one unit of home currency buys $1/a$ units of foreign currency. Now the home exchange rate depreciates to $b > a$, and one unit of home currency buys $1/b$ units of foreign currency, with $1/b < 1/a$. The size of the depreciation D of the home currency is

$$D = \left(\frac{1}{a} - \frac{1}{b}\right) \Big/ \left(\frac{1}{a}\right) = \left(1 - \frac{a}{b}\right) = \left(\frac{b-a}{b}\right).$$

Symmetrically, the foreign currency was initially worth a units of home currency but is now worth b. Thus, the size of the appreciation A of the foreign currency is

$$A = \frac{(b-a)}{a} = \frac{b}{a}D$$

Thus, the percentage appreciation A will be approximately equal to the percentage depreciation D when b/a is close to 1, which is when b is approximately equal to a, that is, when the change in the exchange rate is small.

FIGURE 13-1

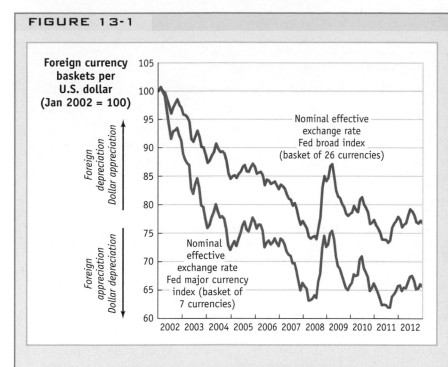

Effective Exchange Rates: Change in the Value of the U.S. Dollar, 2002–2012 The chart shows the value of the dollar measured by the U.S. Federal Reserve using two different baskets of foreign currencies, starting with the index set to 100 foreign baskets in January 2002. Against a basket of 7 major currencies, the dollar had depreciated by more than 25% by late 2004, and 35% by early 2008. But against a broad basket of 26 currencies, the dollar had lost only 15% of its value by 2004, and 25% by 2008. This is because the dollar was floating against the major currencies, but the broad basket included important U.S. trading partners (such as China and other Asian economies) that maintained fixed or tightly managed exchange rates against the dollar. These trends only briefly reversed during the global financial crisis of 2008 before continuing up to 2012.

Source: U.S. Federal Reserve.

the U.S. dollar has steadily fallen in value against a basket of other currencies. It lost quite a lot of value against many well-known major currencies, such as the euro, the pound sterling, the Canadian dollar, and the Swiss franc. But on average, the weakening of the dollar was not as pronounced when measured against *all* U.S. trading partners. The simple reason for this was the fact that Japan and China, along with several other developing countries in Asia, sought to peg or control their exchange rates to limit their appreciation against the dollar. Thus, in the figure the downward trend for the broad basket of currencies is not as steep as that for the basket of seven major currencies.

Example: Using Exchange Rates to Compare Prices in a Common Currency

To make comparisons of prices across nations, we must convert prices to a common currency. The following examples show how we use exchange rates to accomplish this task.

James Bond is back from another mission and, what with all the explosions and shootouts, his wardrobe is looking ragged. He needs a new tuxedo. Bond will be in numerous cities as part of Her Majesty's Secret Service in the next few days, so he can shop around the globe. Although style is important, price is a key factor in Bond's choice, given the meager MI6 clothing allowance. Should he visit a new tailor in Manhattan? Go back to his favorite cutter in Hong Kong? Or simply nip around the corner to Savile Row in London?

The London tailor sells a tux for £2,000; the Hong Kong shop is asking HK$30,000; and in New York, the going rate is $4,000. In the near future, when the decision must be made, these prices are fixed in their respective home currencies. Which tux will 007 choose?

TABLE 13-2

Using the Exchange Rate to Compare Prices in a Common Currency Now pay attention, 007! This table shows how the hypothetical cost of James Bond's next tuxedo in different locations depends on the exchange rates that prevail.

Scenario		1	2	3	4
Cost of the tuxedo in local currency	London	£2,000	£2,000	£2,000	£2,000
	Hong Kong	HK$30,000	HK$30,000	HK$30,000	HK$30,000
	New York	$4,000	$4,000	$4,000	$4,000
Exchange rates	HK$/£	15	16	14	14
	$/£	2.0	1.9	2.1	1.9
Cost of the tuxedo in pounds	London	£2,000	£2,000	£2,000	£2,000
	Hong Kong	£2,000	£1,875	£2,143	£2,143
	New York	£2,000	£2,105	£1,905	£2,105

To choose among goods priced in different currencies, Bond must first convert all the prices into a common currency; for this he uses the exchange rate (and a calculator disguised as a toothbrush). Table 13-2 shows the prices, in local currency and converted into pounds, under different hypothetical exchange rates.

Scenario 1 In the first column, the Hong Kong suit costs HK$30,000 and the exchange rate is HK$15 per £. Dividing HK$30,000 by 15, we find that this suit costs £2,000 in British currency. The U.S. suit has a price of $4,000, and at an exchange rate of $2 per pound we obtain a British currency price of £2,000. Here the exchange rates are such that all prices are the same when measured in a common currency (pounds). Bond has a difficult choice.

Scenario 2 Moving to the next column, the Hong Kong dollar has depreciated against the pound compared with scenario 1: it takes more HK$ (16 instead of 15) to buy £1. In contrast, the U.S. dollar has appreciated against the pound: it takes fewer dollars (1.9 instead of 2.0) to buy £1. At the new exchange rates, the cost of the New York tux has gone up to £2,105 (4,000/1.9), and the Hong Kong tux has fallen to £1,875 (30,000/16). Hong Kong now has the lowest price.

Scenario 3 Compared with scenario 1, the Hong Kong dollar has appreciated: it takes fewer $HK to buy £1 (14 instead of 15), and the price of the Hong Kong tux has risen to £2,143 (30,000/14). The U.S. dollar, on the other hand, has depreciated: it takes more dollars (2.1 instead of 2) to buy £1. With the dollar's depreciation, New York now has the best price of £1,905 (4,000/2.1).

Scenario 4 In this case, compared with scenario 1, the pound has depreciated against both of the other currencies, and they have each appreciated against the pound. It takes fewer Hong Kong dollars (14 instead of 15) and fewer U.S. dollars (1.9 instead of 2.0) to buy £1. Now London has the bargain price of £2,000 and the other cities have higher prices.

This example illustrates a key point. We assumed that while exchange rates may change, the prices of goods in each country are fixed in the short run (in domestic-currency terms). An economist would say the prices are *sticky* in the short run, and, as we see later, this is not an unreasonable assumption. Given that assumption, changes in exchange rates will cause changes in the common-currency prices of goods from different countries.

Generalizing The same logic applies to any exchange rate. All else equal, when the prices of goods are constant in each country, the following conclusions will apply:

■ *Changes in the exchange rate cause changes in prices of foreign goods expressed in the home currency.*

■ *Changes in the exchange rate cause changes in the relative prices of goods produced in the home and foreign countries.*

■ *When the home country's exchange rate depreciates, home exports become less expensive as imports to foreigners, and foreign exports become more expensive as imports to home residents.*

■ *When the home country's exchange rate appreciates, home exports become more expensive as imports to foreigners, and foreign exports become less expensive as imports to home residents.*

2 Exchange Rates in Practice

Having seen Table 13-1, it might be tempting to use the same figures as a guide to today's exchange rates between countries, but this would be a big mistake. Exchange rates fluctuate. They depreciate and appreciate. A lot. On a single day, in a matter of hours or even minutes, they can change substantially. Over a year, they may move considerably in one direction or another. Any complete theory of exchange rate determination must account for the various exchange rate movements and patterns we see.

Exchange Rate Regimes: Fixed Versus Floating

Economists group different patterns of exchange rate behavior into categories known as **exchange rate regimes.** These regimes reflect choices made by governments, and the causes and consequences of exchange rate regimes are a major focus of our study.
There are two major regime types:

■ **Fixed** (or **pegged**) **exchange rate regimes** are those in which a country's exchange rate fluctuates in a narrow range (or not at all) against some *base currency* over a sustained period, usually a year or longer. A country's exchange rate can remain rigidly fixed for long periods only if the government intervenes in the foreign exchange market in one or both countries.

■ **Floating** (or **flexible**) **exchange rate regimes** are those in which a country's exchange rate fluctuates in a wider range, and the government makes no attempt to fix it against any base currency. Appreciations and depreciations may occur from year to year, each month, by the day, or every minute.

For example, earlier in the book we saw data for two of the most talked about exchange rates in the world today: the U.S. dollar–euro and the Chinese yuan–U.S. dollar rates. The dollar–euro rate fluctuated considerably and was said to be floating; the yuan–dollar rate held steady or changed very slowly and was said to be fixed.

However, the "fixed versus floating" classification is not without its problems. First, to determine whether a regime is fixed or floating, we have to decide where we draw the line between "narrow" and "wide" fluctuations. One rule of thumb is to use the size of annual variations (say, within ±2% or ±1%) as the sign of a fixed regime. Second, "fixed versus floating" is only a very broad description of exchange rate regimes. In reality, the distinctions are not so cut and dried. Fixed and floating provide important benchmarks throughout this book and deliver great insights, but we sometimes need more precise ways of describing *intermediate regimes*, as the following application illustrates.

APPLICATION

Recent Exchange Rate Experiences

If we spend a moment looking at recent exchange rate experiences in a variety of countries, we see not only some helpful illustrations of the differences between floating and fixed rate regimes but also some of the different varieties of fixed and floating behavior. We also see examples of regime change, in which one type of regime gives way to another, either smoothly or catastrophically.

Evidence from Developed Countries Figure 13-2 shows the daily exchange rates from 1996 to 2012 for various currency pairs. The top row shows the U.S. dollar exchange rate against two major currencies (the Japanese yen, the British pound sterling) and against the currency of a neighboring country (the Canadian dollar, also called the *loonie*, because it bears the image of a common loon). The bottom row shows the exchange rate of the euro against the yen, the pound, and the Danish krone. In all six charts, the vertical scale varies by a factor of 2 from maximum to minimum, so all of these charts are comparable in terms of their representation of these exchange rates' volatility.

We can clearly see that the U.S. dollar is in a floating relationship with all three foreign currencies shown in the top row—the yen, pound, and loonie. How volatile are the exchange rates? The range of variation in each case is about the same, with the maximum being about one and a half times the minimum: the yen ranges from about $0.007 to $0.013, the pound from $1.3 to almost $2.1, the loonie from $0.6 to about $1.1. The movements between these peaks and troughs may take many months or years to occur, but the exchange rate also shows much short-run volatility, with lots of up-and-down movement from day to day. A floating regime of this sort is called a **free float.** Similarly, the bottom row of Figure 13-2 shows that the euro floats against the yen and the pound.

In the sixth and final chart, the Danish krone provides a clear contrast—an example of a fixed exchange rate in a developed country. Denmark is part of the European Union, but like Britain, it has kept its own national currency, at least for now, and does not use the euro as its currency. Unlike Britain, however, Denmark has fixed its exchange rate against the euro, keeping it very close to 7.44 krone per euro (0.134 euro per krone). There is only a tiny variation around this rate, well within plus or minus 2%. This type of fixed regime is known as a **band.**

Evidence from Developing Countries Figure 13-3 shows the daily exchange rates against the U.S. dollar from 1996 to 2012 for some developing countries. Exchange rates in developing countries can be much more volatile than those in developed countries. The charts in the top row illustrate exchange rate behavior in three Asian

FIGURE 13-2

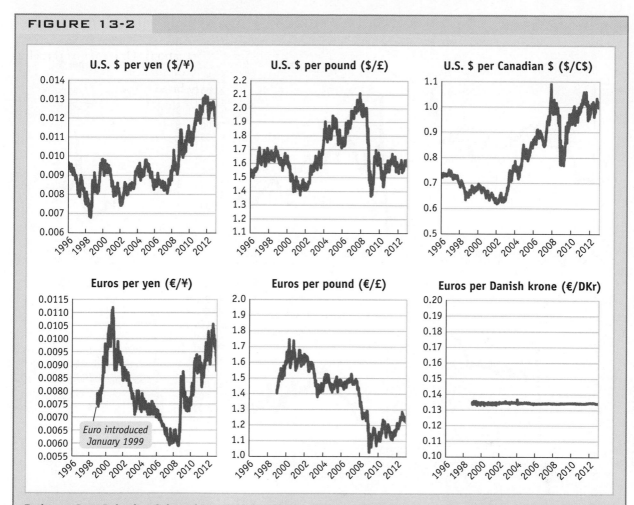

Exchange Rate Behavior: Selected Developed Countries, 1996–2012 This figure shows exchange rates of three currencies against the U.S. dollar and three against the euro. The euro rates begin in 1999 when the currency was introduced. The yen, pound, and Canadian dollar all float against the U.S. dollar. The pound and yen float against the euro. The Danish krone is fixed against the euro. The vertical scale ranges by a factor of 2 on all charts.

Source: FRED, oanda.com.

countries (India, Thailand, and South Korea); the maximum on the vertical axis is three times the minimum.

India had what looked like a fixed rate of about 35 rupees per dollar until a depreciation in 1997; there was then a period of pronounced movement more like a float. However, the government still acted to prevent abrupt currency movements even after 1997. This middle ground, somewhere between a fixed rate and a free float, is called a **managed float** (also known as a *dirty float*, or a policy of *limited flexibility*).

Thailand and South Korea show more extreme versions of the same pattern, except that in these cases the depreciation in 1997 was large and sudden, with the baht and the won exchange rates more than doubling in a matter of weeks. Such dramatic depreciations are called *exchange rate crises* and they are more common in developing countries than in developed countries. Indeed, South Korea had another mini-crisis in 2008.

FIGURE 13-3

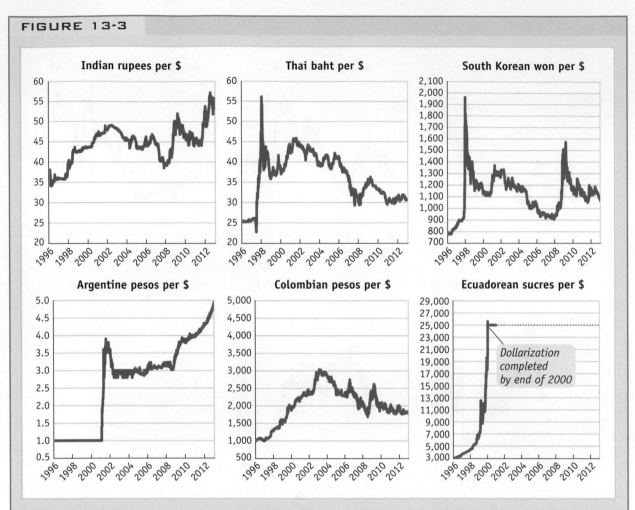

Exchange Rate Behavior: Selected Developing Countries, 1996–2012 Exchange rates in developing countries show a wide variety of experiences and greater volatility. Pegging is common but is punctuated by periodic crises (you can see the effects of these crises in graphs for Thailand, South Korea, and Argentina). Rates that are unpegged may show some flexibility (India). Some rates crawl gradually (Colombia). Dollarization can occur (Ecuador). The vertical scale ranges by a factor of 3 on the upper charts and by a factor of 10 on the lower charts.

Source: FRED, oanda.com.

The bottom row of Figure 13-3 shows some Latin American countries and more varieties of exchange rate experience. The maximum on the vertical scale is now 10 times the minimum, a change made necessary by the even more volatile exchange rates in this region.

Argentina initially had a fixed rate (of one peso per dollar), followed in 2001 by an exchange rate crisis. After a period of limited flexibility, Argentina returned to an almost fixed rate with a band that appeared to be centered at about 3 pesos per dollar, before drifting higher after 2008.

Colombia presents an example of a different kind of fixed exchange rate. Here the authorities did not target the level of the Colombian peso but allowed it to steadily depreciate at an almost constant rate for several years from 1996 to 2002 (before then switching to a managed float). This type of fixed arrangement is called a **crawl** (if the exchange rate follows a simple trend, it is a *crawling peg*; if some variation about the trend is allowed, it is termed a *crawling band*).

In the bottom right corner, Ecuador displays a different crisis pattern. Here a period of floating was followed by a fixed rate rather than the other way around. Episodes of very rapid depreciation like this represent a distinct form of exchange rate behavior; some economists have suggested, not jokingly, that these regimes be identified separately as *freely falling* exchange rate regimes.[5] The Ecuadorean currency stabilized at a fixed rate of 25,000 sucres per dollar, but then the sucre ceased to be. Ecuador took the remarkable step of dollarizing: abolishing its own national currency and adopting the U.S. dollar as its legal tender.

Currency Unions and Dollarization Almost every economy issues its own currency and jealously guards this sovereign right. There are only two exceptions: groups of economies that agree to form a currency or monetary union and adopt a common currency and individual economies that dollarize by adopting the currency of another country as their own.

Under a **currency union** (or **monetary** union), there is some form of transnational structure such as a single central bank or monetary authority that is accountable to the member nations. The most prominent example of a currency union is the Eurozone. Other currency unions include the CFA and CFP Franc zones (among some former French colonies in Africa and the Pacific) and the Eastern Caribbean Currency Union of six member states.

Under **dollarization** one country unilaterally adopts the currency of another country. The reasons for this choice can vary. The adopting country may be very small, so the costs of running its own central bank and issuing its own currency may be prohibitive. Such is the case, for example, for the 60 or so Pitcairn Islanders (who use the New Zealand dollar as their standard currency). Other countries may have a poor record of managing their own monetary affairs and may end up "importing" a better policy from abroad. The currency changeover could be a de jure policy choice; or it may happen de facto if people are so fed up that they stop using the national currency and switch en masse to an alternative. Many of these economies use the U.S. dollar, but other popular choices include the euro, and the Australian and New Zealand dollars.

Exchange Rate Regimes of the World To move beyond specific examples, Figure 13-4 shows a classification of exchange rate regimes around the world, which allows us to see the prevalence of different regime types across the whole spectrum from fixed to floating.[6]

The classification covers 179 economies for the year 2010, and regimes are ordered from the most rigidly fixed to the most freely floating. The first 51 countries are those

---

[5] Carmen M. Reinhart and Kenneth S. Rogoff, 2004, "The Modern History of Exchange Rate Arrangements: A Reinterpretation," *Quarterly Journal of Economics*, 119(1), 1–48.

[6] Up until 2008 the IMF provided an unofficial classification based on observed exchange rate behavior. Most economists prefer this type of classification to the often misleading official classifications that were based on countries' official policy announcements. For example, as we saw in Figure 13-3, Thailand pegged to the dollar before the 1997 crisis, even though official statements denied this and the Thai authorities claimed the baht was floating. On unofficial or de facto classifications, see Carmen M. Reinhart and Kenneth S. Rogoff, 2004, "The Modern History of Exchange Rate Arrangements: A Reinterpretation," *Quarterly Journal of Economics*, 119(1), 1–48. Jay C. Shambaugh, 2004, "The Effect of Fixed Exchange Rates on Monetary Policy," *Quarterly Journal of Economics*, 119(1), 301–352. Eduardo Levy Yeyati and Federico Sturzenegger, 2005, "Classifying Exchange Rate Regimes: Deeds vs. Words," *European Economic Review*, 49(6), 1603–1635.

FIGURE 13-4

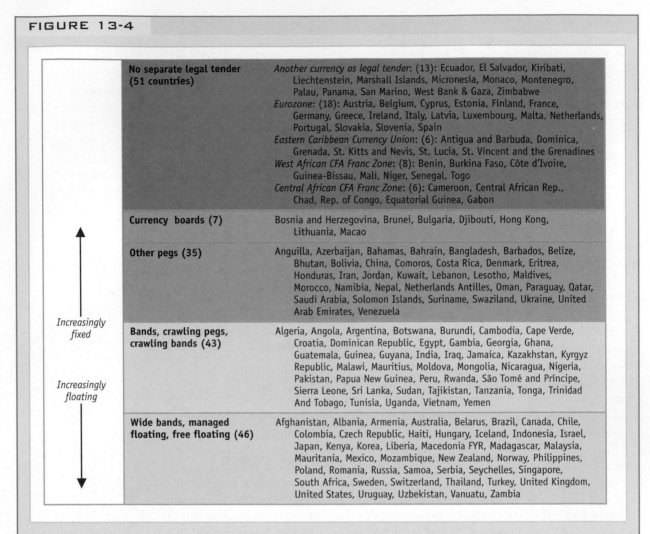

No separate legal tender (51 countries)	*Another currency as legal tender*: (13): Ecuador, El Salvador, Kiribati, Liechtenstein, Marshall Islands, Micronesia, Monaco, Montenegro, Palau, Panama, San Marino, West Bank & Gaza, Zimbabwe *Eurozone*: (18): Austria, Belgium, Cyprus, Estonia, Finland, France, Germany, Greece, Ireland, Italy, Latvia, Luxembourg, Malta, Netherlands, Portugal, Slovakia, Slovenia, Spain *Eastern Caribbean Currency Union*: (6): Antigua and Barbuda, Dominica, Grenada, St. Kitts and Nevis, St. Lucia, St. Vincent and the Grenadines *West African CFA Franc Zone*: (8): Benin, Burkina Faso, Côte d'Ivoire, Guinea-Bissau, Mali, Niger, Senegal, Togo *Central African CFA Franc Zone*: (6): Cameroon, Central African Rep., Chad, Rep. of Congo, Equatorial Guinea, Gabon
Currency boards (7)	Bosnia and Herzegovina, Brunei, Bulgaria, Djibouti, Hong Kong, Lithuania, Macao
Other pegs (35)	Anguilla, Azerbaijan, Bahamas, Bahrain, Bangladesh, Barbados, Belize, Bhutan, Bolivia, China, Comoros, Costa Rica, Denmark, Eritrea, Honduras, Iran, Jordan, Kuwait, Lebanon, Lesotho, Maldives, Morocco, Namibia, Nepal, Netherlands Antilles, Oman, Paraguay, Qatar, Saudi Arabia, Solomon Islands, Suriname, Swaziland, Ukraine, United Arab Emirates, Venezuela
Bands, crawling pegs, crawling bands (43)	Algeria, Angola, Argentina, Botswana, Burundi, Cambodia, Cape Verde, Croatia, Dominican Republic, Egypt, Gambia, Georgia, Ghana, Guatemala, Guinea, Guyana, India, Iraq, Jamaica, Kazakhstan, Kyrgyz Republic, Malawi, Mauritius, Moldova, Mongolia, Nicaragua, Nigeria, Pakistan, Papua New Guinea, Peru, Rwanda, São Tomé and Príncipe, Sierra Leone, Sri Lanka, Sudan, Tajikistan, Tanzania, Tonga, Trinidad And Tobago, Tunisia, Uganda, Vietnam, Yemen
Wide bands, managed floating, free floating (46)	Afghanistan, Albania, Armenia, Australia, Belarus, Brazil, Canada, Chile, Colombia, Czech Republic, Haiti, Hungary, Iceland, Indonesia, Israel, Japan, Kenya, Korea, Liberia, Macedonia FYR, Madagascar, Malaysia, Mauritania, Mexico, Mozambique, New Zealand, Norway, Philippines, Poland, Romania, Russia, Samoa, Serbia, Seychelles, Singapore, South Africa, Sweden, Switzerland, Thailand, Turkey, United Kingdom, United States, Uruguay, Uzbekistan, Vanuatu, Zambia

Increasingly fixed ↑

Increasingly floating ↓

A Spectrum of Exchange Rate Regimes The chart shows a recent classification of exchange rate regimes around the world.

Source: With the exception of Estonia and Latvia (which joined the Eurozone in 2011 and 2014, and are classified as such) all classifications are for 2010 and based on Ethan Ilzetzki, Carmen M. Reinhart and Kenneth S. Rogoff, 2010, "Exchange Rate Arrangements Entering the 21st Century: Which Anchor Will Hold?" and the author's calculation. See the next chapter for more details.

that have no currency of their own—they are either dollarized or in a currency union. Next are seven countries using an ultrahard peg called a **currency board,** a type of fixed regime that has special legal and procedural rules designed to make the peg "harder"—that is, more durable. Then come 35 other pegs, with variations of less than ±1%, some fixed to a single currency and a few pegging against a basket of currencies. These are followed by 43 bands, crawling pegs, and crawling bands. We then encounter the more flexible regimes: 46 cases of wide bands, managed floating rates, and freely floating regimes.

Looking Ahead This brief look at the evidence motivates the analysis in the remainder of this book. First, the world is divided into fixed and floating rate regimes, so we need to understand how *both* types of regime work. Studying fixed and floating regimes side by side will occupy much of our attention for the next few chapters. Second, when we look at who is fixed and who is floating, we start to notice patterns. Most of the floaters are advanced countries and most of the fixers are developing countries (the major exception is the euro area). The important question of why some countries fix while others float is covered in more detail in later chapters. ■

3 The Market for Foreign Exchange

Day by day, and minute by minute, exchange rates the world over are set in the **foreign exchange market** (or **forex** or **FX** market), which, like any market, is a collection of private individuals, corporations, and some public institutions that buy and sell. When two currencies are traded for each other in a market, the exchange rate is the price at which the trade was done, a price that is determined by market forces.

The forex market is not an organized exchange: each trade is conducted "over the counter" between two parties at numerous interlinked locations around the world. The forex market is massive and has grown dramatically in recent years. According to the Bank for International Settlements, in April 2010 the global forex market traded $4.0 trillion per day in currency, 20% more than 2007, twice as much as in 2004, and almost five times as much as in 1992. The three major foreign exchange centers—the United Kingdom ($1,854 billion per day, almost all in London), the United States ($904 billion, mostly in New York), and Japan ($312 billion, principally in Tokyo)—played home to more than 75% of the trade.[7] Other important centers for forex trade include Hong Kong, Singapore, Sydney, and Zurich. Thanks to time-zone differences, when smaller trading centers are included, there is not a moment in the day when foreign exchange is not being traded somewhere in the world. This section briefly examines the basic workings of this market.

The Spot Contract

The simplest forex transaction is a contract for the immediate exchange of one currency for another between two parties. This is known as a **spot contract** because it happens "on the spot." Accordingly, the exchange rate for this transaction is often called the **spot exchange rate.** In this book, the use of the term "exchange rate" always refers to the spot rate. Spot trades are now essentially riskless: technology permits settlement for most trades in real time, so that the risk of one party failing to deliver on its side of the transaction (*default risk* or *settlement risk*) is essentially zero.[8]

Most of our personal transactions in the forex market are small spot transactions via retail channels, but this represents just a tiny fraction of the activity in the forex market each day. The vast majority of trading involves commercial banks in major financial centers around the world. But even there the spot contract is the

---

[7] Data from BIS, *Triennial, Central Bank Survey: Foreign exchange and derivatives market activity in April 2010* (Basel, Switzerland: Bank for International Settlements, September 2010).

[8] Spot trades formerly took two days for settlement. If a bank failed in that period, spot trades could suffer occasional settlement failure. However, since 1997 a *continuously linked settlement* system has been used by the major trading banks and now covers a substantial majority of cross-currency transactions all over the world.

most common type of trade and appears in almost 90% of all forex transactions, either on its own as a single contract or in trades where it is combined with other forex contracts.

Transaction Costs

When individuals buy a little foreign currency through a retail channel (such as a bank), they pay a higher price than the midrange quote typically seen in the press; and when they sell, they are paid a lower price. The difference or **spread** between the "buy at" and "sell for" prices may be large, perhaps 2% to 5%. These fees and commissions go to the many middlemen that stand between the person on the street and the forex market. But when a big firm or a bank needs to exchange millions of dollars, the spreads and commissions are very small. Spreads are usually less than 0.1%, and for actively traded major currencies, they are approximately 0.01% to 0.03%.

Spreads are an important example of **market frictions** or **transaction costs.** These frictions create a wedge between the price paid by the buyer and the price received by the seller. Although spreads are potentially important for any microeconomic analysis of the forex market, macroeconomic analysis usually proceeds on the assumption that, in today's world of low-cost trading, the transaction-cost spreads in markets are so low for the key investors that they can be ignored for most purposes.

Derivatives

The spot contract is undoubtedly the most important contract in the forex market, but there are many other related forex contracts. These contracts include *forwards*, *swaps*, *futures*, and *options*. Collectively, all these related forex contracts are called **derivatives** because the contracts and their pricing are derived from the spot rate.

With the exception of forwards, the forex derivatives market is small relative to the entire global forex market. According to the most recent April 2010 survey data from the Bank for International Settlements, the trade in spot contracts amounted to $1,490 billion per day (37% of trades), the trade in forward contracts was $475 billion per day (12% of trades), and the trade in swaps (which combine a spot and a forward) accounted for $1,765 billion per day (44% of trades). The remaining derivative trades amounted to $250 billion per day (7% of trades).

For the rest of this chapter, we focus on the two most important contracts—the spot and the forward. Figure 13-5 shows recent trends in the spot and forward rates in the dollar–euro market. The forward rate tends to track the spot rate fairly closely, and we will explore this relationship further in a moment.

The full study of derivative markets requires an in-depth analysis of risk that is beyond the scope of this book. Such topics are reserved for advanced courses in finance that explore derivative contracts in great detail. The following application, however, will provide you with a basic guide to derivatives.

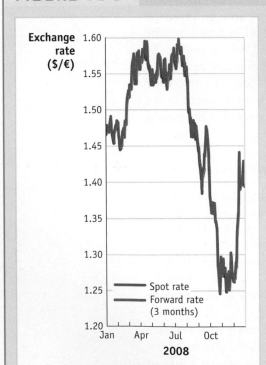

FIGURE 13-5

Spot and Forward Rates The chart shows typical movements in the U.S. spot and three-month forward exchange rates for the euro in dollars per euro using the year 2008 as an example. The spot and forward rates closely track each other.

Source: Federal Reserve Bank of New York.

Foreign Exchange Derivatives

There are many derivative contracts in the forex market, of which the following are the most common.

Forwards A **forward** contract differs from a spot contract in that the two parties make the contract today, but the *settlement date* for the delivery of the currencies is in the future, or forward. The time to delivery, or *maturity*, varies—30 days, 90 days, six months, a year, or even longer—depending on the contract. However, because the price is fixed as of today, the contract carries no risk.

Swaps A **swap** contract combines a spot sale of foreign currency with a forward repurchase of the same currency. This is a common contract for counterparties dealing in the same currency pair over and over again. Combining two transactions reduces transactions costs because the broker's fees and commissions are lower than on a spot and forward purchased separately.

Futures A **futures** contract is a promise that the two parties holding the contract will deliver currencies to each other at some future date at a prespecified exchange rate, just like a forward contract. Unlike the forward contract, however, futures contracts are standardized, mature at certain regular dates, and can be traded on an organized futures exchange. Hence, the futures contract does not require that the parties involved at the delivery date be the same two parties that originally made the deal.

Options An **option** contract provides one party, the buyer, with the right to buy (*call*) or sell (*put*) a currency in exchange for another at a prespecified exchange rate at a future date. The other party, the seller, must perform the trade if asked to do so by the buyer, but a buyer is under no obligation to trade and, in particular, will not exercise the option if the spot price on the expiration date turns out to be more favorable.

All of these products exist to allow investors to trade foreign currency for delivery at different times or with different contingencies. Thus, derivatives allow investors to engage in *hedging* (risk avoidance) and *speculation* (risk taking).

■ Example 1: Hedging. As chief financial officer of a U.S. firm, you expect to receive payment of €1 million in 90 days for exports to France. The current spot rate is $1.20 per euro. Your firm will incur losses on the deal if the euro weakens (dollar strengthens) to less than $1.10 per euro. You advise the firm to buy €1 million in call options on dollars at a rate of $1.15 per euro, ensuring that the firm's euro receipts will sell for at least this rate. This locks in a minimal profit even if the spot exchange rate falls below $1.15 per euro. This is hedging.

■ Example 2: Speculation. The market currently prices one-year euro futures at $1.30 per euro, but you think the euro will strengthen (the dollar will weaken) to $1.43 per euro in the next 12 months. If you wish to make a bet, you would buy these futures, and if you are proved right, you will realize a 10% profit. In fact, any spot rate above $1.30 per euro will generate some profit. If the spot rate is at or below $1.30 per euro a year from now, however, your investment in futures will generate a loss. This is speculation. ■

Private Actors

The key actors in the forex market are the traders. Most forex traders work for **commercial banks.** These banks trade for themselves in search of profit and also serve clients who want to import or export goods, services, or assets. Such transactions usually involve a change of currency, and commercial banks are the principal financial intermediaries that provide this service.

For example, suppose Apple Computer Inc. has sold €1 million worth of computers to a German distributor and wishes to receive payment for them in U.S. dollars (with the spot rate at $1.30 per euro). The German distributor informs its commercial bank, Deutsche Bank, which then debits €1 million from the distributor's bank account. Deutsche Bank then sells the €1 million bank deposit in the forex market in exchange for a $1.3 million deposit and credits that $1.3 million to Apple's bank in the United States, which, in turn, deposits $1.3 million into Apple's account.

This is an example of **interbank trading.** This business is highly concentrated: about 75% of all forex market transactions globally are handled by just 10 banks, led by names such as Deutsche Bank, UBS, Citigroup, HSBC, and Barclays. The vast majority of forex transactions are profit-driven interbank trades, and it is the exchange rates for these trades that underlie quoted market exchange rates. Consequently, we focus on profit-driven trading as the key force in the forex market that affects the determination of the spot exchange rate.

Other actors are increasingly participating directly in the forex market. Some **corporations** may trade in the market if they are engaged in extensive transactions either to buy inputs or sell products in foreign markets. It may be costly for them to do this, but by doing so, they can bypass the fees and commissions charged by commercial banks. Similarly, some **nonbank financial institutions** such as mutual fund companies may invest so much overseas that they can justify setting up their own forex trading operations.

Government Actions

We have so far described the forex market in terms of the private actors. Our discussion of the forex market is incomplete, however, without mention of actions taken by government authorities. Such activities are by no means present in every market at all times, but they are sufficiently frequent that we need to fully understand them. In essence, there are two primary types of actions taken by governments in the forex market.

At one extreme, it is possible for a government to try to completely control the market by preventing its free operation, by restricting trading or movement of forex, or by allowing the trading of forex only through government channels. Policies of this kind are a form of **capital control,** a restriction on cross-border financial transactions. In the wake of the 1997 Asian exchange rate crisis, for example, the Malaysian government temporarily imposed capital controls, an event that prompted Prime Minister Mahathir Mohamad to declare that "currency trading is unnecessary, unproductive and totally immoral. It should be stopped, it should be made illegal."[9] In more recent years, capital controls have been seen in countries such as China, Argentina, Iceland, and Cyprus.

---

[9] From a speech at the World Bank meeting in Hong Kong, September 20, 1997, in which Mr. Mohamad also referred to the legendary currency trader George Soros as a "moron." See Edward A. Gargan, "Premier of Malaysia Spars with Currency Dealer; Mahathir Says Soros and His Ilk Are 'Impoverishing Others' for Profit," *New York Times*, September 22, 1997, p. A1.

Capital controls are never 100% successful, however. Illegal trades will inevitably occur and are almost impossible to stop. The government may set up an **official market** for foreign exchange and issue a law requiring people to buy and sell in that market at officially set rates. But illicit dealings can persist "on the street" in **black markets** or *parallel markets* where individuals may trade at exchange rates determined by market forces and not set by the government. For example, in Italy in the 1930s, the Mussolini regime set harsh punishments for trading in foreign currency that gradually rose to include the death penalty, but trading still continued on the black market.

A less drastic action taken by government authorities is to let the private market for forex function but to fix or control forex prices in the market through **intervention,** a job typically given to a nation's central bank.

How do central banks intervene in the forex market? Indeed, how can a government control a price in any market? This is an age-old problem. Consider the issue of food supply in medieval and premodern Europe, one of the earliest examples of government intervention to fix prices in markets. Rulers faced a problem because droughts and harvest failures often led to food shortages, even famines—and sometimes political unrest. Governments reacted by establishing state-run granaries, where wheat would be stored up in years of plenty and then released to the market in years of scarcity. The price could even be fixed if the government stood ready to buy or sell grain at a preset price *and if the government always had enough grain in reserve to do so*. Some authorities successfully followed this strategy for many years. Others failed when they ran out of grain reserves. Once a reserve is gone, market forces take over. If there is a heavy demand that is no longer being met by the state, a rapid price increase will inevitably follow.

Government intervention in the forex market works in a similar maner. To maintain a fixed or pegged exchange rate, the central bank must stand ready to buy or sell its own currency, in exchange for the base foreign currency to which it pegs, at a fixed price. In practice, this means keeping some foreign currency reserves as a buffer, but having this buffer raises many problems. For one thing, it is costly—resources are tied up in foreign currency when they could be invested in more profitable activities. Second, these reserves are not an unlimited buffer, and if they run out, then market forces will take over and determine the exchange rate. In later chapters, we explore why countries peg, how a peg is maintained, and under what circumstances pegs fail, leading to an exchange rate crisis.

So, as we've seen, the extent of government intervention can vary. However, even with complete capital controls, including the suppression of the black market, private actors are always present in the market. Our first task is therefore to understand how private economic motives and actions affect the forex market.

4 Arbitrage and Spot Exchange Rates

The most basic of activities pursued by private actors in any market is **arbitrage,** a trading strategy that exploits any profit opportunities arising from price differences. Understanding arbitrage is one of the keys to thinking like an economist in any situation and is essential in studying exchange rates.

In the simplest terms, arbitrage means to buy low and sell high for a profit. If such profit opportunities exist in a market, then it is considered to be out of equilibrium.

If no such profit opportunities exist, there will be no arbitrage; the market is in **equilibrium** and satisfies a **no-arbitrage condition.**

Arbitrage with Two Currencies

Suppose you trade dollars and pounds for a bank with branches in New York and London. You can electronically transfer the funds cost free between the two branch locations. Forex trading commissions are the same in each city and so small as to be negligible. Suppose the exchange rate in New York is $E_{\pounds/\$}^{\text{N.Y.}} = \pounds 0.50$ per dollar, in London $E_{\pounds/\$}^{\text{London}} = \pounds 0.55$ per dollar. Can you make a profit for the bank?

Yes. You can buy \$1 for £0.50 in New York and sell it for £0.55 in London for an instant, riskless profit. Indeed, everyone would buy in New York and sell in London.

In general, one of the three outcomes can occur in the forex market. The spot rate can be higher in London: $E_{\pounds/\$}^{\text{N.Y.}} < E_{\pounds/\$}^{\text{London}}$; the spot rate can be higher in New York: $E_{\pounds/\$}^{\text{N.Y.}} > E_{\pounds/\$}^{\text{London}}$; or the spot rate can be the same in both locations: $E_{\pounds/\$}^{\text{N.Y.}} = E_{\pounds/\$}^{\text{London}}$. Arbitrage occurs in the first two cases. Only in the last case, in which spot rates are equal, does no arbitrage occur. Hence, the no-arbitrage condition for spot rates is

$$E_{\pounds/\$}^{\text{N.Y.}} = E_{\pounds/\$}^{\text{London}}$$

Figure 13-6 shows the no-arbitrage condition. Following both sets of arrows (AB and ACDB), we see that on each path we start with a dollar and end up with pounds, but we are indifferent between these paths only when the end result is identical. This situation would be an equilibrium, in which no arbitrage is possible.

If the market is out of equilibrium, arbitrage would drive up the price in the low-price market and drive down the price in the high-price market. In our example,

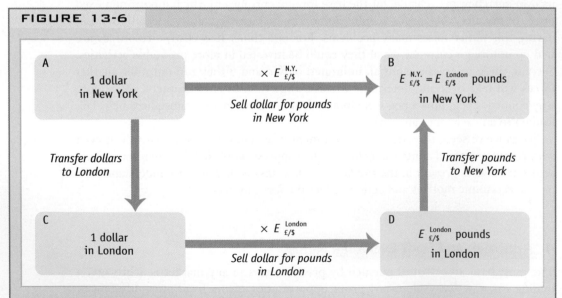

FIGURE 13-6

Arbitrage and Spot Rates Arbitrage ensures that the trade of currencies in New York along the path AB occurs at the same exchange rate as via London along path ACDB. At B the pounds received must be the same. Regardless of the route taken to get to B, $E_{\pounds/\$}^{\text{N.Y.}} = E_{\pounds/\$}^{\text{London}}$.

everyone buying dollars in New York and selling them in London would bid up the spot rate in New York from £0.50 and would bid down the spot rate in London from £0.55. This process would continue until the prices converged, arbitrage ceased, and equilibrium was reached. In forex markets, these adjustments happen nearly instantaneously, whether in the high-tech electronics markets of world financial centers or in the markets on street corners in the developing world.

Forex traders at their desks in London and money changers on the street in Kabul.

Arbitrage with Three Currencies

The same logic that we just applied to transactions between two currencies can also be applied to transactions involving three currencies. Again, as the trader in New York, you are considering trading dollars and pounds, but you also consider indirect or "triangular" trade via a third currency, say, the euro. Triangular arbitrage works as follows: you sell dollars in exchange for euros, then immediately sell the same euros in exchange for pounds. This roundabout way to acquire pounds is feasible, but is it sensible? Perhaps.

For example, suppose euros can be obtained at $E_{€/\$} = €0.8$ per dollar, and pounds can be obtained at $E_{£/€} = £0.7$ per euro. Starting with $1, you can obtain 0.8 euros, and with those 0.8 euros, you can obtain 0.7×0.8 pounds. Thus, setting aside the negligibly small commissions, the resulting pound–dollar exchange rate on the combined trade is $E_{£/€} \times E_{€/\$} = 0.7 \times 0.8 = 0.56$ pounds per dollar. If, say, the exchange rate on the direct trade from dollars to pounds is a less favorable $E_{£/\$} = 0.5$, we can trade $1 for £0.56 via the euro, and then trade the £0.56 for $1.12 by way of a direct trade (because $1.12 = 0.56/0.5$), a riskless profit of 12 cents.

In general, three outcomes are again possible. The direct trade from dollars to pounds has a better rate: $E_{£/\$} > E_{£/€}E_{€/\$}$; the indirect trade has a better rate: $E_{£/\$} < E_{£/€}E_{€/\$}$; or the two trades have the same rate and yield the same result: $E_{£/\$} = E_{£/€}E_{€/\$}$. Only in the last case are there no profit opportunities. This no-arbitrage condition can be written in two ways:

$$\underbrace{E_{£/\$}}_{\substack{\text{Direct}\\ \text{exchange rate}}} = E_{£/€}E_{€/\$} = \underbrace{\frac{E_{£/€}}{E_{\$/€}}}_{\text{Cross rate}}$$

The right-hand expression, a ratio of two exchange rates, is called a **cross rate**. Examine the units carefully and notice how the two € cancel out. This no-arbitrage condition applies to all currency combinations and is illustrated by the paths AB and ACB in Figure 13-7 (you can see why it is called *triangular arbitrage*).

The cross rate formula is very convenient. It means that we do not need to keep track of the exchange rate of every currency at all times. For example, if we know the exchange rates against, say, the dollar, for every currency, then for *any* pair of currencies A and B we can use the dollar rates of each currency and the cross rate formula to work out the rate at which the two currencies will trade: $E_{A/B} = E_{A/\$}/E_{B/\$}$. In practice, this is how most exchange rates are calculated.

FIGURE 13-7

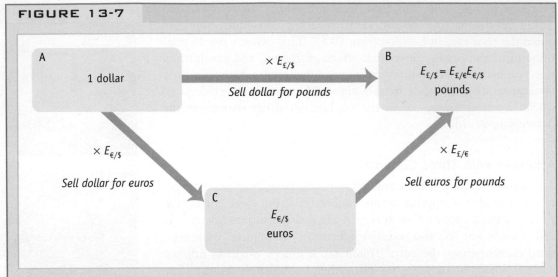

Arbitrage and Cross Rates Triangular arbitrage ensures that the direct trade of currencies along the path AB occurs at the same exchange rate as via a third currency along path ACB. The pounds received at B must be the same on both paths, and $E_{£/\$} = E_{£/€}E_{€/\$}$.

Cross Rates and Vehicle Currencies

The study of cross rates is not a meaningless exercise because the vast majority of currency pairs are exchanged for each other through a third currency. There are 164 distinct currencies in the world at the time of this writing. If you write down every possible currency pair, then count them up, there would be 13,366 active forex markets in operation. In reality, however, there are only a tiny fraction of this number. Why?

The vast majority of the world's currencies trade directly with only one or two of the major currencies, such as the dollar, euro, yen, or pound, and perhaps a few other currencies from neighboring countries. This is not too surprising. After all, to take some obscure examples, how often does somebody want to trade a Kenyan shilling for a Paraguayan guaraní? Or a Mauritanian ouguiya for a Tongan pa'anga? These are small, far-apart countries between which there is very little international trade or investment. It is hard to find counterparties for forex trade in these currencies—so hard that the costs of trading become prohibitive. And there is no need to bear these costs because, to continue our example, Kenya, Paraguay, Mauritania, and Tonga conduct a lot of business in major currencies such as the U.S. dollar, so individuals always have the option to engage in a triangular trade at the cross rate to convert shillings to dollars to guaranís (or ouguiyas to dollars to pa'angas), all for a reasonable commission.

When a third currency, such as the U.S. dollar, is used in these transactions, it is called a **vehicle currency** because it is not the home currency of either of the parties involved in the trade. Market data illustrate the importance of vehicle currencies. According to the 2010 survey data from the Bank for International Settlements, the most common vehicle currency is the U.S. dollar, which appears on one side of 85% of all global trades. The euro is next, playing a role in 39% of all trades (many of them with the U.S. dollar). The yen appears in 19% of all trades and the British pound in 13%.

5 Arbitrage and Interest Rates

So far, our discussion of arbitrage has shown how actors in the forex market—for example, the banks—exploit profit opportunities if currencies trade at different prices. But this is not the only type of arbitrage activity affecting the forex market.

An important question for investors is in which currency they should hold their liquid cash balances. Their cash can be placed in bank deposit accounts denominated in various currencies where it will earn a modest interest rate. For example, a trader working for a major bank in New York could leave the bank's cash in a euro deposit for one year earning a 2% euro interest rate or she could put the money in a U.S. dollar deposit for one year earning a 4% dollar interest rate. How can she decide which asset, the euro or the dollar deposit, is the best investment?

This is the final problem that we address in this chapter, and this analysis provides the tools we need to understand the forex market in the rest of this book. The analysis again centers on arbitrage. Would selling euro deposits and buying dollar deposits make a profit for the banker? Decisions like these drive the demand for dollars versus euros and the exchange rate between the two currencies.

The Problem of Risk A key issue for the trader is the exchange rate risk. The trader is in New York, and her bank cares about returns in U.S. dollars. The dollar deposit pays a known return, in dollars. But the euro deposit pays a return in euros, and one year from now we cannot know for sure what the dollar–euro exchange rate will be. Thus, how we analyze arbitrage in the sections that follow depends on how exchange rate risk is handled by the investor.

As we know from our discussion of derivatives, an investor may elect to cover or hedge their exposure to exchange rate risk by using a forward contract, and their decision then simplifies to a case of *riskless arbitrage*. On the other hand, an investor may choose not to use a forward, and instead wait to use a spot contract when their investment matures, whereupon their decision is a case of *risky arbitrage*. These two ways of doing arbitrage lead to two important implications, called *parity conditions*, which describe equilibria in the forward and spot markets. We now examine each one in turn.

Riskless Arbitrage: Covered Interest Parity

Suppose that contracts to exchange euros for dollars in one year's time carry an exchange rate of $F_{\$/\euro}$ dollars per euro. This is known as the **forward exchange rate** and it allows investors to be absolutely sure of the price at which they can trade forex in the future.

Assume you are trading for the bank in New York, and you have to decide whether to invest \$1 for one year in either a dollar or euro bank deposit that pays interest. The interest rate offered in New York on dollar deposits is $i_\$$ and in Europe the interest rate offered on euro deposits is $i_\euro$. Which investment offers the higher return?

If you invest in a dollar deposit, your \$1 placed in a U.S. bank account will be worth $(1 + i_\$)$ dollars in one year's time. The dollar value of principal and interest for the U.S. dollar bank deposit is called the *dollar return*. Note that we explicitly specify in what currency the return is measured, so that we may compare returns.

If you invest in a euro deposit, you first need to convert the dollar to euros. Using the spot exchange rate, \$1 buys $1/E_{\$/\euro}$ euros today. These $1/E_{\$/\euro}$ euros would be placed in a euro account earning $i_\euro$, so in a year's time they would be worth $(1 + i_\euro)/E_{\$/\euro}$ euros.

You would then convert the euros back into dollars, but you cannot know for sure what the future spot rate will be. To avoid that risk, you engage in a forward contract today to make the future transaction at a forward rate $F_{\$/\euro}$. The $(1 + i_\euro)/E_{\$/\euro}$ euros you will have in one year's time can then be exchanged for $(1 + i_\euro)F_{\$/\euro}/E_{\$/\euro}$ dollars, the dollar value of principal and interest, or the dollar return on the euro bank deposit.[10]

Three outcomes are possible when you compare the dollar returns from the two deposits. The U.S. deposit has a higher dollar return, the euro deposit has a higher dollar return, or both deposits have the same dollar return. In the first case, you would advise your bank to sell its euro deposits and buy dollar deposits; in the second case, you would advise the bank to sell its dollar deposits and buy euro deposits. Only in the third case is there no expected profit from arbitrage, so the corresponding no-arbitrage condition can be written as follows:

$$\text{Covered interest parity (CIP): } \underbrace{(1 + i_\$)}_{\substack{\text{Dollar return on} \\ \text{dollar deposits}}} = \underbrace{(1 + i_\euro)\frac{F_{\$/\euro}}{E_{\$/\euro}}}_{\substack{\text{Dollar return on} \\ \text{euro deposits}}} \qquad (13\text{-}1)$$

This expression is called **covered interest parity (CIP)** because all exchange rate risk on the euro side has been "covered" by use of the forward contract. We say that such a trade employs *forward cover*. The condition is illustrated in Figure 13-8.

What Determines the Forward Rate? Covered interest parity is a no-arbitrage condition that describes an equilibrium in which investors are indifferent between the returns on interest-bearing bank deposits in two currencies and exchange risk has been eliminated by the use of a forward contract. Because one of the returns depends on the forward rate, covered interest parity can be seen as providing us with a theory of what determines the forward exchange rate. We can rearrange the above equation and solve for the forward rate:

$$F_{\$/\euro} = E_{\$/\euro}\frac{1 + i_\$}{1 + i_\euro}$$

Thus, if covered interest parity holds, we can calculate the forward rate if we know all three right-hand side variables: the spot rate $E_{\$/\euro}$, the dollar interest rate $i_\$$, and the euro interest rate $i_\euro$. For example, suppose the euro interest rate is 3%, the dollar interest rate is 5%, and the spot rate is \$1.30 per euro. Then the preceding equation says the forward rate would be $1.30 \times (1.05)/(1.03) = \$1.3252$ per euro.

In practice, this is exactly how the forex market works and how the price of a forward contract is set. Traders at their computers all around the world can see the interest rates on bank deposits in each currency, and the spot exchange rate. We can now also see why the forward contract is called a "derivative" contract: to establish the price of the forward contract (the forward rate F), we first need to know the price of the spot contract (the spot rate E). That is, the pricing of the forward contract is derived from the pricing of the underlying spot contract, using additional information on interest rates.

This result raises a new question: How are the interest rates and the spot rate determined? We return to that question in a moment, after looking at some evidence to verify that covered interest parity does indeed hold.

---

[10] Note that this arbitrage strategy requires a spot and a forward contract. The two can be combined in a swap contract, and this helps explain the prevalence of swaps in the forex market.

FIGURE 13-8

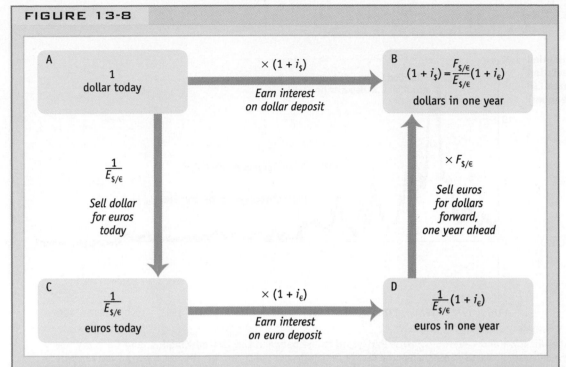

A 1 dollar today

$\times (1 + i_\$)$

Earn interest on dollar deposit

B $(1 + i_\$) = \dfrac{F_{\$/€}}{E_{\$/€}}(1 + i_€)$

dollars in one year

$\dfrac{1}{E_{\$/€}}$

Sell dollar for euros today

$\times F_{\$/€}$

Sell euros for dollars forward, one year ahead

C $\dfrac{1}{E_{\$/€}}$ euros today

$\times (1 + i_€)$

Earn interest on euro deposit

D $\dfrac{1}{E_{\$/€}}(1 + i_€)$ euros in one year

Arbitrage and Covered Interest Parity Under CIP, returns to holding dollar deposits accruing interest going along the path AB must equal the returns from investing in euros going along the path ACDB with risk removed by use of a forward contract. Hence, at B, the riskless payoff must be the same on both paths, and $(1 + i_\$) = \dfrac{F_{\$/€}}{E_{\$/€}}(1 + i_€)$.

APPLICATION

Evidence on Covered Interest Parity

Does covered interest parity hold? We expect returns to be equalized only if arbitrage is possible. But if governments impose capital controls, there is no way for traders to exploit profit opportunities and no reason for the returns on different currencies to equalize. Historical examples of such policies can provide illustration.

For example, Figure 13-9 shows that covered interest parity held for the United Kingdom and Germany after the two countries abolished their capital controls in the period from 1979 to 1981. (The German deposits shown here were denominated in marks prior to 1999; after 1999, the euro replaced the mark as the German currency.)

The chart shows the profit that could have been made (measured in percent per annum in British currency, before transaction costs) if the investor had been able to move funds from the United Kingdom to Germany with forward cover (or, when the line is in negative territory, the profit from moving funds from Germany to the United Kingdom). From Equation (13-1), we know that the profit from this riskless arbitrage would be

$$\text{Profit} = \underbrace{(1 + i_{GER}) \frac{F_{UK/GER}}{E_{UK/GER}}}_{\substack{\text{Pound return on} \\ \text{German deposits}}} - \underbrace{(1 + i_{UK})}_{\substack{\text{Pound return on} \\ \text{U.K. deposits}}}$$

FIGURE 13-9

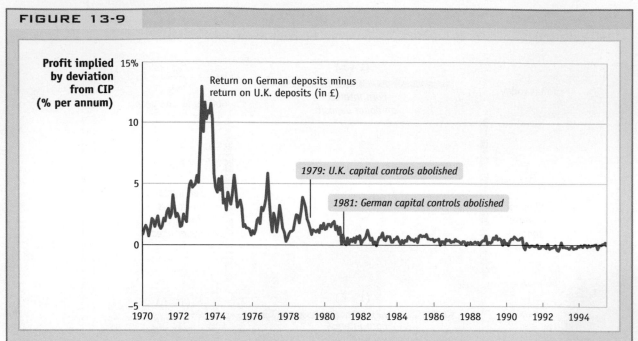

Financial Liberalization and Covered Interest Parity: Arbitrage between the United Kingdom and Germany The chart shows the difference in monthly pound returns on deposits in British pounds and German marks using forward cover from 1970 to 1995. In the 1970s, the difference was positive and often large: traders would have profited from arbitrage by moving money from pound deposits to mark deposits, but capital controls prevented them from freely doing so. After financial liberalization, these profits essentially vanished, and no arbitrage opportunities remained. The CIP condition held, aside from small deviations resulting from transactions costs and measurement errors.

Source: Maurice Obstfeld and Alan M. Taylor, 2004, Global Capital Markets: Integration, Crisis, and Growth, *Japan–U.S. Center Sanwa Monographs on International Financial Markets (Cambridge, UK: Cambridge University Press).*

This profit would be zero only if covered interest parity held. In the 1960s and 1970s, the *hypothetical* profits implied by this expression were large—or would have been had arbitrage been allowed. Instead, capital controls in both countries prevented arbitrage. Covered interest parity therefore failed to hold. Following the financial liberalization from 1979 to 1981, arbitrage became possible. From that time until the present, profits have been essentially zero (not exactly zero because of regulations, fees, other transaction costs, and measurement error). Once we allow for these factors, there are no profit opportunities left. Covered interest parity holds when capital markets are open, and, using similar calculations, this can be confirmed for all freely traded currencies today. ■

Risky Arbitrage: Uncovered Interest Parity

As we noted above, the second way to engage in arbitrage is to use spot contracts, and accept that the future exchange rate is then subject to risk. We now examine this case, and by doing so, we will arrive at an understanding of how the exchange rate is determined in the spot market.

To keep things simple, let us suppose, for now, that investors focus *exclusively* on the expected dollar return of the two bank deposits and not on any other characteristics of the investment. (See **Side Bar: Assets and Their Attributes.**) Imagine you are once again trading for a bank in New York, and you must decide whether to invest $1 for one year in a dollar or euro bank deposit that pays interest. This time, however, you use spot contracts only and make no use of the forward contract to hedge against the riskiness of the future exchange rate.

The $1 invested in a dollar deposit will be worth $(1 + i_\$)$ in one year's time; this is the dollar return, as before.

If you invest in a euro deposit, a dollar buys $1/E_{\$/€}$ euros today. With interest, these will be worth $(1 + i_€)/E_{\$/€}$ euros in one year. At that time, you will convert the euros back into dollars using a spot contract at the exchange rate that will prevail in one year's time. In this case, traders like you face exchange rate risk and must make a *forecast* of the future spot rate. We refer to the forecast as $E^e_{\$/€}$, which we call the **expected exchange rate.** Based on the forecast, you expect that the $(1 + i_€)/E_{\$/€}$ euros you will have in one year's time will be worth $(1 + i_€)E^e_{\$/€}/E_{\$/€}$ when converted into dollars; this is the *expected dollar return* on euro deposits, that is, the expected dollar value of principal and interest for euro deposits.

SIDE BAR

Assets and Their Attributes

The bank deposits traded in the forex market pay interest and are part of the wider portfolio of assets held by banks and other private actors. As we have argued, the forex market is heavily influenced by the demand for these deposits as assets.

An investor's entire portfolio of assets may include stocks, bonds, real estate, art, bank deposits in various currencies, and so on. What influences the demand for all these different kinds of assets? Viewed from a financial viewpoint (i.e., setting aside the beauty of a painting or seaside mansion), all assets have three key attributes that influence demand: return, risk, and liquidity.

An asset's **rate of return** is the total net increase in wealth (measured in a given currency) resulting from holding the asset for a specified period, typically one year. For example, you start the year by buying one share of DotBomb Inc., a hot Internet stock, for $100. At year's end, the share is worth $150 and has paid you a dividend of $5. Your total return is $55: a $50 capital gain from the change in the stock price plus a $5 dividend. Your total annual rate of return is 55/100, or 55%. The next year, the stock falls from $150 to $75 and pays no dividend. You lose half of your money in the second year: your rate of return for that year equals −75/150, or −50%. All else equal, investors prefer investments with high returns.

The **risk** of an asset refers to the volatility of its rate of return. The **liquidity** of an asset refers to the ease and speed with which it can be liquidated, or sold. A stock may seem to have high risk because its rate of return bounces up and down a lot, but its risk must be considered in relation to the riskiness of other investments. Its degree of risk could be contrasted with the rate of interest your bank offers on a money market deposit, a return that is usually very stable over time. You will lose your bank deposit only if your bank fails, which is unlikely. Your bank deposit is also very liquid. You can go to a cash machine or write a check to instantly access that form of wealth. In contrast, a work of art, say, is much less liquid. To sell the art for the greatest amount, you usually need the services of an auctioneer. Art is also risky. Works by different artists go in and out of fashion. All else equal, investors prefer assets with low risk and high liquidity.

This discussion of an asset's attributes allows us to make two observations. First, because all else is never equal, investors are willing to trade off among these attributes. You may be willing to hold a relatively risky and illiquid asset if you expect it will pay a relatively high return. Second, what you expect matters. Most investments, like stocks or art, do not have a fixed, predictable, guaranteed rate of return. As a result, all investors have to forecast. We refer to the forecast of the rate of return as the **expected rate of return.**

Again, three outcomes are possible: the U.S. deposit has a higher expected dollar return, the euro deposit has a higher expected dollar return, or both deposits have the same expected dollar return.

We have assumed that traders like you are indifferent to risk and care only about expected returns. Thus, in the first two cases, you have expected profit opportunities and risky arbitrage is possible: you would sell the deposit with the low expected return and buy the deposit with the higher expected return. Only in the third case is there no expected profit from arbitrage. This no-arbitrage condition can be written as follows:

$$\text{Uncovered interest parity (UIP):} \quad \underbrace{(1 + i_\$)}_{\substack{\text{Dollar return on} \\ \text{dollar deposits}}} = \underbrace{(1 + i_€) \frac{E^e_{\$/€}}{E_{\$/€}}}_{\substack{\text{Expected dollar return} \\ \text{on euro deposits}}} \qquad (13\text{-}2)$$

This expression is called **uncovered interest parity (UIP)** because exchange rate risk has been left "uncovered" by the decision not to hedge against exchange rate risk by using a forward contract and instead simply wait to use a spot contract in a year's time. The condition is illustrated in Figure 13-10.

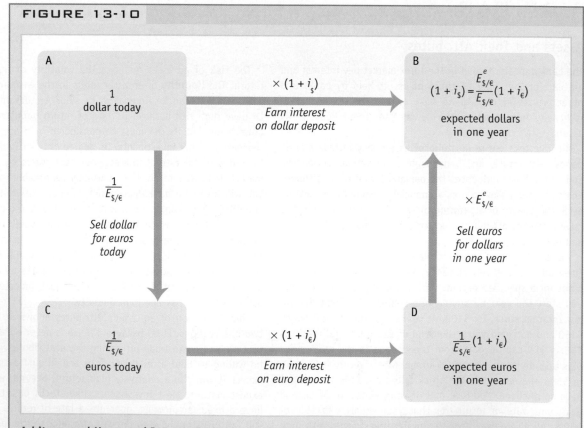

FIGURE 13-10

Arbitrage and Uncovered Interest Parity Under UIP, returns to holding dollar deposits accruing interest going along the path AB must equal the *expected* returns from investing in euros going along the risky path ACDB. Hence, at B, the expected payoff must be the same on both paths, and $(1 + i_\$) = \frac{E^e_{\$/€}}{E_{\$/€}}(1 + i_€)$.

What Determines the Spot Rate? Uncovered interest parity is a no-arbitrage condition that describes an equilibrium in which investors are indifferent between the returns on unhedged interest-bearing bank deposits in two currencies (where forward contracts are not employed). Because one of the returns depends on the spot rate, uncovered interest parity can be seen as providing us with a theory of what determines the spot exchange rate. We can rearrange the above equation and solve for the spot rate:

$$E_{\$/€} = E^e_{\$/€} \frac{1 + i_€}{1 + i_\$}$$

Thus, if uncovered interest parity holds, we can calculate today's spot rate if we know all three right-hand-side variables: the expected future exchange rate $E^e_{\$/€}$; the dollar interest rate $i_\$$; and the euro interest rate $i_€$. For example, suppose the euro interest rate is 2%, the dollar interest rate is 4%, and the expected future spot rate is $1.40 per euro. Then the preceding equation says today's spot rate would be 1.40 × (1.02)/(1.04) = $1.3731 per euro.

However, this result raises more questions: How can the expected future exchange rate $E^e_{\$/€}$ be forecast? And, as we asked in the case of covered interest parity, how are the two interest rates determined?

In the next two chapters, we address these unanswered questions, as we continue to develop the building blocks needed for a complete theory of exchange rate determination. We start by looking at the determinants of the expected future exchange rate $E^e_{\$/€}$, and developing a model of exchange rates in the long run, and then by looking at the determinants of the interest rates $i_\$$ and $i_€$. We will soon learn that future expectations make the solution of forward-looking economic problems tricky: we have to solve backward from the future to the present, and this motivates the order of the material in this textbook—we must understand exchange rates in the long run before we can understand them in the short run.

APPLICATION

Evidence on Uncovered Interest Parity

Does uncovered interest parity hold? The two interest parity equations seen previously are very similar. Equation (13-1), the CIP equation, uses the forward rate; Equation (13-2), the UIP equation, uses the expected future spot rate:

$$\text{CIP: } (1 + i_\$) = (1 + i_€) \frac{F_{\$/€}}{E_{\$/€}}$$

$$\text{UIP: } (1 + i_\$) = (1 + i_€) \frac{E^e_{\$/€}}{E_{\$/€}}$$

To allow us to see what this implies about the relationship between the expected future spot rate and the forward rate, we divide the second equation by the first, to obtain

$$1 = E^e_{\$/€}/F_{\$/€}, \text{ or}$$

$$F_{\$/€} = E^e_{\$/€}$$

The expected future spot rate and the forward rate are distinct concepts. They are also the instruments employed in two different forms of arbitrage—risky and riskless. But, in equilibrium, *under the assumptions we have made*, we now see that they should not differ at all; they should be exactly the same!

Thus, if *both* covered interest parity *and* uncovered interest parity hold, an important relationship emerges: *the forward rate $F_{\$/\epsilon}$ must equal the expected future spot rate $E^e_{\$/\epsilon}$*. The result is intuitive. In equilibrium, and *if investors do not care about risk* (as we have assumed in our presentation of UIP), then they have no reason to prefer to avoid risk by using the forward rate, or to embrace risk by awaiting the future spot rate; for them to be indifferent, as market equilibrium requires, the two rates must be equal.

With this result we can find an approach to testing UIP that is fairly easy to describe and implement. Because the evidence in favor of CIP is strong, as we have seen, we may assume that it holds. In that case, the previous equation then provides a test for whether UIP holds. But if the forward rate equals the expected spot rate, then we can also express this equivalence relative to today's spot rate, to show that the **expected rate of depreciation** (between today and the future period) equals the **forward premium** (the proportional difference between the forward and spot rates):

$$\underbrace{\frac{F_{\$/\epsilon}}{E_{\$/\epsilon}} - 1}_{\substack{\text{Forward} \\ \text{premium}}} = \underbrace{\frac{E^e_{\$/\epsilon}}{E_{\$/\epsilon}} - 1}_{\substack{\text{Expected rate} \\ \text{of depreciation}}}$$

For example, if the spot rate is \$1.00 per euro, and the forward rate is \$1.05, the forward premium is 5%. But if $F_{\$/\epsilon} = E^e_{\$/\epsilon}$, the expected future spot rate is also \$1.05, and there is a 5% expected rate of depreciation.

We can easily observe the left-hand side of the preceding equation, the forward premium, because both the current spot and forward rates are data we can collect in the market. The difficulty is on the right-hand side: we typically cannot observe expectations. Still, the test can be attempted using surveys in which traders are asked to report their expectations. Using data from one such test, Figure 13-11 shows a strong correlation between expected rates of depreciation and the forward premium, with a slope close to 1. Because expected depreciation does not always equal the interest differential, the points do not lie exactly on the 45-degree line. Does this mean that arbitrage is not working? Not necessarily. The deviations may be caused by sampling errors or noise (differences in opinion of individual traders). In addition, there may be limits to risky arbitrage in the real world because of various factors such as transactions costs (market frictions) and aversion to risk, which we have so far neglected, but which we discuss in more detail in later chapters. That the slope "on average" is close to 1 provides some support for UIP. ■

Uncovered Interest Parity: A Useful Approximation

Because it provides a theory of how the spot exchange rate is determined, the uncovered interest parity equation (13-2) is one of the most important conditions in international macroeconomics. Yet for most purposes, a simpler and more convenient concept can be used.

FIGURE 13-11

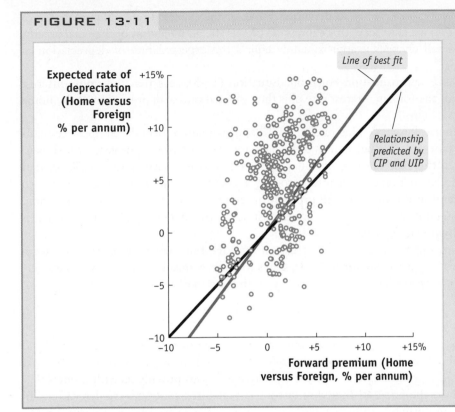

Evidence on Interest Parity When UIP and CIP hold, the 12-month forward premium should equal the 12-month expected rate of depreciation. A scatterplot showing these two variables should be close to the diagonal 45-degree line. Using evidence from surveys of individual forex traders' expectations over the period 1988 to 1993, UIP finds some support, as the line of best fit is close to the diagonal.

Notes: Line of best fit is through the origin. Data are monthly for the German mark, Swiss franc, Japanese yen, British pound, and Canadian dollar against the U.S. dollar from February 1988 to October 1993.

Source: Menzie Chinn and Jeffrey A. Frankel, 2002, "Survey Data on Exchange Rate Expectations: More Currencies, More Horizons, More Tests." In W. Allen and D. Dickinson, eds., Monetary Policy, Capital Flows and Financial Market Developments in the Era of Financial Globalisation: Essays in Honour of Max Fry *(London: Routledge), pp. 145–167.*

The intuition behind the approximation is as follows. Holding dollar deposits rewards the investor with dollar interest. Holding euro deposits rewards investors in two ways: they receive euro interest, but they also receive a gain (or loss) on euros equal to the rate of euro appreciation that approximately equals the rate of dollar depreciation. Thus, for UIP to hold, and for an investor to be indifferent between dollar deposits and euro deposits, any interest shortfall (excess) on the euro side must be offset by an expected gain (loss) in the form of euro appreciation or dollar depreciation.

We can write the approximation formally as follows:

$$\text{UIP approximation:}\quad \underbrace{i_\$}_{\substack{\text{Interest rate} \\ \text{on dollar} \\ \text{deposits} = \\ \text{Dollar rate} \\ \text{of return on} \\ \text{dollar deposits}}} = \underbrace{\underbrace{i_\euro}_{\substack{\text{Interest rate on} \\ \text{euro deposits}}} + \underbrace{\frac{\Delta E^e_{\$/\euro}}{E_{\$/\euro}}}_{\substack{\text{Expected rate of} \\ \text{depreciation of the} \\ \text{dollar}}}}_{\substack{\text{Expected dollar rate of return on} \\ \text{euro deposits}}} \qquad (13\text{-}3)$$

There are three terms in Equation 13-3. The left-hand side is the interest rate on dollar deposits. The first term on the right is the interest rate on euro deposits. The second term on the right can be expanded as $\Delta E^e_{\$/\euro}/E_{\$/\euro} = (E^e_{\$/\euro} - E_{\$/\euro})/E_{\$/\euro}$ and is the expected fractional change in the euro's value, or the expected rate of appreciation of the euro. As we have seen, this expression equals the appreciation of the euro exactly, but for small changes it approximately equals the expected rate of depreciation of the dollar.[11]

The UIP approximation equation, Equation (13-3), says that the home interest rate equals the foreign interest rate plus the expected rate of depreciation of the home currency.

A numerical example illustrates the UIP approximation formula. Suppose the dollar interest rate is 4% per year and the euro interest rate is 3% per year. If UIP is to hold, then the expected rate of dollar depreciation over a year must be 1%. In that case, a dollar investment put into euros for a year will grow by 3% because of euro interest and in dollar terms will grow by an extra 1% because of euro appreciation, so the total dollar return on the euro deposit is approximately equal to the 4% that is offered by dollar deposits.[12]

To sum up, the uncovered interest parity condition, whether in its exact form (13-2) or its approximate form (13-3), states that there must be parity between expected returns, *expressed in a common currency*, in the two markets.

Summary

All economic models produce an output (some unknown or *endogenous* variable to be explained) and require a set of inputs (some known or *exogenous* variables that are treated as given). The two interest parity conditions provide us with models that explain how the prices of the two most important forex contracts are determined in market equilibrium with no arbitrage possibilities. Uncovered interest parity applies to the spot market and determines the spot rate, based on interest rates and exchange rate expectations. Covered interest parity applies to the forward market and determines the forward rate based on interest rates and the spot rate. Figure 13-12 sums up what we have learned.

6 Conclusions

The forex market has a long and often tumultuous record and, in today's globalized world, exchange rates matter more than ever. They affect the prices of international transactions, can be a focus of government policy, and often play a major role in economic and political crises.

---

[11] To derive Equation (13-3), we can write $E^e_{\$/€}/E_{\$/€} = (1 + \Delta E^e_{\$/€}/E_{\$/€})$, so Equation (13-2) becomes

$$1 + i_\$ = (1 + i_€)\left(1 + \frac{\Delta E^e_{\$/€}}{E_{\$/€}}\right) = 1 + i_€ + \frac{\Delta E^e_{\$/€}}{E_{\$/€}} + \left[i_€\frac{\Delta E^e_{\$/€}}{E_{\$/€}}\right]$$

When the euro interest rate and the expected rate of depreciation are small, the last term in brackets is very small and may be neglected in an approximation. We can then cancel out the 1 that appears in the first and third terms of the above equation to obtain Equation (13-3).

[12] Note that the $1 investment in euros will be worth $(1.03) \times (1.01) = \$1.0403$ after one year, which is very close to $1.04, the value of the dollar deposit after one year. The difference is just the approximation error. See the previous footnote.

FIGURE 13-12

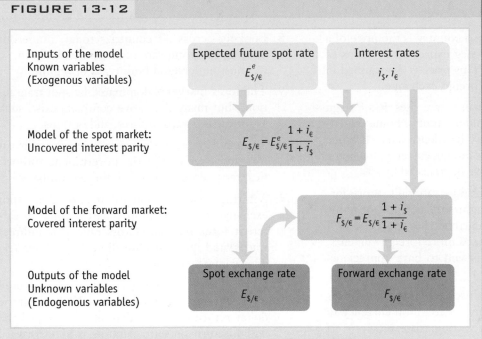

How Interest Parity Relationships Explain Spot and Forward Rates In the spot market, UIP provides a model of how the spot exchange rate is determined. To use UIP to find the spot rate, we need to know the expected future spot rate and the prevailing interest rates for the two currencies. In the forward market, CIP provides a model of how the forward exchange rate is determined. When we use CIP, we derive the forward rate from the current spot rate (from UIP) and the interest rates for the two currencies.

This chapter has set the stage for our study of exchange rates. We learned what exchange rates are and how they are used. We have also seen how they have behaved in reality under different exchange rate regimes. History shows a vast range of past experiences, and this experimentation continues.

These observations underscore the importance of understanding different regimes and their causes and consequences. We have prepared ourselves by examining the workings of the forex market in some detail. Government intervention (or its absence) in this market determines the nature of the exchange rate regime in operation, from fixed to floating. The workings of actors in the forex market then ultimately determine equilibrium values of exchange rates.

How is forex market equilibrium determined? We can now see that two key forces operate in the forex market: arbitrage and expectations. Through expectations, news about the future can affect expected returns. Through arbitrage, differences in expected returns are equalized, as summed up by the two important interest parity conditions, covered interest parity and uncovered interest parity. In the next two chapters, we build on these ideas to develop a complete theory of exchange rates.

KEY POINTS

1. The exchange rate in a country is the price of a unit of foreign currency expressed in terms of the home currency. This price is determined in the spot market for foreign exchange.

2. When the home exchange rate rises, less foreign currency is bought/sold per unit of home currency; the home currency has depreciated. If home currency buys $x\%$ less foreign currency, the home currency is said to have depreciated by $x\%$.

3. When the home exchange rate falls, more foreign currency is bought/sold per unit of home currency; the home currency has appreciated. If home currency buys $x\%$ more foreign currency, the home currency is said to have appreciated by $x\%$.

4. The exchange rate is used to convert the prices of goods and assets into a common currency to allow meaningful price comparisons.

5. Exchange rates may be stable over time or they may fluctuate. History supplies examples of the former (fixed exchange rate regimes) and the latter (floating exchange rate regimes), as well as a number of intermediate regime types.

6. An exchange rate crisis occurs when the exchange rate experiences a sudden and large depreciation. These events are often associated with broader economic and political turmoil, especially in developing countries.

7. Some countries may forgo a national currency to form a currency union with other nations (e.g., the Eurozone), or they may unilaterally adopt the currency of another country ("dollarization").

8. Looking across all countries today, numerous fixed and floating rate regimes are observed, so we must understand both types of regime.

9. The forex market is dominated by spot transactions, but many derivative contracts exist, such as forwards, swaps, futures, and options.

10. The main actors in the market are private investors and (frequently) the government authorities, represented usually by the central bank.

11. Arbitrage on currencies means that spot exchange rates are approximately equal in different forex markets. Cross rates (for indirect trades) and spot rates (for direct trades) are also approximately equal.

12. Riskless interest arbitrage leads to the covered interest parity (CIP) condition. CIP says that the dollar return on dollar deposits must equal the dollar return on euro deposits, where forward contracts are used to cover exchange rate risk.

13. Covered interest parity says that the forward rate is determined by home and foreign interest rates and the spot exchange rate.

14. Risky interest arbitrage leads to the uncovered interest parity (UIP) condition. UIP says that when spot contracts are used and exchange rate risk is not covered, the dollar return on dollar deposits must equal the expected dollar returns on euro deposits.

15. Uncovered interest parity explains how the spot rate is determined by the home and foreign interest rates and the expected future spot exchange rate.

KEY TERMS

exchange rate, p. 436
appreciation, p. 438
depreciation, p. 438
effective exchange rate, p. 440
exchange rate regimes, p. 443

fixed (or pegged) exchange rate regime, p. 443
floating (or flexible) exchange rate regime, p. 443
free float, p. 444
band, p. 444
managed float, p. 445

crawl, p. 446
currency (or monetary) union, p. 447
dollarization, p. 447
currency board, p. 448
foreign exchange (forex or FX) market, p. 449

PROBLEMS

1. Refer to the exchange rates given in the following table:

| Country (currency) | June 25, 2010 | | June 25, 2009 | |
	FX per $	FX per £	FX per €	FX per $
Australia (dollar)	1.152	1.721	1.417	1.225
Canada (dollar)	1.037	1.559	1.283	1.084
Denmark (krone)	6.036	9.045	7.443	5.238
Euro	0.811	1.215	1.000	0.703
Hong Kong (dollar)	7.779	11.643	9.583	7.750
India (rupee)	46.36	69.476	57.179	48.16
Japan (yen)	89.35	134.048	110.308	94.86
Mexico (peso)	12.697	18.993	15.631	13.22
Sweden (krona)	7.74	11.632	9.577	7.460
United Kingdom (pound)	0.667	1.000	0.822	0.609
United States (dollar)	1.000	1.496	1.232	1.000

Source: U.S. Federal Reserve Board of Governors, H.10 release: Foreign Exchange Rates.

Based on the table provided, answer the following questions:

a. Compute the U.S. dollar–yen exchange rate $E_{\$/¥}$ and the U.S. dollar–Canadian dollar exchange rate $E_{\$/C\$}$ on June 25, 2010, and June 25, 2009.

b. What happened to the value of the U.S. dollar relative to the Japanese yen and Canadian dollar between June 25, 2009, and June 25, 2010? Compute the percentage change in the value of the U.S. dollar relative to each currency using the U.S. dollar-foreign currency exchange rates you computed in (a).

c. Using the information in the table for June 25, 2010, compute the Danish krone–Canadian dollar exchange rate $E_{krone/C\$}$.

d. Visit the website of the Board of Governors of the Federal Reserve System at http://www.federalreserve.gov/. Click on "Economic Research and Data" and then "Statistics: Releases and Historical Data." Download the H.10 release Foreign Exchange Rates (weekly data available). What has happened to the value of the U.S. dollar relative to the Canadian dollar, Japanese yen, and Danish krone since June 25, 2010?

e. Using the information from (d), what has happened to the value of the U.S. dollar relative to the British pound and the euro? *Note:* The H.10 release quotes these exchange rates as U.S. dollars per unit of foreign currency in line with long-standing market conventions.

2. Consider the United States and the countries it trades with the most (measured in trade volume): Canada, Mexico, China, and Japan. For simplicity, assume these are the only four countries with which the United States trades. Trade shares and exchange rates for these four countries are as follows:

Country (currency)	Share of Trade	$ per FX in 2009	$ per FX in 2010
Canada (dollar)	36%	0.9225	0.9643
Mexico (peso)	28%	0.0756	0.0788
China (yuan)	20%	0.1464	0.1473
Japan (yen)	16%	0.0105	0.0112

a. Compute the percentage change from 2009 to 2010 in the four U.S. bilateral exchange rates (defined as U.S. dollars per unit of foreign exchange, or FX) in the table provided.

b. Use the trade shares as weights to compute the percentage change in the nominal effective exchange rate for the United States between 2009 and 2010 (in U.S. dollars per foreign currency basket).

c. Based on your answer to (b), what happened to the value of the U.S. dollar against this basket between 2009 and 2010? How does this compare with the change in the value of the U.S. dollar relative to the Mexican peso? Explain your answer.

3. Go to the website for Federal Reserve Economic Data (FRED): http://research.stlouisfed.org/fred2/. Locate the monthly exchange rate data for the following:

a. Canada (dollar), 1980–2012
b. China (yuan), 1999–2004, 2005–2009, and 2009–2010
c. Mexico (peso), 1993–1995 and 1995–2012
d. Thailand (baht), 1986–1997 and 1997–2012
e. Venezuela (bolivar), 2003–2012

Look at the graphs and make your own judgment as to whether each currency was fixed (peg or band), crawling (peg or band), or floating relative to the U.S. dollar during each time frame given.

4. Describe the different ways in which the government may intervene in the forex market. Why does the government have the ability to intervene in this way, while private actors do not?

5. Suppose quotes for the dollar–euro exchange rate $E_{\$/€}$ are as follows: in New York $1.50 per euro, and in Tokyo $1.55 per euro. Describe how investors use arbitrage to take advantage of the difference in exchange rates. Explain how this process will affect the dollar price of the euro in New York and Tokyo.

6. Consider a Dutch investor with 1,000 euros to place in a bank deposit in either the Netherlands or Great Britain. The (one-year) interest rate on bank deposits is 2% in Britain and 4.04% in the Netherlands. The (one-year) forward euro–pound exchange rate is 1.575 euros per pound and the spot rate is 1.5 euros per pound. Answer the following questions, using the *exact* equations for UIP and CIP as necessary.

a. What is the euro-denominated return on Dutch deposits for this investor?
b. What is the (riskless) euro-denominated return on British deposits for this investor using forward cover?
c. Is there an arbitrage opportunity here? Explain why or why not. Is this an equilibrium in the forward exchange rate market?
d. If the spot rate is 1.5 euros per pound, and interest rates are as stated previously, what is the equilibrium forward rate, according to covered interest parity (CIP)?
e. Suppose the forward rate takes the value given by your answer to (d). Compute the forward premium on the British pound for the Dutch investor (where exchange rates are in euros per pound). Is it positive or negative? Why do investors require this premium/discount in equilibrium?
f. If uncovered interest parity (UIP) holds, what is the expected depreciation of the euro (against the pound) over one year?
g. Based on your answer to (f), what is the expected euro–pound exchange rate one year ahead?

7. You are a financial adviser to a U.S. corporation that expects to receive a payment of 40 million Japanese yen in 180 days for goods exported to Japan. The current spot rate is 100 yen per U.S. dollar ($E_{\$/¥} = 0.01000$). You are concerned that the U.S. dollar is going to appreciate against the yen over the next six months.

   a. Assuming the exchange rate remains unchanged, how much does your firm expect to receive in U.S. dollars?

   b. How much would your firm receive (in U.S. dollars) if the dollar appreciated to 110 yen per U.S. dollar ($E_{\$/¥} = 0.00909$)?

   c. Describe how you could use an options contract to hedge against the risk of losses associated with the potential appreciation in the U.S. dollar.

8. Consider how transactions costs affect foreign currency exchange. Rank each of the following foreign exchanges according to their probable spread (between the "buy at" and "sell for" bilateral exchange rates) and justify your ranking.

   a. An American returning from a trip to Turkey wants to exchange his Turkish lira for U.S. dollars at the airport.

   b. Citigroup and HSBC, both large commercial banks located in the United States and United Kingdom, respectively, need to clear several large checks drawn on accounts held by each bank.

   c. Honda Motor Company needs to exchange yen for U.S. dollars to pay American workers at its Ohio manufacturing plant.

   d. A Canadian tourist in Germany pays for her hotel room using a credit card.

NET WORK

Visit the ft.com website (or another financial website such as oanda.com or xe.com), and download the same exchange rates shown in Table 13-1 for today's date. For all currencies (other than the dollar), compute the one-year percentage appreciation or depreciation against the dollar. For the dollar, compute the one-year percentage appreciation or depreciation against each currency. (*Hint:* Search for "cross rates" on ft.com.)

NET WORK

Visit the OANDA website (oanda.com) to explore recent exchange rate trends for any pair of countries in the world. Download some series to a spreadsheet for manipulation, or use the online graphing tools to plot trends (*Hint:* Try searching "historical exchange rates" on oanda.com.) Try to plot examples of some fixed and floating rates. See whether you can locate data for an exchange rate crisis during recent years. Can you tell from the data which countries are fixed and which are floating?

14

Exchange Rates I: The Monetary Approach in the Long Run

Our willingness to pay a certain price for foreign money must ultimately and essentially be due to the fact that this money possesses a purchasing power as against commodities and services in that foreign country.

Gustav Cassel, of the Swedish school of economics, 1922

The fundamental things apply / As time goes by.
Herman Hupfeld, songwriter, 1931 (featured in the film *Casablanca*, 1942)

The cost of living is usually rising, but it rises in some places more than others. From 1970 to 1990, for example, a standardized Canadian basket of consumer goods rose in price considerably. In 1970 a Canadian would have spent C$100 (100 Canadian dollars) to purchase this basket; by 1990 the same basket cost C$392. Thus, Canadian prices rose by 292%. Over the same period, in the United States, a basket of goods that initially cost $100 in 1970 had risen in cost to $336 by 1990. Thus, U.S. prices rose by only 236%. Both countries witnessed serious inflation, but Canadian prices rose more.

Did these price changes cause U.S. goods to appear relatively cheaper? Would they have caused Canadians to start spending more on U.S. goods, or Americans to spend less on Canadian goods?

The answer to these questions is no. In 1970 C$1 was worth almost exactly $1 (1 U.S. dollar). So in 1970 both baskets cost the same *when their cost was expressed in a common currency*, about C$100 = $100. By 1990, however, the Canadian dollar had depreciated relative to its 1970 value and C$1.16 was needed to buy $1.00. Thus, the $336 U.S. basket in 1990 actually cost $336 × 1.16 = C$390 when expressed in Canadian currency—almost the same price as the C$392 Canadian basket! (Conversely, expressed in U.S. currency, the Canadian basket cost about 392/1.16 = $338, almost the same as the $336 U.S. basket.)

In this example, although Canadian prices rose about 16% more than U.S. prices, U.S. residents also found that each of their U.S. dollars could buy about 16% more loonies. From the U.S. point of view, the cost of the baskets in each country *expressed in U.S. dollars* rose by about the same amount. The same was true from the Canadian perspective with all prices expressed in loonies. Economists (such as Gustav Cassel, quoted previously) would say that the relative *purchasing power* of each currency (in terms of U.S. versus Canadian goods) had remained the same.

Is it a coincidence that the changes in prices and exchange rates turned out that way? One of the oldest and most fundamental macroeconomic hypotheses, dating back to the sixteenth century, asserts that this outcome is *not* a coincidence at all—and that *in the long run*, prices and exchange rates will always adjust so that the purchasing power of each currency remains comparable over baskets of goods in different countries (as here, where $100 and C$100 could purchase comparable amounts of goods in 1970, and also in 1990). This hypothesis, which we explore in this chapter, provides another key building block in the theory of how exchange rates are determined. In the last chapter, uncovered interest parity provided us with a theory of how the spot exchange rate is determined, given knowledge of three variables: the expected future exchange rate, the home interest rate, and the foreign interest rate. In this chapter we look at the long run to see how the expected future exchange rate is determined; then, in the next chapter, we turn to the short run and discuss how interest rates are determined in each country. When all the pieces are put together, we will have a complete theory of how exchange rates are determined in the short run and the long run.

If investors are to make forecasts of future exchange rates, they need a plausible theory of how exchange rates are determined in the long run. The theory we develop in this chapter has two parts. The first part involves the theory of purchasing power, which links the exchange rate to price levels in each country in the long run. This theory provides a partial explanation of the determinants of long-run exchange rates, but it raises another question: How are price levels determined? In the second part of the chapter, we explore how price levels are related to monetary conditions in each country. Combining the monetary theory of price level determination with the purchasing power theory of exchange rate determination, we emerge with a *long-run* theory known as the **monetary approach to exchange rates.** The goal of this chapter is to set out the long-run relationships between money, prices, and exchange rates.

1 Exchange Rates and Prices in the Long Run: Purchasing Power Parity and Goods Market Equilibrium

Just as arbitrage occurs in the international market for financial assets, it also occurs in the international markets for goods. An implication of complete goods market arbitrage would be that the prices of goods in different countries expressed in a common currency must be equalized. Applied to a single good, this idea is called the *law of one price*; applied to an entire basket of goods, it is called the theory of *purchasing power parity*.

Why should these "laws" hold? If the price of a good is not the same in two locations, buyers will rush to buy at the cheap location (forcing prices up there) and avoid buying from the expensive location (forcing prices down there). Some factors, such as the costs of transporting goods between locations, may hinder the process of arbitrage, and more refined models take such *frictions* into account. For now, our goal is to develop a simple yet useful theory based on an idealized world of *frictionless trade* where transaction costs can be neglected. We start at the microeconomic level with single goods and the law of one price. We then move to the macroeconomic level to consider baskets of goods and purchasing power parity.

The Law of One Price

The **law of one price (LOOP)** states that in the absence of trade frictions (such as transport costs and tariffs), and under conditions of free competition and price flexibility (where no individual seller or buyer has the power to manipulate prices and prices can freely adjust), identical goods sold in different locations must sell for the same price *when prices are expressed in a common currency*.

To see how the law of one price operates, consider the trade in diamonds that takes place between the United States and the Netherlands. Suppose that a diamond of a given quality is priced at €5,000 in the Amsterdam market, and the exchange rate is $1.20 per euro. If the law of one price holds, the same-quality diamond should sell in New York for (€5,000 per diamond) × (1.20 $/€) = $6,000 per diamond.

Why will the prices be the same? Under competitive conditions and frictionless trade, arbitrage will ensure this outcome. If diamonds were more expensive in New York, arbitragers would buy at a low price in Holland and sell at a high price in Manhattan. If Dutch prices were higher, arbitragers would profit from the reverse trade. *By definition*, in a market equilibrium there are no arbitrage opportunities. If diamonds can be freely moved between New York and Amsterdam, both markets must offer the same price. Economists refer to this situation in the two locations as an *integrated market*.

We can mathematically state the law of one price as follows, for the case of any good g sold in two locations, say, Europe (EUR, meaning the Eurozone) and the United States (US). The *relative price* (denoted $q^g_{US/EUR}$) is the ratio of the good's price in Europe relative to the good's price in the United States where both prices are expressed in a common currency.

Using subscripts to indicate locations and currencies, the relative price can be written

$$\underbrace{q^g_{US/EUR}}_{\substack{\text{Relative price of good } g \\ \text{in Europe versus U.S.}}} = \underbrace{(E_{\$/€} P^g_{EUR})}_{\substack{\text{European price} \\ \text{of good } g \text{ in } \$}} / \underbrace{P^g_{US}}_{\substack{\text{U.S. price of} \\ \text{good } g \text{ in } \$}}$$

where P^g_{US} is the good's price in the United States, P^g_{EUR} is the good's price in Europe, and $E_{\$/€}$ is the dollar-euro exchange rate used to convert euro prices into dollar prices.

Notice that $q^g_{US/EUR}$ expresses the rate at which goods can be exchanged: it tells us how many units of the U.S. good are needed to purchase one unit of the same good in Europe (hence, the subscript uses the notation US/EUR). This contrasts with the nominal exchange rate $E_{\$/€}$ which expresses the rate at which currencies can be exchanged ($/€).

The law of one price may or may not hold. Recall from Chapter 13 that there are three possibilities in an arbitrage situation of this kind: the ratio exceeds 1 and the good is costlier in Europe; the ratio is less than 1 and the good is cheaper in Europe; or $E_{\$/€} P^g_{EUR} = P^g_{US}$, the ratio is $q^g_{US/EUR} = 1$, and the good is the same price in both locations. Only in the final case is there no arbitrage, the condition that defines market equilibrium. In equilibrium, European and U.S. prices, expressed in the same currency, are equal; the relative price q equals 1, and the law of one price holds.

How does the law of one price further our understanding of exchange rates? We can rearrange the equation for price equality, $E_{\$/€}P_{EUR}^g = P_{US}^g$, to show that if the law of one price holds, then the exchange rate must equal the ratio of the goods' prices expressed in the two currencies:

$$\underbrace{E_{\$/€}}_{\substack{\text{Exchange} \\ \text{rate}}} = \underbrace{P_{US}^g/P_{EUR}^g}_{\substack{\text{Ratio of} \\ \text{goods' prices}}}$$

One final word of caution: given our concerns in the previous chapter about the right way to define the exchange rate, we must take care when using expressions that are ratios to ensure that the units on each side of the equation correspond. In the last equation, we know we have it right because the left-hand side is expressed in dollars per euro and the right-hand side is also a ratio of dollars to euros (\$ per unit of goods divided by € per unit of goods).

Purchasing Power Parity

The principle of **purchasing power parity (PPP)** is the macroeconomic counterpart to the microeconomic law of one price (LOOP). The law of one price relates exchange rates to the relative prices of an individual good, while purchasing power parity relates exchange rates to the relative prices of a basket of goods. In studying international macroeconomics, purchasing power parity is the more relevant concept.

We can define a *price level* (denoted P) in each location as a weighted average of the prices of all goods g in a basket, using the same goods and weights in both locations. Let P_{US} be the basket's price in the United States and P_{EUR} the basket's price in Europe. *If the law of one price holds for each good in the basket, it will also hold for the price of the basket as a whole.*[1]

To express PPP algebraically, we can compute the relative price of the two baskets of goods in each location, denoted $q_{US/EUR}$:

$$\underbrace{q_{US/EUR}}_{\substack{\text{Relative price of} \\ \text{basket in Europe} \\ \text{versus U.S.}}} = \underbrace{(E_{\$/€}P_{EUR})}_{\substack{\text{European} \\ \text{price of basket} \\ \text{expressed in \$}}} / \underbrace{P_{US}}_{\substack{\text{U.S. price} \\ \text{of basket} \\ \text{expressed in \$}}}$$

Just as there were three possible outcomes for the law of one price, there are three possibilities for PPP: the basket is cheaper in United States; the basket is cheaper in Europe; or $E_{\$/€}P_{EUR} = P_{US}$; the basket is the same price in both locations, and $q_{US/EUR} = 1$. In the first two cases, the basket is cheaper in one location and profitable arbitrage on the baskets is possible. Only in the third case is there no arbitrage. PPP holds *when price levels in two countries are equal when expressed in a common currency.* This statement about equality of price levels is also called **absolute PPP.**

---

[1] For example, if the law of one price holds and $P_{US}^g = (E_{\$/€}) \times (P_{EUR}^g)$ for all goods g, this implies that for N goods, the *arithmetic* weighted average satisfies $\sum_{g=1}^{N}\omega^g P_{US}^g = (E_{\$/€}) \times \sum_{g=1}^{N}\omega^g P_{EUR}^g$ for any set of weights ω^g that sum to 1, so PPP holds. The same is also true for *geometric* averages. Technically speaking, this follows for *any* price index definition that satisfies the usually required property that the index be homogeneous of degree 1 in the individual goods' prices.

For example, suppose the European basket costs €100, and the exchange rate is $1.20 per euro. For PPP to hold, the U.S. basket would have to cost $1.20 \times 100 = \$120$.

The Real Exchange Rate

The relative price of the two countries' baskets (denoted q) is the macroeconomic counterpart to the microeconomic relative price of individual goods (q^g). The relative price of the baskets is one of the most important variables in international macroeconomics, and it has a special name: it is known as the **real exchange rate.** The real exchange rate $q_{US/EUR} = E_{\$/€}P_{EUR}/P_{US}$ tells us how many U.S. baskets are needed to purchase one European basket.

As with the nominal exchange rate, we need to be careful about what is in the numerator of the real exchange rate and what is in the denominator. According to our definition (based on the case we just examined), we will refer to $q_{US/EUR} = E_{\$/€}P_{EUR}/P_{US}$ as the home country, or the U.S. real exchange rate: it is the price of the European basket in terms of the U.S. basket (or, if we had a Home-Foreign example, the price of a Foreign basket in terms of a Home basket).

To avoid confusion, it is essential to understand the difference between nominal exchange rates (which we have studied so far) and real exchange rates. The exchange rate for currencies is a *nominal* concept; it says how many dollars can be exchanged for one euro. The real exchange rate is a *real* concept; it says how many U.S. baskets of goods can be exchanged for one European basket.

The real exchange rate has some terminology similar to that used with the nominal exchange rate:

- If the real exchange rate rises (more Home goods are needed in exchange for Foreign goods), we say Home has experienced a **real depreciation.**
- If the real exchange rate falls (fewer Home goods are needed in exchange for Foreign goods), we say Home has experienced a **real appreciation.**

Absolute PPP and the Real Exchange Rate

We can restate absolute PPP in terms of real exchange rates: *purchasing power parity states that the real exchange rate is equal to 1.* Under absolute PPP, all baskets have the same price when expressed in a common currency, so their relative price is 1.

It is common practice to use the absolute PPP-implied level of 1 as a benchmark or reference level for the real exchange rate. This leads naturally to some new terminology:

- If the real exchange rate $q_{US/EUR}$ is below 1 by $x\%$, then Foreign goods are relatively cheap: $x\%$ cheaper than Home goods. In this case, the Home currency (the dollar) is said to be *strong*, the euro is *weak*, and we say the euro is **undervalued** by $x\%$.
- If the real exchange rate $q_{US/EUR}$ is above 1 by $x\%$, then Foreign goods are relatively expensive: $x\%$ more expensive than Home goods. In this case, the Home currency (the dollar) is said to be weak, the euro is strong, and we say the euro is **overvalued** by $x\%$.

For example, if a European basket costs $E_{\$/€}P_{EUR} = \$550$ in dollar terms, and a U.S. basket costs only $P_{US} = \$500$, then $q_{US/EUR} = E_{\$/€}P_{EUR}/P_{US} = \$550/\$500 = 1.10$, the euro is strong, and the euro is 10% overvalued against the dollar.

Absolute PPP, Prices, and the Nominal Exchange Rate

Finally, just as we did with the law of one price, we can rearrange the no-arbitrage equation for the equality of price levels, $E_{\$/€}P_{EUR} = P_{US}$, to allow us to solve for the exchange rate that would be implied by absolute PPP:

$$\text{Absolute PPP:} \quad \underbrace{E_{\$/€}}_{\substack{\text{Exchange} \\ \text{rate}}} = \underbrace{P_{US}/P_{EUR}}_{\substack{\text{Ratio of} \\ \text{price levels}}} \tag{14-1}$$

This is one of the most important equations in our course of study because it shows how PPP (or absolute PPP) makes a clear prediction about exchange rates: *Purchasing power parity implies that the exchange rate at which two currencies trade equals the relative price levels of the two countries.*

For example, if a basket of goods costs \$460 in the United States and the same basket costs €400 in Europe, the theory of PPP predicts an exchange rate of \$460/€400 = \$1.15 per euro.

Thus, if we know the price levels in different locations, we can use PPP to determine an implied exchange rate, subject to all of our earlier assumptions about frictionless trade, flexible prices, free competition, and identical goods. The PPP relationship between the price levels in two countries and the exchange rate is therefore a key building block in our theory of how exchange rates are determined, as shown in Figure 14-1. Moreover, the theory is not tied to any point in time: if we can forecast future price levels, then we can also use PPP to forecast the expected future exchange rate implied by those forecasted future price levels, which is the main goal of this chapter.

Relative PPP, Inflation, and Exchange Rate Depreciation

PPP in its absolute PPP form involves price levels, but in macroeconomics we are often more interested in the rate at which price levels change than we are in the price levels themselves. The rate of growth of the price level is known as the *rate of inflation*, or simply **inflation.** For example, if the price level today is 100, and one year from now it is 103.5, then the rate of inflation is 3.5% (per year). Because inflation is such an important variable in macroeconomics, we examine the implications of PPP for the study of inflation.

To consider changes over time, we introduce a subscript t to denote the time period, and calculate the rate of change of both sides of Equation (14-1) from period t to

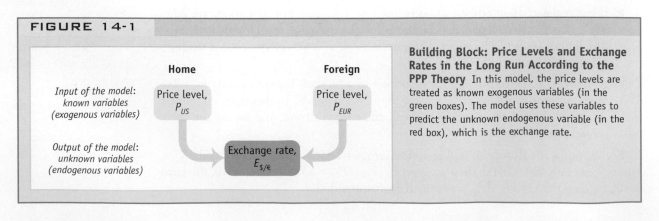

FIGURE 14-1

Building Block: Price Levels and Exchange Rates in the Long Run According to the PPP Theory In this model, the price levels are treated as known exogenous variables (in the green boxes). The model uses these variables to predict the unknown endogenous variable (in the red box), which is the exchange rate.

Input of the model: known variables (exogenous variables)

Home
Price level, P_{US}

Foreign
Price level, P_{EUR}

Output of the model: unknown variables (endogenous variables)

Exchange rate, $E_{\$/€}$

period $t + 1$. On the left-hand side, the rate of change of the exchange rate in Home is the rate of exchange rate depreciation in Home given by [2]

$$\frac{\Delta E_{\$/€,t}}{E_{\$/€,t}} \quad = \quad \underbrace{\frac{E_{\$/€,t+1} - E_{\$/€,t}}{E_{\$/€,t}}}_{\text{Rate of depreciation of the nominal exchange rate}}$$

On the right of Equation (14-1), the rate of change of the ratio of two price levels equals the rate of change of the numerator minus the rate of change of the denominator:[3]

$$\frac{\Delta(P_{US}/P_{EUR})}{(P_{US}/P_{EUR})} = \frac{\Delta P_{US,t}}{P_{US,t}} - \frac{\Delta P_{EUR,t}}{P_{EUR,t}} = \underbrace{\left(\frac{P_{US,t+1} - P_{US,t}}{P_{US,t}}\right)}_{\substack{\text{Rate of inflation in} \\ \text{U.S. } \pi_{US,t}}} - \underbrace{\left(\frac{P_{EUR,t+1} - P_{EUR,t}}{P_{EUR,t}}\right)}_{\substack{\text{Rate of inflation in} \\ \text{Europe } \pi_{EUR,t}}} = \pi_{US} - \pi_{EUR}$$

where the terms in brackets are the inflation rates in each location, denoted π_{US} and π_{EUR}, respectively.

If Equation (14-1) holds for levels of exchange rates and prices, then it must also hold for rates of change in these variables. By combining the last two expressions, we obtain

$$\text{Relative PPP:} \quad \underbrace{\frac{\Delta E_{\$/€,t}}{E_{\$/€,t}}}_{\substack{\text{Rate of depreciation of the} \\ \text{nominal exchange rate}}} \quad = \quad \underbrace{\pi_{US,t} - \pi_{EUR,t}}_{\text{Inflation differential}} \qquad (14\text{-}2)$$

This way of expressing PPP is called **relative PPP,** and it *implies that the rate of depreciation of the nominal exchange rate equals the difference between the inflation rates of two countries (the inflation differential).*

We saw relative PPP in action in the example at the start of this chapter. Over 20 years, Canadian prices rose 16% more than U.S. prices, and the Canadian dollar depreciated 16% against the U.S. dollar. Converting these to annual rates, Canadian prices rose by 0.75% per year more than U.S. prices (the inflation differential), and the loonie depreciated by 0.75% per year against the dollar. Relative PPP held in this case.[4]

Two points should be kept in mind about relative PPP. First, unlike absolute PPP, relative PPP predicts a relationship between *changes* in prices and *changes* in exchange rates, rather than a relationship between their levels. Second, remember that relative PPP is *derived from* absolute PPP. Hence, the latter always implies the former: *if absolute PPP holds, this implies that relative PPP must hold also.* But the converse need not be true: *relative PPP does not necessarily imply absolute PPP* (if relative PPP holds, absolute PPP can hold or fail). For example, imagine that all goods consistently cost 20% more in country A than in country B, so absolute PPP fails; however, it still can be the case that the inflation differential between A and B (say, 5%) is always equal to the rate of depreciation (say, 5%), so relative PPP will still hold.

---

[2] The rate of depreciation at Home and the rate of appreciation in Foreign are approximately equal, as we saw in the previous chapter.
[3] This expression is exact for small changes and otherwise holds true as an approximation.
[4] Note that the rates of change are approximate, with $1.0075^{20} = 1.16$.

Summary

The purchasing power parity theory, whether in the absolute PPP or relative PPP form, suggests that price levels in different countries and exchange rates are tightly linked, either in their absolute levels or in the rates at which they change. To assess how useful this theory is, let's look at some empirical evidence to see how well the theory matches reality. We can then reexamine the workings of PPP and reassess its underlying assumptions.

APPLICATION

Evidence for PPP in the Long Run and Short Run

Is there evidence for PPP? The data offer some support for relative PPP most clearly over the long run, when even moderate inflation mounts and leads to large cumulative changes in price levels and, hence, substantial cumulative inflation differentials.

The scatterplot in Figure 14-2 shows average rates of depreciation and inflation differentials for a sample of countries compared with the United States over three decades from 1975 to 2005. If relative PPP were true, then the depreciation of each country's currency would exactly equal the inflation differential, and the data would line up on the 45-degree line. We see that this is not literally true, but the correlation

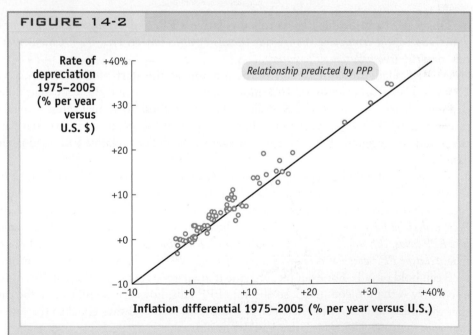

FIGURE 14-2

Inflation Differentials and the Exchange Rate, 1975–2005 This scatterplot shows the relationship between the rate of exchange rate depreciation against the U.S. dollar (the vertical axis) and the inflation differential against the United States (horizontal axis) over the long run, based on data for a sample of 82 countries. The correlation between the two variables is strong and bears a close resemblance to the theoretical prediction of PPP that all data points would appear on the 45-degree line.

Source: IMF, International Financial Statistics.

is close. Relative PPP is an approximate, useful guide to the relationship between prices and exchange rates in the long run, over horizons of many years or decades.

But the purchasing power theory turns out to be a fairly useless theory in the short run, over horizons of just a few years. This is easily seen by examining the time series of relative price ratio and exchange rates for any pair of countries, and looking at the behavior of these variables from year to year and not just over a long period. If absolute PPP held at all times, then the exchange rate would always equal the relative price ratio. Figure 14-3 shows 35 years of data for the United States and United Kingdom from 1975 to 2010. This figure confirms the relevance of absolute and relative PPP in the long run because the price-level ratio and the exchange rate have similar levels and drift together along a common trend. In the short run, however, the two series show substantial and persistent differences. In any given year the differences can be 10%, 20%, or more. These year-to-year differences in levels and changes show that absolute and relative PPP fail in the short run. For example, from 1980 to 1985, the pound depreciated by 45% (from $2.32 to $1.28 per pound), but the cumulative inflation differential over these five years was only 9%. ■

How Slow Is Convergence to PPP?

If PPP were taken as a strict proposition for the short run, then price adjustment via arbitrage would occur fully and instantaneously, rapidly closing the gap between common-currency prices in different countries for all goods in the basket. This doesn't happen. The evidence suggests that PPP works better in the long run. But how long is the long run?

Research shows that price differences—the deviations from PPP—can be persistent. Estimates suggest that these deviations may die out at a rate of about 15% per year. This kind of measure is often called a *speed of convergence:* in this case, it implies that after one year, 85% (0.85) of an initial price difference persists; compounding, after two years, 72% of the gap persists ($0.72 = 0.85^2$); and after four years, 52%

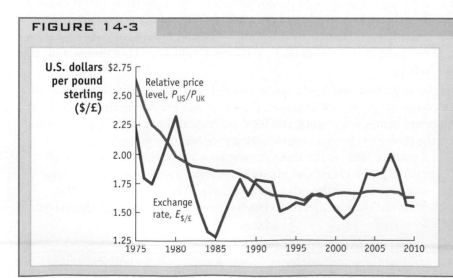

FIGURE 14-3

Exchange Rates and Relative Price Levels Data for the United States and United Kingdom for 1975 to 2010 show that the exchange rate and relative price levels do not always move together in the short run. Relative price levels tend to change slowly and have a small range of movement; exchange rates move more abruptly and experience large fluctuations. Therefore, relative PPP does *not* hold in the short run. However, it is a better guide to the long run, and we can see that the two series do tend to drift together over the decades.

Source: Penn World Table, version 7.1.

$(0.52 = 0.85^4)$. Thus, approximately half of any PPP deviation still remains after four years: economists would refer to this as a four-year *half-life*.

Such estimates provide a rule of thumb that is useful as a guide to forecasting real exchange rates. For example, suppose the home basket costs $100 and the foreign basket $90, in home currency. Home's real exchange rate is 0.900, and the home currency is overvalued, with foreign goods less expensive than home goods. The deviation of the real exchange rate from the PPP-implied level of 1 is –10% (or –0.1). Our rule of thumb tells us that next year 15% of this deviation will have disappeared (i.e., 0.015), so the new deviation will be only –0.085, meaning that Home's real exchange rate would be forecast to be 0.915 after one year and thus end up a little bit closer to 1, after a small depreciation. Similarly, after four years, all else being equal, 52% of the deviation (or 0.052) would have been erased, and the real exchange rate would by then be 0.952, only –4.8% from PPP. (See **Side Bar: Forecasting When the Real Exchange Rate Is Undervalued or Overvalued.**)

What Explains Deviations from PPP?

If it takes four years for even half of any given price difference to dissipate, as research has indicated, it is no surprise that PPP does not hold in the short run. But how can arbitrage take so long to eliminate price differences? Economists have found a variety of reasons why PPP fails in the short run.

- *Transaction costs.* Trade is not frictionless as we have assumed thus far because the costs of international transportation are significant for most goods and because some goods also bear additional costs, such as tariffs and duties, when they cross borders. By some recent estimates, transportation costs may add about 20% on average to the price of goods moving internationally, while tariffs (and other policy barriers) may add another 10%.[5] Other costs arise due to the time it takes to ship goods, and the costs and time delays associated with developing distribution networks and satisfying legal and regulatory requirements in foreign markets.

- *Nontraded goods.* Some goods are inherently nontradable; one can think of them as having infinitely high transaction costs. Most goods and services fall somewhere between tradable and nontradable. Consider a restaurant meal; it includes traded goods, such as some raw foods, and nontraded goods, such as the work of the chef. As a result, PPP may not hold. (See **Headlines: The Big Mac Index.**)

- *Imperfect competition and legal obstacles.* Many goods are not simple undifferentiated commodities, as LOOP and PPP assume, but are differentiated products with brand names, copyrights, and legal protection. For example, consumers have the choice of cheaper generic acetaminophen or a pricier brand-name product such as Tylenol, but these are not seen as perfect substitutes. Such differentiated goods create conditions of *imperfect competition* because firms have some power to set the price of their good. With this kind of *market power*, firms can charge different prices not just across brands but also across

---

[5] There is also evidence of other significant border-related barriers to trade. See James Anderson and Eric van Wincoop, 2004, "Trade Costs," *Journal of Economic Literature*, 42, 691–751.

SIDE BAR

Forecasting When the Real Exchange Rate Is Undervalued or Overvalued

When relative PPP holds, forecasting exchange rate changes is simple: just compute the inflation differential. But how do we forecast when PPP doesn't hold, as is often the case? Even if the real exchange rate is not equal to 1, knowing the real exchange rate and the convergence speed may still allow us to construct a forecast of real and nominal exchange rates.

To see how, let's take an example. Start with the definition of the real exchange rate: $q_{US/EUR} = E_{\$/€} P_{EUR}/P_{US}$. Rearranging, we find $E_{\$/€} = q_{US/EUR} \times (P_{US}/P_{EUR})$. By taking the rate of change of that expression, we find that the rate of change of the nominal exchange rate equals the rate of change of the real exchange rate plus home inflation minus foreign inflation:

$$\underbrace{\frac{\Delta E_{\$/€,t}}{E_{\$/€,t}}}_{\substack{\text{Rate of depreciation} \\ \text{of the nominal} \\ \text{exchange rate}}} = \underbrace{\frac{\Delta q_{US/EUR,t}}{q_{US/EUR,t}}}_{\substack{\text{Rate of depreciation} \\ \text{of the real exchange} \\ \text{rate}}} + \underbrace{\pi_{US,t} - \pi_{EUR,t}}_{\text{Inflation differential}}$$

When the real exchange rate q is constant, the first term on the right is zero and we are back to the simple world of relative PPP and Equation (14-2). For forecasting purposes, the predicted nominal depreciation is then just the second term on the right, the inflation differential. For example, if the forecast is for U.S. inflation to be 3% next year and for European inflation to be 1%, then the inflation differential is +2% and we would forecast a U.S. dollar depreciation, or rise in $E_{\$/€}$, of +2% next year.

What if q isn't constant and PPP fails? If there is currently a deviation from absolute PPP, but we still think that there will be convergence to absolute PPP in the long run, the first term on the right of the formula is not zero and we can estimate it given the right information.

To continue the example, suppose you are told that a U.S. basket of goods currently costs $100, but the European basket of the same goods costs $130. You would compute a U.S. real exchange rate $q_{US/EUR}$ of 1.30 today. But what will it be next year? If you expect absolute PPP to hold in the long run, then you expect that the U.S. real exchange rate will move toward 1. How fast? At this point, you need to know the convergence speed. Using the 15% rule of thumb, you estimate that 15% of the 0.3 gap between 1 and 1.3 (i.e., 0.045) will dissipate over the coming year. Hence, you forecast that the U.S. real exchange will fall from 1.3 to 1.255, implying a change of −3.46% in the coming year. In this case, adding the two terms on the right of the expression given previously, you forecast that the approximate change in E next year will be the change in $q_{US/EUR}$ of −3.46% plus the inflation differential of +2%, for a total of −1.46%; that is, a dollar appreciation of 1.46% against the euro.

The intuition for the result is as follows: the U.S. dollar is undervalued against the euro. If convergence to PPP is to happen, then some of that undervaluation will dissipate over the course of the year through a real appreciation of the dollar (predicted to be 3.46%). That real appreciation can be broken down into two components:

1. U.S. goods will experience higher inflation than European goods (we have predicted that the inflation differential will be +2%).

2. The remainder of the real appreciation will be accomplished via a 1.46% nominal dollar appreciation (predicted based on a convergence speed of 15% per year).

---

countries (pharmaceutical companies, for example, charge different prices for drugs in different countries). This practice is possible because arbitrage can be shut down by legal threats or regulations. If you try to import large quantities of a firm's pharmaceutical and resell them as an unauthorized distributor, you will probably hear very quickly from the firm's lawyers and/or from the government regulators. The same would apply to many other goods such as automobiles and consumer electronics.

■ *Price stickiness.* One of the most common assumptions of macroeconomics is that prices are "sticky" in the short run—that is, they do not or cannot adjust quickly and flexibly to changes in market conditions. PPP assumes that arbitrage can force prices to adjust, but adjustment will be slowed down by price stickiness. Empirical evidence shows that many goods' prices do not adjust quickly in the short run. For example, in Figure 14-3, we saw that the nominal exchange rate moves up and down in a very dramatic fashion but that price levels are much more sluggish in their movements and do not fully match exchange rate changes.

Despite these problems, the evidence suggests that as a long-run theory of exchange rates, PPP is still a useful approach.[6] And PPP may become even more relevant in the future as arbitrage becomes more efficient and more goods and services are traded. Years ago we might have taken it for granted that certain goods and services (such as pharmaceuticals, customer support, and health-care services) were strictly nontraded and thus not subject to arbitrage at the international level. Today, many consumers shop for pharmaceuticals overseas to save money. If you dial a U.S. software support call center, you may find yourself being assisted by an operator in another country. In some countries, citizens motivated by cost considerations may travel overseas for dental treatment, eye care, hip replacements, and other health services (so-called medical tourism or health tourism). These globalization trends may well continue.

HEADLINES

The Big Mac Index

For more than 25 years, The Economist *newspaper has engaged in a whimsical attempt to judge PPP theory based on a well-known, globally uniform consumer good: McDonald's Big Mac. The over- or undervaluation of a currency against the U.S. dollar is gauged by comparing the relative prices of a burger in a common currency, and expressing the difference as a percentage deviation from one:*

$$\text{Big Mac Index} = q^{\text{Big Mac}} - 1 = \left(\frac{E_{\text{\$/local currency}}P_{\text{local}}^{\text{Big Mac}}}{P_{\text{US}}^{\text{Big Mac}}}\right) - 1$$

Home of the undervalued burger?

Table 14-1 shows the July 2012 survey results, and some examples will illustrate how the calculations work. Row 1 shows the average U.S. dollar price of the Big Mac of $4.33. An example of undervaluation appears in Row 2, where we see that the Buenos Aires correspondent found the same burger cost 19 pesos, which, at an actual exchange rate of 4.57 pesos per dollar, worked out to be $4.16 in U.S. currency, or 4%

less than the U.S. price. So the peso was 4% undervalued against the U.S. dollar according to this measure, and Argentina's exchange rate would have had to appreciate to 4.39 pesos per dollar to attain the level implied by a burger-based PPP theory. An example of overvaluation appears in Row 4, in the case of neighboring Brazil. There a Big Mac cost 10.08 reais, or $4.94 in U.S. currency at the prevailing exchange

rate of 2.04 reais per dollar, making the Brazilian burgers 14% more expensive than their U.S. counterparts. To get to its PPP-implied level, and put the burgers at parity, Brazil's currency would have needed to depreciate to 2.33 reais per dollar. Looking through the table, burger disparity is typical, with only 7 countries coming within ±5% of PPP.

[6] Alan M. Taylor and Mark P. Taylor, 2004, "The Purchasing Power Parity Debate," *Journal of Economic Perspectives*, 8, 135–158.

TABLE 14-1

The Big Mac Index The table shows the price of a Big Mac in July 2012 in local currency (column 1) and converted to U.S. dollars (column 2) using the actual exchange rate (column 4). The dollar price can then be compared with the average price of a Big Mac in the United States ($4.33 in column 1, row 1). The difference (column 5) is a measure of the overvaluation (+) or undervaluation (−) of the local currency against the U.S. dollar. The exchange rate against the dollar implied by PPP (column 3) is the hypothetical price of dollars in local currency that would have equalized burger prices, which may be compared with the actual observed exchange rate (column 4).

| | Big Mac Prices | | Exchange rate (local currency per U.S. dollar) | | Over (+)/ under (−) valuation against dollar, % (5) |
	In local currency (1)	In U.S. dollars (2)	Implied by PPP (3)	Actual, July 25th (4)	
United States	$ 4.33	4.33	—	—	—
Argentina	Peso 19	4.16	4.39	4.57	−4
Australia	A$ 4.56	4.68	1.05	0.97	8
Brazil	Real 10.08	4.94	2.33	2.04	14
Britain	£ 2.69	4.16	0.62	0.65	−4
Canada	C$ 3.89	3.82	0.90	1.02	−12
Chile	Peso 2050	4.16	473.71	493.05	−4
China	Yuan 15.65	2.45	3.62	6.39	−43
Colombia	Peso 8600	4.77	1987.29	1804.48	10
Costa Rica	Colones 1200	2.40	277.30	501.02	−45
Czech Republic	Koruna 70.33	3.34	16.25	21.05	−23
Denmark	DK 28.5	4.65	6.59	6.14	7
Egypt	Pound 16	2.64	3.70	6.07	−39
Euro area	€ 3.58	4.34	0.83	0.83	0
Hong Kong	HK$ 16.5	2.13	3.81	7.76	−51
Hungary	Forint 830	3.48	191.80	238.22	−19
India	Rupee 89	1.58	20.57	56.17	−63
Indonesia	Rupiah 24200	2.55	5592.00	9482.50	−41
Israel	Shekel 11.9	2.92	2.75	4.08	−33
Japan	Yeo 320	4.09	73.95	78.22	−5
Latvia	Lats 1.69	2.94	0.39	0.57	−32
Lithuania	Litas 7.8	2.74	1.80	2.85	−37
Malaysia	Ringgit 7.4	2.33	1.71	3.17	−46
Mexico	Peso 37	2.70	8.55	13.69	−38
New Zealand	NZS 5.1	4.00	1.18	1.27	−7
Norway	Kroner 43	7.06	9.94	6.09	63
Pakistan	Rupee 285	3.01	65.86	94.61	−30
Philippines	Peso 118	2.80	27.27	42.20	−35
Poland	Zloty 9.1	2.63	2.10	3.46	−39
Russia	Rouble 75	2.29	17.33	32.77	−47
Saudi Arabia	riyal 10	2.67	2.31	3.75	−38
Singapore	S$ 4.4	3.50	1.02	1.26	−19
South Africa	Rand 19.95	2.36	4.61	8.47	−46
South Korea	Won 3700	3.21	855.00	1151.00	−26
Sri Lanka	Rupee 290	2.21	67.01	131.00	−49
Sweden	SKr 48.4	6.94	11.18	6.98	60
Switzerland	SFr 6.5	6.56	1.50	0.99	52
Taiwan	NT$ 75	2.48	17.33	30.20	−43
Thailand	Baht 82	2.59	18.95	31.70	−40
Turkey	Lira 8.25	4.52	1.91	1.83	4
UAE	Dirhams 12	3.27	2.77	3.67	−25
Ukraine	Hryvnia 15	1.86	3.47	8.09	−57
Uruguay	Peso 99	4.53	22.88	21.87	5
Venezuela	Bolivar 34	7.92	7.86	4.29	83

Source: © The Economist Newspaper Limited, London (July 26, 2012). Actual market exchange rates are for July 25, 2012. PPP-implied rate is local currency price divided by price in United States. The U.S. price is average of four cities; China price is average of five cities; Euro area price is weighted average of prices in euro area; India price is the price of a Maharaja Mac.

2   Money, Prices, and Exchange Rates in the Long Run: Money Market Equilibrium in a Simple Model

It is time to take stock of the theory developed so far in this chapter. Up to now, we have concentrated on PPP, which says that in the long run the exchange rate is determined by the ratio of the price levels in two countries. But this prompts a question: What determines those price levels?

Monetary theory supplies an answer: according to this theory, in the long run, price levels are determined in each country by the relative demand and supply of money. You may recall this theory from previous macroeconomics courses in the context of a closed economy. This section recaps the essential elements of monetary theory and shows how they fit into our theory of exchange rates in the long run.

What Is Money?

We recall the distinguishing features of this peculiar asset that is so central to our everyday economic life. Economists think of **money** as performing three key functions in an economy:

1. Money is a *store of value* because, as with any asset, money held from today until tomorrow can still be used to buy goods and services in the future. Money's rate of return is low compared with many other assets. Because we earn no interest on it, there is an opportunity cost to holding money. If this cost is low, we hold money more willingly than other assets (stocks, bonds, and so forth).

2. Money is a *unit of account* in which all prices in the economy are quoted. When we enter a store in France, we expect to see the prices of goods to read something like "100 euros"—not "10,000 Japanese yen" or "500 bananas," even though, in principle, the yen or the banana could also function as a unit of account in France (bananas would, however, be a poor store of value).

3. Money is a *medium of exchange* that allows us to buy and sell goods and services without the need to engage in inefficient barter (direct swaps of goods). The ease with which we can convert money into goods and services is a measure of how *liquid* money is compared with the many illiquid assets in our portfolios (such as real estate). Money is the most liquid asset of all.

The Measurement of Money

What counts as money? Clearly, currency (coins and bills) in circulation is money. But do checking accounts count as money? What about savings accounts, mutual funds, and other securities? Figure 14-4 depicts the most widely used measures of the money supply and illustrates their relative magnitudes with recent data from the United States. The most basic concept of money is currency in circulation (i.e., in the hands of the nonbank public). After that, M0 is typically the narrowest definition of money (also called "base money"), and it includes both currency in circulation and the reserves of commercial banks (liquid cash held in their vaults or on deposit at the Fed). Normally, in recent years, banks' reserves have been very small and so M0 has been virtually identical to currency in circulation. This changed dramatically after the financial crisis of 2008 gave rise to liquidity problems, and banks began to maintain

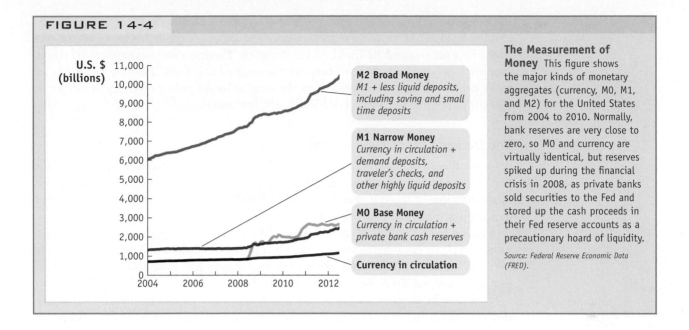

FIGURE 14-4

The Measurement of Money This figure shows the major kinds of monetary aggregates (currency, M0, M1, and M2) for the United States from 2004 to 2010. Normally, bank reserves are very close to zero, so M0 and currency are virtually identical, but reserves spiked up during the financial crisis in 2008, as private banks sold securities to the Fed and stored up the cash proceeds in their Fed reserve accounts as a precautionary hoard of liquidity.

Source: Federal Reserve Economic Data (FRED).

huge reserves at the Fed as a precaution. (When and how this unprecedented hoard of cash will be unwound remains to be seen, and this is a matter of some concern to economists and policy makers.)

A different narrow measure of money, M1, includes currency in circulation plus highly liquid instruments such as demand deposits in checking accounts and traveler's checks, but it *excludes* bank's reserves, and thus may be a better gauge of money available for transactions purposes. A much broader measure of money, M2, includes slightly less liquid assets such as savings and small time deposits.[7]

For our purposes, money is defined as the *stock of liquid assets that are routinely used to finance transactions*, as implied by the "medium of exchange" function of money. So, in this book, when we speak of money (denoted M), we will generally mean M1 (currency in circulation plus demand deposits). Many important assets are excluded from M1, including longer-term assets held by individuals and the voluminous interbank deposits used in the foreign exchange market discussed in the previous chapter. These assets do not count as money in the sense we use the word because they are relatively illiquid and not used routinely for transactions.

The Supply of Money

How is the supply of money determined? In practice, a country's **central bank** controls the **money supply.** Strictly speaking, by issuing notes and coins (and private bank reserves), the central bank controls directly only the level of M0, or base money,

---

[7] There is little consensus on the right broad measure of money. Until 2006 the U.S. Federal Reserve collected data on M3, which included large time deposits, repurchase agreements, and money market funds. This was discontinued because the data were costly to collect and thought to be of limited use to policy makers. In the United Kingdom, a slightly different broad measure, M4, is still used. Some economists now prefer a money aggregate called MZM, or "money of zero maturity," as the right broad measure, but its use is not widespread.

the amount of currency and reserves in the economy. However, it can *indirectly* control the level of M1 by using monetary policy to influence the behavior of the private banks that are responsible for checking deposits. The intricate mechanisms by which monetary policy affects M1 are beyond the scope of this book. For our purposes, we make the simplifying assumption that the central bank's policy tools are sufficient to allow it to control the level of M1 indirectly, but accurately.[8]

The Demand for Money: A Simple Model

A simple theory of household money demand is motivated by the assumption that the need to conduct transactions is in proportion to an individual's income. For example, if an individual's income doubles from $20,000 to $40,000, we expect his or her demand for money (expressed in dollars) to double also.

Moving from the individual or household level up to the aggregate or macroeconomic level, we can infer that the aggregate **money demand** will behave similarly. *All else equal, a rise in national dollar income (nominal income) will cause a proportional increase in transactions and, hence, in aggregate money demand.*

This insight suggests a simple model in which the demand for money is proportional to dollar income. This model is known as the **quantity theory of money:**

$$\underbrace{M^d}_{\substack{\text{Demand} \\ \text{for money (\$)}}} = \underbrace{\overline{L}}_{\text{A constant}} \times \underbrace{PY}_{\substack{\text{Nominal} \\ \text{income (\$)}}}$$

Here, PY measures the total nominal dollar value of income in the economy, equal to the price level P times real income Y. The term $\overline{L}$ is a constant that measures how much demand for liquidity is generated for each dollar of nominal income. To emphasize this point, we assume for now that every $1 of nominal income requires $\overline{L}$ of money for transactions purposes and that this relationship is constant. (Later, we relax this assumption.)

The intuition behind the last equation is as follows: If the price level rises by 10% and real income is fixed, we are paying a 10% higher price for all goods, so the dollar cost of transactions rises by 10%. Similarly, if real income rises by 10% but prices stay fixed, the dollar amount of transactions will rise by 10%. Hence, the *demand for nominal money balances*, M^d, is proportional to the *nominal* income PY.

Another way to look at the quantity theory is to convert all quantities into real quantities by dividing the previous equation by P, the price level (the price of a basket of goods). Quantities are then converted from nominal dollars to real units (specifically, into units of baskets of goods). These conversions allow us to derive the *demand for real money balances*:

$$\underbrace{\frac{M^d}{P}}_{\substack{\text{Demand for} \\ \text{real money}}} = \underbrace{\overline{L}}_{\text{A constant}} \times \underbrace{Y}_{\text{Real income}}$$

Real money balances measure the purchasing power of the stock of money in terms of goods and services. The expression just given says that the demand for

---

[8] A full treatment of this topic may be found in a textbook on money and banking. See Laurence M. Ball, 2012, *Money, Banking, and Financial Markets*, 2nd edition (New York: Worth).

real money balances is proportional to real income. The more real income we have, the more real transactions we have to perform, and the more real money we need.

Equilibrium in the Money Market

The condition for equilibrium in the money market is that the demand for money M^d must equal the supply of money M, which we assume to be under the control of the central bank. Imposing this condition on the last two equations, we find that nominal money supply equals nominal money demand:

$$M = \bar{L}PY$$

and, equivalently, that real money supply equals real money demand:

$$\frac{M}{P} = \bar{L}Y$$

A Simple Monetary Model of Prices

We are now in a position to put together a simple model of the exchange rate, using two building blocks. The first building block, the quantity theory, is a model that links prices to monetary conditions. The second building block, PPP, is a model that links exchange rates to prices.

We consider two locations, or countries, as before; the United States will be the home country and we will treat the Eurozone as the foreign country. We shall refer to the Eurozone, or more simply Europe, as a country in this and later examples. The model generalizes to any pair of countries or locations.

Let's consider the last equation given and apply it to the United States, adding U.S. subscripts for clarity. We can rearrange this formula to obtain an expression for the U.S. price level:

$$P_{US} = \frac{M_{US}}{\bar{L}_{US}Y_{US}}$$

Note that the price level is determined by how much nominal money is issued relative to the demand for real money balances: the numerator on the right-hand side M_{US} is the total supply of *nominal* money; the denominator $\bar{L}_{US}Y_{US}$ is the total demand for *real* money balances.

The analogous expression for the European price level is:

$$P_{EUR} = \frac{M_{EUR}}{\bar{L}_{EUR}Y_{EUR}}$$

The last two equations are examples of the **fundamental equation of the monetary model of the price level.** Two such equations, one for each country, give us another important building block for our theory of prices and exchange rates as shown in Figure 14-5.

In the long run, we assume prices are flexible and will adjust to put the money market in equilibrium. For example, if the amount of money in circulation (the nominal money supply) rises, say, by a factor of 100, and real income stays the same, then there will be "more money chasing the same quantity of goods." This leads to inflation, and

FIGURE 14-5

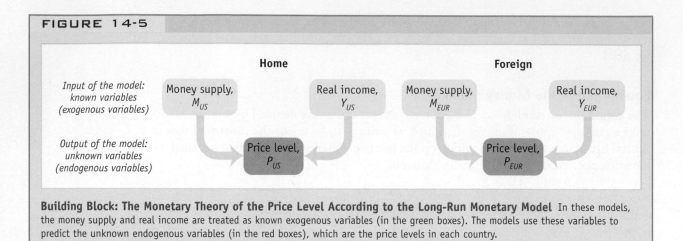

Building Block: The Monetary Theory of the Price Level According to the Long-Run Monetary Model In these models, the money supply and real income are treated as known exogenous variables (in the green boxes). The models use these variables to predict the unknown endogenous variables (in the red boxes), which are the price levels in each country.

in the long run, the price level will rise by a factor of 100. In other words, we will be in the same economy as before except that all prices will have two zeros tacked on to them.

A Simple Monetary Model of the Exchange Rate

A long-run model of the exchange rate is close at hand. If we take the last two equations, which use the monetary model to find the price level in each country, and plug them into Equation (14-1), we can use absolute PPP to solve for the exchange rate:

$$
\underbrace{E_{\$/€}}_{\substack{\text{Exchange}\\\text{rate}}} = \underbrace{\frac{P_{US}}{P_{EUR}}}_{\substack{\text{Ratio of}\\\text{price levels}}} = \underbrace{\frac{\left(\dfrac{M_{US}}{\bar{L}_{US}Y_{US}}\right)}{\left(\dfrac{M_{EUR}}{\bar{L}_{EUR}Y_{EUR}}\right)}}_{} = \underbrace{\frac{(M_{US}/M_{EUR})}{(\bar{L}_{US}Y_{US}/\bar{L}_{EUR}Y_{EUR})}}_{\substack{\text{Relative nominal money}\\\text{supplies divided by relative}\\\text{real money demands}}} \qquad (14\text{-}3)
$$

This is the **fundamental equation of the monetary approach to exchange rates.** By substituting the price levels from the monetary model into PPP, we have put together the two building blocks from Figures 14-1 and 14-5. The implications of this equation are as follows:

■ Suppose the U.S. money supply increases, all else equal. The right-hand side increases (the U.S. nominal money supply increases relative to Europe), causing the exchange rate to increase (the U.S. dollar depreciates against the euro). For example, if the U.S. money supply doubles, then all else equal, the U.S. price level doubles. That is, a bigger U.S. supply of money leads to a weaker dollar. That makes sense—there are more dollars around, so you expect each dollar to be worth less.

■ Now suppose the U.S. real income level increases, all else equal. Then the right-hand side decreases (the U.S. real money demand increases relative to Europe), causing the exchange rate to decrease (the U.S. dollar appreciates against the euro). For example, if the U.S. real income doubles, then all else equal, the U.S. price level falls by a factor of one-half. That is, a stronger U.S. economy leads to a stronger dollar. That makes sense—there is more demand for the same quantity of dollars, so you expect each dollar to be worth more.

Money Growth, Inflation, and Depreciation

The model just presented uses absolute PPP to link the level of the exchange rate to the level of prices and uses the quantity theory to link prices to monetary conditions in each country. But as we have said before, macroeconomists are often more interested in rates of change of variables (e.g., inflation) rather than levels.

Can we extend our theory to this purpose? Yes, but this task takes a little work. We convert Equation (14-3) into growth rates by taking the rate of change of each term.

The first term of Equation (14-3) is the exchange rate $E_{\$/\epsilon}$. Its rate of change is the rate of depreciation $\Delta E_{\$/\epsilon}/E_{\$/\epsilon}$. When this term is positive, say, 1%, the dollar is depreciating at 1% per year; if negative, say, −2%, the dollar is appreciating at 2% per year.

The second term of Equation (14-3) is the ratio of the price levels P_{US}/P_{EUR}, and as we saw when we derived relative PPP at Equation (14-2), its rate of change is the rate of change of the numerator (U.S. inflation) minus the rate of change of the denominator (European inflation), which equals the inflation differential $\pi_{US,t} - \pi_{EUR,t}$.

What is the rate of change of the third term in Equation (14-3)? The numerator represents the U.S. price level, $P_{US} = M_{US}/\overline{L}_{US}Y_{US}$. Again, the growth rate of a fraction equals the growth rate of the numerator minus the growth rate of the denominator. In this case, the numerator is the money supply M_{US}, and its growth rate is μ_{US}:

$$\mu_{US,t} = \underbrace{\frac{M_{US,t+1} - M_{US,t}}{M_{US,t}}}_{\text{Rate of money supply growth in U.S.}}$$

The denominator is $\overline{L}_{US}Y_{US}$, which is a constant $\overline{L}_{US}$ times real income Y_{US}. Thus, $\overline{L}_{US}Y_{US}$ grows at a rate equal to the growth rate of real income g_{US}:

$$g_{US,t} = \underbrace{\frac{Y_{US,t+1} - Y_{US,t}}{Y_{US,t}}}_{\text{Rate of real income growth in U.S.}}$$

Putting all the pieces together, the growth rate of $P_{US} = M_{US}/\overline{L}_{US}Y_{US}$ equals the money supply growth rate μ_{US} minus the real income growth rate g_{US}. We have already seen that the growth rate of P_{US} on the left-hand side is the inflation rate π_{US}. Thus, we know that

$$\pi_{US,t} = \mu_{US,t} - g_{US,t} \tag{14-4}$$

The denominator of the third term of Equation (14-3) represents the European price level, $P_{EUR} = M_{EUR}/\overline{L}_{EUR}Y_{EUR}$, and its rate of change is calculated similarly:

$$\pi_{EUR,t} = \mu_{EUR,t} - g_{EUR,t} \tag{14-5}$$

The intuition for these last two expressions echoes what we said previously: when money growth is higher than real income growth, we have "more money chasing fewer goods" and this leads to inflation.

Combining Equation (14-4) and Equation (14-5), we can now solve for the inflation differential in terms of monetary fundamentals and finish our task of computing the rate of depreciation of the exchange rate:

$$\underbrace{\frac{\Delta E_{\$/€,t}}{E_{\$/€,t}}}_{\substack{\text{Rate of depreciation of the} \\ \text{nominal exchange rate}}} = \underbrace{\pi_{US,t} - \pi_{EUR,t}}_{\text{Inflation differential}} = (\mu_{US,t} - g_{US,t}) - (\mu_{EUR,t} - g_{EUR,t}) \quad (14\text{-}6)$$

$$= \underbrace{(\mu_{US,t} - \mu_{EUR,t})}_{\substack{\text{Differential in} \\ \text{nominal money supply} \\ \text{growth rates}}} - \underbrace{(g_{US,t} - g_{EUR,t})}_{\substack{\text{Differential in real} \\ \text{output growth rates}}}$$

The last term here is the rate of change of the fourth term in Equation (14-3).

Equation (14-6) is the fundamental equation of the monetary approach to exchange rates expressed in rates of change, and much of the same intuition we applied in explaining Equation (14-3) carries over here.

■ If the United States runs a looser monetary policy in the long run measured by a faster money growth rate, the dollar will depreciate more rapidly, all else equal. For example, suppose Europe has a 5% annual rate of change of money and a 2% rate of change of real income; then its inflation would be the difference: 5% minus 2% equals 3%. Now suppose the United States has a 6% rate of change of money and a 2% rate of change of real income; then its inflation would be the difference: 6% minus 2% equals 4%. And the rate of depreciation of the dollar would be U.S. inflation minus European inflation, 4% minus 3%, or 1% per year.

■ If the U.S. economy grows faster in the long run, the dollar will appreciate more rapidly, all else equal. In the last numerical example, suppose the U.S. growth rate of real income in the long run increases from 2% to 5%, all else equal. U.S. inflation equals the money growth rate of 6% minus the new real income growth rate of 5%, so inflation is just 1% per year. Now the rate of dollar depreciation is U.S. inflation minus European inflation, that is, 1% minus 3%, or −2% per year (meaning the U.S. dollar would now appreciate at 2% per year).

With a change of notation to make the United States the foreign country, the same lessons could be derived for Europe and the euro.

3 The Monetary Approach: Implications and Evidence

The monetary approach is the workhorse model in the study of long-run exchange rate movements. In this section, we look at some applications and empirical evidence.

Exchange Rate Forecasts Using the Simple Model

An important application of the monetary approach to exchange rate determination is to provide a forecast of the future exchange rate. Remember from the previous chapter that foreign exchange (forex) market arbitragers need such a forecast to be able to make arbitrage calculations using uncovered interest parity. Using Equation (14-3), we can see that a forecast of future exchange rates (the left-hand side) can be constructed as long as we know how to forecast future money supplies and real income (the right-hand side).

In practice, this is why expectations about money and real income in the future attract so much attention in the financial media, and especially in the forex market. The discussion returns with obsessive regularity to two questions. The first question — What are central banks going to do? — leads to all manner of attempts to decode the statements of central bank officials. The second question — How is the economy expected to grow in real terms? — leads to a keen interest in any economic indicators, such as productivity or investment, that might hint at changes in the rate of income growth.

Any such forecasts come with at least two major caveats. First, there is great uncertainty in trying to answer these questions, and forecasts of economic variables years in the future are inevitably subject to large errors. Nonetheless, this is one of the key tasks of financial markets. Second, whenever one uses the monetary model for forecasting, one is answering a hypothetical question: What path would exchange rates follow from now on *if prices were flexible and PPP held*? As forecasters know, in the short run there might be deviations from this prediction about exchange rate changes, but in the longer run, we expect the prediction will supply a more reasonable guide.

Forecasting Exchange Rates: An Example To see how forecasting might work, let's look at a simple scenario and focus on what would happen under flexible prices. Assume that U.S. and European real income growth rates are identical and equal to zero (0%) so that real income levels are constant. Assume also that the European money supply is constant. If the money supply and real income in Europe are constant, then the European price level is constant, and European inflation is zero, as we can see from Equation (14-5). These assumptions allow us to perform a controlled thought-experiment, and focus on changes on the U.S. side of the model, all else equal. Let's look at two cases.

Case 1: A one-time unanticipated increase in the money supply. In the first, and simpler, case, suppose at some time T that the U.S. money supply rises by a fixed proportion, say, 10%, all else equal. Assuming that prices are flexible, what does our model predict will happen to the level of the exchange rate after time T? To spell out the argument in detail, we look at the implications of our model for some key variables.

  a. There is a 10% increase in the money supply M.

  b. Real money balances M/P remain constant, because real income is constant.

  c. These last two statements imply that price level P and money supply M must move in the same proportion, so there is a 10% increase in the price level P.

  d. PPP implies that the exchange rate E and price level P must move in the same proportion, so there is a 10% increase in the exchange rate E; that is, the dollar depreciates by 10%.

A quicker solution uses the fundamental equation of the monetary approach at Equation (14-3): the price level and exchange rate are proportional to the money supply, all else equal.

Case 2: An unanticipated increase in the rate of money growth. The model also applies to more complex scenarios. Consider a second case in which the U.S. money supply is not constant, but grows at a steady fixed rate μ. Then suppose we learn at time T that the United States will raise the rate of money supply growth from some previously fixed rate μ to a slightly higher rate $\mu + \Delta\mu$. How would people expect the exchange rate to behave, assuming price flexibility? Let's work through this case step by step:

a. Money supply M is growing at a constant rate.

b. Real money balances M/P remain constant, as before.

c. These last two statements imply that price level P and money supply M must move in the same proportion, so P is always a constant multiple of M.

d. PPP implies that the exchange rate E and price level P must move in the same proportion, so E is always a constant multiple of P (and hence of M).

Corresponding to these four steps, the four panels of Figure 14-6 illustrate the path of the key variables in this example. This figure shows that if we can forecast

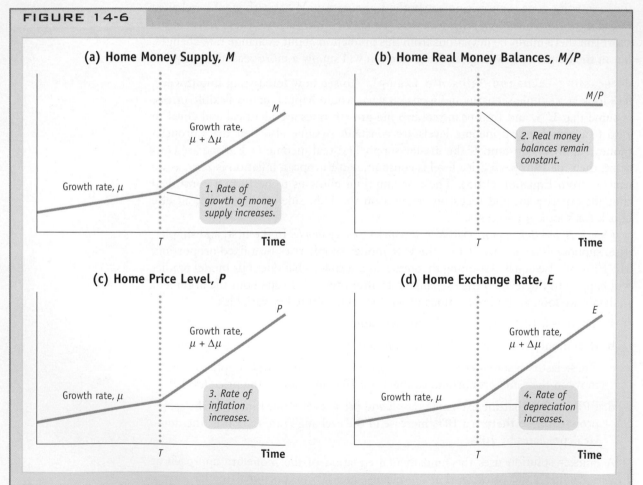

FIGURE 14-6

(a) Home Money Supply, M

(b) Home Real Money Balances, M/P

(c) Home Price Level, P

(d) Home Exchange Rate, E

An Increase in the Growth Rate of the Money Supply in the Simple Model Before time T, money, prices, and the exchange rate all grow at rate μ. Foreign prices are constant. In panel (a), we suppose at time T there is an increase $\Delta\mu$ in the rate of growth of home money supply M. In panel (b), the quantity theory assumes that the level of real money balances remains unchanged. After time T, if real money balances (M/P) are constant, then money M and prices P still grow at the same rate, which is now $\mu + \Delta\mu$, so the rate of inflation rises by $\Delta\mu$, as shown in panel (c). PPP and an assumed stable foreign price level imply that the exchange rate will follow a path similar to that of the domestic price level, so E also grows at the new rate $\mu + \Delta\mu$, and the rate of depreciation rises by $\Delta\mu$, as shown in panel (d).

the money supply at any future period as in (a), and if we know real money balances remain constant as in (b), then we can forecast prices as in (c) and exchange rates as in (d). These forecasts are good in any future period, under the assumptions of the monetary approach. Again, Equation (14-3) supplies the answer more quickly; under the assumptions we have made, money, prices, and exchange rates all move in proportion to one another.

APPLICATION

Evidence for the Monetary Approach

The monetary approach to prices and exchange rates suggests that, all else equal, increases in the rate of money supply growth should be the same size as increases in the rate of inflation and the rate of exchange rate depreciation. Looking for evidence of this relationship in real-world data is one way to put this theory to the test.

The scatterplots in Figure 14-7 and Figure 14-8 show data from 1975 to 2005 for a large sample of countries. The results offer fairly strong support for the monetary theory. All else equal, Equation (14-6) predicts that an $x\%$ difference in money growth rates (relative to the United States) should be associated with an $x\%$ difference in inflation rates (relative to the United States) and an $x\%$ depreciation of the home exchange rate (against the U.S. dollar). If this association were literally true in the data, then each country in the scatterplot would be on the 45-degree line. This is not exactly true, but the actual relationship is very close and offers some support for the monetary approach.

One reason the data do not sit on the 45-degree line is that all else is *not* equal in this sample of countries. In Equation (14-6), countries differ not only in their relative

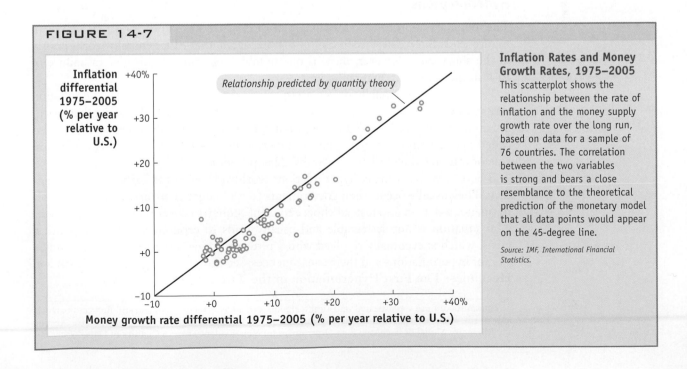

FIGURE 14-7

Inflation Rates and Money Growth Rates, 1975–2005 This scatterplot shows the relationship between the rate of inflation and the money supply growth rate over the long run, based on data for a sample of 76 countries. The correlation between the two variables is strong and bears a close resemblance to the theoretical prediction of the monetary model that all data points would appear on the 45-degree line.

Source: IMF, International Financial Statistics.

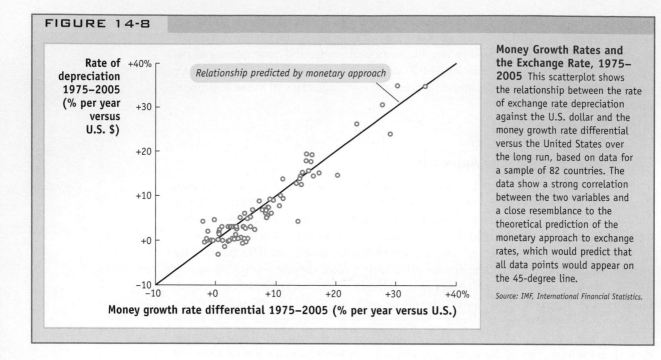

FIGURE 14-8

Rate of depreciation 1975–2005 (% per year versus U.S. $)

Relationship predicted by monetary approach

Money growth rate differential 1975–2005 (% per year versus U.S.)

Money Growth Rates and the Exchange Rate, 1975–2005 This scatterplot shows the relationship between the rate of exchange rate depreciation against the U.S. dollar and the money growth rate differential versus the United States over the long run, based on data for a sample of 82 countries. The data show a strong correlation between the two variables and a close resemblance to the theoretical prediction of the monetary approach to exchange rates, which would predict that all data points would appear on the 45-degree line.

Source: IMF, International Financial Statistics.

money supply growth rates but also in their real income growth rates. Another explanation is that we have been assuming that the money demand parameter L is constant, and this may not be true in reality. This is an issue we must now confront.[9] ■

APPLICATION

Hyperinflations

The monetary approach assumes long-run PPP, which has some support, as we saw in Figure 14-2. But we have been careful to note, again, that PPP generally works poorly in the short run. However, there is one notable exception to this general failure of PPP in the short run: hyperinflations.

Economists traditionally define a **hyperinflation** as occurring when the inflation rate rises to a sustained rate of more than 50% *per month* (which means that prices are doubling every 51 days). In common usage, some lower-inflation episodes are also called hyperinflations; for example, an inflation rate of 1,000% *per year* is a common rule of thumb (when inflation is "only" 22% per month).

There have been many hyperinflations worldwide since the early twentieth century. They usually occur when governments face a budget crisis, are unable to borrow to finance a deficit, and instead choose to print money to cover their financing needs. The situation is not sustainable and usually leads to economic, social, or political crisis, which is eventually resolved with a return to price stability. (For more discussion of hyperinflations and their consequences, see **Side Bar: Currency Reform** and **Headlines: The First Hyperinflation of the Twenty-First Century**.)

---

[9] Economists can use sophisticated statistical techniques to address these issues and still find results favorable to the monetary approach in the long run. See David E. Rapach and Mark E. Wohar, 2002, "Testing the Monetary Model of Exchange Rate Determination: New Evidence from a Century of Data," *Journal of International Economics*, 58(2), 359–385.

SIDE BAR

Currency Reform

Hyperinflations help us understand how some currencies become extinct if they cease to function well and lose value rapidly. Dollarization in Ecuador is a recent example. Other currencies survive such traumas, only to be reborn. But the low denomination bills—the ones, fives, tens—usually become essentially worthless and normal transactions can require you to be a millionaire. The elimination of a few pesky zeros might then be a good idea. A government may then *redenominate* a new unit of currency equal to 10^N (10 raised to the power N) old units.

Sometimes N can get quite large. In the 1980s, Argentina suffered hyperinflation. On June 1, 1983, the *peso argentino* replaced the (old) peso at a rate of 10,000 to 1. Then on June 14, 1985, the *austral* replaced the peso argentino at 1,000 to 1. Finally, on January 1, 1992, the *convertible peso* replaced the austral at a rate of 10,000 to 1 (i.e., 10,000,000,000 old pesos). After all this, if you had owned 1 new peso in 1983 (and had changed it into the later monies), it would have lost 99.99997% of its U.S. dollar value by 2003.

In 1946 the Hungarian *pengö* became so worthless that the authorities no longer printed the denomination on each note in numbers, but only in words—perhaps to avert distrust (unsuccessful), to hide embarrassment (also unsuccessful), or simply because there wasn't room to print all those zeros. By July 15, 1946, there were 76,041,000,000,000,000,000,000,000 pengö in circulation. A stable new currency, the *forint*, was finally introduced on July 26, 1946, with each forint worth 400,000 quadrillion pengö (4×10^{20} = 400,000,000,000,000,000,000 pengö). The dilution of the Zimbabwean dollar from 2005 to 2009 was even more extreme, as the authorities lopped off 25 zeros in a series of reforms before the currency finally vanished from use.

PPP in Hyperinflations Each of these crises provides a unique laboratory for testing the predictions of the PPP theory. The scatterplot in Figure 14-9 looks at the data using changes in levels (from start to finish, expressed as multiples). The change in the exchange rate (with the United States) is on the vertical axis and the change in the price level (compared with the United States) is on the horizontal axis. Because of the huge changes involved, both axes use log scales in powers of 10. For example, 10^{12} on the vertical axis means the exchange rate rose (the currency depreciated) by a factor of a trillion against the U.S. dollar during the hyperinflation.

If PPP holds, changes in prices and exchange rates should be equal and all observations would be on the 45-degree line. The changes follow this pattern very closely, providing support for PPP. What the hyperinflations have in common is that a very large depreciation was about equal to a very large inflation differential. In an economy with fairly stable prices and exchange rates, large changes in exchange rates and prices only develop over the very long run of years and decades; in a hyperinflation, large inflations and large depreciations are compressed into the short run of years or months, so this is one case where PPP holds quite well even in the short run.

Some price changes were outrageously large. Austria's hyperinflation of 1921 to 1922 was the first one on record, and prices rose by a factor of about 100 (10^2). In Germany from 1922 to 1923, prices rose by a factor of about 20 billion (2×10^{10}); in the worst month, prices were doubling on average every two days. In Hungary from 1945 to 1946, pengö prices rose by a factor of about 4 septillion (4×10^{27}), the current record, and in July 1946, prices were doubling on average every 15 hours. Serbia's inflation from 1992 to 1994 came close to breaking the record for cumulative price changes, as did the most recent case in Zimbabwe. In comparison, Argentina's 700-fold inflation and Brazil's 200-fold inflation from 1989 to 1990 look modest.

Above top to bottom are an Argentine 500,000 austral bill of 1990; a 1923 one billion German mark note (1 German billion = 1 U.S. trillion); and a Hungarian 100 Million B-pengö of 1946, with the "B" denoting the Hungarian billion, or a million million: this 100,000,000,000,000,000,000 pengö note is the highest denomination of currency ever issued by any country.

FIGURE 14-9

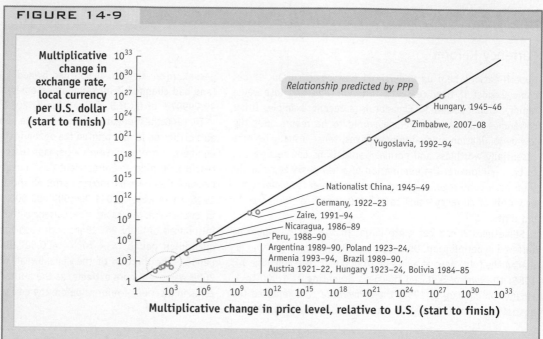

Purchasing Power Parity during Hyperinflations The scatterplot shows the relationship between the cumulative start-to-finish exchange rate depreciation against the U.S. dollar and the cumulative start-to-finish rise in the local price level for hyperinflations since the early twentieth century. Note the use of logarithmic scales. The data show a strong correlation between the two variables and a *very* close resemblance to the theoretical prediction of PPP that all data points would appear on the 45-degree line.

Sources: IMF, International Financial Statistics; Phillip Cagan, 1956, "The Monetary Dynamics of Hyperinflation," in Milton Friedman, ed., Studies in the Quantity Theory of Money (Chicago: University of Chicago Press), pp. 25–117; Pavle Petrovic and Zorica Mladenovic, 2000, "Money Demand and Exchange Rate Determination under Hyperinflation: Conceptual Issues and Evidence from Yugoslavia," Journal of Money, Credit and Banking, 32, 785–806; Teh-Wei Hu, 1971, "Hyperinflation and the Dynamics of the Demand for Money in China, 1945–1949," Journal of Political Economy 79(1), 186–95; Jason Lim II, 2012, "Observations of the Political and Economic Situation in China by the British Mercantile Community during the Civil War, 1945–1949," in Anne-Marie Brady and Douglas Brown, eds., Foreigners and Foreign Institutions in Republican China (Abingdon, U.K.: Routledge), pp. 109–27; Zimbabwe estimate based on author's calculations and Steve H. Hanke and Alex K. F. Kwok, 2009, "On the Measurement of Zimbabwe's Hyperinflation," Cato Journal 29(2), 353–64.

Money Demand in Hyperinflations There is one other important lesson to be learned from hyperinflations. In our simple monetary model, the money demand parameter L was assumed to be *constant* and equal to $\overline{L}$. This implied that real money balances were proportional to real income, with $M/P = \overline{L}\,Y$ as shown in Equation (14-5). Is this assumption of stable real money balances justified?

The evidence shown in Figure 14-10 suggests this assumption is not justified, based on a subset of the hyperinflations. For each point, on the horizontal axis of this figure, we see the peak monthly inflation rate (the moment when prices were rising most rapidly); on the vertical axis, we see the level of real money balances in that month relative to their initial level (in the month just before the hyperinflation began). If real money balances were stable, there should be no variation in the vertical dimension aside from fluctuations in real income. But there is, and with a clear pattern: the higher the level of inflation, the lower the level of real money balances. These declines are far too severe to be explained by just the fall in real incomes experienced during hyperinflations, though such income declines did occur.

This finding may not strike you as very surprising. If prices are doubling every few days (or every few hours), the money in people's pockets is rapidly turning into

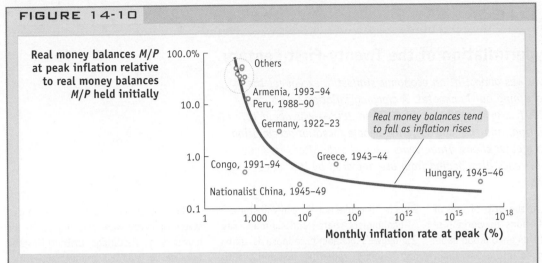

FIGURE 14-10

The Collapse of Real Money Balances During Hyperinflations This figure shows that real money balances tend to collapse in hyperinflations as people economize by reducing their holdings of rapidly depreciating notes. The horizontal axis shows the peak monthly inflation rate (%), and the vertical axis shows the ratio of real money balances in that peak month relative to real money balances at the start of the hyperinflationary period. The data are shown using logarithmic scales for clarity.

Sources: IMF, International Financial Statistics; Phillip Cagan, 1956, "The Monetary Dynamics of Hyperinflation," in Milton Friedman, ed., Studies in the Quantity Theory of Money (Chicago: University of Chicago Press), pp. 25–117; Teh-Wei Hu, 1971, "Hyperinflation and the Dynamics of the Demand for Money in China, 1945–1949," Journal of Political Economy 79(1), 186–95.

worthless pieces of paper. They will try to minimize their money holdings—and will do so even more as inflation rises higher and higher, just as the figure shows. It becomes just too costly to hold very much money, despite one's need to use it for transactions.

If you thought along these lines, you have an accurate sense of how people behave during hyperinflations. You also anticipated the extensions to the simple model that we make in the next section so it is more realistic. Even during "normal" inflations—situations that are less pathological than a hyperinflation—it is implausible to assume that real money balances are perfectly stable. In our extension of the simple model, we will assume that people make the trade-off highlighted previously: comparing the benefits of holding money for transactions purposes with the costs of holding money as compared with other assets. ■

4 Money, Interest Rates, and Prices in the Long Run: A General Model

So far we have a long-run theory that links exchange rates to the price levels in each country: PPP. We also have a simple long-run monetary model that links price levels in each country to money supply and demand: the *quantity theory*.

These building blocks provide some basic intuition for the links between price levels, money, and exchange rates. The trouble is that the quantity theory's assumption — that the demand for money is stable — is implausible. In this section, we explore a more general model that addresses this shortcoming by allowing money demand to vary with

HEADLINES

The First Hyperinflation of the Twenty-First Century

By 2007 Zimbabwe was almost at an economic standstill, except for the printing presses churning out banknotes. A creeping inflation—58% in 1999, 132% in 2001, 385% in 2003, and 586% in 2005—was about to become hyperinflation, and the long-suffering people faced an accelerating descent into even greater chaos. Three years later, shortly after this news report, the local currency disappeared from use, replaced by U.S. dollars and South African rand.

. . . Zimbabwe is in the grip of one of the great hyperinflations in world history. The people of this once proud capital have been plunged into a Darwinian struggle to get by. Many have been reduced to peddlers and paupers, hawkers and black-market hustlers, eating just a meal or two a day, their hollowed cheeks a testament to their hunger.

Like countless Zimbabweans, Mrs. Moyo has calculated the price of goods by the number of days she had to spend in line at the bank to withdraw cash to buy them: a day for a bar of soap; another for a bag of salt; and four for a sack of cornmeal.

The withdrawal limit rose on Monday, but with inflation surpassing what independent economists say is an almost unimaginable 40 million percent, she said the value of the new amount would quickly be a pittance, too.

"It's survival of the fittest," said Mrs. Moyo, 29, a hair braider who sells the greens she grows in her yard for a dime a bunch. "If you're not fit, you will starve."

Economists here and abroad say Zimbabwe's economic collapse is gaining velocity, radiating instability into the heart of southern Africa. As the bankrupt government prints ever more money, inflation has gone wild, rising from 1,000 percent in 2006 to 12,000 percent in 2007. . . . In fact, Zimbabwe's hyperinflation is probably among the five worst of all time, said Jeffrey D. Sachs, a Columbia University economics professor, along with Germany in the 1920s, Greece and Hungary in the 1940s and Yugoslavia in 1993. . . .

Basic public services, already devastated by an exodus of professionals in recent years, are breaking down on an ever larger scale as tens of thousands of teachers, nurses, garbage collectors and janitors have simply stopped reporting to their jobs because their salaries, more worthless literally by the hour, no longer cover the cost of taking the bus to work. . . .

The bodies of paupers in advanced states of decay were stacking up in the mortuary at Beitbridge District Hospital because not even government authorities were seeing to their burial. . . . Harare Central Hospital slashed admissions by almost half because so much of its cleaning staff could no longer afford to get to work.

Most of the capital, though lovely beneath its springtime canopy of lavender jacaranda blooms, was without water because the authorities had stopped paying the bills to transport the treatment chemicals. Garbage is piling up uncollected. Sixteen people have died in an outbreak of cholera in nearby Chitungwiza, spread by contaminated water and sewage. . . .

Vigilantes in Kwekwe killed a man suspected of stealing two chickens, eggs and a bucket of corn. . . . And traditional chiefs complained about corrupt politicians and army officers who sold grain needed for the hungry to the politically connected instead.

the nominal interest rate. But this theory, in turn, brings another variable into play: How is the nominal interest rate determined in the long run? Answering this question will lead us to consider the links between inflation and the nominal interest rate in an open economy. With these new models in hand, we then return to the question of how best to understand what determines exchange rates in the long run.

The Demand for Money: The General Model

The general model of money demand is motivated by two insights, the first of which carries over from the quantity theory, the simple model we studied earlier in this chapter.

■ *There is a benefit from holding money.* As is true in the simple quantity theory, the benefit of money is that individuals can conduct transactions with it, and we continue to assume that transactions demand is in proportion to income, all else equal.

■ *There is a cost to holding money.* The nominal interest rate on money is zero, $i_{money} = 0$. By holding money and not earning interest, people incur the opportunity cost of holding money. For example, an individual could hold an interest-earning asset paying $i_\$$. The difference in nominal returns between this asset and money would be $i_\$ - i_{money} = i_\$ > 0$. This is one way of expressing the opportunity cost.

Moving from the individual or household level up to the macroeconomic level, we can infer that aggregate money demand in the economy as a whole will behave similarly:

All else equal, a rise in national dollar income (nominal income) will cause a proportional increase in transactions and, hence, in aggregate money demand.

All else equal, a rise in the nominal interest rate will cause the aggregate demand for money to fall.

Thus, we arrive at a general model in which money demand is proportional to nominal income, and is a decreasing function of the nominal interest rate:

$$\underbrace{M^d}_{\substack{\text{Demand for}\\\text{money (\$)}}} = \underbrace{L(i)}_{\substack{\text{A decreasing}\\\text{function}}} \times \underbrace{P \times Y}_{\substack{\text{Nominal}\\\text{income (\$)}}}$$

Recall that, formerly, in the quantity theory, the parameter L (the liquidity ratio, the amount of money needed for transactions per dollar of nominal GDP) was a constant. In this general model, we assume that L is a decreasing function of the nominal interest rate i. Dividing by P, we can derive the demand for real money balances:

$$\underbrace{\frac{M^d}{P}}_{\substack{\text{Demand for}\\\text{real money}}} = \underbrace{L(i)}_{\substack{\text{A decreasing}\\\text{function}}} \times \underbrace{Y}_{\substack{\text{Real}\\\text{income}}}$$

Figure 14-11(a) shows a typical **real money demand function** of this form, with the quantity of real money balances demanded on the horizontal axis and the nominal interest rate on the vertical axis. The downward slope of the demand curve reflects the inverse relationship between the demand for real money balances and the nominal interest rate *at a given level of real income* (Y).

Figure 14-11(b) shows what happens when real income increases from Y_1 to Y_2. When real income increases (by $x\%$), the demand for real money balances increases (by $x\%$) at each level of the nominal interest rate and the curve shifts.

Long-Run Equilibrium in the Money Market

The money market is in equilibrium when the real money supply (determined by the central bank) equals the demand for real money balances (determined by the nominal interest rate and real income):

$$\underbrace{\frac{M}{P}}_{\substack{\text{Real money}\\\text{supply}}} = \underbrace{L(i)Y}_{\substack{\text{Real money}\\\text{demand}}} \tag{14-7}$$

FIGURE 14-11

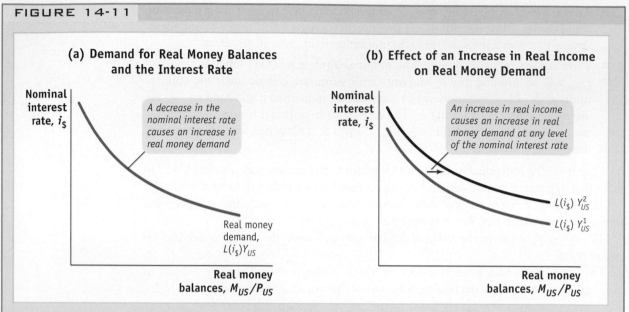

(a) Demand for Real Money Balances and the Interest Rate

Nominal interest rate, $i_\$$

A decrease in the nominal interest rate causes an increase in real money demand

Real money demand, $L(i_\$)Y_{US}$

Real money balances, M_{US}/P_{US}

(b) Effect of an Increase in Real Income on Real Money Demand

Nominal interest rate, $i_\$$

An increase in real income causes an increase in real money demand at any level of the nominal interest rate

$L(i_\$)\, Y_{US}^2$

$L(i_\$)\, Y_{US}^1$

Real money balances, M_{US}/P_{US}

The Standard Model of Real Money Demand Panel (a) shows the real money demand function for the United States. The downward slope implies that the quantity of real money demand rises as the nominal interest rate $i_\$$ falls. Panel (b) shows that an increase in real income from Y_{US}^1 to Y_{US}^2 causes real money demand to rise at all levels of the nominal interest rate $i_\$$.

We will continue to assume that prices are flexible in the long run and that they adjust to ensure that equilibrium is maintained.

We now have a model that describes equilibrium in the money market which will help us on the way to understanding the determination of the exchange rate. Before we arrive at the long-run exchange rate, however, we need one last piece to the puzzle. Under the quantity theory, the nominal interest rate was ignored. Now, in our general model, it is a key variable in the determination of money demand. So we need a theory to tell us what the level of the nominal interest rate i will be in the long run. Once we have solved this problem, we will be able to apply this new, more complex, but more realistic model of the money market to the analysis of exchange rate determination in the long run.

Inflation and Interest Rates in the Long Run

The tools we need to determine the nominal interest rate in an open economy are already at hand. So far in this chapter, we have developed the idea of purchasing power parity (PPP), which links prices and exchange rates. In the last chapter, we developed another parity idea, uncovered interest parity (UIP), which links exchange rates and interest rates. With only these two relationships in hand, PPP and UIP, we can derive a powerful and striking result concerning interest rates that has profound implications for our study of open economy macroeconomics.

Relative PPP, as indicated in Equation (14-2), states that the rate of depreciation equals the inflation differential at time t. When market actors use this equation to forecast future exchange rates, we use a superscript e to denote such expectations. Equation (14-2) is recast to show expected depreciation and inflation at time t:

$$\underbrace{\frac{\Delta E^e_{\$/€}}{E_{\$/€}}}_{\substack{\text{Expected rate of} \\ \text{dollar depreciation}}} = \underbrace{\pi^e_{US} - \pi^e_{EUR}}_{\text{Expected inflation differential}}$$

Next we recall that UIP in the approximate form (Equation 13-3) can be rearranged to show that the expected rate of depreciation equals the interest differential at time t:

$$\underbrace{\frac{\Delta E^e_{\$/€}}{E_{\$/€}}}_{\substack{\text{Expected rate of} \\ \text{dollar depreciation}}} = \underbrace{i_\$}_{\substack{\text{Net dollar} \\ \text{interest rate}}} - \underbrace{i_€}_{\substack{\text{Net euro} \\ \text{interest rate}}}$$

This way of writing the UIP equation says that traders will be indifferent to a higher U.S. interest rate relative to the euro interest rates (making U.S. deposits look more attractive) only if the higher U.S. rate is offset by an expected dollar depreciation (making U.S. deposits look less attractive). For example, if the U.S. interest rate is 4% and the euro interest rate is 2%, the interest differential is 2% and the forex market can be in equilibrium only if traders expect a 2% depreciation of the U.S. dollar against the euro, which would exactly offset the higher U.S. interest rate.

The Fisher Effect

Because the left sides of the previous two equations are equal, the right sides must also be equal. Thus, the nominal interest differential equals the expected inflation differential:

$$\underbrace{i_\$ - i_€}_{\substack{\text{Nominal interest} \\ \text{rate differential}}} = \underbrace{\pi^e_{US} - \pi^e_{EUR}}_{\substack{\text{Nominal inflation rate} \\ \text{differential (expected)}}} \qquad (14\text{-}8)$$

What does this important result say? To take an example, suppose expected inflation is 4% in the United States and 2% in Europe. The inflation differential on the right is then +2% (4% − 2% = +2%). If interest rates in Europe are 3%, then to make the interest differential the same as the inflation differential, +2%, the interest rate in the United States must equal 5% (5% − 3% = +2%).

Now suppose expected inflation in the United States changes, rising by one percentage point to 5%. If nothing changes in Europe, then the U.S. interest rate must also rise by one percentage point to 6% for the equation to hold. In general, this equation predicts that changes in the expected rate of inflation will be fully incorporated (one for one) into changes in nominal interest rates.

All else equal, a rise in the expected inflation rate in a country will lead to an equal rise in its nominal interest rate.

This result is known as the **Fisher effect,** named for the American economist Irving Fisher (1867–1947). Note that because this result depends on an assumption of PPP, it is therefore likely to hold only in the long run.

The Fisher effect makes clear the link between inflation and interest rates under flexible prices, a finding that is widely applicable. For a start, it makes sense of the evidence we just saw on money holdings during hyperinflations (see Figure 14-10). As inflation rises, the Fisher effect tells us that the nominal interest rate i must rise by the same amount; the general model of money demand then tells us that $L(i)$ must fall because it is a decreasing function of i. Thus, for a given level of real income, real money balances must fall as inflation rises.

In other words, the Fisher effect predicts that the change in the opportunity cost of money is equal not just to the change in the nominal interest rate but also to the change in the inflation rate. In times of very high inflation, people should, therefore, want to reduce their money holdings—and they do.

Real Interest Parity

As just described, the Fisher effect tells us something about nominal interest rates, but we can quickly derive the implications for real interest rates, too. Rearranging the last equation, we find

$$i_\$ - \pi^e_{US} = i_€ - \pi^e_{EUR}$$

The expressions on either side of this equation might look familiar from previous courses in macroeconomics. When the inflation rate (π) is subtracted from a *nominal* interest rate (i), the result is a **real interest rate** (r), the inflation-adjusted return on an interest-bearing asset. Given this definition, we can simplify the last equation further. On the left is the expected real interest rate in the United States ($r^e_{US} = i_\$ - \pi^e_{US}$). On the right is the expected real interest rate in Europe ($r^e_{EUR} = i_€ - \pi^e_{EUR}$).

Thus, using only two assumptions, PPP and UIP, we have shown that

$$r^e_{US} = r^e_{EUR} \tag{14-9}$$

This remarkable result states the following: *if PPP and UIP hold, then expected real interest rates are equalized across countries.*

This powerful condition is called **real interest parity** and because it depends on an assumption of PPP, it is therefore likely to hold only in the long run.[10]

We have arrived at a strong conclusion about the potential for globalization to cause convergence in economic outcomes, because real interest parity implies the following: *arbitrage in goods and financial markets alone is sufficient, in the long run, to cause the equalization of real interest rates across countries.*

We have considered two locations, but this argument applies to all countries integrated into the global capital market. In the long run, they will all share a common expected real interest rate, the long-run expected **world real interest rate** denoted r^*, so

$$r^e_{US} = r^e_{EUR} = r^*$$

---

[10] You may have encountered other theories in which real interest rates are equalized across countries by other means. Countries may share common technologies (because of technology diffusion) or might have similar saving behavior (because of similar preferences). Such assumptions could lead to identical real interest rates even in two *closed* economies. But here we have derived the real interest parity condition *only* from UIP and PPP, meaning that, in *open* economies, these are *sufficient* conditions for real interest rates to be equalized. No other assumptions are needed!

From now on, unless indicated otherwise, we treat r^* as a given, exogenous variable, something outside the control of a policy maker in any particular country.[11]

Under these conditions, the Fisher effect is even clearer, because, by definition,

$$i_\$ = r^e_{US} + \pi^e_{US} = r^* + \pi^e_{US} \qquad i_\text{€} = r^e_{EUR} + \pi^e_{EUR} = r^* + \pi^e_{EUR}$$

Thus, in each country, the long-run expected nominal interest rate is the long-run world real interest rate plus that country's expected long-run inflation rate. For example, if the world real interest rate is $r^* = 2\%$, and the country's long-run expected inflation rate goes up by two percentage points from 3% to 5%, then its long-run nominal interest rate also goes up by two percentage points from the old level of 2 + 3 = 5% to a new level of 2 + 5 = 7%.

APPLICATION

Evidence on the Fisher Effect

Are the Fisher effect and real interest parity supported by empirical evidence? One might expect a problem here. We derived them from purchasing power parity. The evidence we have seen on PPP offers support only in the long run. Thus, we do not expect the Fisher effect and real interest parity to hold exactly in the short run, but we might expect them to hold (at least approximately) in the long run.

Figure 14-12 shows that the Fisher effect is close to reality in the long run: on average, countries with higher inflation rates tend to have higher nominal interest rates, and the data line up fairly well with the predictions of the theory. Figure 14-13 shows that, for three developed countries, real interest parity holds fairly well in the long

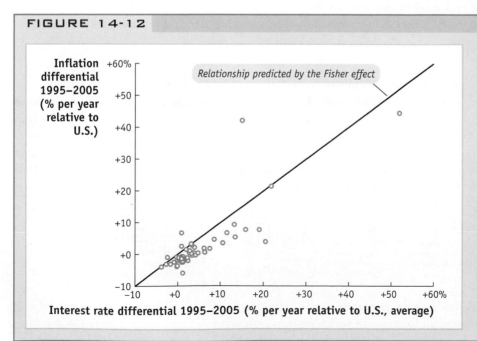

FIGURE 14-12

Inflation Rates and Nominal Interest Rates, 1995–2005 This scatterplot shows the relationship between the average annual nominal interest rate differential and the annual inflation differential relative to the United States over a ten-year period for a sample of 62 countries. The correlation between the two variables is strong and bears a close resemblance to the theoretical prediction of the Fisher effect that all data points would appear on the 45-degree line.

Source: IMF, International Financial Statistics.

Inflation differential 1995–2005 (% per year relative to U.S.)

Relationship predicted by the Fisher effect

Interest rate differential 1995–2005 (% per year relative to U.S., average)

---

[11]Advanced economic theories explore the determinants of the world real interest rate, with reference to consumption preferences of households and the extent to which they discount the future.

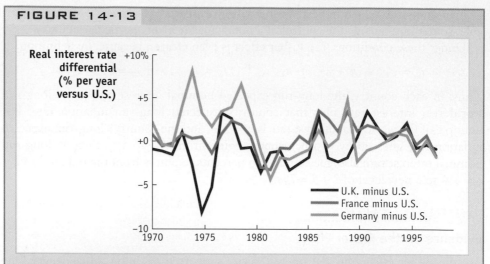

FIGURE 14-13

Real interest rate differential (% per year versus U.S.)

U.K. minus U.S.
France minus U.S.
Germany minus U.S.

Real Interest Rate Differentials, 1970–1999 This figure shows actual real interest rate differentials over three decades for the United Kingdom, Germany, and France relative to the United States. These differentials were not zero, so real interest parity did not hold continuously. But the differentials were on average close to zero, meaning that real interest parity (like PPP) is a general long-run tendency in the data.

Source: Maurice Obstfeld and Alan M. Taylor, 2004, Global Capital Markets: Integration, Crisis, and Growth, *Japan-U.S. Center Sanwa Monographs on International Financial Markets (Cambridge, UK: Cambridge University Press).*

run: real interest differentials are not always zero, but they tend to fluctuate around zero in the long run. This could be seen as evidence in favor of long-run real interest parity. ■

The Fundamental Equation Under the General Model

Now that we understand how the nominal interest rate is determined in the long run, our general model is complete. This model differs from the simple model (the quantity theory) *only* by allowing L to vary as a function of the nominal interest rate i.

We can therefore update our fundamental equations to allow for this change in how we treat L. For example, the fundamental equation of the monetary approach to exchange rates, Equation (14-3), can now be suitably modified:

$$\underbrace{E_{\$/€}}_{\substack{\text{Exchange} \\ \text{rate}}} = \underbrace{\frac{P_{US}}{P_{EUR}}}_{\substack{\text{Ratio of} \\ \text{price levels}}} = \frac{\left(\dfrac{M_{US}}{L_{US}(i_\$)Y_{US}}\right)}{\left(\dfrac{M_{EUR}}{L_{EUR}(i_€)Y_{EUR}}\right)} = \underbrace{\frac{(M_{US}/M_{EUR})}{(L_{US}(i_\$)Y_{US}/L_{EUR}(i_€)Y_{EUR})}}_{\substack{\text{Relative nominal money supplies} \\ \text{divided by relative real money demands}}} \quad (14\text{-}10)$$

What have we gained from this refinement? We know that the simple model will remain valid for cases in which nominal interest rates remain unchanged in the long run. It is only when nominal interest rates change that the general model has different implications, and we now have the right tools for that situation. To put those tools to work, we revisit the example of an exchange rate forecasting problem we encountered earlier in this chapter.

Exchange Rate Forecasts Using the General Model

Earlier in the chapter, we looked at two forecasting problems *under the assumption of flexible prices*. The first was a one-time unanticipated change in an otherwise constant U.S. money supply. Under the assumptions we made (stable real income in both countries and stable European money supply), this change caused a one-time increase in the U.S. price level but did not lead to a change in U.S. inflation (which was zero before and after the event).

The Fisher effect tells us that if inflation rates are unchanged, then, in the long run, nominal interest rates remain unchanged. Thus, the predictions of the simple model remain valid. But in the second and more complex forecasting problem, there was a one-time unanticipated change in the U.S. money growth rate that *did* lead to a change in inflation. It is here that the general model makes different predictions.

Earlier we assumed that U.S. and European real income growth rates are identical and equal to zero (0%), so real income levels are constant. We also assumed that the European money supply is constant, so that the European price level is constant, too. This allowed us to focus on changes on the U.S. side of the model, all else equal.

We now reexamine the forecasting problem for the case in which there is an increase in the U.S. rate of money growth. We learn at time T that the United States is raising the rate of money supply growth from some fixed rate μ to a slightly higher rate $\mu + \Delta\mu$.

For example, imagine an increase from 2% to 3% growth, so $\Delta\mu = 1\%$. How will the exchange rate behave in the long run? To solve the model, we make a provisional assumption that U.S. inflation rates and interest rates are constant before and after time T and focus on the differences between the two periods caused by the change in money supply growth. The story is told in Figure 14-14:

a. The money supply is growing at a constant rate. If the interest rate is constant in each period, then real money balances M/P remain constant, by assumption, because $L(i)Y$ is then a constant. If real money balances are constant, then M and P grow at the same rate. Before T that rate is $\mu = 2\%$; after T that rate is $\mu + \Delta\mu = 3\%$. That is, the U.S. inflation rate rises by an amount $\Delta\mu = 1\%$ at time T.

b. As a result of the Fisher effect, U.S. interest rates also rise by $\Delta\mu = 1\%$ at time T. Consequently, real money balances M/P must fall at time T because $L(i)Y$ will decrease as i increases.

c. In (a) we have described the path of M. In (b) we found that M/P is constant up to T, then drops suddenly, and then is constant after time T. What path must the price level P follow? Up to time T, it is a constant multiple of M; the same applies after time T, but the constant has increased. Why? The nominal money supply grows smoothly, without a jump. So if real money balances drop down discontinuously at time T, the price level must jump up discontinuously at time T. The intuition for this is that the rise in inflation and interest rates at time T prompts people to instantaneously demand less real money, but because the supply of nominal money is unchanged, the price level has to jump up. Apart from this jump, P grows at a constant rate; before T that rate is $\mu = 2\%$; after T that rate is $\mu + \Delta\mu = 3\%$.

d. PPP implies that E and P must move in the same proportion, so E is always a constant multiple of P. Thus, E jumps like P at time T. Apart from this jump, E grows at a constant rate; before T that rate is $\mu = 2\%$; after T that rate is $\mu + \Delta\mu = 3\%$.

FIGURE 14-14

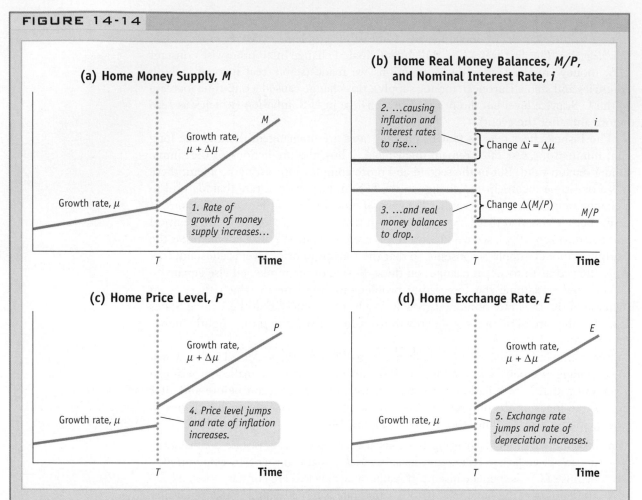

An Increase in the Growth Rate of the Money Supply in the Standard Model Before time T, money, prices, and the exchange rate all grow at rate μ. Foreign prices are constant. In panel (a), we suppose at time T there is an increase $\Delta\mu$ in the rate of growth of home money supply M. This causes an increase $\Delta\mu$ in the rate of inflation; the Fisher effect means that there will be a $\Delta\mu$ increase in the nominal interest rate; as a result, as shown in panel (b), real money demand falls with a discrete jump at T. If real money balances are to fall when the nominal money supply expands continuously, then the domestic price level must make a discrete jump up at time T, as shown in panel (c). Subsequently, prices grow at the new higher rate of inflation; and given the stable foreign price level, PPP implies that the exchange rate follows a similar path to the domestic price level, as shown in panel (d).

Corresponding to these four steps, Figure 14-14 illustrates the path of the key variables in this example. (Our provisional assumption of constant inflation rates and interest rates in each period is satisfied, so the proposed solution is internally consistent.)

Comparing Figure 14-14 with Figure 14-6, we can observe the subtle qualitative differences between the predictions of the simple quantity theory and those of the more general model. Shifts in the interest rate introduce jumps in real money demand. Because money supplies evolve smoothly, these jumps end up being reflected in the price levels and hence—via PPP—in exchange rates. The Fisher effect tells us that these interest rate effects are ultimately the result of changes in expected inflation.

Looking Ahead We can learn a little more by thinking through the market mechanism that produces this result. People learn at time T that money growth will be more rapid in the United States. This creates expectations of higher inflation in the United States. If people believe PPP holds in the long run, they will believe higher future inflation will cause the U.S. currency to depreciate in the future. This prospect makes holding dollars less attractive, by UIP. People try to sell dollars, and invest in euros. This creates immediate downward pressure on the dollar—even though at time T itself the supply of dollars does not change at all! This lesson underlines yet again the importance of expectations in determining the exchange rate. *Even if actual economic conditions today are completely unchanged, news about the future affects today's exchange rate.* This crucial insight can help us explain many phenomena relating to the volatility and instability in spot exchange rates, an idea we develop further in the chapters that follow.

5 Monetary Regimes and Exchange Rate Regimes

The monetary approach shows that, in the long run, all nominal variables—the money supply, interest rate, price level, and exchange rate—are interlinked. Hence, monetary policy choices can radically affect some important economic outcomes, notably prices and inflation, about which policy makers, governments, and the people they represent deeply care. The approach therefore highlights issues that must be taken into account in long-run economic policy design, and we will explore these important connections between theory and policy in this final section of the chapter.

We have repeatedly stressed the importance of inflation as an economic variable. Why is it so important? High or volatile inflation rates are considered undesirable. They may destabilize an economy or retard its growth.[12] Economies with low and stable inflation generally grow faster than those with high or volatile inflation. Inflationary crises, in which inflation jumps to a high or hyperinflationary level, are very damaging indeed.[13]

Thus, an overarching aspect of a nation's economic policy is the desire to keep inflation within certain bounds. The achievement of such an objective requires that policy makers be subject to (or subject themselves to) some kind of constraint in the long run. Such constraints are called **nominal anchors** because they attempt to tie down a nominal variable that is potentially under the policy makers' control.

Policy makers cannot directly control prices, so the attainment of price stability in the *short run* is not feasible. The question is what can policy makers do to promote price stability in the long run and what types of flexibility, if any, they will allow

---

[12] Macroeconomists can list numerous potential costs of inflation. Expected inflation generates a cost of holding money, a tax on transactions that adds friction to the economy; firms and workers use nominal contracts for prices and would have to change prices and rewrite contracts more often; inflation also distorts the economy when a tax system has significant nominal provisions (e.g., fixed deductions and exemptions). Unexpected inflation creates arbitrary redistributions from creditors to debtors, and this introduces risk into borrowing and lending, making interest rates and investment more costly. In short, if inflation is other than low and stable, economic life becomes at best inconvenient and at worst (as in a hyperinflation) dysfunctional. See N. Gregory Mankiw, 2013, *Macroeconomics*, 8th ed., Chap. 5 (New York: Worth).
[13] This evidence is merely suggestive: high inflation and slow growth may each be caused by other factors, such as weak institutions. Some studies have used sophisticated econometrics to address this problem. See Stanley Fischer, 1993, "The Role of Macroeconomic Factors in Growth," *Journal of Monetary Economics*, 32, 485–511; Robert J. Barro, 1997, *Determinants of Economic Growth* (Cambridge, Mass.: MIT Press); Michael Bruno and William Easterly, 1998, "Inflation Crises and Long-Run Growth," *Journal of Monetary Economics*, 41, 3–26.

themselves in the short run. Long-run nominal anchoring and short-run flexibility are the characteristics of the policy framework that economists call the **monetary regime.** In this section, we examine different types of monetary regimes and what they mean for the exchange rate.

The Long Run: The Nominal Anchor

Which variables could policy makers use as anchors to achieve an inflation objective in the long run? To answer this key question, all we have to do is go back and rearrange the equations for relative PPP at Equation (14-2), the quantity theory in rates of change at Equation (14-6), and the Fisher effect at Equation (14-8), to obtain alternative expressions for the rate of inflation in the home country. To emphasize that these findings apply generally to all countries, we re-label the countries Home (H) and Foreign (F) instead of United States and Europe.

The three main nominal anchor choices that emerge are as follows:

■ **Exchange rate target:** Relative PPP at Equation (14-2) says that the rate of depreciation equals the inflation differential, or $\Delta E_{H/F}/E_{H/F} = \pi_H - \pi_F$. Rearranging this expression suggests one way to anchor inflation is as follows:

$$\underbrace{\pi_H}_{\text{Inflation}} = \underbrace{\frac{\Delta E_{H/F}}{E_{H/F}}}_{\substack{\text{Rate of} \\ \text{depreciation} \\ | \\ \boxed{\text{Anchor variable}}}} + \underbrace{\pi_F}_{\substack{\text{Foreign} \\ \text{inflation}}}$$

Relative PPP says that home inflation equals the rate of depreciation plus foreign inflation. A simple rule would be to set the rate of depreciation equal to a constant. Under a fixed exchange rate, that constant is set at zero (a peg). Under a crawl, it is a nonzero constant. Alternatively, there may be room for movement about a target (a band). Or there may be a vague goal to allow the exchange rate "limited flexibility." Such policies can deliver stable home inflation if PPP works well and if policy makers keep their commitment. The drawback is the final term in the equation: PPP implies that over the long run the home country "imports" inflation from the foreign country over and above the chosen rate of depreciation. For example, under a peg, if foreign inflation rises by 1% per year, then so, too, does home inflation. Thus, countries almost invariably peg to a country with a reputation for price stability (e.g., the United States). This is a common policy choice: fixed exchange rates of some form are in use in more than half of the world's countries.

■ **Money supply target:** The quantity theory suggests another way to anchor because the fundamental equation for the price level in the monetary approach says that inflation equals the excess of the rate of money supply growth over and above the rate of real income growth:

$$\underbrace{\pi_H}_{\text{Inflation}} = \underbrace{\mu_H}_{\substack{\text{Money supply growth} \\ | \\ \boxed{\text{Anchor variable}}}} - \underbrace{g_H}_{\text{Real output growth}}$$

A simple rule of this sort is: set the growth rate of the money supply equal to a constant, say, 2% a year. The printing presses should be put on automatic pilot, and no human interference should be allowed. Essentially, the central bank is run by robots. This would be difficult to implement. Again the drawback is the final term in the previous equation: real income growth can be unstable. In periods of high growth, inflation will be below the desired level. In periods of low growth, inflation will be above the desired level. For this reason, money supply targets are waning in popularity or are used in conjunction with other targets. For example, the European Central Bank claims to use monetary growth rates as a partial guide to policy, but nobody is quite sure how serious it is.

■ **Inflation target plus interest rate policy:** The Fisher effect suggests yet another anchoring method:

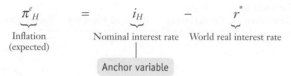

$$\underbrace{\pi^e_H}_{\substack{\text{Inflation} \\ \text{(expected)}}} = \underbrace{i_H}_{\text{Nominal interest rate}} - \underbrace{r^*}_{\text{World real interest rate}}$$

Anchor variable

The Fisher effect says that home inflation is the home nominal interest rate minus the foreign real interest rate. If the latter can be assumed to be constant, then as long as the average home nominal interest rate is kept stable, inflation can also be kept stable. This type of nominal anchoring framework is an increasingly common policy choice. Assuming a stable world real interest rate is not a bad assumption. (And in principle, the target level of the nominal interest rate could be adjusted if necessary.) More or less flexible versions of inflation targeting can be implemented. A central bank could in theory set the nominal interest rate at a fixed level at all times, but such rigidity is rarely seen and central banks usually adjust interest rates in the short run to meet other goals. For example, if the world real interest rate is $r^* = 2.5\%$, and the country's long-run inflation target is 2%, then its long-run nominal interest rate ought to be on average equal to 4.5% (because 2.5% = 4.5% − 2%). This would be termed the *neutral* level of the nominal interest rate. But in the short run, the central bank might desire to use some flexibility to set interest rates above or below this neutral level. How much flexibility is a matter of policy choice, as is the question of what economic objectives should drive deviations from the neutral rate (e.g., inflation performance alone, or other factors like output and employment that we shall consider in later chapters).

The Choice of a Nominal Anchor and Its Implications Under the assumptions we have made, any of the three nominal anchor choices are valid. If a particular long-run inflation objective is to be met, then, all else equal, the first equation says it will be consistent with one particular rate of depreciation; the second equation says it will be consistent with one particular rate of money supply growth; the third equation says it will be consistent with one particular rate of interest. But if policy makers announced targets for all three variables, they would be able to match all three consistently only by chance. Two observations follow.

First, using more than one target may be problematic. Under a fixed exchange rate regime, policy makers cannot employ any target other than the exchange rate. However, they may be able to use a mix of different targets if they adopt an intermediate regime,

TABLE 14-2

Exchange Rate Regimes and Nominal Anchors This table illustrates the possible exchange rate regimes that are consistent with various types of nominal anchors. Countries that are dollarized or in a currency union have a "superfixed" exchange rate target. Pegs, bands, and crawls also target the exchange rate. Managed floats have no preset path for the exchange rate, which allows other targets to be employed. Countries that float freely or independently are judged to pay no serious attention to exchange rate targets; if they have anchors, they will involve monetary targets or inflation targets with an interest rate policy. The countries with "freely falling" exchange rates have no serious target and have high rates of inflation and depreciation. It should be noted that many countries engage in implicit targeting (e.g., inflation targeting) without announcing an explicit target and that some countries may use a mix of more than one target.

	COMPATIBLE EXCHANGE RATE REGIMES				
Type of Nominal Anchor	Countries without a Currency of Their Own	Pegs/ Bands/Crawls	Managed Floating	Freely Floating	Freely Falling (rapid depreciation)
Exchange rate target	✔	✔	✔		
Money supply target			✔	✔	
Inflation target (plus interest rate policy)			✔	✔	
None				✔	✔

such as a managed exchange rate with limited flexibility. Table 14-2 illustrates the ways in which the choice of a target as a nominal anchor affects the choice of exchange rate regime. Obviously, these are not independent choices. But a variety of choices do exist. Thus, *nominal anchoring is possible with a variety of exchange rate regimes.*

Second, whatever target choice is made, a country that commits to a target as a way of nominal anchoring is committing itself to set future money supplies and interest rates in such a way as to meet the target. Only one path for future policy will be compatible with the target in the long run. Thus, *a country with a nominal anchor sacrifices monetary policy autonomy in the long run.*

APPLICATION

Nominal Anchors in Theory and Practice

An appreciation of the importance of nominal anchors has transformed monetary policy making and inflation performance throughout the global economy in recent decades.

In the 1970s, most of the world was struggling with high inflation. An economic slowdown prompted central banks everywhere to loosen monetary policy. In advanced countries, a move to floating exchange rates allowed great freedom for them to loosen their monetary policy. Developing countries had already proven vulnerable to high inflation and now many of them were exposed to even worse inflation. Those who were pegged to major currencies imported high inflation via PPP. Those who weren't pegged struggled to find a credible nominal anchor as they faced economic downturns of their own. High oil prices everywhere contributed to inflationary pressure.

TABLE 14-3

Global Disinflation Cross-country data from 1980 to 2012 show the gradual reduction in the annual rate of inflation around the world. This disinflation process began in the advanced economies in the early 1980s. The emerging markets and developing countries suffered from even higher rates of inflation, although these finally began to fall in the 1990s.

	ANNUAL INFLATION RATE (%)						
	1980–1984	1985–1989	1990–1994	1995–1999	2000–2004	2005–2009	2010–2012
World	14.1%	15.5	30.4	8.4	3.9	4.0	4.2
Advanced economies	8.7	3.9	3.8	2.0	1.8	2.0	2.2
Emerging markets and developing countries	31.4	48.0	53.2	13.1	5.6	6.5	6.4

Source: Kenneth Rogoff, 2003, "Globalization and Global Disinflation," Economic Review, Federal Reserve Bank of Kansas City, IV, 45–78. Updated for the years 2005 to 2012 using the IMF World Economic Outlook database.

In the 1980s, inflationary pressure continued in many developed countries, and in many developing countries high levels of inflation, and even hyperinflations, were not uncommon. Governments were forced to respond to public demands for a more stable inflation environment. In the 1990s, policies designed to create effective nominal anchors were put in place in many countries, and these have endured to the present.

One study found that the use of explicit targets grew markedly in the 1990s, replacing regimes in which there had previously been no explicit nominal anchor. The number of countries in the study with exchange rate targets increased from 30 to 47. The number with money targets increased from 18 to 39. The number with inflation targets increased most dramatically, almost sevenfold, from 8 to 54. Many countries had more than one target in use: in 1998, 55% of the sample announced an explicit target (or monitoring range) for more than one of the exchange rate, money, and inflation. These shifts have persisted. As of 2010, more than a decade later, there were still more than 50 inflation-targeting countries (many now part of the single Eurozone block), and there were more than 80 countries pursuing some kind of exchange rate target via a currency board, peg, band or crawl type arrangement.[14]

Looking back from the present we can see that most, but not all, of those policies have turned out to be credible, too, thanks to political developments in many countries that have fostered **central bank independence.** Independent central banks stand apart from the interference of politicians: they have operational freedom to try to achieve the inflation target, and they may even play a role in setting that target.

Overall, these efforts are judged to have achieved some success, although in many countries inflation had already been brought down substantially in the early to mid-1980s before inflation targets and institutional changes were implemented. Table 14-3 shows a steady decline in average levels of inflation since the early 1980s. The lowest levels of inflation are

---

[14] On the 1990s see Gabriel Sterne, 1999, "The Use of Explicit Targets for Monetary Policy: Practical Experiences of 91 Economies in the 1990s," *Bank of England Quarterly Bulletin,* 39(3), 272–281. Data for circa 2010 from www.centralbanknews.info and from exchange rate classifications in the previous chapter.

seen in the advanced economies, although developing countries have also started to make some limited progress. In the industrial countries, central bank independence is now commonplace (it was not in the 1970s), but in developing countries it is still relatively rare.

Still, one can have too much of a good thing, and the crisis of 2008–2010 prompted some second thoughts about inflation targets. Typically, such targets have been set at about 2% in developed countries, and with a world real interest rate of 2% this implies a neutral nominal interest rate of 4%. In terms of having room to maneuver, this rate permits central banks to temporarily cut their interest rates up to four percentage points below the neutral level. Prior to the crisis this range was considered ample room for central banks to take short-run actions as needed (e.g., to stimulate output or the rate of inflation if either fell too low). In the crisis, however, central banks soon hit the lower bound of zero rates and could not prevent severe output losses and declines in inflation rates to low or, at times, negative levels (*deflation*). As Irving Fisher famously noted, deflation is very damaging economically—it drives up real interest rates when nominal rates can fall no further as an offset, and falling prices make the real burden of nominal debts higher. These problems have led some economists, among them the IMF's Chief Economist, Olivier Blanchard, to question whether inflation targets should be set higher (e.g., at 4% rather than 2%).[15] The idea received a lukewarm reception, however: moving to a higher inflation target is easy in principle, but many feared its potential abuse would risk the hard-won credibility gains that central banks have earned for themselves in the last three decades. Indeed, even as inflation rates fell almost to zero in major economies like the United States and Eurozone, many central bankers continued to speak of their vigilance in guarding against inflation. ■

6 Conclusions

This chapter emphasized the determinants of exchange rates in the long run using the monetary approach. We employed PPP and a simple monetary model (the quantity theory) to study an equilibrium in which goods are arbitraged and prices are flexible. Under these assumptions, in the home country, changes in the money supply pass through into proportional changes in the price level and the exchange rate.

We also found that uncovered interest parity and PPP implied that real interest rates are equalized across countries. This helped us develop a monetary model that was more complex—and more realistic—because it allowed money demand to fluctuate in response to changes in the interest rate. In that setting, increases in money growth lead to higher inflation and a higher nominal interest rate and, hence, via decreases in money demand, to even higher price levels. Still, the same basic intuition holds, and one-time changes in the money supply still lead to proportional changes in prices and exchange rates.

The monetary approach to exchange rates provides a basis for certain kinds of forecasting and policy analysis using the flexible-price model in the long run. But such forecasts matter even in the short run because today's spot exchange rate depends, like all asset prices, on the exchange rate expected to prevail in the future. To make these connections clear, in the next chapter we bring together the key ideas of arbitrage (from the previous chapter) and expectations (from this chapter) to form a complete model of the exchange rate.

---

[15] Olivier Blanchard, Giovanni Dell'Ariccia, and Paolo Mauro, 2010, "Rethinking Macroeconomic Policy," *IMF Staff Position Note*, SPN/10/03.

KEY POINTS

1. Purchasing power parity (PPP) implies that the exchange rate should equal the relative price level in the two countries, and the real exchange rate should equal 1.

2. Evidence for PPP is weak in the short run but more favorable in the long run. In the short run, deviations are common and changes in the real exchange rate do occur. The failure of PPP in the short run is primarily the result of market frictions, imperfections that limit arbitrage, and price stickiness.

3. A simple monetary model (the quantity theory) explains price levels in terms of money supply levels and real income levels. Because PPP can explain exchange rates in terms of price levels, the two together can be used to develop a monetary approach to the exchange rate.

4. If we can forecast money supply and income, we can use the monetary approach to forecast the level of the exchange rate at any time in the future. However, the monetary approach is valid only under the assumption that prices are flexible. This assumption is more likely to hold in the long run, so the monetary approach is not useful in the short run forecast. Evidence for PPP and the monetary approach is more favorable in the long run.

5. PPP theory, combined with uncovered interest parity, leads to the strong implications of the Fisher effect (interest differentials between countries should equal inflation differentials). The Fisher effect says that changes in local inflation rates pass through one for one into changes in local nominal interest rates. The result implies real interest parity (expected real interest rates should be equalized across countries). Because these results rest on PPP, they should be viewed only as long-run results, and the evidence is somewhat favorable.

6. We can augment the simple monetary model (quantity theory) to allow for the demand for real money balances to decrease as the nominal interest rate rises. This leads to the general monetary model. Its predictions are similar to those of the simple model, except that a one-time rise in money growth rates leads to a one-time rise in inflation, which leads to a one-time drop in real money demand, which in turn causes a one-time jump in the price level and the exchange rate.

7. The monetary approach to exchange rate determination in the long run has implications for economic policy. Policy makers and the public generally prefer a low-inflation environment. Various policies based on exchange rates, money growth, or interest rates have been proposed as nominal anchors. Recent decades have seen a worldwide decline in inflation thanks to the explicit recognition of the need for nominal anchors.

KEY TERMS

PROBLEMS

1. Suppose that two countries, Vietnam and Côte d'Ivoire, produce coffee. The currency unit used in Vietnam is the dong (VND). Côte d'Ivoire is a member of Communauté Financière Africaine (CFA), a currency union of West African countries that use the CFA franc (XOF). In Vietnam, coffee sells for 5,000 dong (VND) per pound. The exchange rate is 30 VND per 1 CFA franc, $E_{VND/XOF} = 30$.

   a. If the law of one price holds, what is the price of coffee in Côte d'Ivoire, measured in CFA francs?

   b. Assume the price of coffee in Côte d'Ivoire is actually 160 CFA francs per pound of coffee. Compute the relative price of coffee in Côte d'Ivoire versus Vietnam. Where will coffee traders buy coffee? Where will they sell coffee in this case? How will these transactions affect the price of coffee in Vietnam? In Côte d'Ivoire?

2. Consider each of the following goods and services. For each, identify whether the law of one price will hold, and state whether the relative price $q^g_{US/Foreign}$ is greater than, less than, or equal to 1. Explain your answer in terms of the assumptions we make when using the law of one price.

   a. Rice traded freely in the United States and Canada

   b. Sugar traded in the United States and Mexico; the U.S. government imposes a quota on sugar imports into the United States

   c. The McDonald's Big Mac sold in the United States and Japan

   d. Haircuts in the United States and the United Kingdom

3. Use the table that follows to answer this question. Treat the country listed as the home country, and treat the United States as the foreign country. Suppose the cost of the market basket in the United States is $P_{US} = \$190$. Check to see whether PPP holds for each of the countries listed, and determine whether we should expect a real appreciation or real depreciation for each country (relative to the United States) in the long run. For the answer, create a table similar to the one shown and fill in the blank cells. (*Hint:* Use a spreadsheet application such as Excel.)

Country (currency measured in FX units)	Per $, $E_{FX/\$}$	Price of Market Basket (in FX)	Price of U.S. Basket in FX (P_{US} times $E_{FX/\$}$)	Real Exchange Rate, $q_{COUNTRY/US}$	Does PPP Hold? (yes/no)	Is FX Currency Overvalued or Undervalued?	Is FX Currency Expected to Have Real Appreciation or Depreciation?
Brazil (real)	2.1893	520					
India (rupee)	46.6672	12,000					
Mexico (peso)	11.0131	1,800					
South Africa (rand)	6.9294	800					
Zimbabwe (Z$)	101,347	4,000,000					

4. Table 14-1 in the text shows the percentage undervaluation or overvaluation in the Big Mac, based on exchange rates in July 2012. Suppose purchasing power parity holds in the long run, so that these deviations would be expected to disappear. Suppose the local currency prices of the Big Mac remained unchanged. Exchange rates one year later on July 1, 2013, were as follows (*Source:* ft.com):

Country	Per U.S. $
Australia (A$)	1.08
Brazil (real)	2.23
Canada (C$)	1.05
Denmark (krone)	5.72
Eurozone (euro)	0.77
India (rupee)	59.43
Japan (yen)	99.75
Mexico (peso)	12.89
Sweden (krona)	6.67

Based on these data and Table 14-1, calculate the change in the exchange rate from July 2012 to July 2013, and state whether the direction of change was consistent with the PPP-implied exchange rate using the Big Mac Index. How might you explain the failure of the Big Mac Index to correctly predict the change in the nominal exchange rate between July 2012 and July 2013?

5. You are given the following information. The current dollar-pound exchange rate is $2 per pound. A U.S. basket that costs $100 would cost $120 in the United Kingdom. For the next year, the Fed is predicted to keep U.S. inflation at 2% and the Bank of England is predicted to keep U.K. inflation at 3%. The speed of convergence to absolute PPP is 15% per year.

a. What is the expected U.S. minus U.K. inflation differential for the coming year?
b. What is the current U.S. real exchange rate $q_{US/UK}$ with the United Kingdom?
c. How much is the dollar overvalued/undervalued?
d. What do you predict the U.S. real exchange rate with the United Kingdom will be in one year's time?
e. What is the expected rate of real depreciation for the United States (versus the United Kingdom)?
f. What is the expected rate of nominal depreciation for the United States (versus the United Kingdom)?
g. What do you predict will be the dollar price of one pound a year from now?

6. Describe how each of the following factors might explain why PPP is a better guide for exchange rate movements in the long run versus the short run: (i) transactions costs, (ii) nontraded goods, (iii) imperfect competition, (iv) price stickiness. As markets become increasingly integrated, do you suspect PPP will become a more useful guide in the future? Why or why not?

7. Consider two countries: Japan and Korea. In 1996 Japan experienced relatively slow output growth (1%), while Korea had relatively robust output growth (6%). Suppose the Bank of Japan allowed the money supply to grow by 2% each year, while the Bank of Korea chose to maintain relatively high money growth of 12% per year.

For the following questions, use the simple monetary model (where L is constant). You will find it easiest to treat Korea as the home country and Japan as the foreign country.

a. What is the inflation rate in Korea? In Japan?

b. What is the expected rate of depreciation in the Korean won relative to the Japanese yen (¥)?

c. Suppose the Bank of Korea increases the money growth rate from 12% to 15%. If nothing in Japan changes, what is the new inflation rate in Korea?

d. Using time series diagrams, illustrate how this increase in the money growth rate affects the money supply M_K, Korea's interest rate, prices P_K, real money supply, and $E_{won/¥}$ over time. (Plot each variable on the vertical axis and time on the horizontal axis.)

e. Suppose the Bank of Korea wants to maintain an exchange rate peg with the Japanese yen. What money growth rate would the Bank of Korea have to choose to keep the value of the won fixed relative to the yen?

f. Suppose the Bank of Korea sought to implement policy that would cause the Korean won to appreciate relative to the Japanese yen. What ranges of the money growth rate (assuming positive values) would allow the Bank of Korea to achieve this objective?

8. This question uses the general monetary model, where L is no longer assumed constant, and money demand is inversely related to the nominal interest rate. Consider the same scenario described at the beginning of the previous question. In addition, the bank deposits in Japan pay a 3% interest rate, $i_¥ = 3\%$.

a. Compute the interest rate paid on Korean deposits.

b. Using the definition of the real interest rate (nominal interest rate adjusted for inflation), show that the real interest rate in Korea is equal to the real interest rate in Japan. (Note that the inflation rates you computed in the previous question will be the same in this question.)

c. Suppose the Bank of Korea increases the money growth rate from 12% to 15% and the inflation rate rises proportionately (one for one) with this increase. If the nominal interest rate in Japan remains unchanged, what happens to the interest rate paid on Korean deposits?

d. Using time series diagrams, illustrate how this increase in the money growth rate affects the money supply M_K; Korea's interest rate; prices P_K; real money supply; and $E_{won/¥}$ over time. (Plot each variable on the vertical axis and time on the horizontal axis.)

9. Both advanced economics and developing countries have experienced a decrease in inflation since the 1980s (see Table 14-3 in the text). This question considers how the choice of policy regime has influenced such global disinflation. Use the monetary model to answer this question.

a. The Swiss Central Bank currently targets its money growth rate to achieve policy objectives. Suppose Switzerland has output growth of 3% and money growth of 8% each year. What is Switzerland's inflation rate in this case? Describe how the Swiss Central Bank could achieve an inflation rate of 2% in the long run through the use of a nominal anchor.

b. Like the Federal Reserve, the Reserve Bank of New Zealand uses an interest rate target.

Suppose the Reserve Bank of New Zealand maintains a 6% interest rate target and the world *real* interest rate is 1.5%. What is the New Zealand inflation rate in the long run? In 1997 New Zealand adopted a policy agreement that required the bank to maintain an inflation rate no higher than 2.5%. What interest rate targets would achieve this objective?

c. The central bank of Lithuania maintains an exchange rate band relative to the euro. This is a prerequisite for joining the Eurozone. Lithuania must keep its exchange rate within ±15% of the central parity of 3.4528 litas per euro. Compute the exchange rate values corresponding to the upper and lower edges of this band. Suppose PPP holds. Assuming Eurozone inflation is currently 2% per year and inflation in Lithuania is 5%, compute the rate of depreciation of the lita. Will Lithuania be able to maintain the band requirement? For how long? Does your answer depend on where in the band the exchange rate currently sits? A primary objective of the European Central Bank is price stability (low inflation) in the current and future Eurozone. Is an exchange rate band a necessary or sufficient condition for the attainment of this objective?

10. Several countries that have experienced hyperinflation adopt dollarization as a way to control domestic inflation. For example, Ecuador has used the U.S. dollar as its domestic currency since 2000. What does dollarization imply about the exchange rate between Ecuador and the United States? Why might countries experiencing hyperinflation adopt dollarization? Why might they do this rather than just fixing their exchange rate?

11. You are the central banker for a country that is considering the adoption of a new nominal anchor. When you take the position as chairperson, the inflation rate is 4% and your position as the central bank chairperson requires that you achieve a 2.5% inflation target within the next year. The economy's growth in real output is currently 3%. The world real interest rate is currently 1.5%. The currency used in your country is the lira. *Assume prices are flexible.*

a. Why is having a nominal anchor important for you to achieve the inflation target? What is the drawback of using a nominal anchor?

b. What is the growth rate of the money supply in this economy? If you choose to adopt a money supply target, which money supply growth rate will allow you to meet your inflation target?

c. Suppose the inflation rate in the United States is currently 2% and you adopt an exchange rate target relative to the U.S. dollar. Compute the percent appreciation/depreciation in the lira needed for you to achieve your inflation target. Will the lira appreciate or depreciate relative to the U.S. dollar?

d. Your final option is to achieve your inflation target using interest rate policy. Using the Fisher equation, compute the current nominal interest rate in your country. What nominal interest rate will allow you to achieve the inflation target?

NET WORK

The Big Mac Index isn't the only popular PPP gauge. In 2004, the *Economist* made a Starbucks Tall Latte Index, which you can try to find online. (*Hint:* Search "cnn tall latte index.") In 2007, two new indices appeared: the iPod Index (based on the local prices of Apple's iPod music player) and iTunes Index (based on the local prices of a single song downloaded from Apple's iTunes store). Find those indices online and the discussions surrounding them. (*Hint:* Search "ipod itunes index big mac.") Do you think that either the iPod Index or iTunes Index is a better guide to currency overvaluation/undervaluation than the Big Mac Index? Explain your answer.

Visit the websites of some central banks around the world, for example, the U.S. Federal Reserve (http://www.federalreserve.gov/) and the European Central Bank (http://www.ecb.int/). Read their main statements of policy. Try to find out what their policy goals are *in the long run*. Who sets them? Is there more than one goal? What about a nominal anchor—Is controlling inflation a long-run goal? If so, what policy is used to try to ensure that the long-run inflation goal will be met? In the short run, is the main tool they use for implementing their policy the quantity of money, the exchange rate, or the interest rate?

15

Exchange Rates II: The Asset Approach in the Short Run

The long run is a misleading guide to current affairs. In the long run we are all dead. Economists set themselves too easy, too useless a task if in tempestuous seasons they can only tell us that when the storm is past the ocean is flat again.

John Maynard Keynes, *A Tract on Monetary Reform*, 1923

As we saw in the last chapter, the monetary approach to exchange rates may work in the long run, but it is a poor guide to what happens in the short run. To recap this distinction, let's return to the Canada–U.S. comparison with which we opened the last chapter—only this time we'll focus on developments in the short run.

From March 2005 to March 2006, the Canadian price level (measured by the consumer price index) rose from 126.5 to 129.3, an increase of 2.2%. The U.S. price level rose from 193.3 to 199.8, an increase of 3.4%. U.S. prices therefore increased 1.2% more than Canadian prices. But over the same period, the loonie (Canadian dollar) rose in value from $0.8267 to $0.8568, an appreciation of 3.6%.[1]

Because Canadian baskets cost 2.2% more in loonie terms, *and* because each loonie cost 3.6% more in U.S. dollar terms, the change in the U.S. dollar price of the Canadian basket was approximately the sum of these two changes, or about 5.8%. Over the same period, however, the U.S. dollar price of U.S. baskets rose only 3.4%. Taking the difference, Canadian baskets ended up 2.4% more expensive than U.S. baskets, meaning that the U.S. *real* exchange rate with Canada rose by 2.4%, a real depreciation. This pattern was not unusual. In the previous year from March 2004 to March 2005, the real depreciation had been even larger, at 7.5%, so over two years Canadian goods rose in price by about 10% compared with U.S. goods.

---

[1] Data for this example are taken from the Bank of Canada and U.S. Bureau of Labor Statistics.

As we have already noted, evidence of this kind suggests that substantial deviations from purchasing power parity (PPP) occur in the short run: the same basket of goods generally does not cost the same everywhere at all times. These short-run failures of the monetary approach prompted economists to develop an alternative theory to explain exchange rates in the short run: the **asset approach to exchange rates,** the subject of this chapter.

The asset approach is based on the idea that currencies are assets. The price of the asset in this case is the spot exchange rate, the price of one unit of foreign exchange. To explain the determination of exchange rates in the short run, we can draw on what we learned about arbitrage. Recall from Chapter 13 that arbitrage plays a major role in the foreign exchange (forex, or FX) market by forcing the expected returns of two assets in different currencies to be equal. This insight led us to derive the uncovered interest parity (UIP) condition. Because it characterizes the forex market equilibrium in the short run, UIP is further explored and extensively applied in this chapter.

The asset approach differs from the monetary approach in its time frame and assumptions. The monetary approach applies more to a long run of several years or even decades; the asset approach applies more to a short run of a few weeks or months, or maybe a year or so at most. In the monetary approach, we treat goods prices as perfectly flexible, a plausible assumption in the long run; in the asset approach, we assume that goods prices are sticky, a more appropriate assumption in the short run. Each theory is valid but only in the right context. Thus, rather than supplanting the monetary approach, the asset approach complements it, and provides us with the final building blocks necessary to construct a complete theory of exchange rates.

So far, we have assumed that exchange rates are determined by market forces in the goods, money, and forex markets—so our theory is relevant when the exchange rate floats, and the authorities leave it to find its own market-determined level. Can our theory also tell us anything about fixed exchange rates? Yes. At the end of the chapter, we see how the same theoretical framework can be applied to a fixed exchange rate regime.

1 Exchange Rates and Interest Rates in the Short Run: UIP and FX Market Equilibrium

To begin our study of exchange rates in the short run, let's recap the crucial equilibrium condition for the forex market. In our earlier presentation, we considered a U.S. investor with two alternative investment strategies: a one-year investment in a U.S. dollar account with an interest rate $i_\$$, or a one-year investment in a euro account with an interest rate $i_€$. Here are the essentials.

Risky Arbitrage

For the case of risky arbitrage, the forex market is in equilibrium when there is no expected difference in the rates of return on each type of currency investment in the two countries or locations. As before, we assume Home is the United States (U.S.); and Foreign is Europe (EUR, meaning the Eurozone). As we saw in the approximate uncovered interest parity condition—Equation (13-3), and repeated in this section as Equation (15-1)—this outcome requires that the dollar rate of return on the home investment (the dollar deposit) equal the expected dollar rate of return on the foreign investment (the euro deposit),

$$\underbrace{i_\$}_{\substack{\text{Interest rate}\\\text{on dollar deposits}\\=\\\text{Dollar rate of return}\\\text{on dollar deposits}}} = \underbrace{\underbrace{i_\euro}_{\substack{\text{Interest rate}\\\text{on euro deposits}}} + \underbrace{\frac{(E^e_{\$/\euro} - E_{\$/\euro})}{E_{\$/\euro}}}_{\substack{\text{Expected rate of depreciation}\\\text{of the dollar}}}}_{\substack{\text{Expected dollar rate of return}\\\text{on euro deposits}}} \qquad (15\text{-}1)$$

where each interest rate is an annual rate, $E_{\$/\euro}$ is today's exchange rate (the spot rate), and $E^e_{\$/\euro}$ is the expected future exchange rate that will prevail one year ahead.

The uncovered interest parity (UIP) equation is the **fundamental equation of the asset approach to exchange rates,** and from now on, we use it in the form of Equation (15-1). As we have seen, by rearranging this equation, we can solve it for the spot exchange rate, *if we know all of the other variables.* Thus, the asset approach employs the UIP equation to determine today's spot exchange rate, as illustrated in Figure 15-1. *Note that the theory is useful only if we know the future expected exchange rate and the short-term interest rates.* Where does that knowledge come from?

Short-Term Interest Rates The first assumption is that we know today's interest rates on deposit accounts in each country, the dollar interest rate $i_\$$, and the euro account interest rate $i_\euro$. Market participants can observe these short-term interest rates. But how are these interest rates determined, and, in particular, what is their relation to economic policy? In the next section, we explore that question to develop a fuller understanding of how exchange rates are determined.

Exchange Rate Expectations The second assumption is that we know the forecast of the future level of the exchange rate $E^e_{\$/\euro}$. The asset approach itself does not provide the answer, so we must look elsewhere. Where to look? In the long-run monetary approach to the exchange rate presented in the previous chapter. We can now see how the asset approach and monetary approach fit together.

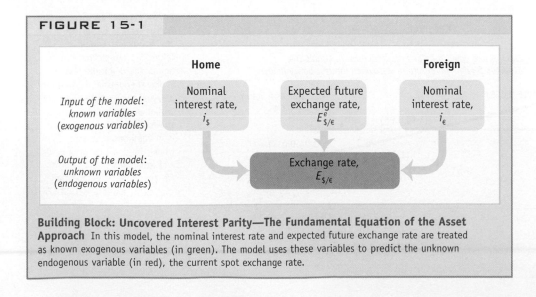

FIGURE 15-1

Building Block: Uncovered Interest Parity—The Fundamental Equation of the Asset Approach In this model, the nominal interest rate and expected future exchange rate are treated as known exogenous variables (in green). The model uses these variables to predict the unknown endogenous variable (in red), the current spot exchange rate.

Equilibrium in the FX Market: An Example

To explore the concepts we've just studied, let's work through a numerical example to show how equilibrium in the forex market is determined.

Suppose that the current European interest rate $i_{\mathbb{e}}$ is 3%, and the current U.S. interest rate $i_{\$}$ is 5%. Suppose also that we have made a forecast (using the long-run monetary model of exchange rates) that the expected future exchange rate $E^e_{\$/\mathbb{e}}$ (in one year's time) is 1.224 dollars per euro.

Now examine Table 15-1 to see how, for various values of the spot exchange rate $E_{\$/\mathbb{e}}$, we can calculate the domestic rate of return and expected foreign rate of return in U.S. dollars. (Remember that 5% = 0.05, 3% = 0.03, etc.) As you work through the table, remember that the foreign returns have two components: one due to the European interest rate $i_{\mathbb{e}}$ and the other due to the expected rate of depreciation of the dollar, as in Equation (15-1).

Figure 15-2 presents an **FX market diagram,** a graphical representation of these returns in the forex market. We plot the expected domestic and foreign returns (on the vertical axis) against today's spot exchange rate (on the horizontal axis). The domestic dollar return (*DR*) (which is Home's nominal interest rate) is fixed at 5% = 0.05 and is independent of the spot exchange rate.

According to Equation (15-1), the foreign expected dollar return (*FR*) depends on the spot exchange rate and it varies as shown in Table 15-1. For example, we can infer from the table that a spot exchange rate of 1.224 implies a foreign return of 3% = 0.03. Hence, the point (1.224, 0.03) is on the *FR* line in Figure 15-2. This is the special case in which there is no expected depreciation (spot and expected future exchange rates equal 1.224), so the foreign return equals the foreign country's interest rate, 3%.

More generally, we see that the foreign return falls as the spot exchange rate $E_{\$/\mathbb{e}}$ increases, all else equal. Why? This is clear mathematically from the right side of Equation (15-1). The intuition is as follows. If the dollar depreciates today, $E_{\$/\mathbb{e}}$ rises; a euro investment is then a more expensive (and, thus, less attractive) proposition, all else

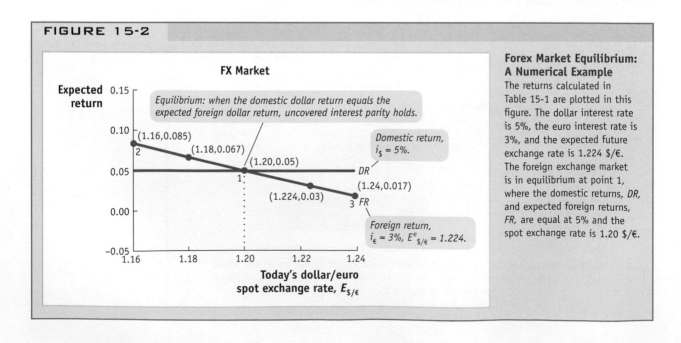

FIGURE 15-2

FX Market

Equilibrium: when the domestic dollar return equals the expected foreign dollar return, uncovered interest parity holds.

Domestic return, $i_{\$}$ = 5%.

Foreign return, $i_{\mathbb{e}}$ = 3%, $E^e_{\$/\mathbb{e}}$ = 1.224.

Forex Market Equilibrium: A Numerical Example
The returns calculated in Table 15-1 are plotted in this figure. The dollar interest rate is 5%, the euro interest rate is 3%, and the expected future exchange rate is 1.224 $/€. The foreign exchange market is in equilibrium at point 1, where the domestic returns, *DR*, and expected foreign returns, *FR*, are equal at 5% and the spot exchange rate is 1.20 $/€.

TABLE 15-1

Interest Rates, Exchange Rates, Expected Returns, and FX Market Equilibrium: A Numerical Example The foreign exchange (FX) market is in equilibrium when the domestic and foreign returns are equal. In the example shown in this table, the dollar interest rate is 5% (column 1), the euro interest rate is 3% (column 2), and the expected future exchange rate (one year ahead) is $E^e_{\$/€} = 1.224$ \$/€ (column 4). The rows in the table correspond to a range of possible spot exchange rates shown in column (3), and these spot rates in turn imply the expected depreciation rates in column (5) and the expected foreign returns in column (6). The unique equilibrium is highlighted, where both domestic and expected foreign returns are 5% in annual dollar terms, and the spot rate is 1.20 \$/€. Figures are rounded in the table. Figure 15-2 plots the domestic and foreign returns (columns 1 and 6) against the spot exchange rate (column 3).

	(1)	(2)	(3)	(4)	(5)	(6) = (2) + (5)
	Interest Rate on Dollar Deposits (annual)	Interest Rate on Euro Deposits (annual)	Spot Exchange Rate (today)	Expected Future Exchange Rate (in 1 year)	Expected Euro Appreciation against Dollar (in 1 year)	Expected Dollar Return on Euro Deposits (annual)
	Domestic Return (\$)					Foreign Expected Return (\$)
	$i_\$$	$i_€$	$E_{\$/€}$	$E^e_{\$/€}$	$\dfrac{E^e_{\$/€} - E_{\$/€}}{E_{\$/€}}$	$i_€ + \dfrac{E^e_{\$/€} - E_{\$/€}}{E_{\$/€}}$
	0.05	0.03	1.16	1.224	0.0552	0.0852
	0.05	0.03	1.18	1.224	0.0373	0.0673
Market equilibrium	0.05	0.03	1.20	1.224	0.02	0.05
	0.05	0.03	1.22	1.224	0.0033	0.0333
	0.05	0.03	1.24	1.224	−0.0129	0.0171

equal. That is, \$1 moved into a European account is worth fewer euros today; this, in turn, leaves fewer euro proceeds in a year's time after euro interest has accrued. If expectations are fixed so that the future euro–dollar exchange rate $E^e_{\$/€}$ is known and unchanged, then those fewer future euros will be worth fewer future dollars. Hence, the foreign return (in dollars) goes down as $E_{\$/€}$ rises, *all else equal*, and the *FR* curve slopes downward.

What is the equilibrium level of the spot exchange rate? According to Table 15-1, the equilibrium exchange rate is 1.20 \$/€. Only at that exchange rate are domestic returns and foreign returns equalized. To illustrate the solution graphically, domestic and foreign returns are plotted in Figure 15-2. The FX market is in equilibrium, and foreign and domestic returns are equal, at point 1 where the *FR* and *DR* curves intersect.

Adjustment to Forex Market Equilibrium

Our forex market equilibrium condition and its graphical representation should now be clear. But how is this equilibrium reached? It turns out that arbitrage automatically pushes the level of the exchange rate toward its equilibrium value.

To see this, suppose that the market is initially out of equilibrium, with the spot $E_{\$/€}$ exchange rate at a level too low, so that the foreign return—the right-hand side of Equation (15-1)—exceeds the domestic return (the left-hand side).

At point 2 in Figure 15-2, foreign returns are well above domestic returns. With the spot exchange rate of 1.16 $/€ and (from Table 15-1) an expected future exchange rate as high as 1.224 $/€, the euro is expected to *appreciate* by 5.5% = 0.055 [=(1.224/1.16) − 1]. In addition, euros earn at an interest rate of 3%, for a whopping foreign expected return of 5.5% + 3% = 8.5% = 0.085, which far exceeds the domestic return of 5%. At point 2, in other words, the euro offers too high a return; equivalently, it is too cheap. Traders want to sell dollars and buy euros. These market pressures bid up the price of a euro: the dollar starts to depreciate against the euro, causing $E_{\$/€}$ to rise, which moves foreign and domestic returns into equality and forces the exchange rate back toward equilibrium at point 1.

The same idea applies to a situation in which the spot exchange rate $E_{\$/€}$ is initially too high. At point 3 in Figure 15-2, foreign and domestic returns are not equal: the exchange rate is 1.24 $/€. Given where the exchange rate is expected to be in a year's time (1.224 $/€), paying a high price of 1.24 $/€ today means the euro is expected to *depreciate* by about 1.3% = 0.013 [=1.224/1.24 − 1]. If euro deposits pay 3%, and euros are expected to depreciate 1.3%, this makes for a net foreign return of just 1.7%, well below the domestic return of 5% = 0.05. In other words, at point 3, the euro offers too low a return; equivalently, it is too expensive today. Traders will want to sell euros.

Only at point 1 is the euro trading at a price at which the foreign return equals the domestic return. At point 1, the euro is neither too cheap nor too expensive—its price is just right for uncovered interest parity to hold, for arbitrage to cease, and for the forex market to be in equilibrium.

Changes in Domestic and Foreign Returns and FX Market Equilibrium

When economic conditions change, the two curves depicting domestic and foreign returns shift. In the case of the domestic return curve, the movements are easy to understand because the curve is a horizontal line that intersects the vertical axis at the domestic interest rate. If the domestic interest changes, the curve shifts up or down. Shifts in the foreign returns curve are a bit more complicated because there are two parts to the foreign return: the foreign interest rate plus any expected change in the exchange rate.

To gain greater familiarity with the model, let's see how the FX market example shown in Figure 15-2 responds to three separate shocks:

- A higher domestic interest rate, $i_\$ = 7\%$
- A lower foreign interest rate, $i_€ = 1\%$
- A lower expected future exchange rate, $E^e_{\$/€} = 1.20$ $/€

These three cases are shown in Figure 15-3, panels (a), (b), and (c). In all three cases, the shocks make dollar deposits more attractive than euro deposits, but for different reasons. Regardless of the reason, however, the shocks we examine all lead to dollar appreciations.

A Change in the Domestic Interest Rate In Figure 15-3, panel (a), when $i_\$$ rises to 7%, the domestic return is increased by 2% so the domestic return curve *DR* shifts up by 2% = 0.02 from DR_1 to DR_2. The foreign return is unaffected. Now, at the initial equilibrium spot exchange rate of 1.20 $/€, the domestic return (point 4) is higher than the foreign return. Traders sell euros and buy dollars; the dollar appreciates to 1.177 $/€ at the new equilibrium, point 5. The foreign return and domestic return are equal once again, and UIP holds once more.

FIGURE 15-3

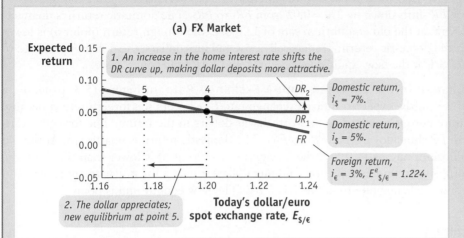

(a) FX Market

1. An increase in the home interest rate shifts the DR curve up, making dollar deposits more attractive.

5   4

DR₂

Domestic return, $i_\$ = 7\%$.

1

DR₁

Domestic return, $i_\$ = 5\%$.

FR

Foreign return, $i_\€ = 3\%$, $E^e_{\$/\€} = 1.224$.

2. The dollar appreciates; new equilibrium at point 5.

Today's dollar/euro spot exchange rate, $E_{\$/\€}$

(a) A Change in the Home Interest Rate A rise in the dollar interest rate from 5% to 7% increases domestic returns, shifting the DR curve up from DR₁ to DR₂. At the initial equilibrium exchange rate of 1.20 $/€ on DR₂, domestic returns are above foreign returns at point 4. Dollar deposits are more attractive and the dollar appreciates from 1.20 $/€ to 1.177 $/€. The new equilibrium is at point 5.

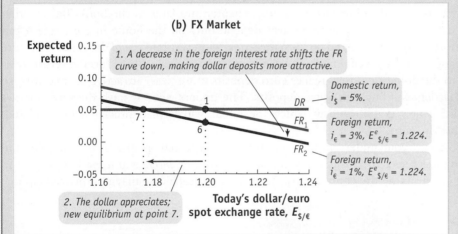

(b) FX Market

1. A decrease in the foreign interest rate shifts the FR curve down, making dollar deposits more attractive.

1

DR

Domestic return, $i_\$ = 5\%$.

7

FR₁

Foreign return, $i_\€ = 3\%$, $E^e_{\$/\€} = 1.224$.

6

FR₂

Foreign return, $i_\€ = 1\%$, $E^e_{\$/\€} = 1.224$.

2. The dollar appreciates; new equilibrium at point 7.

Today's dollar/euro spot exchange rate, $E_{\$/\€}$

(b) A Change in the Foreign Interest Rate A fall in the euro interest rate from 3% to 1% lowers foreign expected dollar returns, shifting the FR curve down from FR₁ to FR₂. At the initial equilibrium exchange rate of 1.20 $/€ on FR₂, foreign returns are below domestic returns at point 6. Dollar deposits are more attractive and the dollar appreciates from 1.20 $/€ to 1.177 $/€. The new equilibrium is at point 7.

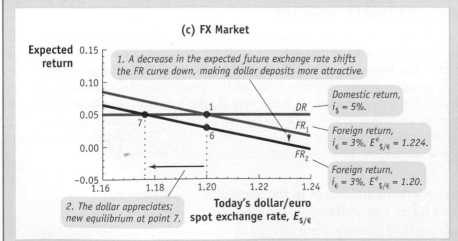

(c) FX Market

1. A decrease in the expected future exchange rate shifts the FR curve down, making dollar deposits more attractive.

1

DR

Domestic return, $i_\$ = 5\%$.

7

FR₁

Foreign return, $i_\€ = 3\%$, $E^e_{\$/\€} = 1.224$.

6

FR₂

Foreign return, $i_\€ = 3\%$, $E^e_{\$/\€} = 1.20$.

2. The dollar appreciates; new equilibrium at point 7.

Today's dollar/euro spot exchange rate, $E_{\$/\€}$

(c) A Change in the Expected Future Exchange Rate A fall in the expected future exchange rate from 1.224 to 1.20 lowers foreign expected dollar returns, shifting the FR curve down from FR₁ to FR₂. At the initial equilibrium exchange rate of 1.20 $/€ on FR₂, foreign returns are below domestic returns at point 6. Dollar deposits are more attractive and the dollar appreciates from 1.20 $/€ to 1.177 $/€. The new equilibrium is at point 7.

A Change in the Foreign Interest Rate In Figure 15-3, panel (b), when i_ϵ falls to 1%, euro deposits now pay a lower interest rate (1% versus 3%). The foreign return curve FR shifts down by $2\% = 0.02$ from FR_1 to FR_2. The domestic return is unaffected. Now, at the old equilibrium rate of 1.20 $/€, the foreign return (point 6) is lower than the domestic return. Traders sell euros and buy dollars; the dollar appreciates to 1.177 $/€ at the new equilibrium, point 7, and UIP holds once more.

A Change in the Expected Future Exchange Rate In Figure 15-3, panel (c), a decrease in the expected future exchange rate $E^e_{\$/\epsilon}$ lowers the foreign return because a future euro is expected to be worth fewer dollars in the future. The foreign return curve FR shifts down from FR_1 to FR_2. The domestic return is unaffected. At the old equilibrium rate of 1.20 $/€, the foreign return (point 6) is lower than the domestic return. Again, traders sell euros and buy dollars, causing the dollar to appreciate and the spot exchange rate to fall to 1.177 $/€. The new equilibrium is point 7.

Summary

The FX market diagram, with its representation of domestic returns and foreign returns, is central to our analysis in this chapter and later in the book. Be sure that you understand that domestic returns depend only on the home interest rate $i_\$$ but that foreign returns depend on both the foreign interest rate i_ϵ *and* the expected future exchange rate $E^e_{\$/\epsilon}$. Remember: any change that raises (lowers) the foreign return relative to the domestic return makes euro deposits more (less) attractive to investors, so that traders will buy (sell) euro deposits. The traders' actions push the forex market toward a new equilibrium at which the dollar will have depreciated (appreciated) against the euro.

To check your understanding, you might wish to rework the three examples and the figures for the opposite cases of a *decrease* in $i_\$$, an *increase* in i_ϵ, and an *increase* in $E^e_{\$/\epsilon}$; constructing the equivalent of Table 15-1 for each case may also prove helpful.

2 Interest Rates in the Short Run: Money Market Equilibrium

The previous section laid out the essentials of the asset approach to exchange rates. Figure 15-1 sums up the uncovered interest parity relationship at the heart of the asset approach. The spot exchange rate is the output (endogenous variable) of this model, and the expected future exchange rate and the home and foreign interest rates are the inputs (exogenous variables). But where do these inputs come from? In the last chapter, we developed a theory of the long-run exchange rate, the monetary approach, which can be used to forecast the future exchange rate. That leaves us with just one unanswered question: How are current interest rates determined?

Money Market Equilibrium in the Short Run: How Nominal Interest Rates Are Determined

Having seen how the supply and demand for money work in the previous chapter, we can build on that foundation here. We consider two money markets in two locations: the United States and Europe. Both markets are in equilibrium with money demand equal to money supply. In both locations, the money supply is controlled by a central bank and is taken as given; the demand for real money balances $M/P = L(i)Y$ is a function of the interest rate i and real income Y.

The Assumptions It is important to understand the key difference between the way we approach money market equilibrium in the short run (in this chapter) and the way we approached it in the long run (in the last chapter).

In the last chapter, we made the following *long-run* assumptions:

- In the long run, the price level P is fully flexible and adjusts to bring the money market to equilibrium.
- In the long run, the nominal interest rate i equals the world real interest rate plus domestic inflation.

In this chapter, we make *short-run* assumptions that are quite different:

- In the short run, the price level is sticky; it is a known predetermined variable, fixed at $P = \overline{P}$ (the bar indicates a fixed value).
- In the short run, the nominal interest rate i is fully flexible and adjusts to bring the money market to equilibrium.

Why do we make different assumptions in the short run?

First, why assume prices are now sticky? The assumption of sticky prices, also called **nominal rigidity,** is common to the study of macroeconomics in the short run. Economists have many explanations for price stickiness. Nominal wages may be sticky because of long-term labor contracts. Nominal product prices may be sticky because of contracts and *menu costs;* that is, firms may find it costly to frequently change their output prices. Thus, although it is reasonable to assume that all prices are flexible in the long run, they may not be in the short run.

Second, why assume that interest rates are now flexible? In the previous chapter, we showed that nominal interest rates are pinned down by the Fisher effect (or real interest parity) in the long run: in that case, the home nominal interest rate was equal to the world real interest rate plus the home rate of inflation. However, recall that this result does not apply in the short run because it is derived from purchasing power parity—which, as we know, only applies in the long run. Indeed, we saw evidence that in the short run real interest rates fluctuate in ways that deviate from real interest parity.

The Model With these explanations of our short-run assumptions in hand, we can now use the same general monetary model of the previous chapter and write down expressions for money market equilibrium in the two countries as follows:

$$\underbrace{\frac{M_{US}}{P_{US}}}_{\substack{\text{U.S. supply of} \\ \text{real money balances}}} = \underbrace{L(i_{\$}) \times Y_{US}}_{\substack{\text{U.S. demand for} \\ \text{real money balances}}} \qquad (15\text{-}2)$$

$$\underbrace{\frac{M_{EUR}}{P_{EUR}}}_{\substack{\text{European supply of} \\ \text{real money balances}}} = \underbrace{L(i_{€}) \times Y_{EUR}}_{\substack{\text{European demand for} \\ \text{real money balances}}} \qquad (15\text{-}3)$$

To recap: In the long run, prices adjust to clear the money market and bring money demand and money supply into line. In the short run, when prices are sticky, such adjustment is not possible. However, nominal interest rates *are* free to adjust. In the short run, the nominal interest rate in each country adjusts to bring money supply and money demand into equilibrium.

Money Market Equilibrium in the Short Run: Graphical Solution

Figure 15-4 represents the U.S. money market (a similar diagram applies to the European market). On the horizontal axis is the quantity of U.S. real money balances M_{US}/P_{US} and on the vertical axis is the U.S. nominal interest rate $i_\$$. The vertical line represents the supply of real money balances; this supply is fixed by the central bank at the level $M_{US}^1/\overline{P}_{US}^1$ and is independent of the level of the interest rate. The downward-sloping line represents the demand for real money balances, $L(i_\$) \times Y_{US}$. Demand decreases as the U.S. nominal interest rate increases because the opportunity cost of holding money rises and people don't want to hold high money balances. The money market is in equilibrium at point 1: the demand and supply of real money balances are equal at $M_{US}^1/\overline{P}_{US}^1$ and at a nominal interest rate $i_\$^1$.

Adjustment to Money Market Equilibrium in the Short Run

If interest rates are flexible in the short run, as we assume they are, there is nothing to prevent them from adjusting to clear the money market. But how do market forces ensure that a nominal interest rate $i_\$^1$ is attained? The adjustment process works as follows.

Suppose instead that the interest rate was $i_\$^2$, so that we were at point 2 on the real money demand curve. At this interest rate, real money demand is less than real money supply. In the aggregate, the central bank has put more money in the hands of the public than the public wishes to hold. The public will want to reduce its cash holdings

FIGURE 15-4

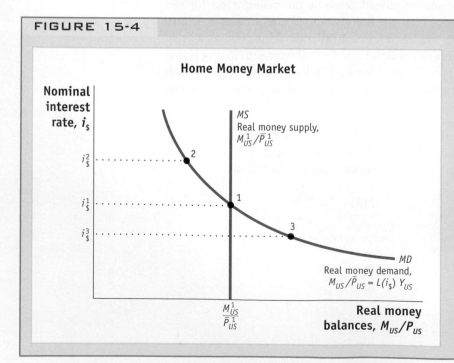

Equilibrium in the Home Money Market The supply and demand for real money balances determine the nominal interest rate. The money supply curve (MS) is vertical at $M_{US}^1/\overline{P}_{US}^1$ because the quantity of money supplied does not depend on the interest rate. The money demand curve (MD) is downward-sloping because an increase in the interest rate raises the cost of holding money, thus lowering the quantity demanded. The money market is in equilibrium when the nominal interest rate $i_\$^1$ is such that real money demand equals real money supply (point 1). At points 2 and 3, demand does not equal supply and the interest rate will adjust until the money market returns to equilibrium.

by exchanging money for interest-bearing assets such as bonds, saving accounts, and so on. That is, they will save more and seek to lend their money to borrowers. But borrowers will not want to borrow more unless the cost of borrowing falls. So the interest rate will be driven down as eager lenders compete to attract scarce borrowers. As this happens, back in the money market, in Figure 15-4, we move from point 2 back toward equilibrium at point 1.

A similar story can be told if the money market is initially at point 3, where there is an excess demand for money. In this case, the public wishes to reduce their savings in the form of interest-bearing assets and turn them into cash. Now fewer loans are extended. The loan market will suffer an excess demand. But borrowers will not want to borrow less unless the cost of borrowing rises. So the interest rate will be driven up as eager borrowers compete to attract scarce lenders. These adjustments end only when point 1 is reached and there is no excess supply of real money balances.

Another Building Block: Short-Run Money Market Equilibrium

This model of the money market may be familiar from previous courses in macroeconomics. The lessons that are important for our theory of exchange rates are summed up in Figure 15-5. We treat the price level in each country as fixed and known in the short run. We also assume that the money supply and real income in each country are known. The equilibrium equations for the money market, Equations (15-2) and (15-3), then tell us the interest rates in each country. Once these are known, we can put them to use in another building block seen earlier: the interest rates can be plugged into the fundamental equation of the asset approach to exchange rate determination, Equation (15-1), along with the future expected exchange rate derived from a forecast based on the long-run monetary model of the previous chapter. In that way, the spot exchange rate can finally be determined.

Changes in Money Supply and the Nominal Interest Rate

Money market equilibrium depends on money supply and money demand. If either changes, the equilibrium will change. To help us better understand how exchange rates are determined, we need to understand how these changes occur.

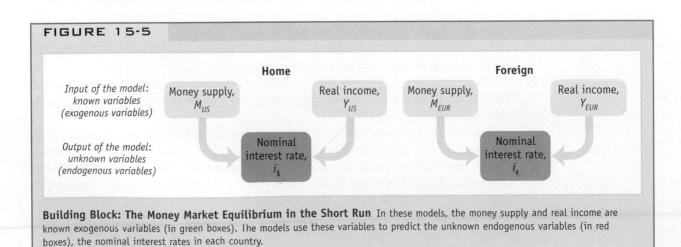

FIGURE 15-5

Building Block: The Money Market Equilibrium in the Short Run In these models, the money supply and real income are known exogenous variables (in green boxes). The models use these variables to predict the unknown endogenous variables (in red boxes), the nominal interest rates in each country.

FIGURE 15-6

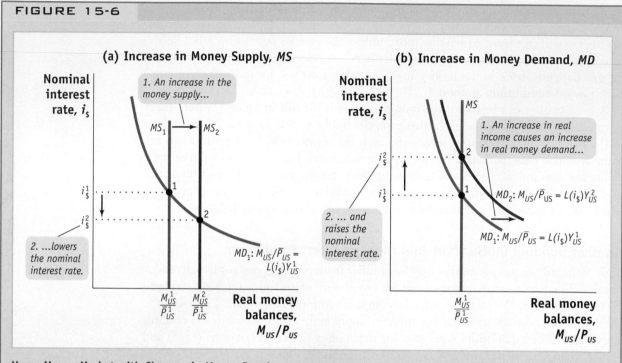

Home Money Market with Changes in Money Supply and Money Demand In panel (a), with a fixed price level $\overline{P}^1_{US}$, an increase in nominal money supply from M^1_{US} to M^2_{US} causes an increase in real money supply from $M^1_{US}/\overline{P}^1_{US}$ to $M^2_{US}/\overline{P}^1_{US}$. The nominal interest rate falls from $i^1_\$$ to $i^2_\$$ to restore equilibrium at point 2. In panel (b), with a fixed price level $\overline{P}^1_{US}$, an increase in real income from Y^1_{US} to Y^2_{US} causes real money demand to increase from MD_1 to MD_2. To restore equilibrium at point 2, the interest rate rises from $i^1_\$$ to $i^2_\$$.

Figure 15-6, panel (a), shows how the money market responds to a monetary policy change consisting of an increase in Home (U.S.) nominal money supply from M^1_{US} to M^2_{US}. Because, by assumption, the U.S. price level is fixed in the short run at $\overline{P}^1_{US}$, the increase in nominal money supply causes an increase in real money supply from $M^1_{US}/\overline{P}^1_{US}$ to $M^2_{US}/\overline{P}^1_{US}$. In the figure, the money supply curve shifts to the right from MS_1 to MS_2. Point 1 is no longer an equilibrium; at the interest rate $i^1_\$$, there is now an excess supply of real money balances. As people move their dollars into interest-bearing assets to be loaned out, the interest rate falls from $i^1_\$$ to $i^2_\$$, at which point the money market is again in equilibrium at point 2. By the same logic, a reduction in the nominal money supply will raise the interest rate.

To sum up, *in the short run, all else equal, an increase in a country's money supply will lower the country's nominal interest rate; a decrease in a country's money supply will raise the country's nominal interest rate.*

Fortunately, our graphical analysis shows that, for a *given* money demand curve, setting a money supply level uniquely determines the interest rate and vice versa. Hence, for many purposes, *the money supply or the interest rate may be used as a policy instrument.* In practice, most central banks tend to use the interest rate as their policy instrument because the money demand curve may not be stable, and the fluctuations caused by this instability would lead to unstable interest rates if the money supply were set at a given level as the policy instrument.

APPLICATION

Can Central Banks Always Control the Interest Rate? A Lesson from the Crisis of 2008–2009

In our analyses so far, we have assumed that central banks can control the money market interest rate, and that they can effectively do so whether they set the interest rate or the money supply. These assumptions are critical in this chapter and in the rest of this book. But are they really true? In general, perhaps, but policy operations by central banks can be undermined by financial market disruptions. Recent events in many countries illustrate the problem.

In the United States, for example, the Federal Reserve sets as its *policy rate* the interest rate that banks charge each other for the overnight loan of the money they hold at the Fed. In normal times, changes in this cost of short-term funds for the banks are usually passed through into the *market rates* the banks charge to borrowers on loans such as mortgages, corporate loans, auto loans, and so forth, as well as on interbank loans between the banks themselves. This process is one of the most basic elements in the so-called *transmission mechanism* through which the effects of monetary policy are eventually felt in the real economy.

In the recent crisis, however, banks regarded other banks and borrowers (and even themselves) as facing potentially catastrophic risks. As a result, they lent much less freely and when they did loan, they charged much higher interest rates to compensate themselves for the risk of the loan suffering a loss or default. Thus, although the Fed brought its policy rate all the way down from 5.25% to 0% in 2007 and 2008, there was no similar decrease in market rates. In fact, market interest rates barely moved at all, and even the credit that was available at more favorable rates was often restricted by tighter lending standards; total credit expanded very little, and refinancings were limited.

A second problem arose once policy rates hit the *zero lower bound* (ZLB). At that point, the central banks' capacity to lower the policy rate further was exhausted. However, many central banks wanted to keep applying downward pressure to market rates to calm financial markets. The Fed's response was a policy of *quantitative easing*.

Usually, the Fed expands base money M0 by either lending to banks which put up safe government bonds as collateral, or by buying government bonds outright in open-market operations—although these actions are taken only in support of the Fed's interest rate target. But in the crisis, and with interest rates stuck at a floor, the Fed engaged in a number of extraordinary policy actions to push more money out more quickly:

1. It expanded the range of credit securities it would accept as collateral to include lower-grade, private-sector bonds.

2. It expanded the range of securities that it would buy outright to include private-sector credit instruments such as commercial paper and mortgage-backed securities.

3. It expanded the range of counterparties from which it would buy securities to include some nonbank institutions such as primary dealers and money market funds.

As a result of massive asset purchases along these lines, M0 in the United States more than doubled to over a trillion dollars. However, there was very little change in M1 or M2, indicating that banks had little desire to translate the cash they were receiving from the Fed into the new loans and new deposits that would expand the broad money supply.

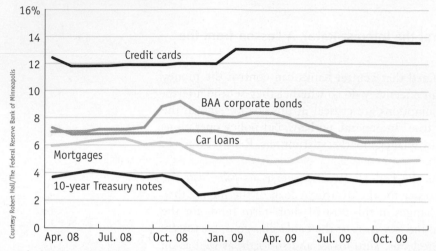

A broken transmission: the Fed's extraordinary interventions did little to change private credit market interest rates from 2008 through 2009.

Similar crisis actions were taken by the Bank of England and, eventually, by the European Central Bank (ECB); both expanded their collateral rules, although their outright purchase programs were more narrowly focused on aggressive use of open-market operations to purchase large quantities of U.K. and Eurozone government bonds (though in the ECB's case this included low-grade bonds from crisis countries such as Greece and Portgual).

To sum up, with the traditional transmission mechanism broken, central banks had to find different tools. In the Fed's case, by directly intervening in markets for different types of private credit at different maturities, policy makers hoped to circumvent the impaired transmission mechanism. Would matters have been much worse if the central banks had done nothing at all? It's hard to say. However, if the aim was to lower market interest rates in a meaningful way and expand broader monetary aggregates, it is not clear that these policies had significant economic effects. ■

Changes in Real Income and the Nominal Interest Rate

Figure 15-6, panel (b), shows how the money market responds to an increase in home (U.S.) real income from Y_{US}^1 to Y_{US}^2. The increase in real income causes real money demand to increase as reflected in the shift from MD_1 to MD_2. At the initial interest rate $i_\$^1$, there is now an excess demand for real money balances. To restore equilibrium at point 2, the interest rate rises from $i_\$^1$ to $i_\$^2$ to encourage people to hold lower dollar balances. Similarly, a reduction in real income will lower the interest rate.

To sum up, *in the short run, all else equal, an increase in a country's real income will raise the country's nominal interest rate; a decrease in a country's real income will lower the country's nominal interest rate.*

The Monetary Model: The Short Run Versus the Long Run

The short-run implications of the model we have just discussed differ from the long-run implications of the monetary approach we presented in the previous chapter. It is important that we look at these differences, and understand how and why they arise.

Consider the following example: the home central bank that previously kept the money supply constant suddenly switches to an expansionary policy. In the following year, it allows the money supply to grow at a rate of 5%.

■ If such annual expansions are expected to be a permanent policy in the long run, the predictions of the long-run monetary approach and Fisher effect are clear. All else equal, a five percentage point increase in the rate of home money growth causes a five percentage point increase in the rate of home inflation and a five percentage point increase in the home nominal interest rate. The home interest rate will then *rise* in the long run when prices are flexible.

■ If this expansion is expected to be temporary, then the short-run model we have just studied in this chapter tells a very different story. All else equal, if the home money supply expands, the immediate effect is an excess supply of real money balances. The home interest rate will then *fall* in the short run when prices are sticky.

These different outcomes illustrate the importance of the assumptions we make about price flexibility. They also point out the importance of the nominal anchor in monetary policy formulation and the constraints that central banks have to confront. The different outcomes also explain some apparently puzzling linkages among money, interest rates, and exchange rates. In both of the previous cases, an expanded money supply leads to a weaker currency. However, in the short run, low interest rates and a weak currency go together, whereas in the long run, high interest rates and a weak currency go together.

What is the intuition for these findings? In the short run, when we study the impact of a lower interest rate and we say "all else equal," we have assumed that expectations have not changed concerning future exchange rates (or money supply or inflation). In other words, we assume (implicitly) a temporary policy that does not tamper with the nominal anchor. In the long run, if the policy turns out to be permanent, this assumption is inappropriate; prices are flexible and money growth, inflation, and expected depreciation now all move in concert—in other words, the "all else" is no longer equal.

A good grasp of these key differences between the short- and long-run approaches is essential to understanding how exchange rates are determined. To cement our understanding, in the rest of the chapter we explore the different implications of temporary and permanent policy changes. To make our exploration a bit easier, we now lay out the short-run model in a succinct, graphical form.

3 The Asset Approach: Applications and Evidence

To simplify the graphical presentation of the asset approach, we focus on conditions in the home economy; a similar approach can be used for the foreign economy. For illustration we again assume that Home is the United States and Foreign is Europe meaning the Eurozone.

The Asset Approach to Exchange Rates: Graphical Solution

Figure 15-7 shows two markets: panel (a) shows the home money market (for the United States), and panel (b) shows the FX market diagram (for the dollar–euro market). This figure summarizes the asset approach in the short run.

The U.S. Money Market Panel (a) depicts equilibrium in the U.S. money market. The horizontal axis shows the quantity of U.S. real money balances demanded or supplied, M_{US}/P_{US}. The vertical axis shows the U.S. nominal interest rate $i_\$$. Two relationships are shown:

1. The vertical line *MS* represents the U.S. real money supply. The line is vertical because (i) the nominal U.S. money supply M_{US} is treated as exogenous (known), because it is set by the home central bank, and (ii) the U.S. price level $\overline{P}_{US}$ is treated as exogenous (known) in the short run because prices are sticky.

FIGURE 15-7

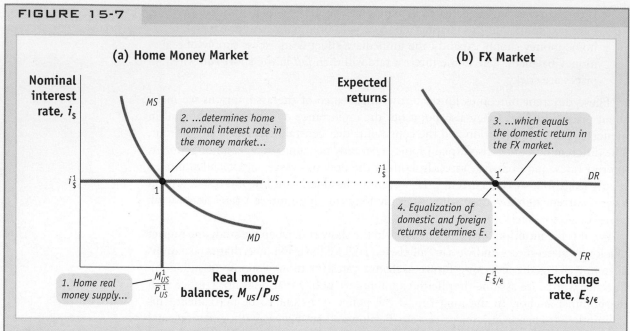

(a) Home Money Market

Nominal interest rate, $i_\$$

MS

2. ...determines home nominal interest rate in the money market...

$i_\$^1$

1

MD

1. Home real money supply...

$\dfrac{M_{US}^1}{\overline{P}_{US}^1}$

Real money balances, M_{US}/P_{US}

(b) FX Market

Expected returns

3. ...which equals the domestic return in the FX market.

$i_\$^1$

1'

DR

4. Equalization of domestic and foreign returns determines E.

FR

$E_{\$/€}^1$

Exchange rate, $E_{\$/€}$

Equilibrium in the Money Market and the FX Market The figure summarizes the equilibria in the two asset markets in one diagram. In panel (a), in the home (U.S.) money market, the home nominal interest rate $i_\$^1$ is determined by the home levels of real money supply *MS* and demand *MD* with equilibrium at point 1.

In panel (b), in the dollar–euro FX market, the spot exchange rate $E_{\$/€}^1$ is determined by foreign and domestic expected returns, with equilibrium at point 1'. Arbitrage forces the domestic and foreign returns in the FX market to be equal, a result that depends on capital mobility.

2. The curve *MD* on the diagram represents the U.S. demand for real money balances, $L(i_\$)Y_{US}$. It slopes down because, when the home nominal interest rate $i_\$$ rises, the opportunity cost of holding money increases, and demand falls. For now, we also assume that the U.S. real income level Y_{US} is exogenous (given) and fixed in the short run.

In equilibrium, money demand equals money supply, the quantity of real money demanded and supplied is $M_{US}^1/\overline{P}_{US}^1$, and the nominal interest rate is $i_\$^1$ (point 1).

The Market for Foreign Exchange Panel (b) depicts equilibrium in the FX market. The horizontal axis shows the spot exchange rate, $E_{\$/€}$. The vertical axis shows U.S. dollar returns on home and foreign deposits. Two relationships are shown:

1. The downward-sloping foreign return curve *FR* shows the relationship between the exchange rate and the expected dollar rate of return on foreign deposits $[i_€ + (E_{\$/€}^e - E_{\$/€})/E_{\$/€}]$. The European interest rate $i_€$ is treated as exogenous (given); it is determined in the European money market, which is not shown in this figure. The expected future exchange rate $E_{\$/€}^e$ is treated as exogenous (given); it is determined by a forecast obtained from the long-run model we developed in the previous chapter.

2. The horizontal domestic return line *DR* shows the dollar rate of return on U.S. deposits, which is the U.S. nominal interest rate $i_\$$. It is horizontal at $i_\$^1$ because this is the U.S. interest rate determined in the home money market in panel (a), and it is the same regardless of the spot exchange rate.

In equilibrium, foreign and domestic returns are equal (uncovered interest parity holds) and the FX market is in equilibrium at point 1′.

Capital Mobility Is Crucial We assume that the FX market is subject to the arbitrage forces we have studied and that uncovered interest parity will hold. But this is true only if there are no capital controls: as long as capital can move freely between home and foreign capital markets, domestic and foreign returns will be equalized. Our assumption that DR equals FR depends on capital mobility. If capital controls are imposed, there is no arbitrage and no reason why DR has to equal FR.

Putting the Model to Work With this graphical apparatus in place, it is relatively straightforward to solve for the exchange rate given knowledge of all the known (exogenous) variables we have just specified.

To solve for the exchange rate, we start in the home money market in panel (a) on the horizontal axis, at the level of real money supply $M_{US}^1/\bar{P}_{US}^1$; we trace upward along MS to MD at point 1, to find the current home interest rate $i_\$^1$. We then trace right and move across from the home money market to the FX market in panel (b), since the home interest rate is the same as domestic return DR in the FX market. We eventually meet the FR curve at point 1′. We then trace down and read off the equilibrium exchange rate $E_{\$/\epsilon}^1$.

Our graphical treatment shows that solving the model is as simple as tracing a path around the diagrams. While we gain in simplicity, we also lose some generality because one market, the foreign money market, has been left out of the analysis. However, the same analysis also applies to the foreign country. As a quick check that you understand the logic of the asset approach to exchange rates, you might try to construct the equivalent of Figure 15-7 under the assumption that Europe is Home and the United States is the Foreign. (*Hint:* In the FX market, you will need to treat the home [European] expected future exchange rate $E_{\epsilon/\$}^e$ and the foreign [U.S.] interest rate $i_\$$ as given. Take care with the currency units of every variable when making the switch.)

Short-Run Policy Analysis

The graphical exposition in Figure 15-7 shows how the asset approach works to determine the exchange rate. This approach can be used to analyze the impacts of economic policy or other shocks to the economy.

The most straightforward shocks we can analyze are temporary shocks because they affect only the current state of the money and foreign exchange markets and do not affect expectations about the future. In this section, we use the model to see what happens when there is a temporary, short-run increase in the money supply by the central bank.

A Temporary Shock to the Home Money Supply We take the model of Figure 15-7 and assume that, apart from the home money supply, all exogenous variables remain unchanged and fixed at the same level. Thus, foreign money supply, home and foreign real income and price levels, and the expected future exchange rate are all fixed.

The initial state of all markets is shown in Figure 15-8. The home money market is in equilibrium at point 1 where home money supply MS and money demand MD are equal at the home nominal interest rate $i_\$^1$. The foreign exchange market is in

FIGURE 15-8

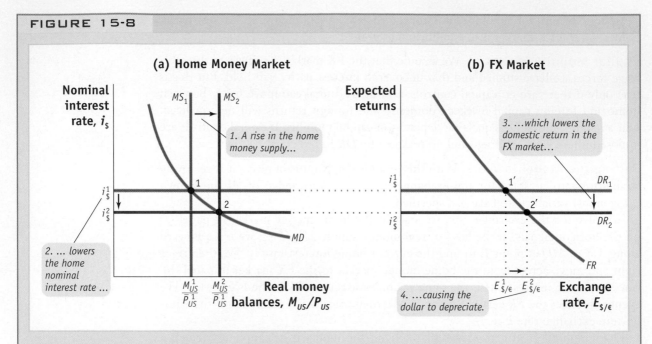

(a) Home Money Market

Nominal interest rate, $i_\$$

MS_1 MS_2

1. A rise in the home money supply...

$i_\$^1$

1

$i_\$^2$

2

MD

2. ... lowers the home nominal interest rate ...

$\dfrac{M_{US}^1}{\overline{P}_{US}^1}$ $\dfrac{M_{US}^2}{\overline{P}_{US}^1}$ **Real money balances, M_{US}/P_{US}**

(b) FX Market

Expected returns

3. ...which lowers the domestic return in the FX market...

$i_\$^1$ 1' DR_1

$i_\$^2$ 2' DR_2

FR

$E_{\$/\epsilon}^1$ $E_{\$/\epsilon}^2$ **Exchange rate, $E_{\$/\epsilon}$**

4. ...causing the dollar to depreciate.

Temporary Expansion of the Home Money Supply In panel (a), in the home money market, an increase in home money supply from M_{US}^1 to M_{US}^2 causes an increase in real money supply from $M_{US}^1/\overline{P}_{US}^1$ to $M_{US}^2/\overline{P}_{US}^1$. To keep real money demand equal to real money supply, the interest rate falls from $i_\$^1$ to $i_\$^2$, and the new money market equilibrium is at point 2. In panel (b), in the FX market, to maintain the equality of domestic and foreign expected returns, the exchange rate rises (the dollar depreciates) from $E_{\$/\epsilon}^1$ to $E_{\$/\epsilon}^2$, and the new FX market equilibrium is at point 2'.

equilibrium at point 1', where domestic return DR equals foreign return FR, where $i_\$^1 = i_\epsilon^1 + (E_{\$/\epsilon}^e - E_{\$/\epsilon}^1)/E_{\$/\epsilon}^1$, and the spot exchange rate is $E_{\$/\epsilon}^1$.

Suppose the U.S. money supply is increased temporarily from M_{US}^1 to M_{US}^2. Under the assumption of sticky prices, $\overline{P}_{US}^1$ does not change, so the U.S. real money supply will increase to $M_{US}^2/\overline{P}_{US}^1$, and the real money supply curve shifts from MS_1 to MS_2 in panel (a). U.S. real money demand is unchanged, so the money market equilibrium shifts from point 1 to point 2 and the nominal interest rate falls from $i_\$^1$ to $i_\$^2$. The expansion of the U.S. money supply causes the U.S. nominal interest rate to fall.

A *temporary* monetary policy shock leaves the long-run expected exchange rate $E_{\$/\epsilon}^e$ unchanged. Assuming all else equal, European monetary policy is also unchanged, and the euro interest rate remains fixed at i_ϵ. If $E_{\$/\epsilon}^e$ and i_ϵ are unchanged, then the foreign return FR curve in panel (b) is unchanged and the new FX market equilibrium is at point 2'. The lower domestic return $i_\$^2$ is matched by a lower foreign return. The foreign return is lower because the U.S. dollar has depreciated from $E_{\$/\epsilon}^1$ to $E_{\$/\epsilon}^2$.

The result is intuitive, and we have seen each of the steps previously. We now just put them all together: a home monetary expansion lowers the home nominal interest rate, which is also the domestic return in the forex market. This makes foreign deposits more attractive and makes traders wish to sell home deposits and buy foreign deposits. This, in turn, makes the home exchange rate increase (depreciate). However, this depreciation makes foreign deposits less attractive (all else equal). Eventually, the equality of foreign and domestic returns is restored, uncovered interest parity holds again, and the foreign exchange market reaches a new short-run equilibrium.

A Temporary Shock to the Foreign Money Supply We now repeat the previous analysis for a shock to the *foreign* money supply. All other exogenous variables remain unchanged and fixed at their initial levels. Thus, home money supply, home and foreign real income and price levels, and the expected future exchange rate are all fixed. The initial state of all markets is shown in Figure 15-9: the home money market is in equilibrium at point 1 and the FX market is in equilibrium at point 2.

Let's see what happens when the foreign money supply increases temporarily. Because changes in the foreign money supply have no effect on the home money market in panel (a), equilibrium remains at point 1 and the home nominal interest rate stays at $i_\$^1$.

The shock is temporary, so long-run expectations are unchanged, and the expected exchange rate $E_{\$/€}^e$ stays fixed in panel (b). However, because the foreign money supply has expanded temporarily, the euro interest rate falls from $i_€^1$ to $i_€^2$. Foreign returns are diminished, all else equal, by a fall in euro interest rates, so the foreign return curve FR shifts downward from FR_1 to FR_2. On the horizontal axis in panel (b), we can see that at the new FX market equilibrium (point 2') the home exchange rate has decreased (the U.S. dollar has appreciated) from $E_{\$/€}^1$ to $E_{\$/€}^2$.

This result is also intuitive. A foreign monetary expansion lowers the foreign nominal interest rate, which lowers the foreign return in the forex market. This makes foreign deposits less attractive and makes traders wish to buy home deposits and sell foreign

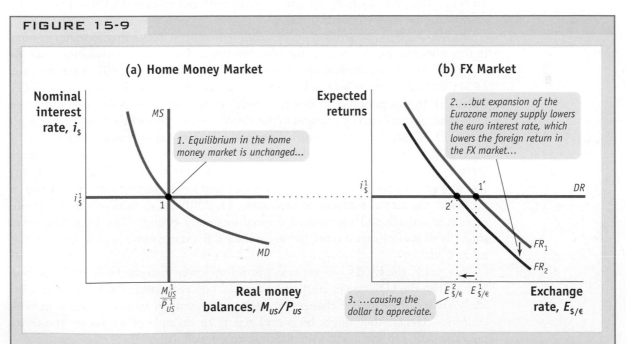

FIGURE 15-9

(a) Home Money Market

Nominal interest rate, $i_\$$

MS

1. Equilibrium in the home money market is unchanged...

$i_\$^1$

1

MD

$\dfrac{M_{US}^1}{P_{US}^1}$ **Real money balances, M_{US}/P_{US}**

(b) FX Market

Expected returns

2. ...but expansion of the Eurozone money supply lowers the euro interest rate, which lowers the foreign return in the FX market...

$i_\$^1$

1'

DR

2'

FR_1

FR_2

3. ...causing the dollar to appreciate.

$E_{\$/€}^2$ $E_{\$/€}^1$ **Exchange rate, $E_{\$/€}$**

Temporary Expansion of the Foreign Money Supply In panel (a), there is no change in the home money market. In panel (b), an increase in the foreign money supply causes the foreign (euro) interest rate to fall from $i_€^1$ to $i_€^2$. For a U.S. investor, this lowers the foreign return $i_€ + (E_{\$/€}^e - E_{\$/€})/E_{\$/€}$, all else equal. To maintain the equality of domestic and foreign returns in the FX market, the exchange rate falls (the dollar appreciates) from $E_{\$/€}^1$ to $E_{\$/€}^2$, and the new FX market equilibrium is at point 2'.

deposits. This, in turn, makes the home exchange rate decrease (appreciate). However, this appreciation makes foreign deposits more attractive (all else equal). Eventually, the equality of foreign and domestic returns is restored, uncovered interest parity holds again, and the foreign exchange market reaches a new short-run equilibrium.

To ensure you have grasped the model fully, you might try two exercises. First, derive the predictions of the model for temporary *contractions* in the home or foreign money supplies. Second, go back to the version of Figure 15-7 that you constructed from the European perspective and generate predictions using that version of the model, first for a temporary expansion of the money supply in Europe and then for a temporary expansion in the United States. Do you get the same answers?

APPLICATION

The Rise and Fall of the Dollar, 1999–2004

In the 1990s, many developed countries adopted monetary policies that established clear, long-run nominal anchors. The European Central Bank, for example, adopted an explicit inflation target. The Federal Reserve in the United States operated with a more implicit target, but nonetheless could claim to have a credible anchor, too.

The Fisher effect tells us that nominal anchoring of this kind ought to keep nominal interest rate differentials between the United States and the Eurozone roughly constant in the long run. But in the short run, this constraint does not apply, so central banks have some freedom to temporarily change their monetary policies. In the years 2000 to 2004, such flexibility was put to use and interest rates in the United States and Europe followed very different tracks.

In later chapters, we study in more detail why central banks alter monetary policy in the short run, but for now we focus on how such changes affect exchange rates. As Figure 15-10 shows, the Fed raised interest rates from 1999 to 2001 faster than the ECB (the Fed was more worried about the U.S. economy "overheating" with higher inflation). In this period of global economic boom, the ECB's policy also tightened over time, as measured by changes in the Euro interest rate—the refinancing rate set by the ECB. But the changes were more restrained and slower in coming.

As Figure 15-10 also shows, the Fed then lowered interest rates aggressively from 2001 to 2004, with rates falling as low as 1% in 2003 to 2004 (the U.S. economy had slowed after the boom and the Fed hoped that lower interest rates would avert a recession; the terrorist attacks of September 11, 2001, led to fears of a more serious economic setback and encouraged further monetary easing). The ECB also acted similarly to lower interest rates, but again the ECB did not move rates as far or as fast as the Fed.

As a result, the ECB's interest rate, previously lower than the Fed's rate, was soon higher than the U.S. rate in 2001 and remained higher through 2004. Investors most likely viewed these policy changes as a temporary shift in monetary policy in both countries. Hence, they might be considered as an example of temporary monetary policy shocks. Do our model's predictions accord well with reality?

Up until 2001, the policy of higher rates in the United States could be seen as a temporary home monetary contraction (relative to foreign), and our model would predict a dollar appreciation in the short run. After 2001 the aggressive reductions in U.S. interest rates could be seen as a temporary home monetary expansion (relative

FIGURE 15-10

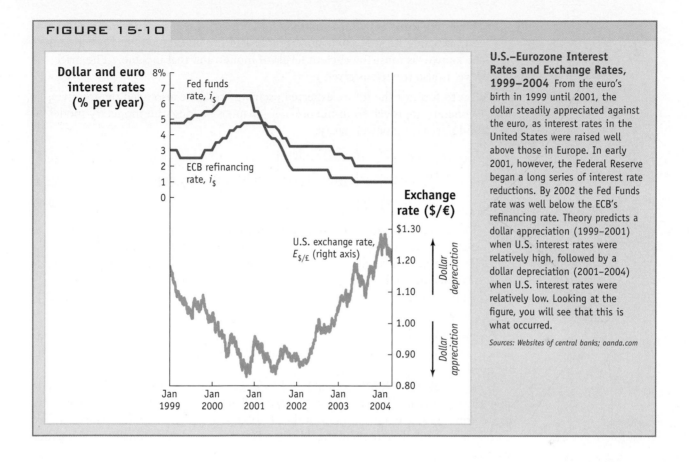

U.S.–Eurozone Interest Rates and Exchange Rates, 1999–2004 From the euro's birth in 1999 until 2001, the dollar steadily appreciated against the euro, as interest rates in the United States were raised well above those in Europe. In early 2001, however, the Federal Reserve began a long series of interest rate reductions. By 2002 the Fed Funds rate was well below the ECB's refinancing rate. Theory predicts a dollar appreciation (1999–2001) when U.S. interest rates were relatively high, followed by a dollar depreciation (2001–2004) when U.S. interest rates were relatively low. Looking at the figure, you will see that this is what occurred.

Sources: Websites of central banks; oanda.com

to foreign), and our model predicts a dollar depreciation in the short run. Looking at the path of the dollar–euro exchange rate in the figure, we can see that the model accords well with reality. ■

4 A Complete Theory: Unifying the Monetary and Asset Approaches

In this section, we extend our analysis from the short run to the long run, and examine permanent as well as temporary shocks. To do this, we put together a complete theory of exchange rates that couples the long-run and short-run approaches, as shown schematically in Figure 15-11:

- We need the asset approach (this chapter)—short-run money market equilibrium and uncovered interest parity:

$$\left.\begin{array}{l} \overline{P}_{US} = M_{US}/[L_{US}(i_\$)Y_{US}] \\[4pt] \overline{P}_{EUR} = M_{EUR}/[L_{EUR}(i_\text{€})Y_{EUR}] \\[4pt] i_\$ = i_\text{€} + \dfrac{E^e_{\$/\text{€}} - E_{\$/\text{€}}}{E_{\$/\text{€}}} \end{array}\right\} \quad \text{The asset approach.} \qquad (15\text{-}4)$$

- There are three equations and three unknowns (two short-run nominal interest rates and the spot exchange rate). The future expected exchange rate must be known, as must the current levels of money and real income. (The price level is also treated as given.)

- But to forecast the future expected exchange rate, we also need the long-run monetary approach from the previous chapter—a long-run monetary model and purchasing power parity:

$$P^e_{US} = M^e_{US}/[L_{US}(i^e_\$)Y^e_{US}]$$
$$P^e_{EUR} = M^e_{EUR}/[L_{EUR}(i^e_{\text{€}})Y^e_{EUR}] \left.\right\} \quad \text{The monetary approach.} \quad (15\text{-}5)$$
$$E^e_{\$/\text{€}} = P^e_{US}/P^e_{EUR}$$

- There are three equations and three unknowns (two price levels and the exchange rate). Note that all variables here have a superscript e to denote future expected values or forecasts. We assume that forecasts of future money, real income, and nominal interest rates are known. This model can then be applied to obtain price forecasts and, hence, a forecast of the future expected exchange rate.[2]

Figure 15-11 sums up all the theory we have learned so far in the past two chapters. It shows how all the pieces fit together. In total we have six equations and six unknowns.

It is only now, with all the building blocks in place, that we can fully appreciate how the two key mechanisms of *expectations* and *arbitrage* operate in a variety of ways to determine exchange rates in both the short run and the long run. Ensure you are comfortable with all of the building blocks—how they work individually and how they connect.

After all our hard work, we have arrived at a complete theory to explain exchange rates in the short run and the long run. The model incorporates all of the key economic fundamentals that affect exchange rates and, in practice, although forex markets exhibit a great deal of turbulence and uncertainty, there is evidence that these fundamentals play a major role in shaping traders' decisions (see **Side Bar: Confessions of a Forex Trader**).

Long-Run Policy Analysis

When and how can we apply the complete model? The downside of working with the complete model is that we have to keep track of multiple mechanisms and variables; the upside is that the theory is fully developed and can be applied to short-run and long-run policy shocks.

The temporary shocks we saw in the last section represent only one kind of monetary policy change, one that does not affect the long-run nominal anchor. The fact that these shocks were temporary allowed us to conduct all of the analysis under

---

[2] Recall that the previous chapter also showed us how real interest parity can be used to solve for the long-run nominal interest rate i in each country, the so-called *neutral level* of the nominal interest rate. For example, restricting our attention to the case of a stable long-run inflation rate (e.g., under nominal anchoring in which an announced inflation target is expected to be hit in each country), we have

$$i_\$ = \pi_{US,target} + r^* \left.\right\}$$
$$i_{\text{€}} = \pi_{EUR,target} + r^* \quad \text{Real interest parity.}$$

FIGURE 15-11

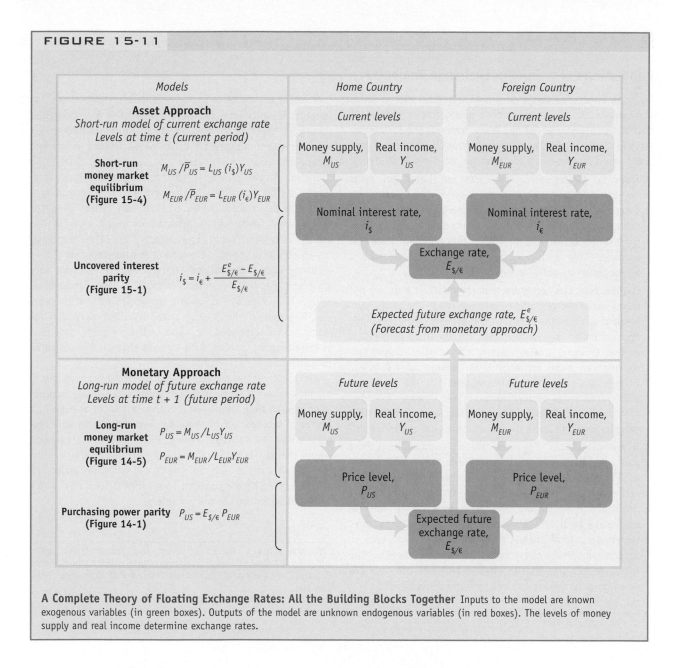

A Complete Theory of Floating Exchange Rates: All the Building Blocks Together Inputs to the model are known exogenous variables (in green boxes). Outputs of the model are unknown endogenous variables (in red boxes). The levels of money supply and real income determine exchange rates.

the assumption that the long-run expected level of the exchange rate remained unchanged.

When the monetary authorities decide to make a *permanent* change, however, this assumption of unchanged expectations is no longer appropriate. Under such a change, the authorities would cause an enduring change in all nominal variables; that is, they would be electing to change their nominal anchor policy in some way. Thus, when a monetary policy shock is permanent, the long-run expectation of the level of the exchange rate has to adjust. This change will, in turn, cause the exchange rate predictions of the short-run model to differ from those made when the policy shock was only temporary.

SIDE BAR

Confessions of a Foreign Exchange Trader

Trying to forecast exchange rates is a major enterprise in financial markets and serves as the basis of any trading strategy. A tour of the industry would find many firms offering forecasting services at short, medium, and long horizons. Forecasts are generally based on three methodologies (or some mix of all three):

1. *Economic fundamentals.* Forecasts are based on ideas developed in the past two chapters. Exchange rates are determined by factors such as money, output, interest rates, and so on; hence, forecasters try to develop long- and short-range predictions of these "fundamental" variables. Example: "The exchange rate will depreciate because a looser monetary policy is expected."

2. *Politics.* Forecasts recognize that some factors that are not purely economic can affect exchange rates. One is the outbreak of war (see the application at the end of this chapter). Political crises might matter, too, if they affect perceptions of risk. Changes in risk interfere with simple interest parity and can move exchange rates. Making such forecasts is more qualitative and subjective, but it is still concerned with fundamental determinants in our theory. Example: "The exchange rate will depreciate because a conflict with a neighboring state raises the probability of war and inflation."

3. *Technical methods.* Forecasts rely on extrapolations from past behavior. Trends may be assumed to continue ("momentum"), or recent maximum and minimum values may be assumed to be binding. These trading strategies assume that financial markets exhibit some persistence and, if followed, may make such an assumption self-fulfilling for a time. Nonetheless, large crashes that return asset prices back to fundamental levels can burst such bubbles. Example: "The exchange rate has hit this level three times this year but never gone further; it will not go further this time."

A recent survey of U.K. forex traders provided some interesting insights into this world.[*] One-third described their trading as "technically based," and one-third said their trades were "fundamentals-based"; others were jobbing or trading for clients.

The survey revealed that insights from economic theory mattered little from one hour to the next. In the very short run, within the day, traders confessed that many factors unrelated to economic fundamentals affected exchange rates in the market: 29% cited "bandwagon effects," and 33% mentioned "overreaction to news." Concerning within-day changes in exchange rates, when asked, "Do you believe exchange rate movements accurately reflect changes in the fundamental value," fully 97% of the traders responded no and only 3% yes. However, in the medium run, described as within six months, 58% responded yes. And in the long run, described as more than six months, 87% thought that changes reflected fundamentals.

Which economic fundamentals mattered? News about money supplies, interest rates, and GDP levels was quickly incorporated into trading, usually in less than a minute or even in a matter of seconds. All of these are key variables in our complete model. As we would expect, PPP was deemed irrelevant within the day, but 16% thought it mattered in the medium run, and 44% in the long run. The lack of unanimity about PPP may reflect legitimate concerns about its shortcomings (which we examined in the previous chapter).

---

[*] Yin-Wong Cheung, Menzie D. Chinn, and Ian W. Marsh, 2004, "How Do UK-Based Foreign Exchange Dealers Think Their Market Operates?" *International Journal of Finance and Economics*, 9(4), 289–306.

These insights guide our analysis of permanent policy shocks. They also tell us that we cannot approach such analysis chronologically. Before we can figure out what happens in the short run, we have to know expectations, that is, what is going to happen in the long run. Thus, we have to use a technique that is common in forward-looking economic problems: we must *solve backward* from the future to the present. (This ordering mirrors the presentation of the material in this textbook—we must understand the long run before we can understand the short run.)

A Permanent Shock to the Home Money Supply We start our analysis of the Home (U.S.) and Foreign (Europe) economies with each economy currently at a long-run equilibrium in which all variables are steady. In this equilibrium, we assume that each country has a fixed real income, a fixed money supply, and a zero rate of inflation. Hence, there is a zero rate of depreciation because the equilibrium is characterized by purchasing power parity, and interest rates in each country are the same because the equilibrium is characterized by uncovered interest parity.

Our analysis is shown Figure 15-12. Panels (a) and (b) show the short-run impacts of a permanent increase in the money supply in the home (U.S.) money and FX markets; panels (c) and (d) show the long-run impacts and the adjustment from the short run to the long run.

As shown in panels (a), (b), (c), and (d), we suppose the home economy starts with initial equilibria in the home money and FX markets shown by points 1 and 1′, respectively. In the money market, in panels (a) and (c), at point 1, the home money market is initially in equilibrium: MS_1 corresponds to an initial real money supply of $M_{US}^1/\overline{P}_{US}^1$; given real money demand MD, the nominal interest rate is $i_{\$}^1$. In the FX market, in panels (b) and (d), at point 1′, the domestic return DR_1 is the nominal interest rate $i_{\$}^1$. Given the foreign return curve FR_1, the equilibrium exchange rate is $E_{\$/€}^1$. If both economies are at a long-run equilibrium with zero depreciation, then this is also the expected future exchange rate $E_{\$/€}^{e1} = E_{\$/€}^1$.

We now start to figure out what happens after the policy shock hits today, working backward from the future to the present.

The Long Run Refer to panels (c) and (d) of Figure 15-12. In the long run, we know from the monetary approach that an increase in the money supply will eventually lead to a proportionate increase in the price level and the exchange rate. If the money supply increases from M_{US}^1 to M_{US}^2 today, then the price level will *eventually* increase by the same proportion from P_{US}^1 to P_{US}^2, and, to maintain PPP, the exchange rate will *eventually* rise by the same proportion (and the dollar will depreciate) from $E_{\$/€}^1$ to its long-run level $E_{\$/€}^4$, in panel (d), where $E_{\$/€}^4/E_{\$/€}^1 = P_{US}^2/P_{US}^1 = M_{US}^2/M_{US}^1 > 1$. (We use "4" to denote long-run exchange rate values because there will be some short-run responses to consider in just a moment.)

Thus, in the long run, in panel (c), if money and prices both rise in the same proportion, then the real money supply will be unchanged at its original level $M_{US}^1/P_{US}^1 = M_{US}^2/P_{US}^2$, the real money supply curve will still be in its original position MS_1, and the nominal interest rate will again be $i_{\$}^1$. In the long run, the money market returns to where it started: long-run equilibrium is at point 4 (which is the same as point 1).

In the FX market, however, a permanent money supply shock causes some permanent changes in the long run. One thing that does not change is the domestic return DR_1, since in the long run it returns to $i_{\$}^1$. But the exchange rate will rise from the initial long-run exchange rate $E_{\$/€}^1$, to a new long-run level $E_{\$/€}^4$. Because $E_{\$/€}^4$ is a long-run stable level, it is also the new expected level of the exchange rate $E_{\$/€}^4$ that will prevail in the future. That is, the future will look like the present, under our assumptions, except that the exchange rate will be sitting at $E_{\$/€}^4$ instead of $E_{\$/€}^1$. What does this change do to the foreign return curve FR? As we know, when the expected exchange rate increases, foreign returns are higher, so the FR curve shifts up, from FR_1 to FR_2. Because in the long run $E_{\$/€}^4$ is the new stable equilibrium exchange rate, and $i_{\$}^1$ is the interest rate, the new FX market equilibrium is at point 4′ where FR_2 intersects DR_1.

FIGURE 15-12

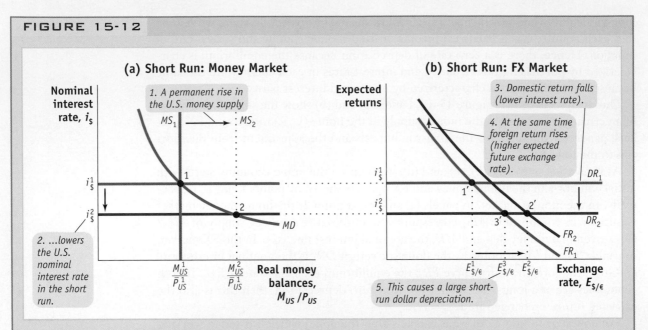

Permanent Expansion of the Home Money Supply, Short-Run Impact: In panel (a), the home price level is fixed, but the supply of dollar balances increases and real money supply shifts out. To restore equilibrium at point 2, the interest rate falls from $i_\$^1$ to $i_\$^2$. In panel (b), in the FX market, the home interest rate falls, so the domestic return decreases and DR shifts down. In addition, the permanent change in the home money supply implies a permanent, long-run depreciation of the dollar. Hence, there is also a permanent rise in $E_{\$/€}^e$, which causes a permanent increase in the foreign return $i_€ + (E_{\$/€}^e − E_{\$/€})/E_{\$/€}$, all else equal; FR shifts up from FR_1 to FR_2. The simultaneous fall in DR and rise in FR cause the home currency to depreciate steeply, leading to a new equilibrium at point 2′ (and not at 3′, which would be the equilibrium if the policy were temporary).

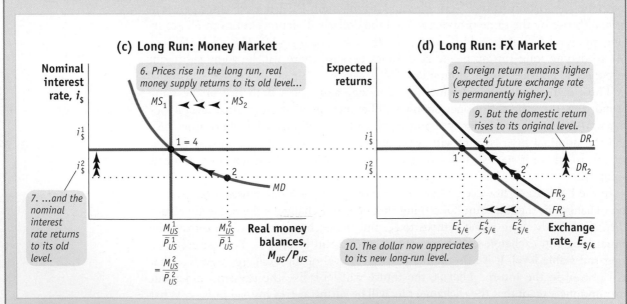

Long-Run Adjustment: In panel (c), in the long run, prices are flexible, so the home price level and the exchange rate both rise in proportion with the money supply. Prices rise to P_{US}^2, and real money supply returns to its original level M_{US}^1/P_{US}^1. The money market gradually shifts back to equilibrium at point 4 (the same as point 1). In panel (d), in the FX market, the domestic return DR, which equals the home interest rate, gradually shifts back to its original level. The foreign return curve FR does not move at all: there are no further changes in the foreign interest rate or in the future expected exchange rate. The FX market equilibrium shifts gradually to point 4′. The exchange rate falls (and the dollar appreciates) from $E_{\$/€}^2$ to $E_{\$/€}^4$. Arrows in both graphs show the path of gradual adjustment.

The Short Run Only now that we have changes in expectations worked out can we work back through panels (a) and (b) of Figure 15-12 to see what will happen in the short run.

Look first at the FX market in panel (b). Because expectations about the future exchange rate have changed with today's policy announcement, the FX market is affected immediately. Everyone knows that the exchange rate will be $E^4_{\$/€}$ in the future. The foreign return curve shifts when the expected exchange rate changes; it rises from FR_1 to FR_2. This is the same shift we just saw in the long-run panel (d). The dollar is expected to depreciate to $E^4_{\$/€}$ (relative to $E^1_{\$/€}$) in the future, so euro deposits are more attractive today.

Now consider the impact of the change in monetary policy in the short run. Look at the money market in panel (a). In the short run, if the money supply increases from M^1_{US} to M^2_{US} but prices are sticky at P^1_{US}, then real money balances rise from M^1_{US}/P^1_{US} to M^2_{US}/P^1_{US}. The real money supply shifts from MS_1 to MS_2 and the home interest rate falls from $i^1_\$$ to $i^2_\$$, leading to a new short-run money market equilibrium at point 2.

Now look back to the FX market in panel (b). If this were a *temporary* monetary policy shock, expectations would be unchanged, and the FR_1 curve would still describe foreign returns, but domestic returns would fall from DR_1 to DR_2 as the interest rate fell and the home currency would depreciate to the level $E^3_{\$/€}$. The FX market equilibrium, after a temporary money supply shock, would be at point 3', as we have seen before.

But this is not the case now. This time we are looking at a permanent shock to money supply. It has *two* effects on today's FX market. One impact of the money supply shock is to lower the home interest rate, decreasing domestic returns in today's FX market from DR_1 to DR_2. The other impact of the money supply shock is to increase the future expected exchange rate, increasing foreign returns in today's FX market from FR_1 to FR_2. Hence, the FX market equilibrium in the short run is where DR_2 and FR_2 intersect, now at point 2', and the exchange rate depreciates all the way to $E^2_{\$/€}$.

Note that the short-run equilibrium level of the exchange rate ($E^2_{\$/€}$) is higher than the level that would be observed under a temporary shock ($E^3_{\$/€}$) and also higher than the level that will be observed in the long run ($E^4_{\$/€}$). To sum up, *in the short run, the permanent shock causes the exchange rate to depreciate more than it would under a temporary shock and more than it will end up depreciating in the long run.*

Adjustment from Short Run to Long Run The arrows in panels (c) and (d) of Figure 15-12 trace what happens as we move from the short run to the long run. Prices that were initially sticky in the short run become unstuck. The price level rises from P^1_{US} to P^2_{US}, and this pushes the real money supply back to its initial level, from MS_2 back to MS_1. Money demand MD is unchanged. Hence, in the home money market of panel (c), the economy moves from the short-run equilibrium at point 2 to the long-run equilibrium, which is again at point 1, following the path shown by the arrows. Hence, the interest rate gradually rises from $i^2_\$$ back to $i^1_\$$. This raises the domestic returns over in the FX market of panel (d) from DR_2 back to DR_1. So the FX market moves from the short-run equilibrium at point 2' to the long-run equilibrium, which is again at point 4'.

An Example Let's make this very tricky experiment a bit more concrete with a numerical example. Suppose you are told that, all else equal, (i) the home money supply permanently increases by 5% today; (ii) prices are sticky in the short run, so this also causes an increase in real money supply that lowers domestic interest rates by four percentage points from 6% to 2%; (iii) prices will fully adjust in one year's time to today's monetary expansion and PPP will hold again. Based on this information, can you predict what will happen to prices and the exchange rate today and in a year's time?

Yes. Work backward from the long run to the short run, as before. In the long run, a 5% increase in M means a 5% increase in P that will be achieved in one year. By PPP, this 5% increase in P implies a 5% rise in E (a 5% depreciation in the dollar's value) over the same period. In other words, over the next year E will rise at 5% per year, which will be the rate of depreciation. Finally, in the short run, UIP tells us what happens to the exchange rate today: to compensate investors for the four percentage point decrease in the domestic interest rate, arbitrage in the FX market requires that the value of the home currency be expected to appreciate at 4% per year; that is, E must fall 4% in the year ahead. However, if E has to fall 4% in the next year and still end up 5% above its level at the start of today, then it must jump up 9% today: it overshoots its long-run level.

Overshooting

Compared with the temporary expansion of money supply we studied before, the permanent shock has a much greater impact on the exchange rate in the short run.

Under the temporary shock, domestic returns go down; traders want to sell the dollar for one reason only—temporarily lower dollar interest rates make dollar deposits less attractive. Under the permanent shock, domestic returns go down and foreign returns go up; traders want to sell the dollar for two reasons—temporarily lower dollar interest rates and an expected dollar depreciation make dollar deposits *much* less attractive. In the short run, the interest rate and exchange rate effects combine to create an instantaneous "double whammy" for the dollar, which gives rise to a phenomenon that economists refer to as exchange rate **overshooting.**

To better visualize the overshooting phenomenon, we show in Figure 15-13 the time path over which the key economic variables change after the permanent shock we just studied using Figure 15-12. We see the following:

a. The nominal money supply is subject to a one-time increase at time T.

b. Real money balances rise instantaneously but revert to their initial level in the long run; the nominal interest rate falls instantaneously but reverts to its initial level in the long run.

c. The price level is sticky in the short run but rises to a new higher level in the long run, increasing in the same proportion as the nominal money supply.

d. The exchange rate rises (depreciates) to a new higher level in the long run, rising in the same proportion as the nominal money supply. In the short run, however, the exchange rate rises even more, overshooting its long-run level, then gradually decreasing to its long-run level (which is still higher than the initial level).

The overshooting result adds yet another argument for the importance of a sound long-run nominal anchor: without it, exchange rates are likely to be more volatile,

FIGURE 15-13

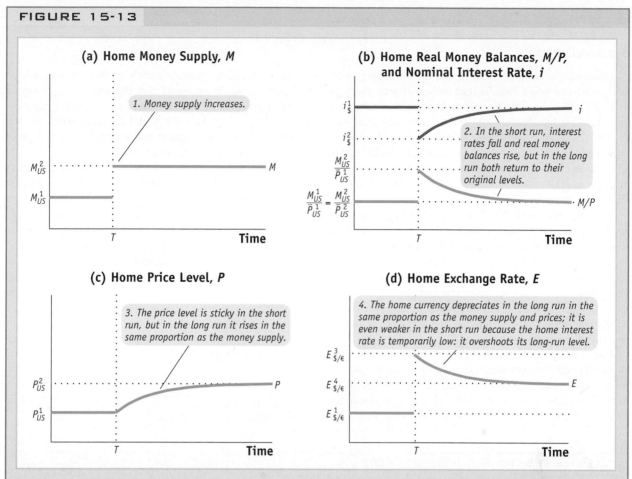

Responses to a Permanent Expansion of the Home Money Supply In panel (a), there is a one-time permanent increase in home (U.S.) nominal money supply at time T. In panel (b), prices are sticky in the short run, so there is a short-run increase in the real money supply and a fall in the home interest rate. In panel (c), in the long run, prices rise in the same proportion as the money supply. In panel (d), in the short run, the exchange rate overshoots its long-run value (the dollar depreciates by a large amount), but in the long run, the exchange rate will have risen only in proportion to changes in money and prices.

creating instability in the forex market and possibly in the wider economy. The wild fluctuations of exchange rates in the 1970s, at a time when exchange rate anchors were ripped loose, exposed these linkages with great clarity (see **Side Bar: Overshooting in Practice**). And new research provides evidence that the shift to a new form of anchoring, inflation targeting, might be helping to bring down exchange rate volatility in recent years.[3]

---

[3] Andrew K. Rose, 2007, "A Stable International Monetary System Emerges: Inflation Targeting Is Bretton Woods, Reversed," *Journal of International Money and Finance*, 26(5), 663–681.

SIDE BAR

Overshooting in Practice

Overshooting can happen in theory, but does it happen in the real world? The model tells us that if there is a tendency for monetary policy shocks to be more permanent than temporary, then there will be a tendency for the exchange rate to be more volatile. Thus, we might expect to see a serious increase in exchange rate volatility whenever a nominal anchoring system breaks down. Indeed, such conditions were seen in the 1970s, which is precisely when the overshooting phenomenon was discovered. How did this happen?

From the 1870s until the 1970s, except during major crises and wars, the world's major currencies were fixed against one another. Floating rates were considered anathema by policy makers and economists. Later in this book, we study the gold standard regime that began circa 1870 and fizzled out in the 1930s and the subsequent "dollar standard" of the 1950s and 1960s that was devised at a conference at Bretton Woods, New Hampshire, in 1944. As we'll see, the Bretton Woods system did not survive for various reasons.

When floating rates reappeared in the 1970s, fears of instability returned. Concern mounted as floating exchange rates proved much more volatile than could be explained according to the prevailing flexible-price monetary approach: the models said that money supplies and real income were simply too stable to be able to generate such large fluctuations (as seen in Figure 15-14). Some feared that this was a case of *animal spirits*, John Maynard Keynes's term for irrational forces, especially in asset markets like that for foreign exchange. The challenge to economists was to derive a new model that could account for the wild swings in exchange rates.

In 1976, economist Rudiger Dornbusch of the Massachusetts Institute of Technology developed such a model. Building on Keynesian foundations, Dornbusch showed that sticky prices and flexible exchange rates implied exchange rate overshooting.[*] Dornbusch's seminal work was a rare case of a theory arriving at just the right time to help explain reality. In the 1970s, countries abandoned exchange rate anchors and groped for new ways to conduct monetary policy in a new economic environment. Policies varied and inflation rates grew, diverged, and persisted. Overshooting helps make sense of all this: if traders saw policies as having no well-defined anchor, monetary policy shocks might no longer be guaranteed to be temporary, so long-run expectations could swing wildly with every piece of news.

---

[*] Rudiger Dornbusch, December 1976, "Expectations and Exchange Rate Dynamics," *Journal of Political Economy,* 84, 1161–1176.

FIGURE 15-14

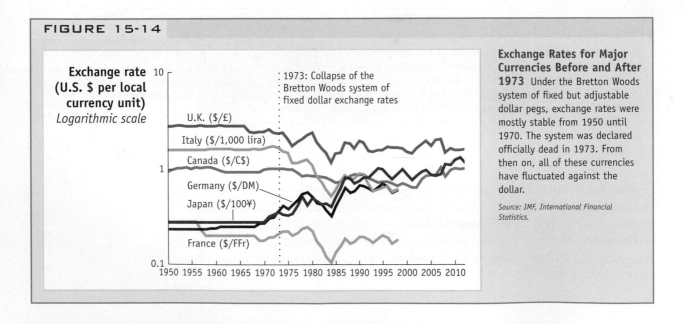

Exchange Rates for Major Currencies Before and After 1973 Under the Bretton Woods system of fixed but adjustable dollar pegs, exchange rates were mostly stable from 1950 until 1970. The system was declared officially dead in 1973. From then on, all of these currencies have fluctuated against the dollar.

Source: IMF, International Financial Statistics.

5 Fixed Exchange Rates and the Trilemma

We have developed a complete theory of exchange rates, based on the assumption that market forces in the money market and the foreign exchange market determine exchange rates. Our models have the most obvious application to the case of floating exchange rate regimes. But as we have seen, not every country floats. Can our theory also be applied to the equally important case of fixed exchange rate regimes and to other intermediate regimes? The answer is yes, and we conclude this chapter by adapting our existing theory for the case of fixed regimes.

What Is a Fixed Exchange Rate Regime?

To understand the crucial difference between fixing and floating, we contrast the polar cases of tight fixing (hard pegs including narrow bands) and free floating, and ignore, for now, intermediate regimes. We also set aside regimes that include controls on arbitrage (*capital controls*) because such extremes of government intervention render our theory superfluous. Instead, we focus on the case of a fixed rate regime without controls so that capital is mobile and arbitrage is free to operate in the foreign exchange market.

Here the government itself becomes an actor in the foreign exchange market and uses intervention in the market to influence the market rate. Exchange rate intervention takes the form of the central bank buying and selling foreign currency at a fixed price, thus holding the market exchange rate at a fixed level denoted $\overline{E}$.

We can explore the implications of that policy in the short run and the long run using the familiar building blocks of our theory. To give a concrete flavor to these analyses, we replace the United States and the Eurozone (whose currencies float against each other) with an example of an actual fixed exchange rate regime. In this example, Foreign remains the Eurozone, but Home is now Denmark.

We examine the implications of Denmark's decision to peg its currency, the krone, to the euro at a fixed rate $\overline{E}_{DKr/€}$.[4]

In the long run, fixing the exchange rate is one kind of nominal anchor. Yet even if it allowed the krone to float but had *some* nominal anchor, Denmark's monetary policy would still be constrained in the long run by the need to achieve its chosen nominal target. We have seen that any country with a nominal anchor faces long-run monetary policy constraints of some kind. *What we now show is that a country with a fixed exchange rate faces monetary policy constraints not just in the long run but also in the short run.*

Pegging Sacrifices Monetary Policy Autonomy in the Short Run: Example

By assumption, equilibrium in the krone–euro forex market requires that the Danish interest rate be equal to the Eurozone interest rate plus the expected rate of depreciation of the krone. But under a peg, the expected rate of depreciation is zero.

---

[4] The actual arrangement is a "narrow band" centered on 7.46038 DKr/€ and officially of width ±2.25%, according to the ERM arrangement between Denmark and the Eurozone that has been in effect since 1999. In practice, the peg is much tighter and krone usually stays within ±0.5% of the central rate.

Here uncovered interest parity reduces to the simple condition that the Danish central bank must set its interest rate equal to $i_\unicode{0x20AC}$, the rate set by the ECB:

$$i_{DKr} = i_\unicode{0x20AC} + \underbrace{\frac{E^e_{DKr/\unicode{0x20AC}} - E_{DKr/\unicode{0x20AC}}}{E_{DKr/\unicode{0x20AC}}}}_{\substack{\text{Equals zero for a credible} \\ \text{fixed exchange rate}}} = i_\unicode{0x20AC}$$

Denmark has lost control of its monetary policy: it cannot independently change its interest rate under a peg.

The same is true of money supply policy. Short-run equilibrium in Denmark's money market requires that money supply equal money demand, but once Denmark's interest rate is set equal to the Eurozone interest rate $i_\unicode{0x20AC}$, there is only one feasible level for money supply, as we see by imposing $i_\unicode{0x20AC}$ as the Danish interest rate in money market equilibrium:

$$M_{DEN} = \overline{P}_{DEN} L_{DEN}(i_{DKr}) Y_{DEN} = \overline{P}_{DEN} L_{DEN}(i_\unicode{0x20AC}) Y_{DEN}$$

The implications are striking. The final expression contains the euro interest rate (exogenous, as far as the Danes are concerned), the fixed price level (exogenous by assumption), and output (also exogenous by assumption). No variable in this expression is under the control of the Danish authorities in the short run, and this is the only level of the Danish money supply consistent with equilibrium in the money and forex markets at the pegged rate $\overline{E}_{DKr/\unicode{0x20AC}}$. If the Danish central bank is to maintain the peg, then in the short run it must choose the level of money supply implied by the last equation.

What's going on? Arbitrage is the key force. For example, if the Danish central bank tried to supply more krone and lower interest rates, they would be foiled by arbitrage. Danes would want to sell krone deposits and buy higher-yield euro deposits, applying downward pressure on the krone. To maintain the peg, whatever krone the Danish central bank had tried to pump into circulation, it would promptly have to buy them back in the foreign exchange market.

Thus, *our short-run theory still applies, but with a different chain of causality:*

- Under a float, the home monetary authorities pick the money supply M. In the short run, the choice of M determines the interest rate i in the money market; in turn, via UIP, the level of i determines the exchange rate E. The money supply is an input in the model (an exogenous variable), and the exchange rate is an output of the model (an endogenous variable).

- Under a fix, this logic is reversed. Home monetary authorities pick the fixed level of the exchange rate E. In the short run, a fixed E pins down the home interest rate i via UIP (forcing i to equal the foreign interest rate i^*); in turn, the level of i determines the level of the money supply M necessary to meet money demand. The exchange rate is an input in the model (an exogenous variable), and the money supply is an output of the model (an endogenous variable).

This reversal of short-run causality is shown in a new schematic in the top part of Figure 15-15.

FIGURE 15-15

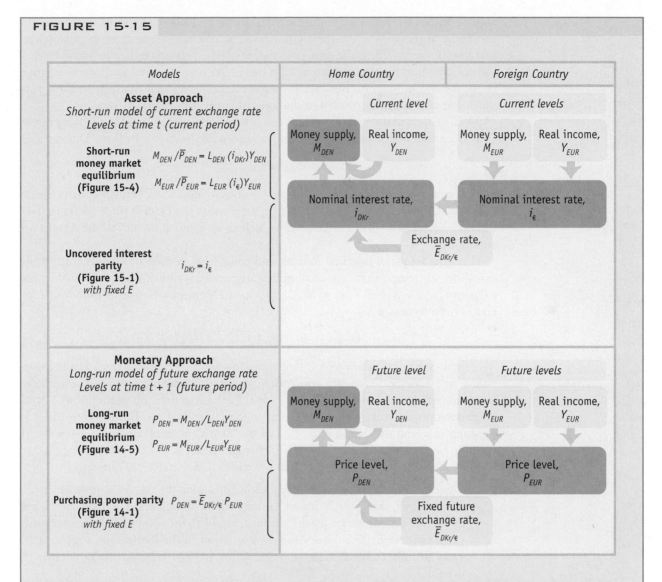

| | Models | Home Country | Foreign Country |

Asset Approach
*Short-run model of current exchange rate
Levels at time t (current period)*

Short-run money market equilibrium (Figure 15-4)
$M_{DEN}/\overline{P}_{DEN} = L_{DEN}(i_{DKr})Y_{DEN}$
$M_{EUR}/\overline{P}_{EUR} = L_{EUR}(i_{\unicode{x20AC}})Y_{EUR}$

Uncovered interest parity (Figure 15-1)
with fixed E
$i_{DKr} = i_{\unicode{x20AC}}$

Current level

Money supply, M_{DEN} Real income, Y_{DEN}

Nominal interest rate, i_{DKr}

Exchange rate, $\overline{E}_{DKr/\unicode{x20AC}}$

Current levels

Money supply, M_{EUR} Real income, Y_{EUR}

Nominal interest rate, $i_{\unicode{x20AC}}$

Monetary Approach
*Long-run model of future exchange rate
Levels at time t + 1 (future period)*

Long-run money market equilibrium (Figure 14-5)
$P_{DEN} = M_{DEN}/L_{DEN}Y_{DEN}$
$P_{EUR} = M_{EUR}/L_{EUR}Y_{EUR}$

Purchasing power parity (Figure 14-1)
with fixed E
$P_{DEN} = \overline{E}_{DKr/\unicode{x20AC}}P_{EUR}$

Future level

Money supply, M_{DEN} Real income, Y_{DEN}

Price level, P_{DEN}

Fixed future exchange rate, $\overline{E}_{DKr/\unicode{x20AC}}$

Future levels

Money supply, M_{EUR} Real income, Y_{EUR}

Price level, P_{EUR}

A Complete Theory of Fixed Exchange Rates: Same Building Blocks, Different Known and Unknown Variables Unlike in Figure 15-10, the home country is now assumed to fix its exchange rate with the foreign country. Inputs to the model are known exogenous variables (in green boxes). Outputs of the model are unknown endogenous variables (in red boxes). The levels of real income and the fixed exchange rate determine the home money supply levels, given outcomes in the foreign country.

Pegging Sacrifices Monetary Policy Autonomy in the Long Run: Example

As we have noted, choosing a nominal anchor implies a loss of long-run monetary policy autonomy. Let's quickly see how that works when the anchor is a fixed exchange rate.

Following our discussion of the standard monetary model, we must first ask what the nominal interest rate is going to be in Denmark in the long run. But we have already answered that question; it is going to be tied down the same way as in the short run, at the level set by the ECB, namely $i_{\text{€}}$. We might question, in turn, where *that* level $i_{\text{€}}$ comes from (the answer is that it will be related to the "neutral" level of the nominal interest rate consistent with the ECB's own nominal anchor, its inflation target for the Eurozone). But that is beside the point: all that matters is that $i_{\text{€}}$ is as much out of Denmark's control in the long run as it is in the short run.

Next we turn to the price level in Denmark, which is determined in the long run by PPP. But if the exchange rate is pegged, we can write long-run PPP for Denmark as

$$P_{DEN} = \overline{E}_{DKr/\text{€}}P_{EUR}$$

Here we encounter another variable that is totally outside of Danish control in the long run. Under PPP, pegging to the euro means that the Danish price level is a fixed multiple of the Eurozone price level (which is exogenous, as far as the Danes are concerned).

With the long-run nominal interest and price level outside of Danish control, we can show, as before, that monetary policy autonomy is out of the question. We just substitute $i_{DKr} = i_{\text{€}}$ and $P_{DEN} = \overline{E}_{DKr/\text{€}}P_{EUR}$ into Denmark's long-run money market equilibrium to obtain

$$M_{DEN} = P_{DEN}L_{DEN}(i_{DKr})Y_{DEN} = \overline{E}_{DKr/\text{€}}P_{EUR}L_{DEN}(i_{\text{€}})Y_{DEN}$$

The final expression contains the long-run euro interest rate and price levels (exogenous, as far as the Danes are concerned), the fixed exchange rate level (exogenous by assumption), and long-run Danish output (also exogenous by assumption). Again, no variable in the final expression is under the control of the Danish authorities in the long run, and this is the only level of the Danish money supply consistent with equilibrium in the money and foreign exchange market at the pegged rate of $\overline{E}_{DKr/\text{€}}$.

Thus, *our long-run theory still applies*, just with a different chain of causality:

- Under a float, the home monetary authorities pick the money supply M. In the long run, the growth rate of M determines the interest rate i via the Fisher effect and also the price level P; in turn, via PPP, the level of P determines the exchange rate E. The money supply is an input in the model (an exogenous variable), and the exchange rate is an output of the model (an endogenous variable).

- Under a fix, this logic is reversed. Home monetary authorities pick the exchange rate E. In the long run, the choice of E determines the price level P via PPP, and also the interest rate i via UIP; these, in turn, determine the necessary level of the money supply M. The exchange rate is an input in the model (an exogenous variable), and the money supply is an output of the model (an endogenous variable).

This reversal of long-run causality is also shown in the new schematic in the bottom part of Figure 15-15.

The Trilemma

Our findings lead to the conclusion that policy makers face some tough choices. Not all desirable policy goals can be simultaneously met. These constraints are summed up in one of the most important principles in open-economy macroeconomics.

Consider the following three equations and parallel statements about desirable *policy goals*. For illustration we return to the Denmark–Eurozone example:

---

1. $\dfrac{E^e_{DKr/\unicode{x20AC}} - E_{DKr/\unicode{x20AC}}}{E_{DKr/\unicode{x20AC}}} = 0$

A fixed exchange rate

- May be desired as a means to promote stability in trade and investment
- Represented here by zero expected depreciation

---

2. $i_{DKr} = i_{\unicode{x20AC}} + \dfrac{E^e_{DKr/\unicode{x20AC}} - E_{DKr/\unicode{x20AC}}}{E_{DKr/\unicode{x20AC}}}$

International capital mobility

- May be desired as a means to promote integration, efficiency, and risk sharing
- Represented here by uncovered interest parity, which results from arbitrage

---

3. $i_{DKr} \neq i_{\unicode{x20AC}}$

Monetary policy autonomy

- May be desired as a means to manage the home economy's business cycle
- Represented here by the ability to set the home interest rate independently of the foreign interest rate

---

For a variety of reasons, as noted, governments may want to pursue all three of these policy goals. But they can't: formulae 1, 2, and 3 show that it is a *mathematical impossibility* as shown by the following statements:

- 1 and 2 imply not 3 (1 and 2 imply interest equality, contradicting 3).
- 2 and 3 imply not 1 (2 and 3 imply an expected change in *E*, contradicting 1).
- 3 and 1 imply not 2 (3 and 1 imply a difference between domestic and foreign returns, contradicting 2).

This result, known as the **trilemma,** is one of the most important ideas in international macroeconomics.[5] It tells us that the three policy goals just outlined are mutually incompatible: you cannot have all three at once. You must choose to drop one of the three (or, equivalently, you must adopt one of three pairs: 1 and 2, 2 and 3, or 3 and 1). Sadly, there is a long history of macroeconomic disasters stemming from the failure of some policy that ignored this fundamental lesson.

The trilemma can be illustrated graphically as in Figure 15-16. Each corner of the triangle represents a viable policy regime choice. For each corner, the label on the opposite edge of the triangle indicates the goal that has been sacrificed, while the labels on the two adjacent edges show the two goals that can be attained under that choice (see **Side Bar: Intermediate Regimes**).

---

[5] A definition: "Trilemma *noun* 1. a quandary posed by three alternative courses of action" (*Collins English Dictionary* online).

FIGURE 15-16

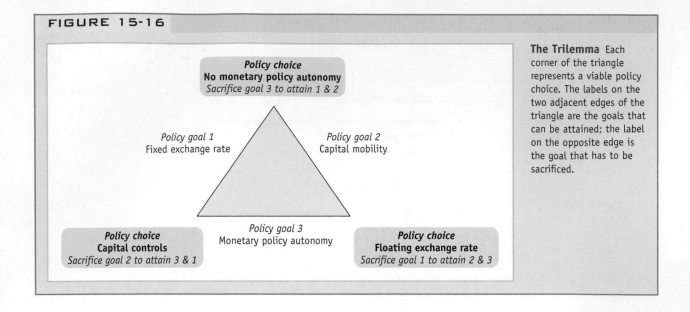

The Trilemma Each corner of the triangle represents a viable policy choice. The labels on the two adjacent edges of the triangle are the goals that can be attained; the label on the opposite edge is the goal that has to be sacrificed.

SIDE BAR

Intermediate Regimes

The lessons of the trilemma most clearly apply when the policies are at the ends of a spectrum: a hard peg or a float, perfect capital mobility or immobility, complete autonomy or none at all. But sometimes a country may not be fully in one of the three corners: the rigidity of the peg, the degree of capital mobility, and the independence of monetary policy could be partial rather than full.

For example, in a band arrangement, the exchange rate is maintained within a range of ±X% of some central rate. The significance of the band is that some expected depreciation (i.e., a little bit of floating) is possible. As a result, a limited interest differential can open up between the two countries. For example, suppose the band is 2% wide (i.e., ±1% around a central rate). To compute home interest rates, UIP tells us that we must add the foreign interest rate (let's suppose it is 5%) to the expected rate of depreciation (which is ±2% if the exchange rate moves from one band edge to the other). Thus, Home may "fix" this way and still have the freedom to set 12-month interest rates in the range between 3% and 7%. But the home country cannot evade the trilemma forever: on average, over time, the rate of depreciation will have to be zero to keep the exchange rate within the narrow band, meaning that the home interest rate must track the foreign interest rate apart from small deviations.

Similar qualifications to the trilemma could result from partial capital mobility, in which barriers to arbitrage could also lead to interest differentials. And with such differentials emerging, the desire for partial monetary autonomy can be accommodated.

In practice, once these distinctions are understood, it is usually possible to make some kind of judgment about which corner best describes the country's policy choice. For example, in 2007 both Slovakia and Denmark were supposedly pegged to the euro as members of the EU's Exchange Rate Mechanism (ERM). But the similarities ended there. The Danish krone was operating in ERM bands of official width ±2.25%, but closer to ±0.5% in practice, a pretty hard peg with almost no movement. The Slovak koruna was operating with ±15% bands and at one point even shifted that band by appreciating its central rate by 8.5% in March 2007. With its perpetual narrow band, Denmark's regime was clearly fixed. With its wide and adjustable bands, Slovakia's regime was closer to managed floating.[*]

---

[*] Note that Slovakia has since joined the euro as of 2009.

The Trilemma in Europe

We motivated the trilemma with the case of Denmark, which has chosen policy goals 1 and 2. As a member of the European Union (EU), Denmark adheres to the single-market legislation that requires free movement of capital within the bloc. It also unilaterally pegs its krone to the euro under the EU's Exchange Rate Mechanism (ERM), an arrangement that ostensibly serves as a stepping-stone to Eurozone membership. Consequently, UIP predicts that the Danish central bank must set an interest rate at the same level as that set by the ECB; it has lost option 3.

The Danes could make one of two politically difficult choices if they wished to gain monetary independence from the ECB: they could abandon their commitment to the EU treaties on capital mobility (drop 2 to get 3), which is extremely unlikely, or they could abandon their ERM commitment and let the krone float against the euro (drop 1 to get 3), which is also fairly unlikely. Floating is, however, the choice of the United Kingdom, an EU country that has withdrawn from the ERM and that allows the pound to float against the euro.

Figure 15-17 shows evidence for the trilemma. Since 1999 the United Kingdom has had the ability to set interest rates independently of the ECB. But Denmark has

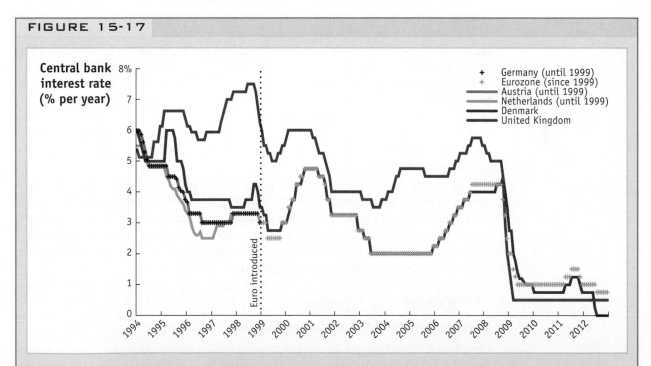

FIGURE 15-17

The Trilemma in Europe The figure shows selected central banks' base interest rates for the period 1994 to 2012 with reference to the German mark and euro base rates. In this period, the British made a policy choice to float against the German mark and (after 1999) against the euro. This permitted monetary independence because interest rates set by the Bank of England could diverge from those set in Frankfurt. No such independence in policy making was afforded by the Danish decision to peg the krone first to the mark and then to the euro. Since 1999 the Danish interest rate has moved almost exactly in line with the ECB rate. Similar forces operated pre-1999 for other countries pegging to the mark, such as the Netherlands and Austria. Until they joined the Eurozone in 1999, their interest rates, like that of Denmark, closely tracked the German rate.

Sources: Websites of the central banks.

not: since 1999 the Danish interest rate has tracked the ECB's rate almost exactly. (Most of the departures from equality reflect uncertainty about the euro project and Denmark's peg at two key moments: at the very start of the euro project in 1999, and during the credibility crisis of the Eurozone since the crisis of 2008.)

These monetary policy ties to Frankfurt even predate the euro itself. Before 1999 Denmark, and some countries such as Austria and the Netherlands, pegged to the German mark with the same result: their interest rates had to track the German interest rate, but the U.K. interest rate did not. The big difference is that Austria and the Netherlands have formally abolished their national currencies, the schilling and the guilder, and have adopted the euro—an extreme and explicit renunciation of monetary independence. Meanwhile, the Danish krone lives on, showing that a national currency can suggest monetary sovereignty in theory but may deliver nothing of the sort in practice. ■

6 Conclusions

In this chapter, we drew together everything we have learned so far about exchange rates. We built on the concepts of arbitrage and equilibrium in the foreign exchange market in the short run, taking expectations as given and applying uncovered interest parity. We also relied on the purchasing power parity theory as a guide to exchange rate determination in the long run. Putting together all these building blocks provides a complete and internally consistent theory of exchange rate determination.

Exchange rates are an interesting topic in and of themselves, but at the end of the day, we also care about what they mean for the wider economy, how they relate to macroeconomic performance, and the part they play in the global monetary system. That is our goal in the next chapters in which we apply our exchange rate theories in a wider framework to help us understand how exchange rates function in the national and international economy.

The theory we've developed in the past three chapters is the first tool that economists and policy makers pick up when studying a problem involving exchange rates. This theory has served well in rich and poor countries, whether in periods of economic stability or turbulence. Remarkably, it has even been applied in wartime, and to round off our discussion of exchange rates, we examine some colorful applications of the theory from conflicts past and present.

APPLICATION

News and the Foreign Exchange Market in Wartime

Our theory of exchange rates places expectations at center stage, but demonstrating the effect of changing expectations empirically is a challenge. However, wars dramatically expose the power of expectations to change exchange rates. War raises the risk that a currency may depreciate in value rapidly in the future, possibly all the way to zero. For one thing, the government may need to print money to finance its war effort, but how much inflation this practice will generate may be unclear. In addition, there is a risk of defeat and a decision by the victor to impose new economic arrangements such as a new currency; the existing currency may then be converted into the new currency at a rate dictated by the victors or, in a worst-case scenario, it may be declared totally worthless, that is, not legal tender. Demand for the currency will then collapse to nothing and so will its value. Investors in the foreign exchange market are continually updating their forecasts about a war's possible outcomes, and, as a result, the path of an exchange rate during wartime usually reveals a clear influence of the effects of news.

The U.S. Civil War, 1861–1865 For four years, beginning April 12, 1861, a war raged between Union (Northern) and Confederate (Southern) forces. An important economic dimension of this conflict was the decision by the Confederate states to issue their own currency, the Confederate dollar, to help gain economic autonomy from the North and finance their war effort. The exchange rate of the Confederate dollar against the U.S. dollar is shown in Figure 15-18.

How should we interpret these data? The two currencies differed in one important respect. If the South had won, and the Confederate states had gained independence, they would have kept their Confederate dollar, and the Northern United States would have kept their U.S. dollar, too. Instead, the South was defeated, and, as expected in these circumstances, the U.S. dollar was imposed as the sole currency of the unified country; the Confederate dollar, like all liabilities of the Confederate nation, was repudiated by the victors and, hence, became worthless.

FIGURE 15-18

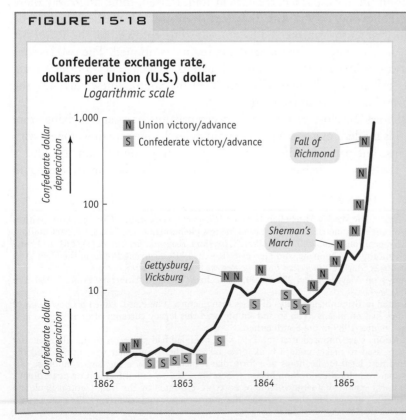

Exchange Rates and News in the U.S. Civil War The value of the Confederate dollar fluctuated against the U.S. dollar and is shown on a logarithmic scale. Against the backdrop of a steady trend, victories and advances by the North (N) were generally associated with faster depreciation of the Confederate currency, whereas major Southern successes (S) usually led to a stronger Confederate currency.

Sources: Wesley C. Mitchell, 1908, Gold, Prices, and Wages under the Greenback Standard *(Berkeley, Calif.: University of California Press), Table 2; George T. McCandless Jr., 1996, "Money, Expectations, and U.S. Civil War,"* American Economic Review, *86(3), 661–671.*

War news regularly influenced the exchange rate.[6] As the South headed for defeat, the value of the Confederate dollar shrank. The overall trend was driven partly by inflationary war finance and partly by the probability of defeat. Major Northern victories marked "N" tended to coincide with depreciations of the Confederate dollar. Major Southern victories marked "S" were associated with appreciations or, at least, a slower depreciation. The key Union victory at Gettysburg, July 1–3, 1863, and the near simultaneous fall of Vicksburg on July 4 were followed by a dramatic depreciation of the Confederate dollar. By contrast, Southern victories (in the winter of 1862 to 1863 and the spring of 1864) were periods when the Southern currency held steady or even appreciated. But by the fall of 1864, and particularly after Sherman's March, the writing was on the wall, and the Confederate dollar began its final decline.

Currency traders in New York did good business either way. They were known to whistle "John Brown's Body" after a Union victory and "Dixie" after Confederate success, making profits as they traded dollars for gold and vice versa. Abraham Lincoln was not impressed, declaring, "What do you think of those fellows in Wall Street, who are gambling in gold at such a time as this? . . . For my part, I wish every one of them had his devilish head shot off."

The Iraq War, 2002–2003 The Civil War is not the only example of such phenomena. In 2003 Iraq was invaded by a U.S.-led coalition of forces intent on overthrowing the regime of Saddam Hussein, and the effects of war on currencies were again visible.[7]

Our analysis of this case is made a little more complicated by the fact that at the time of the invasion there were *two* currencies in Iraq. Indeed, some might say there were two Iraqs. Following a 1991 war, Iraq had been divided: in the North, a de facto Kurdish government was protected by a no-fly zone enforced by the Royal Air Force and U.S. Air Force; in the South, Saddam's regime continued. The two regions developed into two distinct economies, and each had its own currency. In the North, Iraqi dinar notes called "Swiss" dinars circulated.[8] In the South, a new currency, the "Saddam" or "print" dinar, was introduced.[9]

Figure 15-19 shows the close correlation between wartime news and exchange rate movements for this modern episode. We can compare exchange rate movements with well-known events, but panel (a) allows another interesting comparison. In 2002 a company called TradeSports Exchange allowed bets on Saddam's destiny by setting up

---

[6] This correlation was noted by Wesley Mitchell in 1903, (*A History of the Greenbacks*; Chicago: University of Chicago Press). For recent econometric studies that examine this phenomenon, see George T. McCandless, Jr., 1996, "Money, Expectations, and U.S. Civil War," *American Economic Review*, 86(3), 661–671; and Kristen L. Willard, Timothy W. Guinnane, and Harvey S. Rosen, 1996, "Turning Points in the Civil War: Views from the Greenback Market," *American Economic Review*, 86(4), 1001–1018.

[7] This case study draws on Mervyn King, May 2004, "The Institutions of Monetary Policy," *American Economic Review*, 94(2), 1–13.

[8] The notes were printed in Britain using plates of Swiss manufacture. The Kurds issued no new notes of their own; indeed, they had no means to do so and simply used this legacy currency after 1991. No new Swiss dinars were issued after 1989 in the South either.

[9] Once economic sanctions were imposed after the 1991 war, Baghdad had no access to the high-security technology and papers used to make modern banknotes. Instead, the Swiss dinar was retired, and the Saddam regime issued new legal tender notes in a form that it *could* print by using low-technology offset litho techniques that your local printer might use. These were the so-called Saddam or print dinars. Circulation of these notes exploded: a large volume of notes were printed by the Iraqi Central Bank and counterfeits added to this number. For these reasons, the northern currency, the Swiss dinar, was much more stable in the 1990s than the Saddam dinar.

FIGURE 15-19

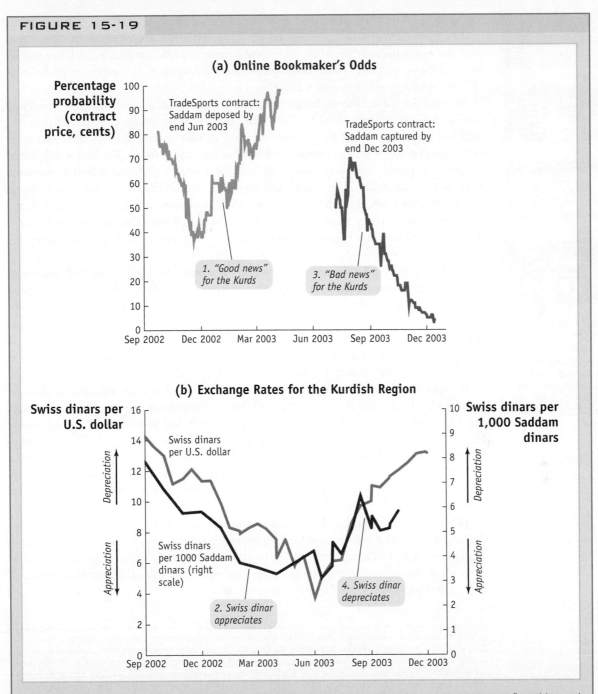

(a) Online Bookmaker's Odds

Percentage probability (contract price, cents)

TradeSports contract: Saddam deposed by end Jun 2003

TradeSports contract: Saddam captured by end Dec 2003

1. "Good news" for the Kurds

3. "Bad news" for the Kurds

(b) Exchange Rates for the Kurdish Region

Swiss dinars per U.S. dollar

Swiss dinars per 1,000 Saddam dinars

Swiss dinars per U.S. dollar

Swiss dinars per 1000 Saddam dinars (right scale)

Depreciation / Appreciation

2. Swiss dinar appreciates

4. Swiss dinar depreciates

Exchange Rates and News in the Iraq War As regime change looked more likely from 2002 to 2003, as reflected in panel (a), the Swiss dinar, the currency used by the Kurds, appreciated against the U.S. dollar and the Saddam dinar, the currency used in the south, as shown in panel (b). When the U.S. invasion ended, the difficult postwar transition began. Insurgencies and the failure to find Saddam Hussein became a cause for concern, as reflected in panel (a). The Swiss dinar depreciated against the dollar until December 2003, as shown in panel (b).

Notes: Panel (a) shows two contract prices: the value in cents of a TradeSports contract that paid 100¢ if Saddam were deposed by the end of June 2003 and 0 otherwise, and the value in cents of a contract that paid 100¢ if Saddam were captured by the end of December 2003 and 0 otherwise.

Source: Mervyn King, 2004, "The Institutions of Monetary Policy," American Economic Review, 94(2), 1–13.

Currencies in wartime:
A Confederate 2 dollar note
of 1864 issued in Richmond;
an Iraqi Swiss 25 dinar
from the Kurdish region;
a widely forged post-1991
Iraqi Saddam 25 dinar note;
a post-2003 250 new Iraqi
dinar note.

a market in contracts that paid $1 if he was deposed by a certain date, and the prices of these contracts are shown using the left scale. After he was deposed, contracts that paid out upon his capture were traded, and these are also shown. If such a contract had a price of, say, 80¢, then this implied that "the market" believed the probability of overthrow or apprehension was 80%.

In panel (b), we see the exchange rates of the Swiss dinar against the U.S. dollar and the Saddam dinar from 2002 to 2003. The Kurds' Swiss dinar–U.S. dollar rate had held at 18 per U.S. dollar for several years but steadily appreciated in 2002 and 2003 as the prospect of a war to depose Saddam became more likely. By May 2003, when the invasion phase of the war ended and Saddam had been deposed, it had appreciated as far as 6 to the dollar. The war clearly drove this trend: the more likely the removal of Saddam, the more durable would be Kurdish autonomy, and the more likely it was that a postwar currency would be created that respected the value of the Kurds' Swiss dinars. Notice how the rise in the value of the Swiss dinar tracked the odds of regime change until mid-2003.

After Baghdad fell, the coalition sought to capture Saddam, who had gone into hiding. As the hunt wore on, and a militant/terrorist insurgency began, fears mounted that he would never be found and his regime might survive underground and reappear. The odds on capture fell, and, moving in parallel, so did the value of the Swiss dinar. The Kurds now faced a rising probability that the whole affair would end badly for them and their currency. (However, when Saddam Hussein was captured on December 14, 2003, the Swiss dinar appreciated again.)

We can also track related movements in the Swiss dinar against the Saddam or print dinar. Before and during the war, while the Swiss dinar was appreciating against the U.S. dollar, it was also appreciating against the Saddam dinar. It strengthened from around 10 Swiss dinars per 1,000 Saddam dinars in early 2002 to about 3 Swiss dinars per 1,000 Saddam dinars in mid-2003. Then, as the postwar operations dragged on, this trend was reversed. By late 2003, the market rate was about 6 Swiss dinars per 1,000 Saddam dinars. Again, we can see how the Kurds' fortunes appeared to the market to rise and fall.

What became of all these dinars? Iraqis fared better than the holders of Confederate dollars. A new dinar was created under a currency reform announced in July 2003 and implemented from October 15, 2003, to January 15, 2004.[10] Exchange rate expectations soon moved into line with the increasingly credible official conversion rates and U.S. dollar exchange rates for the new dinar. ■

---

[10] Under this reform, all the Swiss and Saddam notes were retired and a newly designed, secure currency for Iraq was brought into circulation nationally. As long as this currency reform was seen as credible, and the market believed it would successfully take place, the market rate would have to converge to the fixed rate set in advance by the authorities for note replacement. As the reform date approached, this convergence occurred, except for what appears to be a small "forgery risk premium" on the Saddam notes—detecting a fake among these notes was by no means simple.

KEY POINTS

1. Our theory of exchange rates builds on two ideas: arbitrage and expectations. First, we developed the theory for the case of floating exchange rates.

2. In the short run, we assume prices are sticky and the asset approach to exchange rates is valid. Interest-bearing accounts in different currencies may offer different rates of nominal interest. Currencies may be expected to depreciate or appreciate against one another. There is an incentive for arbitrage: investors will shift funds from one country to another until the expected rate of return (measured in a common currency) is equalized. Arbitrage in the foreign exchange (forex, or FX) market determines today's spot exchange rate, and the forex market is in equilibrium when the uncovered interest parity condition holds. To apply the uncovered interest parity (UIP) condition, however, we need a forecast of the expected exchange rate in the long run.

3. In the long run, we assume prices are flexible and the monetary approach to exchange rates is valid. This approach states that in the long run, purchasing power parity (PPP) holds so that the exchange rate must equal the ratio of the price levels in the two countries. Each price level, in turn, depends on the ratio of money supply to money demand in each country. The monetary approach can be used to forecast the long-run

future expected exchange rate, which, in turn, feeds back into short-run exchange rate determination via the UIP equation.

4. Putting together all of these ingredients yields a complete theory of how exchange rates are determined in the short run and the long run.

5. This model can be used to analyze the impact of changes to monetary policy, as well as other shocks to the economy.

6. A temporary home monetary expansion causes home interest rates to fall and the home exchange rate to depreciate. This temporary policy can be consistent with a nominal anchor in the long run.

7. A permanent home monetary expansion causes home interest rates to fall and the home exchange rate to depreciate and, in the short run, overshoot what will eventually be its long-run level. This permanent policy is inconsistent with a nominal anchor in the long run.

8. The case of fixed exchange rates can also be studied using this theory. Under capital mobility, interest parity becomes very simple. In this case, the home interest rate equals the foreign interest rate. Home monetary policy loses all autonomy compared with the floating case. The only way to recover it is to impose capital controls. This is the essence of the trilemma.

KEY TERMS

asset approach to exchange rates, p. 522

fundamental equation of the asset approach to exchange rates, p. 523

FX market diagram, p. 524

nominal rigidity, p. 529

overshooting, p. 548

trilemma, p. 555

PROBLEMS

1. Use the money market and FX diagrams to answer the following questions about the relationship between the British pound (£) and the U.S. dollar ($). The exchange rate is in U.S. dollars per British pound $E_{\$/£}$. We want to consider how a change in the U.S. money supply affects interest rates and exchange rates. On all graphs, label the initial equilibrium point A.

   a. Illustrate how a *temporary* decrease in the U.S. money supply affects the money and FX markets. Label your short-run equilibrium point B and your long-run equilibrium point C.

   b. Using your diagram from (a), state how each of the following variables changes in the *short run* (increase/decrease/no change): U.S. interest rate, British interest rate, $E_{\$/£}$, $E_{\$/£}^e$, and the U.S. price level P.

   c. Using your diagram from (a), state how each of the following variables changes in the *long run* (increase/decrease/no change relative to their initial values at point A): U.S. interest rate, British interest rate, $E_{\$/£}$, $E_{\$/£}^e$, and U.S. price level P.

2. Use the money market and FX diagrams to answer the following questions. This question considers the relationship between the Indian rupee (Rs) and the U.S. dollar ($). The exchange rate is in rupees per dollar, $E_{Rs/\$}$. On all graphs, label the initial equilibrium point A.

   a. Illustrate how a *permanent* increase in India's money supply affects the money and FX markets. Label your short-run equilibrium point B and your long-run equilibrium point C.

   b. By plotting them on a chart with time on the horizontal axis, illustrate how each of the following variables changes over time (for India): nominal money supply M_{IN}, price level P_{IN}, real money supply M_{IN}/P_{IN}, interest rate i_{Rs}, and the exchange rate $E_{Rs/\$}$.

   c. Using your previous analysis, state how each of the following variables changes in the *short run* (increase/decrease/no change): India's interest rate i_{Rs}, $E_{Rs/\$}$, expected exchange rate $E_{Rs/\$}^e$, and price level P_{IN}.

   d. Using your previous analysis, state how each of the following variables changes in the *long run* (increase/decrease/no change relative to their initial values at point A): India's interest rate i_{Rs}, $E_{Rs/\$}$, $E_{Rs/\$}^e$, and India's price level P_{IN}.

   e. Explain how overshooting applies to this situation.

3. Is overshooting (in theory and in practice) consistent with purchasing power parity? Consider the reasons for the usefulness of PPP in the short run versus the long run and the assumption we've used in the asset approach (in the short run versus the long run). How does overshooting help to resolve the empirical behavior of exchange rates in the short run versus the long run?

4. Use the money market and FX diagrams to answer the following questions. This question considers the relationship between the euro (€) and the U.S. dollar ($). The exchange rate is in U.S. dollars per euro, $E_{\$/€}$. Suppose that with financial innovation in the United States, real money demand in the United States decreases. On all graphs, label the initial equilibrium point A.

   a. Assume this change in U.S. real money demand is temporary. Using the FX/money market diagrams, illustrate how this change affects the money and FX markets. Label your short-run equilibrium point B and your long-run equilibrium point C.

   b. Assume this change in U.S. real money demand is permanent. Using a new diagram, illustrate how this change affects the money and FX markets. Label your short-run equilibrium point B and your long-run equilibrium point C.

   c. Illustrate how each of the following variables changes over time in response to a permanent reduction in real money demand: nominal money supply M_{US}, price level P_{US}, real money supply M_{US}/P_{US}, U.S. interest rate $i_\$$, and the exchange rate $E_{\$/€}$.

5. This question considers how the FX market will respond to changes in monetary policy in South Korea. For these questions, define the exchange rate as South Korean won per Japanese yen, $E_{\text{won}/¥}$. Use the FX and money market diagrams to answer the following questions. On all graphs, label the initial equilibrium point A.

   a. Suppose the Bank of Korea permanently decreases its money supply. Illustrate the short-run (label equilibrium point B) and long-run effects (label equilibrium point C) of this policy.

   b. Now, suppose the Bank of Korea announces it plans to permanently decrease its money supply but doesn't actually implement this policy. How will this affect the FX market in the short run if investors believe the Bank of Korea's announcement?

   c. Finally, suppose the Bank of Korea permanently decreases its money supply, but this change is not anticipated. When the Bank of Korea implements this policy, how will this affect the FX market in the short run?

   d. Using your previous answers, evaluate the following statements:

      • If a country wants to increase the value of its currency, it can do so (temporarily) without raising domestic interest rates.

      • The central bank can reduce both the domestic price level and value of its currency in the long run.

      • The most effective way to increase the value of a currency is through surprising investors.

6. In the late 1990s, several East Asian countries used limited flexibility or currency pegs in managing their exchange rates relative to the U.S. dollar. This question considers how different countries responded to the East Asian currency crisis (1997–1998). For the following questions, treat the East Asian country as the home country and the United States as the foreign country. Also, for the diagrams, you may assume these countries maintained a currency peg (fixed rate) relative to the U.S. dollar. Also, for the following questions, you need consider only the short-run effects.

   a. In July 1997, investors expected that the Thai baht would depreciate. That is, they expected that Thailand's central bank would be unable to maintain the currency peg with the U.S. dollar. Illustrate how this change in investors' expectations affects the Thai money market and FX market, with the exchange rate defined as baht (B) per U.S. dollar, denoted $E_{\text{B}/\$}$. Assume the Thai central bank wants to maintain capital mobility and preserve the level of its interest rate, and abandons the currency peg in favor of a floating exchange rate regime.

   b. Indonesia faced the same constraints as Thailand—investors feared Indonesia would be forced to abandon its currency peg. Illustrate how this change in investors' expectations affects the Indonesian money market and FX market, with the exchange rate defined as rupiahs (Rp) per U.S. dollar, denoted $E_{\text{Rp}/\$}$. Assume that the Indonesian central bank wants to maintain capital mobility and the currency peg.

   c. Malaysia had a similar experience, except that it used capital controls to maintain its currency peg and preserve the level of its interest rate. Illustrate how this change in investors' expectations affects the Malaysian money market and FX market, with the exchange rate defined as ringgit (RM) per U.S. dollar, denoted $E_{\text{RM}/\$}$. You need show only the short-run effects of this change in investors' expectations.

   d. Compare and contrast the three approaches just outlined. As a policy maker, which would you favor? Explain.

7. Several countries have opted to join currency unions. Examples include those in the Euro area, the CFA franc union in West Africa, and the Caribbean currency union. This involves sacrificing the domestic currency in favor of using a single currency unit in multiple countries. Assuming that once a country joins a currency union, it will not leave, do these countries face the policy trilemma discussed in the text? Explain.

8. During the Great Depression, the United States remained on the international gold standard longer than other countries. This

effectively meant that the United States was committed to maintaining a fixed exchange rate at the onset of the Great Depression. The U.S. dollar was pegged to the value of gold, along with other major currencies, including the British pound, French franc, and so on. Many researchers have blamed the severity of the Great Depression on the Federal Reserve and its failure to react to economic conditions in 1929 and 1930. Discuss how the policy trilemma applies to this situation.

9. On June 20, 2007, John Authers, investment editor of the *Financial Times*, wrote the following in his column "The Short View":

> The Bank of England published minutes showing that only the narrowest possible margin, 5–4, voted down [an interest] rate hike last month. Nobody foresaw this. . . . The news took sterling back above $1.99, and to a 15-year high against the yen.

Can you explain the logic of this statement? Interest rates in the United Kingdom had remained unchanged in the weeks since the vote and were still unchanged after the minutes were released. What news was contained in the minutes that caused traders to react? Explain using the asset approach.

10. We can use the asset approach to both make predictions about how the market will react to current events and understand how important these events are to investors. Consider the behavior of the Union/Confederate exchange rate during the Civil War. How would each of the following events affect the exchange rate, defined as Confederate dollars per Union dollar, $E_{C\$/\$}$?

a. The Confederacy increases the money supply by 2,900% between July and December 1861.
b. The Union Army suffers a defeat in Battle of Chickamauga in September 1863.
c. The Confederate Army suffers a major defeat with Sherman's March in the autumn of 1864.

NETWORK

Search the Internet for websites and services offering exchange rate forecasts. (*Hint:* Do an Internet search for "exchange rate forecast.") How far ahead is the forecast made? What do the forecasters say about the methods that they use, if anything? Is the forecast based on fundamentals or technical methods? How much credence would you give to the forecast?

16

National and International Accounts: Income, Wealth, and the Balance of Payments

Money is sent from one country to another for various purposes: such as the payment of tributes or subsidies; remittances of revenue to or from dependencies, or of rents or other incomes to their absent owners; emigration of capital, or transmission of it for foreign investment. The most usual purpose, however, is that of payment for goods. To show in what circumstances money actually passes from country to country for this or any of the other purposes mentioned, it is necessary briefly to state the nature of the mechanism by which international trade is carried on, when it takes place not by barter but through the medium of money.

John Stuart Mill, 1848

In Chapter 13, we encountered George, the hypothetical American tourist in Paris. We learned about his use of exchange rate conversion—but how did he pay for his expenses? He traded some of his assets (such as dollars converted into euros, or charges on his debit card against his bank account) for goods and services (hotel, food, wine, etc.). Every day households and firms routinely trade goods, services, and assets, but when such transactions cross borders, they link the home economy with the rest of the world. In the upcoming chapters, we study economic transactions between countries, how they are undertaken, and the impact they have on the macroeconomy.

To that end, the first task of any macroeconomist is to measure economic transactions. The collection and analysis of such data can help improve research and policymaking. In a closed economy there are important aggregate flows to consider, such as national output, consumption, investment, and so on. When an economy is open to transactions with the rest of the world, there are a host of additional economic transactions that take place across borders. In today's world economy these international flows of trade and finance have reached unprecedented levels.

Beyond barter: International transactions involve not just goods and services but also financial assets.

Cross-border flows of goods, services, and capital are measured in various ways and are increasingly important subjects of discussion for economists and policy makers, for businesses, and for the well-educated citizen. There are debates about the size of the U.S. trade deficit, trade surpluses in emerging economies like China and India, the growing indebtedness of the United States to the rest of the world, and how these trends might be related to national saving and the government's budget. To understand such debates, we must first know what is being talked about. What do all these measures mean and how are they related? How does the global economy actually function?

The goals of this chapter are to explain the international system of trade and payments, to discover how international trade in *goods and services* is complemented and balanced by a parallel trade in *assets*, and to see how these transactions relate to national income and wealth. In the remainder of the book, we use these essential tools to understand the macroeconomic links between nations.

1 Measuring Macroeconomic Activity: An Overview

To understand macroeconomic accounting in an open economy, we build on the principles used to track payments in a closed economy. As you may recall from previous courses in economics, a closed economy is characterized by a *circular flow of payments*, in which economic resources are exchanged for payments as they move through the economy. At various points in this flow, economic activity is measured and recorded in the **national income and product accounts.** In an open economy, however, such measurements are more complicated because we have to account for cross-border flows. These additional flows are recorded in a nation's **balance of payments accounts.** In this opening section, we survey the principles behind these measurements. In later sections, we define the measurements more precisely and explore how they work in practice.

The Flow of Payments in a Closed Economy: Introducing the National Income and Product Accounts

Figure 16-1 shows how payments flow in a closed economy. At the top is **gross national expenditure (GNE),** the total expenditure on final goods and services by home entities in any given period of measurement (usually a calendar year, unless otherwise noted). It is made up of three parts: personal consumption C, investment I, and government spending G. The sum of these variables equals GNE.

FIGURE 16-1

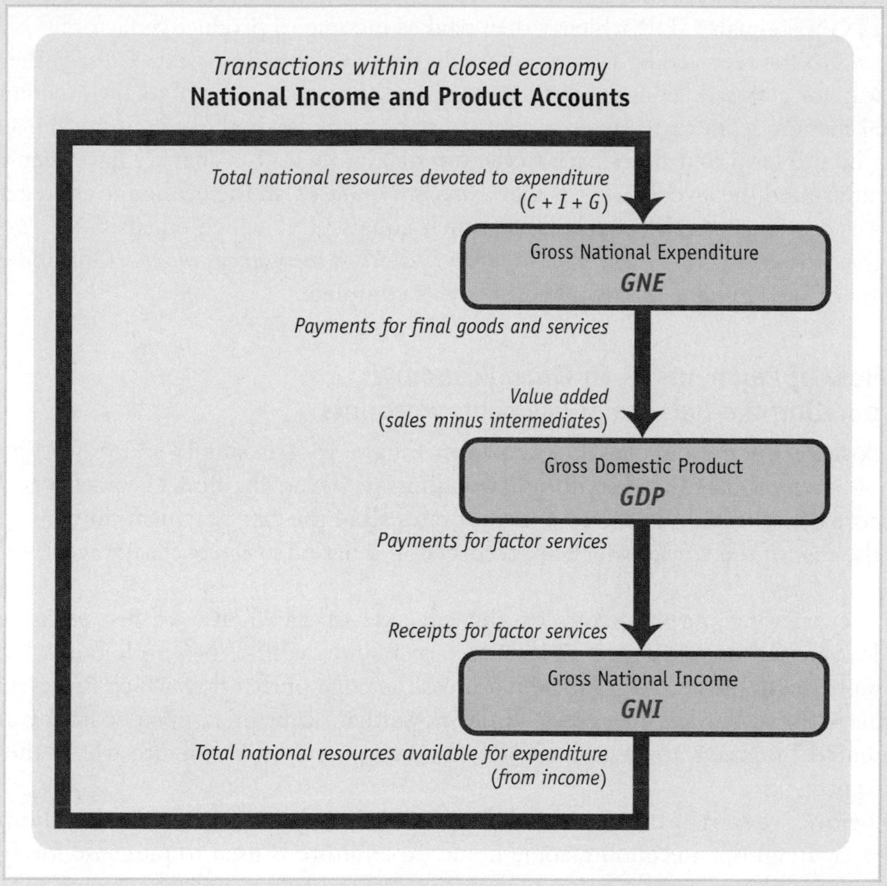

Transactions within a closed economy
National Income and Product Accounts

Total national resources devoted to expenditure
$(C + I + G)$

Gross National Expenditure
GNE

Payments for final goods and services

Value added
(sales minus intermediates)

Gross Domestic Product
GDP

Payments for factor services

Receipts for factor services

Gross National Income
GNI

Total national resources available for expenditure
(from income)

The Closed Economy
Measurements of national expenditure, product, and income are recorded in the national income and product accounts, with the major categories shown. The purple line shows the circular flow of all transactions in a closed economy.

Once GNE is spent, where do the payments flow next? All of this spending constitutes all payments for final goods and services within the nation's borders. Because the economy is closed, the nation's expenditure must be spent on the final goods and services it produces. More specifically, a country's **gross domestic product (GDP)** is the value of all (*intermediate* and *final*) goods and services produced as output by firms, minus the value of all intermediate goods and services purchased as inputs by firms. (GDP is also known as *value added*.) GDP is a product measure, in contrast to GNE, which is an expenditure measure. In a closed economy, intermediate sales must equal intermediate purchases, so in GDP these two terms cancel out, leaving only the value of final goods and services produced, which equals the expenditure on final goods and services, or GNE. Thus, GDP equals GNE.

Once GDP is sold, where do the payments flow next? Because GDP measures the value of firm outputs minus the cost of firm inputs, and this remaining flow is paid by firms as income to factors such as the owners of labor, capital, and land employed by the firms. The factors may, in turn, be owned by households, government, or firms, but such distinctions are not important. The key thing in a closed economy is that all such income is paid to domestic entities. It thus equals the total income resources of the economy, also known as **gross national income (GNI).** By this point in our circular flow, we can see that in a closed economy the expenditure on total goods and services GNE equals GDP, which is then paid as income to productive factors GNI.

Once GNI is received by factors, where do the payments flow next? Clearly, there is no way for a closed economy to finance expenditure except out of its own income, so total income is, in turn, spent and must be the same as total expenditure. This is shown by the loop that flows back to the top of Figure 16-1. What we have seen in our tour around the circular flow is that *in a closed economy*, all the economic aggregate measures are equal: GNE equals GDP which equals GNI which equals GNE. *In a closed economy, expenditure is the same as product, which is the same as income.* Our understanding of the closed economy circular flow is complete.

The Flow of Payments in an Open Economy: Incorporating the Balance of Payments Accounts

The closed-economy circular flow shown in Figure 16-1 is simple and tidy. When a nation opens itself to trade with other nations, however, the flow becomes a good deal more complicated. Figure 16-2 incorporates all of the extra payment flows to and from the rest of the world, which are recorded in a nation's *balance of payments (BOP) accounts.*

The circulating purple arrows on the left side of the figure are just as in the closed-economy case in Figure 16-1. These arrows flow within the purple box, which represents the home country, and do not cross the edge of that box, which represents the international border. The cross-border flows that occur in an open economy are represented by green arrows. There are five key points on the figure where these flows appear.

As before, we start at the top with the home economy's gross national expenditure, $C + I + G$. In an open economy, some home expenditure is used to purchase foreign final goods and services. At point 1, these *imports* are subtracted from home GNE because those goods are not sold by domestic firms. In addition, some foreign expenditure is used to purchase final goods and services from home. These *exports* must be added to home GNE because those goods are sold by domestic firms. (A similar logic applies to intermediate goods.) The difference between payments made for imports and payments received for exports is called the **trade balance (TB),** and it equals net payments to domestic firms due to trade. *GNE* plus *TB* equals *GDP,* the total value of production in the home economy.

At point 2, some home GDP is paid to foreign entities for *factor service imports,* that is, domestic payments to capital, labor, and land owned by foreign entities. Because this income is not paid to factors at home, it is subtracted when computing home income. Similarly, some foreign GDP may be paid to domestic entities as payment for *factor service exports,* that is, foreign payments to capital, labor, and land owned by domestic entities. Because this income is paid to factors at home, it is added when computing home income. The value of factor service exports minus factor service imports is known as **net factor income from abroad (NFIA).** Thus *GDP* plus *NFIA* equals *GNI,* the total income earned by domestic entities from all sources, domestic and foreign.

At point 3, we see that the home country may not retain all of its earned income GNI. Why? Domestic entities might give some of it away—for example, as foreign aid or remittances by migrants to their families back home. Similarly, domestic enti-

FIGURE 16-2

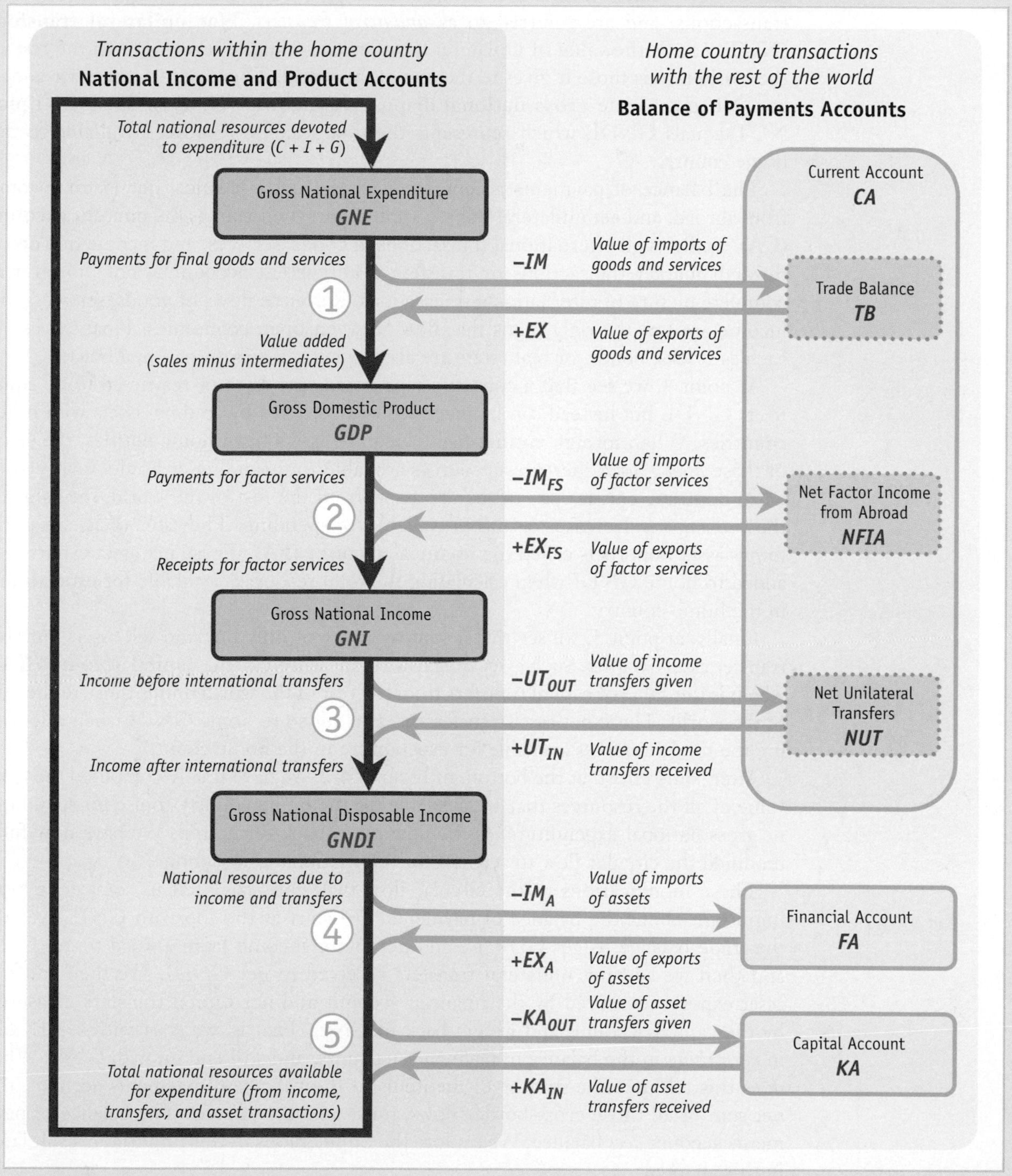

Transactions within the home country
National Income and Product Accounts

Home country transactions with the rest of the world
Balance of Payments Accounts

The Open Economy Measurements of national expenditure, product, and income are recorded in the national income and product accounts, with the major categories shown on the left. Measurements of international transactions are recorded in the balance of payments accounts, with the major categories shown on the right. The purple line shows the flow of transactions within the home economy; the green lines show all cross-border transactions.

ties might receive gifts from abroad. Such gifts may take the form of income transfers or be "in kind" transfers of goods and services. They are considered nonmarket transactions, and are referred to as *unilateral transfers.* **Net unilateral transfers (NUT)** equals the value of unilateral transfers the country receives from the rest of the world minus those it gives to the rest of the world. These net transfers are added to GNI to calculate **gross national disposable income (GNDI).** Thus GNI plus NUT equals GNDI, which represents the total income resources available to the home country.

The balance of payments accounts collect the trade balance, net factor income from abroad, and net unilateral transfers and report their sum as the **current account (CA),** a tally of all international transactions in goods, services, and income that occur through market transactions or transfers. The current account is not, however, a complete picture of international transactions. Resource flows of goods, services, and income are not the only items that flow between open economies. Financial assets such as stocks, bonds, or real estate are also traded across international borders.

At point 4, we see that a country's capacity to spend is not restricted to be equal to its GNDI, but instead can be increased or decreased by trading assets with other countries. When foreign entities pay to acquire assets from home entities, the value of these *asset exports* increases resources available for spending at home. Conversely, when domestic entities pay to acquire assets from the rest of the world, the value of the *asset imports* decreases resources available for spending. The value of asset exports minus asset imports is called the **financial account (FA).** These net asset exports are added to home GNDI when calculating the total resources available for expenditure in the home country.

Finally, at point 5, we see that a country may not only buy and sell assets but also transfer assets as gifts. Such asset transfers are measured by the **capital account (KA),** which is the value of capital transfers from the rest of the world minus those to the rest of the world. These net asset transfers are also added to home GNDI when calculating the total resources available for expenditure in the home country.

After some effort, at the bottom of Figure 16-2, we have finally computed the total value of all the resources that are available for the home country to use for spending, or gross national expenditure, as the flow loops back to the top. We have now fully modified the circular flow to account for international transactions.[1]

These modifications to the circular flow in Figure 16-2 tell us something very important about the balance of payments. We start at the top with GNE. We add the trade balance to get GDP, we add net factor income from abroad to get GNI, and then we add net unilateral transfers received to get GNDI. We then add net asset exports measured by the financial account and net capital transfers measured by the capital account, and we get back to GNE. That is, we start with GNE, add in *everything* in the balance of payments accounts, and still end up with GNE. What does this tell us? The sum of all the items in the balance of payments account, the net sum of all those cross-border flows, must amount to zero! The balance of payments account *does* balance. We explore the implications of this important result later in this chapter.

---

[1] In the past, both the financial and capital accounts were jointly known as "the capital account." This change should be kept in mind not only when consulting older documents but also when listening to contemporary discussion because not everyone cares for the new (and somewhat confusing) nomenclature.

2 Income, Product, and Expenditure

In the previous section, we sketched out all the important national and international transactions that occur in an open economy. With that overview in mind, we now formally define the key accounting concepts in the two sets of accounts and put them to use.

Three Approaches to Measuring Economic Activity

There are three main approaches to the measurement of aggregate economic activity within a country:

- The *expenditure approach* looks at the demand for goods: it examines how much is spent on demand for final goods and services. The key measure is gross national expenditure GNE.

- The *product approach* looks at the supply of goods: it measures the value of all goods and services produced as output minus the value of goods used as inputs in production. The key measure is gross domestic product GDP.

- The *income approach* focuses on payments to owners of factors and tracks the amount of income they receive. The key measures are gross national income GNI and gross national disposable income GNDI (which includes net transfers).

It is crucial to note that in a closed economy the three approaches generate the same number: In a closed economy, $GNE = GDP = GNI$. In an open economy, however, this is not true.

From GNE to GDP: Accounting for Trade in Goods and Services

As before, we start with gross national expenditure, or GNE, which is *by definition* the sum of consumption C, investment I, and government consumption G. Formally, these three elements are defined, respectively, as follows:

- *Personal consumption expenditures* (usually called "consumption") equal total spending by private households on final goods and services, including nondurable goods such as food, durable goods such as a television, and services such as window cleaning or gardening.

- *Gross private domestic investment* (usually called "investment") equals total spending by firms or households on final goods and services to make additions to the stock of capital. Investment includes construction of a new house or a new factory, the purchase of new equipment, and net increases in inventories of goods held by firms (i.e., unsold output).

- *Government consumption expenditures and gross investment* (often called "government consumption") equal spending by the public sector on final goods and services, including spending on public works, national defense, the police, and the civil service. It does *not* include any transfer payments or income redistributions, such as Social Security or unemployment insurance payments—these are *not* purchases of goods or services, just rearrangements of private spending power.

As for GDP, it is *by definition* the value of all goods and services produced as output by firms, minus the value of all intermediate goods and services purchased as inputs by firms. It is thus a product measure, in contrast to the expenditure measure GNE. Because of trade, not all of the GNE payments go to GDP, and not all of GDP payments arise from GNE.

To adjust GNE and find the contribution going into GDP, we *subtract* the value of final goods imported (home spending that goes to foreign firms) and *add* the value of final goods exported (foreign spending that goes to home firms). In addition, we can't forget about intermediate goods: we *subtract* the value of imported intermediates (in GDP they also count as home's purchased inputs) and *add* the value of exported intermediates (in GDP they also count as home's produced output).[2] So, adding it all up, to get from GNE to GDP, we add the value of *all* exports denoted *EX* and subtract the value of *all* imports *IM*. Thus,

$$\underbrace{GDP}_{\substack{\text{Gross domestic} \\ \text{product}}} = \underbrace{C + I + G}_{\substack{\text{Gross national} \\ \text{expenditure} \\ GNE}} + \underbrace{\left(\underbrace{EX}_{\substack{\text{All exports,} \\ \text{final \& intermediate}}} - \underbrace{IM}_{\substack{\text{All imports,} \\ \text{final \& intermediate}}} \right)}_{\substack{\text{Trade balance} \\ TB}} \quad (16\text{-}1)$$

This important formula for GDP says that *gross domestic product is equal to gross national expenditure (GNE) plus the trade balance (TB).*

It is important to understand and account for intermediate goods transactions properly because trade in intermediate goods has surged in recent decades due to globalization and outsourcing. For example, according to the 2010 *Economic Report of the President*, estimates suggest that one-third of the growth of world trade from 1970 to 1990 was driven by intermediate trade arising from the growth of "vertically specialized" production processes (outsourcing, offshoring, etc.). More strikingly, as of 2010, it appears that—probably for the first time in world history—total world trade now consists more of trade in intermediate goods (60%) than in final goods (40%).

The trade balance TB is also called *net exports*. Because it is the net value of exports minus imports, it may be positive or negative.

If *TB* > 0, exports are greater than imports and we say a country has a *trade surplus*.

If *TB* < 0, imports are greater than imports and we say a country has a *trade deficit*.

In 2012, the United States had a trade deficit because exports *X* were $2,184 billion and imports *M* were $2,744 billion. Thus its trade balance was equal to −$560 billion.

From GDP to GNI: Accounting for Trade in Factor Services

Trade in factor services occurs when, say, the home country is paid income by a foreign country as compensation for the use of labor, capital, and land owned by home entities but in service in the foreign country. We say the home country is exporting factor services to the foreign country and receiving factor income in return.

---

[2] Note that intermediate inputs sold by home firms and purchased by other home firms cancel out in GDP, in both closed and open economies. For example, suppose there are two firms A and B, and Firm A makes a $200 table (a final good) and buys $100 in wood (an intermediate input) from Firm B, and there is no trade. Total sales are $300; but GDP or value added is total sales of $300 minus the $100 of inputs purchased; so GDP is equal to $200. Now suppose Firm B makes and exports $50 of extra wood. After this change, GDP is equal to $250. You can see here that GDP *is not equal to* the value of final goods produced in an economy (although it is quite often claimed, mistakenly, that this is a definition of GDP).

An example of a labor service export is a home country professional temporarily working overseas, say, a U.S. architect freelancing in London. The wages she earns in the United Kingdom are factor income for the United States. An example of trade in capital services is *foreign direct investment*. For example, U.S.-owned factories in Ireland generate income for their U.S. owners; Japanese-owned factories in the United States generate income for their Japanese owners. Other examples of payments for capital services include income from overseas *financial* assets such as foreign securities, real estate, or loans to governments, firms, and households.

These payments are accounted for as additions to and subtractions from home GDP. Some home GDP is paid out as *income payments* to foreign entities for factor services imported by the home country IM_{FS}. In addition, domestic entities receive some income payments from foreign entities as *income receipts* for factor services exported by the home country EX_{FS}.

After accounting for these income flows, we see that gross national income (GNI), the total income earned by domestic entities, is *GDP* plus the factor income arriving from overseas EX_{FS}, minus the factor income going out overseas IM_{FS}.[3] The last two terms, income receipts minus income payments, are the home country's *net factor income from abroad*, $NFIA = EX_{FS} - IM_{FS}$. This may be a positive or negative number, depending on whether income receipts are larger or smaller than income payments.

With the help of the GDP expression in Equation (16-1), we obtain the key formula for GNI that says the *gross national income equals gross domestic product (GDP) plus net factor income from abroad (NFIA)*.

$$GNI = \underbrace{\underbrace{C+I+G}_{\substack{\text{Gross national expenditure}\\GNE}} + \underbrace{(EX-IM)}_{\substack{\text{Trade balance}\\TB}}}_{GDP} + \underbrace{(EX_{FS}-IM_{FS})}_{\substack{\text{Net factor income from abroad}\\NFIA}} \quad (16\text{-}2)$$

In 2012 the United States received income payments from foreigners EX_{FS} of $782 billion and made income payments to foreigners IM_{FS} of $539 billion, so the net factor income from abroad *NFIA* was +$243 billion.

APPLICATION

Celtic Tiger or Tortoise?

International trade in factor services (as measured by NFIA) can generate a difference between the product and income measures in a country's national accounts. In the United States, this difference is typically small, but at times NFIA can play a major role in the measurement of a country's economic activity.

In the 1970s, Ireland was one of the poorer countries in Europe, but over the next three decades it experienced speedy economic growth with an accompanying investment boom now known as the Irish Miracle. From 1980 to 2007, Irish real GDP per person grew at a phenomenal rate of 4.1% per year—not as rapid as in some developing countries but extremely rapid by the standards of the rich countries of the European Union (EU) or the

[3] GNI is the accounting concept formerly known as GNP, or *gross national product*. The term GNP is still often used, but GNI is technically more accurate because the concept is a measurement of income rather than product. Note that taxes and subsidies on production and imports are counted in GNE (both) and GDP (production taxes only). This treatment ensures that the tax income paid to the home country is properly counted as a part of home income. We simplify the presentation in this textbook by assuming there are no taxes and subsidies.

Organization for Economic Cooperation and Development (OECD). Comparisons with fast-growing Asian economies—the "Asian Tigers"—soon had people speaking of the "Celtic Tiger" when referring to Ireland. Despite a large recession after the 2008 crisis, real GDP per person in Ireland is still almost three times its 1980 level.

But did Irish citizens enjoy all of these gains? No. Figure 16-3 shows that in 1980 Ireland's annual net factor income from abroad was virtually nil—about €120 per person (in year 2000 real euros) or +0.9% of GDP. Yet by 2000, and in the years since, around 15% to 20% of Irish GDP was being used to make net factor income payments to foreigners who had invested heavily in the Irish economy by buying stocks and bonds and by purchasing land and building factories on it. (By some estimates, 75% of Ireland's industrial-sector GDP originated in foreign-owned plants in 2004.) These foreign investors expected their big Irish investments to generate income, and so they did, in the form of net factor payments abroad amounting to almost one-fifth of Irish GDP. This meant that Irish GNI (the income paid to Irish people and firms) was a lot smaller than Irish GDP.[4] Ireland's net factor income from abroad has remained large and negative ever since.

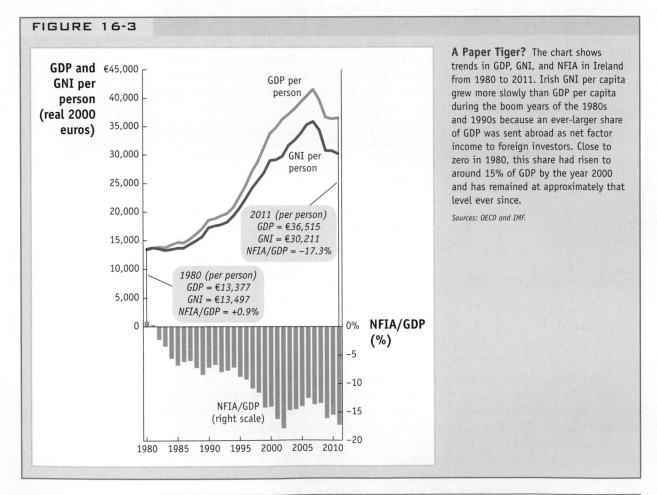

FIGURE 16-3

A Paper Tiger? The chart shows trends in GDP, GNI, and NFIA in Ireland from 1980 to 2011. Irish GNI per capita grew more slowly than GDP per capita during the boom years of the 1980s and 1990s because an ever-larger share of GDP was sent abroad as net factor income to foreign investors. Close to zero in 1980, this share had risen to around 15% of GDP by the year 2000 and has remained at approximately that level ever since.

Sources: OECD and IMF.

[4] Irish GDP might have been inflated as a result of various accounting problems. Some special factors exacerbated the difference between GDP and GNI in Ireland, such as special tax incentives that encouraged foreign firms to keep their accounts in a way which generated high profits "on paper" at their low-tax Irish subsidiaries rather than in their high-tax home country. For these reasons, many economists believe that Irish GNI, despite being more conservative, might be a truer measure of the economy's performance.

This example shows how GDP can be a misleading measure of economic performance. When ranked by GDP per person, Ireland was the 4th richest OECD economy in 2004; when ranked by GNI per person, it was only 17th richest.[5] The Irish outflow of net factor payments is certainly an extreme case, but it serves to underscore an important point about income measurement in open economies. Any country that relies heavily on foreign investment to generate economic growth is not getting a free lunch. Irish GNI per person grew at "only" 3.6% from 1980 to the peak in 2007; this was 0.5% per year less than the growth rate of GDP per person over the same period. Living standards grew impressively, but the more humble GNI figures may give a more accurate measure of what the Irish Miracle actually meant for the Irish. ■

From GNI to GNDI: Accounting for Transfers of Income

So far, we have fully described market transactions in goods, services, and income. However, many international transactions take place outside of markets. International nonmarket transfers of goods, services, and income include such things as foreign aid by governments in the form of *official development assistance* (ODA) and other help, private charitable gifts to foreign recipients, and income remittances sent to relatives or friends in other countries. These transfers are "gifts" and may take the form of goods and services (food aid, volunteer medical services) or income transfers.

If a country receives transfers worth UT_{IN} and gives transfers worth UT_{OUT}, then its net unilateral transfers, NUT, are $NUT = UT_{IN} - UT_{OUT}$. Because this is a net amount, it may be positive or negative. In the year 2012, the United States had net unilateral transfers of $157 billion to the rest of the world. In general, net unilateral transfers play a small role in the income and product accounts for most high-income countries (net outgoing transfers are typically no more than 5% of GNI). But they are an important part of the gross national disposable income (GNDI) for many low-income countries that receive a great deal of foreign aid or migrant remittances, as seen in Figure 16-4.

Measuring national generosity is highly controversial and a recurring theme of current affairs (see **Headlines: Are Rich Countries "Stingy" with Foreign Aid?**). You might think that net unilateral transfers are in some ways a better measure of a country's generosity toward foreigners than official development assistance, which is but one component. For example, looking at the year 2000, a USAID report, *Foreign Aid in the National Interest*, claimed that while U.S. ODA was only $9.9 billion, other U.S. government assistance (such as contributions to global security and humanitarian assistance) amounted to $12.7 billion, and assistance from private U.S. citizens totaled $33.6 billion—for total foreign assistance equal to $56.2 billion, more than five times the level of ODA.

To include the impact of aid and all other transfers in the overall calculation of a country's income resources, we add net unilateral transfers to gross national income. Using the definition of GNI in Equation (16-2), we obtain a full measure of national income in an open economy, known as gross national disposable income (GNDI), henceforth denoted Y:

$$\underbrace{Y}_{GNDI} = \underbrace{C + I + G}_{GNE} + \underbrace{(EX - IM)}_{\substack{\text{Trade balance}\\TB}} + \underbrace{(EX_{FS} - IM_{FS})}_{\substack{\text{Net factor income}\\\text{from abroad}\\NFIA}} + \underbrace{(UT_{IN} - UT_{OUT})}_{\substack{\text{Net unilateral}\\\text{transfers}\\NUT}} \quad (16\text{-}3)$$

$$\underbrace{\phantom{C + I + G + (EX - IM) + (EX_{FS} - IM_{FS})}}_{GNI}$$

[5] Joe Cullen, "There's Lies, Damned Lies, and Wealth Statistics," *Irish Times*, May 1, 2004.

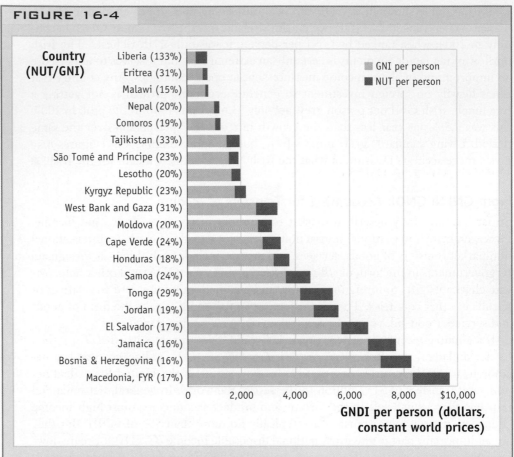

FIGURE 16-4

Major Transfer Recipients The chart shows average figures for the decade 2001 to 2010 for all countries in which average net unilateral transfers exceeded 15% of GNI. Many of the countries shown were heavily reliant on foreign aid, including some of the poorest countries in the world, such as Liberia, Eritrea, Malawi, and Nepal. Some countries with higher incomes also have large transfers because of substantial migrant remittances from a large number of emigrant workers overseas (e.g., Tonga, El Salvador, Honduras, and Cape Verde).

Source: World Bank, World Development Indicators.

In general, economists and policy makers prefer to use GNDI to measure national income. Why? GDP is not a true measure of income because, unlike GNI, it does not include net factor income from abroad. GNI is not a perfect measure either because it leaves out international transfers. GNDI is a preferred measure because it most closely corresponds to the resources available to the nation's households, and national welfare depends most closely on this accounting measure.

What the National Economic Aggregates Tell Us

We have explained all the international flows shown in Figure 16-2 and have developed three key equations that link the important national economic aggregates in an open economy:

■ To get from GNE to GDP, we add TB (Equation 16-1).

HEADLINES

Are Rich Countries "Stingy" with Foreign Aid?

The Asian tsunami on December 26, 2004, was one of worst natural disasters of modern times. Hundreds of thousands of people were killed and billions of dollars of damage was done. Some aftershocks were felt in international politics. Jan Egeland, United Nations Under-Secretary-General for Humanitarian Affairs and Emergency Relief Coordinator, declared, "It is beyond me why we are so stingy." His comments rocked the boat in many rich countries, especially in the United States where official aid fell short of the UN goal of 0.7% of GNI. However, the United States gives in other ways, making judgments about stinginess far from straightforward.

An Indonesian soldier thanks two U.S. airmen after a U.S. Navy helicopter delivered fresh water to Indonesian tsunami victims. The normal operating costs of military assets used for humanitarian purposes are not fully counted as part of official development assistance.

Is the United States stingy when it comes to foreign aid? . . . The answer depends on how you measure. . . .

In terms of traditional foreign aid, the United States gave $16.25 billion in 2003, as measured by the Organization of Economic Cooperation and Development (OECD), the club of the world's rich industrial nations. That was almost double the aid by the next biggest net spender, Japan ($8.8 billion). Other big donors were France ($7.2 billion) and Germany ($6.8 billion).

But critics point out that the United States is much bigger than those individual nations. As a group, member nations of the European Union have a bit larger population than the United States and give a great deal more money in foreign aid—$49.2 billion altogether in 2003.

In relation to affluence, the United States lies at the bottom of the list of rich donor nations. It gave 0.15% of gross national income to official development assistance in 2003. By this measure, Norway at 0.92% was the most generous, with Denmark next at 0.84%.

Bring those numbers down to an everyday level and the average American gave 13 cents a day in government aid, according to David Roodman, a researcher at the Center for Global Development (CGD) in Washington. Throw in another nickel a day from private giving. That private giving is high by international standards, yet not enough to close the gap with Norway, whose citizens average $1.02 per day in government aid and 24 cents per day in private aid. . . .

[Also], the United States has a huge defense budget, some of which benefits

developing countries. Making a judgment call, the CGD includes the cost of UN peacekeeping activities and other military assistance approved by a multilateral institution, such as NATO. So the United States gets credit for its spending in Kosovo, Australia for its intervention in East Timor, and Britain for military money spent to bring more stability to Sierra Leone. . . .

"Not to belittle what we are doing, we shouldn't get too self-congratulatory," says Frederick Barton, an economist at the Center for Strategic and International Studies in Washington.

Source: Republished with permission of Christian Science Monitor, from "Foreign Aid: Is the U.S. Stingy?" Christian Science Monitor/MSN Money, January 6, 2005; permission conveyed through Copyright Clearance Center, Inc.

- To get from GDP to GNI, we add NFIA (Equation 16-2).
- To get from GNI to GDNI, we add NUT (Equation 16-3).

To go one step further, we can group the three cross-border terms into an umbrella term that is called the current account CA:

$$\underbrace{Y}_{GNDI} = \underbrace{C + I + G}_{GNE} + \{\underbrace{(EX - IM)}_{\substack{\text{Trade balance} \\ TB}} + \underbrace{(EX_{FS} - IM_{FS})}_{\substack{\text{Net factor income} \\ \text{from abroad} \\ NFIA}} + \underbrace{(UT_{IN} - UT_{OUT})}_{\substack{\text{Net unilateral} \\ \text{transfers} \\ NUT}}\} \quad (16\text{-}4)$$

$$\underbrace{\hspace{6cm}}_{\substack{\text{Current account} \\ CA}}$$

It is important to understand the intuition for this expression. On the left is our full income measure, GNDI. The first term on the right is GNE, which measures payments by home entities. The other terms on the right, combined into CA, measure all net payments to the home country arising from the full range of international transactions in goods, services, and income.

Remember that in a closed economy, there are no international transactions so TB and NFIA and NUT (and hence CA) are all zero. Therefore, in a closed economy, the four main aggregates GNDI, GNI, GDP, and GNE are exactly equal. In an open economy, however, each of these four aggregates can differ from the others.

Understanding the Data for the National Economic Aggregates

Now that we've learned how a nation's principal economic aggregates are affected by international transactions in theory, let's see how this works in practice. In this section, we take a look at some data from the real world to see how they are recorded and presented in official statistics.

Table 16-1 shows data for the United States in 2012 reported by the Bureau of Economic Analysis in the official national income and product accounts.

Lines 1 to 3 of the table show the components of gross national expenditure GNE. Personal consumption expenditures C were \$11,120 billion, gross private domestic investment I was \$2,062 billion, and government consumption G was \$3,063 billion. Summing up, GNE was \$16,245 billion (line 4).

Line 5 shows the trade balance TB, the net export of goods and services, which was –\$560 billion. (Net exports are negative because the United States imported more goods and services than it exported.) Adding this to GNE gives gross domestic

---

TABLE 16-1

U.S. Economic Aggregates in 2012 The table shows the computation of GDP, GNI, and GNDI in 2012 in billions of dollars using the components of gross national expenditure, the trade balance, international income payments, and unilateral transfers.

Line	Category	Symbol	\$ billions
1	Consumption (personal consumption expenditures)	C	11,120
2	+ Investment (gross private domestic investment)	I	2,062
3	+ Government consumption (government expenditures)	G	3,063
4	= Gross national expenditure	*GNE*	16,245
5	+ Trade balance	*TB*	−560
6	= Gross domestic product	*GDP*	15,685
7	+ Net factor income from abroad	*NFIA*	243
8	= Gross national income	*GNI*	15,928
9	+ Net unilateral transfers	*NUT*	−157
10	= Gross national disposable income	*GNDI*	15,771

Note: Details may not add to totals because of rounding.

Source: U.S. Bureau of Economic Analysis, NIPA Tables 1.1.5 and 4.1, using the NIPA definition of the United States. Data revised as of March 28, 2013.

product GDP of $15,685 billion (line 6). Next we account for net factor income from abroad NFIA, +$243 billion (line 7). Adding this to GDP gives gross national income GNI of $15,928 billion (line 8).

Finally, to get to the bottom line, we account for the fact that the United States received net unilateral transfers from the rest of the world of –$157 billion (i.e., the United States makes net transfers to the rest of the world of $157 billion) on line 9. Adding these negative transfers to GNI results in a gross national disposable income GNDI of $15,771 billion on line 10.

Some Recent Trends Figures 16-5 and 16-6 show recent trends in various components of U.S. national income. Examining these breakdowns gives us a sense of the relative economic significance of each component.

In Figure 16-5, GNE is shown as the sum of consumption C, investment I, and government consumption G. Consumption accounts for about 70% of GNE, while government consumption G accounts for about 15%. Both of these components are relatively stable. Investment accounts for the rest of GNE (about 15%), but investment tends to fluctuate more than C and G (e.g., it fell steeply after the Great Recession in 2008–2010). Over the period shown, GNE grew from $6,000 billion to around $16,000 billion in current dollars.

Figure 16-6 shows the trade balance (TB), net factor income from abroad (NFIA), and net unilateral transfers (NUT), which constitute the current account (CA). In the United States, the trade balance is the dominant component in the current account. For the entire period shown, the trade balance has been in deficit and has grown larger over time. From 2004 to 2008, the trade balance was close to –$800 billion, but it fell during the recession as global trade declined and then rebounded somewhat.

FIGURE 16-5

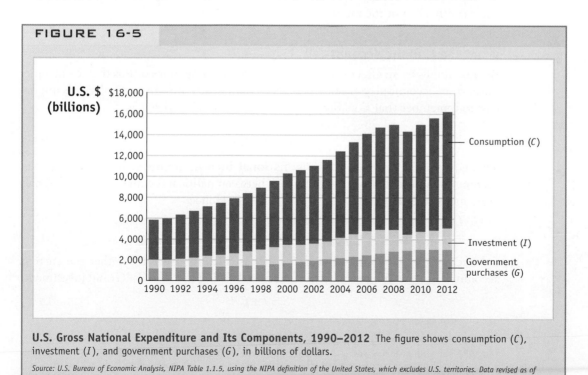

U.S. Gross National Expenditure and Its Components, 1990–2012 The figure shows consumption (C), investment (I), and government purchases (G), in billions of dollars.

Source: U.S. Bureau of Economic Analysis, NIPA Table 1.1.5, using the NIPA definition of the United States, which excludes U.S. territories. Data revised as of March 28, 2013.

FIGURE 16-6

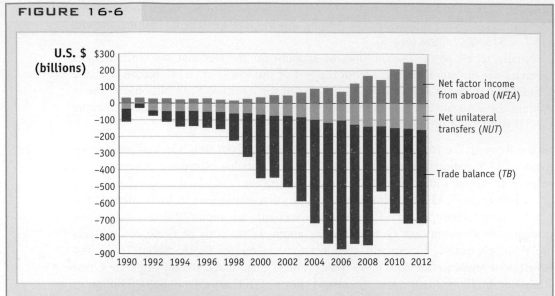

U.S. Current Accounts and Its Components, 1990–2012 The figure shows the trade balance (*TB*), net factor income from abroad (*NFIA*), and net unilateral transfers (*NUT*), in billions of dollars.

Source: U.S. Bureau of Economic Analysis, NIPA Table 4.1, using the NIPA definition of the United States, which includes U.S. territories. Data revised as of March 28, 2013.

Net unilateral transfers, a smaller figure, have been between –$100 and –$150 billion in recent years.[6] Net factor income from abroad was positive in all years shown, and has recently been in the range of $100 to $250 billion.

What the Current Account Tells Us

Because it tells us, in effect, whether a nation is spending more or less than its income, the current account plays a central role in economic debates. In particular, it is important to remember that Equation (16-4) can be concisely written as

$$Y = C + I + G + CA \qquad (16\text{-}5)$$

This equation is the open-economy **national income identity.** It tells us that the current account represents the difference between national income Y (or GNDI) and gross national expenditure GNE (or $C + I + G$). Hence,

GNDI is greater than GNE if and only if CA is positive, or in surplus.

GNDI is less than GNE if and only if CA is negative, or in deficit.

Subtracting $C + G$ from both sides of the last identity, we can see that the current account is also the difference between **national saving** ($S = Y - C - G$) and investment:

$$\underset{Y-C-G}{S} = I + CA \qquad (16\text{-}6)$$

---

[6] In 1991, the United States was in the unusual position of being a net recipient of unilateral transfers: this was a result of transfer payments from other rich countries willing to help defray U.S. military expenses in the Gulf War.

where national saving is defined as income minus consumption minus government consumption. This equation is called the **current account identity** even though it is just a rearrangement of the national income identity. Thus,

S is greater than I if and only if CA is positive, or in surplus.

S is less than I if and only if CA is negative, or in deficit.

These last two equations give us two ways of interpreting the current account, and tell us something important about a nation's economic condition. A current account deficit measures how much a country spends in excess of its income or—equivalently—how it saves too little relative to its investment needs. (A currrent account surplus means the opposite.) We can now understand the widespread use of the current account deficit in the media as a measure of how a country is "spending more than it earns" or "saving too little" or "living beyond its means."

<hr>

APPLICATION

Global Imbalances

We can apply what we have learned to study some remarkable features of financial globalization in recent years, including the explosion in *global imbalances:* the widely discussed current account surpluses and deficits that have been of great concern to policy makers.

Figure 16-7 shows trends since 1970 in saving, investment, and the current account for four groups of industrial countries. All flows are expressed as ratios relative to each region's GDP. Some trends stand out. First, in all four cases, saving and investment have been on a marked downward trend for the past 30 years. From its peak, the ratio of saving to GDP fell by about 8 percentage points in the United States, about 15 percentage points in Japan, and about 6 percentage points in the Eurozone and other countries. Investment ratios typically followed a downward path in all regions, too. In Japan, this decline was steeper than the decline in savings, but in the United States, there was hardly any decline in investment.

These trends reflect the recent history of the industrialized countries. The U.S. economy grew rapidly after 1990 and the Japanese economy grew very slowly, with other countries in between. The fast-growing U.S. economy generated high investment demand, while in slumping Japan investment collapsed; other regions maintained middling levels of growth and investment. Decreased saving in all the countries reflects the demographic shift toward aging populations. That is, higher and higher percentages of these nations' populations are retired, are no longer earning income, and are living on funds they saved in the past.

The current account identity tells us that *CA* equals *S* minus *I*. Thus, investment and saving trends have a predictable impact on the current accounts of industrial countries. Because saving fell more than investment in the United States, the current account moved sharply into deficit, a trend that was only briefly slowed in the early 1990s. By 2003–05 the U.S. current account was at a record deficit level close to −6% of U.S. GDP, only to fall later in the Great Recession. In Japan, saving fell less than investment, so the opposite happened: a very big current account surplus opened up in the 1980s and 1990s, which closed recently. In the euro area and other industrial regions, the difference between saving and investment has been fairly steady, so their current accounts have been closer to balance.

FIGURE 16-7

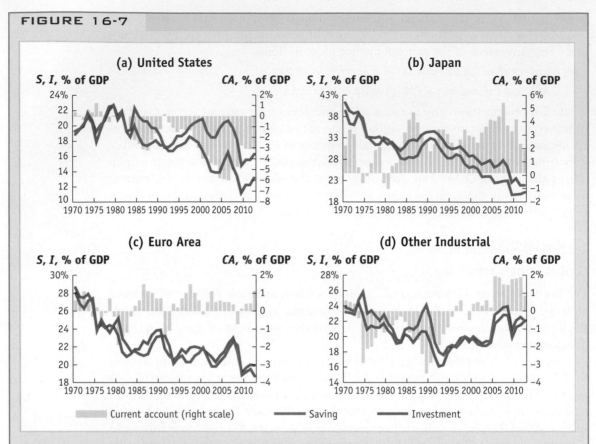

Saving, Investment, and Current Account Trends: Industrial Countries The charts show saving, investment, and the current account as a percent of each subregion's GDP for four groups of advanced countries. The United States has seen both saving and investment fall since 1980, but saving has fallen further than investment, opening up a large current account deficit approaching 6% of GDP in recent years. Japan's experience is the opposite: investment has fallen further than saving, opening up a large current account surplus of about 3% to 5% of GDP, which has narrowed somewhat since the 2008 crisis and recession. The Euro area has also seen saving and investment fall but has been closer to balance overall. Other advanced countries (e.g., non-European EU countries, Canada, Australia, etc.) have tended to run large current account deficits, which have recently moved toward balance.

Source: IMF, World Economic Outlook, September 2005, and updates.

To uncover the sources of the trends in total saving, Figure 16-8 examines two of its components, public and private saving. We define **private saving** as the part of *after-tax* private sector disposable income that is *not* devoted to private consumption C. After-tax private sector disposable income, in turn, is national income Y minus the net taxes T paid by households to the government. Hence, private saving S_p is

$$S_p = Y - T - C \tag{16-7}$$

Private saving can be a positive number, but if the private sector consumption exceeds after-tax disposable income, then private saving is negative. (Here, the private sector includes households and private firms, which are ultimately owned by households.)

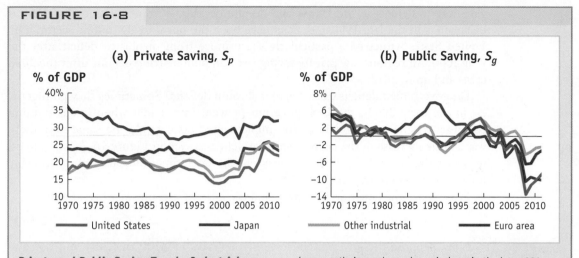

FIGURE 16-8

(a) Private Saving, S_p

% of GDP

(b) Public Saving, S_g

% of GDP

United States — Japan — Other industrial — Euro area

Private and Public Saving Trends: Industrial Countries The chart on the left shows private saving and the chart on the right public saving, both as a percent of GDP. Private saving has been declining in the industrial countries, especially in Japan (since the 1970s) and in the United States (since the 1980s). Private saving has been more stable in the Euro area and other countries. Public saving is clearly more volatile than private saving. Japan has been mostly in surplus and massively so in the late 1980s and early 1990s. The United States briefly ran a government surplus in the late 1990s but then returned to a deficit position. All advanced countries have moved sharply toward lower public saving (in fact, larger deficits) and higher private saving since the 2008 crisis and recession.

Source: IMF, World Economic Outlook, September 2005, and updates.

Similarly, we define **government saving** or **public saving** as the difference between tax revenue T received by the government and government purchases G.[7] Hence, public saving S_g equals

$$S_g = T - G \qquad (16\text{-}8)$$

Government saving is positive when tax revenue exceeds government consumption ($T > G$) and the government runs a *budget surplus*. If the government runs a *budget deficit*, however, government consumption exceeds tax revenue ($G > T$), and public saving is negative.

If we add these last two equations, we see that private saving plus government saving equals total national saving

$$S = Y - C - G = \underbrace{(Y - T - C)}_{\text{Private saving}} + \underbrace{(T - G)}_{\text{Government saving}} = S_p + S_g \qquad (16\text{-}9)$$

In this last equation, taxes cancel out and do not affect saving in the aggregate because they are a transfer from the private sector to the public sector.

One striking feature of the charts in Figure 16-8 is the smooth path of private saving compared with the volatile path of public saving. Public saving is government tax revenue minus spending, and it fluctuates greatly as economic conditions change. The most noticeable feature is the very large public surpluses run up in Japan in the boom of the 1980s and early 1990s which then disappeared during the long slump in the mid- to late 1990s and early 2000s. In other cases, surpluses in the 1970s soon

---

[7] Here, the government includes all levels of government: national/federal, state/regional, local/municipal, and so on.

gave way to deficits in the 1980s, and despite occasional improvements in the fiscal balance (as in the late 1990s), deficits have been the norm in the public sector. The United States witnessed a particularly sharp move from surplus to deficit after the year 2000. All regions saw private saving rise and public saving decline after the 2008 crisis and up to 2012.

Do government deficits cause current account deficits? Sometimes they go together: in the early 2000s, the U.S. government went into deficit when it was fighting two wars (Afghanistan and Iraq) and implemented tax cuts. At the same time there was a large increase in the current account deficit as seen in Figure 16-7. Sometimes, however, the "twin deficits" do not occur at the same time; they are not inextricably linked, as is sometimes believed. Why?

We can use the equation just given and the current account identity to write

$$CA = S_p + S_g - I \qquad\qquad (16\text{-}10)$$

Now, suppose the government lowers your taxes by \$100 this year and borrows to finance the resulting deficit but also says you will be taxed by an extra \$100 plus interest next year to pay off the debt. The theory of *Ricardian equivalence* asserts that you and other households will save the tax cut to pay next year's tax increase, so that any fall in public saving will be fully offset by a rise in private saving. In this situation, the current account—as seen in Equation (16-10)—would be *unchanged*. However, empirical studies do not support this theory: private saving does not fully offset government saving in practice.[8]

How large is the effect of a government deficit on the current account deficit? Research suggests that a change of 1% of GDP in the government deficit (or surplus) coincides with a 0.2% to 0.4% of GDP change in the current account deficit (or surplus), a result consistent with a partial Ricardian offset.

A second reason why the current account might move independently of saving (public or private) is that during the same period there may be a change in the level of investment in the last equation. A comparison of Figures 16-7 and 16-8 shows this effect at work. For example, we can see from Figure 16-7 that the large U.S. current account deficits of the early to mid-1990s were driven by an investment boom, even though total saving rose slightly, driven by an increase in public saving seen in Figure 16-8. Here there was no correlation between government deficit (falling) and current account deficit (rising). Shifts after the 2008 recession illustrate multiple factors at work: U.S. investment collapsed and private saving rose as recession fears increased. The combined effects of lower investment and higher private saving more than offset the decline in public saving and so overall the current account deficit started to decline.

Finally, Figure 16-9 shows global trends in saving, investment, and the current account for advanced countries, emerging and developing economies, and the world economy since 1980. Because the U.S. economy accounts for a large part of the world economy, in aggregate, the industrial countries have shifted into current account deficit over this period, a trend that has been offset by a shift toward current account surplus in the developing countries. The industrialized countries all followed a trend of declining investment and saving ratios, but the developing countries saw the oppo-

---

[8] Menzie D. Chinn and Hiro Ito, 2007, "Current Account Balances, Financial Development and Institutions: Assaying the World 'Saving Glut,'" *Journal of International Money and Finance*, 26(4): 546–569.

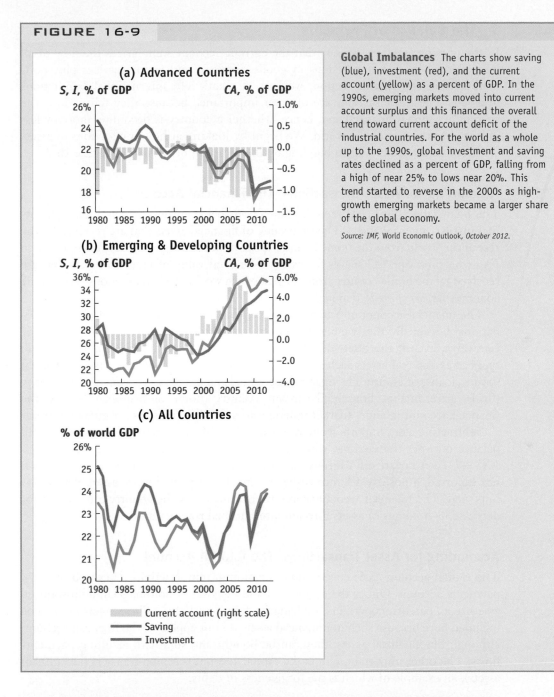

FIGURE 16-9

Global Imbalances The charts show saving (blue), investment (red), and the current account (yellow) as a percent of GDP. In the 1990s, emerging markets moved into current account surplus and this financed the overall trend toward current account deficit of the industrial countries. For the world as a whole up to the 1990s, global investment and saving rates declined as a percent of GDP, falling from a high of near 25% to lows near 20%. This trend started to reverse in the 2000s as high-growth emerging markets became a larger share of the global economy.

Source: IMF, World Economic Outlook, *October 2012.*

site trend: rising investment and saving ratios. For the developing countries, however, the saving increase was larger than the investment increase, allowing a current account surplus to open up. Overall, the industrial country trend of lower saving and investment drove the world trend of lower saving and investment in the 1980s and 1990s. But since the 2000s, the rising share of high-saving emerging and developing countries in the world economy has caused the world trends to reverse. Saving and investment have been on the rise in recent years, but the effects have been felt very unevenly across the globe, leading to the imbalances we have studied. ■

3 The Balance of Payments

In the previous section, we saw that the current account summarizes the flow of all international market transactions in goods, services, and factor services plus non-market transfers. In this section, we look at what's left: international transactions in assets. These transactions are of great importance because they tell us how the current account is financed and, hence, whether a country is becoming more or less indebted to the rest of the world. We begin by looking at how transactions in assets are accounted for, once again building on the intuition developed in Figure 16-2.[9]

Accounting for Asset Transactions: The Financial Account

The financial account (FA) records transactions between residents and nonresidents that involve financial assets. The total value of financial assets that are received by the rest of the world from the home country is the home country's *export of assets*, denoted EX_A (the subscript "A" stands for asset). The total value of financial assets that are received by the home country from the rest of the world in all transactions is the home country's *import of assets*, denoted IM_A.

The financial account measures all "movement" of financial assets across the international border. By this, we mean a movement from home to foreign ownership, or vice versa, even if the assets do not physically move. This definition also covers all types of assets: real assets such as land or structures, and financial assets such as debt (bonds, loans) or equity. The financial account also includes assets issued by any entity (firms, governments, households) in any country (home or overseas). Finally, the financial account includes market transactions as well as transfers, or gifts of assets.

Subtracting asset imports from asset exports yields the home country's net overall balance on asset transactions, which is known as the financial account, where $FA = EX_A - IM_A$. A negative FA means that the country has imported more assets than it has exported; a positive FA means the country has exported more assets than it has imported. The financial account therefore measures how the country can increase or decrease its holdings of assets through international transactions.

Accounting for Asset Transactions: The Capital Account

The capital account (KA) covers some remaining, minor activities in the balance of payments account. One is the acquisition and disposal of nonfinancial, nonproduced assets (e.g., patents, copyrights, trademarks, franchises, etc.). These assets have to be included here because such nonfinancial assets do not appear in the financial account, although like financial assets, they can be bought and sold with resulting payments flows. The other important item in the capital account is capital transfers (i.e., gifts of assets), an example of which is the forgiveness of debts.[10]

---

[9] Officially, following the 1993 revision to the System of National Accounts by the U.N. Statistical Office, the place where international transactions are recorded should be called "rest of the world account" or the "external transactions account." The United States calls it the "international transactions account." However, the older terminology was the "balance of payments account," and this usage persists, so we adopt it here.

[10] The capital account does *not* include involuntary debt cancellation, such as results from unilateral defaults. Changes in assets and liabilities due to defaults are counted as capital losses, or valuation effects, which are discussed later in this chapter.

As with unilateral income transfers, capital transfers must be accounted for properly. For example, the giver of an asset must deduct the value of the gift in the capital account to offset the export of the asset, which is recorded in the financial account, because in the case of a gift the export generates no associated payment. Similarly, recipients of capital transfers need to record them to offset the import of the asset recorded in the financial account.

Using similar notation to that employed with unilateral transfers of income, we denote capital transfers received by the home country as KA_{IN} and capital transfers given by the home country as KA_{OUT}. The capital account, $KA = KA_{IN} - KA_{OUT}$, denotes net capital transfers received. A negative KA indicates that more capital transfers were given by the home country than it received; a positive KA indicates that the home country received more capital transfers than it made.

The capital account is a minor and technical accounting item for most developed countries, usually close to zero. In some developing countries, however, the capital account can at times play an important role because in some years nonmarket debt forgiveness can be large, whereas market-based international financial transactions can be small.

Accounting for Home and Foreign Assets

Asset trades in the financial account can be broken down into two types: assets issued by home entities (home assets) and assets issued by foreign entities (foreign assets). This is of economic interest, and sometimes of political interest, because the breakdown makes clear the distinction between the location of the asset issuer and the location of the asset owner, that is, who owes what to whom.

From the home perspective, a foreign asset is a claim on a foreign country. When a home entity holds such an asset, it is called an **external asset** of the home country because it represents an obligation owed to the home country by the rest of the world. Conversely, from the home country's perspective, a home asset is a claim on the home country. When a foreign entity holds such an asset, it is called an **external liability** of the home country because it represents an obligation owed by the home country to the rest of the world. For example, when a U.S. firm invests overseas and acquires a computer factory located in Ireland, the acquisition is an external asset for the United States (and an external liability for Ireland). When a Japanese firm acquires an automobile plant in the United States, the acquisition is an external liability for the United States (and an external asset for Japan). A moment's thought reveals that all other assets traded across borders have a nation in which they are located and a nation by which they are owned—this is true for bank accounts, equities, government debt, corporate bonds, and so on. (For some examples, see **Side Bar: The Double-Entry Principle in the Balance of Payments.**)

If we use superscripts "H" and "F" to denote home and foreign assets, we can break down the financial account as the sum of the net exports of each type of asset:

$$FA = \underbrace{(EX_A^H - IM_A^H)}_{\substack{\text{Net export of} \\ \text{home assets}}} + \underbrace{(EX_A^F - IM_A^F)}_{\substack{\text{Net export of} \\ \text{foreign assets}}} = \underbrace{(EX_A^H - IM_A^H)}_{\substack{\text{Net export of} \\ \text{home assets} \\ = \\ \text{Net additions to} \\ \text{external liabilities}}} - \underbrace{(IM_A^F - EX_A^F)}_{\substack{\text{Net import of} \\ \text{foreign assets} \\ = \\ \text{Net additions to} \\ \text{external assets}}} \quad \text{(16-11)}$$

In the last part of this formula, we use the fact that net imports of foreign assets are just *minus* net exports of foreign assets, allowing us to change the sign. This reveals to us that FA equals *the additions to external liabilities* (the home-owned assets moving into foreign ownership, net) *minus the additions to external assets* (the foreign-owned assets moving into home ownership, net). This is our first indication of how flows of assets have implications for changes in a nation's wealth, a topic to which we return shortly.

How the Balance of Payments Accounts Work: A Macroeconomic View

To further understand the links between flows of goods, services, income, and assets, we have to understand how the current account, capital account, and financial account are related and why, in the end, the balance of payments accounts must balance as seen in the open-economy circular flow (Figure 16-2).

Recall from Equation (16-4) that gross national disposable income is

$$Y = GNDI = GNE + TB + NFIA + NUT = \underbrace{GNE + CA}_{\substack{\text{Resources available to} \\ \text{home country from income}}}$$

Does this expression represent all of the resources that are available to the home economy to finance expenditure? No. It represents only the income resources, that is, the resources obtained from the market sale and purchase of goods, services, and factor services and from nonmarket transfers. In addition, the home economy can free up (or use up) resources in another way: by engaging in net sales (or purchases) of assets. We can calculate these extra resources using our previous definitions:

$$[\underbrace{EX_A}_{\substack{\text{Value of}\\\text{all assets}\\\text{exported}}} - \underbrace{KA_{OUT}}_{\substack{\text{Value of}\\\text{all assets}\\\text{exported}\\\text{as gifts}}}] - [\underbrace{IM_A}_{\substack{\text{Value of}\\\text{all assets}\\\text{imported}}} - \underbrace{KA_{IN}}_{\substack{\text{Value of}\\\text{all assets}\\\text{imported}\\\text{as gifts}}}] = EX_A - IM_A + KA_{IN} - KA_{OUT} = \underbrace{FA + KA}_{\substack{\text{Extra resources}\\\text{available to the}\\\text{home country due}\\\text{to asset trades}}}$$

Adding the last two expressions, we arrive at the value of the total resources available to the home country for expenditure purposes. This total value must equal the total value of home expenditure on final goods and services, GNE:

$$\underbrace{GNE + CA}_{\substack{\text{Resources available}\\\text{to home country}\\\text{due to income}}} + \underbrace{FA + KA}_{\substack{\text{Extra resources available}\\\text{to the home country}\\\text{due to asset trades}}} = GNE$$

We can cancel GNE from both sides of this expression to obtain the important result known as the balance of payments identity or **BOP identity**:

$$\underbrace{CA}_{\text{Current account}} + \underbrace{KA}_{\text{Capital account}} + \underbrace{FA}_{\text{Financial account}} = 0 \qquad \text{(16-12)}$$

The balance of payments sums to zero: it does balance!

How the Balance of Payments Accounts Work: A Microeconomic View

We have just found that at the macroeconomic level, $CA + KA + FA = 0$, a very simple equation that summarizes, in three variables, every single one of the millions of international transactions a nation engages in. This is one way to look at the BOP accounts.

Another way to look at the BOP is to look behind these three variables to the specific flows we saw in Figure 16-2, and the individual transactions within each flow.

$$CA = (EX - IM) + (EX_{FS} - IM_{FS}) + (UT_{IN} - UT_{OUT})$$

$$KA = (KA_{IN} - KA_{OUT}) \tag{16-13}$$

$$FA = (EX_A^H - IM_A^H) + (EX_A^F - IM_A^F)$$

Written this way, the components of the BOP identity allow us to see the details behind why the accounts must balance. As you can observe from these equations, there are 12 transaction types (each preceded by either a plus or minus sign) and 3 accounts (CA, KA, FA) in which they can appear.

If an item has a plus sign, it is called a balance of payments credit, or **BOP credit.** Six types of transactions receive a plus (+) sign as follows:

Current account (CA):	Exports of goods and services ($+EX$);
	Exports of factor services ($+EX_{FS}$);
	Unilateral transfers received ($+UT_{IN}$).
Capital account (KA):	Capital transfers received ($+KA_{IN}$).
Financial account (FA):	Exports of home and foreign assets ($+EX_A^H$, $+EX_A^F$).

If an item has a minus sign, it is called a balance of payments debit, or **BOP debit.** Six types of transactions receive a minus (−) sign as follows:

Current account (CA):	Imports of goods and services ($-IM$);
	Imports of factor services ($-IM_{FS}$);
	Unilateral transfers given ($-UT_{OUT}$).
Capital account (KA):	Capital transfers given ($-KA_{OUT}$);
Financial account (FA):	Imports of home and foreign assets ($-IM_A^H$, $-IM_A^F$).

Now, to see why the BOP accounts balance overall, we have to understand one simple principle: *every market transaction (whether for goods, services, factor services, or assets) has two parts. If party A engages in a transaction with a counterparty B, then A receives from B an item of a given value, and in return B receives from A an item of equal value.*[11]

---

[11] This principle applies not only to market transactions, but also to nonmarket transactions such as gifts or foreign aid that are entered into the BOP accounts either as "net unilateral transfers" or into the capital account. For example, a $100 export of food aid is not a market transaction, but appears as a credit item in total exports. This credit is offset in the BOP accounts by a −$100 debit in net unilateral transfers. In this way, nonmarket gifts, for which nothing is offered in return, are properly recorded and yet leave the BOP accounts in balance.

Thus, whenever a transaction generates a credit somewhere in the BOP account, it must also generate a corresponding debit somewhere else in the BOP account. Similarly, every debit generates a corresponding credit. (For more detail on this topic, see **Side Bar: The Double-Entry Principle in the Balance of Payments.**)

It might not be obvious where the offsetting item is, but it must exist somewhere *if* the accounts have been measured properly. As we shall see shortly, this is a big "if": mismeasurement can sometimes be an important issue.

SIDE BAR

The Double-Entry Principle in the Balance of Payments

We can make the double-entry principle more concrete by looking at some (mostly) hypothetical international transactions and figuring out how they would be recorded in the U.S. BOP accounts.

1. Recall from Chapter 13 that our friend George was in Paris. Suppose he spent $110 (€100) on French wine one evening. This is a U.S. import of a foreign service. George pays with his American Express card. The bar is owed $110 (or €100) by American Express (and Amex is owed by George). The United States has exported an asset to France: the bar now has a claim against American Express. From the U.S. perspective, this represents an increase in U.S. assets owned by foreigners. The double entries in the U.S. BOP appear in the current account and the financial account:

CA: Drinks in Paris bar	$-IM$	−$110
FA: Bar's claim on AMEX	$+EX_A^H$	+$110

2. George was in the bar to meet his Danish cousin Georg. They both work as wine merchants. After a few bottles of Bordeaux, George enthuses about Arkansas chardonnay and insists Georg give it a try. Georg counters by telling George he should really try some Jutland rosé. Each cousin returns home and asks his firm to ship a case of each wine (worth $36) to the other. This barter transaction (involving no financial activity) would appear solely as two entries in the U.S. current account:

CA: Arkansas wine exported to Denmark	EX	+$36
CA: Jutland wine imported to United States	$-IM$	−$36

3. Later that night, George met a French entrepreneur in a smoky corner of the bar. George vaguely remembers the story: the entrepreneur's French tech company was poised

for unbelievable success with an upcoming share issue. George decides to invest $10,000 to buy the French stock; he imports a French asset. The stock is sold to him through the French bank BNP, and George sends them a U.S. check. BNP then has a claim against Citibank, an export of a home asset to France. Both entries fall within the financial account:

FA: George's French tech stocks	$-IM_A^F$	−$10,000
FA: BNP claim against Citibank	$+EX_A^H$	+$10,000

4. Rather surprisingly, George's French stocks do quite well. Later that year they have doubled in value. George makes a $5,000 donation to charity. His charity purchases U.S. relief supplies that will be exported to a country suffering a natural disaster. The two entries here are entirely in the U.S. current account. The supplies are a nonmarket export of goods offset by the value of the unilateral transfer:

CA: Relief supplies exported	EX	+$5,000
CA: George's charitable gift	$-UT_{OUT}$	−$5,000

5. George was also pleased to see that some poor countries were benefiting from another kind of foreign assistance, debt forgiveness. The U.S. Secretary of State announced that the United States would forgive $1 billion of debt owed by a developing country. This would decrease U.S.-owned assets overseas. The United States was exporting the developing country's assets: it hands the canceled debts back, a credit in the financial account. The double entries would be seen in the capital and financial accounts:

KA: U.S. grant of debt relief	$-KA_{OUT}$	−$1,000,000,000
FA: Decline in U.S. external assets	$-EX_A^F$	+$1,000,000,000

Understanding the Data for the Balance of Payments Account

To illustrate all the principles we've learned, let's look at the United States' balance of payments account. Table 16-2 shows an extract of the U.S. BOP accounts for 2012.[12]

In the current account, in the top part of the table, we look first at the trade in goods and services on lines 1 and 3. Overall exports *EX* were +$2,194 billion (line 1, a credit), and imports *IM* were −$2,734 billion (line 3, a debit). In the summary items,

TABLE 16-2

The U.S. Balance of Payments in 2012 The table shows U.S. international transactions in 2012 in billions of dollars. Major categories are in bold type.

Major Account	Line	Category or Subcategory	Symbol	$ billions
Current Account	1	**Exports of goods and services**	$+EX$	**2,194**
	1a	Of which: Goods		1,564
	1b	Services		630
	2	**Income receipts** [= exports of factor services]	$+EX_{FS}$	**742**
	3	**Imports of goods and services** (−)	$-IM$	**−2,734**
	3a	Of which: Goods (−)		−2,299
	3b	Services (−)		−435
	4	**Income payments** [= imports of factor services (−)]	$-IM_{FS}$	**−543**
	5	**Net unilateral transfers**	NUT	**−134**
Capital and Financial Account	6	**Capital account** net	KA	**6**
	7	**U.S.-owned assets abroad** net increase (−) [= net imports of ROW assets or financial outflow (−)]	$+EX_A^F - IM_A^F$	**18**
	7a	Of which: U.S. official reserve assets		−4
	7b	Other assets		22
	8	**Foreign-owned assets in U.S.** net increase (+) [= net exports of U.S. assets or financial inflow (+)]	$+EX_A^H - IM_A^H$	**385**
	8a	Of which: Foreign official assets		374
	8b	Other assets		11
Statistical Discrepancy	9	**Statistical discrepancy** (sum of 1 to 8, sign reversed)	SD	**+66**
Summary Items		**Balance on current account** (lines 1, 2, 3, 4, and 5)	CA	**−475**
		Of which: Balance on goods and services (lines 1 and 3)	TB	−540
		Balance on income (lines 2 and 4)	$NFIA$	199
		Balance on financial account (lines 7 and 8)	FA	**403**
		Of which: Official settlements balance (lines 7a and 8a)		370
		Nonreserve financial account (lines 7b and 8b)		33

Notes: Details may not add to totals because of rounding. The statistical discrepancy shown here includes financial derivatives not otherwise counted.

Source: U.S. Bureau of Economic Analysis, ITA Table 1, using the ITA definition of the United States. This includes U.S. territories, so these figures are slightly different from those in Table 16-1. Data preliminary as of March 14, 2013.

[12] The BOP account is published each year as the "international transactions account (ITA)" by the BEA. The ITA uses a different geographical definition of the United States territory than the national income and product accounts (NIPA), so these figures do not exactly match those discussed earlier and in Table 16-1.

we see the balance on goods and services, the trade balance TB, was −$540 billion (line 1 plus line 3, or exports minus imports). Exports and imports and the trade balance are also broken down even further into goods and service components (lines 1a, 1b, 3a, and 3b).

The next part of the current account on lines 2 and 4 deals with trade in factor services, also known as the *income account* (referring to the income paid to those factors). Income receipts for factor service exports, EX_{FS}, generated a credit of +$742 billion and income payments for factor service imports, IM_{FS}, generated a debit of −$543 billion. Adding these two items resulted in net factor income from abroad NFIA equal to +$199 billion (line 2 plus line 4), a net credit.

Lastly, we see that net unilateral transfers NUT were −$134 billion, a net debit (line 5); the United States was a net donor as measured by the net transfer of goods, services, and income to the rest of the world. (Typically, in summary tables like these, unilateral transfers are shown only in net form.)

Overall, summing lines 1 through 5, the 2012 U.S. current account balance CA was −$475 billion, that is, a deficit of $475 billion, as shown in the summary items at the foot of the table.

A country with a current account surplus is called a **(net) lender.** By the BOP identity, we know that it must have a deficit in its asset accounts, so like any lender, it is, on net, buying assets (acquiring IOUs from borrowers). For example, China is a large net lender. A country with a current account deficit is called a **(net) borrower.** By the BOP identity, we know that it must have a surplus in its asset accounts, so like any borrower, it is, on net, selling assets (issuing IOUs to lenders). As we can see, the United States is a large net borrower.

Now we move to the capital and financial accounts. Typically, in summary tables like these, the capital account is shown only in net form. The United States in 2012 had a negligible capital account KA of +$6 billion (line 6).

Lastly, we move to the financial account. As explained, this account can be broken down in terms of the exports and imports of two kinds of assets: U.S. assets (U.S. external liabilities) and rest of the world assets (U.S. external assets). In this summary the net trades are shown for each kind of asset.

We see that the United States was engaged in the net sale of foreign assets, so that external assets (U.S.-owned assets abroad) decreased by $18 billion. This net export of foreign assets is recorded as a credit of +$18 billion (line 7). Note that the plus sign maintains the convention that exports are credits.

At the same time, the United States was engaged in the net export of U.S. assets to the rest of the world so that external liabilities (foreign-owned assets in the United States) increased by $385 billion; the net export of U.S. assets is duly recorded as a credit of +$385 billion (line 8).

The sum of lines 7 and 8 gives the financial account balance FA of +$403 billion, recorded in the summary items.

For further information on interventions by central banks, financial account transactions are often also broken down into reserve and nonreserve components. Changes in reserves arise from official intervention in the foreign exchange market—that is, purchases and sales by home and foreign monetary authorities. The balance on all reserve transactions is called the *official settlements balance*, and the balance on all other asset trades is called the *nonreserve financial account*. We see here that U.S. authorities intervened a little: a net import of $4 billion of U.S. official reserves (line 7a) means that the Federal Reserve bought $4 billion in foreign (i.e., nondollar) exchange reserves from foreigners. In contrast, foreign central banks intervened a lot: U.S. entities sold them $374 billion in U.S. dollar reserve assets (line 8a).

Adding up the current account, the capital account, and the financial account (lines 1 through 8), we find that the total of the three accounts was –$66 billion (–$475 + $6 + $403 = –$66). The BOP accounts are supposed to balance by adding to zero—in reality, they never do. Why not? Because the statistical agencies tasked with gathering BOP data find it impossible to track every single international transaction correctly, because of measurement errors and omissions. Some problems result from the smuggling of goods or trade tax evasion. Larger errors are likely due to the mismeasured, concealed, or illicit movement of financial income flows and asset movements (e.g., money laundering and capital tax evasion).

The Statistical Discrepancy To "account" for this error, statistical agencies create an accounting item, the *statistical discrepancy* (SD) equal to minus the error $SD = -(CA + KA + FA)$. With that "correction," the amended version of the BOP identity will hold true in practice, sweeping away the real-world measurement problems. In the table, the statistical discrepancy is shown on line 9.[13] Once the statistical discrepancy is included, the balance of payments accounts always balance.

Some Recent Trends in the U.S. Balance of Payments Figure 16-10 shows recent trends in various components of the U.S. balance of payments. The sharp downward trend of the current account is as previously shown in Figure 16-6, so for the balance of payments identity to hold, there must be an offsetting upward trend in other parts of the BOP accounts. This is indeed the case. We can see that the United States has been financing its growing deficit on the current account primarily by running an expanding surplus on the financial account. In the mid-1990s, there was close to a $100 billion current account deficit and a comparable financial account surplus. A decade later, both figures were in the region of $800 billion, with a substantial decline seen in the period since the global financial crisis of 2008 and up to 2012.

What the Balance of Payments Account Tells Us

The balance of payments accounts consist of the following:

- The current account, which measures external imbalances in goods, services, factor services, and unilateral transfers.
- The financial and capital accounts, which measure asset trades.

Using the principle that market transactions must consist of a trade of two items of equal value, we find that the balance of payments accounts really do balance.

Surpluses on the current account side of the BOP accounts must be offset by deficits on the asset side. Similarly, deficits on the current account must be offset by surpluses on the asset side. By telling us how current account imbalances are financed, the balance of payments connects a country's income and spending decisions to the evolution of that country's wealth, an important connection we develop further in the final section of this chapter.

---

[13] Prior to 2007, the U.S. statistical discrepancy included unmeasured financial derivatives transactions. Starting in 2007, the BEA estimates these transactions, but they are not as yet broken down in detail into home and foreign assets. For clarity, they are not reported here and are included in the statistical discrepancy in Table 16-2.

FIGURE 16-10

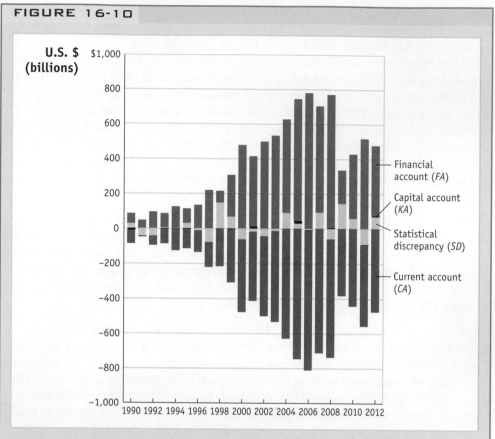

U.S. Balance of Payments and Its Components, 1990–2012 The figure shows the current account balance (*CA*), the capital account balance (*KA*, barely visible), the financial account balance (*FA*), and the statistical discrepancy (*SD*), in billions of dollars.

Source: U.S. Bureau of Economic Analysis, ITA Table 1, using the ITA definition of the United States, which includes U.S. territories. Data revised, and preliminary for 2012, as of March 14, 2013.

4 External Wealth

The measurement of a nation's income flow is not the only important economic variable that must be adapted to the open-economy environment. Economists and policy makers, and the general public, also care about a nation's stock of *wealth*. And so, probably, do you.

For example, Anne has income and expenditures of $50,000 each year and savings in the bank of $10,000. But she also has a credit card debt of $20,000. Beth's life is identical to Anne's in almost every respect: she has income and expenditures of $50,000 each year and savings of $10,000, but she has no credit card debt. Who is better off? Clearly, Beth is. Her income is the same as Anne's. But Anne's wealth or "net worth" is –$10,000 (savings of $10,000 minus debt of $20,000), whereas Beth has a net worth of +$10,000. Anne's wealth is –20% of her income; Beth's wealth is +20% of her income.

Just as a household is better off with higher wealth, all else equal, so is a country. We can calculate a home country's "net worth" or **external wealth (W)** with respect to the rest of the world (ROW) by adding up all of the home assets owned by ROW (foreigners' claims against home) and then subtracting all of the ROW assets owned by the home country (home claims against foreigners). Doing this for the United States at the end of year 2012, we would find that the United States had an external wealth of about –$4,474 billion, according to preliminary BEA estimates. This made the United States the world's biggest debtor in history at the time of this writing. The United States' net debt to the ROW was about $14,250 for every American. Because GDP per person in the United States was about $50,000 in 2012, the external wealth of the U.S. was about –28.5% of GDP.

Why is U.S. external wealth at this level? How did it get there and what will happen next? To understand how the wealth levels of countries evolve, in this final section of the chapter we build on what we have learned from the national income and balance of payments accounts.

The Level of External Wealth

First, we give a definition of the level of a country's external wealth (W):

$$\underbrace{\text{External wealth}}_{W} = \underbrace{\begin{bmatrix} \text{ROW assets} \\ \text{owned by home} \end{bmatrix}}_{A} - \underbrace{\begin{bmatrix} \text{Home assets} \\ \text{owned by ROW} \end{bmatrix}}_{L} \qquad (16\text{-}14)$$

External wealth equals the value of total external assets (A) minus the value of total external liabilities (L). Total external assets is what the rest of the world owes to the home country, and total external liabilities is what the home country owes to the ROW. A country's level of external wealth is also called its *net international investment position* or *net foreign assets*. It is a stock measure, not a flow measure.

> If $W > 0$, *the home country is a* **net creditor** *country: external assets exceed external liabilities, and what the rest of the world owes the home country is greater than what the home country owes to the rest of the world.*

> If $W < 0$, *the home country is a* **net debtor** *country: external liabilities exceed external assets, and what the home country owes to the rest of the world is greater than what the rest of the world owes to the home country.*

External wealth is only one part of a nation's total wealth. The other part of a nation's wealth is internal wealth, which corresponds to the total value of all nonfinancial assets in the home country. (The links between external wealth and total wealth are explored further in the appendix to this chapter.)

Because we are focusing on international economic relationships, our main emphasis is on external wealth because it measures the outstanding obligations of one country to another. Those obligations, and when and how they are paid, can be the source of great economic and political stress. Moreover, the net debts of nations, like those of individuals, ultimately carry a cost. To understand external wealth, let's look at how it is measured and how it evolves.

Changes in External Wealth

There are two reasons a country's level of external wealth changes over time.

1. *Financial flows:* As a result of asset trades, the country can increase or decrease its external assets and liabilities. How? Net exports of foreign assets cause an equal decrease in the level of external assets and hence a corresponding

decrease in external wealth. Net exports of home assets cause an equal increase in the level of external liabilities and hence a corresponding decrease in external wealth. For example, if net exports of assets (whether home or foreign) are +$1 billion, then the change in external wealth is −$1 billion. The net export of assets of all kinds is measured by the financial account (FA), and this has a *negative* effect on external wealth in any period.

2. *Valuation effects:* The value of existing external assets and liabilities may change over time because of capital gains or losses. In the case of external wealth, this change in value could be due to price effects or exchange rate effects. For example, suppose, a U.S. citizen buys 100 shares of BP on the London Stock Exchange at £7 each. Suppose the exchange rate is $1.5 per pound. These U.S. external assets are worth $10.50 each (1.5 times 7), for a total of $1,050. Suppose the price of these shares then falls to £6, and the exchange rate stays the same. Each share is now worth $9.00 (1.5 times 6) and the 100 shares are valued at $900. Their value has fallen in dollar terms by $150 (£1 times 1.5 times 100), which is a capital loss. This is an example of a price effect. Now suppose the exchange rate rises to $1.6 per pound. Each share is still worth £6 in U.K. currency but $9.60 in U.S. currency (1.6 times 6), so the total value of the shares rises to $960, which, relative to the $900 they were previously worth, implies a capital gain of $60. This is an example of an exchange rate effect. Similar effects can change the value of external liabilities.

Adding up these two contributions to the change in external wealth (ΔW), we find

$$\underbrace{\begin{bmatrix} \text{Change in} \\ \text{external wealth} \end{bmatrix}}_{\Delta W} = - \underbrace{\begin{bmatrix} \text{Financial} \\ \text{account} \end{bmatrix}}_{\substack{\text{Net export of assets} \\ = \\ FA}} + \underbrace{\begin{bmatrix} \text{Capital gains on} \\ \text{external wealth} \end{bmatrix}}_{\substack{\text{Valuation effects} \\ = \\ \text{Capital gains minus capital losses}}} \qquad (16\text{-}15)$$

We gain a deeper understanding of this expression if we recall the BOP identity: the current account plus the capital account plus the financial account equals zero. Hence, minus the financial account equals the current account plus the capital account, or $-FA = CA + KA$. Substituting this identity into Equation (16-15), we obtain

$$\underbrace{\begin{bmatrix} \text{Change in} \\ \text{external wealth} \end{bmatrix}}_{\Delta W} = \underbrace{\begin{bmatrix} \text{Current} \\ \text{account} \end{bmatrix}}_{\substack{CA \\ = \\ \text{Unspent} \\ \text{income}}} + \underbrace{\begin{bmatrix} \text{Capital} \\ \text{account} \end{bmatrix}}_{\substack{KA \\ = \\ \text{Net capital} \\ \text{transfers received}}} + \underbrace{\begin{bmatrix} \text{Capital gains on} \\ \text{external wealth} \end{bmatrix}}_{\substack{\text{Valuation effects} \\ = \\ \text{Capital gains} \\ \text{minus capital losses}}} \qquad (16\text{-}16)$$

This fundamental formula tells us that a country can increase its external wealth in one of only three ways:

- Through its own thrift (a CA surplus, so expenditure is less than income)
- By the charity of others (a KA surplus, by receiving net gifts of wealth)
- With the help of windfalls (having positive capital gains)

Similarly, a country can reduce its external wealth by doing any of the opposites.

Understanding the Data on External Wealth

To track external wealth accurately, statisticians apply Equation (16-15). They face the challenge of not only keeping tabs on every trade in assets but also correctly assessing the impact of changing financial market conditions around the world on the value of the country's external assets and liabilities.

Measures of levels and changes in national external wealth are tabulated in an account known as the net international investment position. To illustrate with an example, a simplified version of this account for the United States appears in Table 16-3. The latest detailed data for the year 2012 show a clear distinction between the contribution of financial flows to changes in external wealth—net trade in assets, in column (a)—and the impact of various kinds of valuation effects—columns (b), (c), and (d).

Table 16-3, line 3, column (a), shows that in 2012 the United States, on net, exported $446 billion in assets (net exports of $544 billion of U.S. assets on line 3, minus

TABLE 16-3

U.S. External Wealth in 2011-12 The table shows changes in the U.S. net international investment position during the year 2012 in billions of dollars. The net result in row 3 equals row 1 minus row 2.

Category	Position, end 2011 ($ billions)	Changes in Position during 2012 ($ billions)					Total (a + b + c + d)	Position, end 2012 ($ billions)
			Of Which Valuation Effects					
		Financial Flows (a)	Price Changes (b)	Exchange Rate Changes (c)	Other Changes (d)			
1. External Assets	16,920	97	991	6	4		1,098	18,018
= U.S.-owned assets abroad, of which:								
U.S. official reserve assets	537	4	33	−2	0		35	572
U.S. government assets, other	179	−85	—	0	0		−85	94
U.S. private assets	16,204	178	958	8	4		1,148	17,352
2. External Liabilities	20,736	544	501	1	157		1,203	21,940
= Foreign-owned assets in the United States, of which:								
Foreign official assets in the United States	5,256	394	42	0	0		436	5,692
Other foreign assets	15,480	150	459	1	157		767	16,247
3. External Wealth								
= Line 1 minus Line 2	−3,817	−446	490	5	−153		−105	−3,922
= Net international investment position of the United States								
Symbol	*W* (end 2011)	*−FA*	Capital gains				*ΔW*	*W* (end 2012)

Note: Financial derivatives are excluded.

Source: U.S. Bureau of Economic Analysis, IIP Table 2. Data revised as of June 25, 2013.

net imports of $97 billion of foreign assets on line 1). On their own, these financial flows would have reduced U.S. external wealth by $446 billion in just one year. Yet the actual change in external wealth was much smaller in that year due to positive valuation effects of +$341 billion in columns (b), (c), and (d) which mitigated the decline U.S. external wealth over the same period. These valuation effects were mainly driven by +$490 billion in price change effects and only +$5 billion in exchange rate effects. "Other" changes are recorded as –$153 billion. Thus, while the United States borrowed an additional $446 billion from various nations in 2012, its external wealth actually fell by only $105 billion as shown by the total change on line 3.

So what happened in 2012? The value of the U.S. dollar changed very little against foreign currencies, and hence exchange rate effects were tiny. The main factor was that equity values were rising worldwide (about 15%). However, U.S. external assets include a larger share of higher-risk equities than U.S. external liabilities, which consist of a great deal of lower-risk U.S. debt. This difference in the composition of the two portfolios meant that rising equity markets tended to raise the value of U.S. external assets (which went up about 6% in value) much more than U.S. external liabilities (which went up about 2.5%). In addition, U.S. external liabilities include vast foreign holdings of U.S. Treasury securities, held either as foreign official assets in central banks or as low-risk assets by foreign investors. These dollar-denominated assets tended to have a stable value in 2012 as interest rates on U.S. debt remained low and changed very little from the start to the end of the year.[14]

Some Recent Trends Over the longer run, the changes in external wealth in Equation (16-16) gradually accumulate. In the case of the United States, for the past three decades, the financial account has been almost always in surplus, reflecting a net export of assets to the rest of the world to pay for chronic current account deficits (the capital account has been negligibly small).

If there had been no valuation effects, then Equation (16-15) would make a simple prediction. The change in the level of external wealth between two dates should equal the cumulative net import of assets (minus the financial account) over the intervening period. For example, if we had taken the U.S. external wealth level at the end of 1988 and added to that level all subsequent financial flows for the next 24 years until the end of 2012, we would have estimated U.S. external wealth in 2012 at about –$8,000 billion, which would have been a massive net debtor position (exceeding –50% of GDP). In reality, the actual 2011 figure for external wealth was a lot smaller: only –$4 trillion (–$3,922 billion as shown in Table 16-3).

Why? Valuation effects or capital gains generated the difference of $4 trillion in external wealth over the period from 1988 to 2012, and when added up these effects reduced U.S. net external indebtedness in 2012 by almost one-half compared with the level that financial flows alone would have predicted. The flip side of these valuation effects is that the rest of the world outside the United States suffered an equal and opposite capital loss over the same period. Why? Capital gains always have a "zero sum" property—by symmetry, an increase in the dollar value of the home country's external assets is simultaneously an increase in the dollar value of the rest of the world's external liabilities.

---

[14] Data on the currency composition of U.S. external wealth from Cedric Tille, 2005, "Financial Integration and the Wealth Effect of Exchange Rate Fluctuations," Staff Reports 226, Federal Reserve Bank of New York.

What External Wealth Tells Us

External wealth data tell us the net credit or debit position of a country with respect to the rest of the world. They include data on external assets (foreign assets owned by the home country) and external liabilities (home assets owned by foreigners). A creditor country has positive external wealth, a debtor country negative external wealth.

What drives external wealth? The current account told us about the imbalances in a country's external flows of goods, services, factor services, and income. The balance of payments accounts told us how these imbalances require offsetting financial flows of assets between countries. Countries with a current account surplus (deficit) must be net buyers (sellers) of assets. This buying and selling of assets has implications for external wealth. An increase in a country's external wealth results from every net import of assets; conversely, a decrease in external wealth results from every net export of assets. In addition, countries can experience capital gains or losses on their external assets and liabilities that cause changes in external wealth. All of these changes are summarized in the statement of a country's net international investment position.

5 Conclusions

The science of macroeconomics would be impossible without data, and the vast majority of the data we employ emerge from the efforts of official statisticians around the world. Despite all the statistical discrepancies, and even the occasional errors of omission and commission (see **Side Bar: Beware of Greeks Bearing Statistics**), we would be lost without these measures of macroeconomic activity.

This chapter has illustrated some important accounting concepts and has highlighted some unusual and intriguing features of the current international economic system. We have seen how a consistent system of national income and product accounts allows countries to track international trade flows (including trade in intermediate goods), cross-border factor income flows, and unilateral transfers. We have also seen how these net resource flows of goods and services can be matched against a parallel set of net payment activities involving assets in the balance of payments accounts. Finally, we have seen how the flow of trades in assets can be combined with capital gains and losses to track the evolution of a nation's stock of external wealth, an important part of its total wealth, as recorded in the statement of the net international investment position.

In the remainder of the book, we make extensive use of the concepts introduced in this chapter to develop theories that explore the global macroeconomic links between nations.

SIDE BAR

Beware of Greeks Bearing Statistics

It is important, but rather sad, to note that when it comes to national statistics, we cannot believe everything we read. Over the years numerous governments have been suspected of fiddling with their official data for various purposes, as indicated by the following examples:

- *Greece.* In 2001 Greece was allowed to join the Eurozone. One of the criteria it had to meet in order to join was that its budget deficit could not be more than 3% of its GDP. Greece met this requirement according to its official statistics. In November 2004, after it had been allowed to join

602 PART 7 ■ THE BALANCE OF PAYMENTS

the Eurozone, Greece admitted its 2003 budget deficit was really 3.4%, twice as large as it had previously claimed. In fact, the budget deficit had not been below 3% since 1999. The EU was not amused. Greece continued to publish incorrect or manipulated data (including a 25% upward adjustment to GDP to take into account "black economy" activity such as prostitution). By inflating its GDP, Greece made its budget deficit position look better than it was, which may have allowed Greece to borrow from other countries on favorable terms. When the euro crisis hit in 2008–09, the full horror of Greece's weak economic and fiscal position became clear, by which point the fiasco forced other Eurozone nations and the IMF to provide emergency funding in 2010. Greece eventually defaulted in 2011, went into a deeper depression, and the economic and political ramifications (e.g., austerity policies, the collapse of the Cyprus banking system in 2013, and undermined confidence in other weak economies) have continued to threaten the survival of the euro project itself.

- *Italy.* In 1987 Italy was considered much poorer than northern European countries. But its statisticians also decided to increase GDP by 15% after some guesswork to account for the black economy. Instantly, Italians had a higher official GDP per person than the British, an event known as *il sorpasso*. Not that this made any Italians actually feel richer.

- *Argentina.* After its 2001 crisis, a new populist government took over but faced problems with high and persistent inflation. To "solve" this problem, the government "reorganized" its official statistical bureau, which then started publishing much lower, and highly suspicious, inflation data. Lower inflation also helped the government avoid larger costs of indexed benefits and allowed the government to claim it had solved the inflation problem. Few believed these published data were true.

- *China.* In the 2005 International Comparison Program by the World Bank, the estimate of China's yuan price level came in much higher than had been expected. This had various implications: dividing nominal yuan income by the price level made China look quite a bit poorer. And higher prices made China's real exchange rate less undervalued, or even overvalued. Since poorer countries usually have lower price levels, both of these impacts had the effect of making China's exchange rate look more fairly valued, given its standard of living. This came about at a time when China was under considerable political pressure to appreciate its currency. But skeptics doubted whether the data were totally plausible, because the change in the yuan price level since the previous ICP was much larger than that implied by China's own official inflation data over the same period.

KEY POINTS

1. National flows of expenditure, product, income, and wealth, and international flows of goods, services, income, and assets, together measure important aspects of a country's economic performance and describe its economy's relationship to economies in the rest of the world. The records kept in the national income and product accounts, the balance of payments account, and the net international investment position track these data.

2. The key measures of economic activity are:

   - Gross national expenditure (GNE) measures an economy's total spending on final goods and services. It is the sum of consumption, investment, and government consumption: $GNE = C + I + G$.

   - Gross domestic product (GDP) measures total production (value of all output minus value of all purchased inputs).

   - Gross national income (GNI) measures the total payments to an economy's domestic factors.

   - Gross national disposable income (GNDI, also denoted Y) measures an economy's disposable income including transfers.

   In a closed economy, $GNE = GDP = GNI = GNDI$.

3. In an open economy, GDP need not equal GNE. When nations can trade, the sum of goods and services demanded by domestic residents need not be the same as the sum of goods and services supplied by domestic firms. The difference between GDP and GNE is the trade balance TB: $GDP = GNE + TB$. The trade balance is the difference between a nation's imports and exports of goods and services.

4. In an open economy, GDP need not equal GNI because imports and exports of factor services

(measured by net factor income from abroad or NFIA) imply that factor income received by domestic residents need not be the same as factor payments made by domestic firms. Thus, $GNI = GDP + NFIA$.

5. In an open economy, the true level of disposable income is best measured by gross national disposable income or $Y = GNDI$. GNDI need not equal GNI because net unilateral transfers (NUT) to foreigners may be positive, due to foreign aid and other nonmarket gifts. Thus, $Y = GNDI = GNI + NUT$.

6. The sum of all the aforementioned international transactions, $TB + NFIA + NUT$, is called the current account (CA).

7. From the relationships just outlined, we find that $Y = C + I + G + CA$. This expression is known as the *national income identity*.

8. National saving S is defined as $Y - C - G$. From the national income identity, we can derive the current account identity: $S = I + CA$. The current account equals saving minus investment. Movements in saving or investment, all else equal, feed directly into the current account.

9. All international trades in goods and services and in assets are recorded in an account known as the balance of payments (BOP). As a result of double-entry bookkeeping, and allowing for gifts and transfers, the BOP must sum to zero.

10. The BOP contains the following:
    - Net exports of goods and services, TB, called the trade balance
    - Net exports of factor services, NFIA, called the net factor income from abroad
    - Net unilateral transfers received, NUT, called the net unilateral transfers
    - Net transfers of assets received, KA, called the capital account
    - Net exports of assets, FA, called the financial account

11. The first three items are the current account CA. Since the BOP accounts sum to zero, this implies the balance of payments identity: $CA + FA + KA = 0$.

12. External wealth is a measure of a country's credit or debt position versus the rest of the world. It equals external assets—rest of world (ROW) assets owned by home—minus external liabilities (home assets owned by ROW). The net export (import) of assets lowers (raises) a country's external wealth. External wealth is one part of a country's total wealth.

13. External wealth can change for one of two reasons: the export or import of assets (called financial flows) or changes in the value of existing assets due to capital gains or losses (called valuation effects). Both of these channels affect net external wealth.

KEY TERMS

national income and product accounts, p. 568

balance of payments accounts, p. 568

gross national expenditure (GNE), p. 568

gross domestic product (GDP), p. 569

gross national income (GNI), p. 570

trade balance (TB), p. 570

net factor income from abroad (NFIA), p. 570

net unilateral transfers (NUT), p. 572

gross national disposable income (GNDI), p. 572

current account (CA), p. 572

financial account (FA), p. 572

capital account (KA), p. 572

national income identity, p. 582

national saving, p. 582

current account identity, p. 583

private saving, p. 584

government saving, p. 585

public saving, p. 585

external asset, p. 589

external liability, p. 589

BOP identity, p. 590

BOP credit, p. 591

BOP debit, p. 591

(net) lender, p. 594

(net) borrower, p. 594

external wealth (*W*), p. 596

net creditor, p. 597

net debtor, p. 597

PROBLEMS

1. Below is a partial table of the OECD's 2004 ranking of member countries based on their GDP per capita. Compute the ratio of GNI to GDP in each case. What does this imply about net factor income from abroad in each country? Compute the GNI rankings of these countries. Are there any major differences between the GDP and GNI rankings? What do these differences imply? Indicate?

		GDP per Person	GNI per Person
1	Luxembourg	$64,843	$53,299
2	Norway	$41,880	$42,062
3	United States	$39,660	$39,590
4	Ireland	$36,536	$31,151
5	Switzerland	$34,740	$37,638
6	Netherlands	$33,571	$34,527
7	Iceland	$33,271	$31,897
8	Austria	$33,235	$32,843
9	Australia	$32,643	$31,462
10	Canada	$32,413	$31,751
11	Denmark	$32,335	$32,232
12	Belgium	$31,985	$31,675
13	United Kingdom	$31,780	$32,470
14	Sweden	$31,072	$31,007
15	Germany	$29,916	$28,732
16	Finland	$29,833	$30,361
17	Japan	$29,173	$29,739
18	France	$29,006	$29,287
19	Italy	$27,744	$27,586
20	Greece	$27,691	$27,412
21	Spain	$26,018	$25,672
22	New Zealand	$24,834	$23,205
23	Slovenia	$21,527	$21,268
24	Korea	$20,723	$20,771
25	Czech Republic	$19,426	$18,314
26	Portugal	$19,324	$19,029
27	Hungary	$16,519	$15,548
28	Slovak Republic	$14,651	$14,708
29	Poland	$13,089	$12,511
30	Mexico	$10,145	$9,989
31	Turkey	$7,212	$7,186

2. Note the following accounting identity for gross national income (GNI):

$$GNI = C + I + G + TB + NFIA$$

Using this expression, show that in a closed economy, gross domestic product (GDP), gross national income (GNI), and gross national expenditures (GNE) are the same. Show that domestic investment is equal to domestic savings.

3. Show how each of the following would affect the U.S. balance of payments. Include a description of the debit and credit items, and in each case identify which specific account is affected (e.g., imports of goods and services, IM; exports of assets, EX_A; and so on. (For this question, you may find it helpful to refer to Appendix 1.)

   a. A California computer manufacturer purchases a $50 hard disk from a Malaysian company, paying the funds from a bank account in Malaysia.

   b. A U.S. tourist to Japan sells his iPod to a local resident for yen worth $100.

   c. The U.S. central bank sells $500 million of its holdings of U.S. Treasury bonds to a British financial firm and purchases pound sterling foreign reserves.

   d. A foreign owner of Apple shares receives $10,000 in dividend payments, which are paid into a New York bank.

   e. The central bank of China purchases $1 million of export earnings from a firm that has sold $1 million of toys to the United States, and the central bank holds these dollars as reserves.

   f. The U.S. government forgives a $50 million debt owed by a developing country.

4. In 2010 the country of Ikonomia has a current account deficit of $1 billion and a nonreserve financial account surplus of $750 million. Ikonomia's capital account is in a $100 million surplus. In addition, Ikonomian factories located in foreign countries earn $700 million. Ikonomia has a trade deficit of $800 million. Assume Ikonomia neither gives nor receives unilateral transfers. Ikonomia's GDP is $9 billion.

   a. What happened to Ikonomia's net foreign assets during 2010? Did it acquire or lose foreign assets during the year?

b. Compute the official settlements balance (OSB). Based on this number, what happened to the central bank's (foreign) reserves?

c. How much income did foreign factors of production earn in Ikonomia during 2010?

d. Compute net factor income from abroad (NFIA).

e. Using the identity $BOP = CA + FA + KA$, show that $BOP = 0$.

f. Compute Ikonomia's gross national expenditure (GNE), gross national income (GNI), and gross national disposable income (GNDI).

5. To answer this question, you must obtain data from the Bureau of Economic Analysis (BEA), http://www.bea.gov, on the U.S. balance of payments (BOP) tables. Go to interactive tables to obtain *annual* data for 2008 (the default setting is for quarterly data). It may take you some time to become familiar with how to navigate the website. *You need only refer to Table 1 on the BOP accounts.* Using the BOP data, compute the following for the United States:

a. Trade balance (TB), net factor income from abroad (NFIA), net unilateral transfers (NUT), and current account (CA)

b. Financial account (FA)

c. Official settlements balance (OSB), referred to as "U.S. official reserve assets" and "Foreign official assets in the U.S."

d. Nonreserve financial account (NRFA)

e. Balance of payments (BOP). Note that this may not equal zero because of statistical discrepancy. Verify that the discrepancy is the same as the one reported by the BEA.

6. Continuing from the previous question, find nominal GDP for the United States in 2008 (you can find it elsewhere on the BEA site). Use this information along with your previous calculations to compute the following:

a. Gross national expenditure (GNE), gross national income (GNI), and gross national disposable income (GNDI)

b. In macroeconomics, we often assume the U.S. economy is a closed economy when building models that describe how changes

in policy and shocks affect the economy. Based on the previous data (BOP and GDP), do you think this is a reasonable assumption to make? Do international transactions account for a large share of total transactions (involving goods and services, or income) involving the United States?

7. During the 1980s, the United States experienced "twin deficits" in the current account and government budget. Since 1998 the U.S. current account deficit has grown steadily along with rising government budget deficits. Do government budget deficits lead to current account deficits? Identify other possible sources of the current account deficits. Do current account deficits necessarily indicate problems in the economy?

8. Consider the economy of Opulenza. In Opulenza, domestic investment of $400 million earned $20 million in capital gains during 2012. Opulenzans purchased $120 million in new foreign assets during the year; foreigners purchased $160 million in Opulenzan assets. Assume the valuation effects total $1 million in capital gains.

a. Compute the change in domestic wealth in Opulenza.

b. Compute the change in external wealth for Opulenza.

c. Compute the total change in wealth for Opulenza.

d. Compute domestic savings for Opulenza.

e. Compute Opulenza's current account. Is the CA in deficit or surplus?

f. Explain the intuition for the CA deficit/surplus in terms of savings in Opulenza, financial flows, and its domestic/external wealth position.

g. How would a depreciation in Opulenza's currency affect its domestic, external, and total wealth? Assume that foreign assets owned by Opulenzans are denominated in foreign currency.

9. This question asks you to compute valuation effects for the United States in 2004, using the same methods mentioned in the chapter. Use the bea.gov website to collect the

data needed for this question: look under the "International" heading.

Visit the BEA's balance of payments data page and obtain the U.S. balance of payments for 2004 in billions of dollars. Be sure to get the correct year, and annual data, not quarterly.

Visit the BEA's net international investment position data page and obtain the U.S. net international investment position for end 2003 to end 2004.

a. What was the U.S. current account for 2004?

b. What was the U.S. financial account for 2004?

c. What was the U.S. change in external wealth for 2004?

d. What was the U.S. total valuation effect for 2004?

e. Does the answer to part (d) equal the answer to part (e) minus the answer to part (c)? Why?

f. What do the BEA data indicate was the U.S. valuation effect due to exchange rate changes for 2004?

You may now assume that the U.S. dollar depreciated by 10% against major currencies in 2004, and use this average to estimate valuation effects.

g. What were end-2003 U.S. external liabilities? If 5% of these liabilities were in foreign currency and were subject to a 10% exchange rate appreciation, what decrease in U.S. external wealth resulted?

h. What were end-2003 U.S. external assets? If 65% of these assets were subject to a 10% exchange rate appreciation, what increase in U.S. external wealth resulted?

i. Using the answers to parts (g) and (h), what was the 2004 U.S. valuation effect due to exchange rate changes according to your rough calculation? Is it close to the BEA figure in part (f)?

N E T W O R K

Go to the UN website and find out what the Millennium Development Goals are (http://www.un.org/millenniumgoals). Go to the Gleneagles summit website and examine the promises made (http://www.g8.gov.uk/). Use the Web to check up on how well these G8 promises were kept, such as the UN goal of 0.7% of GDP in official development assistance, the promise to eradicate export subsidies, and the aim to double aid by 2010. (*Hint:* Do an Internet search for sites such as Oxfam or the Jubilee Debt Campaign, or look for the World Bank Tools for Monitoring the Millennium Development Goals.)

N E T W O R K

Use the Web to locate the official macroeconomic statistics for your country. (In the United States, go to http://www.bea.gov.) Find the latest annual data corresponding to the measures discussed in this section. Was your country's GDP higher or lower than its GNE? Why? Was your country's GNI higher or lower than its GDP? Why? What about GNDI—was your country a net giver or net receiver of transfers?

APPENDIX TO CHAPTER 16

External Wealth and Total Wealth

In this chapter, we studied external wealth, but individuals and countries care about their total wealth. How does external wealth relate to total wealth?

External wealth is only part of a country's *total wealth*, the sum of the home capital stock (all nonfinancial assets in the home economy, denoted K) plus amounts owed to home by foreigners (A) minus amounts owed foreigners by home (L):

$$\text{Total wealth} = \underbrace{K}_{\substack{\text{Home nonfinancial} \\ \text{assets}}} + \underbrace{(A - L)}_{\text{External wealth}}$$

In this definition, note that we deliberately exclude financial assets owed by one home entity to another home entity because in the aggregate these cancel out and form no part of a country's total wealth.

Changes in the value of total wealth can then be written as follows:

$$\begin{bmatrix} \text{Change in} \\ \text{total wealth} \end{bmatrix} = \underbrace{\begin{bmatrix} \text{Additions} \\ \text{to } K \end{bmatrix} + \begin{bmatrix} \text{Additions} \\ \text{to } A - L \end{bmatrix}}_{\text{Additions (acquisitions minus disposals)}} + \underbrace{\begin{bmatrix} \text{Capital gains} \\ \text{on } K \end{bmatrix} + \begin{bmatrix} \text{Capital gains} \\ \text{on } A - L \end{bmatrix}}_{\text{Valuation effects (gains minus losses)}}$$

There are two kinds of terms in this expression. The total value of wealth (of a person or a country) may change due to *additions* of assets (such as purchases, sales, or net gifts) or due to valuation effects (capital gains—or, if they are negative, capital losses—arising from changes in the prices of assets).

The previous equation can be simplified by two observations. First, additions to the domestic capital stock K have a simpler expression: they are known as investment, denoted I. (Strictly, this is the gross addition to the capital stock; the net addition would require the subtraction of depreciation, and in the previous notation that would be accounted for under valuation effects since depreciating assets fall in value.)

Second, additions to external wealth, $A - L$, also have a simpler expression: they are equal to net additions to external assets minus net additions to external liabilities, and as we saw in the main chapter, these are equal to *minus* the financial account, $-FA$.

Substituting, we can rewrite the last equations as

$$\begin{bmatrix} \text{Change in} \\ \text{total wealth} \end{bmatrix} = \underbrace{I}_{\substack{\text{Additions to } K \\ = \\ \text{Additions to} \\ \text{assets in the} \\ \text{home economy}}} + \underbrace{(-FA)}_{\substack{\text{Additions to} \\ A - L \\ = \\ \text{Net import of} \\ \text{assets into the} \\ \text{home economy}}} + \underbrace{\begin{bmatrix} \text{Capital gains} \\ \text{on } K \end{bmatrix} + \begin{bmatrix} \text{Capital gains} \\ \text{on } A - L \end{bmatrix}}_{\text{Valuation effects (gains minus losses)}}$$

Now, using the BOP identity, we know that $CA + KA + FA = 0$ so that minus the financial account $-FA$ must equal $CA + KA$; hence, we can rewrite the last equation as

$$\begin{bmatrix} \text{Change in} \\ \text{total wealth} \end{bmatrix} = I + CA + KA + \underbrace{\begin{bmatrix} \text{Capital gains} \\ \text{on } K \end{bmatrix} + \begin{bmatrix} \text{Capital gains} \\ \text{on } A - L \end{bmatrix}}_{\text{Valuation effects (gains minus losses)}}$$

Notice what has happened here. The BOP identity makes the connection between external asset trade and activity in the current account. We take the connection one step further using the current account identity, $S = I + CA$, which allows us to write

$$\begin{bmatrix} \text{Change in} \\ \text{total wealth} \end{bmatrix} = S + KA + \underbrace{\begin{bmatrix} \text{Capital gains} \\ \text{on } K \end{bmatrix} + \begin{bmatrix} \text{Capital gains} \\ \text{on } A - L \end{bmatrix}}_{\text{Valuation effects (gains minus losses)}}$$

The message of this expression is clear. As we all probably know from personal experience, there are only three ways to get more (or less) wealthy: do more (or less) saving (S), receive (or give) gifts of assets (KA), or enjoy the good (bad) fortune of capital gains (losses) on your portfolio. What is true about individuals' wealth is also true for the wealth of a nation in the aggregate.

17

Balance of Payments I: The Gains from Financial Globalization

Save for a rainy day.

Make hay while the sun shines.

Don't put all your eggs in one basket.

How does your household cope with economic shocks and the financial challenges they pose? Let's take an extreme example. Suppose you are self-employed and own a business. A severe storm appears and a flood overwhelms your town. This is bad news on several fronts. As people recover from the disaster, businesses, including yours, suffer and your income is lower for several months. If your business premises are damaged, you must also plan to make new investments to repair the damage.

If you have no financial dealings with anyone, your household, as a little closed economy, faces a difficult trade-off as your income falls. Your household income has to equal its consumption plus investment. Would you try to maintain your level of consumption, and neglect the need to invest? Or would you invest, and let your household suffer as you cut back drastically on consumption? Faced with an emergency like this, most of us look for help beyond our own household, if we can: we might hope for transfers (gifts from friends and family, or emergency relief payments from the government or a charity), or we might rely on financial markets (dip into savings, apply for a loan, rely on an insurance payout, etc.).

What does this story have to do with international economics? If we redraw the boundaries of this experiment and expand from the household unit, to the local, regional, and finally national level, the same logic applies. Countries face shocks all the time, and how they are able cope with them depends on whether they are open or closed to economic interactions with other nations.

To get a sense of how countries can deal with shocks, we can look at data from Caribbean and Central American countries that have faced the same kinds of shock as the household we just described. Every year many tropical storms, some of them of hurricane strength, sweep through this region. The storms are large—hundreds of miles across—and most countries in the region are much smaller in size, some no more than little islets. For them, a hurricane is the town flood blown up to a national scale. The worst storms cause widespread destruction and loss of life.

Hurricanes are tragic human events, but they provide an opportunity for research. Economists study them because such an "act of God"—in economics jargon, a "natural experiment"—provides a laboratory-like test of economic theory. Figure 17-1 shows the average macroeconomic response in these countries after they were hit by a hurricane. In the aftermath, these countries do some of the things we would expect households to do: accept nonmarket gifts (transfers from foreign countries) and borrow (by running a current account deficit). If we subtract nonmarket transfers and examine market behavior alone, the patterns are striking. As a fraction of GDP, investment is typically 3% to 6% higher than normal in the three years after a hurricane, and saving is 1% to 5% lower (excluding transfers). Combining the two effects, the current account (saving minus investment) falls dramatically and is 6% to 10% more in deficit than normal.

Hurricanes are extreme examples of economic shocks. They are not representative of the normal fluctuations that countries experience, but the size and randomness of the hurricanes allow us to look at the nations' macroeconomic responses to such a shock. These responses illustrate some of the financial mechanisms that help open economies cope with all types of shocks, large and small, natural or human in origin.

In this chapter, we see how financially open economies can, in theory, reap gains from financial globalization. We first look at the factors that limit international borrowing and lending. Then, in the remaining sections of the chapter, we see how a nation's ability to use international financial markets allows it to accomplish three different goals:

FIGURE 17-1

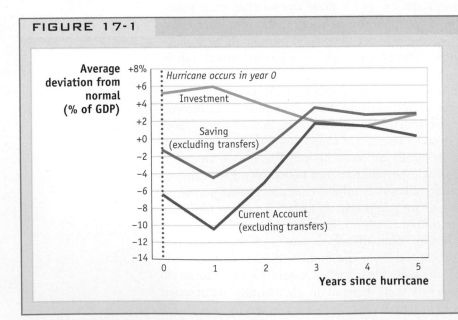

The Macroeconomics of Hurricanes The figure shows the average response (excluding transfers) of investment, saving, and the current account in a sample of Caribbean and Central American countries in the years during and after severe hurricane damage. The responses are as expected: investment rises (to rebuild) and saving falls (to limit the fall in consumption); hence, the current account moves sharply toward deficit.

Note: Transfers are excluded from saving and the current account, and the saving measure is calculated as S − NUT = I + CA − NUT.

Source: John C. Bluedorn, 2005, "Hurricanes: Intertemporal Trade and Capital Shocks," Oxford Economics Working Paper No. 2005-241.

- consumption smoothing (steadying consumption when income fluctuates);
- efficient investment (borrowing to build a productive capital stock); and
- diversification of risk (by trading of stocks between countries).

Along the way, we look at how well the theoretical gains from financial globalization translate into reality (an area of some dispute among economists) and find that many of these gains have yet to be realized. In advanced countries, the gains from financial globalization are often large and more attainable, but in poorer countries the gains may be smaller and harder to realize. We want to understand why these differences exist, and what risks may arise for poor countries that attempt to capture the gains from financial globalization.

Hurricane Mitch battered Central America from October 22, 1998, to November 5, 1998. It was the deadliest hurricane in more than 200 years and the second deadliest ever recorded.

1 The Limits on How Much a Country Can Borrow: The Long-Run Budget Constraint

Our introductory examples show how borrowing can help countries (like households) better cope with shocks. But, also like households, there is a limit to how much a country can borrow (or, how much lenders will lend). Understanding the constraints on how countries might borrow and lend to each other is our critical first task in this chapter. With this understanding we can then examine how financial globalization shapes the economic choices available to a country as economic conditions change over time. The ability to borrow in times of need and lend in times of prosperity has profound effects on a country's well-being.

When we study an economy as it evolves over time, we are taking a *dynamic* approach to macroeconomics—rather than a static approach by looking at the state of the economy at one specific time. The dynamic approach is also known as the *intertemporal approach* to macroeconomics. One key to this approach is that we must keep track of how a country is managing its wealth and whether it is doing so in a way that is within its means, that is, sustainable in the long run. The intertemporal approach makes use of the key lessons from the end of the last chapter, which taught us how to account for the change in a nation's external wealth from one period to the next.

In this section, we use changes in an open economy's external wealth to derive the key constraint that limits its borrowing in the long run: the **long-run budget constraint (LRBC).** The LRBC tells us precisely how and why a country must, in the long run, "live within its means." A country's ability to adjust its external wealth through borrowing and lending provides a buffer against economic shocks, but the LRBC places limits on the use of this buffer.

To develop some intuition, let's look at a simple household analogy. This year (year 0) you borrow $100,000 from the bank at an interest rate of 10% annually. You have no other wealth and inflation is zero. Once you borrow the $100,000, consider two possible different ways in which you can deal with your debt each year.

Case 1 *A debt that is serviced.* Every year you pay the 10% interest due on the principal amount of the loan, $10,000, but you never pay any principal. At the end of each year, the bank renews the loan (a rollover), and your wealth remains constant at −$100,000.

Case 2 *A debt that is not serviced.* You pay neither interest nor principal but ask the bank to roll over the principal plus the interest due on it each year. In year 1, the overdue interest is $10,000, and your debt grows by 10% to $110,000. In year 2, the overdue interest is 10% of $110,000, or $11,000, and your debt grows by 10% again to $121,000. Assuming this process goes on and on, your level of debt grows by 10% every year.

Case 2 is not sustainable. If the bank allows it, your debt level will explode to infinity as it grows by 10% every year forever. This case, sometimes called a rollover scheme, a pyramid scheme, or a *Ponzi game*,[1] illustrates the limits or constraints on the use of borrowing, which implies negative external wealth. In the long run, lenders will simply not allow the debt to grow beyond a certain point. Debts must be paid off eventually. This requirement is the essence of the long-run budget constraint.

How the Long-Run Budget Constraint Is Determined

As is usual when building an economic model, we start with a basic model that makes a number of simplifying assumptions, but yields lessons that can be extended to more complex cases. Here are the assumptions we make about various conditions that affect our model:

- Prices are perfectly flexible. Under this assumption, all analysis in this chapter can be conducted in terms of real variables, and all monetary aspects of the economy can be ignored. (To adjust for inflation and convert to real terms, we could divide all nominal quantities by an index of prices.)

- The country is a **small open economy.** The country trades goods and services with the rest of the world through exports and imports and can lend or borrow overseas, but only by issuing or buying debt (bonds). Because it is small, the country cannot influence prices in world markets for goods and services.

- All debt carries a real interest rate r^*, the **world real interest rate,** which we assume to be constant. Because the country is small, it takes the world real interest rate as given, and we assume it can lend or borrow an unlimited amount at this interest rate.

- The country pays a real interest rate r^* on its start-of-period debt liabilities L and is paid the same interest rate r^* on its start-of-period debt assets A. In any period, the country earns net interest income payments equal to r^*A minus r^*L or, more simply, r^*W, where W is external wealth $(A - L)$ at the start of the period. External wealth may vary over time.

- There are no unilateral transfers $(NUT = 0)$, no capital transfers $(KA = 0)$, and no capital gains on external wealth. Under these assumptions, there are only two nonzero items in the current account: the trade balance TB and net factor income from abroad, r^*W. If r^*W is positive, the country is earning interest and is a lender/creditor with positive external wealth. If r^*W is negative, the country is paying interest and is a borrower/debtor with negative external wealth.

[1] This type of borrowing strategy is named after the infamous swindler Charles Ponzi who engaged in a "pyramid" or "chain letter" operation of this type in Boston in 1919 and 1920, borrowing new money from an expanding base of creditors to pay off past debt.

Calculating the Change in Wealth Each Period In the previous balance of payments chapter, we saw that the change in external wealth equals the sum of three terms: the current account, the capital account, and capital gains on external wealth. In the special case we are studying, our assumptions tell us that the last two terms are zero, and that the current account equals the sum of just two terms: the trade balance TB plus any net interest payments r^*W at the world interest rate on the external wealth held at the end of the last period.

Mathematically, we can write the change in external wealth from end of year $N-1$ to end of year N as follows (where subscripts denote periods, here years):

$$\Delta W_N = \underbrace{W_N - W_{N-1}}_{\substack{\text{Change in external} \\ \text{wealth this period}}} = \underbrace{TB_N}_{\substack{\text{Trade balance} \\ \text{this period}}} + \underbrace{r^* W_{N-1}}_{\substack{\text{Interest paid/received on} \\ \text{last period's external wealth}}}$$

In this simplified world, external wealth can change for only two reasons: surpluses or deficits on the trade balance in the current period, or surpluses and deficits on net factor income arising from interest received or paid.

Calculating Future Wealth Levels Now that we have a formula for wealth changes, and assuming we know the initial level of wealth in year $N-1$, we can compute the level of wealth at any time in the future by repeated application of the formula.

To find wealth at the end of year N, we rearrange the preceding equation:

$$\underbrace{W_N}_{\substack{\text{External wealth at} \\ \text{the end of this period}}} = \underbrace{TB_N}_{\substack{\text{Trade balance} \\ \text{this period}}} + \underbrace{(1 + r^*)W_{N-1}}_{\substack{\text{Last period's external wealth} \\ \text{plus interest paid/received}}}$$

This equation presents an important and intuitive result: it shows that wealth at the end of a period is the sum of two terms. The trade balance this period captures the addition to wealth from net exports (exports minus imports). Wealth at the end of last period times $(1 + r^*)$ captures the wealth from last period plus the interest earned on that wealth. The examples in the following sections will help us understand the changes in a country's external wealth and the role that the trade balance plays here.

The Budget Constraint in a Two-Period Example

We first put these ideas to work in a simplified two-period example. Suppose we start in year 0, so $N = 0$. Suppose further that a country has some initial external wealth from year -1 (an inheritance from the past), and can borrow or lend in the present period (year 0). We also impose the following limit: by the end of year 1, the country must pay off what it has borrowed from other countries and must call in all loans it has made to other countries. That is, the country must end year 1 with zero external wealth.

As we saw in the formula given earlier, $W_0 = (1 + r^*)W_{-1} + TB_0$. Wealth at the end of year 0 depends on two things. At the end of year 0, the country carries over from the last period (year -1) its initial wealth level, plus any interest accumulated on it. In addition, if the country runs a trade deficit it has to run its external wealth down by adding liabilities (borrowing) or cashing in external assets (dissaving); conversely, if the country runs a trade surplus, it lends that amount to the rest of the world.

That's the end of year 0. But next, where do things stand at the end of year 1? We assume the country must have zero external wealth when the world ends at the end of year 1. Applying the preceding formula to year 1, we know that $W_1 = 0 = (1 + r^*)$ $W_0 + TB_1$. We can then substitute $W_0 = (1 + r^*)W_{-1} + TB_0$ into this formula to find that

$$W_1 = 0 = (1 + r^*)^2 W_{-1} + (1 + r^*)TB_0 + TB_1$$

This equation shows that two years later at the end of year 1 the country has accumulated wealth equal to the trade balance in years 0 and 1 ($TB_0 + TB_1$); plus one year of interest earned (or paid) on the year 0 trade balance ($r^* TB_0$); plus the two years of interest and principal earned (or paid) on its initial wealth $(1 + r^*)^2 W_{-1}$.

Because we have stated that the final wealth level W_1 must be zero, the right-hand side of the last equation must be zero, too. For that to be the case, the trade balances in year 0 (TB_0) and in year 1 (TB_1) (plus any accumulated interest) must be equal and opposite to initial wealth (W_{-1}) (plus any accumulated interest):

$$-(1 + r^*)^2 W_{-1} = (1 + r^*)TB_0 + TB_1$$

This equation is the *two-period budget constraint*. It tells us that a creditor country with positive initial wealth (left-hand-side negative) can afford to run trade deficits "on average" in future; conversely, a debtor country (left-hand-side positive) is required to run trade surpluses "on average" in future.

Present Value Form By dividing the previous equation by $(1 + r^*)$, we find a more intuitive expression for the two-period budget constraint:

$$\underbrace{-(1 + r^*)W_{-1}}_{\substack{\text{Minus the present value} \\ \text{of wealth from last period}}} = \underbrace{TB_0 + \frac{TB_1}{(1 + r^*)}}_{\substack{\text{Present value of all present} \\ \text{and future trade balances}}}$$

Every element in this statement of the two-period budget constraint represents a quantity expressed in so-called present value terms.

By definition, the **present value** of X in period N is the amount that would have to be set aside now, so that, with accumulated interest, X is available N periods from now. If the interest rate is r^*, then the present value of X is $X/(1 + r^*)^N$. For example, if you are told that you will receive \$121 at the end of year 2 and the interest rate is 10%, then the present value of that \$121 now, in year 0, is \$100 because $\$100 \times 1.1$ (adding interest earned in year 1) $\times 1.1$ (adding interest earned in year 2) = \$121.

A Two-Period Example Let's put some numbers into the last equation. Suppose a country starts in debt, with a wealth level of −\$100 million at the end of year −1: W_{-1} = −\$100 million. Question: at a real interest rate of 10%, how can the country satisfy the two-period budget constraint that it must have zero external wealth at the end of year 1? Answer: to pay off the \$110 million (initial debt plus the interest accruing on this debt during period 0) on the left-hand side, the country must ensure that the present value of future trade balances TB_1 is +\$110 million on the right-hand side.

The country has many ways to do this.

■ It could pay off its debt at the end of period 0 by running a trade surplus of \$110 million in period 0 and then have balanced trade in period 1.

■ It could wait to pay off the debt until the end of period 1 by having balanced trade in period 0 and then running a trade surplus of \$121 million in period 1.

■ It could pay off the debt and its accumulated interest through any other combination of trade balances in periods 0 and 1, as long as external wealth at the end of period 1 is zero and the budget constraint is satisfied.

Extending the Theory to the Long Run By extending the two-period model to N periods, and allowing N to run to infinity, we can transform the two-period budget constraint into the long-run budget constraint (LRBC). Repeating the two-period logic N times, external wealth after N periods is initial wealth and accumulated interest on that wealth (whether positive or negative) plus all intervening trade balances and accumulated interest on those positive or negative trade balances. If external wealth is to be zero at the end of N periods, then the sum of the present values of N present and future trade balances must equal minus the present value of external wealth. If N runs to infinity, we get an infinite sum and arrive at the equation of the LRBC:[2]

$$\text{LRBC: } \underbrace{-(1 + r^*)W_{-1}}_{\substack{\text{Minus the present value of} \\ \text{wealth from last period}}} = \underbrace{TB_0 + \frac{TB_1}{(1 + r^*)} + \frac{TB_2}{(1 + r^*)^2} + \frac{TB_3}{(1 + r^*)^3} + \frac{TB_4}{(1 + r^*)^4} + \cdots}_{\text{Present value of all present and future trade balances}} \quad (17\text{-}1)$$

This expression for the LRBC says that a debtor country must have future trade balances that are positive in present value terms so that they offset the country's initially negative wealth. Conversely, a creditor country must have future trade balances that are negative in present value terms so that they offset the country's initially positive wealth. The LRBC plays an important role in our analysis of how countries can lend or borrow because it imposes a condition that rules out choices that would lead to exploding positive or negative external wealth.

A Long-Run Example: The Perpetual Loan

The following example helps us understand the long-run budget constraint and we can apply it to various cases that we visit in the rest of the chapter. It shows us how countries that take out an initial loan must make payments to service that loan in the future.

Suppose that today is year 0 and a country is to pay (e.g., to its creditors) a constant amount X every year starting next year, year 1. What is the present value (PV) of that sequence of payments (X)?

$$PV(X) = \frac{X}{(1 + r^*)} + \frac{X}{(1 + r^*)^2} + \frac{X}{(1 + r^*)^3} + \cdots$$

This expression for $PV(X)$ is an infinite sum. If we multiply this equation by $(1 + r^*)$, we obtain

$$PV(X)(1 + r^*) = X + \frac{X}{(1 + r^*)} + \frac{X}{(1 + r^*)^2} + \frac{X}{(1 + r^*)^3} + \cdots$$

---

[2] To get this result, we can take the basic equation for the change in external wealth, $W_0 = (1 + r^*)W_{-1} + TB_0$, and apply it N times with repeated substitution to obtain wealth at the end of period N:

$$W_N = (1 + r^*)^{N+1}W_{-1} + (1 + r^*)^N TB_0 + (1 + r^*)^{N-1}TB_1 + (1 + r^*)^{N-2}TB_2 + \cdots + (1 + r^*)TB_{N-1} + TB_N$$

We can then get toward the LRBC in the text if we divide the previous equation by $(1 + r^*)^N$

$$\frac{W_N}{(1 + r^*)^N} = (1 + r^*)W_{-1} + TB_0 + \frac{TB_1}{(1 + r^*)} + \frac{TB_2}{(1 + r^*)^2} + \cdots + \frac{TB_N}{(1 + r^*)^N}.$$

As we saw earlier, in a Ponzi game, external wealth W_N explodes, growing by a factor $(1 + r^*)$ every period. To prevent this, external wealth W_N (whether positive or negative) must grow more slowly in the long run than the factor $(1 + r^*)^N$. In this case, as N approaches infinity, the left-hand side of the above equation will approach zero. When this is the case, the right-hand side must also approach zero. This tendency of the right-hand side to go to zero in the limit leads directly to the LRBC equation (17-1) in the text.

To find a simple expression for $PV(X)$, we subtract the first equation from the second, cancel out all of the terms on the right except X, then rearrange the remaining equation $r^* PV(X) = X$ to arrive at:

$$\underbrace{\frac{X}{(1+r^*)} + \frac{X}{(1+r^*)^2} + \frac{X}{(1+r^*)^3} + \cdots}_{PV(X)} = \frac{X}{r^*} \qquad (17\text{-}2)$$

This formula helps us compute $PV(X)$ for any stream of constant payments, something we often need to do to verify the long-run budget constraint.

For example, if the constant payment is $X = 100$ and the interest rate is 5% ($r^* = 0.05$), Equation (17-2) says that the present value of a stream of payments of 100 starting in year 1 is $100/0.05 = 2{,}000$:

$$\frac{100}{(1+0.05)} + \frac{100}{(1+0.05)^2} + \frac{100}{(1+0.05)^3} + \cdots = \frac{100}{0.05} = 2{,}000$$

This example, which we will often revisit later in this chapter, shows the stream of interest payments on a **perpetual loan** (i.e., an interest-only loan or, equivalently, a sequence of loans for which *only* the principal is refinanced or rolled over every year). If the amount loaned by the creditor is $2,000 in year 0, and this principal amount is outstanding forever, then the interest that must be paid each year to service the debt is 5% of $2,000, or $100. Under these conditions, wherein the loan payments are always fully serviced, the present value of the future interest payments equals the value of the amount loaned in year 0 and the LRBC is satisfied.

Implications of the LRBC for Gross National Expenditure and Gross Domestic Product

In economics, a budget constraint always tells us something about the limits to expenditure, whether for a person, firm, or government. The LRBC is no different—it tells us that in the long run, a country's national expenditure (GNE) is limited by how much it produces (GDP).

To see why this is true, recall from the previous chapter that the trade balance is the difference between gross domestic product and gross national expenditure, $TB = GDP - GNE$. If we insert this expression into the LRBC equation (17-1) and collect terms, we see that

$$\underbrace{\underbrace{(1+r^*)W_{-1}}_{\substack{\text{Present value of} \\ \text{wealth from} \\ \text{last period}}} + \underbrace{GDP_0 + \frac{GDP_1}{(1+r^*)} + \frac{GDP_2}{(1+r^*)^2} + \cdots}_{\text{Present value of present and future GDP}}}_{\text{Present value of the country's resources}} \qquad (17\text{-}3)$$

$$\underbrace{= \underbrace{GNE_0 + \frac{GNE_1}{(1+r^*)} + \frac{GNE_2}{(1+r^*)^2} + \cdots}_{\text{Present value of present and future } GNE}}_{\substack{= \\ \text{Present value of the country's spending}}}$$

The left side of this equation is the present value of the country's resources in the long run: the present value of any inherited wealth plus the present value of present and future product as measured by GDP. The right side is the present value of all present and future spending ($C + I + G$) as measured by GNE.

We have arrived at the following, very important result: *the long-run budget constraint says that in the long run, in present value terms, a country's expenditures (GNE) must equal its production (GDP) plus any initial wealth.* The LRBC states that an economy must live within its means in the long run.

Summary

The key lesson of our intertemporal model is that a closed economy is subject to a tighter budget constraint than an open economy. In a closed economy, "living within your means" requires a country to have balanced trade each and every year. In an open economy, "living within your means" requires only that a country must maintain a balance between its trade deficits and surpluses that satisfies the long-run budget constraint—they must balance only in a present value sense, rather than year by year.

This conclusion implies that an open economy should be able to do better (or no worse) than a closed economy in achieving its desired pattern of expenditure over time. This is the essence of the theoretical argument that there are gains from financial globalization.

In the next section, we examine this argument in greater detail and consider under what circumstances it is valid in the real world. First, however, we consider some situations in which the assumptions of the model might need to be modified.

APPLICATION

The Favorable Situation of the United States

Two assumptions greatly simplified our intertemporal model. We assumed that the same real rate of interest r^* applied to income received on assets and income paid on liabilities, and we assumed that there were no capital gains on external wealth. However, these assumptions do not hold true for the United States.

"Exorbitant Privilege" Since the 1980s, the United States has been the world's largest ever net debtor with $W = A - L < 0$. Under the model's simplifying assumptions, negative external wealth would lead to a deficit on net factor income from abroad with $r^*W = r^*(A - L) < 0$. And yet as we saw in the last chapter, U.S. net factor income from abroad has been positive throughout this period! How can this be?

The only way a net debtor can earn positive net interest income is by receiving a higher rate of interest on its assets than it pays on its liabilities. The data show that this has been consistently true for the United States since the 1960s. The interest the United States has received on its assets has been higher by about 1.5 to 2 percentage points per year on average (with a slight downward trend) than the interest it pays on its liabilities.

To develop a framework to make sense of this finding, suppose the United States receives interest at the world real interest rate r^* on its external assets but pays interest at a lower rate r^0 on its liabilities. Then its net factor income from abroad is $r^*A - r^0 L = r^*W + (r^* - r^0)L$. The final term, the interest rate difference times total liabilities, is an income bonus the United States earns as a "banker to the world"—like any other bank, it borrows low and lends high.

Understandably, the rest of the world may resent this state of affairs from time to time. In the 1960s French officials complained about the United States' "exorbitant privilege" of being able to borrow cheaply by issuing external liabilities in the form of reserve assets (Treasury debt) while earning higher returns on U.S. external assets such as foreign equity and foreign direct investment. This conclusion is not borne out in the data, however. U.S. Bureau of Economic Analysis (BEA) data suggest that most of the interest rate difference is due not to the low interest paid on Treasury debt, but to the low interest rate on U.S. equity liabilities (i.e., low profits earned on foreign investment in the United States).[3]

"Manna from Heaven" The difference between interest earned and interest paid isn't the only deviation from our simple model that benefits the United States. BEA statistics reveal that the country has long enjoyed positive capital gains (KG) on its external wealth. This gain, which started in the 1980s, comes from a difference of two percentage points between large capital gains on several types of external assets and smaller capital losses on external liabilities.

It is hard to pin down the source of these capital gains because the BEA data suggest that these effects are not the result of price or exchange rate effects, and they just reflect capital gains that cannot be otherwise measured. As a result, the accuracy and meaning of these measurements is controversial. Some skeptics call these capital gains "statistical manna from heaven." Others think these gains are real and may reflect the United States acting as a kind of "venture capitalist to the world." As with the "exorbitant privilege," this financial gain for the United States is a loss for the rest of the world.[4]

Summary When we add the 2% capital gain differential to the 1.5% interest differential, we end up with a U.S. total return differential (interest plus capital gains) of about 3.5% per year on average since the 1980s. For comparison, in the same period, the total return differential was close to zero in every other G7 country.

To include the effects of the total return differential in our model, we have to incorporate the effect of the extra "bonuses" on external wealth as well as the conventional terms that reflect the trade balance and interest payments:

$$\Delta W_N = \underbrace{W_N - W_{N-1}}_{\substack{\text{Change in}\\ \text{external wealth}\\ \text{this period}}} = \underbrace{TB_N}_{\substack{\text{Trade}\\ \text{balance}\\ \text{this period}}} + \underbrace{r^* W_{N-1}}_{\substack{\text{Interest paid/received}\\ \text{on last period's}\\ \text{external wealth}}} + \underbrace{(r^* - r^0)L}_{\substack{\text{Income due to}\\ \text{interest rate}\\ \text{differential}}} + \underbrace{KG}_{\substack{\text{Capital gains}\\ \text{on external}\\ \text{wealth}}}$$

Conventional effects | Additional effects

Too Good to Be True? With this equation, the implications of the final two terms become clearer for the U.S. economy. When positive, they offset wealth losses due to trade deficits. Thus, if these terms increase in value by 1% of GDP, for example, then the United States could run an additional 1% of GDP in trade deficit forever and still satisfy its LRBC.

As Figure 17-2 shows, the United States has seen these offsets increase markedly in recent years, rising from 1% of GDP in the late 1980s to an average of about 4%

[3] John Kitchen, 2007, "Sharecroppers or Shrewd Capitalists? Projections of the U.S. Current Account, International Income Flows, and Net International Debt," *Review of International Economics*, 15(5), 1036–1061; Barry Bosworth, Susan M. Collins, and Gabriel Chodorow Reich, 2007, "Returns on FDI: Does the US Really Do Better?" *Brookings Trade Forum*, 177–210.

[4] William R. Cline, 2005, *The United States as a Debtor Nation* (Washington, D.C.: Institute for International Economics and Center for Global Development); Pierre-Olivier Gourinchas and Hélène Rey, 2007, "From World Banker to World Venture Capitalist: US External Adjustment and the Exorbitant Privilege," in Richard Clarida, ed., *G7 Current Account Imbalances: Sustainability and Adjustment* (Chicago: University of Chicago Press).

of GDP in the 2000s. These large offsets have led some economists to take a relaxed view of the swollen U.S. trade deficit because the offsets finance a large chunk of the country's trade deficit—with luck, in perpetuity.[5] However, we may not be able to count on these offsets forever: longer-run evidence suggests that they are not stable and may be diminishing over time.[6]

Others warn that, given the likely presence of errors in these data, we really have no idea what is going on. In 2006, economist Daniel Gros calculated that the United States had borrowed $5,500 billion over 20 years, even though its external wealth had fallen by "only" $2,800 billion. Have $2.7 trillion dollars been mislaid? Gros argued

FIGURE 17-2

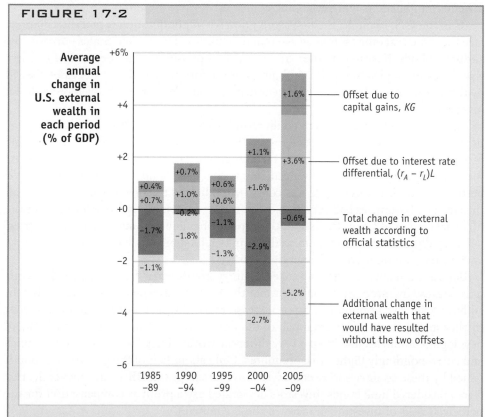

How Favorable Interest Rates and Capital Gains on External Wealth Help the United States The total average annual change in U.S. external wealth each period is shown by the dark red columns. Negative changes were offset in part by two positive effects. One effect was due to the favorable interest rate differentials on U.S. assets (high) versus liabilities (low). The other effect was due to favorable rates of capital gains on U.S. assets (high) versus liabilities (low). Without these two offsetting effects, the declines in U.S. external wealth would have been much bigger.

Notes: Interest rate differential effects are computed assuming that counterfactual liability yields would have been equal to asset yields. Capital gains are computed as the difference between financial flows and changes in external wealth.

Source: U.S. Bureau of Economic Analysis, Balance of Payments Accounts, and Net International Investment Position.

---

[5] Ricardo Hausmann and Federico Sturzenegger, "'Dark Matter' Makes the US Deficit Disappear," *Financial Times*, December 7, 2005.

[6] Christopher M. Meissner and Alan M. Taylor, 2008, "Losing Our Marbles in the New Century? The Great Rebalancing in Historical Perspective," in *Global Imbalances and the Evolving World Economy*, J. S. Little, ed. (Boston: Federal Reserve Bank of Boston).

that most of this difference can be attributed to poor U.S. measurement of the assets foreigners own and investment earnings foreigners receive. Correcting these errors would make all of the additional offset terms disappear—and roughly double the estimated current level of U.S. net indebtedness to the rest of the world.[7] ■

APPLICATION

The Difficult Situation of the Emerging Markets

The previous application showed that the simple intertemporal model may not work for the United States. In this section, we see that its assumptions may also not work for emerging markets and developing countries.

As in the U.S. example, the first assumption we might question is that these nations face the same real interest rate on assets and liabilities. The United States borrows low and lends high. For most poorer countries, the opposite is true. Because of country risk, investors typically expect a risk premium before they will buy any assets issued by these countries, whether government debt, private debt or equity, or foreign direct investments.

Figure 17-3 plots government credit ratings (from Standard & Poor's) against public debt levels using historical data *prior to the financial crisis of 2008* for a large sample of countries. Bond ratings are seen to be highly correlated with risk premiums. At the top of the figure are the advanced countries whose bonds were then rated AA or better. (At the time this sample was constructed, before the financial crisis, almost all the advanced countries had very high credit ratings and moderate debt levels; after the financial crisis and Great Recession, this rapidly changed as some advanced countries' debt rapidly ballooned and their credit ratings fell: some of them even fell quite far and started to look more like emerging markets).

Before the financial crisis, advanced-country bonds carried very small-risk premiums because investors were confident that these countries would repay their debts. In addition, the risk premiums did not increase markedly even as these countries went further into debt. In the bottom half of the figure, we see that emerging markets and developing countries inhabited a very different world. They had worse credit ratings and correspondingly higher-risk premiums. Only about half of the government bonds issued by these countries were considered investment grade, BBB– and above; the rest were considered junk bonds. Investors demanded extra profit as compensation for the perceived risks of investing in many of these countries.

Figure 17-3 also shows that in poorer countries ratings deteriorated rapidly as debt levels rose, an effect that is not as strong in the advanced countries. This observation shows the sharp limits to borrowing for poorer countries: at some stage, the cost of borrowing becomes prohibitive, if it is possible at all.

This example brings us to the other assumption of the simple model that sometimes fails to hold in poorer countries, the assumption that the country can borrow or lend as much as it wants at the prevailing world real interest rate. On the lending side, it usually isn't a problem to save as much as you want. On the borrowing side, however, lenders often tell borrowers that they have reached a debt limit and can borrow no more. When that happens, access to external credit ceases, and anything additional a country wants to consume or invest has to be taken out of its own domestic output.

---

[7] Daniel Gros, "Discrepancies in US Accounts Hide Black Hole," *Financial Times*, June 14, 2006.

FIGURE 17-3

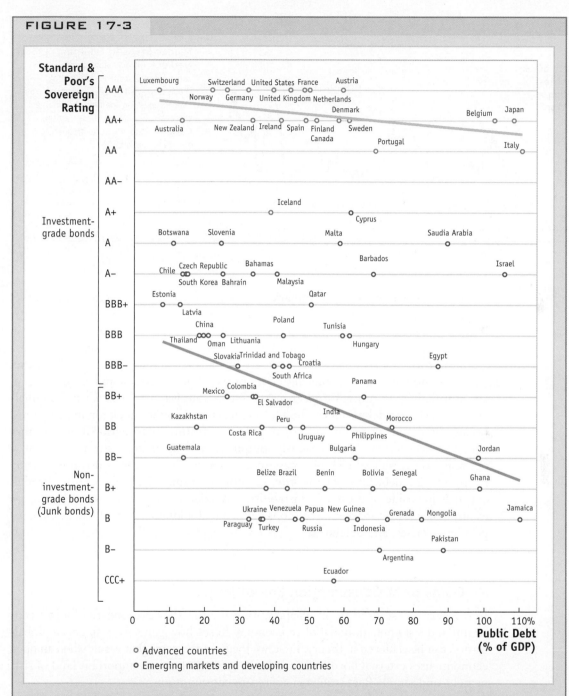

Sovereign Ratings and Public Debt Levels: Advanced Countries Versus Emerging Markets and Developing Countries The data shown are for the period from 1995 to 2005. The advanced countries (green) are at the top of the chart. Their credit ratings (vertical axis) do not drop very much in response to an increase in debt levels (horizontal axis). And ratings are always high investment grade. The emerging markets and developing countries (orange) are at the bottom of the graph. Their ratings are low or junk, and their ratings deteriorate as debt levels rise.

Note: The data shown are from the period before the global financial crisis. Since that event, many advanced countries have seen large increases in public debt and ratings downgrades, and in some cases the impacts have been serious, e.g., Iceland, Ireland, Portugal, and Spain.

Source: Inter-American Development Bank, 2006, "How to Live with Debt," Ideas for Development in the Americas 11 (September–December), Figure 2.

FIGURE 17-4

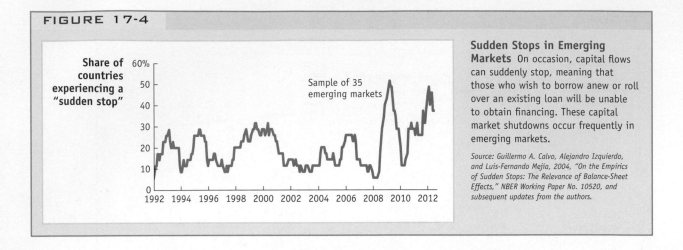

Share of countries experiencing a "sudden stop"

Sample of 35 emerging markets

Sudden Stops in Emerging Markets On occasion, capital flows can suddenly stop, meaning that those who wish to borrow anew or roll over an existing loan will be unable to obtain financing. These capital market shutdowns occur frequently in emerging markets.

Source: Guillermo A. Calvo, Alejandro Izquierdo, and Luis-Fernando Mejía, 2004, "On the Empirics of Sudden Stops: The Relevance of Balance-Sheet Effects," NBER Working Paper No. 10520, and subsequent updates from the authors.

Figure 17-4 illustrates the remarkable frequency with which emerging market countries experience this kind of isolation from global capital markets. Research by economists Guillermo Calvo and Carmen Reinhart has focused attention on sudden stops in the flow of external finance, especially in emerging markets.[8] In a **sudden stop,** a borrower country sees its financial account surplus rapidly shrink (suddenly nobody wants to buy any more of its domestic assets) and so the current account deficit also must shrink (because there is no way to finance a trade imbalance). Reaching a debt limit can be a jolting macroeconomic shock for any economy, because it requires sudden and possibly large adjustments to national expenditure and its composition. Most seriously, output may drop if domestic investment is curtailed as a result of lack of access to external credit. As the constraints arising from hitting a debt limit start to bite, the upside of financial globalization recedes, and the downside of economic instability may take its place. In later chapters, we examine why credit market disruptions happen by looking in more detail at financial problems, crises, and default. ■

2 Gains from Consumption Smoothing

In the next two sections of this chapter, we bring together the long-run budget constraint and a simplified model of an economy to see how gains from financial globalization can be achieved in theory. First, we focus on the gains that result when an open economy uses external borrowing and lending to eliminate an important kind of risk, namely, undesirable fluctuations in aggregate consumption.

---

[8] On the disruptions and costs caused by sudden stops, see Guillermo Calvo and Carmen M. Reinhart, 2000, "When Capital Inflows Suddenly Stop: Consequences and Policy Options," in *Reforming the International Monetary and Financial System*, Peter B. Kenen and Alexander K. Swoboda, eds. (Washington, D.C.: International Monetary Fund), pp. 175–201; Pablo E. Guidotti, Federico Sturzenegger, and Agustín Villar, 2004, "On the Consequences of Sudden Stops," *Economía*, 4(2), 171–214; Michael M. Hutchison and Ilan Noy, 2006, "Sudden Stops and the Mexican Wave: Currency Crises, Capital Flow Reversals and Output Loss in Emerging Markets," *Journal of Development Economics*, 79(1), 225–248.

The Basic Model

We retain all of the assumptions we made when developing the long-run budget constraint. There are no international transfers of income or capital, and the price level is perfectly flexible, so all nominal values are also real values, and so on. We also adopt some additional assumptions. These hold whether the economy is closed or open.

- The economy's GDP or output is denoted Q. It is produced each period using labor as the only input. Production of GDP may be subject to shocks; depending on the shock, the same amount of labor input may yield different amounts of output.

- Households, which consume, are identical. This means we can think of a representative household, and use the terms "household" and "country" interchangeably. The country/household prefers a level of consumption C that is constant over time, or smooth. This level of smooth consumption must be consistent with the country/household's long-run budget constraint.

- To keep the rest of the model simple—for now—we assume that consumption is the only source of demand, and that both investment I and government spending G are zero. Under these assumptions, GNE equals personal consumption expenditures C. In this simple case, if the country is open, the trade balance (GDP minus GNE) equals Q minus C. The trade balance is positive (negative) only if Q, output, is greater (less) than consumption C.

- Our analysis begins at time 0, and we assume the country begins with zero initial wealth inherited from the past, so that W_{-1} is zero.

- When the economy is open, we look at its interaction with the rest of the world (ROW). We assume that the country is small, ROW is large, and the prevailing world real interest rate is constant at r^*. In the numerical examples that follow, we assume $r^* = 0.05 = 5\%$ per year.

Taken all together, these assumptions give us a special case of the LRBC that requires the present value of current and future trade balances to equal zero (because initial wealth is zero):

$$0 = \underbrace{\text{Present value of } TB}_{\text{Initial wealth is zero}} = \underbrace{\text{Present value of } Q}_{\text{Present value of } GDP} - \underbrace{\text{Present value of } C}_{\text{Present value of } GNE}$$

or equivalently,

$$\underbrace{\text{Present value of } Q}_{\text{Present value of } GDP} = \underbrace{\text{Present value of } C}_{\text{Present value of } GNE}. \tag{17-4}$$

Remember, this equation says that the LRBC will hold, and the present value of current and future TB will be zero, if and only if the present value of current and future Q equals the present value of current and future C.

Consumption Smoothing: A Numerical Example and Generalization

Now that we've clarified the assumptions for our model, we can explore how countries smooth consumption by examining two cases:

- A closed economy, in which $TB = 0$ in all periods, external borrowing and lending are not possible, and the LRBC is automatically satisfied

■ An open economy, in which *TB* does not have to be zero, borrowing and lending are possible, and we must verify that the LRBC is satisfied

Let's begin with a numerical example that illustrates the gains from consumption smoothing. We will generalize the result later.

Closed Versus Open Economy: No Shocks Table 17-1 provides a numerical example for our model economy when it is closed and experiences no shocks. Output *Q* is 100 units in each period, and all output is devoted to consumption. The present value of 100 in each period starting in year 0 equals the present value of 100 in year 0, which is simply 100, plus the present value of 100 in every subsequent year, which is 100/0.05 = 2,000 [using Equation (17-2), from the case of a perpetual loan]. Thus, the present value of present and future output is 2,100.

If this economy were open rather than closed, nothing would be different. The LRBC is satisfied because there is a zero trade balance at all times. Consumption *C* is perfectly smooth: every year the country consumes all 100 units of its output, and this is the country's preferred consumption path. There are no gains from financial globalization because this open country prefers to consume only what it produces each year, and thus has no need to borrow or lend to achieve its preferred consumption path.

Closed Versus Open Economy: Shocks The smooth path for the closed economy cannot be maintained if it suffers shocks to output, such as one of the hurricanes discussed at the start of the chapter. Suppose there is a temporary unanticipated output shock of −21 units in year 0. Output *Q* falls to 79 in year 0 and then returns to a level of 100 thereafter. The change in the present value of output is the drop of 21 in year 0. The present value of output falls from 2,100 to 2,079, a drop of 1%.

Over time, will consumption in an open economy respond to this shock in the same way closed-economy consumption does? In the closed economy, there is no doubt what happens. Because all output is consumed and there is no possibility of a trade imbalance, consumption necessarily falls to 79 in year 0 and then rises back to 100 in year 1 and stays there forever. The path of consumption is no longer smooth, as shown in Table 17-2.

In the open economy, however, a smooth consumption path is still attainable because the country can borrow from abroad in year 0, and then repay over time. The country can't afford its original smooth consumption path of 100 every period, because the present value of output is now less. So what smooth consumption path can it afford?

TABLE 17-1

A Closed or Open Economy with No Shocks Output equals consumption. Trade balance is zero. Consumption is smooth.

				Period					Present Value
		0	1	2	3	4	5	...	($r^* = 0.05$)
Output *GDP*	*Q*	100	100	100	100	100	100	...	2,100
Expenditure *GNE*	*C*	100	100	100	100	100	100	...	2,100
Trade balance	*TB*	0	0	0	0	0	0	...	0

Note: All variables take the same values from period 1 onward.

TABLE 17-2

A Closed Economy with Temporary Shocks Output equals consumption. Trade balance is zero. Consumption is volatile.

				Period					Present Value
		0	1	2	3	4	5	...	$(r^* = 0.05)$
Output *GDP*	*Q*	79	100	100	100	100	100	...	2,079
Expenditure *GNE*	*C*	79	100	100	100	100	100	...	2,079
Trade balance	*TB*	0	0	0	0	0	0	...	0

Note: All variables take the same values from period 1 onward.

In the first section of this chapter, we spent some time deriving the LRBC. Now we can see why: the LRBC, given by Equation (17-4), is the key to determining a smooth consumption path in the face of economic shocks. Once we establish the present value of output, we know the present value of consumption, because these must be the same; from this fact we can figure out how to smooth consumption.

In this example, the present value of output Q has fallen 1% (from 2,100 to 2,079), so the present value of consumption must also fall by 1%. How should the country achieve this? Consumption can remain smooth, and satisfy the LRBC, if it falls by 1% (from 100 to 99) in every year. To double-check this logic, we compute the present value of C, using the perpetual loan formula again: 99 + 99/0.05 = 99 + 1,980 = 2,079. Because the present value of C and the present value of Q are equal, the LRBC is satisfied.

Table 17-3 shows the path of all the important macroeconomic aggregates for the open economy. In year 0, the country runs a trade balance of $TB = -20$ (a deficit), because output Q is 79 and consumption C is 99. In subsequent years, when output is 100, the country keeps consumption at 99, and has a trade balance $TB = +1$ (a surplus).

TABLE 17-3

An Open Economy with Temporary Shocks A trade deficit is run when output is temporarily low. Consumption is smooth.

				Period					Present Value
		0	1	2	3	4	5	...	$(r^* = 0.05)$
Output *GDP*	*Q*	79	100	100	100	100	100	...	2,079
Expenditure *GNE*	*C*	99	99	99	99	99	99	...	2,079
Trade balance	*TB*	−20	+1	+1	+1	+1	+1	...	0
Net factor income from abroad	*NFIA*	0	−1	−1	−1	−1	−1	...	—
Current account	*CA*	−20	0	0	0	0	0	...	—
External wealth	*W*	−20	−20	−20	−20	−20	−20	...	—

Note: All variables take the same values from period 1 onward.

Offsetting this +1 trade balance, the country must make net factor payments *NFIA* = −1 in the form of interest paid. The country must borrow 20 in year 0, and then make, in perpetuity, 5% interest payments of 1 unit on the 20 units borrowed.

In year 0, the current account *CA* (= *TB* + *NFIA*) is −20. In all subsequent years, net factor income from abroad is −1 and the trade balance is +1, implying that the current account is 0, with no further borrowing. The country's external wealth *W* is therefore −20 in all periods, corresponding to the perpetual loan taken out in year 0. External wealth is constant at −20; it does not explode because interest payments are made in full each period and no further borrowing is required.

The lesson is clear. When output fluctuates, a closed economy cannot smooth consumption, but an open one can.

Generalizing The lesson of our numerical example applies to any situation in which a country wants to smooth its consumption when confronted with shocks. Suppose, more generally, that output *Q* and consumption *C* are initially stable at some value with *Q* = *C* and external wealth of zero. The LRBC is satisfied because the trade balance is zero at all times.

Now suppose output unexpectedly falls in year 0 by an amount Δ*Q*, and then returns to its prior value for all future periods. The loss of output in year 0 reduces the present value of output (GDP) by the amount Δ*Q*. To meet the LRBC, the country must lower the present value of consumption by the same amount. A closed economy accomplishes this by lowering its consumption by the whole amount of Δ*Q* in year 0. That is its only option! An open economy, however, lowers its consumption uniformly (every period) by a smaller amount, Δ*C* < Δ*Q*. But how big a reduction is needed to meet the LRBC?

Because consumption falls less than output in year 0, the country will run a trade deficit of Δ*Q* − Δ*C* < 0 in year 0. The country must borrow from other nations an amount equal to this trade deficit, and external wealth falls by the amount of that new debt. In subsequent years, output returns to its normal level but consumption stays at its reduced level, so trade surpluses of Δ*C* are run in all subsequent years.

Because the LRBC requires that these surpluses be large enough to service the debt, we know how large the drop in consumption must be. A loan of Δ*Q* − Δ*C* in year 0 requires interest payments of $r^*(\Delta Q - \Delta C)$ in later years. If the subsequent trade surpluses of Δ*C* are to cover these interest payments, then we know that Δ*C* must be chosen so that

$$\underbrace{r^* \times \underbrace{(\Delta Q - \Delta C)}_{\substack{\text{Amount}\\\text{borrowed in}\\\text{year 0}}}}_{\text{Interest due in subsequent years}} = \underbrace{\Delta C}_{\substack{\text{Trade surplus}\\\text{in subsequent}\\\text{years}}}$$

To find out how big a cut in consumption is necessary, we rearrange and find that

$$\Delta C = \frac{r^*}{1 + r^*} \Delta Q$$

Note that the fraction in the above equation is between zero and 1. Thus, the generalized lesson is that an open economy only needs to lower its steady consumption level by a *fraction* of the size of the temporary output loss. [For instance, in the previous numerical example, Δ*C* = (0.05/1.05) × (21) = 1, so consumption had to fall by 1 unit.]

Smoothing Consumption When a Shock Is Permanent We just showed how an open economy uses international borrowing to smooth consumption in response to a temporary shock to output. When the shock is permanent, however, the outcome is different. With a permanent shock, output will be lower by ΔQ in all years, so the only way either a closed or open economy can satisfy the LRBC while keeping consumption smooth is to cut consumption by $\Delta C = \Delta Q$ in all years. This is optimal, even in an open economy, because consumption remains smooth, although at a reduced level.

Comparing the results for a temporary shock and a permanent shock, we see an important point: consumers can smooth out temporary shocks—they have to adjust a bit, but the adjustment is far smaller than the shock itself—but they must adjust immediately and fully to permanent shocks. For example, if your income drops by 50% just this month, you might borrow to make it through this month with minimal adjustment in spending; however, if your income is going to remain 50% lower in every subsequent month, then you need to cut your spending permanently.

Summary: Save for a Rainy Day

Financial openness allows countries to "save for a rainy day." This section's lesson has a simple household analogy. If you cannot use financial institutions to lend (save) or borrow (dissave), you have to spend what you earn each period. If you have unusually low income, you have little to spend. If you have a windfall, you have to spend it all. Borrowing and lending to smooth consumption fluctuations makes a household better off. The same applies to countries.

In a closed economy, consumption must equal output in every period, so output fluctuations immediately generate consumption fluctuations. In an open economy, the desired smooth consumption path can be achieved by running a trade deficit during bad times and a trade surplus during good times. By extension, deficits and surpluses can also be used to finance extraordinary and temporary emergency spending needs, such as the costs of war (see **Side Bar: Wars and the Current Account**).

SIDE BAR

Wars and the Current Account

Our theory of consumption smoothing can take into account temporary and "desired" consumption shocks. The most obvious example of such a shock is war.

Although we assumed zero government spending above, in reality, countries' consumption includes private consumption C and public consumption G. It is simple to augment the model to include G as well as C. Under this circumstance, the constraint is that the present value of GNE $(C + G)$ must equal the present value of GDP. A war means a temporary increase in G.

Borrowing internationally to finance war-related costs goes back centuries. Historians have long argued about the importance of the creation of the British public debt market as a factor in the country's rise to global leadership compared with powerful continental rivals like France. From the early 1700s (which saw rapid financial development led by major financiers like the Rothschilds) to the end of the Napoleonic Wars in 1815, the British were able to maintain good credit; they could borrow domestically and externally cheaply and easily (often from the Dutch) to finance the simultaneous needs of capital formation

for the Industrial Revolution and high levels of military spending.

In the nineteenth century, borrowing to finance war-related costs became more commonplace. In the 1870s, the defeated French issued bonds in London to finance a reparation payment to the triumphant Germans. World War I and World War II saw massive lending by the United States to other Allied countries. More recently, when the United States went to war in Afghanistan (2001) and Iraq (2003), there was a sharp increase in the U.S. current account deficit and in external debt due in part to war-related borrowing.

Better at raising armies than finance, the French fought with one hand tied behind their back.

APPLICATION

Consumption Volatility and Financial Openness

Does the evidence show that countries avoid consumption volatility by embracing financial globalization? A simple test might be to compute the ratio of consumption volatility to output volatility (where volatility equals the standard deviation of the growth rate). If consumption smoothing is achieved, the computed ratio ought to fall. In fact, in our simple model of a small, open economy that can borrow or lend without limit, and that prefers a perfectly smooth path of consumption, this ratio should fall to zero because the economy can take advantage of financial globalization by borrowing and lending to other countries. In practice, this ratio will not be zero if all countries are affected by common global shocks. For example, if every country suffers a negative shock, every country will want to borrow, but that will not be possible: if all countries want to borrow, no countries will want to lend. In practice, however, not all shocks are global, so countries ought to be able to achieve some reduction in consumption volatility through external finance. (We consider the importance of local and global shocks later in this chapter.)

With this in mind, Figure 17-5 presents some discouraging evidence. On the horizontal axis, countries are sorted into 10 groups (deciles) from those that participate least in financial globalization (are least financially liberalized) to those that participate

FIGURE 17-5

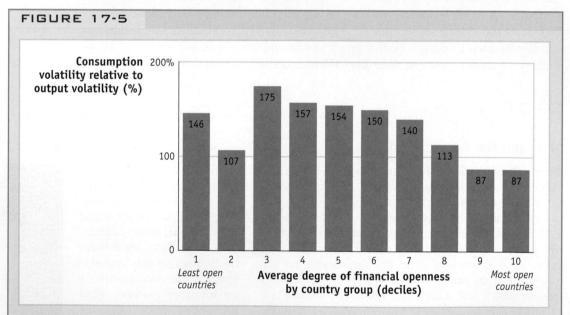

Consumption Volatility Relative to Output Volatility For a very large sample of 170 countries over the period 1995 to 2004, we compute the ratio of consumption volatility to output volatility, expressed as a percentage. A ratio of less than 100% indicates that some consumption smoothing has been achieved. Countries are then assembled into 10 groups (deciles), ordered from least financially open (1) to most financially open (10). The average volatility in each group is shown. Only the most financially open countries have volatility ratios of less than 100%. The high ratios in groups 1 to 8 show, perversely, that consumption is even more volatile than output in these countries.

Note: Volatility is measured by the standard deviation of real output or consumption growth according to the Penn World Tables.

Source: Index of financial openness from Sebastian Edwards, "Capital Controls, Sudden Stops and Current Account Reversals," in Sebastian Edwards, ed., 2007, International Capital Flows (Chicago: University of Chicago Press).

most. On the left are least open countries with tight capital controls (generally poorer countries), on the right are the more open countries that permit free movement of capital (mostly advanced countries). For all these countries, we assess their ability to smooth total consumption $(C + G)$ in the period from 1995 to 2004 using annual data. In closed countries, we would expect that the volatility of consumption would be similar to the volatility of output (GDP) so that the ratio of the two would be close to 100%. But if an open country were able to smooth consumption in line with our simple model, this ratio ought to be lower than 100%.

The figure shows that most groups of countries have an average consumption-to-output volatility ratio of well above 100%. Moreover, as financial liberalization increases, this ratio shows little sign of decrease until fairly high levels of liberalization are reached (around the seventh or eighth decile). Indeed, until we get to the ninth and tenth deciles, all of these ratios are above 100%. Similar findings have been found using a variety of tests, and it appears that only at a very high level of financial liberalization does financial globalization deliver modest consumption-smoothing benefits.[9]

Why are these findings so far from the predictions of our model? In poorer countries, some of the relatively high consumption volatility must be unrelated to financial openness—it is there even in closed countries. In the real world, households are not identical and global capital markets do not reach every person. Some people and firms do not or cannot participate in even domestic financial markets, perhaps because of backward financial systems. Other problems may stem from the way financial markets operate (e.g., poor transparency and regulation) in emerging market countries that are partially open and/or have partially developed their financial systems.

The evidence may not imply a failure of financial globalization, but it does not provide a ringing endorsement either. Consumption-smoothing gains may prove elusive for emerging markets until they advance further by improving poor governance and weak institutions, developing their financial systems, and pursuing further financial liberalization. ■

APPLICATION

Precautionary Saving, Reserves, and Sovereign Wealth Funds

One obstacle to consumption smoothing in poorer countries is the phenomenon of sudden stops, which we noted earlier. If poorer countries can't count on credit lines to be there when they need them, they may fall back on an alternative strategy of engaging in **precautionary saving,** whereby the government acquires a buffer of external assets, a "rainy day fund." That is, rather than allowing external wealth to fluctuate around an average of zero, with the country sometimes being in debt and sometimes being a creditor, the country maintains a higher positive "average balance" in its external wealth account to reduce or even eliminate the need to go into a net debt position. This approach is costly, because the country must sacrifice consumption to build up the buffer. However, poor countries may deem the cost to be worthwhile if it allows them to smooth consumption more reliably once the buffer is established.

In the world economy today, precautionary saving has been on the rise and it takes two forms. The first is the accumulation of **foreign reserves** by central banks. Foreign reserves are safe assets denominated in foreign currency, like U.S. Treasury securities

---

[9] M. Ayhan Kose, Eswar S. Prasad, and Marco E. Terrones, 2007, "How Does Financial Globalization Affect Risk Sharing? Patterns and Channels," IZA Discussion Papers 2903, Institute for the Study of Labor (IZA).

and other low-risk debt issued by governments in rich, solvent countries. They can be used not only for precautionary saving but for other purposes, such as maintaining a fixed exchange rate. As external assets on the nation's balance sheet, these reserves can be deployed during a sudden stop to cushion the blow to the domestic economy. Many economists argue that some part or even the greater part of reserve accumulation in recent years in emerging markets is driven by this precautionary motive.[10]

The second form of precautionary saving by governments is through what are called **sovereign wealth funds,** state-owned asset management companies that invest some government savings (possibly including central bank reserves) overseas. Often, the asset management companies place the government savings in safe assets; increasingly, however, the funds are being placed in riskier assets such as equity and FDI. Some countries, such as Norway (which had an oil boom in the 1970s), use such funds to save windfall gains from the exploitation of natural resources for future needs. Many newer funds have appeared in emerging markets and developing countries (such as Singapore, China, Malaysia, and Taiwan), but these funds have been driven more by precautionary saving than resource booms.

As of March 2013, the countries with the biggest sovereign wealth funds were China ($1.2 trillion), Abu Dhabi ($745 billion), Norway ($716 billion), and Saudi Arabia ($538 billion), with other large funds (more than $75 billion each) in Kuwait, Russia, Singapore, Qatar, Libya, and Australia.[11]

Most observers believe it is likely that sovereign wealth funds will continue to grow in size, and that their use will spread to other countries (see **Headlines: Copper-Bottomed Insurance**). It is interesting that, despite having a legitimate economic rationale, these funds may generate international tensions, as they already have, by attempting to acquire politically sensitive equity and FDI assets from advanced countries. ■

3 Gains from Efficient Investment

Suppose an economy has opened up, and is taking full advantage of the gains from consumption smoothing. Has it completely exploited the benefits of financial globalization? The answer is no, because openness delivers gains not only on the consumption side but also on the investment side by improving a country's ability to augment its capital stock and take advantage of new production opportunities.

The Basic Model

To illustrate these investment gains, we must refine the model we have been using by abandoning the assumption that output can be produced using only labor. We now assume that producing output requires labor and capital, which is created over time by investing output. When we make this change, the long-run budget constraint in

---

[10] Joshua Aizenman and Jaewoo Lee, 2005, "International Reserves: Precautionary versus Mercantilist Views, Theory and Evidence," NBER Working Paper No. 11366; Romain Ranciere and Olivier Jeanne, 2006, "The Optimal Level of International Reserves for Emerging Market Countries: Formulas and Applications," IMF Working Paper No. 06/229; Ceyhun Bora Durdu, Enrique G. Mendoza, and Marco E. Terrones, 2007, "Precautionary Demand for Foreign Assets in Sudden Stop Economies: An Assessment of the New Mercantilism," NBER Working Paper No. 13123.

[11] Data from http://www.swfinstitute.org/fund-rankings/. The Hong Kong Monetary Authority Investment Portfolio ($299 billion) is excluded in the list here as it is not separate from, but part of, the central bank.

HEADLINES

Copper-Bottomed Insurance

Many developing countries experience output volatility. Sovereign wealth funds can buffer these shocks, as recent experience in Chile has shown.

Thousands of government workers marched on downtown Santiago [in November 2008], burning an effigy of Chilean Finance Minister Andres Velasco and calling him "disgusting" as a strike for higher wages paralyzed public services.

Five months later, polls show that Velasco is President Michelle Bachelet's most popular minister. During a three-year copper boom he and central bank President Jose De Gregorio set aside $48.6 billion, more than 30 percent of the country's gross domestic product, that he is now using for tax cuts, subsidies and cash handouts to poor families.

The Chilean peso has risen almost 10 percent against the dollar this year to become the best-performing currency among emerging markets. The country's economy is expected to grow 0.1 percent in 2009, as the region contracts 1.5 percent, according to the International Monetary Fund. . . .

Velasco, 48, applied the lessons learned from decades of economic failure in Latin America—ones he said could also help the U.S. The current crisis followed "a massive regulatory failure in many advanced financial markets over the last decade or so," Velasco said in an interview April 21 [2009] in his office overlooking the presidential palace in downtown Santiago.

"This is a movie that may be novel to some Americans, but this is a movie that people in other places of the world, Chile included, know we have seen," said Velasco, who is scheduled to meet April 25 with Federal Reserve Chairman Ben S. Bernanke in Washington. "We know how it begins, how it unfolds and how it ends." . . .

Commodity-driven swings of boom and bust have defined Latin America's economic history for the past 100 years.

"That is a cycle that needs to be ended," Velasco said. "We have been out to show that a Latin American country can manage properly, and not mismanage, a commodity cycle. You save in times of abundance, and you invest in lean times."

When Velasco joined Bachelet's new cabinet in March 2006, the price of copper had risen by more than half in 12 months to $2.25 a pound. Taxes and profits from state-owned Codelco, the world's largest copper producer, provide about 15 percent of government revenue. Bachelet, 57, Chile's second consecutive socialist president, came under almost immediate pressure to start spending the revenue.

Students went on strike in May of that year, demanding more money for education. More than 800,000 people protested at high schools and universities, and police with water cannons and tear gas arrested more than 1,000. Velasco reiterated his commitment to "prudent fiscal policies" as politicians from the governing coalition demanded he resign. . . .

In his first three years in office, Velasco posted the biggest budget surpluses since the country returned to democracy in 1990. In 2007, Chile became a net creditor for the first time since independence from Spain in 1810.

Last July [2008], copper reached a record of $4.08 a pound. By year-end, the central bank had built $23.2 billion of reserves. The government had $22.7 billion in offshore funds and about $2.8 billion in its own holdings.

After Lehman Brothers Holdings Inc.'s September 15 bankruptcy sparked a global credit freeze, Velasco and De Gregorio had the equivalent of more than 30 percent of GDP available if needed to shore up Chile's banks and defend the peso.

The price of copper plummeted 52 percent from September 30 to year-end, and Velasco dusted off his checkbook. In the first week of January, he and Bachelet unveiled a $4 billion package of tax cuts and subsidies.

"He has been vindicated," said Luis Oganes, head of Latin American research at JPMorgan Chase & Co. in New York, who studied under Velasco. . . .

Velasco's stimulus spending, including 40,000-peso ($68.41) handouts to 1.7 million poor families, has paid off politically. His approval rating almost doubled to 57 percent in March from a low of 31 percent in August.... He is now the most well-liked member of the government, second only to the president at 62 percent.

"People finally understood what was behind his 'stinginess' of early years," said Sebastian Edwards, a Chilean economist at the University of California, Los Angeles. "That explains the rise in his popularity."

Source: Excerpted from Sebastian Boyd, "Harvard Peso Doctor Vindicated as Chile Evades Slump," bloomberg.com, April 23, 2009. Used with permission of Bloomberg L.P. © 2013. All rights reserved.

Equation (17-4) must be modified to include investment I as a component of GNE. For simplicity, however, we still assume that government consumption G is zero. With this change, the LRBC becomes

$$\underbrace{0}_{\text{Initial wealth is zero}} = \text{Present value of } TB$$

Because the TB is output (Q) minus expenditure ($C + I$), we can rewrite this last equation in the following form:

$$\underbrace{\text{Present value of } Q}_{\text{Present value of } GDP} = \underbrace{\text{Present value of } C + \text{Present value of } I}_{\text{Present value of } GNE} \qquad (17\text{-}5)$$

The LRBC will hold if and only if the present value of output Q equals the present value of expenditure ($C + I$).

Using this modified LRBC, we now study investment and consumption decisions in two cases:

- A closed economy, in which external borrowing and lending are not possible, the trade balance is zero in all periods, and the LRBC is automatically satisfied

- An open economy, in which borrowing and lending are possible, the trade balance can be more or less than zero, and we must verify that the LRBC is satisfied

Efficient Investment: A Numerical Example and Generalization

Let's start with a country that has output of 100, consumption C of 100, no investment, a zero trade balance, and zero external wealth. If that state persisted, the LRBC would be satisfied, just as it was in the prior numerical example with consumption smoothing. This outcome describes the optimal path of consumption in both the closed and open economies when output is constant and there are no shocks, that is, nothing happens here that makes the country want to alter its output and consumption.

But now suppose there is a shock in year 0 that takes the form of a new investment opportunity. For example, it could be that in year 0 engineers discover that by building a new factory with a new machine, the country can produce a certain good much more cheaply than current technology allows. Or perhaps there is a resource discovery, but a mine must first be built to extract the minerals from the earth. What happens next? We turn first to a numerical example and then supply a more general answer.

We assume that the investment (in machines or factories or mines) would require an expenditure of 16 units, and that the investment will pay off in future years by increasing the country's output by 5 units in year 1 and all subsequent years (but not in year 0).

The country now faces some choices. Should it make this investment? And if it does, will it make out better if it is open or closed? We find the answers to these questions by looking at how an *open* economy would deal with the opportunity to invest, and then showing why a country would make itself worse off by choosing to be closed, thereby relinquishing at least some of the gains the investment opportunity offers.

As in the previous example, the key to solving this problem is to work with the LRBC and see how the choices a country makes to satisfy it have to change as circumstances do. Before the investment opportunity shock, output and consumption were each 100 in all periods, and had a present value of 2,100. Investment was zero in every period, and the LRBC given by Equation (17-5) was clearly satisfied. If the country decides to not act on the investment opportunity, this situation continues unchanged whether the economy is closed or open.

Now suppose an open economy undertakes the investment. First, we must calculate the difference this would make to the country's resources, as measured by the present value of output. Output would be 100 today and then 105 in every subsequent year. The present value of this stream of output is 100 plus 105/0.05 or 2,200. This is an increase of 100 over the old present value of output (2,100). The present value of the addition to output (of 5 units every subsequent period) is 100.

Can all of this additional output be devoted to consumption? No, because the country has had to invest 16 units in the current period to obtain this future stream of additional output. In this scenario, because all investment occurs in the current period, 16 is the present value of investment in the modified LRBC given by Equation (17-5).

Looking at that LRBC, we've calculated the present value of output (2,200), and now we have the present value of investment (16). We can see that the present value of consumption must equal 2,200 minus 16, or 2,184. This is 4% higher than it was without the investment. Even though some expenditure has to be devoted to investment, the resources available for consumption have risen by 4% in present value terms (from 2,100 without the investment, to 2,184 with it).

We can now find the new level of smooth consumption each period that satisfies the LRBC. Because the present value of C has risen by 4% from 2,100 to 2,184, the country can afford to raise consumption C in all periods by 4% from 100 to 104. (As a check, note that 104 + 104/0.05 = 2,184.) Is the country better off if it makes the investment? Yes—not only does its consumption remain smooth, but it is also 4% higher in all periods.

Table 17-4 lays out the details of this case. In year 0, consumption C is 104, investment I is 16, and *GNE* is 120. The trade balance is −20 because output Q is only 100. The country must borrow 20 units in year 0 to fund the investment of 16 *and* the 4 additional units of consumption the country can afford as a result of the investment. In all future years, consumption C is 104, and because there is no subsequent investment, *GNE* is also 104. Output Q is 105, and the trade balance is +1.

TABLE 17-4

An Open Economy with Investment and a Permanent Shock The economy runs a trade deficit to finance investment and consumption in period 0 and runs a trade surplus when output is higher in later periods. Consumption is smooth.

		\multicolumn{7}{c}{Period}	Present Value
		0	1	2	3	4	5	...	$(r^* = 0.05)$
Output *GDP*	Q	100	105	105	105	105	105	...	2,200
Expenditure *GNE* {	C	104	104	104	104	104	104	...	2,184
	I	16	0	0	0	0	0	...	16
Trade balance	*TB*	−20	+1	+1	+1	+1	+1	...	0
Net factor income from abroad	*NFIA*	0	−1	−1	−1	−1	−1	...	—
Current account	*CA*	−20	0	0	0	0	0	...	—
External wealth	*W*	−20	−20	−20	−20	−20	−20	...	—

Note: All variables take the same values from period 1 onward.

The initial trade deficit of 20 in year 0 results in an external debt of 20. As a perpetual loan, with an interest rate of 5%, this debt of 20 must be serviced by net interest payments of –1 in each subsequent year if the LRBC is to be satisfied. The interest payment of –1 offsets the trade surplus of +1 each period forever. Hence, the current account is zero in all future years, with no further borrowing, and the country's external wealth is –20 in all periods. External wealth does not explode, and the LRBC is satisfied.

This outcome is preferable to any outcome a closed economy can achieve. To attain an output level of 105 from year 1 on, a closed economy would have to cut consumption to 84 in year 0 to free up 16 units for investment. Although the country would then enjoy consumption of 105 in all subsequent years, this is not a smooth consumption path! The open economy *could* choose this path (cutting consumption to 84 in year 0), because it satisfies the LRBC. It won't choose this path, however, because by making the investment in this way, it cannot smooth its consumption and cannot smooth it *at a higher level.* The open economy is better off making the investment *and* smoothing consumption, two goals that the closed economy cannot simultaneously achieve.

Generalizing The lesson of our numerical example applies to any situation in which a country confronts new investment opportunities. Suppose that a country starts with zero external wealth, constant output Q, consumption C equal to output, and investment I equal to zero. A new investment opportunity appears requiring ΔK units of output in year 0. This investment will generate an additional ΔQ units of output in year 1 and all later years (but not in year 0).

Ultimately, consumers care about consumption. In an open economy, they can smooth their consumption, given future output. The constant level of consumption is limited only by the present value of available resources, as expressed by the LRBC. Maximizing the level of consumption is the same as maximizing the present value of consumption. Rearranging Equation (17-5), the LRBC requires that the present value of consumption must equal the present value of output minus the present value of investment. How is this present value maximized?

The increase in the present value of output $PV(Q)$ comes from extra output in every year but year 0, and the present value of these additions to output is, using Equation (17-2),

$$\text{Change in present value of output} = \frac{\Delta Q}{(1 + r^*)} + \frac{\Delta Q}{(1 + r^*)^2} + \frac{\Delta Q}{(1 + r^*)^3} + \cdots = \frac{\Delta Q}{r^*}$$

The change in the present value of investment $PV(I)$ is simply ΔK.

This means the investment will increase the present value of consumption—and hence will be undertaken—if and only if $\Delta Q / r^* \geq \Delta K$. There are two ways to look at this conclusion. Rearranging, investment is undertaken when

$$\underbrace{\Delta Q}_{\substack{\text{Output increase in} \\ \text{subsequent periods}}} \geq \underbrace{r^* \times \Delta K}_{\substack{\text{Interest payment due in} \\ \text{subsequent periods to} \\ \text{finance initial investment}}}$$

The intuition here is that investment occurs up to the point at which the annual benefit from the marginal unit of capital (ΔQ) equals or exceeds the annual cost of borrowing the funds to pay for that capital ($r^* \Delta K$).

Putting it another way, dividing by ΔK, investment is undertaken when

$$\underbrace{\frac{\Delta Q}{\Delta K}}_{\substack{MPK \\ \text{Marginal product of capital}}} \geq \underbrace{r^*}_{\text{World real interest rate}} \qquad (17\text{-}6)$$

This is a standard formula for the optimal or efficient level of investment and may look familiar from other courses in economics. Firms will take on investment projects as long as the **marginal product of capital (MPK)** is at least as great as the real interest rate.

Summary: Make Hay While the Sun Shines

In an open economy, firms borrow and repay to undertake investment that maximizes the present value of output. Households also borrow and lend to smooth consumption, but these borrowing and lending decisions are separate from those of firms.

When investing, an open economy sets its MPK equal to the world real rate of interest. If conditions are unusually good (high productivity), it makes sense to invest more capital and produce more output. Conversely, when conditions turn bad (low productivity), it makes sense to lower capital inputs and produce less output. This strategy maximizes the present value of output minus investment. Households then address the separate problem of how to smooth the path of consumption when output changes. A closed economy must be self-sufficient. Any resources invested are resources not consumed. More investment implies less consumption. This creates a trade-off. When investment opportunities are good, the country wants to invest to generate higher output in the future. Anticipating that higher output, the country wants to consume more today, but it cannot—it must consume less to invest more.

Proverbially, financial openness helps countries to "make hay while the sun shines"—and, in particular, to do so without having to engage in a trade-off against the important objective of consumption smoothing. The lesson here has a simple household analogy. Suppose you find a great investment opportunity. If you have no financial dealings with the outside world, you would have to sacrifice consumption and save to finance the investment.

APPLICATION

Delinking Saving from Investment

The story of the Norwegian oil boom provides a good illustration of our theory about investment and financial openness. North Sea oil was discovered in the 1960s, but the mass exploitation of this resource was unprofitable because cheap and plentiful supplies of oil were being produced elsewhere, primarily in the Persian Gulf. Then came the first "oil shock" in the early 1970s, when the cartel of Oil Producing and Exporting Countries (OPEC) colluded to raise world oil prices dramatically, a shock that was (correctly) viewed as permanent. At these higher oil prices, it suddenly made sense to exploit North Sea oil. Starting in the early 1970s, oil platforms, pipelines, refineries, and terminals were sprouting offshore and along the coast of Norway, causing its capital stock to permanently increase in response to a new productive investment opportunity.

Figure 17-6 shows the path of saving (S) and investment (I) measured as ratios of GDP in Norway from 1965 to 1990. The oil boom is clearly visible in the investment share of GDP, which in the 1970s rose about 10 percentage points above its typical level. Had Norway been a closed economy, this additional investment would have been financed by a decrease in the share of output devoted to public and private consumption. As you can see, no such sacrifice was necessary. Norway's saving rate was flat in this period or even fell slightly. In Norway's open economy, saving and investment were delinked and the difference was made up by the current account, $CA = S - I$, which moved sharply into deficit, approaching minus 15% of GDP at one point. Thus, all of the short-run increase in investment was financed by foreign investment in Norway, much of it by multinational oil companies.

Is Norway a special case? Economists have examined large international datasets to see whether there is general evidence that countries can delink investment decisions from saving decisions as the Norwegians did. One approach follows the pioneering work of Martin Feldstein and Charles Horioka.[12] They estimated what fraction β of each additional dollar saved tended to be invested in the same country. In other words, in their model, if saving rose by an amount ΔS, they estimated that investment would rise by an amount $\Delta I = \beta \Delta S$. In a closed economy, the "savings retention" measure β would equal 1, but they argued that increasing financial openness would tend to push β below 1.

For example, suppose one were to estimate β for the period 1980 to 2000 for three groups of countries with differing degrees of financial integration within the group: in a sample of countries in the European Union, where international financial integra-

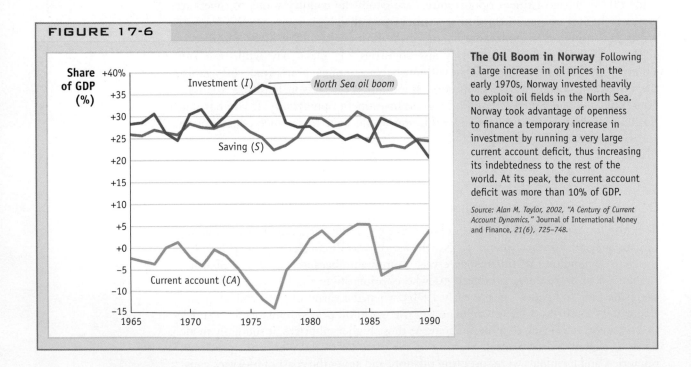

FIGURE 17-6

The Oil Boom in Norway Following a large increase in oil prices in the early 1970s, Norway invested heavily to exploit oil fields in the North Sea. Norway took advantage of openness to finance a temporary increase in investment by running a very large current account deficit, thus increasing its indebtedness to the rest of the world. At its peak, the current account deficit was more than 10% of GDP.

Source: Alan M. Taylor, 2002, "A Century of Current Account Dynamics," Journal of International Money and Finance, 21(6), 725–748.

[12] Martin Feldstein and Charles Horioka, 1980, "Domestic Saving and International Capital Flows," *Economic Journal*, 90(358), 314–329.

tion had advanced furthest, the estimated value of β is 0.26, meaning that 26% of each additional dollar saved tended to be invested in the same country; in a sample of all developed countries with a somewhat lower level of financial integration, the estimate of β is 0.39; and in a sample of emerging markets, where financial integration was lower still, the estimate of β is 0.67.[13] These data thus indicate that financially open countries seem to have a greater ability to delink saving and investment, in that they have a much lower "savings retention" measure β. ■

Can Poor Countries Gain from Financial Globalization?

Our analysis shows that if the world real interest rate is r^* and a country has investment projects for which the marginal product of capital MPK exceeds r^*, then the country should borrow from the rest of the world to finance investment in these projects. Keep this conclusion in mind as we now examine an enduring question in international macroeconomics: Why doesn't more capital flow to poor countries?

Production Function Approach To look at this question carefully, economists must take a stand on what determines a country's marginal product of capital. For this purpose, economists usually employ a version of a **production function** that maps available capital per worker, $k = K/L$, and the prevailing level of **productivity** A to the level of output per worker, $q = Q/L$, where Q is GDP.

A simple and widely used production function takes the form

$$\underbrace{q}_{\substack{\text{Output} \\ \text{per} \\ \text{worker}}} = \underbrace{A}_{\substack{\text{Productivity} \\ \text{level}}} \times \underbrace{k^{\theta}}_{\substack{\text{Capital per} \\ \text{worker}}}$$

where θ is a number between 0 and 1 that measures the contribution of capital to production.[14] Specifically, θ is the elasticity of output with respect to capital (i.e., a 1% increase in capital per worker generates a θ% increase in output per worker). In the real world, θ has been estimated to be approximately one-third, and this is the value we employ here.[15] An illustration is given in the top part of Figure 17-7, panel (a), which graphs the production function for the case in which $\theta = 1/3$ and the productivity level is set at a reference level of 1, so $A = 1$. Thus, for this case $q = k^{1/3}$.

With this production function, what is the marginal product of capital, MPK? It is the slope of the production function, the incremental change in output per worker Δq divided by the incremental change in capital per worker Δk. As we can see from the figure, capital's marginal product MPK (the extra output we get by increasing capital per worker) decreases as k increases. Indeed, from the preceding formula, we can find that MPK, or the slope of the production function, is given by

$$MPK = \frac{\Delta q}{\Delta k} = \underbrace{\theta A k^{\theta-1}}_{\substack{\text{Slope of the} \\ \text{production function}}} = \theta \times \frac{q}{k}$$

[13] Author's calculations based on International Monetary Fund, International Financial Statistics, with investment and saving measured as a share of GDP.
[14] This is called the Cobb-Douglas production function.
[15] Douglas Gollin, April 2002, "Getting Income Shares Right," *Journal of Political Economy*, 110(2), 458–474.

FIGURE 17-7

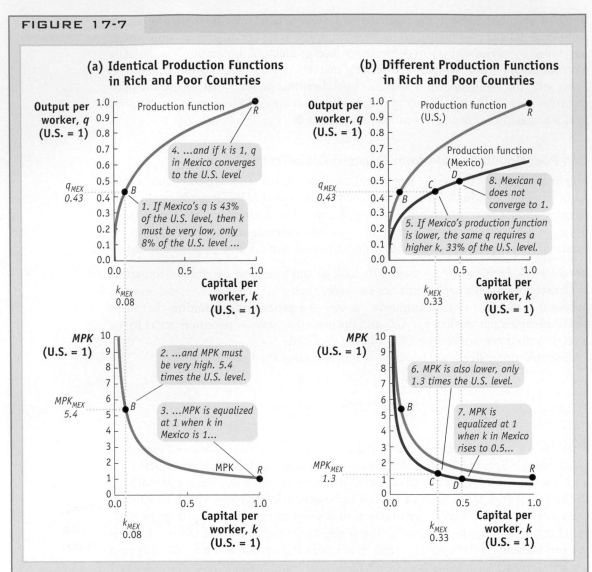

(a) Identical Production Functions in Rich and Poor Countries

Output per worker, q (U.S. = 1)

Production function

4. ...and if k is 1, q in Mexico converges to the U.S. level

q_{MEX} 0.43

B

1. If Mexico's q is 43% of the U.S. level, then k must be very low, only 8% of the U.S. level ...

Capital per worker, k (U.S. = 1)

k_{MEX} 0.08

MPK (U.S. = 1)

2. ...and MPK must be very high. 5.4 times the U.S. level.

MPK_{MEX} 5.4

B

3. ...MPK is equalized at 1 when k in Mexico is 1...

MPK

R

Capital per worker, k (U.S. = 1)

k_{MEX} 0.08

(b) Different Production Functions in Rich and Poor Countries

Output per worker, q (U.S. = 1)

Production function (U.S.)

Production function (Mexico)

q_{MEX} 0.43

B

C

D

8. Mexican q does not converge to 1.

5. If Mexico's production function is lower, the same q requires a higher k, 33% of the U.S. level.

Capital per worker, k (U.S. = 1)

k_{MEX} 0.33

MPK (U.S. = 1)

6. MPK is also lower, only 1.3 times the U.S. level.

B

7. MPK is equalized at 1 when k in Mexico rises to 0.5...

MPK_{MEX} 1.3

C

D

R

Capital per worker, k (U.S. = 1)

k_{MEX} 0.33

Why Doesn't Capital Flow to Poor Countries? If poor and rich countries share the same level of productivity (a common production function), then MPK must be very high in poor countries, as shown in panel (a). For example, if *B* represents Mexico and *R* the United States, we would expect to see large flows of capital to poor countries, until their capital per worker *k* and, hence, output per worker *q* rise to levels seen in the rich world (movement from point *B* to point *R*). The result is convergence. This doesn't happen in reality. Poor and rich countries have different levels of productivity (different production functions) and so MPK may not be much higher in poor countries than it is in rich countries, as shown in panel (b). The poor country (Mexico) is now at *C* and not at *B*. Now investment occurs only until MPK falls to the rest of the world level at point *D*. The result is divergence. Capital per worker *k* and output per worker *q* do not converge to the levels seen in the rich country.

Thus, in this special case, the *marginal product of capital* is proportional to output per worker divided by capital per worker (the output–capital ratio) or the *average product of capital*. The MPK for the case we are studying, in which $\theta = 1/3$ and $A = 1$, is shown in the bottom part of Figure 17-7, panel (a).

A Benchmark Model: Countries Have Identical Productivity Levels To see how a country responds to the possibilities opened up by financial globalization, let's look at what determines the incentive to invest in small open economies of the type we are studying, assuming they all have access to the same level of productivity, $A = 1$.

To understand when such a country will invest, we need to understand how its MPK changes as k changes. For example, suppose the country increases k by a factor of 8. Because $q = k^{1/3}$, q increases by a factor of 2 (the cube root of 8). Let's suppose this brings the country up to the U.S. level of output per worker. Because $MPK = \theta \times q/k$ and because q has risen by a factor of 2, while k has risen by a factor of 8, MPK changes by a factor of 1/4; that is, it falls to one-fourth its previous level.

This simple model says that poor countries with output per worker of one-half the U.S. level have an MPK of four times the U.S level. Countries with one-quarter the U.S. per worker output level have an MPK of 16 times the U.S level, and so on.

To make the model concrete, let's see how well it applies to a comparison of the United States and Mexico in the late 1980s.[16] During this time, the United States produced approximately twice as much GDP per worker as Mexico. Now let's choose units such that all U.S. variables take the value 1, and Mexican variables are proportions of the corresponding U.S. variables. For example, with these units, q was 0.43 in Mexico in the late 1980s (i.e., output per worker in Mexico was 43% of output per worker in the United States).

Now consider the implications of assuming that the economies of Mexico and the United States were described by the same production function with a common productivity level, $A = 1$. In Figure 17-7, panel (a), the United States is at point R (for rich) and Mexico is at point B, and its low output implies a capital per worker k that is only 8% of the U.S. level. What is Mexico's marginal product of capital? It is 5.4 times the U.S. marginal product of capital. Why? As above, MPK is θ (a constant for both countries equal to 1/3) times q/k. In the United States, $q/k = 1$; in Mexico, $q/k = 0.43/0.08 = 5.4$.

We can think of the United States and other rich countries as representing the rest of the world—a large financially integrated region, from Mexico's point of view. The world real interest rate r^* is the opportunity cost of capital for the rest of the world, that is, the rich world's MPK. If the real interest rate r^* is, say, 10% in rich countries like the United States, then their MPK is 10%, and Mexico has an MPK of 54%!

To take an even more dramatic example, we could look at India, a much poorer country than Mexico. India's output per worker was just 8.6% of the U.S. level in 1988. Using our simple benchmark model, we would infer that the MPK in India was 135 times the U.S. level![17]

To sum up, the simple model says that the poorer the country, the higher its MPK, because of the twin assumptions of diminishing marginal product and a common productivity level. Investment ought to be very profitable in Mexico (and India, and all poor countries). Investment in Mexico should continue until Mexico is at point R.

---

[16] In 1985, levels of GDP per worker were $23,256 in Mexico and $48,164 in the United States (in 1996 international dollars), according to the reference source for such data, the Penn World Tables. By 1995 this gap had widened a little. The data in this example are based on Robert E. Hall and Charles I. Jones, 1999, "Why Do Some Countries Produce So Much More Output per Worker Than Others?" *Quarterly Journal of Economics*, 114(1), 83–116.

[17] First solve for the relative level of capital per worker in India: $k_{IND}/k_{US} = [q_{IND}/q_{US}]^{1/\theta} = [0.086]^3 = 0.000636$. The relative MPK in India would then equal $[q_{IND}/q_{US}]/[k_{IND}/k_{US}] = [q_{IND}/q_{US}]^{1/\theta} = [0.086]/[0.086]^3 = 1/[0.086]^2 = 135$.

Economists would describe such a trajectory for Mexico as **convergence.** If the world is characterized by convergence, countries can reach the level of capital per worker and output per worker of the rich country through investment and capital accumulation alone.

The Lucas Paradox: Why Doesn't Capital Flow from Rich to Poor Countries?

Twenty or thirty years ago, a widespread view among economists was that poor countries had access to exactly the same technologies as rich countries, given the flow of ideas and knowledge around a globalizing world. This led economists to assume that if policies shifted to allow greater international movement of capital, foreign investment would flood into poor countries because their very poverty implied that capital was scarce in these countries, and therefore its marginal product was high.

But as Nobel laureate Robert Lucas wrote in his widely cited article "Why Doesn't Capital Flow from Rich to Poor Countries?":

> If this model were anywhere close to being accurate, and if world capital markets were anywhere close to being free and complete, it is clear that, in the face of return differentials of this magnitude, investment goods would flow rapidly from the United States and other wealthy countries to India and other poor countries. Indeed, one would expect no investment to occur in the wealthy countries. . . . The assumptions on technology and trade conditions that give rise to this example must be drastically wrong, but exactly what is wrong with them, and what assumptions should replace them?[18]

What was drastically wrong was the assumption of identical productivity levels A across countries, as represented by the single production function in Figure 17-7, panel (a)? Although this model is often invoked, it is generally invalid. Can we do better?

An Augmented Model: Countries Have Different Productivity Levels

To see why capital does not flow to poor countries, we now suppose that A, the productivity level, is different in the United States and Mexico, as denoted by country subscripts:

$$\underbrace{q_{US}}_{\substack{\text{Output per worker} \\ \text{in the United States}}} = \underbrace{A_{US}k_{US}^{\theta}}_{\text{U.S. production function}} \qquad \underbrace{q_{MEX}}_{\substack{\text{Output per worker} \\ \text{in Mexico}}} = \underbrace{A_{MEX}k_{MEX}^{\theta}}_{\text{Mexican production function}}$$

Countries have potentially different production functions and different MPK curves, depending on their relative levels of productivity, as shown in Figure 17-7, panel (b). The Mexican curves are shown here as lower than the U.S. curves. We now show that this augmented model is a much better match with reality.

The earlier MPK equation holds for each country, so we can compute the ratios of country MPKs as

$$\frac{MPK_{MEX}}{MPK_{US}} = \frac{[\theta q_{MEX}/k_{MEX}]}{[\theta q_{US}/k_{US}]} = \frac{q_{MEX}/q_{US}}{k_{MEX}/k_{US}}$$

---

[18] Robert E. Lucas, Jr., May 1990, "Why Doesn't Capital Flow from Rich to Poor Countries?" *American Economic Review*, 80(2), 92–96. Lucas presented the India example with the assumption that capital's share was 0.4 rather than one-third, and that India's output per worker was one-fifteenth of the U.S. level. In that case, India's MPK is "only" 58 times the U.S. level, an equally absurd conclusion.

Using this equation, we can see the importance of allowing productivity levels to differ across countries. We know that $q_{MEX}/q_{US} = 0.43$, but we can also obtain data on capital per worker that show $k_{MEX}/k_{US} = 0.33$. If we plug these numbers into the last expression, we find that MPK in Mexico is not 5.4 times the U.S. level, as we had earlier determined, but only about 1.3 times (0.43/0.33) the U.S. level. The smaller multiple is due to the lower productivity level that our revised model reveals in Mexico.

Put another way, the data show that Mexico's capital per worker is about one-third that of the United States. If the simple model were true, Mexico would have a level of output level per worker of $(1/3)^{1/3} = 0.69$ or 69% of the U.S. level. However, Mexico's output per worker was much less, only 0.43 or 43% of the U.S. level. This gap can only be explained by a lower productivity level in Mexico. We infer that A in Mexico equals 0.43/0.69 = 0.63, or 63% of that in the United States.

This means that Mexico's production function and MPK curves are lower than those for the United States. This more accurate representation of reality is shown in Figure 17-7, panel (b). Mexico is not at point B, as we assumed in panel (a); it is at point C, on a different (lower) production function and a different (lower) MPK curve. The MPK gap between Mexico and the United States is much smaller, which greatly reduces the incentive for capital to migrate to Mexico from the United States.

The measured MPK differentials in the augmented model do not seem to indicate a major failure of global capital markets to allocate capital efficiently. But the augmented model has very different implications for convergence. Mexico would borrow only enough to move from point C to point D, where its MPK equals r^*. This investment would raise its output per worker a little, but it would still be far below that of the United States.

APPLICATION

A Versus k

In our previous calculations, we found that Mexico did not have a high level of MPK relative to the United States. Hence, we would not expect large flows of capital into Mexico but would expect Mexico to remain relatively poor even with access to global financial markets.

Is this conclusion true in general? What about other developing countries? Table 17-5 repeats the same exercise we just did for many developing countries, including Mexico. In all cases, predicted GDP gains due to financial globalization are large with the benchmark model, but disappointingly small once we augment the model to correct for productivity differences. Moreover, if we were to allow for the fact that gross national income (GNI) gains are less than GDP gains as a result of factor payments to foreign capital that would be due on foreign investment, then the net GNI gains would be smaller still.

This is a profound result. Once we allow for productivity differences, investment will not cause poor countries to reach the same level of capital per worker or output per worker as rich countries. Economists describe this outcome as one of long-run **divergence** between rich and poor countries. Unless poor countries can lift their levels of productivity (raise A), access to international financial markets is of limited use. They may be able to usefully borrow capital, thereby increasing output per worker by some amount, but there are not enough opportunities for productive investment for complete convergence to occur.

TABLE 17-5

Why Capital Doesn't Flow to Poor Countries The table shows data on output and capital per worker (columns 1 and 2). Column 3 shows the level of productivity relative to the United States that is implied by the data. Productivity differences are large for poor countries. If these differences are assumed away, then the gains from financial globalization in poor countries could be large (columns 4, 5). But if they remain, the gains will be small (columns 6, 7).

Country, Group, or Region	(a) Data $\dfrac{q}{q_{us}}$ (1)	(a) Data $\dfrac{k}{k_{us}}$ (2)	(b) Implied Productivity (U.S. = 1) $\dfrac{A}{A_{us}}$ (3)	(c) Outcomes with Financial Globalization — With U.S. Productivity Level, A_{us} Increase in: Capital k (4)	Output q (5)	With Actual Productivity, A Increase in: Capital k (6)	Output q (7)
Latin America							
Argentina	0.42	0.38	0.58	+163%	+139%	+15%	+5%
Brazil	0.32	0.24	0.51	+311	+214	+50	+15
Chile	0.26	0.26	0.41	+289	+280	+4	+1
Mexico	0.43	0.33	0.63	+207	+131	+53	+15
Asia							
China	0.06	0.05	0.17	+2,001	+1,569	+41	+12
India	0.09	0.04	0.24	+2,213	+1,064	+180	+41
Indonesia	0.11	0.09	0.24	+980	+805	+30	+9
Pakistan	0.13	0.04	0.37	+2,202	+679	+408	+72
Africa							
Congo	0.12	0.06	0.32	+1,677	+722	+218	+47
Kenya	0.06	0.03	0.18	+3,078	+1,674	+140	+34
Nigeria	0.05	0.04	0.14	+2,259	+1,970	+22	+7
South Africa	0.25	0.23	0.41	+334	+300	+13	+4
	Group Average			Based on Group Average			
Per Capita Income Quintiles							
1st (Poorest 20% of countries)	0.04	0.02	0.15	+5,371%	+2,474%	+210%	+46%
2nd (2nd Poorest 20%)	0.10	0.07	0.25	+1,426	+907	+86	+23
3rd (Middle 20%)	0.21	0.18	0.38	+463	+368	+32	+10
4th (2nd Richest 20%)	0.40	0.37	0.56	+167	+148	+12	+4
5th (Richest 20%)	0.75	0.85	0.80	+17	+32	−17	−6
Major Groups							
Developing	0.15	0.11	0.31	+836	+572	+65	+18
Emerging	0.29	0.23	0.48	+329	+241	+41	+12

Source: Robert E. Hall and Charles I. Jones, February 1999, "Why Do Some Countries Produce So Much More Output per Worker Than Others?" Quarterly Journal of Economics, 114(1), 83–116.

In the developing world, global capital markets typically are not failing. Rather, low levels of productivity A make investment unprofitable, leading to low output levels that do not produce convergence. But what exactly does A represent?

An older school of thought focused on A as reflecting a country's **technical efficiency,** construed narrowly as a function of its technology and management capabilities. Today, many economists believe there is very little blocking the flow of such knowledge between countries, and that the problem must instead be one of implementation. These economists believe that the level of A may primarily reflect a country's **social efficiency,** construed broadly to include institutions, public policies, and even cultural conditions such as the level of trust. Low productivity might then follow from low levels of human capital (poor education policies) or poor-quality institutions (bad governance, corruption, red tape, and poor provision of public goods including infrastructure). And indeed there is some evidence that, among poorer countries, more capital does tend to flow to the countries with better institutions.[19]

More Bad News? The augmented model shows that as long as productivity gaps remain, investment will be discouraged, and, regrettably, poor countries will not see their incomes converge to rich levels. If we now take some other factors into account, the predictions of the model about convergence are even less optimistic.

■ The model makes no allowance for risk premiums. Suppose the MPK is 10% in the United States and 13% in Mexico. The differential may be a risk premium Mexico must pay to foreign lenders that compensates them for the risk of investing in an emerging market (e.g., risks of regulatory changes, tax changes, expropriation, and other political risks). In this case, no additional capital flows into Mexico. In Figure 17-7, panel (b), Mexico stays at point C and its income does not increase at all.

■ Risk premiums may be large enough to cause capital to flow "uphill" from poor to rich. If world capital markets impose a risk premium higher than 3%, say, 7%, then capital would actually leave Mexico for the United States, moving from the higher to the lower MPK region, in search of a "safe haven" that provides higher risk-adjusted returns. In Figure 17-7, panel (b), Mexico would move left of point C as capital flowed out, and per capita output would fall. Is this a relevant case? Yes. Figure 17-8 shows that risk premiums can be substantial in emerging markets, including Mexico. And U.S. Treasury securities data indicate that from 1994 to 2006, U.S. holdings of Mexican assets rose from $50 billion to $65 billion, but Mexican holdings of U.S. assets rose from $5 billion to $95 billion; on net, capital moved north.

■ The model assumes that investment goods can be acquired at the same relative price in output terms everywhere. In fact, the model treats one unit of investment as the same as one unit of output. But in developing countries, it often costs much more than one unit of output to purchase one unit of capital goods. Poor countries often are ill-equipped to efficiently supply nontraded capital goods (such as buildings or bridges), and their imported capital goods (such as machinery and equipment) are often quite expensive because of trade costs (such as tariffs and transport costs).[20]

[19] James R. Lothian, April 2006, "Institutions, Capital Flows and Financial Integration," *Journal of International Money and Finance*, 25(3), 358–369; Laura Alfaro, Sebnem Kalemli-Ozcan, and Vadym Volosovych, 2008, "Why Doesn't Capital Flow from Rich to Poor Countries? An Empirical Investigation," *Review of Economics and Statistics*, 90(2), 347–368.
[20] Alan M. Taylor, 1998, "On the Costs of Inward-Looking Development: Price Distortions, Growth, and Divergence in Latin America," *Journal of Economic History*, 58(1), 1–28; Jonathan Eaton and Samuel Kortum, 2001, "Trade in Capital Goods," *European Economic Review*, 45(7), 1195–1235.

FIGURE 17-8

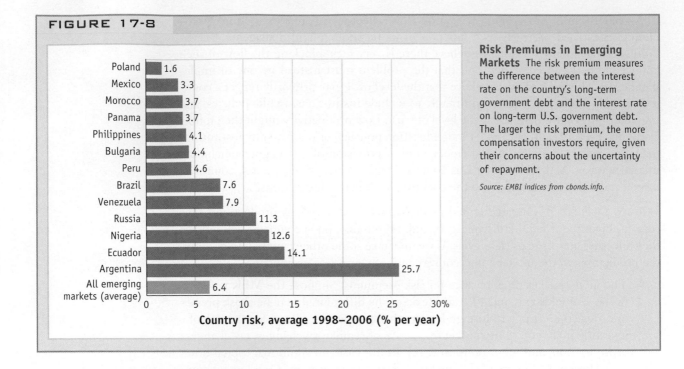

Country risk, average 1998–2006 (% per year)

Poland	1.6
Mexico	3.3
Morocco	3.7
Panama	3.7
Philippines	4.1
Bulgaria	4.4
Peru	4.6
Brazil	7.6
Venezuela	7.9
Russia	11.3
Nigeria	12.6
Ecuador	14.1
Argentina	25.7
All emerging markets (average)	6.4

Risk Premiums in Emerging Markets The risk premium measures the difference between the interest rate on the country's long-term government debt and the interest rate on long-term U.S. government debt. The larger the risk premium, the more compensation investors require, given their concerns about the uncertainty of repayment.

Source: EMBI indices from cbonds.info.

■ The model assumes that the contribution of capital to production is equal across countries. In our estimates, we used 1/3 as the elasticity of output with respect to capital. But recent research suggests that capital's share may be much lower in many developing countries, where a large part of GDP is derived from natural resources with little use of physical capital. This lowers the MPK even more.[21]

■ The model suggests that **foreign aid** may do no better than foreign investors in promoting growth. The model doesn't care where additional capital comes from. Investments paid for by transfers (aid or debt relief) rather than private investments face the same low MPK and the same divergence result holds. Economists dispute whether foreign aid can make a difference to long-term development and growth, or if it is only an act of charity to prop up the poor (or even a total waste of money). The argument also extends to nonmarket and preferential lending offered to poor countries by international financial institutions such as the **World Bank** (see **Side Bar: What Does the World Bank Do?**). In support of the case that aid can make a difference, aid proponents argue that aid can finance public goods that can provide externalities sufficient to jolt a poor country out of a bad equilibrium or "poverty trap"—goods that private markets cannot provide (such as infrastructure, public health, and education). Aid skeptics reply that the evidence for such effects is weak, either because the links are not there or because in practice aid is so bureaucratized and subject to so many diversions and misappropriations that very little of it actually gets spent wisely (see **Headlines: A Brief History of Foreign Aid**).

---

[21] Francesco Caselli and James Feyrer, 2007, "The Marginal Product of Capital," *Quarterly Journal of Economics*, 122(2), 535–568.

SIDE BAR

What Does the World Bank Do?

The World Bank (worldbank.org), based in Washington, D.C., is one of the Bretton Woods "twins" established in 1944 (the other is the International Monetary Fund). Its main arm, the International Bank for Reconstruction and Development, has 188 member countries. Its principal purpose is to provide financing and technical assistance to reduce poverty and promote sustained economic development in poor countries. A country's voting weight in the governance of the World Bank is based on the size of its capital contributions. The World Bank can raise funds at low interest rates and issue AAA-rated debt as good as that of any sovereign nation. It then lends to poor borrowers at low rates. Because the borrower nations could not obtain loans on these terms (or even any terms) elsewhere, the loans are a form of aid or transfer. In return for the preferential rate, the bank may approve a loan for a particular development purpose (building infrastructure, for example) or to support a policy reform package. Controversially, conditions may also be imposed on the borrowing nation, such as changes in trade or fiscal policy. As a result of sovereignty, the implementation of the conditions and the use of the loans have in some cases not turned out as intended, although outright default on these preferential loans is almost unheard of.

HEADLINES

A Brief History of Foreign Aid

Foreign aid is frequently on the political agenda. But can it make any difference?

In 1985, when Bob Geldof organized the rock spectacular Live Aid to fight poverty in Africa, he kept things simple. "Give us your fucking money" was his famous (if apocryphal) command to an affluent Western audience—words that embodied Geldof's conviction that charity alone could save Africa. He had no patience for complexity: we were rich, they were poor, let's fix it. As he once said to a luckless official in the Sudan, after seeing a starving person, "I'm not interested in the bloody system! Why has he no food?"

Whatever Live Aid accomplished, it did not save Africa. Twenty years later, most of the continent is still mired in poverty. So when, earlier this month, Geldof put together Live 8, another rock spectacular, the utopian rhetoric was ditched. In its place was talk about the sort of stuff that Geldof once despised—debt-cancellation schemes and the need for "accountability and transparency" on the part of African governments—and,

instead of fund-raising, a call for the leaders of the G-8 economies to step up their commitment to Africa. (In other words, don't give us your fucking money; get interested in the bloody system.) Even after the G-8 leaders agreed to double aid to Africa, the prevailing mood was one of cautious optimism rather than euphoria.

That did not matter to the many critics of foreign aid, who mounted a lively backlash against both Live 8 and the G-8 summit. For them, continuing to give money to Africa is simply "pouring billions more down the same old ratholes," as the columnist Max Boot put it. At best, these critics say, it's money wasted; at worst, it turns countries into aid junkies, clinging to the World Bank for their next fix. Instead of looking for help, African countries need to follow the so-called Asian Tigers (countries like South Korea and Taiwan), which overcame poverty by pursuing what Boot called "superior economic policies."

Skepticism about the usefulness of alms to the Third World is certainly in order. Billions of dollars have ended up in the pockets of kleptocratic rulers—in Zaire alone, Mobutu Sese Soko stole at least four billion—and still more has been misspent on massive infrastructure boondoggles, like the twelve-billion-dollar Yacyreta Dam, between Argentina and Paraguay, which Argentina's former President called "a monument to corruption." And historically there has been little correlation between aid and economic growth.

This checkered record notwithstanding, it's a myth that aid is doomed to failure. Foreign aid funded the campaign to eradicate smallpox, and in the sixties it brought the Green Revolution in agriculture to countries like India and Pakistan, lifting living standards and life expectancies for hundreds of millions of people. As for the Asian nations that Africa is being told to emulate, they may have pulled themselves up by their bootstraps, but at least they were provided with boots. In the postwar years, South Korea and Taiwan had the good fortune to become, effectively, client states of the U.S. Between 1946 and 1978, in fact, South Korea received nearly as much U.S. aid as the whole of Africa. Meanwhile, the billions that Taiwan got allowed it to fund a vast land-reform program and to eradicate malaria. And the U.S. gave the Asian Tigers more than money; it provided technical assistance and some military defense, and it offered preferential access to American markets.

Coincidence? Perhaps. But the two Middle Eastern countries that have shown relatively steady and substantial economic growth—Israel and Turkey—have also received tens of billions of dollars in U.S. aid. The few sub-Saharan African countries that have enjoyed any economic success at all of late—including Botswana, Mozambique, and Uganda—have been major aid recipients, as has

Costa Rica, which has the best economy in Central America. Ireland (which is often called the Celtic Tiger) has enjoyed sizable subsidies from the European Union. China was the World Bank's largest borrower for much of the past decade.

Nobody doubts that vast amounts of aid have been squandered, but there are reasons to think that we can improve on that record. In the first place, during the Cold War aid was more often a geopolitical tool than a well-considered economic strategy, so it's not surprising that much of the money was wasted. And we now understand that the kind of aid you give, and the policies of the countries you give it to, makes a real difference. A recent study by three scholars at the Center for Global Development found that, on average, foreign aid that was targeted at stimulating immediate economic growth (as opposed to, say, dealing with imminent crises) has had a significantly beneficial effect, even in Africa.

There's still a lot wrong with the way that foreign aid is administered. Too little attention is paid to figuring out which programs work and which don't, and aid still takes too little advantage of market mechanisms, which are essential to making improvements last. There's plenty we don't know about what makes one country succeed and another fail, and, as the former World Bank economist William Easterly points out, the foreign-aid establishment has often promised in the past that things would be different. So we should approach the problem of aid with humility. Yet humility is no excuse for paralysis. In 2002, President Bush created the Millennium Challenge Account, which is designed to target assistance to countries that adopt smart policies, and said that the U.S. would give five billion dollars in aid by 2006. Three years later, a grand total of $117,500 has been handed out. By all means, let's be tough-minded about aid. But let's not be hardheaded about it.

Source: James Surowiecki, "A Farewell to Alms?" New Yorker, July 25, 2005.

Some efforts are now being made to ensure more aid is directed toward countries with better institutional environments: the U.S. Millennium Challenge Corporation has pursued this goal, as has the World Bank. But past evidence is not encouraging: an exhaustive study of aid and growth by economists Raghuram Rajan and Arvind Subramanian concluded: "We find little robust evidence of a positive (or negative) relationship between aid inflows into a country and its economic growth. We also find no evidence that aid works better in better policy or geographical environments, or that certain forms of aid work better than others. Our findings suggest that for aid to be effective in the future, the aid apparatus will have to be rethought."[22] ■

4 Gains from Diversification of Risk

In the second section of this chapter, we studied consumption smoothing using a simplified model. We used a borrowing and lending approach, we considered a small open economy, we assumed that countries owned their own output, and we treated

[22] Raghuram G. Rajan and Arvind Subramanian, 2008, "Aid and Growth: What Does the Cross-Country Evidence Really Show?" *Review of Economics and Statistics*, 90(4), 643–665.

output shocks as given. We then saw how debt can be used to smooth the impact of output shocks on consumption. However, we also discussed the finding that in practice, countries seem to be unable to eliminate the effects of output volatility. The problems seem to be especially difficult in emerging markets and developing countries. We also saw that reliance on borrowing and lending may create problems because there may be limits to borrowing, risk premiums, and sudden stops in the availability of credit.

Are there other ways for a country to cope with shocks to output? Yes. In this final section, we show how **diversification,** another facet of financial globalization, can help smooth shocks by promoting risk sharing. With diversification, countries own not only the income stream from their own capital stock, but also income streams from capital stocks located in other countries. We see how, by using financial openness to trade such rights—for example, in the form of capital equity claims like stocks and shares—countries may be able to reduce the volatility of their incomes (and hence their consumption levels) without *any* net lending or borrowing whatsoever.

Diversification: A Numerical Example and Generalization

To keep things simple and to permit us to focus on diversification, we assume there is no borrowing (the current account is zero at all times). To illustrate the gains from diversification, we examine the special case of a world with two countries, A and B, which are identical except that their respective outputs fluctuate asymmetrically, that is, they suffer equal and opposite shocks.

We now explore how this world economy performs in response to the output shocks. We examine the special case in which there are two possible "states of the world," which are assumed to occur with an equal probability of 50%. In terms of output levels, state 1 is a bad state for A and a good state for B; state 2 is a good state for A and a bad state for B.

We assume that all output is consumed, and that there is no investment or government spending. As we know from the previous chapter, output is distributed to factors in the form of income. We assume output is divided 60–40 between labor income and capital income in each country. The key question for us is who owns this income: domestic residents or foreigners?

Home Portfolios To begin, both countries are closed, and households in each country own the entire capital stock of their own country. Thus, A owns 100% of A's capital, and B owns 100% of B's capital. Under these assumptions, output (as measured by gross domestic product, GDP) is the same as income (as measured by gross national income, GNI) in A and B.

A numerical example is given in Table 17-6, panel (a). In state 1, A's output is 90, of which 54 units are payments to labor and 36 units are payments to capital; in state 2, A's output rises to 110, and factor payments rise to 66 for labor and 44 units for capital. The opposite is true in B: in state 1, B's output is higher than it is in state 2. Using our national accounting definitions, we know that in each closed economy, consumption C, income GNI, and output GDP are equal. In both A and B, all of these quantities are volatile. GNI, and hence consumption, flips randomly between 90 and 110 in both countries. The variation of GNI about its mean of 100 is plus or minus 10 in each country. Because households prefer smooth consumption, this variation is undesirable.

World Portfolios Notice that when one country's capital income is up, the other's is down. World GDP equals world GNI and is always 200. World labor income is always 120 and world capital income is always 80.

TABLE 17-6

Portfolio Diversification Choices: Diversifiable Risks In countries A and B, GDP is allocated 60% to labor income and 40% to capital income. There are two "states of the world": state 1 is bad for A and good for B; state 2 is the opposite. On average, GDP equals 100, but in the good state, GDP is 110, and in the bad state it is only 90. Thus, world GDP and GNI always equal 200, world labor income is always 120, and world capital income is always 80. When each country holds only its own assets as in panel (a), GNI equals GDP and is very volatile. When each country holds a 50% share of the world portfolio as in panel (b), GNI volatility decreases because capital income is now smoothed. When each country holds a portfolio made up only of the other country's capital as in panel (c), GNI volatility falls even further by making capital income vary inversely with labor income.

(a) When Countries Hold 100% Home Portfolios
Each Country Owns 100% of Its Own Capital

	COUNTRY A			COUNTRY B			WORLD		
	Capital Income	Labor Income	GDP = GNI	Capital Income	Labor Income	GDP = GNI	Capital Income	Labor Income	GDP = GNI
State 1	36	54	90	44	66	110	80	120	200
State 2	44	66	110	36	54	90	80	120	200
Variation about mean	∓4	∓6	∓10	±4	±6	±10	0	0	0

(b) When Countries Hold World Portfolios
Each Country Owns 50% A Capital and 50% B Capital with Payoffs as in Panel (a)

	COUNTRY A			COUNTRY B			WORLD		
	Capital Income	Labor Income	GDP = GNI	Capital Income	Labor Income	GDP = GNI	Capital Income	Labor Income	GDP = GNI
State 1	40	54	94	40	66	106	80	120	200
State 2	40	66	106	40	54	94	80	120	200
Variation about mean	0	∓6	∓6	0	±6	±6	0	0	0

(c) When Countries Hold 100% Foreign Portfolios
Each Country Owns 100% of the Other Country's Capital with Payoffs as in Panel (a)

	COUNTRY A			COUNTRY B			WORLD		
	Capital Income	Labor Income	GDP = GNI	Capital Income	Labor Income	GDP = GNI	Capital Income	Labor Income	GDP = GNI
State 1	44	54	98	36	66	102	80	120	200
State 2	36	66	102	44	54	98	80	120	200
Variation about mean	±4	∓6	∓2	∓4	±6	±2	0	0	0

It is apparent from Figure 17-9 that the two countries can achieve partial income smoothing if they diversify their portfolios of capital assets. For example, each country could own half of the domestic capital stock, and half of the other country's capital stock. Indeed, this is what standard portfolio theory says that investors should try to do. The results of this portfolio diversification are shown in Table 17-6, panel (b).

FIGURE 17-9

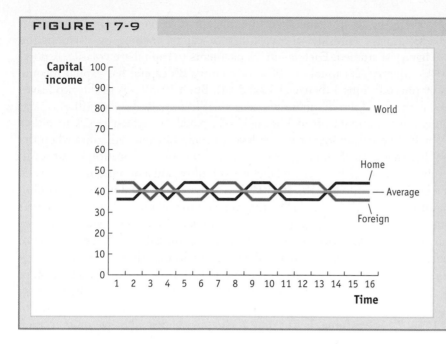

Portfolio Diversification and Capital Income: Diversifiable Risks The figure shows fluctuations in capital income over time for different portfolios, based on the data in Table 17-6. Countries trade claims to capital income by trading capital assets. When countries hold the world portfolio, they each earn a 50–50 split (or average) of world capital income. World capital income is constant if shocks in the two countries are asymmetrical and cancel out. All capital income risk is then fully diversifiable.

Now each country owns one-half of its own capital stock but sells the other half to the other country in exchange for half of the other country's capital stock.[23] Each country's output or GDP is still as it was described in panel (a). But now country incomes or GNI can differ from their outputs or GDP. Owning 50% of the world portfolio means that each country has a capital income of 40 every period. However, labor income still varies between 54 and 66 in the bad and good states, so total income (and hence consumption) varies between 94 and 106. Thus, as Table 17-6, panel (b), shows, capital income for each country is smoothed at 40 units, the average of A and B capital income in panel (a), as also illustrated in Figure 17-9.

How does the balance of payments work when countries hold the world portfolio? Consider country A. In state 1 (bad for A, good for B), A's income or GNI exceeds A's output, GDP, by 4 (94 − 90 = +4). Where does the extra income come from? The extra is net factor income from abroad of +4. Why is it +4? This is precisely equal to the difference between the income earned on A's external assets (50% of B's payments to capital of 44 = 22) and the income paid on A's external liabilities (50% of A's payments to capital of 36 = 18). What does A do with that net factor income? A runs a trade balance of −4, which means that A can consume 94, even when its output is only 90. Adding the trade balance of −4 to net factor income from abroad of +4 means that the current account is 0, and there is still no need for any net borrowing or lending, as assumed. These flows are reversed in state 2 (which is good for A, bad for B).

Note that after diversification, income or GNI varies in A and B by plus or minus 6 (around a mean of 100), which is less than the range of plus or minus 10 seen in Table 17-6, panel (a). This is because 40% of income is capital income and so 40% of the A income fluctuation of 10 can be smoothed by the portfolio diversification.

---

[23] Note that this financial transaction would balance in the financial account, as a pure asset trade, so no borrowing or lending is needed and the current account remains zero, as we have assumed.

Generalizing Let us try to generalize the concept of capital income smoothing through diversification. Consider the volatility of capital income by itself, in the example we have just studied. Each country's payments to capital are volatile. A portfolio of 100% country A's capital or 100% of country B's capital has capital income that varies by plus or minus 4 (between 36 and 44). But a 50–50 mix of the two leaves the investor with a portfolio of minimum, zero volatility (it always pays 40).

This outcome is summed up in Figure 17-10, panel (a), which refers to either country, A or B. There is an identical high level of capital income volatility when the country holds either a 100% home portfolio or a 100% foreign portfolio. However, holding a mix of the two reduces capital income volatility, and a minimum volatility of zero can be achieved by holding the 50–50 mix of the world capital income portfolio.

To generalize this result to the real world, we need to recognize that not all shocks are asymmetric as we have assumed here. The outputs of countries A and B may not be equal and opposite (with correlation −1) as we have assumed here. In general, there will be some common shocks, which are identical shocks experienced by both countries. The impact of common shocks cannot be lessened or eliminated by any form of asset trade. For example, suppose we add an additional shock determined by two new states of the world, X and Y (these states of the world are independent of states of the world 1 and 2). We assume that in state X, the new shock adds five units to each

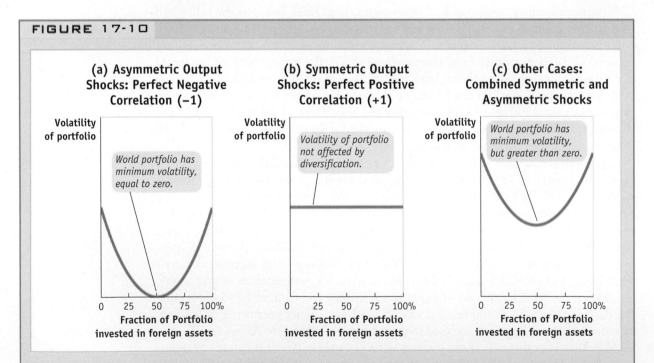

FIGURE 17-10

(a) Asymmetric Output Shocks: Perfect Negative Correlation (−1)

Volatility of portfolio

World portfolio has minimum volatility, equal to zero.

0   25   50   75   100%

Fraction of Portfolio invested in foreign assets

(b) Symmetric Output Shocks: Perfect Positive Correlation (+1)

Volatility of portfolio

Volatility of portfolio not affected by diversification.

0   25   50   75   100%

Fraction of Portfolio invested in foreign assets

(c) Other Cases: Combined Symmetric and Asymmetric Shocks

Volatility of portfolio

World portfolio has minimum volatility, but greater than zero.

0   25   50   75   100%

Fraction of Portfolio invested in foreign assets

Return Correlations and Gains from Diversification The charts plot the volatility of capital income against the share of the portfolio devoted to foreign capital. The two countries are identical in size and experience shocks of similar amplitude. In panel (a), shocks are perfectly asymmetric (correlation = −1), capital income in the two countries is perfectly *negatively* correlated. Risk can be eliminated by holding the world portfolio, and there are large gains from diversification. In panel (b), shocks are perfectly symmetric (correlation = +1), capital income in the two countries is perfectly *positively* correlated. Risk cannot be reduced, and there are no gains from diversification. In panel (c), when both types of shock are present, the correlation is neither perfectly negative nor positive. Risk can be partially eliminated by holding the world portfolio, and there are still some gains from diversification.

country's output; in state Y, it subtracts five units from each. There is no way to avoid this shock by portfolio diversification. The X-Y shocks in each country are perfectly positively correlated (correlation +1). If this were the only shock, the countries' outputs would move up and down together and diversification would be pointless. This situation is shown in Figure 17-10, panel (b).

In the real world, any one country experiences some shocks that are correlated with those of other countries, either positively or negatively, and some that are uncorrelated. As long as some shocks are asymmetric, or country specific, and not common between the home and foreign country, then the two countries can take advantage of gains from the diversification of risk. In this more general case in which symmetric and asymmetric shocks are combined, as depicted in Figure 17-10, panel (c), holding a 100% portfolio of domestic (or foreign) assets generates a volatile income. But holding the 50–50 world portfolio will lower the volatility of income, albeit not all the way to zero (see the appendix at the end of the chapter for a detailed discussion).

Limits to Diversification: Capital Versus Labor Income As we saw in Table 17-6, panel (b), elimination of total income risk cannot be achieved by holding the world portfolio, even in the case of purely asymmetric shocks of capital assets. Why? Because labor income risk is not being shared. Admittedly, the same theory would apply if one could trade labor like an asset, but this is impossible because ownership rights to labor cannot be legally traded in the same way as one can trade capital or other property (that would be slavery).

Although it is true that labor income risk (and hence GDP risk) may not be diversifiable through the trading of claims to labor assets or GDP, this is not quite the end of our story—in theory at least. We saw in Table 17-6, panel (a), that capital and labor income in each country are perfectly correlated in this example: a good state raises both capital and labor income, and a bad state lowers both. This is not implausible—in reality, shocks to production do tend to raise and lower incomes of capital and labor simultaneously. This means that, as a risk-sharing device, trading claims to capital income can substitute for trading claims to labor income.

To illustrate this, imagine an unrealistic scenario in which the residents of each country own no capital stock in their own country but own the entire capital stock of the other country. As shown in Table 17-6, panel (c), owning only the other country's portfolio achieves more risk sharing than holding 50% of the world portfolio.

For example, when A is in the good state (state 2), A's labor income is 66 but A's capital income is 36 (assumed now to be 100% from B, which is in the bad state). This adds up to a portfolio of 102. In the bad state for A (state 2), A's labor income is 54, but A's capital income is 44 (from B, which is in a good state), for a total GNI of 98. So A's income (and consumption) vary by plus or minus 2, between 98 and 102 in panel (c). Compare this fluctuation of ±2 around the mean of 100 to the fluctuations of ±10 (home portfolio) and ±6 (the world portfolio) in panels (a) and (b).

You can see how additional risk reduction has been achieved. A would like to own claims to 50% of B's total income. It could achieve this by owning 50% of B's capital and 50% of B's labor. But labor can't be owned, so A tries to get around the restriction of owning 0% of B's labor by acquiring much more than 50% of B's capital. Because labor's share of income in both countries is more than half in this example—a realistic ratio—this strategy allows for the elimination of some, but not all, risk.

APPLICATION

The Home Bias Puzzle

So much for theory. In practice, we do not observe countries owning foreign-biased portfolios or even the world portfolio. Countries tend to own portfolios that suffer from a strong **home bias**, a tendency of investors to devote a disproportionate fraction of their wealth to assets from their own home country, when a more globally diversified portfolio might protect them better from risk.

To illustrate this, economist Karen Lewis compared the risk and return for sample portfolios from which U.S. investors could have chosen for the period 1970 to 1996. She imagined an experiment in which some assets are allocated to a domestic portfolio (the S&P 500) and the remainder to an overseas portfolio (Morgan Stanley's EAFE fund). In this stylized problem, the question is what weight to put on each portfolio, when the weights must sum to 100%. In reality, U.S. investors picked a weight of about 8% on foreign assets. Was this a smart choice?

Figure 17-11 shows the risk and return for every possible weight between 0% and 100%. Return is measured by the mean rate of return (annualized percent per year); risk is measured by the standard deviation of the return (its root mean square deviation from its mean).

With regard to returns, the foreign portfolio had a slightly higher average return than the home portfolio during this period, so increasing the weight in the foreign

FIGURE 17-11

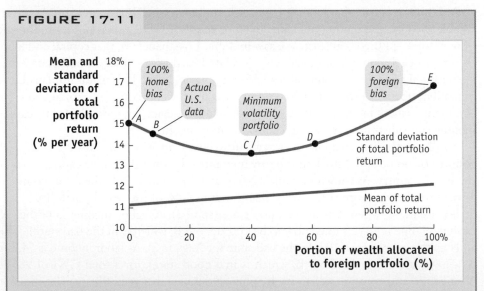

Portfolio Diversification in the United States The figure shows the return (mean of monthly return) and risk (standard deviation of monthly return) for a hypothetical portfolio made up from a mix of a pure home U.S. portfolio (the S&P 500) and a pure foreign portfolio (the Morgan Stanley EAFE) using data from the period 1970 to 1996. U.S. investors with a 0% weight on the overseas portfolio (point A) could have raised that weight as high as 39% (point C) and still raised the return and lowered risk. Even moving to the right of C (toward D) would make sense, though how far would depend on how the investor viewed the risk-return trade-off. The actual weight seen was extremely low at just 8% (point B) and was considered a puzzle.

Source: Karen K. Lewis, 1999, "Trying to Explain Home Bias in Equities and Consumption," Journal of Economic Literature, 37(2), 571–608.

portfolio would have increased the returns: the mean return line slopes up slightly from left to right. What about risk? A 100% foreign portfolio (point E) would have generated higher risk than the home U.S. portfolio (point A); thus, E is above A. However, we know that some mix of the two portfolios ought to produce a lower volatility than either extreme because the two returns are not perfectly correlated. This minimum volatility will not be zero because there are some undiversifiable, symmetric shocks, but it will be lower than the volatility of the 100% home and 100% foreign portfolios: overseas and domestic returns are not perfectly correlated, implying that substantial country-specific diversifiable risks exist.

In fact, Lewis showed that a U.S. investor with a 0% weight on the overseas portfolio (point A) could have raised that weight to as much as 39% (point C), while simultaneously raising the average of her total return and lowering its risk. Even moving to the right of C (toward D) would make sense, though how far would depend on how the investor viewed the risk-return trade-off. Choosing a weight as low as 8% (point B) would seem to be a puzzle.

Broadly speaking, economists have had one of two reactions to the emergence of the "home bias puzzle" in the 1990s. One is to propose many different theories to explain it away: Perhaps it is costly to acquire foreign assets, or get information about them? Perhaps there are asymmetries between home and foreign countries' consumption patterns (due to nontraded goods or trade frictions or even tastes) that make domestic assets a better hedge against domestic consumption risk? Perhaps home investors worry about regulatory barriers and the problems of corporate governance in foreign markets? These and many other solutions have been tried in extremely complex economic models, but none has been judged a complete success.

The other reaction of economists has been to look at the evidence of home bias in the period from the 1970s to the 1990s (the period of the Lewis study) as a legacy of the pronounced deglobalization of financial markets in the postwar period that might slowly disappear. Recent evidence suggests that this might be happening to some degree. There has been a dramatic increase in overseas equity investments in the last 40 years, with a very strong upward trend after 1985 in IMF data. For example, in the United States, the foreign share of the U.S. equity portfolio had risen to 12% by 2001 and 28% in 2010. Over the same period, the U.K. portfolio saw its foreign equity share rise from 28% to 50%. Figure 17-12 shows the massive extent of cross-border holdings of assets in today's global economy. Furthermore, these figures might understate the true extent to which residents have diversified away from home capital because many large multinational firms have capital income streams that flow from operations in many countries. For example, an American purchasing a share of Intel or Ford, or a Briton purchasing a share of BP, or a Japanese person purchasing a share of Sony, is really purchasing shares of income streams from the globally diversified operations of these companies. Technically, Intel is recorded in the data as a 100% U.S. "home" stock, but this makes the home bias puzzle look much worse than it really is because investors do seem to invest heavily in firms such as these that provide an indirect foreign exposure.[24]

---

[24] On trends in home bias since 2001 see Christopher B. Philips, Francis M. Kinniry, Jr., and Scott J. Donaldson, 2012, "The Role of Home Bias in Global Asset Allocation Decisions," Vanguard Research. On the impact of multinationals see Fang Cai and Francis E. Warnock, 2006, "International Diversification at Home and Abroad," NBER Working Paper No. 12220.

FIGURE 17-12

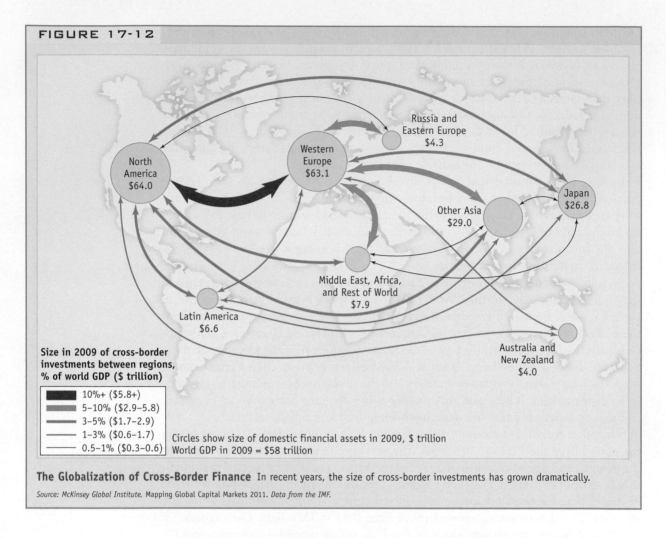

Size in 2009 of cross-border investments between regions, % of world GDP ($ trillion)

▬▬	10%+ ($5.8+)
▬▬	5–10% ($2.9–5.8)
──	3–5% ($1.7–2.9)
──	1–3% ($0.6–1.7)
──	0.5–1% ($0.3–0.6)

Circles show size of domestic financial assets in 2009, $ trillion
World GDP in 2009 = $58 trillion

The Globalization of Cross-Border Finance In recent years, the size of cross-border investments has grown dramatically.

Source: McKinsey Global Institute, Mapping Global Capital Markets 2011. *Data from the IMF.*

Recent trends in diversification within portfolios and within companies may mean that even if the puzzle cannot be explained away, perhaps it will gradually go away. ■

Summary: Don't Put All Your Eggs in One Basket

If countries were able to borrow and lend without limit or restrictions in an efficient global capital market, our discussions of consumption smoothing and efficient investment would seem to suggest that they should be able to cope quite well with the array of possible shocks, in order to smooth consumption. In reality, as the evidence shows, countries are not able to fully exploit the intertemporal borrowing mechanism.

In this environment, diversification of income risk through the international trading of assets can deliver substantial benefits. In theory, if countries were able to pool their income streams and take shares from that common pool of income, all country-specific shocks would be averaged out, leaving countries exposed only to common global shocks to income, the sole remaining undiversifiable shocks that cannot be avoided.

Financial openness allows countries—like households—to follow the old adage "Don't put all your eggs in one basket." The lesson here has a simple household analogy. Think of a self-employed person who owns a ski shop. If the only capital she owns is her own business capital, then her capital income and labor income move together, and go up in good times (winter) and down in bad times (summer). Her total income could be smoothed if she sold some stock in her company and used the proceeds to buy stock in another company that faced asymmetric shocks (a surf shop, perhaps).

In practice, however, risk sharing through asset trade is limited. For one thing, the number of assets is limited. The market for claims to capital income is incomplete because not all capital assets are traded (e.g., many firms are privately held and are not listed on stock markets), and trade in labor assets is legally prohibited. Moreover, even with the traded assets available, investors have shown very little inclination to invest their wealth outside their own country, although that may be slowly changing in an environment of ongoing financial globalization.

5 Conclusions

If a firm or household were to retreat from the national financial markets by keeping its money in a bag in a closet and paying cash for all its purchases (house, cars, appliances, toothpaste, gum, etc.), we would regard it as a strange and potentially costly move. By allowing households to save and borrow, financial markets help households smooth consumption in the face of shocks to their income (such as a debilitating illness, the loss of a job, destruction of property by floods or other acts of nature). Likewise, financial markets allow firms to borrow to invest efficiently in productive projects and permit investors to diversify their portfolios across a wide range of assets.

On the global scale, the same principles apply in theory to countries, subject to the long-run budget constraint. They, too, face income shocks, new investment opportunities, and country-specific risks. We have seen how they can similarly benefit from access to an external capital market—the global capital market.

Theory proves to be far from reality, however: the extent to which countries make use of global financial markets is still limited. Even in the most financially open advanced countries, consumption shocks remain, investment is often financed out of domestic saving, and a home bias persists in investors' portfolios. In poorer countries, we see no consumption smoothing gains realized, and there is little scope for development based on external finance until current low productivity levels are improved.

Are global capital markets failing? To the criticism that financial globalization doesn't work, one could respond that it hasn't really been fully tried yet. Many emerging markets and most developing countries are still on the road to full financial liberalization, and large barriers remain. Even so, deeper institutional weaknesses in these countries may hinder the efficient operation of the mechanisms we have studied. One could argue that such weaknesses may be corrected or diminished by the stimulus to competition, transparency, accountability, and stability that financial openness may provide.[25] But without further institutional improvements, the benefits of financial globalization are likely to be much smaller for these countries, and any benefits must be weighed against potential offsetting costs, such as the risk of crises, which we discuss in later chapters.

---

[25] M. Ayhan Kose, Eswar Prasad, Kenneth S. Rogoff, and Shang-Jin Wei, 2006, "Financial Globalization: A Reappraisal," NBER Working Paper No. 12484.

KEY POINTS

1. Countries can use their external wealth as a buffer to smooth consumption in the face of fluctuations in output or investment. However, this process is not without its limits. The country must service its debts and must not allow debts to roll over and grow without limit at the real rate of interest.

2. The condition that guarantees that debts are serviced is the long-run budget constraint, or LRBC: the present value of future trade deficits must equal minus the present value of initial wealth.

3. The long-run budget constraint can be put another way: the present value of *GDP* plus the present value of initial wealth (the country's resources) must equal the present value of *GNE* (the country's spending).

4. In a closed economy, the country must satisfy *TB* = 0 in every period as there is no external trade in goods or assets. In an open economy, the economy has to satisfy only the long-run budget constraint, which states that *TB* equals minus the present value of initial wealth. The former is a tighter constraint than the latter—implying that there can be gains from financial globalization.

5. The current account may be lower than normal in any period when there is unusually high private or public consumption (such as during a war), unusually low output (such as occurs after a natural disaster), or unusually high investment (such as that following a natural resource discovery).

6. If poor countries had the same productivity as rich countries, there would be substantial gains from investing in poor countries where the marginal product of capital, or MPK, would be much higher. However, this is not the case, and there is little evidence of investment inefficiency at the global level as measured by MPK gaps between countries. What gaps there are may be due to risk premiums. Consequently, large-scale investment (and foreign aid) in poor countries may not accelerate economic growth.

7. In addition to lending and borrowing, a country can reduce its risk by the international diversification of income claims. In practice, only capital income claims (capital assets) are tradable. Labor is not a tradable asset.

8. When assets are traded internationally, two countries can eliminate the income risk arising from country-specific or idiosyncratic shocks; such risk is called diversifiable risk. However, they can do nothing to eliminate the global risk, the shock common to both countries, called undiversifiable risk.

9. In practice, the use of the current account as a buffer and the extent of diversification fall far short of theory's prediction even in advanced countries. Consumption volatility persists, domestic investment is mostly financed from domestic saving, and portfolios display pronounced home bias.

10. In emerging markets and developing countries, financial openness has progressed more slowly and access to global capital markets is more limited and often on worse terms. The gains from financial openness appear weaker, and there is the downside risk of sudden stops and other crises. For gains to be realized, countries may require deeper institutional changes and further liberalization.

KEY TERMS

PROBLEMS

1. Using the notation from the text, answer the following questions. You may assume that net labor income from abroad is zero, there are no capital gains on external wealth, and there are no unilateral transfers.

   a. Express the change in external wealth (ΔW_0) at the end of period 0 as a function of the economy's trade balance (TB), the real interest rate (a constant r^*), and initial external wealth (W_{-1}).

   b. Using (a), write an expression for the stock of external wealth at the end of period 0 (W_0). This should be written as a function of the economy's trade balance (TB_0), the real interest rate, and initial external wealth (W_{-1}).

   c. Using (a) and (b), write an expression for the stock of external wealth at the end of period 1 (W_1). This should be written as a function of the economy's trade balance (TB) each period, the real interest rate, and initial external wealth (W_{-1}).

   d. Using your answers from (a), (b), and (c), write an expression for the stock of external wealth at the end of period 2 (W_2). This should be written as a function of the economy's trade balance (TB) each period, the real interest rate, and initial external wealth (W_{-1}).

   e. Suppose we require that W_2 equal zero. Write down the condition that the three trade balances (in periods 0, 1, and 2) must satisfy. Arrange the terms in present value form.

2. Using the assumptions and answers from the previous question, complete the following:

   a. Write an expression for the *future value* of the stock of external wealth in period N (W_N). This should be written as a function of the economy's trade balance (TB) each period, the real interest rate r^*, and initial external wealth.

   b. Using the answer from (a), write an expression for the *present value* of the stock of external wealth in period N (W_N).

   c. The "no Ponzi game" conditions force the present value of W_N to tend to zero as N

gets large. Explain why this implies that the economy's initial external wealth is equal to the present value of future trade deficits.

   d. How would the expressions in parts (a) and (b) change if the economy had net labor income (positive or negative) to/from abroad or net unilateral transfers? Explain briefly.

3. *In this question, assume all dollar units are real dollars in billions, so, for example, $150 means $150 billion.* It is year 0. Argentina thinks it can find $150 of domestic investment projects with an *MPK* of 10% (each $1 invested pays off $0.10 in every later year). Argentina invests $84 in year 0 by borrowing $84 from the rest of the world at a world real interest rate r^* of 5%. There is no further borrowing or investment after this.

   Use the standard assumptions: Assume initial external wealth W (W in year −1) is 0. Assume $G = 0$ always; and assume $I = 0$ except in year 0. Also, assume $NUT = KA = 0$ and that there is no net labor income so $NFIA = r^*W$.

   The projects start to pay off in year 1 and continue to pay off all years thereafter. Interest is paid in perpetuity, in year 1 and every year thereafter. In addition, assume that if the projects are *not* done, then $GDP = Q = C = \$200$ in all years, so that $PV(Q) = PV(C) = 200 + 200/0.05 = 4,200$.

   a. Should Argentina fund the $84 worth of projects? Explain your answer.

   b. Why might Argentina be able to borrow only $84 and not $150?

   c. From this point forward, assume the projects totaling $84 are funded and completed in year 0. If the MPK is 10%, what is the total payoff from the projects in future years?

   d. Assume this is added to the $200 of GDP in all years starting in year 1. In dollars, what is Argentina's $Q = GDP$ in year 0, year 1, and later years?

   e. At year 0, what is the new $PV(Q)$ in dollars? *Hint:* To ease computation, calculate the value of the increment in $PV(Q)$ due to the extra output in later years.

f. At year 0, what is the new $PV(I)$ in dollars? Therefore, what does the LRBC say is the new $PV(C)$ in dollars?

g. Assume that Argentina is consumption smoothing. What is the percent change in $PV(C)$? What is the new level of C in all years? Is Argentina better off?

h. For the year the projects go ahead, year 0, explain Argentina's balance of payments as follows: state the levels of CA, TB, $NFIA$, and FA.

i. What happens in later years? State the levels of CA, TB, $NFIA$, and FA in year 1 and every later year.

4. Continuing from the previous question, we now consider Argentina's external wealth position.

a. What is Argentina's external wealth W in year 0 and later? Suppose Argentina has a one-year debt (i.e., not a perpetual loan) that must be rolled over every year. After a few years, in year N, the world interest rate rises to 15%. Can Argentina stick to its original plan? What are the interest payments due on the debt if $r^* = 15\%$? If $I = G = 0$, what must Argentina do to meet those payments?

b. Suppose Argentina decides to unilaterally default on its debt. Why might Argentina do this? State the levels of CA, TB, $NFIA$, and FA in year N and all subsequent years. What happens to the Argentine level of C in this case?

c. When the default occurs, what is the change in Argentina's external wealth W? What happens to the rest of the world's external wealth?

d. External wealth data for Argentina and Rest of the World are recorded in the account known as the net international investment position. Is this change in wealth recorded as a financial flow, a price effect, or an exchange rate effect?

5. Using production function and MPK diagrams, answer the following questions. For simplicity, assume there are two countries: a poor country (with low living standards) and a rich country (with high living standards).

a. Assuming that poor and rich countries have the same production function, illustrate how the poor country will converge with the rich country. Describe how this mechanism works.

b. In the data, countries with low living standards have capital-to-worker ratios that are too high to be consistent with the model used in (a). Describe and illustrate how we can modify the model used in (a) to be consistent with the data.

c. Given your assumptions from (b), what does this suggest about the ability of poor countries to converge with rich countries? What do we expect to happen to the gap between rich and poor countries over time? Explain.

Using the model from (b), explain and illustrate how convergence works in the following cases.

d. The poor country has a marginal product of capital that is higher than that of the rich country.

e. The marginal products in each country are equal. Then, the poor country experiences an increase in human capital through government funding of education.

f. The marginal products in each country are equal. Then, the poor country experiences political instability such that investors require a risk premium to invest in the poor country.

6. Assume that Brazil and the United States have different production functions $q = f(k)$, where q is output per worker and k is capital per worker. Let $q = Ak^{1/3}$. You are told that relative to the U.S. = 1, Brazil has an output per worker of 0.32 and capital per worker of 0.24. Can A be the same in Brazil as in the United States? If not, compute the level of A for Brazil. What is Brazil's MPK relative to the United States?

7. Use production function and MPK diagrams to examine Turkey and the EU. Assume that Turkey and the EU have different production functions $q = f(k)$, where q is output per worker and k is capital per worker. Let $q = Ak^{1/3}$. Assume that the productivity level A in Turkey is lower than that in the EU.

a. Draw a production function diagram (with output per worker y as a function of capital per worker k) and MPK diagram (MPK versus k) for the EU. (*Hint:* Be sure to draw the two diagrams with the production function directly above the MPK diagram so that the level of capital per worker k is consistent on your two diagrams.)

b. For now, assume capital cannot flow freely in and out of Turkey. On the same diagrams, plot Turkish production function and MPK curves, assuming that the productivity level A in Turkey is half the EU level and that Turkish MPK exceeds EU MPK. Label the EU position in each chart EU and the Turkish position *T1*.

c. Assume capital can now flow freely between Turkey and the EU and the rest of the world, and that the EU is already at the point where $MPK = r^*$. Label r^* on the vertical axis of the MPK diagram. Assume no risk premium. What will Turkey's capital per worker level k be? Label this outcome point *T2* in each diagram. Will Turkey converge to the EU level of q? Explain.

8. This question continues from the previous problem, focusing on how risk premiums explain the gaps in living standards across countries.

a. Investors worry about the rule of law in Turkey and also about the potential for hyperinflation and other bad macroeconomic policies. Because of these worries, the initial gap between MPK in Turkey and r^* is a risk premium *RP*. Label *RP* on the vertical axis of the MPK diagram. Now where does Turkey end up in terms of k and q?

b. In light of (a), why might Turkey be keen to join the EU?

c. Some EU countries are keen to exclude Turkey from the EU. What might be the *economic* arguments for that position?

9. In this chapter, we saw that financial market integration is necessary for countries to smooth consumption through borrowing and lending. Consider two economies: those of the Czech Republic and France. For each of the following shocks, explain how and to what extent each country can trade capital to better smooth consumption.

a. The Czech Republic and France each experience an EU-wide recession.

b. A strike in France leads to a reduction in French income.

c. Floods destroy a portion of the Czech capital stock, lowering Czech income.

10. Assume that a country produces an output Q of 50 every year. The world interest rate is 10%. Consumption C is 50 every year, and $I = G = 0$. There is an unexpected drop in output in year 0, so output falls to 39 and is then expected to return to 50 in every future year. If the country desires to smooth consumption, how much should it borrow in period 0? What will the new level of consumption be from then on?

11. Assume that a country produces an output Q of 50 every year. The world interest rate is 10%. Consumption C is 50 every year, and $I = G = 0$. There is an unexpected war in year 0, which costs 11 units and is predicted to last one year. If the country desires to smooth consumption, how much should it borrow in period 0? What will the new level of consumption be from then on?

The country wakes up in year 1 and discovers that the war is still going on and will eat up another 11 units of expenditure in year 1. If the country still desires to smooth consumption looking forward from year 1, how much should it borrow in period 1? What will the new level of consumption be from then on?

12. Consider a world of two countries: Highland (H) and Lowland (L). Each country has an average output of 9 and desires to smooth consumption. All income takes the form of capital income and is fully consumed each period.

a. Initially, there are two states of the world: Pestilence (P) and Flood (F). Each happens with 50% probability. Pestilence affects Highland and lowers the output there to 8, leaving Lowland unaffected with an output of 10. Flood affects Lowland and lowers the output there to 8, leaving Highland unaffected with an output of 10. Devise a table with two rows corresponding to each state (rows marked P and F). In three columns, show income to three portfolios: the portfolio of 100% H capital, the portfolio of

100% L capital, and the portfolio of 50% H + 50% L capital.

b. Two more states of world appear: Armageddon (A) and Utopia (U). Each happens with 50% probability but is uncorrelated with the P–F state. Armageddon affects both countries equally and lowers income in each country by a further four units, whatever the P–F state. Utopia leaves each country unaffected. Devise a table with four rows corresponding to each state (rows marked PA, PU, FA, and FU). In three columns, show income to three portfolios: the portfolio of 100% H capital, the portfolio of 100% L capital, and the portfolio of 50% H + 50% L capital.

Compare your answers to parts (a) and (b), and consider the optimal portfolio choices. Does diversification eliminate consumption risk in each case? Explain.

N E T W O R K

1. Go the BEA website (bea.gov). Find the latest annual balance of payments data for the United States.

   a. Compute income earned on (1) external assets and (2) income paid on external liabilities.

   b. Find the latest net international investment position data for the United States. Compute (3) external assets and (4) external liabilities for the end of the prior year.

   c. Divide (1) by (3) and then divide (2) by (4) to find the implied rates of interest on external assets and liabilities. Is the United States still privileged?

2. To learn more about the aid debate, download some of the conflicting arguments made by two prominent figures: Jeffrey Sachs and William Easterly (search: sachs easterly). See, for example, their "Foreign Aid Face Off" in the *Los Angeles Times* (latimes.com, April 30, 2006, and May 7, 2006). See also Nicholas Kristof, "Aid: Can It Work?" *New York Review of Books*, October 5, 2006. After weighing all these arguments, do you feel more or less optimistic about what aid can achieve?

APPENDIX TO CHAPTER 17

. . . .

Common Versus Idiosyncratic Shocks

In reality, home and foreign incomes will not have a perfect inverse correlation as we have assumed in the text. Let us generalize a bit more for our two countries, and focus on capital income.

A More General Case Suppose the shocks to capital income are a and b, for countries A and B, respectively, and that these take a random value each period. The common shock is the *average shock* in the two countries: $\frac{1}{2}(a + b)$. In the chapter, we assumed the average shock was zero, so the shocks were equal and opposite. In the real world, however, this need not be the case.

We can define the A-specific shock as the shock a minus the average shock: $a - \frac{1}{2}(a + b) = \frac{1}{2}(a - b)$. Similarly, the B-specific shock is b minus the average shock: $b - \frac{1}{2}(a + b) = \frac{1}{2}(b - a)$. These *idiosyncratic shocks* are nonzero as long as the A shock is not the same as the B shock, that is, as long as a is not equal to b.

By doing this algebraic manipulation, the A shock can be written as the common shock plus the A-specific shock:

$$a = \underbrace{\frac{1}{2}(a + b)}_{\text{Common shock}} + \underbrace{\frac{1}{2}(a - b)}_{\text{A-specific shock}}$$

Similarly, the B shock can be written as the common shock plus the B-specific shock:

$$b = \underbrace{\frac{1}{2}(a + b)}_{\text{Common shock}} + \underbrace{\frac{1}{2}(b - a)}_{\text{B-specific shock}}$$

We see that the country-specific shocks are the exact opposites of each other: $\frac{1}{2}(a - b)$ and $\frac{1}{2}(b - a)$. The good news is that country-specific shocks are a *diversifiable* risk and satisfy the conditions of the simple case examined in the chapter. So the income risk they generate can be eliminated by diversification: in the world portfolio, the country-specific shocks cancel out, as we can see by adding up the last two equations.

But the common shock is $\frac{1}{2}(a + b)$. As long as this is nonzero, these shocks matter, that is, as long as the shocks are not equal and opposite, pure asymmetric country-specific shocks. The bad news is, the global shocks are an *undiversifiable* risk—no matter which assets you own, you get hit with the global shock, so asset trade offers no escape from these risks.

Numerical Example Figure 17-A1 (an extension of Figure 17-9) provides an illustration of the partial reduction in risk that can be achieved in this case. In Figure 17-9, each country owned 50% of the world portfolio. Thus, capital incomes in each state were as follows: in state 1, A = 36, B = 44; in state 2, A = 44, B = 36. The occurrence of states 1 and 2 was random with 50–50 odds. If A and B diversified by each holding 50% of the world portfolio, they had stable capital income of 40 every period.

In Figure 17-A1, we add an extra "global" shock, which has two states, X and Y, that occur at random with 50-50 odds. However, the random X-Y shock is *independent*

FIGURE 17-A1

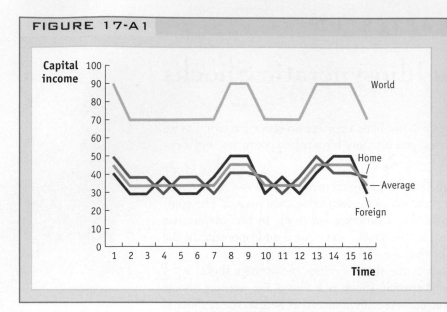

Portfolio Diversification and Capital Income: Undiversifiable Risks We take the example from Table 17-6 and Figure 17-9, and we add a common "global" shock to each country. With probability 50%, each country experiences a five-unit increase in capital income, and with probability 50% experiences a five-unit decrease in capital income. Holding half of the world portfolio reduces *but does not eliminate* capital income risk entirely because the global shock is an undiversifiable risk for the world as a whole.

of the 1-2 shock. We suppose that when the global shock is in state X, both countries receive an extra five units of capital income. When the global shock is in state Y, both countries receive five units less of capital income.

There are now four possible states of the world: 1X, 1Y, 2X, and 2Y. Each has a 25% chance of occurring. For the four states, the capital incomes of the portfolios are as follows:

1X	Home = 41	Foreign = 49	World = 90	Average = 45
2X	Home = 49	Foreign = 41	World = 90	Average = 45
1Y	Home = 31	Foreign = 39	World = 70	Average = 35
2Y	Home = 39	Foreign = 31	World = 70	Average = 35

From this table, and the example shown in Figure 17-A1, we see, as expected, that in this world, holding half of the world portfolio eliminates the risk associated with fluctuations between states 1 and 2. The best that each country can do is to have an income that fluctuates between 45 (half of 90, state X) and 35 (half of 70, state Y). In state X, all income risk associated with states 1 and 2 is gone. And in state Y, all income risk associated with states 1 and 2 is gone. But nothing can be done to eliminate the risk associated with fluctuations between states X and Y.

This more general result does not overturn our basic findings. Holding a 100% home portfolio generates a volatile capital income. So does holding a 100% foreign portfolio. Holding a mix of the two lowers the volatility of capital income, at least when some of the shocks are country-specific shocks, which is always the case in the real world.

18

Balance of Payments II: Output, Exchange Rates, and Macroeconomic Policies in the Short Run

If demand shifts from the products of country B to the products of country A, a depreciation by country B or an appreciation by country A would correct the external imbalance and also relieve unemployment in country B and restrain inflation in country A. This is the most favorable case for flexible exchange rates based on national currencies.

Robert Mundell, 1961

It is easy to understand the dislike . . . for a [fixed exchange rate] system which dictated that a slump must be aggravated by monetary reactions, although, doubtless, [people] had forgotten that the same system served to enhance booms.

Alec Ford, 1962

In the wake of the 2008 Global Financial Crisis, exchange rates have been fluctuating a great deal, and not surprisingly they have once again risen to global prominence in economic, financial, and political debates. In late 2010, the Brazilian finance minister Guido Mantega seemed to invoke the ghosts of the 1930s when he spoke of a new "currency war" as the Brazilian real appreciated; in early 2013, the head of the Deutsche Bundesbank Jens Weidmann used the same term as the euro gained strength. Over the same postcrisis period, however, other central bankers, such as the Chairman of the Federal Reserve Ben Bernanke and the Governor of the Bank of England Mervyn King, managed to display much less anxiety about their currency movements, as the values of the dollar and the pound slipped. Why were the Brazilian and the German economists so fretful? Why were their American and British counterparts so relaxed? Their attitudes reflect the idea that the exchange rate matters for the economy as a whole.

Thus far our study of exchange rates has been largely disconnected from real activity and the rest of the economy. Chapters 13 through 15 developed a theory of exchange rates, in which the economy's level of output was taken as given. To gain a more complete understanding of how an open economy works, we now extend our theory and explore what happens when exchange rates and output fluctuate in the short run. To do this, we build on the accounting framework we learned in the balance of payments chapter to understand how macroeconomic aggregates (including output, income, consumption, investment, and the trade balance) move together and in response to shocks in an open economy.

The model we study is an open-economy variant of the well-known IS-LM model that is widely used in the study of closed-economy macroeconomics. The key assumption of this type of Keynesian model is that prices are "sticky" in the short run so that output is determined by shifts in demand in the goods market. When we are finished, we will have a model that explains the relationships among all the major macroeconomic variables in an open economy in the short run.

Such a model can shed light on many policy issues. We can see how monetary and fiscal policies affect the economy, and discuss how they can be used to stabilize the economy and maintain full employment. One key lesson we learn in this chapter is that the feasibility and effectiveness of macroeconomic policies depend crucially on the type of exchange rate regime in operation.

1 Demand in the Open Economy

To understand macroeconomic fluctuations, we need to grasp how short-run disturbances affect three important markets in an economy: the goods market, the money market, and the foreign exchange (forex) market. In earlier chapters, we studied the forex market and the money market, so we will recap and apply here what we learned in those chapters. But what about the goods market? In the forex chapters, we assumed that output was fixed at a level $\overline{Y}$. We took this to be the full-employment level of output that would be expected to prevail in the long run, when all factor market prices have adjusted to ensure that all factors such as labor and capital are employed. *But these assumptions about output and employment are valid only in the long run.* To understand short-run fluctuations in economic activity, we now develop a short-run, sticky-price Keynesian model and show how fluctuations in demand can create fluctuations in real economic activity. To start building this model, we first make our assumptions clear and then look at how demand is defined and why it fluctuates.

Preliminaries and Assumptions

Our interest in this chapter is to study short-run fluctuations in a simplified, abstract world of two countries. Our main focus is on the home economy. We use an asterisk to denote foreign variables when we need them. For our purposes, the foreign economy can be thought of as the rest of the world. The key assumptions we make are as follows:

- Because we are examining the short run, we assume that home and foreign price levels, $\overline{P}$ and $\overline{P}^*$, are fixed due to price stickiness. As a result of price stickiness, expected inflation is fixed at zero, $\overline{\pi}^e = 0$. If prices are fixed, all quantities can be viewed as both real and nominal quantities in the short run because there is no inflation.

- We assume that government spending $\overline{G}$ and taxes $\overline{T}$ are fixed at some constant levels, which are subject to policy change.

- We assume that conditions in the foreign economy such as foreign output $\overline{Y}^*$ and the foreign interest rate $\overline{i}^*$ are fixed and taken as given. Our main interest is in the equilibrium and fluctuations in the home economy.

■ We assume that income Y is equivalent to output: that is, gross domestic product (GDP) equals gross national disposable income (GNDI). From our study of the national accounts, we know that the difference between the two equals net factor income from abroad plus net unilateral transfers. The analysis in this chapter could easily be extended to include these additional sources of income, but this added complexity would not offer any additional significant insights. We further assume that net factor income from abroad (NFIA) and net unilateral transfers (NUT) are zero, which implies that the current account (CA) equals the trade balance (TB); for the rest of this chapter, we shall just refer to the trade balance.

Our main objective is to understand how output (income) is determined in the home economy in the short run. As we learned from the national accounts, total expenditure or demand for home-produced goods and services is made up of four components: consumption, investment, government consumption, and the trade balance. In the following section, we see how each component is determined in the short run, and use the fact that demand must equal supply to characterize the economy's short-run equilibrium.

Consumption

The simplest model of aggregate private consumption relates household **consumption** C to **disposable income** Y^d. As we learned in Chapter 16, disposable income is the level of total pretax income Y received by households minus the taxes paid by households $\overline{T}$, so that $Y^d = Y - \overline{T}$. Consumers tend to consume more as their disposable income rises, a relationship that can be represented by an increasing function, called the *consumption function:*

$$\text{Consumption} = C = C(Y - \overline{T})$$

A typical consumption function of this form is graphed in Figure 18-1; it slopes upward because consumption increases when disposable income increases.

This equation is known as the *Keynesian consumption function.* In some economic theories, consumption smoothing is both desirable and possible. That is, in any given year consumption need not depend on income in that year, but rather on total lifetime resources (wealth). In contrast, the Keynesian consumption function assumes

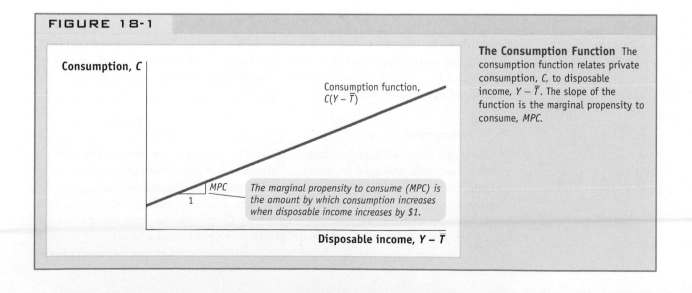

FIGURE 18-1

The Consumption Function The consumption function relates private consumption, C, to disposable income, $Y - \overline{T}$. The slope of the function is the marginal propensity to consume, MPC.

Consumption, C

Consumption function, $C(Y - \overline{T})$

MPC

1

The marginal propensity to consume (MPC) is the amount by which consumption increases when disposable income increases by $1.

Disposable income, $Y - \overline{T}$

that private consumption expenditure *is* sensitive to changes in current income. This assumption seems to be a more reasonable match with reality in the short run: research shows that there is not very much consumption smoothing at the household or national level.

Marginal Effects The consumption function relates the level of consumption to the level of disposable income, but we are more often interested in the response of such variables to small changes in equilibrium, due to policy shocks or other shocks. For that purpose, the slope of the consumption function is called the **marginal propensity to consume (MPC),** and it tells us how much of every extra $1 of disposable income received by households is spent on consumption. We generally assume that *MPC* is between 0 and 1: when consumers receive an extra unit of disposable income (whether it's a euro, dollar, or yen), they will consume only part of it and save the remainder. For example, if you spend $0.75 of every extra $1 of disposable income you receive, your *MPC* is 0.75. The *marginal propensity to save (MPS)* is 1 – *MPC*. In this example *MPS* = 0.25, meaning that $0.25 of every extra $1 of disposable income is saved.

Investment

The simplest model of aggregate investment makes two key assumptions: firms can choose from many possible investment projects, each of which earns a different real return; and a firm will invest capital in a project only if the real returns exceed the firm's cost of borrowing capital. The firm's borrowing cost is the **expected real interest rate** r^e, which equals the nominal interest rate i minus the expected rate of inflation π^e: $r^e = i - \pi^e$. It is important to note that, in general, the expected real interest rate depends not only on the nominal interest rate but also on expected inflation. However, under our simplifying assumption that expected inflation is zero, the expected real interest rate equals the nominal interest rate, $r^e = i$.

When the expected real interest rate in the economy falls, we expect more investment projects to be undertaken. For example, at a real interest rate of 10%, there may be only $1 billion worth of profitable investment projects that firms wish to undertake; but if the real interest rate falls to 5%, there may now be $2 billion worth of profitable projects. Hence, our model assumes that investment I is a decreasing function of the real interest rate; that is, investment falls as the real interest rate rises.

$$\text{Investment} = I = I(i)$$

Remember that this is true only because when expected inflation is zero, the real interest rate equals the nominal interest rate. Figure 18-2 shows a typical investment function of this type. It slopes downward because as the real interest rate falls, the quantity of investment rises.

The Government

To develop a basic model of economic activity in the short run, we assume that the government's role is simple. It collects an amount T of **taxes** from private households and spends an amount G on **government consumption** of goods and services.

Note that the latter includes only actual spending on goods and services bought by the public sector at all levels. For example, G includes military equipment and personnel, transport and infrastructure, public universities and schools, and so forth. Excluded from this concept are the often huge sums involved in government **transfer**

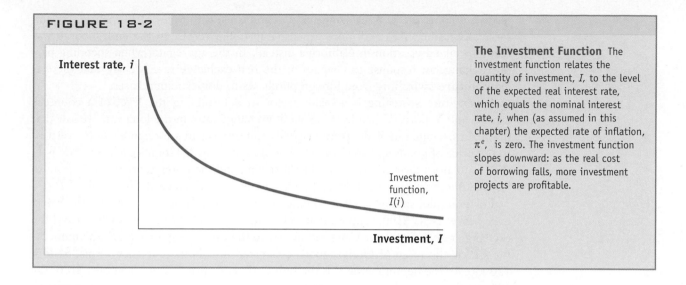

FIGURE 18-2

The Investment Function The investment function relates the quantity of investment, I, to the level of the expected real interest rate, which equals the nominal interest rate, i, when (as assumed in this chapter) the expected rate of inflation, π^e, is zero. The investment function slopes downward: as the real cost of borrowing falls, more investment projects are profitable.

programs, such as social security, medical care, or unemployment benefit systems, that redistribute income between households. Such transfers are excluded because we assume that *in the aggregate* they do not generate any change in the total expenditure on goods and services; they merely change who gets to engage in the act of spending. (Transfers are like negative taxes and, as such, can be seen as a part of T.)

In the unlikely event that $G = T$ exactly, government spending exactly equals taxes and we say that the government has a *balanced budget*. If $T > G$, the government is said to be running a *budget surplus* (of size $T - G$); if $G > T$, a *budget deficit* (of size $G - T$ or, equivalently, a negative surplus of $T - G$).

Fiscal policy is concerned with the levels of taxes T and spending G set by the government. In this chapter, we do not study in detail why or how governments make such policy choices; we make the simple assumption that in the short run the levels of taxes and spending are set exogenously at some fixed levels, denoted by an overbar:

$$\text{Government purchases} = G = \overline{G}$$
$$\text{Taxes} = T = \overline{T}$$

Policy makers may change these levels of taxes and spending at any time. We analyze the impact of such changes on the economy later in this chapter.

The Trade Balance

In the balance of payments chapter, we saw from an accounting standpoint that the trade balance (equal to exports minus imports) measures the impact of foreign trade on the demand for domestic output. To develop a model, however, we need to know what drives these flows, so in our simple model we now explore three key determinants of the trade balance: the real exchange rate, the level of home income, and the level of foreign income.

The Role of the Real Exchange Rate What is the role of the real exchange rate? Recall George, the American tourist we met at the start of our study of exchange rates, who had to deal with a weaker dollar during his visits to Paris over the course of several years. If U.S. and French prices are sticky (constant in euro and U.S. dollar terms), then as the U.S. exchange rate depreciates, the prices of French goods and services became more and more expensive in dollar terms. In the end, George was ready to take a vacation in California instead. In the aggregate, when spending patterns change in response to changes in the real exchange rate, we say that there is **expenditure switching** from foreign purchases to domestic purchases.

Expenditure switching is a major factor in determining the level of a country's exports and imports. When learning about exchange rates in the long run, we saw that the real exchange rate is the price of goods and services in a foreign economy relative to the price of goods and services in the home economy. If Home's exchange rate is E, the Home price level is $\overline{P}$ (fixed in the short run), and the Foreign price level is $\overline{P}^*$ (also fixed in the short run), then the real exchange rate q of Home is defined as $q = E\overline{P}^*/\overline{P}$.

For example, suppose that the home country is the United States, and the reference basket costs $100; suppose that in Canada the same basket costs C$120 and the exchange rate is $0.90 per Canadian dollar. In the expression $q = E\overline{P}^*/\overline{P}$, the numerator $E\overline{P}^*$ is the price of foreign goods converted into home currency terms, $108 = 120 \times 0.90$; the denominator $\overline{P}$ is the home currency price of home goods, $100; the ratio of the two is the real exchange rate, $q = \$108/\$100 = 1.08$. This is the relative price of foreign goods in terms of home goods. In this case, Canadian goods are more expensive than U.S. goods.

A rise in the home real exchange rate (a real depreciation) signifies that foreign goods have become more expensive relative to home goods. As the real exchange rate rises, both home and foreign consumers will respond by *expenditure switching*: the home country will import less (as *home* consumers switch to buying home goods) and export more (as *foreign* consumers switch to buying home goods). These concepts are often seen in economic debates and news coverage (see **Headlines: Oh! What a Lovely Currency War** and **Headlines: The Curry Trade**) and they provide us with the following insight:

■ *We expect the trade balance of the home country to be an increasing function of the home country's real exchange rate. That is, as the home country's real exchange rate rises (depreciates), it will export more and import less, and the trade balance rises.*

The Role of Income Levels The other determinant of the trade balance we might wish to consider is the income level in each country. As we argued earlier in our discussion of the consumption function, when domestic disposable income increases, consumers tend to spend more on all forms of consumption, including consumption of foreign goods. These arguments provide a second insight:

■ *We expect an increase in home income to be associated with an increase in home imports and a fall in the home country's trade balance.*

Symmetrically, from the rest of the world's standpoint, an increase in rest of the world income ought to be associated with an increase in rest of the world spending on home goods, resulting in an increase in home exports. This is our third insight:

■ *We expect an increase in rest of the world income to be associated with an increase in home exports and a rise in the home country's trade balance.*

Combining the three insights above, we can write the trade balance as a function of three variables: the real exchange rate, home disposable income, and rest of the world disposable income:

$$TB = TB(\underbrace{E\overline{P}^*/\overline{P}}_{\substack{\text{Increasing} \\ \text{function}}}, \underbrace{Y - \overline{T}}_{\substack{\text{Decreasing} \\ \text{function}}}, \underbrace{Y^* - \overline{T}^*}_{\substack{\text{Increasing} \\ \text{function}}})$$

HEADLINES

Oh! What a Lovely Currency War

In September 2010, the finance minister of Brazil accused other countries of starting a "currency war" by pursuing policies that made Brazil's currency, the real, strengthen against its trading partners, thus harming the competitiveness of his country's exports and pushing Brazil's trade balance toward deficit. By 2013 fears about such policies were being expressed by more and more policymakers around the globe.

"Devaluing a currency," one senior Federal Reserve official once told me, "is like peeing in bed. It feels good at first, but pretty soon it becomes a real mess."

In recent times, foreign-exchange incontinence appears to have been the policy of choice in capitals from Beijing to Washington, via Tokyo. The resulting mess has led to warnings of a global "currency war" that could spiral into protectionism.

The roll call of forex Cassandras reads like a who's who of global finance and politics: German leader Angela Merkel, Federal Reserve Bank of St. Louis President James Bullard, Bundesbank President Jens Weidmann and Mervyn King, the outgoing governor of the Bank of England. And the list goes on. . .

Currency wars have been a staple of modern finance ever since the collapse of the Bretton Woods system of fixed exchange rates in the early 1970s. As Marc Chandler, global head of currency strategy at Brown Brothers Harriman & Co., says: "Most governments believe that their currencies are too important to be left to the markets." So policy makers have often tried to manipulate the value of their currencies by intervening in the markets.

In recent years, China stands out as the country that has done the most to keep its currency weak in order to boost exports. But it isn't alone. China's efforts have sparked what Fred Bergsten, senior fellow at the Peterson Institute for International Economics, calls "emulation and retaliation."

At their worst, these periodic crosscurrents of intervention have led to "beggarthy-neighbor" policies—self-defeating attempts to improve one country's economy at the expense of everybody else's. . . .

As developed countries like Japan and the U.S. try to kick-start their sluggish economies with ultralow interest rates and binges of money-printing, they are putting downward pressure on their currencies. The loose monetary policies are primarily aimed at stimulating domestic demand. But their effects spill over into the currency world.

Since the end of November, when it became clear that Shinzo Abe and his agenda of growth-at-all-costs would win Japan's elections, the yen has lost more than 10% against the dollar and some 15% against the euro.

These moves are angering export-driven countries such as Brazil and South Korea. But they also are stirring the pot in Europe. The euro zone has largely sat out this round of monetary stimulus and now finds itself in the invidious position of having a contracting economy and a rising currency—making Thursday's meeting of the European Central Bank a must-watch event.

The dirty secret is that using monetary policy to weaken a currency, whether voluntarily or not, is a shortcut to avoid unpopular decisions on fiscal and budgetary issues.

Breakdowns of the global foreign-exchange system have occurred with drastic regularity, but that doesn't mean this currency war will end in tears.

For a start, common sense could prevail, putting an end to the dangerous game of beggar (and blame) thy neighbor. After all, the International Monetary Fund was set up to prevent such races to the bottom, and should try to broker a truce among forex combatants.

If that sounds naive, consider the possibility that this huge bout of monetary stimulus will succeed in engendering a solid recovery driven by domestic demand. Or that fiscal policy will finally be put to work.

Either outcome would take away a big incentive for competitive devaluations and prompt governments to bolster their currencies to avoid stoking inflation.

Growth cures a lot of ills. Even forex incontinence.

Figure 18-3 shows the relationship between the trade balance and the real exchange rate for the home country, all else equal—that is, holding home and foreign disposable income fixed. The trade balance is an *increasing* function of the real exchange rate $E\overline{P}^*/\overline{P}$. Thus, the relationship shown in Figure 18-3 is upward sloping. The reason is that an increase in the real exchange rate (a real depreciation) increases *TB* by raising exports and lowering imports, implying a movement along the curve drawn.

HEADLINES

The Curry Trade

In 2009, a dramatic weakening of the pound against the euro sparked an unlikely boom in cross-Channel grocery deliveries.

If carrying coals to Newcastle is judged a pointless exercise, then importing croissants, baguettes and bottles of claret into France might seem even more absurd. But, due to the strength of the euro against the pound, hundreds of Britons living in France are now using the internet to order their food, including many French specialties, from British supermarkets.

Simon Goodenough, the director of Sterling Shopping, a delivery firm based in Brackley, Northamptonshire, says his company has 2,500 British customers in France and is running five delivery vans full of food to France each week.

"We deliver food from Waitrose, Sainsbury's and Marks and Spencer, but by far the biggest is Asda," said Goodenough ". . . We sit in our depot sometimes looking at the things people have bought and just laugh at the crazi-

ness of it all. We have seen croissants and baguettes in people's shopping bags. And we have delivered bottles of Bergerac wine bought from Sainsbury's to a customer in Bergerac. We even have a few French customers who have now heard about what we do. They love things like curries and tacos, which they just can't get in France.". . .

Goodenough said many of his company's British customers hold pensions or savings in sterling rather than euros: "They have seen a 30% drop in their spending power over the past 18 months."

John Steventon owns La Maison Removals, a delivery company based in Rayleigh, Essex. It takes food from its warehouse to about 1,000 British customers in central France.

"We just can't cope with demand at the moment," he said. . . . "We found

that friends in France were asking us to bring over British food for them so we just thought it made sense to set up a food delivery service. . . . The savings for buying food, in particular, are amazing due to the strength of the euro. Customers tell us that for every £100 they would spend in France buying food, they save £30 buying through us, even with our 15% commission. A lot of people are using us to get things they really miss, such as bacon and sausages."

Nikki Bundy, 41, has lived near Périgueux in the Dordogne with her family for four years. . . . "It's just so much cheaper for us to buy our food this way. . . . The food in France is lovely, but you can come out of a supermarket here with just two carrier bags having spent €100. I still try and buy my fresh fruit and veg in France, but most other things I now buy from Asda."

Source: Excerpted from Leo Hickman, "Expat Orders for British Supermarket Food Surge on Strength of euro," The Guardian, June 9, 2010. Copyright Guardian News & Media Ltd 2010.

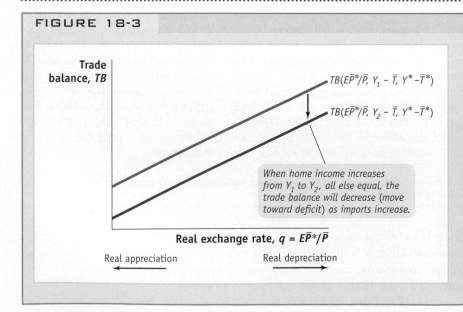

FIGURE 18-3

Trade balance, *TB*

$TB(E\bar{P}^*/\bar{P},\ Y_1 - \bar{T},\ Y^* - \bar{T}^*)$

$TB(E\bar{P}^*/\bar{P},\ Y_2 - \bar{T},\ Y^* - \bar{T}^*)$

When home income increases from Y_1 to Y_2, all else equal, the trade balance will decrease (move toward deficit) as imports increase.

Real exchange rate, $q = E\bar{P}^*/\bar{P}$

Real appreciation ←   → Real depreciation

The Trade Balance and the Real Exchange Rate The trade balance is an increasing function of the real exchange rate, $E\bar{P}^*/\bar{P}$. When there is a real depreciation (a rise in q), foreign goods become more expensive relative to home goods, and we expect the trade balance to increase as exports rise and imports fall (a rise in TB). The trade balance may also depend on income. If home income levels rise, then some of the increase in income may be spent on the consumption of imports. For example, if home income rises from Y_1 to Y_2, then the trade balance will decrease, whatever the level of the real exchange rate, and the trade balance function will shift down.

The effect of the real exchange rate on the trade balance is now clear. What about the effects of changes in output? Figure 18-3 also shows the impact of an increase in home output on the trade balance. At any level of the real exchange rate, an increase in home output leads to more spending on imports, lowering the trade balance. This change would be represented as a downward shift in the trade balance curve, that is, a reduction in TB for a given level of $q = E\overline{P}^*/\overline{P}$.

Marginal Effects Once More The impact of changes in output on the trade balance can also be thought of in terms of the marginal propensity to consume. Suppose home output (which equals home income, because of the assumptions we've made) rises by an amount $\Delta Y = \$1$ and that, all else equal, this leads to an increase in home imports of $\Delta IM = \$MPC_F$, where $MPC_F > 0$. We refer to MPC_F as the *marginal propensity to consume foreign imports*. For example, if $MPC_F = 0.1$, this means that out of every additional $1 of income, $0.10 are spent on imports.

How does MPC_F relate to the MPC seen earlier? After a $1 rise in income, any additional goods consumed have to come from somewhere, home or abroad. The fraction $\$MPC$ of the additional $1 spent on all consumption must equal the sum of the incremental spending on home goods plus incremental spending on foreign goods. Let $MPC_H > 0$ be the *marginal propensity to consume home goods*. By assumption, $MPC = MPC_H + MPC_F$. For example, if $MPC_F = 0.10$ and $MPC_H = 0.65$, then $MPC = 0.75$; for every extra dollar of disposable income, home consumers spend 75 cents—10 cents on imported foreign goods and 65 cents on home goods—and they save 25 cents.[1]

APPLICATION

The Trade Balance and the Real Exchange Rate

Our theory assumes that the trade balance increases when the real exchange rate rises. Is there evidence to support this proposition? In Figure 18-4, we examine the evolution of the U.S. trade balance (as a share of GDP) in recent years as compared with the U.S. real exchange rate with the rest of the world.

By considering the home country to be the United States and the foreign "country" to be the rest of the world, we cannot use data on the *bilateral* real exchange rate q for any individual foreign country. We need a composite or weighted-average measure of the price of goods in all foreign countries relative to the price of U.S. goods. To accomplish this, economists construct *multilateral* measures of real exchange rate movement.

The most common weighting scheme uses a weight equal to that country's share in the home country's trade. If there are N foreign countries, we can write home's total trade as the sum of its trade with each foreign country: $\text{Trade} = \text{Trade}_1 + \text{Trade}_2 + \cdots + \text{Trade}_N$. Applying a trade weight to each bilateral real exchange rate's percentage change, we obtain the percentage change in home's multilateral real exchange rate or **real effective exchange rate**:

$$\underbrace{\frac{\Delta q_{\text{effective}}}{q_{\text{effective}}}}_{\substack{\text{Real effective exchange} \\ \text{rate change (in \%)}}} = \underbrace{\left(\frac{\text{Trade}_1}{\text{Trade}}\frac{\Delta q_1}{q_1}\right) + \left(\frac{\text{Trade}_2}{\text{Trade}}\frac{\Delta q_2}{q_2}\right) + \cdots + \left(\frac{\text{Trade}_N}{\text{Trade}}\frac{\Delta q_N}{q_N}\right)}_{\text{Trade-weighted average of bilateral real exchange rate changes (in \%)}}$$

---

[1] A similar calculation can be applied to the export function, where exports will depend on the marginal propensity to consume imports in the foreign country.

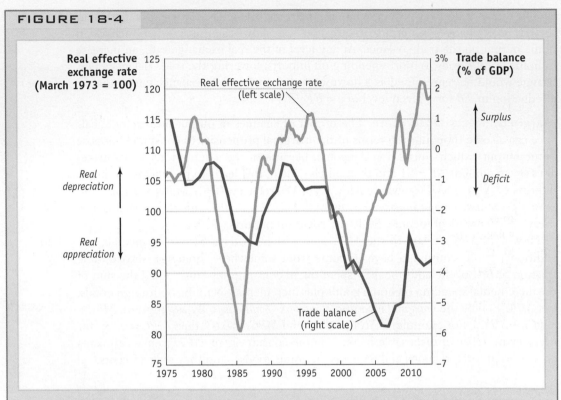

FIGURE 18-4

The Real Exchange Rate and the Trade Balance: United States, 1975–2012 Does the real exchange rate affect the trade balance in the way we have assumed? The data show that the U.S. trade balance is correlated with the U.S. real effective exchange rate index. Because the trade balance also depends on changes in U.S. and rest of the world disposable income (and other factors), and because it may respond with a lag to changes in the real exchange rate, the correlation is not perfect (as seen in the years 2002–07 when the United States had a spending boom).

Source: Federal Reserve Economic Data *(FRED)*.

For example, if we trade 40% with country 1 and 60% with country 2, and we have a real appreciation of 10% against 1 but a real depreciation of 30% against 2, then the change in our real effective exchange rate is $(40\% \times -10\%) + (60\% \times 30\%) = (0.4 \times -0.1) + (0.6 \times 0.3) = -0.04 + 0.18 = 0.14 = +14\%$. That is, we have experienced an effective trade-weighted real depreciation of 14%.

Figure 18-4 shows that the U.S. multilateral real exchange rate and the U.S. trade balance have been mostly positively correlated, as predicted by our model. In periods when the United States has experienced a real depreciation, the U.S. trade balance has tended to increase. Conversely, real appreciations have usually been associated with a fall in the trade balance. However, the correlation between the real exchange rate and the trade balance is not perfect. There appears to be lag between, say, a real depreciation and a rise in the trade balance (as in the mid-1980s). Why? Import and export flows may react only slowly or weakly to changes in the real exchange rate, so the trade balance can react in unexpected ways (see **Side Bar: Barriers to Expenditure Switching: Pass-Through and J Curve**). We can also see that the trade balance and real exchange rate did not move together as much during the years 2000 to 2008 because other factors, such as tax cuts and wartime spending, may have created extra deficit pressures that spilled over into the U.S. current account during this period. ■

SIDE BAR

Barriers to Expenditure Switching: Pass-Through and the J Curve

The basic analysis of expenditure switching in the text assumes two key mechanisms. First, we assume that a nominal depreciation causes a real depreciation and raises the price of foreign imports relative to home exports. Second, we assume that such a change in relative prices will lower imports, raise exports, and increase the trade balance. In reality, there are reasons why both mechanisms operate weakly or with a lag.

Trade Dollarization, Distribution, and Pass-Through

One assumption we made was that prices are sticky in local currency. But what if some *home* goods prices are set in *foreign* currency?

For example, let the foreign country be the United States and suppose a share d of the home-produced basket of goods is priced in U.S. dollars at a sticky *dollar* price $\overline{P}_1$. Suppose that the remaining share, $1 - d$, is priced, as before, in local currency at a sticky *local currency* price $\overline{P}_2$. Hence,

$$\left.\begin{array}{l}\text{Price of foreign goods}\\\text{relative to dollar-priced}\\\text{home goods}\end{array}\right\} = \frac{E \times \overline{P}^*}{E \times \overline{P}_1} = \frac{\overline{P}^*}{\overline{P}_1} \text{ has a weight} = d$$

$$\left.\begin{array}{l}\text{Price of foreign goods}\\\text{relative to local-currency-}\\\text{priced home goods}\end{array}\right\} = \frac{E \times \overline{P}^*}{\overline{P}_2} \text{ has a weight} = 1 - d$$

In this setup, what is the price of all foreign-produced goods relative to all home-produced goods (the real exchange rate)? It is the weighted sum of the relative prices of the two parts of the basket. Hence, we find

$$q = \text{Home real exchange rate} = d\frac{\overline{P}^*}{\overline{P}_1} + (1 - d)\frac{E\overline{P}^*}{\overline{P}_2}$$

The first term with a weight d does not contain E because both numerator and denominator are dollar prices (already expressed in a common currency). Only the second term with a weight $(1 - d)$ contains E, since the prices are in different currencies. Thus, a 1% increase in E will lead to only a $(1 - d)\%$ increase in the real exchange rate.

When d is 0, all home goods are priced in local currency and we have our basic model. A 1% rise in E causes a 1% rise in q. There is full **pass-through** from changes in the nominal exchange rate to changes in the real exchange rate. But as d rises, pass-through falls. If d is 0.5, then a 1% rise in E causes just a 0.5% rise in q. The real exchange rate becomes less responsive to changes in the nominal exchange rate, and this means that expenditure switching effects will be muted.

It turns out that many countries around the world conduct a large fraction of their trade in a currency other than their own, such as U.S. dollars. The most obvious examples of goods with dollar prices are the major commodities: oil, copper, wheat, and

so on. In some Persian Gulf economies, a nominal depreciation of the exchange rate does almost nothing to change the price of exports (more than 90% of which is oil priced in dollars) relative to the price of imports (again, overwhelmingly priced in dollars).

But dollar invoicing—and in Greater Europe, euro invoicing—extends around the world, as shown in Table 18-1. More than 90% of U.S. imports are priced in dollars: all else equal, a U.S. depreciation will hardly change the prices of these imports at

TABLE 18-1

Trade Dollarization The table shows the extent to which the dollar and the euro were used in the invoicing of payments for exports and imports of different countries in the 2002–04 period. In the United States, for example, 100% of exports are invoiced and paid in U.S. dollars but so, too, are 93% of imports. In Asia, U.S. dollar invoicing is very common, accounting for 48% of Japanese exports and more than 75% of exports and imports in Korea, Malaysia, and Thailand. In Europe the euro figures more prominently as the currency used for trade, but the U.S. dollar is still used in a sizable share of transactions.

	Exports Denominated in		Imports Denominated in	
	U.S. Dollar	Euro	U.S. Dollar	Euro
United States	100%	—	93%	—
United Kingdom	26	21%	37	27%
Australia	70	1	50	9
Asia				
Japan	48	10	9	5
Korea	83	7	80	5
Malaysia	90	—	90	—
Thailand	85	3	76	4
Eurozone				
France	34	52	47	45
Germany	24	63	34	55
Italy	18	75	25	70
Greece	46	47	55	40
Spain	30	61	36	60
EU New Accession Countries				
Czech Republic	13	70	18	66
Hungary	12	83	19	73
Latvia	27	57	—	49
Slovakia	12	74	21	60

Source: Selected data from Linda Goldberg and Cédric Tille, "The Internationalization of the Dollar and Trade Balance Adjustment," Federal Reserve Bank of New York Staff Report 255, August 2006.

all. Some Asian countries have trade flows that are 70% to 90% dollarized. Much of this is intra-Asian trade; if, say, a Korean supplier sells to a Japanese manufacturer, very often they conduct the trade not in yen or won, but entirely in U.S. dollars, which is the currency of neither the exporter nor the importer! The table also shows that many new EU member states in Eastern Europe have export shares largely denominated in euros.

Trade dollarization is not the only factor limiting pass-through in the real world. Even after an import has arrived at the port, it still has to pass through various intermediaries. The retail, wholesale, and other distribution activities all add a local currency cost or markup to the final price paid by the ultimate buyer. Suppose the markup is $100 on an import that costs $100 at the port, so the good retails for $200 in shops. Suppose a 10% depreciation of the dollar raises the port price to $110. All else equal, the retail price will rise to just $210, only a 5% increase at the point of final sale. Thus, expenditure switching by final users will be muted by the limited pass-through from port prices to final prices.

How large are these effects? A study of 76 developed and developing countries found that, over the period of one year, a 10% exchange rate depreciation resulted in a 6.5% rise in imported goods prices at the port of arrival but perhaps only a 4% rise in the retail prices of imported goods.[*]

The J Curve

Our model of the trade balance assumes that a real depreciation improves a country's trade balance by increasing exports and reducing imports. In reality, however, these effects may be slow to appear because orders for export and import goods are placed months in advance. Thus, at the moment of depreciation there will be no instantaneous change in export and import volumes.

What does this slow adjustment imply? Exports will continue to sell for a time in the same quantity and at the same domestic price, and so total export earnings remain fixed. What will change is the domestic price paid for the import goods. They will have become more expensive in domestic currency terms. If the same quantity of imports flows in but costs more per unit, then the home country's total import bill will rise.

As a result, if export earnings are fixed but import expenditures are rising, the trade balance will initially *fall* rather than rise, as shown in Figure 18-5. Only after time passes, and export and import orders adjust to the new relative prices, will the trade balance move in the positive direction we have assumed. Because of its distinctive shape, the curve traced out by the trade balance over time in Figure 18-5 is called the **J Curve.** Some empirical studies find that the effects of the J Curve last up to a year after the initial depreciation. Hence, the assumption that a depreciation boosts spending on the home country's goods may not hold in the very short run.

* Jeffrey A. Frankel, David C. Parsley, and Shang-Jin Wei, 2005, "Slow Passthrough Around the World: A New Import for Developing Countries?" National Bureau of Economic Research (NBER) Working Paper No. 11199.

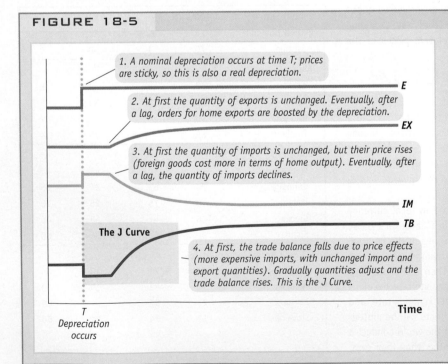

FIGURE 18-5

1. A nominal depreciation occurs at time T; prices are sticky, so this is also a real depreciation. — E

2. At first the quantity of exports is unchanged. Eventually, after a lag, orders for home exports are boosted by the depreciation. — EX

3. At first the quantity of imports is unchanged, but their price rises (foreign goods cost more in terms of home output). Eventually, after a lag, the quantity of imports declines. — IM

— TB

The J Curve

4. At first, the trade balance falls due to price effects (more expensive imports, with unchanged import and export quantities). Gradually quantities adjust and the trade balance rises. This is the J Curve.

T Depreciation occurs — Time

The J Curve When prices are sticky and there is a nominal and real depreciation of the home currency, it may take time for the trade balance to move toward surplus. In fact, the initial impact may be toward deficit. If firms and households place orders in advance, then import and export quantities may react sluggishly to changes in the relative price of home and foreign goods. Hence, just after the depreciation, the value of home exports, *EX*, will be unchanged. However, home imports now cost more due to the depreciation. Thus, the value of imports, *IM*, would actually *rise* after a depreciation, causing the trade balance $TB = EX - IM$ to fall. Only after some time would exports rise and imports fall, allowing the trade balance to rise relative to its predepreciation level. The path traced by the trade balance during this process looks vaguely like a letter J.

Exogenous Changes in Demand

We have already treated as given, or exogenous, the changes or *shocks* in demand that originate in changes to government purchases or taxes. However, other exogenous changes in demand can affect consumption, investment, or the trade balance, and it is important to know how to analyze these, too. Examples of such changes are illustrated in Figure 18-6.

■ *An exogenous change in consumption.* Suppose that at any given level of disposable income, consumers decide to spend more on consumption. After this shock, the consumption function would shift up as in Figure 18-6, panel (a). For example, an increase in household wealth following a stock market or housing market

FIGURE 18-6

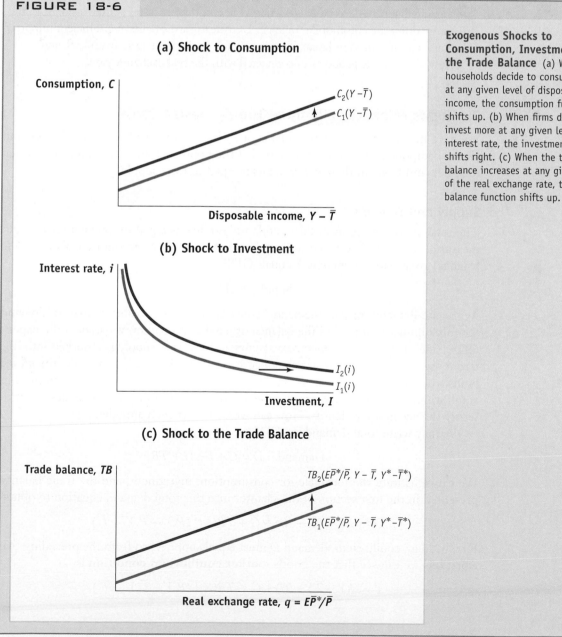

(a) Shock to Consumption

Consumption, C

$C_2(Y - \bar{T})$
$C_1(Y - \bar{T})$

Disposable income, $Y - \bar{T}$

(b) Shock to Investment

Interest rate, i

$I_2(i)$
$I_1(i)$

Investment, I

(c) Shock to the Trade Balance

Trade balance, TB

$TB_2(E\bar{P}^*/\bar{P}, Y - \bar{T}, Y^* - \bar{T}^*)$

$TB_1(E\bar{P}^*/\bar{P}, Y - \bar{T}, Y^* - \bar{T}^*)$

Real exchange rate, $q = E\bar{P}^*/\bar{P}$

Exogenous Shocks to Consumption, Investment, and the Trade Balance (a) When households decide to consume more at any given level of disposable income, the consumption function shifts up. (b) When firms decide to invest more at any given level of the interest rate, the investment function shifts right. (c) When the trade balance increases at any given level of the real exchange rate, the trade balance function shifts up.

boom (as seen in expansions since 1990) could lead to a shift of this sort. This is a change in consumption demand unconnected to disposable income.

■ *An exogenous change in investment.* Suppose that at any given level of the interest rate, firms decide to invest more. After this shock, the investment function would shift up as in Figure 18-6, panel (b). For example, a belief that high-technology companies had great prospects for success led to a large surge in investment in this sector in many countries in the 1990s. This is a change in investment demand unconnected to the interest rate.

■ *An exogenous change in the trade balance.* Suppose that at any given level of the real exchange rate, export demand rises and/or import demand falls. After one of these shocks, trade balance function would shift up as in Figure 18-6, panel (c). Such a change happened in the 1980s when U.S. consumers' tastes shifted away from the large domestic automobiles made in Detroit toward smaller fuel-efficient imported cars manufactured in Japan. This is a switch in demand away from U.S. and toward Japanese products unconnected with the real exchange rate.

2 Goods Market Equilibrium: The Keynesian Cross

We have now studied the determinants of each component of demand. We next put all the components together and show that the goods market is in equilibrium when total demand from all these components is equal to total supply.

Supply and Demand

The total aggregate *supply* of final goods and services is equal to total national output measured by GDP. Given our assumption that the current account equals the trade balance, gross national income Y equals GDP:

$$\text{Supply} = GDP = Y$$

Aggregate demand, or just "demand," consists of all the possible sources of demand for this supply of output. In the balance of payments chapter, we studied the expenditure side of the national income accounts and saw that supply is absorbed into different uses according to the national income identity. This accounting identity *always* holds true. But an identity is not an economic model. A model must explain how, in equilibrium, the observed demands take on their desired or planned values and still satisfy the accounting identity. How can we construct such a model?

We may write total demand for GDP as

$$\text{Demand} = D = C + I + G + TB$$

We can substitute the formulae for consumption, investment, and the trade balance presented in the first section of this chapter into this total demand equation to obtain

$$D = C(Y - \overline{T}) + I(i) + \overline{G} + TB(E\overline{P}^*/\overline{P}, Y - \overline{T}, Y^* - \overline{T}^*)$$

Finally, in an equilibrium, demand D must equal supply Y, so from the preceding two equations we can see that the **goods market equilibrium condition** is

$$Y = \underbrace{C(Y - \overline{T}) + I(i) + \overline{G} + TB(E\overline{P}^*/\overline{P}, Y - \overline{T}, Y^* - \overline{T}^*)}_{D} \tag{18-1}$$

Determinants of Demand

The right-hand side of Equation (18-1) shows that many factors can affect demand: home and foreign output (Y and Y^*), home and foreign taxes (T and T^*), the home nominal interest rate (i), government spending ($\overline{G}$), and the real exchange rate ($E\overline{P}^*/\overline{P}$). Let us examine each of these in turn. We start with home output Y, and assume that all other factors remain fixed.

A rise in output Y (all else equal) will cause the right-hand side to increase. For example, suppose output increases by $\Delta Y = \$1$. This change causes consumption spending C to increase by $+\$MPC$. The change in imports will be $+\$MPC_F$, causing the trade balance to change by $-\$MPC_F$. So the total change in D will be $\$(MPC - MPC_F) = \$MPC_H > 0$, a positive number. This is an intuitive result: an extra \$1 of output generates some spending on home goods (an amount $\$MPC_H$), with the remainder either spent on foreign goods (an amount $\$MPC_F$) or saved (an amount $\$MPS$).

Using this result, Figure 18-7, panel (a), plots demand D, the right-hand side of Equation (18-1), as a function of income or output Y only. For the moment, we hold fixed all other determinants of D. Because D increases as Y increases, the demand function has a positive slope MPC_H, a number between 0 and 1.

Also drawn is the 45-degree line, which represents Y, the left-hand side of Equation (18-1). The 45-degree line has a slope of 1, so it is steeper than the demand function.

This diagram is often called the **Keynesian cross**. It depicts the goods market equilibrium: the goods market is in equilibrium at point 1 where the two lines intersect, for that is the unique point where $D = Y$. This corresponds to an income or output level of Y_1.

Why does the goods market adjust to an equilibrium at this point? To the right of point 1, output tends to fall; to the left of point 1, output tends to rise. Why? At point 2, the output level is Y_2 and demand D exceeds supply Y; as inventories fall, firms expand production and output rises toward Y_1. At point 3, the output level is Y_3 and supply Y exceeds demand; as inventories rise, firms cut production and output falls toward Y_1. Only at point 1 are firms in an equilibrium in which production levels are stable in the short run.

Note the crucial assumptions in this model are that prices are fixed and firms are willing to adjust their production and employment to meet whatever the desired level of demand happens to be. These assumptions may be realistic in the short run, but they do not apply in the long run, when prices can adjust and output and employment are determined by the economy's ability to fully employ its technology and resources.

Factors That Shift the Demand Curve

The Keynesian cross also allows us to examine the impact of the other factors in Equation (18-1) on goods market equilibrium. Let's look at four important cases:

■ *A change in government spending.* An exogenous rise in government purchases $\overline{G}$ (all else equal) increases demand at every level of output, as seen in Equation (18-1). More government purchases directly add to the total demand in the economy. This change causes an upward shift in the demand function D, as in Figure 18-7, panel (b). Goods market equilibrium shifts from point 1 to point 2, to an output level Y_2.

FIGURE 18-7

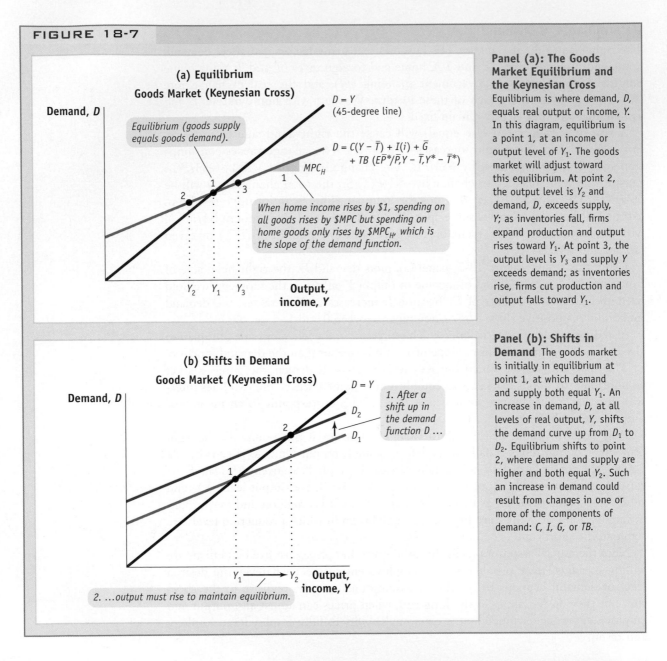

(a) Equilibrium
Goods Market (Keynesian Cross)

Demand, *D*

$D = Y$
(45-degree line)

Equilibrium (goods supply
equals goods demand).

$D = C(Y - \bar{T}) + I(i) + \bar{G}$
$+ TB (E\bar{P}^*/\bar{P}, Y - \bar{T}, Y^* - \bar{T}^*)$

MPC_H

When home income rises by $1, spending on
all goods rises by $MPC but spending on
home goods only rises by MPC_H, which is
the slope of the demand function.

Y_2 Y_1 Y_3 Output,
income, *Y*

(b) Shifts in Demand
Goods Market (Keynesian Cross)

Demand, *D*

$D = Y$

D_2
D_1

1. After a
shift up in
the demand
function D ...

$Y_1 \longrightarrow Y_2$ Output,
income, *Y*

2. ...output must rise to maintain equilibrium.

Panel (a): The Goods Market Equilibrium and the Keynesian Cross Equilibrium is where demand, *D*, equals real output or income, *Y*. In this diagram, equilibrium is a point 1, at an income or output level of Y_1. The goods market will adjust toward this equilibrium. At point 2, the output level is Y_2 and demand, *D*, exceeds supply, *Y*; as inventories fall, firms expand production and output rises toward Y_1. At point 3, the output level is Y_3 and supply *Y* exceeds demand; as inventories rise, firms cut production and output falls toward Y_1.

Panel (b): Shifts in Demand The goods market is initially in equilibrium at point 1, at which demand and supply both equal Y_1. An increase in demand, *D*, at all levels of real output, *Y*, shifts the demand curve up from D_1 to D_2. Equilibrium shifts to point 2, where demand and supply are higher and both equal Y_2. Such an increase in demand could result from changes in one or more of the components of demand: *C, I, G,* or *TB*.

The lesson: any exogenous change in G (due to changes in the government budget) will cause the demand curve to shift.

∎ *A change in taxes (or other factors affecting consumption).* A fall in taxes $\bar{T}$ (all else equal) increases disposable income. When consumers have more disposable income, they spend more on consumption. This change raises demand at every level of output *Y*, because *C* increases as disposable income increases. This is seen in Equation (18-1) and in Figure 18-7, panel (a). Thus, a fall in taxes shifts the demand function upward from D_1 to D_2, as shown again in Figure 18-7, panel (b). The increase in *D* causes the goods market equilibrium to shift from point 1 to point 2, and output rises to Y_2.

The lesson: any exogenous change in C (due to changes in taxes, tastes, etc.) will cause the demand curve to shift.

■ *A change in the home interest rate (or other factors affecting investment).* A fall in the interest rate i (all else equal) will lead to an increase in I, as firms find it profitable to engage in more investment projects, and spend more. This change leads to an increase in demand D at every level of output Y. The demand function D shifts upward, as seen in Figure 18-7, panel (b). The increase in demand causes the goods market equilibrium to shift from point 1 to point 2, and output rises to Y_2.

The lesson: any exogenous change in I (due to changes in interest rates, the expected profitability of investment, changes in tax policy, etc.) will cause the demand curve to shift.

■ *A change in the home exchange rate.* A rise in the nominal exchange rate E (all else equal) implies a rise in the real exchange rate EP^*/P (due to sticky prices). This is a real depreciation, and through its effects on the trade balance TB via expenditure switching, it will increase demand D at any given level of home output Y. For example, spending switches from foreign goods to American goods when the U.S. dollar depreciates. This change causes the demand function D to shift up, as seen yet again in Figure 18-7, panel (b).

The lesson: any change in the exchange rate will cause the demand curve to shift.

■ *A change in the home or foreign price level.* If prices are flexible, then a *rise* in foreign prices or a *fall* in domestic prices causes a home real depreciation, raising $q = E\overline{P}^*/\overline{P}$. This real depreciation causes TB to rise and, all else equal, it will increase demand D at any given level of home output Y. For example, spending switches from foreign goods to American goods when the U.S. prices fall. This change causes the demand function D to shift up, as seen yet again in Figure 18-7, panel (b).

The lesson: any change in P^* or P will cause the demand curve to shift.

Summary

An increase in output Y causes a move along the demand curve (and similarly for a decrease). But any increase in demand that is *not* due to a change in output Y will instead cause the demand curve itself to shift upward in the Keynesian cross diagram, as in Figure 18-7, panel (b). Similarly, any contraction in demand not due to output changes will cause the demand function to shift downward.

To conclude, the main factors that shift the demand curve out are as follows:

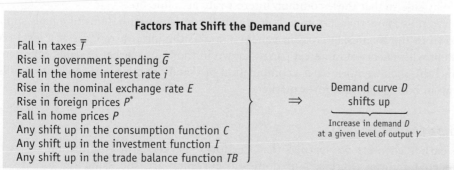

Factors That Shift the Demand Curve	
Fall in taxes $\overline{T}$ Rise in government spending $\overline{G}$ Fall in the home interest rate i Rise in the nominal exchange rate E Rise in foreign prices P^* Fall in home prices P Any shift up in the consumption function C Any shift up in the investment function I Any shift up in the trade balance function TB	$\Rightarrow$ Demand curve D shifts up Increase in demand D at a given level of output Y

The opposite changes lead to a decrease in demand and shift the demand curve in.

3 Goods and Forex Market Equilibria: Deriving the IS Curve

We have made an important first step in our study of the short-run behavior of exchange rates and output. Our analysis of demand shows how the level of output adjusts to ensure a goods market equilibrium, given the levels of each component of demand. Each component, in turn, has its own particular determinants, and we have examined how shifts in these determinants (or in other exogenous factors) might shift the level of demand and, hence, change the equilibrium level of output.

But there is more than one market in the economy, and a *general equilibrium* requires equilibrium in all markets—that is, equilibrium in the goods market, the money market, and the forex market. We need to bring all three markets into the analysis, and we do that next by developing a tool of macroeconomic analysis known as the IS-LM diagram. A version of this may be familiar to you from the study of closed-economy macroeconomics, but in this chapter we develop a variant of this approach for an open economy.

Analyzing equilibria in three markets simultaneously is a difficult task, but it is made more manageable by proceeding one step at a time using familiar tools. Our first step builds on the Keynesian cross depiction of goods market equilibrium developed in the last section and then adds on the depiction of forex market equilibrium that we developed in the earlier exchange rate chapters.

Equilibrium in Two Markets

We begin by defining the **IS curve,** which is one part of the IS-LM diagram.

The IS curve shows combinations of output Y and the interest rate i for which the goods and forex markets are in equilibrium.

In Figure 18-8, panel (b), we derive the IS curve by using the Keynesian cross in panel (a) to analyze goods market equilibrium. In panel (c), we impose the uncovered interest parity relationship that ensures the forex market is in equilibrium.

Before we continue, let's take a closer look at why the various graphs in this figure are oriented as they are. The Keynesian cross in panel (a) and the IS diagram in panel (b) share a common horizontal axis, the level of output or income. Hence, these figures are arranged one above the other so that these common output axes line up.

The forex market in panel (c) and the IS diagram in panel (b) share a common vertical axis, the level of the domestic interest rate. Hence, these figures are arranged side by side so that these common interest rate axes line up.

We thus know that if output Y is at a level consistent with demand equals supply, shown in the Keynesian cross in panel (a), and if the interest rate i is at a level consistent with uncovered interest parity, shown in the forex market in panel (c), then in panel (b), then we must have a combination of Y and i that is consistent with equilibrium in both goods and forex markets.

Forex Market Recap

In earlier chapters we learned that the forex market is in equilibrium when the expected returns expressed in domestic currency are the same on foreign and domestic interest-bearing (money market) bank deposits. Equation (15-1) described this condition, known as uncovered interest parity (UIP), where home and foreign

FIGURE 18-8

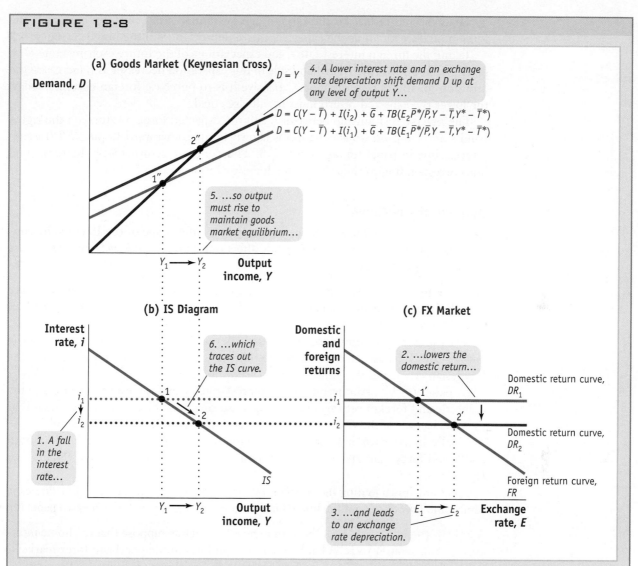

Deriving the IS Curve The Keynesian cross is in panel (a), IS curve in panel (b), and forex (FX) market in panel (c). The economy starts in equilibrium with output, Y_1; interest rate, i_1; and exchange rate, E_1. Consider the effect of a decrease in the interest rate from i_1 to i_2, all else equal. In panel (c), a lower interest rate causes a depreciation; equilibrium moves from 1′ to 2′. A lower interest rate boosts investment and a depreciation boosts the trade balance. In panel (a), demand shifts up from D_1 to D_2, equilibrium from 1″ to 2″, output from Y_1 to Y_2. In panel (b), we go from point 1 to point 2. The IS curve is thus traced out, a downward-sloping relationship between the interest rate and output. When the interest rate falls from i_1 to i_2, output rises from Y_1 to Y_2. The IS curve describes all combinations of i and Y consistent with goods and FX market equilibria in panels (a) and (c).

currencies corresponded to the dollar and the euro; for any currency pair we can write, similarly:

$$\underbrace{i}_{\substack{\text{Domestic} \\ \text{interest rate}}} = \underbrace{i^*}_{\substack{\text{Foreign} \\ \text{interest rate}}} + \underbrace{\left(\frac{E^e}{E} - 1\right)}_{\substack{\text{Expected rate of depreciation} \\ \text{of the domestic currency}}}$$

$$\underbrace{ \qquad \qquad}_{\text{Domestic return}} \qquad \underbrace{\phantom{i^* + \left(\frac{E^e}{E}-1\right)}}_{\text{Expected foreign return}}$$

The expected return on the foreign deposit *measured in home currency* equals the foreign interest rate plus the expected rate of depreciation of the home currency.

Taking the foreign interest rate i^* and expectations of the future exchange rate E^e as given, we know that the right-hand side of this expression decreases as E increases: the intuition for this is that the more expensive it is to purchase foreign currency today, the lower the expected return must be, all else equal.

The inverse relationship between E and the expected foreign return on the right-hand side of the previous equation is shown by the downward-sloping *FR* (foreign returns) line in panel (c) of Figure 18-8. The domestic return *DR* is the horizontal line corresponding to the level of the domestic interest rate i.

Deriving the IS Curve

Using the setup in Figure 18-8, we can now derive the shape of the IS curve by considering how changes in the interest rate affect output *if the goods and forex markets are to remain in equilibrium*.

Initial Equilibrium Let us suppose that the goods market and forex markets are initially in equilibrium at an interest rate i_1, an output or income level Y_1, and an exchange rate E_1.

In panel (a) by assumption, at an output level Y_1, demand equals supply, so the output level Y_1 must correspond to the point 1″, which is at the intersection of the Keynesian cross, and the figure is drawn accordingly.

In panel (c) by assumption, at an interest rate i_1 and an exchange rate E_1, the domestic and foreign returns must be equal, so this must be the point 1′, which is at the intersection of the DR_1 and *FR* curves, and the figure is drawn accordingly.

Finally, in panel (b) by assumption, at an interest rate i_1 and an output level Y_1, both goods and forex markets are in equilibrium. Thus, the point 1 is on the *IS* curve, *by definition*.

Lines are drawn joining the equal output levels Y_1 in panels (a) and (b). The domestic return line DR_1 traces out the home interest rate level from panel (b) across to panel (c).

A Fall in the Interest Rate Now in Figure 18-8, let us suppose that the home interest rate falls from i_1 to i_2. What happens to equilibria in the good and forex markets?

We first look at the forex market in panel (c). From our analysis of UIP in earlier chapters we know that when the home interest rate falls, domestic deposits have a lower return and look less attractive to investors. To maintain forex market equilibrium, the exchange rate must rise (the home currency must depreciate) until domestic and foreign returns are once again equal. In our example, when the home interest rate falls to i_2, the exchange rate must rise from E_1 to E_2 to equalize *FR* and DR_2 and restore equilibrium in the forex market at point 2′.

How do the changes in the home interest rate and the exchange rate affect demand? As shown in panel (a), demand will increase (shift up) for two reasons, as we learned earlier in this chapter.

First, when the domestic interest rate falls, firms are willing to engage in more investment projects, and their increased investment augments demand. The increase in investment, all else equal, *directly* increases demand D at any level of output Y.

Second, the exchange rate E has risen (depreciated). Because prices are sticky in the short run, this rise in the nominal exchange rate E also causes a rise in the real exchange rate $E\overline{P}^*/\overline{P}$. That is, the nominal depreciation causes a real depreciation. This increases demand D via expenditure switching. At any level of output Y consumers switch expenditure from relatively more expensive foreign goods toward relatively less expensive domestic goods. Thus, the fall in the interest rate *indirectly* boosts demand via exchange rate effects felt through the trade balance TB.

One important observation is in order: in an open economy, the phenomenon of expenditure switching operates as an additional element in demand that is not present in a closed economy. *In an open economy, lower interest rates stimulate demand through the traditional closed-economy investment channel and through the trade balance. The trade balance effect occurs because lower interest rates cause a nominal depreciation, which in the short run is also a real depreciation, which stimulates external demand via the trade balance.*

To summarize, panel (a) shows clearly that in response to a decrease in the interest rate, demand has shifted up to D_2 and the Keynesian cross goods market equilibrium is restored by a rise in output to Y_2, which corresponds to point 2″.

In panel (b), we can now derive the shape of the IS curve. At an interest rate i_1 and output level Y_1 and at an interest rate i_2 and an output level Y_2, both the goods and forex markets are in equilibrium. *We have now derived the shape of the IS curve, which describes goods and forex market equilibrium. When the interest rate falls from i_1 to i_2, output rises from Y_1 to Y_2. The IS curve is downward sloping, which illustrates the negative relationship between the interest rate i and output Y.*

Factors That Shift the IS Curve

In deriving the IS curve, we treated various demand factors as exogenous, including fiscal policy, price levels, and the exchange rate. If any factors other than the interest rate and output change, the position of the IS curve would have to change. These effects are central in any analysis of changes in an economy's equilibrium. We now explore several changes that result in an increase in demand, that is, an upward shift in the demand curve in Figure 18-9, panel (a). (A decrease in demand would result from changes in the opposite direction.)

- *A change in government spending.* If demand shifts up because of a *rise in* $\overline{G}$, a fiscal expansion, all else equal, what happens to the IS curve? The initial equilibrium point (Y_1, i_1) would no longer be a goods market equilibrium: if the interest rate is unchanged at i_1, then I is unchanged, as are the exchange rate E and hence TB. Yet demand has risen due to the change in G. That demand has to be satisfied somehow, so more output has to be produced. Some—but not all—of that extra output will be consumed, but the rest can meet the extra demand generated by the rise in government spending. At the interest rate i_1, output must rise to Y_2 for the goods market to once again be in equilibrium. Thus, the IS curve must shift right as shown in Figure 18-9, panel (b).

The lesson: a rise in government spending shifts the IS curve out.

- *A change in taxes.* Suppose taxes were to decrease. With all other factors remaining unchanged, this tax cut makes demand shift up by boosting private consumption, all else equal. We assume that the interest rate i_1, the exchange rate E_1, and government's spending policy are all fixed. Thus, neither I nor TB nor G change. With an excess of demand, supply has to rise, so output must again increase to Y_2 and the IS curve shifts right.

FIGURE 18-9

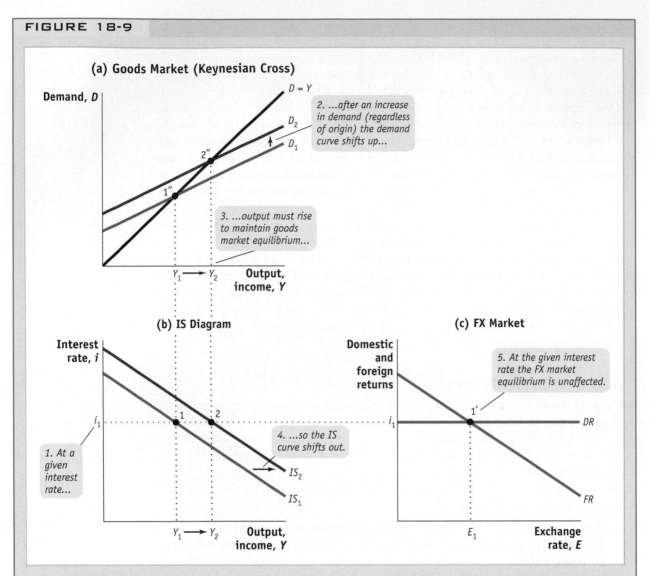

Exogenous Shifts in Demand Cause the IS Curve to Shift In the Keynesian cross in panel (a), when the interest rate is held constant at i_1, an exogenous increase in demand (due to other factors) causes the demand curve to shift up from D_1 to D_2 as shown, all else equal. This moves the equilibrium from 1″ to 2″, raising output from Y_1 to Y_2. In the IS diagram in panel (b), output has risen, with no change in the interest rate. The *IS* curve has therefore shifted right from IS_1 to IS_2. The nominal interest rate and hence the exchange rate are unchanged in this example, as seen in panel (c).

The lesson: a reduction in taxes shifts the IS curve out.

■ *A change in the foreign interest rate or expected future exchange rate.* A *rise* in the foreign interest rate i^* or a *rise* in the future expected exchange rate E^e causes a depreciation of the home currency, all else equal (recall that in the forex market, the FR curve shifts out because the return on foreign deposits has increased; if the home interest rate is unchanged, E must rise). A rise in E causes the real exchange rate to depreciate, because prices are sticky. As a result, *TB* rises via expenditure switching, and demand increases. Because *C*, *I*, and G do not change, there is an excess of demand, and supply has to rise to restore equilibrium. Output Y increases, and the IS curve shifts right.

The lesson: an increase in the foreign return (via i^* or E^e) shifts the IS curve out.

■ *A change in the home or foreign price level.* If prices are flexible, then a *rise* in foreign prices or a *fall* in domestic prices causes a home real depreciation, raising $q = E\overline{P}^*/\overline{P}$. This real depreciation causes TB to rise and, all else equal, demand will rise to a position like D_2. With an excess of demand, supply has to rise to restore equilibrium. Output Y must increase, and the IS curve shifts right.

The lesson: an increase P^* or a decrease in P shifts the IS curve out.

These examples show that the position of the IS curve depends on various factors that we treat as given (or exogenous). We may write this observation using the notation

$$IS = IS(G, T, i^*, E^e, P^*, P)$$

There are many other exogenous shocks to the economy that can be analyzed in a similar fashion—for example, a sudden exogenous change in consumption, investment, or the trade balance. How will the IS curve react in each case? You may have detected a pattern from the preceding discussion.

The general rule is as follows: *any type of shock that increases demand at a given level of output will shift the IS curve to the right; any shock that decreases demand will shift the IS curve down.*

Summing Up the IS Curve

When prices are sticky, the IS curve summarizes the relationship between output Y and the interest rate i necessary to keep the goods and forex markets in short-run equilibrium. The IS curve is downward-sloping. Why? Lower interest rates stimulate demand via the investment channel and, through exchange rate depreciation, via the trade balance. Higher demand can be satisfied in the short run only by higher output. Thus, when the interest rate falls, output rises, and the economy moves along the IS curve.

As for shifts in the IS curve, we have found that any factor which increases demand D at a given home interest rate i must cause the demand curve to shift up, leading to higher output Y and, as a result, an outward shift in the IS curve.

To conclude, the main factors that shift the IS curve out can be summed up as follows:

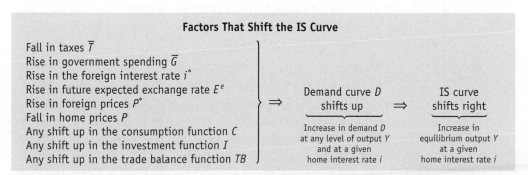

Factors That Shift the IS Curve

Fall in taxes $\overline{T}$		
Rise in government spending $\overline{G}$		
Rise in the foreign interest rate i^*		
Rise in future expected exchange rate E^e	⇒	Demand curve D ⇒ IS curve
Rise in foreign prices P^*		shifts up shifts right
Fall in home prices P		
Any shift up in the consumption function C		Increase in demand D Increase in
Any shift up in the investment function I		at any level of output Y equilibrium output Y
Any shift up in the trade balance function TB		and at a given at a given
		home interest rate i home interest rate i

The opposite changes lead to a decrease in demand and shift the demand curve down and the IS curve to the left.

4 Money Market Equilibrium: Deriving the LM Curve

The IS curve links the forex market and the goods market as depicted by the Keynesian cross. It summarizes combinations of Y and i at which goods demand equals goods supply in a way that is consistent with forex market equilibrium. We have now taken care of equilibria in two out of three markets, so there is only one market left to worry about. In this section, we derive a set of combinations of Y and i that ensures equilibrium in the money market, a concept that can be represented graphically as the **LM curve.**

The LM curve is more straightforward to derive than the IS curve for a couple of reasons. First, the money market is something we have already studied in earlier chapters, so we already have all the tools we need to build the LM curve. Second, unlike the IS curve, the open-economy LM curve is no different from the closed-economy LM curve, so there will be no new material here if you have previously studied the closed-economy IS-LM model in another course.

Money Market Recap

In our earlier study of the money market, we assumed that the level of output or income Y was given. In deriving the LM curve, we now face a new question: What happens in the money market when an economy's output changes?

In the short-run, the price level is assumed to be sticky at a level $\overline{P}$, and the money market is in equilibrium when the demand for real money balances $L(i)Y$ equals the real money supply $M/\overline{P}$:

$$\underbrace{\frac{M}{\overline{P}}}_{\substack{\text{Real} \\ \text{money} \\ \text{supply}}} = \underbrace{L(i)Y}_{\substack{\text{Real} \\ \text{money} \\ \text{demand}}} \qquad (18\text{-}2)$$

Figure 18-10, panel (a), shows that real money demand MD varies inversely with the nominal interest rate. As a result of this relationship, the demand curve for real money balances slopes downward. The real money supply MS is assumed to be fixed for now. Initially, the level of output is at Y_1 and the money market is in equilibrium at $1'$, where real money demand is on MD_1 at $M/\overline{P} = L(i_1)Y_1$.

If output changes, the real money demand curve shifts. For example, if output rises to Y_2 and the real money supply $M/\overline{P}$ remains fixed, then real money demand increases because more output implies a larger number of transactions in the economy for which money is needed. The real money demand curve shifts right to MD_2. To keep money supply and demand equal, $M/\overline{P} = L(i_2)Y_2$, the interest rate rises from $i = i_1$ to $i = i_2$. Equilibrium moves from $1'$ to $2'$.

Deriving the LM Curve

This exercise can be repeated for any level of output Y. Doing so will generate a combination of interest rates i and outputs Y for which the money market is in equilibrium. This set of points, called the LM curve, is drawn in Figure 18-10, panel (b).

For example, if the real money supply is fixed at $M/\overline{P}$, an increase in output from Y_1 to Y_2 generates a rise in the nominal interest rate from i_1 to i_2 in panel (a), as we have just seen. This change can also be depicted as a move from point 1 to point 2 along the LM curve, as shown in panel (b).

FIGURE 18-10

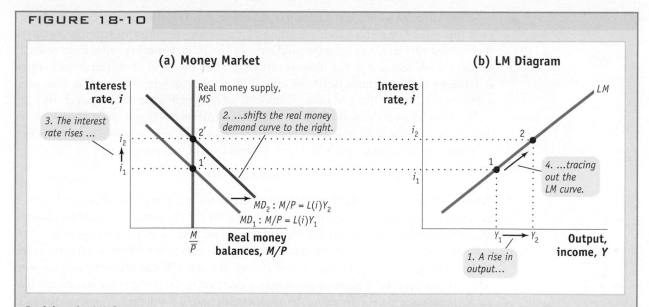

Deriving the LM Curve If there is an increase in real income or output from Y_1 to Y_2 in panel (b), the effect in the money market in panel (a) is to shift the demand for real money balances to the right, all else equal. If the real supply of money, *MS*, is held fixed at $M/\overline{P}$, then the interest rate rises from i_1 to i_2 and money market equilibrium moves from point 1′ to point 2′. The relationship thus described between the interest rate and income, all else equal, is known as the LM curve and is depicted in panel (b) by the shift from point 1 to point 2. The LM curve is upward-sloping: when the output level rises from Y_1 to Y_2, the interest rate rises from i_1 to i_2. The LM curve in panel (b) describes all combinations of *i* and *Y* that are consistent with money market equilibrium in panel (a).

We have now derived the shape of the LM curve, which describes money market equilibrium. When output rises from Y_1 to Y_2, the interest rate rises from i_1 to i_2. The LM curve is an upward-sloping relationship between the interest rate *i* and output *Y*.

The two ways of depicting the money market equilibrium are entirely equivalent. The money market diagram shows the relationship between real money balances demanded and supplied at different interest rates, holding output fixed. The LM curve diagram shows the relationship between output and the interest rate holding real money balances as fixed. Because the LM curve does *not* hold output fixed, it is important to developing our model of how output, interest rates, and exchange rates fluctuate in the short run.

Factors That Shift the LM Curve

An important reason for a shift in the LM curve is a change in the real money supply. (Changes in output result in a move *along* a given LM curve.) The LM curve tells us the interest rate *i* that equilibrates the money market at any given level of output *Y*. Given *Y*, we know that the equilibrium interest rate *i* depends on real money supply $M/\overline{P}$, and so the position of the LM curve depends on $M/\overline{P}$.

The effect of the real money supply on a nation's output or income is important because we are often interested in the impact of monetary policy changes on overall economic activity. To see how this effect operates via the LM curve, we can examine the money market diagram in Figure 18-11, panel (a). An increase in the nominal money supply *M* with sticky prices raises real money supply from $M_1/\overline{P}$ to $M_2/\overline{P}$ and shifts the real money supply curve *MS* to the right.

What happens in the LM diagram if the exogenous real money supply $M/\overline{P}$ changes in this way? For a given level of output Y, the increased supply of real money drives the interest rate down to i_2, and equilibrium in the money market shifts from point 1′ to point 2′. A decrease in the interest rate to i_2 when the level of output is unchanged at Y means that we cannot be on the same LM curve as before. There must have been a downward shift of the LM curve from LM_1 to LM_2 in Figure 18-11, panel (b).

We have shown the following: *an increase in real money supply shifts the LM curve down or to the right; a decrease in the real money supply shifts the LM curve up or to the left.*

Thus, the position of the LM curve is a function of real money supply:

$$LM = LM(M/\overline{P})$$

Remember that in this short-run model of the economy, prices are sticky and treated as given, so any change in the real money supply in the short run is caused by changes in the nominal money supply M, which for now we take as given or exogenous.

Other factors can influence the position of the LM curve. In addition to changes in the money supply, exogenous changes in real money demand will also cause the LM curve to shift. For example, for a given money supply, a decrease in the demand for real money balances (an increase in the L function) at a given level of output Y will tend to lower the interest rate, all else equal, which would be depicted as a shift down or to the right in the LM curve.

Summing Up the LM Curve

When prices are sticky, the LM curve summarizes the relationship between output Y and interest rate i necessary to keep the money market in short-run equilibrium for a given level of the real money supply. The LM curve is upward-sloping. Why? In a money

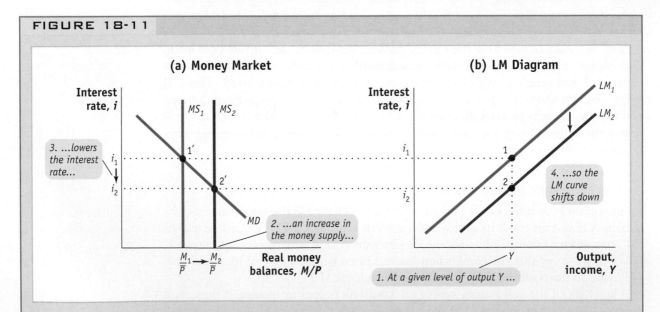

FIGURE 18-11

Change in the Money Supply Shifts the LM Curve In the money market, shown in panel (a), we hold fixed the level of real income or output, Y, and hence real money demand, MD. All else equal, we show the effect of an increase in money supply from M_1 to M_2. The real money supply curve moves out from MS_1 to MS_2. This moves the equilibrium from 1′ to 2′, lowering the interest rate from i_1 to i_2. In the LM diagram, shown in panel (b), the interest rate has fallen, with no change in the level of income or output, so the economy moves from point 1 to point 2. The LM curve has therefore shifted down from LM_1 to LM_2.

market equilibrium, if real money supply is constant, then real money demand must also be constant. If output rises, real money demand rises and to maintain equilibrium, real money demand must contract. This contraction in real money demand is accomplished by a rise in the interest rate. Thus, on the LM curve, when output rises, so, too, does the interest rate.

The following factors shift the LM curve:

Factors That Shift the LM Curve

Rise in (nominal) money supply M ⎱
Any shift left in the money demand function L ⎰ $\Rightarrow$ LM curve <u>shifts down or right</u>

Decrease in
equilibrium home interest rate i
at given level of output Y

The opposite changes lead to an increase in the home interest rate and shift the LM curve up or to the left.

5 The Short-Run IS-LM-FX Model of an Open Economy

We are now in a position to fully characterize an open economy that is in equilibrium in goods, money, and forex markets, as shown in Figure 18-12. This IS-LM-FX figure combines the goods market (the IS curve), the money market (the LM curve), and the forex (FX) market diagrams.

The IS and LM curves are both drawn in panel (a). The goods and forex markets are in equilibrium if and only if the economy is on the IS curve. The money market is in equilibrium if and only if the economy is on the LM curve. Thus, all three markets are in equilibrium if and only if the economy is at point 1, where *IS* and *LM* intersect.

The forex market, or FX market, is drawn in panel (b). The domestic return *DR* in the forex market equals the money market interest rate. Equilibrium is at point 1′ where the foreign return *FR* is equal to domestic return *i*.

In the remainder of this chapter, and in the rest of this book, we make extensive use of this two-panel IS-LM-FX diagram of the open-economy equilibrium to analyze the short-run response of an open economy to various types of shocks. In particular, we look at how government policies affect the economy and the extent to which they can be employed to enhance macroeconomic performance and stability.

Macroeconomic Policies in the Short Run

Now that we understand the open-economy IS-LM-FX model and all the factors that influence an economy's short-run equilibrium, we can use the model to look at how a nation's key macroeconomic variables (output, exchange rates, trade balance) are affected in the short run by changes in government macroeconomic policies.

We focus on the two main policy actions: changes in **monetary policy,** implemented through changes in the money supply, and changes in **fiscal policy,** involving changes in government spending or taxes. Of particular interest is the question of whether governments can use such policies to insulate the economy from fluctuations in output.

We will see that the impact of these policies is profoundly affected by a nation's choice of exchange rate regime, and we will consider the two polar cases of fixed and

FIGURE 18-12

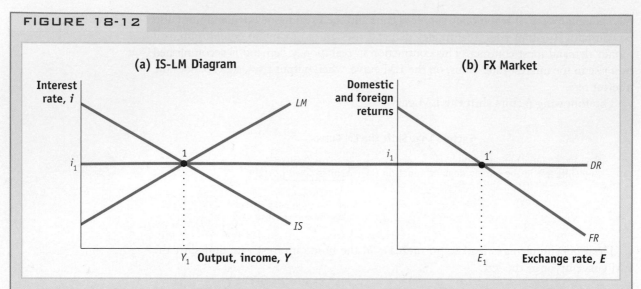

Equilibrium in the IS-LM-FX Model In panel (a), the IS and LM curves are both drawn. The goods and forex markets are in equilibrium when the economy is on the IS curve. The money market is in equilibrium when the economy is on the LM curve. Both markets are in equilibrium if and only if the economy is at point 1, the unique point of intersection of *IS* and *LM*. In panel (b), the forex (FX) market is shown. The domestic return, *DR*, in the forex market equals the money market interest rate. Equilibrium is at point 1′ where the foreign return *FR* equals domestic return, *i*.

floating exchange rates. Many countries are on some kind of flexible exchange rate regime and many are on some kind of fixed regime, so considering policy effects under both fixed and floating systems is essential.

The key assumptions of this section are as follows. The economy begins in a state of long-run equilibrium. We then consider policy changes in the home economy, assuming that conditions in the foreign economy (i.e., the rest of the world) are unchanged. The home economy is subject to the usual short-run assumption of a sticky price level at home *and* abroad. Furthermore, we assume that the forex market operates freely and unrestricted by capital controls and that the exchange rate is determined by market forces.

Temporary Policies, Unchanged Expectations Finally, we examine only *temporary* changes in policies. We will assume that long-run expectations about the future state of the economy are unaffected by the policy changes. In particular, the future expected exchange rate E^e is held fixed. The reason for studying temporary policies is that we are primarily interested in how governments use fiscal and monetary policies to handle temporary shocks and business cycles in the short run, and our model is applicable only in the short run.[2]

The key lesson of this section is that policies matter and can have significant macroeconomic effects in the short run. Moreover, their impacts depend in a big way on the type of exchange rate regime in place. Once we understand these linkages, we will better understand the contentious and ongoing debates about

---

[2] Moreover, permanent changes may not be truly feasible given realistic constraints on governments. For example, a permanent increase in money supply, all else equal, would lead to a permanent increase in the price level, violating a money, exchange rate, or inflation target (the nominal anchor). A permanent increase in government spending, with no increase in taxes, would not be feasible given the government's long-run budget constraint.

exchange rates and macroeconomic policies, including the never-ending arguments over the merits of fixed and floating exchange rates (a topic covered in detail in the next chapter).

Monetary Policy Under Floating Exchange Rates

In this policy experiment, we consider a temporary monetary expansion in the home country when the exchange rate is allowed to float. Because the expansion is not permanent, we assume there is no change in long-run expectations so that the expected future exchange rate remains steady at E^e. This means that there is no change in the expected foreign return curve in the forex market.

Figure 18-13 illustrates the predictions of the model. In panel (a) in the IS-LM diagram, the goods and money markets are initially in equilibrium at point 1. The interest rate in the money market is also the domestic return DR_1 that prevails in the forex market. In panel (b), the forex market is initially in equilibrium at point 1'.

A temporary monetary expansion that increases the money supply from M_1 to M_2 would shift the LM curve to the right in panel (a) from LM_1 to LM_2, causing the interest rate to fall from i_1 to i_2. The domestic return falls from DR_1 to DR_2. In panel (b), the lower interest rate would imply that the exchange rate must depreciate, rising from E_1 to E_2. As the interest rate falls (increasing investment I) and the exchange rate depreciates (increasing the trade balance), demand increases, which corresponds to the move down the IS curve from point 1 to point 2. Output expands from Y_1 to Y_2. The new equilibrium corresponds to points 2 and 2'.

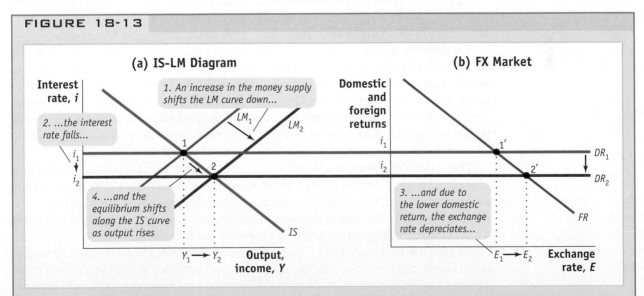

FIGURE 18-13

(a) IS-LM Diagram

(b) FX Market

Monetary Policy Under Floating Exchange Rates In panel (a) in the IS-LM diagram, the goods and money markets are initially in equilibrium at point 1. The interest rate in the money market is also the domestic return, DR_1, that prevails in the forex market. In panel (b), the forex market is initially in equilibrium at point 1'. A temporary monetary expansion that increases the money supply from M_1 to M_2 would shift the LM curve down in panel (a) from LM_1 to LM_2, causing the interest rate to fall from i_1 to i_2. DR falls from DR_1 to DR_2. In panel (b), the lower interest rate implies that the exchange rate must depreciate, rising from E_1 to E_2. As the interest rate falls (increasing investment, I) and the exchange rate depreciates (increasing the trade balance), demand increases, which corresponds to the move down the IS curve from point 1 to point 2. Output expands from Y_1 to Y_2. The new equilibrium corresponds to points 2 and 2'.

The intuition for this result is as follows: monetary expansion tends to lower the home interest rate, all else equal. A lower interest rate stimulates demand in two ways. First, directly in the goods market, it causes investment demand I to increase. Second, indirectly, it causes the exchange rate to depreciate in the forex market, which in turn causes expenditure switching in the goods market, which causes the trade balance TB to increase. Both I and TB are sources of demand and both increase.

To sum up: a temporary monetary expansion under floating exchange rates is effective in combating economic downturns because it boosts output. It also lowers the home interest rate, and causes a depreciation of the exchange rate. What happens to the trade balance cannot be predicted with certainty: increased home output will decrease the trade balance as the demand for imports will rise, but the real depreciation will increase the trade balance, because expenditure switching will tend to raise exports and diminish imports. In practice, economists tend to assume that the latter outweighs the former, so a temporary expansion of the money supply is usually predicted to increase the trade balance. (The case of a temporary contraction of monetary policy has opposite effects. As an exercise, work through this case using the same graphical apparatus.)

Monetary Policy Under Fixed Exchange Rates

Now let's look at what happens when a temporary monetary expansion occurs when the home country fixes its exchange rate with the foreign country at $\overline{E}$. The key to understanding this experiment is to recall the uncovered interest parity condition: *the home interest rate must equal the foreign interest rate under a fixed exchange rate.*

Figure 18-14 puts the model to work. In panel (a) in the IS-LM diagram, the goods and money markets are initially in equilibrium at point 1. In panel (b), the forex market is initially in equilibrium at point 1'.

A temporary monetary expansion that increases the money supply from M_1 to M_2 would shift the LM curve down and to the right in panel (a), and the interest rate would tend to fall, as we have just seen. In panel (b), the lower interest rate would imply that the exchange rate would tend to rise or depreciate toward E_2. This is inconsistent with the pegged exchange rate $\overline{E}$, so the policy makers cannot alter monetary policy and shift the LM curve in this way. They must leave the money supply equal to M_1 and the economy cannot deviate from its initial equilibrium.

This example illustrates a key lesson: under a fixed exchange rate, autonomous monetary policy is not an option. What is going on? Remember that under a fixed exchange rate, the home interest rate must exactly equal the foreign interest rate, $i = i^*$, according to the uncovered interest parity condition. Any shift in the LM curve would violate this restriction and break the fixed exchange rate.

To sum up: monetary policy under fixed exchange rates is impossible to undertake. Fixing the exchange rate means giving up monetary policy autonomy. In an earlier chapter, we learned about the trilemma: countries cannot simultaneously allow capital mobility, maintain fixed exchange rates, and pursue an autonomous monetary policy. We have now just seen the trilemma at work in the IS-LM-FX framework. By illustrating a potential benefit of autonomous monetary policy (the ability to use monetary policy to increase output), the model clearly exposes one of the major costs of fixed exchange rates. Monetary policy, which in principle could be used to influence the economy in the short run, is ruled out by a fixed exchange rate.

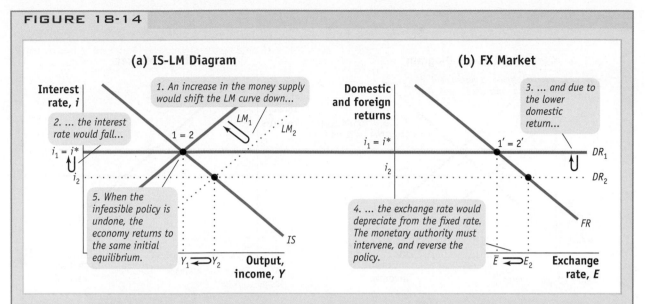

FIGURE 18-14

(a) IS-LM Diagram

(b) FX Market

1. An increase in the money supply would shift the LM curve down...

2. ... the interest rate would fall...

5. When the infeasible policy is undone, the economy returns to the same initial equilibrium.

3. ... and due to the lower domestic return...

4. ... the exchange rate would depreciate from the fixed rate. The monetary authority must intervene, and reverse the policy.

Monetary Policy Under Fixed Exchange Rates In panel (a) in the IS-LM diagram, the goods and money markets are initially in equilibrium at point 1. In panel (b), the forex market is initially in equilibrium at point 1′. A temporary monetary expansion that increases the money supply from M_1 to M_2 would shift the LM curve down in panel (a). In panel (b), the lower interest rate would imply that the exchange rate must depreciate, rising from $\bar{E}$ to E_2. This depreciation is inconsistent with the pegged exchange rate, so the policy makers cannot move LM in this way. They must leave the money supply equal to M_1. Implication: under a fixed exchange rate, autonomous monetary policy is not an option.

Fiscal Policy Under Floating Exchange Rates

We now turn to fiscal policy under a floating exchange rate. In this example, we consider a temporary increase in government spending from $\bar{G}_1$ to $\bar{G}_2$ in the home economy. Again, the effect is not permanent, so there are no changes in long-run expectations, and in particular the expected future exchange rate remains steady at E^e. Figure 18-15 shows what happens in our model. In panel (a) in the IS-LM diagram, the goods and money markets are initially in equilibrium at point 1. The interest rate in the money market is also the domestic return DR_1 that prevails in the forex market. In panel (b), the forex market is initially in equilibrium at point 1′.

A temporary fiscal expansion that increases government spending from $\bar{G}_1$ to $\bar{G}_2$ would shift the IS curve to the right in panel (a) from IS_1 to IS_2, causing the interest rate to rise from i_1 to i_2. The domestic return rises from DR_1 to DR_2. In panel (b), the higher interest rate would imply that the exchange rate must appreciate, falling from E_1 to E_2. As the interest rate rises (decreasing investment I) and the exchange rate appreciates (decreasing the trade balance TB), demand still tends to rise overall as government spending increases, which corresponds to the move up the LM curve from point 1 to point 2. Output expands from Y_1 to Y_2. The new equilibrium is at points 2 and 2′.

What is happening here? The fiscal expansion raises output as the IS curve shifts right. But the increases in output will raise interest rates, all else equal, given a fixed money supply. The resulting higher interest rates will reduce the investment component of demand, and this limits the rise in demand to less than the increase in government spending. This impact of fiscal expansion on investment is often referred to as *crowding out* by economists.

FIGURE 18-15

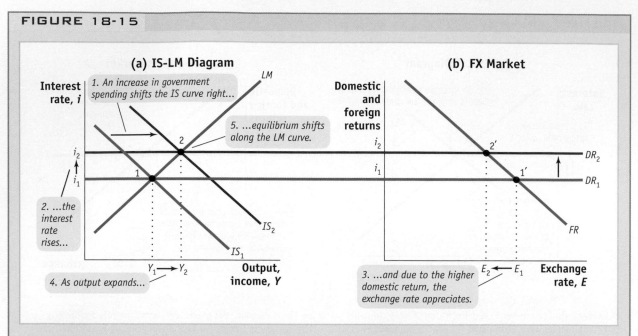

Fiscal Policy Under Floating Exchange Rates In panel (a) in the IS-LM diagram, the goods and money markets are initially in equilibrium at point 1. The interest rate in the money market is also the domestic return, DR_1, that prevails in the forex market. In panel (b), the forex market is initially in equilibrium at point 1'. A temporary fiscal expansion that increases government spending from $\overline{G}_1$ to $\overline{G}_2$ would shift the IS curve to the right in panel (a) from IS_1 to IS_2, causing the interest rate to rise from i_1 to i_2. The domestic return shifts up from DR_1 to DR_2. In panel (b), the higher interest rate would imply that the exchange rate must appreciate, falling from E_1 to E_2. As the interest rate rises (decreasing investment, I) and the exchange rate appreciates (decreasing the trade balance), demand falls, which corresponds to the move along the LM curve from point 1 to point 2. Output expands from Y_1 to Y_2. The new equilibrium corresponds to points 2 and 2'.

The higher interest rate also causes the home currency to appreciate. As home consumers switch their consumption to now less expensive foreign goods, the trade balance will fall. Thus, the higher interest rate also (indirectly) leads to a *crowding out* of net exports, and this too limits the rise in output to less than the increase in government spending. Thus, in an open economy, fiscal expansion not only crowds out investment (by raising the interest rate) but also crowds out net exports (by causing the exchange rate to appreciate).

To sum up: a temporary expansion of fiscal policy under floating exchange rates is effective. It raises output at home, raises the interest rate, causes an appreciation of the exchange rate, and decreases the trade balance. (A temporary contraction of fiscal policy has opposite effects. As an exercise, work through the contraction case using the same graphical apparatus.)

Fiscal Policy Under Fixed Exchange Rates

Now let's see how the outcomes differ when the home country pegs its exchange rate with respect to the foreign country at $\overline{E}$. The key is to recall the parity condition: the home interest rate must remain exactly equal to the foreign interest rate for the peg to hold.

Figure 18-16 shows what happens in this case. In panel (a) in the IS-LM diagram, the goods and money markets are initially in equilibrium at point 1. The interest rate in the money market is also the domestic return DR_1 that prevails in the forex market. In panel (b), the forex market is initially in equilibrium at point 1'.

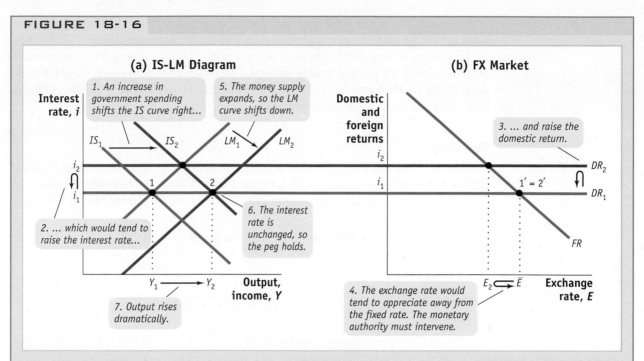

FIGURE 18-16

Fiscal Policy Under Fixed Exchange Rates In panel (a) in the IS-LM diagram, the goods and money markets are initially in equilibrium at point 1. The interest rate in the money market is also the domestic return, DR_1, that prevails in the forex market. In panel (b), the forex market is initially in equilibrium at point 1′. A temporary fiscal expansion on its own increases government spending from $\bar{G}_1$ to $\bar{G}_2$ and would shift the IS curve to the right in panel (a) from IS_1 to IS_2, causing the interest rate to rise from i_1 to i_2. The domestic return would then rise from DR_1 to DR_2. In panel (b), the higher interest rate would imply that the exchange rate must appreciate, falling from $\bar{E}$ to E_2. To maintain the peg, the monetary authority must now intervene, shifting the LM curve down, from LM_1 to LM_2. The fiscal expansion thus prompts a monetary expansion. In the end, the interest rate and exchange rate are left unchanged, and output expands *dramatically* from Y_1 to Y_2. The new equilibrium corresponds to points 2 and 2′.

A temporary fiscal expansion that increases government spending from $\bar{G}_1$ to $\bar{G}_2$ would shift the IS curve to the right in panel (a) from IS_1 to IS_2, causing the interest rate to rise from i_1 to i_2. The domestic return would rise from DR_1 to DR_2. In panel (b), the higher interest rate would imply that the exchange rate must appreciate, falling from $\bar{E}$ to E_2. To maintain the peg, the monetary authority must intervene, shifting the LM curve to the right also, from LM_1 to LM_2. The fiscal expansion thus prompts a monetary expansion. In the end, the interest rate and exchange rate are left unchanged, and output expands *dramatically* from Y_1 to Y_2. The new equilibrium corresponds to points 2 and 2′.

What is happening here? From the last example, we know that there is appreciation pressure associated with a fiscal expansion if the currency is allowed to float. To maintain the peg, the monetary authority must immediately alter its monetary policy at the very moment the fiscal expansion occurs so that the LM curve shifts from LM_1 to LM_2. The way to do this is to expand the money supply, and this generates pressure for depreciation, offsetting the appreciation pressure. If the monetary authority pulls this off, the market exchange rate will stay at the initial pegged level $\bar{E}$.

Thus, when a country is operating under a fixed exchange, fiscal policy is supereffective because any fiscal expansion by the government forces an immediate monetary expansion by the central bank to keep the exchange rate steady. The double, and simultaneous, expansion of demand by the fiscal and monetary authorities imposes a huge stimulus on the economy, and output rises from Y_1 to Y_2 (beyond the level achieved by the same fiscal expansion under a floating exchange rate).

To sum up: a temporary expansion of fiscal policy under fixed exchange rates raises output at home by a considerable amount. (The case of a temporary contraction of fiscal policy would have similar but opposite effects. As an exercise, work through this case using the same graphical apparatus.)

Summary

We have now examined the operation of fiscal and monetary policies under both fixed and flexible exchange rates and have seen how the effects of these policies differ dramatically depending on the exchange rate regime. The outcomes can be summarized as follows:

Responses to Policy Shocks in the IS-LM-FX Model						
Exchange Rate Regime	Policy	i	E	I	TB	Y
Floating	Monetary expansion	↓	↑	↑	↑?	↑
	Fiscal expansion	↑	↓	↓	↓	↑
Fixed	Monetary expansion	0	0	0	0	0
	Fiscal expansion	0	0	0	↓	↑

In this table, an up arrow ↑ indicates that the variable rises; a down arrow ↓ indicates that the variables falls; and a zero indicates no effect. The effects would be reversed for contractionary policies. The row of zeros for monetary expansion under fixed rates reflects the fact that this infeasible policy cannot be undertaken.

In a floating exchange rate regime, autonomous monetary and fiscal policy is feasible. The power of monetary policy to expand demand comes from two forces in the short run: lower interest rates boost investment and a depreciated exchange rate boosts the trade balance, all else equal. In the end, though, the trade balance will experience downward pressure from an import rise due to the increase in home output and income. The net effect on output and investment is positive, and the net effect on the trade balance is unclear—but in practice it, too, is likely to be positive.

Expansionary fiscal policy is also effective under a floating regime, even though the impact of extra spending is offset by crowding out in two areas: investment is crowded out by higher interest rates, and the trade balance is crowded out by an appreciated exchange rate. Thus, on net, investment falls and the trade balance also falls, and the latter effect is unambiguously amplified by additional import demand arising from increased home output.

In a fixed exchange rate regime, monetary policy loses its power for two reasons. First, interest parity implies that the domestic interest rate cannot move independently of the foreign rate, so investment demand cannot be manipulated. Second, the peg means that there can be no movement in the exchange rate, so the trade balance cannot be manipulated by expenditure switching.

Only fiscal policy is feasible under a fixed regime. Tax cuts or spending increases by the government can generate additional demand. But fiscal expansion then requires a monetary expansion to keep interest rates steady and maintain the peg. Fiscal policy becomes ultra-powerful in a fixed exchange rate setting—the reason for this is that if interest rates and exchange rates are held steady by the central bank, investment and the trade balance are never crowded out by fiscal policy. Monetary policy follows fiscal policy and amplifies it.

6 Stabilization Policy

We now have seen that macroeconomic policies can effect economic activity in the short run. These effects open up the possibility that the authorities can use changes in policies to try to keep the economy at or near its full-employment level of output. This is the essence of **stabilization policy.** If the economy is hit by a temporary adverse shock, policy makers could use expansionary monetary and fiscal policies to prevent a deep recession. Conversely, if the economy is pushed by a shock above its full employment level of output, contractionary policies could tame the boom.

For example, suppose a temporary adverse shock such as a sudden decline in investment, consumption, or export demand shifts the IS curve to the left. Or suppose an adverse shock such as a sudden increase in money demand suddenly moves the LM curve up. Either shock would cause home output to fall. In principle, the home policy makers could offset these shocks by using fiscal or monetary policy to shift either the IS curve or LM curve (or both) to cause an offsetting increase in output. When used judiciously, monetary and fiscal policies can thus be used to stabilize the economy and absorb shocks.

The policies must be used with care, however. If the economy is stable and growing, an additional temporary monetary or fiscal stimulus may cause an unsustainable boom that will, when the stimulus is withdrawn, turn into an undesirable bust. In their efforts to do good, policy makers must be careful not to destabilize the economy through the ill-timed, inappropriate, or excessive use of monetary and fiscal policies.

APPLICATION

The Right Time for Austerity?

After the global financial crisis, many observers would have predicted economic difficulties for Eastern Europe in the short run. Most countries had seen a rapid boom before 2008, with large expansions of credit, capital inflows, and high inflation of local wages and prices creating real appreciations: the same ingredients for a sharp economic downturn after the crisis as seen in Greece, Spain, Portugal and Ireland. Yet not all countries suffered the same fate. Here we use our analytical tools to look at two opposite cases: Poland, which fared well, and Latvia, which did not.

In our framework, as the shocks first hit, the demand for Poland's and Latvia's exports declined as a result of a contraction in foreign output Y^* in their trading partners, mainly the rest of Europe. In addition Poland and Latvia faced negative shocks to consumption and investment demand as consumers and investors cut back their expenditures in the face of uncertainty and tighter credit due to financial sector problems. These events would be represented by a leftward shift of Poland's and Latvia's IS curves from IS_1 to IS_2, which we show in Figure 18-17.

But the policy responses differed in each country, illustrating the contrasts between fixed and floating regimes. Because the Poles had a floating exchange rate, they were able to pursue strong monetary expansion and let the currency depreciate. They also maintained their plans for government spending in order to combat the decline in demand. Because the Letts were pegging to the euro, they could not use monetary policy at all, and they had to pursue aggressive austerity and slash government spending in order to satisfy the demands of an EU and IMF assistance program. Our modeling framework makes some predictions about the consequences of these policy choices.

In Figure 18-17, panels (a) and (b), Poland first goes from points 1(1′) to point 2(2′), and the initial shock is partially offset by the induced depreciation of the Polish zloty and increased investment thanks to lower interest rates. Then the equilibrium would be at 2′. In the end, demand would still be below its initial level and a recession would result with output falling from Y_1 to Y_2. However, the central bank responded with expansionary monetary policy, a shift out in the LM curve to LM_3. The economy shifted

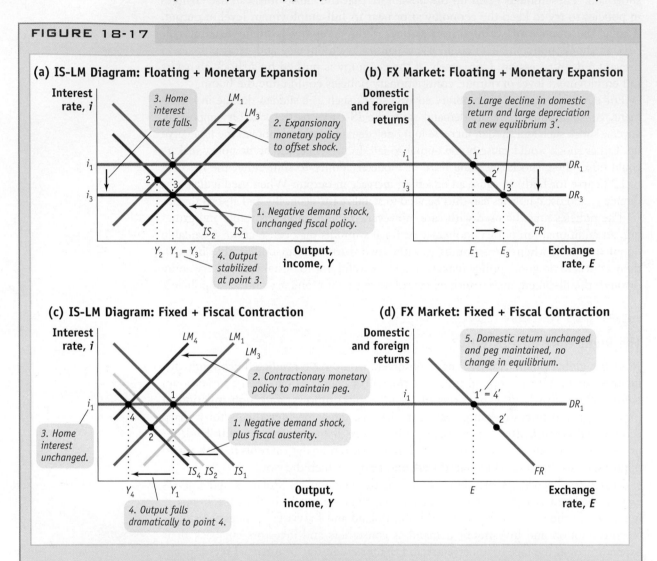

FIGURE 18-17

Examples of Policy Choices Under Floating and Fixed Exchange Rates In panels (a) and (c) in the IS-LM diagram, the goods and money markets are initially in equilibrium at point 1. The interest rate is also the domestic return, DR_1, that prevails in the forex market. In panels (b) and (d), the forex market is initially in equilibrium at point 1′. An exogenous negative shock to demand (e.g., a collapse in foreign income and/or a financial crisis at home) causes the IS curve to shift in from IS_1 to IS_2. Without further action, output and interest rates would fall and the exchange rate would tend to depreciate. In panels (a) and (b), we explore what happens when the central bank can stabilize output at its former level by responding with a monetary policy expansion, increasing the money supply and causing the LM curve to shift out from LM_1 to LM_3. The new equilibrium corresponds to points 3 and 3′. Output is now stabilized at the original level Y_1. The interest rate falls further from i_1 all the way to i_3. The domestic return falls from DR_1 to DR_3, and the exchange rate depreciates all the way from E_1 to E_3. In panels (c) and (d) we explore what happens when the exchange rate is fixed and the government pursues austerity and cuts government spending G. This causes the IS curve to shift in even further from IS_2 to IS_4. If the central bank does nothing, the home interest rate would fall further and the exchange rate would depreciate sharply at point 2 and 2′. To maintain the peg, as dictated by the trilemma, the home central bank must engage in contractionary monetary policy, decreasing the money supply and causing the LM curve to shift in all the way from LM_1 to LM_4. The new equilibrium corresponds to points 4 and 4′. The peg is preserved, but output collapses to the new level Y_4.

to point 3(3′): even lower interest rates amplified the depreciation of the zloty and stimulated demand through investment and expenditure-switching channels. In contrast, as shown in Figure 18-17, panels (c) and (d), Latvia cut government spending, so when their IS curve shifted in, they shifted it *even farther* to IS_4. Bound by the trilemma, Latvia's LM curve had to follow those shifts in lockstep and move in to LM_4 in order to maintain the lat–euro peg. The Latvian economy moved from point 1(1′) to point 4(4′).

The model predicts that a recession might be avoided in Poland, but that there could be a very deep recession in Latvia. What actually happened? Check out the accompanying news item (see **Headlines: Poland Is Not Latvia**). ■

Problems in Policy Design and Implementation

In this chapter, we have looked at open-economy macroeconomics in the short run and at the role that monetary and fiscal policies can play in determining economic outcomes. The simple models we used have clear consequences. On the face of it, if policy makers were really operating in such an uncomplicated environment, they would have the ability to exert substantial control and could always keep output steady with no unemployed resources and no inflation pressure. In reality, life is more complicated for policy makers for a variety of reasons.

Policy Constraints Policy makers may not always be free to apply the policies they desire. A fixed exchange rate rules out any use of monetary policy. Other firm monetary or fiscal policy rules, such as interest rate rules or balanced-budget rules, place limits on policy. Even if policy makers decide to act, other constraints may bind them. While it is always feasible to print money, it may not be possible (technically or politically) to raise the real resources necessary for a fiscal expansion. Countries with weak tax systems or poor creditworthiness—problems that afflict developing countries—may find themselves unable to tax or borrow to finance an expansion of spending even if they wished to do so.

Incomplete Information and the Inside Lag Our models assume that the policy makers have full knowledge of the state of the economy before they take corrective action: they observe the economy's IS and LM curves and know what shocks have hit. In reality, macroeconomic data are compiled slowly and it may take weeks or months for policy makers to fully understand the state of the economy today. Even then, it will take time to formulate a policy response (the lag between shock and policy actions is called the *inside lag*). On the monetary side, there may be a delay between policy meetings. On the fiscal side, it may take even more time to pass a bill through the legislature and then enable a real change in spending or taxing activity by the public sector.

Policy Response and the Outside Lag Even if they finally receive the correct information, policy makers then have to formulate the right response given by the model. In particular, they must not be distracted by other policies or agendas, nor subject to influence by interest groups that might wish to see different policies enacted. Finally, it takes time for whatever policies are enacted to have any effect on the economy, through the spending decisions of the public and private sectors (the lag between policy actions and effects is called the *outside lag*).

Long-Horizon Plans Other factors may make investment and the trade balance less sensitive to policy. If the private sector understands that a policy change is temporary, then there may be reasons not to change consumption or investment expenditure.

HEADLINES

Poland Is Not Latvia

Eastern Europe faced difficult times in the Great Recession. Yet not all countries suffered the same fate, as we see from this story, and the macroeconomic data presented and discussed in Figure 18-18.

. . . Poland and Latvia . . . inherited woefully deficient institutions from communism and have struggled with many of the same economic ills over the past two decades. They have also adopted staggeringly different approaches to the crisis, one of which was a lot more effective than the other.

. . . I don't think it's being radical to say that [since 2004] Poland's performance is both a lot better and a lot less variable and that if you were going to draw lessons from one of the two countries that it should probably be the country which avoided an enormous bubble and subsequent collapse. What is it that caused Poland's economy to be so sound? Was it austerity? Was it hard money?

. . . Both Latvia and Poland actually ran rather substantial budget deficits during the height of the crisis, though Latvia's budgeting in the years preceding the crisis was more balanced and restrained than Poland's. . . . Poland's government spending as a percentage of GDP was also noticeably higher than Latvia's both before the crisis and after it. . . . You can see how, starting in 2008, Latvia starts to make some sharp cuts while Poland continues its steady, modest increases.

FIGURE 18-18

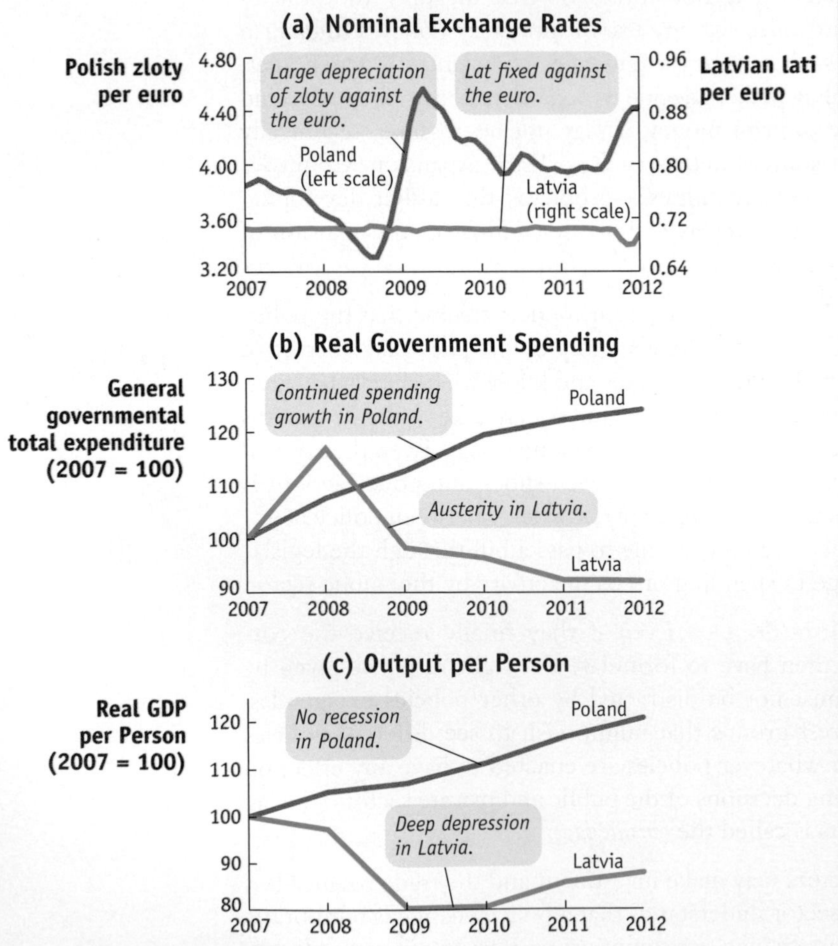

(a) Nominal Exchange Rates

Polish zloty per euro / Latvian lati per euro

Large depreciation of zloty against the euro.

Lat fixed against the euro.

Poland (left scale)

Latvia (right scale)

(b) Real Government Spending

General governmental total expenditure (2007 = 100)

Continued spending growth in Poland.

Poland

Austerity in Latvia.

Latvia

(c) Output per Person

Real GDP per Person (2007 = 100)

No recession in Poland.

Poland

Deep depression in Latvia.

Latvia

Macroeconomic Policy and Outcomes in Poland and Latvia, 2007–2012 Poland and Latvia reacted differently to adverse demand shocks from outside and inside their economies. Panels (a) and (b) show that Poland pursued expansionary monetary policy, let its currency depreciate against the euro, and kept government spending on a stable growth path. Latvia maintained a fixed exchange rate with the euro and pursued an austerity approach with large government spending cuts from 2009 onward. Panel (c) shows that Poland escaped a recession, with positive growth in all years. In contrast, Latvia fell into a deep depression, and real GDP per capita fell 20% from its 2007 peak.

Sources: IMF, International Financial Statistics and World Economic Outlook. Exchange rates are 3-month moving averages; all other data are annual.

So, basically, Poland is a country whose government habitually ran budget deficits before, during, and after the crisis, whose government spends a greater percentage of GDP than Latvia, and which did not cut spending in response to the crisis. Latvia, in contrast, ran balanced budgets, had a very small government as a percentage of GDP, and savagely cut spending in response to the crisis. While I don't think you can call Poland "profligate," if economics really were a morality play you'd expect the Latvians to come out way ahead since they've followed the austerity playbook down to the letter. However, in the real world, Poland's economic performance has been vastly,

almost comically, superior to Latvia's despite the fact that the country didn't make any "hard choices."

All of this, of course, leaves out monetary policy. . . . Part of the reason that Latvia's economic performance has been so awful is that it has pegged its currency to the Euro, a course of action which has made the Lat artificially expensive and which made Latvia's course of "internal devaluation" necessary. . . . Poland did the exact opposite, allowing its currency, the zloty, to depreciate massively against the Euro . . .

Poland did not, in other words, "defend the zloty" because it realized that a devaluation of its currency would be incredibly helpful. And the Polish economy

has continued to churn along while most of its neighbors have either crashed and burned or simply stagnated. . . .

There are plenty of lessons from Poland's economic success, including the need for effective government regulation (Poland never had an out-of-control bubble like Latvia), the need for exchange rate flexibility, and the extreme importance of a country having its own central bank. These lessons are neither left wing nor right wing, Poland's government is actually quite conservative . . . Economics just isn't a morality play, and no matter how often the Latvians cast themselves as the diligent and upstanding enforcers of austerity their economic performance over the past five years has still been lousy.

Source: Excerpted from Mark Adomanis, "If Austerity Is So Awesome Why Hasn't Poland Tried It?" forbes.com, January 10, 2013. Reproduced with Permission of Forbes Media LLC © 2013.

Suppose a firm can either build and operate a plant for several years or not build at all (e.g., the investment might be of an irreversible form). For example, a firm may not care about a higher real interest rate this year and may base its decision on the expected real interest rate that will affect its financing over many years ahead. Similarly, a temporary real appreciation may have little effect on whether a firm can profit in the long run from sales in the foreign market. In such circumstances, firms' investment and export activities may not be very sensitive to short-run policy changes.

Weak Links from the Nominal Exchange Rate to the Real Exchange Rate Our discussion assumed that changes in the nominal exchange rate lead to real exchange rate changes, but the reality can be somewhat different for some goods and services. For example, the dollar depreciated 42% against the yen from 2008 to 2012, but the U.S. prices of Japanese-made cars, like some Toyotas, barely changed. Why? There are a number of reasons for this weak *pass-through* phenomenon, including the dollarization of trade and the distribution margins that separate retail prices from port prices (as we saw in **Side Bar: Barriers to Expenditure Switching: Pass-Through and the J Curve**). The forces of arbitrage may also be weak as a result of noncompetitive market structures: for example, Toyota sells through exclusive dealers and government regulation requires that cars meet different standards in Europe versus the United States. These obstacles allow a firm like Toyota to *price to market:* to charge a steady U.S. price even as the exchange rate moves temporarily. If a firm can bear (or hedge) the exchange rate risk, it might do this to avoid the volatile sales and alienated customers that might result from repeatedly changing its U.S. retail price list.

Pegged Currency Blocs Our model's predictions are also affected by the fact that for some major countries in the real world, their exchange rate arrangements are characterized—often not as a result of their own choice—by a mix of floating and fixed exchange rate systems with different trading partners. For most of the decade 2000–10, the dollar depreciated markedly against the euro, pound, and several other floating currencies, but in the emerging-market "Dollar Bloc" (China, India, and other countries), the monetary authorities have ensured that the variation in the value of their currencies against the dollar was small or zero. When a large bloc of other countries pegs to the U.S. dollar, this limits the ability of the United States to engineer a real effective depreciation.

Weak Links from the Real Exchange Rate to the Trade Balance Our discussion also assumed that real exchange rate changes lead to changes in the trade balance. There may be several reasons why these linkages are weak in reality. One major reason is transaction costs in trade. Suppose the exchange rate is $1 per euro and an American is consuming a domestic good that costs $100 as opposed to a European good costing €100 = $100. If the dollar appreciates to $0.95 per euro, then the European good looks cheaper on paper, only $95. Should the American switch to the import? Yes, if the good can be moved without cost—but there are few such goods! If shipping costs $10, it still makes sense to consume the domestic good until the exchange rate falls below $0.90 per euro. Practically, this means that expenditure switching may be a nonlinear phenomenon: it will be weak at first and then much stronger as the real exchange rate change grows larger. This phenomenon, coupled with the J curve effects discussed earlier, may cause the response of the trade balance in the short run to be small or even in the wrong direction.

APPLICATION

Macroeconomic Policies in the Liquidity Trap

Undoubtedly, one of the most controversial experiments in macroeconomic policy-making began in 2008–10 as monetary and fiscal authorities around the world tried to respond to the major recession that followed the Global Financial Crisis. In this application, we look at the initial U.S. policy response and interpret events using the IS-LM-FX model of this chapter.

The unusual aspect of this crisis was the very rapid realization that monetary policy alone could not fully offset the magnitude of the shock to demand. In the context of our IS-LM-FX model, as consumption and investment fell for exogenous reasons, the shock moved the IS curve very far leftward. One major source of the demand shock was that, as we saw in an earlier chapter, banks were very afraid of taking on risk and sharply reduced their lending to firms and households—and even when they did lend, they were still charging very high interest rates. Thus, even with very expansionary monetary policy, that is, large rightward shifts of the LM curve, low policy interest rates did not translate into cheap borrowing for the private sector. Once the U.S. Federal Reserve had brought its policy rate to zero in December 2008, there was little more it could do to stimulate demand using conventional monetary policies.

This peculiar situation is depicted by the blue lines in Figure 18-19 and differs from the normal IS-LM-FX setup we have seen so far. After the demand shock and the Fed's response to it, the IS curve has moved so far in (to IS_1) and the LM curve has moved so far out (to LM_1), that the IS and LM curves now intersect at a very low interest rate: so low that it is equal to zero. In the money market, nominal interest rates can't fall below zero, so another way of describing this situation is to say that the economy was at an IS-LM equilibrium at which the LM curve was absolutely flat and resting on the horizontal axis (at a 0% interest rate) in the diagram.

(Note that in the FX diagram this would place the domestic return DR at zero. Also, note that interest rates were by this time at zero in all developed countries, for

FIGURE 18-19

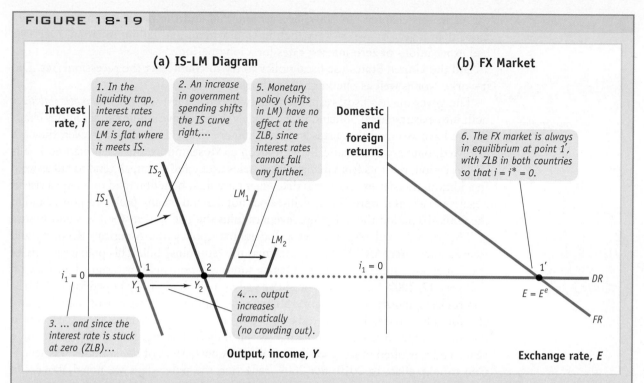

(a) IS-LM Diagram

Interest rate, i

1. In the liquidity trap, interest rates are zero, and LM is flat where it meets IS.

2. An increase in government spending shifts the IS curve right,...

5. Monetary policy (shifts in LM) have no effect at the ZLB, since interest rates cannot fall any further.

IS_2

IS_1

LM_1

LM_2

$i_1 = 0$

1

2

Y_1 Y_2

3. ... and since the interest rate is stuck at zero (ZLB)...

4. ... output increases dramatically (no crowding out).

Output, income, Y

(b) FX Market

Domestic and foreign returns

6. The FX market is always in equilibrium at point 1', with ZLB in both countries so that $i = i^* = 0$.

$i_1 = 0$

DR

1'

$E = E^e$

FR

Exchange rate, E

Macroeconomic Policies in the Liquidity Trap After a severe negative shock to demand, the IS curve may move very far to the left (IS_1). The nominal interest rate may then fall all the way to the zero lower bound (ZLB), with IS_1 intersecting the flat portion of the LM_1 curve at point 1, on the horizontal axis, in panel (a). Output is depressed at a level Y_1. In this scenario, monetary policy is impotent because expansionary monetary policy (e.g., a rightward shift from LM_1 to LM_2) cannot lower the interest rate any further. However, fiscal policy may be very effective, and a shift right from IS_1 to IS_2 leaves the economy still at the ZLB, but with a higher level of output Y_2. (The figure is drawn assuming the ZLB holds in both home and foreign economies, so the FX market is in equilibrium at point 1' with $E = E^e$ at all times.)

similar reasons. Thus, it is also appropriate to think of the foreign (e.g., euro) interest rate as also stuck at zero, which in the FX diagram would lower the foreign return *FR*.)

The situation just described is unusual in several ways. First, monetary policy is powerless in this situation: it cannot be used to lower interest rates because interest rates can't go any lower. In the diagram, moving the LM curve out to LM_2 does not dislodge the economy from the horizontal portion of the LM curve. We are still stuck on the IS_1 curve at a point 1 and a 0% percent interest rate. This unfortunate state of affairs is known as the *zero lower bound* (ZLB). It is also known as a *liquidity trap* because liquid money and interest-bearing assets have the same interest rate of zero, so there is no opportunity cost to holding money, and thus changes in the supply of central bank money have no effect on the incentive to switch between money and interest-bearing assets.

Can anything be done? Yes. The bad news is that fiscal policy is the only tool now available to increase demand. The good news is that fiscal policy has the potential to be super powerful in this situation. The reason is that as long as interest rates are stuck at zero, and the monetary authorities keep them there, government spending will not crowd out investment or net exports, in contrast to the typical situation we studied earlier in this chapter.[3] In 2009, because the Fed and the private sector anticipated more than a year or two of very high unemployment and falling inflation, everyone had expectations of zero interest rates for a long period.

Did the United States use fiscal policy to try to counteract the recession? Yes. Did it work? Not as well as one might have hoped.

The government's fiscal response took two forms. First was the *automatic stabilizer* built into existing fiscal policies. In the models that we have studied so far in this chapter, we have assumed that taxes and spending are fixed. In reality, however, they are not fixed, but vary systematically with income. Most important, when income Y falls in a recession, receipts from income taxes, sales taxes, and so on, all tend to fall as well. In addition, transfer expenditures (like unemployment benefits) tend to go up: a rise in negative taxes, as it were. This decline does not depend on any policy response, and in the 2008–10 period the fall in tax revenues (plus the rise in transfers) was enormous.

The second fiscal response was a discretionary policy, the American Recovery and Reinvestment Act (ARRA), better known as the "stimulus" bill. This policy was one of the first actions undertaken by the Obama administration and it was signed into law on February 17, 2009. Some of the president's advisors had originally hoped for a $1.4 trillion package, mostly for extra government consumption and investment spending, and also for aid to states. This was to be spread over 2 to 3 years from 2009–11. However, the final compromise deal with Congress was only half as big, $787 billion over three years, and was tilted more toward temporary tax cuts. Most of the stimulus was scheduled to take effect in 2010, not 2009, reflecting the policy lags we noted above. On average, the package amounted to about 1.5% of GDP in spending and tax cuts.

Some key outcomes are shown in Figure 18-20. As panel (a) shows, the size of the gap between actual and potential output left a huge hole to be filled by fiscal policy. By mid-2009 this hole was about 6% of potential GDP or over $1 trillion at an annual rate. *Even if the entire stimulus were spent,* the fiscal package could at best have filled only about one-quarter of the collapse in demand or 1.5% of GDP. Policy makers in the government, and many observers, knew the package was too small, but politics stood in the way of a larger package.

The data in panel (a) also show that private consumption fell precipitously. One intention of ARRA was to support private spending through tax cuts. Tax revenues T did fall considerably (largely at the federal level as shown in panel (b), because states were getting some offsetting transfers via ARRA). But tax cuts did not appear to generate much extra private spending, certainly not enough to offset the initial collapse in consumption expenditure. Many consumers were unsure about the economic recovery, worried about the risks of unemployment, and trying to use whatever "extra" money they got from tax cuts to pay down their debts or save. In addition, because people were trying to hold onto their money (precautionary motives were high), the marginal propensity to consume was probably low. Furthermore, for non-Keynesian consumers, the temporary nature of many of the tax cuts meant that anyone following the principles of *Ricardian equivalence* would be likely to save the tax cut to pay off an expected future tax liability.

This left government spending G to do a great deal of the stimulation, but problems arose because of the contrary effects of state and local government policies. As the figure shows, federal expenditures went up, rising by 0.5% of GDP in 2010. Leaving aside the miniscule size of this change, a big source of trouble was that state and local government expenditures went down by just as much. States and localities imposed

---

[3] Note that, at the ZLB, the model resembles the fixed exchange rate model, not the floating exchange rate model, because being stuck at the ZLB pegs the interest rate (in this case at zero, rather than at i^*).

FIGURE 18-20

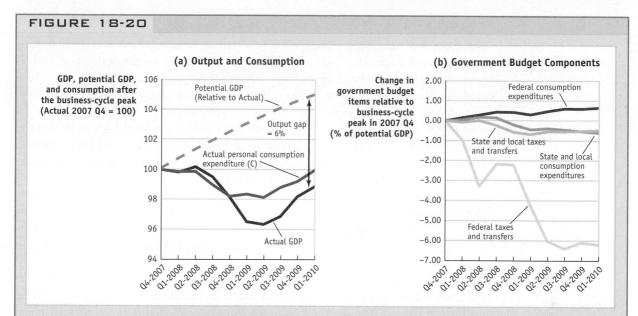

(a) Output and Consumption

GDP, potential GDP, and consumption after the business-cycle peak (Actual 2007 Q4 = 100)

- Potential GDP (Relative to Actual)
- Output gap = 6%
- Actual personal consumption expenditure (C)
- Actual GDP

(b) Government Budget Components

Change in government budget items relative to business-cycle peak in 2007 Q4 (% of potential GDP)

- Federal consumption expenditures
- State and local taxes and transfers
- State and local consumption expenditures
- Federal taxes and transfers

U.S. Fiscal Policy in the Great Recession: Didn't Work or Wasn't Tried? In the U.S. economic slump of 2008–10, output had fallen 6% below the estimate of potential (full-employment) level of GDP by the first quarter of 2009, as seen in panel (a). This was the worst U.S. recession since the 1930s. Policy responses included automatic fiscal expansion (increases in spending and reductions in taxes), plus an additional discretionary stimulus (the 2009 American Recovery and Reinvestment Act). The tax part of the stimulus appeared to do very little: significant reductions in taxes seen in panel (b) were insufficient to prop up consumption expenditure, as seen in panel (a), as consumers saved the extra disposable income. And on the government spending side there was no stimulus at all in the aggregate: increases in federal government expenditure were fully offset by cuts in state and local government expenditure, as seen in panel (b).

Sources: Federal Reserve Economic Indicators (FRED). Potential output from Congressional Budget Office; all other data from the Bureau of Economic Analysis.

austerity spending cuts, which were made necessary by calamitous declines in their tax revenues, by their limited ability (or willingness) to borrow, and by the feeble amount of aid to states authorized in the final ARRA package. The net change in overall government expenditures was thus, in the end, zero.

To sum up, the aggregate U.S. fiscal stimulus had four major weaknesses: it was rolled out too slowly, because of policy lags; the overall package was too small, given the magnitude of the decline in aggregate demand; the government spending portion of the stimulus, for which positive expenditure effects were certain, ended up being close to zero, because of state and local cuts; and this left almost all the work to tax cuts (automatic and discretionary) that recipients, for good reasons, were more likely to save rather than spend. With monetary policy impotent and fiscal policy weak and ill designed, the economy remained mired in its worst slump since the 1930s Great Depression.[4] ■

Construction work on an interstate highway in Cleveland, Ohio, funded by government stimulus money through the ARRA.

---

[4] The size of the output gap was understood early on, even before President Obama took office. At the start of January 2009, the Congressional Budget Office forecast that, without a stimulus, unemployment would rise above 9% by early 2010, and remain there for several years, with an output gap projected to be 6.8% of GDP in 2010 and 2011 (numbers very close to what has transpired). In that context, some economists pointed out the problems with the size and design of the ARRA package, especially the use of temporary tax cuts. See, for example, Martin Feldstein, Statement for the House Democratic Steering and Policy Committee, January 7, 2009; and Paul Krugman, "The Obama Gap," *New York Times*, January 8, 2009.

7 Conclusions

The analysis of macroeconomic policy is different in an open economy than in a closed economy. The trade balance generates an additional source of demand, and its fluctuations are driven by changes in output and the real exchange rate. Expenditure switching is a key mechanism at work here: as international relative prices change, demand shifts from foreign to home goods and vice versa.

The open economy IS-LM-FX framework is a workhorse model for analyzing the macroeconomic responses to shocks and to changes in monetary and fiscal policies. Exploring these responses, in turn, draws out some clear contrasts between the operation of fixed and flexible exchange rate regimes.

Under flexible exchange rates, monetary and fiscal policies can be used. Monetary expansions raise output and also lower the interest rate, which stimulates investment and causes a depreciation, which in turn stimulates the trade balance. Fiscal expansions raise output; raise the interest rate, which depresses investment; and cause an appreciation, which in turn lowers the trade balance.

With two policy tools available, the authorities have considerable flexibility. In particular, their ability to let the exchange rate adjust to absorb shocks makes a strong case for a floating exchange rate. Now we can understand the logic behind Robert Mundell's quote at the start of the chapter.

Under fixed exchange rates, monetary policy cannot be used because the home interest rate has to remain equal to the foreign interest rate in order for the exchange rate to remain fixed. But fiscal policy has great power under a fixed exchange rate. Fiscal expansions raise output and force the monetary authority to expand the money supply to prevent any rise in the interest rate and any appreciation of the exchange rate. In contrast to the floating case, in which interest rate increases and exchange rate appreciation put downward pressure on investment and the trade balance, the demand stimulus is even greater.

With only one policy tool available, the authorities in fixed rate regimes have much less flexibility. They also expose the economy to more volatility because any demand shock will entail an immediate and reinforcing monetary shock. The tendency of fixed exchange rate systems to amplify demand shocks helps us understand the logic behind Alec Ford's quote at the start of the chapter.

Whatever the regime, fixed or floating, our findings suggest that macroeconomic policy can *in principle* be used to stabilize an open economy when it suffers from external shocks. Under floating exchange rates, however, more policy options are available (monetary and fiscal policy responses are feasible) than under fixed exchange rates (only a fiscal policy response is feasible).

Despite these relatively simple lessons, real-world policy design is not straightforward. Policy makers have difficulty identifying shocks, devising the right response, and acting quickly enough to ensure that policy actions have a timely effect. Even then, under some conditions, the economy may respond in unusual ways.

KEY POINTS

1. In the short run, we assume prices are sticky at some preset level P. There is thus no inflation, and nominal and real quantities can be considered equivalent. We assume output GDP equals income Y or GDNI and that the trade balance equals the current account (there are no transfers or factor income from abroad).

2. The Keynesian consumption function says that private consumption spending C is an increasing function of household disposable income $Y - T$.

3. The investment function says that total investment I is a decreasing function of the real or nominal interest rate i.

4. Government spending is assumed to be exogenously given at a level G.

5. The trade balance is assumed to be an increasing function of the real exchange rate EP^*/P, where P^* denotes the foreign price level.

6. The national income identity says that national income or output equals private consumption C, plus investment I, plus government spending G, plus the trade balance TB: $Y = C + I + G + TB$. The right-hand side of this expression is called *demand*, and its components depend on income, interest rates, and the real exchange rate. In equilibrium, demand must equal the left-hand side, supply, or total output Y.

7. If the interest rate falls in an open economy, demand is stimulated for two reasons. A lower interest rate directly stimulates investment. A lower interest rate also leads to an exchange rate depreciation, all else equal, which increases the trade balance. This demand must be satisfied for the goods market to remain in equilibrium, so output rises. This is the basis of the IS curve: declines in interest rates must call forth extra output to keep the goods market in equilibrium. Each point on the IS curve represents a combination of output Y and interest rate i at which the goods and FX markets are in equilibrium. Because Y increases as i decreases, the IS curve is downward-sloping.

8. Real money demand arises primarily from transactions requirements. It increases when the volume of transactions (represented by national income Y) increases, and decreases when the

opportunity cost of holding money, the nominal interest rate i, increases.

9. The money market equilibrium says that the demand for real money balances L must equal the real money supply: $M/P = L(i)Y$. This equation is the basis for the LM curve: any increases in output Y must cause the interest rate to rise, all else equal (e.g., holding fixed real money M/P). Each point on the LM curve represents a combination of output Y and interest rate i at which the money market is in equilibrium. Because i increases as Y increases, the LM curve is upward-sloping.

10. The IS-LM diagram combines the IS and LM curves on one figure and shows the unique short-run equilibrium for output Y and the interest rate i that describes simultaneous equilibrium in the goods and money markets. The IS-LM diagram can be coupled with the forex market diagram to summarize conditions in all three markets: goods, money, and forex. This combined IS-LM-FX diagram can then be used to assess the impact of various macroeconomic policies in the short run.

11. Under a floating exchange rate, the interest rate and exchange rate are free to adjust to maintain equilibrium. Thus, government policy is free to move either the IS or LM curves. The effects are as follows:

    - Monetary expansion: LM shifts to the right, output rises, interest rate falls, exchange rate rises/depreciates.
    - Fiscal expansion: IS shifts to the right, output rises, interest rate rises, exchange rate falls/appreciates.

12. Under a fixed exchange rate, the interest rate always equals the foreign interest rate and the exchange rate is pegged. Thus, the government is not free to move the LM curve: monetary policy must be adjusted to ensure that LM is in such a position that these exchange rate and interest rate conditions hold. The impacts are as follows:

    - Monetary expansion: not feasible.
    - Fiscal expansion: IS shifts to the right, LM follows it and also shifts to the right, output

rises strongly, interest rate and exchange rate are unchanged.

13. The ability to manipulate the IS and LM curves gives the government the capacity to engage in stabilization policies to offset shocks to the economy and to try to maintain a full-employment level of output. This is easier said than done, however, because it is difficult to diagnose the correct policy response, and policies often take some time to have an impact, so that by the time the policy effects are felt, they may be ineffective or even counterproductive.

KEY TERMS

consumption, p. 665
disposable income, p. 665
marginal propensity to consume (MPC), p. 666
expected real interest rate, p. 666
taxes, p. 666
government consumption, p. 666
transfer programs, p. 666
expenditure switching, p. 668
real effective exchange rate, p. 671
pass-through, p. 673
J curve, p. 674
goods market equilibrium condition, p. 676
Keynesian cross, p. 677
IS curve, p. 680
LM curve, p. 686
monetary policy, p. 689
fiscal policy, p. 689
stabilization policy, p. 697

PROBLEMS

1. In 2001, President George W. Bush and Federal Reserve Chairman Alan Greenspan were both concerned about a sluggish U.S. economy. They also were concerned about the large U.S. current account deficit. To help stimulate the economy, President Bush proposed a tax cut, while the Fed had been increasing U.S. money supply. Compare the effects of these two policies in terms of their implications for the current account. If policy makers are concerned about the current account deficit, discuss whether stimulatory fiscal policy or monetary policy makes more sense in this case. Then, reconsider similar issues for 2009–10, when the economy was in a deep slump, the Fed had taken interest rates to zero, and the Obama administration was arguing for larger fiscal stimulus.

2. Suppose that American firms become more optimistic and decide to increase investment expenditure today in new factories and office space.

   a. How will this increase in investment affect output, interest rates, and the current account?

   b. Now repeat part (a), assuming that domestic investment is very responsive to the interest rate so that U.S. firms will cancel most of their new investment plans if the interest rate rises. How will this affect the answer you gave previously?

3. For each of the following situations, use the IS-LM-FX model to illustrate the effects of the shock. For each case, state the effect of the shock on the following variables (increase, decrease, no change, or ambiguous): Y, i, E, C, I, and TB. Assume the government allows the exchange rate to float and makes no policy response.

   a. Foreign output decreases.

   b. Investors expect a depreciation of the home currency.

   c. The money supply increases.

   d. Government spending increases.

4. How would a decrease in the money supply of Paraguay (currency unit is the "guaraní") affect its own output and its exchange rate with Brazil (currency unit is the "real"). Do you think this policy in Paraguay might also affect output across the border in Brazil? Explain.

5. For each of the following situations, use the IS-LM-FX model to illustrate the effects of the shock and the policy response. *Note:* Assume the government responds by using monetary policy to stabilize output, unlike question 3, and assume the exchange rate is floating. For each case, state the effect of the shock on the following variables (increase, decrease, no change, or ambiguous): Y, i, E, C, I, and TB.

   a. Foreign output decreases.
   b. Investors expect a depreciation of the home currency.
   c. The money supply increases.
   d. Government spending increases.

6. Repeat the previous question, assuming the central bank responds in order to maintain a fixed exchange rate. In which case or cases will the government response be the same as in the previous question?

7. This question explores IS and FX equilibria in a numerical example.

   a. The consumption function is $C = 1.5 + 0.75(Y - T)$. What is the marginal propensity to consume MPC? What is the marginal propensity to save MPS?
   b. The trade balance is $TB = 5(1 - [1/E]) - 0.25(Y - 8)$. What is the marginal propensity to consume foreign goods $MPCF$? What is the marginal propensity to consume home goods $MPCH$?
   c. The investment function is $I = 2 - 10i$. What is investment when the interest rate i is equal to $0.10 = 10\%$?
   d. Assume government spending is G. Add up the four components of demand and write down the expression for D.
   e. Assume forex market equilibrium is given by $i = ([1/E] - 1) + 0.10$, where the two foreign return terms on the right are expected depreciation and the foreign interest rate. What is the foreign interest rate? What is the expected future exchange rate?

8. [More Difficult] Continuing the last question, solve for the IS curve: obtain an expression for Y in terms of i, G, and T (eliminate E).

9. Assume that initially the IS curve is given by

$$IS_1: Y = 12 - 1.5T - 30i + 2G$$

and that the price level P is 1, and the LM curve is given by

$$LM_1: M = Y(1 - i)$$

The home central bank uses the interest rate as its policy instrument. Initially, the home interest rate equals the foreign interest rate of 10% or 0.1. Taxes and government spending both equal 2. Call this case 1.

   a. According to the IS_1 curve, what is the level of output Y? Assume this is the desired full-employment level of output.
   b. According to the LM_1 curve, at this level of output, what is the level of the home money supply?
   c. Plot the IS_1 and LM_1 curves for case 1 on a chart. Label the axes, and the equilibrium values.
   d. Assume that forex market equilibrium is given by $i = ([1/E] - 1) + 0.10$, where the two foreign return terms on the right are expected depreciation and the foreign interest rate. The expected future exchange rate is 1. What is today's spot exchange rate?
   e. There is now a foreign demand shock, such that the IS curve shifts left by 1.5 units at all levels of the interest rate, and the new IS curve is given by

$$IS_2: Y = 10.5 - 1.5T - 30i + 2G$$

   The government asks the central bank to stabilize the economy at full employment. To stabilize and return output back to the desired level, according to this new IS curve, by how much must the interest rate be lowered from its initial level of 0.1? (Assume taxes and government spending remain at 2.) Call this case 2.
   f. At the new lower interest rate and at full employment, on the new LM curve (LM_2), what is the new level of the money supply?
   g. According to the forex market equilibrium, what is the new level of the spot exchange rate? How large is the depreciation of the home currency?

h. Plot the new IS_2 and LM_2 curves for case 2 on a chart. Label the axes, and the equilibrium values.

i. Return to part (e). Now assume that the central bank refuses to change the interest rate from 10%. In this case, what is the new level of output? What is the money supply? And if the government decides to use fiscal policy instead to stabilize output, then according to the new IS curve, by how much must government spending be increased to achieve this goal? Call this case 3.

j. Plot the new IS_3 and LM_3 curves for case 3 on a chart. Label the axes, and the equilibrium values.

10. In this chapter, we've studied how policy responses affect economic variables in an open economy. Consider each of the problems in policy design and implementation discussed in this chapter. Compare and contrast each problem as it applies to monetary policy stabilization versus fiscal policy stabilization.

APPENDIX 1 TO CHAPTER 18

....

The Marshall–Lerner Condition

The model developed in this chapter assumes that a depreciation of a country's currency (a rise in q) will cause the trade balance to move toward surplus (a rise in TB). Is this assumption justified?

Let's look at a simple example. Consider a hypothetical two-country world in which trade is initially balanced, so $TB = 0$ or $EX = IM$. The question of how the trade balance changes then simplifies to a question of whether the change in exports is greater or less than the change in imports. Let us consider a small percentage change in the real exchange rate, say, $\Delta q/q = +1\%$, that is, a home real depreciation of 1%. Note that this is, approximately, a foreign real appreciation of 1%, since the foreign real exchange rate $q^* = 1/q$ is simply the inverse of the home real exchange rate, implying that $\Delta q^*/q^* = -1\%$.

As we have argued, when home exports look cheaper to foreigners, the real value of home exports expressed in home units of output will *unambiguously* rise. This effect is described by the elasticity of home exports with respect to the home real exchange rate, denoted η, where

$$\frac{\Delta EX}{EX} = \eta \times \frac{\Delta q}{q} = \eta\%$$

That is, if the home country experiences a 1% real depreciation, its real exports (measured in home units) rise by $\eta\%$.

The same logic applies to the foreign country, with exports EX^*, real exchange rate $q^* = 1/q$, and elasticity η^*, so that

$$\frac{\Delta EX^*}{EX^*} = \eta^* \times \frac{\Delta q^*}{q^*} = \eta^*\%$$

Now consider the trade link between the two countries. Foreign exports must equal home imports, measured in any consistent units. In home, real output units

$$
\begin{array}{l}
\text{Home imports} \\
\text{in units of home output}
\end{array}
= \underbrace{IM(q)}_{\substack{\text{Home imports} \\ \text{(real)}}}
$$

$$
\begin{array}{l}
\text{Foreign exports} \\
\text{in units of home output}
\end{array}
= \underbrace{(1/P)}_{\substack{\text{Divide by home} \\ \text{price level to} \\ \text{convert to home} \\ \text{output units}}} \times \underbrace{E}_{\substack{\text{Exchange} \\ \text{rate converts} \\ \text{foreign to} \\ \text{domestic} \\ \text{currency}}} \times \underbrace{\underbrace{P^* \times \underbrace{EX^*(q^*)}_{\substack{\text{Foreign exports} \\ \text{(real)}}}}_{\substack{\text{Value of foreign exports in} \\ \text{foreign currency}}}}_{}
$$

Value of foreign exports in home currency

where under P^*: _Price of foreign basket in foreign currency_

Equating these two terms, we find that $IM(q) = (EP^*/P) \times EX^*(q^*)$. Thus,

$$IM(q) = q \times EX^*(q^*)$$

This expression makes intuitive sense for the stylized two-country world that we are studying. It states that *IM*, the quantity of home imports (measured in *home* output units), must equal the quantity of foreign exports EX^* (measured in *foreign* output units) multiplied by a factor q that converts units of foreign goods to units of home goods (since q is the relative price of foreign goods, that is home goods per unit of foreign goods).

For a small change, we may write the percentage change in the previous equation as follows. On the left is the percentage change in imports; on the right is the percentage change in q *times* EX^*, which equals the percentage change in q *plus* the percentage change in EX^*:

$$\frac{\Delta IM}{IM} = \frac{\Delta q}{q} + \frac{\Delta EX^*}{EX^*} = \frac{\Delta q}{q} + \left[\eta^* \times \frac{\Delta q^*}{q^*} \right] = 1\% + \left[\eta^* \times (-1\%) \right] = (1 - \eta^*)\%$$

What is going on here? On the home import side, two effects come into play. Foreigners export a lower volume of their more expensive goods measured in foreign output units (a volume effect of $-\eta^*\%$), but those goods will cost more for home importers in terms of home output (a price effect of 1%). The price effect follows because the real exchange rate (the relative price of the foreign goods in terms of domestic goods) has increased (by 1%), and this makes every unit of imports cost more in real terms.

Starting from balanced trade with $EX = IM$, a 1% home real depreciation will cause EX to change by $\eta\%$ and IM to change by $1 - \eta^*\%$. The trade balance (initially zero) will increase (to become positive) if and only if the former impact on EX exceeds the latter impact on IM. This occurs if and only if $\eta > 1 - \eta^*$, or, equivalently,

$$\eta + \eta^* > 1$$

The last expression is known as the *Marshall–Lerner condition:* it says that the trade balance will increase only after a real depreciation if the responsiveness of trade volumes to real exchange rate changes is sufficiently large (or sufficiently elastic) to ensure that the volume effects exceed the price effects.

APPENDIX 2 TO CHAPTER 18

. . . .

Multilateral Real Exchange Rates

How do the predictions of our model change when a country trades with multiple countries or regions? Can our theory be extended to this more realistic case? Can we make a sensible aggregation of trade flows, trade balances, and real exchange rates across, say, N different countries?

Suppose that for trade with any foreign country (say, country 1), the fractional change in home exports EX_1 and imports IM_1 given a small change in the real exchange rate q_1 is

$$\frac{\Delta EX_1}{EX_1} = \varepsilon \times \frac{\Delta q_1}{q_1}; \qquad \frac{\Delta IM_1}{IM_1} = -\varepsilon \times \frac{\Delta q_1}{q_1}$$

The parameter $\varepsilon > 0$ is an *elasticity*. In this case, it is the elasticity of exports and imports with respect to the real exchange rate. When q rises by 1% (a real depreciation), exports rise by $\varepsilon\%$ and imports fall by $\varepsilon\%$. (A more complicated analysis is needed when the import and export elasticities differ; see the first appendix.)

From these relationships, we find the following by rearranging:

$$\Delta TB_1 = \Delta EX_1 - \Delta IM_1 = \varepsilon \frac{\Delta q_1}{q_1} EX_1 + \varepsilon \frac{\Delta q_1}{q_1} IM_1$$

$$= \varepsilon \times (EX_1 + IM_1) \times \frac{\Delta q_1}{q_1}$$

$$= \varepsilon \times \text{Trade}_1 \times \frac{\Delta q_1}{q_1}$$

where $\text{Trade}_i = [EX_i + IM_i]$ is the total trade of the home country with country i.

Adding up this last equation across all countries, the change in the home trade balance is given by $\Delta TB = \Delta TB_1 + \Delta TB_2 + \cdots + \Delta TB_N$, which we can write as

$$\Delta TB = \varepsilon \times \left[\text{Trade}_1 \frac{\Delta q_1}{q_1} + \text{Trade}_2 \frac{\Delta q_2}{q_2} + \cdots + \text{Trade}_N \frac{\Delta q_N}{q_N} \right]$$

We normalize by total trade, where $\text{Trade} = \text{Trade}_1 + \text{Trade}_2 + \cdots + \text{Trade}_N$, to obtain

$$\Delta TB = \varepsilon \times \text{Trade} \times \underbrace{\left[\frac{\text{Trade}_1}{\text{Trade}} \frac{\Delta q_1}{q_1} + \frac{\text{Trade}_1}{\text{Trade}} \frac{\Delta q_2}{q_2} + \cdots + \frac{\text{Trade}_1}{\text{Trade}} \frac{\Delta q_N}{q_N} \right]}_{\text{Trade-weighted average of bilateral real exchange rate changes}}$$

The expression in brackets might look familiar. In Chapter 13, we introduced the concept of a *trade-weighted change in the nominal exchange rate*—the change in the value of a currency against a basket of currencies, where the change in each country-pair's nominal exchange rate was weighted by that particular country-pair's share of trade volume. The preceding expression is similar, only with nominal exchange rates replaced by real exchange rates. The expression shows that (with some assumptions) our model can be extended to more realistic scenarios with many countries by using the change in a trade-weighted real exchange rate covering all trading partners.

Fixed Versus Floating: International Monetary Experience

In truth, the gold standard is already a barbarous relic. All of us, from the Governor of the Bank of England downwards, are now primarily interested in preserving the stability of business, prices, and employment, and are not likely, when the choice is forced on us, deliberately to sacrifice these to the outworn dogma. . . . Advocates of the ancient standard do not observe how remote it now is from the spirit and the requirements of the age.

John Maynard Keynes, 1923

How many more fiascoes will it take before responsible people are finally convinced that a system of pegged exchange rates is not a satisfactory financial arrangement for a group of large countries with independent political systems and independent national policies?

Milton Friedman, 1992

The gold standard in particular—and even pegged exchange rates in general—have a bad name. But the gold standard's having lost her name in the 1920s and 1930s should not lead one to forget her 19th century virtues. . . . Can these lost long-term virtues be retrieved without the world again being in thrall to the barbarous relic? . . . In an integrated world economy, the choice of an exchange rate regime—and thus the common price level—should not be left to an individual country. The spillover effects are so high that it should be a matter of collective choice.

Ronald McKinnon, 2002

A century ago, economists and policy makers may have had their differences of opinion, but—unlike today—almost all of them agreed that a fixed exchange rate was the ideal choice of exchange rate regime. Even if some countries occasionally adopted a floating rate, it was usually with the expectation that they would soon return to a fixed or pegged rate.

The preferred method for fixing the exchange rate was the **gold standard,** a system in which the value of a country's currency was fixed relative to an ounce of gold. As a result, the currency's value was also fixed against all other currencies that were also pegged to gold. The requirements of maintaining the gold standard were strict: although monetary authorities could issue paper money, they had to be willing and able to exchange paper currency for gold at the official fixed rate when asked to do so.

Figure 19-1 documents 140 years of exchange rate arrangements around the world. From 1870 to 1913, most of the world used the gold standard. At the peak in 1913, approximately 70% of the world's countries were part of the gold standard system; a few floated (about 20%) or used other metallic standards (about 10%). Since 1913 much has changed. Adherence to the gold standard weakened during World War I, waxed and waned in the 1920s and 1930s, then was never seen again. In the 1940s, John Maynard Keynes and policy makers from all over the world designed a new system of fixed exchange rates, the Bretton Woods system.

In the period after World War II, the figure shows that many currencies were pegged to the U.S. dollar in this system. Other currencies were pegged to the British pound, the French franc, and the German mark. Because the pound, franc, and mark were all pegged to the dollar at this time, the vast majority of the world's currencies were directly or indirectly fixed on what amounted to a "dollar standard" system.

Like the gold standard, the dollar-based system didn't endure either. Beginning in the early 1970s, floating exchange rates became more common (more than 30% of all

FIGURE 19-1

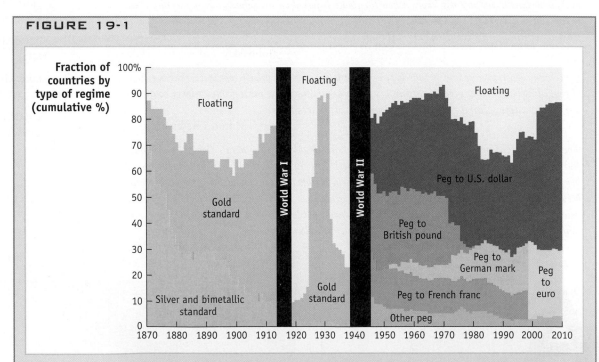

Exchange Rates Regimes of the World, 1870–2010 The shaded regions show the fraction of countries on each type of regime by year, and they add up to 100%. From 1870 to 1913, the gold standard became the dominant regime. During World War I (1914–1918), most countries suspended the gold standard, and resumptions in the late 1920s were brief. After further suspensions in World War II (1939–1945), most countries were fixed against the U.S. dollar (the pound, franc, and mark blocs were indirectly pegged to the dollar). Starting in the 1970s, more countries opted to float. In 1999 the euro replaced the franc and the mark as the base currency for many pegs.

Sources: Christopher M. Meissner, 2005, "A New World Order: Explaining the International Diffusion of the Gold Standard, 1870–1913," Journal of International Economics, 66(2), 385–406; Christopher M. Meissner and Nienke Oomes, 2006, "Why Do Countries Peg the Way They Peg? The Determinants of Anchor Currency Choice," Cambridge Working Papers in Economics 0643, Faculty of Economics, University of Cambridge, and later updates; and extended with Ethan Ilzetzki, Carmen M. Reinhart, and Kenneth S. Rogoff, 2010, "Exchange Rate Arrangements Entering the 21st Century: Which Anchor Will Hold?" unpublished.

currency regimes in the 1980s and 1990s); in recent years, fixed exchange rates have risen again in prominence. Remember that these data count all countries' currencies equally, without any weighting for economic size (measured by GDP). In the larger economies of the world, and especially among the major currencies, floating regimes are more prevalent.

Why do some countries choose to fix and others to float? Why do they change their minds at different times? These are among the most enduring and controversial questions in international macroeconomics and they have been the cause of conflicts among economists, policy makers, and commentators for many years. On one side of the debate are those like Milton Friedman (quoted at the start of this chapter) who in the 1950s, against the prevailing gold standard orthodoxy, argued that floating rates are obviously to be preferred because of their clear economic and political advantages. On the opposing side of the debate are figures such as Ronald McKinnon (also quoted above) who think that only a system of fixed rates can encourage cooperative policy making, keep prices and output stable, and encourage international flows of trade and finance. In this chapter, we examine the pros and cons of different exchange rate regimes.

1 Exchange Rate Regime Choice: Key Issues

In previous chapters, we have examined the workings of the economy under fixed and floating exchange rates. One advantage of understanding the workings of these regimes in such detail is that we are now in a position to address a perennially important macroeconomic policy question: What is the best exchange rate regime choice for a given country at a given time? In this section, we explore the pros and cons of fixed and floating exchange rates by combining the models we have developed with additional theory and evidence. We begin with an application about Germany and Britain in the early 1990s. This story highlights the choices policy makers face as they choose between fixed exchange rates (pegs) and floating exchange rates (floats).

APPLICATION

Britain and Europe: The Big Issues

One way to begin to understand the choice between fixed and floating regimes is to look at countries that have sometimes floated and sometimes fixed and to examine their reasons for switching. In this case study, we look at the British decision to switch from an exchange rate peg to floating in September 1992.

We start by asking, why did Britain first adopt a peg? In the 1970s Britain joined what would later become the European Union and the push for a common currency was part of a larger program, political and economic, to create a single market across Europe. Fixed exchange rates, and ultimately a common currency, were seen as a means to promote trade and other forms of cross-border exchange by lowering transaction costs. In addition, British policy makers felt that an exchange rate anchor might help lower British inflation.

The common currency (the euro) did not become a reality until 1999, and only then in a subset of European Union countries; but the journey started in 1979 with the creation of a fixed exchange rate system called the Exchange Rate Mechanism (ERM). The ERM tied all member currencies together at fixed rates as a step on the way to the adoption of a single currency. In practice, however, the predominant currency in the ERM was the German mark or Deutsche Mark (DM). What this meant was that in the 1980s and 1990s, the German central bank, the Bundesbank, largely retained its monetary autonomy and had the freedom to set its own money supply levels and nominal interest rates. Other countries in the ERM, or looking to join it, in effect had to *unilaterally* peg to the DM. The DM acted like the **base currency** or **center currency** (or Germany was the *base country* or *center country*) in the ERM's fixed exchange rate system.[1]

In 1990, Britain joined the ERM. Based on our analysis of fixed exchange rates in the previous chapter, we can understand the implications of that choice using Figure 19-2. This figure shows the familiar one-country IS-LM-FX diagram for Britain and another IS-LM diagram for the center country, Germany. We treat Britain as the home country and Germany as the foreign country, and denote foreign variables with an asterisk.

Panel (a) shows an IS-LM diagram for Germany, with German output on the horizontal axis and the German DM interest rate on the vertical axis. Panel (b) shows the British IS-LM diagram, with British output on the horizontal axis. Panel (c) shows the British forex market, with the exchange rate in pounds per mark. The vertical axes of panels (b) and (c) show returns in pounds, the home currency.

Initially, we suppose the three diagrams are in equilibrium as follows. In panel (a), at point 1″, German output is Y_1^* and the DM interest rate i_1^*. In panel (b), at point 1, British output is Y_1 and the pound interest rate is i_1. In panel (c), at point 1′, the pound is pegged to the DM at the fixed rate $\overline{E}$ and expected depreciation is zero. The trilemma tells us that monetary policy autonomy is lost in Britain: the British interest rate must equal the German interest rate, so there is uncovered interest parity with $i_1 = i_1^*$.

A Shock in Germany With the scene set, our story begins with a threat to the ERM from an unexpected source. The countries of Eastern Europe began their transition away from Communism, a process that famously began with the fall of the Berlin Wall in 1989. After the wall fell, the reunification of East and West Germany was soon under way. Because the economically backward East Germany required significant funds to support social services, pay unemployment benefits, modernize infrastructure, and so on, the reunification imposed large fiscal costs on Germany, but West Germans were willing to pay these costs to see their country united. As we know from the previous chapter, an increase in German government consumption G^* can be represented as a shift to the right in the German IS curve, from IS_1^* to IS_2^* in panel (a). This shift would have moved the German economy's equilibrium from point 1″ to point 3″. All else equal, the model predicts an increase in German interest rates from i_1^* to i_3^* and a boom in German output from Y_1^* to Y_3^*.[2] This was indeed what started to happen.

The next chapter in the story involves the Bundesbank's response to the German government's expansionary fiscal policy. The Bundesbank was afraid that the boom in German output might cause an increase in German rates of inflation, and it wanted

---

[1] Officially, all currencies in the ERM pegged to a basket of currencies called the ecu (European currency unit).

[2] All else would not have been equal under this shift, given the ERM; Germany's interest rate increase would have been matched by other ERM members to preserve their pegs. For Germany, those shifts would be increases in the foreign interest rate (from Germany's perspective), and those responses would, in turn, have shifted Germany's IS curve a tiny bit farther to the right. These extra effects make no substantive difference to the analysis, so the extra shift is not shown here, for clarity.

FIGURE 19-2

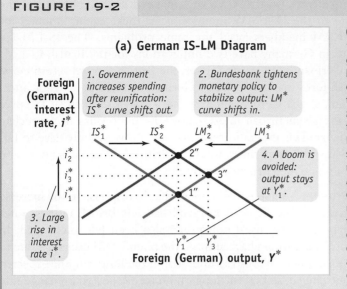

(a) German IS-LM Diagram

Foreign (German) interest rate, i^*

1. Government increases spending after reunification: IS^* curve shifts out.

2. Bundesbank tightens monetary policy to stabilize output: LM^* curve shifts in.

IS_1^* IS_2^* LM_2^* LM_1^*

2''

4. A boom is avoided: output stays at Y_1^*.

i_2^*
i_3^*
i_1^*

3''

1''

3. Large rise in interest rate i^*.

Y_1^* Y_3^*

Foreign (German) output, Y^*

Off the Mark: Britain's Departure from the ERM in 1992 In panel (a), German reunification raises German government spending and shifts IS^* out. The German central bank contracts monetary policy, LM^* shifts up, and German output stabilizes at Y_1^*. Equilibrium shifts from point 1'' to point 2'', and the German interest rate rises from i_1^* to i_2^*. In Britain, under a peg, panels (b) and (c) show that foreign returns, FR, rise and so the British domestic return, DR, must rise to $i_2 = i_2^*$. The German interest rate rise also shifts out Britain's IS curve slightly from IS_1 to IS_2. To maintain the peg, Britain's LM curve shifts up from LM_1 to LM_2. At the same exchange rate and a higher interest rate, demand falls and output drops from Y_1 to Y_2. Equilibrium moves from point 1 to point 2. If the British were to float, they could put the LM curve wherever they wanted. For example, at LM_4 the British interest rate holds at i_1 and output booms, but the forex market ends up at point 4' and there is a depreciation of the pound to E_4. The British could also select LM_3, stabilize output at the initial level Y_1, but the peg still has to break with E rising to E_3.

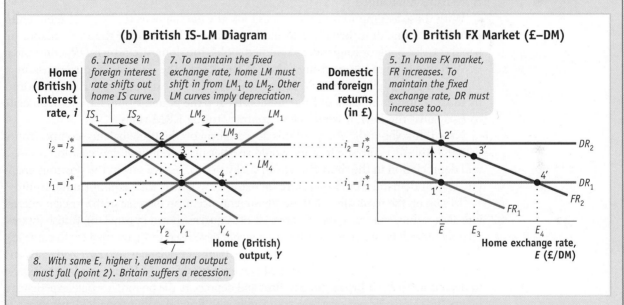

(b) British IS-LM Diagram

Home (British) interest rate, i

6. Increase in foreign interest rate shifts out home IS curve.

7. To maintain the fixed exchange rate, home LM must shift in from LM_1 to LM_2. Other LM curves imply depreciation.

IS_1 IS_2 LM_2 LM_1

LM_3

$i_2 = i_2^*$

2

3

$i_1 = i_1^*$

1

4

LM_4

Y_2 Y_1 Y_4

Home (British) output, Y

8. With same E, higher i, demand and output must fall (point 2). Britain suffers a recession.

(c) British FX Market (£–DM)

Domestic and foreign returns (in £)

5. In home FX market, FR increases. To maintain the fixed exchange rate, DR must increase too.

2'

3'

DR_2

$i_2 = i_2^*$

$i_1 = i_1^*$

1'

4'

DR_1

FR_2

FR_1

$\bar{E}$ E_3 E_4

Home exchange rate, E (£/DM)

to avoid that outcome. Using its policy autonomy, the Bundesbank tightened its monetary policy by contracting the money supply and raising interest rates. This policy change is seen in the upward shift of the German LM curve, from LM_1^* to LM_2^* in panel (a). We suppose that the Bundesbank stabilizes German output at its initial level Y_1^* by raising German interest rates to the even higher level of i_2^*.[3]

---

[3] Interest rate responses in the ERM (described in footnote 2) would, in turn, have moved Germany's IS curve out yet farther, requiring a bit more tightening from the Bundesbank. Again, these indirect effects do not affect the analysis and are not shown, for clarity.

Choices for the Other ERM Countries What happened in the countries of the ERM that were pegging to the DM? We examine what these events implied for Britain, but the other ERM members faced the same problems. The IS-LM-FX model tells us that events in Germany have two implications for the British IS-LM-FX model. First, as the German interest rate i^* rises, the British foreign return curve FR shifts up in the British forex market (to recap: German deposits pay higher interest, all else equal). Second, as the German interest rate i^* rises, the British IS curve shifts out (to recap: at any given British interest rate, the pound has to depreciate more, boosting British demand via expenditure switching). Now we only have to figure out how much the British IS curve shifts, what the British LM curve is up to, and hence how the equilibrium outcome depends on British policy choices.

Choice 1: Float and Prosper? First, let us suppose that in response to the increase in the German interest rate i^*, the Bank of England had left British interest rates unchanged at i_1 and suppose British fiscal policy had also been left unchanged. In addition, let's assume that Britain would have allowed the pound-DM exchange rate to float in the short run. For simplicity we also assume that in the long run, the expected exchange rate remains unchanged, so that the long-run future expected exchange rate E^e remains unchanged at $\overline{E}$.

With these assumptions in place, let's look at what happens to the investment component of demand: in Britain, I would be unchanged at $I(i_1)$. In the forex market in panel (c), the Bank of England, as assumed, holds the domestic return DR_1 constant at i_1. With the foreign return rising from FR_1 to FR_2 and the domestic return constant at DR_1, the new equilibrium would be at 4′ and the British exchange rate rises temporarily to E_4. Thus, if the Bank of England doesn't act, the pound would have to depreciate to E_4 against the DM; it would float, contrary to the ERM rules.

Now think about the effects of this depreciation on the trade balance component of demand: the British trade balance would rise because a nominal depreciation is also a real depreciation in the short run, given sticky prices.[4] As we saw in the previous chapter, British demand would therefore increase, as would British equilibrium output.

To sum up the result after all these adjustments occur, an increase in the foreign interest rate always shifts out the home IS curve, all else equal as shown in panel (b): British interest rates would still be at i_1, and British output would have risen to Y_4, on the new IS curve IS_2. To keep the interest rate at i_1, as output rises, the Bank of England would have had to expand its money supply, shifting the British LM curve from LM_1 to LM_4, and causing the pound to depreciate to E_4. If Britain were to float and depreciate the pound, it would experience a boom. But this would not have been compatible with Britain's continued ERM membership.

Choice 2: Peg and Suffer? If Britain's exchange rate were to stay pegged to the DM because of the ERM, however, the outcome for Britain would not be so rosy. In this scenario, the trilemma means that to maintain the peg, Britain would have to increase its interest rate and follow the lead of the center country, Germany. In panel (b), the pound interest rate would have to rise to the level $i_2 = i_2^*$ to maintain the peg. In panel (c), the domestic return would rise from DR_1 to DR_2 in step with the foreign return's rise from FR_1 to FR_2, and the new FX market equilibrium would be at 2′. The Bank of England would accomplish this rise in DR by tightening its monetary policy

---

[4] This is true in a pure two-country model, and, from the British perspective, Germany is the "rest of the world." With many countries, however, the direction of change is still the same. All else equal, a British real depreciation against Germany will still imply a depreciation of the British real effective exchange rate against the rest of the world.

and lowering the British money supply. In panel (b), under a peg, the new position of the IS curve at IS_2 would imply an upward shift in the British LM curve, as shown by the move from LM_1 to LM_2. So the British IS-LM equilibrium would now be at point 2, with output at Y_2. The adverse consequences for the British economy now become apparent. At point 2, as compared with the initial point 1, British demand has fallen. Why? British interest rates have risen (depressing investment demand I), but the exchange rate has remained at its pegged level $\overline{E}$ (so there is no change in the trade balance). To sum up, what we have shown in this scenario is that the IS curve may have moved right a bit, but the opposing shift in the LM curve would have been even larger. If Britain were to stay pegged and keep its membership in the ERM, Britain would experience a recession.

In 1992 Britain found itself facing a decision between these two choices. As we have noted, if the British pound had been floating against the DM, then leaving interest rates unchanged would have been an option, and Britain could have achieved equilibrium at point 4 with a higher output, Y_4. In fact, floating would have opened up the whole range of monetary policy options. For example, Britain could have chosen a mild monetary contraction by shifting the British LM curve from LM_1 to LM_3, moving equilibrium in panel (b) to point 3, stabilizing U.K. output at its initial level Y_1, and allowing the FX market in panel (c) to settle at point 3' with a mild depreciation of the exchange rate to E_3.

What Happened Next? In September 1992, after an economic slowdown and after considerable last-minute dithering and turmoil, the British Conservative government finally decided that the benefits to Britain of being in ERM and the euro project were smaller than the costs suffered as a result of a German interest-rate hike in response to Germany-specific events. Two years after joining the ERM, Britain opted out.

Did Britain make the right choice? In Figure 19-3, we compare the economic performance of Britain with that of France, a large European Union economy that

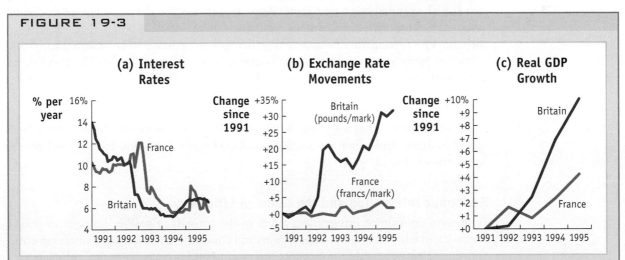

FIGURE 19-3

(a) Interest Rates

(b) Exchange Rate Movements

(c) Real GDP Growth

Floating Away: Britain Versus France after 1992 Britain's decision to exit the ERM allowed for more expansionary British monetary policy after September 1992. In other ERM countries that remained pegged to the mark, such as France, monetary policy had to be kept tighter to maintain the peg. Consistent with the model, the data show lower interest rates, a more depreciated currency, and faster output growth in Britain compared with France after 1992.

Note: Interest rates are three-month LIBOR, annualized rates.

Sources: Data from: econstats.com; IMF, International Financial Statistics and World Economic Outlook databases.

Most Britons are opposed to the euro, some vehemently so.

maintained its ERM peg. After leaving the ERM in September 1992, Britain lowered interest rates [panel (a)] in the short run and depreciated its exchange rate against the DM [panel (b)]. In comparison, France never depreciated and had to maintain higher interest rates to keep the franc pegged to the DM until German monetary policy eased a year or two later. As our model would predict, the British economy boomed in subsequent years panel (c). The French suffered slower growth, a fate shared by most of the other countries that stayed in the ERM.

The British choice stands to this day. Although the option to rejoin the ERM has remained open since 1992, the idea of pegging to (much less joining) the euro is unpopular in Britain. All subsequent British governments have decided that the benefits of increased trade and economic integration with Europe were smaller than the associated costs of sacrificing British monetary autonomy.[5] ■

Key Factors in Exchange Rate Regime Choice: Integration and Similarity

We started this chapter with an application about the policy choice and tradeoffs Britain faced in 1992 when it needed to decide between a fixed exchange rate (peg) and a floating exchange rate (float).

At different times, British authorities could see the potential benefits of participating fully in an economically integrated single European market and the ERM fixed exchange rate system. The fixed exchange rate, for example, would lower the costs of economic transactions among the members of the ERM zone. But, especially in 1992, the British could also see that there would be times when the monetary policy being pursued by authorities in Germany would be out of line with policy that was best for Britain. The fundamental source of this divergence between what Britain wanted and what Germany wanted was that each country faced different shocks. The fiscal shock that Germany experienced after reunification was not felt in Britain or any other ERM country.

To better understand these trade-offs, and the decision to fix or float, we now examine the issues that are at the heart of this decision: economic *integration* as measured by trade and other transactions, and economic *similarity*, as measured by the similarity of shocks.

Economic Integration and the Gains in Efficiency

The term **economic integration** refers to the growth of market linkages in goods, capital, and labor markets among regions and countries. By lowering transaction costs, a fixed exchange rate might promote integration and increase economic efficiency.

---

[5] Even the Liberal Democrats, for a long time pro-euro while just a small party perpetually in opposition, effectively dropped their stance once they had the opportunity to join a coalition government with the Conservatives in 2010.

Trade is the clearest example of an activity that volatile exchange rates might discourage. Stable exchange rates and prices encourage arbitrage and lower the costs of trade. But trade is not the only type of international economic activity likely to be discouraged by exchange rate fluctuations. Currency-related transaction costs and uncertainty also act as barriers to cross-border capital and labor flows.

■ The lesson: *the greater the degree of economic integration between markets in the home country and the base country, the greater will be the volume of transactions between the two, and the greater will be the benefits the home country gains from fixing its exchange rate with the base country. As integration rises, the efficiency benefits of having a fixed exchange rate increase.*

Economic Similarity and the Costs of Asymmetric Shocks

A fixed exchange rate can lead to costs when one country experiences a country-specific shock or **asymmetric shock** that is not shared by the other country.

The application on Britain and Germany showed why an *asymmetric* shock causes problems: it leads to a conflict between the policy goals of the two countries. In our example, German policy makers wanted to tighten monetary policy to offset a boom caused by a positive demand shock due to their expansionary fiscal policy. British policy makers did not want to implement the same policy: because they had not experienced the same shock, following the German monetary policy would have caused a recession in Britain.

Similar or *symmetric* shocks do not cause such problems. Imagine that Germany and Britain experience an identical expansionary demand shock. In this case, German and British monetary authorities would respond identically, raising interest rates by the same amount to stabilize output. This desired symmetric increase in interest rates does not conflict with Britain's fixed exchange rate commitment. If interest rates were initially set at a common level, $i_1 = i_1^*$, they would be raised to a new higher level, $i_2 = i_2^*$. By raising its rates, Britain could stabilize output *and* stay pegged because uncovered interest parity is still satisfied. The exchange rate $\overline{E}$ does not change, and even though Britain is pegging unilaterally to Germany, Britain has the interest rate it would choose even if it were floating and could make an independent monetary policy choice.

When a Home country unilaterally pegs to a Foreign country, asymmetric shocks impose costs on the home country in terms of lost output. When asymmetric shocks hit, the monetary policies that are best for Foreign and for Home will differ, and the peg means that Foreign's policy choice will automatically be imposed on Home. In contrast, symmetric shocks do not impose any costs because the monetary policies that Foreign and Home want to pursue will be the same, and Foreign's imposed choice will suit Home perfectly.

Real-world situations are more complex. Countries are not identical and shocks may be a mix of large and small, symmetric and asymmetric shocks.

■ The lesson: *if there is a greater degree of economic similarity between the home country and the base country (that is, if they face more symmetric shocks and fewer asymmetric shocks), then the economic stabilization costs to home of fixing its exchange rate to the base are smaller. As economic similarity rises, the stability costs of having a fixed exchange rate decrease.*

Simple Criteria for a Fixed Exchange Rate

We can now set out a theory of exchange rate regime choice by considering the *net benefits* (benefits minus the costs) of pegging versus floating. Our discussions about integration and similarity have shown the following:

- *As integration rises, the efficiency benefits of a fixed exchange rate increase.*
- *As symmetry rises, the stability costs of a fixed exchange rate decrease.*

Our theory says that if market integration or symmetry increases, the net benefits of a fixed exchange rate also increase. If the net benefits are negative, the home country should float if the decision is based solely on its economic interests. If the net benefits are positive, the home country should fix.

Figure 19-4 illustrates the theory in a **symmetry-integration diagram** in which the horizontal axis measures the degree of economic integration between a pair of locations, say, A and B, and the vertical axis measures the symmetry of the shocks experienced by the pair A and B.

We use the figure to see whether A should peg unilaterally to B (or vice versa). Suppose conditions change and the pair moves up and to the right, for example, from point 1 toward point 6. Along this path, integration and symmetry are both increasing, so the net benefits of fixing are also increasing. At some critical point (point 2 in the graph), the net benefits turn positive. Before that point, floating is best. After that point, fixing is best.

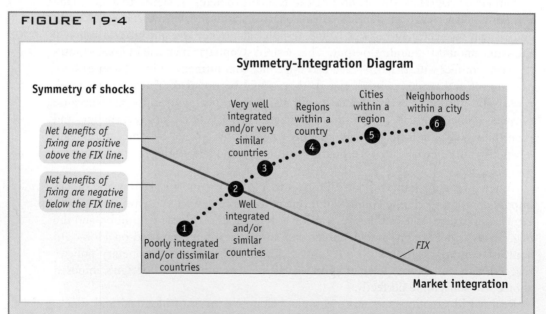

FIGURE 19-4

A Theory of Fixed Exchange Rates Points 1 to 6 in the figure represent a pair of locations. Suppose one location is considering pegging its exchange rate to its partner. If their markets become more integrated (a move to the right along the horizontal axis) or if the economic shocks they experience become more symmetric (a move up on the vertical axis), the net economic benefits of fixing increase. If the pair moves far enough up or to the right, then the benefits of fixing exceed costs (net benefits are positive), and the pair will cross the fixing threshold shown by the *FIX* line. Above the line, it is optimal for the region to fix. Below the line, it is optimal for the region to float.

Our argument is more general: whatever the direction of the path, as long as it moves up and to the right, it must cross some threshold like point 2 beyond which benefits outweigh costs. Thus, there will exist a set of points—a downward-sloping line passing through point 2—that delineates this threshold. We refer to this threshold as the *FIX* line. Points above the *FIX* line satisfy the economic criteria for a fixed exchange rate.

What might different points on this chart mean? If we are at point 6, we might think of A and B as neighborhoods in a city—they are very well integrated and an economic shock is usually felt by all neighborhoods in the city. If A and B were at point 5, they might be two cities. If A and B were at point 4, they might be the regions of a country, and still above the *FIX* line. If A and B were at point 3, they might be neighboring, well-integrated countries with few asymmetric shocks. Point 2 is right on the borderline. If A and B were at point 1, they might be less well-integrated countries with more asymmetric shocks and our theory says they should float.

The key prediction of our theory is this: *pairs of countries above the FIX line (more integrated, more similar shocks) will gain economically from adopting a fixed exchange rate. Those below the FIX line (less integrated, less similar shocks) will not.*

In a moment, we develop and apply this theory further. But first, let's see if there is evidence to support the theory's two main assumptions: Do fixed exchange rates deliver trade gains through integration? Do they impose stability costs by limiting monetary policy options?

APPLICATION

Do Fixed Exchange Rates Promote Trade?

The single most powerful argument *for* a fixed exchange rate is that it may boost trade by eliminating trade-hindering costs. The idea is an old one. In 1878, the United States had yet to re-adopt the gold standard following the Civil War. Policy makers were debating whether going back on gold made sense, and J. S. Moore, a U.S. Treasury official testifying before Congress, was questioned on the subject:

> *Question:* Do you not think that the use of a common standard of value has a tendency to promote a free commercial interchange between the various countries using it?

> *Answer:* If two countries, be they ever so distant from each other, should have the same standard of money . . . there would be no greater harmonizer than such an exchange.

Benefits Measured by Trade Levels As we have noted, this was the conventional wisdom among policy makers in the late nineteenth and early twentieth centuries, and research by economic historians has found strong support for their views: all else equal, two countries adopting the gold standard had bilateral trade levels 30% to 100% higher than comparable pairs of countries that were off the gold standard.[6] Thus, it appears that the gold standard *did* promote trade.

---

[6] J. Ernesto López Córdova and Christopher M. Meissner, March 2003, "Exchange Rate Regimes and International Trade: Evidence from the Classical Gold Standard Era, 1870–1913," *American Economic Review*, 93(1), 344–353; Antoni Estevadeordal, Brian Frantz, and Alan M. Taylor, May 2003, "The Rise and Fall of World Trade, 1870–1939," *Quarterly Journal of Economics*, 118(2), 359–407; Marc Flandreau and Mathilde Maurel, January 2005, "Monetary Union, Trade Integration, and Business Cycles in 19th Century Europe," *Open Economies Review*, 16(2), 135–152. The quotation is cited in an earlier draft of the paper by López Córdova and Meissner.

What about fixed exchange rates today? Do they promote trade? Economists have exhaustively tested this hypothesis using increasingly sophisticated statistical methods. We can look at some evidence from a recent study in which country pairs A–B were classified in four different ways:

a. The two countries are using a *common currency* (i.e., A and B are in a currency union or A has unilaterally adopted B's currency).

b. The two countries are linked by a *direct* exchange rate peg (i.e., A's currency is pegged to B's).

c. The two countries are linked by an *indirect* exchange rate peg, via a third currency (i.e., A and B have currencies pegged to C but not directly to each other).

d. The two countries are not linked by any type of peg (i.e., their currencies *float* against each other, even if one or both might be pegged to some other third currency).

Using this classification and trade data from 1973 to 1999, economists Jay Shambaugh and Michael Klein compared bilateral trade volumes for all pairs under the three pegged regimes (a) through (c) with the benchmark level of trade under a floating regime (d) to see if there were any systematic differences. They also used careful statistical techniques to control for other factors and to address possible reverse causality (that is, to eliminate the possibility that higher trade might have caused countries to fix their exchange rates). Figure 19-5 shows their key estimates, according to which currency unions increased bilateral trade by 38% relative to floating regimes. They also found that the adoption of a fixed exchange rate would promote trade, but only for the case of *direct* pegs. Adopting a direct peg increased bilateral trade by 21% compared with a floating exchange rate. Indirect pegs had a negligible and statistically insignificant effect.[7]

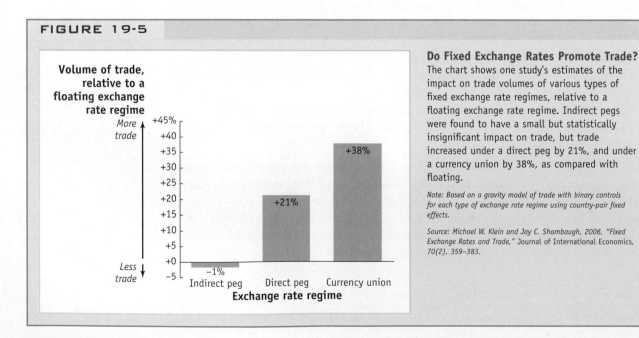

FIGURE 19-5

Do Fixed Exchange Rates Promote Trade? The chart shows one study's estimates of the impact on trade volumes of various types of fixed exchange rate regimes, relative to a floating exchange rate regime. Indirect pegs were found to have a small but statistically insignificant impact on trade, but trade increased under a direct peg by 21%, and under a currency union by 38%, as compared with floating.

Note: Based on a gravity model of trade with binary controls for each type of exchange rate regime using country-pair fixed effects.

Source: Michael W. Klein and Jay C. Shambaugh, 2006, "Fixed Exchange Rates and Trade," Journal of International Economics, 70(2), 359–383.

[7] Michael W. Klein and Jay C. Shambaugh, 2006, "Fixed Exchange Rates and Trade," *Journal of International Economics*, 70(2), 359–383.

Benefits Measured by Price Convergence The effect of exchange rate regimes on trade levels is one way to evaluate the impact of currency arrangements on international market integration, and it has been extensively researched. Another body of research examines the relationship between exchange rate regimes and price convergence. These studies use the law of one price (LOOP) and purchasing power parity (PPP) as criteria for measuring market integration. If fixed exchange rates promote trade by lowering transaction costs, then differences between prices (measured in a common currency) should be smaller among countries with pegged rates than among countries with floating rates. In other words, LOOP and PPP should be more likely to hold under a fixed exchange rate than under a floating regime. (Recall that price convergence underlies the gains-from-trade argument.)

Statistical methods can be used to detect how large price differences must be between two locations before arbitrage begins. Research on prices of baskets of goods shows that as exchange rate volatility increases (as it does when currencies float), price differences widen, and the speed at which prices in the two markets converge decreases. These findings offer support for the hypothesis that fixed exchange rates promote arbitrage and price convergence.[8]

Economists have also studied convergence in the prices of individual goods. For example, several studies focused on Europe have looked at the prices of various goods in different countries (e.g., retail prices of cars and TV sets, and the prices of Marlboro cigarettes in duty-free shops). These studies showed that higher exchange rate volatility is associated with larger price differences between locations. In particular, while price gaps still remain for many goods, the "in" countries (members of the ERM and now the Eurozone) saw prices converge much more than the "out" countries.[9] ■

APPLICATION

Do Fixed Exchange Rates Diminish Monetary Autonomy and Stability?

Probably the single most powerful argument *against* a fixed exchange rate is provided by the trilemma. An economy that unilaterally pegs to a foreign currency sacrifices its monetary policy autonomy.

We have seen the result many times now. If capital markets are open, arbitrage in the forex market implies uncovered interest parity. If the exchange rate is fixed, expected depreciation is zero, and the home interest rate must equal the foreign interest rate. The stark implication is that when a country pegs, it relinquishes its independent monetary policy: it has to adjust the money supply M at all times to

[8] Maurice Obstfeld and Alan M. Taylor, 1997, "Nonlinear Aspects of Goods-Market Arbitrage and Adjustment: Heckscher's Commodity Points Revisited," *Journal of the Japanese and International Economies*, 11(4), 441–479.
[9] Marcus Asplund and Richard Friberg, 2001, "The Law of One Price in Scandinavian Duty-Free Stores," *American Economic Review*, 91(4), 1072–1083; Pinelopi Koujianou Goldberg and Frank Verboven, 2004, "Cross-Country Price Dispersion in the Euro Era: A Case Study of the European Car Market," *Economic Policy*, 19(40), 483–521; Jean Imbs, Haroon Mumtaz, Morten O. Ravn, and Hélène Rey, 2010, "One TV, One Price?" *Scandinavian Journal of Economics* 112(4): 753–781.

ensure that the home interest rate i equals the foreign interest rate i^* (plus any risk premium).

The preceding case study of Britain and the ERM is one more example: Britain wanted to decouple the British interest rate from the German interest rate. To do so, it had to stop pegging the pound to the German mark. Once it had done that, instead of having to contract the British economy as a result of unrelated events in Germany, it could maintain whatever interest rate it thought was best suited to British economic interests.

The Trilemma, Policy Constraints, and Interest Rate Correlations Is the trilemma truly a binding constraint? Economist Jay Shambaugh tested this proposition, and Figure 19-6 shows some evidence using his data. As we have seen, there are three main solutions to the trilemma. A country can do the following:

1. Opt for open capital markets, with fixed exchange rates (an "open peg").

2. Opt to open its capital market but allow the currency to float (an "open nonpeg").

3. Opt to close its capital markets ("closed").

In case 1, changes in the country's interest rate should match changes in the interest rate of the base country to which it is pegging. In cases 2 and 3, there is no need for the country's interest rate to move in step with the base.

FIGURE 19-6

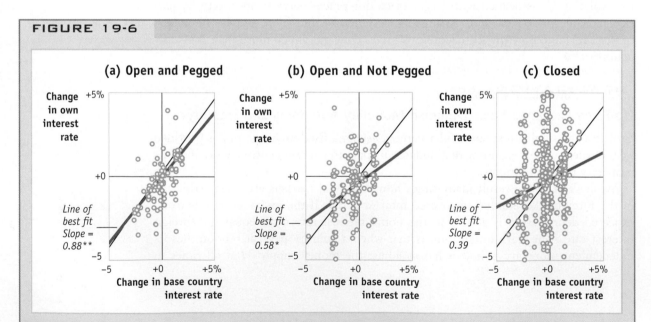

The Trilemma in Action The trilemma says that if the home country is an open peg, it sacrifices monetary policy autonomy because changes in its own interest rate must match changes in the interest rate of the base country. Panel (a) shows that this is the case. The trilemma also says that there are two ways to get that autonomy back: switch to a floating exchange rate or impose capital controls. Panels (b) and (c) show that either of these two policies permits home interest rates to move more independently of the base country.

Notes: ** Statistically significant at 1% level. * Statistically significant at 5% level. Hyperinflations excluded.

Source: Data from Jay C. Shambaugh, 2004, "The Effect of Fixed Exchange Rates on Monetary Policy," Quarterly Journal of Economics, 119(1), 300–351.

Figure 19-6 displays evidence for the trilemma. On the vertical axis is the annual change in the domestic interest rate; on the horizontal axis is the annual change in the base country interest rate. The trilemma says that in an open peg the two changes should be same and the points should lie on the 45-degree line. Indeed, for open pegs, shown in panel (a), the correlation of domestic and base interest rates is high and the line of best fit has a slope very close to 1. There are some deviations (possibly due to some pegs being more like bands), but these findings show that open pegs have very little monetary policy autonomy. In contrast, for the open nonpegs, shown in panel (b), and closed economies, shown in panel (c), domestic interest rates do not move as much in line with the base interest rate, the correlation is weak, and the slopes are much smaller than 1. These two regimes allow for some monetary policy autonomy.[10]

Costs of Fixing Measured by Output Volatility   The preceding evidence suggests that nations with open pegs have less monetary independence. But it does not tell us directly whether they suffer from greater output instability because their monetary authorities cannot use monetary policy to stabilize output when shocks hit. Some studies have found that, on average, the volatility of output growth *is* much higher under fixed regimes.[11] However, a problem in such studies is that countries often differ in all kinds of characteristics that may affect output volatility, not just the exchange rate regime—and the results can be sensitive to how one controls for all these other factors.[12]

In the search for cleaner evidence, some recent research has focused on a key prediction of the IS-LM-FX model: all else equal, an increase in the base-country interest rate should cause output to fall in a country that fixes its exchange rate to the base country. This decline in output occurs because countries that fix have to tighten their monetary policy and raise their interest rate to match that of the base country. In contrast, countries that float do not have to follow the base country's rate increase and can use their monetary policy autonomy to stabilize output, by lowering their interest rate and/or allowing their currency to depreciate. Economists Julian di Giovanni and Jay Shambaugh looked at changes in base-country interest rates (say, the U.S. dollar or euro rates) and examined the correlation of these base interest rate changes with changes in GDP in a large sample of fixed and floating nonbase countries. The results, shown in Figure 19-7, confirm the theory's predictions: when a base country increases

---

[10] The correlation isn't perfect for open pegs, nor is it zero for the other cases. This may not be surprising. Pegs are defined as fixed if they vary within a ±2% band. The band allows central banks a little flexibility with their exchange rates and interest rates that would be lacking in a strict peg (a band of zero width). As for nonpegs and closed countries, there may be reasons why their correlation with the base isn't zero. For example, they may have inflation targets or other monetary policy guidelines that cause their interest rates to follow paths similar to those of the base country. In other words, these countries may be able to change their interest rates a great deal, but how much they choose to change them is another matter.

[11] Atish R. Ghosh, Anne-Marie Gulde, Jonathan D. Ostry, and Holger C. Wolf, 1997, "Does the Nominal Exchange Rate Regime Matter?" NBER Working Paper 5874.

[12] See, for example, Eduardo Levy-Yeyati and Federico Sturzenegger, September 2003, "To Float or to Fix: Evidence on the Impact of Exchange Rate Regimes on Growth," *American Economic Review*, 93(4), 1173–1193; Kenneth Rogoff, Ashoka Mody, Nienke Oomes, Robin Brooks, and Aasim M. Husain, 2004, "Evolution and Performance of Exchange Rate Regimes," IMF Occasional Paper 229, International Monetary Fund.

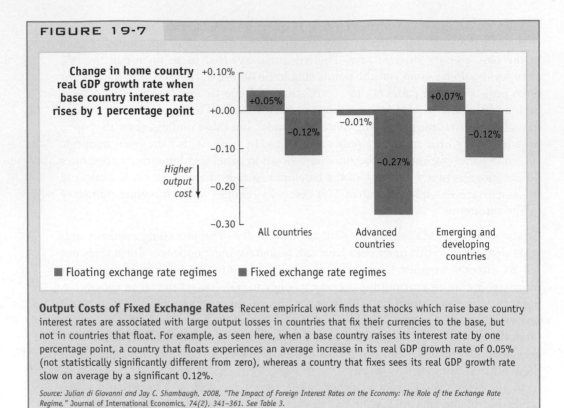

FIGURE 19-7

Change in home country real GDP growth rate when base country interest rate rises by 1 percentage point

+0.10%

+0.00

−0.10

−0.20

−0.30

Higher output cost

+0.05%
−0.12%
−0.01%
−0.27%
+0.07%
−0.12%

All countries
Advanced countries
Emerging and developing countries

■ Floating exchange rate regimes ■ Fixed exchange rate regimes

Output Costs of Fixed Exchange Rates Recent empirical work finds that shocks which raise base country interest rates are associated with large output losses in countries that fix their currencies to the base, but not in countries that float. For example, as seen here, when a base country raises its interest rate by one percentage point, a country that floats experiences an average increase in its real GDP growth rate of 0.05% (not statistically significantly different from zero), whereas a country that fixes sees its real GDP growth rate slow on average by a significant 0.12%.

Source: Julian di Giovanni and Jay C. Shambaugh, 2008, "The Impact of Foreign Interest Rates on the Economy: The Role of the Exchange Rate Regime," Journal of International Economics, 74(2), 341–361. See Table 3.

its interest rate, it spreads economic pain to those countries pegging to it, but not to the countries that float. These findings confirm that one cost of a fixed exchange rate regime is a more volatile level of output. ■

2 Other Benefits of Fixing

We began the chapter by emphasizing two key factors that influence the choice of fixed versus floating rate regimes: economic integration (market linkages) and economic similarity (symmetry of shocks). Other factors can play a role, however, and in this section, we explore some benefits of a fixed exchange rate regime that can be particularly important in emerging markets and developing countries.

Fiscal Discipline, Seigniorage, and Inflation

One common argument in favor of fixed exchange rate regimes in developing countries is that an exchange rate peg prevents the government from printing money to finance government expenditure. Under such a financing scheme, the central bank is called upon to *monetize* the government's deficit (i.e., give money to the government in exchange for debt). This process increases the money supply and leads to high inflation. The source of the government's revenue is, in effect, an inflation tax (called *seigniorage*) levied on the members of the public who hold money (see **Side Bar: The Inflation Tax**).

SIDE BAR

The Inflation Tax

How does the inflation tax work? Consider a situation in which a country with a floating exchange rate faces a constant budget deficit and is unable to finance this deficit through domestic or foreign borrowing. To cover the deficit, the treasury department calls on the central bank to "monetize" the deficit by purchasing an amount of government bonds equal to the deficit.

For simplicity, suppose output is fixed at Y, prices are completely flexible, and inflation and the nominal interest rate are constant. At any instant, money grows at a rate $\Delta M/M = \Delta P/P = \pi$, so the price level rises at a rate of inflation π equal to the rate of money growth. The Fisher effect tells us that the nominal interest rate is $i = r^* + \pi$, where r^* is the real world interest rate.

This ongoing inflation erodes the real value of money held by households. If a household holds M/P in real money balances, then a moment later when prices have increased by an amount $\Delta M/M = \Delta P/P = \pi$, a fraction π of the real value of the original M/P is lost to inflation. The cost of the inflation tax to the household is $\pi \times M/P$. For example, if I hold $100, the price level is currently 1, and inflation is 1%, then after one period the initial $100 is worth only $99 in real (inflation-adjusted) terms, and prices are 1.01.

What is the inflation tax worth to the government? It can spend the extra money printed ΔM to buy real goods and services

worth $\Delta M/P = (\Delta M/M) \times (M/P) = \pi \times (M/P)$. For the preceding example, the expansion of the money supply from $100 to $101, provides financing worth $1 to the government. The real gain for the government equals the real loss to the households.

The amount that the inflation tax transfers from household to the government is called seigniorage, which can be written as

$$\underbrace{\text{Seigniorage}}_{\text{Inflation tax}} = \underbrace{\pi}_{\text{Tax rate}} \times \underbrace{\frac{M}{P}}_{\text{Tax base}} = \pi \times L(r^* + \pi)Y$$

The two terms are often viewed as the tax rate (here, the inflation rate π) and the tax base (the thing being taxed; here, real money balances $M/P = L$). The first term rises as inflation π rises, but the second term goes to zero as π gets large because if inflation becomes very high, people try to hold almost no money, that is, real money demand given by $L(i) = L(r^* + \pi)Y$ falls to zero.

Because of these two offsetting effects, the inflation tax tends to hit diminishing returns as a source of real revenue: as inflation increases, the tax generates increasing real revenues at first, but eventually the rise in the first term is overwhelmed by the fall in the second term. Once a country is in a hyperinflation, the economy is usually well beyond the point at which real inflation tax revenues are maximized.

High inflation and hyperinflation (inflation in excess of 50% *per month*) are undesirable. If nothing else (such as fiscal discipline) can prevent them, a fixed exchange rate may start to look more attractive. Does a fixed exchange rate rule out inflationary finance and the abuse of seigniorage by the government? In principle, yes, but this anti-inflationary effect is not unique to a fixed exchange rate. As we saw in an earlier chapter on the monetary approach to exchange rates, any nominal anchor (such as money, exchange rate, or inflation targets) will have the same effect.

If a country's currency floats, its central bank can print a lot or a little money, with very different inflation outcomes. If a country's currency is pegged, the central bank might run the peg well, with fairly stable prices, or it might run the peg so badly that a crisis occurs, the exchange rate collapses, and inflation erupts.

Nominal anchors imply a "promise" by the government to ensure certain monetary policy outcomes in the long run. However, these promises do not guarantee that the country will achieve these outcomes. All policy announcements including a fixed exchange rate are to some extent "cheap talk." If pressure from the treasury to monetize deficits gets too strong, the commitment to any kind of anchor could fail.

The debate over whether fixed exchange rates improve inflation performance cannot be settled by theory alone—it is an empirical question. What has happened in reality? Table 19-1 lays out the evidence on the world inflation performance from 1970 to 1999. Average inflation rates are computed for all countries and for subgroups of countries:

TABLE 19-1

Inflation Performance and the Exchange Rate Regime Cross-country annual data from the period 1970 to 1999 can be used to explore the relationship, if any, between the exchange rate regime and the inflation performance of an economy. Floating is associated with slightly lower inflation in the world as a whole (9.9%) and in the advanced countries (3.5%) (columns 1 and 2). In emerging markets and developing countries, a fixed regime eventually delivers lower inflation outcomes, but not right away (columns 3 and 4).

	Annual Inflation Rate (%)			
Regime Type	(1) World	(2) Advanced Countries	(3) Emerging Markets and Developing Countries	(4) Emerging Markets and Developing Countries (Excluding the Year after a Regime Change)
Fixed	17.4%	4.8%	19.6%	8.8%
Limited flexibility	11.1	8.3	12.4	10.8
Managed floating	14.0	7.8	15.1	14.7
Freely floating	9.9	3.5	21.2	15.8
Freely falling	387.8	47.9	396.1	482.9

Source: Author's calculations based on the dataset from Kenneth Rogoff, Ashoka Mody, Nienke Oomes, Robin Brooks, and Aasim M. Husain, 2004, "Evolution and Performance of Exchange Rate Regimes," IMF Occasional Paper No. 229, International Monetary Fund.

advanced economies (rich countries), emerging markets (middle-income countries integrated in world capital markets), and developing countries (other countries).

For all countries (column 1), we can see that average inflation performance appears largely unrelated to the exchange rate regime, whether the choice is a peg (17.4%), limited flexibility (11.1%), managed floating (14.0%), or freely floating (9.9%). Only the "freely falling" has astronomical rates of inflation (387.8%). Similar results hold for the advanced countries (column 2) and for the emerging markets and developing countries (column 3). Although average inflation rates are higher in the latter sample, the first four regimes have fairly similar inflation rates, with fixed and freely floating almost the same.

We may conclude that as long as monetary policy is guided by *some* kind of nominal anchor, the particular choice of fixed and floating may not matter that much.[13] Possibly the only place where the old conventional wisdom remains intact is in the developing countries, where fixed exchange rates can help to deliver lower inflation rates after high inflations or hyperinflations. Why? In those situations, people may need to see the government tie its own hands in a very open and verifiable way for expectations of perpetually high inflation to be lowered, and a peg is one way to do that. This can be seen in Table 19-1, column 4. If we exclude the first year after a change in the exchange rate regime, we exclude the periods after high inflations and hyperinflations when inflation (and inflationary expectations) may still persist even after the monetary and exchange rate policies have changed. Once things settle down in years two and later, fixed exchange rates generally do deliver lower (single-digit) inflation rates than other regimes.

---

[13] Kenneth Rogoff, Ashoka Mody, Nienke Oomes, Robin Brooks, and Aasim M. Husain, 2004, "Evolution and Performance of Exchange Rate Regimes," IMF Occasional Paper 229, International Monetary Fund.

■ The lesson: *Fixed exchange rates are neither necessary nor sufficient to ensure good inflation performance in many countries. In developing countries beset by high inflation, an exchange rate peg may be the only credible anchor.*

Liability Dollarization, National Wealth, and Contractionary Depreciations

As we learned in the balance of payments chapter, exchange rate changes can have a big effect on a nation's wealth. External assets and liabilities are never entirely denominated in local currency, so movements in the exchange rate can affect their value. For developing countries and emerging markets afflicted by the problem of *liability dollarization*, the wealth effects can be large and destabilizing, providing another argument for fixing the exchange rate.

Suppose there are just two countries and two currencies, Home and Foreign. Home has external assets A_H denominated in Home currency (say, pesos) and A_F denominated in Foreign currency (say, U.S. dollars). Similarly, it has external liabilities L_H denominated in Home currency and L_F denominated in Foreign currency. The nominal exchange rate is E (with the units being Home currency per unit of Foreign currency—here, pesos per dollar).

The value of Home's dollar external assets and liabilities can be expressed in pesos as EA_F and EL_F, respectively, using an exchange rate conversion. Hence, the Home country's total external wealth is the sum total of assets minus liabilities expressed in local currency:

$$W = \underbrace{(A_H + EA_F)}_{\text{Assets}} - \underbrace{(L_H + EL_F)}_{\text{Liabilities}}$$

Now suppose there is a small change ΔE in the exchange rate, all else equal. This does not affect the values of A_H and L_H, but it *does* change the values of EA_F and EL_F expressed in pesos. We can express the resulting change in national wealth as

$$\Delta W \quad = \quad \underbrace{\Delta E}_{\substack{\text{Change in} \\ \text{exchange rate}}} \quad \times \quad \underbrace{[A_F - L_F]}_{\substack{\text{Net international} \\ \text{credit(+) or debit(−)} \\ \text{position in dollar assets}}} \qquad \text{(19-1)}$$

The expression is intuitive and revealing. After a depreciation ($\Delta E > 0$), the wealth effect is positive if Foreign currency assets exceed Foreign currency liabilities (the net dollar position in brackets is positive) and negative if Foreign currency liabilities exceed Foreign currency assets (the net dollar position in brackets is negative).

For example, consider first the case in which Home experiences a 10% depreciation, with assets of $100 billion and liabilities of $100 billion. What happens to Home wealth if it has $50 billion of assets in dollars and no liabilities in dollars? It has a net credit position in dollars, so it ought to gain. Half of assets and all liabilities are expressed in pesos, so their value does not change. But the value of the half of assets denominated in dollars will rise in peso terms by 10% times $50 billion. In this case, a 10% depreciation increases national wealth by 5% or $5 billion because it increases the value of a net foreign currency credit position.

Now look at the case in which Home experiences a 10% depreciation, as in the preceding example, with zero assets in dollars and $50 billion of liabilities in dollars. All assets and half of liabilities are expressed in pesos, so their value does not change.

But the value of the half of liabilities denominated in dollars will rise in peso terms by 10% times $50 billion. In this case, a depreciation decreases national wealth by 5% or $5 billion because it increases the value of a net foreign currency debit position.

Destabilizing Wealth Shocks Why do these wealth effects have implications for stabilization policy? In the previous chapter, we saw that nominal exchange rate depreciation can be used as a short-run stabilization tool in the IS-LM-FX model. In the face of an adverse demand shock in the Home country, for example, a depreciation will increase Home aggregate demand by switching expenditure toward Home goods. Now we can see that exchange rate movements can influence aggregate demand by affecting wealth.

These effects matter because, in more complex short-run models of the economy, wealth affects the demand for goods. For example,

- Consumers might spend more when they have more wealth. In this case, the consumption function would become $C(Y - T,$ Total wealth$)$, and consumption would depend not just on after-tax income but also on wealth.

- Firms might find it easier to borrow if their wealth increases (e.g., wealth increases the net worth of firms, increasing the collateral available for loans). The investment function would then become $I(i,$ Total wealth$)$, and investment would depend on both the interest rate and wealth.

We can now begin to understand the importance of the exchange rate valuation effects summarized in Equation (19-1). This equation says that countries have to satisfy a special condition to avoid changes in external wealth whenever the exchange rate moves: the value of their foreign currency external assets must exactly equal foreign currency liabilities. If foreign currency external assets do not equal foreign currency external liabilities, the country is said to have a *currency mismatch* on its external balance sheet, and exchange rate changes will affect national wealth.

If foreign currency assets exceed foreign currency liabilities, then the country experiences an increase in wealth when the exchange rate depreciates. From the point of view of stabilization, this is likely to be beneficial: additional wealth will complement the direct stimulus to aggregate demand caused by a depreciation, making the effect of the depreciation *even more* expansionary. This scenario applies to only a few countries, most notably the United States.

However, if foreign currency liabilities exceed foreign currency assets, a country will experience a *decrease* in wealth when the exchange rate depreciates. From the point of view of stabilization policy, this wealth effect is unhelpful because the fall in wealth will tend to offset the conventional stimulus to aggregate demand caused by a depreciation. In principle, if the valuation effects are large enough, the overall effect of a depreciation can be contractionary! For example, while an interest rate cut might boost investment, and the ensuing depreciation might also boost the trade balance, such upward pressure on aggregate demand may well be offset partially or fully (or even outweighed) by decreases in wealth that put downward pressure on demand.

We now see that if a country has an adverse (i.e., negative) net position in foreign currency assets, then the conventional arguments for stabilization policy (and the need for floating) are weak. For many emerging market and developing economies, this is a serious problem. Most of these poorer countries are net debtors, so their external wealth shows a net debit position overall. But their net position in foreign currency is often just as much in debt, or even more so, because their liabilities are often close to 100% dollarized.

Evidence Based on Changes in Wealth When emerging markets experience large depreciations, they often suffer serious collapses in external wealth. To illustrate the severity of this problem, Figure 19-8 shows the impact of exchange rate valuation effects on wealth in eight countries. All the countries experienced exchange rate crises during the period in which the domestic currency lost much of its value relative to the U.S. dollar. Following the 1997 Asian crisis, Korea, the Philippines, and Thailand saw their currencies depreciate by about 50%; Indonesia's currency depreciated by 75%. In 1999 the Brazilian real depreciated by almost 50%. In 2001 Turkey's lira depreciated suddenly by about 50%, after a long slide. And in Argentina, the peso depreciated by about 75% in 2002.

All of these countries also had large exposure to foreign currency debt with large levels of currency mismatch. The Asian countries had borrowed extensively in yen and U.S. dollars; Turkey, Brazil, and Argentina had borrowed extensively in U.S. dollars. As a result of the valuation effects of the depreciations and the liability dollarization all of these countries saw large declines in external wealth. Countries such as Brazil and Korea escaped lightly, with wealth falling cumulatively by only 5% to 10% of annual GDP. Countries with larger exposure to foreign currency debt, or with larger depreciations, suffered much more: in Argentina, the Philippines, and Thailand, the losses were 20% to 30% of GDP and in Indonesia almost 40% of GDP.

Evidence Based on Output Contractions Figure 19-8 tells us that countries with large liability dollarization suffered large wealth effects. But do these wealth effects cause so much economic damage that a country might reconsider its exchange rate regime?

Figure 19-9 suggests that wealth effects are associated with contractions and that the damage is fairly serious. Economists Michele Cavallo, Kate Kisselev, Fabrizio Perri, and Nouriel Roubini found a strong correlation between wealth losses on net foreign currency liabilities suffered during the large depreciations seen after an exchange rate crisis, and a measure of the subsequent fall in real output.[14] For example,

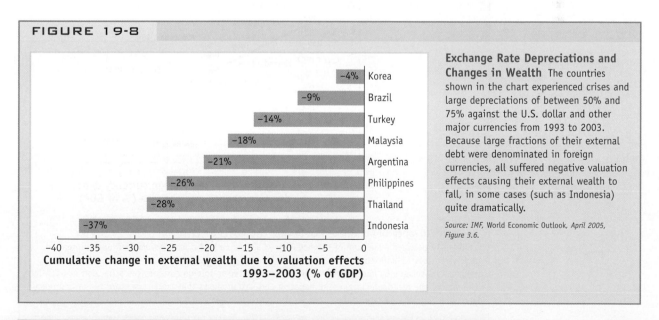

FIGURE 19-8

Exchange Rate Depreciations and Changes in Wealth The countries shown in the chart experienced crises and large depreciations of between 50% and 75% against the U.S. dollar and other major currencies from 1993 to 2003. Because large fractions of their external debt were denominated in foreign currencies, all suffered negative valuation effects causing their external wealth to fall, in some cases (such as Indonesia) quite dramatically.

Source: IMF, World Economic Outlook, April 2005, Figure 3.6.

---

[14] Michele Cavallo, Kate Kisselev, Fabrizio Perri, and Nouriel Roubini, "Exchange Rate Overshooting and the Costs of Floating," Federal Reserve Bank of San Francisco Working Paper Series, Working Paper 2005–07, May 2005.

after 1992 Britain barely suffered any negative wealth effect and, as we noted earlier, did well in its subsequent economic performance: Britain in 1992 sits in the upper left part of this scatterplot (very small wealth loss, no negative impact on GDP). At the other extreme (in the lower right part of this scatterplot), are countries like Argentina and Indonesia, where liability dollarization led to massive wealth losses after the 1997 crisis (large wealth loss, large negative impact on GDP).

Original Sin Such findings have had a powerful influence among international macroeconomists and policymakers in recent years. Previously, external wealth effects were largely ignored and poorly understood. But now, after the adverse consequences of recent large depreciations, macroeconomists recognize that the problem of currency mismatch, driven by liability dollarization, is a key factor in the economic health of many developing countries and should be considered when choosing an exchange rate regime.

Yet these kinds of losses due to currency mismatch are an old problem. In the long history of international investment, one remarkably constant feature has been the inability of most countries—especially poor countries on the periphery of global capital markets—to borrow from abroad in their own currencies. In the late nineteenth century, such countries had to borrow in gold, or in a "hard currency" such as British pounds or U.S. dollars. The same is true today, as is apparent from Table 19-2. In the

FIGURE 19-9

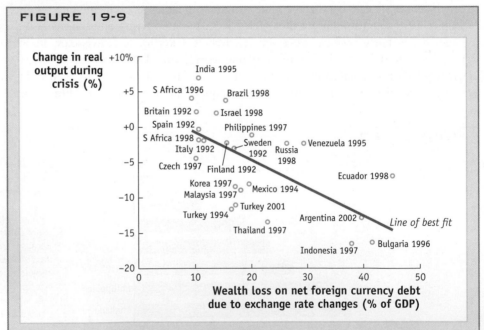

Foreign Currency Denominated Debt and the Costs of Crises This chart shows the correlation between a measure of the negative wealth impact of a real depreciation and the real output costs after an exchange rate crisis (a large depreciation). On the horizontal axis, the wealth impact is estimated by multiplying net debt denominated in foreign currency (as a fraction of GDP) by the size of the real depreciation. The negative correlation shows that larger losses on foreign currency debt due to exchange rate changes are associated with larger real output losses.

Source: Michele Cavallo, Kate Kisselev, Fabrizio Perri, and Nouriel Roubini, "Exchange Rate Overshooting and the Costs of Floating," Federal Reserve Bank of San Francisco Working Paper Series, Working Paper 2005-07, May 2005.

TABLE 19-2

Measures of "Original Sin" Only a few developed countries can issue external liabilities denominated in their own currency. In the financial centers and the Eurozone, the fraction of external liabilities denominated in foreign currency is less than 10%. In the remaining developed countries, it averages about 70%. In developing countries, external liabilities denominated in foreign currency are close to 100% on average.

	External Liabilities Denominated in Foreign Currency (average, %)
Financial centers (United States, United Kingdom, Switzerland, Japan)	8%
Eurozone countries	9
Other developed countries	72
Eastern European countries	84
Middle East and African countries	90
Developing countries	93
Asia/Pacific countries	94
Latin American and Caribbean countries	100

Source: Barry Eichengreen, Ricardo Hausmann, and Ugo Panizza, "The Pain of Original Sin." In Barry Eichengreen and Ricardo Hausmann, eds., 2005, Other People's Money: Debt Denomination and Financial Instability in Emerging-Market Economies (Chicago: University of Chicago Press).

world's financial centers and the Eurozone, only a small fraction of external liabilities are denominated in foreign currency. In other countries, the fraction is much higher; in developing countries, it is close to 100%.

Economists Barry Eichengreen, Ricardo Hausmann, and Ugo Panizza used the term "original sin" to refer to a country's inability to borrow in its own currency.[15] As the term suggests, an historical perspective reveals that the "sin" is highly persistent and originates deep in a country's historical past. Countries with a weak record of macroeconomic management—often due to institutional or political weakness—have in the past been unable to follow prudent monetary and fiscal policies, so the real value of domestic currency debts was frequently eroded by periods of high inflation. Because creditors were mostly unwilling to hold such debt, domestic currency bond markets did not develop, and creditors would lend only in foreign currency which promised a more stable long-term value.

Still, sinners can find redemption. One view argues that the problem is a global capital market failure: for many small countries, the pool of their domestic currency liabilities may be too small to offer any significant risk diversification benefits to foreign investors. In this case, multinational institutions could step in to create markets for securities in the currencies of small countries, or in baskets of such currencies. Another view argues that as such countries improve their institutional quality, design better policies, secure a low-inflation environment, and

---

[15] Barry Eichengreen, Ricardo Hausmann, and Ugo Panizza, 2005, "The Pain of Original Sin." In Barry Eichengreen and Ricardo Hausmann, eds., *Other People's Money: Debt Denomination and Financial Instability in Emerging-Market Economies* (Chicago: University of Chicago Press).

Two Russian bonds: a 100 ruble bond of 1915 and a 1,000 U.S. dollar bond of 1916. Creditors knew the dollar value of the ruble bond could be eroded by ruble depreciation. Only default could erode the value of the dollar bond.

develop a better reputation, they will eventually free themselves from original sin and be able to issue domestic and even external debt in their own currencies. Many observers think this is already happening. Habitual "sinners" such as Mexico, Brazil, Colombia, and Uruguay have recently been able to issue some debt in their own currency. In addition, many emerging countries have been reducing currency mismatch: many governments have been piling up large stocks of foreign currency assets in central bank reserves and sovereign wealth funds and both governments and in some cases the private sectors have been reducing their reliance on foreign currency loans. The recent trends indicate substantial progress in reducing original sin as compared with the 1990s.[16]

Yet any optimism must be tempered with caution. Only time will tell whether countries have really turned the corner and put their "sinful" ways behind them. Progress on domestic-currency borrowing is still very slow in many countries, and this still leaves the problem of currency mismatches in the private sector. While private sector exposure could be insured by the government, that insurance could, in turn, introduce the risk of abuse in the form of *moral hazard*, the risk that insured entities (here, private borrowers) will engage in excessive risk taking, knowing that they will be bailed out if they incur losses. This moral hazard could then create massive political problems, because it may not be clear who, in a crisis, would receive a public-sector rescue, and who would not. Why can't the private sector simply hedge all its exchange rate risk? This solution would be ideal, but in many emerging markets and developing countries, currency derivative markets are poorly developed, many currencies cannot be hedged at all, and the costs are high.

If developing countries cannot avoid currency mismatches, they must try to cope with them. One way to cope is to reduce or stop external borrowing, but countries are not eager to give up all borrowing in world capital markets. A more feasible alternative is for developing countries to minimize or eliminate valuation effects by limiting the movement of the exchange rate. This is indeed what many countries are doing, and evidence shows that the larger a country's stock of foreign currency liabilities relative to GDP, the more likely that country is to peg its currency to the currency in which the external debt is issued.[17]

■ The lesson: *in countries that cannot borrow in their own currency, floating exchange rates are less useful as a stabilization tool and may be destabilizing. Because this outcome applies particularly to developing countries, they will prefer fixed exchange rates to floating exchange rates, all else equal.*

[16] Barry Eichengreen and Ricardo Hausmann, 2005, "Original Sin: The Road to Redemption." In Barry Eichengreen and Ricardo Hausmann, eds., *Other People's Money: Debt Denomination and Financial Instability in Emerging-Market Economies* (Chicago: University of Chicago Press); John D. Burger and Francis E. Warnock, 2003, "Diversification, Original Sin, and International Bond Portfolios," International Finance Discussion Papers 755, Board of Governors of the Federal Reserve System (U.S.); Camilo E. Tovar, 2005, "International Government Debt Denominated in Local Currency: Recent Developments in Latin America," *BIS Quarterly Review*, 109–118; Philip E. Lane and Jay C. Shambaugh, 2010, "Financial Exchange Rates and International Currency Exposures," *American Economic Review* 100(1): 518–40.

[17] Ricardo Hausmann, Ugo Panizza, and Ernesto Stein, 2001, "Why Do Countries Float the Way They Float?" *Journal of Development Economics*, 66(2), 387–414; Christopher M. Meissner and Nienke Oomes, 2006, "Why Do Countries Peg the Way They Peg? The Determinants of Anchor Currency Choice," Cambridge Working Papers in Economics 0643, Faculty of Economics, University of Cambridge.

Summary

We began the chapter by emphasizing the two key factors that influence the choice of fixed versus floating rate regimes: economic integration (market linkages) and economic similarity (symmetry of shocks). But we now see that many other factors can affect the benefits of fixing relative to floating.

A fixed exchange rate may have some additional benefits in some situations. It may be the only transparent and credible way to attain and maintain a nominal anchor, a goal that may be particularly important in emerging markets and developing countries with weak institutions, a lack of central bank independence, strong temptations to use the inflation tax, and poor reputations for monetary stability. A fixed exchange rate may also be the only way to avoid large fluctuations in external wealth, which can be a problem in emerging markets and developing countries with high levels of liability dollarization. These may be powerful additional reasons to fix, and they seem to apply with extra force in developing countries. Therefore, such countries may be less willing to allow their exchange rates to float—a situation that some economists describe as a **fear of floating.**

To illustrate the influence of additional costs and benefits, consider a Home country thinking of pegging to the U.S. dollar as a base currency (Figure 19-10). A Home country with a fear of floating would perceive additional benefits to a fixed exchange rate, and would be willing to peg its exchange at lower levels of integration and similarity. We would represent this choice as an inward shift of the FIX line from FIX_1 to FIX_2. Without fear of floating, based on FIX_1, the Home country would float with symmetry-integration measures given by points 1 and 2, and fix at point 3. But if it had fear of floating, based on FIX_2, it would elect to fix at point 2 because the extra benefits of a fixed rate lower the threshold.

FIGURE 19-10

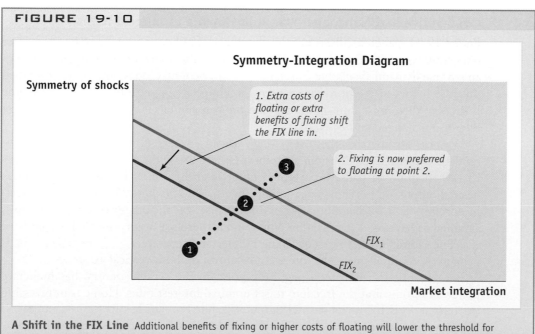

Symmetry-Integration Diagram

Symmetry of shocks

1. Extra costs of floating or extra benefits of fixing shift the FIX line in.

③

2. Fixing is now preferred to floating at point 2.

②

①

FIX_1

FIX_2

Market integration

A Shift in the FIX Line Additional benefits of fixing or higher costs of floating will lower the threshold for choosing a fixed exchange rate. The FIX line moves down. Choosing a fixed rate now makes sense, even at lower levels of symmetry or integration (e.g., at point 2).

3 Fixed Exchange Rate Systems

So far, our discussion has considered only the simplest type of fixed exchange rate: a single home country that unilaterally pegs to a foreign base country. In reality there are more complex arrangements, called **fixed exchange rate systems,** which involve multiple countries. Examples include the global *Bretton Woods system*, in the 1950s and 1960s, and the European *Exchange Rate Mechanism* (ERM), to which all members have to adhere for at least two years as a precondition to euro entry.

Fixed exchange rate systems like these are based on a **reserve currency system** in which N countries $(1, 2, \ldots, N)$ participate. The Nth country, called the center country, provides the reserve currency, which is the base or center currency to which all the other countries peg. In the Bretton Woods system, for example, N was the U.S. dollar; in the ERM, N was the German mark until 1999, and is now the euro.

Throughout this chapter, we have assumed that a country pegs unilaterally to a center country, and we know that this leads to a fundamental asymmetry. The center country has monetary policy autonomy and can set its own interest rate i^* as it pleases. The other noncenter country, which is pegging, then has to adjust its own interest rate so that i equals i^* in order to maintain the peg. The noncenter country loses its ability to conduct stabilization policy, but the center country keeps that power. The asymmetry can be a recipe for political conflict and is known as the *Nth currency problem*.

Are these problems serious? And can a better arrangement be devised? In this section, we show that **cooperative arrangements** may be the answer. We study two kinds of cooperation. One form of cooperation is based on mutual agreement and compromise between center and noncenter countries on the setting of interest rates. The other form of cooperation is based on mutual agreements about adjustments to the levels of the fixed exchange rates themselves.

Cooperative and Noncooperative Adjustments to Interest Rates

Figure 19-11, panel (a), illustrates the possibility of policy conflict between center and noncenter countries. Suppose that Home, which is the noncenter country, experiences an adverse demand shock, but Foreign, the center country, does not. We have studied this case before in the previous chapter: the Home IS curve shifts left and the Home LM curve then must shift up to maintain the peg and ensure that the Home interest rate i is unchanged and equal to i^*.

We now assume that these shifts have already occurred, and we start the analysis with the Home equilibrium at point 1 (where IS_1 and LM_1 intersect) in Home's IS-LM diagram in panel (a). Home output is at Y_1, which is lower than Home's desired output Y_0. Foreign is in equilibrium at point 1′ (where IS_1 and LM_1 intersect) in Foreign's IS-LM diagram in panel (b). Because it is the center country, Foreign is assumed to have used stabilization policy and is therefore at its preferred output level Y_0^*. The Home interest rate equals the Foreign interest rate, $i_1 = i_1^*$, because Home is pegged to Foreign; this is the interest rate shown on both vertical axes.

Because this is a unilateral peg, only Foreign, the center country, has monetary policy autonomy and the freedom to set nominal interest rates. Home is in recession (its output Y_1 is below its desired output Y_0), but Foreign has its desired output. If Foreign makes no policy concession to help Home out of its recession, this would be the noncooperative outcome. There would be no burden sharing between the two countries: Home is the only country to suffer.

FIGURE 19-11

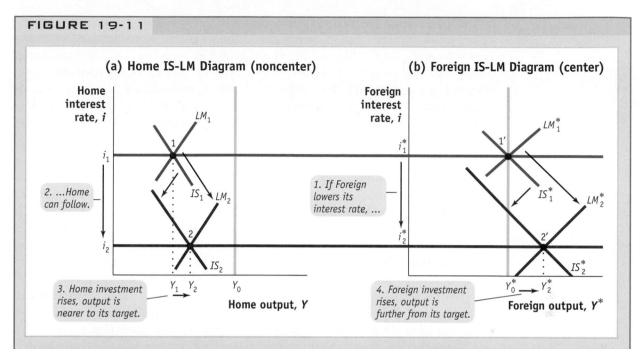

(a) Home IS-LM Diagram (noncenter)

(b) Foreign IS-LM Diagram (center)

Cooperative and Noncooperative Interest Rate Policies by the Center Country In panel (a), the noncenter home country is initially in equilibrium at point 1 with output at Y_1, which is lower than desired output Y_0. In panel (b), the center foreign country is in equilibrium at its desired output level Y_0^* at point 1'. Home and Foreign interest rates are equal, $i_1 = i_1^*$, and Home is unilaterally pegged to Foreign. Foreign has monetary policy autonomy. If the center country makes no policy concession, this is the noncooperative outcome.

With cooperation, the foreign country can make a policy concession and lower its interest rate and home can do the same and maintain the peg. Lower interest rates in the other country shift each country's IS curve in, but the easing of monetary policy in both countries shifts each country's LM curve down. The net effect is to boost output in both countries. The new equilibria at points 2 and 2' lie to the right of points 1 and 1'. Under this cooperative outcome, the foreign center country accepts a rise in output away from its desired level, from Y_0^* to Y_2^*. Meanwhile, Home output gets closer to its desired level, rising from Y_1 to Y_2.

Now suppose we shift to a cooperative outcome in which the center country makes a policy concession. How? Suppose Foreign lowers its interest rate from i_1^* to i_2^*. Home can now do the same, and indeed must do so to maintain the peg. How do the IS curves shift? A lower Foreign interest rate implies that, *all else equal*, Home demand is lower, so the Home IS curve shifts in to IS_2; similarly, in panel (b), a lower Home interest rate implies that, *all else equal*, Foreign demand is lower, so the Foreign IS^* curve shifts in to IS_2^* in panel (b). However, the easing of monetary policy in both countries means that the LM curves shift down in both countries to LM_2 and LM_2^*.

What is the net result of all these shifts? To figure out the extent of the shift in the IS curve, we can think back to the Keynesian cross and the elements of demand that underlie points on the IS curve. The peg is being maintained. Because the nominal exchange rate is unchanged, the real exchange rate is unchanged, so neither country sees a shift in its Keynesian cross demand curve due to a change in the trade balance. But both countries do see a rise in the Keynesian cross demand curve, as investment demand rises thanks to lower interest rates. The rise in demand tells us that new equilibrium points 2 and 2' lie to the right of points 1 and 1': even though the IS curves have shifted in, the downward shifts in the LM curves dominate, and so output in each country will rise in equilibrium.

Compared with the noncooperative equilibrium outcome at points 1 and 1′, Foreign now accepts a rise in output away from its preferred stable level, as output booms from Y_0^* to Y_2^*. Meanwhile, Home is still in recession, but the recession is not as deep, and output is at a level Y_2 that is higher than Y_1. In the noncooperative case, Foreign achieves its ideal output level and Home suffers a deep recession. In the cooperative case, Foreign suffers a slightly higher output level than it would like and Home suffers a slightly lower output level than it would like. The burden of the adverse shock to Home has been shared with Foreign.

Caveats Why would Home and Foreign agree to a cooperative arrangement in the first place? Cooperation might be possible in principle if neither country wants to suffer too much exchange rate volatility against the other—that is, if they are *close* to wanting to be in a fixed arrangement but neither wants to unilaterally peg to the other. A unilateral peg by either country gives all the benefits of fixing to both countries but imposes a stability cost on the noncenter country alone. If neither country is willing to pay that price, there can be no unilateral peg by either country. They could simply float, but they would then lose the efficiency gains from fixing. But if they can somehow set up a peg with a system of policy cooperation, then they could achieve a lower instability burden than under a unilateral peg and this benefit could tip the scales enough to allow the gains from fixing to materialize for both countries.

Cooperation sounds great on paper. But the historical record casts doubt on the ability of countries to even get as far as announcing cooperation on fixed rates, let alone actually backing that up with true cooperative behavior. Indeed, it is rare to see credible cooperative announcements under *floating* rates, where much less is at stake. Why?

A major problem is that, at any given time, the shocks that hit a group of economies are typically asymmetric. A country at its ideal output level not suffering a shock may be unwilling to change its monetary policies just to help out a neighbor suffering a shock and keep a peg going. In theory, cooperation rests on the idea that my shock today could be your shock tomorrow, and we can all do better if we even out the burdens with the understanding that they will "average out" in the long run. But policy makers have to be able to make credible long-run commitments to make this work and suffer short-run pain for long-run gain. History shows that these abilities are often sadly lacking: short-sighted political goals commonly win out over longer-term economic considerations.

For example, consider the European ERM, which was effectively a set of unilateral pegs to the German mark, and now to the euro. The ERM was built around the idea of safeguarding gains from trade in Europe by fixing exchange rates, but the designers knew that it had to incorporate some burden-sharing measures to ensure that the burden of absorbing shocks didn't fall on every country but Germany. The measures proved inadequate, however, and in the crisis of 1992 the German Bundesbank ignored pleas from Italy, Britain, and other countries for an easing of German monetary policy as recessions took hold in the bloc of countries pegging to the German mark. When the test of cooperation came along, Germany wanted to stabilize Germany's output, and no one else's. Thus, even in a group of countries as geographically and politically united as the European Union, it was tremendously difficult to make this kind of cooperation work. (This problem was supposed to be alleviated by true monetary union, with the arrival of the euro and the creation of the European Central Bank in 1999, but even there tensions remain.)

Our main conclusion is that, in practice, the center country in a reserve currency system has tremendous autonomy, which it may be unwilling to give up, thus making cooperative outcomes hard to achieve consistently.

Cooperative and Noncooperative Adjustments to Exchange Rates

We have studied interest rate cooperation. Is there scope for cooperation in other ways? Yes. Countries may decide to adjust the level of the fixed exchange rate. Such an adjustment is (supposedly) a "one-shot" jump or change in the exchange rate at a particular time, which for now we assume to be unanticipated by investors. Apart from that single jump, at all times before and after the change, the exchange rate is left fixed and Home and Foreign interest rates remain equal.

Suppose a country that was previously pegging at a rate $\overline{E}_1$ announces that it will henceforth peg at a different rate, $\overline{E}_2 \neq \overline{E}_1$. By definition, if $\overline{E}_2 > \overline{E}_1$, there is a **devaluation** of the home currency; if $\overline{E}_2 < \overline{E}_1$, there is a **revaluation** of the home currency.

These terms are similar to the terms "depreciation" and "appreciation," which also describe exchange rate changes. Strictly speaking, the terms "devaluation" and "revaluation" should be used only when pegs are being adjusted; "depreciation" and "appreciation" should be used to describe exchange rates that float up or down. Note, however, that these terms are often used loosely and interchangeably.

A framework for understanding peg adjustment is shown in Figure 19-12. We assume now that both Home and Foreign are noncenter countries in a pegged exchange rate system and that each is pegged to a third center currency, say, the U.S. dollar.

(Why this change in the setup compared with the last section? Interest rate adjustment required us to study moves by the center country to help noncenter countries; with exchange rate adjustment, noncenter countries change their exchange rates relative to the center, so in this problem our focus shifts away from the center country.)

We assume that the center (the United States) is a large country with monetary policy autonomy that has set its interest rate at $i_\$$. Home is pegged to the U.S. dollar at $\overline{E}_{\text{home}/\$}$ and Foreign is pegged at $\overline{E}^*_{\text{foreign}/\$}$. In Home's IS-LM diagram in panel (a), equilibrium is initially at point 1 (where IS_1 and LM_1 intersect). Again, because of a prior adverse demand shock, Home output is at Y_1 and is lower than Home's desired output Y_0. In Foreign's IS-LM diagram in panel (b), equilibrium is at Foreign's desired output level Y^*_0 at point 1′ (where IS^*_1 and LM^*_1 intersect). Because Home and Foreign peg to the center currency (here, the U.S. dollar), Home and Foreign interest rates equal the dollar interest rate, $i_1 = i^*_1 = i_\$$.

Now suppose that in a cooperative arrangement, Home devalues against the dollar (and against Foreign) and maintains a peg at a new, higher exchange rate. That is, there is an unanticipated rise in $\overline{E}_{\text{home}/\$}$. The Home and Foreign interest rates remain equal to the dollar interest rate, $i_1 = i^*_1 = i_\$$, because both countries still peg. We can think back to the IS-LM model, or back to the Keynesian cross that we used to construct the IS curve, if necessary, to figure out the effect of the change. Because the nominal depreciation by Home is also a real depreciation, Home sees demand increase: the Home IS curve shifts out to IS_2. Furthermore, the real depreciation for Home is also a real appreciation for Foreign, so Foreign demand *decreases*: the IS^* curve shifts in to IS^*_2. The outcome is cooperative because the burden of the adverse demand shock is being shared: Home output at Y_2 is lower than the ideal Y_0 but not as low as at Y_1; and Foreign has accepted output lower at Y^*_2 than its ideal Y^*_0.

Why might this kind of cooperation work? Home and Foreign could agree that Home would devalue a little (but not too much) so that both countries would jointly feel the pain. Some other time, when Foreign has a nasty shock, Home would "repay" by feeling some of Foreign's pain.

FIGURE 19-12

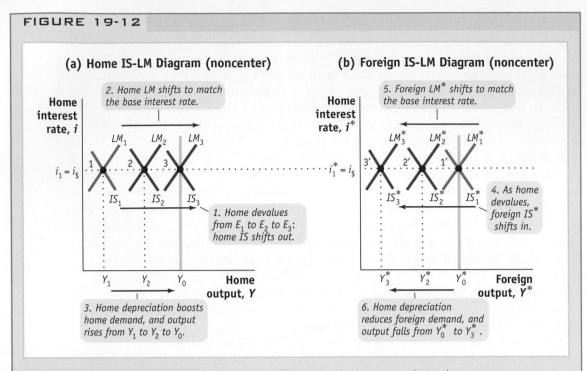

(a) Home IS-LM Diagram (noncenter)

2. Home LM shifts to match the base interest rate.

Home interest rate, i

LM_1 LM_2 LM_3

$i_1 = i_\$$

1. Home devalues from E_1 to E_2 to E_3: home IS shifts out.

IS_1 IS_2 IS_3

Y_1 Y_2 Y_0 **Home output, Y**

3. Home depreciation boosts home demand, and output rises from Y_1 to Y_2 to Y_0.

(b) Foreign IS-LM Diagram (noncenter)

5. Foreign LM^* shifts to match the base interest rate.

Home interest rate, i^*

LM_3^* LM_2^* LM_1^*

$i_1^* = i_\$$

4. As home devalues, foreign IS^* shifts in.

IS_3^* IS_2^* IS_1^*

Y_3^* Y_2^* Y_0^* **Foreign output, Y^***

6. Home depreciation reduces foreign demand, and output falls from Y_0^* to Y_3^*.

Cooperative and Noncooperative Exchange Rate Adjustments by Noncenter Countries In panel (a), the noncenter home country is initially in equilibrium at point 1 with output at Y_1, which is lower than desired output Y_0. In panel (b), the noncenter foreign country is in equilibrium at its desired output level Y_0^* at point 1′. Home and Foreign interest rates are equal to the base (dollar) interest rate and to each other, $i_1 = i_1^* = i_\$$, and Home and Foreign are unilaterally pegged to the base.

With cooperation, Home devalues slightly against the dollar (and against foreign) and maintains a peg at a higher exchange rate. The Home interest and Foreign interest rates remain the same. But the Home real depreciation causes Home demand to increase: IS shifts out to IS_2. This is also a Foreign real appreciation, so foreign demand decreases: IS^* shifts in to IS_2^*. Under this cooperative outcome at points 2 and 2′, foreign accepts a fall in output away from its desired level, from Y_0^* to Y_2^*. Meanwhile, Home output gets closer to its desired level, rising from Y_1 to Y_2.

With noncooperation, Home devalues more aggressively against the dollar. After a large Home real depreciation, IS shifts out to IS_3 and IS^* shifts in to IS_3^*. Under this noncooperative outcome at points 3 and 3′, Home gets its desired output Y_0 by "exporting" the recession to foreign, where output falls all the way to Y_3^*.

Now suppose we shift to a noncooperative outcome in which Home devalues more aggressively against the dollar. After a large real depreciation by Home, Home demand is greatly boosted, and the Home IS curve shifts out all the way to IS_3. Home's real depreciation is also a large real appreciation for Foreign, where demand is greatly reduced, so the Foreign IS^* curve shifts in all the way to IS_3^*. The outcome is noncooperative: Home now gets its preferred outcome with output at its ideal level Y_0; it achieves this by "exporting" the recession to Foreign, where output falls all the way to Y_3^*.

There are two qualifications to this analysis. First, we have only considered a situation in which Home wishes to devalue to offset a negative demand shock. But the same logic applies when Home's economy is "overheating" and policy makers fear that output is above the ideal level, perhaps creating a risk of inflationary pressures. In that case, Home may wish to revalue its currency and export the overheating to Foreign.

Second, we have not considered the center country, here the United States. In reality, the center country also suffers some decrease in demand if Home devalues because the center will experience a real appreciation against Home. However, there is less to worry about in this instance: because the United States is the center country, it has policy autonomy, and can always use stabilization policy to boost demand. Thus, there may be a monetary easing in the center country, a secondary effect that we do not consider here.

Caveats We can now see that adjusting the peg is a policy that may be cooperative or noncooperative in nature. If noncooperative, it is usually called a **beggar-thy-neighbor policy:** Home can improve its position at the expense of Foreign and without Foreign's agreement. When Home is in recession, and its policy makers choose a devaluation and real depreciation, they are engineering a diversion of some of world demand toward Home goods and away from the rest of the world's goods.

This finding brings us to the main drawback of admitting noncooperative adjustments into a fixed exchange rate system. Two can play this game! If Home engages in such a policy, it is possible for Foreign to respond with a devaluation of its own in a tit-for-tat way. If this happens, the pretense of a fixed exchange rate system is over. The countries no longer peg and instead play a new noncooperative game against each other with floating exchange rates.

Cooperation may be most needed to sustain a fixed exchange rate system with adjustable pegs, so as to restrain beggar-thy-neighbor devaluations. But can it work? Consider continental Europe since World War II, under both the Bretton Woods system and the later European systems such as ERM (which predated the euro). A persistent concern of European policy makers in this period was the threat of beggar-thy-neighbor devaluations. For example, the British pound and the Italian lira devalued against the dollar and later the German mark on numerous occasions from the 1960s to the 1990s. Although some of these peg adjustments had the veneer of official multilateral decisions, some (like the 1992 ERM crisis) occurred when cooperation broke down.

APPLICATION

The Gold Standard

Our analysis in this section has focused on the problems of policy conflict in a reserve currency system in which there is one center country issuing a currency (e.g., the dollar or euro) to which all other noncenter countries peg. As we know from Figure 19-1, this is an apt description of most fixed exchange rate arrangements at the present time and going back as far as World War II. A key issue in such systems is the asymmetry between the center country, which retains monetary autonomy, and the noncenter countries, which forsake it.

Are there symmetric fixed exchange rate systems, in which there is no center country and the asymmetry created by the Nth currency problem can be avoided? In theory the ERM system worked this way before the advent of the euro in 1999, but, as the 1992 crisis showed, there was, in practice, a marked asymmetry between Germany and the other ERM countries. Historically, the only true symmetric systems have been those in which countries fixed the value of their currency relative to some commodity. The most famous and important of these systems was the gold standard, and this system had no center country because countries did not peg the exchange rate at $\overline{E}$, the local currency price of some base currency, but instead they pegged at $\overline{P}_g$, the local currency price of gold.

"The best coin that has been struck for two thousand years" declared U.S. President Theodore Roosevelt, on the minting of this beautiful and intricate design to improve artistically on what he saw as the "atrocious hideousness" of American coinage. The U.S. gold parity was $20.67 per troy ounce from 1834 to 1933, so a $20 gold coin like this 1907 Saint Gaudens Double Eagle contained 20/20.67 = 0.9675 ounces of gold.

How did this system work? Under the gold standard, gold and money were seamlessly interchangeable, and the combined value of gold and money in the hands of the public was the relevant measure of money supply (M). For example, consider two countries, Britain pegging to gold at $\overline{P}_g$ (pounds per ounce of gold) and France pegging to gold at $\overline{P}_g^*$ (francs per ounce of gold). Under this system, one pound cost $1/\overline{P}_g$ ounces of gold, and each ounce of gold cost $\overline{P}_g^*$ francs, according to the fixed gold prices set by the central banks in each country. Thus, one pound cost $E_{\text{par}} = \overline{P}_g^*/\overline{P}_g$ francs, and this ratio defined the *par* exchange rate implied by the gold prices in each country.

The gold standard rested on the principle of free convertibility. This meant that central banks in both countries stood ready to buy and sell gold in exchange for paper money at these mint prices, and the export and import of gold were unrestricted. This allowed arbitrage forces to stabilize the system. How?

Suppose the market exchange rate in Paris (the price of one pound in francs) was E francs per pound and deviated from the par level, with $E < E_{\text{par}}$ francs per pound. This would create an arbitrage opportunity. The franc has appreciated relative to pounds, and arbitrageurs could change 1 ounce of gold into $\overline{P}_g^*$ francs at the central bank, and then into $\overline{P}_g^*/E$ pounds in the market, which could be shipped to London and converted into $\overline{P}_g^*/(E\overline{P}_g)$ ounces of gold, which could then be brought back to Paris. Because we assumed that $E < E_{\text{par}}$, $\overline{P}_g^*/(E\overline{P}_g) = E_{\text{par}}/E > 1$, and the trader ends up with more than an ounce of gold and makes a profit.

As a result of this trade, gold would leave Britain and the British money supply would fall (pounds would be redeemed at the Bank of England by the French traders, who would export the gold back to France). As gold entered France, the French money supply would expand (because the traders could leave it in gold form, or freely change it into franc notes at the Banque de France).

We can note how the result tends to stabilize the foreign exchange market (just as interest arbitrage did in the chapters on exchange rates). Here, the pound was depreciated relative to par and the arbitrage mechanism caused the British money supply to contract and the French money supply to expand. The arbitrage mechanism depended on French investors buying "cheap" pounds. This would bid up the price of pounds in Paris, so E would rise toward E_{par}, stabilizing the exchange rate at its par level.

Four observations are worth noting. First, the process of arbitrage was not really costless, so if the exchange rate deviated only slightly from parity, the profit from arbitrage might be zero or negative (i.e., a loss). Thus, there was a small band around the par rate in which the exchange rate might fluctuate without any arbitrage occurring. However, this band, delineated by limits known as the upper and lower "gold points," was typically small, permitting perhaps at most ±1% fluctuations in E on either side of E_{par}. The exchange rate was, therefore, very stable. For example, from 1879 to 1914, when Britain and the United States were pegged to gold at a par rate of $4.86 per pound, the daily dollar–pound market exchange rate in New York was within 1% of its par value 99.97% of the time (and within half a percent 77% of the time).[18]

Second, in our example we examined arbitrage in only one direction, but, naturally, there would have been a similar profitable arbitrage opportunity—subject to transaction costs—in the opposite direction if E had been above E_{par} and the franc had been depreciated relative to parity. (Working out how one makes a profit in that case, and what the net effect would be on each country's money supply, is left as an exercise.)

---

[18] Eugene Canjels, Gauri Prakash-Canjels, and Alan M. Taylor, 2004, "Measuring Market Integration: Foreign Exchange Arbitrage and the Gold Standard, 1879–1913," *Review of Economics and Statistics*, 86(4), 868–882.

Third, gold arbitrage would enforce a fixed exchange rate at E_{par} (plus or minus small deviations within the gold points), thus setting expected depreciation to zero. Interest arbitrage between the two countries' money markets would equalize the interest rates in each country (subject to risk premiums). So our earlier approach to the study of fixed exchange rates remains valid, including a central principle, the trilemma.

Fourth, and most important, we see the inherent symmetry of the gold standard system when operated according to these principles. Both countries share in the adjustment mechanism, with the money supply contracting in the gold outflow country (here, Britain) and the money supply expanding in the gold inflow country (here, France). In theory, if these principles were adhered to, neither country has the privileged position of being able to not change its monetary policy, in marked contrast to a center country in a reserve currency system. But in reality, the gold standard did not always operate quite so smoothly, as we see in the next section. ■

4 International Monetary Experience

A vast diversity of exchange rate arrangements have been used throughout history. In the chapter that introduced exchange rates, we saw how different countries fix or float at present; at the start of this chapter, we saw how exchange rate arrangements have fluctuated over more than a century. These observations motivated us to study how countries choose to fix or float.

To try to better understand the international monetary experience and how we got to where we are today, we now apply what we have learned in the book so far.[19] In particular, we rely on the trilemma, which tells us that countries cannot simultaneously meet the three policy goals of a fixed exchange rate, capital mobility, and monetary policy autonomy. With the feasible policy choices thus set out, we draw on the ideas of this chapter about the costs and benefits of fixed and floating regimes to try to understand why various countries have made the choices they have at different times.

The Rise and Fall of the Gold Standard

As we saw in Figure 19-1, the history of international monetary arrangements from 1870 to 1939 was dominated by one story: the rise and fall of the gold standard regime. In 1870 about 15% of countries were on gold, rising to about 70% in 1913 and almost 90% during a brief period of resumption in the 1920s. But by 1939, only about 25% of the world was pegged to gold. What happened? The analysis in this chapter provides insights into one of the grand narratives of economic history.[20]

The period from 1870 to 1914 was the first era of globalization, with increasingly large flows of trade, capital, and people between countries. Depending on the countries in question, some of these developments were due to technological developments in transport and communications (such as steamships, the telegraph, etc.) and some were a result of policy change (such as tariff reductions). Our model suggests that as the volume of trade and other economic transactions between nations increase, there

---

[19] Barry Eichengreen, 1996, *Globalizing Capital: A History of the International Monetary System* (Princeton, NJ: Princeton University Press); Maurice Obstfeld and Alan M. Taylor, 2004, *Global Capital Markets: Integration, Crisis, and Growth* (Cambridge: Cambridge University Press).

[20] Lawrence Officer, October 1, 2001, "Gold Standard," *EH.Net Encyclopedia*, edited by Robert Whaples, http://eh.net/encyclopedia/article/officer.gold.standard.

will be more to gain from adopting a fixed exchange rate (as in Figure 19-4). Thus, as nineteenth-century globalization proceeded, it is likely that more countries crossed the FIX line and met the economic criteria for fixing.

There were also other forces at work encouraging a switch to the gold peg before 1914. The stabilization costs of pegging were either seen as insignificant—because the pace of economic growth was not that unstable—or else politically irrelevant—because the majority of those adversely affected by business cycles and unemployment were from the mostly disenfranchised working classes. With the exception of some emerging markets, price stability was the major goal and the inflation tax was not seen as useful except in emergencies.

As for the question, why peg to gold? (as opposed to silver, or something else), note that once a gold peg became established in a few countries, the benefits of adoption in other countries would increase further. If you are the second country to go on the gold standard, it lowers your trade costs with one other country; if you are the 10th or 20th country to go on, it lowers your trade costs with 10 or 20 other countries; and so on. This can be thought of as a "snowball effect" (or *network externality*, as economists say), where only one standard can dominate in the end.[21]

This is not to say that all was plain sailing before 1914. Many countries joined gold, only to leave temporarily because of a crisis. Even in countries that stayed on gold, not everyone loved the gold standard. The benefits were often less noticeable than the costs, particularly in times of deflation or in recessions. For example, in the United States, prices and output stagnated in the 1890s. As a result, many people supported

The Granger Collection

Bryan's "cross of gold."

leaving the gold standard to escape its monetary restrictions. The tensions reached a head in 1896 at the Democratic Convention in Chicago, when presidential candidate William Jennings Bryan ended his speech saying: "Having behind us the producing masses of this nation and the world, supported by the commercial interests, the laboring interests and the toilers everywhere, we will answer their demand for a gold standard by saying to them: You shall not press down upon the brow of labor this crown of thorns, you shall not crucify mankind upon a cross of gold." (Bryan lost, the pro-gold McKinley became president, the Gold Standard Act of 1900 was passed to bury any doubts, and tensions defused as economic growth and gold discoveries raised output and prices.)

These trends were upset by World War I. Countries participating in the war needed some way to finance their efforts. The inflation tax was heavily used, and this implied exit from the gold standard. In addition, once the war began in Europe (and later drew in the United States), the majority of global trade was affected by it: trade was almost 100% wiped out between warring nations, and fell by 50% between participants and neutral countries. This effect persisted long after the war ended, and was made worse by protectionism (higher tariffs and quotas) in the 1920s. By the 1930s, world trade had fallen to close to half of its 1914 level. All of these developments meant less economic integration—which in turn meant that the rationale for fixing based on gains from trade was being weakened.[22]

---

[21] Christopher M. Meissner, 2005, "A New World Order: Explaining the International Diffusion of the Gold Standard, 1870–1913," *Journal of International Economics*, 66(2), 385–406.

[22] Reuven Glick and Alan M. Taylor, 2010, "Collateral Damage: Trade Disruption and the Economic Impact of War," *Review of Economics and Statistics*, 92(1), 102–127; Antoni Estevadeordal, Brian Frantz, and Alan M. Taylor, 2003, "The Rise and Fall of World Trade, 1870–1939," *Quarterly Journal of Economics*, 118(2), 359–407.

Then, from 1929 on, the Great Depression undermined the stability argument for pegging to gold. The 1920s and 1930s featured much more violent economic fluctuations than had been seen prior to 1914, raising the costs of pegging. Moreover, politically speaking, these costs could no longer be ignored so easily with the widening of the franchise over time. The rise of labor movements and political parties of the left started to give voice and electoral weight to constituencies that cared much more about the instability costs of a fixed exchange rate.[23]

Other factors also played a role. The Great Depression was accompanied by severe deflation, so to stay on gold might have risked further deflation given the slow growth of gold supplies to which all money supplies were linked. Deflation linked to inadequate gold supplies therefore undermined the usefulness of gold as a nominal anchor.[24] Many countries had followed beggar-thy-neighbor policies in the 1920s, choosing to re-peg their currencies to gold at devalued rates, making further devaluations tempting. Among developing countries, many economies were in recession before 1929 because of poor conditions in commodity markets, so they had another reason to devalue (as some did as early as 1929). The war had also left gold reserves distributed in a highly asymmetric fashion, leaving some countries with few reserves for intervention to support their pegs. As backup, many countries used major currencies as reserves, but the value of these reserves depended on everyone else's commitment to the gold peg, a commitment that was increasingly questionable.

All of these weaknesses undermined the confidence and credibility of the commitment to gold pegs in many countries, making the collapse of the pegs more likely. Currency traders would then speculate against various currencies, raising the risk of a crisis. In the face of such speculation, in 1931 both Germany and Austria imposed capital controls, and Britain floated the pound against gold. The gold standard system then unraveled in a largely uncoordinated, uncooperative, and destructive fashion.

In the language of the trilemma, with its three solutions or "corners," the 1930s saw a movement by policy makers away from the "open capital market/fixed exchange rate" corner, and the other two corners came to dominate. Countries unwilling to close their capital markets by imposing controls opted to abandon the gold peg and moved to the open capital market/floating exchange rate solution, allowing them to regain monetary policy autonomy: Britain and the United States among others made this choice. Countries willing to adopt capital controls but unwilling to suffer the volatility of a floating rate moved to the "closed capital market/fixed exchange rate" solution, allowing them to regain monetary policy autonomy in a different way: Germany and many countries in South America made this choice. Gaining monetary autonomy gave all of these countries the freedom to pursue more expansionary monetary policies to try to revive their economies, and most of them did just that. Finally, a few countries (such as France and Switzerland) remained on the gold standard and did not devalue or impose controls, because they were not forced off gold (they had large reserves) and because they were worried about the inflationary consequences of floating. Countries that stuck with the gold standard paid a heavy price: compared

[23] Barry Eichengreen, 1992, *Golden Fetters: The Gold Standard and the Great Depression* (New York: Oxford University Press).
[24] World gold production more or less kept pace with output growth in the nineteenth century, but output grew much faster than gold stocks in the twentieth century. If gold gets scarcer, its relative price must rise. But if the money price of gold is pegged, the only way for the relative price of gold to rise is for all other prices to fall—that is, by economy-wide price deflation.

with 1929, countries that floated had 26% higher output in 1935, and countries that adopted capital controls had 21% higher output, as compared with the countries that stayed on gold.[25]

Figure 19-13 shows these outcomes. To sum up: although many other factors were important, trade gains and an absence of (or political indifference to) stability costs helped bring the gold standard into being before 1914; reduced trade gains and stability costs that were higher (or more politically relevant) help explain the ultimate demise of the gold standard in the interwar period.

Bretton Woods to the Present

The international monetary system of the 1930s was chaotic. Near the end of World War II, allied economic policy makers gathered in the United States, at Bretton Woods, New Hampshire, to try to ensure that the postwar economy fared better. The architects of the postwar order, notably Harry Dexter White and John Maynard Keynes, constructed a system that preserved one key tenet of the gold standard

FIGURE 19-13

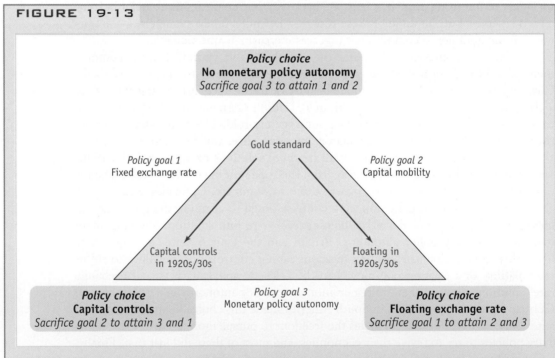

Solutions to the Trilemma Before and After World War I Each corner of the triangle represents a viable policy choice. The labels on the two adjacent edges of the triangle are the goals that can be attained; the label on the opposite edge is the goal that has to be sacrificed. Trade gains and an absence of (or political indifference to) stability costs help explain how the gold standard came into being before 1914 (top corner). Subsequently, reduced trade gains and higher actual (or politically relevant) stability costs help explain the ultimate demise of the gold standard in the 1920s and 1930s. Countries sought new solutions to the trilemma to achieve policy autonomy, either by floating (bottom right corner) or by adopting capital controls (bottom left corner).

[25] Maurice Obstfeld and Alan M. Taylor, 2004, *Global Capital Markets: Integration, Crisis, and Growth* (Cambridge: Cambridge University Press). The output cost estimates are from page 143.

regime—by keeping fixed rates—but discarded the other by imposing capital controls. The trilemma was resolved in favor of exchange rate stability to encourage the rebuilding of trade in the postwar period. Countries would peg to the U.S. dollar; this made the U.S. dollar the center currency and the United States the center country. The U.S. dollar was, in turn, pegged to gold at a fixed price, a last vestige of the gold standard.

In Figure 19-14, the postwar period starts with the world firmly in the "closed capital market/fixed exchange rate" corner on the left. At Bretton Woods, the interests of international finance were seemingly dismissed, amid disdain for the speculators who had destabilized the gold standard in the 1920s and 1930s: U.S. Treasury Secretary Henry Morgenthau pronounced that the new institutions would "drive . . . the usurious money lenders from the temple of international finance." At the time, only the United States allowed full freedom of international capital movement, but this was soon to change.

It was obvious that to have trade one needed to have payments, so some kind of system for credit was needed, at least on a short-term basis. By the late 1950s, after getting by with half measures, many countries in Europe and elsewhere were ready to liberalize financial transactions related to current account transactions to free up the trade and payments system. At the same time, they sought to limit speculative financial transactions that were purely asset trades within the financial account (e.g., interest arbitrage by forex traders).

FIGURE 19-14

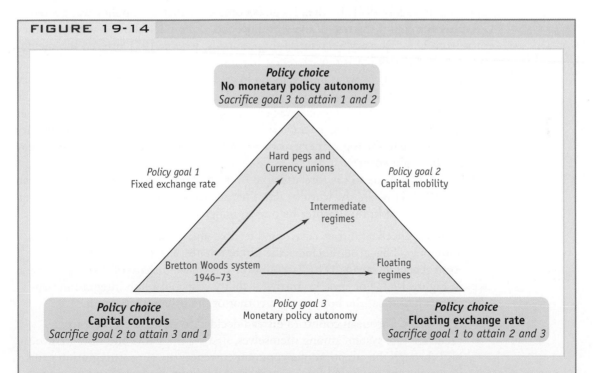

Solutions to the Trilemma Since World War II In the 1960s, the Bretton Woods system became unsustainable because capital mobility could not be contained. Thus, countries could no longer have fixed rates and monetary autonomy (bottom left corner). In the advanced countries, the trilemma was resolved by a shift to floating rates, which preserved autonomy and allowed for the present era of capital mobility (bottom right corner). The main exception was the currency union of the Eurozone. In developing countries and emerging markets, the "fear of floating" was stronger; when capital markets were opened, monetary policy autonomy was more often sacrificed and fixed exchange rates were maintained (top corner).

Unfortunately, in practice it proved difficult then (and has proved so ever since) to put watertight controls on financial transactions. Controls in the 1960s were very leaky and investors found ways to circumvent them and move money offshore from local currency deposits into foreign currency deposits. Some used accounting tricks such as over- or underinvoicing trade transactions to move money from one currency to another. Others took advantage of the largely unregulated offshore currency markets that had emerged in London and elsewhere in the late 1950s.

As capital mobility grew and controls failed to hold, the trilemma tells us that countries pegged to the dollar stood to lose their monetary policy autonomy. This was already a reason for them to think about exiting the dollar peg. With autonomy evaporating, the devaluation option came to be seen as the most important way of achieving policy compromise in a "fixed but adjustable" system. But increasingly frequent devaluations (and some revaluations) undermined the notion of a truly fixed rate system, made it more unstable, generated beggar-thy-neighbor policies, and—if anticipated—encouraged speculators.

The downsides became more and more apparent as the 1960s went on. Other factors included a growing unwillingness in many countries to peg to the U.S. dollar, after inflation in the Vietnam War era undermined the dollar's previously strong claim to be the best nominal anchor currency. It was also believed that this inflation would eventually conflict with the goal of fixing the dollar price of gold and that the United States would eventually abandon its commitment to convert dollars into gold, which happened in August 1971. By then it had become clear that U.S. policy was geared to U.S. interests, and if the rest of the world needed a reminder about asymmetry, they got it from U.S. Treasury Secretary John Connally, who in 1971 uttered the memorable words, "The dollar is our currency, but it's your problem."

Figure 19-14 tells us what must happen in an international monetary system once capital mobility reasserts itself, as happened to the Bretton Woods system in the 1960s. The "closed capital market/fixed exchange rate" corner on the left is no longer an option. Countries must make a choice: they can stay fixed and have no monetary autonomy (move to the top corner), or they can float and recover monetary autonomy (move to the right corner).

These choices came to the fore after the Bretton Woods system collapsed between 1971 and 1973. How did the world react? There have been a variety of outcomes, and the tools developed in this chapter help us to understand them:

- Most advanced countries have opted to float and preserve monetary policy autonomy. This group includes the United States, Japan, United Kingdom, Australia, and Canada. They account for the growing share of floating regimes in Figure 19-1. For these countries, stability costs outweigh integration benefits. They are at the bottom right corner of the trilemma diagram.

- A group of European countries instead decided to try to preserve a fixed exchange rate system among themselves, first via the ERM and now "irrevocably" through the adoption of a common currency, the euro. Integration gains in the closely integrated European market might, in part, explain this choice. This group of countries is at the top corner of the trilemma diagram.

- Some developing countries have maintained capital controls, but many of them (especially the emerging markets) have opened their capital markets. Given the "fear of floating" phenomenon, their desire to choose fixed rates (and sacrifice monetary autonomy) is much stronger than in the advanced countries, all else equal. These countries are also at the top corner of the trilemma diagram.

- Some countries, both developed and developing, have camped in the middle ground: they have attempted to maintain intermediate regimes, such as "dirty floats" or pegs with "limited flexibility." India is often considered to be a case of an intermediate regime somewhere between floating or fixed. Such countries are somewhere in the middle on the right side of the trilemma diagram.

- Finally, some countries still impose some capital controls rather than embrace globalization. China has been in this position, although things are gradually starting to change and the authorities have suggested further moves toward financial liberalization in the future. These countries, mostly developing countries, are clinging to the bottom left corner of the trilemma diagram.

5 Conclusions

Exchange rate regimes have varied greatly across countries and across time and continue to do so. Explaining why this is the case and figuring out the optimal choice of exchange rate regime are major tasks in international macroeconomics.

We began this chapter by studying the main costs and benefits of fixed versus floating regimes. Fixing enhances the economic efficiency of international transactions. Floating allows authorities to stabilize an economy with monetary policy. The clash between these two goals creates a trade-off. Only with enough economic integration (more gains on transactions) and sufficiently symmetric shocks (less need for policy autonomy) do fixed exchange rates make sense, as shown in the symmetry-integration diagram.

However, other factors affect the trade-off, especially in emerging markets and developing countries: fixed exchange rates may provide the only credible nominal anchor after a high inflation, and they insulate countries with net foreign currency debt from the adverse wealth effects of depreciations.

Finally, we examined exchange rate systems in theory and in practice. Over the years, fixed rate systems such as the gold standard and the Bretton Woods system have come and gone, with collapses driven, at least in part, by failures of cooperation. That leaves us today with no real international monetary "system" at all, but rather many countries, and occasionally groups of countries, pursuing their own interests and trying to make the best choice of regime given their particular circumstances. As this chapter has shown, there may be good reasons why "one size fits all" will never apply to exchange rate regimes.

KEY POINTS

1. A wide variety of exchange rate regimes have been in operation throughout history to the present.

2. The benefits for the home country from a fixed exchange rate include lower transaction costs and increased trade, investment, and migration with the base or center country.

3. The costs to the home country from a fixed exchange rate arise primarily when the home and center countries experience different economic shocks and Home would want to pursue monetary policies different from those of the base or center country.

4. The costs and benefits of fixing can be summed up on a symmetry-integration diagram. At high levels of symmetry and/or integration, above the FIX line, it makes sense to fix. At low levels of symmetry and/or integration, below the FIX line, it makes sense to float.

5. A fixed rate may confer extra benefits if it is the only viable nominal anchor in a high-inflation country and if it prevents adverse wealth shocks caused by depreciation in countries suffering from a currency mismatch.

6. Using these tools and the trilemma, we can better understand exchange rate regime choices in the past and in the present. Before 1914 it appears the gold standard did promote integration, and political concern for the loss of stabilization policies was limited. In the 1920s and 1930s, increased isolationism, economic instability, and political realignments undermined the gold standard. After 1945 and up to the late 1960s, the Bretton Woods system of fixed dollar exchange rates was feasible, with strict controls on capital mobility, and was attractive as long as U.S. policies were not at odds with the rest of the world. Since 1973 different countries and groups of countries have gone their own way, and exchange rate regimes reflect the sovereign choice of each country.

KEY TERMS

gold standard, p. 715
base currency, p. 718
center currency, p. 718
economic integration, p. 722
asymetric shock, p. 723
symmetry-integration diagram, p. 724
fear of floating, p. 739
fixed exchange rate systems, p. 740
reserve currency system, p. 740
cooperative arrangements, p. 740
devaluation, p. 743
revaluation, p. 743
beggar-thy-neighbor policy, p. 745

PROBLEMS

1. Using the IS-LM-FX model, illustrate how each of the following scenarios affects the home country. Compare the outcomes when the home country has a fixed exchange rate with the outcomes when the home currency floats.

   a. The foreign country increases the money supply.
   b. The home country cuts taxes.
   c. Investors expect a future appreciation in the home currency.

2. The Lithuanian lita is currently pegged to the euro. Using the IS-LM-FX model for Home (Lithuania) and Foreign (Eurozone), illustrate how each of the following scenarios affect Lithuania:

   a. The Eurozone reduces its money supply.
   b. Lithuania cuts government spending to reduce its budget deficit.
   c. The Eurozone countries increase their taxes.

3. Consider two countries that are currently pegged to the euro: Lithuania and Comoros. Lithuania is a member of the European Union, allowing it to trade freely with other European Union countries. Exports to the Eurozone account for the majority of Lithuania's outbound trade, which mainly consists of manufacturing goods, services, and wood. In contrast, Comoros is an archipelago of islands off the eastern coast of southern Africa that exports food commodities primarily to the United States and France. Comoros historically maintained a peg with the French franc, switching to the euro when France joined the Eurozone. Compare and contrast Lithuania and Comoros in terms of their likely degree of integration symmetry with the Eurozone. Plot Comoros and Lithuania on a symmetry-integration diagram as in Figure 19-4.

4. Use the symmetry-integration diagram as in Figure 19-4 to explore the evolution of international monetary regimes from 1870 to 1939—that is, during the rise and fall of the gold standard.

   a. From 1870 to 1913, world trade flows doubled in size relative to GDP, from about 10% to 20%. Many economic historians believe this was driven by exogenous declines in transaction costs, some of which were caused by changes in transport technology. How would you depict this shift for a pair of countries in the symmetry-integration diagram that started off just below the FIX line in 1870? Use the letter A to label your starting point in 1870 and use B to label the end point in 1913.

b. From 1913 to 1939, world trade flows collapsed, falling in half relative to GDP, from about 20% back to 10%. Many economic historians think this was driven by exogenous increases in transaction costs from rising transport costs and increases in tariffs and quotas. How would you depict this shift for a pair of countries in the symmetry-integration diagram that started off just above the FIX line in 1913? Use the letter B to label your starting point in 1913 and use C to label the end point in 1939.

c. Other economic historians contend that these changes in transaction costs arose endogenously. When countries went on the gold standard, they lowered their transaction costs and boosted trade. When they left gold, costs increased. If this is true, then do points A, B, and C represent unique solutions to the problem of choosing an exchange rate regime?

d. Changes in other factors in the 1920s and 1930s had an impact on the sustainability of the gold standard. These included the following:

   i. An increase in country-specific shocks

   ii. An increase in democracy

   iii. Growth of world output relative to the supply of gold

In each case, explain why these changes might have undermined commitment to the gold standard.

5. Many countries experiencing high and rising inflation, or even hyperinflation, will adopt a fixed exchange rate regime. Discuss the potential costs and benefits of a fixed exchange rate regime in this case. Comment on fiscal discipline, seigniorage, and expected future inflation.

6. In the late 1970s, several countries in Latin America, notably Mexico, Brazil, and Argentina, had accumulated large external debt burdens. A significant share of this debt was denominated in U.S. dollars. The United States pursued contractionary monetary policy from 1979 to 1982, raising dollar interest rates. How would this affect the value of the Latin American currencies relative to the U.S. dollar? How would this affect their external debt in local currency terms? If these countries had wanted to prevent a change in their external debt, what would have been the appropriate policy response, and what would be the drawbacks?

7. Home's currency is the peso and trades at 1 peso per dollar. Home has external assets of $200 billion, all of which are denominated in dollars. It has external liabilities of $400 billion, 75% of which are denominated in dollars.

a. Is Home a net creditor or debtor? What is Home's external wealth?

b. What is Home's net position in dollar-denominated assets?

c. If the peso depreciates to 1.2 pesos per dollar, what is the change in Home's external wealth in pesos?

8. Evaluate the empirical evidence on how currency depreciation affects wealth and output across countries. How does the decision of maintaining a fixed versus floating exchange rate regime depend on a country's external wealth position?

9. Home signs a free-trade agreement with Foreign, which lowers tariffs and other barriers to trade. Both countries are very similar in terms of economic shocks, as they each produce very similar goods. Use a symmetry-integration diagram as in Figure 19-4 as part of your answer to the following questions:

a. Initially, trade rises. Does the rise in trade make Home more or less likely to peg its currency to the Foreign currency? Why?

b. In the longer run, freer trade causes the countries to follow their comparative advantage and specialize in producing very different types of goods. Does the rise in specialization make Home more or less likely to peg its currency to the Foreign currency? Why?

N E T W O R K

Visit the International Monetary Fund's website (http://www.imf.org) and locate the latest classification of exchange rate regimes in all countries around the world. How many countries are fixing and how many are floating?

N E T W O R K

Find the photo of the $20 gold coin on page 746 and the specifications in its caption. Calculate the U.S. dollar price of 1 ounce of gold under the pre-1913 gold standard. Now use the Internet to find details, including gold content, of a British gold sovereign coin worth £1 in the same era. Calculate the British pound price of 1 ounce of gold under the pre-1913 gold standard. Now compute the implied pound–dollar exchange rate. Check your answer against the value given in the text.

20

Exchange Rate Crises: How Pegs Work and How They Break

Global capital markets pose the same kinds of problems that jet planes do. They are faster, more comfortable, and they get you where you are going better. But the crashes are much more spectacular.
Lawrence Summers, U.S. Secretary of the Treasury, 1999

Either extreme: a fixed exchange rate through a currency board, but no central bank, or a central bank plus truly floating exchange rates; either of those is a tenable arrangement. But a pegged exchange rate with a central bank is a recipe for trouble.
Milton Friedman, Nobel laureate, 1998

In the last chapter, we treated the question "fixed or floating?" as a one-time problem of exchange rate regime choice and assumed that, once the choice was made, the chosen regime would be stable and sustainable.

Unfortunately, the reality is different. The typical fixed exchange rate succeeds for a few years, only to break. A recent study found that the average duration of any peg was about five years, and the median duration was only two years.[1] When the break occurs, there is often a large, sudden depreciation accompanied by high economic and political costs. Such a collapse is known as an *exchange rate crisis*. When a country shifts from floating to fixed it is generally smooth and planned, but when a country shifts from fixed to floating it is typically unplanned and catastrophic.

Despite the fragility exposed by recurrent crises, fixed exchange rate regimes are still in use. Typically, after a crisis, a country that prefers to have a fixed exchange rate

---

[1] Michael W. Klein and Jay C. Shambaugh, 2006, "The Nature of Exchange Rate Regimes," NBER Working Paper No. 12729. Since 1970, with the exception of some peculiar countries (the few destined to join the euro, oil exporters like Saudi Arabia and Bahrain, and tiny microstates like Bhutan and Kiribati), only a handful of pegs have lasted longer than a decade, and only one, Hong Kong's peg to the U.S. dollar, was still surviving. See also Maurice Obstfeld and Kenneth Rogoff, 1995, "The Mirage of Fixed Exchange Rates," *Journal of Economic Perspectives*, 9(4), 73–96.

will try to peg again: the cycle of crises may continue. Understanding exchange rate crises is a major goal of international macroeconomics because of the damage they do, not only to the country in which the crisis occurs but often to its neighbors and trading partners. In this chapter we learn about exchange rate crises, their causes, and their consequences.

1 Facts About Exchange Rate Crises

To understand the importance of exchange rate crises, let's examine what crises look like and the costs associated with them.

What Is an Exchange Rate Crisis?

A simple definition of an **exchange rate crisis** would be a "big" depreciation that occurs after a peg breaks.[2] But how big is big enough to qualify as a crisis? In practice, in an advanced country, a 10% to 15% depreciation might be considered large. In emerging markets, the bar might be set higher, say, 20% to 25%.[3] Examples of such crises are shown in Figure 20-1.

Panel (a) shows the depreciation of six European currencies against the German mark after 1992. Four currencies (the escudo, lira, peseta, and pound) were part of the European Exchange Rate Mechanism (ERM); the other two (the markka and krona) were not in the ERM but were pegging to the German mark. All six currencies lost 15% to 25% of their value against the mark within a year.

Panel (b) shows the depreciation of seven emerging market currencies against the U.S. dollar in various crises that occurred from 1994 to 2002. These depreciations, while also very rapid, were much larger than those in panel (a). These currencies lost 50% to 75% of their value against the dollar in the year following the crisis.

The figure illustrates two important points. First, exchange rate crises can occur in advanced countries as well as in emerging markets and developing countries. Second, the magnitude of the crisis, as measured by the subsequent depreciation of the currency, is often much greater in emerging markets and developing countries.

How Costly Are Exchange Rate Crises?

There is much evidence on the potentially damaging effects of exchange rate crises. The economic costs are often large, and the political costs can be even more dramatic (see **Side Bar: The Political Costs of Crises**).

---

[2] Economists sometimes use a broader concept of a *currency crisis* based on other criteria such as reserve losses. See Barry Eichengreen, Andrew K. Rose, and Charles Wyplosz, 1995, "Exchange Market Mayhem: The Antecedents and Aftermath of Speculative Attacks," *Economic Policy*, 10(21), 249–312.

[3] One widely used definition requires at least a 25% depreciation in one year to be sure that such a depreciation is beyond the limits of even a wide band, and a rate of depreciation that is at least 10% higher than in the previous year to ensure that the depreciation is not just part of a broken crawl. Jeffrey A. Frankel and Andrew K. Rose, 1996, "Currency Crashes in Emerging Markets: An Empirical Treatment," *Journal of International Economics*, 41(3-4), 351–366.

FIGURE 20-1

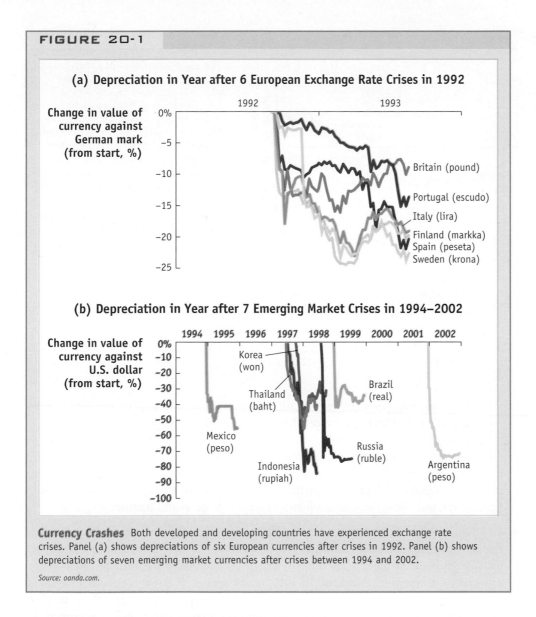

(a) Depreciation in Year after 6 European Exchange Rate Crises in 1992

Change in value of currency against German mark (from start, %)

Britain (pound)
Portugal (escudo)
Italy (lira)
Finland (markka)
Spain (peseta)
Sweden (krona)

(b) Depreciation in Year after 7 Emerging Market Crises in 1994–2002

Change in value of currency against U.S. dollar (from start, %)

Korea (won)
Thailand (baht)
Mexico (peso)
Indonesia (rupiah)
Russia (ruble)
Brazil (real)
Argentina (peso)

Currency Crashes Both developed and developing countries have experienced exchange rate crises. Panel (a) shows depreciations of six European currencies after crises in 1992. Panel (b) shows depreciations of seven emerging market currencies after crises between 1994 and 2002.

Source: oanda.com.

Figure 20-2 presents some evidence on the effects of exchange rate crises. Annual rates of growth of GDP in years close to crises were compared with growth in other (i.e., "normal") years to obtain a measure of how growth differs during crisis periods. The figure shows that just before a crisis all countries have economic growth that is between 0.5% and 1.0% below that in normal years.

After a typical exchange rate crisis, advanced countries and emerging markets react differently. Advanced countries tend to bounce back: growth accelerates and is above normal by the second and third years after the crisis. Emerging markets do not bounce back, and growth usually plummets: it is 2.5% to 3% below normal in the year of the crisis and the two subsequent years, and is still 1% below normal in the third

FIGURE 20-2

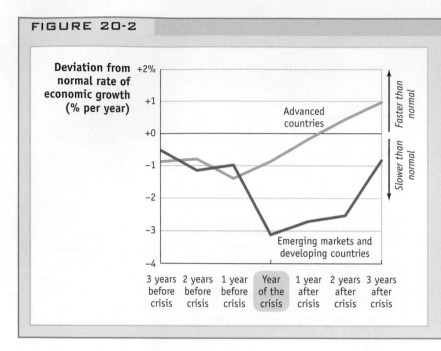

Deviation from normal rate of economic growth (% per year)

The Economic Costs of Crises
Exchange rate crises can impose large economic costs on a country. After a crisis, growth rates in emerging markets and developing countries are, on average, two to three percentage points lower than normal, an effect that persists for about three years. In advanced countries, a depreciation is typically expansionary, and growth is, on average, faster just after the crisis than it was just before.

Source: Maurice Obstfeld and Alan M. Taylor, 2004, Global Capital Markets: Integration, Crisis and Growth (New York: Cambridge University Press).

year. All those reductions in growth add up to about a 10% decline in GDP relative to its typical trend three years after the crisis—a major recession.[4]

The major downturns in emerging markets often have serious economic and social consequences. For example, in the aftermath of the Argentina crisis of 2001 to 2002, news reports were filled with shocking tales of unemployment, financial ruin, rising poverty, hunger, and deprivation. After the Asian crisis of 1997, the recoveries were a little faster, but the economic misfortunes were still deep and painful.

Causes: Other Economic Crises Why are exchange rate crises sometimes so damaging? From the crises of the 1990s, economists learned that exchange rate crises usually go hand in hand with other types of economically harmful financial crises, especially in emerging markets. In the private sector, if banks and other financial institutions face adverse shocks, they may become insolvent, causing them to close or declare bankruptcy: this is known as a **banking crisis.** In the public sector, if the government faces adverse shocks, it may default and be unable or unwilling to pay the principal or interest on its debts: this is known as a *sovereign debt crisis* or **default crisis.** Both banking and default crises can have damaging effects on the economy because they disrupt the flow of credit within and between countries. (In a later chapter, we examine default crises in more detail, including their links to banking and exchange rate crises.)

---

[4] If we were to cumulate these effects over a seven-year time span, we would see that advanced countries typically experience a cycle in which they fall at most 3% below their normal real growth trend but then recover. Emerging markets and developing countries, however, typically suffer a deep downturn, with output at times more than 10% below its normal trend and stuck for some time at a persistently low level.

SIDE BAR

The Political Costs of Crises

Exchange rate crises don't simply have economic consequences—they often have political consequences, too. Figure 20-3 shows that exchange rate crises are often followed by personnel changes at the central bank or finance ministry and not infrequently by a change in a country's leadership as well.

At first, this result might seem odd. As the economist Jeffrey Frankel said, speaking of the Indonesian crisis of 1997: "What is it about devaluation that carries such big political costs? How is it that a strong ruler like Indonesia's Suharto can easily weather 32 years of political, military, ethnic, and environmental challenges, only to succumb to a currency crisis?"*

In emerging markets, we know that the economic costs of exchange rate crises can be large, which helps explain how a Suharto could be undermined. There are many other examples: the Radical Party is the oldest political party in Argentina, but after the exchange rate crisis in 2001 to 2002 under the leadership of President Fernando de la Rúa and Economy Minister Domingo Cavallo, the party faced extinction, polling just 2.3% in the 2003 presidential election.†

Still, why do exchange rate crises carry large political costs in advanced countries where the exit from an exchange rate peg often allows for a depreciation and favorable growth performance? A pertinent example is the decision by Britain's Conservative government to exit the ERM on "Black Wednesday," September 16, 1992. Chancellor Norman Lamont left his job within a year, and Prime Minister John Major tasted defeat at the next general election in 1997, despite faster economic growth after 1992.

Before the crises: Domingo Cavallo, Fernando de la Rúa, Norman Lamont, David Cameron.

The legacy of "Black Wednesday" haunted the Conservatives for years. On the question of economic competence, the polls gave the subsequent Labour government a massive lead for many years. It was not until 2010 that the Conservatives regained power, but only in a coalition, and under their fifth leader in 13 years, David Cameron (who had been a junior minister working under Lamont at the Treasury on that fateful day in 1992).

Even when a depreciation turns out to be good for the economy, the collapse of a peg typically destroys the reputations of politicians and policy makers for credibility and competence. Regaining the trust of the people can take a very long time.

---

*Jeffrey A. Frankel, "Mundell-Fleming Lecture: Contractionary Currency Crashes in Developing Countries," *IMF Staff Papers*, 52(2), 149–192.
†Cavallo had previously served the rival Peronist Party as economy minister in the Menem administration and had presided over the creation of the fixed exchange rate regime, as well as its collapse.

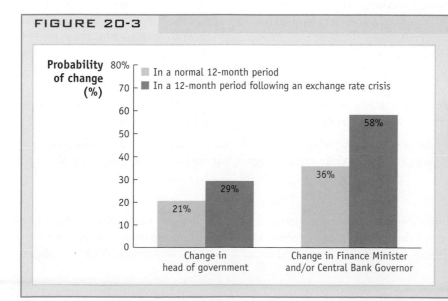

FIGURE 20-3

Probability of change (%)

- In a normal 12-month period
- In a 12-month period following an exchange rate crisis

Change in head of government: 21%, 29%

Change in Finance Minister and/or Central Bank Governor: 36%, 58%

The Political Costs of Crises Exchange rate crises usually impose large political costs on those in power. Compared with what is likely to happen during normal, noncrisis times, it is 22% more likely that one of the two main officials with economic responsibilities (the finance minister and the central bank governor) will be out of a job the year following a crisis. It is also 9% more likely that the head of government (such as a president, prime minister, or premier) will have to depart for one reason or another.

Note: Data on heads of government are from 1971 to 2003, and data on finance ministers and central bank governors are from 1995 to 1999.

Source: Jeffrey A. Frankel, 2005, "Mundell-Fleming Lecture: Contractionary Currency Crashes in Developing Countries," IMF Staff Papers, 52(2), 149–192.

International macroeconomists thus have three crisis types to consider: exchange rate crises, banking crises, and default crises. Evidence shows they can occur one at a time, but they are quite likely to occur simultaneously:

■ *The likelihood of a banking or default crisis increases significantly when a country is having an exchange rate crisis.* One study found that the probability of a banking crisis was 1.6 times higher during an exchange rate crisis (16% versus 10% on average). Another study found that the probability of a default crisis was more than 3 times higher during an exchange rate crisis (39% versus 12% on average).[5] Explanations for these findings focus on valuation effects. As we saw in the last chapter, a big depreciation causes a sudden increase in the local currency value of dollar debts (principal and interest). Because this change in value can raise debt burdens to intolerable levels, exchange rate crises are frequently accompanied by financial distress in the private and public sectors.

■ *The likelihood of an exchange rate crisis increases significantly when a country is having a banking or default crisis.* The same two studies just noted found that the probability of an exchange rate crisis was 1.5 times higher during a banking crisis (46% versus 29% on average). The probability of an exchange rate crisis was more than 5 times higher during a default crisis (84% versus 17% on average).

Explanations for these reverse effects center on the issuance of money by the central bank to bail out banks and governments. Banking crises can be horrendously costly. As can be seen in Table 20-1, countries have to cope not only with direct fiscal costs of fixing a damaged banking sector (e.g., through the bailout and recapitalization of insolvent institutions) but also with typically very long and protracted recessions where output is significantly below trend. These slumps in turn create added cyclical drag on the government's fiscal position (lower taxes, higher spending) leading to a large run up in public debt. Such burdens might be handled purely via future fiscal adjustments, but they can sometimes endanger monetary policy and the nominal anchor. If a country is having a banking crisis, the central bank will be under pressure to extend credit or outright transfers to weak banks to prop them up. If a country is having a default crisis, the government will lose access to foreign and domestic loans and may pressure the central bank to lend to the government. This raises a key question: Why does the extension of credit by the central bank threaten an exchange rate peg? In this chapter, we show how a peg works—and how, if the central bank issues too much money to pay for bailouts and/or government deficits, it can place the peg at risk by causing a loss of reserves.

These findings show how crises are likely to happen in pairs, known as **twin crises,** or all three at once, known as **triple crises,** magnifying the costs of any one type of crisis.

Summary

Exchange rate crises have been recurring for more than 100 years, and we have not seen the last of them. They can generate significant economic costs, and policy makers and scholars are seriously concerned about how to prevent them. What is it about

---

[5] Graciela L. Kaminsky and Carmen M. Reinhart, 1999, "The Twin Crises: The Causes of Banking and Balance-of-Payments Problems," *American Economic Review*, 89(3), 473–500; Carmen M. Reinhart, 2002, "Default, Currency Crises, and Sovereign Credit Ratings," *World Bank Economic Review*, 16(2), 151–170.

TABLE 20-1

Costly Banking Crises The table shows the estimated costs of major banking crises since 1991 in both advanced and emerging economies. Various measures are shown: the loss of output relative to trend, the direct costs to the government of repairing the banking system, and the change in the level of public debt.

Country	Starting Year of the Crisis	Output Loss (% of GDP)*	Direct Fiscal Costs (% of GDP)**	Increase in Public Debt (% of GDP)***
Argentina	2001	71.0%	9.6%	81.9%
Brazil	1994	0.0	13.2	−33.8
China	1998	19.4	18.0	11.2
Denmark	2008	36.0	3.1	24.9
Finland	1991	69.6	12.8	43.6
France	2008	23.0	1.0	17.3
Germany	2008	11.0	1.8	17.8
Greece	2008	43.0	27.3	44.5
Iceland	2008	43.0	44.2	72.2
Indonesia	1997	69.0	56.8	67.6
Ireland	2008	106.0	40.7	72.8
Italy	2008	32.0	0.3	8.6
Japan	1997	45.0	14.0	41.7
Korea	1997	57.6	31.2	9.9
Luxembourg	2008	36.0	7.7	14.6
Malaysia	1997	31.4	16.4	0.2
Mexico	1994	13.7	19.3	16.4
Netherlands	2008	23.0	12.7	26.8
Norway	1991	5.1	2.7	19.2
Portugal	2008	37.0	0.0	33.6
Russia	1998	—	0.1	−7.1
Russia	2008	0.0	2.3	6.4
Sweden	1991	32.9	3.6	36.2
Sweden	2008	25.0	0.7	11.1
Switzerland	2008	0.0	1.1	−0.2
Thailand	1997	109.3	43.8	42.1
Turkey	2000	37.0	32.0	15.3
United Kingdom	2007	25.0	8.8	24.4
United States	2007	31.0	4.5	23.6
Average		*36.9*	*14.8*	*25.6*

* Cumulative, actual relative to trend from crisis start year T until year T+3.
** Restructuring costs including bank recapitalizations but excluding liquidity provision.
*** From year before crisis starts T−1 to year T+3.

Source: Peter Hooper, Michael Spencer, Torsten Sløk, and Thomas Mayer, 2013, "Financial Crises: Past and Present," Global Economic Perspectives, 15 May (Deutsche Bank, Markets Research, Global Economics); based on Fabian Valencia and Luc Laeven, 2012, "Systemic Banking Crises Database: An Update," IMF Working Paper 12/163, International Monetary Fund.

fixed exchange rate regimes that makes them so fragile? Why and how do crises happen? And how can the risks of such crises be mitigated? These are the questions we address in the rest of this chapter.

2 How Pegs Work: The Mechanics of a Fixed Exchange Rate

To start, we must first understand how a pegged exchange rate works. Once we know what policy makers have to do to make a peg work, we will then be in a position to understand the factors that make a peg break.

To help us understand the economic mechanisms that operate in a fixed exchange rate system, we develop a simple model of what a central bank does. We then use the model to look at the demands placed on a central bank when a country adopts a fixed exchange rate.

Preliminaries and Assumptions

We consider a small open economy, in which the authorities are trying to peg to some foreign currency. We make the following assumptions, some of which may be relaxed in later analyses:

- For convenience, and without implying that we are referring to any specific country, we assume that the home currency is called the peso. The currency to which home pegs is the U.S. dollar. We assume the authorities have been maintaining a fixed exchange rate, with E fixed at $\overline{E} = 1$ (one peso per U.S. dollar).

- The country's central bank controls the money supply M by buying and selling assets in exchange for cash. The central bank trades only two types of assets: domestic bonds, often government bonds, denominated in local currency (pesos), and foreign assets, denominated in foreign currency (dollars).

- The central bank intervenes in the forex market to peg the exchange rate. It stands ready to buy and sell foreign exchange reserves at the fixed exchange rate $\overline{E}$. If it has no reserves, it cannot do this and the exchange rate is free to float: the peg is broken.

- Unless stated otherwise, we assume that the peg is credible: everyone believes it will continue to hold. Uncovered interest parity then implies that the home and foreign interest rates are equal: $i = i^*$.

- We also assume for now that the economy's level of output or income is assumed to be exogenous; that is, it is treated as given and denoted Y.

- There is a stable foreign price level $P^* = 1$ at all times. In the short run, the home country's price is sticky and fixed at a level $P = 1$. In the long run, if the exchange rate is kept fixed at 1, then the home price level will be fixed at 1 as a result of purchasing power parity.

- As in previous chapters, the home country's demand for real money balances M/P is determined by the level of output Y and the nominal interest rate i and takes the usual form, $M/P = L(i)Y$. The money market must be in equilibrium, so money demand is always equal to money supply.

- We use the simplest model of a fixed exchange rate, where there is no financial system. The only money is currency, also known as M0 or the monetary base. The monetary base (M0) and broad money (M1) are then the same, so the money supply is denoted M. This assumption allows us to examine the operation of a fixed exchange rate system by considering only the effects of the actions of a central bank.

■ If there is no financial system, we do not need to worry about the role of private banks in creating broad money through checking deposits, loans, and so on. A simple generalization would allow for banks by letting broad money be a constant multiple of the currency.[6] Still, the existence of a banking system is important, and even without formal theory, we will see later in the chapter how it affects the operation of a fixed exchange rate.

The Central Bank Balance Sheet

To understand how the home central bank maintains the peg, we must understand how the home central bank manages its assets in relation to its sole liability, the money in circulation.

Suppose the central bank has purchased a quantity B pesos of domestic bonds. By, in effect, loaning money to the domestic economy, the central bank's purchases are usually referred to as **domestic credit** created by the central bank. These purchases are also called the bank's *domestic assets*. Because the central bank purchases these assets with money, this purchase generates part of the money supply. The part of the home money supply created as a result of the central bank's issuing of domestic credit is denoted B.

Now suppose the central bank has also purchased a quantity R dollars of foreign exchange reserves, usually referred to as **reserves** or foreign assets, and that the exchange rate is pegged at a level $\overline{E} = 1$. The central bank also purchases its reserves with money. Thus, given that the exchange rate has always been 1 (by assumption), the part of the money supply created as a result of the central bank's purchase of foreign exchange reserves is $\overline{E} R = R$.[7]

Because the central bank holds only two types of assets, the last two expressions add up to the total money supply in the home economy:

$$\underbrace{M}_{\text{Money supply}} = \underbrace{B}_{\text{Domestic credit}} + \underbrace{R}_{\text{Reserves}} \tag{20-1}$$

This equation states that the money supply equals domestic credit plus reserves.

This expression is also useful when expressed not in levels but in changes:

$$\underbrace{\Delta M}_{\substack{\text{Change in} \\ \text{money supply}}} = \underbrace{\Delta B}_{\substack{\text{Change in} \\ \text{domestic credit}}} + \underbrace{\Delta R}_{\substack{\text{Change in} \\ \text{reserves}}} \tag{20-2}$$

This expression says that changes in the money supply must result from either changes in domestic credit or changes in reserves.

For example, if the central bank buys additional reserves $\Delta R = 1,000$ dollars, then the money it spends adds $\Delta M = 1,000$ pesos to the money in circulation. If the central bank creates additional domestic credit of $\Delta B = 1,000$ pesos, then it buys 1,000 pesos of government debt, and this also adds $\Delta M = 1,000$ pesos to the money in circulation.

---

[6] Allowing that multiple (the money multiplier) to vary is also possible, but detailed analysis of that mechanism is beyond the scope of this chapter.
[7] In reality, central banks may have acquired reserves in the past at more or less favorable exchange rates, so the current peso value of reserves may be greater than or less than the peso value of the money spent to purchase them. In such cases, the central bank may have positive or negative net worth arising from capital gains or losses on previously purchased reserves (whether such gains are recorded on the central bank's balance sheet depends on its accounting practices and whether it marks reserves at book value or market value). We ignore this problem because it does not greatly affect the analysis that follows.

One common way of depicting Equation (20-1) is to write down each entry and construct the **central bank balance sheet.** The domestic debt and foreign reserves purchased by the central bank are its **assets,** $B + R$. The money supply issued by the central bank M is its **liabilities.**

Following is a hypothetical central bank balance sheet. The central bank has purchased 500 million pesos in domestic government bonds and 500 million pesos in foreign exchange reserves. The total money in circulation resulting from these purchases is 1,000 million pesos. As on any balance sheet, total assets equal total liabilities.

SIMPLIFIED CENTRAL BANK BALANCE SHEET (MILLIONS OF PESOS)			
Assets		**Liabilities**	
Reserves R *Foreign assets (dollar reserves)*	500	**Money supply M** *Currency in circulation*	1,000
Domestic credit B *Domestic assets (peso bonds)*	500		

Fixing, Floating, and the Role of Reserves

The crucial assumption in our simple model is that the central bank maintains the peg by intervening in the foreign exchange market by buying and selling reserves at the fixed exchange rate. In other words, our model supposes that if the central bank wants to fix the exchange rate, it must have some reserves it can trade to achieve that goal. We also assume, for now, that it holds reserves only for this purpose. Thus:

We are assuming that the exchange rate is fixed if and only if the central bank holds reserves; and the exchange rate is floating if and only if the central bank has no reserves.

These assumptions simplify our analysis by clarifying the relationship between the central bank balance sheet and the exchange rate regime. In reality, the relationship may be less clear, but the mechanisms in our model still play a dominant role.

For example, countries may adjust domestic credit as well as reserves, but they never try to maintain a peg by relying *solely* on domestic credit adjustments and zero reserves. Why? In the very short run, forex market conditions can change so quickly that only direct intervention in that market through reserve trading can maintain the peg. In addition, large adjustments to domestic credit may pose problems in an emerging market by causing instability in the bond market as the central bank buys or sells potentially large amounts of government bonds.

Countries can also float and yet keep some reserves on hand for reasons that we ignore in our model so as to keep it simple. They may want reserves on hand for future emergencies, such as war; or as a savings buffer in the event of a sudden stop to financial flows; or so they can peg at some later date.[8] Thus, the minimum level of reserves the central bank will tolerate on its balance sheet may not be at zero, but allowing for some other forms of reserves would not affect our analysis.

---

[8] Some of these functions may be provided by other reserve-holding agencies within the government (such as the Treasury or a sovereign wealth fund). But often all reserves are held by the central bank, which frequently serves as the financial agent of the country.

How Reserves Adjust to Maintain the Peg

We now turn to the key questions we need to answer to understand how a peg works. What level of reserves must the central bank have to maintain the peg? And how are reserves affected by changing macroeconomic conditions? If the central bank can maintain a level of reserves above zero, we know the peg will hold. If not, the peg breaks.

We can rearrange Equation (20-1) to solve for the level of reserves, with $R = M - B$. Why do we do that? It is important to remember that reserves are the unknown variable here: by assumption, reserves change as a result of the central bank's interventions in the forex market, which it must undertake to maintain the peg.

Because (in nominal terms) money supply equals money demand, given by $M = \overline{P}L(i)Y$, we can restate and rearrange Equation (20-1) to solve for the level of reserves:

$$\underbrace{R}_{\text{Reserves}} = \underbrace{\overline{P}L(i)Y}_{\text{Money Demand}} - \underbrace{B}_{\text{Domestic Credit}} \qquad (20\text{-}3)$$

By substituting money demand for money supply, we can investigate how shocks to money demand (say, due to changes in output or the interest rate) or shocks to domestic credit affect the level of reserves.

We can solve this equation. Under our current assumptions, every element on the right-hand side is exogenous and known. The home price level is fixed, the output level is exogenous, interest parity tells us that the home interest rate equals the foreign interest rate, and we can treat domestic credit as predetermined by the central bank's purchases of domestic government debt.

Why is this answer for the reserve level correct and unique? Recall how forex market equilibrium is attained from the chapter on exchange rates in the short run. If the central bank bought more reserves than this, home money supply would expand and the home nominal interest rate would fall, the peso would depreciate, and the peg would break. To prevent this, the central bank would need to intervene in the forex market. The central bank would have to offset its initial purchase of reserves to keep the supply of pesos constant and keep the exchange rate holding steady. Similarly, if the central bank sells reserves for pesos, it would cause the peso to appreciate and would have to reverse course and buy back the reserves. The peg means that the central bank must keep the reserves at the level specified in Equation (20-3).

Graphical Analysis of the Central Bank Balance Sheet

Based on this toolkit, we show the mechanics of a pegged exchange rate in Figure 20-4, which illustrates the central bank balance sheet. On the horizontal axis is the money supply M and on the vertical axis is domestic credit B, both measured in pesos. Money demand is initially at the level M_1, and domestic credit is at B_1.

Two important lines appear in this figure. If reserves R are zero, then all of the money supply is due to domestic credit and Equation (20-1) tells us that $M = B$. The points where $M = B$ are on the 45-degree line. Points on this line, like point Z, correspond to cases in which the central bank balance sheet contains no reserves. By assumption, the country will then have a floating exchange rate, so we call this the **floating line.**

When the assets of the central bank include both reserves and domestic credit, then B and R are both greater than zero and they add up to M. The state of the central bank balance sheet must correspond to a point such as point 1 in this diagram, somewhere

FIGURE 20-4

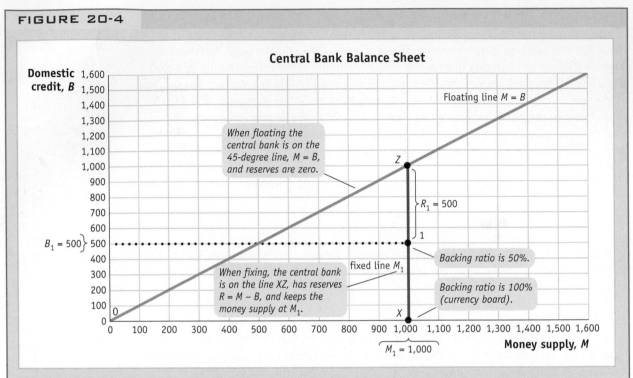

The Central Bank Balance Sheet Diagram On the 45-degree line, reserves are at zero, and the money supply M equals domestic credit B. Variations in the money supply along this line would cause the exchange rate to float. There is a unique level of the money supply M_1 (here assumed to be 1,000) that ensures the exchange rate is at its chosen fixed value. To fix the money supply at this level, the central bank must choose a mix of assets on its balance sheet that corresponds to points on line XZ, points at which domestic credit B is less than money supply M. At point Z, reserves would be at zero; at point X, reserves would be 100% of the money supply. Any point in between on XZ is a feasible choice. At point 1, for example, domestic credit is $B_1 = 500$, reserves are $R_1 = 500$, and $B_1 + R_1 = M_1 = 1,000$.

on the vertical line XZ. We call this the **fixed line** because on this line the money supply is at the level M_3 necessary to maintain the peg.

If domestic credit is B_1, then reserves are $R_1 = M_1 - B_1$, the vertical (or horizontal) distance between point 1 and the 45-degree floating line. Hence, the distance to the floating line tells us how close to danger the peg is by showing how close the central bank is to the point at which reserves run out.[9] The point farthest from danger is X, on the horizontal axis. At this point, domestic credit B is zero and reserves R equal the money supply M. A fixed exchange rate that always operates with reserves equal to 100% of the money supply is known as a **currency board** system.[10]

---

[9] It is important to remember that under our assumptions, all other points in the figure (representing other balance sheet configurations) are ruled out. Floating means having zero reserves and being on the 45-degree line. Other points below the 45-degree line are ruled out because we assume that reserves imply pegging, and these other points would imply a higher or lower level of the money supply and hence an exchange rate other than the pegged rate $\bar{E}$. Points above the 45-degree line are also ruled out: they imply $B > M$ and $R < 0$, which is impossible because reserves cannot be negative.

[10] Strictly speaking, a currency board must satisfy certain other legal and procedural rules. It must own only low-risk interest-bearing foreign assets, not foreign liabilities. It must not perform any function except to exchange domestic currency for foreign currency at the fixed rate. It cannot lend to the domestic banking system to avert banking panics, for example. However, it may hold a bit more than 100% reserve backing, say, 105% to 110%, to guard against fluctuations in the value of its foreign assets. See Kurt Schuler, "Introduction to Currency Boards" (http://users.erols.com/kurrency/intro.htm).

To sum up: if the exchange rate is floating, the central bank balance sheet must correspond to points on the 45-degree floating line; if the exchange rate is fixed, the central bank balance sheet must correspond to points on the vertical fixed line.

The model is now complete, and with the aid of our key tools—the tables and graphs of the central bank balance sheet—we can see how a central bank that is trying to maintain a peg reacts to two types of shocks. We first look at shocks to the level of money demand and then shocks to the composition of money supply.

Defending the Peg I: Changes in the Level of Money Demand

We first look at shocks to money demand and how they affect reserves by altering the level of money supply M. As we saw in Equation (20-3), money supply is equal to money demand, as given by the equation $M = \overline{P} L(i)Y$. If the price level is fixed, then money demand will fluctuate only in response to shocks in output Y and the home interest rate i (which equals the foreign interest rate i^* if the peg is credible). For now, output is exogenous, and a rise in output will raise money demand. The foreign interest rate is also exogenous, and a rise in the foreign interest rate will raise the home interest rate and thus lower money demand. We assume all else is equal, so domestic credit is constant.

A Shock to Home Output or the Foreign Interest Rate Suppose output falls or the foreign interest rate rises. We treat either of these events as an exogenous shock for now, all else equal, and suppose it decreases money demand by, say, 10% at the current interest rate.

For example, suppose we start with a central bank balance sheet as given earlier. Initially, money supply is $M_1 = 1,000$ million pesos. Suppose money demand then falls by 10%. This would lower money demand by 10% to $M_2 = 900$ million pesos. A fall in the demand for money would lower the interest rate in the money market and put depreciation pressure on the home currency. A floating exchange rate would allow the home currency to depreciate in these circumstances. To maintain the peg, the central bank must keep the interest rate unchanged. To achieve this goal, it must sell 100 million pesos ($100 million) of reserves, in exchange for cash, so that money supply contracts as much as money demand. The central bank's balance sheet will then be as follows:

SIMPLIFIED CENTRAL BANK BALANCE SHEET AFTER MONEY DEMAND FALLS (MILLIONS OF PESOS)			
Assets		**Liabilities**	
Reserves R *Foreign assets (dollar reserves)*	400	**Money supply M** *Currency in circulation*	900
Domestic credit B *Domestic assets (peso bonds)*	500		

In Figure 20-5, we can trace the implications of the shock in a graph. The demand for money has fallen, so the *fixed line* is still vertical, but it shifts from the initial money demand level $M_1 = 1,000$ to a new lower level $M_2 = 900$. There is no change to domestic credit, so it remains constant at the level $B_1 = 500$. Thus, the central bank's balance sheet position shifts from point 1 to point 2. This shift takes the balance sheet position closer to the floating line in the diagram: reserves are falling. At point 2, reserves have fallen from $R_1 = 500$ to $R_2 = 400$, as shown.

FIGURE 20-5

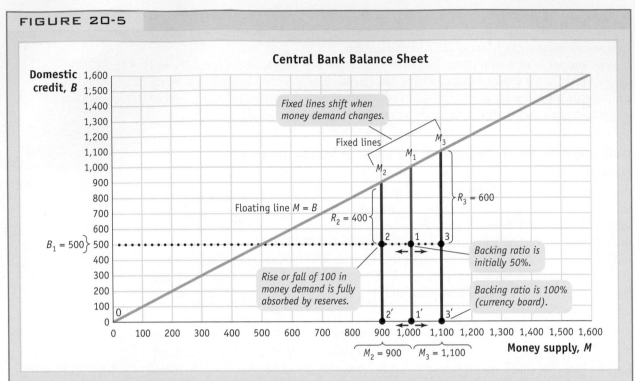

Shocks to Money Demand If money demand falls, interest rates tend to fall, leading to pressure for an exchange rate to depreciate. To prevent this, the central bank must intervene in the forex market and defend the peg by selling reserves and hence lowering the money supply to keep the interest rate fixed and ensure that money supply equals money demand. As shown here, the money supply declines from $M_1 = 1,000$ to $M_2 = 900$. If domestic credit is unchanged at $B_1 = 500$, the change in the central bank balance sheet is shown by a move from point 1 to point 2, and reserves absorb the money demand shock by falling from $R_1 = 500$ to $R_2 = 400$. An opposite positive shock is shown by the move from point 1 to point 3, where $M_3 = 1,100$ and $R_3 = 600$. In a currency board system, a country maintaining 100% reserves will be on the horizontal axis with zero domestic credit, $B = 0$. A currency board adjusts to money demand shocks by moving from point 1' to points 2' or 3'.

Figure 20-5 also shows what would happen with the opposite shock. If money demand increased by 10% from the initial money demand level $M_1 = 1,000$ to a new higher level $M_3 = 1,100$, the central bank would need to prevent an interest rate rise and an appreciation by expanding the money supply by 100 pesos. The central bank would need to intervene and increase the money supply by purchasing $100 of reserves. The central bank's balance sheet position would then shift from point 1 to point 3, moving away from the floating line, with reserves rising from $R_1 = 500$ to $R_3 = 600$.

Equation (20-3) confirms these outcomes as a general result when domestic credit is constant (at B_1 in our example). We know that if the change in domestic credit is zero, $\Delta B = 0$, then any change in money supply must equal the change in reserves, $\Delta R = \Delta M$. This is also clear from Equation (20-2).

We have shown the following: *holding domestic credit constant, a change in money demand leads to an equal change in reserves.*

The Importance of the Backing Ratio In the first example above, money demand and money supply fell by 10% from 1,000 to 900, but reserves fell by 20% from 500 to 400. The proportional fall in reserves was greater than the proportional fall in money because reserves R were initially only 500 and just a fraction (one-half) of the money supply M, which was 1,000. When money demand fell by 100, reserves had to absorb all of the change, with domestic credit unchanged.

The ratio R/M is called the **backing ratio,** and it indicates the fraction of the money supply that is backed by reserves on the central bank balance sheet. It, therefore, tells us the size of the maximum negative money demand shock that the regime can withstand without running out of reserves *if* domestic credit remains unchanged. In our example, the backing ratio was 0.5 or 50% (reserves were 500 and money supply 1,000 initially), so the central bank could absorb up to a 50% decline in the money supply before all of its reserves run out. Because reserves were only 500 to start with, a shock of –500 to money demand would cause reserves to just run out.

In general, *for a given size of a shock to money demand, a higher backing ratio will better insulate an economy against running out of reserves, all else equal.*[11]

In Figure 20-5, the higher the backing ratio, the higher the level of reserves R and the lower the level of domestic credit B, for a given level of money supply M. In other words, the central bank balance sheet position on this figure would be closer to the horizontal axis and farther away from the floating line. This is a graphical illustration of the idea that a high backing ratio makes a peg safer.

Currency Board Operation This maximum backing ratio of 100% is maintained at all times by a currency board. A 100% backing ratio puts the country exactly on the horizontal axis. In Figure 20-5, a currency board would start at point 1′, not point 1. Because reserves would then be 1,000 to start with, a shock of up to –1,000 to money demand could be accommodated without reserves running out. In the face of smaller shocks to money demand such as we have considered, of plus or minus 100, the central bank balance sheet would move to points 2′ or 3′, with reserves equal to money supply equal to money demand equal to 900 or 1,100. These points are as far away from the 45-degree floating line as one can get in this diagram, and they show how a currency board keeps reserves at a maximum 100%. A currency board can be thought of as the safest configuration of the central bank's balance sheet because with 100% backing, the central bank can cope with *any* shock to money demand without running out of reserves. Currency boards are considered a *hard peg* because their high backing ratio ought to confer on them greater resilience in the face of money demand shocks.

Why Does the Level of Money Demand Fluctuate? Our result tells us that to maintain the fixed exchange rate, the central bank must have enough reserves to endure a money demand shock without running out. A shock to money demand is not under the control of the authorities, but they must respond to it. Thus, it is important for policy makers to understand the sources and likely magnitudes of such shocks. Under our assumptions, money demand shocks originate either in shocks to home output Y or the foreign interest rate i^* (because under a credible peg $i = i^*$).

---

[11] To see this, recall that the change in money supply equals the change in reserves, $\Delta M = \Delta R$; hence, for a given *proportional* size of money demand shock $\Delta M/M$, the proportional loss in reserves $\Delta R/R$ can be computed as

$$\% \text{ Change in reserves} = \frac{\Delta R}{R} = \frac{\Delta M}{R} = \frac{\Delta M/M}{R/M} = \frac{\% \text{ Change in money supply}}{\text{Backing ratio}}$$

The higher the backing ratio, the smaller the proportional loss of reserves $\Delta R/R$ for a given size of money demand shock $\Delta M/M$. In our example, the backing ratio was 0.5, so a 10% drop in money supply implied a 10%/0.5 = 20% drop in reserves.

We have studied output fluctuations in earlier chapters, and one thing we observed was that output tends to be much more volatile in emerging markets and developing countries. Thus, the prudent level of reserves is likely to be much higher in these countries. Volatility in foreign interest rates can also be important, whether in U.S. dollars or in other currencies that form the base for pegs.

However, we must also confront a new possibility—that the peg is not fully credible and that simple interest parity fails to hold. In this case, the home interest rate will no longer equal the foreign interest rate, and additional disturbances to home money demand can be caused by the spread between the two. As we now see, this is a vital step toward understanding crises in emerging markets and developing countries.

APPLICATION

Risk Premiums in Advanced and Emerging Markets

So far in the book, we have assumed that uncovered interest parity (UIP) requires that the domestic return (the interest rate on home bank deposits) equals the foreign interest rate plus the expected rate of depreciation of the home currency. However, an important extension of UIP needs to be made when additional risks affect home bank deposits: a **risk premium** is then added to the foreign interest rate to compensate investors for the perceived risk of holding a home domestic currency deposit. This perceived risk is due to an aversion to exchange rate risk or a concern about default risk:

$$ i = i^* + \frac{\Delta E^e_{peso/\$}}{E_{peso/\$}} + \left[\begin{array}{c} \text{Exchange rate} \\ \text{risk premium} \end{array} \right] + \left[\begin{array}{c} \text{Default} \\ \text{risk premium} \end{array} \right] \quad (20\text{-}4) $$

where i is the Peso interest rate, i^* is the Dollar interest rate, and $\frac{\Delta E^e_{peso/\$}}{E_{peso/\$}}$ is the Expected rate of depreciation of the peso. The bracketed terms together with the depreciation form the Interest rate spread (equal to zero if peg is credible and there are no risk premiums).

The left-hand side is still the domestic return, but the right-hand side is now a *risk-adjusted foreign return*. The final three terms are the difference between home and foreign interest rates, and their sum total is known as the **interest rate spread.** What causes these spreads?

The first part of the interest rate spread is the **currency premium:**

$$ \text{Currency premium} = \frac{\Delta E^e_{peso/\$}}{E_{peso/\$}} + \left[\begin{array}{c} \text{Exchange rate} \\ \text{risk premium} \end{array} \right] $$

The currency premium should be zero for a credibly pegged exchange rate: the peso is not expected to change in value relative to the dollar. But if a peg is not credible, and investors suspect that the peg may break, there could be a premium reflecting both the size of the expected depreciation and the currency's perceived riskiness. The currency premium therefore reflects the credibility of monetary policy.

The second part of the interest rate spread is known as the **country premium:**

$$ \text{Country premium} = \left[\begin{array}{c} \text{Default} \\ \text{risk premium} \end{array} \right] $$

The country premium is compensation for perceived default risk (settlement or counterparty risk). It will be greater than zero if investors suspect a risk of losses when they attempt to convert a home (peso) asset back to foreign currency (dollars) in the future. Such a loss might occur because of expropriation, bank failure, surprise taxation, delays, capital controls, other regulations, and so on. The country premium therefore reflects the credibility of property rights.

Why does all this matter? Fluctuations in currency and country premiums have the same effect in Equation (20-4) as fluctuations in the foreign interest rate i^*. Sudden increases in the interest rate spread raise the risk-adjusted foreign return and imply sudden increases in the domestic return, here given by the (peso) interest rate i. In some countries, these spreads can be large and volatile—and even more volatile than the foreign interest rate.

Figure 20-6 presents interest rate spreads for two countries with fixed exchange rates. Panel (a) shows an advanced country, Denmark, which pegs to the euro; panel (b) shows an emerging market, Argentina, which pegged to the dollar from 1991 to 2001.

In Denmark, there was some spread in the early years of the euro from 1999 to 2002 (up to about 0.5% per year), and again some wider spreads in the 2009–10 crisis period, perhaps reflecting a worry that the krone-euro peg might not endure. Otherwise the spread was almost imperceptible (less than 0.1% per year). Overall, the simple correlation between the krone interest rate and the euro interest rate was very high, equal to 0.96. Investors came to see the peg as credible, eliminating the currency premium almost entirely. They also had no fear of default risk if they invested in Denmark, eliminating the country premium almost entirely. Thus one could assume at most times that i was approximately equal to i^* with no spread.

In Argentina the spreads were large: note the bigger vertical scale in panel (b). The annual peso and dollar interest rates were far apart, often differing by 2 or 3 percentage points and sometimes differing by more than 10 percentage points. Most striking is that changes in the spread were usually more important in determining the Argentine interest rate than were changes in the actual foreign (U.S. dollar) interest rate. Overall, the correlation between the peso interest rate i and the dollar interest rate i^* was low, equal to only 0.38. What was going on?

We can separately track currency risk and country risk because Argentine banks offered interest-bearing bank deposits denominated in both U.S. dollars and Argentine pesos. The lower two lines in panel (b) show the interest rate on U.S. dollar deposits in the United States (i^*) and the interest rate on U.S. dollar deposits in Argentina. Because the rates are expressed in the same currency, the difference between these two interest rates cannot be the result of a currency premium. It represents a pure measure of country premium: investors required a higher interest rate on dollar deposits in Argentina than on dollar deposits in the United States because they perceived that Argentine deposits might be subject to a default risk. (Investors were eventually proved right: in the 2001–2002 crisis, many Argentine banks faced insolvency, some were closed for a time, capital controls were imposed at the border, and a "pesification" law turned many dollar assets into peso assets ex post, a form of expropriation and a contractual default.)

The upper line in panel (b) shows the interest rate on peso deposits in Argentina (i), which is even higher than the interest rate on U.S. dollar deposits in Argentina. Because these are interest rates on bank deposits in the same country, the difference between these two rates cannot be due to a country premium. It represents a pure measure of currency premium. Investors required a higher interest rate on peso deposits in Argentina than on dollar deposits in Argentina because they perceived that peso deposits might be subject to a risk of depreciation, that is, a collapse of the

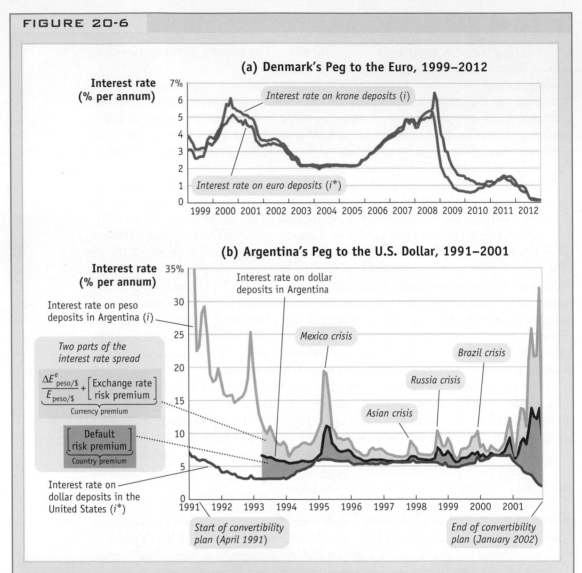

FIGURE 20-6

(a) Denmark's Peg to the Euro, 1999–2012

Interest rate (% per annum)

Interest rate on krone deposits (i)

Interest rate on euro deposits (i*)

(b) Argentina's Peg to the U.S. Dollar, 1991–2001

Interest rate (% per annum)

Interest rate on peso deposits in Argentina (i)

Interest rate on dollar deposits in Argentina

Two parts of the interest rate spread

$$\frac{\Delta E^e_{peso/\$}}{E_{peso/\$}} + \left[\begin{array}{c}\text{Exchange rate}\\\text{risk premium}\end{array}\right]$$

Currency premium

Default risk premium

Country premium

Interest rate on dollar deposits in the United States (i*)

Mexico crisis

Asian crisis

Russia crisis

Brazil crisis

Start of convertibility plan (April 1991)

End of convertibility plan (January 2002)

Interest Rate Spreads: Currency Premiums and Country Premiums When advanced countries peg, the interest rate spread is usually close to zero, and we can assume $i = i^*$. An example is Denmark's peg to the euro in panel (a), where the correlation between the krone and euro interest rates is 0.96. When emerging markets peg, interest rate spreads can be large and volatile, due to both currency and country premiums. An example is Argentina's peg to the U.S. dollar in panel (b), where the correlation between the peso interest rate and the U.S. interest rate is only 0.38.

Note: Three-month interest rates for krone-euro; two-month for peso-dollar.

Source: econstats.com, ft.com, and Danish Bankers Association.

peg. (Investors were eventually proved right again: in the 2001–2002 crisis, the peso depreciated by 75% from $1 to the peso to about $0.25 to the peso, or four pesos per U.S. dollar.)

Summary Pegs in emerging markets are different from those in advanced countries. Because of fluctuations in interest rate spreads, they are subject to even greater interest rate shocks than the pegs of advanced countries, as a result of **credibility** problems.

Currency premiums may fluctuate due to changes in investors' beliefs about the durability of the peg, a problem of the credibility of monetary policy. Country premiums may fluctuate due to changes in investors' beliefs about the security of their investments, a problem of the credibility of property rights.

Still, not every movement in emerging market spreads is driven by economic fundamentals. For example, in Argentina the figure shows that investors revised their risk premiums sharply upward when other emerging market countries were experiencing crises in the 1990s: Mexico in 1994, Asia in 1997, and later Russia and Brazil. With the exception of Brazil (a major trade partner for Argentina), there were no major changes in Argentine fundamentals during these crises. Thus, many economists consider this to be evidence of **contagion** in global capital markets, possibly even a sign of market inefficiency or irrationality, where crises in some parts of the global capital markets trigger adverse changes in market sentiment in faraway places. ■

APPLICATION

The Argentine Convertibility Plan Before the Tequila Crisis

The central bank balance sheet diagram helps us to see how a central bank manages a fixed exchange rate and what adjustments it needs to make in response to a shock in money demand.

We can put this analysis to use with a concrete example: the operation of Argentina's fixed exchange rate system (known as the Convertibility Plan), which began in 1991 and ended in 2002. In this plan, a peg was maintained as one peso per dollar. With the aid of Figure 20-7, we focus first on how the central bank managed its balance sheet during an early phase of the plan, in 1993 and 1994. (We will discuss later years shortly.)

Money Demand Shocks, 1993–1994 The evolution of money supply and reserves is shown in panel (a). From point 1 to point 2 (April 1993 to November/December 1994), all was going well. Argentina had recovered from its hyperinflation in 1989 to 1990, prices were stable, the economy was growing, and so was money demand. Because money demand must equal money supply, the central bank had to increase the money supply. The central bank kept domestic credit more or less unchanged in this period at 4 billion pesos, so reserves had to expand (from 8 billion to 11 billion pesos) as the base money supply expanded (from 12 billion to 15 billion pesos). The backing ratio rose from about 67% (8/12) to about 73% (11/15). In the central bank balance sheet diagram in panel (b), this change is shown by the horizontal move from point 1 to point 2 as the money demand shock causes the fixed line to shift out from M_1 to M_2, so that higher levels of base money supply are now consistent with the peg.

Then an unexpected nasty shock happened: a risk premium shock occurred as a result of the so-called Tequila crisis in Mexico in December 1994. Interest rate spreads widened for Argentina because of currency and country premiums, raising the home interest rate. Argentina's money demand fell. In panel (a), from point 2 to point 3 (November/December 1994 to January/February 1995), base money supply contracted by 1 billion pesos, and this was absorbed almost entirely by a contraction in reserves from 11 billion to 10 billion pesos. The backing ratio fell to about 71% (10/14). In panel (b), this change is shown by the horizontal move from point 2 to point 3 as the money demand shock causes the fixed line to shift in from M_2 to M_3.

FIGURE 20-7

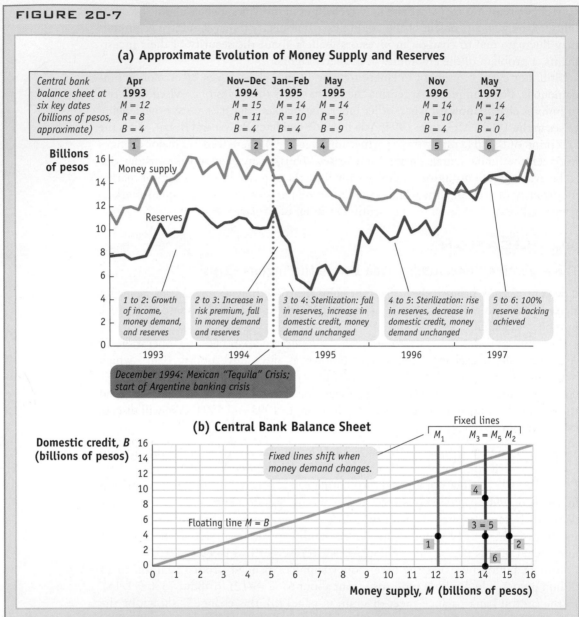

(a) Approximate Evolution of Money Supply and Reserves

Central bank balance sheet at six key dates (billions of pesos, approximate)	Apr 1993		Nov–Dec 1994	Jan–Feb 1995	May 1995		Nov 1996	May 1997
	M = 12		M = 15	M = 14	M = 14		M = 14	M = 14
	R = 8		R = 11	R = 10	R = 5		R = 10	R = 14
	B = 4		B = 4	B = 4	B = 9		B = 4	B = 0

1 to 2: Growth of income, money demand, and reserves

2 to 3: Increase in risk premium, fall in money demand and reserves

3 to 4: Sterilization: fall in reserves, increase in domestic credit, money demand unchanged

4 to 5: Sterilization: rise in reserves, decrease in domestic credit, money demand unchanged

5 to 6: 100% reserve backing achieved

December 1994: Mexican "Tequila" Crisis; start of Argentine banking crisis

(b) Central Bank Balance Sheet

Fixed lines shift when money demand changes.

Fixed lines M_1 $M_3 = M_5$ M_2

Floating line $M = B$

Argentina's Central Bank Operations, 1993–1997 In this period, one peso was worth one U.S. dollar. Panel (a) shows the money supply and reserves. The difference between the two is domestic credit. Six key dates are highlighted before, during, and after the Mexican Tequila crisis. In panel (b), the balance sheet of the central bank at these key dates is shown. Prior to the crisis, domestic credit was essentially unchanged, and reserves grew from $8 billion to $11 billion as money demand grew from M_1 to M_2 in line with rapid growth in incomes (move from point 1 to 2). After the crisis hit in December 1994, interest rate spreads widened, money demand fell from M_2 to M_3, but domestic credit stood still (to point 3) and $1 billion in reserves were lost. In 1995 there was a run on banks and on the currency, and the central bank sterilized by expanding domestic credit by 5 billion pesos and selling $5 billion of reserves as money demand remained constant (to point 4). Reserves reached a low level of $5 billion. By 1996 the crisis had passed and the central bank now replenished its reserves, reversing the earlier sterilization. Domestic credit fell by 5 billion pesos and reserves increased by $5 billion (to point 5, same as point 3). Further sterilized purchases of $4 billion of reserves brought the backing ratio up to 100% in 1997 (to point 6).

Source: IMF, International Financial Statistics. Data compiled by Kurt Schuler.

To Be Continued Through all of these events, the backing ratio remained high and domestic credit remained roughly steady at around 4 billion pesos, corresponding to our model's assumptions so far. People wanted to swap some pesos for dollars, but nothing catastrophic had happened. However, this was about to change. The shock to Argentina's interest rate proved damaging to the real economy and especially the banking sector. Argentines also became nervous about holding pesos. Foreigners stopped lending to Argentina as the economic situation looked riskier. The central bank stepped in to provide assistance to the ailing banks. But we have yet to work out how a central bank can do this and still maintain a peg. After we complete that task, we will return to the story and see how Argentina managed to survive the Tequila crisis. ■

Defending the Peg II: Changes in the Composition of Money Supply

So far we have examined changes to the level of money demand. We have assumed that the central bank's policy toward domestic credit was *passive*, and so B has been held constant up to now. In contrast, we now study shocks to domestic credit B, all else equal. To isolate the effects of changes in domestic credit, we assume that money demand is constant.

If money demand is constant, then so is money supply. Therefore, the key lesson of this section will be that, on its own, a change in domestic credit cannot affect the *level* of the money supply, it can only affect the *composition* in terms of domestic credit and reserves.

A Shock to Domestic Credit Suppose that the central bank increases domestic credit by an amount $\Delta B > 0$ from B_1 to B_2. This increase could be the result of an *open market operation* by the bank's bond trading desk to purchase bonds from private parties. Or it could be the result of a demand by the country's economics ministry that the bank directly finance government borrowing. For now we will not concern ourselves with the cause of this policy decision, and will not discuss whether it makes any sense. We just ask what implications it has for a central bank trying to maintain a peg, all else equal. We assume that domestic output and the foreign interest rate are unchanged.

For example, suppose we start with a central bank balance sheet with money supply at its initial level of $M_1 = 1,000$ million pesos. The bank then expands domestic credit from \$500 million pesos by buying $\Delta B = \$100$ million of peso bonds. All else equal, this action puts more money in circulation, which lowers the interest rate in the money market and puts depreciation pressure on the exchange rate. A floating rate would depreciate in these circumstances. To defend the peg, the central bank must sell enough reserves to keep the interest rate unchanged. To achieve that, it must sell 100 million pesos (\$100 million) of reserves, in exchange for cash, so that the money supply remains unchanged. The central bank's balance sheet will then be as follows:

SIMPLIFIED CENTRAL BANK BALANCE SHEET AFTER EXPANSION OF DOMESTIC CREDIT (MILLIONS OF PESOS)			
Assets		**Liabilities**	
Reserves R Foreign assets (dollar reserves)	400	**Money supply M** Money in circulation	1,000
Domestic credit B Domestic assets (peso bonds)	600		

What is the end result? Domestic credit B changes by +100 million pesos (rising to 600 million pesos), foreign exchange reserves R change by −100 million pesos (falling to 400 million pesos), and the money supply M remains unchanged (at 1,000 million pesos).

The bond purchases expand domestic credit but also cause the central bank to lose reserves as it is forced to intervene in the forex market. There is no change in monetary policy as measured by home money supply (or interest rates) because the sale and purchase actions by the central bank offset each other exactly. This type of central bank action is called **sterilization,** a sterilized intervention, or a sterilized sale of reserves.

In Figure 20-8, we show the implications of sterilization policies. On the vertical axis, domestic credit rises from B_1 to B_2. The balance sheet position of the central bank therefore shifts up the fixed line from point 1 to point 2. Reserves fall by ΔB from $R_1 = \$500$ million to $R_2 = \$400$ million. The central bank has moved closer to point Z, the danger point of zero reserves on the 45-degree line. The backing ratio falls from 50 to 40%.

Figure 20-8 also shows what would happen with the opposite shock. If domestic credit fell by 100 million pesos to 400 million pesos at B_3, with an unchanged money demand, then reserves would rise by $100 million. The central bank's balance sheet ends up at point 3. Reserves rise from $R_1 = 500$ to $R_3 = 600$. The backing ratio now rises from 50% to 60%.

FIGURE 20-8

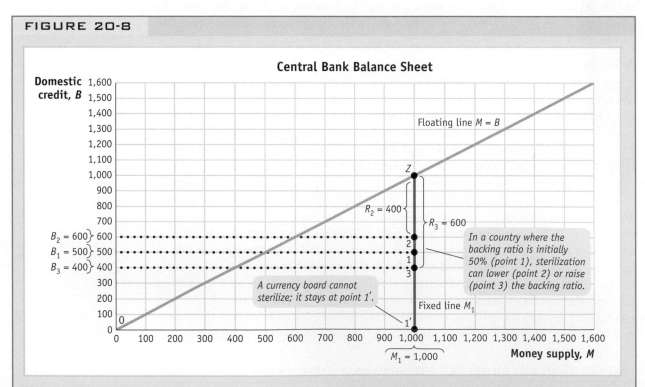

Sterilization If domestic credit rises, money supply rises, all else equal, interest rates tend to fall, putting pressure on the exchange rate to depreciate. To prevent this depreciation, keep the peg, and stay on the fixed line, the central bank must intervene and defend the peg by selling reserves to keep the money supply fixed. As shown here, the money supply is $M_1 = 1,000$. If domestic credit increases from $B_1 = 500$ to $B_2 = 600$, the central bank balance sheet moves from point 1 to point 2, and reserves fall from $R_1 = 500$ to $R_2 = 400$. An opposite shock is shown by the move from point 1 to point 3, where $B_3 = 400$ and $R_3 = 600$. If the country maintains 100% reserves, it has to stay at point 1': a currency board cannot engage in sterilization.

We also see in Figure 20-8 that sterilization is impossible in the case of a currency board because a currency board requires that domestic credit always be zero and that reserves be 100% of the money supply at all times.

Equation (20-3) confirms this as a general result. We know that if the change in money demand is zero, then so is the change in money supply, $\Delta M = 0$; hence, the change in domestic credit, $\Delta B > 0$, must be offset by an equal and opposite change in reserves, $\Delta R = -\Delta B < 0$. This is also clear from Equation (20-2).

We have shown the following: *holding money demand constant, a change in domestic credit leads to an equal and opposite change in reserves, which is called a sterilization.*

Why Does the Composition of the Money Supply Fluctuate? Our model tells us that sterilization has no effect on the level of money supply and hence no effect on interest rates and the rest of the economy. This prompts a question: if sterilization has no effect on these variables, why would central banks bother to do it? In the case of buying and selling government bonds, which is the predominant form of domestic credit, the effects are controversial but are generally thought to be small. The only possible effect would be indirect, via portfolio changes in the bond market. If the central bank absorbs some government debt, it leaves less peso debt for the private sector to hold, and this could change the risk premium on the domestic interest rate. But evidence for that type of effect is rather weak.[12]

However, there is another type of domestic credit that can have very important effects on the wider economy. This is domestic credit caused by a decision by the central bank to lend to private commercial banks in difficulty. Here, the central bank would be fulfilling one of its traditional responsibilities as the protector of the domestic financial system. This action has real effects because a domestic banking crisis, if allowed to happen, can cause serious economic harm by damaging the economy's payments system and credit markets.

In theory, when it comes to banks that are having difficulties, economists distinguish between banks that are illiquid and those that are insolvent. Let's see how loans from the central bank to private commercial banks affect the central bank balance sheet for these two cases. Note that for these cases we can no longer assume that M0 (currency or base money) is the same as M1 (narrow money, which includes checking deposits) or M2 (broad money, which includes saving deposits).

- *Insolvency and bailouts.* A private bank is **insolvent** if the value of its liabilities (e.g., customers' deposits) exceeds the value of its assets (e.g., loans, other securities, and cash on hand). Often, this happens when the bank's assets unexpectedly lose value (loans turn bad, stocks crash). In some circumstances, the government may offer a rescue or **bailout** to banks in such a damaged state, because it may be unwilling to see the bank fail (for political or even for economic reasons, if the bank provides valuable intermediation services to the

---

[12] This argument (which applies also to sterilized interventions under floating rates, which do not alter the level of the money supply) supposes that the central bank trades a large enough amount of the country's government debt that it can affect the default premium. If that were true, then an expansion of domestic credit would lower the amount of government debt that the private sector would have to hold and might convince private investors to tolerate a lower-risk premium. This might then filter through into long- and short-term interest rates in the home economy, with beneficial effects. However, while this line of argument is true in theory, the evidence is often weak and inconsistent and a source of ongoing controversy. See Maurice Obstfeld, 1982, "Can We Sterilize? Theory and Evidence," *American Economic Review*, 72(2), 45–50; Lucio Sarno and Mark P. Taylor, 2001, "Official Intervention in the Foreign Exchange Market: Is It Effective and, If So, How Does It Work?" *Journal of Economic Literature*, 39(3), 839–868.

economy). This bailout could be direct from the finance ministry. But the rescue may happen another way, and even in stages, if the banks ask for a loan from the central bank ostensibly for temporary liquidity purposes, and then (after losses appear) find their loans rolled over for a very long time, or even forgiven with some or all interest and principal unpaid.

Suppose the central bank balance sheet was originally 500 reserves and 500 domestic credit, with base money supply of 1,000. The cash from a bailout (say, 100) goes to the private bank and domestic credit rises (by 100) to 600 on the central bank's balance sheet. Because there has been no increase in base money demand, but more cash has gone into circulation, reserves must fall (by 100) to 400, as in Figure 20-9, panel (a). This central bank action is equivalent to the central bank buying bonds worth 100 directly from the government (a sterilization, as we saw previously) and the government then bailing out the private bank with the proceeds. Bottom line: bailouts are very risky for the central bank because they cause reserves to drain, endangering the peg.

■ *Illiquidity and bank runs.* A private bank may be solvent, but it can still be **illiquid:** it holds some cash, but its loans cannot be sold (liquidated) quickly at a high price and depositors can withdraw at any time. If too many depositors attempt to withdraw their funds at once, the bank is in trouble if it has insufficient cash on hand: this is known as a **bank run.** In this situation, the central bank may lend money to commercial banks that are running out of cash. Suppose, for example, the monetary base is M0 and equals 1,000 as in the last example, but broad money is M2 (including bank deposits) and equals 2,000. The difference of 1,000 is the value of bank checking and saving deposits. If there is a run at a bank, and customers rush in and demand 100 in cash, the bank has to borrow 100 from somewhere to satisfy them. We suppose the bank is at zero cash or at the lowest level permitted by regulation—so it is constrained. Because every other bank is likewise constrained, fearful of lending to the troubled bank, or also experiencing a run, the problem cannot be solved by interbank lending. The central bank is then the **lender of last resort.** Crucially, in addition to the central bank expanding domestic credit (by 100) to 600, base money demand (demand for cash) also rises (by 100) to 1,100. Thus, we have a combination of the two types of shocks we have studied: an increase in domestic credit *and* an increase in (base) money demand, as shown in Figure 20-9, panel (b). Reserves do not change; they stay at 500. Why? The central bank is satisfying a demand for more cash, which absorbs the expansion of domestic credit. The situation will revert to normal when the run ends and the private bank pays back its loan to the central bank. Bottom line: providing liquidity to solvent banks is not risky for the central bank because there is no reserve drain to threaten the peg.

This simple classification of banks as insolvent or illiquid is useful but the reality is more complex. The difference between insolvency and illiquidity is often unclear. If depositors fear that banks have either problem, and that the central bank may bail them out slowly or partially, they will seek to withdraw their deposits and put them in a safe place. If the problems are potentially big, the fear may affect all depositors and all banks, and depositors will not be able to tell which banks are safe, which are illiquid, and which are insolvent. The problem gets more dangerous if the financial system is more complex, when banks have borrowing relationships with each other, for if one suffers losses and fails then it will cause spillover losses for others, and more

FIGURE 20-9

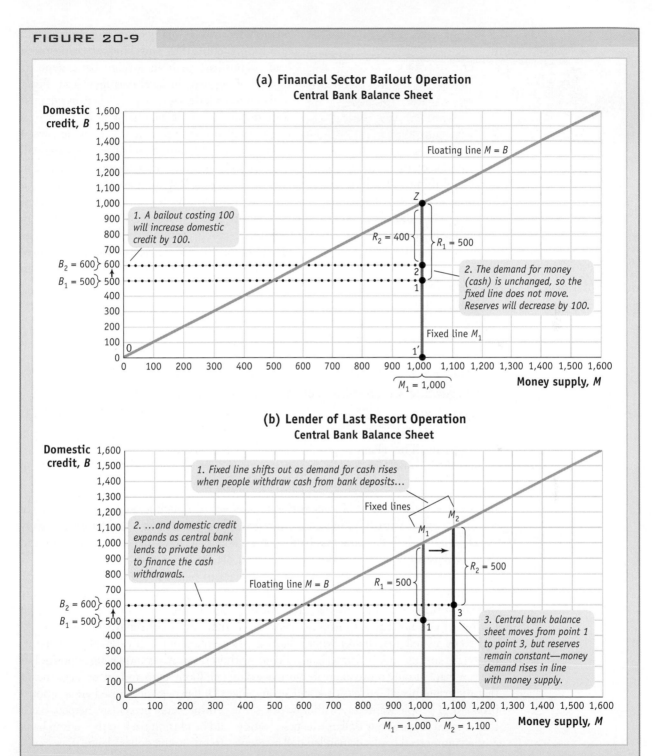

(a) Financial Sector Bailout Operation
Central Bank Balance Sheet

1. A bailout costing 100 will increase domestic credit by 100.

2. The demand for money (cash) is unchanged, so the fixed line does not move. Reserves will decrease by 100.

Floating line $M = B$

Fixed line M_1

$R_2 = 400$

$R_1 = 500$

$M_1 = 1,000$

(b) Lender of Last Resort Operation
Central Bank Balance Sheet

1. Fixed line shifts out as demand for cash rises when people withdraw cash from bank deposits...

2. ...and domestic credit expands as central bank lends to private banks to finance the cash withdrawals.

3. Central bank balance sheet moves from point 1 to point 3, but reserves remain constant—money demand rises in line with money supply.

Fixed lines

Floating line $M = B$

$R_1 = 500$

$R_2 = 500$

$M_1 = 1,000$ $M_2 = 1,100$

The Central Bank and the Financial Sector In panel (a), a bailout occurs when the central bank prints money and buys domestic assets—the bad assets of insolvent private banks. There is no change in demand for base money (cash), so the expansion of domestic credit leads to a decrease of reserves. In panel (b), private bank depositors want to shift from holding deposits to holding cash. If the central bank acts as a lender of last resort and temporarily lends the needed cash to illiquid private banks, both the demand and supply of base money (cash) rise, so the level of reserves is unchanged.

The Old Lady doth protest too much: In September 2007, the Bank of England assured Northern Rock depositors that the bank would not fail. The bank's balance sheet was widely believed to be healthy (solvency), but the bank had run short of cash to fund mortgages (illiquidity). Despite official assurances, there was a run on the bank because depositors preferred cash in hand to government promises.

possible failures. In many emerging markets and developing countries, this kind of panic often leads depositors to hold foreign bank deposits instead of deposits in local currency. This flight to foreign bank deposits happens because depositors do not know if, when, or how much of a bailout will occur. Thus they cannot be sure if the peg will hold, and if their peso deposits will in the end keep their value in dollar terms. In such circumstances, depositors' fears can be self-fulfilling. A bank that faces a run may have to sell illiquid assets in a hurry at a low price, damaging itself and magnifying the problem. As depositors demand foreign currency, they drain reserves and make it more likely that devaluation will happen. A country at risk for devaluation faces a higher-risk premium, which in turn worsens economic conditions and encourages a flight from the domestic currency. If a depreciation happens, then banks and firms that have foreign currency liabilities will be in even worse shape, so running looks even better. And so the vicious circle continues.

To get a sense of the challenges faced by a central bank when confronted with difficulties in the banking sector under a fixed exchange rate, let us return to the case of Argentina after the Mexican Tequila crisis.

APPLICATION

The Argentine Convertibility Plan After the Tequila Crisis

When we left Argentina at the end of the last application, the Mexican Tequila crisis had just hit in December 1994, and Argentina's base money supply had fallen by a billion pesos. This change was shown in Figure 20-7 by the move from point 2 to point 3. With domestic credit steady, this meant that reserves also fell by a billion pesos to a level of 10 billion in January/February 1995.

Banking Crisis, 1995 Higher interest rates were reducing output as the private sector struggled with the high cost of credit. The government's budget deficit grew as tax revenues fell. Commercial bank balance sheets were damaged by bad loans and depressed asset prices. The country now faced the threat of a banking crisis.[13]

The central bank began extending loans, even to banks of questionable solvency. The loans became more abundant and for a much longer duration. Concerns grew that the central bank had stepped up to, or over, the line between acting as a lender of last resort and bailing out insolvent institutions that could not repay.

People feared that banks would fail, but they could not easily tell the difference between a strong bank and a weak one. People withdrew checking and saving deposits, but the run made it only more likely that banks would fail. Contagion and uncertainty meant that the panic hit all banks, weak and strong alike. Dollar deposits caused an additional problem. If people wanted to withdraw pesos, the central bank's peso loans helped, but if they wanted to withdraw dollars, the peso loans would head right back to the central bank as the commercial banks demanded dollar reserves to satisfy the dollar claims.

---

[13] See Laura D'Amato, Elena Grubisic, and Andrew Powell, 1997, "Contagion, Bank Fundamentals or Macroeconomic Shock? An Empirical Analysis of the Argentine 1995 Banking Problems," Working Paper No. 2, Central Bank of Argentina, Buenos Aires; Charles W. Calomiris and Andrew Powell, 2001, "Can Emerging Market Bank Regulators Establish Credible Discipline? The Case of Argentina, 1992–1999," in *Prudential Supervision: What Works and What Doesn't*, Frederic S. Mishkin, ed. (Chicago: University of Chicago Press).

Even as people started to run from bank deposits to cash, higher interest rates and lower output depressed the demand for cash. Reserves drained, casting more doubt on the viability of the fixed exchange rate, raising the currency premium, and draining more reserves. Given the fears of a banking crisis *and* an exchange rate crisis, cash and bank deposits were switched into dollars and moved to banks in Montevideo (Uruguay), Miami, or other offshore locations. People were now starting to run from the currency too.

The consequences for the central bank balance sheet were dramatic. Domestic credit expanded from 4 billion pesos to 9 billion pesos in the first half of 1995, as seen in Figure 20-7 at point 4 in panel (a), even as base money supply remained more or less steady near 14 billion pesos. Cash demand held up, but people were moving bank deposits into pesos and then offshore—and the central bank was providing the peso liquidity (to banks) and then the dollar liquidity (to people) to allow this capital flight to happen. As a result of this sterilization, reserves fell to a low of just 5 billion pesos, with the backing ratio collapsing to a low of about 36% (5/14). In the central bank balance sheet diagram in Figure 20-7, panel (b), the country was now moving vertically up to point 4 and getting perilously close to the floating line, the dangerous place where reserves run out.

Help From the IMF and Recovery In late 1994 Argentina was at the point of being cut off from further official lending by the International Monetary Fund as a result of its failure to reduce its fiscal deficit and pursue other reforms. With private credit markets screeching toward a sudden stop after the Tequila crisis, and the government running a large deficit, the situation looked bleak.

However, after the Tequila crisis, the United States advanced a large assistance package to Mexico, and the IMF took a more lenient view of the Argentine situation, fearing the possibility of a global financial crisis if Argentina crashed too. IMF lending resumed. This was seen as "catalytic" in putting an end to the sudden stop, and a "Patriotic Bond" was issued in private capital markets. The loans provided desperately needed dollars. Some of the dollars could then be poured into the central bank. This replenished reserves, but it also revealed the scale of the bailing out. A substantial fund was set up to salvage insolvent commercial banks, a move that finally erased the stain of the bailouts from the central bank's balance sheet (bad commercial bank debt to the central bank was socialized and then turned into a government debt to foreigners).[14]

The Argentine authorities squeaked through a crisis, the economy recovered, capital flows resumed, and eventually the central bank's emergency loans were paid back. By 1996 economic growth had picked up, interest rate spreads eased, and confidence returned. The central bank reversed its earlier sterilization policies and replenished reserves by contracting domestic credit. By November 1996 domestic credit was back down to 4 billion pesos (its precrisis level), and by May 1997 the central bank had gone further and reduced domestic credit to zero. These steps are shown in the central bank balance sheet diagram in Figure 20-7, panel (b), by the moves from point 4 to point 5 to point 6.

Postscript Argentina's central bank ended up with a 100% backing ratio and was in a position to act as a strict currency board. However, it did not do so and in subsequent turbulent times continued to exercise discretion in its use of sterilization policies. The Convertibility Plan came to an end in 2001, however, when its room for maneuver finally ran out: the economy was in recession, the government was deeper in debt, the IMF and private creditors had reached their lending limits, and the government was reduced

---

[14] For a detailed account of Argentina's travails, see Paul Blustein, 2005, *And the Money Kept Rolling In (and Out): Wall Street, the IMF, and the Bankrupting of Argentina* (New York: Public Affairs).

to raiding the banks and the central bank for resources. The details of that story, which are tied up with the Argentine 2001 default, are taken up in the last chapter. ■

The Central Bank Balance Sheet and the Financial System

We can see from the experiences of Argentina and many other countries that the existence of a financial system affects the operations and balance sheet of the central bank. In particular, whether as a result of its own policy choices, formal laws and regulations, or political pressure, the typical central bank takes on the responsibility for monitoring, regulating, and—in an emergency—protecting a country's commercial banking system.

A More General Balance Sheet As a result of its interactions with banks, the central bank's balance sheet is in reality more complicated than we have assumed in our simplified model. Typically, it looks something like this, with some hypothetical values inserted:[15]

GENERAL CENTRAL BANK BALANCE (MILLIONS OF PESOS)			
Assets		**Liabilities**	
Foreign assets	950	**Foreign liabilities**	50
of which:		of which:	
Foreign reserves (all currencies)	950	*Foreign currency debt issued by the*	50
Gold	0	*central bank*	
Domestic assets	500	**Domestic liabilities**	400
of which:		of which:	
Domestic government bonds bought	300	*Domestic currency debt issued by the*	400
Loans to commercial banks	200	*central bank*	
		Money supply *M*	1,000
		of which:	
		Currency in circulation	900
		Reserve liabilities to commercial banks	100

In the first row, the central bank's *net foreign assets* are worth 900, given by 950 minus 50. We see that foreign assets can include other currencies besides the anchor currency (the dollar) and may also include gold. There may also be offsetting foreign liabilities if the central bank chooses to borrow. In this example, gold happens to be 0, foreign reserves are 950, and foreign liabilities are 50.

In the second row, *net domestic assets* are worth 100, 500 minus 400. We see that domestic assets may be broken down into government bonds (here, 300) and loans to commercial banks (here, 200). All of these assets can be offset by domestic liabilities, such as debt issued in home currency by the central bank. In this example, the central bank has issued 400 in domestic debt, which we shall assume was used to finance the purchase of foreign reserves.

Finally, the money supply is a liability for the central bank worth 1,000, as before. However, not all of that currency is "in circulation" (i.e., outside the central bank, in the hands of the public or in commercial bank vaults). Typically, central banks place *reserve requirements* on commercial banks and force them to place some cash on deposit at the central bank. This is considered a prudent regulatory device. In this case, currency in circulation is 900, and 100 is in the central bank as part of reserve requirements.

---

[15] For simplicity, we assume that the bank has zero net worth, so total assets equal total liabilities. In general, this will not be true from day to day as the central bank can make gains and losses on its assets and liabilities, and it may also have operating profits and losses. However, net worth is typically not very large and, over the longer run, any gains and losses are typically absorbed by the government treasury.

Despite all these refinements, the lessons of our simple model carry over. For example, in the simple approach, money supply (M) equaled foreign assets (R) plus domestic assets (B). We now see that, in general, money supply is equal to *net foreign assets* plus *net domestic assets*. The only real difference is the ability of the central bank to borrow by issuing nonmonetary liabilities, whether domestic or foreign.

Sterilization Bonds Why do central banks expand their balance sheets by issuing such liabilities? To see what the central bank can achieve by borrowing, consider what the preceding balance sheet would look like if the central bank had not borrowed to fund the purchase of reserves.

Without issuing domestic liabilities of 400 and foreign liabilities of 50, reserves would be lower by 450. In other words, they would fall from 950 to their original level of 500 seen in the example at the start of this chapter. Domestic credit would then be 500, as it was in that earlier example, with money supply of 1,000. Thus, what borrowing to buy reserves achieves is not a change in monetary policy (money supply and interest rates are unchanged, given the peg) but an increase in the backing ratio. Instead of a 50% backing ratio (500/1,000), the borrowing takes the central bank up to a 95% backing ratio (950/1,000).

But why stop there? What if the central bank borrowed, say, another 300 by issuing domestic debt and used the proceeds to purchase more reserves? Its domestic liabilities would rise from 400 to 700 (net domestic assets would fall from +100 to −200), and on the other side of the balance sheet, reserves (foreign assets) would rise from 950 to 1,250. Money supply would still be 1,000, but the backing ratio would be 125%. This could go on and on. Borrow another 250, and the backing ratio would be 150%.

As we have seen, these hypothetical operations are all examples of changes in the *composition* of the money supply—in terms of net foreign assets and net domestic assets—holding fixed the *level* of money supply. In other words, this is just a more general form of sterilization. And *sterilization is just a way to change the backing ratio, all else equal*.

What is new here is that the central bank's *net* domestic assets (assets minus liabilities) can be less than zero because the central bank is now allowed to borrow. Many central banks do just this, by issuing bonds—or **sterilization bonds** as they are fittingly described. This allows the backing ratio to potentially exceed 100%.

Looking back at Figure 20-8, we could depict this by allowing reserves R to represent *net* foreign assets, credit B to represent *net* domestic assets, and B to be less than zero. The key equation $M = R + B$ still holds, and the fixed and floating lines work as before, as long as we interpret zero *net* foreign assets as the trigger for a switch from fixed to floating.[16] So we can imagine that the fixed line in Figure 20-8 can extend down below the horizontal axis.

Going below the horizontal axis means that net domestic credit is negative, and the backing ratio is more than 100%. Why might countries want backing to be that high? As we saw, Argentina had high backing of more than 70% on the eve of the Tequila crisis, but this would not have been enough for the peg to survive a major run from the financial system to dollars. In Figure 20-8, the zone below the horizontal axis would be an ultra-safe place, even farther from the floating line. Many countries have recently sought refuge in that direction (see **Side Bar: The Great Reserve Accumulation in Emerging Markets**).

---

[16] As we have argued, the precise level of that trigger may be arbitrary without affecting the insights from this analysis.

The Great Reserve Accumulation in Emerging Markets

An illustration of reserve buildup via sterilization is provided by the activities of the People's Bank of China, whose central bank balance sheet diagram is shown in Figure 20-10 in yuan (¥) units. The vertical distance to the 45-degree line represents net foreign assets R, which were essentially the same as foreign reserves because the bank had close to zero foreign liabilities.*

From 1995 to 2003 net domestic credit in China grew very slowly, from ¥1,409 billion to ¥2,218 billion, but rapid economic growth and financial development caused base money demand to grow rapidly, more than doubling, from ¥2,076 billion to ¥5,284 billion. Thus, most of the base money supply growth of ¥3,208 billion was absorbed by ¥2,399 billion of reserve accumulation. In this period, the backing ratio rose from 32% to 58%.

From 2003 to 2009 net domestic credit fell by ¥6,202 billion and eventually turned negative as the central bank sold large amounts of sterilization bonds. Money supply growth continued, rising from ¥5,284 billion to ¥14,399 billion, an increase of ¥9,115 billion. But the sterilization caused reserves to rise by almost twice as much, by ¥15,317 billion. The backing ratio rose from 58% to 128%. In the years 2009 to 2012 sterilization was not in play, and both reserves and domestic credit increased together; by 2012 money supply was ¥25,235 billion with 95% backing in reserves of ¥23,928.

Given the country's economic (and political) importance, the Chinese case attracts a lot of attention—but it isn't the only example of this type of central bank behavior. Figure 20-11 shows the massive increase in reserves at central banks around the world in recent years: it started in about 1999, it mostly happened in Asia in countries pegging (more or less) to the dollar, and much of it was driven by large-scale sterilization. What was going on?

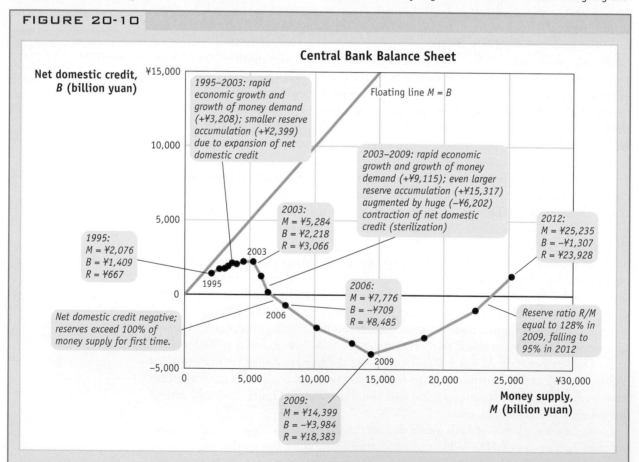

FIGURE 20-10

Central Bank Balance Sheet

Net domestic credit, B (billion yuan)

1995–2003: rapid economic growth and growth of money demand (+¥3,208); smaller reserve accumulation (+¥2,399) due to expansion of net domestic credit

Floating line $M = B$

2003–2009: rapid economic growth and growth of money demand (+¥9,115); even larger reserve accumulation (+¥15,317) augmented by huge (−¥6,202) contraction of net domestic credit (sterilization)

1995:
M = ¥2,076
B = ¥1,409
R = ¥667

2003:
M = ¥5,284
B = ¥2,218
R = ¥3,066

2012:
M = ¥25,235
B = −¥1,307
R = ¥23,928

Net domestic credit negative; reserves exceed 100% of money supply for first time.

2006:
M = ¥7,776
B = −¥709
R = ¥8,485

Reserve ratio R/M equal to 128% in 2009, falling to 95% in 2012

2009:
M = ¥14,399
B = −¥3,984
R = ¥18,383

Money supply, M (billion yuan)

Sterilization in China By issuing "sterilization bonds" central banks can borrow from domestic residents to buy more reserves. With sufficient borrowing of this kind, the central bank can end up with negative net domestic credit and reserves in excess of 100% of the money supply. The chart shows how this has happened in China in some recent years: from 1995 to 2003 net domestic credit in China was steady; reserve growth was almost entirely driven by money demand growth (movement to the right). From 2003 to 2009 sterilization (movement down) sent net domestic credit below zero; sterilization accounted for about 40% of the reserve growth in that period. In 2009–12, sterilization abated and the reserve ratio fell below 100% for the first time in seven years.

Source: IMF, International Financial Statistics.

Causes of the Reserve Accumulation

Why are these countries, most of them poor emerging markets, accumulating massive hoards of reserves? There are various possible motivations for these reserve hoards, in addition to simply wanting greater backing ratios to absorb larger shocks to money demand.** For example, the countries may fear a sudden stop, when access to foreign capital markets dries up. Foreign creditors may cease to roll over short-term debt for a while, but if reserves are on hand, the central bank can temporarily cover the shortfall. This precautionary motive leads to policy guidelines or rules suggesting that an adequate and prudent level of reserves should be some multiple either of foreign trade or of short-term debt. In practice, such ratios usually imply reserve levels less than 100% of M0, the narrow money supply.

An alternative view, illustrated by the case of Argentina that we studied, would tend to focus on a different risk, the fragility of the financial sector. If there is a major banking crisis with a flight from local deposits to foreign banks, then a central bank may need a far greater level of reserves, adequate to cover some or all of M2, the broader measure of money that includes deposits and other liquid commercial bank liabilities. Because M2 can be several times M0, the reserve levels adequate for these purposes could be much larger and well over 100% of M0. Because reserves now far exceed traditional guidelines based on trade or debt levels, fears of financial fragility might be an important part of the explanation for the scale of the reserve buildup, with reserve backing in excess of 100% of M0. As economist Martin Feldstein

pointed out after the Asian crisis, it is unrealistic to expect safe and crisis-free banking sector operations in emerging markets (in 2007 and 2008 we even saw bank runs in "developed countries" like the United Kingdom and the United States). But if countries are pegged, they then need to watch out for the peg: ". . . Sufficient liquidity, either through foreign currency reserves or access to foreign credit, would let a government restructure and recapitalize its banks without experiencing a currency crisis. The more international liquidity a government has, the less depositors will feel that they must rush to convert their currency before the reserves are depleted. And preventing a currency decline can be the best way to protect bank solvency."[†]

Thus, current reserve levels can be seen as a reaction, in part, to the financial crises of the recent past: policy makers have taken a "never again" stance, and have piled up a large war chest of reserves to guard against any risk of exchange rate crises. Is this wise? The benefits may seem clear, but many economists think this "insurance policy" carries too heavy an economic cost as countries invest in low-interest reserves and forsake investments with higher returns.

---

* In this period, foreign liabilities were just 1% of foreign assets.
** For a survey of the various possible explanations of the reserve buildup, see Joshua Aizenman, 2008, "Large Hoarding of International Reserves and the Emerging Global Economic Architecture," *Manchester School*, 76(5): 487–503; Olivier Jeanne, 2007, "International Reserves in Emerging Market Countries: Too Much of a Good Thing?" *Brookings Papers on Economic Activity*, 38(1): 1–80.
[†]See Martin S. Feldstein, March 1999, "A Self-Help Guide for Emerging Markets," *Foreign Affairs*. 78(2), 93–109.

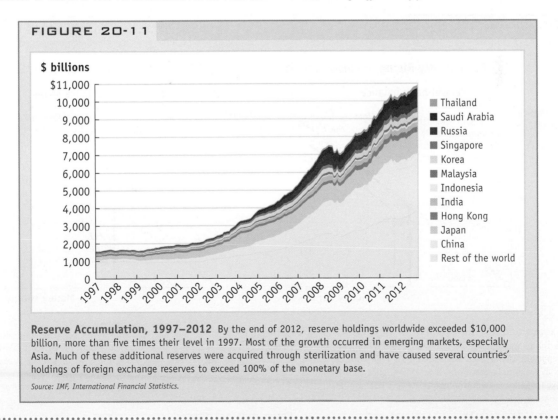

FIGURE 20-11

Reserve Accumulation, 1997–2012 By the end of 2012, reserve holdings worldwide exceeded $10,000 billion, more than five times their level in 1997. Most of the growth occurred in emerging markets, especially Asia. Much of these additional reserves were acquired through sterilization and have caused several countries' holdings of foreign exchange reserves to exceed 100% of the monetary base.

Source: IMF, International Financial Statistics.

Summary

In this section, we examined the constraints on the operations of the central bank when a fixed exchange rate is in operation. We focused on the central bank balance sheet, which in its simplest form describes how the narrow money supply (monetary base) is backed by foreign assets (reserves) and domestic assets (domestic credit). We have seen how, in response to money demand shocks, the central bank buys or sells reserves, to defend the peg. The central bank can also change the composition of the money supply through sterilization operations, which keep the money supply constant.

Two Types of Exchange Rate Crises When reserves go to zero, the country is floating, changes in domestic credit cause changes in the money supply, and the peg breaks. The central bank balance sheet diagrams in Figure 20-12 show two ways in which pegs can break:

- In panel (a), in the first type of crisis, domestic credit is constantly expanding, so the central bank is pushed up the fixed line until reserves run out. At this point, the currency floats, the money supply then grows without limit, and, in the long run, the exchange rate depreciates.
- In panel (b), in the second type of crisis, no long-run tendency exists for the money supply to grow, but there is a short-run temptation to expand the money supply temporarily, leading to a temporarily lower interest rate and a temporarily depreciated exchange rate.

FIGURE 20-12

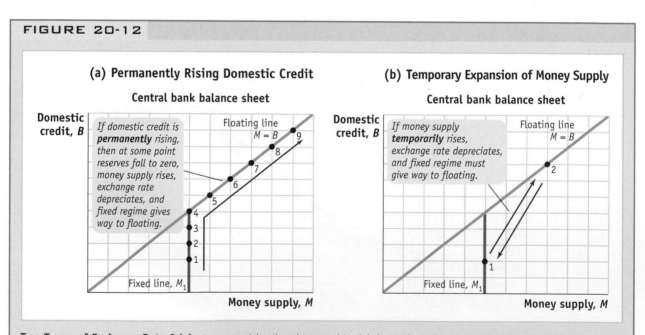

(a) Permanently Rising Domestic Credit

Central bank balance sheet

*If domestic credit is **permanently** rising, then at some point reserves fall to zero, money supply rises, exchange rate depreciates, and fixed regime gives way to floating.*

(b) Temporary Expansion of Money Supply

Central bank balance sheet

*If money supply **temporarily** rises, exchange rate depreciates, and fixed regime must give way to floating.*

Two Types of Exchange Rate Crisis In our model, using the central bank balance sheet diagram, we can see what actions will cause the peg to break. Two types of crisis are highlighted here. In panel (a), a permanent and ongoing expansion of domestic credit is incompatible with a fixed exchange rate regime because, sooner or later, reserves will be reduced to zero, and then the money supply starts to expand. In panel (b), a temporary expansion of domestic credit and the money supply will lower interest rates and depreciate the exchange rate, even if a reversal of this policy is expected in the future. Both policies take the country off the fixed line and onto the floating line.

In the next two sections, we develop models of these two types of crisis. Although the descriptions just given appear simple, a deeper examination reveals some peculiar features that illustrate the powerful role played by market expectations in triggering crises.

3 How Pegs Break I: Inconsistent Fiscal Policies

We begin with a so-called **first-generation crisis model** of inconsistent fiscal policies in a country with a fixed exchange rate, a model proposed by economist Paul Krugman.[17] This kind of crisis model has been successfully applied to many historical cases, including a series of Latin American crises in the 1980s.

The Basic Problem: Fiscal Dominance

In this model, the level of output plays no role, so we assume output is fixed at some level Y. However, the price level P plays an important role, and we allow the price level to be flexible and determined by purchasing power parity (PPP), as in the chapter on the long-run monetary model. For now we keep all our earlier assumptions from this chapter.

In this model, the government is running a persistent deficit DEF because of insufficient tax revenue, and the government's situation is so dire that it is unable to borrow from any creditor. It therefore turns to the central bank for financing. In this type of environment, economists speak of a situation of **fiscal dominance** in which the monetary authorities ultimately have no independence. The treasury hands over bonds in the amount DEF to the central bank, receives cash in the amount DEF in return, and uses the cash to fund the government deficit. As a result, domestic credit B increases by an amount $\Delta B = DEF$ every period. For simplicity, we assume that domestic credit B is growing at a constant positive rate, $\Delta B/B = \mu$. For example, if $\mu = 0.1$, then domestic credit B is growing at 10% per period.

Given our previous graphical analysis of the central bank balance sheet, we can see that the fixed exchange rate is doomed. As in Figure 20-12, panel (a), every change in the level of domestic credit leads to an equal and opposite change in the level of reserves. This process can't go on forever because reserves must eventually run out. At that point, the peg breaks and the central bank shifts from a fixed exchange rate regime to a floating regime, in which the money supply equals domestic credit, $M = B$. We note a key point:

Once reserves run out, the money supply M, which was previously fixed, grows at the same rate as domestic credit, $\Delta M/M = \Delta B/B = \mu$.

The reason the peg breaks in this situation is simple. There is an inconsistency between the authorities' commitment to a monetary policy of a fixed exchange rate and a fiscal policy of continuously monetizing deficits through an endless expansion of domestic credit. On the face of it, crisis results from elementary incompetence on the part of the authorities; to be more generous, we might say that the crisis happens because authorities are willing to let it happen because of overriding fiscal priorities.

A Simple Model

In many ways, this situation is familiar. We have already seen the implications of long-run money growth. In the chapter on exchange rates in the long run, we learned what

---

[17] Paul Krugman, 1979, "A Model of Balance-of-Payments Crises," *Journal of Money, Credit and Banking*, 11(3), 311–325.

happens in response to an *unexpected* increase in the rate of money supply growth: if prices can adjust flexibly, then, after the increase, the economy ends up with all nominal values growing at the rate μ, the rate of growth of domestic credit. There will be inflation as prices P rise at a rate μ, and depreciation as the exchange rate E rises at a rate μ.

The Myopic Case Figure 14-14 (p. 508) described a case in which the rate of growth of the money supply unexpectedly increased by a fixed amount. We apply the same analysis here and assume that investors are *myopic* and do not see the crisis coming. (To be more realistic, we relax this assumption in a moment, but the myopic case provides useful insights.)

Drawing on what we know, Figure 20-13 describes this kind of crisis scenario, assuming that prices are stable in the foreign country, that the foreign interest rate is $i^* = 5\%$, and that all variables change continuously through time. For simplicity, we start with $M = P = E = 1$, and at all times we assume the foreign price level is 1, $P^* = 1$.

Starting at time 1, in the fixed regime, domestic credit is less than the money supply, $B < M$, and reserves are positive, $R > 0$. But because of the monetization of deficits, B is gradually rising, and, as a result, R is steadily falling. Eventually, reserves run out, and thereafter $B = M$ and $R = 0$. We assume for now that the regime change occurs at time 4. In the fixed regime, up to that point, money supply M is fixed, but when floating starts, M grows at a rate μ as shown in panel (a).

Because prices are flexible, the monetary model of exchange rates in the long run tells us that P will be fixed until time 4 and then it will grow at a rate μ. Thus, inflation rises by an amount μ at time 4. The Fisher effect tells us that an increase in the home inflation rate causes a one-for-one increase in the home interest rate. So the home interest rate i must rise by an amount μ as we move from the fixed to the floating regime as shown in panel (b).

An increase in the home interest rate i at time 4 lowers the demand for real money balances, $M/P = L(i)Y$, because in the money demand function, L is a decreasing function of i. Thus, M/P "jumps" down as we change from fixed to floating. Because the money supply M does not change at time 4, the drop in M/P can be accommodated only by a jump in the flexible price level P at time 4. Because, by assumption, PPP holds continuously (and because $P^* = 1$), then we can just compute $E = P/P^* = P$. So the discontinuous rise in P also implies a discontinuous rise in E at time 4, and a depreciation of the home currency. Both E and P jump up and start to grow at rate μ at time 4, as shown in panel (c).

To sum up, in Figure 20-13, the exchange rate crisis occurs at time 4, but the exchange rate doesn't drift continuously away from its previous fixed level. It *jumps* away discontinuously. The new floating path of the exchange rate rises at a growth rate μ, which is above the old fixed rate at time 4.

For example, if the money growth rate is 10% after the crisis, as assumed, then there is a 10 percentage point increase in the interest rate from 5% to 15%. Now suppose this reduces real money demand by 20%, from 1.00 to 0.80. Because the nominal money supply M equals 1 just before and just after the crisis, it does not jump at time 4. To get M/P to fall from 1.00 to 0.80, P must jump up, from 1.0 to $(1/0.80) = 1.25$, implying an instantaneous 25% increase in P. To maintain purchasing power parity, there must also be a 25% increase in the exchange rate E, to 1.25, followed by growth at 10%.

One significant implication of the jump in nominal values is that anyone holding a peso that was worth 1 dollar will suddenly be left holding a peso that is worth only $1/1.25 = 0.80$ dollar. Investors holding pesos at the moment of crisis will suffer a capital loss (in dollar terms) if this model accurately describes their behavior.

FIGURE 20-13

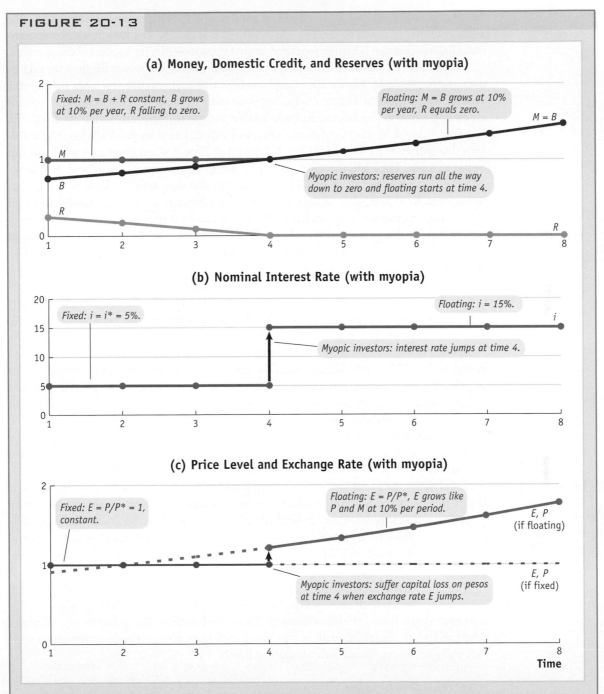

(a) Money, Domestic Credit, and Reserves (with myopia)

Fixed: M = B + R constant, B grows at 10% per year, R falling to zero.

Floating: M = B grows at 10% per year, R equals zero.

M = B

M

B

Myopic investors: reserves run all the way down to zero and floating starts at time 4.

R

R

(b) Nominal Interest Rate (with myopia)

Floating: i = 15%.

Fixed: i = i* = 5%.

i

Myopic investors: interest rate jumps at time 4.

(c) Price Level and Exchange Rate (with myopia)

Floating: E = P/P*, E grows like P and M at 10% per period.

Fixed: E = P/P* = 1, constant.

E, P (if floating)

E, P (if fixed)

Myopic investors: suffer capital loss on pesos at time 4 when exchange rate E jumps.

Time

An Exchange Rate Crisis Due to Inconsistent Fiscal Policies: Myopic Case In the fixed regime, money supply M is fixed, but expansion of domestic credit B implies that reserves R are falling to zero. Suppose the switch to floating occurs when reserves run out at time 4. Thereafter, the monetary model tells us that M, P, and E will all grow at a constant rate (here, 10% per period). The expected rates of inflation and depreciation are now positive, and the Fisher effect tells us that the interest rate must jump up at period 4 (by 10 percentage points). The interest rate increase means that real money demand $M/P = L(i)Y$ falls instantly at time 4. The money supply does not adjust immediately, so this jump in M/P must be accommodated by a jump in prices P. To maintain purchasing power parity, E must also jump at the same time. Hence, myopic investors face a capital loss on pesos at time 4.

The Forward-Looking Case There is good reason to believe that investors will not be as shortsighted (myopic) as we have just assumed. It is usually well known when a government has a deficit that is being monetized, even if the authorities try to conceal the problem.

Let us move to the other extreme, *forward-looking* behavior, which for now we take to mean *perfect foresight*. Figure 20-14 explains how this scenario departs from the myopic version we just saw in Figure 20-13. Suppose peso holders see that domestic credit is rising and reserves are falling. Knowledgeable people will speculate that the fixed rate is going to break in the near future. They will expect pesos to suddenly lose their dollar value if they hold them until the bitter end at time 4 when reserves would run out under myopia. They will therefore decide to dump pesos sooner. But when? And how?

When investors sell all their holdings of a particular currency, it is known as a **speculative attack.** When such an attack occurs, the economy must *immediately* switch to the floating regime we have already studied, since once it has zero reserves, the money supply M will always equal domestic credit B—which has been and will be growing at the constant rate μ. At that same time, the nominal interest rate will also jump up, when the Fisher effect kicks in, and there will be a jump down in both money demand (as the interest rise hits) and in money supply (as the attack drains all remaining reserves).

In our example, the key lesson is that once an attack occurs, the economy completely switches over to the floating regime. Under myopia the switch occurred at time 4. But now, the switch happens well before time 4, and at the time of the attack the economy's inflation, exchange rates, prices, and interest rates all jump to their new (and rising) paths. This leaves one question: When does the speculative attack occur? From Figure 20-14, the answer must be at time 2. In this case, the path of the price level P and the exchange rate E are continuous as we switch from fixed to floating. Only then can the switch occur without any expected dollar gains or losses on holding pesos.

How does this pin down the attack at time 2? Suppose the attack were at any time later than 2, such as time 3. As we can see from the diagram, this requires a jump up in the exchange rate, a *discontinuous depreciation*. If peso holders wait to attack until time 3, they still suffer a capital loss because they have waited too long. What if the attack is before time 2, say, at time 1? An attack at time 1 implies a *discontinuous appreciation* of the peso. But if that happened, any individual peso holder would enjoy capital gains (in dollars) from holding on to pesos rather than exchanging them for reserves at the central bank at the prior fixed rate. They would rather wait, let everyone else attack, and pocket the gains. But if one person thinks like that, all do, and the attack cannot materialize.

The speculative attack model teaches an important lesson. One moment, a central bank may have a pile of reserves on hand, draining away fairly slowly, giving the illusion that there is no imminent danger. The next moment, the reserves are all gone. The model can therefore explain why fixed exchange rates sometimes witness a sudden collapse rather than a long, lingering death.

APPLICATION

The Peruvian Crisis of 1986

An example of a crisis driven by inconsistent fiscal policies and excessive expansion of domestic credit is provided by the events in Peru from 1985 to 1986, illustrated in Figure 20-15.

In the early 1980s, Peru's political and economic conditions were highly unfavorable. The country had endured a period of social unrest and military rule in the 1970s, and the government had an enormous external debt burden. World commodity prices fell, exports and economic growth slowed, and government deficits grew. At the same time, world interest rates sharply increased.

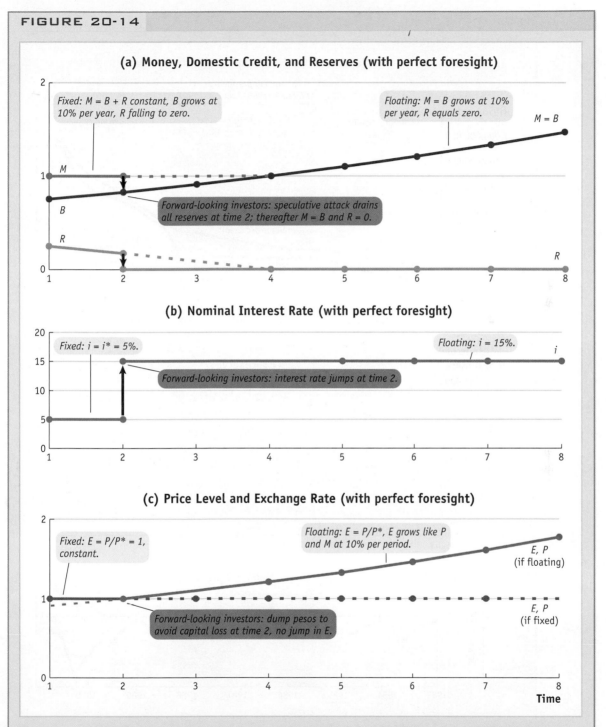

An Exchange Rate Crisis Due to Inconsistent Fiscal Policies: Perfect-Foresight Case Compare this figure with Figure 20-13. If investors anticipate a crisis, they will seek to avoid losses by converting the pesos they are holding to dollars before period 4. The rational moment to attack is at time 2, the point at which the switch from fixed to floating is achieved without any jumps in E or P. Why? At time 2, the drop in money demand (due to the rise in the interest rate) exactly equals the decline in the money supply (the reserve loss), and money market equilibrium is maintained without the price level having to change.

FIGURE 20-15

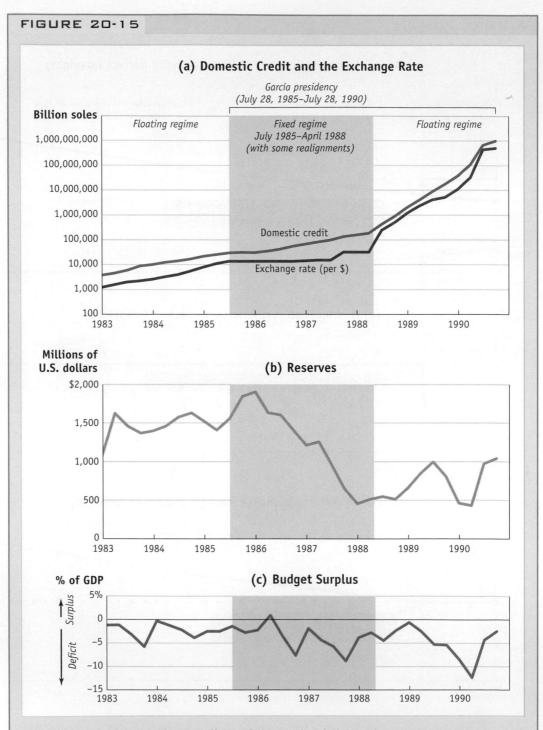

A Crisis in Peru: The Inconsistent Policies of the García Administration From 1985 to 1986 the Peruvian government implemented a fixed exchange rate regime, but government budget problems required significant monetization of budget deficits. Monetary and fiscal policies were inconsistent: a peg was in place, but domestic credit grew exponentially (note that the exchange rate and domestic credit are shown on logarithmic scales). The central bank lost three-quarters of its reserves in two years, and the peg had to be abandoned.

Source: IMF, International Financial Statistics.

The Peruvian government defaulted on its debt obligations and began negotiations with the IMF and other creditors. Denied fresh loans from world capital markets, and with low tax receipts that could not cover rising spending, government financing came to rely on money printing by the central bank—that is, the inflation tax. Domestic credit grew by 65% in 1982, 165% in 1983, and 93% in 1984—a rough doubling every year, on average. The dollar value of Peru's currency, the sol, rapidly sank.

As economic conditions deteriorated further and political violence by guerilla groups intensified, President Alan García Pérez was elected to office in 1985. One important economic measure he instituted immediately was a fixed exchange rate. This stopped the depreciation and was intended to give Peru a firm nominal anchor. But, as we now know, its durability would depend on whether García's administration could solve its fiscal problems and put an end to the monetization of government deficits.

Some fiscal reform was attempted, and the economy recovered slightly: the government budget improved at first. But the administration could not get the government budget out of the red for long. The deficit fell from 2% to 3% of GDP to near zero in early 1986, but by mid-1986 it was growing again, averaging over 5% and peaking at 8% to 9% of GDP in late 1986 and 1987. The printing presses of the central bank kept running, and domestic credit grew 84% in 1985, 77% in 1986, and 146% in 1987—roughly doubling every year.

Under a fixed exchange rate, something had to give. With domestic credit exploding, the central bank was continually selling reserves to defend the peg.[18] Reserves fell from a peak of $2,000 million in early 1986 to $500 million in early 1988. The authorities gave up in April 1988 before the attack was complete and so avoided losing all their dollar reserves. The sol began to float and depreciation was rapid: the sol hit 250,000 sol/$ in September, 500,000 in November, and 1,200,000 by March 1989, and Peru was heading into a hyperinflation.[19]

The data closely match the predictions of the model. Under the peg, reserves drain as domestic credit grows, and the exchange rate is stable. Under the float, reserves are stable, and the exchange rate grows as domestic credit expands.

By the time García left office, Peru was in economic shambles. García's popularity sank. The 1990 presidential election was won by a political newcomer, Alberto Fujimori, who would struggle with the problems created by his predecessor (and problems of his own). Yet, remarkably, in 2006 Alan García Pérez was elected president of Peru for a second time. Twenty years is a long time in politics. ■

Expectations and the Critical Level of Reserves What determines the *critical level of reserves* R_c at which the crisis occurs? In the speculative attack model, the size of the sudden reserve loss, and hence the timing of the crisis, depend critically on market expectations about the future growth rate of domestic credit. The reserves R_c lost at the moment of crisis will depend on how much money investors want to convert into reserves when they attack. This, in turn, depends on how much money demand shrinks as we move from fixed to floating, and that is driven by the change in the interest rate.

Let's assume that each percentage point increase in the interest rate causes a ϕ% fall in real money balances.[20] At the moment of attack, the interest rate rises by an amount

[18] The peg spent most of its time close to 17,300 sol/$. Various realignments to 20,000 and then 33,000 sol/$ in late 1987 bought a little time at the end.
[19] A common currency unit is used throughout this case study for consistency and commensurability. In reality, there were two currency reforms in Peru as a result of inflationary finance. The inti replaced the sol on February 1, 1985, at 1 inti per 1,000 soles, and on July 1, 1991, the nuevo sol replaced the inti at a rate of 1,000,000 nuevos soles per inti.
[20] The constant parameter ϕ is called the *interest semi-elasticity of money demand*.

$\Delta i = \mu$, so the proportional fall in money demand is given by ϕ times that change. Thus, the change in money demand is given by $-\Delta M / M = \phi \times \mu$.

But we also know that the change in the money supply at the moment of attack $-\Delta M$ has to correspond exactly to the size of the reserve drain at the moment of attack, which equals the critical level of reserves R_c that are lost at that instant. Thus,

$$\underbrace{\frac{R_c}{M}}_{\substack{\text{Critical backing ratio} \\ \text{when attack occurs}}} = \frac{-\Delta M}{M} = \underbrace{\phi}_{\substack{\text{Responsiveness} \\ \text{of money demand} \\ \text{to interest rate changes}}} \times \underbrace{\mu}_{\substack{\text{Future} \\ \text{rate of growth of} \\ \text{domestic credit}}}$$

This expression tells us the ratio of the critical level of reserves R_c to the money supply M. It depends on the sensitivity of money demand to the interest rate and on the *expected future rate of growth* of domestic credit μ (remember, investors are *forward-looking*).

To illustrate, and continue our previous example, if the growth rate of domestic credit is expected to be $\mu = 10\%$, and if $\phi = 1.5$, then the fall in money demand and money supply at the moment of attack is 10% times 1.5, or 15%. Thus, when reserves have drained so far that the backing ratio falls to the critical level $R_c = 15\%$, the peg will break. But if μ rises to 20%, the critical level R_c would be twice as large, 30%.

We can now see that if people *expect* a fiscal problem to worsen (expect the deficit to increase, and thus domestic credit to grow faster to finance it), then reserves drain away faster, and the crisis hits sooner, at a higher critical level of reserves R_c. Thus, an increase in the *expected* rate of deficit monetization shortens the length of time that the peg will survive.

This result emphasizes the importance of market beliefs. Suppose a country has reserves well above the critical level. There is no imminent crisis. Then market beliefs change, perhaps because news or rumors emerge about a budget problem. Investors now expect a higher growth rate of domestic credit. Suppose that, as a result of this change in expectations, the critical level of reserves rises so much as to equal the current level of reserves. With the change in expectations, the time for a speculative attack is now. A crisis will happen immediately, *even though there has been no change in the economic situation as of today!*

Summary

The first-generation crisis model tells us that inconsistent fiscal policies can destroy a fixed exchange rate. Yet it is not actual fiscal policy that matters, but *beliefs* and *expectations* about future fiscal policy. Because beliefs about future deficits may or may not be justified, the model opens up the possibility that countries will be punished for crimes they do not intend to commit.

For example, some economists have argued that expected future deficits were a factor in the Asian currency crisis of 1997: the countries were affected by "crony capitalism" and the banking sectors were insolvent because of bad loans to insiders. Once the scale of these problems became known, investors believed that the monetary authorities would bail out the banks. Fears of a rapid future expansion of domestic credit thus undermined the pegs.[21]

---

[21] See, for example, the discussion of Korea's precrisis weaknesses in the operation and regulation of the banking sector, and the central bank's willingness to furtively channel dollar reserves to bail out the banks, in Frederic Mishkin, 2006, *The Next Great Globalization: How Disadvantaged Nations Can Harness Their Financial Systems to Get Rich* (Princeton, NJ: Princeton University Press). See also Craig Burnside, Martin Eichenbaum, and Sergio Rebelo, 2001, "Prospective Deficits and the Asian Currency Crisis," *Journal of Political Economy*, 109(6), 1155–1197.

4 How Pegs Break II: Contingent Monetary Policies

In the previous section, we found that inconsistent fiscal policies under a fixed exchange rate regime eventually cause an exchange rate crisis. However, the crises of the 1990s often did not conform to a model based on deficit monetization because budget problems were absent in many cases. In particular, the Exchange Rate Mechanism (ERM) crisis of 1992 affected developed countries in Europe, most of which were unlikely to monetize deficits. In countries with apparently sound economic policies, foreign currency speculators went for the attack and pegs broke.[22]

Economists therefore developed alternative models of crises, with the pioneering work on the **second-generation crisis model** being done by Maurice Obstfeld. These types of models can explain how, even when policy making is rational and purposeful—rather than incompetent and inconsistent—there may still be situations in which pegs break for no apparent reason.[23]

The Basic Problem: Contingent Commitment

The essence of the model is that policy makers are not committed to the peg under all circumstances. Defending the peg is therefore a **contingent commitment** (a slight oxymoron): if things get "bad enough," the government will let the exchange rate float rather than put the country through serious economic pain. The problem is that everyone—especially, investors in the forex market—knows this and will adjust their expectations accordingly.

To develop some intuition, we return to Britain and Germany in 1992, the example we saw at the start of the previous chapter when we studied fixed and floating regimes. Let's recap the basic story: the German central bank raised interest rates to deal with a domestic shock, the fiscal expansion arising from German unification after 1989. This left Britain with a higher interest rate and a lower output level than it wanted. What would Britain do in response?

If German interest rates are fairly low, so too are British interest rates, output costs in Britain are low, and nobody expects Britain to leave the peg. The peg is *credible*. But if German interest rates rise to high levels, output in Britain falls to an intolerably low level, and nobody expects Britain to stay on the peg for long. Instead, everyone thinks Britain will float and use expansionary monetary policy to boost output and depreciate the pound. The peg is *not credible*, and the market now expects a depreciation in the future.

The problem for Britain is that an expected depreciation will introduce a *currency premium*, as we saw earlier in this chapter. Investors will demand even higher interest rates in Britain to compensate for the imminent depreciation—and this will mean even lower output and even higher pain for Britain!

This creates a gray area. How? It is quite possible that the German interest rate can be at some "intermediate" level at which pegging is tolerable with no expected depreciation: people would expect the peg to hold and the peg would hold. But if there is an expected depreciation and a currency premium, pegging might be intolerable: people would expect the peg to fail and the peg would fail. Crucially, in both scenarios, ex ante market expectations are validated ex post, and hence would be considered "rational."

---

[22] A helpful survey is provided by Sweta C. Saxena, 2004, "The Changing Nature of Currency Crises," *Journal of Economic Surveys*, 18(3), 321–350.
[23] Maurice Obstfeld, 1986, "Rational and Self-Fulfilling Balance-of-Payments Crises," *American Economic Review*, 76(1), 72–81.

FIGURE 20-16

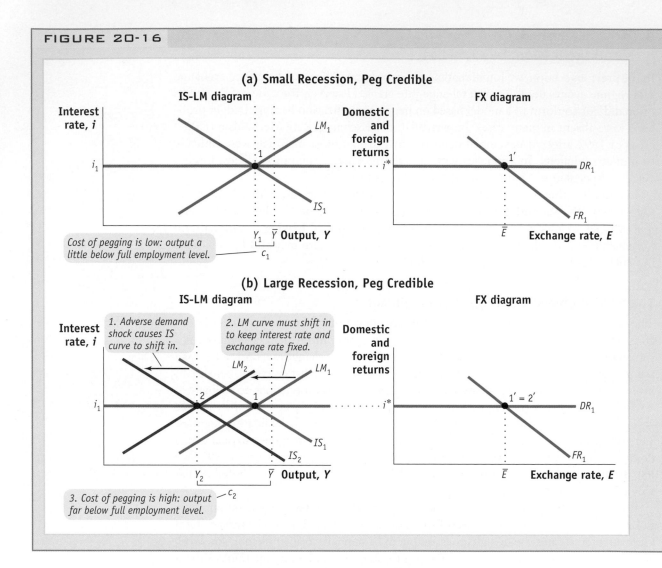

(a) Small Recession, Peg Credible

IS-LM diagram

FX diagram

Cost of pegging is low: output a little below full employment level. — c_1

(b) Large Recession, Peg Credible

IS-LM diagram

FX diagram

1. Adverse demand shock causes IS curve to shift in.

2. LM curve must shift in to keep interest rate and exchange rate fixed.

3. Cost of pegging is high: output far below full employment level. — c_2

Based on these insights from the Britain-Germany example, we now develop an economic model with such *self-fulfilling expectations.* In this model we may not always find a single, unique equilibrium but rather **multiple equilibria.** Whether there is a crisis depends entirely on market sentiment, and not simply economic fundamentals.

A Simple Model

In this type of model, we need a measure of the cost of maintaining the peg. The simplest cost measure is the deviation of output Y in the short run below its full employment level. To allow output to vary, we need to use the IS-LM-FX model introduced in the chapter on macroeconomic policy, which means that we reverse some of the assumptions we made before. From now on, output Y will be variable rather than fixed, and it will be determined by the model. And from now on, prices will be sticky, not flexible, and treated as given.[24]

---

[24] The reason for this change in assumptions is that at the heart of this model the crisis is not driven by a set of policies that will ultimately break the nominal anchor—inflation plays no role here, so prices can be assumed steady; instead, the key mechanism in this model is the desire *in certain circumstances* to stabilize output by using temporary shifts in monetary policy, which means that the exchange rate must be allowed to float.

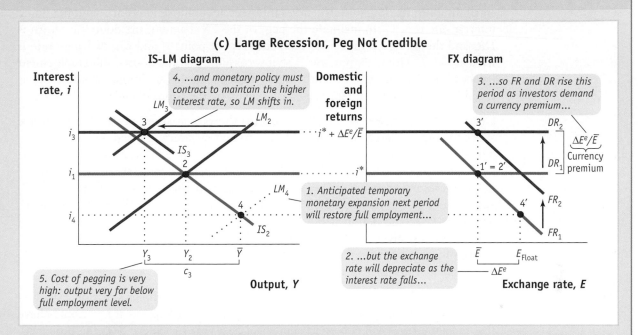

Contingent Commitments and the Cost of Maintaining a Peg This figure describes how the IS-LM-FX equilibrium changes as demand shocks occur and as the credibility of the peg weakens. The economy is pegging at a fixed exchange rate $\bar{E}$. In panel (a), the economy is at IS-LM equilibrium at point 1, with the FX market at point 1′. Output is a little below desired output, so the cost of pegging c_1 is small. In panel (b), there is an adverse shock to domestic demand, and the IS curve shifts in. LM shifts in, too, to maintain the peg. The new IS-LM equilibrium occurs at point 2, with FX market equilibrium at point 2′ (same as 1′). The cost of pegging c_2 is higher. Panel (c) shows that if the country wants to attain full employment output next period, it must move to point 4, shifting the LM curve out and allowing the FX market to settle at point 4′ with the exchange rate depreciating to E_{float}. The peg would still be in operation today, but, by definition, it would no longer be credible if such a policy change were anticipated. Because of the lack of credibility, investors would insist on receiving a positive currency premium *today*, and the home interest rate would rise to i_3, squeezing demand even more and moving the IS-LM equilibrium to point 3 and the FX market to point 3′. Now the cost of pegging c_3 is even higher: having a noncredible peg is more costly than having a credible peg.

For simplicity, we assume there are *some* benefits from pegging, say, the gains from increased trade. Let these benefits be $b > 0$ and constant. Against the benefits of pegging, the government weighs costs c that equal the "output gap": full-employment $\bar{Y}$ output minus current output Y. If costs exceed benefits, we assume that the government will elect to float next period and use monetary policy to restore full employment output. For simplicity, we assume each period lasts one year. (Restricting attention to this type of rule keep things simple while illustrating the key trade-offs.)

In Figure 20-16, we use the home IS-LM-FX diagram to look at how outcomes under the peg can depend on both economic fundamentals and market expectations. We assume foreign output is fixed at Y^*, and we also assume there is no fiscal policy change, so we can focus only on home monetary policy choices. Most important, we assume that investors are aware of the contingent commitment to the peg.

In this setup, it does not matter where adverse output shocks originate. They could result from increases in the foreign interest rate (as in the ERM example). Or they could be caused by a decline in the demand for home goods overseas. All that matters is that the home economy is in some kind of pain with output below the desired level.

Small Recession, Peg Credible Panel (a) shows a situation in which the pain is small. Initially, the IS_1 and LM_1 curves intersect at equilibrium point 1, and the home interest rate is $i_1 = i^*$ to maintain the peg. In the FX diagram, the domestic return is DR_1 and the foreign return FR_1. They intersect at point 1′ and the exchange rate is fixed at $E_1 = \bar{E}$. Home output is at Y_1, but we assume that the desired full employment level of home output is $\bar{Y}$, slightly higher than Y_1. In this situation, when the peg is credible, the economy suffers a small cost given by the "output gap": $c_1 = \bar{Y} - Y_1$.

Large Recession, Peg Credible Panel (b) shows a situation in which the adverse shock to output is large. The IS_2 and LM_2 curves now intersect at equilibrium point 2. The IS curve has moved left by assumption: it is the source of the adverse shock. The LM curve has moved in to maintain the peg and preserve interest parity, so that the home interest rate remains at $i_1 = i^*$. In the FX diagram, the domestic return is still DR_1 and the foreign return is still FR_1, and they intersect at point 2′, the same as point 1′, with $E_1 = \bar{E}$. Home output is now much lower at Y_2. Here, the economy suffers an even larger cost given by the "output gap": $c_2 = \bar{Y} - Y_2$.

We obtain our first important result: *if the market believes that the peg is credible, the output gap (cost) increases as the size of the adverse shock increases.*

Large Recession, Peg Not Credible This is the most complex situation. Panel (c) assumes a large recession as in panel (b), but shows what happens if investors believe that the authorities will choose to depreciate next year to achieve desired output. We suppose exchange rate expectations are unchanged next year at the pegged rate. The IS curve will still be at IS_2, and the required monetary expansion next year will shift the LM curve to LM_4 so that the new equilibrium will be at point 4 with output at the desired level $\bar{Y}$, and a low interest rate of i_4. This will lead to a temporary depreciation next year, the peg will break, and the exchange rate will rise from $\bar{E}$ to E_{float}. We can also see that to achieve full employment output, the lower that Y_2 is, the larger the required shift in the LM curve will be next year and the larger the resulting depreciation.

However, the government's response *next year* will be anticipated by investors. If they know that output is low enough to prompt a depreciation, they will expect a depreciation over the coming year of a size given by $\Delta E^e/\bar{E} = (E_{\text{float}} - \bar{E})/\bar{E} > 0$. This expected depreciation will appear *today* as a currency premium in the FX market of panel (c). The current period's risk-adjusted foreign return curve shifts up to FR_2 by an amount equal to the currency premium.

If the central bank wants to maintain the peg, even though it is not credible, it has to ensure forex market equilibrium at point 3′, so it must raise the home interest rate to i_3. At today's pegged rate $\bar{E}$, uncovered interest parity now requires a higher home interest rate $i_3 = i^* + \Delta E^e/\bar{E}$. Graphically, this means the domestic return curve must also shift up (to DR_2) by an amount equal to the currency premium.

As we know from the earlier chapters on policy and regimes, this shift will depress home demand and lead to even lower home output today, which is shown at Y_3.

In more detail, today the IS curve moves out slightly to IS_3 due to expected depreciation, but the LM curve moves in a long way to LM_3 to defend the peg. The latter effect dominates, because we know that demand and output have to be lower today given the combination of the same exchange rate (no change in the trade balance) and a higher interest rate (lower investment demand). So the new IS-LM equilibrium is at point 3, to the *left* of point 2.

We also note that to achieve this monetary contraction, the central bank must sell reserves—and the drain can take the form of a speculative attack if the currency premium appears suddenly as a result of a switch in beliefs.

The loss of credibility makes a bad recession even worse. If the peg is not credible, a higher interest rate causes the costs of pegging to rise to $c_3 = \overline{Y} - Y_3$. Finally, we note that this cost will be higher when the output gap is higher, because a larger output gap implies a larger depreciation to restore full employment.

Our second important result: *if the forex market switches to believing that the peg is not credible, then reserves drain, the interest rate rises, and the output gap (cost) increases; also, the cost increases more if the output gap is larger to begin with.*

The Costs and Benefits of Pegging Our IS-LM-FX analysis is now complete, and all we need to do is consider the implications.

Figure 20-17 sums up the cost–benefit analysis. The horizontal axis measures the output gap, or the cost of pegging, *when the peg is credible.* We denote these costs $c(\overline{E})$. This notation indicates that this is the cost c when the exchange rate is expected to be

FIGURE 20-17

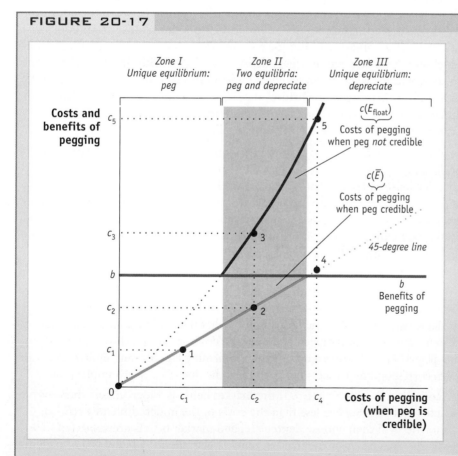

Contingent Policies and Multiple Equilibria Building on Figure 20-16, this figure shows how the costs of pegging depend on whether the peg is credible, and how that affects the game between the authorities and investors. The costs of pegging when the peg is credible are shown on the horizontal axis. To measure these costs on the vertical axis, we can read off from the 45-degree line. We know that the costs of pegging when the peg is not credible will be even higher. Costs rise when investors do not believe in the peg. We assume the government believes the benefits of pegging (e.g., lower trade costs) are fixed and equal to b. In this world, the peg is always credible in Zone I, where benefits always exceed costs: the government never wants to depreciate and investors know it. The peg is always noncredible in Zone III, where costs always exceed benefits: the government always wants to depreciate and investors know it. Zone II is the gray area: if investors believe the peg is credible, costs are low and the peg will hold; if investors believe the peg is noncredible, costs are higher and the peg will break.

at $\overline{E}$ next period. The first of our results showed that this cost rises, and we move right along the horizontal axis, whenever the country suffers an adverse shock under the peg.

The vertical axis measures and compares the costs and benefits of pegging. Benefits are constant at b. The costs when the peg is credible are equal to $c(\overline{E})$ so these will fall on the 45-degree line, since $c(\overline{E})$ is measured on the horizontal axis.

Finally, the cost of pegging when the peg is not credible is denoted $c(E_{\text{float}})$. This notation indicates that this is the cost c when the exchange rate is expected to be at E_{float} next period.

The second of our results showed that the costs of pegging when the peg is not credible are always greater than the costs when the peg is credible, due to the rise in the currency premium associated with an expected depreciation. In other words, the $c(E_{\text{float}})$ line is above the $c(\overline{E})$ line, as shown. We also saw that the difference gets larger as the costs grow larger. In Figure 20-17, this means that the $c(E_{\text{float}})$ curve diverges from the $c(\overline{E})$ curve, as shown.

Corresponding to the previous analysis in Figure 20-16, point 1 (cost c_1) represents a small recession with a credible peg; point 2 (cost c_2) represents a large recession with a credible peg; point 3 (cost c_3) represents the same large recession with a noncredible peg.

With this basic apparatus, we can now analyze the "game" between the authorities and investors. To keep it simple, we suppose investors can choose from two beliefs about what the government will do: {peg, depreciate}. And we suppose the authorities then choose from two actions: {peg, depreciate}. Faced with this type of problem, economists search for what might be considered a rational outcome of the game. We look for a **self-confirming equilibrium,** that is, combinations of investor beliefs and government actions for which the ex post outcome validates the ex ante beliefs.

We can identify several such equilibria using Figure 20-17:

■ In Zone I, $b > c(E_{\text{float}}) > c(\overline{E})$, so the benefits b of pegging always outweigh both kinds of costs, no matter what the market believes. The authorities will always choose to "peg." Anticipating this, the market belief will also be peg, and this is the only ex ante belief that will be validated ex post. Benefits are always given by b, and costs are always those of a credible peg $c(\overline{E})$. There is a unique self-confirming equilibrium: peg, with costs corresponding to the solid portion of the line $c(\overline{E})$. (Example: point 1.)

■ In Zone III, $c(E_{\text{float}}) > c(\overline{E}) > b$, so both kinds of costs of pegging always outweigh the benefits b, no matter what the market believes. The authorities will always choose to "depreciate." Anticipating this, the market belief will also be depreciate, and this is the only ex ante belief that will be validated ex post. Benefits are then always given by b, and the costs are always those of a noncredible peg $c(E_{\text{float}})$. There is a unique self-confirming equilibrium: depreciate, with costs corresponding to the solid portion of the line $c(E_{\text{float}})$. (Example: point 5.)

■ In Zone II, $c(E_{\text{float}}) > b > c(\overline{E})$. If the market belief is "depreciate," then the benefits b of pegging are less than the costs of the noncredible peg $c(E_{\text{float}})$; authorities will then choose depreciate, and market beliefs are validated for this case. Conversely, if the market belief is peg, then the benefits b of pegging are greater than the costs of a credible peg $c(\overline{E})$; authorities will then choose peg, and the market beliefs are also validated for this case. There are two self-confirming equilibria in this zone. Zone II is shown as a gray area in the diagram. And appropriately so! In this range, there is no unique equilibrium, and depending on market beliefs, costs may correspond to the solid portions of either line $c(\overline{E})$ or line $c(E_{\text{float}})$. (Examples: points 2 and 3.)

The Man Who Broke the Bank of England

Our analysis of contingent policies is highly simplified but advances our understanding of the potential for capricious outcomes driven by shifts in market sentiment. Changes in market sentiment, often called "animal spirits," emerge here from a model based on rational actors.

In some circumstances, the instability problem is much worse than we have suggested, for a couple of reasons. First, we have assumed that the government does not exit the peg immediately when it suffers pain, so expectations of depreciation are slow. If a 10% devaluation is feared in one year, this causes a 10% currency premium. But if it is expected to happen in three months (next quarter), then the expected rate of depreciation on an *annualized* basis is much higher and is given by a fourfold compounding of a 10% increase: this is 46% (because 1.10 to the power 4 equals 1.46). So the currency premium would be approximately 46%, a heavy penalty. If the 10% devaluation were expected in one month, the premium would be more than 200% on an annualized basis.[25] As the time frame shrinks, the currency premium explodes!

For example, in 1992 Swedish interest rates climbed astronomically as investors speculated on the imminent demise of the krona's peg to the German mark. The annualized short-term (overnight) lending rate climbed to 75% on September 8 and 500% on September 19. Such an interest rate was not politically tenable for very long. Investors knew this, and they were proved right.

A second issue is how beliefs form in the first place. Suppose we are in Zone II at the "no crisis" self-confirming equilibrium, with beliefs and actions corresponding to "peg." A mass switch in beliefs to "depreciate" would also be a self-confirming equilibrium. How does the market end up in one equilibrium or the other?

If traders are a group of many individuals, spread diffusely throughout the market, then it is unclear how they could all suddenly coordinate a switch to a new set of beliefs. And if each trader can place only a small bet, then it would be irrational for any trader to switch beliefs—unless all traders switch, and without coordination the switch is not going to happen and the peg stands a chance of holding.

But what if there are only a few traders? Or even just one very large trader who can make very big bets? If that single trader changes beliefs, the entire market goes from believing "peg" (no bets) to believing "depreciate" (making as big a bet against the home currency as possible). The coordination problem is solved. This is illustrated by the British ERM crisis of 1992. The large trader was the Quantum Fund, owned

George Soros: "Reflexivity is, in effect, a two-way feedback mechanism in which reality helps shape the participants' thinking and the participants' thinking helps shape reality."

---

[25] In these cases, the rate of depreciation is not small, so the UIP approximation formula is not appropriate. For precision, the exact UIP formula should be used: $1 + i = (1 + i^*)E^e/E$. For example, to use this formula, if the foreign interest rate is 2%, but a 10% devaluation is expected after one quarter, then the formula says that on an annual basis the home interest rate will be given by $1 + i = (1.02) \times (1 + 0.10)^4 = 1.4934$. So the home interest rate is about 49.3%, and subtracting the foreign rate of 2%, we find a currency premium of 47.3%, still close to the 46% given by the approximation formula. In the case of a 10% depreciation expected after 1 week, with 52 weeks per year, the home interest rate will be given by $1 + i = (1.02) \times (1 + 0.10)^{12} = 3.2012$, so the home interest rate is 220% and the currency premium is 218%.

by the famous (to some, infamous) investor George Soros, who likes to use the term "reflexivity" to describe how markets shape events, as well as vice versa.

Soros's firm placed one big bet after another, until he had borrowed billions of pounds and parked all the money in German mark deposits. "It was an obvious bet, a one-way bet," he later recalled.[26] If the pound held, he could convert his marks back to pounds, having paid a small interest cost (the difference between pound and mark interest rates for a few days); if the peg broke, he made billions as the pound fell. And who sold him the marks in exchange for pounds? The Bank of England, under orders from the U.K. Treasury, was intervening furiously, selling marks to prop up the pound at the limits of the ERM band.

The sudden increase in the currency premium was inducing a massive reserve drain. On the morning of September 16, 1992, the pressure on the pound became intense. The government made a feeble defense, raising the Bank's interest rates too little, too late, from 10% to 12% and, at the last gasp, to 15%. Pessimistic investors were unimpressed. With bearish sentiment so strong, reserve outflow was unlikely to halt without stronger measures, such as the Swedes had taken the week before. But with the British economy performing weakly, the government had little stomach for triple-digit interest rates—something investors well knew.

It was all over by lunchtime, with the bulk of the reserves lost, and an estimated £4 billion spent in a futile defense. The event has gone down in history as one more legendary British exchange rate fiasco. ■

Summary

Our results are striking. If government policies are contingent, then they will depend on market sentiment. But market sentiment, in turn, depends on what the market believes the government will do. If costs of pegging are "low," then pegs hold when they "should"—when the government has no desire to exit. If costs of pegging are "high," then crises happen when they "should"—when the government clearly wants to exit. But in between these extremes, an ambiguity arises in the form of multiple equilibria because for some "medium" range of costs, a crisis occurs if and only if the market expects a crisis.

5 Conclusions

Fixed exchange rates exhibit no signs of disappearing. Despite all their potential benefits, however, history shows another persistent feature—the recurrent crises that mark the collapse of fixed regimes.

In this chapter, we studied two kinds of crises. Adverse fiscal conditions can send the money supply out of control. And changes in the real economy can weaken the commitment to a peg. Expectations matter in each case—shifts in investor sentiment can make the crises occur "sooner" (i.e., when economic fundamentals are better), leading to worries that some crises are an unnecessary and undeserved punishment.

Can We Prevent Crises?

With these insights, we can now confront the major policy problem: How can these crises be prevented? A number of solutions have been proposed that merit mention:

---

[26] Ashley Seager, "Black Wednesday Still Haunts Britain," *Reuters*, September 16, 2002.

■ *The case for capital controls.* Crises occur in the forex market when investors see an arbitrage opportunity in shifting from one currency to another. If a nation could shut down its forex market, the risk of a crisis occurring would be lower. However, experience shows that capital controls, which are used to limit or prevent cross-border arbitrage by investors, are hard to implement and never watertight. Empirically, there seems to be no consistent evidence that capital controls work to decrease crisis frequency or enhance growth. In addition, countries tend to want to maintain financial openness as a way to obtain some of the economic gains described in the chapter on financial globalization. Controls could be instituted as a temporary policy, but, given the speed with which crises can unfold, the controls often end up taking effect after the reserves have disappeared. In a few countries (Malaysia after 1997, Spain after 1992), capital controls may have improved a crisis situation, but in many cases controls had only weak or negative effects.[27]

■ *The case against intermediate regimes.* One lesson of the models presented in this chapter is that a change in market expectations today can trigger "unnecessary" crises, with no deterioration today in economic fundamentals (e.g., GDP, inflation, etc.). After the experience of the 1990s, many leading economists began to see that intermediate regimes (such as dirty floats and soft pegs) are very risky when fluid market expectations are taken into account. Under such regimes, the extent of the authorities' commitment to the exchange rate target would be seen as questionable, meaning that departures from the target to monetize deficits or pursue monetary autonomy might be suspected, leading to potentially self-fulfilling crises. How can a nation avoid this outcome? In the trilemma diagram, countries should get out of the middle and move to the corners. This view came to be known as the **corners hypothesis** or the *missing middle*. Given the prevailing view that controls are not a viable option, this reduces the trilemma to a dilemma: in this "bipolar" view, only the two extremes of a hard peg or a true float can be recommended (an idea dating back to Milton Friedman, quoted at the start of this chapter). Evidence has mounted that intermediate regimes have been more crisis-prone in the past (up to five times as likely to have a crisis than a hard peg, according to one study), but the move away from such regimes appears to be very slow.[28]

[27] See, for example, Sebastian Edwards and Jeffrey A. Frankel, eds., 2002, *Preventing Currency Crises in Emerging Markets*, National Bureau of Economic Research Conference Report (Chicago: University of Chicago Press); Sebastian Edwards, ed., 2007, *Capital Controls and Capital Flows in Emerging Economies: Policies, Practices, and Consequences*, National Bureau of Economic Research Conference Report (Chicago: University of Chicago Press); Reuven Glick, Xueyan Guo, and Michael Hutchison, 2006, "Currency Crises, Capital-Account Liberalization, and Selection Bias," *Review of Economics and Statistics*, 88(4), 698–714; Rawi Abdelal and Laura Alfaro, 2003, "Capital and Control: Lessons from Malaysia," *Challenge*, 46(4), 36–53.
[28] After Friedman, the corners hypothesis gained new life in the 1990s and became influential in the minds of leading international economists and policy makers, such as Andrew Crockett, Barry Eichengreen, Stanley Fischer, and Lawrence Summers. For surveys of the intellectual history and arguments for and against the bipolar views, see Morris Goldstein, 2002, *Managed Floating*, Policy Analyses in International Economics, No. 66 (Washington, D.C.: Peterson Institute for International Economics); Thomas D. Willett, 2007, "Why the Middle Is Unstable: The Political Economy of Exchange Rate Regimes and Currency Crises," *World Economy*, 30(5), 709–732. On crisis frequency and evidence for a trend away from the middle, see Andrea Bubula and Inci Otker-Robe, *The Continuing Bipolar Conundrum*, IMF Finance and Development, March 2004. Evidence of no such trend is given by Kenneth Rogoff, Ashoka Mody, Nienke Oomes, Robin Brooks, and Aasim M. Husain, 2004, "Evolution and Performance of Exchange Rate Regimes," IMF Occasional Paper No. 229.

■ *The case for floating.* In a crisis, a peg breaks. If there isn't a peg, there is nothing to break. It might be desirable for all countries to float from that perspective. However, in the chapter on fixed and floating regimes, we saw that there are powerful reasons to peg, especially in emerging markets and developing countries with *fear of floating*. And empirically, there is no overwhelming trend toward floating regimes in recent years. Thus, the floating corner has not attracted all that many countries in practice.

■ *The case for hard pegs.* If floating is out, then the "bipolar view" suggests that (short of dollarizing) countries should go the other way and adopt a really hard peg like a currency board. Only a few countries have ever taken this route, including such examples as Hong Kong (still operative), Estonia (now in the euro), and Argentina (until its 2001–2002 crisis). Not all of these regimes were *strict* currency boards, but they could all be considered hard pegs, with high reserve ratios and some rules to try to limit domestic credit. Did they work? Some worked very well. Although the Hong Kong Monetary Authority wasn't following the strict rules, the system has worked, and the massive reserves have kept the peg alive even in times of financial market turmoil. But hard pegs can also break like any other kind of government commitment, if the authorities deem it necessary, as they did in Argentina. Lesson: all fixed exchange rates can be broken, no matter how strong they appear to be.[29]

■ *The case for improving the institutions of macroeconomic policy and financial markets.* If hard pegs are not a panacea, then risks to pegged regimes might be minimized if the rest of the macroeconomic and financial structure in a country could be endowed with greater strength, increased stability, and enhanced transparency. Admittedly, these goals are always desirable no matter what the exchange rate regime, but they take on added importance when a country is pegging because fiscal and banking problems have emerged as the root cause of so many crises. The steps involved may be slow, incremental, bureaucratic, and unglamorous. But their defenders would claim that, although they lack the "quick-fix" appearance of currency boards and other schemes, these improvements are the foundations on which any successful fixed exchange rate regime must be built.

■ *The case for an international lender of last resort.* We have seen that the adequate level of reserves to avert a crisis can depend on market sentiment. Why not borrow more reserves? This solution is not possible if lenders worry about an imminent crisis and you face a sudden stop. This is where the **International Monetary Fund (IMF)** can help. The IMF may lend to countries in difficulty if it thinks they can restore stability in a timely fashion with the help of a loan. But making the right judgments is far from easy. The IMF may impose unwelcome loan conditions that require policy change, including, for example, stricter control of budget deficits. If the conditions are ignored, the IMF may suspend the loan program. The IMF has also been criticized on occasion for being too hard (Korea in 1997) or too soft (Argentina in 2001). Moreover, its

---

[29] With the exception of Bosnia and Estonia, most modern "currency boards" have violated the strict rule against using domestic credit and have not kept the backing ratio close to 100%. See "Measures of Activism in Monetary Policy for Currency Board-Like Systems," by Kurt Schuler, June 2005 (http://www.dollarization.org/), based on data from the IMF, International Financial Statistics.

capacity to lend is limited and is increasingly dwarfed by private capital flows, causing concerns that future attacks may be too large for any IMF program to contain. Not that larger rescue capacity is necessarily good—at a basic level, many worry that the prospect of IMF bailouts, like any kind of insurance, may encourage lax behavior (*moral hazard*), which could worsen the crisis problem. Not surprisingly, the role of the IMF has been constantly questioned in the current era of globalization.[30]

■ *The case for self-insurance.* What if a country wants to peg, but none of the above ideas offers much comfort? What if capital controls are unattractive or porous, floating too risky, and currency boards too much of a straightjacket? What if a country knows that its domestic macroeconomic and financial architecture is still in a state of remodeling? What if the country looks back at the 1990s and worries that IMF programs will be too small, too late, too full of conditions, or not available when they are most needed? In some ways, this describes many of the Asian countries, and other emerging markets, in the 2000s. The vast reserve buildup of recent years seen in these countries may be an exercise in saving for a rainy day to protect themselves against unpredictable shifts in global financial market conditions.

After what happened in 1997, some Asian countries may not turn to the IMF again—and with their reserve accumulation, they may not need to.

KEY POINTS

1. An exchange rate crisis is a large and sudden depreciation that brings to an end a fixed exchange rate regime.

2. Such crises are common. The typical fixed exchange rate lasts only a few years. History shows that crises can affect all types of countries—advanced, emerging, and developing.

3. Crises have economic costs that tend to be very large in emerging markets and developing countries. Political costs are also large.

4. To avoid a crisis, the central bank in a country with a fixed exchange rate regime must have the ability to peg the exchange rate. In practice, this means the central bank needs foreign currency reserves, which can be bought or sold in the forex market at the fixed rate.

5. In a simple model of a central bank, the money supply consists of domestic credit and foreign reserves. Money demand is exogenous and is determined by interest rates and output levels that we assume are beyond the control of the authorities when the exchange rate is pegged. In this model, reserves are simply money demand minus domestic credit.

6. If money demand rises (falls), holding domestic credit fixed, reserves rise (fall) by the same amount.

7. If domestic credit rises (falls), holding money demand fixed, reserves fall (rise) by the same amount and the money supply is unchanged. The combined result is called sterilization.

[30] For a critical and nontechnical appraisal of IMF actions from 1994 to 2002, see Paul Blustein, 2001, *The Chastening: Inside the Crisis That Rocked the Global Financial System and Humbled the IMF* (New York: Public Affairs); and Paul Blustein, 2005, *And the Money Kept Rolling In (and Out): Wall Street, the IMF, and the Bankrupting of Argentina* (New York: Public Affairs).

8. When the central bank gives assistance to the financial sector, it expands domestic credit. If it is a bailout, money demand is unchanged, and reserves drain. If it is a loan to satisfy depositors' demand for cash, then reserves stay constant.

9. A first-generation crisis occurs when domestic credit grows at a constant rate forever, usually due to the monetization of a chronic fiscal deficit. Eventually, reserves drain and the money supply grows at the same rate, causing inflation and depreciation. Myopic investors do not anticipate the drain, and when reserves run out, they see a sudden jump (depreciation) in the exchange rate. Investors with foresight will try to sell domestic currency before that jump happens and by doing so will cause a speculative attack and a sudden drain of reserves.

10. A second-generation attack occurs when the authorities' commitment to the peg is contingent. If the domestic economy is suffering too high a cost from pegging, the authorities will consider floating and using expansionary monetary policy to boost output by allowing the currency to depreciate, thus breaking the peg. If investors anticipate that the government will break the peg, they will demand a currency premium, making interest even higher under the peg and raising the costs of pegging still further. In this setup, at some intermediate costs, the authorities will maintain the peg as long as investors find the peg credible, but they will allow their currency to depreciate if investors find the peg not credible. This creates multiple equilibria and self-fulfilling crises.

KEY TERMS

PROBLEMS

1. The economic costs of currency crises appear to be larger in emerging markets and developing countries, than they are in advanced countries. Discuss why this is the case, citing the interaction between the currency crisis and the financial sector. In what ways do currency crises lead to banking crises in these countries? In what ways do banking crises spark currency crises?

2. Using the central bank balance sheet diagrams, evaluate how each of the following shocks affects a country's ability to defend a fixed exchange rate.

   a. The central bank buys government bonds.
   b. Currency traders expect an appreciation in the home currency in the future.
   c. An economic expansion leads to a change in home money demand.
   d. The foreign interest rate increases.

3. Consider the central bank balance sheet for the country of Riqueza. Riqueza currently has $1,800 million escudos in its money supply, $1,100 million of which is backed by domestic government bonds; the rest is backed by foreign exchange reserves. Assume that Riqueza maintains a fixed exchange rate of one escudo per dollar, the foreign interest rate remains unchanged, and money demand takes the usual form, $M/P = L(i)Y$. Assume prices are sticky.

   a. Show Riqueza's central bank balance sheet, assuming there are no private banks. What is the backing ratio?
   b. Suppose that Riqueza's central bank sells $200 million in government bonds. Show how this affects the central bank balance sheet. Does this change affect Riqueza's money supply? Explain why or why not. What is the backing ratio now?
   c. Now, starting from this new position, suppose that there is an economic downturn in Riqueza, so that real income contracts by 10%. How will this affect money demand in Riqueza? How will forex traders respond to this change? Explain the responses in the money market and the forex market.

   d. Using a new balance sheet, show how the change described in (c) affects Riqueza's central bank. What happens to domestic credit? What happens to Riqueza's foreign exchange reserves? Explain the responses in the money market and the forex market.
   e. How will the change above affect the central bank's ability to defend the fixed exchange rate? What is the backing ratio now? Describe how this situation differs from one in which the central bank buys government bonds, as in part (b).

4. What is a currency board? Describe the strict rules about the composition of reserves and domestic credit that apply to this type of monetary arrangement.

5. What is a lender of last resort and what does it do? If a central bank acts as a lender of last resort under a fixed exchange rate regime, why are reserves at risk?

6. Suppose that a country's money supply is $1,200 million and its domestic credit is equal to $800 million in the year 2005. The country maintains a fixed exchange rate, the central bank monetizes any government budget deficit, and prices are sticky.

   a. Compute total reserves for the year 2005. Illustrate this situation on a central bank balance sheet diagram.
   b. Now, suppose the government unexpectedly runs a $100 million deficit in the year 2006 and the money supply is unchanged. Illustrate this change on your diagram. What is the new level of reserves?
   c. If the deficit is unexpected, will the central bank be able to defend the fixed exchange rate?
   d. Suppose the government runs a deficit of $100 million each year from this point forward. What will eventually happen to the central bank's reserves?
   e. In what year will the central bank be forced to abandon its exchange rate peg and why?
   f. What if the future deficits are anticipated? How does your answer to part (e) change? Explain briefly.

7. Consider two countries with fixed exchange rate regimes. In one country, government authorities exert fiscal dominance. In the other, they do not. Describe how this affects the central bank's ability to defend the exchange rate peg. How might this difference in fiscal dominance affect the central bank's credibility?

8. The government of the Republic of Andea is currently pegging the Andean peso to the dollar at $E = 1$ peso per dollar. Assume the following:

   In year 1 the money supply M is 2,250 pesos, reserves R are 1,250 pesos, and domestic credit B is 1,000 pesos. To finance spending, B is growing at 50% per year. Inflation is currently zero, prices are flexible, PPP holds at all times, and initially, $P = 1$. Assume also that the foreign price level is $P^* = 1$, so PPP holds. The government will float the peso if and only if it runs out of reserves. The U.S. nominal interest rate is 5%. Real output is fixed at $Y = 2,250$ at all times. Real money balances are $M/P = 2,250 = L(i) \, Y$, and L is initially equal to 1.

   a. Assume that Andean investors are myopic and do not foresee the reserves running out. Compute domestic credit in years 1, 2, 3, 4, and 5. At each date, also compute reserves, money supply, and the growth rate of money supply since the previous period (in percent).

   b. Continue to assume myopia. When do reserves run out? Call this time T. Assume inflation is constant after time T. What will that new inflation rate be? What will the rate of depreciation be? What will the new domestic interest rate be? (*Hint:* Use PPP and the Fisher effect.)

   c. Continue to assume myopia. Suppose that at time T, when the home interest rate i increases, then $L(i)$ drops from 1 to 2/3. Recall that Y remains fixed. What is M/P before time T? What will be the new level of M/P after time T, once reserves have run out and inflation has started?

   d. Continue to assume myopia. At time T, what is the price level going to be right before reserves run out? Right after? What is the percentage increase in the price level? In the exchange rate? [*Hint:* Use the answer to part (c) and PPP.]

   e. Suppose investors know the rate at which domestic credit is growing. Is the path described above consistent with rational behavior? What would rational investors want to do instead?

   f. Given the data presented in the question so far, when do you think a speculative attack would occur? At what level of reserves will such an attack occur? Explain your answer.

9. A peg is not credible when investors fear depreciation in the future, despite official announcements. Why is the home interest rate always higher under a noncredible peg than under a credible peg? Why does that make it more costly to maintain a noncredible peg than a credible peg? Explain why nothing more than a shift in investor beliefs can cause a peg to break.

10. You are the economic advisor to Sir Bufton Tufton, the prime minister of Perfidia. The Bank of Perfidia is pegging the exchange rate of the local currency, the Perfidian albion. The albion is pegged to the wotan, which is the currency of the neighboring country of Wagneria. Until this week both countries have been at full employment. This morning, new data showed that Perfidia was in a mild recession, 1% below desired output. Tufton believes a downturn of 1% or less is economically and politically acceptable but a larger downturn is not. He must face the press in 15 minutes and is considering making one of three statements:

    a. "We will abandon the peg to the wotan immediately."

    b. "Our policies will not change unless economic conditions deteriorate further."

    c. "We shall never surrender our peg to the wotan."

    What would you say to Tufton concerning the merits of each statement?

11. What steps have been proposed to prevent exchange rate crises? Discuss their pros and cons.

21

The Euro

There is no future for the people of Europe other than in union.
Jean Monnet, a "founding father" of the European Union

This Treaty marks a new stage in the process of creating an ever closer union among the peoples of Europe, in which decisions are taken as closely as possible to the citizen.
Maastricht Treaty (Treaty on European Union), 1992, Title 1, Article A

Political unity can pave the way for monetary unity. Monetary unity imposed under unfavorable conditions will prove a barrier to the achievement of political unity.
Milton Friedman, Nobel laureate, 1997

In 1961, the economist Robert Mundell wrote a paper discussing the idea of a *currency area*, also known as a **currency union** or *monetary union*, in which states or nations replace their national monies with a single, common currency.

At the time, almost every country was a separate currency area, so Mundell wondered whether his research would have any practical relevance: "What is the appropriate domain of a currency area? It might seem at first that the question is purely academic since it hardly appears within the realm of political feasibility that national currencies would ever be abandoned in favor of any other arrangement."[1]

Almost 40 years later, on January 1, 1999, 11 nations in Europe joined together to form such a currency area, now known as the *Euro area*, or **Eurozone.** Later that year, Mundell found himself the recipient of a Nobel Prize.

The Eurozone has since expanded and continues to expand. By January 1, 2014, it comprised 18 of the 28 member states of the European Union. They use the notes and coins bearing the name **euro** and the symbol € that have taken the place of former national currencies (francs, marks, liras, and others).

[1] Robert Mundell, 1961, "A Theory of Optimum Currency Areas," *American Economic Review*, 51, 657–665.

The euro remains one of the boldest experiments in the history of the international monetary system. It is a new currency that is used by more than 330 million people in one of the world's most prosperous economic regions. The euro is having enormous economic impacts that will be felt for many years to come.

The goal of this chapter is to understand as fully as possible the euro project: its economic as well as political logic, its institutional form and how it actually operates. We first examine the euro's economic logic by exploring and applying theories that seek to explain when it makes economic sense for different economic units (nations, regions, states) to adopt a common currency and when it makes economic sense for them to have distinct monies. To spoil the surprise: based on the current evidence, most economists judge that the Eurozone may not make sense from a purely economic standpoint, at least for now.

We then turn to the historical and political logic of the euro and discuss its distant origins and recent evolution within the larger political project of the European Union. Looking at the euro from these perspectives, we can see how the euro project unfolded as part of a larger enterprise. In this context, the success of the euro depends on assumptions that the European Union functions smoothly as a political union and adequately as an economic union—assumptions that are constantly under question.

The Ins and Outs of the Eurozone Before we begin our discussion of the euro, we need to familiarize ourselves with the EU and the Eurozone. Way back at the start of the euro project policy makers imagined that the euro would end up as the currency of the **European Union (EU).** The EU is a mainly economic, but increasingly political, union of countries that is in the process of extending across—and some might argue beyond—the geographical boundaries of Europe. The main impetus for the euro project came in 1992 with the signing of the Treaty on European Union, at Maastricht, in the Netherlands. Under the **Maastricht Treaty,** the EU initiated a grand project of *Economic and Monetary Union* (EMU). A major goal of EMU was the establishment of a currency union in the EU whose monetary affairs would be managed cooperatively by members through a new European Central Bank (ECB).[2]

The map in Figure 21-1 shows the state of play at the time of this writing in late 2013. The map depicts some of the EU's main political and monetary alignments. The two are not the same: different countries choose to participate in different aspects of economic and monetary integration, a curious feature of the EU project known as *variable geometry*.

- As of 2014, the EU comprised 28 countries (EU-28). Ten of these had joined as of 2004, Romania and Bulgaria joined in 2007, and Croatia in mid-2013. Five more official candidate countries were formally seeking to join—Iceland, Macedonia, Montenegro, Serbia, and Turkey.[3]

- A country can be in the EU but not in the Eurozone. It is important to remember who's "in" and who's "out." In 1999, just 3 of 15 EU members

---

[2] Some very small non-EU, non-Eurozone states and territories also use the euro. Four micro-states outside the EU, Monaco, San Marino, Vatican City, and Andorra, have legal agreements allowing them to use the euro as their de jure currency (they had previously used the national currencies of their neighbors). All these countries except Andorra can mint their own euro coins. Some other economies also use the euro as their de facto currency, notably Montenegro and Kosovo, plus four French and one UK overseas dependent territory (Mayotte, Saint Barthélemy, Saint Pierre and Miquelon, the French Southern and Antarctic Lands, and Akrotiri and Dhekelia).

[3] Until a naming dispute with Greece is resolved, Macedonia is often referred to in official communications as "the Former Yugoslav Republic of Macedonia" or, if you prefer acronyms, FYROM.

FIGURE 21-1

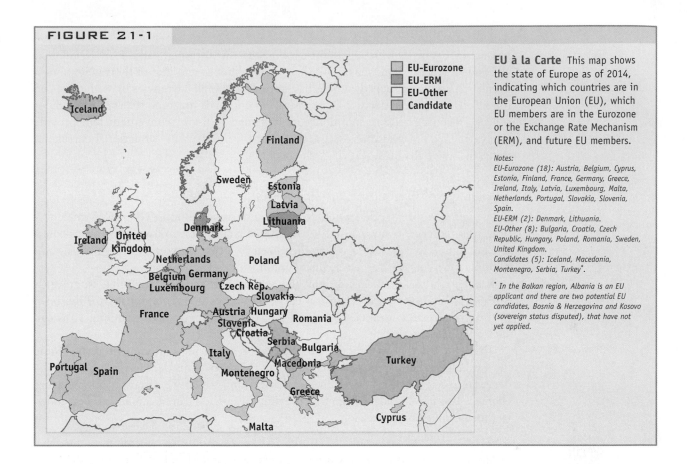

Legend:
- EU-Eurozone
- EU-ERM
- EU-Other
- Candidate

EU à la Carte This map shows the state of Europe as of 2014, indicating which countries are in the European Union (EU), which EU members are in the Eurozone or the Exchange Rate Mechanism (ERM), and future EU members.

Notes:
EU-Eurozone (18): Austria, Belgium, Cyprus, Estonia, Finland, France, Germany, Greece, Ireland, Italy, Latvia, Luxembourg, Malta, Netherlands, Portugal, Slovakia, Slovenia, Spain.
EU-ERM (2): Denmark, Lithuania.
EU-Other (8): Bulgaria, Croatia, Czech Republic, Hungary, Poland, Romania, Sweden, United Kingdom.
Candidates (5): Iceland, Macedonia, Montenegro, Serbia, Turkey.*

* In the Balkan region, Albania is an EU applicant and there are two potential EU candidates, Bosnia & Herzegovina and Kosovo (sovereign status disputed), that have not yet applied.

opted to stay out of the Eurozone and keep their national currencies: these "out" countries were Denmark, Sweden, and the United Kingdom. The other 12 all went "in" by 2001. From then until 2013, a total of 13 new entrants joined the EU, with all of them initially "out" of the euro. Then, on January 1, 2007, the first of these countries, Slovenia, became a member of the Eurozone, followed by Cyprus and Malta (2008), Slovakia (2009), Estonia (2011), and Latvia (2014). As of 2014, the other 7 new entrants still remained "out" of the Eurozone.

■ Most of the "outs" want to be "in." The official procedure to join the Eurozone requires that those who wish to get "in" must first peg their exchange rates to the euro in a system known as the *Exchange Rate Mechanism* (ERM) for at least two years and must also satisfy certain other qualification criteria. Two countries were part of the ERM as of 2014: Denmark and Lithuania. Participation in the ERM is usually taken as an indication of the intent to adopt the euro shortly (Latvia left the ERM to join the euro in January 2014). We discuss the ERM, the qualification criteria, and other peculiar rules later in this chapter.

Euro notes and coins.

1 The Economics of the Euro

In the nineteenth century, economist John Stuart Mill thought it a "barbarism" that all countries insisted on "having, to their inconvenience and that of their neighbors, a peculiar currency of their own." Barbaric or not, national currencies have always been the norm, while currency unions are rare.[4] Economists presume that such outcomes reflect a deeper logic. A common currency may be more convenient and provide other benefits, but it also has some costs. For the "barbarism" of national currencies to persist, the costs must outweigh the benefits.

The Theory of Optimum Currency Areas

How does a country decide whether to join a currency union? To answer this question, let's see if one country, Home, should join a currency union with another country, Foreign. (Our analysis can be generalized to a case in which Foreign consists of multiple members of a larger currency union.)

If countries make a decision that best serves their self-interest—that is, an optimizing decision—when they form a currency union, then economists use the term **optimum currency area (OCA)** to refer to the resulting monetary union. How can such a decision be made?

To decide whether joining the currency union serves its economic interests, Home must evaluate whether the benefits outweigh the costs. This decision is similar to the decision to select a fixed or floating exchange rate, which we discussed in an earlier chapter. Two familiar ideas from that previous discussion can be applied and extended to the currency union decision.

Market Integration and Efficiency Benefits Adopting a common currency implies that the two regions will have an exchange rate fixed at 1. Hence, the same market integration criterion we used to discriminate between fixed and floating regimes can be applied to the case of an OCA:

If there is a greater degree of economic integration between the home region (A) and the other parts of the common currency zone (B), the volume of transactions between the two and the economic benefits of adopting a common currency due to lowered transaction costs and reduced uncertainty will both be larger.

Economic Symmetry and Stability Costs When two regions adopt a common currency, each region will lose its monetary autonomy, and the monetary authorities who have control of the common currency will decide on a common monetary policy and set a common interest rate for all members. Hence, the similarity criterion we used to discriminate between fixed and floating regimes can be applied to the case of an OCA:

If a home country and its potential currency union partners are more economically similar or "symmetric" (they face more symmetric shocks and fewer asymmetric shocks), then it is less costly for the home country to join the currency union.

---

[4] Many currency unions involve the unilateral adoption of a foreign currency by a country that plays no role in managing the common currency (e.g., Panama's use of the U.S. dollar). Even when a foreign country adopts a currency other than the dollar, this situation is often called *dollarization*. In only a few cases are currency unions multilateral in which all member countries participate in the monetary affairs of the union. The Eurozone is the most notable example of a multilateral currency union.

Simple Optimum Currency Area Criteria

We are now in a position to set out a theory of an optimum currency area by considering the *net benefits* of adopting a common currency. The net benefits equal the benefits minus the costs. The two main lessons we have just encountered suggest the following:

■ *As market integration rises, the efficiency benefits of a common currency increase.*

■ *As symmetry rises, the stability costs of a common currency decrease.*

Summing up, the OCA theory says that if either market integration or symmetry increases, the net benefits of a common currency will rise. If the net benefits are negative, the home country would stay out based on its economic interests. If the net benefits turn positive, the home country would join based on its economic interests.

Figure 21-2 illustrates the OCA theory graphically, using the same symmetry-integration diagrams used in the previous chapter on fixed and floating exchange rates. The horizontal axis measures market integration for the Home-Foreign pair. The vertical axis measures the symmetry of the shocks experienced by the Home-Foreign pair. If the Home-Foreign pair moves up and to the right in the diagram, then the benefits increase, the costs fall, and so the net benefit of a currency union rises. At some point, the pair crosses a threshold, the OCA line, and enters a region in which it will be optimal for them to form a currency union based on their economic interests.

The figure looks familiar. The derivation of the OCA line here is identical to the derivation of the FIX line in a previous chapter, which raises an important question.

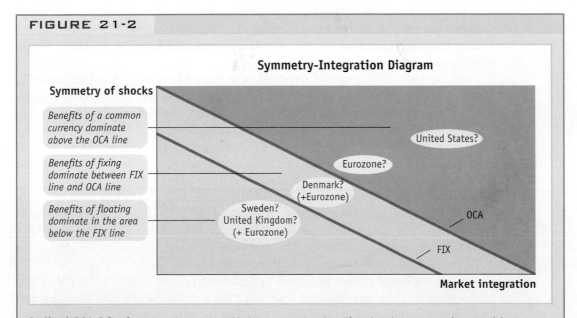

FIGURE 21-2

Symmetry-Integration Diagram

Stylized OCA Criteria Two regions are considering a currency union. If markets become more integrated (a move right on the horizontal axis), the net economic benefits of a currency union increase. If the economic shocks they experience become more symmetric (a move up the vertical axis), the net economic benefits of a currency union also increase. If the parts of the region move far enough up or to the right, benefits exceed costs, net benefits are positive, and they cross the OCA threshold. In the shaded region above the line, it is optimal for the parts of the region to form a currency union. In practice, the OCA line is likely to be above and to the right of the FIX line.

What's the Difference Between a Fix and a Currency Union?

If choosing to fix and choosing to form a currency union were identical decisions, then the FIX and OCA lines would be one and the same. In reality, we think they are likely to differ—and that the OCA line is likely to be above the FIX line, as drawn in Figure 21-2. Thus, when countries consider forming a currency union, the economic tests (based on symmetry and integration) set a higher bar than they set for judging whether it is optimal to fix.

Why might this be so? To give a concrete example, let's consider the case of Denmark, which we studied in an earlier chapter on exchange rates, as an example of the trilemma in Europe. The Danes are in the ERM, so the krone is pegged to the euro. But Denmark has spent a long time in the ERM and shows no signs of taking the next step into the Eurozone. This preference has been democratically expressed—proposals to join the Eurozone have been defeated by referendum. The Danish position looks slightly odd at first glance. Denmark appears to have ceded monetary autonomy to the ECB because its interest rate tracks the euro interest rate closely. Yet the Danes do not gain the full benefits of a currency union because transactions between Denmark and the Eurozone still require a change of currency.

Still, one can make a logical case for Denmark to keep its own currency. By doing so, it better preserves the *option* to exercise monetary autonomy at some future date, even if the option is not being used currently. For one thing, even under the ERM, although the krone is pegged very tightly to the euro within ±2% by choice, the Danes could employ the full ±15% band allowed by ERM and give themselves much more exchange rate flexibility. (A ±15% band isn't a very hard peg—recall that the standard de facto threshold for a peg is no more than ±2% variation in one year.) And because they have only gone as far as pegging to—and not joining—the euro, the Danes are always free to leave the ERM at some future date (as Sweden and the United Kingdom have done) if they want the even greater flexibility of a more freely floating exchange rate.

Now, contrast the position of Denmark with that of Italy, one of several countries in which rumors of departure from the Eurozone have surfaced from time to time (Greece is another example). Compared with a Danish exit from the ERM, an Italian exit from the euro would be messy, complicated, and costly. The actual process of retiring euros and reprinting and reintroducing new lira as money would be difficult enough. More seriously, however, all Italian contracts would have to be switched from euro to lira, in particular the private and public debt contracts. There would be a monumental legal battle over the implicit defaults that would follow from the "lirification" of such euro contracts. Some countries have tried these kinds of strategies, but the examples are not too encouraging. In the 1980s Liberia de-dollarized (and descended into economic crisis) and in 2002 Argentina legislated the "pesification" of its dollar contracts (and descended into economic crisis).

Because the future cannot be known with certainty, countries may value the option to change their monetary and exchange rate regime in the future. Exit from a peg is easy—some might say too easy—and happens all the time. Exit from a common currency is much more difficult (the Eurozone has *no* exit procedure) and is expected to be costly. We conclude that because a country's options are more limited after joining a common currency than after joining a peg, the country will set tougher conditions for the former; thus, the smaller OCA region must lie within the larger optimal fixing region (below and to the left), as shown in Figure 21-2.

Other Optimum Currency Area Criteria

Our simple model in Figure 21-2 illustrated two basic motives for joining a currency union, but there could be many other forces at work. These other considerations can still be examined using the same framework, which allows us to consider several additional arguments for joining a currency union.

Labor Market Integration In the analysis so far, the home and foreign countries trade goods and services, but labor is immobile between the two countries. But what if we suppose instead that Home and Foreign have an integrated labor market, so that labor is free to move between them: What effect will this have on the decision to form an optimum currency area?

Labor market integration allows for an alternative adjustment mechanism in the event of asymmetric shocks. For example, suppose Home and Foreign initially have equal output and unemployment. Suppose further that a negative shock hits Home, but not Foreign. If output falls and unemployment rises in Home, then labor will start to migrate to Foreign, where unemployment is lower. If this migration can occur with ease, the impact of the negative shock on Home will be less painful. Furthermore, there will be less need for Home to implement an independent monetary policy response for stabilization purposes. With an excess supply of labor in one region, adjustment can occur through migration.

This reasoning suggests that the cost to Home of forming a currency union with Foreign, due to the loss of monetary policy autonomy, will be lower when the labor market integration between Home and Foreign is higher, because labor mobility provides an alternative mechanism through which Home can adjust to the shock. All else equal, the possibility of gains of this sort would lower the OCA threshold, as reflected in the shift down of the OCA line from OCA_1 to OCA_2 in Figure 21–3. This shift expands the shaded zone in which currency union is preferred: countries are more likely to want to form a currency union when their labor markets are more integrated.

Fiscal Transfers We have now examined two possible mechanisms through which countries in an OCA can cope with asymmetric shocks: monetary policy and labor markets, the key OCA trade-off emphasized by Robert Mundell. We have ignored fiscal policy. All else equal, one might argue that a country's fiscal policy is autonomous and largely independent of whether a country is inside or outside a currency union. But there is one important exception: fiscal policy will not be independent when a currency union is built on top of a federal political structure with fiscal mechanisms that permit interstate transfers—a system known as *fiscal federalism*.

If a region also has fiscal federalism, then a third adjustment channel is available: when Home suffers a negative shock, the effects of the shock can be cushioned by fiscal transfers from Foreign, allowing more expansionary fiscal policy in Home than might otherwise be the case. For this argument to be compelling, however, the fiscal transfers must be large enough to make a difference. They must also help overcome some limit on the exercise of Home's fiscal policy, that is, the transfers must finance policies that Home could not finance in some other way (e.g., by government borrowing).

If these conditions are satisfied, then the presence of fiscal transfers will lower the costs of joining a currency union. We show the possibility of gains of this sort in Figure 21-3, where, all else equal, enhanced fiscal transfers mean a lower OCA threshold and a shift down from OCA_1 to OCA_2. This shift expands the shaded zone in which currency union is preferred: the better the fiscal transfer mechanisms, the more the countries are likely to want to form a currency union, an alternative but important OCA criterion stressed by the international economist Peter Kenen.[5]

Monetary Policy and Nominal Anchoring One important aspect of Home joining a currency union is that Home's central bank ceases to manage monetary policy (or ceases to exist altogether). Monetary policy is then carried out by a common central bank, whose policies and actions may be subject to different designs, objectives, and political oversight. This may or may not be a good thing, depending on whether the overall monetary policy performance of Home's central bank is (or is expected to be) as good as that of the common central bank.

For example, suppose that Home suffers from chronic high inflation that results from an **inflation bias** of Home policy makers—the inability to resist the political pressure to use expansionary monetary policy for short-term gains. In the long run, on average, inflation bias leads to a higher level of expected inflation and actual inflation. But average levels of unemployment and output are unchanged because higher inflation is expected and inflation has no real effects in the long run.

Suppose that the common central bank of the currency union would be a more politically independent central bank that could resist political pressures to use expansionary monetary policy for short-term gains. It performs better by delivering low inflation on average, and no worse levels of unemployment or output. In this case, joining the currency union improves economic performance for Home by giving it a better nominal anchor: in this scenario, loss of monetary autonomy can be a good thing.

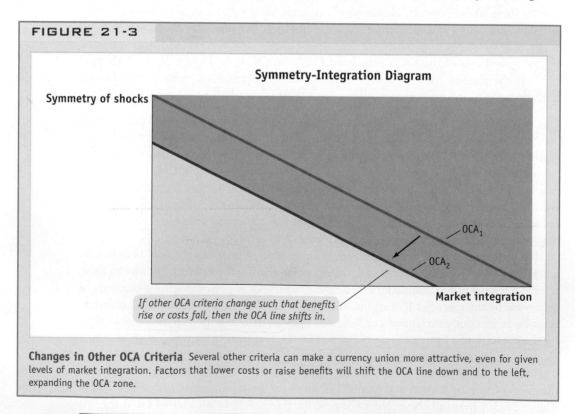

FIGURE 21-3

Symmetry-Integration Diagram

Symmetry of shocks

OCA₁

OCA₂

Market integration

If other OCA criteria change such that benefits rise or costs fall, then the OCA line shifts in.

Changes in Other OCA Criteria Several other criteria can make a currency union more attractive, even for given levels of market integration. Factors that lower costs or raise benefits will shift the OCA line down and to the left, expanding the OCA zone.

[5] Peter Kenen, 1969, "The Theory of Optimum Currency Areas: An Eclectic View," in *Monetary Problems in the International Economy*, edited by Robert A. Mundell and Alexander K. Swoboda (Chicago: University of Chicago Press), pp. 41–60.

There is a possibility that this criterion was important for several Eurozone member states that historically have been subject to high inflation—for example, Italy, Greece, and Portugal. We can represent the possibility of monetary policy gains of this sort in Figure 21-3, where, all else equal, a worsening in the home nominal anchor (or an improvement in the currency union's nominal anchor) shifts the OCA line down. For countries with a record of high and variable inflation, the OCA threshold will fall, so again the OCA line moves down from OCA_1 to OCA_2. This shift also expands the shaded zone in which currency union is preferred: given levels of market integration and symmetry, high-inflation countries are more likely to want to join the currency union and the larger are the monetary policy gains of this sort. (Later on we consider the concerns of the low-inflation countries in this scenario.)

Political Objectives Finally, we turn to noneconomic gains and the possibility that countries will join a currency union even if it makes no pure economic sense for them to do so. For instance, one can imagine that Home's "political welfare" may go up, even if pure economic welfare goes down. How?

Suppose a state or group of states is in a situation in which forming a currency union has value for political, security, strategic, or other reasons. For example, when the United States expanded westward in the nineteenth century, it was accepted, without question, that new territories and states would adopt the U.S. dollar. In recent times, eastward expansion of the EU comes with an assumption that, in the end, accession to the union will culminate in monetary union. These beliefs, assumptions, and accords did not rest very much, if at all, on any of the OCA criteria we have discussed so far. Instead, they were an act of political faith, of a belief in the states' common political future, a statement about destiny.

Political benefits can also be represented in Figure 21-3 by the OCA line shifting down from OCA_1 to OCA_2. In this scenario, for countries between OCA_1 and OCA_2, there are *economic costs* to forming a currency union, but these are outweighed by the *political benefits*. The political dimension has played a significant part in EU and Eurozone history, a topic we discuss later in the chapter.

APPLICATION

Optimum Currency Areas: Europe Versus the United States

At first glance, the theory of optimum currency areas helpfully sets out the important criteria by which we can judge whether it is in a country's interest to join a currency union. But while the OCA criteria work well in theory, in reality, the costs and benefits of a currency union cannot be measured with any great accuracy.

Recognizing this, we can try an alternative approach and use comparative analysis to shed some light on the issue by answering a slightly different question: How does Europe compare with the United States on each of the OCA criteria? Clearly, if one took the view that the United States works well as a common currency zone, and if we find that Europe performs as well as or better than the United States on the OCA criteria, then these findings would lend indirect support to the economic logic of the euro.

Goods Market Integration European countries trade a lot with one another. But as far as we can tell (the available data are not entirely comparable), the individual states within the United States trade even more with one another. For the 50 U.S. states shown in Figure 21-4, panel (a), inter-state trade is about 66% of U.S. GDP.

FIGURE 21-4

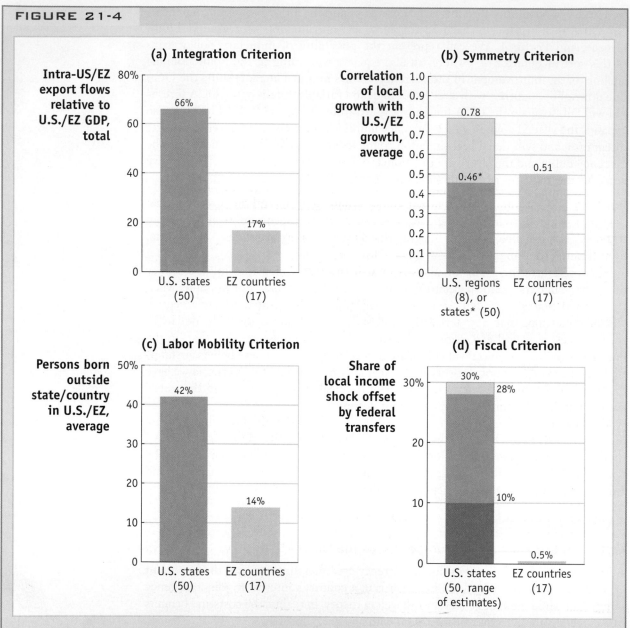

OCA Criteria for the Eurozone and the United States Most economists believe that the United States is much more likely to satisfy the OCA criteria than the EZ is. Why? Data in panel (a) show that interregional trade in the United States rises to levels much higher than those seen among EZ countries. Data in panel (b) show that U.S. and EZ shocks are comparably symmetric. Data in panel (c) show that U.S. labor markets are very integrated compared with those of the EZ. Data in panel (d) show that interstate fiscal stabilizers are large in the United States, but essentially nonexistent in the EZ.

Sources and Notes: Kevin H. O'Rourke and Alan M. Taylor, 2013, "Cross of Euros," Journal of Economic Perspectives, 27(3): 167–92. Data are based on up to at most 17 EZ members in the period up to 2013.

The figure for 17 Eurozone countries is typically much smaller, and their trade with one another is only about 17% of Eurozone GDP. At best, it might be argued that the creation of a "single market" in the EU is still a work in progress (as we see in the next section), and so these intra-EU trade flows will likely rise further as the EU's internal market becomes more integrated. On this test, Europe is probably behind the United States for now.

Symmetry of Shocks A direct way to look at the symmetry of shocks is to compare the correlation of a state or region's GDP annual growth rate with the annual GDP growth of the entire zone. These data are shown in Figure 21-4, panel (b), and the Eurozone countries compare more favorably with the U.S. states and regions on this test: for 50 U.S. states and 17 Eurozone countries, the average correlation with the entire zone's GDP growth rate is close to 0.5 (the much larger 8 U.S. census regions show a much higher correlation with the nation, of course). This result is not too surprising: there is no strong consensus that EU countries are more exposed to local shocks than the regions of the United States. However, as we see in a moment, one potential problem for the EU is what happens in the future: one effect of greater EU goods market integration could be that EU countries start to specialize more, and thus become more dissimilar. In that case, the risk of asymmetric shocks will increase and the EU will be less likely to satisfy the OCA criteria.

Labor Mobility The data in Figure 21-4, panel (c), show what is well known: labor in Europe is much less mobile between states than it is in the United States. More than 40% of U.S. residents were born outside the state in which they live. In the Eurozone, only 14% of people were born in a different country than the one in which they live. (The same is true, as one would expect, of the year-to-year flow of people between regions: it is also an order of magnitude larger in the United States than in Europe.) There are obvious explanations for this: differences in culture and language present obstacles to intra-EU migration that are largely absent in the United States. In addition, although the EU is working to ease such frictions, the local regulatory environment and red tape make it difficult for Europeans to live and work in another EU country, even if they have a legal right to do so. Finally, labor markets in Europe are generally less flexible, making it harder to hire and fire workers, something that may dissuade workers from moving from one place to another in search of better opportunities. Economists have found that differences in unemployment across EU regions tend to be larger and more persistent than they are across the individual states of the United States. In short, the labor market adjustment mechanism is weaker in Europe. On this test, Europe is far behind the United States.

Fiscal Transfers The data in Figure 21-4, panel (d), from a survey of the literature, show that when a U.S. state goes into a recession, for every $1 drop in that state's GDP, the federal government compensates with an offsetting transfer of between 10 cents and 30 cents (this range may be too low: the 28-cent figure is the most recent and is based on Federal income tax variation alone). Stabilizing transfers of this kind are possible only when states agree to engage in fiscal federalism, whereby substantial taxing and spending authority are given to the central authority. The United States has such stabilizing transfers, but the EU and the Eurozone do not. Although individual states in the Eurozone achieve similar results within their own borders, at the level of the Eurozone as a whole, the fiscal transfer mechanism is nonexistent, offsetting less then 1 cent for every €1 of a nation's GDP decline. (The EU budget is little more than 1% of EU GDP and is devoted to other purposes, notably agricultural subsidies, which do not vary much over the business cycle).

FIGURE 21-5

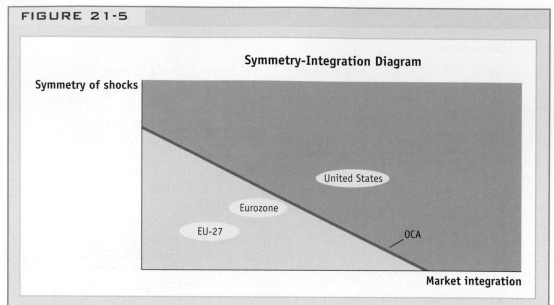

Symmetry-Integration Diagram

Symmetry of shocks

United States

Eurozone

EU-27

OCA

Market integration

Stylized OCA View of the EU and the United States Most economists consider that the Eurozone and EU countries do not satisfy the OCA criteria—they have too little market integration and their shocks are too asymmetric. The Eurozone may be closer to the OCA line since integration runs deeper there, but it is still far behind the United States on the OCA criteria. If we expand to the EU of 27, it is likely that this larger zone fails to meet OCA criteria by an even larger margin, with lower integration and higher asymmetry than the current Eurozone.

Summary On the simple OCA criteria, the EU falls short of the United States as a successful optimum currency area, as shown in Figure 21-5. Goods market integration is a little bit weaker, fiscal transfers are negligible, and labor mobility is very low. At best, one can note that economic shocks in the EU are fairly symmetric, but this fact alone gives only limited support for a currency union given the shortcomings in other areas.

Some economists argue that the economic stability costs are exaggerated: they have doubts about stabilization policy in theory (e.g., the Keynesian view that prices are sticky in the short run) or in practice (e.g., the caveats about policy activism noted in the chapter on short-run macroeconomic policies). But most economists think there are still costs involved when a country sacrifices monetary autonomy. They worry that some or all Eurozone countries now have an inappropriate one-size-fits-all monetary policy, and that there are additional risks such as the absence of a well-defined lender of last resort mechanism in the Eurozone.

On balance, economists tend to believe that the EU, and the current Eurozone within it, were not an optimum currency area in the 1990s when the EMU project took shape and that nothing much has happened yet to alter that judgment. ■

Are the OCA Criteria Self-Fulfilling?

Our discussion so far has taken a fairly static view of the OCA criteria. Countries treat all of the conditions just discussed as given, and, assuming they have adequate information, they can then judge whether the costs of forming a currency union outweigh the benefits. However, another school of thought argues that some of the OCA criteria are not given (i.e., exogenous) and fixed in stone, but rather they are economic outcomes (i.e., endogenous) determined by, among other things, the creation of the currency union itself. In other words, even if the Eurozone isn't an OCA now, by adopting a common currency, it might become an OCA in the future.

Consider goods market integration, for example. The very act of joining a currency union might be expected to promote more trade, by lowering transaction costs. Indeed, that is one of the main supposed benefits. In that case, if the OCA criteria were applied *ex ante* (before the currency union forms), then many countries might exhibit low trade volumes. Their low integration might mean that the OCA criteria are not met, and the currency union might not be formed based on those characteristics. However, if the currency union went ahead anyway, then it might be the case that *ex post* (after the currency union is up and running) countries would trade so much more that in the end the OCA criteria would indeed be satisfied.

This kind of argument is favored by euro-optimists, who see the EU single-market project as an ongoing process and the single currency as one of its crucial elements. This logic suggests that the OCA criteria can be self-fulfilling, at least for a group of countries that are ex ante close to—but not quite—fulfilling the OCA requirements. For example, suppose the EU started out at point 1 in Figure 21-6, just below the OCA line. If the EU countries would only "just do it" and form a monetary union,

FIGURE 21-6

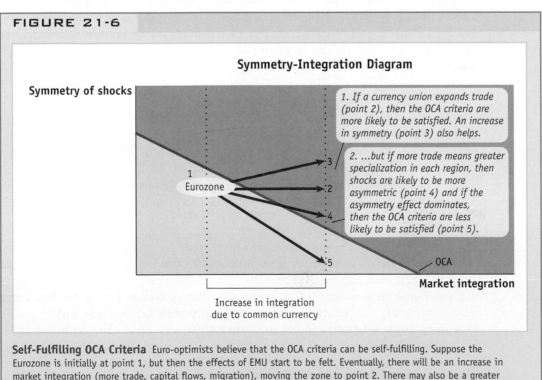

Symmetry-Integration Diagram

1. If a currency union expands trade (point 2), then the OCA criteria are more likely to be satisfied. An increase in symmetry (point 3) also helps.

2. ...but if more trade means greater specialization in each region, then shocks are likely to be more asymmetric (point 4) and if the asymmetry effect dominates, then the OCA criteria are less likely to be satisfied (point 5).

Increase in integration due to common currency

Self-Fulfilling OCA Criteria Euro-optimists believe that the OCA criteria can be self-fulfilling. Suppose the Eurozone is initially at point 1, but then the effects of EMU start to be felt. Eventually, there will be an increase in market integration (more trade, capital flows, migration), moving the zone to point 2. There may also be a greater synchronization of shocks in the Eurozone, moving the zone to point 3. However, euro-pessimists note that market integration and more trade might also lead to more specialization by each country in the EU. In that case, the shocks to each country are likely to become more *asymmetric*, implying a move toward point 4 or point 5. In the case of point 5, the case for an OCA grows weaker, not stronger, after the long-run effects of the currency union have been worked out.

then they would wake up and discover that they had jumped to point 2 once the common currency had boosted trade among them, and, hey, presto: while monetary union didn't make sense beforehand, it does after the fact. Thus, even if the EU or the Eurozone does not look like an OCA now, it might turn out to be an OCA once it is fully operational. However, Euro-pessimists doubt that this self-fulfilling effect will amount to much. Evidence is mixed, and the exact magnitude of this effect is subject to considerable dispute (see **Headlines: Currency Unions and Trade**).[6]

A further argument made by optimists is that greater integration under the EU project might also enhance other OCA criteria. For example, if goods markets are better connected, a case can be made that shocks will be more rapidly transmitted within the EU and will be felt more symmetrically. Thus, creating the Eurozone will not only boost trade but also increase the symmetry of shocks, corresponding to a shift from point 1 to point 3 in Figure 21-6. Such a process would strengthen the OCA argument even more.

Set against this optimistic view is the pessimistic prospect that further goods market integration might also lead to more specialization in production. According to this argument, once individual firms can easily serve the whole EU market, and not just their national market, they will exploit economies of scale and concentrate production. Some sectors in the EU might end up becoming concentrated in a few locations. Whereas in the past trade barriers and other frictions allowed every EU country to produce a wide range of goods, in the future we might see more clustering (the United States provides many examples, such as the auto industry in Detroit, financial services in New York City, entertainment in Los Angeles, or technology in Silicon Valley and San Francisco). If specialization increases, each country will be less diversified and will face more asymmetric shocks. In Figure 21-6, this might correspond to a move from point 1 to point 4, where the case for OCA would strengthen, though not by much; or even a move to point 5, where the costs of asymmetric shocks are so large that they dominate the gains from market integration, so that the case for an OCA is weakened.

Some speculate that certain other OCA criteria could be affected by the adoption of the euro: maybe the common currency will encourage greater labor and capital mobility? Maybe it will encourage more fiscal federalism? As with the arguments about the effects on trade creation and specialization, evidence for these claims is fuzzy. We cannot make a definitive judgment until the Eurozone experiment has run for a few more years and there are sufficient data to make reliable statistical inferences.

Summary

We have seen how a calculation of economic costs and benefits can help us decide whether a common currency makes sense. Based on these criteria alone, it appears that the Eurozone is almost certainly not an optimum currency area, nor the larger EU. Admittedly, this conclusion does not apply with equal force to the entire Eurozone. Some subgroups of countries may satisfy the OCA criteria. For decades Luxembourg has, in fact, used the Belgian franc as a currency; and the Dutch guilder has been closely tied to the German mark. The BeNeLux countries, and maybe Austria too, have always been well integrated with Germany and therefore stronger

---

[6] Some believe a common currency will have other effects, perhaps also encouraging labor and capital mobility within the Eurozone. These might also change the OCA calculus, but significant evidence on these effects has not been found as yet.

HEADLINES

Currency Unions and Trade

Will Eurozone trade rise as a result of the adoption of the euro? The effects seen so far do not appear to be very large.

In the continuing controversies about Europe's bold experiment in monetary union, there has at least been some agreement about where the costs and benefits lie. The costs are macroeconomic, caused by forgoing the right to set interest rates to suit the specific economic conditions of a member state. The benefits are microeconomic, consisting of potential gains in trade and growth as the costs of changing currencies and exchange-rate uncertainty are removed.

A recent . . . study[*] by Richard Baldwin, a trade economist at the Graduate Institute of International Studies in Geneva, scythes through [previous] estimates. He works out that the boost to trade within the euro area from the single currency is much smaller: between 5% and 15%, with a best estimate of 9%. Furthermore, the gain does not build up over time but has already occurred. And the three European Union countries that stayed out—Britain, Sweden and Denmark—have gained almost as much as founder members, since the single currency has raised their exports to the euro zone by 7%.

Interest in the potential trade gains from the euro was primed . . . by a startling result from research into previous currency unions. In 2000 Andrew Rose, an economist at the University of California, Berkeley, reported that sharing a currency boosts trade by 235%.[**] Such a number looked too big to be true. It clashed with earlier research that found exchange-rate volatility reduced trade only marginally. . . .

Despite such worries, researchers continued to find large trade effects from currency unions. Mr. Baldwin explains why these estimates are unreliable. The main problem is that most of the countries involved are an odd bunch of small, poor economies that are in unions because of former colonial arrangements. Such is their diversity that it is impossible to model the full range of possible influences on their trade. But if some of the omitted factors are correlated with membership of a monetary union, the estimate of its impact on trade is exaggerated. And causality is also likely to run the other way: small, open economies, which would in any case trade heavily, are especially likely to share a currency. . . .

The intractable difficulties in working out the trade effect from previous currency unions means that previous estimates are fatally flawed. But the euro has now been in existence since the start of 1999, with notes and coins circulating since January 2002, so there is an increasing body of evidence based on its experience. That has certainly highlighted the macroeconomic disadvantages for its 12 member states. The loss of monetary sovereignty has hobbled first Germany and, more recently, Italy.

Despite these drawbacks, some studies have pointed to a substantial increase in trade within the euro area arising from monetary union, for example, by 20–25% in the first four years. As with the previous currency unions, however, many other explanatory influences might have come into play. Fortunately, unlike those earlier unions, there is a "control" group: the three countries that stayed out. This is particularly useful because they have shared other relevant aspects of membership of the EU, such as trade policy. It is on the basis of this that Mr. Baldwin reaches his best estimate of a 9% increase in trade within the euro area because of monetary union.

As important, he establishes that the boost to trade did not occur, as expected, by lowering the transaction costs for trade within the euro area. Had it done so, the stimulus would have been a fall in the prices of goods traded between euro-zone members relative to those traded with countries outside the currency union. However, Mr. Baldwin fails to find either this expected relative decline or the trade diversion it would have generated from the three countries that stayed out. He argues that another mechanism was at work. The introduction of the euro has in effect brought down the fixed cost of trading in the euro area. This has made it possible for companies selling products to just a few of the 12 member states to expand their market across more or all of them. This explains why the boost to trade has essentially been a one-off adjustment; and why countries that stayed out have benefited almost as much as those that joined.

[T]here is also an important lesson for the 12 members of the euro area. Even if their economies were insufficiently aligned to be best suited for a currency union, one hope has been that the euro would make them converge as they trade much more intensively with one another. The message from Mr. Baldwin's report is that this is too optimistic. Countries in the euro area will have to undertake more reforms, such as making their labour markets more flexible, if they are to make the best of life with a single monetary policy.

[*]Richard Baldwin, *In or Out: Does It Matter? An Evidence-Based Analysis of the Euro's Trade Effects* (London: Centre for Economic Policy Research, 2006).
[**]Andrew K. Rose, 2000, "One Money, One Market: The Effect of Common Currencies on Trade," *Economic Policy*, 30, April, 7–45.

Source: Excerpted from "Economics Focus: The Euro and Trade," Economist, June 22, 2006. © The Economist Newspaper Limited, London (June 22, 2006).

candidates for a currency union. Other countries also had strong criteria for joining: for Italy, perhaps, where monetary policy was often more erratic, a better nominal anchor might have outweighed other negatives.

So if the EU is not an OCA, then why does the euro exist? The euro project was seen as something bigger. This was a currency designed to unify a whole continent of disparate economies, to include France and Germany, Italy and the United Kingdom, to run from west to east, from Scandinavia to the Mediterranean—and it developed with very little reference to the OCA criteria. To understand why the euro happened, we need to study political logic, the topic of the next section.

2 The History and Politics of the Euro

The political origins of the European Union and the euro project can be found in the past. As long ago as 1861, the eminent French writer and statesman Victor Hugo could imagine that "a day will come in which markets open to commerce and minds open to ideas will be the sole battlefields." The timeline in Table 21-1 provides a summary of some of the most important events that have shaped European economic history since 1870. The course of events reveals a European project guided by politics as well as economics.

A Brief History of Europe

The table shows major political and economic events since 1870 and highlights the most important developments affecting monetary policy over the same period. The table is divided into two periods: panel (a) sketches the more distant history that shaped the creation of the EU and progress toward EMU, culminating in the Maastricht Treaty of 1991; panel (b) supplies more detail on important recent events affecting the EU and the EMU project.

The EU project emerged as a cooperative response to a history of noncooperation among nations on the continent, which twice in the twentieth century spilled over into violent military conflict, in World War I (1914–1919) and World War II (1939–1945). Even during the interwar years, political tensions ran high and economic cooperation suffered. The situation was not helped by the punishing economic burdens placed on Germany by the Allied powers after World War I.[7] Matters only became worse during the severe economic downturn that was the Great Depression of the 1930s: protectionism surged again and the gold standard collapsed amid beggar-thy-neighbor devaluations (as discussed in the chapter on fixed and floating regimes).

In 1945, as a weak Europe emerged from the devastation of World War II, many feared that peace would only bring about a return to dire economic conditions. More economic suffering might also sow the seeds of more conflict in the future. At an extreme, some feared it would undermine the legitimacy of European capitalism, with the neighboring Soviet bloc all too eager to spread its alternative Communist model.

What could be done? In a speech in Zurich, on September 19, 1946, Winston Churchill presented his vision:

---

[7] John Maynard Keynes, 1919, *The Economic Consequences of the Peace* (London: Macmillan).

And what is the plight to which Europe has been reduced? . . . Over wide areas a vast quivering mass of tormented, hungry, care-worn and bewildered human beings gape at the ruins of their cities and their homes, and scan the dark horizons for the approach of some new peril, tyranny or terror. . . . That is all that Europeans, grouped in so many ancient states and nations . . . have got by tearing each other to pieces and spreading havoc far and wide. Yet all the while there is a remedy. . . . It is to recreate the European family, or as much of it as we can, and to provide it with a structure under which it can dwell in peace, in safety and in freedom. We must build a kind of United States of Europe.

Back from the Brink: Marshall Plan to Maastricht, 1945–1991 Into this crisis stepped the United States, to offer what has gone down in history as the most generous and successful reconstruction plan ever undertaken, the **Marshall Plan.**[8] From 1947 to 1951 Americans poured billions of dollars worth of aid into the war-torn regions of Western Europe to rebuild economic infrastructure (the Soviet bloc refused to take part in the plan).

The Marshall Plan required that the funds be allocated and administered by a European High Authority, composed of representatives of all countries, which encouraged collective action to solve common problems. Many cooperative arrangements were soon established: to smooth international payments and help trade (European Payments Union, or EPU, in 1950); to encourage trade and diminish rivalries in key goods like coal and steel (European Coal and Steel Community, or ECSC, in 1954); and to promote atomic and nuclear science without military rivalry (Euratom, in 1957).

In 1957 the **Treaty of Rome** was signed by six countries—France, West Germany, Italy, Belgium, Netherlands, and Luxembourg. They agreed to create the *European Economic Community*, or EEC, with plans for deeper economic cooperation and integration. In 1967 they went further and merged the EEC, the ECSC, and Euratom to create a new organization referred to as the *European Communities*, or EC. Two supranational bodies were created: the Council of Ministers, a decision-making body formed of national ministers, and an administrative body, the European Commission.

The dropping of the word "economic" (in the move from EEC to EC) was significant. By the 1960s two future paths had emerged. Would the EC create just a zone of economic integration? Or would it go further and aspire to a political union or a federal system of states—and if so, how far? The question has been hotly debated ever since.

In the 1970s, two major challenges to the EC project emerged: problems of expansion and problems of monetary affairs. The expansion problem involved deciding when and how to admit new members. By 1973 the first enlargement added Denmark, Ireland, and the United Kingdom. The EC (i.e., the Council of Ministers) viewed these states as the right type to gain entry—they had solid credentials in terms of economic development and stability, and all were established democracies. In contrast, the second and third enlargements included countries with weaker economic and

A poster created by the Economic Cooperation Administration, an agency of the U.S. government, to promote the Marshall Plan in Europe.

Courtesy of the Center for the Study of Political Graphics

---

[8] George C. Marshall (1880–1959), American military leader during World War II and named U.S. Secretary of State in 1947, proposed the postwar reconstruction effort for Europe in a speech after he was awarded an honorary degree at Harvard University, on Thursday, June 5, 1947.

TABLE 21-1

(a) European Integration through 1993 This table shows major political and economic events over the past century or more.

	Major Political and Economic Events	Monetary Developments
1870–1914	Largely peaceful era; economic growth and stability.	The **gold standard** system of fixed exchange rates prevails.
1914–1945	World Wars I and II; economic malaise, Great Depression.	Collapse of gold standard, floating exchange rates with instability; capital controls widespread.
1946	Period of postwar rapid growth begins, and will last until 1970s.	The **Bretton Woods system** of fixed exchange rates established.
1947–1951	**Marshall Plan** reconstruction financed by United States and overseen by the **European High Authority.**	**European Payments Union** is created to free up the European payments system and facilitate trade.
1954–1965	In 1954, France, West Germany, Italy, Belgium, Netherlands, Luxembourg form **European Coal and Steel Community** (ECSC). In 1957 they sign **Treaty of Rome** to form **European Economic Community** (EEC). In 1967 the **European Communities** (EC) merges EEC, ECSC, and Euratom; **Council of Ministers** and **European Commission** established.	
1971–1973	**First enlargement:** Denmark, Ireland, and United Kingdom join (1973) to form an EC of 9 countries.	The **Bretton Woods system** of fixed exchange rates collapses.
1973–1979	**European Parliament** directly elected (1979).	**European Monetary System** (EMS) of monetary cooperation creates a currency basket called the **ecu** (a precursor of euro) and the **Exchange Rate Mechanism** (ERM), a system of quasi-fixed exchange rates (1979). Belgium, Luxembourg, Denmark, Germany, France, Ireland, Italy, and Netherlands join EMS/ERM; United Kingdom joins EMS only.
1981–1986	**Second and Third enlargements:** Greece (1981), Portugal and Spain (1986) expand EC to 12 countries.	Greece, Portugal, and Spain join EMS but not ERM.
1987–1990	**Single European Act** (1987) has goal of EC "single market" by 1992.	Spain (1989) and United Kingdom (1990) join ERM.
1990	**German reunification** in 1990 creates new unified German state, adding former East Germany to the EC.	Capital controls abolished in EC.
1991	**Maastricht Treaty** transforms EC into **European Union** (EU); to take effect in 1993. EU citizenship and EU enlargement process established. Plan for **Economic and Monetary Union** (EMU) adopted.	Plan for EMU includes a common currency (Britain and Denmark retain right to opt out), with ERM seen as an entry route. Rules for membership and **convergence criteria** established.
1992		Portugal joins ERM. **ERM crisis:** Britain exits ERM; ERM bands eventually widened.
1993	EU sets out **Copenhagen Criteria,** the political and economic conditions that future EU applicants must satisfy.	Applicants are expected to enter ERM/EMS and achieve the requirements for monetary union in a given period.

political claims—but all the same, Greece (1981), Portugal (1986), and Spain (1986) were soon admitted to the growing club.

The problem of monetary affairs was precipitated by the collapse of the Bretton Woods system of fixed exchange rates in the early 1970s. As we saw in the fixed-floating chapter, the world had been operating since 1946 under a system of fixed

(b) European Integration since 1995 This table shows major political and economic events in recent years.

	Major Political and Economic Events	Monetary Developments
1995	**Fourth enlargement:** Austria, Finland, and Sweden expand EU to 15 countries. **Treaty of Schengen** will create common border system, immigration policies, and free travel zone (Ireland and UK opt out; non-EU countries Iceland, Norway, and Switzerland opt in.)	Austria, Finland, and Sweden join EMS. Austria (1995) and Finland (1996) join ERM.
1997	**Treaty of Amsterdam** addresses EU citizenship, rights, powers of European Parliament, employment, and common foreign and security policy.	**Stability and Growth Pact** (SGP) is adopted to further enforce the Maastricht budgetary rules.
1998	Eleven countries say they will adopt the euro: France, Germany, Italy, Belgium, Netherlands, Luxembourg, Ireland, Portugal, Spain, Austria, Finland	The **European Central Bank** (ECB) is created. The 11 euro countries freeze their bilateral exchange rates on December 31.
1999		The **euro** is introduced as a unit of account on January 1. Euro notes and coins appear in 2002 and replace national currencies. Greece, Denmark join ERM.
2000		In Denmark voters reject euro adoption in a referendum.
2001	**Treaty of Nice** addresses EU expansion, amends and consolidates Rome and Maastricht treaties, and modifies voting procedures.	Greece becomes the twelfth country to join the Eurozone.
2003		In Sweden voters reject euro adoption in a referendum.
2004	**Fifth enlargement:** Cyprus, the Czech Republic, Estonia, Hungary, Latvia, Lithuania, Malta, Poland, Slovakia, and Slovenia expand EU to 25 countries.	Estonia, Lithuania, and Slovenia join ERM.
2005	Ratification of EU **Constitutional Treaty** postponed indefinitely following rejection by voters in French and Dutch referenda. Controversial EU accession talks start for Turkey (candidate since 1999 and an associate member of EEC/EC/EU since 1963).	Cyprus, Latvia, Malta, and Slovakia join ERM. 12 out of 25 Eurozone members are in violation of the Stability and Growth Pact rules.
2007	**Sixth enlargement:** Bulgaria and Romania expand EU to 27 countries.	Slovenia becomes the 13th country to join the Eurozone.
2008–2011	**Global financial crisis** (2008); peripheral countries (Greece, Ireland, Portugal, Spain) in deep recession and at risk of default (2009–); The troika (ECB/EU/IMF) **bailout programs** begin in crisis countries (2010).	Cyprus and Malta (2008), Slovakia (2009), and Estonia (2011) expand Eurozone to 17 countries; ECB (with the EU) takes extraordinary steps to support banks and governments.
2012–2014	Fiscal contraction in EU and harsh **austerity** measures in periphery. Eurozone enters **double-dip** recession (2012). Unemployment climbs over 12%, youth unemployment over 24%; in 2013, a majority of people **distrust the EU** in 15 of 17 Eurozone countries; Croatia joins EU (2013).	ECB President Draghi promises (2012) to do **"whatever it takes"** to save the euro. Cyprus banking crisis (2013) is fifth troika program; de facto break in monetary union as **capital controls** imposed. Latvia joins the euro in 2014.

dollar exchange rates with monetary autonomy, with the trilemma being resolved through the imposition of capital controls. In the 1970s, this system broke down and floating exchange rates became the norm in the advanced economies. At that time, except for wars and crises, Europe had spent roughly a century under some form of a fixed exchange rate system, and European policy makers worried that exchange rate instability might compromise their goals for economic union. Indeed, as early as 1969, the EC's visionary Werner Report anticipated a path via a transitional fixed exchange rate system toward a single currency within 10 years, although the process would take much longer than that. European leaders did take the first and fateful step down this road when they announced that they would create essentially a new mini–Bretton Woods of their own, the *European Monetary System*, or EMS, which began operation in 1979.

The centerpiece of the EMS was the **Exchange Rate Mechanism (ERM),** a fixed exchange rate regime based on bands. The ERM defined each currency's central parity against a basket of currencies, the so-called *ecu* (European currency unit), the precursor to the euro. In practice, the non-German currencies ended up being pegged to the German mark, the central reserve currency in the system (just as the U.S. dollar had been the central reserve currency in the Bretton Woods system).

The ERM permitted a range of fluctuation on either side of the central value or *parity*: a narrow band of ±2.25% for most currencies (the escudo, lira, peseta, and pound were at times permitted a wider band of ±6%). In 1979 all EC countries except the United Kingdom joined the ERM; later, Spain joined in 1989, the United Kingdom in 1990, and Portugal in 1992. In principle, it was a "fixed but adjustable" system and the central parities could be changed, giving potential encouragement to speculators (also like Bretton Woods).

Crises and Opportunities: EMU and Other Projects, 1991–1999 The EC entered the 1990s with the drive for further integration still going strong. Since 1979 a directly elected European parliament had been at work. In 1987 the Single European Act was passed with the goal of reducing further the barriers between countries through the creation of a "single market" by 1992.

If, within the EC, the political momentum was still strong, it was soon given another push by the end of the Cold War in 1989. The Soviet Union disintegrated and Communist rule in Eastern Europe came to an end, symbolized by the fall of the Berlin Wall. What was the EC going to do in response? The Germans had no doubts—East and West Germany would be reunited quickly, to form Germany again. German reunification was formally completed on October 3, 1990. For the EC as a whole, though, there was the question of how to react to the new states on their eastern flank.

The countries of Eastern Europe were eager to move quickly and decisively away from Communism and autocracy and toward capitalism and democracy, and they saw joining the EC as a natural means to that end. From a political and security standpoint, the EC could hardly say no to the former Communist countries, and so plans for further eastern enlargement had to be made rather quickly. Other countries also waited in the wings. In the early 1990s wars broke out in the Balkans, forcing the EC to confront the big hole in its map between Italy and Greece. Did the former Yugoslav states and Albania belong in "Europe," too? And discussion of the eastern frontier of the EC soon brought to the fore the question of Turkey, a country that has had EC associate member status since 1963 and yet had to wait until 2005 for formal admission talks to begin.

In the face of these political challenges, the EC needed to act with purpose, and the grandest treaty to date, the 1991 Treaty on European Union, or the Maastricht Treaty, was the response, reasserting more than ever the goal of creating an "ever closer union among the peoples of Europe." Adding more federal flavor, the treaty gave the EC a new name, the European Union, or EU, and created a notion of EU citizenship. The treaty also laid down the process for enlargement that would eventually take the EU, via three further enlargements to 15 in 1995, 25 in 2004, and 27 in 2007.

Later political developments in the 1990s built on Maastricht. The 1993 Copenhagen Criteria provided formal conditions for new members wanting admission, such as rule of law, human rights, democracy, and so on. The 1995 Schengen Treaty established a zone for the free movement of people (though Ireland and the United Kingdom opted out). The 1997 Amsterdam Treaty forged ahead in EU foreign and security policy and strengthened the rights of EU citizenship and the powers of the European parliament.

The most ambitious part of the Maastricht Treaty was its economic element: the EU-wide goal of **Economic and Monetary Union (EMU).** The economic union would take the idea of a single market even further—to all goods and services, to capital markets, to labor markets—and would call on the European Commission to ensure that national laws and regulations did not stand in the way. But more than this, monetary union would propose a new currency (soon given the name "euro") for the entire EU. Under the plan for the euro, countries would transition from their pegged rates within the ERM into an *irrevocable peg* with the euro at an appointed date. But this plan almost immediately came into doubt.

The ERM proved to be a typically fragile fixed exchange rate system. As we saw in the last chapter, its worst moment came in 1992. In the **ERM crisis,** several ERM countries suffered exchange rate crises and their pegs broke: the British pound, Italian lira, Portuguese escudo, and Spanish peseta. (Other non-ERM currencies such as the Swedish krona and the Finnish markka pegged to the mark also experienced crises and broken pegs.) Even the currencies that stayed within the ERM had to have their bands widened so much as to make their pegs look more like floats for a while. The whole system was reduced to a near shambles.

As we saw in the past two chapters, the fundamental cause of these crises was a tension between the macroeconomic objectives of the center country, Germany (tight monetary policy to prevent overheating after a large fiscal shock caused by reunification), and the objectives of the pegging countries (whose authorities wanted to use expansionary monetary policy to boost output during a period of global slowdown).

The ghosts of the 1992 crisis still roam today. Many countries rejoined the ERM, some at a new rate or with a wider band: Spain, Italy, and Portugal all regrouped, reentered ERM, and ultimately adopted the euro. But Britain permanently left the ERM and turned its back on the common currency. Sweden, officially committed to the euro, has never shown any interest in joining even the ERM. Today, in both Britain and Sweden, public opposition to the euro remains high. And there is always the fear that another ERM crisis could erupt in new EU members that are pegging to the euro as part of their preparation for joining the common currency.

Still, despite the exchange rate crisis in 1992, the ERM was patched up, and most countries remained committed to the plan to launch the euro. The ERM bands were widened in 1993 to a very slack ±15%, and most were happy to live within those limits and get ready for euro admission.

The Eurozone Is Launched: 1999 and Beyond The euro was launched in 11 countries on January 1, 1999, and administered by a newly created central bank, the **European Central Bank (ECB)**.[9] The ECB took control of monetary policy in all Eurozone countries on that date from each national central bank.[10] The national central banks still have responsibilities. They represent their country on the ECB Council, and still supervise and regulate their own country's financial system. The euro immediately became the unit of account in the Eurozone, and a gradual transition took place as euros began to enter circulation and national currencies were withdrawn.

Table 21-2 shows the history and current state of the EU at the time of this writing in 2014. The table shows the dates of membership in the EU, the ERM, and the Eurozone. Also shown are the fixed exchange rate parities of all ERM and euro members—for the latter, these were frozen upon euro entry and became obsolete once the national currencies were retired.[11]

As of 2014, the Eurozone contains 18 "in" countries. Eleven made the switch to the euro in 1999, Greece entered in 2001, Slovenia in 2007, Cyprus and Malta in 2008, Slovakia in 2009, Estonia in 2011, and Latvia in 2014. There are 10 "out" countries. In the ERM "waiting room," there are 2 countries; one of them, Denmark, has been waiting a long time. There are 8 countries not in ERM, although all except the United Kingdom and Sweden are expected to join the ERM and the euro in the medium term of five to 10 years. Of the "out" countries, only Denmark and the United Kingdom can legally opt out of the euro indefinitely, although Sweden is acting as if it can, too; all of these last three countries have popular opposition to the euro and are not expected to adopt the euro anytime soon.

Summary

History shows that the countries of Europe have some deep tendency to prefer fixed exchange rates to floating rates. Apart from brief crisis episodes in times of turmoil (during wars, the Great Depression, and the early 1970s), most European countries have maintained pegged exchange rates against each other since the 1870s. They have now taken the additional step of adopting a common currency.

There have certainly been some economic changes in Europe that make it more likely to satisfy the OCA criteria now than at anytime in the past. The EU project has pushed forward a process of deep economic integration, with major steps such as EMU and the Schengen Treaty bringing Europe closer to the ideal of a single market. But integration is still very much a work in progress, and the OCA criteria are unlikely to be met soon.

Instead, European history leads us to the conclusion that the common currency fits as part of a political project rather than as a purely economic choice. To consider some of the implications of this conclusion, in the remainder of this chapter we consider some of the operational issues and problems faced by the Eurozone during its first decade of existence.

---

[9] The European Central Bank was established on June 1, 1998. It succeeded a prototype monetary authority, the European Monetary Institute (EMI), which for four and a half years had undertaken much of the groundwork for the euro project.

[10] All EU central banks cooperate as a group in the European System of Central Banks (ESCB). Within that group, the central banks of Eurozone member states (known, confusingly, as the Eurosystem banks) have a much closer relationship with the ECB. Only Eurosystem banks have representation on the ECB's Council.

[11] Since 1999 the original ERM has been replaced with a modified ERM II, with the euro replacing its predecessor, the ecu, as the base currency for pegging. Notwithstanding the Maastricht Treaty, all ERM members now operate in a de jure ±15% band (although Denmark sticks to the old, narrow ±2.25% band).

TABLE 21-2

The EU-28 and the Euro Project in 2014 This table shows the progress of each country through EU membership, ERM membership, and adoption of the euro (as of 2014). The euro parities of Eurozone members and ERM members are also shown, although the former have now abolished their national currencies. Dates for future euro adoption are in most cases uncertain or unknown (shown by a question mark).

		YEAR JOINED				
		EU	ERM	Eurozone	Euro Parity (€1 =)	National Currency (Current or Former)
Countries in the Eurozone	Austria	1995	1995	1999	13.7603	schilling
	Belgium	1959	1979	1999	40.3399	frank
	Cyprus	2004	2005	2008	0.585274	pound
	Estonia	2004	2004	2011	15.6466	kroon
	Finland	1995	1996	1999	5.94573	markka
	France	1959	1979	1999	6.55957	franc
	Germany	1959	1979	1999	1.95583	mark
	Greece	1981	1999	2001	340.75	drachma
	Ireland	1973	1979	1999	0.787564	pound
	Italy	1959	1979	1999	1936.27	lira
	Latvia	2004	2005	2014	0.702804	lats
	Luxembourg	1959	1979	1999	40.3399	franc
	Malta	2004	2005	2008	0.4293	lira
	Netherlands	1959	1979	1999	2.20371	guilder
	Portugal	1986	1992	1999	200.482	escudo
	Slovakia	2004	2005	2009	30.126	koruna
	Slovenia	2004	2004	2007	239.64	tolar
	Spain	1986	1989	1999	166.386	peseta
Countries in the ERM	Denmark*	1973	1999	?	7.46038	krone
	Lithuania	2004	2004	2015?	3.4528	litas
Other EU Countries	Bulgaria	2007	?	?	?	lev
	Croatia	2013	?	?	?	kuna
	Czech Republic	2004	?	?	?	koruna
	Hungary	2004	?	?	?	forint
	Poland	2004	?	?	?	zloty
	Romania	2007	?	?	?	leu
	Sweden*	1995	?	?	?	krona
	United Kingdom*	1973	1990–92	?	?	pound

*The United Kingdom and Denmark can legally opt out of the euro. Sweden is opting out de facto by not joining the ERM. All other countries are expected to join at some point.

3 Eurozone Tensions in Tranquil Times, 1999–2007

From its launch in 1999 until 2007 or so, the Eurozone was considered a success. Compared to what came next, this was a time of economic growth and stability for the Eurozone—a period with no recession and with the ECB untroubled by problems either with its explicit inflation target goal or its broader responsibility to support Eurozone economic and financial stability.

The ECB Tower and euro logo, Frankfurt.

In this section we review this fortunate period, focusing on the way in which the ECB's monetary policy rules were devised, and the broader concerns about fiscal stability. This period will be remembered for a somewhat narrow and limited policy focus and a general complacency concerning some of the ultimately more dangerous macroeconomic trends that we discuss in the section which follows.

The European Central Bank

Suppose some German economists from the 1950s or 1960s, after having traveled forward in time to the present day, pop up next to you on a Frankfurt street corner, and say, "Take me to the central bank." They are surprised when you lead them to the gleaming glass and steel Eurotower at Kaiserstrasse instead of the old Bundesbank building.

It is no coincidence that the European Central Bank is located in Frankfurt. It is a testament to the strong influence of German monetary policy makers and politicians in the design of the euro project, an influence they earned on account of the exemplary performance of the German economy, and especially its monetary policy, from the 1950s to the 1990s. To see how German influence has left its mark on the euro, we first examine how the ECB operates and then try to explain its peculiar goals and governance.

For economists, central banks have a few key features. To sum these up, we may ask: What policy instrument does the bank use? What is it supposed to do (goals) and not do (forbidden activities)? How are decisions on these policies made given the bank's governance structure? To whom is the bank accountable, and, subject to that, how much independence does the bank have? For the ECB, the brief answers are as follows:

- *Instrument and goals.* The instrument used by the ECB is the interest rate at which banks can borrow funds. According to its charter, the ECB's primary objective is to "maintain price stability" in the euro area. Its secondary goal is to "support the general economic policies in the Community with a view to contributing to the achievement of the objectives of the Community." (Many central banks have similar instruments and goals, but the ECB has a relatively strong focus on inflation.)

- *Forbidden activities.* To prevent the use of monetary policy for other goals, the ECB may not directly finance member states' fiscal deficits or provide bailouts to member governments or national public bodies. In addition, the ECB has no mandate to act as a lender of last resort by extending credit to financial institutions in the Eurozone in the event of a banking crisis. (Most central banks are not so constrained, and they typically can act as a lender of last resort.)

- *Governance and decision making.* Monetary policy decisions are made at meetings of the ECB's Governing Council, which consists of the central bank governors of the Eurozone national central banks and six members of the ECB's executive board. In practice, policy decisions are made by consensus rather than by majority voting. Meetings are usually held twice each month.

- *Accountability and independence.* No monetary policy powers are given to any other EU institution. No EU institution has any formal oversight of the ECB, and the ECB does not have to report to any political body, elected or otherwise. The ECB does not release the minutes of its meetings. The ECB has independence not only with respect to its instrument (it sets interest rates) but also with respect to its goal (it gets to define what "price stability" means). (A small but growing number of central banks around the world has achieved some independence, but the ECB has more than most.)

On all four points, the working of the ECB has been subject to strong criticisms.

Criticisms of the ECB There is controversy over the price stability goal. The ECB chooses to define price stability as a Eurozone consumer price inflation rate of less than but "close to" 2% per year over the medium term. This target is vague (the notions of "close to" and "medium term" are not defined). The target is also asymmetrical (there is no lower bound to guard against deflation), a characteristic that became a particular worry as inflation rates fell toward zero during the Great Recession following the global financial crisis of 2008.

There is controversy over having only price stability as a goal. On paper, the ECB technically has a secondary goal of supporting and stabilizing the Eurozone economy. But in practice, the ECB has acted as if it places little weight on economic performance, growth, and unemployment, and where the real economy is in the business cycle. In this area, the ECB's policy preferences are different from, say, those of the U.S. Federal Reserve, which has a mandate from Congress not only to ensure price stability but also to achieve full employment. The ECB also differs from the Bank of England, whose former Governor Mervyn King once famously used the term "inflation nutter" to describe a policy maker with an excessive focus on price stability. The ECB's early obsessive focus on money and prices was thought to reflect a combination of its Germanic heritage and its relative lack of long-term reputation.

There is controversy over the ECB's way of conducting policy to achieve its goal. In addition to the "first pillar," which uses an economic analysis of expected price inflation to guide interest rate decisions, the bank has a "second pillar" in the form of a reference value for money supply growth (4.5% per annum). As we saw in the chapter on exchange rates in the long run, however, a fixed money growth rate can be consistent with an inflation target only by chance. For example, in the quantity theory model, which assumes a stable level of nominal interest rates in the long run, inflation equals the money growth rate minus the growth rate of real output. So the ECB's twin pillars will make sense only if real output just happens to grow at less than 2.5% per year, for only then will inflation be, at most, $4.5 - 2.5 = 2$% per year. Perhaps aware of the inconsistency of using two nominal anchors, the ECB has given the impression that most of the time it ignores the second pillar; nonetheless, concern about money supply growth is occasionally expressed.

There is controversy over the strict interpretation of the "forbidden activities" rules. What happens in the event of a large banking crisis in the Eurozone? When banking crises hit other nations, many central banks would choose to extend credit to specific troubled banks or to relax lending standards to the banking sector as a whole, and they could print money to do so. In the Eurozone, officially the ECB can print the money but it cannot implement either type of additional lending; the national central banks of countries in the Eurozone can do the lending but can't print the money. National central banks can devise limited, local credit facilities or arrange private consortia to manage a small crisis, or they can hope for fiscal help from their national treasuries. Big crises could therefore prove more difficult to prevent or contain. (In a discussion that appears later in the chapter, we look at how the ECB reacted during and after the Global Financial Crisis of 2008 and eased these rules somewhat.)

There is controversy over the decision-making process and lack of transparency. Votes are not formally required, and no votes of any kind are reported. Consensus decisions are preferred but these may favor the status quo, causing policy to lag when it ought to move. Minutes are recorded but can be kept secret for 30 years and their level of detail is not known. Some parts of meetings are private without any record being kept at all. Insistence on having all central bank governors on the Council leads to a very large body where consensus may be more difficult to achieve. This design will become even more cumbersome as more countries join the euro, but the structure of the Council is set in the Maastricht Treaty and would be impossible to change without revising the treaty.

There is controversy over the ECB's lack of accountability. Because so much of its operation is secret and it answers to no political masters, some fear that people in the Eurozone will conclude that the ECB lacks legitimacy. Although the EU is a collection of democratic states, many of its decisions are made in places that are far from the people in these states. Many EU bodies suffer a perceived "democratic deficit," including the work of the unelected Commission and the treaties pursued at the intragovernmental level with no popular ratification and little consultation. The ECB can appear to be even further removed at a supra-governmental level. There is nothing akin to the U.S. requirement that the Federal Reserve chairman regularly answer questions from Congress. Rather, the ECB has a more informal dialogue and consultations with the Council, Commission, and Parliament. In response, the finance ministers of the Eurozone have ganged up to form the *Eurogroup*, which meets and opines about what is happening in the Eurozone and what the ECB is (or should be) doing. Occasionally, national heads of governments weigh in to attack the ECB's policy choices or to defend them. Along with the EU's commissioner for economic and monetary affairs, heads of government can make pronouncements and lobby, but they can do little more unless a treaty revision places the ECB under more scrutiny.

The German Model Some of these criticisms are valid and undisputed, but others are fiercely contested. Supporters of the ECB say that strong independence and freedom from political interference are exactly what is needed in a young institution that is struggling to achieve credibility and that the dominant problem in the Eurozone in the recent past has been inflation not deflation. For many of these supporters, the ECB is set up the right way—almost a copy of the Bundesbank, with a strong focus on low inflation to the exclusion of other criteria and a complete separation of monetary policy from politics. Here, German preferences and German economic performance had been very different from those for the rest of the Eurozone, yet they prevailed. How can this be understood?

German preferences for a low-inflation environment have been extremely strong ever since the costly and chaotic interwar hyperinflation (discussed in the chapter on exchange rates in the long run). It was clear that the hyperinflation had been driven by reckless fiscal policy, which had led politicians to take over monetary policy and run the printing presses. After that fiasco, strong anti-inflation preferences, translated from the people via the political process, were reflected in the conduct of monetary policy by the Bundesbank from 1958 until the arrival of the euro in 1999. To ensure that the Bundesbank could deliver a firm nominal anchor, it was carefully insulated from political interference.

Today, as we learned when studying exchange rates in the long run, a popular recipe for sound monetary policy is a combination of central bank independence and an inflation target. Sometimes, the inflation target is set by the government, the so-called *New Zealand model*. But the so-called *German model* went further and faster: the Bundesbank was not only the first central bank to be granted full independence, it was also given both *instrument independence* (freedom to use interest rate policy in the short run) and *goal independence* (the power to decide what the inflation target should be in the long run). This became the model for the ECB, when Germany set most of the conditions for entering a monetary union with other countries where the traditions of central bank independence were weaker or nonexistent.

Monetary Union with Inflation Bias We can see where Germany's preferences came from. But how did it get its way? A deep problem in modern macroeconomics concerns the *time inconsistency* of policies.[12] According to this view, all countries have a problem with inflation bias under discretionary monetary policy. Policy makers would like to commit to low inflation, but without a credible commitment to low inflation, a politically controlled central bank has the temptation to use "surprise" monetary policy expansions to boost output. Eventually, this bias will be anticipated, built into inflation expectations, and hence, in the long run, real outcomes—such as output and unemployment—will be the same whatever the extent of the inflation bias. Long-run money neutrality means that printing money can't make an economy more productive or create jobs.

The inflation bias problem can be solved if we can separate the central bank from politics and install a "conservative central banker" who cares about inflation and nothing else. This separation was strong in Germany, but not elsewhere. Hence, a historically low-inflation country (e.g., Germany) might be worried that a monetary union with a high-inflation country (e.g., Italy) would lead to a monetary union with on average a tendency for middling levels of inflation—that is, looser monetary policies on average for Germany and tighter on average for Italy. In the long run, Germany and Italy would still get the same real outcomes (though in the short run, Germany might have a monetary-led boom and Italy a recession). But, while Italy might gain in the long run from lower inflation, Germany would lose from the shift to a high-inflation environment. Germany would need assurances that this would not happen, and because Germany was such a large and pivotal country in the EU, a Eurozone without Germany was unimaginable (based on simple OCA logic or on political logic). So Germany had a lot of bargaining power.

Essentially, the bargaining over the design of the ECB and the Eurozone boiled down to this: other countries were content to accept that in the long run their real outcomes would not be any different even if they switched to a monetary policy run by the ECB under the German model, and thus had to settle for less political manipulation of monetary policy.

Or so they said at the time. But how could one be sure that these countries did in fact mean what they said? One could take countries' word for it—trust them. Or one

---

[12] Finn E. Kydland and Edward C. Prescott, 1977, "Rules Rather Than Discretion: The Inconsistency of Optimal Plans," *Journal of Political Economy*, 87, 473–492; Guillermo Calvo, 1978, "On the Time Consistency of Optimal Policy in a Monetary Economy," *Econometrica*, 46, 1411–1428; Robert J. Barro and David B. Gordon, 1983, "Rules, Discretion and Reputation in a Model of Monetary Policy," *Journal of Monetary Economics*, 12, 101–121.

could make them prove it—test them. In a world of inflation bias, trust in monetary authorities is weak, so the Maastricht Treaty established some tests—that is, some rules for admission.

The Rules of the Club

The Maastricht Treaty established five rules for admission to the euro zone, as shown in Table 21-3. All five of these **convergence criteria** need to be satisfied for entry. Two of the five rules also serve as ongoing requirements for membership. The rules can be divided into two parts: three rules requiring convergence in nominal measures closely related to inflation and two rules requiring fiscal discipline to clamp down on the deeper determinants of inflation.

Nominal Convergence In the chapters on short- and long-run exchange rates, we explored some of the central implications of a fixed exchange rate, implications that also apply when two countries adopt a common currency (i.e., a fixed exchange rate of 1). Let's consider three implications:

- Under a peg, the exchange rate must be fixed or not vary beyond tight limits.
- Purchasing power parity (PPP) then implies that the two countries' inflation rates must be very close.
- Uncovered interest parity (UIP) then implies that the two countries' long-term nominal interest rates must be very close.

In fact, we may recall that the Fisher effect says that the inflation differential must equal the nominal interest rate differential—so if one is small, the other has to be small, too.

These three conditions all relate to the nominal anchoring provided by a peg, and they roughly correspond to the first three Maastricht criteria in Table 21-3.

TABLE 21-3

Rules of Euro Membership The Maastricht Treaty of 1991 established five conditions that aspiring members of the Eurozone must satisfy prior to entry. The last two fiscal rules are also supposed to be obeyed by members even after entry.

Rule (*prior to entry only)	Criterion
Exchange rate*	Two consecutive years in ERM band with no devaluation (no change in central parity).
Inflation rate*	No more than 1.5 percentage points above the level in the three member states with the lowest inflation in the previous year.
Long-term nominal interest rate*	No more than 2 percentage points above the level in the three member states with the lowest inflation in the previous year.
Government deficit	No more than 3% of GDP in previous financial year.[1]
Government debt	No more than 60% of GDP in previous financial year.[2]

Notes:
The ERM bands in effect at the time of the Maastricht Treaty were narrow (±2.25% or ±6%); since 1993 they have been wide (±15%). The first rule is now applied using the wide bands. Escape clauses are included in the last two fiscal rules, as follows:
[1] Or "the ratio must have declined substantially and continuously and reached a level close to 3% or, alternatively, must remain close to 3% while representing only an exceptional and temporary excess."
[2] Or "the ratio must have sufficiently diminished and must be approaching the reference value at a satisfactory pace."

The rules say that a country must stay in its ERM band (with no realignment) for two years to satisfy the peg rule.[13] It must have an inflation rate "close to" that of the three lowest-inflation countries in the zone to satisfy the inflation rule. And it must have a long-term interest rate "close to" that in the three low-inflation countries.[14] All three tests must be met for a country to satisfy the admission criteria.

What is the economic sense for these rules? They appear, in some ways, superfluous because if a country credibly pegged to (or has adopted) the euro, theory says that these conditions would have to be satisfied in the long run anyway. For that reason they are also difficult to criticize—except to say that, if the rules are going to be met anyway, why not "just do it" and let countries join the euro without such conditions? The answer relates to our earlier discussion about inflation bias. If two countries with different inflation rates adopt a common currency, their inflation rates must converge—but to what level, high or low?

The way the rules were written forces countries to converge on the lowest inflation rates in the zone. We have argued that this outcome is needed for low-inflation countries to sign up, although it will require possibly painful policy change in the high-inflation countries. The Maastricht criteria ensure that high-inflation countries go through this pain and attain credibility by demonstrating their commitment to low inflation before they are allowed in. This process supposedly prevents governments with a preference for high inflation from entering the Eurozone and then trying to persuade the ECB to go soft on inflation. These three rules can thus be seen as addressing the credibility problem in a world of inflation bias. All current euro members successfully satisfied these rules to gain membership, and the end result was marked inflation convergence as shown in Figure 21-7. Current and future ERM members are required to go through the same test.

Fiscal Discipline The Maastricht Treaty wasn't just tough on inflation, it was tough on the causes of inflation, and it saw the fundamental and deep causes of inflation as being not monetary, but fiscal. The other two Maastricht rules are openly aimed at constraining fiscal policy. They are applied not just as a condition for admission but also to all member states once they are in. The rules say that government debts and deficits cannot be above certain reference levels (although the treaty allows some exceptions). These levels were chosen somewhat arbitrarily: a deficit level of 3% of GDP and a debt level of 60% of GDP. However arbitrary these reference levels are, there still exist economic rationales for having some kinds of fiscal rules in a monetary union in which the member states maintain fiscal sovereignty.

Why might inflation ultimately be a fiscal problem? Consider two countries negotiating the treaty, one with low debt levels (e.g., Germany) and one with high debt levels

---

[13] The two-year requirement for the ERM means a country can't cheat by stabilizing its currency at the last minute, possibly in an opportunistic way to get in at a favorable (depreciated) rate that boosts demand for the country's output. Still, as currently interpreted, the ERM rule means that a currency only has to stay within the wide (post-1993) ±15% ERM bands, so the constraint is not all that tight. Also, following the exchange rate crises of 1992 in the United Kingdom and Sweden that gave the ERM a bad name, the two-year ERM membership rule might be waived if either of these two countries wishes to adopt the euro.
[14] The interest rate rule relates to the long-term interest rate for government borrowing, not the short-term rate that is central to UIP. Over the long run, the two move together and on average are generally separated by a positive *term premium*. Under a peg, then, countries will share identical *long-term* interest rates if and only if (1) there is no risk premium difference between them and (2) there is no term premium difference either. In practice, risk premiums and term premiums are higher for riskier borrowers, so in some ways this rule is also related to fiscal discipline (discussed in the next section).

FIGURE 21-7

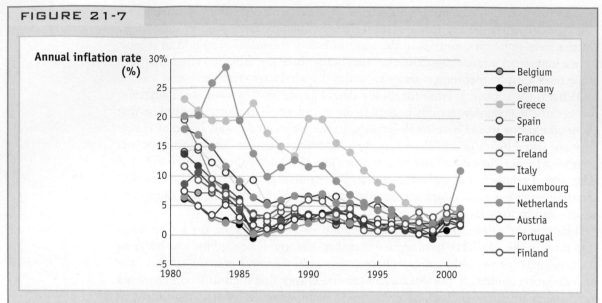

Inflation Convergence To meet the Maastricht Treaty's convergence criteria, the first 12 members of the Eurozone had to reduce their inflation level below a moving target. This target was equal to average inflation in the three lowest-inflation countries in the bloc plus 1.5 percentage points. This process ensured that the Eurozone began with a low inflation rate. The countries currently in the ERM must pass the same test before they can adopt the euro.

Source: European Economy, Statistical Annex, *Autumn 2005.*

(e.g., Italy). Germany has several possible fears in this case. One is that if Italy has high nominal debt (measured in lira, but soon to be measured in euros), Italy will lobby for high inflation once in the union (because inflation destroys the real value of the government's debt). Another fear is that Italy has a higher default risk, which might result in political pressure for the ECB to break its own rules and bail out Italy in a crisis, which the ECB can do only by printing euros and, again, generating more inflation.

The main arguments for the fiscal rules are that any deal to form a currency union will require fiscally weak countries to tighten their belts and meet criteria set by fiscally strong countries in order to further ensure against inflation.

Criticism of the Convergence Criteria Because these rules constitute the main gatekeeping mechanism for the Eurozone, they have been carefully scrutinized and have generated much controversy.

First, these rules involve asymmetric adjustments that take a long time. In the 1980s and 1990s, they mostly involved German preferences on inflation and fiscal policy being imposed at great cost on other countries. Germany had lower inflation and larger surpluses than most countries, and the criteria were set close to the German levels, not surprisingly. To converge on these levels, tighter fiscal and monetary policies had to be adopted in countries like France, Italy, Portugal, and Spain while they tried to maintain the peg (to obey rule 1: staying in their ERM bands). As we saw in the chapter on output, exchange rates, and macroeconomic policy, fiscal contractions are even more contractionary under a peg than under a float. Such policies are politically costly, and hence the peg may not be fully credible. As we saw in the chapter on crises, foreign exchange traders often have doubts about the resolve of the authorities to stick with contractionary policies, and these doubts can increase the risk of self-fulfilling exchange rate crises, as happened in 1992. The same costs and risks now weigh on current Eurozone applicants seeking to pass these tests.

Second, the fiscal rules are seen as inflexible and arbitrary. The numerical targets have little justification: Why 3% for the deficit and not 4%? Why 60% and not 70% for the debt level? As for flexibility, the rules in particular pay no attention to the stage of the business cycle in a particular applicant country. A country in a recession may have a very large deficit even if on average the country has a government budget that is fairly balanced across the whole business cycle. In other words, the well-established arguments for the prudent use of countercyclical fiscal policy (including even nondiscretionary automatic stabilizers) are totally ignored by the Maastricht criteria. This is an ongoing problem, as we shall see in a moment.

Third, whatever good might result from the painful convergence process, it might be only fleeting. For example, the Greek or French governments of the 1990s may have subjected themselves to budgetary discipline and monetary conservatism. Have their preferences really changed or did they just go along with the rules (or pretend to) merely as a way to get in? The same question applies to current Eurozone applicants. As Figure 21-8 shows, once the original dozen members of the Eurozone were in the club, their commitment to fiscal discipline (as reflected in their fiscal deficits) started to weaken in the subsequent decade, in some cases dramatically so.

The problems just noted do not disappear once countries are in the Eurozone. Countries continue to have their own fiscal policies as members of the Eurozone, and they all gain a share of influence on ECB policy through the governance structure of the central bank. Countries' incentives are different once the carrot of EMU membership has been eaten.

FIGURE 21-8

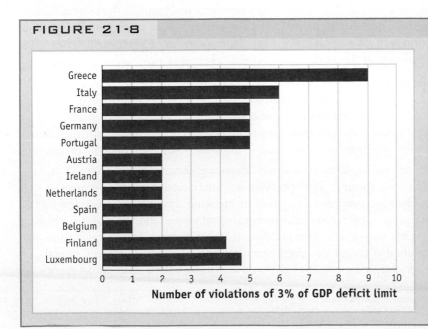

Breaking of Fiscal Rules The fiscal convergence criteria laid down by the Maastricht Treaty and affirmed by the Stability and Growth Pact have been widely ignored. This figure shows the number of times that each of the original 12 members of the Eurozone violated the 3% of GDP government deficit limit from accession until 2010. After the global financial crisis and double-dip recession, the frequency of these violations increased even further.

Source: Martin Wolf, "Implications of the Crisis for Stability and Growth in the Eurozone," World Bank Workshop on Inclusive Growth in Advanced Countries, New York University, October 8, 2010.

Sticking to the Rules

If "in" countries desire more monetary and fiscal flexibility than the rules allow, and being "in" means they no longer risk the punishment of being excluded from the Eurozone, then a skeptic would have to expect more severe budgetary problems and more lobbying for loose monetary policy to appear once countries had entered the Eurozone.

On this point, as we see, the skeptics were to some extent proved right, but the problems they identified were not entirely ignored in the Eurozone's design. On the monetary side, success (low and stable Eurozone inflation) would rest on the design of the ECB as an institution that could withstand political pressure and act with independence to deliver low inflation while ignoring pleas from member governments. In that respect, we have already noted the formidable efforts to make the ECB as independent as possible. On the fiscal side, however, success (in the shape of adherence to the budgetary rules) would rest on the mechanisms established to enforce the Maastricht fiscal criteria. This did not turn out quite so well.

The Stability and Growth Pact Within a few years of the Maastricht Treaty, the EU suspected that greater powers of monitoring and enforcement would be needed. Thus, in 1997 at Amsterdam, the EU adopted the **Stability and Growth Pact (SGP),** which the EU website has described as "the concrete EU answer to concerns on the continuation of budgetary discipline in Economic and Monetary Union." In the end, this provided no answer whatsoever and even before the ink was dry, naysayers were unkind enough to term it the "stupidity pact."

Throwing another acronym into the mix, the SGP was aimed at enforcing the 3% deficit rule and proposed the following to keep states in line: a "budgetary surveillance" process that would check on what member states were doing; a requirement to submit economic data and policy statements as part of a periodic review of "stability and convergence programs"; an "early warning mechanism" to detect any "slippage"; a "political commitment" that "ensures that effective peer pressure is exerted on a Member State failing to live up to its commitments"; and an "excessive deficits procedure" with "dissuasive elements" in the event of failure to require "immediate corrective action and, if necessary, allow for the imposition of sanctions."[15]

The shortcomings of the SGP, which became clear over time, were as follows:

- Surveillance failed because member states concealed the truth about their fiscal problems. Some hired private-sector accounting firms to make their deficits look smaller via accounting tricks (a suspiciously common deficit figure was 2.9%). In the case of Greece, the government simply falsified deficit figures for the purpose of gaining admission to the euro in 2001 and owned up once it was in.

- Punishment was weak, so even when "excessive deficits" were detected, not much was done about it. Peer pressure was ineffective, perhaps because so many of the governments were guilty of breaking the pact that very few had a leg to stand on. Corrective action was rare and states "did their best," which was often not very much. Formal SGP disciplining processes often started but never resulted in actual sanctions because heads of government in Council proved very forgiving of each other and unwilling to dispense punishments.

---

[15] European Commission, Directorate General for Economic and Financial Affairs, "The Stability and Growth Pact." Published online. For a copy of this document, go to http://www.eubusiness.com/Finance/eu-stability-growth-pact/.

- Deficit limits rule out the use of active stabilization policy, but they also shut down the "automatic stabilizer" functions of fiscal policy. Recessions automatically lower government revenues and raise spending, and the resulting deficits help boost aggregate demand and offset the recession. This makes deficit limits tough to swallow, even if monetary policy autonomy is kept as a stabilization tool. In a monetary union, where states have also relinquished monetary policy to the ECB, the pain of hard fiscal rules is likely to be intolerable.

- Once countries joined the euro, the main "carrot" enticing them to follow the SGP's budget rules (or to pretend to follow them) disappeared. Hence, surveillance, punishment, and commitment all quite predictably weakened once the euro was up and running.

These failures of the SGP came to light only gradually, but by 2003 the pact was in ruins, once it became clear that France and (ironically) Germany would be in breach of the pact and that no serious action would be taken against them. As we see next, fiscal problems in the Eurozone have only gotten worse, although whether the principles of the SGP can, or should, be reinstated is the subject of ongoing disagreement.

4 The Eurozone in Crisis, 2008–2013

For almost 10 years, Eurozone policy making focused on two main macroeconomic goals: the ECB's monetary policy credibility and inflation target, seen as a broad success given low and stable inflation outcomes; and the Eurozone governments' fiscal responsibility, seen as a failure given the general disregard for the SGP rules. However, policy makers (like their counterparts all over the world) failed to spot key macroeconomic and financial developments that were to plunge the Eurozone into crisis in 2008 and beyond.

Boom and Bust: Causes and Consequences of an Asymmetrical Crisis With a fanatical devotion to inflation targeting, the ECB (and its constituent central banks) paid insufficient attention to what was historically a primary responsibility of central banks, namely, financial stability. Within some parts of the Eurozone (as elsewhere) borrowers in the private sector were engaged in a credit-fueled boom. In other parts of the Eurozone, savers and banks funneled ever more loans toward those borrowers. The creditors were core Northern European countries like Germany and the Netherlands; the debtors were fast-growing *peripheral* nations such as Greece, Ireland, Portugal, and Spain (so called because they are located geographically on the periphery of Europe).

In Greece, much of the borrowing was by a fiscally irresponsible government that was later found to be falsifying its accounts. In the other peripheral nations, however, the flow of loans funded rapid investment and consumption surges, including a residential construction boom that in places (e.g., Dublin and Barcelona) rivaled the property bubble in parts of the United States. In Ireland and Spain, even as this boom took place, the governments had maintained a fiscal position close to balance, or even surplus; the asymmetric boom helped them at that time. The trouble was to come when the boom gave way to a severe asymmetric bust.

Growth slowed sharply when the global boom turned to a bust that dragged Europe down with it. Much of the construction and overconsumption in the peripheral economies turned out to be unjustified and unsustainable. Along the way, however, the boom had bid up the prices of assets (notably houses) and of many nontraded services (and thus wages), and had left households in the peripheral nations saddled with high debts and uncompetitive, high wage levels that could not be sustained once the artificially high demand of the boom years was exhausted. These events were bad enough, but other factors made things worse.

A vicious spiral began in the peripherals. Construction and nontraded sectors started to collapse, which lowered demand. House prices fell, as did the value of firms. Wealth collapsed, lowering demand further. Output fell in the short run, as did tax revenues. Households cut spending further, and the governments also tightened their belts. With everyone suffering lower incomes and wealth, and the economy contracting, banks tightened lending, which hurt demand still more. As the spiral continued, banks found that their loans were often turning bad, and that many debts would be repaid only partially if at all. Because much of the periphery's lending came from banks connected to the Northern European core, these developments triggered tighter credit everywhere in the Eurozone as banks turned cautious. Lending growth for the whole Eurozone was virtually frozen for five years.

The Policymaking Context The Eurozone faced hard choices after the crisis hit in 2008, but the policy measures taken were more timid and quickly reversed, as compared with actions in other countries.

Why? The choices made can potentially be explained by considering the unique features of the European monetary union. We highlight six points.

- **Limited Lender of Last Resort** The Eurozone is a monetary union, and has a common central bank, but the ECB is highly inflation averse, is restricted from direct government finance, and is required not to engage in lender of last resort actions to banks lacking good collateral. It is therefore unwilling to intervene with emergency liquidity in weak local banks, except with strict guarantees from the local sovereign government; and it has been generally unwilling (with some exceptions) to intervene to ensure weak sovereigns remain funded at sustainable interest rates.

- **No Fiscal Union** The Eurozone lacks a political-fiscal union, and has no fiscal policy tools, because there is no central budget that can be used to engage in cross-country stabilization of shocks. This is in large part due to the absence of a central European government (executive power) standing above the sovereigns (the member states). In contrast, in the United States, with a strong center, substantial federal-level automatic transfers between states act as a significant buffer. In fact, the Eurozone has the reverse problem: when the national sovereigns lose credit market access on reasonable terms, they must beg for assistance from the EU, ECB, and the International Monetary Fund (IMF). As a condition for granting assistance, these organizations have imposed harsh terms that require the countries to undertake fiscal contractions during their slumps, amplifying their business cycle. Overall, even for countries not in a rescue program, the EU authorities have sought even stricter fiscal rules and monitoring since the crisis, adding new stringencies for all countries on top of the Maastricht and SGP protocols.

■ **No Banking Union** The Eurozone also lacks even the minimal political-fiscal cooperation to create a banking union, meaning that responsibility for supervising banks, and resolving or rescuing them when they are insolvent, rests with national sovereigns. In the United States, in contrast, the Federal Deposit Insurance Corporation and other institutions underpin a true federal-level banking union with a common pool of fiscal and monetary resources. Critically, the insurance of an individual U.S. state's banking system does not depend at all on the fiscal position of the state itself.

■ **Sovereign-Bank Doom Loop** Because there isn't a banking union or a political-fiscal union, a Eurozone country's national banks tend to hold the local national sovereign's debt; but, in turn, these sovereigns can end up bearing large fiscal costs to repair banking systems and protect depositors from losing their money. The banks and the sovereign can then enter into a so-called "doom loop": weak banks' losses can damage the sovereign's creditworthiness just when it may need funds to resolve a crisis; simultaneously, a weak sovereign's debt can decline in value, damaging the balance sheets of local banks where such local debt is predominantly held. In contrast, there is no local U.S. doom loop: a California bank does not hold California debt, and a California bank failure would not burden the state itself.

■ **Labor Immobility** Because the Eurozone is especially weak on labor mobility (one of the OCA criteria), a local economic slump (say, in Spain) is likely to persist for longer because unemployed workers cannot migrate easily to another country where there are better opportunities. After the crisis, local long-term unemployment rates (especially among the youth) rose to very high levels in some countries, despite stronger economic conditions in the core Eurozone countries. The United States saw more labor migration between asymmetrically affected areas in its slump.

■ **Exit Risk** We know that after barely more than a decade, the credibility of the Eurozone as permanent, with no possibility of exit, is not 100% certain. Events have shown that the risk of a country's exit can put financial pressure on that country. If investors suspect that a country will exit the Eurozone, they will want to pull their money out of the country's banks and sell its debt, to avoid potential losses. The result is capital flight to safe havens, and higher risk premiums on local interest rates. These reflect the nonzero "redenomination risk" of local assets out of euro and into a new, and much depreciated, local currency plus the risk of losses of depositors via bank restructuring. This dynamic was much in evidence in Cyprus in 2013, for example.

Many of the events in the timeline of 2008–13 can be better understood if we keep these six major points in mind. We now take a closer look at this period, with some key macroeconomic data present for reference in Figure 21-9.

Timeline of Events The first big problem occurred in April 2010 when Greece requested help as its country risk premium spiked and it could no longer borrow at sustainable rates, an action that roiled global financial markets. The EU/ECB/IMF troika jointly devised a plan to stave off the disaster of an uncontrolled default–cum–banking crisis. Together, the troika would provide €110 billion of loans that would give Greece two to three years of guaranteed funding. This help would only be provided under strict conditions that the Greek government radically cut its spending. Financial market

FIGURE 21-9

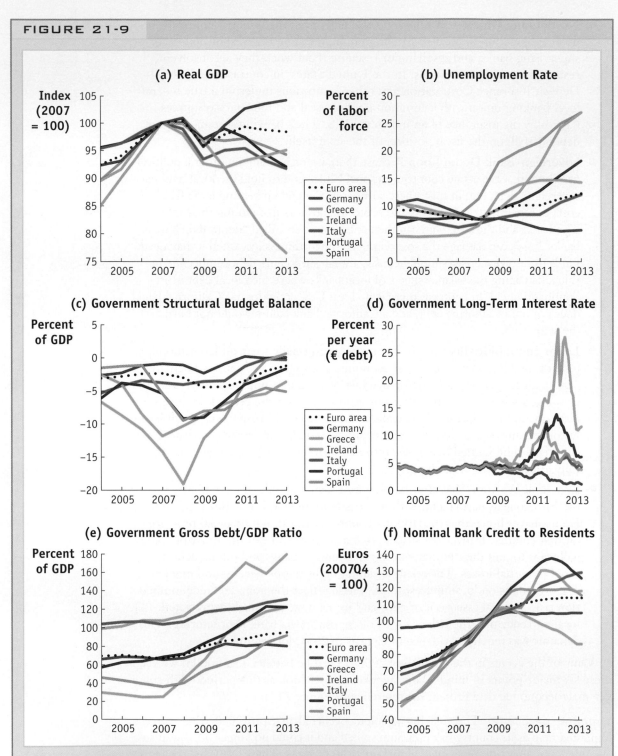

Key Macroeconomic Data for the Eurozone Crisis These six charts cover the Eurozone in the period 2004 to 2013 and show the evolution of output, unemployment, government deficits, interest rates and public debt, and the supply of credit by banks. The divergent fortunes of Germany and the five peripheral countries are clearly visible.

Sources: IMF, Eurostat, OECD.

turmoil continued, however, and the troika announced further measures for Greece on May 7, 2010.

To help other troubled nations (Ireland, Spain, Portugal, and Italy were all at risk), all EU countries established a fund to provide loans of up to €440 billion. This fund, now known as the *European Stability Mechanism* (ESM), was founded on the good credit of the other EU members and was backed by a once unimaginable bond-buying commitment from the ECB. In addition, funds of up to €60 billion from the EU budget provided a theoretical credit line of up to €500 billion. A further sum of €250 billion was pledged by the IMF. The troika believed that these funds would be large enough to cope with any financing problems that might arise in Ireland and Portugal. If financing problems had occurred in larger countries like Spain (or, even worse, Italy), the troika would have had to come up with more resources.

The announcement of these measures kept the panic under control only for a time. The risk premiums of the peripherals spiked again in November 2010, after EU leaders said they wanted to possibly impose losses on bondholders in any future rescues. When the EU leaders made this announcement, financial markets realized that they could suffer losses not only on their Greek bonds but on their bonds issued by other weak countries on the periphery. Even though the EU officials backtracked, the financial markets continued to worry and the borrowing costs for all peripherals started to climb. As their borrowing costs rose, they too lined up to seek official bail-out programs from the troika, often under some duress.

The troika thought their official funding would help keep the periphery countries governments afloat until they could get back on their feet again. But Greece's debt was so high that it eventually had to impose a partial default in February 2012. During May and June of 2012, many thought that Greece was on the verge of exiting the Eurozone and there was further turmoil in financial and political circles. Greece remained in the Eurozone, but by 2013 the Greek unemployment rate was 27%; among youths, the unemployment rate was 58%.

By mid-November 2010, Ireland approached the troika to ask for an ESM program, which further shook confidence in the peripherals and in the euro itself. The Irish had a self-made problem. In 2008–09 Ireland guaranteed the safety of deposits in their private banks to prevent bank runs by bank debt holders that would cause even more economic pain. This method of preventing bank failures did not solve the problem of the private losses, it just transferred the financial sector's massive losses to the government. By late 2010, the Irish government had to admit a loss of about 20% of GDP just to cover the banks' bad debts. The overall fiscal deficit for Ireland that year was an unheard-of 32% of GDP. Financial markets got scared, and the Irish government's interest rate climbed astronomically. They too were pushed into a program of harsh austerity involving public sector cuts and higher taxes. Unemployment rose from 4% in 2006 to 15% by 2012, and among youths it rose to 30%. Ireland was not able to borrow affordably in financial markets again until July 2012, but the economy remained weak.

Spain also faced a banking crisis, and although the Spanish government did not intervene as quickly or as generously as the Irish government, the losses could not be hidden forever, and the country's economy suffered. Banking systems in countries like Spain and Ireland have become so impaired that they do not lend much, and when they do, they do not pass on the ECB's low interest rates to local borrowers: the monetary policy transmission mechanism is broken as low ECB interest rates are not passed through to local firms and consumers. The banks may try to survive as "zombie banks," but they do not help the real economy very much. Similar banking stresses occurred in Portugal and Italy, and by 2013 the interest rates at which Spanish, Portuguese, and Italian firms could borrow from their countries' banks were 2 to 3 percentage points higher than the rates available to German or Austrian firms, causing even greater asymmetry.

Even though Portugal and Spain were not initially as damaged as Greece and Ireland, they shared in the collapse of economic growth in the Eurozone periphery. Spain's banking losses were continually revealed to be larger than previously admitted, and Portugal's growth rate—already bad before the crisis—got even worse. The continuing deterioration in fiscal conditions caused their lending rates to rise, so that in 2011 and 2012 Portugal and Spain, respectively, also reluctantly entered into bailout programs. By 2013 Spanish unemployment reached 27%, and 56% among youths; in Portugal the rates reached 11%, and 38%, respectively.

As of mid-2013, the latest country to enter an official bailout program was Cyprus, a small but telling example of how the Eurozone might cope with further distress. Cyprus had its own boom and bust, a housing bubble of sorts that had been fueled by an influx of foreign wealth (much of it Russian) seeking a safe, offshore tax haven. Cyprus's economy stalled in 2011 after its government credit rating had been downgraded. By 2012, banking problems in Cyprus were apparent: Cypriot banks still held significant Greek debt, and were badly hit when the troika decided to allow a Greek default. As early as July 2012 Cyprus began months of confusing and contentious negotiations with the troika. As rumors emerged that bank depositors might suffer losses, a slow bank run developed in late 2012 and early 2013.

As it turns out, the rumors were well founded. On an extraordinary weekend in March 2013 the troika and the Cyprus government talked long into the night and finally made a deal that would impose significant "taxes" on all bank deposits, including those below the EU's legally guaranteed level of €100,000. All hell broke loose: angry protests began, people tried to get their money out of the banks and out of the country, parliament rejected the deal, and it took another weekend to sort out a different compromise that protected those with less than €100,000 in the bank, but imposed losses on everyone else. Along the way, the government maneuvered around other laws and treaties: it imposed capital controls on banks and at the border, and also shunted aside the priority of depositors and creditors at Laiki Bank and Bank of Cyprus (so that the ECB would be made a preferred creditor ex post—its loans to Laiki, secured with specific collateral, would be transferred whole, without losses, and the losses would be forced onto other secured and unsecured debts of the bank's large creditors, and, remarkably, those of the impaired-yet-acquiring Bank of Cyprus, too). Even though the entire operation was widely judged a political and economic disaster, the President of the Eurogroup (the organization of Eurozone finance ministers) described the outcome as a "template" for handling future crises, a view echoed by ECB President Mario Draghi some days later.

Who Bears the Costs? The view that countries should bear all of the pain for their crises is a consequence of the weak level of cooperation and collective burden-sharing in the Eurozone project. As we have noted, this is very different from the U.S. monetary union where political, fiscal, and banking union structures work together to help spread risks and absorb shocks. The core countries of the Eurozone have made little effort to provide assistance to the peripherals, beyond lending them money which will supposedly have to be paid back one day. The belief has been that every country is responsible for its own fiscal position.

But there is some inconsistency in the Eurozone's approach. Note that in principle the governments (and the banks) of the peripherals could have been allowed to default, and resume operation in a more creditworthy state. Instead, the EU decided on a "moral hazard" or "bailout" approach of trying to ensure that no bank or government creditors were ever hurt. This controversial step had several motivations, many of them understandable, including the desire to protect core EU banks, to protect the collateral of the ECB, to avoid further contagion and panic in financial markets, and perhaps to defend the reputation of the euro as a serious global currency. These decisions cast aside the prior notion that every Eurozone country was responsible unto itself and the idea that the ECB would not go along in any bailouts. Politically, this course of action would bring about much greater centralization of power, with the European and/or IMF authorities dictating more and more terms on which periphery countries in official bailout programs could run their economic policies.

Since the EU leadership desperately wanted to prevent any country from defaulting, the ECB (like central banks in centuries past) became the only Eurozone institution willing and able to lend a hand. The ECB continued to lend to the private banks against the ever-weaker collateral of the peripheral governments' bonds. Prior to the crisis, the ECB had supposedly said it would refuse to lend against such government bonds when their ratings fell, but when push came to shove, the ECB relaxed its lending criteria again and again, because to do otherwise would have triggered a funding crisis for both the banks and their respective governments. By 2012, new ECB President Mario Draghi was promising to do "whatever it takes" to save the euro, but it isn't clear what he meant by that statement. We still do not know, for example, the exact scope and terms of the Outright Monetary Transactions program, a proposed ECB bond-buying program. But some Eurozone officials, such as German Bundesbank head Jens Weidmann, are not eager for the ECB to act as a backstop in government bond markets. He and others fear that undertaking such programs will lead to fiscal dominance, money printing, and inflationary budget financing.

What Next? To the skeptical, the Eurozone/ECB approach has been a giant "extend and pretend" refinancing scheme to postpone tough choices at the nexus of monetary, fiscal, and banking policies. Given the dismal growth path that is expected to continue into the future, the approach will likely fail unless it makes a plan to write down or restructure the underlying losses of banks and governments in the periphery, and even some in the core. The Eurozone needs to have plans and policies in place that will allow it to recapitalize failing banks and restore fiscal health to the governments.

The EU, ECB, IMF, and all of the Eurozone's member governments have been slow to understand (or even agree on) what is happening, and so it has been difficult for them to figure out what to do. As a result of this confusion, they send different signals to different program countries at different times. As of 2013 it remains unclear how these losses will be finally recognized, and the uncertainty created by the Cyprus crisis has done nothing to clarify the matter, as now even humble bank depositors feel themselves to be in the firing line. In addition, political and social unrest remains high, which is hardly surprising given the persistently high levels of unemployment and stagnant living standards. New loans continue to roll out, or rollover, in the program countries, but their debt-to-GDP levels remain high and rising. Yet one way or another, through cuts in public spending, losses for depositors, levies for taxpayers, defaults or inflation for bondholders, or all of the above, the losses will eventually be felt and dealt with. We just don't know how the story will end yet.

A sudden growth miracle could quickly erase all of these problems. But many even doubt whether the current policies will be enough to maintain stability and prevent a continued long depression in the short to medium term. The ECB monetary policy stance changed little in 2010–13, but the governments of the Eurozone turned very hard in the direction of fiscal austerity, which led to a change in the total Eurozone government structural budget surplus of between 3 and 4 percentage points of GDP from 2010 to 2013.

Not coincidentally, in late 2011 the Eurozone went into a double-dip recession, and by early 2013 had recorded six straight quarters of negative growth. Measured from the last peak in output, the slump had dragged on in Europe for about as long as the Great Depression of the 1930s. To service their large euro-denominated debt, program countries like Greece, Ireland, Portugal, Spain, and Cyprus need to see their economies recover and their nominal GDP grow (as measured in euros). In the near term, however, growth forecasts for these economies are dismal. Their real economies continue to shrink, and neither private nor government consumption will provide any relief. Investment might eventually pick up a little and bring about some economic growth (after all, the capital stock is slowly wearing out). A rise in net exports would seem the best hope, but this would normally require a real depreciation in a nation's currency. Because peripherals have no currencies to depreciate (they use the euro), the only way they can restore competitiveness and output is by a large decline in wages and costs, a tough process that is rarely successful, and which is being forced along by high unemployment. In addition to severe social and political pain, this harsh deflation may keep nominal GDP low

In 2010 the debt problems in Greece and elsewhere were symptoms of deeper macro-economic and financial con-flicts that put the Eurozone at risk. German Chancellor Merkel and French President Sarkozy are shown watching from the ramparts.

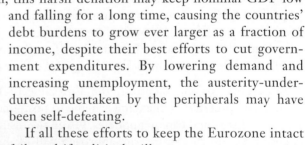

and falling for a long time, causing the countries' debt burdens to grow ever larger as a fraction of income, despite their best efforts to cut govern-ment expenditures. By lowering demand and increasing unemployment, the austerity-under-duress undertaken by the peripherals may have been self-defeating.

If all these efforts to keep the Eurozone intact fail, and if political will evaporates, one or more peripheral countries may default, and even exit the Eurozone. In that event, huge economic sacrifices and deep social damage will have been imposed on their populations, seemingly for nothing. Core countries may also take large losses if they attempt to prop up the system, and they could balk at a "transfer union" based on payments to a group of peripherals to defend the honor of their single currency project. If uncontained, the potentially serious side effects of such an event would surely be an adverse shock for the global economy, but they would be an incredibly serious crisis for Europe itself. Should a scenario like this unfold, tensions will rise, and the Eurozone in its present form might be in peril (see **Headlines: A Bad Marriage?**).

5 Conclusions: Assessing the Euro

The euro project must be understood at least as much in political terms as in economic terms. We have seen how the OCA criteria can be used to examine the logic of currency unions, but in the case of the EU these are not the whole story: Europe does not appear to satisfy the narrow definition of an optimum currency area. In contrast, some of the most important criteria for the survival of the euro may relate to the non-OCA criteria that were included in the Maastricht Treaty. How well can the euro hold up in the future? Even after the crisis, both optimistic and pessimistic views persist.

Euro-optimists For true optimists, the euro is already something of a success: it has functioned in a perfectly adequate way (apart from a crisis that has troubled many other countries too) and can be expected to become only more successful as time goes by. More countries are lining up to join the Eurozone. Even if there are costs in the short run, the argument goes, in the long run the benefits will become clear.

Optimists tend to stress that the OCA criteria might be self-fulfilling. In the long run, they believe the euro will create more trade in the Eurozone. It may also create more labor and capital mobility. They downplay the risk that shocks will become more asymmetric, or at least think this will be outweighed by greater market integration. This will enhance the Eurozone's claim to be an OCA. Since the euro is only a few years old, data are scarce, and these claims can be neither proved nor refuted decisively at present. However, the little evidence we have suggests that although labor mobility has not changed much, goods and services trade in the Eurozone is rising (even if no faster than outside) and that capital market integration has perhaps improved even more dramatically, as measured by the increase in cross-border asset trade and FDI flows in the Eurozone.[16]

Optimists also tend to believe that the ECB will prove to be a strong, credible, independent central bank that can resist political interference or the temptation to print money for the sake of expediency. On paper, the ECB certainly has such characteristics, with a very high degree of independence compared with other central banks. Again, the costs of a common currency may be large in the short run, but as long as the ECB can deliver on its low-inflation target, the optimists reckon it will, in the end, command the respect of the peoples and politicians of the Eurozone.

At a global level, optimists note that the euro is increasingly becoming a reserve currency for foreign central banks, a vehicle currency for trade, and is now the dominant currency used in international bond markets. These developments show the market's confidence in the currency and also augur well for the future, since trade and financing costs may be expected to fall as the euro becomes more widely used around the globe.

Finally, like the "father" of the European Union, Jean Monnet, the optimists believe that the adoption of the euro, like entry to the EU itself, means "no going back": there is simply no imaginable political future for Europe apart from union. Neither the euro nor the EU has exit mechanisms. Perhaps such an idea was inconceivable to the institutional designers. For true believers, the EU project ultimately rests on a deep belief in the political logic of the process and in a presumed common destiny for the peoples of Europe. For them, the great crisis and economic suffering

---

[16] For an excellent survey, see Philip R. Lane, 2006, "The Real Effects of European Monetary Union," *Journal of Economic Perspectives*, 20(4), 47–66.

HEADLINES

A Bad Marriage?

As the Eurozone crisis continued into 2013, Martin Wolf of The Financial Times *summarized the dismal situation.*

Is the eurozone crisis over? The answer is: "yes and no". Yes, risks of an immediate crisis are reduced. But no, the currency's survival is not certain. So long as this is true, the possibility of renewed stress remains.

The best indicator of revived confidence is the decline in interest-rate spreads between sovereign bonds of vulnerable countries and German Bunds. Irish spreads, for example, were just 205 basis points on Monday, down from 1,125 points in July 2011. Portuguese spreads are 465 basis points, while even Greek spreads are 946 basis points, down from 4,680 points in March 2012. Italian and Spanish spreads have been brought to the relatively low levels of 278 and 362 basis points, respectively. [1 basis point = 0.01 percentage points.]

If all members of the eurozone would rejoin happily today, they would be extreme masochists. It is debatable whether even Germany is really better off inside: yes, it has become a champion exporter and runs large external surpluses, but real wages and incomes have been repressed. Meanwhile, the political fabric frays in crisis-hit countries. Anger at home and friction abroad plague both creditors and debtors. Behind this improvement lie three realities. The first is Germany's desire to keep the eurozone intact. The second is the will of vulnerable countries to stick with the policies demanded by creditors. The third was the decision of the European Central Bank to announce bold initiatives—such as an enhanced longer-term refinancing operation for banks and outright monetary transactions for sovereigns—despite Bundesbank opposition. All this has given speculators a glorious run.

Yet that is not the end of the story. The currency union is supposed to be an irrevocable monetary marriage. Even if it is a bad marriage, the union may still survive longer than many thought because the costs of divorce are so high. But a bad romance is still fragile, however large the costs of breaking up. The eurozone is a bad marriage. Can it become a good one?

A good marriage is one spouses would re-enter even if they had the choice to start all over again. Surely, many members would refuse to do so today, for they find themselves inside a nightmare of misery and ill will. In the fourth quarter of last year, eurozone aggregate gross domestic product was still 3 per cent below its pre-crisis peak, while US GDP was 2.4 per cent above it. In the same period, Italian GDP was at levels last seen in 2000 and at 7.6 per cent below its pre-crisis peak. Spain's GDP was 6.3 per cent below the pre-crisis peak, while its unemployment rate had reached 26 per cent. All the crisis-hit economies, save for Ireland's, have been in decline for years. The Irish economy is essentially stagnant. Even Germany's GDP was only 1.4 per cent above the pre-crisis peak, its export power weakened by the decline of its main trading partners.

What, then, needs to happen to turn this bad marriage into a good one? The answer has two elements: manage a return to economic health as quickly as possible, and introduce reforms that make a repeat of the disaster improbable. The two are related: the more plausible longer-term health becomes, the quicker should be today's recovery.

A return to economic health has three related components: write-offs of unpayable debt inherited from the past; rebalancing; and financing of today's imbalances. In considering how far all this might work, I assume that the risk-sharing and fiscal transfers associated with typical federations are not going to happen in the eurozone. The eurozone will end up more integrated than before, but far less integrated than Australia, Canada or the US.

On debt write-offs, more will be necessary than what has happened for Greece. Moreover, the more the burden of adjustment is forced on to crisis-hit countries via falling prices and wages, the greater the real burden of debt and the bigger the required write-offs. Debt write-offs are likely to be needed both for sovereigns and banks. The resistance to recognising this is immensely strong. But it may be futile.

The journey towards adjustment and renewed growth is even more important. It is going to be hard and long. Suppose the Spanish and Italian economies started to grow at 1.5 per cent a year, which I doubt. It would still take until 2017 or 2018 before they returned to pre-crisis peaks: 10 lost years. Moreover, it is also unclear what would drive such growth. Potential supply does not of itself guarantee actual demand.

Fiscal policy is contractionary. Countries suffering from private sector debt overhangs, such as Spain, are unlikely to see a resurgence in lending, borrowing and spending in the private sector. External demand will be weak, largely because many members are adopting contractionary policies at the same time. Not least because it is far from clear that the competitiveness of crisis-hit countries has improved decisively, except in the case of Ireland, as Capital Economics explains in a recent note. Indeed, evidence suggests that Italian external competitiveness is worsening, relative to Germany's.

Yes, the external account deficits have shrunk. But much of this is due to the recessions they have suffered.

Meanwhile, the financing from the ECB, though enough to prevent a sudden collapse into insolvency of weak sovereigns and the banks to which they are tied, required rapid fiscal tightening. The results have been dismal. In a recent letter to ministers, Olli Rehn, the European Commission's vice-president in charge of economics and monetary

affairs, condemned the International Monetary Fund's recent doubts on fiscal multipliers as not "helpful". This, I take it, is an indication of heightened sensitivities. Instead of listening to the advice of a wise marriage counsellor, the authorities have rejected it outright.

Those who believe the eurozone's trials are now behind it must assume either an extraordinary economic turnround or a willingness of those trapped in deep recessions to soldier on, year after grim

year. Neither assumption seems at all plausible. Moreover, prospects for desirable longer-term reforms—a banking union and enhanced risk sharing—look quite remote. Far more likely is a union founded on one-sided, contractionary adjustment. Will the parties live happily ever after or will this union continue to be characterised by irreconcilable differences? The answer seems evident, at least to me. If so, this unhappy story cannot yet be over.

Source: Martin Wolf, "Why the euro crisis is not yet over," Financial Times, February 19, 2013. From the Financial Times © The Financial Times Limited 2013. All Rights Reserved.

of the present are not a major concern: even if there are large costs to be shouldered in the short run, optimists believe that the long-run gains will make it all worthwhile.

Euro-pessimists For true pessimists, the preceding arguments are not convincing. Market integration will not radically change because the impact of the euro on (already high) intra-EU trade levels will be small. Because cultural and linguistic barriers will persist, labor migration will be limited and held back even more by inflexible labor market institutions in most countries. In all markets, regulatory and other frictions will remain.

Moreover, there is resistance to further economic integration. In 2005 an EU directive to liberalize services proved unpopular in many countries and contributed to the failure of referenda on the proposed EU Constitutional Treaty in France and the Netherlands. In many countries, the implications of a single market in all dimensions (goods, services, labor, capital) are only now being dimly understood. Governments and the Commission disagree about how far the process should go.

If integration stops for lack of political support, a key economic rationale for the euro unravels. If political support for the EU stalls, then the political logic is weakened. If some countries press ahead for a closer, more highly integrated union of countries while others stand aside, the sense of a common destiny among all EU nations will be undermined.

On the other key OCA criterion, pessimists note that there is often wide divergence in the countries of the Eurozone. Low-growth, low-inflation countries tend to want looser monetary policy. High-growth, high-inflation countries tend to want tighter monetary policy. If different countries desire very different policies from the ECB, tensions may rise and governments may lose respect for the ECB's independence.

The euro could also be threatened by fiscal problems. The rules say governments cannot lobby the ECB for low interest rates or high inflation to make their debt payments lower or to reduce the real value of their debts, nor can they urge a weaker euro to promote growth. But as history has typically shown, governments tend to trump central banks and will push them around if times get tough. Pessimists note that the Maastricht fiscal rules have evaporated and the Stability and Growth Pact has been emptied of meaning. If some states lobby for loose money, more fiscally prudent or inflation-averse nations will object, and the resulting fight will cause uncertainty and undermine the credibility of the euro. As the fiscal problems of countries mount after the 2008 crisis and double-dip recession in 2011–13 these tensions may rise.

Prior to the crisis, the ECB was continually voicing its concerns about fiscal dangers, but with seemingly little effect on member states' behavior. For example, in November 2005 the ECB asserted its power to deny Eurozone banks the right to use government bonds as collateral if those bonds' credit rating fell too low; but as soon as this vow was put to the test after the 2008 crisis, the ECB caved in and continued to lend against peripheral country government debt of declining quality to prevent crises. The ECB then joined in the fiscal rescue of May 2010 by pledging to fund part of the rescue program, thus stepping farther away from its "no bailout" position. In 2012 the ECB said it would do "whatever it takes" to save the euro, launching the Outright Monetary Transaction bond-buying program, which has yet to be deployed. However, the extent of the Outright Monetary Transaction commitments, their terms, and the conditions under which they will be undertaken remain unclear, and such bond-buying programs are still viewed by some policy makers with suspicion, especially in Germany.

As the crisis drags on, pessimists see no end to the monetary and fiscal policy tensions inherent in trying to impose a monetary union on a region with too many economic, political, cultural, and linguistic differences. At best, even if the euro survives, pessimists believe the region will suffer slow growth and ongoing internal policy conflicts. At worst, the tensions could cause the breakup of the Eurozone into blocs or the reintroduction of the former national currencies.

Summary On the upside, the political dimension of the EU might yet carry the day in the long run, despite current setbacks; in the medium run, the OCA criteria might turn out better than one might think; and even if they don't in the short run, the Eurozone can still survive and function, a workable albeit economically costly currency union.

On the downside, EU enlargement undercuts the OCA logic in the short run and could make the ECB's governance more cumbersome and make resolution of conflicts more difficult. As the member states of the Eurozone cope with severe fiscal problems, there is a significant risk of a clash between the fiscal goals of the governments and monetary goals of the ECB; and should the current crisis intensify (e.g., should any member country default or desire to leave the euro) the project would be in uncharted waters.

What do the people think? The results of successive Eurobarometer polls indicate that at the best of times only about 50% to 60% of the citizens of the Eurozone have thought that the euro has been beneficial. In some countries that figure is higher, in some lower. Since the crisis began, support has fallen from even these lukewarm levels, especially in the hard-hit peripheral countries. The euro remains an experiment—its arrival did not mark the end point of European monetary history, and its long-run fate is not entirely certain.

KEY POINTS

1. A currency union occurs when two or more sovereign nations share a common currency. Sometimes these arrangements are unilateral, such as when a country like Ecuador adopts the U.S. dollar. But some are multilateral, the most prominent example being the Eurozone.

2. The euro is (as of 2014) the currency of 18 European Union (EU) countries, and they manage it collectively by a common monetary authority, the European Central Bank (ECB). Most of the EU's 28 countries are expected to join the euro eventually.

3. According to the theory of optimum currency areas (OCAs), regions should employ a common currency only if they are well integrated and face fairly similar (symmetric) economic shocks. If these criteria are met, efficiency gains from trade should be large, and the costs of forgone monetary autonomy small.

4. A currency union is usually a more irreversible and costly step than simply fixing the exchange rate. The OCA threshold is therefore higher than the threshold for a fixed exchange rate.

5. Additional economic factors can strengthen the case for an OCA. If regions have high labor mobility or large fiscal transfers, these mechanisms may make the costs of a currency union smaller for any given asymmetric shock. In addition, countries with a poor nominal anchor may be eager to join a currency union with a country with a better reputation for inflation performance.

6. Political considerations can drive monetary unions, as when countries feel they have a common destiny and wish to treat monetary union as part of a broader goal of political union.

7. The Eurozone has fairly high trade integration, although not quite as high as that of the United States. The Eurozone might or might not pass this OCA test.

8. The Eurozone has fairly symmetric shocks for most countries. The Eurozone probably does pass this OCA test.

9. The Eurozone has very low labor mobility between countries. The Eurozone almost certainly fails this OCA test.

10. The OCA criteria may fail ex ante, but they may be self-fulfilling: thanks to the common currency, after some years, trade and labor mobility may increase, tipping the balance in favor of an OCA ex post. But increasing specialization due to trade may cause more asymmetric shocks, which would push in the opposite direction.

11. The lack of compelling economic arguments for the euro leads us to study its historical and political origins. The EU must be understood as a political project, and the euro is an important part of the conception of the EU. Although many EU citizens have trust in this project, polls show that such a view is held by only a bare majority.

12. The ECB plays the pivotal role in securing the future of the euro. If it can deliver low inflation and economic stability comparable with the German central bank, after which it was designed, the euro is more likely to succeed as a currency in the EU and as a global currency.

13. Attempts to exert political influence on the ECB continue and the Council of Ministers has often proved weak at punishing countries that break the rules of the Eurozone (the Maastricht criteria and the Stability and Growth Pact).

14. The global financial crisis of 2008 and Great Recession were the first real test of the euro, and a stern test at that. Like other economies, the Eurozone suffered from excessive lending and financial bubbles in some countries, fiscal indiscipline in other countries, bailouts of banks, and (as a result) pressure on the central bank to deviate from established policies to support the real economy, banks, and governments. These problems were difficult to handle because they affected Eurozone countries in an asymmetric fashion. As a result, ECB and EU authorities struggled to devise effective policy responses based on broad cooperation except in the direst moments. The economic and political situation remains fragile, especially in the hard-hit peripheral economies of Greece, Ireland, Portugal, and Spain.

15. A double-dip recession began in 2011 making matters even worse: slow growth damaged fiscal positions, government ambitions were limited, the ECB was reluctant to try aggressive or unconventional tactics, and the European banking system remains fragile.

KEY TERMS

currency union, p. 811
Eurozone, p. 811
euro, p. 811
European Union (EU), p. 812
Maastricht Treaty, p. 812
optimum currency area (OCA),
p. 814

inflation bias, p. 818
Marshall Plan, p. 827
Treaty of Rome, p. 827
Exchange Rate Mechanism
(ERM), p. 830
Economic and Monetary Union
(EMU), p. 831

ERM crisis, p. 831
European Central Bank (ECB),
p. 832
convergence criteria, p. 838
Stability and Growth Pact (SGP),
p. 842

PROBLEMS

1. One could view the United States as a currency union of 50 states. Compare and contrast the Eurozone and the United States in terms of the optimum currency area (OCA) criteria.

2. After German reunification and the disintegration of Communist rule in Eastern Europe, several countries sought to join the European Union (EU) and later the Economic and Monetary Union (EMU). Why do you believe these countries were eager to integrate with Western Europe? Do you think policy makers in these countries believe that OCA criteria are self-fulfilling? Explain.

3. The Maastricht Treaty places strict requirements on government budgets and national debt. Why do you think the Maastricht Treaty called for fiscal discipline? If it is the central bank that is responsible for maintaining the fixed exchange rate, then why does fiscal discipline matter? How might this affect the gains/losses for joining a currency union?

4. The following figure shows some hypothetical OCA criteria with the Eurozone for selected countries. *Assume that these are based solely on economic criteria*—that is, without reference to other political considerations. Refer to the diagram in responding to the questions that follow.

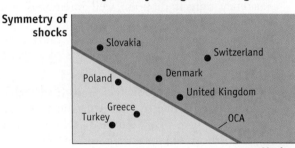

Symmetry-Integration Diagram

a. Which of the countries satisfy the OCA criteria for joining a monetary union?

b. Compare Poland and the United Kingdom in terms of the OCA criteria regarding *market integration* with the Eurozone. Discuss one possible source of differences in integration (with the EU) in the two countries.

c. Compare Poland and the United Kingdom in terms of the OCA criteria regarding *symmetric versus asymmetric shocks* (relative to the Eurozone). Discuss one possible source of differences in symmetry (with the EU) in the two countries.

d. Suppose that policy makers in both Poland and the United Kingdom care only about being able to use policy in response to shocks. Which is more likely to seek membership in the EMU and why?

e. What did the ERM crises reveal about the preferences of the United Kingdom? Why has the United Kingdom sought membership only in the EU without seeking membership in the Eurozone? Consider other costs and benefits not in the diagram, both economic and political.

f. What did membership in the Eurozone reveal about the preferences of Greece? Consider other costs and benefits not in the diagram, both economic and political.

5. Congress established the Federal Reserve System in 1914. Up to this point, the United States did not have a national currency; Federal Reserve notes are still the paper currency in circulation today. Earlier attempts at establishing a central bank were opposed on the grounds that a central bank would give the federal government monopoly over money. This was a reflection of the historic debate between maintaining states' rights versus establishing a strong centralized authority in the United States. That is, the creation of the Fed and a national currency would mean that states would no longer have the authority to control the money supply on a regional level. Discuss the debate between states' rights versus centralized authority in the context of the EMU and the European Central Bank.

6. In recent years there have been reports that a group of six Gulf countries (Bahrain, Kuwait, Oman, Qatar, Saudi Arabia, and the United Arab Emirates) were considering the introduction of a single currency. Currently, these countries use currencies that are effectively pegged to the U.S. dollar. These countries rely heavily on oil exports to the rest of the world, and political leaders in these countries are concerned about diversifying trade. Based on this information, discuss the OCA criteria for this group of countries. What are the greatest potential benefits? What are the potential costs?

7. Before taking office as the new Federal Reserve chairman, Ben Bernanke advocated for the adoption of an inflation target to promote price stability in the United States. Compare and contrast the Fed and the European Central Bank in terms of their commitment to price stability and economic stability. Which central bank has more independence to pursue price stability as a primary objective? Explain.

8. Why do countries with less independent central banks tend to have higher inflation rates? Is it possible for the central bank to increase output and reduce unemployment in the long run? In the long run, is the German model a good one? Explain why or why not.

9. Compare the Maastricht Treaty convergence criteria with the OCA criteria. How are these convergence criteria related to the potential benefits and costs associated with joining a currency union? If you were a policy maker in a country seeking to join the EMU, which criterion would you eliminate and why?

N E T W O R K

Do some research on the Internet to construct an updated version of the map in Figure 21-1. You can find membership information on the websites of the European Union (europa.eu) and the European Central Bank (www.ecb.int). Since 2014, have any new countries joined the European Union, or applied to join? Have any countries entered the Exchange Rate Mechanism, or exited from it? Have any new countries adopted the euro?

Topics in International Macroeconomics

Economics is a science of thinking in terms of models joined to the art of choosing models which are relevant to the contemporary world.

John Maynard Keynes, 1938

Like other fields of economics, international macroeconomics is evolving continually. New empirical analyses are constantly appearing, deepening our understanding, and bringing attention to new phenomena. New theoretical models are always being developed, to better explain long-standing puzzles or to confront new ones. The fast-changing global economic environment of recent years has pushed forward research faster than ever.

In the four stand-alone sections of this final chapter, we examine several important topics that have occupied researchers for many years and that remain at the cutting edge. In these "mini-chapters" we explore new issues as well as important extensions to the core models presented earlier in the book:

- We ask whether purchasing power parity really works as a long-run theory of exchange rates. Evidence shows that a better theory has to explain why price levels are higher in richer countries. We develop such a theory and show how it can be applied to improve exchange rate forecasts.

- We ask whether uncovered interest parity really works as a short-run theory of exchange rates. We show that forex traders often make massive profits (and also losses) and that such profits may be somewhat predictable. If arbitrage operates to support uncovered interest parity in an efficient market, such profits ought to be eliminated. One explanation might be that there are limits to arbitrage, such as an aversion to the extreme riskiness of profits in the forex market.

■ We study the problem of defaults by governments on their debt. Some of the facts to be explained are why any lenders lend given the risk of default, why borrowers choose to default when they do, and what price they pay for defaulting. We develop a model in which adverse economic shocks (low output) make countries more likely to default. The bigger such shocks are, the more the countries default, and the less willing lenders are to lend, unless they receive a higher interest rate. The model fits various facts: poorer countries have more volatile output, are charged higher interest rates, default more often even at lower levels of debt, and lenders don't make much profit.

■ We look at the performance of the global macroeconomy before, during, and after the 2007–2009 Global Financial Crisis and subsequent Great Recession. We look to understand some of the causes and consequences of this event using the tools we have developed throughout the book, even as the repercussions of this event continue to unfold.

1 Exchange Rates in the Long Run: Deviations from Purchasing Power Parity

According to the most recent data from the World Bank, in 2012 gross national income per capita in the United States was $50,120, but by converting incomes using the exchange rate, it was found that gross national income per capita in China was only $5,740, about 11.5% of the U.S. level. Were the Chinese really that poor in terms of material living standards? No.

When the calculations were repeated by comparing dollar incomes with the dollar prices of baskets of consumer goods, Chinese gross national income per capita was found to be about $9,210 in terms of U.S. consumer goods, so that nation's living standards were now seen to be almost twice as high, at 18.4% of the U.S. level. The reason: in dollar terms, most goods cost a lot less in China than in the United States. The dollar price level in China was lower than in the United States. The implication: purchasing power parity (PPP) does not hold, and the real exchange rate is a long way from 1.

These adjustments have many implications: for example, they affect calculations of living standards, poverty, allocations of aid, and projections of growth, consumption, demographics, pollution, and so on. So we need to understand these deviations from PPP for many reasons, including the need to refine our theory of exchange rates. When we learned about long-run exchange rates, we showed that we could predict the expected future exchange rate using the monetary approach to exchange rates, *if* purchasing power parity holds, that is, if baskets of goods sell for the same price in all locations. This theory provided a workable model of real exchange rates, but it was far from perfect. In this section, we address a major deficiency in PPP theory: its assumption that all goods are costlessly tradable.

Limits to Arbitrage

One way to set up a more realistic economic model would be to introduce costs of trading, which is now an important area of research in international economics.

To gain familiarity with trade costs and to see how they matter, let's assume that the cost of trading the good equals some fraction c of the unit cost of the good at its source. For example, suppose there is one good, and it sells for $P = \$100$ in Home. It costs \$10 to ship the good from Home to another country, Foreign. The **trade cost** is $c = 0.1 = 10\%$. The cost of the good on arrival in Foreign, including the trade cost, would be $P \times (1 + c) = \$110$.

How do trade costs affect arbitrage? If you were considering trying to make an arbitrage profit by shipping a \$100 widget from Home to Foreign, then you wouldn't even think of doing it unless the Foreign price converted into dollars EP^* was at least \$110 (where E is Home's exchange rate, and P^* is the Foreign price in Foreign currency). Otherwise, you make a loss once the trading costs are taken into account. Similarly, going from Foreign to Home, you wouldn't ship goods unless the Home price P was at least 10% above the foreign price EP^*.

Formally, the ratio of the prices in the two locations can be written in proportional terms as $q = EP^*/P$. As we learned in our study of long-run exchange rates, for any basket of goods, q is also known as the *real exchange rate* of the home country. Thus, if $P = \$100$ and $EP^* = \$110$, then this relative price ratio would be $(110/100) = 1.1$.

As we have just seen, arbitrage from Home to Foreign is profitable only if the Foreign price is higher than the Home price adjusted for the trade cost, which requires $q = EP^*/P > 1 + c$. Conversely, arbitrage the other way is profitable only if the Home price is sufficiently higher than the Foreign price, with $1/q = P/(EP^*) > 1 + c$.

Thus, if q is below $1 + c$, there will be no arbitrage from Home to Foreign. And if q is above $1/(1 + c)$, there will be no arbitrage from Foreign to Home. So we have shown that, taking trade costs into account, the *no arbitrage condition* for market equilibrium is

$$\frac{1}{1 + c} \leq \underbrace{\frac{EP^*}{P}}_{\substack{\text{Real exchange rate} \\ q}} \leq 1 + c$$

Let's look at what this condition implies for various levels of trading costs.

- *Zero costs.* With $c = 0$, the no arbitrage equilibrium condition reduces to an equality because both left- and right-hand sides equal 1, implying that $q = 1$. This equality is the condition for the law of one price (LOOP), which we expect to hold when arbitrage is costless. An illustration is shown in Figure 22-1, panel (a), which plots the hypothetical relative price q over time for Home and Foreign.

- *Low costs.* Suppose c is low, say, 10%, as in our example. If the price difference between source and destination is less than 10%, then there is no arbitrage. Hence, q is free to wander in what is called a **no-arbitrage band** between $1/(1 + c) = (100/110)$ and $1 + c = (110/100)$. For values of q between 0.91 and 1.1, then, the market is considered to be in equilibrium. This is shown in Figure 22-1, panel (b). Small deviations from LOOP are possible, but LOOP is still approximately true.

- *High costs.* Suppose c is high, say, 50%. If the price difference is less than 50%, there will be no arbitrage. There is a wider no-arbitrage band between $1/(1 + c) = (100/150)$ and $1 + c = (150/100)$ in which the market is in equilibrium and no arbitrage is possible. This is shown in Figure 22-1, panel (c). Deviations from LOOP are possible in the range 0.67 to 1.5, and LOOP no longer applies.

This analysis shows that when trade costs or *costs of arbitrage* are higher, arbitrage will not happen for small price deviations, and the possible deviations from LOOP

FIGURE 22-1

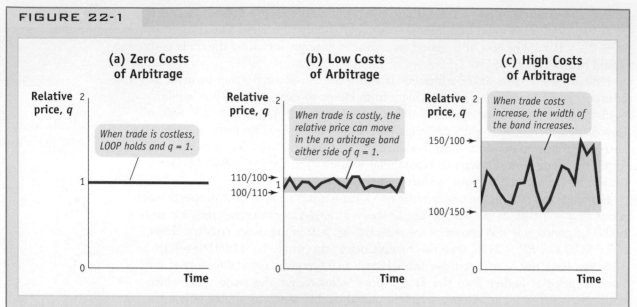

(a) Zero Costs of Arbitrage

When trade is costless, LOOP holds and q = 1.

(b) Low Costs of Arbitrage

When trade is costly, the relative price can move in the no arbitrage band either side of q = 1.

(c) High Costs of Arbitrage

When trade costs increase, the width of the band increases.

No Arbitrage Bands The hypothetical relative price ratio q is shown in three cases. In panel (a), trade costs are zero, so the law of one price (LOOP) holds and q has to equal 1. In panel (b), trade costs are small, say, 10%, so the prices in the two locations can differ. The high price can exceed the low price by up to 10%, so q can range between 100/110 (0.91) and 110/100 (1.1). In panel (c), trade costs are high, say, 50%, so the high price may exceed the low price by up to 50%, so q can range between 150/100 and 100/150. Thus, as costs of arbitrage increase, deviations from simple LOOP and PPP become larger, and these "laws" become less useful.

become greater. If the prices of many goods deviated from LOOP, this would imply deviations from PPP. If costs are huge, then arbitrage is practically impossible and the prices of the same good in two locations need not bear any relation to one another and can be very far apart. Under such conditions, goods are almost always nontraded, and LOOP and PPP will not apply.

Trade Costs in Practice These results show that when evaluating LOOP for one good or PPP for a basket of goods, we must take into account trade costs and consider how they affect deviations from price equality. Empirical research suggests that trade costs are affected by economic policies, as well as by characteristics of goods and their markets.[1]

An important part of trade costs is costs of transportation. For U.S. imports, for example, estimated freight rates vary from 1% of the good's price (for transport equipment) to 27% (for fertilizer). In many countries with worse transport infrastructure, these costs can be much higher: one estimate suggests that the average landlocked country has transport costs 55% higher than the average coastal country.

[1] Charles Engel and John H. Rogers, 1996, "How Wide Is the Border?" *American Economic Review*, 86(5), 1112–1125; Maurice Obstfeld and Alan M. Taylor, 1997, "Nonlinear Aspects of Goods-Market Arbitrage and Adjustment: Heckscher's Commodity Points Revisited," *Journal of the Japanese and International Economies*, 11(4), 441–479; David C. Parsley and Shang-Jin Wei, 2001, "Explaining the Border Effect: The Role of Exchange Rate Variability, Shipping Costs, and Geography," *Journal of International Economics*, 55(1), 87–105; James E. Anderson and Eric van Wincoop, 2004, "Trade Costs," *Journal of Economic Literature*, 42(3), 691–751.

Another major factor that influences trade costs is a country's trade policy. Average tariffs of 5% (rich countries) or more than 10% (developing countries) constitute an additional cost, and such tariffs vary widely by type of good. Quotas (limits to import quantities) and regulatory barriers (such as health and environmental regulations) also add to trade costs, but the costs they add are difficult to compute. In addition to transport and policy costs, economists have found statistical evidence of other causes of price gaps between markets, including distance between markets, crossing international borders, having different currencies, having floating exchange rates, and so on.

The illustration that follows shows the magnitudes of international trade costs for advanced countries.[2] Like the variable c above, these costs are expressed as a percentage markup over the pre-shipment price of the goods. The data are averaged over all types of goods and based on direct measurements and econometric estimates:[3]

	Transport costs, 21%	Freight costs, 11%
		Transit costs (time), 9%
Total international trade costs, 74%		
	Costs at the border, 44%	Tariffs and nontariff barriers, 8%
		Language barrier, 7%
		Different currencies, 14%
		Security and other costs, 9%

(Note that the subcosts are aggregated by compounding: e.g., a 21% markup on top of a 44% markup on a $1 good in the middle column results in a 74% markup in the left column, because $1.21 \times 1.44 \times \$1 = \$1.74$.)

These data show that trade costs are large—and typically, they are even larger outside the advanced countries and create a very wide no-arbitrage band. This observation has led economists to incorporate trade costs into our economic models, so we can develop a more realistic theory of what goes on in the real world.

APPLICATION

It's Not Just the Burgers That Are Cheap

If real exchange rates can deviate from the PPP-implied value of 1, the next question to ask is, how do they vary, and why? One place to find a clue is in the pattern of deviations from PPP. For example, look at the *Economist* newspaper's Big Mac index by searching the Internet for "economist big mac index." If deviations from PPP were random, they might easily be dismissed as an approximation error. However, deviations from PPP in the Big Mac index are not entirely random: burgers tend to be cheaper in poorer countries. In July 2012, for example, the *Economist* found that, expressed in U.S. dollars, a Big Mac cost 38% less in Mexico and 46% less in Malaysia than it did in the United States.

---

[2] From Prabir De, 2006, "Why Trade Costs Matter?" Working Papers 706, Asia-Pacific Research and Training Network on Trade (ARTNeT), an initiative of UNESCAP and IDRC, Canada. Based on James E. Anderson and Eric van Wincoop, 2004, "Trade Costs," *Journal of Economic Literature*, 42(3), 691–751.

[3] Another important trade cost element is the *intranational* distribution and retail costs that are incurred as a good moves within a country from the sellers/importers to buyers/exporters. Intranational distribution costs may be around 35 to 50% of a good's cost in developed countries, but there is wide variation. In the United States, for example, distribution costs can be as low as 14% (electronic equipment) or as high as 216% (ladies' clothing).

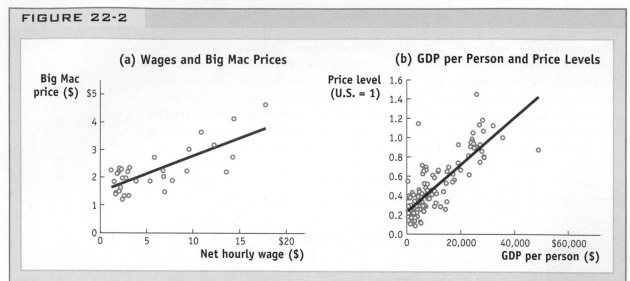

FIGURE 22-2

(a) Wages and Big Mac Prices

Big Mac price ($)

(b) GDP per Person and Price Levels

Price level (U.S. = 1)

Big Mac Price Levels in Rich and Poor Countries Panel (a) shows that richer countries (measured by higher wages) tend to have higher Big Mac prices (measured in a common currency). Panel (b) shows that richer countries (measured by higher GDP per person) tend to have higher overall price levels (measured in a common currency).

Source: Michael R. Pakko and Patricia S. Pollard, November 2003, "Burgernomics: A Big Mac™ Guide to Purchasing Power Parity," Review, Federal Reserve Bank of St. Louis, 9–28.

It isn't too difficult to think of a reason for this finding—the presence of nontraded goods. A Big Mac is a combination of some traded goods (such as flour, beef, and special sauce) and some nontraded goods (such as cooks and cleaners). Local labor wages are a large percentage of the costs of nontraded goods, so such goods tend to cost less in a poor country where wages are lower. The evidence in Figure 22-2, panel (a), supports this logic. This scatterplot shows that the dollar price of the Big Mac is strongly correlated with the local hourly wage in dollars.

Why stop here? The argument shouldn't apply only to burgers, and indeed in 2004 the *Economist* did a parallel experiment and compared the prices of another globally uniform and omnipresent consumer product: the Starbucks tall latte. Similar patterns emerged: in dollar terms (adjusting for international variations in the size of the cups) the latte cost 15% less in Mexico and 25% less in Malaysia than it did in the United States.

The argument applies to most goods that are included in calculations of national price levels. Almost all goods have some local, nontraded component—some local value added or some local retail and distribution costs. Thus, the general price level should vary systematically in the same way, and it does. Figure 22-2, panel (b), shows that a country's price level is strongly correlated with the level of GDP per person. Rich countries have higher price levels; their baskets cost more. In other words, the real exchange

Latte disparity: Starbucks in the Forbidden City, Beijing.

rate $q = EP^*/P$ does *not* equal 1 for all countries, and PPP does not hold, even in the long run. The remainder of this section explores this pattern using economic theory and considers what effect the lack of PPP has on the exchange rate models and predictions we developed earlier in the book. ■

Nontraded Goods and the Balassa-Samuelson Model

Trade costs have major implications for international macroeconomics. In fact, by expanding our analysis from one good that is traded to two goods—one traded and one not traded—we can explain price level differences and deviations from PPP.

We assume there are two countries: Home and Foreign (values for Foreign are denoted by an asterisk). Thus, w denotes the Home wage and w^* denotes the Foreign wage, each measured in the respective currencies. The Home exchange rate is E (units of Home currency per unit of Foreign currency). There are two goods. Each good is produced competitively and labor is the only input needed. One is a nontraded, service good (say, a haircut), denoted N, and its trade costs are effectively infinite. The other is a costlessly tradable good (say, a DVD player), denoted T, that has no trade costs at all. Prices of goods will be denoted p and p^*, each measured in the respective currencies, with subscripts T and N to denote traded and nontraded goods.

A Simple Model The model can be solved in three steps, with assumptions as follows:

1. *The traded good has the same price in both countries.* This is true because trade costs are zero. For simplicity, we assume that the traded good has a price of 1 when measured in Home currency (say, dollars). This is its price in Home and Foreign, so

$$p_T = 1 \qquad Ep_T^* = 1$$

   In our example, the DVD player sells for \$1 everywhere.

2. *Productivity in traded goods determines wages.* Suppose that one Home worker can make A units of the traded good (the DVD player) per hour. Then the worker's hourly wage w will be equal to \$$A$ because each unit of the good sells for \$1 and competition means that the wage will equal the value of the output produced by each hour of labor input. Similarly, if Foreign workers can make A^* units of the traded good per hour, their dollar wage Ew^* will be equal to \$$A^*$. Thus, wage levels in each country are equal to productivity levels:

$$w = A \qquad Ew^* = A^*$$

   In our example, if Home workers make ten \$1 DVD players per hour, their hourly wage is \$10 per hour. If Foreign workers make only five per hour, their hourly wage is \$5.

3. *Wages determine the prices of nontraded goods.* Crucially, we assume that the level of productivity in nontraded goods is a fixed constant, the same everywhere, equal to 1. In our example, it always takes one hour to get a haircut in Home and Foreign, but with the wages given previously, this means the cost of a haircut will equal exactly one hour of labor. In general, the dollar price of the nontraded good in each country equals the wage, so $p_N = w$ and $Ep_N^* = Ew^*$. Because these wages are given by productivity (as we saw in the second step),

$$p_N = A \qquad Ep_N^* = A^*$$

   To continue our example, if the productivities are 10 and 5 in Home and Foreign, the hourly wages must be \$10 and \$5, respectively, and Home haircuts will cost \$10 and Foreign haircuts \$5.

The conclusion from these three assumptions? Countries with higher traded goods productivity will have relatively high wages and hence relatively high prices of nontraded goods. This means they will also have relatively higher overall price levels, depending on how large the share of nontraded goods in the consumption basket is. To see this, suppose the nontraded goods share of consumption is n (so the traded share is $1 - n$).

Changes in Productivity Now suppose Home productivity A increases, with the proportional change given by $\Delta A/A$. What happens to the Home price level? The price of traded goods is unchanged and stays at 1, but the price of nontraded goods is equal to A and it rises. Taking the weighted average, we can compute the (percentage) change in the Home price level as

$$\underbrace{\frac{\Delta P}{P}}_{\substack{\text{Change in} \\ \text{Home price level}}} = \underbrace{(1-n)}_{\substack{\text{Share of} \\ \text{traded goods}}} \times \underbrace{\left(\frac{\Delta p_T}{p_T}\right)}_{\substack{\text{Change in} \\ \text{Home traded} \\ \text{goods price} \\ = \text{zero}}} + \underbrace{n}_{\substack{\text{Share of} \\ \text{nontraded goods}}} \times \underbrace{\left(\frac{\Delta p_N}{p_N}\right)}_{\substack{\text{Change in} \\ \text{Home nontraded} \\ \text{goods price} \\ = \Delta A/A}} = n\frac{\Delta A}{A}$$

By the same logic, the same is true for Foreign: a change in its dollar price level will result from a change in foreign productivity:

$$\underbrace{\frac{\Delta(EP^*)}{(EP^*)}}_{\substack{\text{Change in} \\ \text{Foreign price level}}} = \underbrace{(1-n)}_{\substack{\text{Share of} \\ \text{traded goods}}} \times \underbrace{\left(\frac{\Delta(Ep^*_T)}{(Ep^*_T)}\right)}_{\substack{\text{Change in} \\ \text{Foreign traded} \\ \text{goods price} \\ = \text{zero}}} + \underbrace{n}_{\substack{\text{Share of} \\ \text{nontraded goods}}} \times \underbrace{\frac{\Delta(Ep^*_N)}{(Ep^*_N)}}_{\substack{\text{Change in} \\ \text{Foreign nontraded} \\ \text{goods price} \\ = \Delta A^*/A^*}} = n\frac{\Delta A^*}{A^*}$$

The last two equations are intuitive. For our example, a 1% rise in Home DVD player productivity A will raise Home wages w by 1%; therefore, Home haircut prices rise 1% and, because these haircuts have a weight $n < 1$ in the overall basket, the overall price index rises by n%.

By putting together these last two results, we can solve for the change in the real exchange rate q. Recall that q is equal to EP^*/P, so the percentage change in q is given by the percentage change in the numerator EP^* minus the percentage change in the denominator P. *But we have just computed those changes in the last two equations.* Hence, subtracting the first equation above from the second, the change in the real exchange rate is given by

$$\underbrace{\frac{\Delta q}{q}}_{\substack{\text{Change in} \\ \text{real exchange} \\ \text{rate} \\ (\text{Foreign price level } EP^* \\ \text{relative to Home } P)}} = \underbrace{n}_{\substack{\text{Share of} \\ \text{nontraded goods}}} \times \underbrace{\left(\frac{\Delta A^*}{A^*} - \frac{\Delta A}{A}\right)}_{\substack{\text{Change in} \\ \text{Foreign traded} \\ \text{productivity level} \\ \text{relative to Home}}} \qquad (22\text{-}1)$$

Thus, relative productivities in the traded goods sector drive relative prices, through their effects on wages and prices in the nontraded sector.

Generalizing In this example, we examined the effects of productivity and wages on the prices of DVD players and haircuts. The analysis applies to all goods, however, and it can explain the cheap Big Mac story told earlier. A country has relatively low wages because it has relatively low labor productivity in traded goods. Low productivity and wages hold down the prices of nontraded goods and the nontraded part of the overall price level.

This equation describes a relationship between productivity and the real exchange rate known as the **Balassa-Samuelson effect,** named for the economists Bela Balassa and Paul Samuelson:

When compared with other countries, a country experiencing an increase in productivity will see wages and incomes rise and will see its real exchange rate appreciate, meaning that its price level will rise.[4]

Overvaluations, Undervaluations, and Productivity Growth: Forecasting Implications for Real and Nominal Exchange Rates

The Balassa-Samuelson model makes a firm prediction that is supported strongly by evidence: price levels are higher in rich countries. The scatterplot in Figure 22-2, panel (b), showed this fact, and we zoom in to examine a part of it in Figure 22-3.

In such a figure, a point on the line of best fit is the predicted **equilibrium real exchange rate** $\tilde{q}$ of the Balassa-Samuelson model. Figure 22-3 plots the U.S. real exchange rate against each foreign country—it shows foreign dollar prices EP^* relative to U.S. prices P. So an increase on the vertical axis is a rise in the relative price of foreign goods: it is a U.S. real depreciation, or a foreign real appreciation. The actual data do not sit precisely on the line of best fit. That is, the observed real exchange rate q may differ from its equilibrium value $\tilde{q}$.

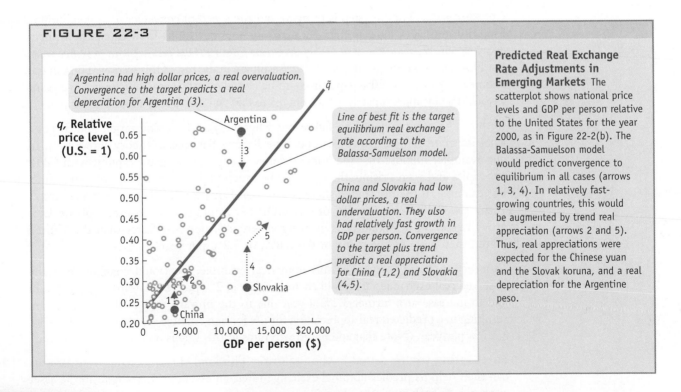

FIGURE 22-3

Argentina had high dollar prices, a real overvaluation. Convergence to the target predicts a real depreciation for Argentina (3).

Line of best fit is the target equilibrium real exchange rate according to the Balassa-Samuelson model.

China and Slovakia had low dollar prices, a real undervaluation. They also had relatively fast growth in GDP per person. Convergence to the target plus trend predict a real appreciation for China (1,2) and Slovakia (4,5).

Predicted Real Exchange Rate Adjustments in Emerging Markets The scatterplot shows national price levels and GDP per person relative to the United States for the year 2000, as in Figure 22-2(b). The Balassa-Samuelson model would predict convergence to equilibrium in all cases (arrows 1, 3, 4). In relatively fast-growing countries, this would be augmented by trend real appreciation (arrows 2 and 5). Thus, real appreciations were expected for the Chinese yuan and the Slovak koruna, and a real depreciation for the Argentine peso.

---

[4] Note that the traded goods sector is the *only* sector in which productivity can vary, so the only way for a country to get richer is by raising the productivity level in that sector, leading to higher wages and output. Also, in this model, GDP is equal to wages times the supply of labor. Thus, high wages are also synonymous with high output per person.

As we saw in the long-run exchange rates chapter, the typical real exchange rate q can from time to time experience an overvaluation or undervaluation relative to its equilibrium value $\tilde{q}$. But there we assumed that the equilibrium value was 1, as predicted by PPP theory. Here, the equilibrium $\tilde{q}$ isn't necessarily 1, and is given the Balassa-Samuelson theory.

Here, we judge deviations from equilibrium by looking at the distance from the equilibrium, that is, from the line of best fit. For example, if actual q is 10% above predicted $\tilde{q}$, then foreign prices are "too high": we would say that the U.S. real exchange rate is *undervalued* and the foreign real exchange rate *overvalued* relative to the equilibrium level $\tilde{q}$.

We can now begin to see how the Balassa-Samuelson theory can improve our theory of exchange rates in the long run and the forecasts that depend on such a theory.

Forecasting the Real Exchange Rate By comparing actual exchange rates with their predicted equilibrium values, forecasting the real exchange rate can be broken down into two problems: (1) how quickly q will return toward its equilibrium value $\tilde{q}$ and (2) how quickly the equilibrium value $\tilde{q}$ will change over time as a result of productivity changes. In other words, q may be heading toward a target level $\tilde{q}$, but our model tells us that it might be a moving target that is moving along a trend. This means that real exchange rate prediction must be broken down into two parts.

For example, suppose q is currently 0.5 but the Balassa-Samuelson model says the equilibrium value of $\tilde{q}$ is 0.6. Clearly, q is predicted to rise by 0.1, or by 20%, to return to equilibrium (0.1/0.5 = 20%). How long will this take?

Convergence The first step is to figure out the speed of convergence to equilibrium. Empirical estimates indicate that real exchange rate deviations from equilibrium might decay slowly: *the consensus "half life" of deviations from PPP has been reported to be five years.* For illustration, we adopt this *rule of thumb* estimate in the rest of this section. Thus, in our example, if half of the 20% gap is likely to be closed over five years, then over five years, q would rise by approximately 10% from 0.5 to 0.55, an increase of about 2% per year.

Trend The second step is to figure out whether $\tilde{q}$ is a moving target and forecast what its trend rate of growth will be. The Balassa-Samuelson theory shows how. In our example, suppose that the home country is expected to grow rapidly, with GDP per capita and wages rising; then $\tilde{q}$ could be much higher than 0.6 in five years' time. For example, if the nontraded share is 0.4, then Equation (22-1) says that a country's $\tilde{q}$ will rise 0.4% for every 1% of real GDP per capita growth in excess of the U.S. growth rate. So if a country is growing at, say, 8% per year faster than the United States, then $\tilde{q}$ should be rising by $0.4 \times 8\%$, or 3.2% per year.

Convergence + Trend For this numerical example, we would conclude that the observed real exchange rate q is likely to increase at 2% per year toward its equilibrium and to increase at a further 3.2% a year due to the upward drift of that equilibrium, resulting in a predicted real appreciation for the foreign country at a rate of about 2 + 3.2 = 5.2% per year. (Note that adding growth rates in this way is only an approximation.)

Forecasting the Nominal Exchange Rate This kind of real exchange rate forecast can then help us predict nominal exchange rates, an essential component in the asset approach to exchange rates. How?

By definition, the real exchange rate is $q = EP^*/P$; by rearranging, we find $E = qP/P^*$, and we have an expression for the nominal exchange rate. When PPP holds, this equation becomes $E = P/P^*$: under PPP, the real exchange rate q equals 1, and the exchange rate is equal to the ratio of national price levels.

When PPP *doesn't hold*, however, we have to worry about possible changes in q. Since $E = qP/P^*$, then taking rates of change, we find

$$\underbrace{\frac{\Delta E}{E}}_{\substack{\text{Rate of} \\ \text{nominal depreciation}}} = \underbrace{\frac{\Delta q}{q}}_{\substack{\text{Rate of} \\ \text{real depreciation}}} + \underbrace{\left(\frac{\Delta P}{P} - \frac{\Delta P^*}{P^*}\right)}_{\substack{\text{Inflation differential} \\ \text{(home minus foreign)}}} \qquad (22\text{-}2)$$

In the long-run exchange rates chapter, we saw a simpler version of this expression: PPP forced q to be constant and equal to 1, and the first term on the right vanished. We were left with a result, known as *relative PPP*, which says that changes in nominal exchange rates depend on inflation differentials alone. Taken literally, forecasters can then focus just on inflation forecasts.

When the Balassa-Samuelson effect is present, PPP fails, but we can still forecast future exchange rate changes using Equation (22-2). In using this equation, however, we not only have to forecast inflation, we have to forecast changes in the real exchange rate, too. Thus, in real-world financial markets, foreign exchange traders have to pay attention to many macroeconomic forecasts before forming an expectation about how E is likely to evolve over time.

Adjustment to Equilibrium Finally, we note that the Balassa-Samuelson model does not tell us how the real exchange rate will adjust. Suppose we have forecast a 1% real appreciation (−1% change in q). In Equation (22-2), this could imply either a 1% nominal appreciation (−1% on the left) or an extra 1% of home inflation over and above foreign inflation (+1% on the right), or some combination of the two.

Thus:

■ *If the model says there is currently a real undervaluation, either home goods prices have to rise or the value of the home currency has to rise—there is no other way to make home goods more expensive.*

■ *If the model says there is currently a real overvaluation, either home goods prices have to fall or the value of the home currency has to fall—there is no other way to make home goods less expensive.*

APPLICATION

Real Exchange Rates in Emerging Markets

To see how we can use these ideas to make forecasts of real and nominal exchange rates, we examine three cases in Figure 22-3 that were in the news a few years ago. The data we use are for the year 2000, which allows us to look at subsequent events and see how well the predictions of the model turned out in the following years.

China: Yuan Undervaluation? The Balassa-Samuelson model predictions: in 2000 the real exchange rate with China was $q = 0.231$, well below (0.088 below) the predicted equilibrium level of $\tilde{q} = 0.319$. The yuan was undervalued according to the model and would have to experience a 38% real appreciation (0.088/0.231) against the U.S. dollar to close the gap. Using our old rule of thumb, half of this gap or 19% would be eliminated in five years, implying an approximate 3.5% annual increase in q due to convergence.

However, in addition, China was a fast-growing economy at this time and its GDP per capita was growing about 6% per annum faster than U.S. GDP per capita. So the real exchange rate would have to appreciate *even more* due to Balassa-Samuelson effects.

Figure 22-3 suggests that every 1% gain in GDP per capita is associated with an approximate 0.4% real appreciation (as expected if the nontraded share were 0.4). So a 6% differential growth rate per year (China minus United States) would imply a further $0.4 \times 6 = 2.4\%$ per year real appreciation in the yuan due to the trend of the moving target.[5]

What actually happened: Adding up both effects, the model predicts a real yuan appreciation of $3.5 + 2.4 = 5.9\%$ per year. As noted previously, this would imply either a nominal appreciation of the yuan against the dollar, or higher inflation in China. Inflation did start to rise in China, up to as much as 4.1% in 2004, although the data are not considered terribly accurate. This was not that much higher than U.S. inflation. Until mid-2005 China pegged the yuan to the dollar but then decided to switch to an unofficial crawling peg, allowing the yuan to appreciate gradually against the dollar, but very slowly. Many commentators saw this as a response to protectionist pressure in the United States, where cheap Chinese imports were raising hackles. But the Chinese had reasons of their own to let the yuan rise: to keep domestic inflation at a reasonable level.

Argentina: Was the Peso Overvalued? The Balassa-Samuelson model predictions: Figure 22-3 clearly shows that Argentina's currency was overvalued in 2000: Argentina's price level was 0.656, but the predicted equilibrium level of $\tilde{q}$ was 0.512. For a country at that level of GDP per capita, Argentina's dollar prices would have had to fall by 22% to reach that equilibrium. Argentina's growth had slowed after 1998, so, unlike in the China case, very little rise in the equilibrium $\tilde{q}$ could have been expected (which would have mitigated the need for a fall in actual q).

What actually happened: Argentina was pegging the peso to the dollar at 1:1, so adjustment had to come through a fall in Argentine prices relative to U.S. prices. With U.S. inflation at only 2%, this would happen slowly unless Argentine prices actually dropped. Unfortunately, this deflation process was slow and politically painful, involving wage and price cuts in an economy that was far from liberalized and competitive. The overvalued exchange rate was also hurting the demand for Argentine goods. Although the peg held for a long time, the country was driven into crisis by fiscal and financial sector problems. In the crisis of 2001–02, the peso depreciated to three per dollar: the overvaluation was eliminated, and then some.

Slovakia: Obeying the Rules? The Balassa-Samuelson model predictions: Figure 22-3 also shows Slovakia. Like China, Slovakia was a fast-growing country, part of a group of countries in Eastern Europe lined up to join the European Union (EU) and ultimately the Eurozone. Slovakia's real exchange rate was $q = 0.282$ in 2000 and undervalued relative to the predicted equilibrium $\tilde{q} = 0.534$. Here, q needed to rise by 89% to reach equilibrium. Using our rule of thumb, half of this gap, or 45%, would be closed in five years, implying a real appreciation of about 7.5% per year. In addition, fast GDP per capita growth relative to the EU probably added another 1% to 2% on top of that, as in the China case, as a result of the moving target. Thus, the expected real appreciation would have been 8% to 10% per year.

What actually happened: Slovakia notched up high rates of real appreciation of between 5% and 10% per annum from 1992 to 2004, as did many other countries in Eastern Europe.[6] The situation was like that in China: it required some

---

[5] Jeffrey A. Frankel, "The Balassa-Samuelson Relationship and the Renminbi," Harvard University, December 2006.

[6] Balázs Égert, Kirsten Lommatzsch, and Amina Lahrèche-Révil, 2006, "Real Exchange Rates in Small Open OECD and Transition Economies: Comparing Apples with Oranges?" *Journal of Banking and Finance*, 30(12), 3393–3406.

combination of nominal appreciation and inflation. But Slovakia (and many of its neighbors) also wanted to join the euro. As we saw in the chapter on the euro, the Maastricht criteria would require Slovakia to peg to the euro (no appreciation) and keep its inflation within limits (within 2% of the "best" in the EU). Our model suggests this would be impossible: the koruna would have to appreciate or Slovakia's inflation would have to accelerate! As an exercise, you may wish to explore in more detail what actually happened. (See the second **Net Work** problem at the end of this chapter.) ■

Conclusion

In general, PPP does not hold. Goods prices are not the same in all countries. Arbitrage fails, most likely because of trade costs. The Balassa-Samuelson theory can explain how prices vary when goods are not traded and why rich countries have higher price levels. As countries get richer, their wages rise, driving up the prices of their nontraded goods (which use local labor as an input). This will drive up the overall price index and will cause the real exchange rate to fall—that is, a real appreciation. The theory finds strong empirical support and can be used to make better models of real and (hence) nominal exchange rates, with improved predictions, in situations in which an assumption of PPP is inappropriate.

2 Exchange Rates in the Short Run: Deviations from Uncovered Interest Parity

When we studied exchange rates in the short run, we examined interest arbitrage in the forex market and introduced uncovered interest parity (UIP), the fundamental condition for forex market equilibrium. Recall that UIP states the expected return on foreign deposits should equal the return on domestic deposits when both are expressed in domestic currency.

For such an important foundation of exchange rate theory, however, UIP remains subject to considerable debate among international macroeconomists. The topic is important because any failure of UIP would affect our theories about exchange rates and the wider economy. For that reason, in this section we further explore the UIP debate to better understand the mechanism of arbitrage in the forex market.

APPLICATION

The Carry Trade

Uncovered interest parity (UIP) implies that the home interest rate should equal the foreign interest rate plus the rate of depreciation of the home currency. If UIP holds, it would seem to rule out the naive strategy of borrowing in a low interest rate currency and investing in a high interest rate currency, an investment referred to as a **carry trade.** In other words, UIP implies that the expected profit from such a trade is zero:

$$\text{Expected profit} = \underbrace{i_F}_{\substack{\text{Interest rate} \\ \text{on foreign currency}}} + \underbrace{\frac{\Delta E^e_{H/F}}{E_{H/F}}}_{\substack{\text{Expected rate of depreciation} \\ \text{of the home currency}}} - \underbrace{i_H}_{\substack{\text{Interest rate} \\ \text{on home currency}}} \quad (22\text{-}3)$$

$$\underbrace{\phantom{i_F + \frac{\Delta E^e_{H/F}}{E_{H/F}}}}_{\text{Expected home currency rate of return on foreign deposits}} \quad \underbrace{}_{\text{Cost of carry}}$$

From the home perspective, the return to an investment in the foreign currency (the foreign return) consists of the first two terms on the right-hand side of the preceding equation. Let's suppose the foreign currency (that of Australia, say) has a high interest rate of 6%. Now suppose the home country (Japan, say) has a low interest rate of 1%. The final term in the preceding equation is the cost of borrowing funds in local currency (Japanese yen) or, in financial jargon, the *cost of carry*. The interest rate differential, 5%, would be the profit on the carry trade *if the exchange rate remained unchanged*. If UIP is true, however, it would be pointless to engage in such arbitrage because the low-yield currency (the yen) would be expected to appreciate by 5% against the high-yield currency (the Australian dollar). The exchange rate term would be −5%, leaving zero expected profit.

The Long and Short of It In the past decade or two, the predominant low interest rate currencies in the world economy have been the Japanese yen and the Swiss franc, and carry traders have often borrowed ("gone short") in these currencies and made an investment ("gone long") in higher interest rate major currencies such as the U.S. dollar, pound sterling, euro, Canadian dollar, Australian dollar, and New Zealand dollar. The profits from these trades have been very large. Has UIP failed?

To grasp how a carry trade functions, Figure 22-4, panel (a), shows actual monthly profits (in percent per month) from a carry trade based on borrowing low-interest yen in the Japanese money market and investing the proceeds in a high-interest Australian dollar money market account for one month. Also shown are the cumulative profits (in yen) that would have accrued from a ¥100 carry trade initiated on January 1, 1992. Panel (b) shows the underlying data used to calculate these returns. We see that over this entire period, the annual Australian dollar interest rate exceeded the Japanese yen interest rate, often by five or six percentage points. Thus, returns would be positive for this strategy if the yen depreciated or even appreciated only slightly against the Australian dollar. But if the yen appreciated more than slightly in any month, returns would be negative, and losses would result.

Panel (a) shows that in many months the high interest being paid on the Australian dollar was not offset by yen appreciation, and the carry trade resulted in a profit; this pattern was seen frequently in the period from 1995 to 1996, for example. There were other periods, however, when a sharp yen appreciation far exceeded the interest differential, and the carry trade resulted in a loss; this pattern occurred quite a bit in late 1998 and again during the global financial crisis of 2008. In 1998, for example, in each of three months, in fact—August, October, and December 1998—the Australian dollar lost about 10% in value, wiping out the profits from *two years' worth of interest differentials* in all three cases. Overall, we see that the periods of positive and negative returns were driven not by the fairly stable interest differential seen in panel (b), but by the long and volatile swings in the exchange rate.

To sum up, the carry trade strategy was subject to a good deal of volatility, and over the decade from the start of 1992 to the end of 2001, the highs and lows canceled each other out in the long run. On November 1, 2001, for example, the average return on this carry trade was virtually zero. Cumulative interest since 1992 on the two currencies expressed in yen was virtually the same, about 13%. Over that period, 100 yen placed in either currency at the start would have been worth 113 yen by the end.

What happened after that date? Subsequent trends again caused the value of Australian investment to pull ahead, as can be seen in panel (a) by the mostly positive returns registered month after month from 2002 to 2006. By June 2007

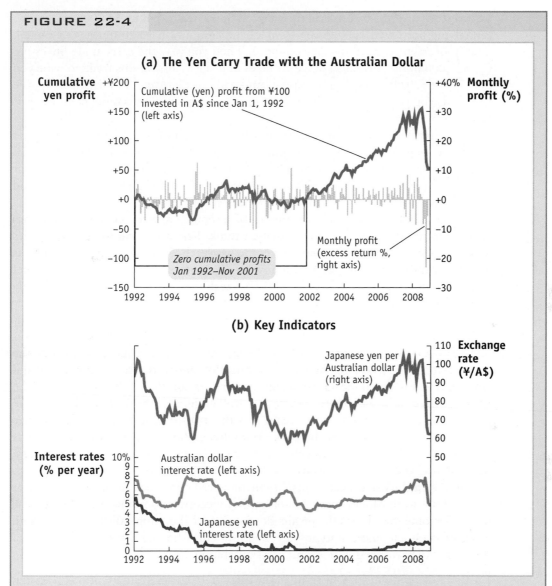

FIGURE 22-4

(a) The Yen Carry Trade with the Australian Dollar

Cumulative yen profit

Cumulative (yen) profit from ¥100 invested in A$ since Jan 1, 1992 (left axis)

Zero cumulative profits Jan 1992–Nov 2001

Monthly profit (excess return %, right axis)

Monthly profit (%)

(b) Key Indicators

Japanese yen per Australian dollar (right axis)

Exchange rate (¥/A$)

Interest rates (% per year)

Australian dollar interest rate (left axis)

Japanese yen interest rate (left axis)

Carry Trades In the 1990s and 2000s, the yen had a lower interest rate than many other currencies. Carry trades borrow in low-yield yen to invest in higher-yield currencies like the Australian dollar. Such trades can be profitable for long periods, but dramatic reversals, though rare, can quickly undermine profits.

Sources: oanda.com and econstats.com.

cumulative profits were well over ¥100. The reason? As panel (b) shows, the yen persistently weakened against the Australian dollar over this five-year period (by about 6% to 7% per year), reinforcing the interest differential (about 6% to 7% also) rather than offsetting it. Adding up, from 2002 to 2006 the cumulative return on the carry trade was about 15% per year! Would that trend continue or was there to be another sudden swing resulting from yen appreciation? As we can see, another wipeout came along in 2008. This question brings us to a consideration of the role of risk in the forex market.

Investors face very real risks in this market. Suppose you put up $1,000 of your own capital and borrow $19,000 in yen from a bank. You now have 20 times your capital, a ratio, or *leverage*, of 20 (not uncommon). Then you play the carry trade, investing the $20,000 in the Australian dollar. It takes only a 5% loss on this trade to wipe you out: 5% of $20,000 eats all your capital. And without that *margin* to back you up, the bank bids you goodbye. As we have seen, losing 5% in a month is quite possible, as is losing 10% or even 15%.

For policy makers and market participants, the broader fear is that while big losses for households would be bad enough, big losses at large, high-leverage financial institutions could have damaging spillover effects in the global macroeconomy. For example, in June 2007, Jim O'Neill, Goldman Sachs chief global economist, said investment firms had been caught on the wrong side of huge bets against the Japanese yen: "There has been an amazing amount of leverage on currency markets that has nothing to do with real economic activity. I think there are going to be dead bodies around when this is over. The yen carry trade has reached 5% of Japan's GDP. This is enormous and highly risky, as we are now seeing."[7] Days later Steven Pearson, chief currency strategist at HBOS bank, said, "A sizeable reversal at some point is highly likely, but the problem with that statement is the 'at some point' bit, because carry trades make money steadily over long periods of time."[8]

In the carry trade, as history shows, a big reversal can always happen as everyone rushes to exit the carry trades and they all "unwind" their positions at the same time. The answer to the dangling question above is yes, a big reversal did come along for the trade in question: after rising another 10% against the yen from January to July 2007, the Australian dollar then fell by 15% in the space of a month, eating up about three years' worth of interest differential for anyone unlucky enough to buy in at the peak. Many hedge funds and individual investors who made ill-timed or excessively leveraged bets lost a bundle (see **Headlines: Mrs. Watanabe's Hedge Fund**).

Still, given the persistence of profits, anyone predicting such reversals may appear to be crying wolf. Money managers often face incentives to follow the herd and the market's momentum keeps the profits flowing—until they stop. All this ensures high levels of stress and uncertainty for anyone in the forex trading world and for some of the households engaged in this kind of risky arbitrage.

Carry Trade Summary Our study of the carry trade focuses our attention on several facts. First, even if expected returns from arbitrage are zero, actual realized returns are often not zero. Second, such returns appear to be persistent. Third, the returns are also very volatile, or risky. All of these issues need to be addressed as we judge the success or failure of UIP. ■

APPLICATION

Peso Problems

The example of carry trades between the Japanese yen and the Australian dollar shows how actual returns from interest arbitrage may be nonzero (but risky) for a pair of currencies that are floating. But the same can be true for two currencies that are fixed.

---

[7] Ambrose Evans-Pritchard, "Goldman Sachs Warns of 'Dead Bodies' after Market Turmoil," telegraph. co.uk, June 3, 2007.
[8] Veronica Brown, "Carry Trade Devotees Keep Faith in Testing Times," Reuters, June 12, 2007.

HEADLINES

Mrs. Watanabe's Hedge Fund

The OECD estimated the total yen carry trade at $4 trillion in 2006. This trade involves not just large financial institutions but increasing numbers of Japanese individual investors, who place money in high-yielding foreign currency deposits or uridashi *bonds.*

"FX Beauties" founder Mayumi Torii

TOKYO—Since the credit crisis started shaking the world financial markets this summer, many professional traders have taken big losses. Another, less likely group of investors has, too: middle-class Japanese homemakers who moonlight as amateur currency speculators.

Ms. Itoh is one of them. Ms. Itoh, a homemaker in the central city of Nagoya, did not want her full name used because her husband still does not know. After cleaning the dinner dishes, she would spend her evenings buying and selling British pounds and Australian dollars.

When the turmoil struck the currency markets last month, Ms. Itoh spent a sleepless week as market losses wiped out her holdings. She lost nearly all her family's $100,000 in savings.

"I wanted to add to our savings, but instead I got in over my head," Ms. Itoh, 36, said.

Tens of thousands of married Japanese women ventured into online currency trading in the last year and a half, playing the markets between household chores or after tucking the children into bed. While the overwhelmingly male world of traders and investors here mocked them as kimono-clad "Mrs. Watanabes," these women collectively emerged as a powerful force, using Japan's vast wealth to sway prices and confound economists. . . .

Now Japan's homemaker-traders may become yet another casualty of the shakeout hitting the debt, credit and stock markets worldwide. . . . Most analysts estimate that Japanese online investors lost $2.5 billion trading currency last month. . . .

Some of the women used their own money, some used their husband's, and some used a combination of both. But by trading, they challenged deeply held social prohibitions in Japan against money, which is often seen here as dirty, especially when earned through market speculation.

"There are strict taboos against money that isn't earned with sweat from the brow," said Mayumi Torii, a 41-year-old mother of one who said she earned $150,000 since she started margin trading in currencies early last year.

Ms. Torii is one of Japan's most famous housewife-traders. She has written a book on her investing strategies and founded a support group for home traders, the FX Beauties Club, which now has 40 members. (FX is financial shorthand for "foreign exchange.") . . .

One reason Japan's homemakers can move markets is that they hold the purse strings of the nation's $12.5 trillion in household savings. For more than a decade, that money languished in banks here at low interest rates. But as the rapid aging of Japan's population has brought anxiety about the future, households are starting to move more of it overseas in search of higher returns.

A tiny fraction of this has flowed into risky investments like online currency accounts. Most of these accounts involve margin trading, in which investors place a cash deposit with a brokerage that allows them to borrow up to 20 or even 100 times their holdings for trading.

The practice has been popular not only because it vastly raises the level

of potential profits, but also because it allowed wives to trade at home, said Hiroshi Takao, chief operating officer of TokyoForex, an online trading firm.

The housewife-traders were so secretive that many market analysts did not realize how widespread the trend had become until this summer, when the police arrested a Tokyo housewife accused of failing to pay $1.1 million in taxes on her foreign exchange earnings. . . .

For a time, margin trading seemed like a surefire way to make money, as the yen moved only downward against the dollar and other currencies. But last month, in the midst of the credit turmoil, the yen soared as hedge funds and traders panicked.

Ms. Itoh recalled that she had wanted to cry as she watched the yen jump as much as 5 percent in value in a single day, Aug. 16.

"But I had to keep a poker face, because my husband was sitting behind me," Ms. Itoh said.

She did not sell her position, thinking the yen would fall again. But by the next morning, only $1,000 remained in her account, she said. . . .

[M]ost of the half dozen homemaker-traders interviewed for this article said they were already trading again, and the rest said they soon would be—including Ms. Itoh, who said she would probably invest her remaining $1,000 in savings.

"There's no other way to make money so quickly," she said.

To illustrate this case, we turn to recent data involving the U.S. dollar pegs of two emerging market countries, Hong Kong and Argentina.

As we saw in the chapter on fixed and floating regimes, in the case of a credibly fixed peg with no risk of a depreciation or any other risks (no currency premium and no default risk premium), the UIP condition states that the home interest rate should equal the foreign interest rate because investors treat domestic and foreign currency as perfect substitutes that always have been and always will be interchangeable at a fixed rate. Thus, the interest differential between the two currencies should be zero. Again, if true, this outcome would seem to rule out any desire on the part of investors to engage in arbitrage (e.g., via the carry trade). But there is an important exception: when pegs are not credible, risk premiums can cause large interest differentials—and cause investors to smell a profit.

Figure 22-5, panel (a), shows data for Hong Kong from 1990 to 2001, including the crucial period in 1997 when many Asian countries were in crisis and their exchange rate pegs were breaking. Most of the time, the interest differential between the Hong Kong dollar and the U.S. dollar was zero, as one would expect for what was perceived to be a credible peg. Hong Kong was operating a quasi-currency board with reserves

FIGURE 22-5

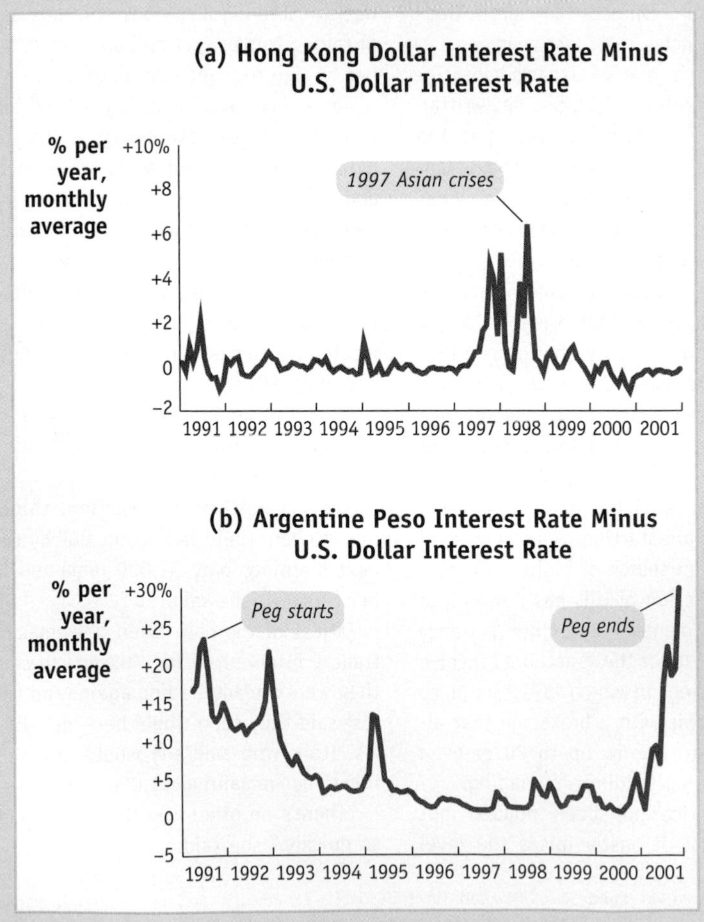

(a) Hong Kong Dollar Interest Rate Minus U.S. Dollar Interest Rate

(b) Argentine Peso Interest Rate Minus U.S. Dollar Interest Rate

Peso Problems If exchange rates are fixed (and credible), then the interest rate on the home currency and the base currency should be the same. As seen here, however, the Hong Kong dollar and Argentina peso often had large currency premiums. Hong Kong's peg held, and carry trade profits were made. Argentina's peg broke, and losses were massive.

Source: Hong Kong Monetary Authority and econstats.com.

of approximately 300% of the (base) money supply. Short of dollarization, this was considered about the most bulletproof peg around.

Nonetheless, in late 1997 investors started to fear that Hong Kong might suffer the same fate as other Asian economies. Expecting a future depreciation of the Hong Kong dollar, they started to demand a currency premium. At its peak, the Hong Kong interest rate rose almost 20 percentage points per year above the U.S. interest rate in late October, and the spread exceeded 5 percentage points for over three weeks.. However, *the expected depreciation never happened*. The Hong Kong dollar's peg to the U.S. dollar survived. Investors may have been reasonable to fear a crisis and demand a premium beforehand (ex ante), but after the fact (ex post), these unrealized expectations became realized profits. As a result, there was a lot of money to be made from the carry trade for those willing to park their money in Hong Kong dollars during all the fuss.

Should you always bet on a peg to hold in a crisis? No. Figure 22-5, panel (b), shows data for Argentina from 1991 to 2001. This includes the period of looming crisis for the Argentine economy in 2001, as the likelihood of default and depreciation grew. The country was in fiscal trouble with an ailing banking sector. It no longer had the ability to borrow in world capital markets and was about to be cut off from International Monetary Fund assistance. A recession was deepening. All of this was raising the pressure on the government to use monetary policy for purposes other than maintaining the peg. Investors began to demand a huge currency-plus-default premium on Argentine peso deposits to compensate them for the risk of a possible depreciation and/or banking crisis. Peso interest rates at one point were more than 25% above the U.S. interest rate. But in this case, investors' fears were justified: in December 2000 to January 2001 the Argentine government froze bank deposits, imposed capital controls, and the peg broke. The peso's value plummeted, and soon the exchange rate exceeded three pesos to the dollar, erasing more than two-thirds of the U.S. dollar value of peso deposits. In retrospect, the precrisis interest differentials had been too small: the carry traders who gambled and left their money in peso deposits eventually lost their shirts.

We can now see how expectations may not be realized, even when exchange rates are fixed. Fixed exchange rates often break, and investors may reasonably demand currency premiums at certain times. However, after the fact, such premiums may lead to returns from interest arbitrage that are positive (when pegs hold, as in the Hong Kong case) or negative (when pegs break, as in the Argentine case).

International economists refer to this phenomenon as the **peso problem** (given its common occurrence in a certain region of the world). But again, it is far from clear that the profits seen are a sign that UIP fails or that investors are acting irrationally. The collapse of a peg can be seen as a rare event, an extreme occurrence that is hard to predict but that will lead to large changes in the values of assets. This situation is not unlike, say, fire or earthquake insurance: every year that you pay the premium and nothing happens, you make a "loss" on the insurance arrangement, a pattern that could go on for years (hopefully, for your entire life), but you know that the insurance will pay off to your advantage in a big way if disaster strikes. ■

Peso problems: a man hammers on the door of a bank in a protest over frozen accounts, Buenos Aires, June 2002.

ALI BURAFI/AFP/Newscom

The Efficient Markets Hypothesis

Do carry trade profits disprove UIP? To explore this question further, let us rewrite Equation (22-3), which calculates expected profits, by replacing *expected* or *ex ante* values of the exchange rate with *actual* or *ex post* realized values.

$$\text{Actual profit} = \underbrace{i_F}_{\substack{\text{Interest rate} \\ \text{on foreign currency}}} + \underbrace{\frac{\Delta E_{H/F}}{E_{H/F}}}_{\substack{\text{Actual rate of depreciation} \\ \text{of the home currency}}} - \underbrace{i_H}_{\substack{\text{Interest rate} \\ \text{on home currency}}} \qquad (22\text{-}4)$$

$$\underbrace{\hphantom{i_F + \frac{\Delta E_{H/F}}{E_{H/F}}}}_{\text{Actual home currency rate of return on foreign deposits}} \qquad \underbrace{\hphantom{i_H}}_{\text{Cost of carry}}$$

Note the one subtle difference: the disappearance of the superscript "*e*," which denoted expectations of future exchange rate depreciation. This expression can be computed only after the fact: although interest rates are known in advance, the future exchange rate is not. We know actual profits only after the investment strategy has run its course.

Thus, the sole difference between actual and expected profits is a **forecast error** that corresponds to the difference between actual depreciation and expected depreciation. (Again, the importance of exchange rate forecasts is revealed!) This forecast error is the difference between Equation (22-3) and Equation (22-4), that is,

$$\text{Forecast error} = \begin{pmatrix} \text{Actual} \\ \text{profit} \end{pmatrix} - \begin{pmatrix} \text{Expected} \\ \text{profit} \end{pmatrix} = \frac{\Delta E_{H/F}}{E_{H/F}} - \frac{\Delta E_{H/F}^e}{E_{H/F}} \qquad (22\text{-}5)$$

Armed with this way of understanding *unexpected* profits, we can now confront an important and controversial puzzle in international macroeconomics: What can the behavior of this forecast error tell us about UIP and the workings of the forex market? One way to attack that question is to study expected and actual profits side by side to see the size of the forecast error and its pattern of behavior.

Expected Profits On the one hand, strictly speaking, UIP itself says nothing about the forecast error. It says only that before that fact, or *ex ante*, expected profits should be zero. Expectations are not directly observable in markets, but we can recall the evidence presented in the chapter on exchange rates in the short run based on surveys of traders' expectations for major currencies from 1988 to 1993. As a recap, Figure 22-6, panel (a), presents this evidence again. The figure plots the expected depreciation against the interest differential for several major currencies.[9]

On the 45-degree line, these two terms are equal, and expected profits will be zero, according to Equation (22-3). As in several studies of this sort, on average, the data are aligned close to, but not exactly on, the 45-degree line, so they are not wildly inconsistent with UIP. The line-of-best-fit slope is close to 1. But the survey data are probably prone to error and cover only some (but not all) of the traders in the market. Even using formal statistical tests, it is difficult to reject UIP based on shaky evidence of this sort. The hypothesis that UIP holds can typically survive this kind of test.

Actual Profits On the other hand, we know that actual profits are made. It is enlightening to see exactly how they are made by replacing the expected depreciation in panel (a) with actual depreciation, after the fact, or *ex post*. This change is made in

---

[9] Recall that given *covered* interest parity, which does hold, the interest differential also equals the forward premium.

FIGURE 22-6

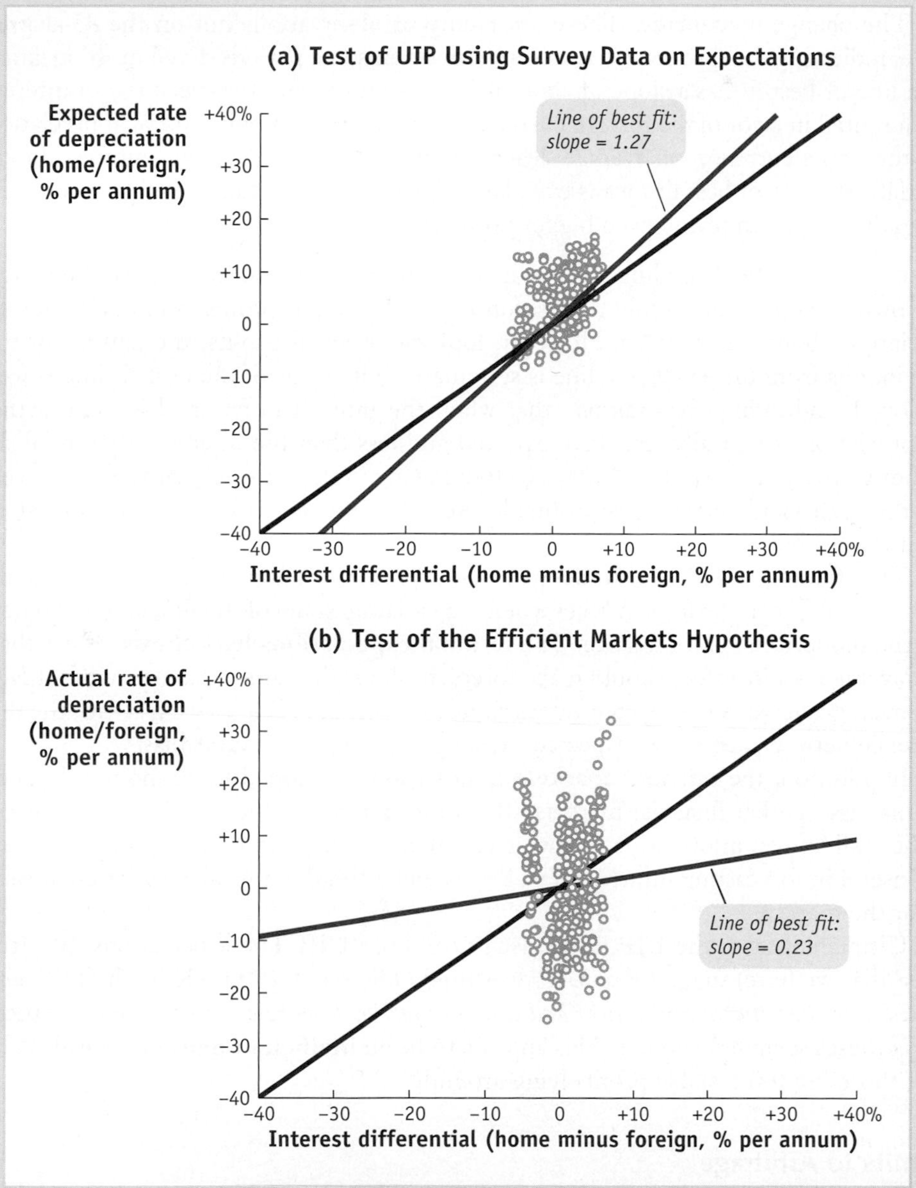

(a) Test of UIP Using Survey Data on Expectations

Expected rate of depreciation (home/foreign, % per annum)

Line of best fit: slope = 1.27

Interest differential (home minus foreign, % per annum)

(b) Test of the Efficient Markets Hypothesis

Actual rate of depreciation (home/foreign, % per annum)

Line of best fit: slope = 0.23

Interest differential (home minus foreign, % per annum)

UIP and the Efficient Markets Hypothesis Each dot represents an actual 12-month period for a given currency versus the U.S. dollar. According to trader surveys, expected depreciations were, *on average*, more or less in line with UIP, as seen in panel (a), where the slope is not far from 1. But panel (b) shows that, after the fact, these forecasts were not very good, and systematically wrong, in this sample. Actual depreciations were far out of line with expectations: the slope is only 0.23. On average, high-yield currencies systematically depreciated only 23% as much as the interest differential would have forecast under UIP.

Notes: Line of best fit is through the origin. Data shown are monthly for the German mark, Swiss franc, Japanese yen, British pound, and Canadian dollar against the U.S. dollar from February 1988 to October 1993.

Source: From Menzie Chinn and Jeffrey A. Frankel, "Survey Data on Exchange Rate Expectations: More Currencies, More Horizons, More Tests," in W. Allen and D. Dickinson, eds., 2002, Monetary Policy, Capital Flows and Financial Market Developments in the Era of Financial Globalisation: Essays in Honour of Max Fry (London: Routledge), pp. 145–167.

panel (b), which, to be consistent, shows actual profits for the same currencies over the same period.

The change is dramatic. There are plenty of observations not on the 45-degree line, indicating that profits and losses were made in some periods. Even more striking, the line of best fit has a slope of about 0.2. This means that for every 1% of interest differential in favor of the foreign currency, we would expect only a 0.2% appreciation of the home currency, on average, leaving a profit of 0.8%. At larger interest differentials, the line of best fit means even larger profits. (Some studies find zero, or even negative slopes, implying even bigger profits!)

The UIP Puzzle A finding that profits can be made needs careful handling. On its own, this need not imply a violation of UIP: random profits could arise due to variation about a zero mean. However, looking at actual profits, the pattern of the deviations from the 45-degree line is systematic. The slope of the best-fit line is well below 1, indicating, for example, that when the interest differential is high, actual depreciation is typically less than expected and less than the interest differential. In other words, *on average*, the carry trade (borrowing in the low-yield currency to invest in the high-yield currency) is profitable. Actual profits are risky, but they appear to be forecastable.

This finding is widely considered to be a puzzle or anomaly. If such profits are forecastable, then the forex market would be violating some of the fundamental tenets of the modern theory of finance. The **rational expectations hypothesis** argues that, on average, all investors should make forecasts about the future that are without *bias*: on average, actual and expected values should correspond. But, as we just saw, the difference between actual and expected exchange rates reveals a clear bias.

In addition, the **efficient markets hypothesis,** developed by economist Eugene Fama, asserts that financial markets are "informationally efficient" in that all prices reflect all known information at any given time. Hence, such information should not be useful in forecasting future profits: that is, one should not be able to systematically beat the market.

Ultimately then, the UIP puzzle isn't just about UIP. The expectations data (the best that we have) suggest that UIP does hold. The real UIP puzzle is why *UIP combined with the rational expectations and efficient markets hypotheses* fails to hold. Yet these hypotheses seemingly do fail. This appears to be an **inefficient market** instead. Why are those big forecastable profits lying around?

Limits to Arbitrage

Economists have proposed a number of ways to resolve these puzzles, and at some level all of these can be described as explanations based on a **limits to arbitrage** argument. What does this mean? In the first section of this chapter, we argued that there were limits to arbitrage, in the form of trade costs, that can help explain the PPP puzzle: purchasing power parity will not hold if there are frictions such as transport costs, tariffs, and so on that hamper arbitrage in goods markets.

Limits to arbitrage arguments can also be applied in the world of finance. But how? And can they help explain the UIP puzzle?

Trade Costs Are Small It is tempting but ultimately not fruitful to look for the same kinds of frictions that we saw in goods markets. Conventional trade costs in financial markets are simply too small to have an effect that is large enough to explain the puzzle. There are bid-ask spreads between currencies, and there may be other technical trading costs, for example, associated with when a forex trade is placed during the day and which financial markets are open. But none of these frictions provides a sufficient explanation for the forecastable profits and the market's inefficiency.

There is also the problem that if one wishes to make a very large transaction, especially in a less liquid currency, the act of trading itself may have an adverse impact on the exchange rate and curtail profitable trades. For example, an order for $1 billion of more liquid yen is more easily digested by the market than an order for $1 billion of less liquid New Zealand dollars. But again, this possibility is not likely to explain the UIP puzzle because investors can avert such a situation by breaking their trades up into small pieces and spreading them out over time. So even though these trading costs are real, they may not be large enough to offset the very substantial profits we have seen.

If trading costs are the sole limit to arbitrage, there is still a puzzle. We must look elsewhere.

Risk Versus Reward A promising approach to the puzzle examines traders' alternative investment strategies, draws on other puzzles in finance, is based less on introspection and more on observations of actual trading strategies, and connects with the frontiers of the emerging field of behavioral economics.

To approach this research and to make the investment problem facing the trader a little clearer, we can reconsider the data shown in Figure 22-6. In panel (b) we saw that the slope was only 0.23, meaning that for every 1% of interest differential, we would predict only 0.23% of offsetting depreciation, leaving a seemingly predictable profit of 0.77%. Suppose we followed a carry trade strategy of borrowing in the low interest rate currency and investing in the high-interest currency. If the interest differential were 1%, then we would expect to net a profit of 0.77%; if the interest differential were 2%, we would expect to double that profit to 1.54%; a differential of 3% would yield 2.31% profit, and so on, if we simply extrapolate that straight line.

This strategy would have delivered profits. However, there are two problems with it. First, profits do not, in fact, grow linearly with the interest differential. The straight-line model is a poor fit. At high-interest differentials there are times when profits are very good, and other times when the carry trade suffers a reversal, and large losses accrue, as we have seen. The second problem is a related one. At all levels of the interest differential, Figure 22-6 clearly shows the extreme volatility or riskiness of these returns due to the extreme and unpredictable volatility of the exchange rate. Actual rates of depreciation can easily range between plus or minus 10% per year, and up to plus or minus 30% in some cases.

One measure of the volatility of returns used by economists is the standard deviation, which we can now put to use to explore why these positive but risky profits are left unexploited.

The Sharpe Ratio and Puzzles in Finance Carry trade profits are the difference between a risky foreign return and a safe domestic interest rate. This kind of return difference is called an **excess return,** and to analyze it further, we can draw on one of the standard tools of financial economics.

The **Sharpe ratio** is the ratio of an asset's average annualized excess return to the annualized standard deviation of its return:

$$\text{Sharpe ratio} = \frac{\text{Mean (annual excess return)}}{\text{Standard deviation (annual excess return)}}$$

The ratio was invented by William Forsyth Sharpe, a Nobel laureate in economics. As a ratio of "rewards to variability," the Sharpe ratio tells us how much the returns on an asset compensate investors for the risks they take when investing in it.

Figure 22-7 displays data on returns to the simple carry trade strategy for several major currencies against the British pound for the period 1976 to 2005. For each pair of currencies, it is assumed that each month a trader would have borrowed in the low interest rate currency and invested in the high interest rate currency. Details on the returns to a portfolio of all such trades (equally weighted) are also shown.

In panel (a) we see that the returns to these strategies were positive for all currencies (they were also statistically significant), and, on average, they were about 4% per year. However, the volatility of the returns was even larger in all cases, as measured by the standard deviation. On average, this was about 10% on an annual basis, although falling to 6% for the portfolio (due to gains from diversification). In panel (b) the corresponding Sharpe ratios are shown, and we can see that they fall below 1 in all cases. The average for all currencies is 0.4 and, thanks to a reduction in volatility due to diversification, the equally weighted portfolio has a modestly higher Sharpe ratio of 0.6.

We now must ask: Should Sharpe ratios of around 0.5 be considered "big" or "small"? Do they signal that investors are missing a profit opportunity? Should people be rushing to take profits in investments that offer this mix of risk and reward? If this can be judged to be a "big" Sharpe ratio, then we have a puzzle as the market would seem to be failing in terms of efficiency.

FIGURE 22-7

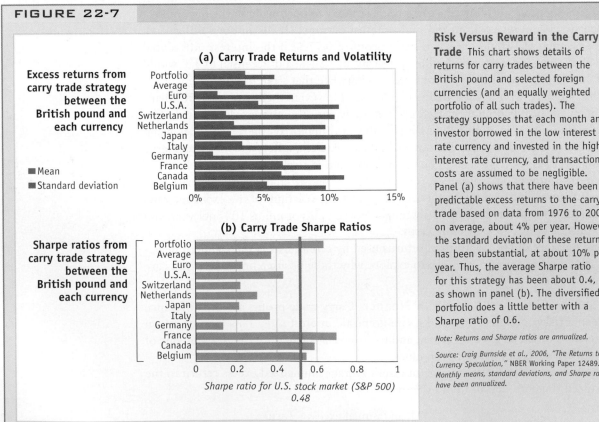

(a) Carry Trade Returns and Volatility

Excess returns from carry trade strategy between the British pound and each currency

■ Mean
■ Standard deviation

Portfolio
Average
Euro
U.S.A.
Switzerland
Netherlands
Japan
Italy
Germany
France
Canada
Belgium

0%   5%   10%   15%

(b) Carry Trade Sharpe Ratios

Sharpe ratios from carry trade strategy between the British pound and each currency

Portfolio
Average
Euro
U.S.A.
Switzerland
Netherlands
Japan
Italy
Germany
France
Canada
Belgium

0   0.2   0.4   0.6   0.8   1

Sharpe ratio for U.S. stock market (S&P 500) 0.48

Risk Versus Reward in the Carry Trade This chart shows details of returns for carry trades between the British pound and selected foreign currencies (and an equally weighted portfolio of all such trades). The strategy supposes that each month an investor borrowed in the low interest rate currency and invested in the high interest rate currency, and transaction costs are assumed to be negligible. Panel (a) shows that there have been predictable excess returns to the carry trade based on data from 1976 to 2005, on average, about 4% per year. However, the standard deviation of these returns has been substantial, at about 10% per year. Thus, the average Sharpe ratio for this strategy has been about 0.4, as shown in panel (b). The diversified portfolio does a little better with a Sharpe ratio of 0.6.

Note: Returns and Sharpe ratios are annualized.

Source: Craig Burnside et al., 2006, "The Returns to Currency Speculation," NBER Working Paper 12489. Monthly means, standard deviations, and Sharpe ratios have been annualized.

It turns out that many investors in the forex market would consider that 0.5 is a fairly small Sharpe ratio. To see why, and to understand how this approach may "solve" the UIP puzzle, we note that historically, as shown in panel (b), the annual Sharpe ratio for the U.S. stock market has been about 0.48, based on the excess returns of the broad S&P 500 index over and above risk-free U.S. Treasury bonds. This reference level of 0.48 might be thought of as a hurdle that competing investment strategies must beat if they are to attract additional investment. But we can see from panel (b) that forex carry trades either fall below this bar, or just barely surmount it.

There are indeed excess returns in the stock market, but investors are not rushing to borrow money to buy stocks to push that Sharpe ratio any lower. Admittedly, many economists consider the stock market finding to be a puzzle (called the *equity premium puzzle*) because under various standard theories and assumptions about risk aversion, it is hard to understand why investors sit back and leave such excess returns on the table. And yet they do, a fact that leads other economists to postulate that some very nonstandard assumptions, some drawn from psychology, may now need to be included in models to properly explain investor behavior. Research in *behavioral finance*, a branch of behavioral economics, attempts to explain such seemingly irrational market outcomes using various principles such as rational action under different preferences (e.g., strong aversion to loss) or more limited forms of rationality (e.g., models with slow or costly learning).

To sum up, there are now theories that might explain why nobody arbitrages the stock market when its Sharpe ratio is 0.48. That just isn't a high enough reward-risk ratio to attract investors. But in our forex market data, the Sharpe ratio is about the same, and most other studies find carry trade Sharpe ratios that are little larger than the stock market's 0.48.[10] So we may have an answer to the question why arbitrage does not erase all excess returns. The ratio of rewards to risk is so very small that investors in the market are simply uninterested. Indeed, surveys of trader behavior in major firms by economist Richard Lyons suggest that, in the forex market, if the predicted Sharpe ratio of a strategy falls below even 1, then this is enough to discourage investor interest.[11]

Predictability and Nonlinearity Can we do better than a straight-line model or linear predictions of returns and crude carry trade strategies? More complex and diversified forex trading strategies may be able to jack up the Sharpe ratio a little, but not too much. As an alternative way of describing the data, for example, we can use nonlinear models that fit the data quite well.[12]

Nonlinear models show that at low interest differentials (say, 0% to 2%), profits are inherently low, and nobody has been much interested in arbitrage given the risks; conversely, at high differentials (say, 5% or more), the rewards have often vanished as investors have rushed in, bid up the high-yield currency to its maximum value, causing a reversal that wipes out carry trade profits. At the extremes, arbitrage has tended to

---

[10] Furthermore, in illiquid markets, traders may be concerned that the act of trading itself will cause adverse price movements, eliminating profits. In that case, observed Sharpe ratios may overstate the size of unexploited profits.

[11] Richard K. Lyons, 2001, *The Microstructure Approach to Exchange Rates* (Cambridge, Mass.: MIT Press). Lyons also found carry trade Sharpe ratios of about 0.4 using a historical sample of currencies.

[12] Jerry Coakley and Ana-Maria Fuertes, 2001, "A Non-Linear Analysis of Excess Foreign Exchange Returns," *Manchester School*, 69(6), 623–642; Lucio Sarno, Giorgio Valente, and Hyginus Leon, 2006, "Nonlinearity in Deviations from Uncovered Interest Parity: An Explanation of the Forward Bias Puzzle," *Review of Finance*, 10(3), 443–482; Òscar Jordà and Alan M. Taylor, 2012, "The Carry Trade and Fundamentals: Nothing to Fear but FEER Itself," *Journal of International Economics*, 88(1), 74–90."

work when it should (or shouldn't). Only in the middle do moderate, positive Sharpe ratios emerge, it seems, for investors willing to take some risks. Thus, our "small" average Sharpe ratios are a mix of these low and high returns, suggesting more sophisticated strategies should ensure that the investment decision depends on the size of the expected return. But the rewards relative to risk are still quite meager and Sharpe ratios are still fairly low even when arbitrage looks most promising.

Conclusion

The main lesson here is that risky arbitrage is fundamentally different from riskless arbitrage. Based on this sort of standard financial analysis, many economists conclude that although there may be excess returns, even *predictable* excess returns, in the forex market, the risk-reward ratio is typically too low to attract additional investors.[13] In that sense, there is no puzzle left and arbitrage has not failed—it has just gone as far as might be reasonably expected, at least given investor behavior in equity markets and elsewhere. In forex market research, nobody has yet proved that there are large amounts of low-risk money lying on the table (though if they did, they might not publish the result).

What are the implications? Here, there is common ground between the UIP and PPP puzzles. In the case of the PPP puzzle studied earlier in the chapter, limits to arbitrage in the goods market (mainly due to transaction costs) may create a band of inaction allowing for deviations from parity in purchasing prices. In the case of the UIP puzzle, limits to arbitrage in the forex market (mainly due to risk) may allow for deviations from interest parity in some situations.

3 Debt and Default

In the chapter on the gains from financial globalization, when global capital markets work well, they can deliver gains in the form of consumption smoothing and investment efficiency. Yet international financial relations are often disrupted by **sovereign default,** which occurs when a sovereign government (i.e., one that is autonomous or independent) fails to meet its legal obligations to make payments on debt held by foreigners.

Sovereign default has a long history. Perhaps the first recorded default was in the fourth century BC, when Greek municipalities defaulted on loans from the Delos Temple.[14] Many of today's advanced countries have defaulted in the past. In 1343 a war-weary Edward III of England defaulted on short-term loans which ruined the major merchant banks of Florence, Italy. In 1557, Phillip II of Spain defaulted on short-term loans principally from South German bankers.[15] Spain defaulted six more times before 1800 and another seven times in the nineteenth century. France defaulted eight times between 1558 and the Revolution in 1789. A group of German states, Portugal,

---

[13] There may be a few exceptions to this general statement, and indeed, some currency hedge funds and other large firms with deep pockets and an appetite for risk may be able to eke out worthwhile profits through complex trading strategies, but only time will tell whether these players will whittle down the Sharpe ratio any further.

[14] Federico Sturzenegger and Jeromin Zettelmeyer, 2007, *Debt Defaults and Lessons from a Decade of Crises* (Cambridge, Mass.: MIT Press), Chapter 1.

[15] Meir G. Kohn, "Merchant Banking in the Medieval and Early Modern Economy," February 1999, Dartmouth College, Department of Economics Working Paper No. 99-05.

Austria, and Greece defaulted at least four times each in the 1800s, and across Europe as a whole, there were at least 46 sovereign defaults between 1501 and 1900.[16] The United States has maintained a clean sheet during its brief existence, although several U.S. states defaulted when they were emerging markets in the 1800s.[17]

The advanced countries of today tend not to default, although the large debts they have incurred during the Global Financial Crisis may put some of them at greater risk (from 2010 to 2013 countries such as Ireland, Portugal, Spain, Italy, Slovenia, and Cyprus have been under strain, and Greece actually defaulted). In contrast, default has been, and remains, a recurring problem in emerging markets and developing countries. One count shows that countries such as Argentina, Brazil, Mexico, Turkey, and Venezuela have defaulted between five and nine times since 1824 (and at least once since 1980) and have spent 30% of the time failing to meet their financial obligations. Another count lists 48 sovereign defaults in the period from 1976 to 1989, many in Latin America but others dotted throughout the world, and 16 more in the period from 1998 to 2002, including headline crises in Russia (1998) and Argentina (2002).[18]

One of the most puzzling aspects of the default problem is that emerging markets and developing countries often get into default trouble at much lower levels of debt than advanced countries. Yet default is a serious macroeconomic and financial problem for these countries. Because they attract so few financial flows of other kinds, government debt constitutes a large share (more than 30%) of these nations' external liabilities.[19]

To understand the workings of sovereign debt and defaults, we must first look at some of the peculiar characteristics of this form of borrowing.

A Few Peculiar Facts About Sovereign Debt

The first important fact about sovereign debt is that debtors are almost never forced to pay. Using the military to enforce repayment is always costly, and is certainly out of fashion in the modern world. Legal actions are also largely futile: when developing country debt is issued in a foreign jurisdiction (e.g., in London or New York), there is practically no legal way to enforce a claim against a sovereign nation, and the recent increase in sovereign default litigation has done very little to change this state of affairs.[20]

---

[16] Carmen M. Reinhart, Kenneth S. Rogoff, and Miguel A. Savastano, 2003, "Debt Intolerance," *Brookings Papers on Economic Activity*, 1, 1–74.
[17] For example, see Section 258 of the Mississippi state constitution. The American colonies did default, for example, on the paper bills known as *continentals*, issued from 1775 to 1779 to finance the Revolutionary War. However, in an attempt to make good, the colonies' bad debts were assumed by the United States in 1790 on the urging of the first U.S. Secretary of the Treasury, Alexander Hamilton, a statesman with an acute understanding of the importance of good credit.
[18] Carmen M. Reinhart, Kenneth S. Rogoff, and Miguel A. Savastano, 2003, "Debt Intolerance," *Brookings Papers on Economic Activity*, 1, 1–74; Federico Sturzenegger and Jeromin Zettelmeyer, 2007, *Debt Defaults and Lessons from a Decade of Crises* (Cambridge, Mass.: MIT Press), Chapter 1.
[19] About 50% of the external liabilities of these countries consist of debt, and of that, approximately 75% is government debt. Data for 2004 from the World Bank; Global Development Finance database; and Gian Maria Milesi-Ferretti and Philip R. Lane, 2006, "The External Wealth of Nations Mark II: Revised and Extended Estimates of Foreign Assets and Liabilities, 1970–2004," IMF Working Paper No. 06/69.
[20] On litigation, see Federico Sturzenegger and Jeromin Zettelmeyer, "Has the Legal Threat to Sovereign Debt Restructuring Become Real?" CIF Working Paper, Universidad Torcuato Di Tella, April 2006. In theory, foreign assets of defaulters can be legally seized, but defaulting nations naturally avoid this by repatriating such assets shortly before going into default. In contrast, advanced country debt is usually issued at home, in the country's own jurisdiction, where creditors (domestic and foreign) have stronger legal claims against the sovereign. Even so, the winds could change, and the still ongoing battle in the New York courts in the case of *NML Capital Ltd. v. Republic of Argentina* exposes the stubborn, but as yet fruitless, efforts of creditors in their eternal efforts to pare back sovereign immunity and enforce their contracts.

The repayment of a sovereign debt is thus a matter of choice for the borrowing government. Economists are therefore inclined to look for a rational explanation in which default is triggered by economic conditions: how painful does repayment have to become before default occurs?

To answer this question, we must evaluate the costs and benefits of default. The benefits are clear: no repayment means the country gets to keep all that money. Are there costs? While not as apparent as the benefits, there must be costs to default—if there were no costs, countries would never pay their debts, and, as a result, no lending would happen in the first place! Thus economists (ignoring sentimental motives for repayment such as honor and honesty) have focused on two types of costs that act as a "punishment" for defaulters and provide the incentive for nations to repay their debts.[21]

- *Financial market penalties.* Empirical evidence shows that debtors are usually excluded from credit markets for some time after a default. This exclusion could expose them to greater consumption risk and other disadvantages. However, economic theory casts doubt on whether avoiding these costs is enough of an incentive to repay the loans. Repayment is less likely when the exclusion period is short or when borrowers have other ways to smooth consumption (such as investing previously borrowed wealth, purchasing insurance, or going to a different set of financial intermediaries).

- *Broader macroeconomic costs.* These could include lost investment, lost trade, or lost output arising from adverse financial conditions in the wake of a default. These adverse conditions include higher risk premiums, credit contractions, exchange rate crises, and banking crises. If these costs are high enough, they can encourage nations to repay, even if financial market costs are insufficient.

Old-style punishment: In response to a default, the French invaded and occupied Mexico in 1862, suffering only one major defeat at the battle of Puebla (now commemorated by the Mexican holiday Cinco de Mayo).

Summary Sovereign debt is a **contingent claim** on a nation's assets: governments will repay depending on whether it is more beneficial to repay than to default. With a simple model of how a country makes the decision to default, we can better understand why borrowers default some of the time and repay some of the time; what ultimately causes these contingent outcomes; why some borrowers get into default trouble even at low levels of debt, while others do not; and how lenders respond to this state of affairs and why they continue to lend to defaulting countries. The model we develop is simple, but it provides useful insights on all of these questions.[22]

A Model of Default, Part One: The Probability of Default

In this section, we present a static, one-period model of sovereign debt and default. The first part of the model focuses on default as a contingent claim that will be paid only under certain conditions.

[21] Jonathan Eaton and Mark Gersovitz, 1981, "Debt with Potential Repudiation: Theoretical and Empirical Analysis," *Review of Economic Studies*, 48(2), 289–309; Jeremy Bulow and Kenneth Rogoff, 1989, "A Constant Recontracting Model of Sovereign Debt," *Journal of Political Economy*, 97(1), 155–178; Kenneth M. Kletzer and Brian D. Wright, 2000, "Sovereign Debt as Intertemporal Barter," *American Economic Review*, 90(3), 621–639; Laura Alfaro and Fabio Kanczuk, 2005, "Sovereign Debt as a Contingent Claim: A Quantitative Approach," *Journal of International Economics*, 65(2), 297–314.
[22] The model is based on Luis Catão and Sandeep Kapur, 2006, "Volatility and the Debt-Intolerance Paradox," *IMF Staff Papers*, 53(2), 195–218.

Assumptions The model focuses on the desire of borrowers to default in hard times, when output is relatively low, so that they may smooth their consumption. Thus, for now we ignore any investment motives for borrowing and concentrate on the consumption-smoothing or "insurance" benefits that a country derives from having the option to default on its debt and consume more than it otherwise would.

If repayment is to be contingent in our model, on what will it be contingent? To introduce some exogenous fluctuations, we assume, realistically, that a borrowing country has a fluctuating level of output Y. Specifically, Y is equally likely to take any value between a minimum $\overline{Y} - V$ and a maximum $\overline{Y}$. The difference between the minimum and maximum is a measure of the volatility of output, V. Although the level of output Y is not known in advance, we assume that everyone understands the level of V and the probability of different output levels Y. We suppose the government is the sole borrower and it takes out a one-period loan in the previous period, before the level of output is known. The debt will be denoted L for loan (or liability, which it is) and carries an interest rate r_L, which we call the *lending rate*. We suppose this loan is supplied by one or more competitive foreign creditors who have access to funds from the world capital market at a risk-free interest rate r, which we assume is a constant.

We suppose the loan is due to be paid off after the country finds out what output Y is in the current period. The problem we have is as follows: to figure out the lending terms (the debt level and lending rate) and to understand what the country chooses to do when the loan comes due (default versus repayment). As in many problems in economics, we must "solve backward" to allow for expectations.

The Borrower Chooses Default Versus Repayment We assume the sovereign borrower faces some "punishment" or cost for defaulting. There are debates about what forms these costs could take, and we discuss this later in this section. For now we do not take a stand on exactly what these costs are but assume that if the government defaults, then it faces a cost equivalent to a fraction c of its output: that is, cY is lost, leaving only $(1 - c)Y$ for national consumption. Note that these costs are unlike debt payments: they are just losses for the debtor with no corresponding gains for the creditors.

Now that we have established some costs of defaulting, the choice facing the country becomes clearer. For simplicity, we assume two possible courses of action: repay or default.[23] If the government repays the debt, the country will be able to consume only output Y minus the principal and interest on the loan $(1 + r_L)L$. If the government defaults, the country can consume output Y minus the punishment cY. Thus, the government will act as follows:

$$\text{Repay if} \quad \underbrace{Y - (1 + r_L)L}_{\substack{\text{Consumption after} \\ \text{repayment (line RR)}}} \quad > \quad \underbrace{Y - cY}_{\substack{\text{Consumption after nonrepayment} \\ \text{and default (line NN)}}}$$

Figure 22-8 plots both sides of this inequality against Y for the case in which both repayment and default will occur within the range of possible output levels between maximum output $\overline{Y}$ and minimum output $\overline{Y} - V$. At some critical level of output, called the **repayment threshold**, the government will switch from repayment to default. At this critical level, the two sides of the preceding inequality have to be equal; that is, the debt payoff amount $(1 + r_L)L$ must equal the punishment cost cY.

---

[23] Intermediate cases of partial default are possible in theory and in reality, as is renegotiation, but we focus on a binary default versus repayment choice for simplicity.

By rearranging the preceding inequality, we can find the level of Y at the repayment threshold Y_T and can restate the government's choice as

$$\text{Repay if} \quad Y \geq \underbrace{\frac{(1 + r_L)L}{c}}_{\substack{\text{Repayment threshold} \\ = \\ Y_T}}$$

For the case shown in Figure 22-8, we assume that this repayment threshold, $Y_T = (1 + r_L)L/c$, is within the range of possible outputs between the minimum $\overline{Y} - V$ and the maximum $\overline{Y}$.

The value of consumption after repayment, $Y - (1 + r_L)L$, is shown by the repayment line RR, which has a slope of 1: every extra \$1 of output goes toward consumption, net of debt repayments. The value of consumption after nonrepayment and default, $Y - cY$, is shown by the nonrepayment line NN, which has a slope of $(1 - c)$, which is less than 1: when a country has decided to default, from every extra \$1 of output gained by not repaying the country's debts, only \$$(1 - c)$ goes toward consumption, allowing for the net punishment cost.

The lines RR and NN intersect at the critical point T, and the corresponding level of output Y_T is the repayment threshold. Given that the slope of NN is less than the

FIGURE 22-8

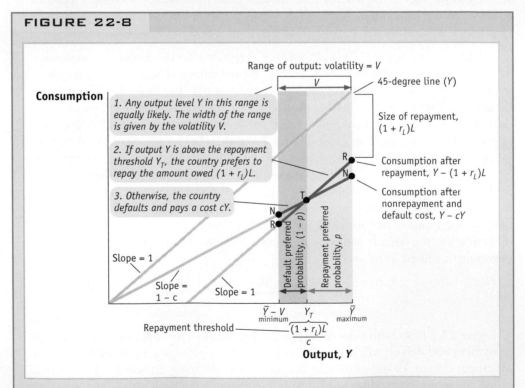

Repayment Versus Default When output is high, the country repays its debt with probability p (the fraction of the shaded area that is light) because the cost of defaulting is greater than the cost of repayment. In this region, consumption after repayment (shown by line RR) is greater than consumption after defaulting (line NN). When output is low, the country defaults with probability $1 - p$ (the fraction of the shaded area that is dark). In this region, the cost of defaulting is less than the cost of repayment because line NN is above line RR. The switch from default to repayment occurs at point T, where the critical level of output reaches the repayment threshold Y_T.

slope of RR, we can see that the country will choose to repay when output is above the repayment threshold Y_T (i.e., to the right of T) and to default when output is below the repayment threshold Y_T (i.e., to the left of T).

Note that the size of the repayment region relative to the default region tells us how likely repayment is to occur relative to default. Let the probability of repayment be p. The key piece of the puzzle is to figure out what determines p. We now show how it depends on two factors: how volatile output is and how burdensome the debt repayment is.

An Increase in the Debt Burden The first variation on the model in Figure 22-8 that we consider is an exogenous increase in the level of debt payments, which we suppose increase from the original level $(1 + r_L)L$ to a new higher level $(1 + r'_L)L'$. This increase could be due to a change in the debt level, a change in the lending rate, or some combination of the two. This case is shown in Figure 22-9.

The value of consumption after repayment, $Y - (1 + r_L)L$, must fall as $(1 + r_L)L$ rises, so line RR will shift down to R'R'. The costs of repayment are higher, and the country will find it beneficial to default more often. We can see this in the figure because after the RR curve shifts down, a greater part of the line NN will now sit above the line R'R', and the new critical intersection point T will move to the right at T', corresponding to the new higher repayment threshold, $Y'_T = (1 + r'_L)L'/c$.

What does this mean for the probability of repayment? It must fall. The repayment region on the right is now smaller, and the default region on the left is larger. With all

---

FIGURE 22-9

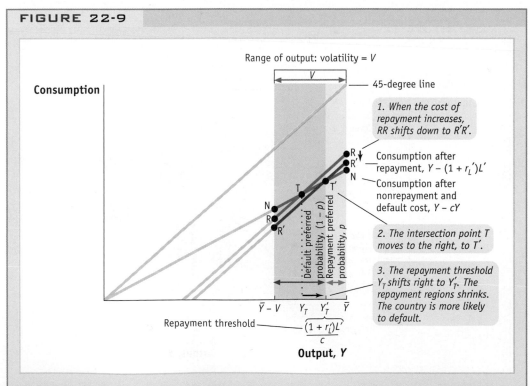

An Increase in the Debt Burden An increase in the level of debt or the lending rate raises the repayment sum and so reduces consumption after repayment at all levels of Y, causing RR to shift down. This shift makes repayment less likely (the light shaded area gets smaller) and default more likely (the dark shaded area gets larger). The probability of repayment p falls. The switch from default to repayment occurs at a higher critical level of output at T', the new repayment threshold Y'_T.

output levels in the two regions equally likely, the probability p that output is in the repayment region must now be lower.

We have considered only a small change in the debt burden, so the repayment region hasn't vanished. But if the debt burden increases sufficiently, RR will shift down so far that the critical point T will shift all the way to the right, to the maximum level of output, the repayment region will disappear, and the probability of repayment will be zero (or 0%). If the debt burden is high enough, the country is always better off taking the punishment.

Conversely, if the debt burden *decreases* sufficiently, RR will shift up so far that the critical point T will shift all the way to the left, to the minimum level of output, the default region will disappear, and the probability of repayment will be 1 (or 100%). If the debt burden is low enough, the country will always repay.

Thus, the outcome shown in Figure 22-8 applies only when the debt burden is at some intermediate level such that the repayment threshold is between the minimum and maximum levels of output.

An Increase in Volatility of Output The second variation on the model in Figure 22-8 that we consider is an increase in the volatility of output, which we suppose increases from its original level V to a new higher level V'. This case is shown in Figure 22-10. There could be many reasons why a country is subject to higher output volatility: weather shocks to agricultural output, political instability, fluctuations in the prices of its exports, and so on.

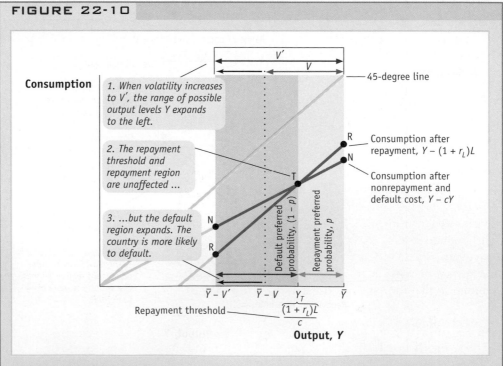

FIGURE 22-10

1. When volatility increases to V', the range of possible output levels Y expands to the left.

2. The repayment threshold and repayment region are unaffected ...

3. ...but the default region expands. The country is more likely to default.

Consumption after repayment, $Y - (1 + r_L)L$

Consumption after nonrepayment and default cost, $Y - cY$

Repayment threshold — $\dfrac{(1 + r_L)L}{c}$

Default preferred probability, $(1 - p)$

Repayment preferred probability, p

45-degree line

Output, Y

An Increase in Volatility An increase in volatility expands the range of low output possibilities. The repayment threshold Y_T stays the same because it is unrelated to V and depends only on the cost of defaulting and the size of the repayment burden. Even though the repayment region (light shaded area) remains the same size, the increased volatility makes default more likely because the default region (dark shaded area) is now relatively larger. The probability of repayment p falls.

In this case, the consumption levels after repayment on line RR and after default on line NN are unchanged because the debt burden is unchanged. What has changed is that there is now a much wider range of possible output levels. Higher volatility V means that output can now fall to an even lower minimum level, $\overline{Y} - V'$, but can only attain the same maximum $\overline{Y}$.

Thus, an increase in V makes default more likely. In Figure 22-8, the country wanted to default whenever output fell below the critical level T, so it will certainly want to default in the wider range of low outputs brought into play by higher volatility. The default region gets larger and now includes all these new possible levels of output to the left of T. Conversely, the range of outputs to the right of T where repayment occurs is unchanged because the repayment threshold, $Y_T = (1 + r_L)L/c$, is unaffected by a change in V. Hence, the probability p that output is in the repayment region must fall because the repayment region is now smaller relative to the default region.

To sum up, a rise in volatility lowers the level of debt L at which default becomes a possibility and after that point makes default more likely at any given level of L, up to the point at which default occurs with probability 100%.

The Lender Chooses the Lending Rate All of the preceding results assume a given interest rate on the loan. But now that we know how the likely probability of repayment p is determined, we can calculate the interest rate that a competitive lender must charge. Competition will mean that lenders can only just break even and make zero expected profit. Thus, the lender will set its lending rate so that the expected revenues from each dollar lent, given by the probability of repayment p times the amount repaid $(1 + r_L)$, equal the lender's cost for each dollar lent, which is given by $(1 + r)$, the principal plus the risk-free interest rate at which the lender can obtain funds.

$$\text{Break-even condition for lender:} \quad \underbrace{p}_{\substack{\text{Probability} \\ \text{of repayment}}} \times \underbrace{\underbrace{(1 + r_L)}_{\substack{\text{Lender's revenue} \\ \text{if repaid}}} = \underbrace{(1 + r)}_{\text{Lender's costs}}}_{\text{Lender's expected revenue}}$$

What do we learn from this expression? The right-hand side is a constant, determined by the world risk-free rate of interest r. Thus, the left-hand side must be constant, too. If p were 1 (100% probability of repayment), the solution would be straightforward: with no risk of default and competitive lenders, the borrower will rightly obtain a lending rate equal to the risk-free rate r. But as the probability of repayment p falls, to keep the left-hand side constant, the lenders must raise the lending rate r_L. That is, to compensate for the default risk, the lenders charge a risk premium so that they still just break even.

APPLICATION

Is There Profit in Lending to Developing Countries?

Our break-even assumption may seem a little odd. A popular belief is that rich country creditors, like loan sharks, are making huge profits from lending to developing countries. But the long-run empirical evidence suggests otherwise.

Economists Christoph Klingen, Beatrice Weder, and Jeromin Zettelmeyer looked at how lenders fared in emerging markets from the 1970s to the 2000s by computing the returns on government debt in 22 borrower countries.[24] They did not look at the *ex ante returns* that consisted of the promised repayments in the original loan contracts. Instead, they looked at the *ex post returns*, the realized rates of interest actually paid on the loans, allowing for any defaults, suspensions of payments, reschedulings, or other deviations from the contractual terms.

The results were striking, as shown by Figure 22-11. The average returns on emerging market bonds in this period were 9.1% per year. This was barely above the three-year U.S. government bond returns of 8.6% over the same period and below returns on 10-year U.S. government bonds (9.2%) and U.S. corporate bonds (10.5%). This is not because the borrowers were charged low interest rates beforehand. They were charged typical risk premiums. But if the loans had been paid off *according to those terms*, we would have expected that lenders would have reaped much larger returns ex post. For example, based on the typical risk premiums seen in emerging markets in the period 1998 to 2007, an extra 2.8% return would have been demanded as a risk premium ex ante, pushing ex post returns up to around 12% to 13%. But such high *ex post* returns were not seen, as Figure 22-11 shows: defaults ate up the risk premiums and the lenders barely broke even.

Considering the highly risky nature of emerging market debt, as compared with U.S. corporate debt, this finding is remarkable and it suggests that the break-even assumption of our simple model is not far wrong. Admittedly, there were periods when emerging market bonds paid off handsomely. In the early 1990s there were few defaults and lenders were repaid at high interest rates. But there were also periods with massive defaults, like the early 1980s, in which repeated postponements and restructurings meant that creditors got back only pennies on each dollar they had lent to the defaulting countries. Defaults are rare but cataclysmic

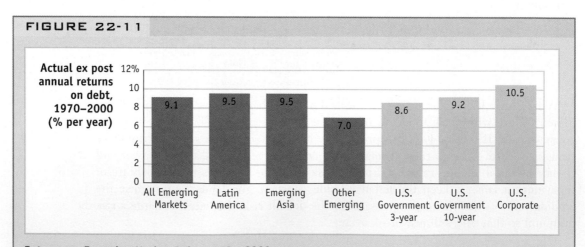

FIGURE 22-11

Actual ex post annual returns on debt, 1970–2000 (% per year)

Returns on Emerging Market Debt, 1970s–2000s The *ex post* annual realized returns on emerging market debt have been 9.1% on average, as high as 9.5% in Latin America and Asia, but as low as 7% elsewhere (columns 1–4). Given their riskiness, these returns compare unfavorably with returns on safe U.S. government debt and U.S. corporate debt (columns 5–7). Whatever *ex ante* risk premiums were charged to emerging markets, defaults ate them all up and lenders only just broke even.

Source: Ex post returns from Christoph Klingen, Jeromin Zettelmeyer, and Beatrice Weder, 2004, "How Private Creditors Fared in Emerging Debt Markets, 1970–2000," IMF Working Paper No. 04/13.

---

[24] Christoph Klingen, Jeromin Zettelmeyer, and Beatrice Weder, 2004, "How Private Creditors Fared in Emerging Debt Markets, 1970–2000," IMF Working Paper No. 04/13.

events for creditors, so only a long-run sample can be informative. But judging from the data in Figure 22-11, lenders to emerging markets have only just broken even, if that. ■

A Model of Default, Part Two: Loan Supply and Demand

The first steps we took in constructing the model were to understand the problem from the lender's standpoint. Knowing the probability p that borrowers will default when output is low, lenders adjust the lending rate r_L they charge depending on the volatility of output V and the level of debt L. Knowing the lending rate and the debt amount determines the loan supply curve for a country, which, combined with an understanding of loan demand, will allow us to determine equilibrium in the loan market.

Loan Supply Suppose output volatility is at some low level V. The probability of repayment is shown in Figure 22-12, panel (a). The loan supply curve $LS(V)$ is shown in panel (b).

At low levels of debt, as we saw, the probability of repayment is 100%, so a loan of size L in this range will be made at a lending rate r_L that equals the risk-free rate. In this debt range, the loan supply curve is flat between points 1 and 2. Then, as debt rises above some loan size L_V that depends on the volatility of the borrowing country's output, the probability of repayment starts to fall below 1 (100%), and the break-even condition tells us that lenders will have to start increasing the lending rate so they don't lose their shirts. At point 2 (the point at which the probability of repayment falls below 100%), the supply curve starts to slope up. For any given increase in loan size L, lenders must decide how much to increase the lending rate r_L to ensure that the break-even condition is met. In making this decision, the lenders must take into account that any increases in L and/or r_L will adversely affect the repayment probability p (as we saw earlier). Finally, as the loan size approaches its maximum L_{MAX}, the rising repayment burden (higher L *and* higher r_L) will cause the probability of repayment to approach zero. The lending rate will have to approach infinity to ensure that the loan will break even, so the loan supply curve becomes vertical as the debt limit L_{MAX} is reached. No loans are supplied above this level of debt.

Loan Demand The equilibrium market outcome must be somewhere on the lender's loan supply curve. But it must also be on the borrower's loan demand curve. How is that determined? The formal derivation of borrowing demand depends on the country's consumption preferences, including its aversion to risk; this is mathematically complex, but we can sum up the results intuitively by drawing a loan demand curve $LD(V)$ that depends on two factors: the lending rate charged, r_L, and the volatility of output, V. We restrict our attention to the normal case in which the demand curve slopes down so that an increase in the interest cost of the loan (a rise in r_L) causes a decrease in the size of loan demanded (a fall in L).

We can now finish our graphical representation of the loan market equilibrium, and in Figure 22-12, panel (b), equilibrium is at point 3, where loan supply LS and loan demand LD intersect. Note that this intersection will be, as shown, between L_V and L_{MAX}. Why? Below debt level L_V, the country never defaults and so debt provides no consumption-smoothing insurance in this range, and the country will want to borrow more and move up and to the right along the loan supply curve. As the cost

FIGURE 22-12

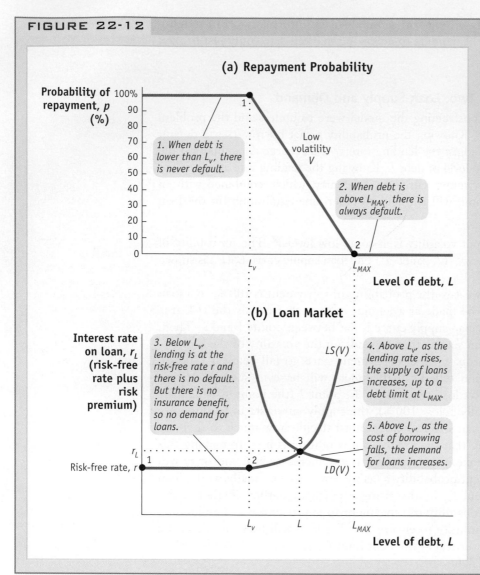

(a) Repayment Probability

Probability of repayment, p (%)

1. When debt is lower than L_v, there is never default.

Low volatility V

2. When debt is above L_{MAX}, there is always default.

Level of debt, L

(b) Loan Market

Interest rate on loan, r_L (risk-free rate plus risk premium)

3. Below L_v, lending is at the risk-free rate r and there is no default. But there is no insurance benefit, so no demand for loans.

4. Above L_v, as the lending rate rises, the supply of loans increases, up to a debt limit at L_{MAX}.

5. Above L_v, as the cost of borrowing falls, the demand for loans increases.

$LS(V)$

$LD(V)$

Risk-free rate, r

Level of debt, L

Loan Market Equilibrium When Volatility Is Low A higher level of debt means the probability of repayment falls (and the probability of default increases) between points 1 and 2 in panel (a), starting at the debt level L_v. As the probability of repayment falls, lenders increase the lending rate as the quantity of debt increases, so the loan supply curve LS slopes up in panel (b). As the lending rate falls, more debt is demanded by the country as insurance against consumption risk, so the loan demand curve LD slopes down. The equilibrium is at point 3 where demand and supply intersect.

of borrowing rises, however, the country must consider the trade-off between the amount of insurance it obtains from the debt and the rising cost of that insurance. At some point, this trade-off evens out and we reach the loan quantity the country desires. In Figure 22-12 the quantity of loans supplied and demanded will be equal at equilibrium point 3 with debt level L and lending rate r_L.

An Increase in Volatility What happens if the country has a higher level of volatility V'? We now show how the loan supply and demand curves will shift to $LS(V')$ and $LD(V')$, as shown in Figure 22-13.

In panel (a), higher volatility means that default starts to become a possibility at a low level of debt compared with the low volatility case, as we saw previously. Once above that level of debt, repayment is less likely than when volatility is low. This means that the lending rate rises more quickly to ensure the lenders break even, and

FIGURE 22-13

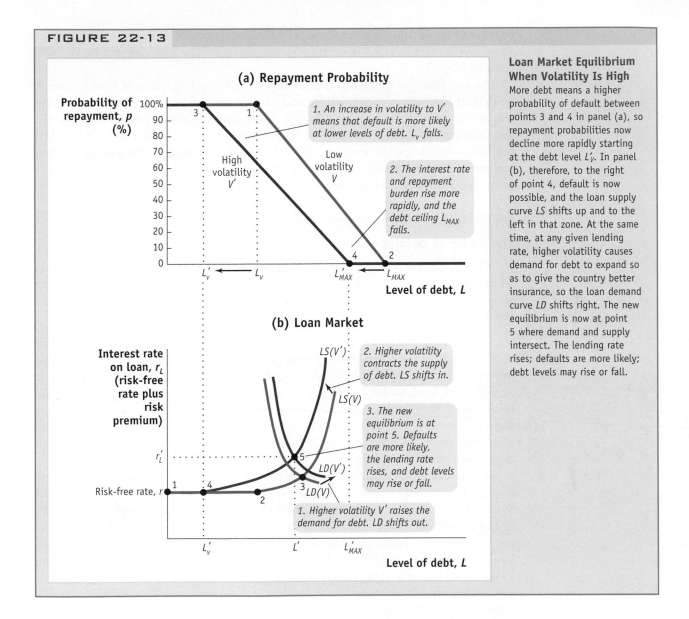

(a) Repayment Probability

Probability of repayment, p (%)

1. An increase in volatility to V' means that default is more likely at lower levels of debt. L_V falls.

High volatility V'

Low volatility V

2. The interest rate and repayment burden rise more rapidly, and the debt ceiling L_{MAX} falls.

L_V' ← L_V L_{MAX}' ← L_{MAX}

Level of debt, L

(b) Loan Market

Interest rate on loan, r_L (risk-free rate plus risk premium)

$LS(V')$

2. Higher volatility contracts the supply of debt. LS shifts in.

$LS(V)$

3. The new equilibrium is at point 5. Defaults are more likely, the lending rate rises, and debt levels may rise or fall.

r_L'

$LD(V')$

Risk-free rate, r

$LD(V)$

1. Higher volatility V' raises the demand for debt. LD shifts out.

L_V' L' L_{MAX}'

Level of debt, L

Loan Market Equilibrium When Volatility Is High More debt means a higher probability of default between points 3 and 4 in panel (a), so repayment probabilities now decline more rapidly starting at the debt level L_V'. In panel (b), therefore, to the right of point 4, default is now possible, and the loan supply curve LS shifts up and to the left in that zone. At the same time, at any given lending rate, higher volatility causes demand for debt to expand so as to give the country better insurance, so the loan demand curve LD shifts right. The new equilibrium is now at point 5 where demand and supply intersect. The lending rate rises; defaults are more likely; debt levels may rise or fall.

the probability of repayment reaches zero at a lower level of debt. The debt ceiling falls to a lower level L_{MAX}', because higher interest rates mean that the repayment burden will rise more quickly in this case as debt increases.

Consequently, in panel (b), the interest rate is higher at every debt level, and debt hits a ceiling at a lower level of debt. That is, we have shown that the loan supply curve shifts left and up. The lending rate starts to rise at point 4, at a lower debt level L_V', because higher volatility can lead to the possibility of defaults at lower levels of debt. Second, at higher debt levels, higher volatility always means a higher probability of default, so higher interest rates are imposed by lenders, all the way up to the ceiling at L_{MAX}'.

What about loan demand? When volatility rises, the loan demand curve also shifts. With typical preferences (which include risk aversion), higher volatility means that the country will want more insurance, or more consumption smoothing, all else equal.

In this model, defaultable debt is the only form of insurance a country can get, so, at any given lending rate, it will want to have more debt. The loan demand curve shifts right to $LD(V')$.

The net result of the shifts in loan supply and demand is a new equilibrium at point 5. If loan supply moves left/up and loan demand moves right, the lending rate will definitely increase. The net effect on the amount of debt is ambiguous, however, and depends on whether the demand shift is larger than the supply shift. If the supply effect dominates, the country will end up with less debt, higher-risk premiums, and more frequent defaults—the very characteristics we see in emerging markets as compared with advanced countries.

APPLICATION

The Costs of Default

Our model of default, like many others, relies on punishment costs to give debtors an incentive to repay. Is this realistic? How big are the costs? Defaulters do not get away scot-free, and to see why, we consider evidence from a Bank of England study and other research.[25]

Financial Market Penalties First, defaulters are excluded from further borrowing until the default is resolved though negotiations with the creditors. These exclusion periods may vary. The Bank of England study found that in the 1980s defaulters were denied market access for an average of four and a half years; however, in the easy credit atmosphere of the 1990s and 2000s, that figure dropped to an average of three and a half months. Exclusion from credit markets can create future consumption costs when the cushion of borrowing is no longer there to smooth consumption. Exclusion may impair investment, too.

Second, default is associated with a significant downgrade in credit ratings and corresponding increases in risk premiums.[26] The Bank of England study found that 7 of 8 nondefaulters had credit ratings of BBB+ or better (the exception was India), but 12 of 13 past defaulters were ranked BB+ or worse (the one exception was Chile). These results applied to countries with a variety of income per capita and debt-to-GDP levels. This kind of penalty has a long history: in the first wave of globalization before 1914, defaulters on average paid an extra 1% per year in interest rate risk premiums, controlling for other factors.[27]

Finally, defaulters may face another major inconvenience when borrowing: an inability to borrow in their own currency. The Bank of England study found that non-defaulting countries, including India, China, Korea, Czech Republic, Malaysia, and Hungary, were able to issue between 70 and 100% of their debt in domestic currency; in contrast, a group of past defaulters, including Brazil, Mexico, Philippines, Chile, and Venezuela, only issued between 40 and 70% of their debt in their own currency. In studying fixed and floating regimes, we learned that the disadvantage of liability dollarization is that depreciations increase the costs of debt principal and interest

---

[25] This application is based on Bianca De Paoli, Glenn Hoggarth, and Victoria Saporta, 2006, "Costs of Sovereign Default," *Bank of England Quarterly Bulletin*, Fall.

[26] Carmen M. Reinhart, Kenneth S. Rogoff, and Miguel A. Savastano, 2003, "Debt Intolerance," *Brookings Papers on Economic Activity* (1), 1–74.

[27] Maurice Obstfeld and Alan M. Taylor, 2003, "Sovereign Risk, Credibility and the Gold Standard: 1870–1913 versus 1925–31," *Economic Journal*, 113(487), 241–275.

in domestic currency terms. These changes can lead to destabilizing wealth effects because these impacts amplify debt burdens on the balance sheets of households, firms, and governments.

Broader Macroeconomic Costs and the Risk of Banking and Exchange Rate Crises The financial penalties are not the only cost that would-be defaulters must weigh. Default may trigger additional output costs, including the serious threats of twin or triple crises.

A default can do extensive damage to the domestic financial system because domestic banks typically hold a great deal of government debt—and they may have been coerced to hold even more such debt in the period right before a default.[28] The banks will likely call for help, putting further fiscal strain on the government. But the government usually has no resources to bail out the banks at a time like this (often, it has been trying to persuade the banks to help out the government). A default crisis can then easily spawn a banking crisis. At best, if the banks survive, prudent management requires the banks to contract domestic lending to rebuild their capital and reduce their risk exposure. At worst, the banks fail. The disappearance of their financial intermediation services will then impair investment activity, and negative wealth effects will squeeze the consumption demand of depositors who lose their access to their money, temporarily or permanently, in a bank that is closed or restructured. The result is lower demand and lower output in the short run and hence more risk for banks because debtors find it harder to pay back their bank loans in recessions. Financial disruption to the real economy also disrupts a nation's international trade. Default can disrupt the short-term credit (provided by domestic and foreign lenders) that is used to finance international trade, and there is some evidence that large and persistent trade contractions follow a default.[29]

In addition to a banking crisis, a default can trigger an exchange rate crisis if the country (like many emerging markets) is trying to preserve a fixed exchange rate. An increase in risk premiums on long-term loans to the government may be matched by a similar increase in risk premiums on bank deposits, especially if a banking crisis is feared. A risk premium shock of this sort, as we learned when we studied exchange rate crises, contracts money demand and causes a drain of foreign exchange reserves at the central bank as the peg is defended. At the same time, if the pleading of banks for fiscal help is ignored, the central bank will be under pressure to do a sterilized sale of reserves to allow it to act as a lender of last resort and expand domestic credit. But such activity will cause reserve levels to fall even further. The reserve drain may be large enough to break the peg, or at least damage the peg's credibility. Expected depreciation will then enlarge the risk premium further, compounding the reserve drain. In the meantime, interest rate increases further dampen investment in the home economy, lowering output and making it harder for debts to be serviced, which hurts the banks again, lowers output again, and compounds all of the problems just outlined.

Lower output and higher-risk premiums can be expected during a default crisis, but they can also trigger banking and exchange rate crises. Low output and high-interest

---

[28] Although some governments, notably Argentina in 2002, have shown great cunning in trying to honor debt held by domestic creditors while defaulting on foreigners, this kind of discrimination strategy may be difficult to execute legally and technically. Anna Gelpern and Brad Setser, 2004, "Domestic and External Debt: The Doomed Quest for Equal Treatment," *Georgetown Journal of International Law*, 35, 795.

[29] Andrew K. Rose, 2005, "One Reason Countries Pay Their Debts: Renegotiation and International Trade," *Journal of Development Economics*, 77(1), 189–206.

rates can break a contingent commitment to a peg; as we have seen in this chapter, they can generate a greater incentive to default; and we also know they can only worsen domestic financial conditions by making it harder for everyone to service their debt to banks and by damaging bank balance sheets.

From all these circuitous descriptions, presented schematically in Figure 22-14, the potential for a "vicious circle" of interactions should now be clear, explaining why so often the three types of crisis are observed together.

The consequences of default are therefore not pleasant. As Table 22-1 shows, when default crises occur *on their own*, there appear to be no costs; unfortunately, that applies in only 4 of 45 cases, less than 10% of all defaults in the sample. In every

FIGURE 22-14

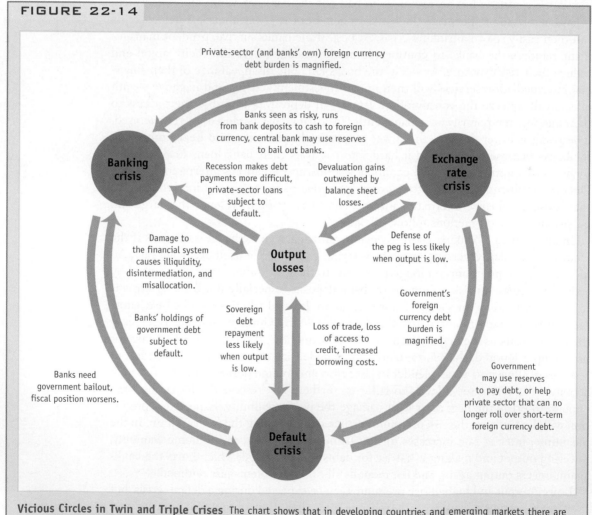

Vicious Circles in Twin and Triple Crises The chart shows that in developing countries and emerging markets there are complex feedback linkages between banking crises, default crises, and exchange rate crises. A depreciation magnifies foreign currency debt burdens, weakening the financial position of the government, private sector, and banks. A default weakens banks and cuts off foreign credit, leaving reserves as the only remaining buffer. A banking crisis can lead to costly bailouts, undermining either the government's fiscal position or the central bank's reserve. All three types of crisis can have serious output costs, which exacerbate the problem.

Source: Based on Bianca De Paoli, Glenn Hoggarth, and Victoria Saporta, 2006, "Costs of Sovereign Default," Bank of England Quarterly Bulletin, Fall.

TABLE 22-1

Costs of Sovereign Defaults, 1970–2000 Output losses can be very large after a default, as measured by deviation from trends. While a default-only crisis may be short and not costly, the more common twin and triple crises last much longer and have very high costs.

Type of Crisis	Number of Crises	Average Length (years)	Mean Cost per Year (% of GDP)
Default only	4	3	–1.0
Default and exchange rate crisis	13	5	10.3
Default and banking crisis	7	8	13.2
Triple crisis	21	10	21.7
All crises	45	8	15.1

Source: Bianca De Paoli, Glenn Hoggarth, and Victoria Saporta, 2006, "Costs of Sovereign Default," Bank of England Quarterly Bulletin, Fall.

other case, there is either a twin default/exchange rate crisis (13 cases), a twin default/banking crisis (7 cases), or a triple default/exchange rate/banking crisis (21 cases). In all these other cases (more than 90% of defaults), the output losses associated with the crisis are significant, measured by deviation from trend output growth: on average, around 15% of GDP per year for eight years. That is a large cost, even if comparisons with normal trends may be misleading, because it is difficult to estimate the costs that the countries would have faced had they not defaulted.[30]

To sum up, if financial penalties and legal action provide insufficient motives for repayment, there is reason to believe that many other costs of default exist that provide enough incentive for contingent debt repayment. ■

Conclusion

We have developed a simple model in which sovereign debt is a contingent claim that will not be paid in hard times. In equilibrium borrowers obtain consumption-smoothing via debt (a form of insurance against volatile consumption levels) at a price—the risk premium—that compensates lenders for default risk. The model is too simple to capture all aspects of the default problem, such as the tendency of borrowing to move in volatile cycles, and the scope for contagion and "animal spirits" in this asset market as in any other.

Nonetheless, the model provides valuable insights and leads us to deeper questions. For example, the model assumes that output volatility is the root cause of default, and we know that output volatility is high in poorer countries. But what is behind that? In some developing countries, it could be a result of commodity specialization, terms-of-trade shocks, climate, and other economic disturbances. Yet an alternative explanation might be the poor institutional framework in these countries, which is correlated with

---

[30] That is to say, output may have fallen anyway because of the economic shocks that preceded the observed default. Obtaining more precise estimates of default costs remains a goal of ongoing research. See Eduardo Levy-Yeyati and Ugo Panizza, "The Elusive Costs of Sovereign Defaults," Research Department Working Paper 581, Inter-American Development Bank, November 2006.

both low incomes and high volatility. Thus, the default problem may be, deep down, a reflection of poor institutions. Poor institutions may also be generating default at lower debt levels through nonvolatility channels: they may obscure financial transparency, generate weak property rights, prevent credit monitoring, encourage corruption and bribery, allow for the misuse of loans, lead politicians to focus on the short term (with risky overborrowing), and so on—all of which add to the risk premium, all else equal.

How did advanced countries eventually find a way to avoid these outcomes? Our model suggests that all countries want to default at some debt level, but for advanced countries, that level might be very high. Why? The model says it must be that the costs of default in such countries are much higher. There may be truth to this on two dimensions: economic and political. Economically, a sovereign default in an advanced country would wreck a highly developed financial system, whereas in poorer countries the very lack of financial sophistication probably keeps such costs lower. In addition, the political costs are higher in advanced countries, in that a large, democratically empowered, and wealth-holding middle class is likely to punish governments that take such actions; in poorer countries, the political costs may be smaller if the losers are fewer or political accountability is weaker.

Every few years, in a tranquil time, some expert predicts that there will not be any more sovereign defaults. They can't be taken very seriously. History does suggest that many of the deep and intertwined underlying political-economy problems can be solved, but it may take an awfully long time for countries to overcome these impediments and emerge from the serial default club.[31]

APPLICATION

The Argentina Crisis of 2001–2002

In this section we focused on the problem of default. But we also emphasized (as in Figure 22-14) the feedback mechanisms at work in twin and triple crisis situations in which default crises, exchange rate crises, and banking crises may simultaneously occur. Just as in the case of self-fulfilling exchange rate crises (explained in the chapter on crises), these "vicious circles" may lead to self-fulfilling twin and triple crises where, as the economist Guillermo Calvo puts it, "If investors deem you unworthy, no funds will be forthcoming and, thus, unworthy you will be." In general, theory and empirical work suggest that bad fundamentals only make the problem of self-fulfilling crises worse, and disentangling the two causes can be difficult, leading to ongoing controversy over who or what is to blame for any given crisis. The Argentina crisis of 2001–02 dramatically illustrates these problems.[32]

Background Argentina successfully ended a hyperinflation in 1991 with the adoption of a rigidly fixed exchange rate system called the Convertibility Plan, and a 1-to-1

[31] Philip T. Hoffman, Gilles Postel-Vinay, and Jean-Laurent Rosenthal, 2007, *Surviving Large Losses: Financial Crises, the Middle Class, and the Development of Capital Markets* (Cambridge, MA: Harvard University Press).
[32] For further reading about the Argentine crisis, see Michael Mussa, 2002, *Argentina and the Fund: From Triumph to Tragedy* (Washington, D.C.: Institute for International Economics); Gerardo della Paolera and Alan Taylor, 2003, "Gaucho Banking Redux," *Economía*, 3(2), 1–42; Andrew Powell, 2003, "Argentina's Avoidable Crisis: Bad Luck, Bad Economics, Bad Politics, Bad Advice," in Susan M. Collins and Dani Rodrik, eds., *Brookings Trade Forum 2002* (Washington, D.C.: The Brookings Institution), pp. 1–58; Paul Blustein, 2005, *And the Money Kept Rolling In (and Out): Wall Street, the IMF, and the Bankrupting of Argentina* (New York: Public Affairs).

peg of the peso to the U.S. dollar. As we noted in a previous chapter, this system operated with high reserve backing ratios and (in theory) strict limits on central bank use of sterilization policy. The Convertibility Plan was a quasi currency board.

With a firm nominal anchor, Argentina's economy grew rapidly up to 1998, apart from a brief slowdown after the Mexican (Tequila) crisis in 1994. The country was able to borrow large amounts at low-interest rates in the global capital market. The only troubling sign at this point was that despite boom conditions the government ran persistent deficits every year, increasing the public debt to GDP ratio. Most of this debt was held by foreigners, which increased Argentina's net external debt relative to GDP. Given the long-run budget constraints (for the government, and for the country) these deficits were unsustainable.

In 1997 crises in Asia were followed by increases in emerging market risk premiums, and these shocks were magnified by crises in 1998 in Russia and Brazil. The Brazil crisis also led to a slowdown and depreciation in one of Argentina's major trading partners. At the same time, the U.S. dollar started to appreciate, dragging the Argentina peso into a stronger position against all currencies. Higher interest rates, lower demand abroad, and an appreciated exchange rate put the Argentine economy into a recession.

Dive With these changes in external conditions, Argentina's macroeconomic regime started to unravel. The recession worsened an already bad fiscal situation. Because no surpluses had been run in the good times, there was no cushion in the government accounts, and the red ink grew. Public debt, which had been 41% of GDP in 1998, grew to 64% of GDP in 2001. Foreign creditors began to view these debt dynamics as possibly explosive and inconsistent with the long-run budget constraint, implying a risk of default. The creditors demanded higher interest rates for new loans and refinancings, which only increased the rate of debt explosion. Risk premiums on long-term government debt blew up, from 3% to 4% in late 1997 to 7% to 8% in late 2000.

The fiscal situation thus damaged the economy and the banking sector, as higher interest rates depressed aggregate demand in the short run, and caused a deterioration of banks' balance sheets (as loans went bad and other assets declined in value). This deterioration, in turn, made the fiscal situation worse, because in a recession tax revenues tend to fall and government social expenditures tend to rise. The government needed to borrow more, even as the lenders started to withdraw.

In addition, the situation posed a threat to the monetary regime and the Convertibility Plan. People were worried that if the government accounts worsened further, then all public credit would be turned off, and if the government were then unwilling to impose the austerity of spending cuts in mid-recession, it would have had to finance the deficit using the inflation tax. Finally, even if the government did not use inflationary finance, it still might want to use temporary monetary policy autonomy to relieve the recession through a devaluation and lower interest rates, both of which would make the peg not credible. Either or both of these threats would expose the peg to the risk of a speculative attack.

In addition, people knew that if the banks got into trouble, they would need to call on the central bank to act as a lender of last resort, as they had in 1994 (when reserves had plummeted and a crisis was averted only by a last-minute lifeline from the International Monetary Fund [IMF]). If people felt that their deposits would be safer in Miami or Montevideo, there would be a massive run from deposits to peso cash to dollars, overwhelming even the substantial foreign exchange reserves at the central bank.

Crash In 2001 all of these forces gathered in a perfect storm. Politically, fiscal compromise proved impossible between the two main political forces (the weak President Fernando de la Rúa of the Radical Party and the powerful Peronist provincial governors). The provinces collected and spent large amounts of national tax revenue and were not willing to make sacrifices to help de la Rúa, a political opponent. They gambled, correctly, that a crisis would bring them to power (even at the cost of destroying the country).

By mid-2001, private creditors had almost walked away from Argentina and the last-gasp effort involved a swap of short-term high interest rate debt for long-term *very high* interest rate debt, with an annual yield near 15%. Markets were unimpressed—this scheme bought a few months of breathing space on principal payments, but left Argentina with an even worse debt service problem down the road. Private lending dried up and despite a (noncredible) announcement of a zero deficit rule in July, the risk premium on government debt exploded, from 10% in June to 15% in August, and approached 20% in October. As the debt burden grew and the economy sank, we know from this chapter that default would be increasingly likely.

There was only one lender left now, the IMF. But they were increasingly as unimpressed with Argentina's policy shenanigans as everyone else. In a move that it doubted at the time and regretted soon thereafter, the IMF made one last big loan to Argentina in August 2001. The money was poured into the government's coffers and into the Central Bank's dwindling pot of reserves, but it didn't last very long.

The banks were in a very weak state. Economic conditions were raising the number of nonperforming loans anyway. But banks had also been coerced or persuaded that it would be a good idea for them to buy large amounts of the government's debt in 2001. This dollar debt carried a high interest rate, but was also risky, because of the possibility of default and/or exchange rate depreciation after a crisis. Depositors knew this and they also knew that banks would probably fail if the central bank and the government could not protect them.

The End The three crises were all now shaping up to happen, encouraged by output contractions, consistent with the "vicious circle" dynamics shown in Figure 22-14. The final act came in November. The IMF concluded that the economy was not being turned around by any of the policies in place and that further loans were therefore a waste of time unless Argentina made radical adjustments, including considering the possibilities of devaluing, defaulting, and even dollarizing. The government would have none of it, and when the IMF announced no more credit, the public knew the game was up, and seeking to put their assets in a safe haven, they started a massive run on the banks. To stem the flow, the government imposed capital controls (*corralito*) to stop such activity, and also froze the majority of bank deposits.

This triggered a political explosion, violence and unrest, and within days de la Rúa was history, airlifted from the Casa Rosada by helicopter. His numerous successors over the following weeks initiated a default on the public debt (the world's biggest-ever default at the time) and allowed the exchange rate to float (it fell to 4 pesos to the dollar very quickly). The private sector was awash with unserviceable dollar liabilities, so the government "pesified" them, causing utter chaos in the courts and grave economic uncertainty. The banks were barely functional for several months, and the savings of many Argentines vanished. Taxes were raised and government spending cut. The economy went from a bad recession to total meltdown, amid scenes of previously unimaginable poverty and deprivation.

Argentina's policies were inconsistent. When the government chose a fixed exchange rate, it had to accept its pros and cons, including the risk of larger recessions when external conditions were unfavorable. But they also had to accept that a fixed exchange rate ruled out the inflation tax and placed limits on the lender of last resort capacity of a central bank faced with capital flight. Such concerns would not have been as important if the country had kept its fiscal policy in check and maintained access to credit, but in 2001 the country simply had no more room for maneuver. ■

Postscript As of 2007, there had been no major crisis since 2001, world economic conditions had been fairly benign, and many countries had built up large exchange reserves. This led many observers to call into question the need for the IMF, given its perceived failings in the 1997–2001 crises, and the small size of its lending capabilities in the face of growing private sector financial flows. On the other hand, international economic crises have been around for a very long time, so to more seasoned observers, it seemed a little premature for some to be calling for dismantling the only emergency service we have (see **Headlines: Is the IMF "Pathetic"?**). They were proved right when during and after the global financial crisis in 2008, the IMF was called to the scene of many macroeconomic accidents, including in several so-called advanced countries, to provide rescue funding.

4 The Global Macroeconomy and the 2007–2013 Crisis

The **Global Financial Crisis** of 2007–09 and the associated **Great Recession** constitute one of the most significant global macroeconomic events of modern history. Even now, when the full implications are as yet unclear, we may anticipate that when these times are assessed by economic historians in the distant future, they will probably rank in the memory not far behind such momentous events as the 1930s Great Depression. And already, looking only to the very near future, in terms of the economic damage created, the current recessions will not be forgotten quickly by our generation of households, firms, banks, or governments, all of whom have been affected by the downturn, and many of whom have endured serious suffering.

In this section of the chapter, we look at the crisis using the tools of international macroeconomics developed throughout this book. We begin by looking at the origins of the crisis not only in events of the previous decade, but also as part of longer-term trends in the U.S. and global economies. We then look at the Great Recession itself, how events unfolded, and what we can learn about the economic shocks and policy responses. Next, we look at how the global economy can recover from this shock, a process that was under way, but still fragile and with a long way to go as this chapter was written in late 2013.

Macroeconomists have much to learn from the crisis. Some key macro-financial and policy issues have been known about since the early 1800s, but they had been ignored or forgotten by many economists, and more future research is likely to focus on these important issues.

Backdrop to the Crisis

Several features of the precrisis global economy can help us understand some of the calamitous events that were to follow. Keep in mind, however, that the benefits of hindsight should not cause us to underestimate the difficulties observers had in

HEADLINES

Is the IMF "Pathetic"?

The IMF is the closest thing to a global lender of last resort. When times are calm, it may be tempting to think of abolishing the institution. As this precrisis column pointed out, to have done so would have been a remarkably complacent idea.

Meral Karasulu did what any seasoned International Monetary Fund staffer would do: She grinned and, for the umpteenth time, listened to suggestions that the institution was to blame for the 1997 Asian financial crisis.

"Thank you for your question," she replied to an audience member at a May 14 EuroMoney conference in Seoul. Then, she launched into a defense of the IMF's actions.

As the IMF's representative in South Korea, Karasulu is used to the drill. After all, many Koreans routinely refer to the "IMF crisis." It's a reminder that a decade after Asia's turmoil, the IMF is still explaining itself wherever it goes.

Three weeks after the Seoul conference, there was similar griping at an event I attended in Buenos Aires. The mood had barely changed since March 2005, when President Nestor Kirchner scored points with many of Argentina's 40 million people by calling the IMF "pathetic." He has been demanding that the institution stop criticizing the Latin American country.

Korea and Argentina have little in common. Yet Korea is among the nations stockpiling currency reserves to avoid having to go to the IMF for a bailout ever again. Argentina, meanwhile, continues to tout the end of its IMF-backed program last year as an economic victory.

This column isn't a defense of the IMF's actions during the Asian crisis or Argentina's in the early 2000s. The Washington-based fund has a small army of well-compensated people to do that. And the IMF has had its fair share of blunders, including telling Asian countries to tighten fiscal policy during a crisis.

Yet all this talk of IMF irrelevance is overdone. What's more, the chatter suggests the creation of a new bubble called complacency.

"It's ironic to my mind that people say the fund isn't needed anymore because nothing in the global financial system is broken at the moment," John Lipsky, the IMF's first deputy managing director, said in an interview last month in Tokyo. "It strikes me we are trying to anticipate and prepare for when things may go wrong again." . . .

Sure, Asia has insulated itself from markets with trillions of dollars of currency reserves. The IMF's phones may be ringing off the hook if China's economy hits a wall, the U.S. dollar plunges, the so-called yen-carry trade blows up, a major terrorist attack occurs, oil prices approach $100 a barrel or some unexpected event roils world markets.

The thing is, the IMF and its Bretton Woods sister institution, the World Bank, have scarcely been more necessary. How

efficient and cost-effective they are is debatable; what's not is that today's global economy needs the buffering role that both of them play. . . .

The IMF was never set up to play the role it did during crises in Mexico, Asia and Russia in the 1990s and turmoil in Latin America since then. Even so, it will be called upon the instant a crisis in one country spreads to another. As imperfect as the IMF is, the world needs the economic equivalent of a fire brigade when markets plunge.

There's much chatter about how global prosperity is reducing the need for billion-dollar IMF bailouts. As of March, IMF lending had shriveled to $11.8 billion from a peak of $81 billion in 2004. A single nation, Turkey, accounted for about 75 percent of the IMF's portfolio.

Isn't that a good thing? The IMF is like a paramedic: You hope you won't need one, but it's great that one is just a phone call away. Plenty of things could still go awry and necessitate a call to the IMF. . . .

Complacency looms large in today's world. All too many investors think the good times are here to stay and all too many governments are ignoring their imbalances for similar reasons. . . .

All this means that, far from being irrelevant, the IMF may be in for a very busy couple of years.

understanding these developments as they were unfolding at the time. Although a number of these trends were recognized by some observers as problematic, opinions were split as to whether any one of these issues was serious enough to justify any corrective action prior to the crisis.

Preconditions for the Crisis The global financial crisis was primarily a story of investments turned bad, that is, of savings unwisely allocated. To get a sense of what fueled the boom and bust cycle, it is worth asking where those savings materialized at a global and macroeconomic level and where they ended up.

As we saw in the chapter on crises, a large source of global saving in the ten years prior to the crisis was the group of *emerging market* (EM) countries that consistently ran surpluses on their current accounts, as their investment rates (quite high) were consistently exceeded by their saving rates (even higher). Because the world as a whole has to have a current account equal to zero, these EM surpluses had to be offset by equal and opposite *developed market* (DM) current account deficits, as shown in Figure 22-15, panel (a). Given their sheer size, the largest surplus and deficit countries—China and the United States, respectively—often came to dominate the discussion, but when we adjust for country size, the trends were much broader than that. Most EMs ran significant current account surpluses (along with some DMs like Japan and Germany) and many DMs ran current account deficits of a size comparable to or exceeding those in the United States (e.g., the United Kingdom, Spain, Ireland, Portugal, and Greece).

This unusual situation soon drew the attention of economists and policy makers, and began to generate its own vocabulary. The unidirectional flow from EM to DM was referred to as the problem of **global imbalances;** the high level of savings in the EMs that was a part of it was referred to as the **savings glut.** Because real interest rates had fallen in this era, analysts recognized that even if the global level of savings supply and investment demand had risen in parallel, the fall in interest rates suggested that, on net, it was an increase in the supply of savings (relative to investment demand) that had upset the global equilibrium. What were the causes and consequences of this shift? To understand the causes, we need to assess policies in the EM economies where the flows originated; to grasp the consequences, we need to focus on the DM economies where the funds were put to use.

On the EM side, at the broadest level, economists understand the dramatic increase in savings after 1997 as a conscious act of self-insurance. Many of these countries (especially those in Asia) had been very high saving societies for many, many years, and much of this was private saving. However, the new twist was the rapid increase in public (government) saving. As we saw in the balance of payments chapter, holding fixed private saving and investment, an increase in government saving necessarily sends the current account toward more surplus. Why did governments want to save? As we saw in the chapter on crises, and even in the introduction to macroeconomics, EM countries pay a high economic and political cost for crises. This outcome became painfully clear in the 1990s, starting with the Mexican crisis of 1994, but the lesson was rammed home by the chaos in Asian economies unleashed by the 1997 crisis, when currencies collapsed, deep recessions took hold, and governments were overturned when access to external financing dried up.

Looking back on those bleak times and on the inability of private capital markets or multilateral agencies such as the IMF to offer financial help that was both constructive and sufficient, many EM policy makers reached two key conclusions. First, they knew that they did not want to be the next Suharto, the Indonesian president humiliated by having to do the bidding of the IMF in exchange for funding; and they knew that to avoid being put in that position, they would have to take responsibility for their own financial security and, instead of relying on access to borrowed funds, would instead have to build up a war chest of liquid savings that could be drawn down in the event of a crisis.

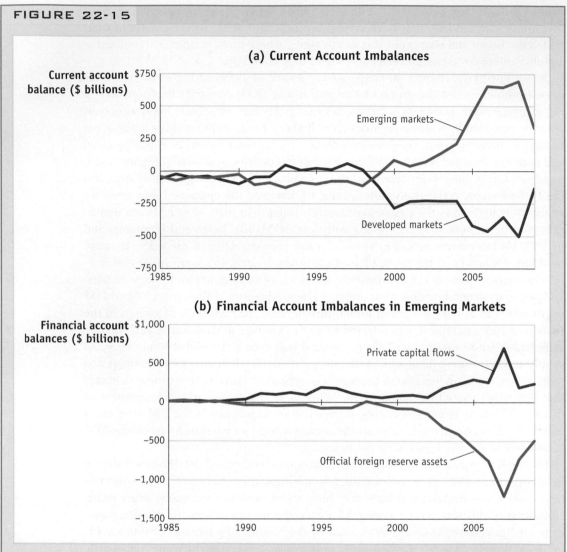

FIGURE 22-15

(a) Current Account Imbalances

Current account balance ($ billions)

Emerging markets

Developed markets

(b) Financial Account Imbalances in Emerging Markets

Financial account balances ($ billions)

Private capital flows

Official foreign reserve assets

Global Imbalances and Their Composition from the 1980s to the Global Financial Crisis Panel (a) shows that from the late 1990s the chronic current account deficits of developed markets were offset by chronic surpluses in emerging markets. Looking just at the emerging markets, panel (b) shows that the emerging markets' financial accounts were in deficit due to massive official foreign reserve accumulation, offset somewhat by private capital flows. In the crisis period of 2007–09 these patterns were somewhat dampened.

Sources: IMF and Haver.

The private sectors in EM countries also learned and made some changes to their behavior after the 1990s crises: for example, there was typically a shift toward less borrowing in foreign currency to reduce the liability dollarization problem that we noted in the chapter on global financialization as one of the peculiar risks for EM countries. However, EM policymakers first began a large, concerted accumulation of public external assets in their central bank or treasury accounts. That is, policymakers increased the purchase of official foreign assets as recorded in the Official Settlements Balance of the balance of payments (described in the first balance of payments chapter). In balance of payments terms, these large-scale imports of official assets by EMs were the Financial Account counterpart to their large Current Account (CA) surpluses, as seen in Figure 22-15, panel (b).

Thus, official capital was flowing from EM to DM economies. Indeed, the official savings dwarfed the private sector capital flows that were generally moving in the opposite direction, from DM and into EM. On net, as some described it, capital was flowing *uphill* from poor to rich countries, an outcome viewed as odd by some observers because capital is generally expected to flow *downhill* from rich to poor countries, given the need for poor countries to invest in finance growth and economic development. As we saw in the chapter on the gains from financial globalization, economists have identified many reasons (summed up in the catch-all term "productivity") to explain why capital might not flow from rich to poor countries. But there was a new development in the first decade of the new century: the flows had not simply stopped, they had reversed! As we have argued, however, this change might have been for good reason.

What impact did these flows have on the rich DM countries? First let us note that although the EM economies were largely engaged in the purchase of official assets like U.S. Treasuries, the effect of the massive purchase programs was felt in all credit markets. Buying a large amount of U.S. government debt bids down the yield on that debt (as the prices of the bonds are bid up). A result is that other holders of Treasuries now decide, on the margin, that they don't find the asset so attractive anymore, and they seek higher returns from other assets. This change in portfolio balance lowers yields on other forms of debt such as corporate debt, loans, mortgages, and so on. This large flow of EM savings thus created a large wave of liquid funds in global capital markets seeking profitable investment opportunities, and allowing borrowers access to capital on some of the most generous terms that had been seen in a very long time.

On the face of it, access to a large flow of credit on extremely favorable terms sounds like a fantastically beneficial opportunity for the DM economies. However, behind that view is the assumption that given such an increase in economic opportunities, DM economies would use the funds wisely, with due regard to the risk and return on each project. In theory, good investments would be supported, and the benefits realized from those investments (the marginal product of capital) would be positive and high enough to exceed the real costs of borrowing. In other words, if the financial systems of the world, and particularly those in the DM economies, had been efficient in their allocation of such capital flows, and if all projects by private or public borrowers had been a wise use of funds, then all would have been well.

Unfortunately, such an outcome, often assumed in theory, is not guaranteed in practice. Many observers of emerging economies, and of the deeper history of the developed countries, were acutely aware of this possibility because they had seen repeated episodes of credit booms and busts that ended in tears for developing economies. These busts usually led to some combination of banking/currency/default crises, as we saw in the earlier chapters on crises. These observers saw that the DM countries now risked a similar fate, as the decade of the 2000s witnessed the expansion of credit in developed economies rise to a level not seen before in the entire recorded history of financial capitalism, as revealed by the trends shown in Figure 22-16.

The view that the DM world could absorb these savings and put them to good use, and do so at ever higher levels of debt, depended on a particularly presumptive, some might say arrogant, view that despite the lessons from emerging economies, somehow the developed economies were "different." The DM optimists' argument could be summed up along

FIGURE 22-16

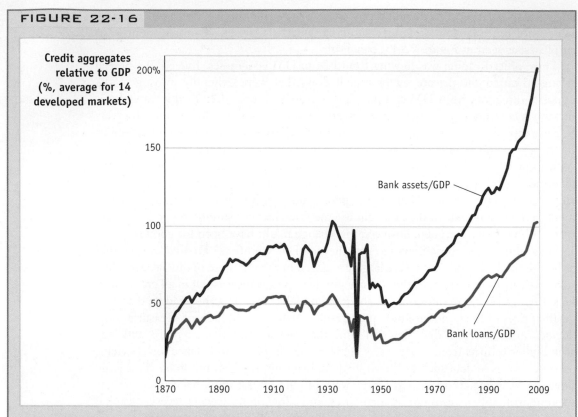

Developed Market Credit Trends over 140 Years This chart shows average data for fourteen developed markets since 1870. The ratio of bank loans and total bank assets to GDP was stable in the early twentieth century and fell during the 1930s following the Great Depression. In the postwar period these ratios surpassed their previous peaks around 1980 and kept on growing as modern economies built their economic model around more and more debt.

Source: Moritz Schularick and Alan M. Taylor, 2013, "Credit Booms Gone Bust: Monetary Policy, Leverage Cycles and Financial Crises, 1870–2008," American Economic Review 102(2), 1029–61.

the following lines: "Sure, those rather backward emerging countries with all their political problems and unsophisticated financial systems are inevitably going to have banking crises now and then and all the resulting problems, but we'll never see that sort of thing here, because we are developed, and that sort of thing doesn't happen to us anymore." A period of relatively stable economic performance in the 1990s and early 2000s lent support to the claim that even if occasional financial shocks hit the economy, policy makers had developed the tools needed to contain such problems and ensure that this "Great Moderation" of the business cycle could continue. However, for a few skeptical observers (including, notably, some economists at the Bank for International Settlements), this attitude appeared overconfident, and it was soon exposed as such in a rather spectacular way.

Exacerbating Policies and Distortions The discussion of the longer-run forces behind capital flows from DM to EM countries provides a backdrop to the crisis, but as an explanation, it is incomplete. Many other questions remain. Why did these flows accelerate so rapidly in the years 2004 to 2007? Why did these capital flows result in such poor economic outcomes in places as diverse as the United States, Ireland, Latvia, or Greece? Was the problem generated by failures in economic policy making and regulation, or was it primarily a result of mistakes by market participants themselves? At the time of writing, these remain contested issues, but we can summarize some of the more influential and persuasive viewpoints.

■ Some observers believe that monetary policies in the EM economies, particularly China and other Asian economies, made the problem worse by pursuing a policy of deliberately **undervalued exchange rates.** This policy promoted an overly rapid, export-led growth strategy highly dependent on the Western (mainly U.S.) consumer being willing to go deeper into debt to purchase a growing supply of manufactured goods. However, it is hard to find robust evidence that, given their stage of development, these economies' exchange rates were drastically out of line with normal historical or cross-country levels. These countries might just have been saving more for the precautionary reasons noted above.

■ Some argue that much of the blame for the crisis resides with monetary policy makers in the DM economies, and especially the **too-easy monetary policy** of the U.S. Federal Reserve. These critics feel that under former Chairman Alan Greenspan, the Fed kept interest rates too low for too long in the period after the 9/11 terrorist attacks. These low interest rates encouraged lending across all credit markets at a time when the wave of savings from EMs hit the system, and facilitated bubbles at least in some places (e.g., the California and Florida housing markets). A similar argument can be leveled at the ECB, which also pursued rates that were "too low" for some euro member countries where similar bubbles were ignited (e.g., Ireland and Spain). However, it can be argued that the Fed was following its legal dual mandate of low inflation and high employment, with no sign of failure on either target. It can also be argued that, in theory, a low interest rate policy should not necessarily compromise a good financial system's ability to do proper credit risk evaluation when properly regulated and left to itself.

■ Others would argue that the problem was a **failure of regulation and supervision** in that the Fed, the ECB, the Bank of England, and countless other central banks, as well as national regulatory bodies and lawmakers, simply allowed the financial systems to run out of control. This process had much deeper roots, going back to the trend toward financial deregulation seen around the world since the 1970s. This view is supported by the telling observation that under the more stringent regulatory regimes created after the 1930s disaster (e.g., legislation such as the U.S. Glass-Steagall Act, and more proactive regulators employing stricter standards), no developed country witnessed any banking crises whatsoever from 1945 to 1970. A slightly different take would argue that regulations did not shift, so much as they were simply outpaced by the scale of financial innovation, which both allowed the system to take on greater risks through new products (e.g., the securitization of credit with a reliance on rating agencies and the use of unregulated derivatives) and to expand so much as to create large, complex, "too big to fail" (or in some countries "too big to save") banks. Either way, regulators share some of the blame either for relaxing rules too much or not keeping up with the times.

■ Some analysts believe that **government failure** is to blame because governments distorted private incentives in various ways, over and above any impact of easy monetary policies noted above. For example, in the United States, the government gave implicit backing to quasi-official organizations like Fannie Mae and Freddie Mac, which purchased or guaranteed large shares of the mortgage market, and ended up effectively bankrupt. The government was also seen as offering implicit backstops to many "too big to fail" banks. When this happens, the implicit insurance gives people an incentive to take too much risk, knowing that they will be bailed out of some or all losses, a problem known as *moral hazard*. Similar concerns arose about European banks, which in some countries were larger than those in the United States, and even more leveraged when the crisis struck. In addition, the central banks stood accused of offering some kind of similar downside protection, by seeming to declare, when asked, that their doctrine concerning asset price bubbles was not to pop them or lean against them, but rather to wait for them to collapse and then step in to fix any problems. Yet against these points, it could be noted that large swathes of credit market excess—indeed, the majority—flowed through channels quite distant from the government's reach, and that ex post, whatever the perceived bailouts the bankers thought they might get, in practice most of those exposed found themselves with a lot of "skin in the game," of which they lost a great deal (or, in the case of Lehman Brothers and many other entities around the world, almost all of it).

■ Many other observers see widespread evidence of **market failure,** in which irrational investors, herding, imperfect information, and asymmetric information all created serious inefficiencies in financial systems. According to this view, which is hundreds of years old, the financial markets are capable of sustained bouts of euphoria followed by revulsion, a kind of mood swing where investors switch from being willing to take on lots of risk, only to then switch quickly to avoid the same risks, an oscillation between greed and fear that has no real connection to market fundamentals and that creates unnecessary and unwelcome volatility in the economy. Yet even if this view often looks persuasive after the fact, spotting the bubble or the imminent crisis beforehand is a very different matter: even if we can now agree that there was a U.S. housing bubble, as it unfolded, it took an awfully long time for more than just a few observers to voice their concerns.

Summary History shows that economies based on financial capitalism have experienced banking crises throughout the modern era. This is true whether one is speaking of developed markets or emerging markets, with the possible exception of a brief interlude of calm during the financially repressed post-1945 era, as shown in Figure 22-17. However, as the financial sector was deregulated in the last three or four decades, it regrouped and expanded, and we have once again found ourselves in what is, to the economic historian, if not the economist, a very familiar place characterized by periodic episodes of financial instability. With some success, policy makers mitigated some of these shocks, but after credit and leverage grew to unprecedented levels, there came a shock so large that it defied control and sent the world economy into the most severe slump since the 1930s Great Depression.

Panic and the Great Recession

In 2007 the Global Financial Crisis started to unfold quickly from a set of potential risks into a massive catastrophe that would wreak havoc on the global economy for the next several years (see the timeline in Table 22-2).

FIGURE 22-17

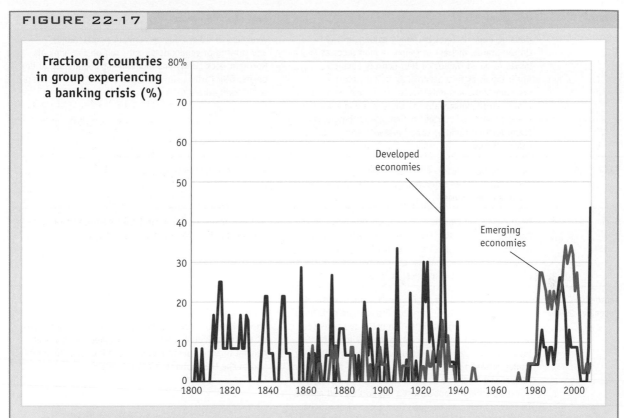

Banking Crises in History This chart tracks the frequency of banking crises each year in both developed (high-income) and emerging (middle- to low-income) economies.

Source: Rong Qian, Carmen M. Reinhart, and Kenneth S. Rogoff, 2011. "On Graduation from Default, Inflation and Banking Crises: Elusive or Illusion?" In NBER Macroconomics Annual 2010 edited by Daron Acemoglu and Michael Woodford, pp. 1–36.

Like almost all financial crashes seen over the course of modern economic history, some particular event triggered a flight from risk to safety in capital markets. In this case, the trigger was a deterioration in the quality of U.S. residential mortgages. As house prices stalled, and then fell, and mortgage delinquencies rose in 2006 and 2007, problems quickly became evident, especially in the more risky subprime mortgages. Similar stresses also erupted in the financial and housing markets in other countries such as the United Kingdom and Ireland.

The losses were centered on major financial institutions in the United States and overseas including commercial banks (some of the very largest like Citibank or Bank of America in the United States, and RBS in the United Kingdom), investment banks (which held some of the mortgage risk), and insurance companies (like AIG, which had provided lucrative but ultimately underpriced default insurance policies on many mortgage products that it was ill-equipped to honor).

A Very Modern Bank Run Once the problems of bad mortgages had spread, and given the very thin (some would later say, too thin) capitalization of the financial system in general, it became very difficult not only for outsiders to borrow from banks, but also for banks to borrow from outsiders and from each other. People feared that banks might end up unable to repay their loans. With one or two exceptions, deposit

TABLE 22-2

Timeline for the Global Financial Crisis This table highlights key events in the 2007–13 period.

Date	U.S. events	Rest of world events
2007	Housing price declines becoming evident in the United States, distress in subprime mortgages as losses revealed (failure of New Century Financial, April; losses at Bear Stearns, June/July, etc.), economy slows and enters recession; credit spreads widen; stock market falls; by the year's end the Fed is easing and has started its first special programs (Term Auction Facility; swap lines with some foreign central banks)	Weakness in other housing markets (e.g. Ireland) and slowing of economic growth; run on the bank at Northern Rock (U.K.) and government guarantees all deposits; BNP Paribas suffers losses (August); stocks start to fall everywhere
Early 2008	Failure of Bear Stearns investment bank (taken over by JPMorgan with Fed support); more Fed facilities and expanded swap lines	Recession spreads to Europe.
Summer 2008	Fannie Mae and Freddie Mac (U.S. government housing agencies) get Treasury credit lines; IndyMac bank fails; widespread mortgage distress evident; creditworthiness of banks and other financial entities decline since much of mortgage risk is dispersed via securitization	Distress in several European banks exposed to same mortgage risk is dispersed via securitization.
September–December 2008	Full financial panic starts; Fannie Mae and Freddie Mac go into government conservatorship; Failure of Lehman Brothers investment bank (bankruptcy) and takeover of Merrill Lynch (by Bank of America); failure of AIG insurance company, supported by Fed; Reserve Primary money market fund shares "break the buck"; Washington Mutual and Wachovia banks taken over in distress; start of extraordinary financial sector support by Fed and US Treasury (TARP plan changed from toxic asset purchases to capital injections; money market fund guarantees; Fed buys mortgage-backed securities); extra support for megabanks Bank of America and Citigroup; stock market collapses further	Bank failures in several countries (RBS, Lloyds TSB and some UK building societies; Fortis, Dexia, ING, German regional banks, etc.). Government of Ireland guarantees all of its bank debt. Global stock market collapse and general financial panic everywhere, flight to safe assets and to the U.S. dollar until March 2010.
2009	Large fiscal stimulus program ($700 billion over 3 years). Stock market bottoms in March, at less than half its previous peak; credit crisis continues; unemployment rises to 10%. Fed starts QE program. Massive government support to auto industry. Banks subject to stress tests and begin recapitalization.	Europe and Japan in recession. Recession in developed markets turns out to be largest since 1930s. Variety of fiscal stimulus measures, longer term monetary easing. But emerging markets suffer no banking/currency/default crises and quickly recover, notably China and India, but also Brazil.
2010	U.S. recovery remains sluggish, especially in mid-year. Unemployment remains near 10% and inflation falls to near 1%. Fed begins QE2 program in the fall, with no prospect for any further fiscal stimulus.	Core Europe recovering, strongly in Germany; UK pursuing strong austerity; European peripherals in grip of debt deflation, unemployment, budget deficits and exploding debt. Both Greece and Ireland take EU-IMF rescue packages. Midyear bank stress tests not so rigorous (no sovereign stress) and bank recapitalization slow. Intra-EU tensions over who should absorb losses in current and future crises
2011–13	U.S. recovery continues slowly, but another spring/summer slowdown occurs. Fed begins QE3 program in the fall of 2011, and fiscal stimulus continues to go into reverse, especially at the state and local level. By 2013 there are signs of housing market recovery; and unemployment dips below 8%. Long-term interest rates rise as market anticipates a return to normal in the near future, but Fed remains cautious with rates on hold.	Fiscal austerity programs take hold in much of Europe and the UK. Europe goes into recession again in late 2011, a double dip, and records 6 straight quarters of negative real GDP growth, with Eurozone unemployment at a record 12% by 2013. UK records three consecutive quarters of negative or zero growth in 2011–12. Monetary policy still stuck at zero interest rates can do little to help in these cases. Emerging markets growth remains fairly strong, but falters in 2013.

runs were mostly avoided thanks to deposit insurance. But in today's economy banks also fund themselves by short-term loans, and it was these funding facilities that shrank in size, or became prohibitively expensive, when the creditworthiness of banks came into question.

This inability to borrow had the same effect as a run on deposits: banks had to shrink their balance sheets and scramble for liquid funds to fill the funding gap left by their inability to borrow. To free up and conserve cash, they had to stop making new loans and/or allow old loans to "roll off" their books. They also had to sell their securities starting with the most liquid, but as the crisis took its toll, they then had to sell more illiquid assets (such as hard-to-value mortgages and derivatives) into collapsing markets at what would later turn out to have been "fire sale" prices precipitated by the usual lack of buyers in a panic. Because the banks were taking steep losses not only on their loan books but also now on securities, their capital was soon depleted. As their share values fell, many banks were on the edge of bankruptcy. Several huge banks, including the investment banks Bear Stearns and Lehman Brothers and retail banks such as Washington Mutual, either failed outright or were bought in a takeover for pennies. In September 2008 the financial systems in the United States and all over the world were plagued with a banking panic of a magnitude not seen since the early 1930s.

Financial Decelerators As always, the financial crisis had the effect of depressing real economic activity, through the so-called financial accelerator mechanism (or in this case, decelerator). Much of business depends on a reliable financial system to fund day-to-day activities and the massive problems in the financial system added a real friction to the economy. Also, when wealth is destroyed by a panic, the impaired households and firms tend to rebuild their wealth by saving to pay off liabilities or accumulate assets, thus dampening the demand for goods and services. Lost wealth also impedes access to credit, making recovery slower than it otherwise would be. In 2008 and 2009 there was also policy uncertainty as authorities in the United States and throughout the world tried to devise a sequence of monetary, financial, and fiscal policies to stem the crisis.

A curious side effect of the crisis was the effect on the dollar and the unusually high spread between U.S. government interest rates and private sector interest rates: at the height of panic, investors sought out U.S. dollar assets as a safe haven (a typical experience for a reserve currency). This caused the dollar to appreciate markedly and the yields on U.S. government bills to approach zero. That is to say, risk premiums became a factor in all currency and asset markets, not just in emerging countries, and these forces rather than, say, policy interest rates, became for a while the major drivers of market rates and currency values.

The End of the World Was Nigh It took until March 2009 for the collapse of U.S. stock markets to end (the S&P 500 Index hit a low point of 666). By this time three of the big five U.S. specialist investment banks had failed or been taken over and a $700 billion bank recapitalization scheme had been created by the U.S. Treasury in fits and starts during the last days of the Bush administration and the first days of the Obama administration. Confidence in the ability of the economic and financial situation to recover was low, to put it mildly. Bank recapitalization projects took shape in other countries, too (the United Kingdom took the lead on this front), and a greater sense of calm was restored by the April 2009 G-20 summit in London, at which a united front of global leaders pledged greater support and cooperation. Fiscal policy makers had by then stepped in with large-scale stimulus plans in most countries (see Table 22-3) and monetary policy had been eased everywhere, in many countries all the way down

TABLE 22-3

Discretionary Fiscal Policies in the Great Recession After the crisis, as output growth slowed or turned negative, many countries increased government spending or cut taxes to try to provide additional macroeconomic stimulus. The table shows data on discretionary fiscal stimulus measures for the G-20 taken in 2008–10 relative to a 2007 baseline, as a percent of GDP.

	2008	2009	2010
Argentina	0.0	1.5	—
Australia	0.7	2.1	1.7
Brazil	0.0	0.6	0.8
Canada	0.0	1.9	1.7
China	0.4	3.1	2.7
France	0.0	0.7	0.8
Germany	0.0	1.6	2.0
India	0.6	0.6	0.6
Indonesia	0.0	1.3	0.6
Italy	0.0	0.2	0.1
Japan	0.3	2.4	1.8
Korea	1.1	3.9	1.2
Mexico	0.0	1.5	—
Russia	0.0	4.1	1.3
Saudi Arabia	2.4	3.3	3.5
South Africa	1.7	1.8	−0.6
Turkey	0.0	0.8	0.3
United Kingdom	0.2	1.4	−0.1
United States	1.1	2.0	1.8
G-20 PPP-GDP weighted average	0.5	2.0	1.5
G-20 discretionary impulse	0.5	1.5	−0.5

Source: IMF, "Update on Fiscal Stimulus and Financial Sector Measures," April 26, 2009.

to zero interest rates. Credit was still tight, but for those who could get it, costs had fallen. Despite fears of a return to 1930s-style protectionism, world trade policies stayed open, thanks in part to countries' commitments to and oversight by the World Trade Organization, and trade volumes started to pick up.

As these efforts took hold, the freefall of the world economy halted, and the sharp downward trends in GDP and trade (similar to those seen after 1929) hit bottom. But by now the economic costs of the financial meltdown had reached unfathomable heights (see Figure 22-18 for U.S. evidence).

Despite initial concerns, it was not the actual direct costs of financial bailouts that were the main problem. In the United States, the terms obtained in the depths of the crisis were so favorable that taxpayers made a small profit; in other countries, such as the United Kingdom, and especially Ireland, the costs to the public purse of bailing out the banks were huge. Instead, the main problem was that in the United States and elsewhere output was 5% or more below capacity and unemployment near to or above 10%, conditions that were likely to persist for years. In terms of lost output and

FIGURE 22-18

The Crisis and Recession in the United States These charts show key U.S. economic trends from 2003 through 2013.

(a) Output and Unemployment

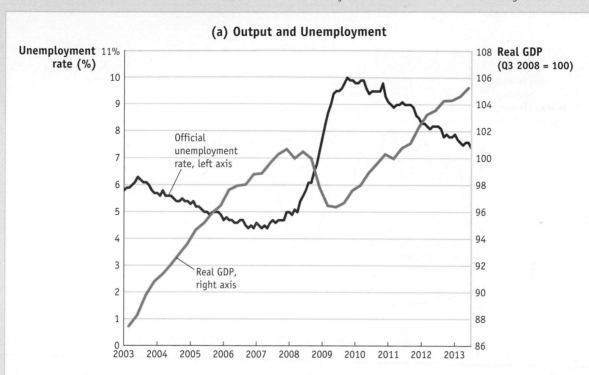

(b) Banking and Finance

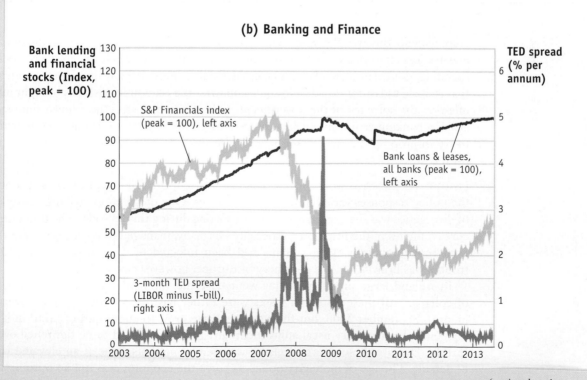

(continued on the next page)

FIGURE 22-18   *Continued*

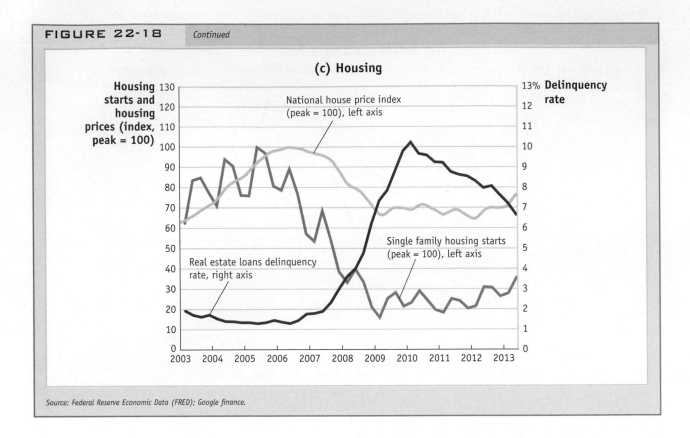

(c) Housing

Housing starts and housing prices (index, peak = 100)

National house price index (peak = 100), left axis

Delinquency rate

Single family housing starts (peak = 100), left axis

Real estate loans delinquency rate, right axis

Source: Federal Reserve Economic Data (FRED); Google finance.

employment, this was the worst U.S. and global slump in 80 years. In terms of the massive lost tax revenues for governments, along with some much smaller increases in spending, this event blew a large hole in the fiscal stability of many developed countries that is likely to last for decades. In some countries the economic crisis has brought into question the solvency of the government itself. Thus, as history has shown time and again, a banking crisis can quickly mutate into a sovereign debt crisis as governments, to try to prop up the system, socialize the losses of the financial system at significant fiscal cost.

Europe As the crisis wore on, and recovery started, the full extent of the shock and the policy responses varied in different countries. One of the most striking examples of divergence was the experience of the Eurozone during this episode. The traditional core countries of the Eurozone, especially Germany, managed to escape quite lightly, even though their banking systems had been infected by U.S. toxic assets. Deep trouble was brewing on the periphery of Europe, however (see Figure 22-19).

In Ireland large property booms went bust and the banking system was at risk of collapse. All these potential losses were rather hastily absorbed by the government in September 2008, but their eventual size grew to about half of GDP in late 2010 and the necessary fiscal adjustment, already austere, had to be tightened even further. Despite these efforts, Ireland was seen by markets to be at an elevated risk of default. The use of monetary policy to boost the economy was not an option: the Irish had joined the euro and could pull no policy lever but the one marked "fiscal," which was hard in reverse. By 2009 real GDP had fallen by 13% from its 2007 peak

FIGURE 22-19

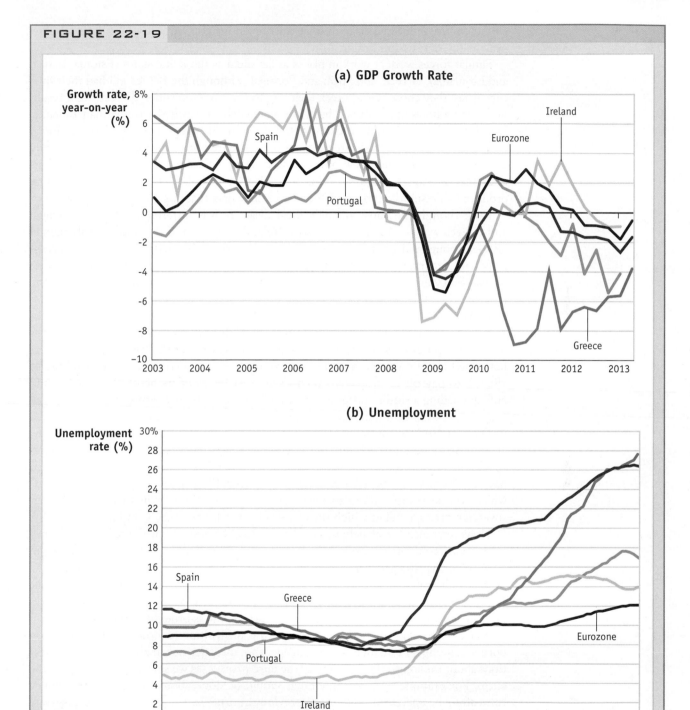

The Crisis and Recession in the Eurozone These charts show key Eurozone economic trends from 2003 through 2013, with an emphasis on the four peripheral countries: Portugal, Ireland, Greece, and Spain.

Source: Eurostat.

and unemployment had risen dramatically; even in 2013 output was still 10% below peak as the depression dragged on.

Similar forces were at work in places as far afield as the Baltic states (Estonia, Latvia, and Lithuania), Greece, and Spain and Portugal. Although the Baltics still had their own currencies, they chose not to break their peg to the euro and suffered greatly as a result. Spain had a housing boom and bust, but fortunately, it was less extreme than Ireland's. Less exposed to a housing meltdown and domestic banking crisis, the less-developed economies of Portugal and Greece faced the more traditional problem of a chronically large budget deficit that blew out to a massive gap in 2009 and 2010 once recessions caused tax revenues to evaporate. Greece faced an additional and long-standing credibility problem as a result of reporting falsified economic data that disguised its true problems.

Even though the cause of their fiscal disasters was different, however, Portugal and Greece were lumped together with Ireland and Spain in the uncharitably named "PIGS" group, and given low (near-junk) credit ratings. By 2010 this group had access to financial markets, if at all, only at very high interest rates. They skirted very close to insolvency and had avoided default only through funds advanced by the ECB, the EU, and the IMF (the "troika").

In March 2010, for example, Greece needed a special EU-IMF loan rescue package. But this only staved off the problems for a while. By October 2010 the peripherals were facing punitive market interest rates, and in November the Irish government was persuaded to follow Greece into a very contentious EU-IMF loan rescue package to allow it to pay off (at taxpayer expense) the vast losses of its banks. Portugal would end up needing a similar program. Eventually, even under the terms of the new Greek program, the debt burden remained too high and Greece defaulted and restructured its debts in 2012, to lower the debt burden (by this time most of the debt was in official, not private, hands). Again, peripheral countries like Spain and, more important, Italy came under funding pressure, which was only relieved when new ECB President Mario Draghi said "the ECB is ready to do whatever it takes to preserve the euro" which has been interpreted to mean that the ECB will step in to prevent further sovereign crises, a belief which thus far has been self-reinforcing and not tested.

However, much Greek debt was held by banks in Cyprus, and with the banks' solvency in question a bank run developed there slowly at first then building up to a massive crisis in early 2013. Cyprus's government and the troika then imposed capital controls, suspended bank withdrawals, and imposed losses on large depositors and other bank creditors. Cyprus was de facto outside the Eurozone and the problem of how to resolve failed banks in a monetary union without a fiscal or banking union was brought to the fore.

Needless to say, this debacle exposed the difficulties of how to regulate cross-border banking and finance within Europe, and, most serious of all, raised many questions about the long-term viability of the euro project (as we saw in the chapter on the euro). For example: What, if anything, should be done about Eurozone fiscal policy rules after the spectacular failure of previous efforts? Is it possible for such disparate economies to be safely put into a common currency given the asymmetric shocks they face? Can a way be found for European cross-border banks to operate safely? How can the "global imbalance" problem *within* the Eurozone microcosm be resolved to temper the flow of capital from sober and restrained high-savers in Germany and elsewhere to persistent-deficit, credit-bubble, and crisis-prone low-saving peripheral countries? Can the Eurozone tolerate a default by either a state or a banking system, or will moral hazard prevail? Will the ECB be left to pick up the bill? Or will it be the taxpayers, and if so, which ones? The resolution of these Eurozone problems may require shifts to greater banking, fiscal, or even political union, but as of now any meaningful steps in these various directions have yet to appear.

The Rest of the World What about the rest of the world? Outside of the United States and the Eurozone, the impacts were less catastrophic. Japan escaped lightly for the rather depressing reason that its economy had already been in a quasi-slump for over 15 years, had already seen its banking system collapse, and had very slow growth and near-zero rates of inflation and interest.

The most remarkable outcome was, however, in the emerging market world where rapid growth quickly resumed. These countries had experienced strong precrisis economic growth, were not exposed so much to financial sector risk at home (or to problems in the developed market's financial world), carried less debt in their economies, and had also amassed large war chests of reserves. In many cases, these nations spent their reserves to support fiscal policy expansions that buffered their economies from the global shock, without necessitating new borrowing (when credit markets were impaired) or placing their exchange rate regimes at risk. These nations had saved for a rainy day, and now it was pouring.

The main locus of this rapid EM recovery was in Asia (except for Japan), which was buttressed by strong support measures in China, including a large-scale public spending program. Latin America also turned around very quickly, led by boom conditions in Brazil and deft deployment of reserves in Chile. Only Mexico, more closely tied to the economic disaster in the United States, had to contend with macroeconomic difficulties. The luck of Brazil, as a commodity exporter, was also shared by a few DM countries, like Australia, Canada, and Norway, whose valuable natural resources were quickly in demand again after the resumption of growth in China and other EM countries.

In this way, a remarkable "two-track" economic recovery started to take shape in 2009 (see Figure 22-20). It was something never witnessed before: the DM countries were unable to kick start a true recovery, but the EM countries powered ahead regardless, largely under their own steam. The "decoupling" of the EM fate from the DM trend was unusual. From a historical point of view, however, it was even more striking that the world had gone through its greatest synchronized global financial crisis ever and not a single EM country had experienced a banking, currency, or sovereign default crisis. Had anyone suggested this outcome before the fact, they would surely have been greeted with incredulity.

The Road to Recovery The question going forward is how long this state of affairs can persist. When, if ever, will the DM countries, and especially the United States and the Eurozone, return to "normal" (whatever that means)? As of late 2013, the U.S. recovery was further along, with output creeping above its previous peak; but Europe and the U.K. remained stuck in deep depressions exceeded in severity only by the downturns of the 1930s. Several risks (some of them remote) still lurked in the background:

■ In most DM countries, fiscal policies were tightened in 2010 and later years, via the withdrawal of U.S. fiscal stimulus, or as part of U.K. and European austerity programs. There were also sequestrations and government shutdowns in the United States. Countries tightened in peripheral Europe, when they were forced to do so by the troika after they could not borrow in markets, but for others it was a choice, as in core Europe, the United Kingdom and the United States. Critics argued that austerity slowed growth and exacerbated public debt levels.

FIGURE 22-20

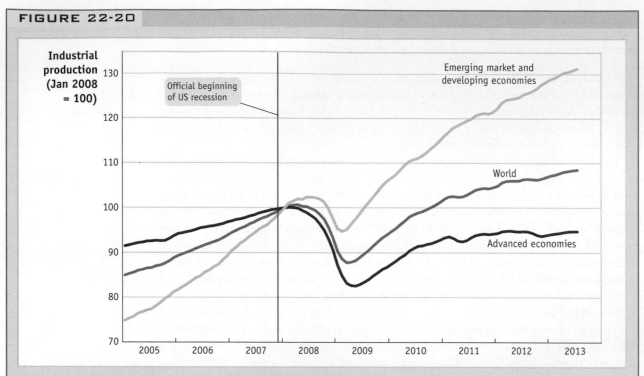

The "Two-Track" Global Recovery Using data on industrial production, these two charts contrast the sluggish recovery in developed markets with the rapid resumption of growth in emerging markets.

Source: IMF, World Economic Outlook, *October 2013.*

- Monetary policy had hit the zero interest rate lower bound at the Fed and other central banks. This left no further room for easing using conventional tools when such easing was badly needed (especially when fiscal stimulus started to be withdrawn in conditions of still-high unemployment and below-target inflation). In addition, the conventional transmission mechanisms through which monetary policy affects economic activity remained impaired as many banks continued to struggle with damaged balance sheets. Many small and medium-size firms were unable to borrow at low rates. Many households held little or negative equity in their homes and were unable to borrow or refinance at low rates.

- The Fed had instituted unconventional measures such as quantitative easing (QE) used in the crisis and QE2 and QE3, additional rounds undertaken in 2010 and 2012, causing the Fed's balance sheet to expand. These unsterilized *large-scale asset purchases* could provide stimulus through a variety of channels to lower interest rates throughout the market, support asset prices and wealth, and also weaken the U.S. dollar. The latter effect was not always welcomed by trading partners and has sparked concerns of a global "currency war" that could then mutate into a protectionist battle or trade war. And supporting asset markets in such an open and sustained way marked a controversial new step for the Fed.

- How the Fed or Bank of England or Bank of Japan would exit from QE-type measures and how the ECB would pull back its special liquidity support and (sterilized) bond purchase programs are, as of late 2013, future problems still to be resolved. Can these steps be taken without igniting inflation if liquidity isn't contracted sharply enough? Can they be done without sparking bankruptcies or defaults if interest rates rise too quickly and hurt those on floating interest rates? It is hard to find precedents for these unusual monetary experiments, and even a hint of the Fed scaling back its QE program spooked markets in mid-2013.

■ As of 2013, the Eurozone remained in a fragile state: growth was dismal, with weak banks and fiscal positions, especially in the periphery. There was still no grand strategy apart from liquidity provided by the ECB. Fiscal austerity continued to bite, especially in the periphery as a required condition of the bailout programs. Greece's debt levels continued to climb into unsustainable ranges, making a second default more likely. Europe's new European Stability Mechanism cannot be used for legacy problems, but even going forward it would be too small to cope with crises in multiple countries all at once. Beyond this scheme no larger or more permanent arrangements to handle Eurozone financial instability and sovereign crises had yet been determined.

■ Almost all of the advanced economies emerged from the crisis with still historically high private debt levels (debts of households and firms) as well as rapidly rising public debt levels. The emerging countries grew more strongly, with less fiscal strain, but on the back of rapid private credit growth of their own. By 2013 even that engine of growth was faltering. How much this burden of public and private debt will continue to weigh on DM and EM prospects for future economic growth and complete global recovery remains unclear, but such levels have not been seen before. Here again, we are in uncharted waters and economic research is active in these areas.

We should hope that the world will discover how or if some of the conditions that helped shape the crisis might be avoided in the future. Can better financial regulation prevent damaging credit booms? Can improved bankruptcy procedures help countries deal with failing banks quickly and with less damage to the economy or the taxpayer? Can more EM economies find alternative insurance mechanisms, or else accumulate an adequate level of reserves? Can the Eurozone develop a more stable political and economic architecture than the half-built structure currently in place? Will global imbalances persist at the levels seen in the last decade, or will they moderate either through smooth market adjustments, or in response to more direct policy activism?

Conclusion: Lessons for Macroeconomics

The above description of the global financial crisis and its aftermath is necessarily incomplete. The event itself is far from over, and it represents a massive shock to the world economy, both economically and politically. Its full repercussions will unfold over many years and are impossible to predict with certainty.

What is more certain is that the crisis is already causing serious intellectual repercussions and is profoundly changing our thinking with respect to the way that macroeconomists do their research and teaching. It is now clear that many defects of existing, standard macroeconomic models need to be fixed. It is not enough to model the real side of the economy and ignore the financial sector. Deeper thinking will be needed to integrate finance and macroeconomics and to modernize the neglected area of money and banking, once a core subject of macroeconomics. In this respect, economists will need to think carefully about what drives the demand for money and other safe assets when markets fail, and how to understand and incorporate rival views of crises, such as irrational herding, limits to arbitrage, imperfect information, moral hazard, and so forth.

The scope of policy objectives will have to be carefully scrutinized to determine whether and how the authorities can develop sufficient (and sufficiently sharp) instruments to meet their targets of not just price stability and, possibly, maximum employment, but also financial stability (an original, but somewhat forgotten, responsibility of central banks). Here, a narrow focus on interest rate policy will be joined by a broader investigation of what a sensible *macroprudential policy* for the financial sector might look like.

Lastly, the challenges will require new evidence to guide theory and refute or confirm hypotheses. Financial shocks of the kind we have just witnessed are rare events. For the purposes of empirical study, a sample of comparable episodes can be found, but only if one looks deep into economic history. The calm and prosperity of the world economy from the mid-1980s up to 2007, the so-called Great Moderation, lulled many into thinking that we had entered a new era, in which "this time is different"; it turned out to be an illusion. Greater attention to the lessons of economic history might have counteracted some of that complacent and naïve thinking. In the end, economists and policy makers face the task of better linking aggregate economic outcomes to financial conditions, a task that will surely take economic research down some new and interesting paths. There is much work to do.

KEY POINTS

1. Purchasing power parity does not hold between rich and poor countries, in either relative or absolute form. Prices of goods are systematically higher in rich countries. As countries become relatively richer, we can therefore expect their price levels to rise and, hence, their real exchange rates to appreciate. Exchange rate forecasts (real and nominal) need to be adjusted accordingly, as do judgments as to whether a country's exchange rate is under- or overvalued.

2. The Balassa-Samuelson theory explains price differences across countries as a result of differences in the wage (labor) costs embodied in nontraded goods. It assumes that nontraded goods have zero (or small) productivity differences. Under those assumptions, large differences in traded goods productivity are associated with large differences in income per capita, wages, and the prices of nontraded goods.

3. Uncovered interest parity (UIP) appears to hold when market expectations are measured directly using data from surveys of traders. But the joint hypothesis of UIP and rational expectations (the efficient markets hypothesis) appears to be invalid because exchange rate forecasts seem to be systematically and predictably wrong.

4. On average, exchange rate movements have been smaller than predicted by UIP, so a carry trade strategy of borrowing in the low-yield currency and investing in the high-yield currency delivers profits or excess returns. However, these excess returns are risky, with a Sharpe ratio well below 1, and typically close to 0.4 to 0.5. As with the stock market, few investors are willing to devote speculative capital to such risky investments.

5. Default is as old as capital markets. Sovereign defaults on international lending have been widely documented for several centuries. In the modern era, defaults are associated with economic downturns, and a good deal of this pain seems to be a result of default. This "punishment" for the defaulter creates one important benefit—it makes lending possible in the first place, since sovereigns otherwise face no incentive to repay.

6. A simple model of default can explain why countries default in bad times. They need to insure

against really painful outcomes and default allows them to do this. The price of such insurance is the risk premium they must pay on top of the risk-free rate when they borrow, so that the lender breaks even. This kind of model explains the existence of default as an equilibrium outcome. Nonetheless, many other factors can precipitate default crises, including complex feedback between default, banking crises, and exchange rate crises.

7. Before 2008, large capital flows from EM to DM created global imbalances, and some similar imbalances could be found within the DM world. Some of these flows ended up financing unsustainable private or public consumption or failed housing investments in certain DM economies (United States, Britain, Ireland, Spain, etc.) and as the malinvestment contaminated balance sheets of banks globally the stage was set for the Global Financial Crisis.

8. The subsequent Great Recession saw contractions in aggregate demand and credit, and ballooning government debts and deficits in many DM countries. The financial crisis now created a fiscal problem, and in some cases, brought governments to a near-insolvent position, in some cases necessitating rescue packages (the euro periphery). EM economies bounced back quickly, but the DM economies had a deep slump, making the global recovery weak and doubtful.

KEY TERMS

trade cost, p. 861
no-arbitrage band, p. 861
Balassa-Samuelson effect, p. 867
equilibrium real exchange rate, p. 867
carry trade, p. 871
peso problem, p. 877
forecast error, p. 878
rational expectations hypothesis, p. 880

efficient markets hypothesis, p. 880
inefficient market, p. 880
limits to arbitrage, p. 880
excess return, p. 881
Sharpe ratio, p. 881
sovereign default, p. 884
contingent claim, p. 886
repayment threshold, p. 887
Global Financial Crisis, p. 903

Great Recession, p. 903
global imbalances, p. 905
savings glut, p. 905
undervalued exchange rates, p. 909
too-easy monetary policy, p. 909
failure of regulation and supervision. p. 909
government failure, p. 909
market failure, p. 910

PROBLEMS

1. (PPP) Richland and Poorland each have two industries: traded TVs and nontraded house maintenance. The world price of TVs is R$100 (R$ = Richland dollar). Assume for now that the exchange rate is R$1 = 1 PP (PP = Poorland peso) and that prices are flexible. It takes 1 day for a worker in each country to visit and maintain 1 house. It takes 1 day for a Richland worker to make a TV, and 4 days for a Poorland worker.

    a. What is the Richland wage in R$ per day? What is the Poorland wage in PP per day? In R$ per day? What is the ratio of Poorland to Richland wages in a common currency?

    b. What is the price of a house maintenance visit in each country?

    c. Assume people in each country spend half their income on TVs and half on house maintenance. Compute the CPI (consumer price index) for each country given by the square root of (TV price) times (house maintenance price).

    d. Compute the standard of living in each country by dividing local currency wages by the CPI from part (c)? Is Poorland really as poor as suggested by the last answer in part (a)?

e. Productivity now doubles in the Poorland TV industry, all else equal. How many days does it now take for Poorland workers to make a TV? What happens to the wage in Poorland? The price of house maintenance? The CPI?

f. If the central bank of Poorland wants to avoid inflation in this situation, how would it like to adjust the exchange rate?

2. (PPP) "Some fast-growing poorer countries face a conflict between wanting to maintain a fixed exchange rate with a rich country and wanting to keep inflation low." Explain the logic behind this statement. Use the examples of Slovakia and China to illustrate your argument.

3. (UIP) What is a peso problem? In the case of fixed exchange rates, explain how peso problems can account for persistent interest rate differentials. Study the U.S.–Britain short-term (end-of-month) nominal interest rate differentials shown below for the year 1896 (from NBER series 13034). Both countries were on the gold standard at a fixed exchange rate of $4.86 throughout this year. Did the United States have a peso problem? When did it become really big? When did it go away? (*Extra Credit*: Do some research on the Web and discover the political reasons for the timing of this peso problem.)

Jan 1896	3.84%
Feb 1896	2.94%
Mar 1896	2.76%
Apr 1896	2.40%
May 1896	1.63%
Jun 1896	1.20%
Jul 1896	1.43%
Aug 1896	3.77%
Sep 1896	3.70%
Oct 1896	8.51%
Nov 1896	2.60%
Dec 1896	−1.39%

4. (UIP) You are in discussion with a forex trader.

a. She reveals that she made a 10% annual rate of return last year. Based on these data, can we say that the forex market in question violates the efficient markets hypothesis (EMH)?

b. The trader reveals that she can make predictable 10% annual rates of return on forex trades for a pair of currencies, with a standard deviation of 25%, and has been doing so for a long time. Calculate the Sharpe ratio for these trades. Based on these data, does the forex market in question satisfy EMH?

c. Can the trader's predictable profits be explained by trading frictions? By risk aversion?

5. (Default) "Poor countries are exploited when they borrow in global capital markets, because they are charged an extortionate rate of interest." Explain how empirical evidence and theoretical arguments might counter this assertion.

6. (Default) The Republic of Delinquia has a nondisaster output level of $100 each year. With 10% probability each year, output falls to a disaster level of $80, and the country will feel so much pain that it will default and pay neither principal nor interest on its debts. The country decides to borrow $20 at the start of the year, and keep the money under the mattress. It will default and keep the money in the event that output is low, but this will entail sacrificing $4 in punishment costs. Otherwise, it pays back principal and interest due. Lenders are competitive and understand these risks fully.

a. What is the probability of default in Delinquia?

b. The interest rate on safe loans is 8% per annum, so a safe loan has to pay off 1.08 times $20. What is the lending rate charged by competitive lenders on the risky loan to Delinquia?

c. What does Delinquia consume in disaster years? In nondisaster years?

d. Repeat part (c) for the case where Delinquia cannot borrow. Is Delinquia better off with or without borrowing?

7. (Global Crisis) When emerging markets elected to accumulate vast sums of reserves in the 2000s decade, did this create a problem in developed markets? How might this problem be resolved, or resolve itself, going forward? Does the EM decision to accumulate the reserves look like a wise one, after the fact?

8. (Global Crisis) In 2010 there was a risk that the state of Ireland was at risk of going broke because it had poured too much money into its insolvent banks to try to keep them alive, but already incomes had fallen massively and public services were being cut harshly too. Describe the trade-offs involved in the various options: (a) increasing austerity (raising taxes and cutting spending) even more to keep the banks alive; (b) letting the State default on its external debt to keep the banks alive and limit austerity; (c) allow the banks to fail to save the State's creditworthiness and limit austerity. Consider the problem from a purely Irish national interest perspective first. Now think of an EU level perspective: how is your analysis of who should foot the bill affected by the fact that many of the Irish bank creditors were foreign (many in the EU), and that many of the risks of financial damage were due to contagion to other (principally EU) foreign countries.

N E T W O R K

1. (PPP) Find the price of some of your favorite books or CDs on Amazon.com in the United States. Now find the price of the same items at Amazon.co.uk in the United Kingdom. Are there arbitrage opportunities? What if you ordered 100 or 1,000 items? What are the shipping costs as a fraction of the cost of your order? How would you determine the tariffs and duties you would need to pay? Are there any other barriers to trade?

2. (PPP) In certain years, the EU accession countries faced appreciation and/or inflation pressure. In March 2007 a step was taken to resolve these problems in the case of the Slovak koruna. The EU gave permission for Slovakia to "bend the rules" a bit. Which one of the Maastricht criteria was relaxed? Use the Internet to find out (*Hint*: Search the Internet for "Slovak koruna"). What does this say about the importance that EU authorities attach to low inflation? Suppose Slovakia was still relatively poor but in the Eurozone. The Balassa-Samuelson effect would still be present even with a common currency, so how would inflation rates differ in the rich and poor parts of Europe? Why could that be a problem for ECB policy makers?

3. (UIP) Imagine you are a carry trader. Go to the ft.com site and locate the "Market data" part of the site. Find one-month LIBOR interest rates for some major currencies: U.S. dollar, pound, euro, Japanese yen, Swiss franc, Canadian dollar, and Australian dollar (*Hint*: Search "ft.com money rates"). Find the lowest-yield currency, and call it X. How much interest would you pay in X units after borrowing $100X$ for one month? (*Hint*: The raw data are annualized rates.) Compute the exchange rate between X and every other higher-yield currency Y (*Hint*: Search "ft.com cross rates"). For each Y, compute how much $100X$ would be worth in Y units today, and then in a month's time with Y-currency interest added. Revisit this question in a month's time, find the spot rates at that moment, and compute the resulting profit from each carry trade. Did all your imaginary trades pay off? Any of them?

Index

in China, 860
in Ireland (1980–2011), 576f,
576n4
transfers of income, GNDI
and, 577–578, 578f
in U.S. (2012), 860
Gross national product (GNP),
575n3
Gross private domestic investment, 573
Group of Eight (G8), 338–340,
339n4, 645
GSP. *See* Generalized System of
Preferences
Guest workers. *See Gastarbeiters*
Gulf War, 582n6

H

H1B visa program, 131, 158,
160
H-2A visa program, 130
Haiti, 429
Hamilton, Alexander, 885n17
Hamlet (Shakespeare), 411
Harley, William, 310–311
Harley-Davidson, 308,
310–314, 313n18. *See also*
Motorcycles, heavyweight
Harmon, Nkenge, 362
Harris, Richard, 178
Hausmann, Ricardo, 737
Hawley, Willis C., 12
Heckscher, Eli, 87–88
**Heckscher-Ohlin (HO)
model,** 10, 87–88, 118,
119, 124, 139n8, 205n6
assumptions of, 89–91
with differing productivities
across countries, 102–106,
104f, 106t
with effects of trade on factor
prices, 110–119
factor endowments in 2010,
100–102, 101f
factor intensities across countries, 91–92
free-trade equilibrium, 94–98
labor intensity of each
industry and, 90f
Leontief's paradox and,
99–100, 99t, 107–109,
107f, 108f
no-trade equilibrium, 92–94
testing of, 98–109
**Heckscher-Ohlin (HO)
theorem,** 97–98, 99
Hedge fund, 875, 884n13
Hedging (risk avoidance), 451
Helpman, Elhanan, 178

High costs of arbitrage, 861,
862f
High-technology export
subsidies, 351
Airbus strategy and, 354,
355–356, 357
Airbus subsidy and, 354,
355–357, 356f
Boeing and subsidy with cost
advantage, 354, 357–358,
357f, 358f
Boeing strategy and, 354,
356, 357–358
with China and rare earth
minerals, 352
commercial aircraft and,
358–361
multiple equilibria, 355
Nash equilibrium and, 354
payoff matrix and, 352–353
payoff matrix between two
firms, 354f
strategies, 352–358
Himes, Christopher, 83
Hines, James, 224
H&M, 386
HO model. *See* Heckscher-
Ohlin model
HO theorem. *See* Heckscher-
Ohlin theorem
Home bias, 652–654, 652f, 654f
Home country
export subsidies in large,
334–340, 335f, 338f
export subsidies in small,
331–334, 332f
gains for, 153–154
home equilibrium and, 35–36
home equilibrium with no
trade and, 35f
home indifference curve and,
34–35
no-trade equilibrium in, 93f
opportunity cost and prices
with, 36
PPF and, 33–34, 34f
Ricardian model and, 33–37
specific-factors model and,
61–64
wages in, 36–37
Home equilibrium
with consumption, production
and trade, 42f
with free trade, 94–95, 95f
home country and, 35–36
with no trade and home
country, 35f
Home export supply curve
foreign import demand and,
50–51, 50f

with home export supply, 49f
international prices and,
47–51
with labor productivity and
wages over time, 48f
Home firms
import quotas and, 265, 266
no-trade equilibrium for, 214f
offshoring equilibrium for,
215f
Home import demand curve,
241–242, 241f
Home interest rates, 527f
Home labor
demand and relative wage,
203–204, 203f
increase in, 127f, 127n4,
127n5, 137–138, 137f, 139f
market, 126f
Home loss
home quotas and, 287–288
home tariff and, 285–286
threat of duty and, 302f
Home money market
with changes in money supply
and money demand, 532f
equilibrium in, 530f
Home money supply
with long-run adjustment,
546f
permanent shock to, 544–545
responses to permanent
expansion of, 549f
short-run impact of permanent expansion of, 546f
temporary expansion of, 538f
temporary shock to, 537–539
Home monopoly, 320
free-trade equilibrium and,
283–284, 283f
home quota and, 286–288,
287f
home tariff and, 284–286,
285f
no-trade equilibrium and,
282–283
tariffs and quotas with,
281–291
U.S. imports of Japanese
automobiles and, 288–291
Home portfolios, risk diversification and, 647
Home price, tariffs and,
291–292
Home quotas, 286–288, 287f
Home tariff, 284–286, 285f
Home welfare
export subsidies in large home
country and influence on,
335–336

export subsidies in small
home country and
influence on, 333–334
with free trade for small
country, 239–240
with gains from free trade at
home, 240f
gains from trade and,
239–241
no trade and, 239
production subsidies and, 342
tariffs and influence on,
258–259, 293
Homemaker-traders, 875
Honda, 311
Honduras, 578f
Hong Kong, 11n3, 757n1
agreements made at Hong
Kong WTO meeting (Dec.
2005), 329t, 330–331
Big Mac index and, 485t
exports, 269
FDI stocks in, 22
foreign capital in, 149n12
FX market in, 449
golf club trade and, 166t
household workers in, 157
labor productivity and wages
in, 108f
snowboard exports, 28
trade/GDP ratio for, 11t
Hong Kong Monetary
Authority Investment
Portfolio, 630n11
Horizontal FDI, 20
Household workers, 157
HSBC, 452
Hufbauer, Gary Clyde, 255n12
Hugo, Victor, 826
Hume, David, 87
Hungary, 8n2
Big Mac index and, 485t
EU and, 158n16
pengö and forint in, 497, 497f
per capita income of, 18
PPP and hyperinflation in, 498f
trade dollarization and, 67f
trade/GDP ratio for, 11t
Hunger
food security and, 340
G8 and, 339
Hupfeld, Herman, 473
Hurricanes
macroeconomics of, 610f
Mitch, 611f
Hussein, Saddam, 560, 560n9,
562
Hyperinflation, 496, 731
collapse of real money
balances during, 499f